THESAURUS

The National Thesaurus

A KEVIN WELDON PRODUCTION

The Little Macquarie
THESAURUS

General Editor
Richard Tardif

THE MACQUARIE LIBRARY

Published by The Macquarie Library Pty Ltd
The Macquarie Dictionary, Macquarie University NSW 2109
First published 1987
Reprinted 1989, 1992, 1993, 1995 (twice), 1996, 1997 (twice), 1999, 2000, 2001

© Copyright Macquarie University NSW, 1987

Produced in Australia for the Publisher

Typeset by Photoset Computer Service Pty Ltd

Printed in Australia by McPherson's Printing Group

National Library of Australia Cataloguing-in-Publication Data

The Little Macquarie Thesaurus
Includes Index
ISBN 0 949757 42 X.

1. English language — Synonyms and antonyms.
2. English language — Australia.
I. Tardif, Richard, 1956–.

423'.1

All rights reserved. No part of this publication may be reproduced, stored in a retrieval system, or transmitted in any form, or by any means electronic, mechanical, photocopying, recording, or otherwise without the prior permission of the publisher.

A number of words entered in this thesaurus are derived from trademarks. However, the presence or absence of this indication of derivation should not be regarded as affecting the legal status of any trademark.

Contents

Preface vi
How to use this book x
Abbreviations used in the Thesaurus xi

The Little Macquarie Thesaurus 1

Editorial Staff

General Editor Richard Tardif
Special Consultants Brenda McPhee, M.B.B.S.
  Tony Press, B.Sc., Ph.D.
  Tony Rodd, B.Sc.
  J. Simons, M.Sc., Ph.D.
Computer Systems William E. Smith
  Robert Mannell

with thanks to the Speech, Hearing and Language Research Centre, Macquarie University

Preface

1. What use is a thesaurus?

Mainly, it is a place for finding words. Turn to a thesaurus if you have lost a word, if you are tired of some word and want another like it, if you think a word ought to exist but don't yet know it, or if you simply would like to read all the words there are about an idea, feeling or object.

A thesaurus is a kind of dictionary-in-reverse. Dictionaries try to keep words apart. They pin words down and hold them in place with precise definitions, making a point of their differences. So the distinctions between say, *big, huge* and *substantial* are spelt out, and the spaces between each are made clearly visible.

In a thesaurus, on the other hand, all the words associated with a particular idea come together, overflowing the boundaries of their dictionary definitions. It is this sense of the flow of language that contributes to the pleasure, and often the humour, of reading a thesaurus. Attached to this sense of flow, as well, is an element of danger.

Scarcely any word in the English language can be replaced by another without some change in meaning — that is, there are hardly any true *synonyms*. If you find a word listed here with another word that you know, you can be sure both have a *similar* meaning. But if you are not certain of the exact meaning of the new word, you should check in a dictionary to see that it is appropriate for your use.

2. The origins of the thesaurus.

Thesauruses arrange language into broad areas of meaning — concepts like *heat* and *cold, land* and *sea, big* and *small*. This seems largely to follow the way language is arranged in people's minds. It seems, in other words, a natural way to list the words of a language, as opposed to the strict alphabetical order of modern dictionaries.

In fact some of the earliest known dictionaries do group words under general concepts such as *fire* and *sea*. It was not until the second half of the 16th century that it became usual to arrange dictionaries alphabetically. The earliest dictionaries, then, resemble the modern thesaurus in structure, but their general purpose is still to define or translate the individual words they list.

3. Roget's Thesaurus.

The first person to produce a book with the sole aim of providing lists of words associated by meaning was Peter Mark Roget (1779-1869). Roget's *Thesaurus* first appeared in 1852, and his name has been associated with the idea of the thesaurus ever since.

Roget himself was an English physician and scientist, active in public service as well as scholarly life. The word he chose as the title for his book was, at the time, a relatively obscure term in archaeology used to mean 'a storehouse for treasure', though it also had linguistic associations.

His book is indeed a treasure-house of linguistic riches. It divides the language into about 1000 key concepts. These keys themselves are organised according to an abstract classificatory system, modelled in many ways on the great descriptive catalogues of the 18th century. Such catalogues were intended to systematise knowledge in fields as diverse as biology, economics and grammar, and it seems that Roget's classification was produced, similarly, as an analysis of meaning in language.

However, the revolutions in understanding that have taken place in the sciences of biology and economics have also overtaken Roget's classification of meaning. His systematic arrangement now seems more the point of view of a particular person living in a particular time and place, rather than a general truth about language. It is none the less interesting for that, though. And its usefulness at the more mundane level as a general 'wordfinder' is undisputed.

4. The Little Macquarie Thesaurus.

Much has happened to the English language since Roget devised his thesaurus, especially with its migration to Australia. Social forces have wrought changes to individual words and their meaning, to the multitudinous relations between words, to general attitudes towards style in language, and to the way language itself is perceived and understood. All these have demanded a fresh approach to writing a thesaurus.

The Little Macquarie Thesaurus presents a far greater number of keywords than Roget's original 1000, all much smaller in size. This is done for the sake of simplicity and ease of use. At the same time a larger range is given under each keyword than would be found in a typical dictionary of synonyms, since one of the main tasks of a thesaurus is to introduce new and diverse words to the reader.

The Little Macquarie Thesaurus derives most of its material from the complete *Macquarie Thesaurus*, while *The Macquarie Dictionary* itself naturally provides the ultimate word base for this work, since it remains the most thorough record of the English language as it is currently used in Australia.

A thesaurus and dictionary go hand in hand. In a dictionary you can find the precise shade of meaning of a word, whether the word is acceptable in formal usage, how it is pronounced, and so on. While relying on a dictionary to convey all these things, a thesaurus is ideally shaped to present to the reader the rich resources of a language.

The Little Macquarie Thesaurus aims to present the language characteristics of the community of Australian speakers and writers, and in so doing to express something of the nature of that community itself. As a greater thinker from Roget's own time, Karl Marx, wrote: 'Language is just as much the product of a communal way of life as it is in another respect the existence of the communal way of life — its self-expressing existence.'

Richard Tardif

How to use this book

What do you do when you want to describe a book you have read, and the only word you can think of is **'good'**?

... Simple! Look up **'good'** in the front section of this thesaurus and there you will find the *keyword* **GOOD**, with a range of words you could use to describe your book.

If the word you are trying to avoid is not **'good'**, but **'nice'**, which does not appear as a keyword, look it up in the back section of the book. At **'nice'** you will find several senses of the word:

nice *adj* **1** accomplished **2** delicious **3** discriminating **4** good **5** kind **6** modest **7** pleasant **8** precise **9** promiscuous

Choose the word closest in meaning to your own idea of **'nice'** and look up this keyword in the front section.

Abbreviations used in this Thesaurus

adj. adjective
adv. adverb
Aeron. Aeronautics
Agric. Agriculture
Alg. Algebra
Amer. Ind. American Indian
Anat. Anatomy
Anc. Hist. Ancient History
Anglican Ch. Anglican Church
Anthrop. Anthropology
Archaeol. Archaeology
Archit. Architecture
Astrol. Astrology
Astron. Astronomy
Aust. Australia, Australian

Biochem. Biochemistry
Biol. Biology
Bot. Botany
Bldg Trades. Building Trades
Brit. British

Carp. Carpentry
Chem. Chemistry
Class. Myth. Classical Mythology
Colloq. Colloquial
Comm. Commerce

Ecol. Ecology
Econ. Economics
Educ. Education
Egypt. Egyptian
Elect. Electronics, Electrical
Eng. Hist. English History
Engin. Engineering
Europ. Hist. European History

Geog. Geography
Geol. Geology
Geom. Geometry
Gk Greek

Govt Government

Hist. History

interj. interjection
Internat. Law. International Law
It. Italian

joc. jocular
Journal. Journalism

Lit. Literature

Mech. Mechanics
Med. Medicine
Mediev. Hist. Medieval History
Metall. Metallurgy
Mil. Military
Mineral. Mineralogy
Myth. Mythology

n. noun
Naut. Nautical
NSW New South Wales
N.T. Northern Territory
N.Z. New Zealand

obs. obsolete

Parl. Parliament
Pharm. Pharmacy
Philos. Philosophy
Photog. Photography
Phys. Physics
prep. preposition
pron. pronoun
Psychiat. Psychiatry
Psychol. Psychology

Qld Queensland

R. League Rugby League

Rom. Cath. Ch. Roman Catholic Church
R. Union Rugby Union

S.A. South Australia
Stats. Statistics
Surf. Surfing
Surg. Surgery

Tas. Tasmania
Tech. Drawing. Technical Drawing

Theat. Theatre
Theol. Theology

U.S. United States of America

v. verb
Vet. Sci. Veterinary Science
Vic. Victoria

W.A. Western Australia

Zool. Zoology

Aa

ABANDON v defect from, desolate, discontinue *(Law)*, dish, disown, ditch, forsake, give over, give up, give up as a bad job, hand over, jettison, leave someone to their own devices, let down, let go, throw up, wash one's hands of, write off, yield; **renounce**, abjure, abnegate, discard, disclaim, dismiss, dispense with, forgo, have done with, reject, relinquish, repudiate, waive; **jilt**, cast off, drop, throw over; **strand**, expose, maroon; **desert**, bugger off, decamp, leave someone holding the baby, leave someone in the lurch, pike on, rat on, run out on, shoot through, squib on, walk out on

ABANDONED adj abject *(Obs.)*, derelict, deserted, desolate, destitute *(Obs.)*, forlorn, forsaken, high and dry, like a shag on a rock, lorn *(Archaic)*, lovelorn, stranded, unredeemed, vacant *(Law)*

ABANDONER n defector, deserter, evacuator, quitter, rat, relinquisher, seceder; **jilt**, jilter; **abnegator**, forgoer

ABANDONMENT n defection, dereliction, desertion, desolation, evacuation, exposure, relinquishment, resignation, surrender, vacation, waiver; **renunciation**, abdication, abnegation, rejection, shedding; **forsakenness**, desolateness, forlornness, lovelornness

ABATEMENT n assuagement, attenuation, mitigation, moderation, modulation, palliation, relaxation, relief, remission, remittence, remittency, temperament *(Obs.)*, wane; **pacification**, mollification, tranquillisation

ABBEY n cell, chartreuse, cloister, convent, hermitage, monastery, nunnery, priorate, priory; **ashram.** See also PLACE OF WORSHIP; CHURCH; SHRINE

ABBREVIATE v abridge, condense, cut a long story short, epigrammatise, precis, sum up, summarise, telescope; **abstract**, boil down, digest, encapsulate, formularise, formulate, formulise, make a synopsis of, outline, precis

ABDOMEN n belly, gut, hypochondrium, hypogastrium, middle, midriff, pubes, puku *(N.Z.)*, venter, waist, waistline, womb *(Obs.)*; **stomach**, bingie, breadbasket, inner man, maw, tum, tummy; **paunch**, bay window, beer gut, bow window, corporation, pot, potbelly, pukunui *(N.Z.)*, spare tyre; **solar plexus**, mark *(Boxing)*, wind *(Colloq.)*; **entrails**, comic cuts, gizzard, guts, innards, insides, internals, intestines, viscera, vitals; **alimentary canal**, appendix, bowel, bowels, caecum, colon, duodenum, enteron, epigastrium, foregut, ileum, jejunum, large intestine, midgut, oesophagus, omentum, pylorus, rectum, small intestine, vermiform appendix; **navel**, bellybutton, omphalos, umbilicus

ABOUND v bristle, crowd, flock, formicate, mass, swarm, teem, throng, troop; **oversupply**, congest, overman, overwhelm, snow under

ABOVE adv atop, over, overhead

ABRASIVE n abradant, abrader, bath brick *(Metall.)*, emery board, emery cloth, emery paper, emery wheel,

abrasive   2   **abstain**

floatstone, oilstone, sandblast, sander, sandpaper, steel wool, stone, strop, wet and dry, whetstone; **rasp**, broach, grattoir, rasper, scraper; **scratcher**, back scratcher, strigil

ABRASIVE *adj* abradant, erodent, erosive, grating, scratchy; **frictional**, non-skid, non-slip, tractional

ABRIDGMENT *n* abbreviation, compression, condensation, encapsulation, shortened version; **abstract**, analysis, argument, compendium, digest, epitome, formularisation, formulation, formulisation, highlights, outline, precis, résumé, run-down, summarisation, summary, summing up, synopsis; **epigram**, cameo, capsule, epitaph, essay, haiku, limerick, monostich, mot, news item, novella, short story, vignette; **jottings**, adversaria; **ellipsis**, abbreviation, acronym, blend, brachylogy, elision, portmanteau word, syncope

ABSENCE *n* blank, blankness, default, dumbness, emptiness, lack, lacuna, loss, non-access, short, vacuity, want, wantage *(U.S.)*; **leave**, furlough, leave of absence, sabbatical, sickie; **absenteeism**, exile, non-appearance, truancy, voidance

ABSENT *adj* A.W.L., A.W.O.L., absent without leave, ack-willie, away, missing, off, truant; **bereft**, bankrupt, blank, dry, dumb, empty-handed, minus, unprovided for, vacant, wanting; **used up**, out of stock

ABSENTEE *n* absenter, exile, interstater, truant, wag

ABSENTLY *adv* blankly, dumbly, vacantly; **off**, out

ABSORB *v* assimilate, blot, digest, occlude, soak up, sop up, sponge up, swab; **consume**, devour, down, drink, eat, engorge, gobble, goof, gulf, gulp, imbibe, ingest, ingurgitate, lap, manducate *(Rare)*, raven *(Obs.)*, sip, sup, swallow, take, taste, whet one's whistle; **take in**, drink, drink in, embrace, engulf, import, receive, ship *(Naut.)*; **respire**, aspirate, gasp, inbreathe, inhale, suck in, whiff

ABSORBENT *adj* absorptive, bibulous, hygroscopic, leachy, leaky, pervious, porous, receptive, recipient, spongelike, suctorial; **ingestive**, aspiratory, assimilative, assimilatory, digestive, edacious, inspiratory; **diathermanous**, diathermic; **assimilable**, consumable, digestible, respirable

ABSORBER *n* absorbent, consumer, devourer, digester, embracer, inhiber, inhaler, recipient, soak; **sucker**, aspirator, haustellum *(Crustacean Entomol.)*; **sponge**, activated charcoal, blotting paper, mop, pounce, sanitary napkin, tampon, wettex

ABSORPTION *n* consumption, engorgement, imbibition, importation, ingestion, ingurgitation, occlusion, suction; **assimilation**, digestion, embracement, engulfment; **intake**, gasp, in-draught, inhalation, inrush, in-rushing, inspiration, puff, pull, suck, whiff; **receptiveness**, absorbency, absorptiveness, absorptivity, receptivity, recipience

ABSTAIN *v* deny oneself, forbear, forgo, hold back, mortify oneself, refrain, resist, restrain oneself; **give up**, be on the wagon, be on the water wagon, cold-turkey, cut, eschew, forswear, kick the habit, renounce, swear off, take the pledge; **fast**, count calories, diet, reduce, watch one's waistline

ABSTAINER *n* abstinent, eschewer, faster, forgoer, Lysistratan, monk, nun, old maid, Spartan, Victorian; **ascetic**, mortifier, penitent, puritan; **celibate**, cherry, vestal, vestal virgin, virgin, virgo intacta; **dieter**, weight watcher; **teetotaller**, coldwater man *(Obs.)*, lemon avenue, prohibitionist, total abstainer, waterbag, wowser

ABSTINENCE *n* austerities, cold-turkey, denial, eschewal, fasting, mortification, penance, self-abnegation, self-denial; **asceticism**, austereness, austerity, monachism, monasticism, puritanism; **abstemiousness**, abnegation, abstention, forbearance, frugality, refrainment, sparingness, Spartanism, temperateness; **celibacy**, chastity, continence, honesty *(Archaic)*, intactness, maidenhead, maidenhood, non-access, virginity; **teetotalism**, Prohibition, soberness, sobriety, temperance, the pledge; **dieting**, banting, weight reduction. *See also* FAST

ABSTINENT *adj* abstemious, abstentious, puritanical, self-denying, steady, temperate, Victorian, wowserish; **ascetic**, ascetical, austere; **celibate**, chaste, clean, continent, honest, moral, pure; **virgin**, intact, vestal, virginal; **frugal**, spare, sparing, Spartan; **teetotal**, dry, off the grog, on the square, on the wagon, on the water wagon, sober, sober as a judge, stone-cold sober

ABSTINENTLY *adv* abstemiously, frugally, sparingly; **ascetically**, austerely, self-denyingly; **chastely**, continently, virginally; **teetotally**, soberly, temperately

ABUNDANCE *n* ampleness, bounteousness, bountifulness, copiousness, foison *(Archaic)*, fulsomeness, plenitude, plenteousness, plentifulness, prodigality, prolificacy, prolificness; **plenty**, bonanza, cornucopia, flood, lashings, milk and honey, more where it came from, outpouring, profusion; **generousness**, heartiness, lavishness

ABUNDANT *adj* ample, bounteous, bountiful, copious, cornucopian, enough and to spare, overabundant, plenteous, plentiful, polycarpic *(Bot.)*, profuse, prolific, rampant, superabundant, teeming, wealthy; **hearty**, fulsome, generous, lavish; **fat**, bumper, pregnant, prodigal, rich

ABUNDANTLY *adv* affluently, amply, copiously, innumerably, multitudinously, numerously, plenteously, plentifully, thickly; **manyfold**, manifoldly, variously

ACCELERATE *v* give it herbs, gun *(Aeron.)*, race *(Motor Vehicles)*, rap, rev, step on it, step on the gas *(U.S.)*; **quicken**, pick up, rally *(Theat.)*

ACCELERATOR *n* pedal, quickener, tandem generator, throttle

ACCENT *n* brogue, burr, inflection; **drawl**, drone, gutturalness, hoarseness, monotone, nasality, rhotacism, snuffle, trachyphonia, trill, twang; **dialect**, cockneyism, dialecticism, foreignism, localism, patois; **Received Standard English**, BBC English, cockney, the King's English, the Queen's English; **Australian English**, Broad Australian, Cultivated Australian, General Australian, Modified Australian

ACCESS *n* fairway, gate *(Archaic)*, pass, passage, thoroughfare, way; **right of way**, dedication of way; **way in**, adit, doorway, dromos, entrance, gateway; **way through**, cluse, defile, ghat *(India)*, notch *(U.S.)*, strait *(Archaic)*; **way out**, débouché, exit; **driveway**, approach, avenue *(Brit.)*, drive; **runway**, airstrip, flare-path, tarmac, taxiway

ACCOMPANY *v* associate with, assort *(Archaic)*, bear company with, chaperone, companion, company *(Archaic)*, consort, join with, keep company with, run with; **escort**, arm, conduct, convoy, guide, walk; **follow**, dangle, go around with, hang about, hang round, run around with, string along with; **partner**, see, squire, take out

ACCOMPANYING *adj* appendant, attached, attendant, collateral; **companionate**, associate, associational

ACCOMPLICE *n* abettor, accessory, camorrist, colluder, conspirator, particeps criminis, partner in crime; **ally**, affiliate, aligner, confederate, friend at court; **collaborator**, fellow traveller, fifth columnist, quisling, sympathiser; **factionary**, champion, cultist, factionist, partisan, votary; **follower**, hanger on, henchman, parasite, satellite, stooge, yes-man. *See also* PARTNER

ACCOMPLISH *v* achieve, act up to, attain, break the back of, compass, deliver the goods, discharge, dispatch, dispose of, do, effect, effectuate, execute, expedite, fulfil, perform, procure, produce, produce the goods, realise, transact, turn the trick; **bring off**, bang over, bring about, button up, carry out, carry through, chalk up, fix up, get over, hurdle, knock off, make, make a good job of, make short work of, pull off, put over, put through, surmount, work, work the oracle; **complete**, bring to a head, cap, cast off *(Knitting)*, clinch, conclude, consummate, crown, culminate, finish, put the capper on *(N.Z.)*, round off, succeed

ACCOMPLISHED *adj* a dab hand at, a good hand at, artful, artistic, fine, handsome *(U.S.)*, hot-shot, lighthanded, master, masterful, masterly, nice, notable *(Archaic)*, specialistic, stylish, subtle, virtuoso; **experienced**, au fait, blooded, educated, old, practised, pragmatic, professional, qualified, sure-footed, thoroughbred, thoroughpaced, up-to-date, versed, veteran. *See also* COMPETENT

ACCOMPLISHER *n* achiever, completer, concluder, discharger, effecter, expediter, finisher, fulfiller, succeeder

ACCOMPLISHMENT *n* achievement, attainment, discharge, dispatch, effectuation, execution, implementation, performance, procurance, production, time, transaction; **feat**, blow, coup, deed, effort, exploit, fait accompli, masterstroke, res gestae, stroke, success; **completion**, arrival, close, conclusion, culmination, effect, finish, fruition, rounding off, wind-up; **realisation**, consummation, entelechy, fulfilment

ACCORDING TO RULE *adv* according to Hoyle, bureaucratically, constitutionally, preceptively, prescriptively

ACCOUNT *n* bank account, budget account, capital account, cash account, debtor and creditor account, deposit account, drawing account *(U.S.)*, expense account, joint account, running account, suspense account; **passbook**, bank passbook, bankbook, tally *(Hist.)*; **balance sheet**, bank statement, contract note, group certificate, profit and loss statement, return, statement; **entry**, balance, credit, debit, double entry *(Obs.)*, item, minute, note, record, single entry, tally, trial balance, write-off; **bill**, bills of lading, invoice, itemised bill, reckoning, score, statement, tab, tally, ticket; **receipt**, warrant; **ledger**, budget, cashbook, daybook, folio, inventory, journal, receipt book, register, the books

ACCOUNT *v* audit, bank, budget, inventory, keep accounts, keep books, take stock; **balance**, balance the books, cast up, make accounts square, make square, make up, settle, square, tally, tot up, wind up; **enter**, bill, capitalise, credit, debit, journalise, log, note, post, record, ring up, set off; **write off**, liquidate

ACCOUNTABILITY *n* accountableness, answerableness, avouchment, blamableness, responsibility; **assignability**, attributiveness, imputativeness; **blameworthiness**, blamefulness, culpability, culpableness, guilt

ACCOUNTANT *n* chartered accountant, cost accountant, public accountant; **bookkeeper**, balancer, purser, tallier; **auditor**, auditor-general, comptroller, controller

ACCOUNTING *n* accountancy, bookkeeping, cost accounting, money matters, reckoning; **budgeting**, allocation, batch costing, costing, factoring, job costing, periodising, process costing; **audit**, auditing

ACCUMULATION *n* agglomerate, agglomeration, aggregate, aggregation, collective, conglomerate, cumulation, deposit, glomeration; **collection**, budget, hoard, miscellanea, miscellanies, odds and sods, omnium gatherum, paraphernalia, rhapsody *(Archaic)*, sundries; **hoardings**, gleanings; **backlog**, bank-up, pile-up; **bundle**, bale, faggot, fardel *(Archaic)*, fascicle, sheaf, wisp; **heap**, congeries, cumulus, drift, haymow, hayrick, haystack, hill, mound, pile, pyre, stack; **cluster**, bob, bunch, clump, clutch, knot, whisk; **batch**, battery, crop; **lot**, boodle *(U.S.)*, book, caboodle, nest, set; **package**, packet, parcel, shiralee, truss; **mass**, forest, wilderness; **accumulativeness**, amassment, crowdedness, cumulativeness

ACCUMULATIVE *adj* agglomerative, aggregative, cumulative; **collective**, congregate, congregational, gregarious; **clustered**, aciniform, agminate; **cumulate**, aggregate; **clustery**, clumpish, clumpy; **conglomerate**, agglomerate, conglomeratic, conglomeritic, glomerate

ACCUMULATIVELY *adv* aggregately, collectively, cumulatively, in the aggregate; **together**, crowdedly, en masse, tout ensemble; **gregariously**

ACCUSATION *n* attack, bill, denunciation *(Obs.)*, impeachment, personal action, prosecution; **charge**, arraign *(Obs.)*, arraignment, blame, complaint, count, crimination, frame-up, gravamen, imputation, incrimination, inculpation, indictment, laying of charges, matter, plaint, quantum meruit, rap, reproach; **countercharge**, appeal *(Obs.)*, recrimination, retort; **denunciation**, delation, denounce-

accusation   6   **acrimonious**

ment; **allegation**, implication, innuendo, insinuation

ACCUSATORY *adj* accusatorial, accusing, condemnatory, criminative, denunciatory, inculpatory, invective, recriminative, recriminatory; **incriminatory**, incriminating, inculpatory

ACCUSE *v* complain about, oppugn, tax with; **denounce**, delate, denunciate, hammer *(Stock Exchange)*, put someone's pot on, turn queen's evidence against, turn state's evidence against; **criminate**, crust; **finger**, fit, frame, have the wood on, point the bone at, put the finger on; **allege**, imply, insinuate. *See also* LAY CHARGES

ACCUSED *n* appellee, co-defendant, co-respondent, defendant, prosecutor, respondent, suspect

ACCUSER *n* alleger, arraigner, attacker, charger, complainant, complainer, demandant, impeacher, incriminator, indicter, plaintiff, public prosecutor, taxer; **recriminator**, countercharger; **denouncer**, approver, delator, denunciator, framer, oppugner

ACHE *n* pain, pang, qualm, throb, throe, twinge, twitch; **headache**, hemicrania *(Obs.)*, migraine, sick headache, splitting headache; **earache**, toothache; **backache**, Lebanese back, Mediterranean back, shagger's back; **stomach-ache**, colic, collywobbles, gastralgia, gripes, hunger pain, pain in the gut; **afterpains**, growing pains, phantom limb pains, referred pain, teething pains; **cardialgia**, angina; **hyperalgesia**, arthralgia, brachialgia, causalgia, hemialgia, neuralgia, neuritis. *See also* PAIN

ACOUSTIC *adj* phonic, sonant, sonantal, soniferous, vocal, voiced; **audible**, clear, distinct, heard, plain; **sonic**, infrasonic, subsonic, supersonic; **homophonic**, polyphonic

ACOUSTICS *n* audio, phonics, subsonics, supersonics, tonometry, ultrasonics; **monophonic sound**, mono, quadrophony, stereo, stereophony; **sound wave**, envelope, wave train; **audio frequency**, amplitude, wavelength; **diffraction**, dispersion, equalisation; **sonagraph**, optical sound, Rayleigh disc, spectrograph, tonometer; **bel**, decibel, phon

ACQUIESCENCE *n* compliance, obedience; **amenability**, amenableness, corrigibility, ductility, tractability; **passivity**, meekness, non-resistance, passiveness, resignation, resignedness, tameness, yieldingness

ACQUIT *v* assoil *(Archaic)*, compound, discharge, exonerate, forgive, let off, pardon, purge, remit, reprieve, spare; **absolve**, clear, exculpate, excuse, justify, let out, vindicate; **turn up**, compurge, testify for; **get off**, get up

ACQUITTAL *n* absolution, acquittance, clearance, discharge, dismissal, exoneration, pardon, purgation, quittance, release, remission, reprieve; **excusal**, exculpation, vindication; **nolle prosequi**, autrefois acquit, autrefois attaint, non prosequitur; **amnesty**, immunity

ACQUITTED *adj* clear, exonerated, not guilty, uncondemned; **absolvable**, exculpable, excusable, vindicable

ACRIMONIOUS *adj* acerbate, bitter, caustic, fierce, heated, maenadic, passionate, peppery, rancorous, shrewish, stinging, vehement, virulent, warm; **resentful**, aggrieved, hurt,

acrimonious   7   **act of war**

indignant, peeved, shat off, sulky, sullen

ACRIMONY *n* acrimoniousness, asperity, bitterness, ill feeling, intolerance, rancorousness, rancour, sourness, verjuice; **sullenness**, sulkiness

ACROSS *adv* athwart, o'er *(Poetic)*, over, through, thwart, traverse *(Obs.)*

ACROSS *prep* along, athwart *(Naut.)*, o'er *(Poetic)*, over, per, round, through, thwart

ACT *n* afterpiece, catastasis, drop scene, episode, induction, love-scene, scena, scene, sequence; **routine**, number, show stopper, showpiece; **interlude**, antic *(Archaic)*, antimasque, ballet, curtain-raiser, entr'acte, episode, hokum *(U.S.)*, inset, intermezzo, lollipop, waits; **character sketch**, duologue, impersonation, monologue, monology *(Obs.)*, personation, rendition, representation, sketch, skit; **curtain call**, curtain speech, epilogue, prologue, protasis

ACT DISCOURTEOUSLY *v* commit a solecism, drop a brick, forget oneself, speak out of turn, speak with one's foot in one's mouth, take a liberty, tread on someone's corns, tread on someone's toes; **talk back**, answer back, give someone a short answer, give someone lip

ACT FOR *v* act on behalf of, deputise for, represent, stand in for, subcontract

ACTING *n* mummery, rendering; **characterisation**, portrayal, representation; **Stanislavsky Method**, epic theatre, the Method; **dramatics**, histrionics, staginess, theatricals; **showmanship**, stagecraft, stardom, theatrecraft

ACTION *n* act, deed, delaying action, factum, manoeuvre, move, proceeding, stroke, transaction; **feat**, execution, exploit, gest *(Archaic)*, jest *(Obs.)*, performance, stunt; **practice**, exercitation, hands-on experience, praxis, run-through; **process**, function, progress, unit process; **reaction**, reflex

ACTIVATE *v* action, actuate, energise, galvanise, initiate, provoke, put into commission; **animate**, arouse, excite, rouse, wake up, waken; **revive**, reactivate, reanimate, recrudesce, repeat; **crack the whip**, get things moving

ACTIVATION *n* actuation, animation, arousal, galvanisation, initiation, institution, provocation, reanimation, recrudescence, revival

ACT OF WAR *n* aggression, armed intervention, casus belli, declaration of war, invasion; **battle**, action, armed conflict, brush, charge, clash, combat, contest, dogfight, engagement, fight, fray, incident, melee, pitched battle, raid, rencounter, skirmish, stonk *(Colloq.)*, stoush *(Colloq.)*, toil *(Archaic)*; **war manoeuvre**, combined operations, framework operations, operation, siege, tactic; **campaign**, anabasis, crusade, expedition, mission; **call to arms**, battle cry, cry, marching orders, summons, war cry; **strategy**, battle-orders, commander's concept, concept of operations, deployment, generalship, manoeuvres, orders of the day, plan, tactics; **war game**, field day, naumachia, naumachy; **fortune of war**, outcome of battle; **massacre**, bloodshed, mayhem, pillage; **militarisation**, armament, mobilisation, rearmament, war footing, war measures. *See also* WAR; BATTLEGROUND

ACTOR *n* actress, artist, artiste, character actor, ham, method actor, portrayer, quick-change artist, stager *(Archaic)*, straight man, Thespian, tragedian, tragedienne, trouper; **star**, choragus, co-star, coryphaeus *(Gk. Antiq.)*, film star, lead, leading lady, leading man, matinee idol, megastar, premiere, principal, principal boy, solo, soloist, starlet, superstar; **extra**, bit-player, chorus member, spear-carrier, supernumerary, support, supporting actor, walk-on; **understudy**, double, stand-in, stuntman, substitute; **baddie**, black hat, villain; **feed**, endman; **dame**, figurant, figurante, foil, heavy, ingenue, interlocutor, interlocutress, interlocutrice, interlocutrix, juvenile, pantomime dame, soubrette

ACT PRETENTIOUSLY *v* bung on an act, bung on side, give oneself airs, pile on the agony, put on dog, put on jam, put on the dog, show off, swank; **bedizen**, dandify, lairise; **dramatise**, overdress, overwrite, theatricalise

ACT RASHLY *v* count one's chickens before they are hatched, go at something baldheaded, go off half-cocked, go off the deep end, have a deathwish, plunge in, rush in, rush in where angels fear to tread, rush one's fences; **live dangerously**, adventure, buy a pig in a poke, buy into trouble, chance one's arm, give a hostage to fortune, play a dangerous game, play with fire, put all one's eggs in one basket, ride for a fall, risk, stick one's neck out, take a risk, tempt providence; **go to any length**, be extreme, stick at nothing; **burn one's fingers**, get out of one's depth

ACTUALISE *v* crystallise, give rise to, hypostatise, objectify, objectivise, realise

ACTUALITY *n* actualness, concreteness, entelechy, here, here and now, immediacy, objectivity, reality, realness, solidity, substance, substantiveness, the real, truth, verity; **object**, entity, fact, noumenon, realia, subject, substantial, substratum, thing, thing-in-itself. *See also* REALITY

ACTUALLY *adv* as a matter of fact, concretely, existentially, factually, for real, in fact, in reality, in substance, in truth, indeed, solidly, substantively

ACT UNFAIRLY *v* be on the grouter, come in on the grouter, take advantage, take unfair advantage; **discriminate**, discriminate against, favour, gerrymander, load the scales, rig, rob Peter to pay Paul, stack; **not play the game**, break the rules, commit a foul, hit below the belt

ACT UNKINDLY *v* bear malice towards, cut, disoblige, do someone a bad turn, offend, put someone's nose out of joint; **bully**, abuse, browbeat, hector, victimise; **torment**, bedevil, harry, hound, persecute, play cat and mouse with, torture; **harm**, come the acid over *(N.Z.)*, give no quarter to, give someone hell, hurt, maltreat, ride roughshod over, spitchcock *(Rare)*; **brutalise**, brutify, dehumanise

ADD *v* admix, annex, append, attach, enlarge, heap, lend, piggyback, postfix, subjoin, suffix, superinduce, tack on, tag, throw in; **add to**, accessorise; **supplement**, accrete, round out,

add   9   adhesive

superadd, superimpose on; **interpolate,** grangerise, intercalate, interject, interpose; **footnote,** note; **be additional,** advene, supervene

ADDITION *n* accession, accruement, additive, adjunct, affix, alts and adds, annexation, annexe, appendance, appendant, appurtenance, appurtenant, attachment, bonus, enlargement, interpolation, mixture, postfix, postscript, prolongation, streak, subjunction, superaddition, superimposition, superinducement, superinduction, supplementation; **total,** subtotal, sum, summation; **appendage,** appendicle, arm, fin, flap, label, lapel, lappet, tab, tag, tailpiece, wing; **accompaniment,** accessory, accretion, accrual, accumulation, admixture, extension, increase, increment, makeweight, trappings. *See also* MORE; POSTSCRIPT

ADDITIONAL *adj* another, appendiculate, codicillary, follow-up, fresh, incidental, more, new, second, supernumerary; **additive,** accretive, adjunctive, incremental, interpolative; **annexed,** accessorial, accessory, appendant, appertaining, appurtenant, attached, belonging, incident; **supplementary,** ancillary, auxiliary, subsidiary, supplemental; **extra,** bonus, further, over, plus, surplus

ADDITIONALLY *adv* adjunctively, caudally, extensionally, in addition, subscriptively, supplementally, supplementarily; **moreover,** at that, beyond, by the way, farther, further, furthermore, incidentally, more, yea *(Archaic);* **as well,** also, and all, beside, besides, either, eke *(Archaic),* else, even, for good measure, into the bargain, item *(Obs.),* likewise, nay, to boot, too, withal *(Archaic);* yet; **and so on,** and all that, and all that jazz, and so forth, and then some, and what have you, and what not, et al, et cetera, etc.

ADDRESS *n* box number, direction, postcode, redirection, superscript *(Obs.),* superscription, zipcode *(U.S.)*

ADEQUACY *n* adequateness, all that could be desired, enough, full measure, reasonableness, satisfaction, store, sufficiency; **quorum,** right number; **repletion,** bellyful, one's fill; **minimum,** least one can do, no less; **competence,** competency, effectuality, effectualness, worthiness; **one's due,** one's just deserts

ADEQUATE *adj* enough, equal to one's needs; **sufficient,** self-sufficient; **satisfactory,** decent, fair, reasonable; **barely sufficient,** bare, scant, scanty; **competent,** effectual, equal to the task

ADEQUATELY *adv* due *(Archaic),* duly, enough, reasonably, sufficiently; **abundantly,** amply, bounteously, bountifully, copiously, fulsomely, plenteously, plentifully; **generously,** lavishly; **effectually,** competently

ADHESIVE *n* adherer, agglutinant, binding, cohesive, fixative, goo, stick; **binder,** bind, bond, bonder; **uniter,** binder, bonder, gluer; **burr,** clinger; **adhesive tape,** durex, Scotch tape, Sellotape, sticky tape, wafer; **glue,** araldite, arming, birdlime, clag, clearcole, contact cement, contact glue, dextrin, fish glue, gluten, glyptal resin, glyptol, gum, mucilage, original gum, paste, propolis, size, solder, spirit gum, starch-gum; **grout,** luting, putty, sealant, sealing wax, wax; **cement,** compo, concrete, mortar, mud, plaster, ready-mix

adjudicator — advance

ADJUDICATOR *n* arbitrator, arbitress, concluder, condemner, decider, determiner, disposer, judge, judger, judicator, juror, jury; **referee**, central umpire, field umpire, goal umpire, ref, third man, touch judge, ump, umpie, umpire

ADJUST *v* adapt, correct *(Physics)*, phase in, regularise, shape; **accommodate**, attune, get it together, move with the times, reconcile; **match**, find one's level, register, synchronise, track

ADJUSTMENT *n* accommodation, compromise, conformation, reconcilement, reconciliation, settlement, settling, standardisation, synchronisation

ADMINISTRATIVE AREA *n* canton *(Switzerland)*, city, commonwealth, constituency, county, department *(France)*, division, electorate, municipality, oblast *(Russia)*, precinct *(U.S.)*, province, riding, satrapy *(Obs.)*, shire, state, subdivision, town, ward

ADMIRABLENESS *n* acceptability, commendableness, exemplariness, favourableness, laudability, laudableness, praiseworthiness, splendidness, unobjectionableness

ADOLESCENT *n* grommet, juvenile, spring chicken, teenager, teenybopper, youngling, youth; **lad**, colt, cub, debutant, fledgling, hobbledehoy, pup, puppy, sapling, shaveling *(Archaic)*, shaver, sprig, stripling, younker *(Archaic)*; **hoodlum**, larrikin, yob; **bodgie**, mod, punk, rocker, skinhead, surfie, ted, teddy boy; **lass**, damsel, debutante, filly, mademoiselle, maid, maiden; **nymphette**, carnie; **widgie**, bobbysoxer *(U.S.)*, bud;

youthful person, evergreen, Peter Pan, young blood

A DRINK *n* drop of the old religion *(Brit.)*, aperitif, bracer, charge, chaser, chug-a-lug, coaster *(Obs.)*, dram, drop, drop of the doings, drop of the needle, gargle, hair of the dog that bit you, heart-starter, hooker, Jimmy Woodser, lace, lacing, leg opener, mickey, Mickey Finn, nightcap, nip, nobbler, one for the bitumen, one for the gutter, one for the road, pipe-opener, potation, quickie, reviver, rosiner, shot *(U.S.)*, slug, snifter, snort, snorter, spot, sting, stirrup cup, sundowner, swig, the other half, tipple, toast, tot

ADVANCE *n* advancement, course, distance, going forwards, headway, march, movement, passage, process, progress, progression, race *(Archaic)*, way *(Naut.)*; **encroachment**, invasion, trespass; **surge**, effluxion, floodtide, flow, flux, onrush, press, push, rush, stream, sweep, wave, whirlwind; **forward position**, forefront, forwardness, front, head, head, lead, van, vanguard; **head start**, lead, lead time, start

ADVANCE *v* amble, continue, cover the ground, follow, go on, jog, make headway, make one's way, make progress, make strides, move, nose forward, precede, press forward, proceed, progress, push forward, shoot along, shoot through, stalk, take, thread, travel ahead, travel on, walk, wend *(Archaic)*; **come up to**, arrive at, breast, come abreast of; **close in**, approach, draw in; **bring up**, bring on, march forward, track in *(Film)*; **encroach**, advance on, head into, head towards, impinge on, impinge upon, invade, make tracks for; **pull ahead,**

burn ahead, gain ground, lose, make up leeway, outstrip, overhaul, overtake, pass, plough through *(Naut.)*, stem; **advance relentlessly,** forge ahead, juggernaut, steamroller; **crowd,** hustle, press; **surge,** flood, roll, rush, sweep

ADVANCED *adj* first, foremost, forward, leading, up; **advancing,** coming, forward moving, go-ahead, ongoing, onward, proceeding, processional, progressing, progressional, progressive, sweeping

ADVANTAGE *n* benefit, profit, vantage; **upper hand,** command, high ground, trump card, vantage ground, vantage point; **flying start,** edge, jump, lead, odds, pull, start; **privilege,** favour; **advantageousness,** desirability, preferability, preferableness

ADVANTAGEOUS *adj* beneficial, desirable, preferable

AERATED *adj* aeriferous, bubbly, carbonated, oxygenated; **inflated,** blown up, puffy; **well-ventilated,** air-conditioned

AERIAL *n* antenna, dipole, direction-finder, ferrite-rod aerial, rabbit ears, Yagi aerial

AEROLOGY *n* aerodynamics, aerography, aeromechanics, aerometry, aerostatics, anemometry, barometry, pneumatics, pneumatology *(Obs.),* pneumovinometry, spherics

AEROPLANE *n* air ambulance, air-taxi, airbus, airliner, biplane, bird, canard, cantilever, charter plane, convertiplane, fixed-wing aircraft, flying wing, freighter, glider-tug, goony bird, jet, jetliner, jumbo, jump-jet, monocoque, monoplane, penguin, plane, propjet, pusher, semi-monocoque, ski-plane, STOL, stratocruiser, stressed skin, swing-wing, tanker, tractor, transport, triplane, turbojet, turboprop, VTOL, wing; **air force,** bomber, dive-bomber, fighter, fighter-bomber, helicopter gunship, interceptor, pathfinder, spotter, spotter plane, troop-carrier, warplane *(U.S.)*

AESTHETE *n* artist, cognoscente, connoisseur, critic, culture-vulture, culturist, epicure, fusspot, gentleman, gourmet, highbrow, judge, lady, virtuoso

A FEW *n* a handful, just one or two, trickle, two men and a dog; **the few,** minority, remnant

AFFAIR *n* business, concern, job; matter, piece, present *(Obs.),* spin *(Colloq.),* thing. See also OCCURRENCE; SITUATION

AFFECTATION *n* beau geste, dramatisation, frill, mannerism, postiche, pretence, pretension; **airs,** airs and graces, dramatics, graces, histrionics; **act,** attitude, manner, pose, side; **schmalz,** bathos, crocodile tears, simper, snivel, sob-stuff, treacle; **varnish,** shoddy, veneer

AFFECTED *adj* all piss 'n' wind, artificial, arty, dramatic, exhibitionistic, factitious, forced, hammy, histrionic, laboured, mannered, missish, over-produced, studied, theatrical, unnatural; **pretentious,** arty-crafty, arty-farty, bombastic *(Obs.),* bombastical *(Obs.),* flatulent, piss-elegant, prestige, swank, up-market; **snobbish,** condescending, gracious, grand, grandiose, high-sounding, highfalutin, jumped-up, la-di-da, la-di-dady, Pecksniffian, snooty, snotnosed, snotty, snotty-nosed, toffee-nosed

(Brit.); **dandyish,** all ponced up, buckish, coxcombical, mincing, minikin, peacockish, peacocky, poncy, sparkish, strutting; **precious,** coy, fallal *(Obs.)*, foppish, niminy-piminy, rosewater, simpering, twee; **schmalzy,** crocodilian, sawney, soppy, soupy, treacly, unctuous; **donnish,** hypercorrect, pedantic, pedantical, precise; **priggish,** dandy, fine, genteel, goody-goody, mealy-mouthed, old-maidish, prim, prissy, proper, prudish, superfine; **hypocritical,** tongue-in-cheek

AFFECTEDLY *adv* artificially, factitiously, forcedly, histrionically, studiedly, theatrically, unnaturally; **pretentiously,** bombastically *(Obs.)*, flatulently; **foppishly,** coyly, gingerly *(Obs.)*, mincingly, prancingly, preciously, simperingly; **donnishly,** pedantically; **priggishly,** genteelly, primly

AFFECTEDNESS *n* artificiality, artificialness, factitiousness, forcedness, hype, hypocrisy, overelaborateness, studiedness, theatricality, theatricalness, unnaturalness; **pretentiousness,** bombast, condescendence, flatulence, flatulency, graciosity, grandiosity, magniloquence, pomposity, snobbery, stiltedness; **soppiness,** treacliness, unctuosity, unctuousness; **foppery,** coquetry, coxcombry, foppishness; **preciosity,** coyness, preciousness; **pedantry,** donnishness, preciseness, precision; **genteelness,** piss-elegance; **priggery,** priggishness, primness, sanctimony

AFFECTED PERSON *n* actor, actress, affecter, artiste, attitudiniser, drama queen, dramatiser, hypocrite, poser, poseuer; **dandy,** adonis, beau, buck, coxcomb, dude *(U.S.)*, exquisite, fop, gay, gay blade, jackanapes, lair, macaroni, masher *(Obs.)*, peacock, ponce, prancer, prig *(Archaic)*, show pony, spark, turkey cock, two-bob lair, ultra; **arty,** culture-vulture; **snob,** buckeen, bunyip aristocracy, his Lordship, Lady Muck, Lord Muck, snoot, snot, snotnose, snotty nose, stuffed shirt; **Grand Pooh-Bah,** panjandrum; **pedant,** bush-lawyer; **sniveller,** crocodile, simperer; **pharisee,** holy Joe, pietist, religionist, Tartuffe

AFFIRMATION *n* attestation, confirmation, corroboration, endorsement, homologation, ratification; **approval,** accession, assent, consent, okay, Royal assent, sanction, support; **avowal,** acknowledgment, cognovit, confession, recognition; **acceptance,** accession, acquiescence, adoption, resignation, sanctification, subscription; **the affirmative,** affirmative, amen, ay, placet, pro, the nod, yea, yes. *See also* AGREEMENT

AFTER *adv* next, proximately, proximo, second, secondarily, secondly; **afterwards,** since, thereon, thereupon, therewith; **behind,** in the tracks of, in the wake of, posteriorly, postpositively, ulteriorly; **hereunder,** below, et seq, hereinafter, thereinafter; **consequently,** ex post facto, in consequence, subsequently, thus

AFTERNOON *n* afto, arvo, midafternoon, p.m.

AFTERWORLD *n* afterlife, beyond, hereafter, other world, the other side; **underworld,** Hades, limbo, lower world, nether regions, nether world, Shades, Sheol; **Dreamtime,** alchera, alcheringa; **nirvana,** atman, Brahma. *See also* HEAVEN; HELL

AGE *n* chronological age, life-span, longevity, three score and ten; **old age,** eighties, elderliness, Indian summer, nineties, seventies, sixties; **agedness,** ancientness, oldness, senescence; **senility,** anecdotage, dotage, second childhood; **middle age,** certain age, change of life, climacteric, menopause; **autumn,** autumn of life, mellowness; **adulthood,** adultness, age of consent, age of discretion, drinking age, driving age, full age, legal age, majority, manhood, matronage, maturity, prime, prime of life, summer, voting age, womanhood; **maturity,** matureness, ripeness; **marriageability,** marriageableness, nubility; **geratology,** geriatrics, gerontology, nostology; **geriatrician,** gerontologist; **age-group,** generation, peer group

AGE *v* flower, grow old, grow out of, grow up, mature, mellow, number, ripen; **have had a good innings,** have one foot in the grave; **decline,** wane; **outlive,** overlive *(Obs.)*

AGED *adj* advanced in years, ancient, autumnal, elderly, frosty, grey, grey-headed, hoary, in the sere and sallow, long in the tooth, long-lived, longeval, of a ripe old age, old, old as Methuselah, old as the hills, white-haired, white-headed; **anile,** haggish; **senile,** burnt out, decrepit, doddering, doting, gaga, over the hill, past it, past one's prime, run to seed; **ageing,** declining, failing, getting on, in one's declining years, oldish, senescent, with one foot in the grave; **venerable,** matriarchal, patriarchal; **retired,** pensioned off, superannuated; **geriatric,** nostologic; **centenarian,** nonagenary, octogenary, quinquagenary, septu-

agenary, sexagenary; **mature,** adult, full-grown, fully-fledged, grown, grown-up, mellowed, of age, over-age; **middle-aged,** of a certain age; **menopausal,** menopausic; **marriageable,** nubile, ripe and ready; **elder,** aîné, eldest, major *(Brit.)*, senior

AGEDLY *adv* mellowly, autumnally, maturely, ripely; **on the shady side of,** upwards of

AGENCY *n* instrument, instrumentation, machine, operation, procuration *(Obs.)*; **mission,** brevet, commission, errand; **embassy,** chancellery, consulate, legation, viceconsulate; **assignment,** delegacy

AGENDA *n* docket *(U.S.)*, notice paper *(Parl. Proc.)*, program, schedule, timetable; **repertoire,** repertory, stock *(Theat.)*; **menu,** range of options, set of alternatives; **bill of fare,** carte, diet chart, menu, table d'hôte, tariff; **questionnaire,** ballot paper, survey, unity ticket

AGENT *n* apparatchik, clerk of works, depositary, mandatary, proctor, receiver, representative, subagent, vicar; **deputy,** appointee, fill-in, spokesman, spokesperson, spokeswoman, substitute, surrogate, vice-chairman; **actor,** coexecutor, coexecutrix, contractor, doer, executor, executor de son tort, executrix, factotum, palatine, performer, practitioner, subcontractor; **viceroy,** crown agent, governor-general, lieutenant governor, state governor, vice-regent, vicegerent. *See also* DELEGATE: AMBASSADOR

AGENTIAL *adj* proctorial, representational, representative, vice-regal, vicegeral; **acting,** deputy; **ambassadorial,** commissarial, consular, diplo-

agential   14   **aim at**

matic, legatine, legationary, official, proconsular, vice-consular, **vicarious,** delegated, vicarial

AGGRESSIVE *adj* aggro *(Colloq.),* assailant, belligerent, combative, hawkish, militant, persecutive, persecutory, spoiling for a fight, truculent; **predatory,** depredatory, incursive, offensive

AGGRESSIVELY *adv* belligerently, harassingly, offensively, truculently

AGITATE *v* disturb, startle, tempest *(Obs.),* traumatise, trouble, unfix, unsettle, wimple; **shake,** jiggle, joggle, succuss, toss about, vex *(Archaic);* **ferment,** hot up; **beat,** cheddar, churn, cream, mill, move, muddle *(U.S.),* popple, stir, stoke, whip, whisk; **torment,** disturb, roil, stir, vex, worry

A GOOD TIME *n* ball, feast, field day, high time, idyll, picnic, time of one's life; **pastime,** amusement, dissipation, hobby, sport; **red-letter day,** special occasion; **dolce vita,** gracious living, high life, life of Riley; **paradise,** Eden, Elysium, heaven, land of milk and honey, lucky country; **a place in the sun,** a bed of roses, a good scene, clover, featherbed, lap of luxury, the primrose path

AGREE *v* arrange, close up on, close with, consent *(Obs.),* cotton *(Colloq.),* harmonise, meet, run parallel, see eye to eye, settle, shake, shake hands, unite; **sympathise,** empathise; **accord,** act together, attune, concert

AGREEABILITY *n* agreeableness, compliableness, conformability, conformableness, reconcilability, reconcilableness

AGREEABLE *adj* agreeably disposed, amenable, bent upon, complacent *(Archaic),* complaisant, compliant, desirous, disposed, easygoing, favourably disposed, inclined, minded, of a mind to, predisposed, willing; **happy to,** apt *(Archaic),* content, fain *(Archaic),* glad, lief *(Archaic),* nothing loath, ready; **wholehearted,** ungrudging, unmurmuring; **prompt,** alacritous, spontaneous; **voluntary,** gratuitous, ultroneous *(Rare),* unasked for, unforced, volunteer

AGREEMENT *n* accord, complaisance, compliance, concord, concurrence, consensus, covenant, facility, general agreement, unanimity; **harmony,** accord, accordance, amity, arrangement, common ground, compatibility, concert, concord, congeniality, consent *(Archaic),* consentaneity, consentaneousness, consentience, consonance, empathy, esprit de corps, fellow feeling, meeting point, rapport, settlement, solidarity, sympathy, team spirit, understanding, unity; **compliance,** coexistence, conformance, conformity; **reconciliation,** accommodation, atonement *(Obs.),* détente, rapprochement, reconcilement. *See also* AFFIRMATION

AIM *n* ambition, be-all and end-all, errand, ideal, mecca, mission, object, target, view; **goal,** bourn, butt *(Obs.),* destination; **target,** bird, butt, chase, checkpoint, clay pigeon, dartboard, inner, mark, pin, popinjay, tee; **purpose,** end, intention, purport, sake

AIM AT *v* affect *(Archaic),* aspire to, intend, meditate, premeditate, pretend to, purpose

AIR *n* air-mass; **fresh air**, open, open air, out-of-doors, ozone, sea air, the great outdoors; **sky**, ether, the blue, the heavens; **thin air**, ethereality, etherealness, rarity; **gas**, compressed air, nitrogen, oxygen

AIR *v* expose, give an airing; **ventilate**, air-condition; **aerate**, activate, carbonate, oxygenate; **blow up**, inflate; **puff up**, balloon out, blouse out

AIRCRAFT *n* aerodyne, craft, delta wing, flying machine, kite, ship; **helicopter**, autogyro, chopper, copter, egg-beater, gyrocopter, gyroplane, ornithopter, rotary wing aircraft, rotorcraft, whirlybird *(U.S.)*; **flying boat**, amphibian, float plane, hydroplane, seaplane; **glider**, box kite, hang-glider, kite, sailplane, soarer; **parachute**, brolly *(Brit.)*, canopy, chute, drogue; **aerostat**, airship, balloon, blimp, captive balloon, dirigible, kite balloon, montgolfier, sausage, zeppelin; **gondola**, car, nacelle; **UFO**, bogy, flying saucer, magic carpet

AIRFLOW *n* advection, air-cushion, current, down draught, in-draught, jet stream, slipstream, thermal, up draught, wind; **turbulence**, air-pocket, airhole, backwash, backwind, bump, burble *(Aeron.)*, dirty wind, downwash, pocket, wash

AIRING *n* air-conditioning, flow-through ventilation, ventilation

AIRPORT *n* aerodrome, hangar; **runway**, apron, landing strip, tarmac, threshold; **air traffic control**, control tower, ground control

AIRWAY *n* air-drive, air-duct, air-intake, airshaft, louvre, vent, ventilator; **air-conditioner**, demister, exhaust fan, fan; **inflator**, aerator, bicycle pump, pump; **air-chamber**, air-jacket

AIRY *adj* elemental, elementary, ethereal; **pneumatic**, aerologic, aeromechanic, aeromechanical, aerometric, aerostatic; **aerobiotic**, aerobic; **aerial**, airborne, flying

ALARM *v* consternate, disquiet, distress, unhinge, unnerve, unsettle, unstring; **worry**, eat, exercise, trouble

ALAS *interj* alack *(Archaic)*, deary-me, heigh-ho, lack a day *(Archaic)*, misery me, oh dear, oh no, wellaway *(Archaic)*, woe, woe is me

ALCOHOL *n* aqua vitae, ardent spirits, bombo, bootleg *(U.S.)*, booze, brewage, cordial *(U.S.)*, drink, ethanol, ethyl alcohol, firewater, grain alcohol, grave-digger *(Brit. Mil.)*, grog, gutrot, hard stuff, home-brew, hooch *(U.S.)*, ink, juice, La Perouse, Lady Blamey, liquor, lunatic soup, lush, plonk, pot, purge *(N.Z.)*, rotgut, rum *(U.S.)*, shicker, skinful, slosh *(Brit.)*, snake juice, spirits of wine, stagger juice, swipes, the bottle, turps, waipiro *(N.Z.)*, wallop; **intoxicant**, inebriant, stimulant; **sly grog**, hooch *(U.S.)*, moonshine, mountain dew, Old Hokanni *(N.Z.)*, poteen *(Irish)*; **methylated spirits**, bush champagne, jungle juice, metho, musical milk, white angel, white lady. *See also* A DRINK: BEER: WINE

ALCOHOL CONTAINER *n* balthazar, eighteen, keg, nine, pig *(N.Z.)*, pipe, wineskin; **beer glass**, bobby *(W.A.)*, bumper, butcher *(S.A.)*, cruiser, half, handle, jar, lady's waist, long-sleever, middy, pint, pixie *(Vic.)*, pony, pot, pottle, schooner, tankard; **stubby**, baby, Darwin stubby, echo *(S.A.)*, frostie, glass can; **wine measure**, jigger, noggin, tot; **can**, tinnie, tube

ALCOTEST *n* Alcolmeter, bag test, blue balloon, booze bus, breathalyser

ALLERGY *n* hay fever, hypersensitivity, idiosyncrasy, photoallergy, pollinosis

ALLEVIANT *adj* alleviating, assuasive, balmy, balsamaceous, balsamic, emollient, lenient *(Archaic)*, lenitive, palliative, sooth, soothing; **analgesic**, anodyne, paregoric, sedative; **soothed**, comfortable, easeful, easy

ALLEVIATE *v* adduce *(Obs.)*, allay, assuage, ease, lighten, mitigate, palliate, sweeten; **soothe**, attemper, comfort, give comfort to, hush, mollify, pat on the back, pour oil on troubled waters, salve, set at ease, solace; **relieve**, disburden, disembarrass, disencumber, free, reprieve, rescue, respite; **clear the air**, get off someone's back, lay off, smooth the ruffled brow of care, temper the wind to the shorn lamb

ALLEVIATION *n* abatement, assuagement, easement, easing, mitigation, palliation, relaxation, relief, remission; **deliverance**, disburdenment, disembarrassment, reprieve, rescue, respite, rest, truce; **solace**, appeasement, comfort, consolation, mollification, solacement, soothing; **ease**, analgesia, lightness, sedation

ALLEVIATOR *n* allayer, assuager, comforter, easer, mitigator, pacifier, palliator, reliever, solacer, soother; **salve**, alleviant, alleviative, balm, balsam, comfort, lenitive *(Rare)*, palliative; **analgesic**, anodyne, paregoric, sedative

ALLIANCE *n* coalition, combine, confederacy, confederation, league, pie

ALLOWANCE *n* beer money, expenses, housekeeping, maintenance, pin money, pocket-money, spending money, tip, viaticum; **subsidy**, deficiency payment; **scholarship**, bursary, exhibition; **alms**, charity, collection, maundy *(Brit.)*, maundy money *(Brit.)*, offering; **expenditure**, disbursement. *See also* FUNDS

ALL THAT GLITTERS IS NOT GOLD *phr* don't judge a sausage by its shiny overcoat, you can't judge a book by its cover

ALLURE *n* amiability, animal magnetism, appeal, attraction, charisma, charm, cynosure, fascination, glam, glamour, it, magic, oomph, sex appeal, sunny disposition, winning ways, zest; **draw**, drawcard; **lure**, allurement, attraction, bait, captivation, come-on, counterattraction, enchantment, engagement, enticement, fascination, inducement, magnetism, spell; **seduction**, cajolery, honeyed words, inveiglement, invitation, solicitation, temptation; **entanglement**, ensnarement, entrapment; **trap**, birdlime, booby trap, butterfly net, drawnet, hook, lure, mesh, rat-trap, snare, springe, tin hare, toils, wire

ALLURE *v* attempt *(Archaic)*, attract, becharm, beguile, captivate, charm, court, enamour, enmesh, entice, fascinate, intrigue, inveigle, invite, magnetise *(Obs.)*, make *(Colloq.)*, mesmerise, seduce, smite, tantalise, titillate, toll *(Obs.)*, trepan *(Archaic)*, vamp, wheedle, witch; **lure**, bait, catch, ensnare, entrap, mesh, waylay

allurer *n* attractor, bewitcher, captivator, charmer, desirable, dish, dreamboat, enchanter, engager, enthraller, enticer, fascinator, forbidden fruit, inviter, lady-killer, magnet, magnetiser, object of desire, object of lust, seducer, sex object, sex symbol, tempter; **siren**, a bit of fluff, Circe, Delilah, enchantress, femme fatale, mantrap, Mata Hari, nymphette, pin-up, seductress, temptress, twat, vamp, vamper, witch; **stud**, Don Juan, masher *(Archaic)*, rake, sheikh *(Archaic)*, sugar daddy, wolf; **gold-digger**, inveigler; **ensnarer**, entrapper, spider, trapper, waylayer

alluring *adj* amorous, appealing, appetising, attractive, bed-worthy, buxom, Circean, come-hither, cuddlesome, cuddly, delectable, desirable, enticing, flirtatious, glam, glamorous, intriguing, inviting, kinky, kissable, kittenish, lush, much in demand, oomphy, pin-up, piquant, provocative, racy, ravishing, seductive, sensual, sexy, siren, stimulating, tantalising, tempting, thrilling, voluptuous, well-endowed, well-hung, well-proportioned, well-rounded, winsome, zesty; **charismatic**, bewitching, captivating, catching, charming, enchanting, engaging, fascinating, fetching, impressive, interesting, irresistible, magic, magnetic, prepossessing, striking, taking, winning, witching

alluringly *adv* attractively, buxomly, desirably, enticingly, glamorously, intriguingly, invitingly, kittenishly, piquantly, ravishingly, seductively, sexily, temptingly, witchingly, zestily; **appealingly**, bewitchingly, charismatically, enchantingly, engagingly, fascinatingly, fetchingly, irresistibly, magically, magnetically, strikingly

alluringness *n* attractiveness, bedworthiness, buxomness, desirability, desirableness, engagingness, invitingness, irresistibility, irresistibleness, kittenishness, lushness, seductiveness, sexiness, sugariness, temptingness, winsomeness, witchery

allusion *n* hint, implication, innuendo, insinuation, intimation, rumour, suggestion, undercurrent, word; **connotation**, overtone, predication, sub-text, subaudition; **indication**, adumbration, prefigurement

allusive *adj* allusory, insinuative, oblique, suggestive; **implicational**, connotative, implicative, indicative, predicative; **implicit**, half-spoken, implied, tacit, undeclared, understood, unexpressed, unspoken, unvoiced, unwritten; **latent**, below the surface, dormant, potential, sleeping, underlying, undeveloped, unsuspected; **obscure**, arcane, esoteric, unexplored

allusiveness *n* implicitness, obliqueness, obliquity, suggestiveness, tacitness; **latency**, more than meets the eye, potentiality

almost *adv* about, all but, approximately, chock, for all practical purposes, give or take, most *(U.S.)*, nearly, practically, proximately, pushing, rising, thereabouts, upon the point of, wellnigh. *See also* CLOSELY

almshouse *n* refuge, settlement, shelter, social settlement

alone *adv* like a bandicoot on a burnt ridge, like a country dunny, like a lily on a dirt box, like a lily on a dustbin, like a petunia in an onion

alone   18   **amount**

patch, like a shag on a rock, on one's ace, on one's own, on one's Pat, on one's Pat Malone, single-handedly, solitarily, solo, solus, with the flies

ALPHABETICAL *adj* abecedarian, alphabetic, alphanumeric

ALTERNATE *v* interchange, intermit, reciprocate, recur, take turns, vary; **cycle**, circulate, revolve, roll round, rotate, run, turn

ALTIMETER *n* almucantar, cathetometer, ceilometer, hypsometer, orometer, radio altimeter, water-gauge; **altimetry**, hypsography, hypsometry, isometry

AMALGAMATION *n* consolidation, embodiment, federalisation, fusion, integration, merger, unification; **affiliation**, filiation, membership; **institutionalism**, officialism, regimentation

AMBASSADOR *n* ambassador extraordinary, ambassador plenipotentiary, ambassador-at-large *(U.S.)*, ambassadress, career diplomat, chargé d'affaires, diplomat, diplomatist, high commissioner, minister resident, resident *(Brit.)*; **attaché**, commissioner, consular agent, cultural attache, first secretary, minister, second secretary; **consul**, consul general, proconsul, representative, vice-consul; **papal nuncio**, ablegate, commissary, internuncio, legate, nuncio, vicar; **diplomatic corps**, corps diplomatique; **persona grata**, persona non grata. *See also* AGENT; DELEGATE

AMBASSADORSHIP *n* commissionership, consulate, consulship, executorship, legateship, nunciature, surrogateship, vicarship, vice-chairmanship, vice-consulship, vice-regency, vicegerency, viceroyship

AMENABLY *adv* plastically, pliably, pliantly, sensitively, susceptibly

AMID *prep* amidst, mid, midst

AMMUNITION *n* ammo, munitions; **bullet**, cannonball, cartouche, cartridge, dumdum, magazine, pellet, projectile, rubber bullet, slow bullet, slug, torpedo, tracer bullet; **gunpowder**, cordite, dynamite, explosive, gelignite, guncotton, high explosive, propellant, salt-petre, smokeless powder, T.N.T.; **shot**, canister, cannon shot, case shot, chain-shot, drop shot, dust-shot, grape, grapeshot, langrage, lead, load, round-shot, shrapnel; **percussion cap**, ball, cap, pineapple *(Colloq.)*; **shell**, gas shell, grenade, hand grenade, hang-fire, incendiary, rifle grenade, sabot, whiz-bang; **detonator**, booster; **cannelure**, twist; **nuclear warhead**, nose-cone, war nose, warhead; **chemical weapon**, blister gas, diphosgene, fireball, gas, lewisite, liquid fire, mustard gas, napalm, nerve gas, phosgene, poison gas, stinkpot, vesicant, yellow rain. *See also* BOMB; ARSENAL

AMOUNT *n* complement, matter, number, proportion, quantity, quantum, sum; **batch**, boiling, brewing, cast *(Metall.)*, churning, lot, make, making, measure, pour, shear, shower; **haul**, catch, draught, take; **load**, boatful, cartload *(Obs.)*, keel, lift, pack, pitch, shipload, shipment, wagonload; **supply**, flow, output, yield; **dose**, dosage, overdose; **bagful**, armful, barrelful, basinful, boxful, dipperful, dishful, fistful, forkful, glassful, handful, hatful, kettleful, lapful, pipeful, plateful, pocketful, potful, sackful, shovelful, spadeful; **miscellaneous quantities**, butt, cordage, escort return, frail, haymow, job lot, pocket *(Tas.)*, reel. *See also* BIT

AMPHIBIAN *adj* amphibiotic, amphibious, batrachian; **froglike**, anuran, toadlike

AMULET *n* charm, Christopher medal, force-field, palladium, phylactery *(Archaic)*, scarab, scarabaeus, talisman

AMUSE *v* distract, divert, tickle

AMUSED *adj* distracted, diverted, entertained; **sportive**, frisky, frolicsome, gamesome, larksome, playful, rompish, sportful

AMUSEMENT *n* disport *(Archaic)*, distraction, diversion, divertissement, entertainment, game, pastime, recreation, relaxation, sport; **toy**, plaything, puzzle; **romp**, buffoonery, buster *(U.S.)*, frolic, horseplay, jinks, lark, shine, spree; **sportiveness**, frolicsomeness, gamesomeness, rompishness, sportfulness; **fun and games**, beer and skittles, bobsy-die, enjoyment, fun, play, pleasure; **revelry**, carnival, merrymaking, whoopee; **bush week**, capping day *(N.Z.)*, festivities, gaieties, gaudy *(Brit.)*, revels; **playtime**, break

AMUSEMENT PARK *n* carnival, fair, fun park, funfair; **fairground amusements**, Aunt Sally *(Brit.)*, big dipper, carousel, coaster *(U.S.)*, coconut shy, Ferris wheel, helter-skelter, merry-go-round, river caves, roller-coaster, roundabout, scenic railway, sideshow, swing boat, switchback, whirlabout, whirligig; **play centre**, creative leisure centre, day centre; **fun parlour**, amusement arcade, casino, midway *(U.S.)*, penny arcade, poolroom; **playroom**, cubbyhouse, nursery, playhouse, rumpus room, Wendy house;

playground, adventure playground, park, sandpit; **swing**, jungle gym, monkey bars, seesaw, slide, slippery dip

AMUSE ONESELF *v* disport oneself, have fun, play, recreate, sport; **trifle**, dabble, dally, toy, toy with; **romp**, fool around, frisk, frolic, gambol, horse about, play silly buggers, play up, skylark

AMUSING *adj* distractive, diversionary, diverting, divertive, entertaining, fun, light, recreational

ANAESTHESIA *n* anaesthetisation, etherisation, thermanaesthesia; **analgesia**, abirritation, deadening, desensitisation; **sedation**, narcotisation, narcotism, twilight sleep. *See also* UNCONSCIOUSNESS; INSENSIBILITY

ANAESTHETIC *n* abirritant, anaesthesin, benzocaine, ether, etheriser, ethyl ether, eucaine, fluothane, general anaesthetic, halothane, knockout drop, local, local anaesthetic, novocaine, palfium, pethidine, phenacaine, phencyclidine, procaine, tribromoethanol, trichlorethylene; **analgesic**, anodyne, deadener, painkiller; **laughing gas**, gas, nitrous oxide; **sedative**, chloral, hypnotic, laudanum, Mickey Finn, narcotic, opiate, sleeping-draught, sleeping-drug, sleeping-pill, stupefacient, stupefier, truth drug

ANAESTHETIC *adj* abirritant, analgesic, anodyne, deadening, knockout, sedative

ANAESTHETISE *v* chloroform, etherise, freeze, keep under; **narcotise**, dope, drug, hocus, opiate, stupefy; **knock out**, concuss, daze, flatten, K.O., kayo, king-hit, knock endwise *(N.Z.)*, knock endways, stun; **desensitise**, abirritate, benumb, blur, deaden, dull, numb

ANALOG *adj* digital; **programmable,** dedicated, intelligent, interactive, user-friendly

ANALYSIS *n* appraisal, assay, assessment, breakdown, criticism, critique, diagnosis, methodology; **analytical procedure,** classification, exhaustive study, graphing, ordering, random sampling, reductionism, sifting, sorting, systematisation, tabulating; **microanalysis,** destructive distillation, gas chromatography, gas-liquid chromatography, on-stream analysis, paper chromatography; **dissection,** anatomisation, anatomy, autopsy, biopsy, segmentation; **inquiry,** investigation, review, reviewal, scan, scrutiny, study; **analytics,** critical-path analysis, input-output analysis, marginalism, operations research, principal components analysis, systems analysis, variable rule analysis; **analytical display,** frequency distribution, graph, histogram, record, register, table

ANALYST *n* analyser, appraiser, assayer, assessor, deriver, dissector, nuts-and-bolts man, prosector, reductionist, scanner

ANARCHIC *adj* anarchistic, disobedient, insurgent, mutinous, nihilistic, seditionary, seditious; **lawless,** disorderly, headless, helmless, illegal, riotous, unattended, unchartered, unregulated; **unruly,** libertine, licentious, pandemoniac, pandemonic, turbulent; **irresponsible,** ruffian, runaway, tearaway, unbitted, unbridled; **arbitrary,** unilateral, unwarranted

ANARCHICALLY *adv* arbitrarily, high-handedly, irresponsibly, lawlessly, out of hand, out of order, seditiously, unwarrantedly, without book

ANARCHISE *v* destabilise, disobey, mutiny, rebel, ride roughshod over the law, run riot, take the law into one's own hands

ANARCHIST *n* destructionist, nihilist; **despiser of the law,** hell's angel, irresponsible, mad mullah, outlaw, revolutionary, ruffian, seditionary, urban guerilla

ANARCHY *n* blackboard jungle, civil disobedience, pandemonium, tumult, turbulence, turmoil; **lawlessness,** brute force, disorderliness, lynch law, misgovernment, misrule, unruliness, Wild West; **irresponsibility,** arbitrariness, irresponsibleness; **anarchism,** nihilism, ruffianism, seditiousness

ANCESTRALLY *adv* genealogically; **hereditarily,** lineally; **genetically,** hereditably, heritably, inheritably

ANCESTRY *n* descent, extraction; **generation,** birth, origin; **genealogy,** family tree, genealogical tree, stemma, tree; **herd-book,** studbook; **pedigree,** blood, heredity, heritance *(Archaic),* inheritance, line, lineage; **pure line,** straight line; **breed,** strain, type; **stock,** root, rootstock, stem, stirps; **branch,** moiety, offshoot, side; **matriline,** distaff side, matriarchy, spear side; **patriline,** patriarchy; **clan,** breed, family, gens, house, kith and kin, nation, race, stock, team *(Obs.),* tribe; **legitimacy; illegitimacy,** bastardy, unlawfulness; **polygenesis,** difference *(Her.).* See also GENETICS

ANCHOR *n* bower, dead man, dogstick, drag-anchor, kedge anchor, kellick, mudhook, pick *(Colloq.),*

anchor 21 **angry**

sheet anchor, sprag; **hook,** grapnel, grapple, grappler, grappling hook, grappling iron, tenterhook; **clevis,** hame, lunette, ottfur hook

AND *conj* along with, as well as, eke *(Archaic),* in addition to, let alone, together with, with; **plus,** beside *(Rare),* besides, not to mention, over and above

ANGEL *n* archangel, cherub, cherubim, guardian angel, ministering spirit, morning star, pure spirit, seraph, seraphim; **celestial hierarchy,** celestial beings, choir, dominations, dominions, hierarchy, order, powers, princedoms, principalities, thrones, virtues; **angelhood,** divinity

ANGER *n* blood and thunder, choler, dudgeon, fury, ill temper, indignation, infuriation, ire, pique, rage, resentment, temper, the Jimmy Brits, the shits, vexation, wrath; **angriness,** crankiness, furiousness, furore, hastiness, incensement, irefulness, lividity, lividness, passion, resentfulness, savageness, savagery, vehemence, wrathfulness; **irascibility,** irascibleness, passionateness, prickliness, shrewishness

ANGER *v* enrage, huff, incense, inflame, infuriate, pique, put someone's back up, rouse, vex; **irritate,** get on someone's goat, give someone the Jimmy Brits, give someone the shits, provoke, shit

ANGLE *n* inflection, oblique angle, obtuse angle, reflex angle, right angle, spherical angle, straight angle; **adjacent angle,** allied angles, alternate angles, cant, co-interior angles, complementary angle, corresponding angles, exterior angle, plane angle, re-entrant angle, supplementary angle, vertical angle; **angle of incidence,** angle of reflection, angle of refraction, angular diameter, critical angle; **inclination,** altitude, angle of attack, attitude, azimuth, bank, bearing, camber angle, codeclination, declination, depression, deviation, dip, elevation, elongation, grid magnetic angle, heading, magnetic declination, magnetic variation, solar parallax, stalling angle; **axil,** beam *(Radio),* bite *(Dentistry),* fleam *(Tools),* quarter point, quirk, steeve *(Naut.),* stop *(Zool.),* wedge; **degree,** centigrade, complement, mil, minute, pitch, radian, second, steradian, supplement.   *See also* BEND

ANGRILY *adv* apoplectically, furiously, in a fury, in a huff, in a rage, in high dudgeon, indignantly, infuriately *(Archaic),* irately, irefully, lividly, rampantly, red-facedly, shrewishly, with one's hackles up, wrathfully; **crankily,** hastily, irascibly; **acrimoniously,** rancorously, virulently; **gloweringly,** loweringly, tough; **resentfully,** huffily, sulkily, sullenly, umbrageously; **fiercely,** passionately, savagely, vehemently, warmly; **infuriatingly,** provocatively, provokingly; **invidiously,** odiously

ANGRY *adj* ablaze, blazing, cheesed-off, cross as a cat, cross as a dog, cross as crabs, cross as two sticks, dirty, fit to be tied, full up *(N.Z. Colloq.),* furious, hairy, hopping, hopping mad, hot under the collar, indignant, infuriate *(Archaic),* infuriated, irate, ireful, like a bear with a sore head, livid, mad, mad as a hornet, mad as a maggot, mad as a meat-axe, mad with rage, on the warpath, rampant, ranting, red-faced, red-hot, ropeable, shitty-livered, snaky, steamed-up, up in arms, uptight, vexed, wally *(Brit.)*, wood *(Obs.)*, wrath *(Archaic)*, wrathful, wroth, wrought; **fed up**, brassed off, fed up to the back teeth, fed up to the gills, huffy, pissed-off, sick, sick to death; **mean**, apoplectic, black-browed, choleric, cranky, cursed, easily aroused, evil, hasty, irascible, ornery, prickly, quick-tempered, savage, umbrageous *(Rare)*; **glaring**, lowering, wild-eyed

ANGRY ACT *n* flaw *(Obs.)*, huff, paddy, paddywhack, pelter, rage, ramp, rampage, tantrum, tear, wax, wobbly *(N.Z.)*; **fireworks**, act, blow-up, explosion, flare, flare-up; **dirty look**, glare, glower, lour; **sulk**, sulks; **diatribe**, rant, yap

ANGRY PERSON *n* angry young man, hellcat, maenad, ranter, shrew, spitfire, thunderbolt, wildcat

ANGULARLY *adv* antrorsely, crookedly, diagonally, forkedly, obliquely, orthogonally, perpendicularly, rectangularly; **at an angle**, abeam, athwart, athwartships, cornerways, cornerwise, crabways, crabwise, square, zigzag; **aslant**, akimbo, askew, out of square

ANIMAL *n* beast, brute, creature, zooid

ANIMAL CALL *n* cry; **talk**, language, utterance; **roar**, bell, bellow, roaring, trumpet; **howl**, caterwaul, hoot, screech, ululation; **growl**, grunt, snarl; **drone**, buzz, hum, whine; **bark**, bay, bow-wow, woof, yap, yip *(U.S.)*; **mew**, miaow, purr; **bray**, heehaw; **bleat**, baa; **whinny**, neigh; **moo**, low; **whimper**, whine. *See also* BIRD-CALL

ANIMAL DWELLING *n* doghouse, kennel; **cattery; cowshed**, byre, cowhouse, crib, stall; **stable**, livery stable, loosebox, mews, riding stables, stabling; **pigsty**, piggery, pigpen, sty; **coop**, cage, hutch, terrarium; **beehive**, apiary, hive, vespiary; **dovecot**, henhouse, pigeonhole; **nest**, aerie, aviary, eyrie, hatchery, heronry, nide, nidus, perch, rookery; **ant bed**, ant hill, termitarium; **lair**, den, form, foxhole, home, lodge; **warren**, burrow, crabhole, earth, hole, rabbit-warren, sett, tunnel

ANIMAL-LIKE *adj* beastlike, bestial, brutal, brute, brutish, faunal, zooid, zoological, zoomorphic; **subhuman**, theriomorphic, theroid; **animalcular**, rotiferal; **wild**, ferae naturae *(Law)*, feral, untamed; **mammalian**, mammiferous; **bovine**, canine *(dogs)*, cervine *(deer)*, equine *(horses)*, erinaceous *(hedgehogs)*, feline *(cats)*, hircine *(goats)*, leonine *(lions)*, lupine *(wolves)*, ovine *(sheep)*, phocine *(seals)*, sciurine *(squirrels)*, simian *(apes and monkeys)*, taurine *(bulls)*, ursine *(bears)*, vaccine *(cows)*, vituline *(calves)*

ANIMAL OFFSPRING *n* cub, juvenile, pup, puppy, whelp, wolf cub; **kitten**, kitty, ligon, tigon; **colt**, fawn, filly, foal, yearling; **calf**, bobby calf, heifer, maverick, poddy, slink, staggering bob, weaner, weanling; **lamb**, kid, lambkin, yeanling; **piglet**, piggie, pigling, shoat, sucker, sucking-pig; **joey; chicken**, chick, cygnet, duckling, eaglet, fledgling, gosling, green duck, juvenal, juvenile, nestling, owlet, poult; **tiddler**, alevin, cercaria, codling, fingerling, fry, poddy mullet; **larva**, caseworm, maggot, miracidium, planula, polliwog, tadpole; **pupa,** chrysalid, chrysalis, nymph; **spiderling,** money spider; **dragonet; litter,** drop, farrow, team; **brood,** clutch, hatch, nide; **spawn,** culch, spat

ANIMAL PART *n* proboscis, snout, trunk; **horn,** antler, attire, hartshorn, ivory, point, scur, spike; **pincers,** chela, forceps, nipper; **tooth,** carnassial, denticle, fang, tush, tusk; **cheek pouch,** bell, dewlap, jowl, pouch; **forelimb,** arm, brachium, foreleg; **paw,** foot, forefoot, forepaw, pad, pettitoes, podium; **hoof,** unguis, ungula; **claw,** nail, unguis; **tail,** brush, bush, flag *(Hunting),* fox brush, scut; **shell,** plastron, scutcheon, scute, shuck *(U.S.),* tortoiseshell, turbinate

ANIMAL'S COAT *n* coat, fleece, jacket, pelage; **fur,** badger, beaver, blue fox, broadtail, caracul, chinchilla, cony, deerskin, ermine, fisher, fitch, galyak, hamster, kolinsky, lapin, miniver, mink, monkey, muskrat, nutria, pointed fox, puma, sable, seal, skunk, squirrel, vair, wolf, zibeline; **wool,** alpaca, angora, astrakhan, camelhair, cashmere, horsehair, mohair, mother hair, Persian lamb; **crest,** coma, foretop; **bellies,** belly-wool, underfur; **dag,** abb, dagging, daglock, dagwool, tag; **tuft,** fetlock, floccus, flock, switch; **mane,** collar, frill, hackle, torques; **eyeclip,** eyewool, moustache

ANNIHILATE *v* abrogate, annul, disannul, exterminate, extirpate, nullify, wipe out; **expunge,** blank, blot out, void *(Archaic),* wipe off the map

ANNIVERSARY *n* bicentenary, bicentennial *(U.S.),* biennial, birthday, centenary, decennial, ides, jubilee, millennium, quatercentenary, quincentenary, quindecennial, quinquennial, quotidian *(Archaic),* sabbatical year *(Rabbinical Law),* sesquicentenary, tercentenary, tricentennial, triennial

ANNOY *v* aggravate, chafe, get across, get in someone's hair, get on one's goat, get on one's nerves, get on one's wick, get to someone, get under one's skin, give someone the pip, give someone the shits, importune *(Obs.),* irk, nettle, pip, put out, raise a bite, rankle, rub up the wrong way, ruffle; **exasperate,** acerbate, chevy, chivvy, drive someone up the wall, exacerbate, fray, gall, infuriate, madden, piss someone off, rile, roil, sting; **irritate,** antagonize, bug, fret, nark, niggle, offend, play cat and mouse, provoke, try the patience of; **harass,** badger, bait, bedevil, bullyrag, devil, get on someone's back, get on someone's hammer, gig, haggle *(Archaic),* harry, hassle, haze, keep at, nag, needle, persecute, pester, pick on, plague, rag, rib, stir, tease, torment; **trouble,** bother, fuss, worry

ANNOYANCE *n* chafe, exacerbation, exasperation, fret, infuriation, irritation, peeve, trouble, vexation; **annoyingness,** importunacy, importunateness, irksomeness, offensiveness, troublesomeness; **harassment,** bedevilment, persecution, pinpricking, tease; **irritant,** aggravation, annoy *(Archaic),* pinprick, torment, vexation; **nuisance,** bind, bore, bother, face-ache, menace, pain, pain in the arse, pain in the neck, pest, plague, terror, thorn, thorn in one's flesh, thorn in one's side, trial

ANNOYED *adj* aggravated, bushwhacked, irritated, vexed; **exasperated,** browned off, fed up, fed up to the

annoyed

back teeth, fed up to the gills; **harassed,** hassled, hot and bothered, tormented

ANNOYER *n* aggravator, exasperator, stirrer; **harasser,** baiter, nagger, niggler, persecutor, plaguer, tease, teaser, tormentor, troubler; **trouble,** difficulty, problem, the dizzy limit, the last straw, the limit, worry

ANNOYING *adj* abrasive, aggravating, irritating, offensive, plaguy *(Archaic),* tiresome, trying, vexatious; **troublesome,** bothersome, important *(Obs.),* importunate, importune, irksome, narky, niggling, pesky *(U.S.),* pestiferous, pestilent, thorny, troublous *(Archaic),* worrisome; **exasperating,** galling, infuriating, insupportable, maddening, mother-fucking *(U.S.),* wicked

ANNOYINGLY *adv* aggravatingly, irksomely, offensively, tiresomely, tryingly; **exasperatingly,** gallingly, infuriatingly, insupportably, maddeningly

ANOMALY *n* anomalism *(Obs.),* discrepancy, irreconcilable, variance; **misfit,** mismatch, mockery, ring-in, square peg in a round hole

ANSWER *n* acknowledgment, countersign, echo, password, rejoinder, repartee, replication, reply, report, rescript, respondence, response, return; **reaction,** bite, comeback, contradiction, counter charge, counterclaim, defence

ort, riposte; **conditioned response,** conditioned reflex; **responsive singing,** antiphon, antiphony, gradual *(Eccles.).* See also SOLUTION

anthropology

ANSWER *v* acknowledge, rejoin, reply, respond, return; **retort,** bite back, confute, contradict, counter charge, counterclaim, rebut, repartee *(Obs.),* riposte; **reduce to silence,** cut the ground from under someone's feet, not leave someone a leg to stand on, silence

ANSWERER *n* rebutter, replier, respondent

ANSWERING *adj* respondent, responsive; **providing a final answer,** conclusive, decisive, definitive; **answerable,** capable of being answered, extractable, resolvable, soluble, solvable; **antiphonal,** amoebaean

ANTECEDENCE *n* anteriority, coming before, lead, precedence, precession, prevenance, priority, right of way; **head start,** advantage, handicap, law *(Sport),* start

ANTECEDENT *n* archetype, exemplar, model, original, protoplast, prototype; **prefix,** forepart; **leader,** promo, run-in groove, trailer *(Film).* See also FORERUNNER

ANTHROPOLOGICAL *adj* anthropogenic, anthropologic, palae-ethnologic, somatological; **ethnologic,** ethnographic, ethnographical, ethnological; **humanistic,** anthropocentric, anthropomorphic, manward, personal, personalistic

ANTHROPOLOGY *n* anthropogenesis, anthropogeography, anthropography, anthropometry, ethnogeny, ethnography, ethnology, palae-ethnology, somatology; **social studies,** demography, social anthropology, social science

ANTICIPATE v look ahead, pre-empt, preconceive, see how the cat will jump, see how the land lies, sniff the morning air; **prepare**, lay in stocks, make allowance for, prepare for; **foresee**, feel in one's bones, forefeel, foreknow, foretaste, prefigure, see one's way ahead; **foreshadow**, adumbrate; **forewarn**, bode *(Archaic)*, forebode, predict, presage, previse

ANTICIPATION n aforethought, calculation, forecast, forefeel, foretaste, forethought, hunch, longsightedness, premeditation; **prudence**, forward planning, looking ahead, precaution, preparation, providence *(Rare)*; **foresight**, clairvoyance, divination, ESP, foreknowledge, precognition, prediction, prescience, prevision, second sight; **foreboding**, adumbration, bodement, boding, forewarning, forshadowing, premonition, presage, presentiment

ANTICIPATIVELY adv adumbratively, against the time when, anticipatorily, designingly, far-sightedly, foreknowingly, presciently, providently, prudently

ANTICIPATORY adj aforethought, precautionary, premeditated; **anticipative**, adumbrative, anticipant of, precognitive; **prudent**, designing, pre-emptory, precautious, prepared, provident, thrifty; **foresighted**, clairvoyant, far-seeing, far-sighted, longsighted, longheaded, onlooking, prescient, psychic

ANTIQUE adj antiquarian, classic, obsolete, old-world, olde-worlde, period, veteran, vintage; **outdated**, antiquated, archaic, backward, behind the times, dated, old hat, old-fashioned, old-line *(U.S.)*, out-of-date, outworn, passé; **expired**, elapsed, extinct, lapsed, run out

ANY n anybody, anyone, anything, what have you, what not, whoever; **everybody**, everyman, everyone, everything; **all and sundry**, every man jack, every Tom Dick and Harry, one and all; **thingummyjig**, sundries, thing, whatnot

APATHETIC adj ambitionless, bloodless, dead-and-alive, depressed, depressive, lackadaisical, mopey, mopish, passive, perfunctory, phlegmatic, purposeless, spiritless, unaspiring, viewless; **torpid**, benumbed, comatose, dreamy, dull, inert, languid, lethargic, listless, moony, numb, sluggish, supine; **uninterested**, aloof, disinterested, distanced, impassive, insensible, insusceptible, switched-off, turned off, unaffected, unmoved, unresponsive, unruffled, unsympathetic, untouched, withdrawn; **uncommitted**, apolitical, uninvolved; **indifferent**, detached, easy, half-hearted, half-pie, incurious, irresponsive, lukewarm, uncaring; **nonchalant**, airy, careless, casual, cavalier, easygoing, insouciant, off-hand, pococurante, throwaway, unconcerned

APATHETICALLY adv bloodlessly, languidly, listlessly, lukewarmly, mopingly, mopishly, perfunctorily, spiritlessly; **nonchalantly**, casually, cavalierly, phlegmatically, unconcernedly; **indifferently**, aloofly, by halves, half-heartedly, impassively, incuriously, uninterestedly

APATHETIC PERSON n indifferentist, mope, moper, no-hoper, Norm, pococurante, yawner, zombie; **nonchaser**

APATHY *n* accidie, acedia, depression, mopishness, phlegm *(Obs.)*, purposelessness, spiritlessness; **torpor**, inertia, languidness, lethargy, listlessness, numbness, stupor, torpidity; **indifference**, aloofness, bloodlessness, detachment, disinterest, half-heartedness, impassiveness, impassivity, incuriosity, incuriousness, indifferentism, lack of involvement, lukewarmness, perfunctoriness, unconcern, unconcernedness, uninterestedness; **nonchalance**, carelessness, casualness, easiness, insouciance, jemenfoutisme, pococurantism

APEX *n* apogee, apolune, ceiling, critical altitude, upper, vertex, zenith; **summit**, brow, cop *(Obs.)*, crest, crown, head, top; **edge**, brink, verge; **high-water mark**, benchmark *(Survey)*, bush-line, floodmark, timber line, water-level, waterline, watermark. *See also* HEIGHT; MOUNTAIN; TOWER

APPARENT *adj* external, manifest, ostensible, outward, seeming, semblable *(Archaic)*, specious, superficial, surface

APPARENTLY *adv* at first sight, at the first blush, from the look of the thing, manifestly, on the face of it, ostensibly, prima facie, seemingly, superficially, to all appearances, to the eye

APPEAR *v* arise, bob up, come, come into view, come to light, come up, crop up, drop in, emerge, figure, front up, gleam, heave in sight, loom, materialise, peep, peer, present, report, rise, shoot *(Bot.)*, show, show a leg, show one's face, show the flag *(Colloq.)*, show through, show up, spring *(Archaic)*, surface, turn up, unroll, uprise *(Archaic);* **seem,** appear, look, look like, sound

APPEARANCE *n* air, apparel *(Archaic)*, aspect, bearing, cast, clip, colour, complexion, cut of someone's jib, facies *(Ecol.)*, figure, garment, image, light, look, looks, mien, outward, presence; **face,** cheer *(Archaic)*, contour, countenance, facade, features, lineament, physiognomy, profile, visage; **phenomenon,** mode *(Philos.)*, phase; **apparition,** emergence, emersion, fade-in, forthcoming, loom, manifestation, materialisation

APPEARANCES *n* apparentness, colouring, externals, face value, gloss, guise, pretence, seeming, semblance, show, superficiality, superficialness, superficies, surface, surface structure

APPLAUSE *n* acclaim, bouquet, cheer, clap, curtain call, eclat, hand, handclap, ovation, plaudit, round of applause, salvo, three cheers; **tribute,** compliment, encomium, eulogium, eulogy, hymn, laud, paean, panegyric, toast; **admiring look,** eye-service. *See also* APPROVAL

APPOINTEE *n* administrator, heir-designate, nominee, office-bearer, officer, official, receiver *(Law)*

APPRAISE *v* assess, capitalise, esteem, price, prize, quote, rate, revalue, tag, value; **offer,** bid

APPROVAL *n* a good press, admiration, appreciation, appreciativeness, approbation, endorsement, esteem, opinion, sympathy; **recommendation,** a good word, advocacy, commendation, endorsement, espousal, rave, support, testimonial, wrap-up *(Colloq.);* **praise,** acclamation, celebration, emblazonment, exaltation,

approval   27   **aptly**

extolment, glory, laudation; **sanction,** acceptance, acceptation, countenance, recognition; **personality cult.**
See also APPLAUSE

APPROVE *v* accept, advocate, approbate, bless, countenance, endorse, hand it to, hold a brief for, hold with, recognise, sanction, set one's seal on, sympathise; **acclaim,** big-mouth, carol, celebrate, cry up, emblazon, eulogise, exalt, extol, hail, hymn, laud, magnify *(Archaic)*, panegyrise, plug, polish, praise, rap up; **compliment,** commend, recommend, sing someone's praises, sing the praises of, speak well of; **admire,** appreciate, favour, prize, smile on, take to, think the world of, value; **give full marks,** give points, give someone a good mark, pass, throw a bouquet; **applaud,** clap, huzza *(Archaic)*; **cheer,** barrack for, root for *(U.S.)*; **toast,** bumper, raise one's glass

APPROVED *adj* commended, recommended; **praiseworthy,** admirable, approvable, commendable, exemplary, laudable, prepossessing; **acceptable,** all right, cleared, okay, passed, uncensored; **favourite,** darling, favoured, in favour, in high favour, in someone's good books, popular

APPROVER *n* acclaimer, admirer, amateur *(Obs.)*, applauder, appreciator, caroller, fan, favourer, follower, groupie, supporter, sympathiser; **praiser,** encomiast, eulogiser, eulogist, exalter, lauder, panegyrist, tributary, tributer; **barracker,** cheerer, claque *(Theat.)*, rooter; **recommender,** advocate, advocator, countenancer, extoller, promoter; **following,** fan club

APPROVING *adj* applauding, applausive, approbative, approbatory, commendatory, favourably disposed, lost in admiration, plausive *(Rare)*, recommendatory, shook on; **praising,** acclamatory, complimentary, encomiastic, eulogistic, laudatory, panegyrical, rapt, rave, tributary; **favourable,** acceptant, appreciative, appreciatory, recognitive, recognitory, susceptive, sympathetic, tolerant, uncritical

APPROVINGLY *adv* admiringly, appreciatively, appreciatorily, complimentarily, encouragingly; **eulogistically,** panegyrically, **favourably,** in a good light, smilingly, sympathetically, sympathisingly; **tolerantly,** uncritically; **in favour of,** pro; **commendably,** admirably, exemplarily, laudably, praiseworthily

APT *adj* applicable, apposite, appropriate, fit, german *(Obs.)*, germane, in point, pertinent, relevant, to the point; **up one's street,** congenial, to one's taste, unobjectionable; **fitting,** apropos, becoming, befitting, condign, due, felicitous, just the job, meet *(Archaic)*, perfect, proper, ready-made, right, suitable, toward *(Obs.)*, towardly *(Archaic)*; **compatible,** assorted, coherent, consistent, en rapport, self-consistent, typical

APTLY *adv* applicably, appositely, appropriately, apropos, felicitously, pertinently, relevantly; **fittingly,** becomingly, befittingly, coherently, condignly, congruously, duly, in order, meetly *(Archaic)*, properly, right, rightly, suitably; **in accordance,** in chime, in compliance, in concert, in keeping, in phase, in register, in step, in tram *(Mech.)*; **adjustably,** reconcilably; **thereunder,** according to, pursuant, pursuantly

APTNESS *n* applicability, applicableness, application, appositeness, appropriateness, aptitude, becomingness, competency *(Law)*, consonance, eligibility, felicitousness, fitness, fittingness, happiness, pertinence, pertinency, relevance, relevancy, suitability; **propriety,** decorum, rightness, suitableness, towardliness, towardness; **horses for courses; compatibility,** compatibleness, reconcilability, reconcilableness, togetherness

ARBOREAL *adj* arborescent, arborous, silvan, sylvan; **beechen,** cedarn, citrus, olive, palmy, piny, willowy, withy; **arboricultural,** floricultural

ARCANE *adj* cabalistic, covert, esoteric, mystic, occult, recondite

ARCANUM *n* esotericism, esotery, invisibility, mystery, mystique, occult

ARCH *n* arching, archlet, archway, extrados, flying buttress, haunch, intrados, ogive, Roman arch, skew arch, squinch; **dome,** arcade, barrel vault, calotte, cloche, cupola, fornix, geodesic dome, hemicycle, hemisphere, hemispheroid, radome, semidome, tholus, vault, vaulting; **beading,** bead, echinus, ovolo, quad, quadrant moulding; **foil,** foliation

AREA *n* circumference, circumscription, compass, extent, spread; **hectare,** acre, are, hide *(Old Eng. Law),* pole, square; **square measure,** acreage, floor space, floorage. *See also* SPACE

ARGUE *v* altercate, argy-bargy, contend, dispute, have it out, quarrel, row, strive, war; **conflict,** clash, collide; **confront,** antagonise *(U.S.),* assail, encounter, face, front, frustrate, get on the wrong side of, lead someone a chase, lead someone a dance, meet, oppugn, pit oneself against, subvert, thwart, turn against

ARGUMENT *n* altercation, argy-bargy, assailment, catfight, clash, collision, combat, confrontation, confrontment, disagreement, dispute, encounter, hassle, imbroglio, miff, quarrel, row, ruckus *(U.S.),* ruction, run-in, set on, showdown, tangle, vendetta, war, yike; **rebuttal,** con, counterargument, crossing

ARGUMENTATIVE *adj* belligerent, contradictious, contradictive, contradictory, contrary, contrasuggestible, contrasuggestive, disputant, disputatious, disputative; **dissenting,** anti, dissentient, dissident, divergent, remonstrant. *See also* CONTENTIOUS

ARGUMENTATIVELY *adv* belligerently, contentiously, controversially, disputatiously, divisively; **contradictorily,** contrarily

ARGUMENTATIVENESS *n* cantankerousness, combativeness, contentiousness, disputatiousness, divisiveness, quarrelsomeness

ARISTOCRACY *n* ancien régime, daimio, elite, ermine, high society, nobility, patriciate, peerage, purple, ruling class, the haves, top drawer, upper class, upper crust; **gentry,** county, gentlefolk, squattocracy, squirearchy, squiredom; **noble birth,** blue blood, ennoblement, gentility, gentle birth, grandeur, noblesse; **pedigree,** ancestry, descent, durbar, line, lineage, succession, witan; **royalty,** kingliness, majesty, princeliness, queenliness; **lordship,** baronage, barony, dukedom, earldom, emperor-

aristocracy

ship, kingship, ladyship, marquisate, princedom, queenhood, sultanship, thanage, viscountcy. *See also* ARISTOCRAT

ARISTOCRAT *n* blue blood, boyar, Brahman, childe *(Archaic)*, eupatrid, hidalgo, life peer, nob *(Brit.)*, noble, nobleman, patrician, peer, swell *(Brit.)*; **Lord,** archduke, atheling, baron, count, count palatine, daimio, dauphin, donzel *(Archaic)*, duke, earl, emir, grand duke, grandee, jarl, Junker, landgrave, lord, lord temporal, lordling, magnifico, marchese, margrave, marquess, marquis, monseigneur, prince, prince consort, prince imperial, prince regent, prince royal, princeling, rangatira *(N.Z.)*, robber baron, seigneur, sir, sire *(Obs.)*, thane, tsarevitch, viscount; **Lady,** archduchess, baroness, countess, dame, dauphiness, don, donzella *(Archaic)*, dowager, grand duchess, landgravine, life peeress, marchesa, marchioness, margravine, marquise, miladi, milady, noblewoman, peeress, princess, princess royal, sultana, tsarevna, viscountess; **sovereign,** emperor, king, majesty, queen, rajah, rani, rex, sultan, tsar, tsarina; **squire,** armiger, country gentleman *(Brit.)*, laird, landlord, landowner, squatter; **lady-in-waiting,** maid of honour; **dynasty,** noble family. *See also* UPPER CLASS

ARISTOCRATIC *adj* blue-blooded, highborn, highbred, noble, patrician, pedigreed, thoroughbred, toffee-nosed *(Brit. Colloq.)*, toney, tonky *(N.Z. Colloq.)*, topdrawer, upper, upper-class, well-born; **titled,** archducal, baronial, coroneted, ducal, lordly, seigneurial; **royal,** every inch a king, imperial, kingly, princely, purple, queenly, regal

ARISTOCRATICALLY *adv* imperially, lordly *(Archaic)*, nobly

ARM *n* brachium, fin, forearm, shoulder, warwicks, wing; **armpit,** axilla; **elbow,** ancon, crazy bone *(U.S.)*, funny bone; **hand,** bunch of fives, carpus, duke, fin, fist, flipper, knuckle, metacarpus, mauley, mitt, mutton-fist, palm, paw, thenar, wrist; **finger,** annular, digit, forefinger, hooks, index finger, lifeline, little finger, onka, pinkie, pollex, ring finger, thumb; **nail,** claw, fingernail, onyx, talon, unguis

ARMED *adj* armoured, capital, heavy-armed, helmeted, mailed, under arms

ARMED FORCES *n* armed services, army, artillery, cavalry, foot, general staff, horse, infantry, light horse, military, musketry *(Obs.)*, rifles, soldiery; **navy,** flotilla, marine, R.A.N., senior service; **airforce,** Kamikaze, R.A.A.F., R.A.F.; **nation in arms,** army of occupation, host *(Archaic)*, land power, Sabaoth, standing army; **unit,** arm, battalion, battery, battle *(Archaic)*, brigade, century, cohort, column, command, contingent, division, force, garrison, legion, maniple, regiment, section; **squad,** cadre, company, element, escadrille *(U.S.)*, group, platoon, squadron, sub-unit, troop; **detachment,** detail, party; **array,** line, square, wedge. *See also* SERVICEMAN: HIGH COMMAND: SOLDIER: COMBAT TROOPS

ARMLIKE *adj* brachial, caudal, finlike, twiglike, winglike; **caudate,** cirrate, cirriped, cirrose, finny, flagellate, winged; **appendicular,** extensional

ARMOUR *n* brigandine, chain mail, harness *(Archaic)*, mail, panoply; **shield**, buckler, escutcheon, hielamon *(Aborig.)*, mulga *(Aborig.)*, scutum, targe *(Archaic)*, target; **testudo**, tortoise; **bard**, chamfrain, chanfron; **helmet**, basinet, beaver, burgonet, headpiece, morion; **gauntlet**, basket hilt, coquille *(Fencing)*, glove, palm *(Naut.)*; **breastplate**, box *(Cricket)*, byrnie, codpiece, corslet, cuirass, culet, gorget, habergeon, hauberk, jack, lorica, plastron; **armguard**, bracer *(Archery)*, brassard, palette, rerebrace; **greave**, chausses, cuisse, kneecap, kneepad, kneepiece, pad, tasset; **faceguard**, beaver, eyeshade, goggles, gum-shield, mask, mouthguard, mouthpiece, nasal, nosepiece, visor, vizard *(Obs.)*

ARMOURER *n* ballistics expert, bowyer, fletcher

AROUSE *v* actuate, bestir, call forth, goad, instigate, kick up, kindle interest, kittle *(Brit.)*, prompt, provoke, roust, rout out, spur, stir up, tickle, titillate; **incite**, agitate, enkindle, fan, fire, flesh *(Archaic)*, inflame, inspirit, rouse, set on fire, skitch, sool; **stir the possum**, cook up a storm, trail a coat; **goad**, force on, get on someone's back, hound, hurry along, hurry up, hustle, needle, prick, prod, push, scrub *(Horseracing)*, spur, sting, stockwhip

ARRANGE *v* fix, manipulate, route, settle, work it; **prearrange**, arrange to meet, ask someone out, invite, make a date, preconcert, prefix *(Rare)*; **rendezvous**, date, tryst

ARRANGED *adj* agreed, decided upon, planned, prearranged, set-up

ARRANGEMENT *n* accord, agreement, composition, deal, pact, pair, set-up, settlement, settling, understanding

ARREST *v* apprehend, bag, bounce, capture, do, give in charge, knock off, lumber, nick, pick up, pinch, pull in, recapture, seize, trap. See also IMPRISON

ARRIVAL *n* advent, coming, homecoming, incoming, influx; **disembarkation**, landfall, landing, set-down; **check-in**, registration

ARRIVE *v* bob up, come, fetch up, lob in, roll in, roll up, surface, turn up; **reach**, arrive at, attain, come to, end up at, fetch *(Naut.)*, get to, hit, join, lob at, make, put in at, regain, strike, top; **check in**, register; **pull in**, arrive *(Obs.)*, beach, berth, bring up, cast anchor, come in, drop anchor, land, make land, make landfall, touchdown; **settle on**, light on; **disembark**, alight, debus, detrain, dismount, get down, get off, get out, go ashore, jump ship

ARRIVER *n* comer, landing party; **new chum**, bine *(W.A. Colloq.)*, black hat *(Archaic)*, blow-in, boat people, immigrant, migrant, new arrival, New Australian, refugee; **immigrant**, Jimmy Grant, pomegranate, pommie; **newcomer**, griffin *(East India)*, stranger

ARROGANCE *n* airs, airs and graces, arrogancy, disdainfulness, haughtiness, hubris, loftiness, pride, self-importance, smugness, stuffiness, superciliousness, toploftiness, uppishness; **disdain**, affectation, hauteur, pomposity, scorn, vainglory; **insolence**, assumption, assurance, hide, impertinence, impudence, nerve, presumption, sauce; **self-assertion**, brass,

arrogance   31   **artistry**

cheek, conceit, face, front, hide, nerve, pretension, side, swagger, swank, swashbuckling; **insult**, contumely; **snobbery**, elitism, ethnocentrism, inverted snobbery, superiority complex; **dogmatism**, opinionatedness

ARROGANT *adj* assured, autocratic, barefaced, cavalier, full of oneself, high and mighty, high-hat, impertinent, impudent, insolent, loudmouthed, overweening, proud, puffed-up, saucy, smug; **disdainful**, conceited, haughty, highfalutin, hoity-toity, lofty, off-hand, sniffy, supercilious, superior, toffee-nosed *(Brit.)*, too big for one's britches, unashamed; **overconfident**, cockish, cocky, smart-arse; **snobbish**, elitist, ethnocentric; **self-important**, stuffy, toney, tonky *(N.Z.)*, toplofty, uppish, uppity

ARROGANTLY *adv* assuredly, autocratically, barefacedly, impertinently, impudently, overweeningly, swaggeringly, swashingly; **audaciously**, bumptiously, forwardly, presumedly, presumptuously, self-importantly, shamelessly, vaingloriously; **cavalierly**, cockily, cockishly, saucily; **high-handedly**, dictatorially, dogmatically, domineeringly, imperiously, magisterially, overbearingly, patronisingly; **superciliously**, disdainfully, haughtily; **snobbishly**, stuffily, uppishly

ARROGANT PERSON *n* assumer, loudmouth, peacock, presumer, swaggerer, upstart; **bully**, bastard from the bush, fascist *(Colloq.)*, hector, pusher, rugger-bugger, swashbuckler, tin god, two-bob boss, upstart; **smart alec**, clever dick, dogmatiser, dogmatist, smart arse; **cock sparrow**, buck, cockalorum, cut-lunch commando, squirt; **snob**, boiled shirt, elitist, his nibs, inverted snob, pannikin snob, patroniser, snoot, snot, snotnose, snotty nose

ARSENAL *n* armory *(U.S.)*, armoury, arms chest, caisson, dump, garderobe *(Archaic)*, gun rack, pile, stack; **gun-carriage**, caisson, limber; **magazine**, powder keg; **holster**, pistol-case; **bandolier**, cartridge belt, clip; **scabbard**, sheath; **arrow-case**, quiver; **rifle range**, practice range, rocket range; **bomb bay**, bomb rack, gun emplacement

ARTIST *n* depicter, limner, old master; **painter**, aquarellist, colourist, dauber, frescoer, genre painter, landscape painter, marine painter, watercolourist; **illustrator**, caricaturist, commercial artist, copyist, illuminator, vignettist; **designer**, cartoonist, delineator, drafter, draftsman, draughtsman, sign-painter, signwriter; **drawer**, crayoner, crayonist, pastellist, penciller, sketcher; **black-and-white artist**, monochromist; **bohemian**, dilettante. *See also* CRAFTSMAN; ENGRAVER

ARTISTIC *adj* aesthetic, painterly; **pictorial**, graphic, illustrated, picturesque, vivid; **illustrative**, figurative; **abstract**, non-objective, non-representational, surrealistic; **naturalistic**, impressionist, objective, realist, representational; **formal**, dry; **colouristic; in perspective**, axonometric, cabinet, to scale; **stippled**, daubed, flown, hard-edge, malerisch

ARTISTRY *n* accomplishment, art, artifice *(Obs.)*, craft, delicacy, delicateness, felicity, fineness, finesse, lightness, niceness, power, savoir-faire,

ARTLESS *adj* blue-eyed, childlike, dewy-eyed, dupable, green, gullible, inartificial, ingenuous, innocent, naive, natural, simple, simple-minded, single-hearted, single-minded, trusting, unaffected, uncalculating, undesigning, unguarded, unpretentious, unsophisticated, unsuspecting, unsuspicious, untutored, unvarnished, unworldly, verdant, wide-eyed; **hick**, arcadian, backwoods, provincial, rustic, up-country *(Derog.)*

ARTLESSLY *adv* guilelessly, gullibly, ingenuously, naively, naturally, simple-mindedly, simply, unaffectedly, unpretentiously, unsophisticatedly

ARTLESSNESS *n* childlikeness, dupability, greenness, guilelessness, gullibility, inartificiality, ingenuousness, innocence, lack of sophistication, literality, naivety, naturalness, rusticity, simple heart, simple-mindedness, simplicity, unaffectedness, unpretentiousness, unsophisticatedness, unsophistication, unworldliness, viridity

ARTLESS PERSON *n* babe, dupe, fall guy, gudgeon, gull, ingenue, innocent, lamb, lamb to the slaughter, patsy, primitive, shlemiel, sitting duck, sucker; **hick**, backwoodsman *(U.S.)*, hayseed, rough diamond, rube *(U.S.)*, rustic

artistry 32 asker

subtleness, subtlety; **style**, elegance, grace, handsomeness *(U.S.)*; **technique**, execution, technic; **virtuosity**, bravura, brilliantness, display, fireworks, sparkle, technical skill; **verve**, dash, elan, panache, pizzazz, zest; **know-how**, stock-in-trade, the first string in one's bow

ASCEND *v* arise, levitate, rise, uprise *(Archaic)*, upswing; **gain height**, jump, mount, skyrocket, soar, take off, zoom; **tower**, ramp, rear, rear up, spire, stand up; **surmount**, culminate, top; **climb**, clamber, escalade, scale, shin, shinny, swarm up, walk up, work one's way up; **mount**, back *(Archaic)*, get up, horse, remount; **mountaineer**, back up, herringbone, sidestep, sidle *(N.Z.)*

ASCENDIBLE *adj* climbable, scalable, surmountable

ASCENDING *adj* ascendant, assurgent, emergent, orient *(Archaic)*, rising, up; **climbing**, epigeous, positively geotropic, running, scandent; **uplifting**, anabatic; **upward**, heavenward, skyward

ASCENT *n* ascension, assurgency, climb, escalade, escalation, mount, rise, rising, up, uprise *(Archaic)*, uprising, upswing; **upthrust**, upstroke, upthrow; **upsurge**, ridge lift, zoom; **slope**, acclivity, gradient, ramp; **climbing**, alpinism, clambering, layback, mountaineering, rockclimbing

ASHAMED *adj* conscience-smitten, conscience-stricken, contrite, embarrassed, guilt-stricken, penitent, repentant, sorry

ASKER *n* adjurer, beseecher, conjurer, impetrator *(Rare)*, implorer, importuner, pleader, postulant, requester, suppliant, supplicant; **applicant**, appealer, appellant, canvasser, imprecator, invoker, petitionary *(Archaic)*, petitioner; **interceder**, intercessor, interpellant, interpellator, lobbyist, urger; **beggar**, bummer, bludger, cadger, craver, hum, mendicant, panhandler *(U.S. Colloq.)*

ASLEEP *adj* dead, dead to the world, fast asleep, not awake, out to it, sleeping, sound asleep; **dormant**, dormient; **torpid**, comatose, lethargic, narcoleptic; **sleepy**, heavy with sleep, slumberous, somnolent; **drowsy**, dozy, oscitant, out of it, switched-off; **somnambulant**, somnambulistic

ASLEEP *adv* abed (*Obs.*), bedward, in the arms of Morpheus; **sleepily**, dozily, drowsily, somnolently; **soporifically**, hypnotically, lethargically, somnolently, soporiferously

ASSENTER *n* acceder, accepter, accorder, acknowledger, admitter, affirmant, affirmer, approver, attestor, conceder, conformer, consenter, covenanter, endorser, ratifier, rubber stamp, sanctifier, signatory, signer, subscriber, upholder, yes-man; **reconciler**, arranger, compounder, compromiser

ASSENTING *adj* consenting, signatory; **acquiescent**, agreeable, agreed, compliant, conventional (*Law*), resigned, willing; **affirmative**, confirmatory, ratifying, recognitive, recognitory. *See also* IN AGREEMENT

ASSENTINGLY *adv* affirmably, affirmatively, approvingly, concededly, consensually, consentingly, reconcilably, agreeably, accordingly, at one with, compliantly, conformably, congenially, consentaneously, empathically, in agreement, nem. con., nem. diss., pro, sympathetically, unanimously, with one accord

ASSENT TO *v* accede to, accept, accord with, acknowledge, admit, agree to, approbate (*Scot. Law*), be a sport, buy (*Colloq.*), come to terms with, concede, concur, embrace, fall in with, give one's vote to, give the nod to, go along with, grant, grant consent to, hear, lend oneself to, recognise, say yes to, turn a willing ear to, wear (*Colloq.*); **confirm**, adopt, affirm, amen, approve, attest, authorise, bear out, corroborate, countersign, endorse, fortify, homologate, ratify, sanction, sign, subscribe to, uphold; **okay**, initial, rubber-stamp, seal; **come to terms with**, acquiesce in, be resigned to, come around to, give in to, have no objection to, lie down under

ASSERT *v* affirm, allege, argue, asseverate, aver, avouch (*Archaic*), avow, claim, contend, declare, dogmatise, enunciate, insist, maintain, pose, posit, predicate, profess, pronounce, protest, protest, state, submit, swear, vouch, vow; **propose**, advance, move, put forward, suggest; **assert oneself**, be confident, maintain a high profile

ASSERTER *n* affirmant, affirmer, alleger, assurer, claimer, declarer, dogmatiser, dogmatist, enunciator, insister, maintainer, protester, submitter

ASSERTION *n* admission, affirmation, allegation, asseveration, assurance, averment, avouchment, avowal, claim, contention, declaration, dogmatisation, enouncement, enunciation, ipse dixit, offer, pretension, profession, pronouncement, protestation, restatement, statement, submission, vouch (*Obs.*); **proposition**, predicate, predication, premise; **affidavit**, statutory declaration

ASSERTIVE *adj* assertory, assured, outspoken, positive, strong; **insistent**, categorical, dogmatic, emphatic, peremptory, urgent; **declaratory**, declarative

ASSERTIVENESS n peremptoriness, positive thinking; **emphasis**, accent, avowedness, dogmatism, insistence, insistency, stress; **assertiveness training**, positive thinking course, self-development course

ASSESS v appraise, appreciate, esteem, estimate, evaluate, gauge, rank, rate, reckon, size up, sum up, valorise, valuate, value, weigh, weigh up; **take stock**, meditate, ponder; **review**, survey; **judge**, adjudicate, arbitrate, criticise, deem, doom, have an eye for, hear, pronounce on, sit in judgment on, try

ASSESSABLE adj appraisable, arbitrable, decidable, determinable, estimable, gaugeable, judicable, judiciable

ASSESSMENT n appraisal, appreciation, comment, critic *(Obs.)*, criticism, critique, esteem *(Archaic)*, estimate, estimation, evaluation, judgment, marking, measurement *(Survey)*, notice, opinion, rating, report, revaluation, review, reviewal, stocktaking, textual criticism, valorisation, valuation, value

ASSESSOR n appraiser, appreciator, estimator, gauger, judge, valuator, valuer, valuer general; **commentator**, critic, reviewer

ASSESSORIAL adj critical, estimative, valuational; **judgmental**, moralising, moralistic, sententious; **adjudicative**, arbitral, arbitrational, arbitrative, decretal, decretive, decretory, determinant, determinative, judicative, judicatory, judicial, judiciary

ASSIGNATION n appointment, blind date, date, double date, engagement, interview, introduction, invitation, meeting, note in one's diary, prearrangement, rendezvous, tryst; **place of assignation**, meeting place, trysting place

ASSOCIATE v bear company, consociate, familiarise *(Obs.)*, forgather with, hobnob, keep company, keep in touch, mingle, pal up with, partner, socialise, stay in touch, take up with, troop with; **rally**, forgather, meet, rendezvous; **club**, band together, cartelise, clique, gang, hang together, hold together, league, squadron; **affiliate**, align, ally, filiate, identify with, nail one's colours to the mast, take sides; **federate**, confederate, federalise, pull together; **unite**, combine, enter into, merge, pool; **organise**, embody, incorporate, institutionalise; **join up**, enlist, sign on, take out membership; **jump on the band wagon**, climb on the band wagon, get with the strength

ASTONISH v amaze, astound, flabbergast, overwhelm, surprise, throw; **dumbfound**, benumb, petrify, stun, stupefy; **awe**, dazzle, take one's breath away; **stagger**, knock someone bandy, make someone sit up and take notice, make someone's hair curl, strike all of a heap, take by surprise

ASTONISHED adj agog, bug-eyed, goggle-eyed, marvelling, open-eyed, open-mouthed, wondering; **astounded**, aghast, astound *(Archaic)*, confounded, dumbfounded, flabbergasted, staggered, stupefied, thunderstruck, unable to believe one's eyes, unexpressive *(Obs.)*; **awe-struck**, overwhelmed, struck dumb, wonderstruck

ASTONISHING *adj* amazing, astounding, remarkable, staggering, stupendous; **awesome,** awe-inspiring, awful, inexpressible, mind-boggling, overwhelming; **wonderful,** extraordinaire, extraordinary, fabulous, fantabulous, fantastic, fazzo, fearful, incredible, insane, marvellous, miraculous, phenomenal, prodigious, wondrous; **superb,** gallant *(Archaic),* massive, singular, splendid, sublime, tremendous

ASTONISHINGLY *adv* amazingly, astoundingly, remarkably, to one's astonishment, wondrous, wondrously; **wonderfully,** awesomely, extraordinarily, fabulously, fantastically, incredibly, inexpressibly, marvellously, miraculously, phenomenally; **sublimely,** dazzlingly, singularly, superbly

ASTONISHMENT *n* amaze *(Archaic),* amazedness, amazement, awe, stupefaction, surprise, wondering, wonderment

ASTRONOMER *n* astrologer, astrophysicist, lunarian, selenographer, selenologist, stargazer, uranographer, uranographist, uranologer

ASTRONOMICAL *adj* areodetic, astrophysical, radioastronomical, selenodetik, selenographic, uranographic, uranographical, uranological, zodiacal; **areocentric,** geocentric, heliocentric; **epicyclic,** equinoctial, evectional, nodical, perigeal, perigean, periodic, solstitial, syzygial

ASTRONOMIC POINT *n* aberration, annual parallax, diurnal parallax, evection, geocentric parallax, heliocentric parallax, inequality; **brightness,** magnitude; **arc,** azimuth, ecliptic, epycycle, southing; **declination,** celestial latitude, celestial longitude, elongation, emersion, galactic latitude, galactic longitude, latitude, magnetic declination; **degree,** galactic coordinate, trigon, variation; **node,** syzygy; **octant,** opposition, quadrature, quartile, quintile, sextile, trine; **perigee,** pericynthion, perihelion, perilune; **apogee,** aphelion, apocynthion; **precession,** precession of the equinoxes; **solstice,** solstitial point, summer solstice, vertical circle; **equinox,** equinoctial point; **eclipse,** annual eclipse, dichotomy, occultation, total eclipse; **rise,** proper motion, right ascension; **orbit,** apsis, line of apsides, revolution, rotation, synchronous equatorial; **equinoctial,** celestial equator, equinoctial line; **galactic circle,** colure, galactic equator, galactic plane; **tropic,** Tropic of Cancer, Tropic of Capricorn; **pole,** celestial pole, galactic pole, North Pole, South Pole; **zenith,** nadir, radiant, solar apex, vertex; **aclinic line,** magnetic equator

ASTRONOMY *n* almagest, areodesy, astrology, astrometry, astrophysics, radioastronomy, selenodesy, selenography, selenology, stargazing, uranography, uranology *(Obs.),* uranometry *(Obs.);* **astrobiology,** astrobotany, astrogeology; **big bang theory,** expanding universe, nebular hypothesis, steady state theory, superdense theory; **Copernican System,** Ptolemaic system

AT *prep* before, by, chez, in the teeth of, through, with

ATHLETIC *adj* agile, flippant *(Obs.),* nimble; **gymnastic,** aerobic, callisthenic, isometric

AT ISSUE *adv* before the house, in mind, in question, on the table, under discussion

AT LIBERTY *adv* at large, loose, on the loose, out of the wood

ATMOSPHERIC *adj* aerographic, aerographical, meteoric *(Obs.)*, meteorological, stratospheric; **high-pressure**, anticyclonic, hyperbaric; **low-pressure**, cyclonic; **barometric**, barographic

ATMOSPHERIC PRESSURE *n* air-pressure, free air overpressure; **high**, anticyclone; **low**, cyclone, low area; **cold front**, depression; **warm front**, heatwave, warm sector; **occluded front**, occlusion; **eye**, front, ridge, storm centre, trough, vortex, wedge; **convergence**, divergence, frontogenesis, frontolysis

ATOM *n* corpuscle, exotic atom, molecule, nuclide, radionuclide, Rutherford-Bohr atom; **ion**, anion, cation, free radical, negative ion, positive ion, radical, thermion, zwitterion; **atomic structure**, electron orbit, nucleus; **atomic mass**, atomic number, equivalent, isotopic number, mass number, neutron excess, packing fraction, weight; **quantum number**, charm, colour, flavour, isotopic spin, spin, strangeness

ATOMIC *adj* corpuscular, molecular, nuclear; **intermolecular**, interatomic, intra-atomic, intramolecular, subatomic

ATOMIC BOMB *n* A-bomb, atom bomb, fission bomb, nuclear bomb; **hydrogen bomb**, fusion bomb, H-bomb; **neutron bomb**, clean bomb, clean weapon; **nuclear weapon**, nuclear warhead

ATOMIC RADIATION *n* alpha radiation, beta radiation, cascade shower, colorescence, delta radiation, gamma radiation, rays, re-radiation, secondary emission, soft shower, twenty-one centimetre line; **ray**, alpha ray, beta ray, electron beam, molecular beam; **radioactivity**, alpha decay, artificial radioactivity, beta decay, induced radioactivity, photodisintegration, stimulated emission; **radiation level**, absorbed dose, ambient dose, background count, background radiation, chronic dose, gray count, rad count, rem count, strontium unit; **fallout**, fallout contour, fallout pattern, rainout, yield; **half-life**, becquerel, curie *(Physics)*, roentgen; **X-rays**, roentgen rays, thermal X-rays, X-radiation.
See also NUCLEAR ENERGY; RADIOACTIVATION; ATOMIC BOMB

ATOMIC THEORY *n* atomics, microphysics, nuclear physics, nucleonics, quantum electrodynamics, quantum mechanics, quantum theory

ATONE FOR *v* assoil *(Archaic)*, confess, purge, shrive; **reform**, apologise, be on good behaviour, conciliate, heal, live down, make one's peace, pray, propitiate, repair; **excuse**, condone

ATONEMENT *n* expiation, penance, penitence, purgation, purge, shrift *(Archaic)*

AT SEA *adv* overseas, undersea; **offshore**, inshore, outward, seaward, seawards

ATTACK *n* assailment, assault, attempt on one's life, battery, blow, cannonade, feint, field-gunnery, fire, firing, mining, offence, onset, onslaught, potshot, salvo, shot, volley; **counter-attack**, counteroffensive, escalation of violence, retaliation; **foray**, drive, excursion *(Obs.)*, forage, interdiction, offensive, pillage, push, raid, rush, sally, sortie, storm, surprise, thrust; **incursion**, bust, infiltration, ingress, inroad, invasion, irruption; **ambush**, ambuscade, stake-out; **air-raid**, air strike, blitz, blitzkrieg, bombardment, broadside, first strike, plastering, prang, stoush, strafe; **charge**, career *(Obs.)*, course, flèche; **indecent assault**, rape

ATTACK *v* assail, assault, attempt someone's life, beat up, carry the fight, fall on, fall upon, fly at, get, get into, get stuck into, go at, go for, have at *(Archaic)*, hit, hoe into, horsewhip, jump down someone's throat, knuckle, lace into *(Brit.)*, let someone have it, make at, make mincemeat of, mug, pelt, pitch into, prey on, put the boot into, round on, sabre, savage, set about, set on, set upon, sic onto, take the offensive, tear into, turn on, visit, wade into, weigh into, whale into; **counterattack**, retaliate; **strike the first blow**, aggress, draw first blood; **beset**, beleaguer, declare open season on, gang up on, harass, invest, leaguer, mob, press, rabble; **charge**, advance, advance against, advance on, bear down on, erupt, remise *(Fencing)*, run at, rush, sally, tilt; **besiege**, blockade, invade, lay seige to, move in, siege, stake out; **ambush**, ambuscade, bushwhack; **spring**, descend on, jump *(U.S.)*, surprise, swoop on; **depredate**, forage, foray, pillage, plunder, raid.   *See also* FIRE ON

ATTACK *interj* banzai, charge, geronimo, go for it, up there Cazaly; **on guard**, have at you

ATTACKER *n* aggressor, assailant, assailer, assaulter, bludgeoner, harasser, hawk; **raider**, air-raider, invader, space invader; **ambusher**, ambuscader; **forager**, forayer, pillager;

front line, advance party, shock troops, spearhead, storm troops

ATTAINABLE *adj* compassable, dischargeable, doable, performable, surmountable

ATTEMPT *n* adventure, assay, bid, effort, endeavour, essay, experiment, fetch *(Archaic)*, first-up, go, long shot, offer, shot, speculation, try, try-on, venture; **whack**, burl, crack, fling, fly, pop, run-through, stab, stroke, two bites at the cherry; **striving**, assailment, conation, struggle, trial

ATTEMPT *v* assail, assay, carve out, endeavour, essay, have a lash at it, take on, try; **try for**, aim at, aim for, offer at *(Obs.)*, seek, study, tackle, undertake; **strive for**, attack, exert oneself, grasp, push hard for, put effort into, scrabble for, struggle for, work towards; **audition for**, apply, read for, throw one's hat in the ring, try out for; **venture on**, experiment, gamble, hazard, push one's luck, speculate, take one's chance, tempt fortune, try one's fortune, try one's hand, try one's luck; **try one's hand at**, chance one's arm, give it a bash, give it a buck, give it a go, give it a nudge, give it a whirl, have a bash, have a buck, have a crack, have a go, have a punt, have a smack, make an attempt, take time out to; **keep on trying**, battle on, hammer away at; **go all out**, do one's level best, give it everything one has, go for the doctor, move heaven and earth, put one's best foot forward, shoot one's bolt, sink or swim; **seek to**, get to grips with, make bold to, settle down to

ATTEMPTER *n* aimer, assailant *(Rare)*, assailer, assayer, battler, endeavourer, essayer, essayist, mover, seeker,

attempter

trier; **struggler**, do-it-yourselfer, goer, striver; **gambler**, hazarder, punter; **candidate**, apellant, applicant, applier, aspirant, postulant, pretender, probationer

ATTEND TO *v* address oneself to, advert, be all ears, be all eyes, be on the alert, concentrate, consider, dig *(Colloq.)*, focalise, focus, get down to, hang on the lips of, hang upon, have an eye to, heed, keep an eye on, listen, look at, look to, mark, mind, note, reck, regard, see about, sink into, stand by, study, watch; **notice**, animadvert *(Obs.)*, be awake-up, enter into, eye, get with it, observe, remark, sit up and take notice

ATTENTIVE *adj* advertent, alert, alerted, argus-eyed, awake, curious, heedful, interested, mindful, observant, open-eyed, watchful; **aware**, alive to, on the ball, sharp, witting *(Archaic)*; **assiduous**, careful, painful *(Archaic)*, painstaking, sedulous, serious; **fastidious**, finical, finicky; **absorbed**, concerned, deep in, earnest, engrossed, intent, rapt, spellbound, wrapped up in

ATTENTIVELY *adv* absorbedly, advertently, alertly, fixedly, heedfully, interestedly, mindfully, on the edge of one's chair, regardfully, with one's ears flapping; **assiduously**, carefully, earnestly, intently; **sharp**, hard

ATTENTIVENESS *n* advertence, advertency, alertness, curiousness, heedfulness, mindfulness, regardfulness, watchfulness; **engrossment**, absorbedness, absorption, fascination, intentness, interestedness; **assiduousness**, application, assiduity, carefulness, sedulity, sedulousness; **fastidiousness**, finicality; **attention**, awareness, engagement, focalisation, heed, interest, note, notice, regard, remark

ATTITUDINISE *v* act, affect, emote, feign, go through the motions, peacock, play-act, pose, posture, posturise, prance; **simper**, be affected, mince, prim, smirk; **snivel**, snuffle, turn on the waterworks

ATTRACT *v* adduce, allure, bring towards, decoy, draw to, engage, gather, lure, magnetise, pull; **gravitate**, cluster

ATTRACTION *n* adduction, allurement, appetence, attractiveness, counter-attraction, draw, pull; **gravity**, gravitation; **chemical affinity**, chemotaxis, Van der Waals' forces. *See also* MAGNETISM

ATTRACTIVE *adj* adducent, adductive, alluring, appetent, appetising, arresting, seductive; **magnetic**, aeromagnetic, electromagnetic, geomagnetic, ionised, magneto-chemical, magnetomotive, magnetostatic, polar, pyromagnetic; **ferromagnetic**, diamagnetic, ferrimagnetic, paramagnetic; **gravitational**, gravitative

ATTRACTOR *n* bait, centre of attraction, decoy, draw, lure, teaser; **magnet**, electromagnet, lodestone, magnetite, permanent magnet; **magnetiser**, keeper

AUDACIOUSNESS *n* assuredness, audacity, barefacedness, bumptiousness, effrontery, forwardness, hardihood, presumptuousness, shamelessness; **cockiness**, cockishness, sauciness; **high-handedness**, dictatorialness, domineeringness, high-mindedness, imperiousness, officiousness

AUDIBLY *adv* within earshot, within hail

AUDIENCE *n* captive audience, claque, full house, theatre, turnout; **playgoer**, cineaste, cinemagoer, concert-goer, fan, film freak, first-nighter, groundling *(Archaic)*

AUDIO *adj* hi-fi, high-fidelity, laser, mono, monophonic, quadraphonic, stereo, stereophonic; **gramophonic**, phonautographic, phonographic; **megaphonic**, microphonic

AUDITORIUM *n* amphitheatre, circus *(Rom. Antiq.)*, colosseum; house; **theatre**, big top, chamber of horrors, circus, concert-hall, hippodrome, house, music hall, music theatre, nickelodeon *(U.S.)*, odeum, opera house, palace, playhouse, showboat *(U.S.)*, strip joint, theatre in the round, three-ring circus; **picture theatre**, biograph *(Obs.)*, drive-in, drive-it-in, film theatre, fleas-'n'-itches *(Colloq.)*, flicks *(Colloq.)*, hardtop, passion pit *(Colloq.)*, picture house *(Obs.)*, picture palace *(Obs.)*, theatre; **seating**, balcony, box, circle, dress circle, front of house, gallery, loge, lounge, parquet *(U.S.)*, stalls, the gods, upper circle

AUSTRALIA *n* down-under, God's own country, Godzone, Oz, the lucky country; **the mainland**

AUSTRALIAN *n* antipodean, Aussie, Aussielander, dinkum Aussie, dinky-di Aussie, ocker, ockerina, skippy, sullivan; **New Australian**, Balt, black hat *(Obs.)*, new chum, reffo, wog *(Derog.)*; t'othersider, Eastern Stater *(W.A.)*, mainlander *(Tas)*; **New South Welshman**, cornstalk; **Victorian**, cabbage-gardener, cabbage-lander, cabbage-patcher, gumsucker, Mexican; **Tasmanian**, apple islander, Derwent duck *(Obs.)*, Derwenter *(Obs.)*, mutton-bird, mutton-bird eater, Tasmaniac, Tassie, Tassielander, Taswegian, Vandemonian *(Obs.)*; **Queenslander**, bananabender, kanakalander *(Obs.)*, sugarlander; **Territorian**, top-ender; **Western Australian**, groper, groperlander, sandgroper, Westralian; **South Australian**, crow-eater, magpie, wheatlander

AUTHENTICATE *v* authorise, certify, endorse, notarise, validate; **prove**, approve *(Obs.)*, bear out, confirm, corroborate, demonstrate, document, establish, make good, manifest, reprove, show, substantiate, sustain, try *(Obs.)*, verify, vouch

AUTHENTICATION *n* accreditation, approbation *(Obs.)*, certificate *(Law)*, certification, confirmation, jurat *(Law)*, manifestation, probate, probation *(Rare)*, testamur *(Educ.)*, validation, verification, voucher, warrant; **identification**, exequatur, ID, papers; **medical certificate**, aegrotat; **grounds**, corpus delicti *(Law)*, data, document *(Obs.)*, exhibit, gist; **reference**, adduction, authority, chapter and verse, citation, locus classicus

AUTHORIAL *adj* auctorial, subeditorial; **under one's hand**, holographical; manuscript; **clerical**, scribal, secretarial

AUTHORISE *v* accredit, crown, empower, enable, establish, mandate, revest, sanction, seal, swear in, warrant

AUTHORITATIVE *adj* commanding, competent, dominant, dominative, imperial, master, predominant, prepotent, sceptred, sovereign, superintendent, supreme; **official**, authentic *(Obs.)*, cathedral, ex-cathedra, ex-officio, oracular

AUTHORITY n accreditation, carte blanche, commission, jurisdiction, mandate, officiation, power, prerogative, procuration, roving commission; **authoritativeness**, arbitrament, dominance, dominancy, masterfulness, potence, potency, supremacy, supremeness; **authoritarianism**, absolutism, bumbledom, despotism, divine right of kings, domination, domineeringness, fascism, officialism, peremptoriness, totalitarianism, tyranny; **dominion**, command, commission, condominium, dominium, franchise, imperium, reign, rule, sway; **government**, headship, hegemony, kingship, leadership, lordship, magistracy, masterdom, mastery, seigniory, sovereignty, suzerainty; **rule**, a firm hand, command, governance, law, martial law, say-so, sway; **emblem of authority**, arm, chair, crown, diadem, fasces, mayoral chain, rod, sceptre, throne

AUTOCRATIC adj authoritarian, domineering, fascist, feudal, feudalistic, imperious, lordly, masterful, peremptory, totalitarian

AVARICIOUS adj acquisitive, covetous, extortionate, grasping, greedy, hungry, insatiable, insatiate, rapacious, selfish

AVENGER n kadaicha man, nemesis, requiter, revenger, vendettist

AVERAGE n arithmetic mean, centroid, geometric mean, harmonic mean, indifference point, mean, median, moment, normal, root mean square; **middlings**, intergrade; **golden mean**, compromise, happy medium, middle course

AVERAGE v compromise, equalise, even up, iron out differences, split the difference, standardise

AVOID v avert, back away from, blench from, blink at, dip out on, duck, evade, fight shy of, give a wide berth, jib, miss, not touch with a barge pole, shrink from, shy away from, steer clear of; **bypass**, boycott, cold-shoulder, ditch, eschew, fob off, get off, leave, let sleeping dogs lie, put on one side, shun; **shirk**, bilk, bludge, dingo, dodge, funk, pass the buck, sell the dump *(Colloq.)*, shuffle out of; **equivocate**, avoid the issue, beat about the bush, beg the question, deflect, fence, hedge, hem and haw, parry, prevaricate, procrastinate, quibble, shelve, sidestep, skate over, skate round, stall, temporise

AVOIDANCE n buck-passing, escapism, evasion, evasiveness, obliqueness, prevention, tokenism; **abstention**, abstinence, eschewal; **act of avoidance**, dodge, duck, escape, flight, flit, shuffle, sidestep

AVOIDER n absconder from public labour *(Archaic)*, abstainer, averter, chicaner, deserter, dodger, draft dodger, escaper, escapist, eschewer, evader, shunner, truant; **fleer**, blencher, boggler, ducker, fly-by-night, fugitive, runaway; **shirker**, bilker, bludger, buck-passer, coaster, dingo, hedger, malingerer, quitter, shirk, skulker, slacker; **quibbler**, equivocator, fencer, prevaricator, procrastinator, temporiser

AVOWED adj declared, predicate, predicative, professed, sworn

AWAKE *adj* wide-awake; **astir**, about, up and about; **wakeful**, insomniac, insomnious, restless, sleepless, watchful *(Archaic)*

AWARD *n* a feather in one's cap, accolade, blue riband, blue ribbon, cordon bleu, credit, distinction, laurels; **laurel wreath**, bay, crown, garland, palm; **prize**, booty, spoils, stakes, sweepstake, tern; **entertainment award**, Awgie, BAFTA, Emmy, gold record, Grammy, Logie, Mo, Oscar, platinum record, Sammy; **writing award**, Age Book Award, Booker Prize, Miles Franklin Award, Patrick White Award, Pulitzer Prize, Vogel Award, Walkley Award; **painting award**, Archibald Prize, Blake Prize, Sulman Prize, Wynn Prize; **general award**, Churchill Fellowship, Fulbright Fellowship, Harkness Fellowship, Nobel Prize, Rhodes Scholarship, Rotary Scholarship, ZONTA Fellowship; **sporting award**, America's Cup, Davis Cup, F.A. Cup, Melbourne Cup, Sheffield Shield, Stawell Gift, the Ashes, The Auld Mug, World Cup; **best and fairest**, Brownlow Medal *(Vic.)*, Dally M. Award *(N.S.W.)*, Magarey Medal *(S.A.)*, Sandover Medal *(W.A.)*; **trophy**, belt, black belt, blue, bronze medal, colours, cup, first prize, gold medal, Grand Prix, loving-cup, pendant, pennant, pot, premium, ribbon, silver medal; **honours list**, birthday honours, honour roll; **medal**, bar, citation, decoration, fruit salad *(Mil. Colloq.)*, gong *(Colloq.)*, honour, medallion; **knighthood**, dubbing; **booby prize**, wooden spoon

AWARD *v* adjudge, bestow, grant, present; **decorate**, crown, distinguish *(Archaic)*, garland, laurel, reward; **diploma**, cap *(N.Z.)*; **knight**, dub

AWARD WINNER *n* diplomate, laureate, licentiate, prizewinner; **medallist**, gold medallist

AWAY *adv* afield, awa *(Scot.)*, interstate, off *(Naut.)*, o.s., out, overseas; **behind someone's back**, in absentia

AXE *n* broadaxe, celt, chopper, cleaver, fasces, hack, hatchet, kelly, meataxe, mogo, palstave, sax, scutch, tomahawk, tommyaxe, tommyhawk, twibill

Bb

BABY-SITTING *n* child-care, day care

BACK *n* dorsum, paddywhack, small of the back; **spine**, backbone, chine, rachis, spinal column, spinal cord, vertebral column; **hunchback**, dowager's hump, humpback, widow's hump

BACK OUT *v* back down, back off, back-pedal, backtrack, chuck it, chuck one's hand in, flunk out, scratch, sling it in, stand down, throw in one's hand; **bale out**, bolt *(U.S.)*, cut one's losses; **withdraw from**, evacuate, give the game away, quit, resign, secede from, surrender, throw in the towel, vacate

BACK TO BASICS *phr* back to taws, back to the drawing-board, here we go again

BAD *adj* abject, baleful, dismal, egregious, grievous, hopeless, ill, mean, measly, miserable, not much chop, not much cop, paltry, pathetic, pernicious, poor, sad, shameful, sorry, woeful, wretched; **worthless**, base, bodgie, botchy, brum, brummy, bum, cheap, cheapjack, crook, crummy, el cheapo, grotty, inferior, losel *(Archaic)*, low, mean, mongrel, nogood, not worth a pinch of shit, not worth a whoop, onkus, punk, queer, rubbishy, scrubby, scummy, shoddy, sleazy, tacky, tin, tin-pot, unacceptable, unsatisfactory, unworthy, up to putty; **awful**, abominable, abysmal, abyssal, appalling, atrocious, chronic, contemptible, deplorable, despicable, detestable, disastrous, disgraceful, dreadful, enormous, execrable, God-awful, grievous, ignominious, inexcusable, inexpiable, lamentable, monstrous, outrageous, pitiful, rotten, shocking, terrible, unforgivable, ungodly, unholy, unmentionable, unreal, unspeakable, vile; **adverse**, detrimental, dire, direful, hard, impossible, malevolent, malign, opposite *(Obs.)*, portentous, undesirable, unfavourable, unfortunate; **evil**, sinful, wicked; **worst**, of the blackest dye, of the deepest dye; **devilish**, diabolic, diabolical, helluva, infernal; **damned**, cursed, curst, damnable; **squalid**, insalubrious, seamy; **stinking**, cankerous, filthy, foul, lousy, noisome, odious, putrid, R.S., rank, ratshit, rotten, septic, shithouse, shitty

BAD DEBT *n* counterfeit notes, debt, forged notes; **dishonoured cheque**, bad cheque, bogus cheque, boomerang, bouncing cheque, floater, rubber cheque; **stop order**, abatement *(Law)*, days of grace, moratorium, protest *(Comm.)*, stop, stop payment, suspension

BADLY *adv* bad, dismally, ill, miserably, shamefully, undesirably, unfortunately, woefully; **awfully**, abominably, abysmally, appallingly, atrociously, damnably, deplorably, despicably, dreadfully, egregiously, execrably, shockingly, terribly, unspeakably

BADLY-BEHAVED *adj* disobedient, ill-behaved, ill-mannered, naughty, pert, perverse, problem, sullen, uncooperative; **rascally**, blackguardly, knavish, pestilent, ratbaggy, roguish, sly; **mischievous**, arch, elfin, elfish, frolicsome, gamin, impish, kittenish, puckish, scampish, tricksy; **disorderly,** destructive, hooligan, larrikinish, rough, rough-and-tumble, rude, undisciplined; **irresponsible,** fly-by-night, improper, wayward, wrong; **uncontrollable,** hyperactive, incorrigible, obstreperous, overactive, rambunctious *(U.S. Colloq.),* restive, restless, unruly

BADLY-DONE *adj* angular, bad, botched, botchy, crappy, faulty, hopeless, ill; **ill-contrived,** ill-chosen, ill-conceived, ill-devised, infelicitous, unhappy, unplanned. *See also* INCOMPETENT

BAD MOOD *n* dismals, fit of depression, fit of the blues, joes, languish *(Obs.),* lousy, low spirits, megrims, moods, mopes, vapours *(Archaic);* **tears,** waterworks

BADNESS *n* dismalness, egregiousness, grievousness, lousiness, miserableness, peccancy, preciousness, shamefulness, sinfulness, woefulness, wretchedness; **awfulness,** abominableness, atrociousness, contemptibility, deplorability, deplorableness, despicability, despicableness, detestableness, devilishness, diabolicalness, dreadfulness, fiendishness, infernality, monstrousness, terribleness, vileness; **adverseness,** direfulness, pestilence, portentousness, sinisterness, undesirableness; **squalidity,** insalubrity, seaminess, shoddiness, sleaziness, unhealthiness; **worthlessness,** paltriness, unworthiness

BAD PERSON *n* bad apple, bad egg, bad hat, bad lot, bad penny, black sheep, bodgie, good-for-nothing, idler, losel *(Archaic),* ne'er-do-well, poor white trash, punk, rag, scum, trash, undesirable, waster, wastrel, whatnot; **bastard,** arse, arsehole, bathplug, bathtub, berk, blister *(Brit.),* bugger, bum, companion *(Obs.),* coyote *(U.S.),* cunt, cunthook *(N.Z.),* cur, deadshit, dog, drop kick *(N.Z.),* dunghill, fucker, hound, mongrel, mother *(U.S.),* mother-fucker *(U.S.),* pimp, rattler, shit, shithead, so-and-so, sod, son of a bitch, stinker, swine, the end, the living end, turd; **louse,** blighter, cad, caitiff *(Archaic),* dastard, dingo, heel, insect, poon, prick, rat, rat-fink, reptile, rotter *(Brit.),* runt, serpent, skulk, skunk, snake, sneak, sneaker, squib, swab, toad, varmint, vermin, viper, wretch; **creep,** creeping Jesus, drip, fink, jerk; **bloodsucker,** bushranger, vampire; **bitch,** cow, fleabag, hag, harpy, hellcat, scold, witch; **fiend,** demon, devil, hellhound, lost soul; **monster,** Frankenstein, ogre, ogress, savage, terror

BAD THING *n* abomination, arsehole, atrocity, bad apple, bad news, bane, bastard, blemish, botch, brummy, bungle, detestation, devil, dirty word, dunghill, fizzer, fucker, horror, mother *(Colloq.),* mother-fucker *(Colloq.),* scandal; **trash,** garbage, goats, mess of pottage, pulp, quickie, rag, rubbish; **the pits,** low tide, the end, the living end; **jonah,** evil omen, evil star, hex, hoodoo, jinx

BAG *n* billum, blister pack, carpetbag, carrier bag, carry bag, carryall, cod, dillybag, ditty-bag, duffle bag, garbag, gladbag, grip, gunny, holdall, jiffy bag, kitbag *(Mil.),* musette bag *(U.S.),* paper bag, plastic bag, poke *(Obs.),* seabag, shoulder-bag, string bag, tote bag, workbag; **swag,** bluey, frame pack, haversack, knapsack, matilda, pack, packsack *(U.S.)*, rucksack, satchel, scrip *(Archaic)*; **saddlebag**, dosser, pannier; **sack**, cornsack, flourbag, gamebag, mailbag, ragbag, sugarbag; **package**, Christmas stocking, packet, parcel, sachet; **doggie bag**, feedbag, nosebag, tuckerbag, waterbag; **sac**, conceptacle, crop, cupule, cyst, cystoid, utricle, vesica, vesicle; **bladder**, air-chamber, air-cushion, air-sac, balloon, gasbag; **pod**, capsule, peasecod, shell, skin, theca

BALD *adj* bald as a bandicoot, bald-headed, balding, baldish, baldpated, eggshell blond, thatchless, tonsured; **hairless**, beardless, clean-shaven, furless, glabrate, glabrous, smooth, smooth-faced; **featherless**, callow, impennate; **depilatory**, exfoliative

BALL *n* bomb *(Geol.)*, crystal ball, globe, globoid, moon, orb, sphere, spheroid, toroid, torus; **celestial globe**, celestial sphere; **playing ball**, baseball, basketball, beach ball, billiard ball, bowl, bowling ball, colour, cricket ball, cue ball, eight ball, football, golf ball, medicine ball, pill, ping-pong ball, pioneer ball *(Croquet)*, pushball, rubber ball, shot, six-stitcher, soccer ball, softball, spotball *(Billiards)*, squash ball, tennis ball, volleyball; **balloon**

BANK *n* acceptance house, building society, central bank, clearing house, discount house, finance company, merchant bank, mutual savings bank, reserve bank, savings bank, terminating building society, trading bank; **stock exchange**, Bourse, exchange, kerb, pit *(U.S.)*; **market**, bear market, bull market, buy-back market, commercial bill market, contango, futures exchange, futures market, grey market, inter-company market, seller's market, short-term money market, spot market, stock market; **books closing date**, ex date, spot month

BAR *n* arch bar, bail, capstan bar, crossbar, drawbar, flat, jack, rail, sliprail; **metal bar**, angle iron, channel iron, roll bar, T-bar, U-bolt; **crowbar**, handspike, heaver, jemmy, pinch, pinch-bar, sweep, swipe, tiller, tommy bar

BARE *v* clear out, debark, disfurnish, dismantle, divest, expose, open, uncase, uncover, undrape, unshroud, unswathe, unveil, unwrap; **strip**, clear, deplume, disfurnish, dismantle, undress, unshroud, unswathe; **depilate**, clip, deplume, epilate, fleece, grain, pink, pull, tonsure, unhair; **defoliate**, deflower, denudate, denude, exfoliate, strip; **moult**, exuviate, mew, shed; **clear**, burn off, bush *(Agric.)*, bushwhack *(N.Z.)*, deforest, disafforest, disforest; **pare**, decorticate, excoriate, excorticate, hull, peel, pod, skin, unhusk

BARE *adj* bleak, defoliate, denudate, exposed, hypaethral, leafless, nudicaul, open, uncovered; **featureless**, blank, open; **unpainted**, unvarnished; **nude**, full-frontal, naked, stark, stark-naked, unclad, uncovered; **undressed**, barefaced, barefoot, barefooted, barehanded, bareheaded, barelegged, topless; **revealing**, décolleté, low, low-cut, low-necked, peekaboo

BARENESS *n* blankness, bleakness, denudation, leaflessness; **hairlessness**, alopecia, alopecia areata, baldness, beardlessness, calvities, expos-

bareness   45   **bay**

edness, exposure, mange, manginess, tonsure; **nudity**, birthday suit, décolletage, dishabille, nakedness, nudeness, undress; **nudism**, naturism

BARGAIN *n* buy, dicker, go *(U.S.)*, special, steal; **cheapie**, brummy, button, catchpenny, el cheapo, rip; **sale**, garage sale, jumble sale, rummage sale

BARGAINER *n* chafferer, shaver

BARGAINING *n* chaffer, haggling

BARKER *n* bellower, bleater, brayer, growler, grunter, howler, roarer, snarler, yelper; **croaker**, honker, squawker, whooper; **chirruper**, cackler, chirper, hooter, twitterer

BARRACKS *n* casern, hut, lines, quarters, station; **college**, hall, hall of residence, inn *(Brit.)*; **dormitory**, sleeping quarters; **mess**, long house, pueblo, roundhouse; **selamlik**, seraglio, harem

BARREL *n* breaker *(Naut.)*, butt, cask, eighteen, firkin, hogshead, keg, kilderkin, nine, pin, puncheon, quarter cask, scuttlebutt, tierce, tun, water-butt, wood; **vat**, bin, churn, drum, hopper, keeve, kier, lauter tun, tank. *See also* BASIN; BOTTLE; VESSEL

BARRENLY *adv* aridly, desolately, sterilely; **unproductively**, fruitlessly, in vain, ineffectively, nonproductively, unfruitfully, unprofitably, vainly

BASIN *n* baptistery, font, lavabo, lavatory, laver, piscina; **laundry tub**, copper, dolly pot, trough; **bath**, bathtub, footbath, tub; **tank**, boiler, cistern, reservoir, sump, well; **inkwell**, inkhorn; **eyebath**, eyeglass. *See also* VESSEL

BASKET *n* basketry, breadbasket, chip basket, clothes basket, creel, flasket, frail, gondola, hamper, hanaper, kit *(N.Z.)*, linen basket, Maori basket *(N.Z.)*, punnet, scuttle, sewing basket, shopping basket, skep, trug, workbasket; **bassinette**, car-basket, carry basket, carry cot, cradle, crib, Moses basket. *See also* BOX; BAG; CASE

BATH *n* basin, bidet, birdbath, bush shower, douche, footbath, hand basin, hipbath, jacuzzi, lavatory, shower, sink, sitz bath, spa, tub, washbasin, washbowl, washtub; **washstand**, commode, vanity unit; **font**, laving, laver; **laundry**, laundrette, laundromat, washhouse; **steriliser**, autoclave; **sluice**, banjo, cradle, launder, strake, V-box; **copper**, kier, trough, tub; **carwash**; **sheep dip**, plunge dip, washpool

BATHROOM *n* bagnio, bathhouse, baths, comfort station, facilities, sauna, shower room, steam bath, sudatorium, thermae, toilet facilities, washroom

BATTLEGROUND *n* Armageddon, cockpit, field, field of battle, firezone, trenches; **enfilade**, action stations, echelon, firing line, front, front line, line, line of battle; **minefield**; **beachhead**, bridgehead; **headquarters**, base, camp, general headquarters, GHQ, HQ, operations room

BATTLER *n* grind, ironside, plodder, stayer, sticker, the walking wounded

BAY *n* bight, embayment, gulf, hole, indentation, ria; **inlet**, arm, armlet, canal, cove, creek, estuary, fiord, firth, flow, frith, lough, tidal inlet; **passage**, sound, strait; **tidal basin**, embouchure, tide-lock. *See also* SEA; LAKE

be   **be annoyed**

BE *v* exist, pre-exist; **live,** keep body and soul together, subsist; **occur,** be situated at, happen, lie, take place; **continue,** abide, endure, go on, last, prevail, remain, survive

BE ABLE *v* admit of, bear, can, have a chance, may, stand a chance, stand the strain

BE ABSENT *v* be nowhere, exile, flex, flexi, flex off, give something a miss, go bush, miss out on, shoot through; **go missing,** beg off, jig, jig it, jig school, jump bail, play hooky, play the wag, play truant, shoot the moon, truant, wag, wag it

BE ACCUSTOMED TO *v* be always at, be given to, be in the habit of, be used to, be wont to, do regularly, go in for, make a habit of, make a practice of, perform regularly, practise, take to, take up

BEAD *n* ball-bearing, bullet, button, gibber, globule, grain, granule, pearl, pellet, pill, pilule, spherule, stone *(Games)*; **nut,** acinus, berry, boll, corn; **bobble,** poi *(N.Z.)*, pompom; **clew; drop,** dewdrop, droplet, gutta; **bubble,** blob

BE ADEQUATE *v* be sufficient, cover, last, offset, run to; **suffice,** answer, be enough, do, make do, serve; **qualify,** fill the bill, make the grade, measure up to, pass, pass muster

BEAM *n* arch bar, bar, baulk, bellcast batten, bolster, box girder, cleat, crossbar *(Gymnastics)*, crossbeam, crosstree *(Naut.)*, fascine, fish *(Naut.)*, flying shore, gallows top *(Naut.)*, girder, hammerbeam, hydrofoil, I-beam, jack, joist, lintel, manteltree, needle beam, nogging, outrigger, plate, principal, purlin, rafter, rood beam, shore, shoring, sill, sleeper *(Railways)*, splat, straining beam, stretcher, stringer, strut, subprincipal *(Carp.)*, supporter, tie beam, transom, trestletree, trimmer, trussed beam, trussing, upholder

BE ANGRY *v* blow a fuse, blow a gasket, blow one's cool, blow one's top, blow up, boil, boil over, bung on an act, do a slow burn, do one's block, do one's bun, do one's cruet, do one's lolly, do one's nana, do one's nut, do one's quince, do one's scone, flip one's lid, fly off the handle, fly out, foam at the mouth, fume, get off one's bike, get one's back up, get one's dander up, get one's Irish up, get one's monkey up, go bananas, go crook, go hostile *(N.Z.)*, go off one's brain, go off pop, hit the ceiling, hit the roof, let fly, let go, let off steam, let rip, lose one's block, lose one's cool, lose one's temper, lose one's wool, perform, rage, ramp, rampage, rant, rear up, sound off, spit chips, stack on an act, storm, tear one's hair out, throw a fit, throw a willy; **get the shits,** broil, grudge, have a skinful, have the shits; **darken,** glare, glower, lour, sulk; **flare up,** bite, bite back, bridle, bristle, flame, flare out, flash, growl, jangle *(Archaic)*, see red, thunder, yap

BE ANGRY WITH *v* be crooked on, be dirty on, come the acid over *(N.Z.)*, get one's knife into, go butcher's, go butcher's hook at, go crook at, look daggers at, roar someone up, snap someone's head off, take it out on, tell off; **resent,** stomach *(Obs.)*, sweat, take amiss, take exception

BE ANNOYED *v* be sick of, go off the deep end, have had a bellyful, have had an eyeful, have had it, have the pip, have the shits, have the tomtits

BE APPOINTED *v* be promoted, get on, get the nod

BE APPROVED *v* get the nod, pass muster; **grow on**, be in big with, get in good with, prepossess; **impress**, bring down the house, grab them by the balls, knock their eyes out, lay them in the aisles, take them by storm, wow them

BEARABLE *adj* endurable, livable, sufferable, supportable, sustainable, swallowable, tolerable

BEARD *n* barb, bumfluff, burnsides *(U.S.)*, down, face fungus, five o'clock shadow, goatee, imperial, Vandyke beard, whiskers, ziff; **moustache**, dundreary, handlebar moustache, lice ladders, mo, muttonchops, side-whiskers, sideboard, sideburns *(U.S.)*, sidelevers, walrus moustache, whiskers

BE ARROGANT *v* be too big for one's boots, be up oneself, cavalier, cock *(Obs.)*, flaunt, get a big head, get a swelled head, get on one's high horse, have more front than Mark Foys, have tickets on oneself, lord it over, overween, put on jam, queen it, swagger, swank, swash, swell; **presume**, assume, have a nerve, have oneself on, have the cheek, horn in, perk; **patronise**, high-hat, overbear; **disdain**, cock a snook at, despise, scorn, sneer at; **dogmatise**, lay down the law about; **bully**, bullyrag, domineer, lord it over, overlord

BEAT *v* batter, belabour, clobber, cob, cream, curry, fib, hammer, lace *(Brit.)*, lam, lambaste, larrup, lather, paste, pelt, plaster, pommel *(U.S.)*, pummel, thrash, towel, trounce, wallop, whale; **beat up**, bash up, beat hell out of, beat the living daylights out of, beat the tripe out of, do for, do over, give someone Bondi *(Obs.)*, give someone Larry Dooley, lam into, lay hands on, tan someone's hide, whale into. *See also* HIT: CUDGEL

BEAT A PATH *v* pave a way, trail *(U.S.)*; **leave a trail**, lay down a track, track *(U.S.)*; **chart**, navigate, plot, track

BEATEN *adj* battered, creamed, smitten, stricken; **knocked over**, floored, unloaded

BEAT TIME *v* keep time; **syncopate**

BEAUTIFUL *adj* Adonic, angelic, apollonian, beauteous, comely, dreamy, gorgeous, heavenly, lovely, nymphal, nymphean, ornamental, personable, pulchritudinous, sheen *(Archaic)*, statuesque, stunning; **attractive**, becoming, bonzer, boshter, decorative, easy on the eye, good, jaunty, sightly, smart, soignée, spunky, trig; **good-looking**, brave *(Archaic)*, fine, handsome, proper *(Archaic)*, seemly, well-favoured; **pretty**, blooming, bonny, bright-eyed, dinky, dishy, dollish, fair, mignon, minion, pretty-pretty, prettyish, rosy, rosy-cheeked, ruddy, specious *(Obs.)*; **elegant**, exquisite, polished, refined, silken, thoroughbred; **voluptuous**, bosomy, buxom, callipygian, curvaceous, curvy, long-limbed, pneumatic, sensuous, sexy, shapely, sonsy *(Scot. Irish)*, well-proportioned; **picturesque**, aesthetic, aesthetical, artistic, charming, pleasant; **glorious**, brilliant, flamboyant, grand, grandiose, imperial, lustrous, magnific *(Archaic)*, magnificent, regal, resplendent, splendid, splendorous, stately, sumptuous, superb, triumphant *(Obs.)*; **graceful**, aerial, ethereal, flowing, fluent, gracile, lissom,

beautiful

lithe, supple; **radiant**, blooming, bright, ravishing, splendent; **delicate**, dainty, minikin

BEAUTIFULLY *adv* angelically, beauteously, becomingly, gorgeously, stunningly; **decoratively**, attractively, bravely *(Archaic)*, handsomely; **prettily**, bonnily, dollishly; **gloriously**, grandiosely, grandly, imperially, lustrously, resplendently; **splendidly**, regally, statuesquely, sumptuously, superbly; **gracefully**, aerially, daintily, delicately, elegantly, ethereally, exquisitely, flowingly, fluently; **radiantly**, bright, brightly; **voluptuously**, buxomly

BEAUTIFUL PERSON *n* Adonis, angel, Aphrodite, Apollo, bathing beauty, bathing belle, beau ideal, beauty, belle, bombshell, corpus delicti, dish, doll, dolly, dolly bird, dream, dreamboat, English rose, eyeful, goddess, good looker, houri, knockout, looker, nymph, peri, phoenix, picture, smasher, spunk, stunner, swan, Venus

BEAUTIFY *v* brave *(Obs.)*, decorate, glamorise, prettify, pretty, refine, set off; **smarten up**, brighten up, chamfer up, slick up *(U.S.)*, tart up, trig up

BEAUTY *n* beauteousness, comeliness, gorgeousness, heavenliness, loveliness, pulchritude; **good looks**, attractiveness, beauty spot, handsomeness, jauntiness, picturesqueness, seemliness, sexiness, smartness, spunkiness; **prettiness**, bonniness, fairness; **grandeur**, braveness *(Archaic)*, bravery *(Archaic)*, brilliance, gloriousness, glory, grandiosity, grandness, lustrousness, magnificence, resplendence, splendidness, splendour, sumptuousness, superbness; **radi-**

48

be cautious

ance, bloom, brightness, brilliance, gloss; **elegance**, charm, exquisiteness, fluency, grace, gracefulness, gracility, style, symmetry; **delicacy**, daintiness, lightness; **voluptuousness**, buxomness, shapeliness, voluptuosity; **aesthetics**

BE BORED WITH *v* be fed up with, be sick of, be weary of, tire, tire of; **pass the leaden hours**, be in the doldrums, while away the time

BE BUSY *v* burn the candle at both ends, burn the midnight oil, have a number of irons in the fire, have one's hands full, have other fish to fry, not have a moment to call one's own; **be active**, bustle, busy oneself, buzz about, hum, hum with activity, rush, rush around; **gad about**, have one's fling; **be cooking**

BE CALLOUS *v* couldn't care less, give short shrift, have no heart, have no mercy, have no pity, know no mercy, not be moved, stick to the letter of the law, turn a deaf ear; **be ruthless**, give no quarter, have one's pound of flesh; **be insensitive**, have a hide like a rhinocerous, have a thick skin; **harden**, case-harden, deaden, dehumanise, sear

BECAUSE *conj* along of, as, because of, by reason of, for, forwhy *(Archaic or Joc.)*, in the light of, in view of, on account of, owing to, since, sith *(Archaic)*; **for the sake of**, for the love of, in order to; **consequently**, hence, in consequence, so, so as, so that, then, therefore; **thereat**, hereat

BE CAUTIOUS *v* be on the safe side, look twice, mind one's tongue, play safe, take care, take no risks, think twice, tread warily, watch one's step; **feel one's way**, be tentative, tiptoe, tread on eggs, tread softly; **beware**, be on one's guard, guard against, keep a weather eye open, mind, ware (*Archaic*), watch out; **cover oneself**, insure; **play it cool**, go easy with, let well alone

BE CERTAIN *v* be sure, bet London to a brick, bet your boots; **dare say**, believe, have no doubt; **lay down the law**, dogmatise, know all the answers

BE CHEAP *v* cost little; **slump**, collapse, fall in price

BE CLOSE *v* appose, border, burn, juxtapose, lie off, neighbour, subjoin

BE COLD *v* do a freeze, do a perish, freeze, go blue with cold, go numb with cold; **chill**, freeze the balls off a brass monkey, frost, glaciate, ice, regelate, rime; **snow**, hail, sleet; **shiver**, get goose pimples, shudder, tremble; **become cold**, cloud over, freshen

BECOME CONFUSED *v* blunder, blush, dither, flap, flounder, fuss, get one's knickers in a knot, get one's knickers in a twist, go off the deep end, lose one's head, not know which way to look, wander

BECOME GREATER *v* accumulate, bank up, gain, gather, grow, regenerate, snowball, thrive; **increase**, advance, appreciate, blow out (*Horseracing*), boom, develop, gain, harden, jump, lengthen, mount, multiply, proliferate, pullulate, rise, rocket, shoot up, take off, upswing, wax; **intensify**, branch out, concentrate, escalate, fade up (*Television*), gain strength, make greater, rise; **swell**, bag, belly, blouse out, dilate, fill, fill out, hypertrophy, inflate, intumesce, puff up, stretch, tumefy

BECOME IRRITATED *v* bung it on, bung on an act, chuck a mental, cut off one's nose to spite one's face, frown, get the shits, get up on the wrong side of bed, glower, go to market, look black, lour, pack a shitty, pout, scowl

BECOME KNOWN *v* circulate, get about, get around, get out, percolate, turn out; **dawn on**, dawn upon, sink in, soak in

BECOME SLEEPY *v* begin to nod, one's eyelids become heavy, rub one's eyes, yawn

BECOME UNCONSCIOUS *v* black out, faint, pass out, swoon, swound (*Archaic*), throw a seven; **conk out**, go out like a light, sleep

BE CONTENT *v* be a box of birds, be in heaven, make no complaint, purr, tread on air, walk on air

BE CONTINGENT ON *v* depend on, hang on, hinge on, rest on

BE CURIOUS *v* dig into, make inquiries, nose about, nose after, nose into, nose out, poke about, poke around, poke one's nose into, pry, root around, rubberneck, stickybeak, wonder

BED *n* bassinette, berth, box bed, bunk, charpoy (*India*), cot, couch, cradle, day bed, doss, folding bed, four-poster, humidicrib, pad, shakedown, stretcher; **sleeping-bag**, fart sack; **mattress**, air mattress, pallet, palliasse; **sleeping quarters**, crash pad, crew's quarters, dorm, dormer (*Archaic*), dormitory, doss house, forecastle, glory hole (*Naut.*); **sleeping car**, campervan, camping body, couchette, overnight caravan, sleeper

bedclothes   50   **beer**

BEDCLOTHES *n* bed linen, bed-roll, bedding, nap, pillowcase, pillowslip, sheet, slip; **blanket,** afghan, bunny-rug, electric blanket, kaross, rug, throw *(U.S.)*; **eiderdown,** bedspread, comfort *(U.S.)*, comfortable *(U.S.)*, comforter *(U.S.)*, continental quilt, counterpane, coverlet, doona, duvet, quilt, spread; **swagman's blanket,** bagman's two-up, wagga; **sleeping-bag,** fart sack, fleabag; **saddlecloth,** caparison, housing, trappings

BE DEAF *v* have a hearing problem, not hear; **turn a deaf ear,** not listen; **fall on deaf ears; deafen,** split the eardrums

BE DIFFICULT *v* be no picnic, be uphill, run one hard, try one's patience

BE DISMISSED *v* be given the golden handshake, fall, get one's ticket, get the boot, get the chop, get the sack, get the shunt, get the spear

BE DISSONANT *v* clang, clash, jangle; **blare,** bray; **hoarsen,** crack, croak, snore; **groan,** creak; **grate,** graunch, gride, grind, grit, jar, rasp, saw, scrape, scratch, scoop

BEDROOM *n* bedchamber *(Archaic)*, boudoir, bower *(Poetic)*, cabinet, camera, chamber, closet, cubicle, den, dormitory, garderobe *(Archaic)*, pad, passion pit *(Colloq.)*; **cabin,** berth, billet, cabinet, double room, guestroom, roomette *(U.S.)*, single room, sleep-out, sleeper, stateroom; **guardroom,** billet, quarters, rooms, tollbooth

BEDS *n* bed base, bedstead, berth, box bed, brass bed, bunk, charpoy *(India)*, couch, day bed, doss, double bed, double-bunk, ensemble, featherbed, fold-away bed, folding bed, four-poster, head-board, king-size bed, night-and-day, queen-size bed, roll-away bed, sack, shakedown, sickbed, single bed, sofa-bed, tester bed, three-quarter bed, twin bed, waterbed; **stretcher,** air-bed, camp bed, camp stretcher, hammock, trestle bed, truckle bed, trundle bed; **cot,** baby basket, bassinette, carry basket, carry cot, child's bed, cradle, crib; **mattress,** air mattress, Dutch wife, fart sack, foam mattress, futon, inner-spring mattress, li-lo, palliasse, quilt *(Obs.)*, rubber mattress, sleeping-bag. *See also* COUCH

BE EARLY *v* abort, be premature, go off at half-cock, go off half-cocked, miscarry; **take an early mark,** put the clock forward; **antedate; jump the gun,** beat the gun, break, break away, steal a march on

BE EASY *v* be a breeze, be a piece of cake, be no object, be nothing to it

BE ENERGETIC *v* brace up, effervesce, feel one's oats, perk up; **bustle,** hustle, make an effort, strive; **get into,** get cracking, get stuck into, hoe into, hop into, put one's shoulder to the wheel, take the bit between one's teeth, warm to

BEER *n* ale, amber fluid, amber liquid, ball of malt *(Brit.)*, Bishop Barker, bitter *(Brit.)*, bock beer, brown ale, brownie, catch up, chicha, coldie, cruiser, draught beer, fifty-fifty, handle, hops, ice-cold, ketchup, lager, light ale, liquid lunch, lube, malt, malt liquor, mild, mild ale, new beer, nog *(Brit.)*, old, old beer, packaged beer, pale ale *(Brit.)*, paroo sandwich, pilsener, piss, porter, pertergaff, poultry lunch *(W.A.)*, rabbit, senator, shandy, shandygaff *(Obs.)*, she-oak *(Obs.)*, shearer's joy, sheep-wash, sherbet, shypoo *(W.A.)*, slops, small beer, stout, stringybark, suds, swipes *(Brit.)*, tap, tapping, wassail. *See also* ALCOHOL

BE EXCESSIVE *v* gild the lily, go too far, lay it on, lay it on thick, make a welter of it, overdrive, overshoot the mark, overstep the mark, pile it on, push it; **burn the candle at both ends,** overdo it, overtax oneself

BE EXCITED *v* boil over, cream one's jeans, galumph, go ape over, go wild, hot up, rave, take off, take on, throw a fit, throw a willy; **flutter,** flap, tremble, twitter

BE EXPEDIENT *v* advantage, befit, beseem, suit one's purpose; **fill the bill,** answer, deliver the goods, do, produce results, serve

BE EXPENSIVE *v* be at a premium, be at a price, cost the earth

BE FAITHFUL TO *v* abide by, adhere to, be true to, stand by, stay with, stick by, stick to, stick with, support, uphold; **owe loyalty,** bear allegiance, homage, render; **stick together,** hang together

BE FASHIONABLE *v* be in, be in the swim, be U, be with it, catch on; **dress up,** gussy up, perk up, spruce up; **dandify,** caparison, primp, prink; **set a trend**

BE FASTENED *v* be fixed, fay, tail *(Bldg Trades)*

BE FERTILE *v* bloom, blossom, burgeon, flourish; **produce,** bear, crop, fruit, overbear, overcrop, overproduce, spawn, yield; **abound,** overabound, proliferate, superabound, swarm, teem

BE FEW AND FAR BETWEEN *v* be thin on the ground, be weak in numbers, diminish, run short; **be in the minority,** be too few, be without a quorum

BEFORE *adv* afore, antecedently, anteriorly, erewhile *(Archaic)*, fore *(Obs.)*, heretofore, previously, prior to; **hereinbefore,** above, thereinbefore, ubi supra; **yesterday,** ult., ultimo, ulto., yesteryear

BEFORE *prep* afore, ere *(Archaic)*, fore *(Obs.)*, or *(Archaic)*

BE FORGETFUL *v* have a head like a sieve

BE FRIENDS *v* associate with, be hand in glove with, be mates with, familiarise *(Obs.)*, fraternise, get along with, get on with, go around with, go out with, go with, hobnob, knock around with, neighbour with, see, stick together, track with; **befriend,** ally, brother, care for, chum up with, fall in with, make friends with, pal, pal up with; **warm to,** click, cotton on to

BE FRIGHTENED *v* be at panic stations, freak out, get cold feet, get the wind up, go off the deep end, have a willy, have kittens, have one's heart in one's boots, have one's heart in one's mouth, have the breeze up, hit the panic button, jump out of one's skin, lose one's nerve, pack death, pack it, pack shit, panic, press the panic button, take a willy, turn to jelly; **fear,** doubt *(Archaic)*, dread, funk, misdoubt *(Archaic)*, misgive, squib; **tremble,** blanch, blench, boggle, cower, quail, shake, shudder, shy, start

BEG *v* accost, bite, bludge, cadge, fang, hum, panhandle *(U.S. Colloq.)*, put the acid on, put the fangs into, put the hard word on, put the nips

beg   52   **be healthy**

into, sting, touch; **take up a collection,** hold a barrel, hold a benefit, levy, pass round the hat, whip round

BE GENEROUS *v* bestow, do someone proud, do the handsome thing, do the right thing, give carte blanche, give one's all, lavish, shower, spare no expense

BEGGING *adj* adjuratory, beseeching, impetrative, imploratory, importunate, imprecatory, invocatory, petitionary, precatory, rogatory, suppliant, supplicant, supplicating, supplicatory; **cap in hand,** on bended knees; **intercessional,** intercessory

BE GRATEFUL *v* say ta, say thankyou, thank; **appreciate,** bless, praise; **be full of gratitude,** be overwhelmed by someone's generosity; **acknowledge,** acknowledge one's debt to, give credit where credit is due; **thank God,** praise Heaven, thank one's lucky stars; **be grateful for small mercies,** be grateful for what you can get; **accept gratefully,** not look a gift horse in the mouth, receive with open arms

BEGUILE *v* bluff, con, delude, wrongfoot; **hook,** catch, catch out, mislead, rope in; **duckshove,** finagle; **outsmart,** circumvent, outfox, outjockey, outmanoeuvre, outwit, pull a fast one, steal a march on, undercut; **machinate,** compass, contrive, engineer, feint, manipulate, mastermind, wangle; **insinuate,** fish, wheedle; **intrigue,** plot, scheme; **know a thing or two,** live by one's wits, never miss a trick, not miss a trick; **cheat,** doublecross; **ambush,** crimp, ensnare, entrap

BE GUILTY *v* have a skeleton in the cupboard, have something to hide; **be ashamed,** blush, feel guilty, feel small, hang one's head, hide one's head; **confess,** admit one's guilt, avouch *(Archaic),* come clean, go to press *(Prison Colloq.),* own up

BE HAD *v* be sold a pup, bite, fall for, have oneself on

BE HAPPY *v* be full of beans, be in good spirits; **cheer up,** brighten, buck up, ginger up, lighten, liven up, perk up, rise, take heart; **breeze along,** feel one's oats, keep one's chin up, keep one's pecker up, look on the bright side, sparkle, tread on air, walk on air; **make merry,** frolic, kick up one's heels, racket, rollick

BEHAVE *v* acquit oneself, act, bear oneself, behave oneself, carry oneself, comport oneself, conduct oneself, deal, demean oneself, deport oneself, do, do by; **perform,** paddle one's own canoe, play one's part, play the game, shift for oneself; **live,** lead one's life, run one's race; **react,** respond, treat

BEHAVIOUR *n* actions, conduct, conversation *(Archaic),* course, dealing, form, front, goings-on, manner, manners, mode of conduct, observance, play *(Obs.),* proceedings, treatment; **behaviour pattern,** collective behaviour, course of action, culture complex, method, modus operandi, path, procedure, response, standards; **custom,** living, mannerism, role, trick, way, way of acting, ways; **bearing,** air, carriage, comportment, countenance *(Obs.),* demeanour, deportment, mien; **breeding,** finish

BE HEALTHY *v* be a box of birds, be alive and kicking, feel good; **thrive,** bloom, flourish; **keep fit,** condition, tone up; **recover,** convalesce, feel oneself again, get over, lick one's wounds, pick up, pull round, pull

be healthy through, rally, recruit, recuperate, rehabilitate, turn the corner

BEHIND *adv* after; **backwards,** back, hindwards, rearward, sternwards; **aback,** abaft, aft, astern; **posteriorly,** epaxially, retrorsely; **backstage,** upstage

BE HONEST *v* go straight, have clean hands, keep faith, keep one's promise, play fair, play the game, play with a straight bat, turn an honest penny; **call a spade a spade,** lay it on the line, make no bones, nail one's colours to the mast, plump out *(Brit.)*, sound off, speak one's mind, speak out; **confess,** make a clean breast of, own up, put one's cards on the table, reveal all, tell the truth

BE HOT *v* blaze, boil, broil, burn, roast, swelter; **flush,** glow, run a temperature

BE HUNGRY *v* famish, have a good appetite, have the munchies, raven *(Obs.)*, starve

BE IGNORANT *v* be none the wiser, have come down in the last shower, have come up by parcel-post, not have a clue, not have an earthly, not have the faintest, not have the foggiest, not know B from a bull's foot, not know someone from Adam; **become ignorant,** lose track

BE ILL *v* ail, have one foot in the grave, sicken; **come down with,** catch, get, go down with, take; **present with,** complain of, suffer from; **relapse; faint,** collapse, lose consciousness, swoon; **waste away,** decay, dwine *(Archaic)*, fall away, invalid, peak, pine

BE IMMORAL *v* err, offend, sin, stray, transgress, trespass; **backslide,** fall, fall from grace, go to the bad, go to the devil, lapse, slip, spoil one's record

BE IMPENITENT *v* be fixed in one's ways, be seared, brazen it out, die game, harden one's heart, have no shame, not give a damn

BE IMPERFECT *v* fall short of perfection, have a fault

BE IMPORTANT *v* carry, import *(Obs.)*, matter, reck *(Archaic)*, signify, tell, weigh; **carry weight,** be in big on, bulk (large); **concern,** affect, interest

BE IMPULSIVE *v* go at something baldheaded, lose one's head, not think twice, take it into one's head; **extemporise,** adlib, improvise; **talk off the top of one's head,** say the first thing that comes into one's mind

BE INACTIVE *v* bide one's time, kill time, not lift a finger, rest on one's laurels, sit, sit tight, sleep, slumber, stagnate, tick over, vegetate, warm a seat, wile away; **become inactive,** cop out, corpse, flag, give up, languish, leave someone to it, rest, slacken, slake, stand, stop, throw in the sponge, throw in the towel, throw it in, wind down; **hibernate,** aestivate, hole up; **sit it out,** leave be, let it be, let sleeping dogs lie, sit on the fence; **hold off,** default, forbear, hold one's peace, pocket *(U.S.)*, refrain, refuse, resist, strike. *See also* IDLE

BE INATTENTIVE *v* be lost in, daydream, dream, have one's head in the clouds, let one's thoughts wander, lose oneself in, moon, muse, nap, nod, sleep, stargaze, switch off, wander; **be distracted,** lose the thread, lose track, pay no attention; **disre-**

be inattentive   54   **belief**

gard, blink at, forget, let pass, let slide, miss, overlook, pretermit; **fiddle**, doodle, fool around, play at, toy with; **skim**, pass over, slip, slur over

BE IN DEBT *v* be indebted, be under obligation to pay, have insufficient funds, owe, take the knock *(Horseracing)*; **get into debt**, borrow, dishonour a cheque, incur a debt, overdraw, run up a bill; **go bankrupt**, be gazetted, collapse, crash, go bust, go to the wall

BE INDEPENDENT *v* be one's own boss, be one's own master, be one's own person, call no man master, do one's own thing, fend for oneself, go it alone, go one's own way, paddle one's own canoe, pull oneself up by the bootstraps, shift for oneself; **kick over the traces**, kick against the pricks

BE INDIFFERENT *v* be left cold, blink at, not bat an eye, not care a straw, not give a damn, not give a fuck, not give a hang, not give a shit, not give a stuff, not give a tinker's cuss, not give a tinker's damn, not give a twopenny damn, not give a twopenny dump, shrug off, take for granted; **mope**, dream, moon, switch off

BE INFERIOR *v* be below standard, fall short, not hold a candle to, not measure up, not pass muster, not shape up; **play second fiddle**, bow before, depend, take a back seat

BE INFERTILE *v* go to waste, lie fallow, shrivel, stagnate; **abort**, miscarry, spike

BE INFORMAL *v* let one's hair down, not stand on ceremony, relax, underdress

BEING *n* ens, existence, incidence, life, pre-existence, presence, self-existence, ubiquity; **origin**, category, first principle; **subsistence**, survival, sustentation. *See also* ACTUALITY

BE INNOCENT *v* have a clear conscience, have clean hands, have nothing to hide

BE JEALOUS OF *v* envy, **covet**, crave, eat one's heart out, long for, lust after; **begrudge**, be put out, grudge, have one's nose out of joint, take a jaundiced view, view with a jaundiced eye

BE KILLED *v* get hers, get his, go for a burton, hasten one's end, shorten one's life, take years off one's life

BE LATE *v* miss the boat, miss the bus; **sleep in**, lie over; **delay**, be slow of the mark, dillydally, gain time, play for time, postdate, procrastinate, tarry

BE LENIENT *v* baby, bear with, fondle *(Obs.)*, go easy on, humour, indulge, mollycoddle; **relent**, come round, give quarter, go soft, take the acid off, take the heat off, yield; **relax**, liberalise, loosen, stretch a point, unbend, unbutton; **dispense**, exempt, indulgence, remit, reprieve

BELIEF *n* acceptance, acceptation, assumption, confidence, credence, credit, credulity, credulousness, dependence, faith, fondness *(Archaic)*, presumption, trust, trustfulness, trustingness; **popular belief**, bug *(Colloq.)*, folk myth, folklore, old wives' tale, superstition; **credibility**, accreditation, credential, credibleness, credit; **creed**, articles of faith, canon, catechism, credendum, credo, doctrine, dogma, doxy, faith, gospel, ideology, ism, philosophy, plank

BELIEVABLE *adj* authentic, credent *(Obs.)*, credible, fiducial, plausible, plausive *(Obs.)*, swallowable, trustworthy, worthy of belief

BELIEVE *v* accept, assume, credit, deem, hold, imagine, opine, pin one's faith on, profess, put one's trust in, put stock in, swallow, take for, take for granted, take someone at their word, take stock in, think, trow *(Archaic)*, trust, understand; **misbelieve**; **ascribe to, accredit with, attribute to**

BELIEVER *n* convert, devotee, good liver, initiate, Marian, pietist, puritan, the faithful, votary; **zealot**, Bible Belt, bible-banger, bible-basher, bibliolater, born-again Christian, bush Baptist, fanatic, hot-gospeller, Jesus-freak, Salvationist; **ecstatic**, penitent, spiritualist; **ascetic**, anchorite, contemplative, flagellant, hermit, mystic, stylite, sufi; **pilgrim**, alhaji *(Islam)*, hajji

BELIEVING *adj* bold *(Obs.)*, confident, confiding, credent, credulous, faithful *(Obs.)*, fond *(Archaic)*, superstitious, trustful, trusting, trusty *(Rare)*; **credal**, creedal, doctrinal, ideological, mythical

BELIEVINGLY *adv* confidently, credulously, superstitiously, trustfully, trustingly; **in my opinion**, to the best of one's belief

BE LIFTED *v* scend

BE LIKELY *v* be odds-on favourite, be sure to win, seem probable; **think likely**, believe, count on, dare say, expect, have reason to believe, presume, suppose, take for granted; **seem likely**, bid fair, have a strong probability, imply, lend colour to, point to, promise; **have every chance of winning**, be favoured to win, be the favourite, run a good chance, stand a good chance

BELITTLE *v* debunk, make light of, minify, minimise, set at naught, slight, trivialise, vilipend; **subordinate**, overshadow; **trifle**, coquet, dally

BELONG *v* appertain

BE LOUD *v* be enough to wake the dead, be noisy, belt, brawl, broil, clamour, crow, deafen, go hammer and tongs, hoot, racket, roister, rough-house, row, shatter the silence; **shout**, raise the roof, roar, scream blue murder; **vociferate**, ballyhoo, bluster, give tongue, haw-haw, hawk, loudmouth, pipe up, rave, shout down, speak up, stress, talk down, yammer, yap; **bang**, boom, clang, clangour, crash, fulminate, peal, pound, thump, thunder; **resound**, pierce, rattle, ring, volley; **blare**, bell, bellow, bray; **howl**, hoot, shriek, ululate, wail; **blubber**, blub, brattle, snort

BELOVED *adj* darling, dear, honey, lief *(Archaic)*, precious, sweet, well-beloved; **favourite**, blue-eyed, white-haired, white-headed

BELOW *adv* infra, thereunder, underneath; **low, down**; **basally**, underfoot, underground, ventrally

BELT *n* band, belting, cestus, cinch, cincture, girth, strap, surcingle; **ribbon**, aglet, apron-strings, cordon, fillet, string, tie; **lace**, bootlace, latchet *(Archaic)*; **garter**, suspender; **watch-chain**, albert, watch-guard, watchband, watchstrap; **elastic band**, keylock closure, lacker band, rubber band, twist-tie; **octopus strap**, ockie strap, spider; **metal strap**, astrigal

BELT INTO v buckle down to, bury oneself in work, dig into, get cracking at, get into the swim, get into the swing, get stuck into, go all out to, go at something, go at something bald-headed, go in for, go to town, have a go at, lay about oneself mightily, make short work of, make the most of one's time, not let the grass grow under one's feet, peg away at, pull one's finger out, pull one's weight, stick at nothing; **fuss**, carry on, fidget, make a fuss, make a song and dance about, run riot; **activate**, bring on stream, bring into production

BE MAD v be a shingle short, have bats in the belfry, have the ha-has, need one's head read, not play with a full deck; **take a fit**, chuck a mental, have a turn, run amuck; **go mad**, crack, get the Darling pea, go haywire, lose one's marbles

BE MEEK v bow and scrape, creep, eat crow, eat dirt, eat humble pie, eat one's words, eat out of someone's hand, get off one's high horse, grovel, hide one's head, kiss the dust, know one's place, lick the dust, lose face, not dare to show one's face again, pull in one's horns, sing small, submit; **crawl**, brown-nose, lick someone's arse, lick someone's boots, piss in someone's pocket, pull one's forelock, toady to, touch one's forelock, tug one's forelock; **humble oneself**, condescend, deign, demean oneself, stoop, vouchsafe; **be humbled**, be made to look foolish, receive a snub

BE MISERLY v begrudge, dole out, have a death adder in one's pocket, have short arms and long pockets, hold back, pinch, scrimp, skimp, stay at home on a button day, stint, throw money around like a man with no hands, withhold

BE MODEST v draw in one's horns, hide one's light under a bushel, keep in the background, keep one's distance, not big-note oneself, not give oneself airs, not put on side, sell oneself short, undersell oneself; **blush**, shrink, withdraw

BE MOTIVATED v become carried away, become fired with enthusiasm, follow another's lead, obey a call, yield to temptation; **have an axe to grind**, be driven on

BEND n angle, corner, dogleg, elbow, flection, flexure, fold, fork, hairpin bend, inflection, notch, zigzag; **angularity**, acuteness, angularness, bifurcation, crookedness, flexure, forkedness, obliqueness, obliquity, perpendicularity. See also ANGLE

BEND v couch, crouch, flex, incline, jackknife, spring, turn; **angle**, square, square away, stagger

BE NEGLECTED v go by the board, go to rack and ruin, go to waste, lapse; **neglect oneself**, let oneself go, not care how one looks, not take care of oneself, waste away

BE NEUTRAL v abstain, abstain from voting, avoid, have no hand in, have nothing to do with, not take sides, pull one's head in, sit on the fence, stand aloof, steer a middle course, take no part, trim one's course; **neutralise**, defuse, depoliticize, keep the peace

BENT *adj* antrorse, biflex, crooked, flectional, flexional, flexural, forked; **angular**, angulated, equiangular, isogonic; **acute**, cant, oblique, orthogonal, skew; **perpendicular**, normal, on the beam, square; **angled**, contrary, decussate, inclined, inflexed, jagged, notched, serrated, zigzag

BE OBVIOUS *v* go without saying, speak for itself, stand to reason, tell its own tale; **be prominent**, be right under one's nose, loom large, stand out, stand out a mile, stare one in the face, stick out, stick out like a sore toe, stick out like dogs' balls; **show up**, keep a high profile, maintain a high profile, shine

BE OF NO REPUTE *v* be at a discount, not be thought much of, stink; **be in disgrace**, be in bad odour with, be in bad with, be in disfavour with, be in dutch with, be in somebody's black books, be in the doghouse, be in wrong with, be on somebody's black list, be persona non grata, be under a cloud, sleep under the house; **fall from grace**, blot one's copybook, come down, fall, go into eclipse, lose ground, stoop

BE OF SERVICE *v* boot *(Obs. Poetic)*, come in handy, come into use, serve, stand in good stead, stead *(Archaic)*, subserve

BE OLD *v* be ancient, have seen its day, have whiskers on it; **age**, fossilise, get on, get on in years, go to seed, run to seed; **stale**, crumble, fade

BE OUT OF LUCK *v* be for it, be in the wars, be up against it, draw the short straw, feel the pinch, go downhill, go through the hoop, go through the mill, hit a bad patch, hit bad times, lead a dog's life, stew in one's own juice; **come to grief**, come a buster, come a cropper, come a stumer, come unstuck, cruel one's pitch, feel the draught, go for a sixer, go for six, slump, take a knock; **cop the lot**, catch a packet, cop a basinful; **ail**, distress

BE PATIENT *v* bide one's time, play a waiting game, sit tight, stand by, sweat it out, wait

BE PATIENT *interj* don't get your knickers in a knot, don't get your knickers in a twist, half a mo, hang on, hold on, hold your horses, hold your water, just a minute, just a tick, simmer down, slow down, steady on, wait a minute

BE PENITENT *v* confess, have learnt one's lesson, mend one's ways, reform, repent, turn over a new leaf; **apologise**, make up, say one is sorry, shake hands; **regret**, cry over spilt milk, deplore, kick oneself, rue, rue the day

BE PERMITTED TO *v* be allowed to, can, may; **get the nod**, clear with, get the Murray cod

BE PLEASANT *v* appeal to, attract, charm, charm the pants off, delight, endear oneself to, please

BE PLEASED *v* congratulate oneself, laugh, purr, rejoice, smile; **have a good time**, enjoy oneself, jet set, kick up one's heels, let one's hair down, live, live it up, rage; **luxuriate**, bask, indulge, wallow

BE PRECISE *v* dot one's i's and cross one's t's, mind one's p's and q's, take care; **get it right**, hit the nail on the head; **elaborate**, emendate, quote chapter and verse, refine; **literalise**; **formulate**, formularise, formulise;

regulate, emend, get technical, nick, tram *(Mach.)*; **pinpoint**, bring into focus, define, register *(Print.)*, true

BE PREJUDICED AGAINST *v* have a bias against, have a derry on, have a down on, see one side only; **ossify**, become set in one's ways, congeal *(U.S.)*, fossilise

BE PRESENT *v* assist *(Obs.)*, attend, frequent, front *(Colloq.)*, gatecrash, hang on, lie at, lie in, occupy, sit in on, take one's place; **habituate**, hang about, hang around, haunt, mooch, stick around; **stay**, stick on, stop, tarry

BE PROMISCUOUS *v* go on the streets, prostitute oneself, put out, rig, run around, sleep around, swing, swing the bag, wanton; **philander**, fornicate, sow one's wild oats, wench, whore, womanise; **seduce**, debauch, deflower, ruin; **rape**, force, ravish, violate

BE PUNISHED *v* answer for, catch it, cop it, face the music, get it in the neck, get one's just deserts, get what is coming, take one's medicine, take the rap; **take the high jump**, dance, run the gauntlet, swing

BE REALISTIC *v* face facts, get wise, have one's feet on the ground, keep one's feet on the ground, know which side one's bread is buttered; **make realistic**, bring to the light of day, deglamourise, demystify, make come true, realise

BEREFT *adj* beggared, deprived, dispossessed, impoverished, pillaged, ravished, stripped, stripped bare

BE RELIEVED *v* breathe more freely, draw comfort, respire, take a deep breath, take comfort

BE RETICENT *v* clam up, hold aloof, hold off, interiorise, internalise; **underplay**, not give anything away, underact; **suffer in silence**, pocket one's pride, swallow one's pride, swallow one's words; **withhold**, hold back, keep back, keep close, keep dark, keep under one's hat, laugh in one's sleeve, laugh up one's sleeve, reserve, restrain, suppress

BE REVEALED *v* come out in the wash, come to light, leak out, ooze out, see the light of day, transpire

BE SELFISH *v* care about number one, feather one's nest, have an axe to grind, keep an eye to the main chance, not care about anyone else, push one's barrow

BE SILENT *v* ace it, ace it up, belt up, can it, cut the cackle, cut the cake, hold one's peace, hold one's tongue, keep one's mouth shut, pipe down, put a cork in it, put a sock in it, rest, shut one's mouth, shut up, stow it; **refuse comment**, button the lip, keep mum, keep one's counsel, stand mute; **lose one's tongue**, save one's breath, waste no words on

BE SIMILAR *v* agree, be all one, be birds of a feather, be in the same boat, be much of a muchness, be nothing in it, be twins, conform, correspond, match, parallel; **approximate**, approach, border on, come close to, remind of, resemble, savour of, smack of, take after

BE SMELLY *v* honk like a gaggle of geese, hum, pong, reek, smell, smell like Dead Horse gully, stink, stink out

BE SOCIABLE *v* accost, bow, gladhand, greet, have the flags out, hello, palm *(Obs.)*, recognise, rub noses

be sociable   59   **betrayer**

(N.Z.), salaam, shake hands with, tin kettle *(N.Z.)*, welcome, wring someone's hand; **meet,** bump into, rencounter, run across, run into, run up against; **introduce,** bring out, present; **associate,** go out, keep company, neighbour with, rub elbows with, rub shoulders with; **ask out,** date; **entertain,** do the honours, give a party, host a party, keep open house, receive, throw a party; **invite,** cultivate, have in, have over; **regale,** dine, do someone proud, serve, sup; **party on,** make whoopee, racket, rage; **socialise,** circulate, come out of one's shell, get about, get around, go around, mix, step out *(U.S.)*, table-hop

BE STRICT *v* bear down on, clamp down on, come down on like a ton of bricks, crack down on, get technical with, give it heaps, give no quarter, rule with a rod of iron, stand no nonsense; **discipline,** gruel, take in hand, tear strips off, tutor, use severely; **harden,** indurate, put one's foot down, stiffen

BE STUPID *v* have come down in the last shower, have kangaroos in the top paddock, have no brains, have slipped one's trolley, have whiteants, not know if it's Bourke Street or Tuesday, not know if it's Pitt Street or Christmas, not know the time of day, not know what day it is, take leave of one's senses

BE SURPLUS *v* go begging, go to waste, overabound, run over, superabound; **overflow,** brim over, burst at the seams, run a bunker, well over

BE SURPRISED *v* hit the ceiling, hit the roof, jump out of one's skin, not know what hit one, sit up, start

BE THIRD *v* come third, get a bronze, show *(U.S.)*

BE THIRSTY *v* be dry, feel parched, thirst

BE TIMELY *v* make hay while the sun shines, strike while the iron is hot, take time by the forelock; **catch,** make

BE TIRED *v* droop, faint, feel like a greasespot, languish, sink, stagger; **collapse,** be fagged out, crack up, drop, pack up; **do one's dash,** have shot one's bolt, knock oneself out

BE TRANSPARENT *v* allow light, show through; **make transparent,** clarify, clear

BETRAY *v* collaborate, doublecross, give away, knife in the back, sell down the river, sell out; **dob in,** blow the whistle on, dingo on, dob on, grass on, put in, rat on, scab on, shop, snitch on, turn king's evidence on, weasel; **belie,** fall away from, play fast and loose with, play someone false; **two-time,** cheat on, deceive

BETRAYAL *n* breach of promise, breach of trust, give-away, sell-out; **defection,** collaboration, double-dealing, foul play, high treason, perfidy, treachery, treason; **adultery,** a bit on the side, extramarital sex. *See also* UNFAITHFULNESS

BETRAYER *n* apostate, backstabber, belier, blackleg, changeling *(Archaic)*, Delilah, double-crosser, double-dealer, fairweather friend, fink, grasser, Iscariot, judas, Mata Hari, ratter, recreant, renegade, scab, snake, snake in the grass, snitch, snitcher, stool pigeon, tergiversator, traditor, viper, weasel; **collaborator,** collaborationist, fifth column, fifth colum-

betrayer   60   **be unselfish**

nist, quisling, security risk, silvertail, traitor, traitress, Trojan Horse, welsher; **adulterer**, adulteress, two-timer

BETROTHED *n* fiancé, fiancée, intended

BE TRUE *v* be a fact, be the case, conform to fact, hold good, hold true, hold water, ring true, stand the test; **prove to be fact**, authenticate, verify

BE TRUTHFUL *v* be in earnest, mean what one says, stick to the facts, tell the truth

BETWEEN *prep* amid, amidst, among, betwixt *(Archaic)*, 'tween, 'twixt *(Archaic)*

BE UNABLE TO PAY *v* fail, go bankrupt, go bung, go to the wall, take the knock *(Horseracing)*; **postpone payment**, charge, defer payment, put on account, put on the slate; **stop payment**, protest, refuse payment, repudiate, scale down, suspend

BE UNCERTAIN *v* be in a quandary, dither, doubt, flounder, hesitate, lose the scent, lose the trail, misgive, not know which way to turn, vacillate, wonder; **take a chance**, bet, buy a pig in a poke, wager; **hang in the balance**, depend, suspend

BE UNFRIENDLY *v* bear ill will, bear malice, grudge, gun for, have it in for; **quarrel**, come to blows, rencounter; **hound**, oppress, persecute, spite; **snub**, cut someone dead, give someone the deep freeze, give the cold shoulder to, ignore, keep at arm's length, turn one's back on; **ostracise**, boycott, excommunicate, have nothing to do with, send to Coventry, treat as a leper; **alienate**, antagonize, cause bad blood, dissocialise, estrange, rupture, set at odds; **sulk**, have a hate on, have a snout on, have the sulks

BE UNGRATEFUL *v* look a gift-horse in the mouth, take as one's due, take for granted, turn one's nose up; **grumble**, complain, whinge; **omit to thank**, forget to thank; **begrudge a thankyou**, not be beholden to, see no reason to thank; **forget a kindness**, return evil for good

BE UNHAPPY *v* be sad, have a face as long as a fiddle, have a face as long as a wet week, have a lump in the throat, have one's heart in one's boots, sorrow; **droop**, languish, slump; **brood**, chew the rag, moan, mope; **cry**, cry one's eyes out, have a good cry, have a good moan, pipe one's eye *(Brit.)*, snivel, weep; **pine**, eat one's heart out, grieve

BE UNIMPORTANT *v* be no great shakes, be not worth a cracker, be not worth two bob, be nothing to boast about, make no odds, not be a row of beans, not matter a twopenny damn, not matter a twopenny dump; **be all the same**, be neither here nor there; **play second fiddle**, take a back seat

BE UNLIKELY *v* be improbable, not have a ghost of a chance, stand no chance

BE UNPALATABLE *v* nauseate, turn, turn one's stomach; **pall**, cloy, lose its appeal, lose its savour

BE UNREADY *v* be caught napping, be caught short, be caught with one's pants down; **go off half-cocked**

BE UNSELFISH *v* be altruistic, be disinterested, bend over backwards, do as you would be done by, go out of one's way, live for others, make a sac-

be unselfish   61   **big**

rifice, observe the golden rule, put oneself out, sacrifice oneself

BE UNWILLING *v* back off, baulk, baulk at, be disinclined, be reluctant, boggle, boggle at, disincline, fight shy of, have no stomach for, hesitate, jib, jib at, nill *(Archaic)*, not be in the mood for, pussyfoot, scruple, shake one's head, shy away from; **hang back,** drag the chain, not cooperate, not pull one's weight, shirk, slack, slack off; **grudge,** begrudge

BE VIOLENT *v* be on the rampage, go on the rampage, lash out, rage, ramp, rampage, rant, swash; **bluster,** roar, storm, thunder; **run wild,** break away, break bounds, run amuck, stampede; **riot,** run riot; **see red,** get up, go berserk; **brutalise,** barbarise, bestialise; **assault,** attack, go bull-headed at, tear into; **manhandle,** bemaul, do violence to, knock about, knock around, tousle; **bully,** bullyrag, chuck one's weight about, give someone the shock treatment, strongarm *(U.S.)*; **violate,** outrage

BE WANTING *v* be lacking, not suffice, run dry, run low, run out, run short

BEWARE *interj* action stations, care *(Brit. Colloq.)*, caveat emptor, look out, watch it, watch out

BE WEALTHY *v* be born with a silver spoon in one's mouth, be rolling in it, have a quid, have money to burn; **make money,** clean up, coin; **prosper,** coin it, mint it, strike it rich, thrive; **enrich oneself,** accumulate wealth, aggrandise, batten on, feather one's nest, line one's pocket, stash it away

BE WILLING *v* be disposed, be inclined, be of a mind to, enthuse, have a mind to, have no scruples, lean towards, see fit, think fit; **agree,** acquiesce, concur, give one's consent, go along with, lend a willing ear, make no bones about, turn a willing ear; **volunteer,** offer oneself

BE WISE *v* have a good head on one's shoulders, have a lot of nous, have one's head screwed on the right way

BEWITCH *v* charm, enchant, fascinate *(Obs.)*, mesmerise, spellbind; **cast a spell on,** hex, overlook, point the bone at, put the mozz on, voodoo, witch

BEWITCHED *adj* away with the fairies, enchanted, fey, mesmerised, spellbound, under a spell

BEWITCHER *n* carline *(Scot.)*, charmer, enchanter, enchantress, sorcerer, sorceress, warlock, witch, wizard; **alchemist,** chemist *(Obs.)*, philosopher *(Obs.)*; **witchdoctor,** bone-pointer *(Aborig.)*, fetishist, gulli-gulli man, kadaicha man *(Aborig.)*, koradji, medicine man, voodooist; **miracle-worker,** magus, thaumaturge, theurgist; **conjurer,** magician, prestidigitator

BICYCLE *n* bike, BMX, boneshaker, chopper, coaster, cycle, dragster, high-riser, penny-farthing, pushbike, safety bicycle, tandem, treadle, velocipede; **tricycle,** dinky, pedicab, quadricycle, three-wheeler, trike, unicycle; **skateboard,** roller skate, scooter; **motorcycle,** ag-bike, agricultural bike, easy rider, grid, iron horse *(Archaic)*, moped, motor scooter, motorbike, solo, trail bike; **sidecar,** chair *(Colloq.)*, combination

BIG *adj* biggish, bull, decuman, double, family-size, great, large, mickle *(Scot.)*, queen-size, sizeable; **bulky,** cyclopean, elephantine, gross, heavy, massive, massy, megalithic,

big 62 **bird part**

monumental; **ample,** capacious, expansive, voluminous; **huge,** broad, enormous, jumbo, king, king-size, mammoth, mighty, old-man, titanic; **gigantic,** Brobdingnagian, colossal, Gargantuan, giant, gigantean, gigantesque, immense, monster, monstrous, prodigious, strapping; **extensive,** palatial, spacious, sweeping; **vast,** cosmic, vasty *(Poetic);* **walloping,** slashing, smacking, swingeing, thumping, whopping

BILL *n* blister, demand, dun, final notice, invoice, Jack-'n'-Jill; **IOU,** marker; **promissory note,** bill *(Obs.),* bond, calabash, certificate of deposit, debenture, debenture stock. *See also* DEBT

BINGE *n* bacchanalia, barney, bash, bat, beanfeast, bender, blow-out, bust, debauch, gorge, jag, lost weekend, orgy, saturnalia, splurge, spree, wallow

BINOMIAL *adj* biquadratic, quadratic, quadric, quintic, trinomial

BIOLOGIST *n* bacteriologist, cytologist, ecologist, histologist, microbiologist

BIOLOGY *n* autoecology, bacteriology, biochemistry, biodynamics, biogeny, bionics, bionomics, biophysics, cryobiology, cytology, ecology, histology, histopathology, karyology, marine biology, microbiology, molecular biology, radiobiology, synecology

BIRD *n* birdie, cock, dickybird, feathered friend, hen; **songbird,** songster; **birds,** Aves, avifauna, ornis; **poultry,** Australorp, Aylesbury duck, bantam, brahma, broiler, capon, chicken, cochin, cockerel, fowl, leghorn, Muscovy duck, Orpington, Pekin, Plymouth Rock, poulard, poussin, pullet, quail, Rhode Island Red, rooster, rumper, Sussex, turbit, turkey, turkey cock, white leghorn, Wyandotte; **chick,** flapper, fledgling; **flock,** gaggle, murmuration, wisp; **kookaburra,** alarm bird, breakfast bird, brown kingfisher, bushman's clock, clockbird, giant kingfisher, great brown kingfisher, ha-ha duck, ha-ha pigeon, Jack, jackass, Jacko, Jacky, John, Johnny, kooka, laughing Jack, laughing jackass, laughing John, laughing Johnass, laughing Johnny, laughing kingfisher, laughing kookaburra, settler's clock, settler's kingfisher, shepherd's clock, woop woop pigeon

BIRDCALL *n* birdsong, boom, charm, cheep, chirm, chirp, chirr, chirrup, chorus, coo, cuckoo, roll, screech, squawk, toot, trill, tweet, twitter, warble; **cackle,** caw, clack, clang, clink, croak; **song,** note, pipe, piping, woodnote; **dawn chorus,** matin, matin song; **crowing,** cock-a-doodle-doo, cockcrow, gobble, honk, quack, swan song. *See also* ANIMAL CALL

BIRDLIKE *adj* ornithoid; **avian,** avifaunal, ornithic; **winged,** alar, alary, alate, aliform, pennate, volant; **anatine,** anserine *(geese),* aquiline *(eagles),* columbine *(doves),* corvine *(crows),* gallinaceous *(fowl),* grallatorial *(wading birds),* halcyon *(kingfishers),* hirundine *(swallows),* larine *(gulls),* pavonine *(peacocks),* rasorial *(fowl),* strigiform *(owls),* struthious *(ostriches),* turdine *(thrushes),* vulturine *(vultures)*

BIRD PART *n* beak, bill, neb, nib; **comb,** caruncle, cockscomb, crest, crown, rose-comb; **snood,** crop, wattle; **wing,** ala; **talon,** claw, pounce; **wishbone,** fourchette, furcula, furculum

BIRTH *n* accouchement, childbed, confinement, delivery, lying-in, time; **child-bearing,** childbirth, parturiency, parturition; **Leboyer birth,** breech birth, breech delivery, caesarean section, homebirth, natural childbirth; **labour,** pains, throes, travail; **false labour,** couvade, pre-labour; **puerperium; abortion,** miscarriage, stillbirth; **delivery room,** labour ward; **farrowing house,** hatchabator, hatchery, nest, rookery, springer paddock, stud-farm

BISECTOR *n* diagonal, diameter, divider, dividing line, equator

BIT *n* cut, dab, deal, jot, minim, ounce, peck, pennyworth, piece, pinch, portion, rap, snip, snippet, tittle; **drop,** draught, dreg, dribble, dribs and drabs, drink, droob, sup, thimbleful; **mouthful,** bite, chew, gulp; **block,** cube, nugget, slab; **clod,** clot, divot, divvy, sod, turf. *See also* AMOUNT

BLACK *n* blue-black, crow, jet, jet black, raven, sable, sloe; **blackness,** darkness, inkiness, lividness, nigritude, obscurity, pitchiness, sootiness, swarthiness; **nigrescence,** nigrification; **shading,** shadow; **black and white,** chiaroscuro

BLACK *adj* black as jet, black as pitch, black as the ace of spades, coal-black, dark, dusky, inky, livid, piceous *(Zool.),* pitch-black, pitchy, raven, sable *(Poetic),* sombre, swart *(Archaic),* swarthy; **blackish,** coaly, fuliginous, nigrescent; **blackened,** burnt, corked, japanned, sooty, ustulate; **ebony,** jet, jetty; **black-browed,** black-headed, brunette

BLACKEN *v* black, blot, darken, nigrify, smudge; **black-lead,** charcoal, cork, smoke; **ebonise,** japan

BLACKENER *n* animal black, black, blacking, carbon black, ivory black, lampblack, nigrosine; **Indian ink,** japan, kohl, printer's ink

BLADDER *n* ureter, urethra, vesica, waterworks; **vesicle,** bursa, capsule, cistern, cyst, sinus; **duct,** tube, vas, vessel

BLADED *adj* bladelike, carinal, carinate, ensiform, gladiate, serrated, two-edged, xiphoid; **knife-edged,** cutthroat; **incisive,** carnassial, keen, mordacious, sharp; **sectorial,** incisory, laniary

BLATANCY *n* flagrance, obviousness, openness; **demonstrativeness,** expressiveness, showiness

BLATANT *adj* flagrant, glaring, striking; **manifest,** apparent, clear as day, evincible, obvious, patent, unmistakable, visible; **in the limelight,** conspicuous, in the foreground, pronounced; **unconcealed,** barefaced, brazen, flaunting, naked

BLEED *v* haemorrhage; **menstruate,** be leaking, be on the rags, have George visiting, have one's period, have the flags out, see the flowers, see the roses, see the visitors

BLEEDER *n* haemophiliac

BLEEDING *n* bleed, epistaxis, gush, haemorrhage, nosebleed; **menstruation,** catamenia, flowers, girl's week, menses, menstrual flow, monthly, period, the curse

BLIND *v* bedazzle, blear, hoodwink, put another's eyes out, seel *(Archaic),* throw dust in another's eyes; **be**

blind — go blind, lose one's sight; **blindfold**, darken, dazzle, hood

BLIND *adj* amaurotic, blind as a bat, blind as a wombat, blinded, eyeless, moon-blind, sightless, stone-blind, visionless; **temporarily blind**, bedazzled, blind drunk, nyctalopic, snow-blind

BLINDNESS *n* amaurosis, blackout, moon blindness *(Vet. Sci.)*, retrolental fibroplasia; **temporary blindness**, day blindness, dazzle, flash blindness, hemeralopia, snow blindness. *See also* FAULTY SIGHT

BLIND PERSON *n* four-eyes, myope, protanope, squinter, the blind, tritanope; boko

BLOOD *n* claret, plasma, serum; **blood cell**, corpuscle, erythrocyte, haemocyte, haemoglobin, haemoleucocyte, leucocyte, lymphocyte, neutrophil, phagocyte, platelet, red cell, white cell

BLOOD VESSEL *n* arteriole, artery, capillary, vein, vena, venule

BLOW *v* blast, blaze *(Obs.)*, bluster, howl, overblow, rage, squall, storm *(U.S.)*

BLUE *n* azure, bluebell, caerulean, cerulean, cornflower, forget-me-not, lapis lazuli, sapphire, sky blue; **light blue**, Copenhagen blue, pearl blue, pearl grey, powder blue, Wedgwood blue; **deep blue**, anil, Bristol blue, gentian blue, indigo, perse, royal blue, ultramarine, violet; **navy**, blue-black, navy blue; **electric blue**, peacock blue; **slate**, steel blue; **blue-green**, aqua, aquamarine, beryl, Nile blue, saxe blue, sea, turquoise

BLUE *adj* cold, cyanic, ice-blue, pavonine, sapphirine, woaded; **azure**, azury, cerulean, sky-blue, skyey *(Poetic)*; **bluish**, blue-green, bluey, glaucous; **blue-grey**, cyanotic, livid, slaty

BLUENESS *n* bluishness; **lividness**, cyanosis, lividity

BLUE PIGMENT *n* bice, Brunswick blue, cobalt blue, cyanin, indican, indophenol, induline, Prussian blue, smalt, Thenard's blue, true blue, verditer, viridian, woad, zaffre; **washing blue**, blue-bag; **blue light**, Bengal light, Bengal match; **blueing**

BLUNT, *v* dull, hebetate, obtund, turn

BLUNT *adj* dull, dullish, flat, flat as a tack, obtundent, obtuse, pointless, worn; **rounded**, hebetate *(Bot.)*, obtuse; **club-shaped**, clavate, claviform

BLUNTLY *adv* dully, obtusely

BLUNTNESS *n* dullness, obtuseness, pointlessness; **blunting**, hebetation

BODILY *adj* animal, corporal, corporeal, fleshly, physical, skeletal, systemic; **anatomical**, audiological, gastrological, ophthalmological, topical; **anterior**, inferior, posterior, sagittal, superior; **organic**, biliary, cardiac, hepatitic, lymphatic, pancreatic, renal, splenetic, thyroid

BODILY DISCHARGE *n* eccrisis, egestion, excretion; **discharge**, defluxion, flow, gleet, ichor, lochia, matter, maturation, pus, suppuration, swab; **perspiration**, diaphoresis, exudate, exudation, foam, lather, sudor, sweat, transpiration; **menstruation**, catamenia, dysmenorrhoea, friends, George, girls' week, menses, monthly, period, the curse; **gore**, cruor, grume; **excrement**, excreta; **sewage**, effluent, nightsoil, soil. *See also* SECRETION; DEFECATION; URINATION

BODY *n* bulk *(Rare)*, carcass *(Joc.)*, corpse *(Obs.)*, corpus, corpus delicti *(joc.)*, corse *(Archaic)*, soma, system, the body beautiful; **anatomy**, physique, vital statistics; **corporality**, corporeity, corporealness, physicality; **physiology**, endocrinology, neuroanatomy, neurology, neurophysiology, organology, otology

BOLT *n* barrel bolt, cap screw, dzus, explosive bolt, eye bolt, fishbolt, panic bolt, ringbolt; **nut**, butterfly nut, castellated nut, locknut, wing nut; **lock**, ball catch, catch, cylinder lock, dead latch, deadlock, night latch, padlock, safety catch, springlock, steering lock, yale lock; **latch**, hasp; **tumbler**, broach, snib, talon

BOMB *n* A-bomb, atomic bomb, blockbuster, bombshell, booby trap, buzzbomb, depth charge, doodlebug *(Colloq.)*, fire bomb, fission bomb, flying bomb, fragmentation bomb, fusion bomb, H-bomb, hydrogen bomb, ICBM, incendiary, letter bomb, Mills bomb, Molotov cocktail, neutron bomb, nuclear bomb, petard, pineapple *(Colloq.)*, plastic bomb, rocket bomb, smokebomb, stick, time bomb; **missile**, aerodynamic missile, air to air missile, air to surface missile, ballistic missile, barrage rocket, cruise missile, guided missile, intercontinental ballistic missile, intermediate range ballistic missile, mangonel, Polaris, rocket, SAM, surface-to-air missile, surface-to-surface missile, theatre missile, torpedo; **mine**, acoustic mine, antenna mine, contact mine, girandole, influence mine; **landmine**; **magnetic mine**; **launcher**, anti-aircraft gun, anti-tank gun, bazooka, rocket gun, rocket-launcher, silo

BOMBAST *n* bad speaking, balderdash, blah, bluff, boasting, bravado, bunkum *(U.S.)*, fanfaronade, fustian, gasconade, hot air, Johnsonese, rodomontade, wind; **turgidity**, grandiloquence, magniloquence, orotundity, pomposity, pompousness, pretentiousness, sesquipedalianism, swollenness, tumidity; **demagoguery**, demagoguism, demagogy, oratory, rhetoric

BOMBASTIC *adj* all piss'n'wind, circumlocutory, demagogic, fustian, grandiose, infelicitous, inflated, orotund, overblown, pompous, swollen, tub-thumping, tumid, turgid; **affected**, flamboyant, flashy, highfalutin, high-flown, pretentious, stilted; **sententious**, Johnsonian, pedantic, rhetorical

BOMBASTICALLY *adv* loftily, pretentiously, tumidly, turgidly, windily

BOND *n* bind, hitch, ligament, link, tie, vinculum; **yoke**, fetter; **bandage**, ligature

BOND ENERGY *n* chemical affinity, ionisation potential, work function; **ionic bond**, chemical bond, cohesion, covalent bond, dative bond, donor-bond, double bond, duplet, exchange force, semipolar bond, strong nuclear interaction, triple bond, weak nuclear interaction; **energy state**, ground state, stationary state

BONE *n* atomy *(Obs.)*, frame, os, skeleton; **caput**, capitulum, condyle, diaphysis; **joint**, articulation, ball-and-socket joint, diarthrosis, enarthrosis, ginglymus, gomphosis, hinge, pivot joint, symphysis

BOO *n* brickbat, Bronx cheer, catcall, groan, handclap, hiss, raspberry, slow handclap, the bird, thumbs down; **sneer**, frown, scowl; **demerit**, black mark, blackball

BOOK *n* publication, rare book, title, tome, volume; **work**, autonym, classic, magnum opus; **codex**, manuscript, MS, palimpsest; **edition**, casebound, coedition, conflation, hardback, hardcover, limited edition, paperback, three-decker, trade edition, vanity edition, yearly; **first edition**, Aldine, incunabula; **series**, collection, library, set; **bestseller**, potboiler; **reprint**, reissue; **slim volume**, booklet, brochure, chapbook, fascicle, fascicule, fasciculus, pamphlet, part work; **remaindered volume**; **library book**, floater *(Colloq.)*; **novel**; **penny dreadful**, dime novel *(U.S.)*, dreadful, shocker, thriller; **pillow book**, curiosa *(U.S.)*, erotica, facetiae, yellowback; **cookery book**, cookbook, recipe book; **storybook**, picture book, pop-up book; **compilation**, anthology, collectanea, festschrift, garland, memoirs, miscellanea, miscellany, omnibus, Parnassus, potpourri, recollections, sketchbook, travels; **notebook**, album, diary

BOOKBINDING *n* blocking, border, carpet page, coat of arms, crest, dinkus, doublure, fillet, frontispiece, headpiece, illumination, initial, logo, marbling, panel, rib, tailpiece, tooling, vignette

BOOKLOVER *n* bibliomaniac, bibliophile; **book collector**, antiquarian, **librarian**, acquisitions librarian, bibliographer, cataloguer; **bibliomania**, bibliophilism

BOOK PART *n* binding, board, half-binding, half-leather, rib, thermoplastic binding, three-quarter binding, yapp; **jacket**, cover, wrapper; **page**, bastard title, blocking, centrefold, centrespread, contents page, doublure, endpaper, flyleaf, frontispiece, half-title page, imprint page, leaf, recto, reverso, titlepage, verso; **gathering**, quire, section, signature; **quarto**, eighteenmo, eightvo, elephant, folio, sextodecimo, sixteenmo, thirty-twomo, twenty-fourmo, twentymo, vigesimo, vigesimoquarto; **addendum**, appendix, colophon, corrigendum, end matter, foreword, index, induction *(Archaic)*, introduction, preface, prelims, subindex

BOOK TRADE *n* proofreading, publishing; **publisher**; **bookseller**, newsagent; **bookshop**, book store, newsagency, second-hand bookshop; **printer**, book designer, bookbinder, compositor, copytaker, layout artist, proofreader, reader, typesetter

BOOM *n* bang, clank, clonk, clump, knock, thud, thump, wham, whop; **rumble**, growl, grumble, gurgle, thunder; **drumbeat**, beat, drumming, dub, rap, rappel, rataplan, roll, rub-a-dub, ruffle, tap, tapping, tom-tom; **tantara**, blare, honk

BOOM *v* bang, beat, clank, clonk, thud, thump; **rumble**, roll, thunder

BOOT *n* Bill Masseys *(N.Z. Colloq.)*, blucher, bovver boot *(Brit. Colloq.)*, buskin, elastic sides, gambado, half-boot, jack boot, riding boot, shoe *(U.S.)*, surgical boot, top-boot, ug boot; **gumboot**, galosh *(Obs.)*, galoshes, gumshoe, overshoes *(U.S.)*, rubbers *(U.S.)*, wellies, wellington boot. *See also* FOOTGEAR

BORDER *v* march upon, skirt, verge on

BORE *n* alf, bromide, drip, fish head, humdrum, pain, pain in the neck, pill, shmo, vegetable, wet blanket; **pedant**, Dryasdust, lugger, sermoniser; **bind**, a big yawn, annoyance, bore, drag, nuisance, yawn; **cliché**, banality, commonplace, platitude; **sermon**, litany; **stodge**, purple prose; **dullsville**, daily grind, grindstone, the nine to five, treadmill, wet weekend; **culture desert**

BORE *v* bore the pants off, irk, leave cold, leave flat, make one yawn, pall on, send one to sleep, tire, try, try one's patience, weary; **be tedious**, cloy, dull, glut, jade, pall, stale; **protract**, do to death, drag out, outstay one's welcome, overdo; **drag on**, jog along, jog on, linger on, wear thin

BORED *adj* blasé, full of ennui, hipped *(U.S.)*, hippish *(U.S.)*, indifferent, jaded, melancholy, tired of, world-weary; **listless**, lethargic, weary; **fed up**, browned off, cheesed-off, fed up to the back teeth, jack of, pissed-off, sick to death of

BOREDOM *n* discontent, ennui, indifference, languor, lethargy, listlessness, satiety, seven-year itch, taedium vitae, weariness

BOREHOLE *n* artesian bore, artesian well, bore, wellpoint; **funnel**, tundish; **sinkhole**, pothole, sink, swallow-hole

BORING *adj* dull, dull as dishwater, featureless; **tedious**, everlasting, stale, unrelieved, weariful, wearing, wearisome; **insipid**, flat, ho-hum, humdrum, incurious, ineffective, institutional, lifeless, pointless, sapless, tame, undramatic, unsatisfying; **pedantic**, dry, pedantical, platitudinous, sentermonic, sermonic, stodgy, stuffy; **irksome**, bolshie, distasteful, stultifying, tiresome; **slow**, dragging; **commonplace**, banal, clichéd, common, hackneyed, jejune, pedestrian, prosaic, prosy, stupid, trite, uninspired, uninspiring, unreadable, vapid; **monotonous**, monotone, repititious, uniform; **arid**, barren, blank, bovine, desolate, soul-destroying; **drab**, dreary; **leaden**, leady, plodding, ponderous, sodden, soggy; **soulless**, tasteless; **bucolic**, isolated, provincial, small-time

BORINGNESS *n* drabness, dreariness, dullness, pointlessness, stupidness, tedium, wearifulness, wearisomeness; **monotonousness**, everlastingness, humdrum, sameness, uniformity; **insipidity**, insipidness, jejuneness, lifelessness, staleness, sterility, tameness, vapidity, vapidness; **aridity**, aridness, barrenness, blankness, desolation, soullessness, tastelessness; **pedantry**, pedestrianism, prosaicness, prosaism, prosiness, sententiousness, stodginess, stuffiness, unreadability, unreadableness; **leadenness**, ponderosity, ponderousness, sogginess

BORROW *v* charter, gear *(Econ.)*, hire, lease, rent; **bludge**, bot, bum, cadge, fang, put in the fangs, put in the hooks, put in the nips, put in the screws, put the acid on, put the bite on, put the fangs into, put the hooks into, put the nips into, scrounge, snip, touch

borrower 68 **bounce**

BORROWER n debtor, mortgagor; lessee, hirer, renter, sublessee, tenant, under-lessee, undertenant; leaser, underletter; **bludger,** bastard from the bush, bloodsucker, bot, bumzack *(W.A.),* cadger, scrounger

BOSS n baas, boss cocky, boss of the board, bossboy, bwana, cock of the walk, cove *(Archaic),* employer, foreman, forewoman, ganger, gov. *(Brit.),* governor, guv, head, head serang, himself *(Colloq.),* joss, maluka, manager, master, missus, mistress, number one, numero uno, old man, overseer, padrone *(U.S.),* pannikin boss, sahib, senior, skip *(Sport),* skipper, straw boss *(U.S.),* supervisor, the man, top dog, tycoon; **gang boss,** capo, don, gang leader, godfather

BOTTLE n aristotle, balthazar, dead marine, demijohn, double magnum, echo, flagon, half-bottle, jeroboam, magnum, methuselah, nebuchadnezzar, pig *(N.Z.),* plagon, rehoboam, stubby; **flask,** canteen, carafe, costrel, decanter, feeding bottle, fiasco, flasket, glass can, hipflask, phial, waterbottle, water-monkey; **retort,** alembic, matrass, still; **measuring cup,** burette, dispenser, Erlenmeyer flask, graduate *(Rare), (measuring cylinder)*

BOTTLE n aristotle, balthazar, dead marine, demijohn, double magnum, echo, flagon, half-bottle, jeroboam, magnum, methuselah, nebuchadnezzar, pig *(N.Z.),* plagon, rehoboam, stubby; **flask,** canteen, carafe, costrel, decanter, feeding bottle, fiasco, flasket, glass can, hipflask, phial, waterbottle, water-monkey; **retort,** alembic, matrass, still; **measuring cup,** burette, dispenser, Erlenmeyer flask, graduate *(Rare),* measuring cylinder,

pipette, pycnometer; **vacuum flask,** Dewar flask, thermos; **hot water bottle,** hottie, warming pan; **cylinder,** aerosol container, aqualung, gas cylinder, plenum, pressure pack, soda siphon. *See also* VESSEL; DRINKING VESSEL; BARREL

BOTTOM n base, bed, bedrock, floor, seat; **foundation,** baseboard, basis, bedding, bottom board, ceiling *(Naut.),* cordon, deck head, flooring, groundsel *(Obs.),* groundwork, podium, roadbed, rock, sea-floor, stereobate, sub-base, substratum, substructure, tholobate, understratum; **bottom part,** culet, exergue, foot, footing, heel, heelpiece, predella, skirt, stairfoot, strip footing, tail; **stump,** pedestal, plinth; **underside,** bilge, bulge *(Obs.),* sole, underbody, undercarriage, underlay, underlayer, underneath, underpart, undersurface; **basement,** downstairs, undercroft, underground; **low level,** base level, baseline, invert, low, low-water mark, nadir, rock bottom

BOTTOM adj basal, base, basic, basilar, bottommost, downstairs, ground, lowermost, lowest, nethermost, radical, rock-bottom, stereobatic, subbasal, submontane, sunken, underfoot, underground, underlaid, undermost; **underlying,** inferior *(Bot.),* lower, nether, subjacent, under, ventral; **low,** depressed, lowly, prostrate, repent, reptant, subased

BOTTOMS UP interj cheers, chug-a-lug, down the hatch, here's looking at you, here's mud in your eye, here's to you, prost, skol, your health

BOUNCE v rebound, resile, spring

BOUNDARY *adj* circumferential, circumscriptive, limbic, perimetric, perimetrical; **peripheral**, frontier, outmost, riverside, terminal; **marginal**, limbate, submarginal; **roadside**, wayside; **coastal**, littoral, seaboard, seaside

BOW *v* bend the knee, bob, curtsy, genuflect, kow-tow, make obeisance, salaam

BOWL OVER *v* barrel, bottle, bowl down, deck, lay low, skittle; **fell**, flatten, floor, ground, iron out, knock down, knock endways, knock endwise, level, spread-eagle, tackle; **knock out**, concuss, king-hit, lay out, wooden; **overturn**, roll, tip over, tip up

BOX *n* can, carton, crate, packing case, tea-chest; **trunk**, imperial, portmanteau; **hatbox**, bandbox; **casket**, cartouche, chest, coffer; **safe**, money-box, peter, piggy bank, strongbox, till; **locker**, glove box, glove compartment, medicine box, medicine chest; **letterbox**, ballot-box, mailbox, pillar-box, post-box; **snuffbox**, pillbox; **matchbox**, tinderbox, window box, fernery, flowerbox, flowerpot, jardinière, planter box, polyhouse, terrarium; **woodbox**, coalscuttle, hod, woodbin; **lunch box**, canteen, crib-box, crib-tin *(N.Z.)*, tuckerbox; **canister**, breadbin, caddy, firkin, tea caddy; **icebox**, car fridge, chillybin *(N.Z.)*, cool safe, cooler, Coolgardie safe, esky, frig, ice bucket, ice chest, refrigerator, stubby cooler. *See also* CASE: BASKET: BAG

BOYCOTT *v* bar, blackball, de-list, fence *(Archaic)*, keep out, ward off; **disqualify**, count out, debar, disenfranchise, disfranchise, suspend; proscribe, forbid, outlaw, taboo. *See also* ISOLATE: EXCLUDE

BRACE *n* batten, cleat, stair-rod, stretcher, truss; **plate**, chill, cog, fish-plate, gang nail, tang

BRACHIAL *adj* carpal, clavicular, digital, humeral, index, manual, metacarpal, palmar, scapular; **pedal**, astragalgar, femoral, fibibular, geniculate, patellar, tarsal, tibial

BRAG *v* big-mouth, bluster, boast, bounce, brave *(Obs.)*, bull, bulldust, crack up *(Obs.)*, crow, gasconade, pitch a line, puff, rodomontade, shoot a line, shoot off one's mouth, skite, swagger, talk big, trumpet, vapour, vaunt; **ego-trip**, big-note oneself, blow one's own trumpet, exult, glory, glory in, grandstand, sell oneself; **have a swelled head**, have tickets on oneself, think oneself Christmas, think oneself someone, think oneself something

BRAGGART *n* big noter, big-mouth, bighead, boaster, brag, braggadocio, fanfaron, grandstander, name-dropper, pup, puppy, skite, skiter, vaunter; **blusterer**, blower, bouncer, bull artist, bullshit artist, tinhorn *(U.S.)*; **egoist**, egomaniac, egotist, narcissist

BRAGGART *adj* blustering, boasting, bragging, vainglorious; **boastful**, blustery, spread-eagle *(U.S.)*, swanky, thrasonical; **big-headed**, swelled-headed, swollen headed; **egoistic**, egoistical, egotistic, egotistical, narcissistic

BRAGGARTISM *n* egoism, egomania, egotism, narcissism, vainglory; **boastfulness**, swankiness, vaingloriousness

bragging — breathless

BRAGGING *n* blustering, boasting, ego-tripping, namedropping, skiting, vapouring; **bluster,** blow, bounce, bravado, puff, self-advertisement, swagger; **braggadocio,** bull, bullshit, fanfaronade, gasconade, jactation, rodomontade; **brag,** boast, ego trip, vaunt

BRAGGINGLY *adv* big *(Colloq.)*, blusteringly, boastfully, boastingly, swankily, thrasonically, vapouringly, vauntingly; **egoistically,** egotistically

BRANCH *n* anabranch, arm, embranchment, ramus, side road; **fork,** crotch, crutch, elbow; **radius,** spoke, sprag; **diverter,** divaricator. *See also* DIVERGENCE

BRASS INSTRUMENT *n* brass, brass wind; **trumpet,** Bach trumpet, bugle, clarino, clarion, cornet, flugelhorn, horn, trump *(Poetic)*; **trombone,** sackbut, slush pump; **French horn,** mellophone, Wagner tuba; **tuba,** baritone, bombardon, euphonium, helicon, saxtuba, sousaphone; **cornet,** bass horn, ophicleide, serpent; **saxhorn,** althorn, alto, alto horn, tenor horn, tenor saxhorn; **hand-horn,** alpenhorn, alphorn, coach-horn, shophar; **conch,** murex

BRAVE *v* bite the bullet, face up to, grasp the nettle, look in the face, outbrave, square up to; **dare,** bell the cat, go through fire and water, venture; **put on a bold front,** crack hardy, crack hearty, keep a stiff upper lip, keep the flag flying, put on a brave face, take it on the chin, **pluck up courage,** take heart

BREAK *n* chink, cleat, cleavage plane, cleft, columnar jointing, crack, crevasse, crevice, cut, divide, fault, fault line, fault plane, fissure, fracture, grain, hair parting, joint, rent, rip, rupture, schism, slip, split, tear, transcrystalline fracture; **divorce,** breakup, bust-up, cut-out, rift; **detachment,** fork, fragment, orphan *(Print.)*, outbuilding, outlier, part, split; **breakaway,** cave

BREAK *v* burst, bust, crack, crash, ding, hole, prang, smash, snap, stave, stave in, tear, wrench; **crush,** chew up, smash

BREATHE *v* breathe in, draw breath, inbreathe, inhale, inspire, insufflate, respire, suck the breath, suspire *(Archaic)*; **exhale,** breathe out; **puff,** aspirate, huff, snuffle; **sniff,** snuff, whiff, whiffle; **wheeze,** cough, hiccup, sneeze; **gasp,** blow, breathe hard, breathe heavily, pant

BREATHING *n* aspiration, expiration, inspiration, insufflation, respiration; **rough breathing,** snoring, spiritus asper, stertor, windedness; **smooth breathing,** spiritus lenis; **artificial respiration,** kiss of life; **inhalation,** draw, puff, toke, whiff; **exhalation,** aspirate, blow, halitus, hiccups, hiss, pant, sibilation, sigh, steam, suspiration; **gasp,** cough, croup, graveyard bark, graveyard cough, rattle, sneeze, sniff, sniffle, snore, snort, snuff, snuffle, sternutation, wheeze; **the breath,** atman, wind; **breathing apparatus,** aqualung, octopus regulator, SCUBA, self-contained underwater breathing apparatus; **oxygen tent,** iron lung, oxygen mask

BREATHLESS *adj* apnoeal, apnoeic, asphyxiated, choked, gasping, panting, puffed, short-winded, smothered, suffocated, winded

breeder   71   **bright**

BREEDER *n* eugenicist, eugenist, grafter, grower, hybridiser, propagator, stirpiculturist, stockbreeder

BREEDING GROUND *n* incubator, womb; **cradle**, nursery; **hotbed**, fertile soil, good soil, seedbed; **hothouse**, conservatory, garden, glasshouse, greenhouse, terrarium; **auxanometer**, crescograph

BREVIARY *n* antiphonary, bible, catechism, ceremonial, diurnal, family Bible, gradual, hours, hymnal, hymn-book, missal, passional, polyglot, pontifical, prayer book, Psalter, service book, testament, vesperal

BREW *v* malt, rack, still *(Obs.)*, work; **alcoholise**, lace, spike

BREWER *n* distiller, stiller *(Obs.)*, wet *(U.S.)*; **sly grogger**, bootlegger, moonshiner; **oenologist**, wine-taster, wine-grower, winemaker

BRIBABILITY *n* corruptibility, purchasability, venality

BRIBABLE *adj* all right *(Colloq.)*, buyable, corrupt, for sale, on the market, purchasable, Tammany-Hall, venal

BRIBE *n* backhander, bonus *(Colloq.)*, boodle *(U.S.)*, consideration, fix, oil, palm oil, sling, sop, under-the-table payment; **hush money**, drugola, inducement allowance, kickback, payola, protection, protection money, slush fund, subsidisation; **inducement**, bait, douceur, incentive, sweetener

BRIBE *v* blackmail, buy, buy off, cross someone's palm, get at, grease someone's palm, have in one's pay, make it right with, oil, oil someone's palm, pay off, purchase, sling, suborn, subsidise, sweeten, tamper with, throw a sop to

BRIBER *n* bagman, bent cop, blackmailer, boodler, crooked politician, embraceor, suborner, subsidiser

BRIBERY *n* corruption, dollar diplomacy, embracery, jobs for the boys, pork *(U.S.)*, pork barrel, protection, protection racket, subornation, watergate

BRIDGE *n* Bailey bridge, box-girder bridge, chain-bridge, clapper bridge, drawbridge, embracery, floating bridge, flyover *(Brit.)*, humpback bridge, overbridge, overfly, overpass, pivot bridge, span, suspension bridge, swing bridge, toll bridge, transporter bridge, traversing bridge, trestle bridge, truss bridge; **gangplank; crossover**, covered way, covert way, footbridge, pedestrian crossing, scramble crossing, zebra crossing; **conduit**, aqueduct, course, lockage, viaduct; **pass**, access, defile; **tunnel**, corridor, creek *(Obs.)*, crosscut, passage, passageway, shaft; **pontoon**, float; **ford**, stepping stone

BRIGHT *adj* aureate, brilliant, effulgent, flashy *(Rare)*, fulgent, gleaming, illustrious *(Obs.)*, irradiate, lambent, lightsome, lively, lucent *(Archaic)*, lucid, radiant, refulgent, relucent, resplendent, sheer *(Obs.)*, shimmery, shining, splendent, splendorous, transparent *(Obs.)*, vivid; **sparkling**, agleam, aglimmer, aglitter, asteriated, aventurine, chatoyant, clinquant, diamanté, glittery, rutilant *(Rare)*, scintillant, scintillating; **glaring**, blinding, garish, glary, lurid; **flashing**, fulgurant, fulgurous, fulminous; **shiny**, ganoid, glare, glassy, glossy, polished, satin, satiny, sheen *(Archaic)*, sheeny, silk, silken, silky, silvery, sleek, slick, waxlike, waxy, wet-look; **lustrous**, iridescent, lus-

bright   72   **brown**

tred, nacreous, opalescent, opaline, orient, oriental, pearl, pearly; **clear,** crystal, empyreal, empyrean, glass, mild; **cloudless,** shadeless, shadowless, unshadowed; **sunny,** sundrenched, sunlit, sunshine, sunshiny; **moonlit,** moonlight, moonshiny, moony, star-studded, starlight, starlit, starry; **lamplit,** lamplight, torchlight, torchlit; **light,** illuminative, photic; **luminous,** fluorescent, irradiant, irradiative, luciferous, luminescent, luminiferous, noctilucent, phosphorescent, photogenic *(Biol.),* radiative

BRIGHTLY *adv* bright, brilliantly, clear, clearly, illuminatingly, lucidly, resplendently, vividly; **glowingly,** candescently, effulgently, fulgently, incandescently, lambently, lustrously, radiantly, refulgently; **glitteringly,** flickeringly, glimmeringly, glisteningly, starrily; **glossily,** silkily, sleekly, slickly; **fierily,** flamingly; **glaringly,** blindingly, dazzlingly; **garishly,** luridly

BRIGHTNESS *n* bright *(Archaic),* brilliance, brilliantness, dazzle, effulgence, fieriness, fire, flame, flashiness, garishness, glare, glaringness, irradiance, irradiancy, lambency, liveliness, lucence *(Archaic),* lucency *(Archaic),* luridness, resplendence, silveriness, splendour, starriness, vividness; **luminescence,** asterism, bioluminescence, chemiluminescence, electroluminescence, fluorescence, luminosity, luminousness, noctilucence, phosphorescence, photoluminescence, radioluminescence, thermoluminescence, triboluminescence; **polish,** burnish, gloss, glossiness, lustrousness, sheen, shine, shininess, sleekness, slickness, varnish; **iridesc-**

ence, highlights, lustre, opalescence, orient, pearl, reflet, schiller. *See also* LIGHT

BRITTLE *adj* calcareous, china, crisp, crispy, crispy-crunchy, crunchy, crusty, eggshell, glass, glasslike, glassy, red-short, semivitreous, shivery, splintery, vitreous; **breakable,** brashy, crumbly, fragile, frail, frangible, friable, shatterable, short, tender *(Wool)*

BRITTLENESS *n* crispness, glassiness, vitreosity, vitreousness, vitrification; **breakability,** fragileness, fragility, frailness, frailty, frangibility, tenderness *(Wool)*

BROADCAST *adj* beamed, on the air, transmitted

BROTHEL *n* bagnio, bawdy house, bordello, cathouse, disorderly house, drum, escort agency, house of ill fame, house of ill repute, knocking shop, massage parlour, stews *(Archaic),* whorehouse; **red light district**

BROWN *n* beige, dun; **brownness,** rustiness, suntan, tawniness; **brunette,** bitumen blonde, brunet *(Obs.);* **browning,** tanning; **brown pigment,** bistre, burnt sienna, burnt umber, henna, raw sienna, raw umber, rust, sienna, sinopia, umber; **melanin**

BROWN *v* blanco, bronze, embrown, tan, toast; **rust**

BROWN *adj* brown as a berry, brownish, brunette, nutbrown, spadiceous; **suntanned,** bronzed, sunburned, sunburnt, tanned; **dark brown,** chocolate, cocoa, coffee-coloured, fuscous, mocha, puce, seal brown, sepia, umber, Vandyke brown; **mahogany,** maple, oak, teak, walnut; **light brown,**

almond, amber, bisque, camel, khaki, tan; **tawny**, cacky-coloured, cervine, musteline; **buff**, fallow, fawn; **beige**, biscuit, café au lait, caramel, ecru, unbleached; **dun**, drab, fulvous, putty; **snuff-coloured**, nicotine-stained; **reddish-brown**, auburn, bronze, bronzy, cinnamon, copper, coppery, cupreous, ferruginous, foxy, ginger, gingery, hazel, hepatic, liver, rubiginous, russet, rust-coloured, rusty, terracotta, testaceous, titian; **chestnut**, bay, dapple-bay, roan, sorrel

BRUSH *n* banister brush, bootbrush, currycomb, dandy-brush, duster, feather duster, fitch, hairbrush, nailbrush, scrubbing-brush, wire brush; **comb**, bug rake, flea rake, hatchel, heckle; **broom**, besom, Turks' head broom; **carpet-sweeper**, floor polisher, hoover, vacuum cleaner; **mop**, floorcloth, scrim, squeegee; **scraper**, nail-file, strigil; **fibre cleaner**, gin, linter, rippler, scutch

BRUTAL *adj* bestial, boarish, brute, bull, bullish, ferocious, hubristic; **barbaric**, barbarian, barbarous, loutish, rude, vandal, vandalic; **ruffianly**, piratical, plug-ugly *(U.S.)*, thuggish, tough. *See also* VIOLENT

BUBBLE *n* air-bell, bead, bleb *(Rare)*, blob; **blister**, bulla, phlyctena, seed; **artificial horizon; bubble chamber**

BUBBLE *v* boil, burble, effervesce, fizz, fizzle, foam, froth, intumesce, lather, mantle, prickle, sparkle, spume; **gargle**, guggle, gurgle; **ferment**, aerate, carbonate, yeast

BUBBLINESS *n* effervescence, effervescency, foaminess, frothiness, gassiness, life, liveliness, prickle, spumescence, yeastiness; **carbonation**, carbon dioxide, carbonic acid gas, fermentation, zyme *(Obs.)*

BUBBLING *n* burble, burbling, cavitation; **foam**, barm, bead, collar, froth, head *(Alc. Bev.)*, lather, sea-foam, spindrift, spray, spume, suds, surf, yeast; **bubbler**, carbonator, fountain, latherer, soda syphon; **fizzy drink**, bubbly, sherbet; **bubble bath; bubble gum**

BUBBLINGLY *adv* ebulliently, effervescently, foamily, foamingly, frothily, yeastily

BUBBLY *adj* aerated, carbonated, ebullient, effervescent, fizzy, foamy, frothing, frothy, gassy, lathery, spumescent, spumous, spumy, sudsy, with a head on, yeasty; **sparkling**, brisk, lively, petillant, prickly, spritzig; **blistered**, blebby, blistery

BUILD *v* construct, engineer, erect, make, put up, raise; **mason**, brick, carpenter, riprap; **prefabricate**, precast, preform

BUILDER *n* architect, checker *(U.S.)*, civil engineer, draughtsman, engineer, erecter, landscape architect, master builder; **mason**, brickie, bricklayer, carpenter, cowan, lather; **rigger**, scaffolder

BUILDING *n* construction, erection, fabric, facility, structure, superstructure, work; **edifice**, complex, dome, megastructure, pile; **outbuilding**, addition, annexe, dependency, extension, finger, outhouse, wing; **substructure**, chassis, foundation, infrastructure, shell, substruction; **framework**, cage, casing, cradling, frame, gantry, roll cage, scaffold, scaffolding, skeleton, truss, trussing, undercarriage; **trellis**, espalier, lattice, pergola

BUILDING MATERIALS *n* bricks and mortar, lath and plaster, wattle and daub; **brick**, adobe, ashlar, cement, concrete, plaster, stone; **mortar**, binder; **roofing**, shingle, slate, thatch, tile; **flooring**, boarding, decking, panelling, paving, planking, studding; **insulation**, asbestos, batt, fibreglass, fireproofing, rockwool; **rubble**, backfill, ballast, bedding, fill, filler, riprap. *See also* TIMBER

BULGE *n* ball, billow, mushroom, pout, swell; **belly**, bay window *(Colloq.)*, beer gut, bloat, potbelly, venter; **hump**, dowager's hump, gibbosity, humpback, hunch, hunchback, widow's hump; **bud**, button, lobation, lobe, lobule, mamilla, nipple, stud, tit, titty; **protuberance**, bridge, cusp, excrescence, outgrowth, shoulder, snout, spine, spur, tenon, tentacle, torus; **crest**, comb; **swelling**, bump, bunion, chondroma, desmoid, goitre, hernia, puff, scrofula, struma, tumescence, tumour, turgescence; **lump**, air-sac, anbury, bedeguar, boss, capped hock, cheloid, condyloma, cyst, diverticulum, fibroid, fibroma, ganglion, keloid, knot, macrocyst, node, nodule, papilla, papilloma, polyp, sebaceous cyst, spavin, tuber, verruca, wart, wen; **blister**, barb, bighead, blain, bleb *(Rare)*, blood blister, bog spavin, boil, bulla, carbuncle, gathering, head, pimple, pock, pustule, tubercle, vesicle; **goose pimples**, heat rash, horripilation; **welt**, wale, weal, wheal. *See also* KNOB

BULGE *v* bag, balloon, belly, bilge, billow, bloat, fill, fill out, heave, mushroom, puff up, swell, tumefy; **hump**, hunch, lump, pod; **butt**, dome, peak, point; **blister**, gather, vesicate, vesiculate; **emboss**, pounce, raise, stud; **knot**, lump; **extrude**, evaginate, herniate. *See also* JUT

BULL ARTIST *n* babbler, bilge artist, jabberer, joker, magger, magpie, maunderer, patterer, piffler, raver, twaddler, verbalist, yawper

BULLSHIT *interj* all my eye and Betty Martin, apple sauce, arseholes, balls, bull, bullswool, don't make me laugh, eh, fiddle-de-dee, fiddlesticks, get along with you, go on, humph, like fun, my foot, my sainted aunt, oh yeah, pah, phooey, pig's arse, pig's bum, pigs, pigs might fly, pshaw, pull the other one (it has bells), sure, tell that to the horse marines, tell that to the marines, that'll be the day, that's a good one, try another, um, what

BUNGLE *n* boggle, botch, botch-up, clambake *(U.S. Colloq.)*, cock-up, flub, fumble, mistake; **muddle**, dawdling, flounder, potter; **blunder**, a foot in the mouth, fluff, malapropism; **botchery**, piece of incompetence, slopwork; **bad shot**, cow shot, foozle, miscue, misfield *(Cricket)*, mishit

BUNGLE *v* arse up, blow it, boggle, botch, botch up, butcher, cock up, crap up, flub, fluff, foozle, hash, hash make a hash of, make a mess of, make a poor fist of, maladminister, misconduct, misdo, mishandle, mismanage, muck up, muff; **blunder**, be slipping, bumble, flounder, fumble, get in the road, goof, grope, muddle, put one's foot in it, stumble; **arse about**, arse around, arsehole about, bugger around, bugger about, clown, fool around, muck about, muck around; **dabble**, dawdle, piddle, piss about, piss around, potter, tinker; **be incapacitated**, have two left feet; **jerry-**

build, cobble, mullock, slum; **charge at**, charge like a bull at a gate, go bull-headed at; **fumble**, catch a crab *(Rowing)*, duff *(Sport)*, miscue, misfield *(Cricket)*, mishit, misthrow, pull, slice

BUOYANT *adj* afloat, floatable, floating, floaty, natant

BUREAUCRAT *n* administrator, civil servant, legislator, mandarin, official, palatine, public servant

BURNING *n* baking, calcination, carbonisation, decrepitation, firing, flashing, roasting, scorching, singeing, ustulation; **combustion**, ignition, kindling; **pyrography**, branding, cauterisation, cautery, galvanocautery

BURN OUT *v* die down, expire

BURP *n* belch, eructation, retch; **fart**, braff, flatulence, flatus, fluff, gas, smelly, wind

BURP *v* belch, eruct, eructate, repeat; **fart**, braff, break wind, drop a bundle, drop one's lunch, fluff, go off, let off, lunch, make a smell, shoot a fairy

BURY *v* coffin, entomb, immure, inhume, inter, inurn, lay to rest, pit, sepulchre, tomb; **lay out**, cere, embalm, mummify, shroud; **lie buried**, lie six feet under, push up daisies

BUSILY *adv* hectically; **actively**, energetically, lively, pertly, spiritedly, warmly, with might and main; **sprightly**, bustlingly, dapperly, hurriedly, hurryingly, racily, spryly; **vigorously**, dashingly, dynamically; **restlessly**, exhaustlessly, skittishly, unquietly, unrestingly; **flat out**, at full tilt, flat out like a lizard drinking, full blast, in everything bar a bath, in full swing, in the swim, like a cut snake, like nobody's business, on a hurdy-gurdy, on the hop, on the trot, on the wing, up to one's ears, up to one's elbows, up to one's eyes; **in the press of business**, in medias res, in the middle of things, in the thick of it all; **in action**, in use, on active service, on the job

BUSY *adj* active, alive, engaged, hard at work, hearty, hectic, humming, lissom, renascent, smart, warm; **sprightly**, agile, animated, brisk, dapper, fast, full of go, hurried, live, lively, prompt, quick *(Rare)*, racy, spry; **vigorous**, bustling, energetic, go-ahead, jazzy, pert, pushing, red-blooded, slick, spirited, spiritoso, wide-awake; **dashing**, dashy, dynamic, slashing; **tireless**, exhaustless, indefatigable, never-tiring, persevering, sedulous, unresting, unstinting, wearilless; **hard-working**, businesslike, industrious, painstaking, practical, pragmatic, unresting, vigilant

BUSYNESS *n* activeness, aliveness, lissomness, pertness, warmness; **activity**, exertion, goings-on, movement at the station, much ado, to-do; **bustle**, coil, hustle, merry-go-round, razzamatazz, razzle-dazzle, rush, song and dance, stir; **much ado about nothing**, all froth and bubble, boondoggle, sound and fury signifying nothing; **burst of activity**, flurry, sally, sprint, spurt, start, tornado; **fuss**, bother, stink

BUTLER *n* maitre d'hôtel, majordomo, sewer; **valet**, bearer, body-servant, boots, boy, buttons, cabin boy *(Naut.)*, callboy, fag, garcon, gentleman, gillie, groom, knave, lackey, man, manservant, page, pageboy,

butler   76   **byroad**

valet de chambre, varlet *(Archaic)*; **porter,** bellboy, bellhop, night porter; **flunkey,** chasseur, footboy, footman, yeoman *(Archaic);* **stableboy,** equerry, groom, horsetailer, ostler, strapper. See also SERVANT

BUTT *n* April fool, Aunt Sally, buffoon, byword, easy prey, fair game, fall guy, figure of fun, guy, laughing stock, object of ridicule, patsy, stooge, zany; **gullible person,** admass, country bumpkin, hick, innocent, innocent abroad, local yokel, rube *(U.S.),* Simple Simon. See also VICTIM

BUTTOCKS *n* acre, arse, backside, base, beam, behind, big A, bot, bottom, breech, bum, butt, can, cheeks, chuff, coit, derrière, ding, dinger, fanny, jacksy *(N.Z.),* Khyber, nates, posterior, rear, rump, seat, slats, tail; **haunch,** ham, hip, hock, hunkers, loins; **anus,** arsehole, back passage, blot, blurter, breezer, bronze, bronzo, brown-eye, crack, date, freckle, fundament, hole, quoit, ring; natal cleft

BUTTON *n* Anzac button, collar stud, cufflink, dome, hook and eye, pearl button, popper, press-stud, snap, snap fastener, stud, tuft; **buckle,** clasp, ouch *(Archaic),* tache *(Archaic);* **toggle,** frog; **ring,** woggle; **zipper,** slide fastener, zip, zip-fastener; **buttonhook**

BUY *v* acquire, bulk buy, buy into, forestall, get, have, hive off, mailorder, make a purchase, obtain, overbuy, pay for, pre-empt, procure, purchase, take, traffic in, underbuy; **monopolise,** buy out, buy up, corner the market, engross, gridiron *(U.S.),* peacock; **redeem,** buy back, ransom; **buy on credit,** hire-purchase, lay-by, pay C.O.D., pay cash; **be in the market for**; **hire,** book, rent; **shop,** bargain, drive a hard bargain, get one's money's worth, go on a shopping spree, go shopping, market, patronise, shop around; **be in the chair,** shout; **buy a pig in a poke**

BUYABLE *adj* convertible, purchasable; **redemptory,** redeemable

BUYER *n* consignee, consumer, consumer society, hire purchaser, impulse buyer, peacocker, purchaser, transferee, vendee; **customer,** bargainer, bearer, chap *(Obs.),* client, haggler, marketer, patron, shopper; **clientele,** carriage trade, clientage; **patronage,** custom

BUYING *n* consumption, mail order, pre-emption, purchase, retirement *(Comm.),* shopping, shopping spree; **monopolisation,** coemption, engrossment; **repurchase,** redemption; **hire-purchase,** H.P., lay-away, lay-by; **buy,** a good buy, acquisition, bargain, purchase, short covering

BY CHANCE *adv* accidentally, adventitiously, arbitrarily, at a venture, at hazard, bechance, casually, coincidentally, desultorily, haphazard, haphazardly, perchance *(Archaic),* perhaps *(Rare),* promiscuously, without rhyme or reason; **whatever happens,** in any event; **luckily,** fortuitously, fortunately, providentially; **unluckily,** sadly

BY NAME *adv* baptismally, nominally, pseudonymously, titularly; **generically,** terminologically

BYROAD *n* bypass, bypath, bystreet, byway, crossroad, detour, side road, turn-off; **sidetrack,** shunt, siding, tram pinch

Cc

CABIN n bach (N.Z.), beach hut, box (Brit.), cabana (U.S.), casino, crannog, holiday house, lodge, shooting lodge (Brit.), villa, weekender; **hut**, bothy (Scot.), cabane, caboose, chalet, cot, crib, hutch, rancho, slab hut; **humpy**, goondie, mia-mia, wurley; **lean-to**, skillion, **hovel**, badger-box, hutch, lodge, shack, shanty, shebang, slum, whare (N.Z.); **dump**, den, dog-box (N.Z. Colloq.), doghouse, dugout, hole; **slums**, rabbit-warren, squats, warren. See also HOUSE

CALAMITOUS adj catastrophic, dire, disastrous, dreadful, evil, ruinous, tragic; **adverse**, difficult, ill, rough, rugged, stiff, thwart, troublesome; **inauspicious**, ill-boding, ill-omened, ill-starred, ominous, sinister, sinistrous, unfavourable; **agonising**, distressful, distressing

CALAMITOUSLY adv disastrously, ruinously; **inauspiciously**, evilly; **distressingly**, agonisingly, distressfully

CALL ATTENTION TO v agitate, engage, enkindle, point out, publicise, ram down someone's throat; **upstage**, do a hollywood, draw attention to oneself, draw the crabs, feature, make a splash; **call after**, catch someone's eye, hello, hist, yoo-hoo

CALL (OF ANIMALS) v cry, laugh, sing, speak, talk, whistle; **roar**, bell, bellow, blare, trumpet; **howl**, caterwaul, hoot, screech, ululate, wail; **bark**, bay, bay at the moon, challenge (Hunting), give tongue, growl, grunt, snap, snarl, woof, yap, yelp; **bray**, heehaw, **baa**, bleat; **drone**, buzz, hum, whine; **whinny**, neigh, snicker, whicker; **mew**, miaow, purr; **moo**, low. See also CHIRP

CALLOUS adj cold-blooded, conscienceless, hard, hard-hearted, hard-nosed, hardened, heartless, indurated, inhumane, inured, loveless, obdurate, rocky, steely, stony, stony-hearted, tough, unfeeling, unsqueamish; **cold-hearted**, bloodless, clinical, cold, frigid, frosty, frozen, icy, marble, marbly, rigid, soulless, uncompassionate, unsympathetic; **ruthless**, harsh, iron-fisted, merciless, pitiless, severe, unpitying; **brutal**, cruel, inhuman; **unrelenting**, implacable, inexorable, inflexible, relentless, remorseless; **unmoved**, dry-eyed, impassible, impassive, impervious, passionless, stoic, stoical, tearless, unemotional; **insensitive**, clumsy, heavy-footed, insensible, outspoken, tactless, thick-skinned, unconsidered

CALLOUSLY adv brutally, hard-heartedly, heartlessly, inhumanely, inhumanly, lovelessly, obdurately, pitilessly, soullessly, stonily, unfeelingly, unsympathetically; **cold-heartedly**, bloodlessly, clinically, cold-bloodedly, coldly, cruelly, frigidly, frostily, frozenly, icily, in cold blood, without turning a hair; **ruthlessly**, harshly, mercilessly, relentlessly, unrelentingly; **insensitively**, clumsily, tactlessly

CALLOUSNESS n cold-turkey, hard-heartedness, hardness of heart, heartlessness, induration, lovelessness, obduracy, obdurateness, pitilessness, rockiness, severity, steeliness, stoni-

callousness — ness, tactlessness, unfeelingness; **ruthlessness,** barbarity, cold-bloodedness, cruelty, inhumanity, mercilessness, savagery; **relentlessness,** inexorability, remorselessness; **coldness,** frigidity, frostiness, iciness; **insensitivity,** a thick hide, impassiveness, impassivity, indifference, insensitiveness, irresponsiveness, Stoicism, unconcern; **unfeeling person,** block, emotional cripple, Stoic

CAMERA *n* box brownie, box camera, camera obscura, continuous strip camera, instamatic, magic eye, miniature camera, polaroid camera, reflex camera, single-lens reflex camera, SLR camera, stop-action camera; **heliograph,** nephograph, photochronograph, spectroheliograph; **optical printer,** sensitometer, vignetter; **projector,** bioscope, magic lantern, viewer

CAMERA FILM *n* carbon paper, contact paper, emulsion, plate; **film strip,** reel, roll film; **microfilm,** biblio film, fast film, fine-grain film, high-speed film, infra-red film, isochromatic film, orthochromatic film, slow film, X-ray film; **darkroom; photographic chemical,** Amidol, cyanine, developer, reducer, stop bath

CAMERA PART *n* cable release, gate, lens turret, magazine; **lens,** amplifier, fish-eye lens, telephoto lens, wide-angle lens, zoom lens; **exposure meter,** extinction meter, light meter, photoelectric meter; **viewfinder,** finder, focuser, rangefinder, telemeter; **shutter,** focal plane shutter; **filter,** colour-filter, diffuser, UV filter; **flash,** flashbulb, flashcube, flashgun, flashlight, photoflash lamp, strobe; **aperture,** depth of field, depth of focus, f number, hyperfocal distance, stop; **shutter speed,** acutance, ASA/BS, density, DIN, latitude, opacity

CAMP *n* bivouac, bivvy, fly-camp *(N.Z.),* tentage, transit camp, transit site; **camp site,** camping ground, camping site, caravan park, encampment; **tent,** bell tent, bivvy, canvas, fly; **wigwam,** tepee, tipi, whare *(N.Z.),* yurt

CANCEL *v* abolish, annul, break off, defeat, dele *(Print.),* delete, derecognise, deregister, dissolve, infirm *(Archaic),* invalidate, nullify, quash, rescind, scrub, void; **revoke,** abjure, avoid, climb down, countermand, eat one's words, renounce, repudiate, retract, reverse, unsay, unspeak, unswear; **repeal,** abate, abolish, abrogate; **recall,** call back, recede, undo, withdraw

CANCELLATION *n* annulment, cancel, countermand, delenda, deletion, deregistration, dissolution, invalidation, nullification, recision, rescission, reversal, voidance; **revocation,** discontinuance, disuse, recall, repudiation, suspension, undoing, withdrawal; **repeal,** abatement, abolishment, abolition, abrogation, ademption, avoidance, bar, suppression; **renunciation,** abdication, abjuration; **abolitionism**

CANCELLER *n* abator, abjurer, abolisher, abrogator, invalidator, repealer, rescinder, revoker, withdrawer

CANCER *n* growth, Spanish dancer, Jimmy dancer, the big C, tumour; **carcinogenesis,** oncogenesis, sarcomatosis; **cancer form,** adenoma, cancroid, carcinoma, carcinomatosis, encephaloma, enchondroma, endotheliomia, epithelioma, fibroid, fibroma, glioma, granuloma, haemangioma, leiomyoma, leukaemia, melanoma, molluscum, myoma, osteoma, rhabdomyoma, sarcoma, scirrhus, scleroma

CANDLE *n* bougie, dip, taper; **candlestick**, candelabrum, girandole, menorah, pricket; **torch**, brand *(Poetic)*, fire, flambeau, flame, flare, Hawaiian flare, link, luau light

CAP *n* balmoral, beanie, beaver, beret, billycock *(Colloq.)*, biretta, black cap *(Law)*, bonnet *(Scot.)*, calotte, Cossack hat, coxcomb *(Obs.)*, dunce's cap, fez, fool's cap, forage cap *(Mil.)*, gigglehat *(Mil.)*, glengarry *(Scot.)*, jockey cap, kalpak, kepi, nightcap, sailor hat, shako *(Mil.)*, skullcap, sou'wester *(Naut.)*, tam, tam-o'-shanter, tarboosh, tricorn, tuque, yarmulke, zucchetto *(Rom. Cath. Ch.)*; **bonnet**, blue-bonnet, bluecap, capote, cloche, coif, mob-cap *(Obs.)*; **bathing cap**, shower cap. *See also* HEADGEAR; HAT; HELMET

CAPABILITY *n* ability, capableness, capacity, faculty, power; **effectiveness**, cogency, effectuality, effectualness, efficaciousness, efficacy, forcefulness, forcibility, forcibleness, operation, operativeness, virtuousness *(Archaic)*

CAPABLE *adj* able; **effective**, cogent, effectual, efficacious, forceful, forcible, mean *(Colloq.)*, operative, unstoppable, virtual *(Archaic)*, virtuous *(Archaic)*

CAPABLY *adv* ably; **effectively**, cogently, effectually, efficaciously, forcefully, forcibly, operatively, tellingly, virtuously *(Archaic)*

CAPITAL *n* asset backing, authorised capital, capital expenditure, capital stock, circulating capital, corpus, fixed capital, issued capital, paid-up capital, principal, risk capital, shareholders' funds, working capital; **fund**, loan fund, revolving fund; **assets**, current assets, goodwill, intangibles, liquid assets; **bill**, allonge, bank bill, bill of exchange, bill of sale, demand bill, documentary bill, foreign bill, sight bill, Treasury bill *(Brit.)*, Treasury note; **deposit**, fixed deposit, statutory reserve deposit, time deposit; **bank rate**, bond rate, differential rate, dividend rate, interest, rediscount rate; **credit**, credit note, credit rating, credit slip, credit transfer; **charge card**, bank card, credit card, credit plate, plastic, plastic money; **bond**, acceptance, certificate of deposit, security, unsecured note. *See also* STOCKS AND SHARES

CAPITAL PUNISHMENT *n* death penalty, execution, lynching; **electrocution**, electric chair; **fusillade**, firing squad; **hanging**, halter, high jump, long drop; **strangulation**, bow-stringing, garrotte; **crucifixion**, impalement; **beheading**, decapitation; **flaying**, cut, hanging drawing and quartering; **burning at the stake**, auto-da-fé, fire, the stake

CAPITULATE *v* back down, bend the knee, buckle under, cave in, cede, condescend *(Obs.)*, defer to, fall, give ground, give in, give way, go under, haul down the flag, knuckle under, lay down one's arms, lose ground, lower the flag, run scared, sag, sky the rag, sky the towel, strike the flag, succumb, surrender, throw in one's hand, throw in the sponge, throw in the towel, throw it in, throw up, yield; **submit**, accede, acquiesce, appease, comply, concede, draw in one's horns, lump it, remit *(Obs.)*, resign oneself, temporise, turn the other cheek

CAPRICE *n* caper, capriccio, dash, megrim *(Archaic)*, prank, vagary; **impulse**, fancy, fantasy, humour, hunch, inspiration, maggot *(Rare)*, notion, spurt of imagination, sudden thought, whim, whimsy; **extemporisation**, ad lib, fantasia, impromptu, improvisation

CAPRICIOUS *adj* artistic, dashing, dashy, fanciful, freakish, giddy, harebrained, hasty, impetuous, impulsive, maggoty *(Rare)*, notional *(Chiefly U.S.)*, promiscuous, reckless, spirited, undisciplined, vagarious, wanton, whimsical; **wilful**, arbitrary, fly-away, headstrong, wayward; **extemporary**, ad hoc, ad lib, extemporal *(Obs.)*, extemporaneous, extempore, impromptu, improvised, spontaneous, unpremeditated

CAPRICIOUSLY *adv* arbitrarily, capriccioso, giddily, impulsively, lightly, like an artist, notionally *(Chiefly U.S.)*, on the spur of the moment, promiscuously, waywardly, whimsically, without a second thought, without arrière-pensée, without rhyme or reason, without thinking; **impetuously**, at the drop of a hat, dashingly, feet first; **extemporaneously**, ad lib, ad libitum, extemporarily, extempore

CAPRICIOUSNESS *n* arbitrariness, giddiness, impulsiveness, knee-jerk reaction, promiscuousness, spontaneity, weak-mindedness, whimsicality, whimsicalness; **extemporaneousness**, adhockery, extemporariness; **wilfulness**, self-will, waywardness

CAPTIVATED *adj* carried away, enthralled, fascinated, much taken by, overcome, seduced, smitten, spellbound, struck by, tempted; **aroused**, horny, lustful, randy, sexually excited

CAPTURE *n* apprehension, arrest, conquest, occupation, seizing, seizure; **pillage**, looting, ravishment, theft; **abduction**, beguilement, enticement

CAPTURE *v* apprehend, arrest, attach *(Obs.)*, carry, conquer, extend *(Obs.)*, get *(Obs.)*, jump *(Draughts)*, possess *(Archaic)*, surprise, swoop down on, take, take by storm, take by surprise, take possession of, take prisoner; **abduct**, abstract, bear off, carry off, convey *(Obs.)*, kidnap, make away with, run away with, spirit away, tear off with; **grab**, bag, catch up, clasp, clutch, collar, fang *(Obs.)*, fist, foot *(Falconry)*, gobble, grip, gripe, help oneself to, hook, jump at, lay by the heels, lay hold of, lay hold on, make a grab for, nab, nail, pocket, pounce on, reach for, scrag, seize, snaffle, snap up, snatch, strip, swoop up, tail, take, take hold of, whisk, wrench, wrest

CAR *n* auto *(U.S.)*, automatic, automobile *(U.S.)*, brougham, buggy *(Colloq.)*, bus *(Colloq.)*, courtesy car, demonstrator, electric car, four-door, hatchback, horseless carriage, manual, motor car, plagon wagon *(Derog.)*, rod, steamer, two-door, wheels *(Colloq.)*, Z-car; **runabout**, beetle *(Colloq.)*, bubble car, three-wheeler; **sports car**, fastback, G.T., gran turismo, hardtop, roadster, tourer, two-seater; **convertible**, cabriolet, coupé, landau *(Archaic)*, landaulet *(Obs.)*; **jalopy**, bomb, chaffcutter, crate, crock, flivver, rattletrap, rust bucket, shandrydan, tin lizzie; **limousine**, berline, limmo, phaeton, saloon, saloon car, sedan, touring car, V8, yank tank; **station wagon**, brake, estate car *(Brit.)*, shooting brake *(Brit.)*; **utility**, buckboard, pick-up, tilly, ute, utility truck; **four-wheel drive**, beach buggy, bobcat, dune buggy, four-wheeler, Landrover, off-road vehicle, oversnow vehicle, snowcat, snowmobile; **panel van**, carnal car, fuck truck, shaggin' wagon, sin-bin; **campervan**, camper, kombi; **police car**, black maria, bull car, bun wagon, paddy-wagon, patrol wagon, patrol-car, prowl car *(U.S.)*, squad car, wagon; **racing car**, altered, dragster, go-kart, hot rod, kart, stock car; **taxicab**, cab, hack, jitney *(U.S. Colloq.)*, taxi

CARAVAN *n* camper, campervan, mobile home, relocatable home, trailer *(U.S.)*; **caravanserai**, serai

CARE *n* attendance, ministration, tendance, tender loving care, thoughtfulness, TLC; **thought**, attention, deliberation; **carefulness**, attentiveness, deliberativeness, diligence, fussiness, jealousness, mindfulness, solicitousness, vigilance, wariness; **charge**, adoption, care, fosterage, guardianship, keeping, ministry, providence *(Relig.)*, trust, ward; **upbringing**, bringing-up, upkeep

CARE FOR *v* keep an eye on, minister to, shepherd, take care of, tend; **keep**, look after, save, sit on; **foster**, bring up, fetch up *(U.S.)*, groom, raise, rear; **mind**, attend, baby-sit, sit, take care of, watch; **take pains**, be at pains to, be sure, bother, look out for, look to one's laurels, make sure; **nurse**, fondle, lap, mollycoddle, mother, room in, suckle; **fuss over**, dance attendance on, make a fuss of, wait on hand and foot

CAREFUL *adj* attentive, diligent, heedful, intent, measured, mindful; **ministrant**, clucky, ministrative, regardful, serviceable *(Archaic)*, solicitous, thoughtful; **fussy**, jealous, laboured, old-womanish, overconscientious, pernickety

CAREFULLY *adv* attentively, diligently; **solicitously**, on tiptoe, soft, thoughtfully

CARGO CONTAINER *n* container, I.S.O., seatainer, tank, tanker, W-box

CARRIAGE *n* American buggy, barouche, berlin, britzka, brougham, buckboard *(U.S.)*, buggy, cabriolet, calash, car *(Poetic)*, cariole, caroche, carromata, chaise, chariot, coach-and-four, cobb *(Obs.)*, coupé, curricle, diligence, dogcart, drag, droshky, equipage, fiacre, fly, four-in-hand, gharry, gig, hackney, hackney-carriage, hackney-coach, hansom, jaunting car, jingle, landau, phaeton, post-chaise, rig, shay, spider, stage, stagecoach, stanhope, sulky, surrey *(U.S.)*, tally-ho, tandem, tilbury, trap, unicorn, victoria, vis-a-vis, wagonette; **caravan**, covered wagon *(U.S.)*, prairie schooner *(U.S.)*. *See also* WAGON

CASE *n* attaché case, beauty case, briefcase, dispatch box, dispatch case, papeterie, portfolio, skippet, sponge bag, vanity case, writing case; **suitcase**, port, valise; **purse**, billfold *(U.S.)*, budget *(Obs.)*, burse, cardcase,

case 82 **cause**

handbag, moneybag, notecase, pochette, pocket-book, pouch, reticule, wallet, whippy, willy; **compact,** smelling bottle; **workbox,** ditty-bag, ditty-box, etui, housewife, kit; **sheath,** encasement, holster, quiver, sabretache, scabbard; **magazine,** cartridge, cassette; **specimen case,** solander, vasculum. See also BOX; BAG; BASKET

CASH *n* argent *(Obs.)*, big bickies, brass, bread, cabbage, chaff, chips, circulating medium, currency, dibs, dosh, dough, gelt, gold, hard cash, hard-earned, hay, ill-gotten gains, kale *(U.S.)*, l.s.d., legal tender, loot, lucre, mazuma, mintage, money, moolah, oscar, pelf, ready, shekels, splosh, spon, spondulicks, stuff, tender, wampum *(U.S.)*; **banknote,** bill *(U.S.)*, double-header, greenback *(U.S.)*, money order, note, order, paper, shin plaster *(Obs.)*; **pound,** fiddley, frog, iron man, jim, quid, seine; **dollar,** buck, Oxford, plunk *(U.S.)*, seine, smacker; **folding money,** bankroll, lettuce, paper money, roll, scoop. See also COINAGE; FUNDS; ALLOWANCE; TREASURY; CURRENCY

CASH *v* change, collect, draw, draw on, float a loan, go liquid, liquidate, overdraw, raise the wind, realise, run, tap, withdraw from

CASH *adj* financial, fiscal, hippocket, monetary, pecuniary; **convertible,** hard, liquid, realisable, utterable; **numismatic,** numismatical, nummary, nummular; **money-minded**

CASUALTY *n* the walking wounded, the wounded; **amputee; handicapped person,** cripple, defective, paraplegic, quadriplegic, slow worker; **wreck,** bomb, tin lizzie, write-off

CASUISTIC *adj* deceptive, elenctic, illegitimate, Jesuitical, misleading, paralogistic, perverse, sophistic; **quibbling,** fine-spun, inconsequent, over subtle, pettifogging

CAT *n* ballarat, feline, grimalkin, kitten, marmalade cat, mog, moggy, mouser, puss, pussy, tabby, tom, tomcat, tortoiseshell; **Abyssinian,** Angora, Archangel, Burmese, Cheshire, Egyptian, Havana brown, Himalayan, Maltese, Manx, Persian, Russian blue, Siamese, Turkish

CATCH FIRE *v* blaze, burn ahead, deflagrate, go up in smoke, sweal, take fire; **flame,** conflagrate, flare up, flash, spark; **smoke,** smoulder

CATTLE *n* beef, beef cattle, beefalo, beefer, bobby calf, bovine, buffalo, bull, bullock, catalo, cow, dairy cattle, four-legged kangaroo *(Joc.)*, heifer, kine *(Archaic)*, longhorn, micky, moo-cow, muley, neat *(Obs.)*, ox, poddy, ruminant, Russians, snaily, sook, sookie, springer, steer, vealer

CAUSAL *adj* aetiological, determinant, efficient, evocable, occasional; **causative,** ergative, inductive; **provocative,** catalytic, deterministic, evocative, instigative, provoking

CAUSALITY *n* aetiology, determinism, final causes, finalism, teleology

CAUSALLY *adv* aetiologically, causatively

CAUSE *n* causation, determinant, evocation, ground, matter, occasion; **reason,** factor, secret, skill *(Obs.)*, wherefore, why; **engenderment,** beginning, breeding; **catalysis,** induction, precipitation

CAUSE *v* bring about, bring to bear, bring to pass, do, induce, occasion; **produce**, awaken, bring on, catalyse, conduce, evoke, excite, give rise to, incur, inspire, kick up, precipitate, provoke, spark off, waken; **make**, get, have, let; **engender**, be responsible for, beget, breed, bring forth, create, play a part in

CAUSE DIFFICULTIES *v* complicate, embarrass, entangle, harry, involve, mire, perplex; **mess someone around**, fuck someone about, fuck someone around, lead someone a chase, lead someone a merry dance, make it hot for, mess someone about, put through the hoops, tree

CAUSER *n* evoker, mainspring, pivot, prime mover, primum mobile, principle; **provoker**, begetter, beginner, breeder, engenderer, inducer, inspirer, producer; **catalyst**, casus belli, catalyser, precipitator; **causative**, incentive, instigation, provocative

CAUTIOUS *adj* canny, careful, chary, circumspect, circumspective, deliberate, discreet, heedful, measured, ware *(Archaic)*, wary; **guarded**, close, conservative, safe, safety-conscious; **prudent**, forethoughtful; **tentative**, gingerly

CAUTIOUSLY *adv* cannily, carefully, charily, circumspectively, conservatively, discreetly, measuredly, warily; **guardedly**, on one's guard, safely; **tentatively**, gingerly; **prudently**, forethoughtfully

CAUTIOUSNESS *n* caution, circumspection, circumspectness; **care**, caginess, carefulness, chariness, conservativeness, guardedness, heedfulness, wariness, watchfulness; **prudence**, canniness, discretion, forethought; tentativeness, gingerliness, hesitation; **instinct of self-preservation**

CAVE *n* cavern, cove, dugout, grot *(Poetic)*, grotto; **chamber**, catacomb, columbarium, hypogeum, tomb; **burrow**, cubbyhole, foxhole, wormhole. *See also* HOLLOW; EXCAVATION

CELEBRATION *n* festivities, jollities, revels, silly season; **party**, carouse, chavoo, corroboree, do, hootenanny *(U.S.)*, jamboree, love-in, rage, rave, riot, rort, shindig, shindy, shivaree *(U.S.)*, turn, wayzgoose, wing-ding; **function**, levee, reception; **feasting**, banquet, beanfeast, beano, bunfight, feast, fete, hangi, junket, love feast, midnight feast, prawn night, umu; **garden party**, annual picnic; **spree**, a night on the tiles, a night on the town, bacchanal, bash, bat, piss-up, stag party. *See also* JOY; FESTIVAL

CELEBRATORY *adj* commemorational, commemorative, commemoratory; **revelling**, bacchanal, bacchanalian, bacchic, convivial, mad, noise-making, on the loose, on the town, roisterous, rollicking, saturnalian; **triumphant**, exultant, jubilant, jubilatory, triumphal; **congratulatory**, gratulatory

CELESTIALLY *adv* blissfully, divinely, paradisiacally, supernally

CELL *n* black hole, black peter, calaboose *(U.S.)*, circle, condemned cell, death cell, death row, digger *(N.Z.)*, dummy *(N.Z.)*, dungeon, glasshouse *(Brit.)*, go-slow, oubliette, peter, pound, slot, slough, sweatbox; **penalty box**, sin-bin; **pen**, crib, pound, stabling; **cage**, coop, kennel, Skinner Box; **stocks**, pillory; **black maria**, bun

cell

wagon, paddy-wagon, wagon. *See also* PRISON

CELLULAR *adj* alveolate, amygdaloidal, cellulous, faveolate, geodic, honeycombed, lacunal, lacunar, lacunose, vacuolate; **porous,** poriferous, spongy; **chambered,** ventricular

CEMETERY *n* boneyard, burial ground, churchyard, field of Mars, garden of remembrance, God's acre, graveyard, marble orchard, necropolis, potter's field; **crematorium,** cinerarium, mortuary, charnel, charnel-house, funeral parlour, morgue. *See also* GRAVE

CENTRAL *adj* axial, centric, nuclear, nucleate, pivotal, umbilical; **epicentral,** epifocal *(Geol.);* centrifugal, focal; **concentric,** homocentric; **intermediate,** intermediary, medium; **middle,** halfway, medial, median, mid, middlemost, midmost, midway; **pivotal,** axial

CENTRALISE *v* centre, concentrate, concentre, focalise, focus, middle

CENTRALLY *adv* axially, centrically, centrifugally, centripetally, focally; **intermediately,** amidships, medially, medianly, midmost; **in midstream, in** medias res, in the middle; **dead-centre,** bang on

CENTRE *n* centrum, core, heart, heartwood, hub, kern, kernel, marrow, nave, node, nucellus, nucleor, nucleus, pith, yolk; **middle,** golden mean, halfway house, hey-diddle-diddle, mean, media, median, mid-point, midriff, midst, midway, waist; **navel,** omphalos, umbilicus; **bullseye,** blank, bull; **centre of gravity,** barycentre, centre of inertia, centre of mass, centroid, dead centre; **centre of buoyancy,** metacentre; **focus,** bunt

84

certainly

(Naut.), epicentre *(Geol.),* eye, fess point *(Her.),* focal point; **nerve centre,** ganglion, H.Q., headquarters; **storm centre,** eye of the storm

CENTRE-LINE *n* axis, caudex *(Bot.),* columella, fulcrum, hinge, newel *(Bldg Trades),* pivot, polar axis

CENTRE OF ACTIVITY *n* beehive, hive, hive of activity, madding crowd, madhouse, Mecca, thick of things; **peak hour,** rush hour; **period of activity,** session, shift, spell

CERAMICS *n* agateware, basaltware, belleek, biscuit, bisque, bucchero, cameo ware, celadon, china, crackle, crackleware, delft, Dresden, earthenware, faïence, graniteware, ironstone, Ming, murrhine glass, nankeen, porcelain, pottery, raku, scraperboard, Sevres, terracotta, ware, Wedgwood, willow-ware; **enamelwork,** champlevé, cloisonné, majolica; **clay,** glaze, slip

CERTAIN *adj* apodictic, doubtless, incontrovertible, indubitable, irrefragable, irrefutable, unchallengeable, undeniable, undoubted, unimpeachable, unquestionable, unquestioned; **sure-fire,** dead set, in the bag; **cast-iron,** absolute, perfect *(Obs.),* unfailing; **unequivocal,** unambiguous, unmistakable; **self-evident,** axiomatic; **inevitable,** bound to happen, unavoidable; **sure,** decided, definite, determinate, positive; **confident,** assured, secure, self-assured, self-confident, self-sufficient; **cocksure,** cool as a cucumber, overconfident; **doctrinaire,** bigoted, dogmatic, opinionated, thetic, unshakeable

CERTAINLY *adv* abso-bloody-lutely, absolutely, assuredly, beyond a shadow of doubt, beyond question, bound

certainly to be, clearly, decidedly, doubtless, doubtlessly, for a certainty, for a monte, for certain, for sure, indubitably, iwis *(Obs.)*, no doubt, rightly, sure as death and taxes, surely, undoubtedly, unimpeachably, unmistakably, unquestionably; **definitely**, by all means, no risk, of course, questionless, sure, without question; **without doubt,** all right, very well; **incontestably,** apodictically, demonstrably, determinately, positively, undeniably; **inevitably, sure** *(U.S.)*, without fail

CERTAIN THING *n* bird *(Horseracing)*, bird in the hand, cert, dead certainty, inevitable, knocktaker, monte, moral, open and shut case, safe bet, sure cop, sure thing; **clincher,** convincer; **dictum,** gospel

CERTAINTY *n* certitude, decidedness, positivism, sureness, surety; **assurance,** aplomb, assuredness, cocksureness, self-assurance, self-confidence, self-sufficiency; **conviction,** belief, confidence, secureness; **doctrinarism,** bigotry, dogmatism; **idée fixe,** obsession

CERTIFICATE *n* birth certificate, death certificate, group certificate, land certificate, lines *(Brit. Colloq.)*, marriage certificate, navicert; **casebook,** bill of health; **licence,** driving licence, learner's permit, miner's right, pass, passport, trading certificate, visa; **ship's papers,** clearance papers, maygo. *See also* RECORD

CHAIN-REACTING *adj* multiplicational, subcritical, supercritical; **radioactive,** charged, hot, irradiated, radiogenic, radiological; **fissile,** fertile, fissionable, scissile; **nuclear,** atomic, endo-ergic, endothermic, exoergic, exothermic, thermonuclear

CHAIR *n* banquette, basket chair, bentwood chair, butterfly chair, camp chair, camp stool, cane chair, captain's chair, carver, commode, deck chair, dining chair, director's chair, dos-à-dos, fan-back chair, fiddle-back, folding chair, garden chair, garden seat, highchair, kitchen chair, ladder-back chair, lavatory seat, love seat, Morris chair, occasional chair, pull-up chair, seat, sociable, stacking chair, straight-backed chair, swivel chair, tete-a-tete, throne *(Colloq.)*, toilet seat, tubchair, upholstered chair, vis-a-vis, Windsor chair, wing chair; **easychair,** armchair, club chair, hanging chair, lounge chair, recliner, rocker, rocking chair, squatter's chair, steamer chair, swing chair, TV chair; **stool,** bar stool, bedroom stool, dressing stool, footrest, footstool, kitchen stool, milking stool, music stool, piano stool, taboret, vanity stool; **highchair,** bouncer, bouncinette, cuddle seat, high seat; **bench,** bar top, bench top, form, ingle seat, pulvinar *(Rom. Antiq.)*, window seat, working top. *See also* COUCH

CHALLENGE *n* boast, brave *(Archaic)*, cry of defiance, dare, gage, taunt, threat, war cry, whoop; **outcry,** protest

CHAMPIONSHIP *n* ascendancy, mastery

CHANCE ON *v* fluke, happen on, hit on, hit upon, light on, stumble on; **happen,** fall to one's lot

CHANGE *n* alteration, alts and adds, amendment, arrangement, fluctuation, flux, metamorphism, metamorphosis, modification, permutation, perversion, radicalisation, reaction, reformation, rehash, renounce, reorganisation, revisal, revise, revision, sea change, sfumato *(Art)*, shake-up, shift, switch, switch-over, switcheroo, transit, transition, turn, twist, variation, vicissitude; **sudden change**, break, cataclysm, crisis, cut, jump cut, metastasis, revolution; **transformation**, alchemy, bioconversion, conversion, denaturation, denaturisation, differentiation, diversification, endomorphism, fossilisation, heteromorphism, heteromorphy, metaplasm, transfiguration, transfigurement, transmogrification, transmutation, transubstantiation, xenogenesis; **modification**, adaptation, adjustment, dialectic, dissimilation, inflection, modulation, mutation, rectification, saltation; **morphosis**, anabolism, carbonisation, catabolism, cytokinesis, karyokinesis, metabolism, metaplasia, oxidation; **turning point**, climacteric, climacterical, climax, crisis

CHANGE v acculturate, affect, alter, amend, catalyse, chequer, counterchange, dissimilate, launder *(Finance)*, leave one's mark on, leaven, make over, manipulate, modify, mutate, permute, pervert, rehash, remodel, revise, revolutionise, touch, twist, vary; **modulate**, adapt, adjust, edit, fair *(Shipbuilding)*, finetune, qualify, recast, reshape, specialise, trim *(Naut.)*; **permutate**, permute, ring the changes; **adapt**, lend oneself to; **differentiate**, diversify, jump, mutate, switch, turn; **grade**, glide, gradate, graduate, melt, range, shade, slide; **change into**, become; **convert**, arrange, colour, deform, metamorphose, radicalise, rectify, transcribe, transfigure, transform, translate, transmogrify, turn; **transmute**, alchemise, alkalise, denature, elaborate, fossilise, metabolise, transpose *(Obs.)*, transubstantiate

CHANGEABLE *adj* alterable, ambulatory, changeful, mutable, transmutable; **adaptable**, adaptive, elastic, light, mobile, protean, supple, variform, versatile, volatile; **allomorphous**, allomerous, metastable; **unstable**, insecure, instable, rootless, treacherous, unsound, unsteady; **wavering**, fluctuant, fluctuating, roller-coaster, up-and-down, vacillating, vacillatory; **fluky, variable; fluidic**, astatic, floating, fluent *(Rare)*, fluid, fluidal, labile, sandy, slippery, unsettled, vagrant; **capricious**, amphibolic, crank, errant, erratic, fickle, flighty, freakish, freaky, Jekyll-and-Hyde, mercurial, slippery, temperamental, variable, varying, wayward, whimsical; **vacillatory**, acrobatic, meandering, uncertain, unsettled, vacillating, wavering; **chameleon-like**, chameleonic, kaleidoscopic, phantasmagorical; **inconstant**, indefinite, indeterminate, movable, vertiginous; **transitory**, caducous, short-life, shortlived

CHANGEABLENESS *n* alterableness, changeability, changefulness, mutability, mutableness, transmutability, variability, variableness; **unsteadiness**, astaticism, fluidity, fluidness, insecurity, instability, lability, sandiness, treacherousness, unsettledness, unsoundness, unstableness; **adaptability**, adaptableness, adaptiveness, alterability, elasticity, mobility, suppleness; **volatility**, versatility; **allom-**

erism, allomorphism, metastability; **inconstancy,** indefiniteness, indeterminacy, indeterminateness, indetermination, unsteadiness, vertiginousness; **uncertainness,** fickleness, flightiness, freakiness, freakishness, levity, mercurialness, waywardness; **vacillation,** fluctuation, tergiversation; **transitoriness,** caducity, temporality; **unsettledness,** flukiness

CHANGEABLY *adv* alterably, changefully, mutably, transmutably, variably; **unstably,** astatically, fluidly, treacherously, uncertainly, unsoundly, unsteadily; **capriciously,** errantly, erratically, fickly, flightily, freakishly, mercurially, temperamentally, uncertainly, waywardly; **indefinitely,** inconstantly, indeterminately, unsteadily, vertiginously; **waveringly,** acrobatically, meanderingly, vacillatingly; **adaptively,** elastically, supplely, supply, versatilely

CHANGELESS *adj* invariable, invariant, typecast, unchanging, unfading, unfailing, unflagging, unregenerate; **unchangeable,** immovable, immutable, inadaptable, inalterable, incommutable, indecomposable, indissoluble, irrecoverable, irreducible, unshakeable; **hard-core,** deep-rooted, deep-seated, dyed-in-the-wool; **constant,** endless, enduring, eternal, eterne *(Archaic),* hard-wearing, indefeasible, indelible, ineffaceable, ineradicable, inerasable, interminable, irremovable, irrepealable, irreversible, lasting, perdurable, perennial, permanent, persistent, quenchless, regular *(Mil.),* stable, staid *(Rare),* standing, unending; **fixed,** confirmed, determined, immovable, inexorable, inflexible, infrangible, steadfast; **deathless,** immortal, imperishable, incorruptible, undying

CHANGELESSLY *adv* immovably, immutably, inalterably, incommutably, incorruptibly, indissolubly, inexorably, inflexibly, infrangibly, invariably, irrecoverably, irreducibly, irrepealably, irreversibly, unfadingly, unfailingly, unflaggingly, unregenerately, unshakeably; **constantly,** consistently, persistently, steadfastly; **eternally,** alway *(Arch.),* always, enduringly, for keeps, immortally, imperishably, interminably, perdurably, perennially, undyingly, unendingly; **permanently,** indefeasibly, indelibly, ineffaceably, ineradicably, inerasably, irremovably, stably

CHANGELESSNESS *n* immutability, immutableness, inadaptability, inalterability, incommutability, incommutableness, invariability, **inflexibility,** inexorability, inexorableness, inflexibleness, infrangibility, infrangibleness; **constancy,** continuance, enduringness, eternalness, permanence; **immortality,** deathlessness, imperishability, imperishableness, **permanency,** indefeasibility, indelibility, indelibleness, indissolubility, indissolubleness, ineffaceability, irreducibility, irreducibleness, irremovability, irreversibility, irreversibleness, stability, stableness, unfadingness, unfailingness; **immortalisation;** **fixedness,** consistency, determinateness, fixity, steadfastness; **entrenchment,** establishment, fixation, ossification, settlement, settling

CHANGER *n* alembic, alterant, catalyser, catalyst, catalytic, converter, modifier, modulator, philosopher's stone, transducer, transformer; **adaptor**, adjuster, finetuner; **converter**, alchemist, transmuter; **varier**, amender, manipulator, perverter, reviser, revisionist

CHANGING *adj* heteromorphic, on the turn, transformative, transmutative, variant, vicissitudinary, vicissitudinous, xenogenetic, xenogenic; **adaptive**, acculturative, modificatory; **modulative**, alterant, alterative, amendatory *(U.S.)*, manipulative, manipulatory, revisionary, revisory

CHANNEL *n* aqueduct, canal, conduit, ditch, duct, dyke, irrigator, lane, lead, navigable water, navigation, reach, river, runnel, seaway, ship canal, stream channel, swash, thoroughfare, tideway, trench, trough, wash, watercourse, waterway; **stormwater channel**, floodway, gutter, spillway; **moat**, fosse; **tunnel**, water-tunnel, windtunnel; **donga**, dry creek, wadi, winterbourne; **strait**, euripus, gat, neck, sound; **valley**, arroyo, gulch *(U.S.)*, gullet, gully, nullah, pass *(U.S.)*, water-gap

CHANNEL *v* canal; **canalise**; **pipe**, siphon, spile; **irrigate**, subirrigate; **reticulate**, vein

CHANNELLED *adj* ducted, vascular, veined; **villiform**, funnel-like, gutter-like, pipy, wormlike; **irrigational**, irrigative

CHARACTER *n* complexion *(Obs.)*, constitution, genius, identity, image, nature, persona, personality, psychology, self; **temperament**, cue *(Archaic)*, disposition, ethos, frame of mind, grain, humour, mind, mood, spirit, temper, tone; **type**, blood, breed, cast, colour, complexion, cut, feather, hue, kidney, make, make-up, manner *(Obs.)*, mien, mould, quality, sort, stamp, style, timber, worth; **grain**, strain, streak, stripe *(U.S.)*, vein; **habit**, idiolect, idiosyncrasy, peculiarity, trait

CHARACTERISTIC *n* attribute, character, difference *(Logic)*, differentia, distinction, distinctive feature, distinguishing feature, essence, flavour, form *(Philos.)*, genius, idiom, idiosyncrasy, individualism, individuality, lineament, mannerism, mark, particularity, parts, peculiarity, personality, singularity, speciality, specific, trait, way

CHARACTERISTIC *adj* attitudinal, complexional, constitutional, dispositional, inherited, invariant, temperamental, typical; **fundamental**, basic, congenital, essential, idiosyncratic, inborn, inbred, inherent, innate, inner, native; **aural**, atmospheric

CHARACTERISTICALLY *adv* at bottom, au fond, idiosyncratically, in character, out of character, temperamentally, to the manner born, typically

CHARACTERISTICS *n* aspects, attributes, endowments, expression, features, inheritance, instincts, physiognomy, properties, qualities, streak, stuff, touch; **soul**, anima, animus, essence, heart, inner man, inner nature, inner woman, inscape, inside; **backbone**, calibre, fibre, mettle, pith, principle, strength; **air**, atmosphere, aura

CHARGE *n* corkage, cover charge, fixed charge, flag fall, floating charge; **service charge**, breakage, brokerage, cranage, drayage, ferriage, footage *(Mining)*, lockage, quayage; **admission**, admission fee, doormoney, entrance, fare, fee; **gate money, appearance money, attendance money

CHARGE v levy, reverse charges, tax, tithe

CHARITY n aid, alms, gate money, relief; **subsidy,** allowance, bounty, expense account, grant, handout, scholarship, studentship, subsidisation; **foreign aid,** economic aid; **benefit,** family allowance, legal aid, meals on wheels, pension, repatriation, social bandaid, social security, social welfare, state aid; **relief work,** casework, social service, social work, welfare work; **appeal,** bottle drive, button day, door knock, drive, flag day, fundraiser, tarpaulin muster, telethon, war effort, whip-around; **fund,** collection plate, community chest *(U.S. Canada),* kitty, poor box, the tin; **alimony,** keep, maintenance, palimony, supplies *(Obs.),* support

CHEAP adj affordable, cheap at the price, dirt-cheap, economic, economical, frugal, inexpensive, low-priced, no-frills, sixpenny; **marked down,** cut-price, cut-rate, depreciated, discounted, half-price, nominal, on special, reduced; **free,** buckshee, complimentary, costless, gratis, gratuitous, honorary, interest-free; **untaxed,** duty-free, scot-free, tax-free; **worthless,** fustian, not worth a bumper, not worth a cracker, not worth a crumpet, unvalued, valueless; **cheap and nasty,** brum, brummy, catchpenny, el cheapo, gimcrack, tawdry, tinhorn *(U.S.),* tinsel, tinselly, trashy, trumpery; **depreciative,** depreciatory, depressive; **economy-class,** third-class, tourist-class

CHEAPEN v beat down, depreciate, depress, devalue, discount, knock down, reduce, undervalue; **underbuy,** buy for a song, go offshore; **undercharge,** underquote, undercut, undersell

CHEAPLY adv at a discount, cheap, for a song, for next to nothing, inexpensively, on the cheap; **for free,** for nothing, gratis, gratuitously

CHEAPNESS n inexpensiveness; **valuelessness,** worthlessness; **depreciation,** devaluation, price-cutting, undervaluation; **concession,** cut rate, discount, discount rate, trade discount, undercharge; **depression,** recession, slump

CHEAT v beat *(U.S.),* bilk, brass, bubble *(Archaic),* chisel, clip, cog, con, cozen, cully *(Archaic),* defraud, diddle, do, do down, do in the eye, do out of, finagle, flim-flam, fob off *(Archaic),* fudge, gyp, hoozle, hotpoint, jockey, mountebank, nick, overreach, palm, point, quack, ringbolt *(N.Z.),* rogue, rook, shortchange, smuggle, sting, suck in, swindle, swizzle, take down, take the palm, trepan *(Archaic),* trick out of, work a slanter

CHEMICAL adj alchemic, alchemical, biochemic, biochemical, biophysical, chemic *(Archaic),* chemurgic, chemurgical, electrochemical, enzymological, inorganic, microchemical, organic, stoichiometric, thermochemical

CHEMICAL AGENT n biocatalyst, carrier, catalyst, inhibitor, metabolite, negative catalyst, promoter, reactant, reagent, sequestrating agent; **chemical component,** fraction, reaction product; **oxidant,** oxidiser, oxidising agent, oxygenation; **deoxidiser,** re-

chemical agent

ducing agent; **precipitate**, condensate, flocculent precipitate, sediment, settlings, solute, sublimate; **crystal**, dimorph, tree, trimorph; **solution**, colloidal solution, saturated solution, sol, spirit; **chemical reaction**, degradation, metathesis, synthesis; **valency**, bivalency, covalency, quadrivalency, trivalency

CHEMICAL ELEMENT *n* actinide, allotrope, dyad, element, halogen, isotope, metal, non-metal, radioelement, terbium metals, transition element, transuranic element; **atom**, monad, nuclide; **chemical compound**, binary compound, clathrate compound, earth, epimer; gas hydrate, isomer, salt, tautomer; **isomerism**, cis-trans isomerism, dimorphism, enantiomorphism, enantiotropy, epimerisation, isotopy, racemism, tautomerism

CHEMISTRY *n* alchemy, biochemistry, biophysics, chemurgy, electrochemistry, enzymology, gravimetry, inorganic chemistry, magneto-chemistry, microchemistry, molecular biology, organic chemistry, oxidimetry, photochemistry, physical chemistry, stereochemistry, stoichiometry, surface chemistry, thermochemistry, topochemistry, zoochemistry, zymurgy

CHEQUE *n* bank cheque, bank-draft, banker's draft, blank cheque, certified cheque, counter cheque; **voucher**, coupon, gift token, IOU

CHEST *n* breast, brisket, bust, front, thorax; **torso**, trunk; **rib**, costa, slat; **bosom**, boob, breast, Bristols, bub, bust, charlies, cleavage, dug, fun bags, knockers, norks, tits; **nipple**, areola, diddy, dug, mamilla, pap, teat, tit, titty

CHILD *n* affiliate, descendant, scion, sprig *(Joc.)*, sprout; **son**, daughter; **grandchild**, grand-daughter, grandson, great-grandchild, great-granddaughter, great-grandson; **foster-child**, daughter-in-law, foster-daughter, foster-son, fosterling, godchild, goddaughter, godson, son-in-law, stepchild, stepdaughter, stepson

CHILDLESS FEMALE *n* gilt, nullipara, virgin

CHILDREN *n* grandchildren, kiddiewinks, small fry, the young; **child**, ankle-biter, bambino, elf, innocent, joey, junior, kid, kiddie, Little Johnny, little vegemite, littlie, moppet, nipper, piccaninny, slip, sprog, subteen, tiddler, weeny-bopper, youngie; **kindergartener**, preschooler; **prodigy**, child wonder, hopeful, wunderkind; **changeling**, elfchild; **brat**, bantling *(Archaic)*, enfant terrible, jackanapes, little bugger, perisher, pickle, tyke, Young Turk; **urchin**, gamin, latchkey child, ragamuffin, street Arab, waif; **girl**, bint, chick, chicken, girlie, lassie, miss, moppet; **minx**, chit, missy; **tomboy**, gamine, hoyden; **boy**, buster *(U.S.)*, junior, laddie, master, smacker, sonny. *See also* ADOLESCENT; OFFSPRING

CHIRP *v* bill and coo, cheep, chirm, chirrup, coo, cuckoo, peep, pip, squeak, trill, tweet, twitter, warble; **cackle**, caw, clang, gabble, gaggle, gobble, squawk, waul; **crow**, cock-a-doodle-doo, croak, gobble, honk, quack, whoop; **cluck**, chuckle, clack. *See also* CALL (OF ANIMALS)

CHISEL *n* adze, boaster, bolster, cold chisel, crosscut chisel, drove, firmer chisel, gouge, graver, hack hammer, hardy, icebreaker, leilira, neolith, os-

chisel 91 **circuitousness**

teotome, pitching tool, quarrel, set chisel, sett, spud

CHOICE *n* alternative, discretion, druthers, elective, first refusal, option, refusal; **preference**, fancy, favourite, predilection; **selection**, adoption, cull, pick; **preselection**, co-option, nomination, preferment, selectness; **free will**, preferentialism, self-determination, voluntariness, will; **smorgasbord**, menu *(Computers)*, variety; **eclecticism**

CHOOSE *v* fix on, fix upon, handpick, mark out, pick, pick and choose, pick out, pitch on, pitch upon, select, set on, take; **prefer**, fancy, favour, have rather, like best, opt for, plump for, single out; **pick the eyes out of**, arbitrate, decide, resolve; **suit oneself**, work one's will. *See also* ELECT

CHOOSER *n* endorser, nominator, plumper, preferentialist, preferrer, selector; **voter**, ballotter, black-baller, caster, constituent, elector, electoral college *(U.S.)*, electorate, floating voter, quorum, swinging voter; **suffragist**, suffragette; **decider**, determiner, resolver; **eclectic**

CHOSEN *adj* choice, elect, favourite, hand-picked, pet, picked, select; **eligible**, adoptable, votable

CHRONOMETRIC *adj* chronogrammatic, chronographic, datal, horary, horologic

CHURCH *n* fane *(Archaic)*, House of God, kirk *(Scot.)*; **cathedral**, basilica, minster, procathedral, title; **temple**, conventicle, joss house, mosque, naos, pagoda, pantheon, synagogue, tabernacle, ziggurat; **meeting house**, bethel *(U.S.)*, chapel, chapterhouse; **vicarage**, manse, parsonage, presbytery, rectory; **nave**, ambulatory, apse, choir, clerestory, cloister, confessional, decanal, decani, epistle side, gospel side, precinct, retrochoir, rood loft, transept, tribune, triforium; **corona**, Jesse window, tambour; **pulpit**, ambo, lectern, minbar, reading desk, rostrum, tribune; **pew**, faldstool, propitiary, sedile, tribune; **crypt**, Easter sepulchre, sepulchre, undercroft; **steeple**, minaret, spire. *See also* PLACE OF WORSHIP; ABBEY; SHRINE

CHURCH *adj* basilic, synagogical, tabernacular

CHUTE *n* chinaman, feed, feedpipe, gravity feed; **sluice**, flash, lock, penstock, weir; **race**, flume *(U.S.)*, headrace, leat, millrace, millrun, raceway, sluiceway, spillway, tailrace

CINEMATISE *v* cinematograph, dissolve, fade, film, flashback, pan, shoot, strip in

CIRCLE *n* circumference, cirque *(Phys. Geog.)*, compass *(Obs.)*, epicycle, orbit, radius, roundel, roundlet, spiral; **round**, circuit, gyre *(Poetic)*, lap *(Racing)*, loop, turn; **rim**, felloe, tread; **annual ring**, annulation; **cromlech**, fairy ring; **equator**, celestial equator, ecliptic, equinoctial line, galactic circle, galactic equator, meridian; **disc**, bezant *(Archit.)*, button, coin, plate, slug; **discus**, puck; **bullseye**. *See also* RING; WHEEL; OVAL

CIRCUITOUSNESS *n* anfractuosity, circuity, circularity, circumvolution, convolution, flexuosity, meander, sinuation, sinuosity, sinuousness, tortuosity, tortuousness, wriggle; **intorsion**, circumnutation, koru *(N.Z.)*; **curliness**, crispation, crispness, frizz; **torsion**, wring, writhe; **entwinement**, twine, winding; **volution**, dextrality, verticillation

CIRCULAR *adj* clypeate, cycloid, full, revolving, rounded, spiral, spirelike, spiriferous; **ringed**, annulate, annulose, armillary, circinate *(Bot.)*, hooped, ringleted, torquated; **ringlike**, annular, areolar, areolate, circinate, coronary, coronate, cricoid; **cyclic**, bicyclic, tricyclic

CIRCULATE *v* coin, counterfeit, forge, issue, mint, monetise, utter; **revalue**, demonetise, devalue

CIRCUS PERFORMER *n* acrobat, aerialist, balancer, bareback rider, clown, equilibrist, flier, highwire artist, juggler, lion tamer, slackwire artist, strongman, sword-swallower, tightrope walker, trapeze artist, tumbler; **snake-charmer**; **fire-eater**, fire-swallower, pyrotechnist

CITIZEN *n* burgher, townsfolk, townsman, townspeople, townswoman; **cityite**, city slicker, dude *(U.S.)*, suburbanite, townie

CITY *n* Babylon, big smoke, burg *(U.S.)*, burgh *(Chiefly Scot.)*, capital, concrete jungle, conurbation, federal capital, free city, megalopolis, metropolis, open city, state capital, system city; **inner city**, business area, business section, central business district, civic centre, downtown, residential district, riverfront, shopping area, the docks, uptown, waterfront, waterfrontage; **suburb**, barrio, borough, built-up area, dormitory, dormitory suburb, faubourg, municipality, parish, precinct *(U.S.)*, subdivision, ward; **suburbia**, commuter belt, exurbia, ribbon development; **slum area**, ruins, shanty-town, skid row, slums, tin pan alley; **native quarter**, chinatown, ghetto, kasbah. *See also* TOWN

CLARIFICATION *n* elucidation, illumination, illustration; **explanation**, appendix, elaboration, exegesis, explication, exposé, exposition, interpretation; **decipherment**, cryptanalysis, decryption, demystification, unravelment; **annotation**, adversaria, apostil, comment, commentary, crib, epexegesis, footnote, gloss, marginalia, note, schedule, scholium; **key**, caption, cipher, legend; **reductionism**, oversimplification

CLARIFIER *n* elucidator, explainer, exponent, expositor, expounder, illustrator, luminary; **decipherer**, cryptanalyst, decoder, solver, unraveller, unscrambler; **annotator**, commenter, exegete, glossator, scholiast

CLARIFY *v* clear, clear up, demystify, elucidate, rationalise, shed light on, speak for itself, speak plainly, throw light on; **explain**, amplify, bring home to, elaborate, explicate, expound, flesh out, illuminate, illumine, illustrate, set out, spell out; **decipher**, decode, decrypt, puzzle out, resolve, see, solve, unravel, unscramble, untangle; **annotate**, comment, interpret

CLARITY *n* clearness, legibility, limpidity, limpidness, lucidity, lucidness, pellucidness, perspicuity, perspicuousness, plainness, preciseness, precision, transparency; **intelligibility**, apprehensibility, cognisability, comprehensibility, comprehensibleness, intelligibleness, interpretability, luminousness

CLASS *n* bracket, branch, category, denomination, description, fashion, gender *(Obs.)*, genre, group, kidney, kind, persuasion *(Colloq.)*, range, set, sort, strain *(Rare)*, subcategory, subgroup, subset, subtype, type, variety; **taxon,** alliance, class, family, genus, kingdom, life form, order, phylum, species, strain, subclass, subfamily, subgenus, subkingdom, suborder, subphylum, subspecies, superclass, superfamily, superorder, variety; **tribe,** breed, brood, group, phratry, race, social class, stirps, stock; **rank,** caste, degree, estate, grade, league, place, standard, stratum, stream; **miscellaneous classes,** blood group, Dan *(Judo)*, genotype, phenotype, suit *(Cards)*, weight *(Boxing)*. *See also* CLASSIFICATION

CLASS *v* assort, categorise, classify, code, codify, coordinate, digest, distinguish, distribute, divide, fire-rate, gradate, grade, identify, label, lemmatise, mark, methodise, order, pigeonhole, range, rank, rate, reclassify, schematise, size, sort, staple, stratify, stream, systematise, systemise, zone

CLASSER *n* adjuster, categorist, classifier, codifier, digester, grader, identifier, indexer, ranger, ranker, sorter, systematiser, systematist, tabulator; **typologist,** systemiser, taxonomer, taxonomist; **wool classer,** con man, fleece-oh, fleece-picker, fleecy, guesser, piece-picker, stapler, wool sorter

CLASSIFICATION *n* assortment, categorisation, codification, coordination, dichotomisation, distribution, rating, reclassification, schematisation, systematisation, systematism, systemisation, tabularisation; **typology,** architectonics, systematics, systematology; **miscellaneous classifications,** bulk classing, decimal classification, Dewey decimal classification, multiplication table, nosology, periodic table, petrography, physiography, wool classing; **system,** hierarchy, ladder, method, nomenclature, syntax *(Obs.)*, tabulation, taxonomy; **table,** catalogue, code, digest, index, inventory, key, schedule, sequence, subject catalogue, synchronism, timetable. *See also* CLASS

CLASSIFICATORY *adj* categorical, diachronic, hierarchical, Linnean, physiographical, synchronic, systematic, tabular, taxonomic, taxonomical, typological; **classifiable,** classable, identifiable, sortable; **generic,** assorted, class, classified, coordinative, ordinal, phyletic, subgeneric, subordinal, subspecific, typical, varietal

CLEAN *v* char, clean out, clean up, cleanse, furbish, mop up, muck out, police *(U.S. Mil.)*, polish, scavenge, sponge, spot, spot-clean, spring-clean; **wash,** flush, gargle, kier, shampoo, swill, syringe, wash down, wash out, wash up; **bathe,** bath, lave *(Poetic)*, rinse, shower, tub; **sweep,** broom, brush, hoover, mop, swab, swingle, vacuum, vacuum-clean; **scrub,** black, buff, dust, rub, scour; **degrease,** ajax, soap, soft-soap; **comb,** card, hatchel; **launder,** dry-clean; **filter,** cohobate, distil, elutriate, filtrate, refine; **purify,** baptise, heal, lustrate, purge, sanctify; **sluice,** cradle, hush, pan, surface; **scrub a gas,** pickle *(Metall.)*, scavenge *(Metall.)*; **decarbonise,** decarburise, decoke; **sandblast,** careen, grave *(Naut.)*, holystone; **currycomb,** curry; **dag,** chase marguerites, ring *(Agric.)*. *See also* DISINFECT

clean

CLEAN *adj* clean as a whistle, dustless, immaculate, spick-and-span, spotless, squeaky-clean, unspotted; **pure,** blameless, candid, chaste, clean, fresh, innocent, irreproachable, lily, pristine, spotless, stainless, uncorrupted, undefiled, unmixed, unsoiled, unstained, unsullied, untainted, virgin, virginal; **uncontaminated,** alembicated, aseptic, axenic, refined, sterile; **sanitary,** antiseptic, hygienic

CLEANER *n* char, charlady, charwoman, cleaner upper *(Colloq. Joc.),* cleaning lady, daily, duster, greasy, old Dutch; **sweeper,** broomie, chimneysweep, street sweeper; **launderer,** drycleaner, laundress, laundryman, laundrywoman, spotter, washerman, washerwoman; **purifier,** clarifier, purger, refiner; **washer,** careener, currier, depurator, scourer; **sanitary inspector,** sanitarian

CLEANLINESS *n* cleanness, freshness, immaculacy, immaculateness, pureness, purity, spotlessness; **asepsis,** disinfection, hygiene, sanitariness

CLEANLY *adv* cleanlily, immaculately, spotlessly; **aseptically,** antiseptically, hygienically, sanitarily, sterilely; **purely,** fresh, immaculately, virginally

CLEANSER *n* amole, Bob Hope, cold cream, quillai bark, shampoo, soap, soap flakes, soapbark, toiletry, Windsor soap; **detergent,** abluent, abstergent, cleaner, degreaser, detersive, rinser, saddle-soap, sugar soap, washing powder, washing soda; **mouthwash,** gargle, rinse; **purge,** aperient, catharsis, depurative, physic, purgation, purgative; **disinfectant,** antiseptic, argyrol, boric acid, chlorination, chlorine, Dakin's solution, eusol, fumigant, hexachlorophene, hexylresorcinol, Javel water, lysol, orthoboric acid, phenol, silver fluoride, surgical spirit; **cleansing agent,** antifouling, borax, flux, whiting; **sandblast,** holystone, sandsoap; **facepack,** face mask, facial mask; **purifier,** chlorinator, disinfecter, fumigator; **separator,** alembic, distilling apparatus, elutriator, filter, filter bed, filter cloth, filter paper, filter press, filter tip, still

CLEANSING *n* ablutions, annual, bath, bubble bath, douche, footbath, lavage, lavation, pommy wash *(Joc.),* rinse, rinsing, sauna, shampoo, shower, sitz bath, sluice, splash, sponge, sponge bath, sponge-down, toilet *(Surg.),* Turkish bath, wash; **quick wash,** a lick and a promise, APC, Mary Pickford in three acts; **scour,** brush, careen, careenage, decarb, decarbonisation, decarburisation, decoke, scrub, ultrasonic cleaning; **housework,** sweep, sweeping, washing-up; **cleaning of clothes,** bull *(Mil.),* dry-cleaning, shoeshine; **clean-up,** blitz, emu parade, police *(U.S. Mil.),* spring-clean, springcleaning; **washing,** banjoing, box sluicing, surfacing; **purification,** depuration, elutriation, filtration; **sterilisation,** antisepsis, fumigation; **religious cleansing,** ablution, baptism, expurgation, lavabo, lustration, lustrum

CLEANSING *adj* abluent, abstergent, aperient, depurative, detergent, detersive, disinfectant, purgative, purging, saponaceous; **ablutionary,** balneal, cleanly, lavational, sudatory; **self-cleaning,** antifouling, dirt repel-

cleansing 95 **cloak**

lant, dust repellant, dustproof; **purificatory**, baptismal, expiatory, lustral, purgatorial, purgatory

CLEAR *adj* apparent, articulate, crystal clear, easily grasped, easy, explicit, fair, legible, limpid, lucid, luculent, obvious, pellucid, perspicuous, plain, precise, readable, straightforward, transparent, unambiguous; **intelligible**, apprehensible, cognisable, cognoscible, comprehendible, comprehensible, decipherable, explainable, explicable, fathomable, graspable, interpretable, knowable, luminous, perceivable, perceptible, recognisable, scrutable

CLEARANCE *n* circumdenudation, clearage, defloration, defoliation, deforestation, denudation, disforestation, disfurnishment, excoriation; **burn-off**, burn, burn-back, bush-burn *(N.Z.)*; **paring**, decortication, excortication, exfoliation; **clearing**, clears *(N.Z.)*

CLEARLY *adv* articulately, clear, fairly, limpidly, lucidly, luculently, perspicuously, plain, plainly, precisely; **intelligibly**, cognisably, comprehensibly, in plain words, luminously, perceivably, perceptibly, recognisably

CLICK *n* chink, clink, crack, flick, snap, snick, snip, tick, tick-tock; **clatter**, brattle, chatter, clackety-clack, clop, clutter, death-rattle, pitapat, pitter-patter, rattle, trot-trot; **buzz**, bray, drone, hum, purr, skirr, stertor, whine, whirr, whiz, woof, zoom; **twang**, ping, plonk, plunk, thrum, zing; **clap**, flap, flip-flop, flop, flump, flutter, whack; **footfall**, crunch, footstep, pad, plod, step, tramp, tread

CLICK *v* clip-clop, crunch, smack, snap, snick, tick; **rattle**, brattle, chatter, clack, clatter, clutter, drum, rataplan; **ping**, pink *(Motor Vehicles)*; **flap**, flop; **buzz**, drone, hum, purr, whirr, whiz

CLIMATIC *adj* climatologic, climatological; **fair**, balmy, calm, fairweather; **intemperate**, gusty, inclement, rough, stormy, tornadic, unsettled; **weathered**, weather-beaten; **weatherwise**

CLIMATOLOGY *n* bioclimatology, hygrometry, microclimatology; **meteorology**, met report, meteorological report, micro-meteorology, synoptic meteorology, weather forecasting; **weather map**, aerograph, synoptic chart, weather chart; **isobar**, isallobar, isochor, isopiestic; **isotherm**, isallotherm, isocheim, isothere, isothermal; **isoneph**

CLIMBER *n* ascender, clamberer, escalader; **mountaineer**, alpinist, cragsman, mountain-climber

CLIP *n* alligator clip, bicycle clip, binding *(Skiing)*, bulldog clip, clothes peg, crocodile clip, paperclip, peg, staple; **hairclip**, bobby pin, butterfly clip, hair slide, hairgrip, hairpin; **clamp**, agraffe, brace, clam, cramp, head, vice

CLIQUE *n* bunch, coterie, crowd, outfit, smart set; **cult**, push, sect; **cell**, cabal, cadre, inner circle, inside; **connections**, old boy network, old school tie; **salon**, conversazione, reunion

CLOAK *n* aba, blanket *(North America)*, burnous, cape, capote, chador *(Islam)*, chrisom *(Obs.)*, chuddar, cope, cowl, dolman, joseph, kaross, korowai *(N.Z.)*, manta, manteau *(Archaic)*, mantelet, mantle, mantua, mat *(N.Z.)*, mozzetta, muffle, opera-cloak, palatine, pall *(Obs.)*, pallium, pelerine, pelisse, plaid, pluvial, poncho, serape, shawl, stole, surplice, tallith, wrap.   *See also* OVERCOAT; RAINCOAT

CLOSE *v* shut, slam; **shutter,** board up; **blockade,** clench, occlude, shut in, shut up, stop down *(Photog.)*, wall in, wall up; **stop,** airproof, bung, cork, obturate, plug, spile, stem, stop up, stopper, stopple *(Archaic)*, top; **seal,** plumb, seel *(Falconry)*, wafer, weather-strip; **gag,** stuff, tampon, wad

CLOSE *adj* approximate, dead *(Golf)*, gimme *(Golf)*, hither, hithermost, hot *(Games)*, near, nearby, nigh, proximate, silly *(Cricket)*, warm *(Colloq.)*; **adjacent,** appositional, approximal, bumper-to-bumper, circumlittoral, close-order, connivent, conterminous, contiguous, end on, immediate, neighbour *(U.S.)*, neighbouring, next, next-door, proximate, ringside, surrounding, vicinal; **approaching,** coming, oncoming; **accessible,** approachable, attainable

CLOSED *adj* barred, blind, close, drawn, fast, occluded, occludent, occlusive, shut, unopened; **stopped,** corked, ventless; **impenetrable,** airproof, airtight, gastight, hermetic, hermetically sealed, impermeable, impervious, proof

CLOSELY *adv* a hop step and a jump away, a step away, as near as damn it, as near as makes no difference, at close quarters, at hand, at one's elbow, at one's fingertips, at one's heels, bumper-to-bumper, cheek by jowl, close, eyeball to eyeball, hard by, just round the corner, near at hand, on the back of, on the heels of, on the point of, on the tip of one's tongue, right on top of, to hand, under one's nose, within a hair's breadth, within a stone's throw, within an inch of, within cooee, within earshot, within hearing, within range, within reach, within spitting distance; **together,** adjacently, appositionally, chock, conterminously, contiguously, next-door, nigh; **nearby,** around, by, here, hereabout, hereby *(Archaic)*, hither, in view, near.   *See also* ALMOST

CLOSENESS *n* adjacency, contact, contiguousness, immediacy, immediateness, nearness, propinquity, proximity; **close position,** neighbourhood, presence, vicinage, vicinity; **accessibility,** approachability, approachableness, attainability; **approach,** approximation, coming, oncoming; **conjunction,** apposition, cluster, juxtaposition; **a near thing,** close call, dead draw, gimme *(Golf)*, photo finish, squeaker *(Shooting)*; **closest point,** pericynthion, perigee, perilune, periphelion

CLOSURE *n* blockade, close, obstruction, obturation, occlusion, shut, slam, stop; **impenetrability,** impenetrableness, impermeability, impermeableness, imperviousness

CLOTHE *v* apparel *(Archaic)*, array, attire, costume, deck out, dress, endue with, equip, frock, garb, habit, invest, rig out, rig up, robe, swaddle, tire *(Archaic)*, tog, tog out, tog up; **style,** tailor, trim *(Obs.)*

CLOTHED *adj* apparelled, arrayed, done up, dressed, tricked out; **well-dressed,** all done up like a sore toe, all dressed up, dollish, dressed to kill, dressed to the nines, dressed up like a pox doctor's clerk, smart, Sunday-go-to-meeting *(U.S.)*

CLOTHES *n* apparel, array, attire, caparison, cladding *(Obs.)*, clobber, clothing, dress, garb, garment, gear, get-out, get-up, habiliment, habiliments, maternity clothes, menswear, mocker, raiment *(Archaic)*, rig, rig-out, robes, slip-on, things, tire *(Archaic)*, toggery, trappings, trim, vest *(Archaic)*, vesture *(Archaic)*, wardrobe, wear, wearables, wearing apparel; **clothwork**, dart, fly, gore, peplum, tuck. See also FINERY; OUTFIT

CLOTHIER *n* cobbler, corsetiere, costumier, couturière, couturier, dresser, dressmaker, equipper, fashion designer, fashioner *(Obs.)*, furrier, glover, haberdasher *(U.S.)*, hatter, hosier, milliner, modiste, outfitter, sewer, slopworker, stylist, tailor; **clothing store**, furriery, haberdashery, hosiery, jeanery, millinery, slopshop

CLOUD *n* clag, cloudbank, cloudlet, hogsback *(N.Z.)*, low cloud, mare's-tail, rack, rain cloud, sky *(Obs.)*, storm-cloud, thundercloud, woolpack; **cloud-type**, altocumulus, altostratus, cirrocumulus, cirrostratus, cirrus, cu-nim, cumulonimbus, cumulus, cumulus fractus, false cirrus, fractocumulus, fractostratus, funnel cloud, nimbostratus, nimbus *(Obs.)*, orographic clouds, stratocumulus, stratus, stratus fractus; **puff**, scud, whiff; **mist**, brume, gauze, haze; **steam**, effluvium, fumes, vaporescence, vapour, wet steam; **vapour trail**, contrail; **fog**, aerosol *(Physics)*, brume, fogbank, pea soup, pea souper, sea-fog; **smoke**, dust, fug, nuclear cloud, pother, smog, smother, smoulder, smudge

CLOUD *v* becloud, cloud over, overcast, overcloud, shadow; **smoke**, reek; **mist**, fog, gauze; **vaporise**, steam, vapour; **fumigate**, smoke out

CLOUDILY *adv* nebulously, sullenly, sunlessly; **foggily**, hazily, mistily; **smokily**, dustily, murkily, smudgily; **steamily**, vaporously

CLOUDINESS *n* fogginess, gauziness, haziness, hydrometeor, mackerel sky, mistiness, nebulosity, nebulousness, steaminess; **smokiness**, dustiness, murkiness; **vaporousness**, vaporosity, vapourishness; **vaporisation**, fumigation; **sunlessness**, sullenness

CLOUD STUDY *n* hydrometeorology, nephanalysis, nephology; **isoneph**, nephogram, nephograph, nephoscope

CLOUDY *adj* heavy, nubilous, overcast; **cirrose**, cirrostrative, cumuliform, cumulous, mammatus, stratiform; **cloud-like**, nebulose, nebulous; **sunless**, sullen; **steamy**, vaporescent, vaporific, vaporous, vapour-like, vapouring, vapourish, vapoury; **misty**, gauzelike, hazy; **smoggy**, dusty, fuggy, murky, smudgy, soupy, thick; **foggy**, brumous; **smoky**, fuliginous, fumy

CLUB *n* blackjack, bludgeon, cosh, cudgel, donger, knobkerrie, leangle, life-preserver, maul *(Obs.)*, mere, nightstick, nulla-nulla *(Aborig.)*, patu, shillelagh, stave, truncheon, waddy; **staff**, prodder, quarterstaff, rod, shakuhachi, singlestick, stick, taiaha; **whip**, birch, cane, cat, cat-o'-nine-tails, flagellum, lash, rawhide, scourge, strap, switch, whiplash; **flail**, swingle, swipple, thresher; **flyswat**, flapper, swat, swatter; **bat**, battledore, bumble puppy, crosse, racquet, willow; **golf club**, brassy, bulger, cleek, iron, lofting iron, putter; **hammer**, ballpein hammer, claw hammer, club hammer, drop hammer, flatter, fuller, gavel, jackhammer, knapping hammer, lump hammer, mallet, maul, plexor, sledge-hammer, steam hammer, tilt hammer, trip hammer, water-hammer; **ram**, battering ram, beetle, pile-driver, pounder, rammer

COASTLINE n bank, coast, littoral, rivage *(Archaic)*, seafront, seashore, seaside, shore, the coast; **waterfront**, lakefront, ocean beach, riverfront, shoreline, strand, strandline, waterside; **continental shelf**, embayment

COAT v anoint, bedaub, besmear, flock, lather, powder, smear, spread, wipe *(Plumbing)*; **batter**, breadcrumb, candy, frost, glair, glaze, ice; **paint**, calcimine, clobber, distemper, duco, japan, kalsomine, lacquer, prime, shellac, undercoat, varnish, whitewash; **plate**, anodise, braze, copper, electroplate, ferrotype, foil, galvanise, nickel, nickel-plate, oxidise, platinise, sherardise, silver-plate, sputter *(Physics)*, tin, veneer, zinc; **gild**, foliate, overgild; **bituminise**, asphalt, pave, seal, tarmac, underseal; **cement-render**, bag, cement, clay, daub, flush, impaste, paper, parget, paste, pay, plaster, puddle, putty, render, roughcast. *See also* COVER

COATED adj chromed, copper-bottomed, electroplated, galvanised, gilded, gilt, plated, tinned; **bituminised**, sealed, tar, tarred, tarry; **sugar-coated**, candied, farinose, frosted, glacé, glairy, iced, powdery, sugared. *See also* COVERED

COATING n backing, carapace, cladding, coat, collodion, colouring, covering, deposit, double glazing, frost, glaze ice, impasto, integument, macadamisation, mother-of-pearl, nacre, petrifying liquid, plating, pricking coat, respray, rind, sheathing, sheet, shell, shield, shingle, silver frost, skin, slate, stucco, test, tile, top dressing, veneering, wash, washing; **facing**, chemise, crib, cribbing, fireback, leaf, liner, lining, overlay, revetment, veneer; **panel**, board, flag, foil, lath, plank, plate, shale, shaving, slab, slat, strip, wafer; **sheeting**, aponeurosis, carpet, dust sheet, endoperidium, endopleura, endothelium, epidermis, epithelium, exoperidium, membrane, mesothelium, peridium, skin, squama, tissue; **stripe**, section, vitta, zone; **shoe lining**, heeltap, insole, lift, sole, welt; **underlay**, underfelt

CODE n arcanum, character *(Obs.)*, cipher, cryptograph, enigma, morse code, riddle, secret; **gabble**, double-dutch, gibberish, splutter

CODIFY v code, conventionalise, institutionalise, prescribe, ritualise, subsume

COFFIN n casket, cist, columbarium, ossuary, sarcophagus, urn; **bier**, catafalque, hearse, pall

COINAGE n change, cobar, Kembla, loose change, rouleau, shrapnel, silver, small change, specie; **coin**, bean, billon, bit *(Obs.)*, brown *(Obs.)*, copper, mite, picayune *(U.S.)*; **numismatics**, coin collector, numismatologist, numismatology; **counterfeit coin**, grey, jack, nob, rap, slug. *See also* CASH

COLD *n* chill, coryza, flu, grippe, rheum, the dog's disease, the sniffles, the snuffles, URTI; **cold symptom**, catarrh, cough, hacking cough, rhonchus, sneezing, the bot, tussis, wheeziness; **septic throat**, adenoids, laryngitis, pharyngitis, quinsy, relaxed throat, rhinitis, sinusitis, strep throat, tonsillitis, tracheitis, uvulitis; **ear infection**, glue ear, labyrinthitis, Ménière's syndrome, otalgia, otitis, tinnitus, tympanitis, utriculitis

COLD *adj* Antarctic, Arctic, freezing, frigid, frigorific, frosty, glacial, hyperborean, ice-cold, icy, nipping, perishing; **stone-cold**, marble; **cool**, coldish, coolish, fresh, nippy, sharp; **chilled**, agued, algid, clammy, hypothermal, shivering, trembly; **blue**, frostbitten; **wintry**, bleak, brumal, chill, chilly, raw, winter; **snowy**, niveous, white; **sleety**, slushy; **frosted**, frostlike, frosty, hoar, iced, rimy; **frozen**, gelid, glacé (*U.S.*), icicled; **glacial**, englacial, glaciered, glaciological, sub- glacial, superglacial

COLDLY *adv* bleakly, fresh, freshly, wintrily; **icily**, chillily, chillingly, frigidly, frostily, gelidly, glacially; **tremblingly**, aguishly

COLDNESS *n* bleakness, cold, coolness, wintriness; **chilliness**, chillness, nip, nippiness, sharpness; **frozenness**, clamminess, frigidity, frostiness, gelation, gelidity, geliness, glaciation, iciness, regelation; **chill**, ague, algidity, algor, rigour; **shiver**, shudder, tremble, tremor; **goose pimples**, cold shivers, goose bumps, horripilation, the shivers; **frostbite**, chillblains; **cold snap**, brass monkey weather, cold change, cold front, cold wave, perisher; **winter**, the big freeze, the dead, the dead of winter; **ice age**, glacial epoch

COLLAPSE *v* be history, bite the dust, come undone, come unstuck, crash, crumple, fall, give way, go by the board, go for a burton, go phut, go to the dogs, go under, go up in smoke, have had it, have had the dick, have had the sword, perish; **disintegrate**, dissipate, dissolve

COLLECTIVELY *adv* associatively, communally, mutually, shoulder to shoulder, together, unitedly; **federally**, corporately; **clannishly**, cliquishly, fraternally, tribally

COLLEGE *n* Academe, academy, athenaeum, college of advanced education, institute, institution, lyceum, poly, polytechnic (*Brit. U.S.*), seminary, teacher's college, university college; **university**, campus, Ivy League, open university, state university (*U.S.*), the shop, varsity; **technical college**, tech, trade school, training college, training school, vocational school, W.E.A.; **evening college**, mechanics' hall, mechanics' institute, night school, school of arts; **business college**, commercial college; **agricultural college**, agricultural high school; **naval college**, arsenal, military college, training ship; **conservatorium**, conservatoire; **teaching hospital**, medical school. *See also* SCHOOL

COLLIDE *v* clash, connect, crash, fall foul of each other, hurtle (*Rare*), impact, impinge, jostle, smash together; **bump**, barge into, cannon into, foul, knock, push; **crash**, crack up, pile up, prang, smash, stack

COLORIFIC *adj* chromatic, chromogenic, tinctorial; **monochromatic,** monochroic, monochrome, monochromic, unicolour; **isochromatic,** isochroous; **metachromatic,** amphichroic, apatetic, panchromatic, polychromatic

COLOUR *n* complementary colour, primary colour, prismatic colours, secondary colour, tertiary colour; **hue,** cast, grain *(Obs.),* nuance, patina, taint *(Obs.),* tainture *(Obs.),* tinct *(Obs.),* tinge, tint, undertint, undertone; **spectrum,** palette, prism, rainbow; **areola,** areolation, sunbow, sundog; **colour-scheme,** colour coordination, decorator colours, fashionable colours; **colours,** military colours, national colours, racing colours, strip, team colours; **complexion,** bloom, rubicundity, skin colour; **skin pigmentation,** chloasma, freckle, melanin, melanism; **chromophore,** chlorophyll, chromatoplasm, chromogen, chromoplasm, chromoplast, chromoprotein, haemoglobin; **camouflage,** countershading, protective colouring; **colouring,** colouration, pigmentation; **colour quality,** chroma, gradation, intensity, purity, saturation, tone, value. *See also* DYE

COLOUR *v* chrome, counterstain, distemper, dye, ink, mordant, ochre, overdye, paint, pencil, reddle, stain, umber; **tint,** sickly *(Obs.),* taint *(Obs.),* tinct *(Obs.),* tincture, tinge, wash; **brighten,** highlight, tone up; **tone,** tone down

COLOURED *adj* florid, high-coloured, hued, roseate, rosy, rubicund, self-coloured; **dyed,** double-dyed, fumed, piece-dyed, tinct *(Poetic);* **mordant,** sunfast; **colourable,** stainable

COLOURFUL *adj* deep, glowing, iridescent, purple, rich, saturated, strong; **bright,** brilliant, colouristic, fiery, gay, hot, jazzy, live, lively, psychedelic, snazzy, technicolour, vivid; **gaudy,** garish, glaring, loud, lurid

COLOURFULLY *adv* fierily, floridly, gaudily, glaringly, glowingly, iridescently, richly, vividly

COLOURFULNESS *n* floridity, floridness, iridescence, richness; **brightness,** brilliance, fieriness, gaudiness, glaringness, liveliness, vividness; **glow,** blare, flame, highlights

COLOURIST *n* brightener, chromolithographer, colourer, dyer, painter, seagull *(Colloq.),* stainer, tinter, toner

COLOURLESS *adj* achromatic, achromatous, achromic, untinged; **neutral,** delicate, light, mousy, pastel, thin; **black-and-white,** sepia; **anaemic,** green, mealy, pallid, pasty, pasty-faced, sallow, sallowish, sick, sickly, wan, wannish, washed-out, whey-faced, white, white-faced, white-livered; **cadaverous,** bloodless, ghastly, ghostlike, lurid; **pale,** ashy, blank, palish; **dull,** dullish, muddy, old, sad, sober, sombre, subdued; **watery,** wheyish, wheylike; **bleached,** etiolated, faded

COLOURLESSNESS *n* achromatism, lack of colour; **fading,** blanching, decolouration, discolouration, etiolation, tarnish; **paleness,** delicateness, lightness, thinness, whiteness; **dullness,** soberness, sobriety, sombreness; **pallor,** anaemia, bloodlessness, cadaverousness, ghastliness, mealiness, pallidness, pastiness, sallow-

colourlessness, sickliness, wanness; **albinism**, alphosis

COMBAT TROOPS *n* cannon fodder, field army, firing line, front line, ranks, troops; **task force**, advance *(U.S.)*, advance guard, chasseur, flying column, sally, sortie, spearhead, van, vanguard; **outpost**, flank, post *(U.S.)*, rear, rearguard, screen, wing; **storm troops**, commando, paras, paratroops, perdu *(Obs.)*, shock troops, SS; **guerilla**, ambusher, freedom fighter, irregular, partisan, skirmisher, terrorist, urban guerrilla; **fighter pilot**, ace, aircraftman, aircraftwoman, airman. *See also* SOLDIER; SERVICEMAN; ARMED FORCES

COMBINATION *n* addition, aggregation, amalgamation, assemblage, association, coalescence, coalition, commixture, composition, confection, conglomeration, conjunction, conjuncture *(Obs.)*, consolidation, coordination, flux, fusion, incorporation, interfusion, intermingling, interweaving, mergence, mixture, polysynthesis, summation, symbiosis, synergism, synergy, synthesisation, synthesism, synthetisation, totalisation, unification, union, unity, zygosis; **desegregation**, assimilation, integration

COMBINATIVE *adj* aggregative, amalgamative, collective, combinational, conjunctional, conjunctive, federative, integrative; **connective**, copulative, syndetic

COMBINE *n* aggregate, amalgam, assemblage, assembly, collective, combination, compound, condensate, consolidation, ensemble, fusion, melting pot, merger, mix, synthesis, system, tie, union, web

COMBINE *v* associate, club, commingle, compound, confect *(Obs.)*, conjoin, consolidate, decompound, merge, organise, synergise, unify; **synthesise**, assemble, compose, make, synthetise; **blend**, commix, fuse, incorporate, interfile, interfuse, mix, temper *(Archaic)*; **amalgamate**, coalesce, compact, conflate, conglomerate, consolidate, coordinate, hang together, join; **desegregate**, assimilate, integrate

COMBINED *adj* allied, associate, associated, coalescent, confederate, conjoint, coordinate, joint, synthetic, tight-knit, unified, unsegregated; **composite**, aggregate, coalition, complex, compound

COMBINER *n* amalgamator, assembler, blender, catalyst, compounder, conjoiner, consolidator, coordinator, fusionist, incorporator, synthesiser, synthesist, synthetiser, unifier, unionist; **mingler**, integrationist, integrator; **weaver**, interweaver, twiner

COMBUSTIBILITY *n* combustibleness, flammability, ignitability, inflammability, inflammableness

COME BETWEEN *v* intercept, interlope, interpose, intervene, punctuate; **partition**, bar, blockade, cordon off, curtain off, obstruct, rope off; **intercept**, cut off, occult

COME CLOSE *v* approach, bear down, close, close in, close with, come near, confront, congress *(Rare)*, draw near, draw on, gain on, lay aboard *(Naut.)*, near, overtake, reach, rise *(Naut.)*, sap *(Fort.)*, shave, trench on, verge, walk up; **approximate**, be in the neighbourhood of, be in the vicinity of, be on the point of, border on

COMEDY *n* comic opera, farce, high comedy, sitcom, situation comedy, sketch, skit; **burlesque**, antimasque, buffoonery, caricature, clownery, commedia dell'arte, harlequinade, low comedy, mime, parody, slapstick; **practical joking**, prankery; **black comedy**, gallows humour, graveyard humour, sly humour, tragicomedy; **sarcasm**, irony, lampoon, lampoonery, satire. *See also* HUMOUR; JOKE

COME TO ONE'S SENSES *v* cease to be irrational, have all one's marbles

COMING AFTER *n* consecutiveness, posteriority, postposition, subsequence, successiveness; **consequentiality**, consequentialness; **supersedure**, follow, supersession, supervenience, supervention; **consequence**, aftereffect, corollary, flow-on, result, resultant, secondary, sequel, sequent

COMMAND *n* adjuration, behest, bidding, call, calling, caution, charge, commission, demand, dictate, enjoinment, hest *(Archaic)*, imperative, injunction, instruction, order, order of the day, placet, prescript, prescription, request, requisition, rubric, sanction, say-so, testament, threat, ultimatum, will, word, word of command; **decree**, act, appointment, brevet, bull, commandment *(Obs.)*, decretal, dictum, directive, dispensation, edict, fiat, instruction, law, mandate, mitzvah, ordinance, precept, prescript, regulation, rescript, rule, ukase; **countermand**, caveat, recall, revocation. *See also* LEGAL ORDER

COMMAND *v* acquisition, adjure, appoint, bid, bung, call upon, charge, commission, conjure, demand, dictate, direct, enjoin, give orders, give the command, insist on, instruct, order, prescribe, require, send for, tell; **summon**, commit, remand, subpoena; **decree**, appoint, enact, legislate, ordain, set

COMMANDER *n* adjurer, bidder, demander, enjoiner, exacter, mandator, orderer, prescriber

COMMANDING *adj* adjuratory, authoritative, decisive, decretal, decretive, decretory, edictal, imperatival, imperative, injunctive, instructional, mandatory, official, preceptive, prescriptive; **jussive**; **dictatorial**, authoritarian, imperious, in command, masterful, peremptory

COMMANDINGLY *adv* at the stroke of a pen, imperatively, officially, preceptively, prescriptively

COMMAND RESPECT *v* awe, dazzle, impress, inspire respect, overawe; **sanctify**, consecrate, enshrine; **stand on one's dignity**, observe due decorum, stand on ceremony; **commemorate**, celebrate, do honour to, observe, remember

COMMEMORATE *v* immortalise, memorialise, monumentalise, preserve

COMMEMORATION *n* ceremonial parade, fly-past, honour board, honour book, honour guard, honour roll, march-past, procession; **commemorative**, memorial, retrospective, war memorial; **honour**, decoration, honourable mention, honours list, knighthood, medal, wreath. *See also* TRIBUTE

COMMEMORATIVE *adj* commemorational, commemoratory, epitaphic, memorial

COMMENTARY *n* comment, criticism, critique, discussion, editorial, press, review; **caption**, inscription, legend; **footnote**, adversaria, annotation, appendix, critical apparatus, excursus, gloss, glossary, marginalia, notes, scholium

COMMERCIALLY *adv* on the market, retail, wholesale; **by auction**, by mail order, door-to-door, over the counter

COMMITTEE *n* caucus, comitia, commission, panel, quango, shop committee, vigilance committee, works council; **conference**, colloquium, convention, round table, summit, symposium, think-tank, workshop; **forum**, chamber, court, curia, diet, duma, General Assembly, moot, parliament; **quorum**, plenum; **faction**, arm, left wing, right wing, the Opposition; **conclave**, conventicle; **gang**, camorra, Mafia, tong; **picket line**, line-up

COMMOTION *n* bobberie, bovver *(Brit. Colloq.)*, breach of the peace, brouhaha, bunfight, bust-up, clamour, clatter, corroboree, distraction, disturbance, hoo-ha, hubble-bubble, hurly-burly, pandemonium, pell-mell, squall, tempest, three-ring circus; **riot**, broil, merry hell, outbreak, race riot, rout, rumpus, scrimmage, sedition *(Archaic)*, trouble, tumult, uproar; **hullabaloo**, bobsy-die, fuss, hubbub, pother, rhubarb, to-do; **free-for-all**, dust, dust-up, fracas; **jungle**, no-man's-land, wilderness; **babel**, bear garden, bloodhouse; **troubled waters**

COMMUNICATE *v* broadcast, convey, disseminate, get across, give, impart, pass on, project, put across, put over, relay, rumour, transmit; **link up with**, be in touch with, converse with, get in touch with, get on to, intercommunicate, keep in touch with, liaise with, look up, normalise relations with, stay in touch with, telephone; **contact**, connect with, get, get through to, make contact with, raise; **signal**, flag, tick-tack *(Horseracing)*, wave to

COMMUNICATION *n* commerce, communion, congress, connection, contact, converse, dialogue, fellowship, impartation, impartment, information transmission, intelligence *(Obs.)*, interchange, intercommunication, intercommunion, intercourse, liaison, propagation, transmittal, transmittance; **nonverbal communication**, body language, semaphore, sign language, signalling, tick-tack; **code**, cryptosystem; **telepathy**, thought transference, thought-reading; **afflatus**, afflation, gift of tongues

COMMUNITY *n* hamlet, kraal, street, town; **clan**, colony, house, people, primary group, race, rod; **commune**, ashram, collective, cooperative, kibbutz, kolkhoz; **class**, caste, order, stratum; **social system**, matriarchate, matriarchy, patriarchate, patriarchy

COMPANION *n* associate, beau, bedfellow, collaborator, colleague, commensal, compeer, comrade, consort *(Obs.)*, fellow traveller, helpmate, helpmeet *(Archaic)*, partner, running mate *(U.S.)*; **follower**, camp follower, hanger-on, inseparable, satellite, shadow; **bridesmaid**, best man, maid of honour, matron of honour, paranymph; **accompanist**, accompanist, backing group, backing musician

COMPANIONSHIP *n* coexistence, commensalism, commensality, comradeship, partnership, presence, togetherness; **accompaniment**, backing, obbligato, support, vamp; **company,** association, concomitance, conjunction

COMPANY *n* holding company, joint-stock company, limited company, private company, private enterprise, proprietary limited company, straw company, subsidiary company, unlimited company; **conglomerate,** amalgamation, cartel, concern, cooperative, cooperative society, empire, firm, group, house, industry, interest, mixed business, mixed industry, multinational, pool *(U.S.),* pyramid, syndicate, transnational; **commercial centre,** entrepot, fort, marketplace, mart, office; **chamber of commerce**

COMPARABLE *adj* analogous, assimilable; **comparative,** allegorical, collative, parallel, relative, typological; **contrastable,** compared with, contrasted with, contrastive, contrasty

COMPARABLY *adv* by analogy, comparatively, in proportion, relatively

COMPARE *v* balance, cf., collate, confer *(Obs.),* draw a parallel, liken, resemble *(Archaic),* weigh up

COMPARER *n* collator, comparator, measurer, standardiser, typologist

COMPARISON *n* allegory, analogy, balance, collation, compare, likening, parallel, proportion *(Archaic),* simile, similitude

COMPARTMENT *n* booth, caisson, cell, chamber, closet, crib; **niche,** cranny, cubbyhole, nook, pigeonhole

COMPENSATE *v* expiate, indemnify, make amends, make good, overcompensate, pay back, ransom, recompense, redeem, render, render back, repay, requite, restitute, satisfy, square off with; **offset,** allow for, countervail, cover; **recoup,** catch up on, get back, recover, replevy, retrieve; **reward,** guerdon, reimburse, remit, remunerate, replace, restore, return, revest

COMPENSATION *n* amends, apology, guerdon *(Poetic),* indemnity, recession, redress, reparation, requital, requitement, restitution, restoration, satisfaction; **recoupment,** poundbreach, recaption, recoup, recovery, replevin, resumption, retrieval; **remuneration,** attachment, golden handshake, meed *(Archaic),* offset, pay-off, payment, refund, reimbursement, repayment, return, reward, salvage; **damages,** blood money, distrainment, hoot *(N.Z.),* indemnification, recompense, square-off; **penalty rate,** allowance, climatic allowance, compo, dirt money, disability allowance, district allowance, isolation allowance, shift allowance, subsistence allowance, time allowance, tool allowance, workers' compensation

COMPENSATORY *adj* apologetic, conciliatory, offset, propitiatory, reparative, restoring; **redemptive,** expiatory, Lenten, lustral, piacular, purgatorial, purgatory, redemptory; **penitent,** reformed, repentant

COMPETENCE *n* accomplishment, capableness, competency, completeness *(Archaic),* efficiency, goodness, handiness, nimbleness, proficiency, resourcefulness, skilfulness, skill, workmanship; **adeptness,** adroitness, craft, craftiness, cunning, cunningness, deftness, dexterity, dexterousness, facility, featliness *(Archaic);* **expertise,** address, craftsmanship, expertness, masterfulness, masterliness, mastery, professionalism, science; **ability**, capability, control, endowment, flair, grasp, grip, knowledge, prowess, talent, verve *(Rare)*; **aptitude**, bent, faculty, flair, forte, genius, gift, innate ability, knack, metier, sense, strong point, talent, the right stuff, the stuff; **skills**, abilities, capabilities, capacity, cleverness, colonial experience, creativity, giftedness, powers; **versatility**, enterprise, resource, versatileness; **dexterity**, ambidexterity, ambidextrousness, dexterousness; **athleticism**, ball sense, gross motor skills, suppleness, surefootedness

COMPETENT *adj* able, adept, adroit, capable, clean, complete *(Archaic)*, efficient, expert, extraordinaire, fully-fledged, good, good at, practical, proficient, resourceful, skilled, sure, together, workmanlike; **dexterous**, crafty *(Archaic)*, deft, feat *(Archaic)*, fit, habile, handy, nimble, quaint *(Archaic)*, smart, sure-footed, wristy; **cunning**, curious *(Archaic)*, daedal *(Poetic)*, neat, slick; **versatile**, all-round, ambidexter *(Archaic)*, ambidextrous; **clever**, gifted, heavenborn, peart; talented; **best**, gun, top. *See also* ACCOMPLISHED

COMPETITIVE *adj* agonistic, combatant, combative, conflictive, dog-eat-dog, emulative, emulous, gladiatorial, vying; **hand-to-hand**, fistic, stand-up; **knockout**, elimination, sudden-death

COMPETITIVELY *adv* agonistically, combatively, vyingly; **hand to hand**

COMPETITIVENESS *n* combativeness, emulation, keenness, rivalry

COMPETITOR *n* adversary, backmarker, challenger, combatant, combater, concurrent *(Rare)*, contender, contestant, contester, drag-racer, dueller, duellist, emulator, entrant, entry, field, logomachist, principal, racer, rival, selection, starter, striver, struggler, tourneyer, vendettist; **finalist**, quarterfinalist, semifinalist; **dark horse**, also-ran, front-runner, hotpot, outsider, roughie, runner-up, skinner

COMPLAIN *v* belly-ache, bitch, bitch and bind, bleat, carp, chew the rag, croak, fratch, fret, fuss, gripe, grizzle, grouch, grouse, growl, grumble, moan, murmur, mutter, plain *(Archaic)*, repine, seethe, squawk, scream blue murder, squeal, whine, whinge, yammer; **be discontented**, feel blue, feel sad, get upset, take in bad part, take on

COMPLAINER *n* bitch, bite *(N.Z.)*, bleater, carper, fault-finder, fussbudget *(U.S.)*, fusspot, griper, grizzleguts, grouch, grouser, growler, grumblebum, grumbler, grump, lemon, malcontent, miseryguts, moaner, mopoke, murmurer, mutterer, nark, sorehead, squawker, squealer, whiner, whingeing Pom, whinger, yammerer

COMPLAINT *n* beef, belly-ache, bleat, cavil, chip on the shoulder, dissent, gravamen, grievance, gripe, grouse, grumble, kick, lamentation, moan, murmur, peeve, plaint, regret, repining, squawk, squeal, whine, whinge, yammer

COMPLETER *n* clincher, closer, finisher, fulfiller, supplementer; **integrator**, synthesist, synthetiser

complex *adj* complicate, complicated, higher *(Biol.)*, involved, sophisticated; **intricate**, convolute, curious *(Obs.)*, elaborate, Gordian, involute, involutional, labyrinthine, perplexing, reticular, winding; **compound**, composite, decompound; **overelaborate**, fussy, Heath Robinson, over-produced *(Music)*, overworked, overwrought; **elaborated**, developed, elaborative. *See also* TANGLED

complexity *n* complexness, complicacy, complicatedness, complicity, convolution, fussiness, intricacy, intricateness, involution, knottiness, overelaborateness, overelaboration, perplexity, sophistication, winding; **inextricability**, inextricableness; **compositeness**, composition, multifariousness; **maziness**, mazement, tortuousness; **complication**, embellishment, embranglement, enmeshment, entanglement. *See also* TANGLE

complexly *adv* complicatedly, elaborately, intricately, involutedly, kaleidoscopically, overelaborately, perplexingly

complicate *v* develop, elaborate, embarrass, embellish, involve, overelaborate, overwork, thicken; **confound**, confuse, perplex

composed *adj* controlled, cool, cool-headed, dégagé, deliberate, detached, imperturbable, level-headed, poised, self-composed, self-contained, self-possessed, stable, steady, take-it-or-leave-it, unflappable, unfussed, unhurried, unruffled; **placid**, ataractic, bland, calm, clear, equal *(Archaic)*, even, impassionate *(Rare)*, level, secure, sedate, subdued, tranquil, tranquillo *(Music)*, undisturbed, untouched; **easygoing**, balanced, easy, equable, even-minded, even-tempered, lackadaisical, lenient, mild, philosophical; **impassive**, dead-pan, inscrutable; **phlegmatic**, dull, fireless, flat, passive, phlegmy, spiritless, stoic, stolid, torpid, unemotional, unfired, unimpassioned; **blasé**, jaded, smooth, sophisticated, suave, unblinking, world-weary; **reposeful**, docile, easeful, sedative

compose oneself *v* calm down, recover oneself, relax, simmer down, unbend, unwind; **keep calm**, get a hold of oneself, get the better of one's feelings, get the better of oneself, hold on, keep one's hair on, keep one's shirt on, keep one's temper; **be indifferent**, not bat an eyelid, not turn a hair, play it cool; **be unenthused**, be left cold, keep one's cool, not go nap on; **endure**, be patient, submit

composure *n* balance, cool *(Colloq.)*, coolness, equanimity, equilibrium, even-mindedness, level-headedness, levelness, poise, sang-froid, savoir-faire, self-possession, steadiness, unflappableness; **imperturbability**, blandness, equability, equableness, imperturbableness, stoicism, stolidity, stolidness; **ease**, confidence, easefulness, repose, reposefulness, secureness, security; **calmness**, ataraxia, calm, imperturbation, placidity, placidness, sedateness, tranquillity, tranquilness; **restraint**, control, docility, self-control, temperance; **mildness**, clemency, lenience, leniency, lenity; **patience**, submission; **detachment**, dispassionateness, impassiveness, impassivity, in-

COMPROMISE *v* coexist, come to terms, compound, live and let live, meet halfway, split the difference, strike a bargain; **go with the fashion,** bend with the breeze, jump on the band wagon, swim with the stream

COMPUTATION *n* calculation, compute, figure work, figures, numeration, reckoning, workings; **count,** aggregate, headcount, re-count, sum, summation, tale *(Archaic),* tally, tot, total; **estimate,** approximation, cast-off *(Print.),* guess, guesstimate; **demography,** capitation, census, demographics

COMPUTE *v* cast up, figure, find, reckon, recount, work out; **count,** add up, card *(Golf),* cash up, cast, differentiate, enumerate, number, numerate, re-count, reach, sum, sum up, tally, tell, tell off, tot up, total; **divide,** add, cube, factorise, integrate, multiply, permute, quantise *(Physics),* raise, rationalise, reduce, square, subtract, transpose; **borrow,** carry, dot and carry one *(Colloq.);* **estimate,** guesstimate, make

COMPUTER *n* analog computer, artificial intelligence, control computer, data-handling system, digital computer, digital controller, electronic computer, macrocomputer, mainframe computer, microcomputer, PC, personal computer, processor, supercomputer, synchronous computer, Turing Machine, word processor; **adding machine,** cash register, comptometer, tab, tabulator, taximeter, totalisator, totaliser *(U.S.);* **slide rule,** difference engine, ready reckoner; **abacus,** cuisenaire rods, Napier's bones (rods), quipu

COMPUTER CONTROLS *n* cursor box, joystick, light-pen, mouse

COMPUTER PROGRAMMER *n* liveware, logical designer, operator, programmer, systems analyst, systems engineer

COMPUTER RECORD *n* core memory, core store, counter, disc file, disc storage, file, hard copy, location, memory, memory bank, record, register, registration, store, working memory

COMPUTING *n* ADP, automatic data processing, batch processing, data capture, data processing, data retrieval, electronic data processing, number crunching *(Colloq.),* systems analysis, systems engineering

CONATIVE *adj* appetent, appetitive, orectic

CONCEIVE *v* fall, teem *(Obs.);* **be pregnant,** be with child, carry, expect, gestate, have a bun in the oven; **make pregnant,** duff *(Colloq.),* get with child, impregnate, inseminate, knock up *(Colloq.),* pot; **be at stud,** service, stand; **rut,** be on heat

CONCEPTION *n* fecundation, impregnation; **polyembryony,** superfecundation, superfetation, twinning; **fertilisation,** artificial insemination, crossfertilisation, crosspollination, in-vitro fertilisation, insemination, IVF, pollination, self-fertilisation, self-pollination; **breeding,** artificial selection, crossing, dysgenics, engraftation, engraftment, eugenics, fancy, genetic engineering, grafting, hybridisation, hybridism, interbreeding, intercross, layering, mongrelisation, natural selection, outbreeding, outcrossing, propagation, selection, stirpiculture, thremmatology; **seedbed**; **birthrate**, hatchability. *See also* PREGNANCY: BIRTH: REPRODUCTION

CONCERNING *prep* about, after, anent *(Scot.)*, apropos of, as for, as regards, as to, in point of, in respect, of, on, regarding, respecting, touching on, towards, vis-a-vis, with reference to, with regard to, with respect to

CONCERT *n* chamber concert, gig, prom concert, recital, soirée, subscription concert; **eisteddfod**, festival; **musicale**, blow, community singing, jam, jam session, rockfest, singsing, singsong; **serenade**, shivaree *(U.S.)*; **item**, bracket, number

CONCISE *adj* brief, compact, compressed, exact, laconic, precise, short, short-spoken, short-winded, succinct; **abbreviated**, abridged, condensed, elliptical, potted, telescoped; **abstractive**, compendious, epitomic, epitomical, summarised, synoptic; **epigrammatic**, crisp, pithy, pointed, pregnant, sententious, straight, terse, trenchant

CONCISELY *adv* briefly, compendiously, laconically, summarily, synoptically; **in brief**, in a few words, in a nutshell, in a word, in fine, in short; **epigrammatically**, crisply, directly, elliptically, pithily, shortly, straight out, straightly, tersely, to the point, trenchantly

CONCISENESS *n* brevity, briefness, compactness, compendiousness, concision, crispness, curtness, economy, shortness, succinctness, terseness; **epigrammatism**, Atticism, laconism, pithiness, sententiousness, straightness, trenchancy

CONDITION *n* affection *(Archaic)*, fettle, kilter, shape, state, state of repair, strain, temper, trim *(Naut.)*; **situation**, case, clinical picture, conjuncture, fare *(Archaic)*, lot, pass, pickle, place, plight, position, posture, predicament; **phase**, appearance, aspect, facies, phasis; **dimension**, plane; **status**, estate, footing, place, quality, rank, situation, standing, station, status quo; **circumstance**, circs, how it is, how things stand, terms, the state of affairs, the state of play, the state of the nation, the way of it; **mode**, feel *(Music)*, modality, phase, phasis, state, way

CONDITIONAL *adj* contingent, dependent, eventual, hypothetical, interlocutory *(Law)*, nisi, provisional, provisory

CONDITIONALLY *adv* provisionally, qualifiedly; **but**, however, though

CONDUCTOR *n* bandmaster, choirmaster, choragus, kapellmeister, maestro, timekeeper; **leader**, band leader, concertmaster, first violinist, principal; **pipe major**, drum-major, trumpet-major

CONFESS *v* acknowledge, admit, betray oneself, break cover, come clean, come one's guts, get something off one's chest, make a clean breast of, out with, own up, shrive, spit it out, unbosom oneself, unburden oneself, wash one's dirty linen in public; **declare one's hand**, give oneself away, give the game away, give the show away, have egg on one's face, lay one's cards on the table, put one's foot in one's mouth, show one's true colours, wear one's heart on one's sleeve; **express**, come out on, declare,

CONFORM *v* accommodate, act one's age, adapt oneself, agree, be guided by, be one's age, behave properly, bend with the breeze, comply, do as others do, fall into line, follow, follow the beaten track, follow the precedents, go by the book, keep up appearances, obey, observe conventions, observe proprieties, observe the rules, play the game, quadrate, run with the herd, run with the mob, swim with the tide, toe the line

CONFORMER *n* Babbitt, capitalist roader, classicist, conformist, conservative, conventionalist, dag *(Colloq.)*, formalist, observer of conventions, reactionary, right wing, right winger, schoolmarm, silvertail, stick-in-the-mud, stickler, straight, suburbanite, suburbia, WASP; **normaliser**, adjuster, aligner, regulator, styliser; **yesman**, company man, party man

CONFORMIST BEHAVIOUR *n* a matter of form, accepted behaviour, convention, conventionalism, custom, form, formality, good form, orthodoxy, usage; **stereotype**, cliche, set piece, type *(Biol.)*, type genus, yardstick; **clannishness**, desire to conform, herd instinct; **conservatism**, Babbittry, conservativeness, conventionality, reaction, WASP-ishness

CONFORMITY *n* agreement, assimilation, coincidence, conformability, conformableness, conformation, correspondence, straightness, uniformity, uniformness; **conformance**, abidance, appropriateness, felicitousness, good form, observance, order, propriety; **typicalness**, commonness, normalcy, normality, ordinariness, regularity, the ordinary; **rightness**, fitness, legitimacy, legitimateness; **classicism**, academicism, classicalism, classicality, formalism; **adaptation**, adjustment

CONFUSE *v* amaze *(Obs.)*, baffle, becloud, bedazzle, befog, bewilder, bother, bowl over, buffalo, confound, daze, dazzle, discombobulate *(Colloq.)*, discomfit, discompose, disconcert, discountenance, disorientate, distract, disturb, dizzy, faze, floor, flummox, flurry, fluster, flutter, fog, hobble, maze *(Archaic)*, muddle, mystify, nonplus, obfuscate, perplex, perturb, puddle, puzzle, rattle, shake up, stick, stumble, stump, stun, throw

CONFUSED *adj* adrift *(Colloq.)*, aflutter, at a loss, at one's wits end, at sea, bemused, bewildered, boxed, bushed, confounded, disconcerted, distracted, distrait, distraught, fluttery, mixed-up, muddled, perplexed, up a gumtree, up the wall; **muddle-headed**, dithering, dithery, dizzy, unbalanced; **blank**, in limbo, lost

CONFUSEDLY *adv* bewilderedly, discomposedly, disconcertedly, distractedly, distraughtly, dizzily, flutteringly, hectically, perplexedly, wanderingly, wildly

CONFUSING *adj* bewildering, clear as mud, distracting, distractive, perplexing; **mazelike**, labyrinthine, mazy

CONFUSINGLY *adv* bewilderingly, blunderingly, discomposingly, disconcertingly, disturbingly, perplexingly

CONFUSION *n* amazement *(Obs.)*, bamboozlement, bedevilment, bewilderment, daze, discomfiture, discomposure, disconcertedness, disconcertion, disconcertment, dismay, dis-

confusion orientation, distraction, dizziness, embarrassment, fog, mazement *(Archaic)*, muddle-headedness, muzziness, mystification, nonplus, obfuscation, perplexity, perturbation, wilderment *(Archaic)*, wooziness; **dither**, bother, flap, flat spin, flurry, fluster, flustration, flutter, fuss, ruffle, spin, tail spin, tizz, tizzy

CONGRATULATE *v* cheer, compliment, drink to, felicitate, gratulate *(Archaic)*, pat on the back; **wish someone joy**, wish happy returns; **show one's respect**, dip one's lid, shake someone's hand; **honour**, duchess, fête, lionise, make much of; **congratulate oneself**, thank one's lucky stars, thank one's stars

CONGRATULATION *n* compliment, compliments, compliments of the season, congratulations, felicitation; **best wishes**, good wishes, happy returns, regards; **toast**, a pat on the back, cheer, handshake, health, salute, salvo

CONGRATULATIONS *interj* congrats; **bravo**, cheers, hooray

CONGRATULATORY *adj* congratulant, gratulatory, well-wishing

CONGRUITY *n* accord *(Archaic)*, accordance, affinity, agreement, coherence, concurrence, concurrency, conformableness, conformance, conformity, congruence, congruousness, consentaneity, consentaneousness, consistency, consonance, correspondence, fit; **harmony**, accord, balance, concinnity, congeniality, harmoniousness, harmonisation, sympathy, syntonisation, syntony; **unity**, oneness, unison; **equivalence**, coincidence, commensurability, correspondence, parallelism, parity, sameness; **homology**, homonymy, homophony, isomerism, synonymity, synonymousness

CONGRUOUS *adj* accordable, accordant, agreeing, answerable to, commeasurable, concurrent, conformable, consentaneous, consistent, consonant, corroborant, felicitous, happy, natural, pursuant to, sympathetic; **harmonious**, at one, cosmic, harmonic, homophonic, homophonous, one, true, unisonous; **equivalent**, actinomeric, correspondent, homologous, isomeric, parallel, same, synonymous; **congruent**, coincident, coincidental

CONGRUOUSLY *adv* accordantly, accordingly, answerably, compatibly, concurrently, conformably, congenially, consentaneously, consistently, consonantly, happily, harmoniously, sympathetically, sympathisingly, thereafter *(Obs.)*, unobjectionably, **correspondingly**, coincidentally, coincidently, commensurably, correspondently; **equivalently**, just the same, the same, typically, uniformly

CONJECTURAL *adj* abstract, academic, baseless, doctrinaire, hypothetical, notional, speculative, theoretical; **supposed**, assumptive, axiomatic, ballpark, estimated, presumptive, putative, quasi, reputed, so-called, suppositional, suppositious, supposititious, suppositive; **conjecturable**, assumable, guessable, supposable, surmisable; **assumed**, conjectured, given, mooted, postulated, presumed

CONJECTURALLY *adv* academically, doctrinally, hypothetically, on paper, presumptively, putatively, speculatively, suppositionally, suppositively, theoretically

CONJECTURE *n* aim *(Obs.)*, bush reckoning, extrapolation, forecast, guess, guesstimate, guesswork, hunch, inkling, intuition, shot, shot in the dark, surmisal, surmise, suspicion; **theory**, abstraction, ideology, ism, philosophy, principle, school of thought, view; **assumption**, axiom, hypothesis, postulate, postulation, premise, presumption, presupposition, presurmise, proposition, speculation, supposal, supposition

CONJECTURE *v* expect *(Colloq.)*, extrapolate, guess, guesstimate, imagine, smell a rat, suppose, surmise, suspect, trow *(Archaic)*; **assume**, give, posit, postulate, presume, presuppose

CONNECTING *adj* conjugative, conjunctional, conjunctive, connective, copulative, intercommunicative, syndetic; **unitive**, integrative

CONSECRATE *v* dedicate, hallow, sanctify; **saint**, beatify, canonise

CONSERVATION *n* conservancy, environmentalism; **green ban**; **preservation**, bottling, canning, cold storage, dehydration, desiccation, ensilage, freeze-drying, hydro-cooling, pickling, refrigeration; **insulation**, insulator, lagging, mineral wool, rockwool; **proofing**, fireproofing, resist, waterproofing; **embalmment**, mummification, taxidermy

CONSERVATIONIST *n* environmentalist, greenie, preservationist; **caretaker**, aquarist, archivist, conservator, curator, gamekeeper, guard, guardian, keeper, nightwatchman, warden, watchman; **preserver**, embalmer, salter, taxidermist

CONSERVATIVE *adj* Biedermeier, blue-rinse, daggy, reactionary, straight, straight-arrow, suburban, twin-set and pearls, uptight, WASP; **clannish**, closely adhering, loyal; **right-wing**, arbitrary, overbearing, procrustean, right; **orthodox**, canonical, classic, classical, conformist, fundamentalist, law-abiding, strict

CONSERVE *v* keep, preserve, put away, salt away, salt down; **refrigerate**, bottle, brine, can, corn, cure, dehydrate, desiccate, dry, ensile, freeze-dry, jerk, kipper, lyophilise, pickle, pot, salt, silo, smoke, tin; **proof**, fireproof, prove, rainproof, showerproof, waterproof; **plate**, cellulose, underseal; **embalm**, fix *(Microscopy)*, mummify, stuff

CONSPIRACY *n* cabal, collusion, complot, conjuration *(Obs.)*, countermine, counterplot, frame, frame-up, intrigue, machinations, plant, plot, practices *(Archaic)*, ready. *See also* PLAN

CONSPIRE *v* cabal, complot, conjure *(Obs.)*, contrive, counterplot, intrigue *(Obs.)*, lay heads together, lay plans, machinate, plot, practise *(Archaic)*, put heads together, scheme, work one's nut. *See also* PLAN

CONSTITUENT *adj* cantonal, component, elemental, elementary, fractional, integral, integrant

CONSTRUCTION *n* building, civil engineering, prefabrication, public works, reconstruction, restoration; **architecture**, architectonics, draughtsmanship, landscape architecture, tectonics; **bricklaying**, indenting, infilling, masonry, rubblework, stonework, toothing; **carpentry**, post-and-beam construction, timber-framing

CONSULT *v* cite, refer to; **wise up on**, gen up on, get a line on, get the good guts on, scout, scout out

CONTACT *n* attaint *(Obs.)*, brush, contingence, dab, graze, interface, kiss, osculation, taction *(Obs.)*, tag, touch; **junction**, abutment, abuttal; **meeting**, link-up, occlusion; **meshing**; **contiguity**, contiguousness, tangency

CONTACT *v* apply, hit, join, make contact, meet, touch; **abut**, adjoin, border on, impinge, juxtapose, subjoin; **intertwine**, be in mesh, dovetail, fay, mesh, tooth, twist; **hit**, alight upon, chance upon; **brush**, button *(Fencing)*, dab, graze, kiss, nose, nuzzle, tongue; **join**, be tangent to, board, butt, link up, occlude, touch

CONTACTING *adj* adjoining, valvate; **contiguous**, conterminous, impingent, meeting, osculatory, striking, tangent, tangential, touching

CONTAINER *n* case, frame, holder, receiver, receptacle; **cover**, enclosure, wrapper; **cupboard**, cabinet, dresser, filing cabinet, locker, press, wardrobe; **reliquary**, ark, burse, chrismatory, cist, monstrance, phylactery, pyx, pyxis, shrine, tabernacle; **cage**, beehive, coop, enclosure, fishbowl, goldfish-bowl, hutch, pen, skep. *See also* BASKET: BOX: CASE: BAG: BASIN: BARREL: VESSEL: BOTTLE

CONTENT *adj* contented, easy, satisfied; **comfortable**, comfy, cottonwool, dégagé, satisfactory, snug, well-off, well-to-do; **complacent**, relaxed, self-complacent, self-content, self-satisfied, sitting pretty; **happy**, eudemonic, felicific, happy as a lark, happy as Larry, joyful

CONTENTEDLY *adv* at home, at one's ease, comfortably, in one's element; **complacently**, self-complacently

CONTENTEDNESS *n* content, contentment, peace of mind; **comfortableness**, featherbed, heavenliness; **comfort**, cottonwool, ease, weal *(Archaic)*; **happiness**, bliss, blissfulness, eudemonia, felicity, glory, honeymoon, seventh heaven; **complacency**, gratification, satisfaction, self-satisfaction

CONTENTIOUS *adj* conflictive, controversial, dissentious, divisive, eristic; **at variance**, inconsonant; **arguable**, contestable, contradictable, disputable, exceptionable. *See also* ARGUMENTATIVE

CONTENTIOUSNESS *n* argumentativeness, contrariness, disputatiousness, divisiveness, negativeness, negativity, pettifoggery; **discord**, disunion, disunity

CONTENTS *n* cargo, content, fraught *(Obs.)*, freight, lading, load, pack, payload, wealth; **capacity**, capaciousness, cubature, mass, tonnage, volume

CONTEST *n* agony *(Rare)*, comp, competition, concurrence *(Rare)*, conflict, conflictation, contention, contestation, engagement, game, infighting, match, prize *(Archaic)*, stakes *(Joc.)*, struggle, toil *(Archaic)*, trial, tug of war, war; **tournament**, carnival, challenge, grudge match, local derby, meet, meeting; **boxing match**, arm-wrestling, duello, prize fight, sciamachy, spar; **bullfighting**, cockfighting, main, tauromachy; **rodeo**, buckjumping, bulldogging, camp draft, carousel, gymkhana; **jousts**, lists, pool *(Fencing)*, tilting, tournament *(Hist.)*, tourney *(Archaic)*; **panel game**, game show, quiz, spelling bee; **boatrace**, stew; **miscellaneous contest**, eisteddfod, roller derby, sheepdog trial, shoot, shooting match, spider *(Bowling)*, surf carnival, woodchop; **championship**, cup, cup final, cup tie, decider, final, finals, grand final, match-of-the-day, open, preliminary final, premiership, quarterfinal, replay, run-off, semi, semifinal, test, test match, tie breaker. *See also* FIGHT; RACE

CONTEST *v* compete, contend, emulate, play, race, rival, run, run close, run hard, strive, try out, vie; **challenge**, draw, throw down the gauntlet, throw down the glove; **enter the lists**, take up the cudgels, take up the gauntlet, take up the glove, throw one's hat into the ring; **walk over,** run rings round; **bandy words**, argy-bargy, bicker, chaffer, chop *(Obs.)*, debate *(Archaic)*, haggle, have words, jangle *(Archaic)*, join issue, make the fur fly, row, squabble, tiff, wrangle. *See also* FIGHT

CONTINUAL *adj* abiding, constant, continuative, continuous, enduring, lasting, ongoing, persistent, standing; **everlasting**, ceaseless, continuing, endless, incessant, non-stop, perennial, perpetual, round-the-clock, unceasing, unending, uninterrupted, unrelenting, unrelieved, year-round; **assiduous**, unfailing, unflagging, unremitting, unresting, unwearied; **extended**, continued, drawn-out, interminable, long-term, longstanding, prolonged, protracted, protractive; **continuable**, maintainable, retainable, sustainable

CONTINUALLY *adv* all along, constantly, continuatively, continuously, incessantly, momently, non-stop, persistently, sempre *(Music)*; **unremittingly**, abidingly, assiduously, at a run, ceaselessly, on end, unceasingly, unfailingly, unflaggingly, unrelentingly, unrelievedly, unrestingly, unswervingly, unweariedly; **always**, alway *(Archaic)*, e'er *(Poetic)*, ever, still *(Poetic)*, yet; **successively**, consecutively, in succession, one after another, sequentially, serially, seriately, seriatim; **unbrokenly**, flowingly, on, solidly, steadily, straight, uninterruptedly; **forever**, day in day out, endlessly, ever and again, ever and anon, everlastingly, evermore, on and on, perennially, perpetually, week in week out, without a break, year in year out

CONTINUATION *n* abidance, abidingness, continuance, continuativeness, continuity, continuousness, duration, long standing, maintenance, progress, progression, subsistence, sustainment; **protraction**, prolongation, prolongment; **incessantness**, endlessness, incessancy, uninterruptedness, unremittingness; **successiveness**, consecutiveness, perseverance, seriation; **unbrokenness**, solidity, solidness

CONTINUE *v* endure, flow, go on, keep the ball rolling, keep up, kick on, last, proceed, push on, soldier on, survive, wear, weather; **attacca**, segue *(Music)*; **abide**, bide *(Archaic)*, dwell, remain, rest, stay; **persist**, hold on, hold out, keep going, persevere, sit out, stick around, stick on

CONTINUER *n* continuator, maintainer, prolonger, protractor; **survivor**, abider, laster, perennial, survivalist

CONTRACEPTION n birth control, family planning; **rhythm method,** safe period, Vatican roulette; **sterilisation,** castration, tubal ligation, vasectomy; **abortion,** aborticide, D and C, dilation and curettage, embryectomy, vacuum aspiration; **contraceptive,** cap, combination pill, condom, contraceptive sheath, copper 7, diaphragm, durex *(Brit.)*, Dutch cap, French letter, Frenchy, frog, I.U.D., intra-uterine device, loop, minipill, once a month pill, pessary, preventive, prophylactic, raincoat, rubber *(U.S.)*, sequential pill, sheath, skin, spermicide, the pill; **abortifacient,** morning-after pill

CONTRACT n agreement, arrangement, bargain, bond, compact, convention, covenant, deal, dicker, gentlemen's agreement, mise, settlement, testament, truck, understanding; **promise,** assurance, commitment, engagement, gage, guarantee, guaranty, Hippocratic oath, homage, insurance, oath, obligation, parole, pledge, sacrament, simple vow, swear, troth *(Archaic)*, undertaking, vote *(Obs.)*, vow, wager *(Archaic)*, warranty, word of honour; **pact,** concord, concordat, entente, league, protocol, treaty, truce; **bond,** cartel, charter; **booking,** gig, pre-engagement; **type of contract,** affreightment *(Comm.)*, aleatory contract, assumpsit, binder, bottomry *(Marine Law)*, carryover, collateral agreement, collective agreement, consent agreement, futures contract, immoral contract, implied contract, knock-for-knock agreement *(Insurance)*, lend-lease, mandate *(Roman and Civil Law)*, nudum pactum, quasi contract, quit claim deed, restrictive covenant, social contract, subcontract, sweetheart deal, turnkey contract, wagering contract. See also DEED

CONTRACT v astringe, constrict, constringe; **shrink,** atrophy, blast, blight, draw in, dwindle, retract, shrivel, waste, wither, wizen; **crumple,** corrugate, crush, rumple, wrinkle; **take in,** pleat, tuck

CONTRACTED adj constricted, cramped, straitlaced *(Archaic)*, tense; **withered,** atrophied, blasted, marasmic, shrivelled, shrunken, stunted, tabescent, tabetic, tabid, wasted, wizened; **retractive,** astringent, constrictive, constringent, contractile, contractive, retractile; **spasmodic,** spastic; **systolic,** systaltic; **retractable,** contractible, foldaway

CONTRACTION n constriction, gather, intake, retraction, shrink, shrinkage; **spasm,** peristalsis, plasmolysis, systole, tetanus, vaginismus, vasoconstriction; **atrophy,** marasmus, tabefaction, wasting; **astringency,** constringency; **contractedness,** contractibility, contractibleness, contractility, contractiveness, retractility

CONTRACTOR n agent of necessity, arranger, bargainer, binder, covenantor, engager, indenter, obligor *(Law)*, subcontractor, undertaker; **promiser,** pledger, swearer, vower

CONTRAST n antithesis, contradiction, contrariety, discrepancy, disparity, dissimilarity, inversion, oppositeness; **contrary,** antonym, counterpart, foil, opposite, opposite pole, reverse, the other side

CONTRAST v invert, oppose, reverse, set against

CONTRAVENE v break, infract, infringe; **offend; racketeer,** traffic; **trespass,** encroach

CONTROL v curb, damp, govern, keep in check, keep under control, manage, monitor, regulate, restrain, size *(Obs.)*; **monopolise,** collar, corner the market, engross, rort, take over

CONTROLLED *adj* automated, computer-controlled, monitored, regulated

CONTROLLING *adj* checking, dedicated *(Computers)*, governing, regulating, regulative, regulatory

CONTROLLING DEVICE n checker, controller, curb, damper, dedicated computer, governor, guide, monitor, regulator, rein, the controls; **automatic control,** auto, automation, computer control, process control, remote control, servocontrol

CONVENTIONAL *adj* academic, accepted, appropriate, common-or-garden, customary, decorous, felicitous, habitual, prosaic, set, usual; **commonplace,** copybook, household, normal, ordinary, ready-made, stereotyped, unexceptional, unremarkable; **typical,** entopic, in character, stereotyped, stereotypical, true *(Biol.)*; **conformable,** acquiescent, adjustable, agreeable, assimilative, assimilatory, complacent, pliable

CONVENTIONALLY *adv* appropriately, as a matter of course, as a matter of form, in line, in step, pro forma, rightly, true; **conservatively,** classically, formally, straightly; **orthodoxly,** according to, by rule, conformably, in accordance with, in conformity with, in keeping with, strictly; **commonly,** as usual, in the natural order of things, invariably, normally, ordinarily, regularly, typically, unexceptionally, uniformly, unremarkably

CONVERGE v be on a collision course with, come together, come up to, cut off, focus, intercept, join, unite, unite with; **meet,** bump into, collide with, come across, come upon, encounter, fall in with, meet up with; **concentrate,** assemble, bring together, gather together

CONVERGENCE n accession, afflux, assembly, coming together, concentration, concourse, confluence, conflux, congress, encounter, flection, flexion, flocking together, huddling together, junction; **meeting,** collision, encounter

CONVERGENT *adj* asymptotic, asymptotical, flexional, synclinal; **confluent,** centring, centripetal, cusped, cuspidal, cuspidate

CONVERT v bring over, bring round, episcopise, reclaim, reform, regenerate; **teach,** brainwash, evangelise, missionise, proselytise; **corrupt,** heathenise, paganise

CONVEYOR n apron, beef chain, belt, chainpump, conveyor belt, shiploader, the chain (*Butchering*); **escalator,** moving pathway, moving staircase, travelator; **lift,** dumb waiter, elevator, goods lift, service lift

COOEE *interj* ahoy, halloo, hallow, ho, hoy, yo-ho, yoo-hoo; **oyez,** hear ye; **hurray,** banzai *(Japan)*, bravo, hosanna, huzza, tiger *(U.S.)*; **carn,** have a go; **tally-ho,** tantivy, view halloo, yoicks

COOK n baker, chief, confectioner, doctor *(Naut.)*, kitchen hand, pastrycook, restaurateur; **bush cook,** bab-

cook v fix, get, microwave, pan (*U.S.*), pick, precook, prepare; **grill**, barbecue, broil, carbonado, griddle, toast; **bake**, plank (*U.S.*), roast, shirr; **fry**, brown, deep-fry, French-fry, frizzle, pan fry, parch, sauté, scramble, sear, shallow-fry, stir-fry; **boil**, coddle, hard-boil, parboil, poach, simmer; **braise**, casserole, fricassee, ragout, scallop, stew; **blanch**, scald; **steep**, brew, draw, infuse, percolate, seethe (*Obs.*); **dredge**, bread, breadcrumb, coat, crumb, egg, flour; **mince**, bone, chip, chop, dice, filet, fillet, spatchcock, spitchcock; **tenderise**, hang, macerate, marinate, soak; **crackle**, decrepitate; **strain**, tammy, **season**, flavour, pepper, spice; **curry**, devil, korma; **preserve**, brandy, brew, corn, jug, kipper, pickle, pot, salt, smoke, souse; **garnish**, dress, sauce, stuff; **baste**, bard, lard; **make tea**, boil the billy; **truss**, collar; **cream**, blend, puree, whip, whisk; **candy**, caramelise, conserve (*Obs.*), crystallise, sugar, thread; **prove**, raise, shorten; **deglaze**

COOKED adj baked, billy, boiled, broiled, en brochette, en cocotte, en daube, flambé, fried, grilled, roast, sauté, stewed; **underdone**, blue, half-baked, medium, rare, raw, soft-boiled; **done**, done to a turn, hard-boiled, overdone, well-done; **rich**, short, shortcrust, suety, unleavened; **sugared**, glacé; **cured**, dried, pickled, potted, salt, smoked, soused, suncured; **culinary**, cordon bleu, home-cooked; **au bleu**, à la chasseur, au bleu, au citron, au gratin, au jus, au lait, au naturel, au poivre, au vin, bonne femme, cacciatore, catalane, chasseur, julienne, lyonnaise, maître d'hôtel, marengo, marinara, mariniere, orly, parmentier, paysanne, soufflé

COOKERY n catering, cooking, cordon bleu cookery, cuisine, domestic science, gastrology, haute cuisine, nouvelle cuisine; **baking**, boiling, broiling, grilling, infusion, marination, red cooking, roasting, simmering, stewing, toasting; **peeling**, KP (*U.S.*), paring, spud-bashing; **cookbook**, cookery book, recipe book; **recipe**, receipt

COOKWARE n enamelware, kitchenware, ovenware, pyrex; **pressure cooker**, autoclave, olla, steamer; **frying pan**, banjo, deep-frier, frypan, pan, popper, sizzle plate, skillet, wok; **casserole**, bedourie, camp oven, cocotte, crock-pot, Dutch oven, fondu dish, marmite, ramekin, terrine; **egg coddler**, poacher; **griddle**, gem iron, jaffle iron, waffle-iron; **baking dish**, roaster; **saucepan**, bainmarie, billy, billycan, broiler, cauldron, double boiler, double saucepan, fish kettle, goashore (*N.Z.*), kettle, pot, steam-boiler, steamboat, steamer, stockpot; **mess tin**, dixie; **cake tin**, dariole, patty pan, patty paper, ring tin; **bombe**, coquille, scallop; **blender**, egg-beater, food processor, rotary beater, vitamiser, whisk; **skewer**, brochette; **percolator**, dripolator

COOL v air-condition, air-cool, fan, water-cool; **refrigerate**, chill, ice, supercool; **freeze**, deep freeze, quick-freeze, snap-freeze

COOLED *adj* chilled, iced; **refrigerative**, refrigerant, thermolytic; **air-conditioned**, aircooled, water-cooled; **frozen**, frappé, quick-frozen, snap-frozen

COOLER *n* coolant, cooling tower, radiator, ultracooler *(Winemaking)*, water-cooler, water-jacket; **refrigerator**, creamer, crisper, fridge, frost-free refrigerator, reefer; **freezer**, chiller, deep freeze, freezing chamber, ice chest, ice machine, icebox; **Coolgardie safe**, bush refrigerator, cool safe; **ice bucket**, chillybin, esky, wine-cooler; **freezing works**, icehouse; **freezing mixture**, carbon dioxide snow, cryogen, cryohydrate, isobutane, rhigolene; **ice-cubes**, iceblocks, rocks; **air-conditioner**, fan

COOLING *n* cold storage, cryonics, refrigeration, thermolysis, ventilation; **air-conditioning**, regenerative cooling; **cryogenics**

COOPERATE *v* club together, collaborate, combine, confederate, coordinate, go hand in hand, pull together, synergise, team up, unite, work as a team, work together; **conspire**, connive, plot, tick-tack with; **participate**, club in, contribute, pitch in; **concur**, go along with, help, play ball, string along with

COOPERATION *n* consensus, cooperativeness, give-and-take, helpfulness, reciprocity; **team spirit**, clannishness, esprit de corps, fellowship, party spirit, solidarity, unitedness; **collaboration**, combined operation, concurrence, concurrency, connivance, coordination, joint effort, participation, synergism, synergy, teamwork, working together

COOPERATIVE *adj* coefficient, collaborative, concurrent, coordinative, solidary, synergetic, synergic, synergistic; **allied**, coalition, cobelligerent, confederate, confederative, united, unitive

COOPERATIVELY *adv* collaboratively, concurrently, coordinately, hand-in-glove, in cahoots, in league; **unitedly**, jointly, together

COOPERATOR *n* collaborator, co-operationist, coworker, fellow worker, participant, participator, partner; **ally**, cobelligerent, confederate; **conspirator**, accessory, accessory after the fact, accessory before the fact, accomplice, conniver, plotter; **coordinator**, combiner, organiser, uniter

COPIED *adj* duplicate, duplicative, ectypal, facsimile, reproductive; **transcriptive**, word for word

COPIER *n* imitator, reproducer; **transcriber**, copyist, exemplifier *(Law)*; **manifolder**, cyclostyle, diagraph, electrotyper, fordigraph, gestetner, hectograph, mimeograph, pantograph, photocopier, polygraph, tracer

COPY *n* blind copy, clone, ditto, double, dubbing, dummy, duplicate, ectype, facsimile, fax, match, model, moulding, repeat, replica, reproduction; **counterfeit**, forgery, semblance; **tracing**, transfer; **transcript**, engrossment, estreat, exemplification *(Law)*, fair copy, transcription, typescript; **carbon copy**, flimsy, manifold; **plate**, electro, electrotype, offset, zincograph; **photocopy**, autotype, blueprint, gestetner, microcopy, photostat, xerograph, xerox, zincograph; **offprint**, decal, galley, galley proof, print, proof; **woodblock**, intaglio, wood engraving, woodcut; **cast**, death mask, mould, squeeze; **magnification**, reduction

COPY *v* ditto, dub, duplicate, facsimile, imitate, match, replicate, reproduce, simulate; **transcribe**, engross, estreat, exemplify *(Law)*, take down word for word; **trace**, calk, cyclostyle, generate *(Maths)*; prick; **mould**, squeeze; **photostat**, autotype, blueprint, decal, electrotype, fordigraph, gestetner, hectograph, manifold, mimeograph, offprint, roneo, xerox

COPYING *n* duplication, repetition, replication, reproduction, transcription; **reprography**, autography, autotypy, decal, decalcomania, intaglio, zincography

CORD *n* bond, cable, cablet, line, rope; **leash**, lariat *(U.S.)*, lashing, lasso *(Agric.)*, lead, leading rein, leg rope, lune, lunge, lunging rein, tether; **towrope**, guide rope, lifeline, tow, towline; **tightrope**, highwire, slackwire; **whip**, cat-o'-nine-tails, knout, lash, quirt *(U.S.)*, rawhide, rope's end, sjambok, stockwhip, tawse *(Scot.)*; **rigging**, bight, boltrope, brail, breeching, buntline, cable, cablet, clew line, colt, cordage, downhaul, earing, gantline, grabrope, guestrope, halliard, halyard, handy billy, hawser, inhaul, jackstay, knife lanyard, lanyard, lashing, messenger, monkey rope, outhaul, painter, pendant, preventer, ratline, reef point, sennit, sheet, shroud, slings, spring, standing rigging, stay, stirrup, stop, stopper, sweep, swifter, tack, tackle, traveller, triatic stay, tripping line, vang, warp; **miscellaneous cords**, baulk, bellpull, chalk-line *(Building Trades)*, clothes line, creance, dragline, dragrope, footrope, guide rope, heddle, marline, match, mooring, ripcord, sashcord, skipping-rope, stringline, surfline, tagrope, topping lift, trail rope, trip-wire, wick. *See also* STRING; TAPE; THREAD; WIRE

CORD *v* rope, string, wire; **fibrillate**, rove, sleave; **tie**, lace; **thread**, interweave, thrum; **rein in**, lasso, rope in; **spin**, strand, wiredraw

CORDED *adj* corduroy, funicular, ropy, stringed; **right-handed**, cable-laid, hawser-laid, shroud-laid, twice-laid; **stringy**, desmoid, sinewy, wiry; **fibrous**, fibred, fibriform, fibrillar, fibrilliform, fibrillose, fibroid, filamentary, filamentous, filar, filiform, filose, piled, piliform, tendrillar, tentacular, threadlike, thready, unifilar, wirewove; **silky**, byssaceous, cobwebbed, cobwebby, silk

CORPORAL PUNISHMENT *n* flogging, lashing, strapping, the cuts, whipping; **beating**, bastinado, belting, doing, drubbing, flagellation, fustigation *(Archaic)*, hiding, running the gauntlet, scourging, thrashing, trouncing, walloping; **Botany Bay dozen**, bob, bull, canary, tester; **blow**, buffet, clout, cuff, domino *(Obs.)*, pandy, stripe, stroke; **smack**, blanketing, box on the ear, dusting, going-over, paddle, paddywhack, rap over the knuckles, slap, spank, spanking, wallop; **torture**, breaking on the wheel, Chinese burn, Chinese water torture, excruciation, sensory deprivation, strappado, third degree, torment *(Obs.)*

CORPORATION *n* body corporate, business house, enterprise, no-liability company, unincorporated association, unlimited company; es-

corporation **tablishment**, aunty, organisation; **cartel**, combine, conference *(Shipping)*, consortium, monopoly, pool, ring, syndicate; **trading bloc**, co-op, common market, EEC, farmers' cooperative, OPEC; **company**, cast, firm, line-up, outfit; **partnership**, duumvirate, group practice, triumvirate; **team**, rink, side

CORRECT *v* blue-pencil, copyedit, crosscheck, edit, emend, proofread, red-pencil, revise, subedit; **rectify**, amend, disabuse, edify, expurgate, set to rights, straighten; **check**, authenticate

CORRECT *adj* exact, just, lawful, right as rain, unerring, unimpeachable; **authorised**, canonical, orthodox, recognised; **true**, authentic, factual, fiducial, genuine, historical, infallible, real, ridge, ridgy-didge, sooth *(Archaic)*, veracious, veritable, very; **right**, becoming, comme il faut, decent, decorous, fair and above board, family *(Films Television)*, fitting, incorrupt, irreproachable, just, moral, principled, proper, reproachless, right-minded, righteous, rightful, savoury, scrupulous, seemly, squeaky-clean, straight, true, unspotted, up to the mark, upright, viceless, virtuous

CORRECTION *n* emendation, proofreading, recension, redaction, revision; **rectification**, amendment, edification, reform, reformation

CORRECTIVE *adj* amendatory *(U.S.)*, rectifying, reformational, reformative, reformatory

CORRECTLY *adv* aright, by the book, exactly, orthodoxly, scrupulously, unerringly; **rightly**, by right, fairly, incorruptly, irreproachably, lawfully, morally, righteously, straight, truly, unimpeachably, uprightly, virtuously; **decorously**, decently, in reason, properly, seemly, within bounds, within reason

CORRECTNESS *n* becomingness, decency, decentness, decorousness, decorum, irreproachableness, irreproachableness, propriety, right-mindedness, savouriness, seemliness, the conventionalities, the conventions, the thing; **right**, ethicality, justness, morality, principle, rectitude, righteousness, rightness, the straight and narrow, virtue, virtuousness, welldoing; **straightness**, a step in the right direction, lawfulness, orthodoxy, scrupulosity, the right track, the ticket, trueness, unerringness

CORRECTOR *n* book editor, checker, copyeditor, emendator, proofreader, redactor, reviser, subeditor; **righter of wrongs**, amender, edifier, rectifier

CORRESPONDENT *n* addressee, consignee, epistler, letter writer, penfriend

CORRUGATED *adj* carinal, carinate, corduroy, knurled, ribbed, striate, strigose

COSMETICS *n* beauty spot, blusher, court plaster, eye shadow, eyeliner, face powder, foundation, foundation cream, greasepaint, highlighter, kohl, liner, lippie, lipstick, mascara, nail polish, nail varnish, pancake, pencil, rouge, vanishing cream; **make-up**, face, face paint, war paint

COSMIC *adj* cosmical, galactic, macrocosmic, universal; **heavenly**, celestial, empyreal, firmamental, sphery, superlunary, supernal, superterrestrial, uranian, uranic; **extragalactic**, intergalactic, interlunar, interplan-

cosmic   120   **counterbalance**

etary, intersidereal, interstellar; **ethereal**, skyey *(Poetic)*

COSMICALLY *adv* ethereally, supernally; **geocentrically,** heliacally, heliocentrically, stellately

COST *n* charge, damage, differential rate, expenditure, expense, price, rate, score; **cost price;** floor price, net price, trade price, wholesale price; **unit cost,** cost unit, operating cost, unit price; **market price,** going price, market, retail price, spot price; **asking price,** knockdown price, reserve price, upset price; **offer,** ante, bid, nearest offer, o.n.o.; **admission,** entrance fee, footing, gate, gate money, gate-takings; **overheads,** burden, oncost, outlay; **production fee,** prime cost; **corkage,** service charge; **commission,** bank charge, cut, percentage; **fee,** contract sum, cost-plus, honorarium, most common fee *(Med.),* refresher, transfer fee *(Football),* tuition, tutorage; **brassage,** seigniorage. See also FREIGHT; VALUE

COST *v* bring, fetch, sell for, set one back; **be worth,** close at *(Stock Exchange);* **amount to,** add up to, come to, run to; **valorise,** bull, fix a price, set; **change in value,** down-value, fall, rise, transvalue, upvalue

COSTUME *n* cap and bells, domino, drag, fancy dress, masquerade, motley

COUCH *n* banana bed, banana chair, canapé, chaise longue, chesterfield, cuddle seat, davenport *(U.S.),* day bed, divan, fauteuil, lounge, lounge suite, night-and-day, ottoman, settee, settle, sofa, sofa-bed, studio couch. See also CHAIR; BED

COUNCIL *n* divan, junta, politburo, presidium, soviet, zemstvo; **board,** board of reference, directorate, syndicate; **forum,** discussion group, panel, round table, workshop; **parliament,** agora, assembly, chamber, congress, diet, gemot, house, House of Assembly, senate; **cabinet,** camarilla, council of war, court, genro, Privy Council, shadow cabinet; **committee,** select committee, sessional committee, standing committee, steering committee, subcommittee; **consistory,** conference, convocation, ecumenical council, parish council, presbytery, Sanhedrin, synod, Vatican Council, vestry

COUNTERACT *v* antagonise *(Physiol.),* counter, countercheck, countermand, countervail, counterwork, frustrate, neutralise, overturn, remedy, slap down, undo; **balance,** counterpoise, counterweigh, equiponderate, match, offset, write off

COUNTERACTING *adj* antidotal, counter-revolutionary, counteractive, diriment, remedial, rescissory, revocatory

COUNTERACTION *n* counter, counter-reformation, counter-revolution *(Politics),* counterattack, counterblast, countercheck, counterclaim, countermove, counterpressure, neutralisation, reaction, recoil, retroaction

COUNTERBALANCE *n* balancer, check, counterpoise, counterweight, counterwork, equilibrant, offset, tare *(Chem.);* **antidote,** antacid, antalkali, buffer, counterirritant, counterpoison, neutraliser

COUNTRY DWELLER n backcountryman, bushman, bushranger, bushwhacker, country cousin, countryman, countrywoman, plainsman, provincial, ruralist, rustic, villager, wench; **peasant,** bogtrotter, boor, bumpkin, bushie, churl, clown, hayseed, hillbilly, muzhik, ploughboy, ploughman, yeoman *(Brit.)*; **country people,** country folk, peasantry; **bucolic,** swain *(Poetic)*

COURAGE n braveness, bravery, courageousness, crest, fortitude, guts, prowess, valiance, valiantness, valorousness, valour; **daring,** adventurousness, daringness, derring-do, emprise *(Archaic)*, enterprise, liveliness, venturesomeness, venturousness; **heroism,** chivalrousness, chivalry, gallantness, gallantry, knight-errantry; **boldness,** audaciousness, audacity, chutzpah, gall, moxie *(U.S.)*, nerve; **fearlessness,** dauntlessness, doughtiness, great-heartedness, intrepidity, stoutness; **hardiness,** game, gameness, gaminess, grit, hardihood, pluck, pluckiness; **spirit,** heart, mettle, spiritedness, sportsmanship, spunk, spunkiness, stomach *(Obs.)*; **undauntedness,** heart of oak, unshrinkingness; **stalwartness,** manliness, Spartanism, virtue *(Obs.)*; **pot-valiance,** Dutch courage

COURAGEOUS adj brave, mentioned in dispatches, proud *(Obs.)*, valiant, valorous; **daring,** adventuresome, adventurous, venturesome, venturous; **heroic,** chivalric, chivalrous, epic, gallant, herculean, lion-hearted; **bold,** audacious, defiant, nervy; **fearless,** dauntless, doughty, great-hearted, inapprehensive, indomitable, intrepid, stout, stout-hearted; hardy, game, game as a pissant, game as Ned Kelly, gamy, gritty, plucky, pretty *(Scot. Archaic)*; **spirited,** full of fight, high-spirited, mettled, mettlesome, spunky; **undaunted,** fortitudinous, unblinking, unflinching, unshrinking; **stalwart,** gutsy, manly, Spartan, strong; **pot-valiant**

COURAGEOUSLY adv bravely, nobly, valiantly, valorously; **daringly,** adventurously, venturesomely, venturously; **heroically,** chivalrously, epically, gallantly; **boldly,** audaciously, defiantly, fearlessly; **fearlessly,** dauntlessly, doughtily, indomitably, intrepidly, stalwartly, stoutheartedly, stoutly; **hardily,** gamely, gamily, grittily, pluckily, spiritedly, spunkily; **undauntedly,** unblinkingly, unflinchingly, unshrinkingly

COURSE n correspondence course, extension course, external course, in-service course, internship, novitiate, postgraduate course, refresher course, sandwich course; **introductory course,** ABC's, elementary course, elements, initiation, isagogics, propaedeutics, rudiments, three R's; **curriculum,** program, syllabus; **discipline,** area, elective, field, honours, major, minor *(U.S.)*, speciality, study; **arts,** classics, humanities, liberal arts, manual arts, quadrivium, the sciences, trivium. *See also* LESSON: LEARNING

COURTEOUS adj attentive, chivalric, chivalrous, civil, debonair, decent, decorous, fair, fair-spoken, gallant, gracious, polite, proper; **well-mannered,** civilised, couth, cultivated, mannered, mannerly, refined, tasteful, well brought up, well-behaved, well-bred, well-

courteous 122 cover

educated, well-spoken, well-tried; **gentlemanlike**, gentlemanly; **ladylike**, gentlewomanly, lady; **genteel**, euphemistic, euphemistical, gentle *(Archaic)*, mild *(Obs.)*, soft-spoken; **suave**, polished, sleek, slick, smooth, smooth-spoken, sophisticated, urbane

COURTEOUSLY *adv* attentively, chivalrously, civilly, debonairly, decently, decorously, fairly *(Obs.)*, gallantly, graciously, mannerly *(Archaic)*, politely, properly, well, with good grace; **gently**, genteelly, mildly; **suavely**, sleekly, slickly, urbanely

COURTEOUSNESS *n* decorousness, diplomacy, gentility, gentleness *(Archaic)*, graciousness, graciousness, hypocorism, mannerliness, mildness, politeness, politesse; **attentiveness**, chivalrousness, debonairness, decentness, errantry, gallantness; **suaveness**, breeding, decorum, sleekness, slickness, suavity, urbaneness, urbanity

COURTEOUS PERSON *n* cavalier, chevalier, diplomatist, gentleman, gentlewoman, lady

COURTESY *n* civility, comity, complacency *(Obs.)*, decency, good manners, manners, respect; **chivalry**, gallantry; **attentions**, attention, complacency *(Obs.)*, devoir, devoirs; **deference**, regard; **curtsy**, bob, bow, cheese *(Obs.)*, kow-tow, salaam; **salutation**, greetings, red carpet, respects, salute, welcome; **suavities**, urbanities

COURT OF LAW *n* assizes *(Brit.)*, bar, bench, board, board of enquiry, closed court, court, divan, durbar *(Indian)*, forum, inquest, judicatory, law court, open court, tribunal; **arbitration court**, Chancery *(Brit.)*, common court, Conciliation and Arbitration Commission, coroner's court, County Court, court leet *(Obs.)*, court martial, Court of Appeal, Court of Common Pleas *(Brit.)*, Court of Disputed Returns, Court of Petty Sessions, Court of Quarter Sessions, court of record, crown court *(Brit.)*, District Court, drumhead court martial, Exchequer, Family Court, high court, High Court of Australia, High Court of Justice *(Brit.)*, higher court, industrial court, inferior court, juvenile court, leet *(Obs.)*, Magistrate's Court, moot *(Obs.)*, moot court, oyer and terminer, police court, probate court, quarter sessions, sessions, Star Chamber, superior court, Supreme Court; **courthouse**, cells, courtroom, dock, judge's chambers, jury-box, witness box

COURT SESSION *n* high jump *(Colloq.)*, oyer *(Obs. Brit.)*, session, sitting, woodpeckers' day *(Prison Colloq.)*

COVER *v* face, invest, pall, throw something over, web; **shroud**, drape; **jacket**, blanket, caparison, cloak, cushion, mantle, trap *(Obs.)*, tuck, vest; **mask**, blindfold, cowl, hood; **swathe**, bandage, cocoon, enfold, enswathe, enwrap, insulate, involve, muffle, smother, swaddle; **wrap**, bundle, gift-wrap, pack, package; **bind**, fother *(Naut.)*, parcel, serve *(Naut.)*, whip; **overlay**, bespread, carpet, litter, perfuse; **line**, brattice, face, fettle, resurface, revet; **upholster**, overstuff *(Furnit.)*, trim; **roof**, canopy, cope, embower, plash, rafter, shade, shingle, thatch, tile; **grass**, loam, sod, sward, top, top-dress, topsoil, turf.

See also COAT

COVERED *adj* covert; **hooded**, cowled, cucullate, veiled; **tegminal**, tegumental; **jacketed**, armour-plated, ermined, ironclad, loricate, panoplied. *See also* COATED

COVERING *n* carpet, cladding, cloak, clothing, cover, covert, gilding, housing, involucre, mantle, overlay, pall, panoply, sheet, shroud, skin, tegmen, tegument, umbrella, veil; **sheath**, case, casing, casing shoe, jacket, scabbard, sheathing; **capsule**, husk, integument, pod, rind, seed capsule, seed vessel, shell; **hatch**, booby hatch *(Naut.)*, calash, grate, lid, shutter; **coating**, coat, crust, encrustation, film, plaque *(Dentistry)*, scale, skin; **icing**, spread, topping; **scum**, dusting, fur, fuzz, fuzziness, head *(Winemaking)*, scurf; **antimacassar**, facings, lambrequin *(Armour)*, loose cover, pall, pallium, pillow sham, runner, shower, slip cover, throwover, tidy *(U.S.)*, trim; **placemat**, damask, duchesse set, tablecloth; **drapery**, dossal *(Archaic)*, dosser, frontal, frontlet, lambrequin, scrim; **cover glass**, bell glass, bell jar, cloche, crystal, watchglass; **tea-cosy**, eggcosy

COWARD *n* chicken, chocolate soldier, cowardly custard, craven, creamer, cry-baby, dastard, dingo, faint-heart, fraidy-cat, funk, gutless wonder, milksop, nervous Nellie, niddering *(Archaic)*, poltroon, poofter, recreant, scaredy-cat, sheep, sissy, skulk, skulker, softie, sook, sop, squib, weakie, wheyface, wimp, yellow streak, yellow-belly

COWARDICE *n* baseness, cowardliness, cravenness, dastardliness, faintheartedness, fearfulness, nervelessness, poltroonery, pusillanimity, recreance, spinelessness

COWARDLY *adj* base, chicken, chicken-hearted, coward, craven, dastard, dastardly, faint, fainthearted, fearful, fearsome, frightened, gritless, gun-shy, gutless, lily-livered, mealy-mouthed, milky, nerveless, niddering *(Archaic)*, pissweak, poor, poor-spirited, pusillanimous, recreant, sooky, spineless, spiritless, tame, terrified, timid, unheroic, unknightly, unmanly, white-livered, yellow, yellow-bellied

CRACKLE *n* crackling, crepitation, decrepitation, rattle; **sputter**, fizz, fizzing, hizz, snort

CRACKLE *v* crepitate, decrepitate, fizz, fizzle, spatter, splutter, sputter

CRACKLY *adj* fizzy, snappy, sputtering, sulphury

CRAFTSMAN *n* artisan *(Obs.)*, handicraftsman, mosaicist, technician; **woodworker**, ebonist, woodcraftsman; **sculptor**, carver, modeller, sculptress; **potter**, ceramist; **metalworker**, brazier, goldsmith, silversmith; **jeweller**, lapidary; **enameller**, enamelist; **photographer**, retoucher. *See also* ARTIST; ENGRAVER

CRAMP *n* charley horse *(U.S.)*, cork knee (leg), coxalgia, sprain, stiffness, stitch, strain, subluxation, tic, writer's cramp; **slipped disc**, spondylitis, spondylolisthesis; **rheumatism**, ankylosis, arthritis, bursitis, gout, housemaid's knee, lumbago, osteoarthritis, podagra, rheumatoid arthritis, synovitis, tennis elbow, tenosynovitis, tophus; **fibrositis**, tenonitis; **repetition strain injury**, carpal tunnel syndrome, repetitive strain injury, RSI

CRANIAL *adj* auralicular, buccal, cerebral, facial, frontal, mandibular, maxillary, narial, nasal, ocular, ophthalmic, parietal, temporal; **oral**, alveolar, dental, faucal, gingival, labial, lingual, palatal, uvular, velar

CRAWLER *n* arse-licker, brown-nose, bumboy, creeping Jesus, fawner, flunkey, groveller, lackey, lickspittle *(Brit.)*, spaniel, sponger, sycophant, toady; **doormat**, earthworm, groveller, the muck of the earth, worm

CREATE *v* author, bring into being, call into being, compose, conceive, father, form, give rise to; **concoct**, brew, contrive, cook up, make up, throw together; **invent**, coin, compose, extemporise, fabricate, forge, improvise, innovate, mint, originate, toss, turn; **develop**, be responsible for, beat out, bring about, contrive, design, devise, engineer, evolve, excogitate, formulate, frame, incubate, stage, think out, think up; **establish**, constitute, found, inaugurate, institute, institutionalise, open the door to, plant, set up, stablish *(Archaic)*; **breed**, bring forth, engender, generate, germinate, ingenerate *(Archaic)*, procreate; **re-create**, re-form, recast, reconstitute, regenerate. *See also* MAKE

CREATION *n* coinage, composition, conception, cross-fertilisation, design, devisal, excogitation, fabrication, generation, genesis, innovation, invention, origin, origination, procreation, production, reproduction; **spontaneous generation**, abiogenesis, autogenesis, autogeny, continuous creation, parthenogenesis; **improvisation**, extemporisation; **establishment**, constitution, engenderment, institution; **re-creation**, destructive distillation, recast, reconstitution, reconstruction, regeneracy, regeneration. *See also* MAKING

CREATIVE *adj* excogitive, generative, groundbreaking, innovational, innovative, innovatory, inventive, omnific, original, originative, Promethean; **seminal**, primordial, procreative, productive; **industrial**, factorial, factory-like, handcrafted, handmade; **constructive**, formative, tectonic; **creational**, authorial, conceptional, genetic, institutive, parturient

CREATIVELY *adv* institutively, inventively, originally, originatively, productively; **constructively**, formatively, tectonically; **industrially**, technologically

CREATIVITY *n* creativeness, formativeness, innovation, inventiveness, originality, parturiency, productivity; **workmanship**, craftsmanship, fashion *(Obs.)*, handicraft; **authorship**, creatorship

CREATOR *n* architect, author, authoress, coiner, composer, conceiver, constituter, designer, deviser, engenderer, excogitator, fabricator, framer, generator, hatcher, inventor, original *(Archaic)*, originator, procreator, source; **maker**, artificer, artisan, builder, constituter, constructor, contriver, craftsman, developer, erecter, fabricant, fabricator, former, framer, manufacturer, producer, smith, wright; **innovator**, idea-monger, innovationist, mastermind; **founder**, establisher, father, first cause, fons et origo, fountainhead, institutor, mainspring, mother, parent, prime mover;

creator / **crowd**

improviser, extemporiser, improvisator

CRESCENT *n* half-moon, lune, lunette, lunula, meniscus, semicircle

CRIME *n* capital crime, felony, inside job, malfeasance, malversation, misdeed, misprision, racket; **crime wave**; **extortion**, collusion, collusiveness, fraud, protection racket, solicitation; **infringement**, breach, contravention, dereliction, encroachment, infraction, misdemeanour, offence, transgression, trespass; **wrong**, injury, injustice, offence, tort; **atrocity**, malpractice, outrage, war crime. *See also* UNLAWFULNESS

CRIMINAL *n* accessory, bandit, bushranger, conman, crim, crook, demon, desperado, felon, gangster, gunnie, hood, hoodlum, outlaw, principal, punk, standover man, torch; **lawbreaker**, contravener, encroacher, infractor, malfeasant, offender, trespasser; **convict**, hardnose, incorrigible *(Obs.)*, lag, old chum, old hand, prisoner of the crown, recidivist; **racketeer**, black marketeer, colluder, mobster *(U.S.)*; **Mafia**, Cosa Nostra, crime ring, family *(U.S.)*, Honourable Society; **underworld**, gangland

CROOK *n* adventurer, adventuress, corrupter, dodger, fake, faker, fraud, judas, knave, racketeer, rascal, ratbag, rogue, shark, twister, wangler, wrong 'un; **swindler**, ambidexter *(Archaic)*, bilker, chicaner, doubledealer, front man, pettifogger, sharp dealer, shicer, shyster, twicer; **cheat**, blackleg, cardsharper, cheater, gypper, gypster, kite, palmer, rook, sharp, sharper, short-changer, spieler; **self-seeker**, company politician, sycophant; **corrupt official**, bent cop, dishonest politician, jobber, security risk

CROSS *n* ankh, crosslet *(Heraldry)*, crux ansata, flyfot, swastika, tau cross, tee; **crucifix**, Celtic cross, Greek cross, Holy Rood, Jerusalem cross, Maltese cross, papal cross, Saint Andrew's Cross, Saint George's Cross, Saint Patrick's Cross, tree *(Eccles. Archaic)*; **decussation**, chiasm, chiasma, X-shape

CROSS *v* cross, cut, decussate, gauntlet *(Railways)*, intersect, overlap, traverse; **crisscross**, craze; **bestraddle**, bestride, overstride

CROSSED *adj* crisscross, crossgrained, cross-legged; **netlike**, arachnoid, clathrate, crazed, cross-grained, mesh, meshy, net, reticulate

CROSSING *n* intersection, junction, overlapping

CROSSING *adj* equitant, overlapping; **intersectional**, secant; **transversal**, athwart, cross, jessant *(Heraldry)*, thwart, transverse, traverse; **cruciform**, chiasmal, chiasmic, crucial, cruciate, decussate, tee-shaped, X-shaped

CROSSPIECE *n* buttock line *(Naut.)*, crossbar, crossbeam, crosstree, thwart, transversal, transverse, traverse

CROSSWAY *n* circus *(Brit.)*, crossstreet, crossroad, level crossing, roundabout, traffic circle

CROSSWISE *adv* crisscross, fesswise *(Heraldry)*; **transversally**, on the cross, transversely, traverse *(Obs.)*; **cruciformly**, crucially, decussately

CROWD *n* army, cohort, galaxy, host; **band**, caravan, choir, chorus, company, consort *(Obs.)*, flock *(Rare)*,

crowd 126 **cunning**

rout *(Archaic)*, squad, tribe, troop *(Rare)*, troupe; **corps**, body, brigade, phalanx, regiment; **meeting**, assembly, jamboree, mass meeting, muster, parade, rally, unlawful assembly; **congregation**, communion, ecclesia, parish council, vestry; **reception**, audience, durbar, levee

CROWDED *adj* mobbish, multitudinous *(Poetic)*, serried, thronged; **congregational**, colonial, convocational

CRUCIAL MOMENT *n* appropriate moment, climacteric, crisis, high time, moment of truth, one's hour, psychological moment, the fullness of time, tide *(Archaic)*, turning point, watershed; **deadline**, crunch *(Colloq.)*, crux, eleventh hour, last minute, term day; **time**, day, hour, minute, moment, opportunity, turn

CRY *n* bawl, blubber, boohoo, howl, snivel, sob, wail, weep, whimper, whine; **keen**, croon *(Scot. Irish)*, ululation; **groan**, sigh

CUDGEL *v* baste, bastinado, drub, fustigate *(Archaic)*, pistol-whip; **bludgeon**, blackjack, club, cosh, sledge, sledge-hammer, truncheon, waddy; **belt**, cane, ferule, pandy *(Scot.)*, strap, welt; **whip**, birch, breech *(Archaic)*, cat, cowhide *(U.S.)*, cut, flagellate, flail, flog, horse *(Obs.)*, horsewhip, knout, lash, leather, scourge, scratch, see (someone's) backbone, slash, swinge *(Archaic)*, swish, switch, taw *(Obs.)*, thresh; **pelt**, catapult, lapidate, pebble, pellet, pip. *See also* HIT: BEAT

CULTISM *n* cargo cult, dendrolatry, divinisation, druidism, fertility cult, fetishism, firewalking, heliolatry, hero-worship *(Antiq.)*, idolism, Magianism, paganism, phallicism, ritualism, shamanism, sun-dance, sun-worship; **Satanism**, black mass, demonism, demonolatry, diabolism; **snake-worship**, ophiolatry, zombiism; **zoolatry**, animal worship; **Rastafarianism**

CULTIVATED *adj* a cut above, appreciative, Attic, cultured, discriminating, educated, fine, polished, polite, refined, seemly, well-bred; **aesthetic**, aesthetical, delicate, exquisite, pretty *(Archaic)*, rarefactive, sensitive

CUNNING *n* art, artifice, chicanery, craft, double-dealing, finesse, gimmickry, guile, guilefulness, hanky-panky, Jesuitism, Jesuitry, Machiavellianism, Machiavellism, nimbleness, sharp practice, subtleness, subtlety, supersubtlety, trickery; **machination**, engineering, enginery, insinuation, manipulation, politicking; **politics**, fancy footwork, intrigue, manoeuvring, strategy; **craftiness**, archness, cleverness, deviousness, diabolicalness, insidiousness, shiftiness, slyness, trickiness, trickishness, tricksiness, wiliness, wryness; **astuteness**, cuteness, knowingness, sharpness, shrewdness

CUNNING *adj* calculating, diabolic, diabolical, guileful, insidious, insinuative, Machiavellian, mephistophelian, subtle, supersubtle, wily; **crafty**, artful, artificial *(Obs.)*, carney, clever, cute, daedal *(Poetic)*, deep, deep-laid, devious, dodgy, hard-headed, Jesuitical, nimble, serpentine, slim *(Obs.)*, smart, wry; **astute**, all there, fly *(Colloq.)*, foxy, sharp, shrewd; **underhand**, arch, leery, shifty, sleeky, slick, sly, spivvy, weaselly; **trick**, catchy, gimmicky, rorty, trickish, tricksy, tricky; **diversionary**, distracting, feinting; **politic**, manipulative, strategic

CUNNING PERSON *n* artful dodger, bag of tricks, dodger, Jesuit, shrewdie, wangler; **con man**, bluffer, con woman, entrapper, faker, fraud, rorter, spiv; **machinator**, carpetbagger *(U.S.)*, downy bird, insinuator, political animal, shaver; **fox**, duckshover, finagler, gamesman, serpent, slyboots, trepan *(Archaic)*, trepanner, tricker, trickster, weasel; **cheat**, cardsharp, double-dealer, sharper; **intriguer**, plotter, politician, schemer

CUPBOARD *n* almery *(Archaic)*, ambry *(Archaic)*, armoire, base unit, bookcase, cabinet, cellaret, chiffonier, china cabinet, closet, cocktail cabinet, corner cabinet, display unit, filing cabinet, glory hole, hutch, kitchen cupboard, larder, linen closet, linen cupboard, locker, medicine cabinet, pantry, press, safe, wall unit, Welsh dresser; **sideboard**, buffet, credence, credenza, dresser; **wardrobe**, built-in wardrobe, clothes cupboard, clothes press, garderrobe *(Archaic)*, lowboy, robe, tallboy, walk-in wardrobe; **chest of drawers**, chiffonier, dressing-table, glory box, hope chest

CURIOSITY *n* curiousness, inquisitiveness, nosiness

CURIOUS *adj* agog, inquiring, questioning; **inquisitive**, nosy, prying, rubberneck

CURL *n* braid, crimp, crimps, frizz, frizzle, ringlet; **permanent wave**, cold wave, marcel; **curler**, braider, crimper, crisper, frizzler

CURRENCY *n* exchange, floating currency, foreign currency, foreign exchange, forward exchange, fractional currency, managed currency; **standard**, bimetallism, gold bullion standard, gold standard, gold-exchange standard, monometallism, silver standard, symmetallism; **sterling**, decimal currency, Eurodollars, gold reserve, petrodollars; **mintage**, monetisation. *See also* CASH; COINAGE

CURRENT *n* backwash, bombora, countercurrent, cross-current, drift, ebb and flow, flood, flux, overfall, rip, tidal current, tide-rip, underset, undertow; **tide**, dodge tide, ebb tide, flood tide, half-tide, high tide, lee tide, low tide, low water, neap, neap tide, rip-tide, spring tide; **flash flood**, eustatic movement, freshet, stormwater, tidal wave; **surge**, disemboguement, ground swell, surf, wash; **race**, millrace, millrun, tide-race, tideway; **eddy**, maelstrom, vortex, whirlpool. *See also* FLOW; STREAM; SPRING

CURRENT *adj* live *(Broadcasting)*, now happening, passing, present, running; **immediate**, instant, latest; **existing**, actual; **contemporary**, current, living, modern-day, present-day, rife; **modern**, in fashion, up-to-date, up-to-the-minute, up-to-the-moment, with-it

CURRIER *n* fellmonger, flesher, skinner

CURRIERY *n* skinnery, tannery

CURSED *adj* accursed, b., bally, blamed *(U.S.)*, blank *(euph.)*, blankety, blasted, bleeding, bloody, blooming *(euph.)*, buggered, confounded, cussed, damned, darned, doggone *(U.S.)*, dratted, f'ing, flaming, frigging, fucking, plurry

CURVATURE *n* arcuation, bent, concaveness, concavity, convexity, convexness, curvedness, spiling; **curling**, assurgency, curl, flexure, incurvation, incurvature, resupination, retroflexion; **waviness**, damascene, damask, sinuosity

CURVATURE OF THE SPINE *n* crouchback *(Archaic)*, gibbousness, hunchback, kyphosis, roach back, scoliosis, stoop, sway-back

CURVE *n* arc, bow, camber, crispation, roll, scallop, scoop, undulation, wave; **arithmetic curve**, cardioid, catenary, cissoid, conchoid, conic section, cycloid, envelope *(Geom.)*, epicycloid, folium, geodesic line, gradient *(Physics)*, hyperbola, hypocycloid, locus, parabola, quadrant, rhumb, segment, sine wave, sinusoid, synergic curve, trajectory, trochoid; **caustic**, catacaustic, diacaustic; **figure 8**, lemniscate; **bend**, bight, flexure, gooseneck, heel *(Golf)*, inflection, inturn, offset, ogee, quirk, S-bend, sheer, sigmoid flexure, swan neck, turn, twist; **loop**, hank, picot; **horseshoe**, U-bolt; **hook**, crook, crotchet, falx, fleshhook, sickle, uncinus, uncus

CURVE *v* arch, bend, bow, camber, curl, flex, hog, incurve, loop, overarch, sag, stoop, sweep, turn; **recurve**, retroflect; **hook**, crook, incurvate; **wave**, scallop, undulate

CURVED *adj* bent, bow, bowed, bowlike, cambered, incurvate, loopy, saddle-backed, sigmoid; **U-shaped**, horseshoe; **hooked**, crooked, crotchety, falcate, falciform, hamate, hooky, quirky, scorpioid, unciform, uncinate; **convex**, biconcave, biconvex, concave, lenticular; **crescent**, horned, lunar, lunarian, lunate, lunular, lunulate, meniscoid, semilunar; **heart-shaped**, bell-shaped, cordate, flabellate, pear-shaped; **semicircular**, hemicyclic, semielliptical

CURVEDLY *adv* fully, wavily; **convexly**, archwise, concavely

CURVILINEAR *adj* conchoidal, epicycloidal, hypocycloidal; **geodesic**, caustic, geodetic, toric, toroidal; **wavy**, damascene, gyrose, repand, undulative, undulatory, wavelike; **parabolic**, catenarian, catenary, hyperbolic, paraboloidal, sinusoidal, trochoidal; **blunt**, lobate, obtuse; **recurvate**, assurgent, resupinate, retroflex, retroussé, revolute, tip-tilted, turned up

CUSTOM *n* common practice, constitution, consuetude, convention, established custom, habit, habitude, institute, institution, matter of course, practice, praxis, second nature, usage, usance *(Obs.)*, usual practice, wont; **routine**, beaten track, daily grind, daily round, groove, rut, the ordinary, the usual; **protocol**, etiquette, good form, manners, the done thing; **mores**, the conventionalities, the proprieties, ways; **tradition**, culture, culture complex *(Sociol.)*, folklore, folkways, survival, unwritten law, way of our forebears; **procedure**, manner, mode, way, way of doing things; **ceremony**, ceremonial, observance, rite, rite of passage, ritual

CUSTOMARILY *adv* as a rule, generally, in general, ordinarily, regularly, usually; **habitually**, by force of habit, by habit, inveterately, wontedly; **as usual**, according to habit, as can be expected

CUSTOMARINESS *n* accustomedness, generalness, normality, ordinariness, regularity, staidness, triteness, usual-

customariness   129   **cutter**

ness; **habitualness**, inveteracy, inveterateness, wontedness

CUSTOMARY *adj* accustomed, consuetudinary, habitual, habituated, usual, wonted *(Archaic)*; **traditional**, accepted, conventional, time-honoured, traditive; **approved**, de rigueur, established, recognised, settled; **regular**, common, commonplace, general, normal, ordinary, stock; **stereotyped**, clichéd, hackneyed, trite, unoriginal; **rooted in tradition**, folkloristic, passed on by word of mouth, unwritten

CUT *n* gash, incision, kerf, laceration, lancination, score, scotch, slash, slit, snick, snip, stab, tear; **notch**, box, chip, cleft, crenature, crop, dap, gain, hack, incisure, indent, indentation, nock, undercut; **scarification**, chatter marks, graze, scoring; **cross-section**, crosscut, exsection, microtomy, section, transection; **haircut**, Dad'n'Dave, shave; **shear**, long blow, second cut

CUT *v* bite into, chine, gash, gride, heckle, knife, lance, prick, scissor, scotch, shear *(Archaic)*, slit, snip, tool, trench *(Obs.)*, vivisect; **sliver**, dice, flitch, hash, mince, ribbon; **axe**, adze, chip, chop, swing kelly, tomahawk; **fell**, clear-cut, clear-fell, coppice, hew, knock down *(N.Z.)*, log, poll, pollard; **scratch**, carbonado, claw, crimp, graze, hack, hackle, overscore, raze *(Obs.)*, scarify, score, scribe; **ringbark**, girdle; **notch**, blaze, chase, crenel, crenellate, gain, indent, jag, nick, nock, pink, serrate, snick, trench, undercut; **slice**, cross-section, crosscut, section, skive, thickness, transect; **saw**, break down, crosscut, lumber, quartersaw, rip, stave, whipsaw; **carve**, chisel, engrave, etch, gouge, grave *(Archaic)*, incise, rough-hew, whittle; **thread**, die, rifle, tap; **mutilate**, give someone a facial, grangerise, lacerate, mangle, rip, slash; **barber**, cut, poll, scalp, shingle; **mow**, head, make hay, reap, scythe; **shear**, barrow, channel, dag, razor, shave, undress; **clip**, abscind, bang, bobtail, crop, curtail, cut short, disbranch, guillotine, hog, pinch, poll, prune, sever, trim; **whittle**, edge, snig; **cut out**, excide, excise, exscind, exsect; **bevel**, cant, chamfer, countersink, facet, rake; **circumcise**, decerebrate, resect; **behead**, decapitate

CUT *adj* cleft, cloven, incised; **clipped**, trimmed; **diced**, brunoise, fine-cut, julienne; **carved**, carven *(Poetic)*, chiselled, engraved, graven, step-cut, table-cut; **clear-cut**, clear-felled

CUT OFF *v* amputate, decapitate, dehorn, head, mutilate, pinion, poll, tail; **disembowel**, eviscerate, exenterate, gut; **epilate**, depilate, shave; **sterilise**, alter, castrate, de-sex, deknacker, do, doctor, emasculate, geld, mark, spay, unman. *See also* SUBTRACT

CUTTER *n* cheese-cutter, cigar-cutter, glass-cutter, guillotine, microtome; **cutting machine**, burr, capstan lathe, chaser, chipper, decapitator, dicer, die, lathe, machine tool, milling machine, mincer, scarificator, scarifier, scorer, skiver tap; **mower**, header, lawn-mower, mowing machine, reaper, reaping machine, slasher. *See also* AXE; KNIFE; SAW; SCISSORS; CHISEL

CUTTING *n* bushing, clipping, mowing, pruning, rod pruning, xylotomy; **severance,** curtailment, decapitation, decerebration, dissection, disseverance, disseveration, disseverment; **carving,** engraving, rifling, tapping, trepanation, turnery, whittling; **surgery,** abscission, amputation, circumcision, excision, microsurgery, necrotomy, nephrotomy, vivisection; **timber-getting,** bush bashing, bush-falling, clear-felling, logging, lumbering

CUTTING *adj* slashing; **jagged,** jaggy, lacerate, lacerated, laciniate, retuse; **scissile,** cleavable, dissectible, fellable, lacerable, sectile, severable

CUTTINGLY *adv* incisively, keenly, sharply

Dd

DAILY *adj* diurnal, quotidian; **dawn,** auroral; **morning,** antemeridian, breakfast-time, forenoon, matin, matutinal, midmorning; **midday,** lunchtime, meridian, noonday; **afternoon,** postmeridian

DAILY *adv* all day, diurnally, morning noon and night, overday; **a.m.,** ante meridiem; **p.m.,** post meridiem

DAM *n* conduit, floodgate, gate, levee, lock, lock-gate, penstock, retaining wall, revetment, sluice, sluicegate, spillway, tide-gate, water-gate, weir

DAMAGE *n* defacement, disablement, disfeaturement, disfigurement, ill-treatment, molestation; **wounding,** concision, forging *(Horseracing),* maiming, mutilation; **wreckage,** arson, breakage, ruination, sabotage, vandalism, wreck; **wear,** wear and tear; **disrepair,** brokenness, disruption, rack and ruin, ruin, ruination, unsoundness; **shabbiness,** dilapidation, raggedness, seediness, worminess, wornness. *See also* HARM; INJURY

DAMAGE *v* annoy, damnify, grangerise, hack, ill-treat, ill-use, impair, mar, pinch, play hell with, play the devil with, prejudice, scathe *(Archaic),* vandalise, vex *(Archaic),* wrong; **devastate,** eat, ravage, smite; **undermine,** put the skids under, sabotage, white-ant. *See also* INJURE; BREAK; SPOIL

DAMAGED *adj* broken, buggered, bung, bust, busted, cactus, clapped-out, cracked, defective, disrupt, disserviceable, foxy, fucked, impaired, in dock, kaput, no good to Gundy, on the blink, on the fritz, on the skids, on the turn, out of joint, out of order, pakaru *(N.Z.),* R.S., ratshit, ruined, worn-out; **unsound,** affected, sick, stricken, unhealthy. *See also* INJURED; DILAPIDATED

DAMAGER *n* blinder, maimer, mangler, molester, mutilator, ravager, ruiner, vandal, wrecker; **spoiler,** adulterator, contaminator, tarnisher, vitiator; **saboteur,** marplot, underminer

DANCE *n* ball, fandango, formal, knees-up, prom *(U.S.),* ridotto; **barndance,** b. and s., country dance, hoedown, hop, moondance, square dance, woolshed hop; **breakdance,** rapdance; **routine,** phrase, set

DANCE *v* cut a rug *(U.S. Colloq.),* dance the night away, frisk, have a bop, hoof it, hop, jig, prance, shuffle, tread, trip, trip the light fantastic; **jive,** bop, bump and grind, frug, jazz, jitterbug, rock, shimmy, stomp, twist; **foxtrot,** cakewalk, dosido, mambo, polka, square-dance, tango, twostep, waltz; **pirouette,** balance, chassé, glissade, promenade, set; **breakdance,** break, rapdance, rap; **choreograph**

DANCE HALL *n* ballroom, disco, discotheque, palais de danse

DANCER *n* belly dancer, breakdancer, frisker, glider, go-go girl, hoofer *(U.S.),* jitterbug, prancer, rapdancer, rope-dancer, shuffler, square-dancer, stripper, tangoist, tap-dancer, terpsichorean, wiredancer; **ballet-dancer,** ballerina, corps de ballet, coryphée,

dancer danseur, danseuse, figurant, figurante; **partner,** gigolo, taxi dancer *(U.S.);* **choreographer,** choreologist, dance arranger

DANCING *n* ballet, ballroom dancing, belly dancing, breaking, breakdancing, disco dancing, eurhythmics, exhibition dancing, flamenco, jazz dance, light fantastic, modern dance, nautch *(India)*, rapdancing, rapping, street dancing, tap dancing, wiredancing; **folk dancing,** bush dancing, clogdancing, morris dancing, square dancing; **caper,** frisk, gambol, leap, saltation, skip; **choreography,** choreology

DANGER *n* a matter of life and death, jeopardy, peril; **risk,** adventure *(Obs.)*, chance, venture *(Archaic);* **threat,** dynamite, menace, shadow, sword of Damocles; **hazard,** a trap for young players, awkwardness, hot seat, hot spot, pit, pitfall, predicament, three-day night; **trap,** black spot *(Brit.)*, deathtrap, fire hazard, fire risk, firetrap, snorter, vigia; **minefield,** no-man's-land

DANGEROUS *adj* critical, forbidding, parlous, perilous, precarious, touch-and-go, unhealthy, unsafe; **risky,** awkward, chancy, dicey, equilibristic, hard-hat, hazardous, kittle *(Brit.)*, touchy, tropical *(Colloq.)*, unreliable, venturesome; **ominous,** imminent, malignant, menacing, serious, threatening; **suicidal,** breakneck, desperate, Kamikaze

DANGEROUSLY *adv* adventurously, critically, desperately, ominously, parlously, perilously, precariously; **riskily,** at hazard, awkwardly, hazardously, on the spot, on thin ice, venturously; **threateningly,** forbiddingly, malignantly, menacingly; **vulnerably,** indefensibly, insecurely, unguardedly, unwarily

DANGEROUSNESS *n* chanciness, criticalness, desperateness, forbiddingness, imperilment, ominousness, perilousness, precariousness, seriousness, venturesomeness; **endangerment,** imperilment, obnoxiousness; **weak spot,** Achilles heel, chink in one's armour, hazardousness, incertitude, insecurity, soft underbelly

DARK *n* moonset, night, the dead of night; **nightfall,** crepuscule, dusk, evening, gloaming, half-light, sundown, sunset, twilight; **eclipse,** annular eclipse, lunar eclipse, solar eclipse, total eclipse; **blackout,** brownout, dim-out *(U.S.)*, lights out, outage

DARK *adj* aphotic, benighted, cimmerian, darkling *(Poetic)*, darksome *(Poetic)*, lightless, midnight, obscurant, obscure, pitch-dark, rayless, starless, stygian, thick; **dark-coloured,** black, blackish, dusky, grey, infuscate *(Entomol.)*, pitchy, sable *(Poetic)*, sooty, swart, swarthy; **ecliptic,** blackout, blinding, ecliptical, opaque, umbral. *See also* SHADOWY

DARKEN *v* blacken, dark *(Obs.)*, embrown, opaque; **become dark,** darkle, dim, dusk, fade, fog, grow dark, lour; **obscure,** adumbrate, becloud, blind, blot, cloud, cover, eclipse, obfuscate, overcast, overcloud, overshade, overshadow; **black out,** brown out, turn down the lights, turn out the lights; **shade,** crosshatch, hatch, shadow, silhouette

DARKENER *n* blackener, dimmer, eclipser, fader, opaque; **blind,** blinder, holland blind, jalousie, shade, venetian, venetian blind; **sunglasses**, dark glasses, polaroids, shades

DARKENING *n* obfuscation, obscuration, occultation, overshadowing, shadowing; **shading**, chiaroscuro *(Painting)*, crosshatching, hatching

DARKLY *adv* blackly, greyly; **in the dark**, darkling *(Poetic)*, in the shadows; ecliptically, blindingly; dimly, duskily; **murkily**, cloudily, foggily, loweringly, smokily, **obscurely**, opaquely

DARKNESS *n* blackness, gloom, greyness, pitchiness, sootiness; **opacity**, obscureness, obscurity, opaqueness; **shadiness**, sunlessness, umbrageousness; **dimness**, bleariness, cloudiness, dullness, duskiness, sombreness; **murkiness**, dirtiness, fogginess, mistiness, smokiness. *See also* SHADE

DAYDREAMER *n* doodler, stargazer, wool-gatherer

DEAD *adj* breathless *(Archaic)*, cold, dead as a dodo, dead as a doornail, deceased, defunct, departed, done for, exanimate, fallen, gone, inanimate, lifeless, no more, parted *(Archaic)*, stillborn, stone-cold, stone-dead; **deceased**, lamented, late, mourned, regretted, sainted; **asleep**, at rest; **mortal**, ephemeral, perishable, short-lived, transitory; **doomed**, condemned to death, done for, fey; **dying**, far gone, moribund, sick unto death; **drowned**, asphyxiate, frozen, strangled, suffocated; **extinct**, defunct, moribund

DEADLY *adj* deathful, deathly, fatal, fateful, feral *(Archaic)*, lethal, malignant, mortal, sublethal, terminal

DEAF *adj* deaf and dumb, deaf as a doorpost, deaf as a post, deaf-mute, hard of hearing, stone-deaf, tone-deaf; **deafened**, unable to hear; **deaf to**, not listening, unhearing

DEAFNESS *n* anacusis, deaf-mutism, faulty hearing, tone-deafness; **deaf person**, deaf-mute

DEAL FAIRLY *v* deal honestly, do justice to, right, see that justice is done; **give someone a go**, give a person his due, give someone a break, give someone a fair go, give the devil his due; **play the game**, be a sport

DEATH *n* biolysis, curtains, decease, demise *(Obs.)*, depart *(Obs.)*, departure *(Archaic)*, dissolution, dying, end, ending, expiration *(Obs.)*, great divide, megadeath, mort *(Obs.)*, one's hour, parting, release, sticky end, supreme sacrifice, time, utterance *(Obs.)*; **lifelessness**, cadaverousness, coldness, deadness, defunctness, exanimation, inanimateness, moribundity, mortification, rigor mortis; **asphyxiation**, brain death, cot death, crucifixion, euthanasia, famishment, martyrdom, natural death, race suicide, starvation, stillbirth, strangulation, sudden-death syndrome, suicide; **doom**, bane, fate, Götterdämmerung, sentence of death; **Death**, the grim reaper; **death's-head**, black, crossbones, marrowbones, skull and crossbones; **dance of death**, danse macabre; **deathwatch**, death bell, death knell, passing bell, wake; **death throes**, death-rattle, deathbed, dying day, last agony, last gasp (breath), last hour, last words, swan song; **death-wish**, thanatophobia, thanatopsis;

death 134 **decorative**

necromania, necrophilia, necrophilism, necrophobia

DEATHLIKE *adj* biolytic, deathful, deathly, funeral, ghastly, macabre; **corpselike,** cadaveric, cadaverous; **posthumous,** defunctive, post-mortem, post-obit

DEBT *n* a dead horse, a dog tied up, bad debt, book debt, debit, debt of honour, deficit, funded debt, interminable debt, national debt, outstanding account, set-off *(Finance);* **liability,** charges, current liabilities, dues, fixed liability, insury, interest; **credit,** advance, house loan, mortgage, overdraft, personal loan, second mortgage; **hire-purchase,** H.P., lay-by, never-never. *See also* BILL

DEBTOR *n* arrestee, bankrupt, borrower, contributory, defaulter, garnishee, mortgagee

DECEITFUL *adj* crafty, deceptive, delusive, devious, dishonest, dissimulative, double, double-faced, double-tongued, fast, fraudulent, hollow, insidious, Janus-faced, lying, mendacious, misleading, mythomaniac, tortuous, two-faced, untruthful; **hypocritical,** pharasaical, sanctimonious; **plausible,** disingenuous, evasive, fast-talking, insincere, smooth, tricksy; **unfaithful,** double-dealing, perfidious, two-timing; **perjured,** forsworn

DECISIVELY *adv* earnestly, in earnest, resolvedly, seriously, stably, steadfastly, steadily; **resolutely,** immovably, risoluto *(Music),* single-mindedly, unbendingly, uncompromisingly; **wilfully,** wantonly

DECOLOURANT *n* blancher, bleacher, decolouriser, diluter; **bleach,** chlorine, hydrogen peroxide, oxalic acid

DECORATE *v* adorn, beautify, boss, embellish, enrich, frost, furbish, garnish, mould, ornament, titivate; **array,** apparel *(Archaic),* bedeck, bedight *(Archaic),* bedizen, bespangle, deck, dight *(Archaic),* dress up, prank, preen, primp, tire *(Archaic),* trim; **bejewel,** bespangle, powder, set, stud; **overelaborate,** pansy up, tart up; **pattern,** detail, dice, figure, trace, vermiculate, wreathe; **festoon,** dress ship, flag; **pink,** engrail

DECORATION *n* adornment, beautification, bedecking, blazonry, decor, embellishment, embossment, encrustation, enrichment, figure, frost, frostwork, garnish, garnishment, garniture, moiré, motif, openwork, ornament, ornamentation, pattern, pride *(Archaic);* **figuration,** arabesque, cuspidation, foliation, gammadion, toreutics, vermiculation; **decorativeness,** ornamentality; **floridness,** floridity, overelaborateness, overelaboration; **interior decoration,** paperhanging; **bunting,** Christmas tree, festoonery, paperchain, streamer; **pokerwork,** pyrography; **scroll,** curlicue, flourish, quirk, volute; **fretwork,** fret, meander, scrollwork; **iron lace;** **centrepiece,** epergne; **figurehead,** fiddlehead

DECORATIVE *adj* Christmassy, dressy, elaborate, embroidered, fancy, fine, frosted, highly-wrought, non-functional, ornamental, rich, worked, wrought; **florid,** alhambresque, baroque, clinquant, luxuriant, ornate, overelaborate, overwrought, platersque, rococo, trumpery; **bannered,** beribboned, cockaded; **annular,** floriated, foliate, foliated, geometric, multifoil, runic; **enamelled,** champlevé, cloisonné; **gilt,** chrysel-

decorative   **defaulter**

ephantine, gilded, gilt-edged, ormolu; **cut**, engraved, glyptic, incised, step-cut, toreutic, trap-cut; **fluted**, repoussé; **inlaid**, inwrought

DECORATIVELY *adv* adorningly, dressily, glitteringly, ornamentally, richly; **luxuriantly**, floridly, over-elaborately

DECORATOR *n* adorner, beautifier, detailer, dresser, embellisher, garnisher; **interior decorator**, interior designer, paperer, paperhanger; **carver**, embosser, engraver, medallist; **jeweller**, enameller, enamellist, goldsmith, silversmith

DECREASE *n* abatement, contraction, damping, decrement, depletion, detumescence, diminution, lessening, maceration, miniaturisation, minimisation, reduction, shrinkage, shrinking, taper; **depreciation**, break, cut, deflation, devaluation, discount, disinflation, drop, markdown, sag, subtraction; **mitigation**, alleviation, attenuation, extenuation; **decline**, downswing, downturn, ebb, fall, subsidence, wane; **abridgment**, abbreviation, curtailment; **cutback**, depression, recession, redundancy, retrenchment, short-time, the axe

DECREASE *v* abate, bate, diminish, lessen, lower, miniaturise, minify, minimise, reduce; **depreciate**, belittle, bring down, deflate, degrade, derogate, devalue, discount, down-value, downgrade, hammer, laugh away, laugh off, lower, make little of, mark down, play down, pooh-pooh, pull down, sink; **mitigate**, allay, alleviate, ease, extenuate, moderate; **weaken**, attenuate, damp, depress, dilute, relax, slack, underdamp *(Physics)*; **shorten**, abridge, axe, cut, precis; **cut back**, downsize, draw one's horns in, pare, prune, pull one's horns in, retrench, scale down, scant, slash, step down, taper, whittle, whittle down, wind down; **shrink**, contract, sanforise *(Textiles)*. See also WANE

DECREASED *adj* diminished, less, lesser, miniature, miniaturised, under; **reduced**, abridged, censored, cut, expurgated, watered-down

DECREASING *adj* decrescent, detumescent, dwindling, reducing, waning; **depreciative**, deflationary, depreciatory; **mitigatory**, alleviant, alleviative, extenuatory, mitigative

DECREASINGLY *adv* diminishingly; **less**, at a discount, down, off, under; **on the wane**, at low ebb, decrescendo, in decline, less and less

DEED *n* articles, escrow, guarantee, indent, indenture, instrument, memorandum, memorandum of association, specialty *(Law)*, statute, submission *(Law)*, trust deed, written contract; **article**, clause, condition, condition precedent, condition subsequent, consideration *(Law)*, provision, small print, stipulation; **escalation clause**, escalator clause, exclusion clause *(Insurance)*, habendum, reddendum, roll-over provision, wet-weather clause. *See also* CONTRACT

DEEP *adj* abysmal, abyssal, bottomless, cavernous, profound, unsounded, yawning

DEEPLY *adv* profoundly

DEFAULTER *n* absconder, bankrupt, bilker, dishonourer, fly-by-night, insolvent, scaler, stag *(Stock Exchange)*, welsher, wife starver

DEFEAT v afflict *(Obs.)*, annihilate, break, come all over, conquer, dish up, do for, go through like a dose of salts, go through like a packet of salts, overcome, overmaster, overthrow, overturn, overwhelm, piss all over, piss over, prostrate, rout, shit all over, slaughter, subdue, subjugate, take by storm, tame, triumph over, whelm *(Archaic)*; **beat,** beat the stuffing out of, beat the tripe out of, clobber, do like a dinner, down, drub, fight down, floor, give someone Bondi *(Obs.)*, knock into a cocked hat, knock someone bandy, knock the bejesus out of, knock the bottom out of, knock the stuffing out of, pulverise, punish, thrash, towel, trim *(U.S. Colloq.)*, trounce, wallop, whop; **checkmate,** confute, euchre, master, mate, outargue, outplay, outstare, shoot down, stump, whipsaw *(U.S.);* **stop,** foil *(Archaic)*, ignore *(U.S. Law)*, upset; **best,** better, bowl over, bump, dismiss, donkey-lick, get ahead of, get the best of, get the drop on, have the best of, have the drop on, knock off, knock spots off, lick, outbox, peg *(Baseball)*, polish off, roll, shout down, skunk *(U.S. Colloq.)*, whip *(U.S. Colloq.)*, whitewash, wipe the floor with, worst

DEFEATER n bester, conqueror, conquistador, drubber, subjugator

DEFECATE v bog, cack, choke a darkie, crap, crash, do a job, drop a darkie, evacuate, lay an egg, loosen, move the bowels, open the bowels, pass, pass excrement, see a man about a dog, see a man about a job, shit; **go to the toilet,** be caught short, kangaroo, spend a penny, visit aunty, visit Mary

DEFECATION n big jobs, bog, business, crash, Edgar Britt, evacuation, jobbies, movement, number two, passage, shit; **faeces,** blind mullet, business, cack, crap, darkie, egesta, faecal pellets, gruff nuts, Henry the Third, meconium, motion, ordure, poo, poop, Richard the Third, scat, shit, stool, turd, weenies; **scatology,** coprology. See also DUNG

DEFECT v change one's allegiance, change one's mind, change one's spots, change one's tune, do an about-face, go back on one's word, renege, sing a different tune, sing another tune, tergiversate, unthink, unwill; **see the light,** change one's ways, convert, go over, go straight, mend one's ways, regenerate, repent, turn, turn over a new leaf; **apostatise,** fall away, renegade, throw over; **err,** fall from grace, fall into evil ways, go to the bad, turn away from God

DEFECTION n about-face, apostasy, backsliding, change of allegiance, changeover, desertion, renunciation, secession, transfer *(Football)*, treason, turnabout; **conversion,** proselytism, rebirth, redemption, reformation, regeneracy, regeneration, renascence; **rehabilitation,** re-education, reconditioning, repatriation; **brainwashing,** alienation, indoctrination

DEFECTOR n apostate, deserter, renegade, reneger, transfer *(Football)*, turncoat; **tergiversator,** acrobat, tergiversant; **convert,** born-again, catechumen, changed person, disciple, neophyte, new man, new woman, novice, proselyte; **degenerate,** sinner

DEFENCE n resistance, security, self-defence, self-preservation, self-protection; **protection,** armour, buffer, bulwark, safeguard, shield; **civil defence,** national service; **defence policy,** Fortress Australia, forward defence, scorched earth policy; **air cover,** air picket, umbrella; **barrage,** balloon barrage, flak, screen, smokescreen; **early warning system,** dumaresq, radar

DEFEND *v* fence, fend *(Archaic),* forfend, stand up for, take someone's part; **entrench,** dig in, retrench, sap, trench; **barricade,** bulwark, crenellate, embattle *(Archaic),* fortress *(Rare),* garrison, palisade, rampart, rearm, stockade; **repel,** ward off; **be on the defensive,** man, steel oneself

DEFENDED *adj* armed, armoured, bastioned, battlemented, entrenched, fortified, protected, walled; **defendable,** bombproof, bullet-proof, defensible, proof; **alerted,** warned; **defensive,** protective

DEFENDER *n* bastion, champion, crusader, protector; **sentry,** bodyguard, coast-watcher, lifeguard, sentinel; **army reserve,** Dad's army, Home Guard; **deliverer,** rescuer, saviour

DEFER *v* adjourn, carry over, continue *(Law),* count out *(Brit.),* enlarge *(Law),* hold over, postpone, prorogue, put off, put over *(U.S.),* remit, sleep on it, suspend, wait *(Colloq.);* **retard,** hold up, leg-rope

DEFERMENT *n* abeyance, adjournment, continuance *(Law),* deferral, postponement, raincheck, respite

DEFERRED *adj* abeyant, adjourned, postponed, prorogued, suspended

DEFERRER *n* delayer, postponer, procrastinator, tarrier; **detainer,** retarder

DEFIANTLY *adv* antagonistically, eyeball to eyeball, in someone's teeth, in the teeth of the wind, insurrectionally, obstructively, perversely, rebelliously, resistently, tauntingly; **combatively,** militantly; **controversially,** argumentatively, cantankerously, contentiously, disputatiously, divisively, protestingly, quarrelsomely; **contrariwise,** au contraire, by contraries, con, contrarily, crosswise *(U.S.),* incompatibly; **unyieldingly,** implacably, irreconcilably, persistently, unshrinkingly

DEFICIENCY *n* default, defect, deficit, depletion, insufficiency, lack, missing link, need, omission, requirement, shortage, shortcoming, shortfall, want, wantage; **incompleteness,** incompletion, incomprehensiveness; **perfunctoriness,** paucity, scrappiness, sketchiness, superficiality

DEFICIENT *adj* half-and-half, in short supply, insufficient, meagre, out of, rationed, short, short of, strapped for, wanting; **incomplete,** bitty, fragmental, fragmentary, imperfect, incomprehensive, on the anvil, perfunctory, scant, scrappy, sketchy, superficial, touch-and-go; **unfinished,** cut short, partial, truncated, uncompleted; **unaccomplished,** blank, unbegun, undone, unexecuted, unfinalised, unrealised; **rudimentary,** abortive

DEFICIENTLY *adv* by halves, imperfectly, incompletely, partially, partly, rudimentarily, scrappily, sketchily

DEFLECT *v* deviate, perturb *(Astron.);* **reflect,** backscatter, refract; **hook,** cut, edge, seam, slice, swing; **deviate,** depart from, digress, divagate, diverge, fly off at a tangent, pull over, sheer,

deflect

shunt, sidetrack, turn off; **sidle**, move aside, oblique *(Mil.)*

DEFLECTION *n* aberration, declension, departure, deviation, digression, divergence, excursion, perturbation *(Astron.)*, variation *(Astron.)*; **reflection**, backscatter *(Physics)*, refraction, refringence; **diversion**, circumvention, circumvolution, divagation, indirection

DEFLECTIVE *adj* aberrant, aberrational, deviating, divergent, inflective, sideward, sideways, tangential, transverse, veering; **refractive**, reflectional, refractional, refringent; **indirect**, anfractuous, circuitous, circular, circumventive, devious, diversionary, doglegged, errant, erratic, roundabout, sinuous, tortuous, twisting, winding, wry; **off-course**, askew, oblique, sharp, skew, squiffy, straggly, wide

DEFLECTIVELY *adv* across, aside, athwart, athwartships, away, collaterally, divergently, obliquely, off, sidelong, sideward, sidewards, sideways, transversely; **astray**, afield, agley *(Scot.)*, awry, indirectly, off the track, off to billyo, off to buggery, wide, wide of the mark, wild; **circuitously**, circularly, deviously, eccentrically, round, tortuously, wryly

DEFLECTOR *n* circumventor, deviator, diverter, inflector, refractor, shyer, swerver, switcher, tacker

DELEGATE *n* delo *(Colloq.)*, emissary, envoy, go-between, intermediatory, mediator, middle man, negotiator, plenipotentiary, proxy; **delegation**, deputation, mission. *See also* AGENT; AMBASSADOR

democratisation

DELICIOUS *adj* ambrosial, ambrosian, delish, epicurean, fit for the gods, goluptious, luscious, more-ish, mouth-watering, nice, nummy, scrumptious, succulent, yum, yummy; **delicate**, dainty; **savoury**, appetizing, flavoursome, palatable, sapid, savorous *(U.S.)*, tangy, tasty, tempting, toothsome, zesty

DELUDE ONESELF *v* deceive oneself, have oneself on, labour under a false impression, misapprehend, wank; **dream**, daydream, feign, imagine, make as if, make as though, make believe, pretend; **hallucinate**, flashback, hear things, see pink elephants, see things

DELUSION *n* error, false impression, misconception, superstition, warped notion; **illusion**, bubble, dream, figment, fixed idea, hallucination, mirage, myth, reverie; **daydream**, chimera, idle fancy, imagining, make-believe, phantasm, phantasmagoria, play-acting, vision; **dream world**, castle in the air, cloud-cuckoo-land, cloudland, dreamland, fool's paradise, pie in the sky; **will-o'-the-wisp**, ignis fatuus. *See also* ILLUSION

DELUSIVE *adj* airy, dreamlike, dreamy, fatuous, illusional, illusionary, illusive, illusory, quixotic, spurious, unreal; **delusional**, barmecidal, chimerical, feigned, fictitious, imaginary, imagined, make-believe, phantasmagorical, phantasmal, visional, visionary; **phantom**, apparitional, ghostly, shadowy, spectral; **hallucinative**, psychedelic, spaced, spaced-out, spacey, transcendental

DEMOCRATISATION *n* communisation, socialisation; **populism**, communism

democratise / **depart**

DEMOCRATISE *v* communise, give to the people, socialise; **popularise**, vernacularise, vulgarise

DEMOGRAPHY *n* demographics, ekistics; **demographer**, demographist, town planner

DEMOTE *v* abase, break, bust, debase, declass, degrade, disrate, relegate, shaft

DEMOTION *n* abasement, debasement, degradation, relegation

DENIAL *n* apophasis *(Rhet.)*, contradiction, disclaimer, nay, negative, non est factum, rebuttal, traverse *(Law)*; **repudiation**, disaffirmance, disaffirmation, disavowal, disclamation, disownment, negation, palinode, recarnation, renouncement, renunciation, retraction; **nullification**, abolishment, abolition, abrogation, annulment, avoidance *(Law)*, cancellation, cassation, countermand, disaffirmance, discharge *(Law)*, frustration, repeal, rescission, revocation, self-contradiction, voidance

DENIER *n* contradictor, controverter, gainsayer, negativist; **repudiator**, abjurer, disavower, disclaimer, disowner, forswearer; **nullifier**, abrogator, annihilator, canceller, counterclaimant, counterworker, dissolver *(Law)*, repealer, revoker, voider

DENIGRATION *n* disparagement, stigmatisation, vilification; **reproach**, censure, derogation; **defilement**, corruption, pollution; **taint**, attaint *(Obs.)*, blot, brand, cloud, slur, smear, smirch, stain, stigma; **skeleton in the cupboard**, badge of infamy, blot on the escutcheon, dirty linen, family skeleton, mark of Cain

DENIGRATOR *n* stigmatiser; **disgracer**, defiler, dishonourer, low joint; **scandal sheet**, gutter press, rag, yellow press

DEN OF VICE *n* cesspool, cloaca, den of iniquity, sewer, sink; **Babylon**, cities of the plain, iron age, Sodom and Gomorrah

DENY *v* contradict, controvert, disaffirm, gainsay, give the lie to, negate, negative, rebut, traverse *(Law)*; **repudiate**, abjure, disavow, disclaim, disown, forswear, recant, renege *(Archaic)*, renounce, retract; **annul**, annihilate, avoid *(Law)*, cancel, derecognise, disaffirm *(Law)*, dissolve, do away with *(Colloq.)*, invalidate, nullify *(Law)*, repeal, rescind, set aside, think better of, vacate, void

DENYING *adj* abjuratory, adversative, contradictious, contradictive, contradictory, negative, negatory, repudiative

DEODORISE *v* freshen the air; **ventilate**, air a room

DEPART *v* alley, avoid *(Obs.)*, beat a retreat, beat it, blow, buzz along, buzz off, chuff off, clear out, disappear, eloign, evacuate, exit, flit *(Obs.)*, get along, get away, get lost, get nicked, go, go away, go bush, go off, hook it, hop, hop it, leave, lob off, make off, mooch off, move, move out, nick out, part, pull out, push along, push off, quit, remove oneself, retire, retreat, shove off, shuffle off, take an early mark, tie a knot in one's bluey, tootle off, void *(Archaic)*; **set off**, blast off, cast off, get under way, hit the road, make sail, put forth, put off *(Naut.)*, put out *(Naut.)*, put to sea, sail, sally forth, set forth, set out, set sail, shake the dust from one's feet, sling one's hook, step out, take off, take to the road, take wing, weigh anchor; **embark**, embus, entrain, go on board; **storm out**, bounce out, flounce out, vote with one's feet, walk out; **break camp**, check out, decamp, make tracks, pull up stakes, saddle up; **run off**, arsehole off, beat a hasty retreat, bugger off, cut, cut and run, flee, fuck off, hightail, light out, micky quick, nip, piss off, pop off, rack off, run out, scat, scram, shoot off, shoot through like a Bondi tram, skedaddle, skid-doo, split, strike, take a powder, take flight, take to flight, take to one's heels, tear, turn tail, vamoose, zot; **abscond**, absent oneself, blow through, decamp, desert, do a bunk, do a getaway, do a moonlight flit, do a sneak, get off, go A.W.O.L., leave in the lurch, make oneself scarce, nick off, play truant, run away, run off, run out on, scarper, shoot the moon, shoot through, skip, slope off, take French leave, take to the bush, take to the hills; **withdraw from**, abandon, evacuate, leave, pull back from, quit, vacate; **withdraw**, bow out, fall back, fall off, go down *(Brit. Educ.)*, make an exit, retire *(Sport)*, take one's leave; **emigrate**, migrate, transmigrate

DEPARTING *adj* farewell, going, goodnight, now loading, parting, recessional, valedictory; **retired**, outgoing, retiring; **emigrating**, emigrant, emigrational, outbound, outward bound

DEPARTURE *n* debarkation, embarkation, emigration, exodus, going, issue; **withdrawal**, decampment, exit, pullout, retirement, walkout; **take-off**, blast-off, lift-off, sailing, start; **moonlight flit**, French leave, moonlight flitting, skedaddle *(U.S. Colloq.)*; **dismissal**, congé, congee *(Obs.)*, nunc dimittis, retrenchment; **early mark**, early minutes, nick

DEPENDANT *n* camp-follower, client, clientèle, hanger-on, parasite, satellite; **ward**, charge, foster-child, mother's boy, protégé; **vassal**, feudatory, henchman, liegeman; **pensioner**; **contingent**, appendant *(Law)*, contingency

DEPENDENCE *n* clientship, dependency, entrustment, reliance; **guardianship**, tutelage, wardship

DEPENDENT *adj* at the mercy of, in chancery, in the hands of, parasitic, reliant, semiparasitic, tied to the apron-strings; **contingent**, appendant

DEPEND ON *v* hang on, hinge on, turn on; **bank on**, bargain on, figure on, lean on, pend *(Obs.)*, reckon, rely on, repose; **live for**, hope *(Archaic)*, swear by, trust to

DEPICT *v* depicture, limn, portray, represent; **draw**, design, draft, illustrate, outline, profile, sketch; **paint**, blot, colour, daub, illuminate, scumble, tint, touch up; **pencil**, charcoal, crayon, crosshatch, hachure, hatch, ink, shade, shadow *(Obs.)*, stipple; **glaze**, decorate; **model**, cast, mould; **sculpt**, carve, chip, chisel, sculpture; fecit, sculpsit

DEPICTIVE *adj* delineative, descriptive, imitative, pictorial; **graphic**, diagrammatic; **cartographic**, cartographical, cosmographic, cosmographical

DEPILATION *n* deplumation, ecdysis *(Zool.)*, epilation, exuviation, moulting

DEPTH *n* deepness, lowness, profoundness, profundity; **depths**, abysm, abyss, gulf, profound; **sounding**, bathometry, cast, echo sounding, plumbing; **bathometer**, echo sounder, flashboard, lead line; **mark**, isobath

DEPUTE *v* accredit, appoint, authorise, charge, commission, commit into the hands of, commit into the keeping of, delegate, employ, empower, entrust with, hire, name, nominate, place in charge

DERIVE FROM *v* come from, grow out of, hail from, originate in, stem from

DESCEND *v* coast, drop, glissade, go down, lapse, set, slip down; **free-fall**, bale out, jump, parachute; **abseil**, climb down, rappel; **land**, bellyland, crash, ditch, flop, put down, touch down

DESCENDANT *n* chip off the old block, heir, heritor *(Archaic)*, heritress, inheritor, inheritress, inheritrix; **offshoot**, root, scion; **full blood**, purebred; **half-blood**, bronze-wing *(N.T. W.A.)*, half-breed, half-caste, ladino, métis, métisse, mestiza, mestizo, mulatto, muleteer, mustee, octoroon, quadroon, quartes caste; **hybrid**, crossbred, crossover, mongrel, top cross; **throwback**, atavist, reverter

DESCENT *n* decadence, declension, declination, down, downswing, downwardness, drop, dropping, gravitation; **landing**, bellylanding, crash-landing, dead-stick landing, instrument landing, soft landing, three-point landing, touchdown; **slide**, chute, ramp, slippery dip; **abseil**, rappel; **bow**, droop, sag, stoop; **prolapse**, lapse

DESERVE *v* be entitled to, merit, rate; **be hoist with one's own petard**, have it coming to one, reap the whirlwind, serve one right; **be right**, be only natural justice

DESIDERATUM *n* ambition, attraction, big game, consummation greatly to be desired, desiderata, desire, fantasy, goal, lure, magnet, Mecca, object of desire; **torment of Tantalus**

DESIRABLE *adj* appetising, covetable, eligible, enviable, in demand, inviting, mouth-watering, popular, preferable, succulent, tantalising, top

DESIRE *n* achage, ache, affectation *(Obs.)*, appetence, appetite, craving, demand, eagerness, famishment, hunger, hungriness, keenness, longing, mania, need, passion, pine *(Obs. Archaic)*, rage, thirst, thirstiness, will, yearning; **ardour**, ardency, concupiscence, fire, flame, libido, lust, passion, passionateness; **obsession**, compulsion, insane desire; **desires**, sighs, wishes; **wish**, conation, desideration, fancy, hankering, itch, mind, urge, velleity, volition, want, whim, whimsy, willingness, yen; **partiality**, bent, inclination, leaning, penchant, predilection, propensity; **aspiration**, ambition, ambitiousness, arrivisme, zeal; **languishing**, nostalgia, wistfulness; **fondness**, liking, love, relish, stomach, taste; **avarice**, acquisitiveness, avariciousness, avidity, covetousness, cupidity, graspingness, greed, greediness, insatiability, insatiableness, insatiateness, mammonism, rapaciousness, rapacity, selfishness, voracity; **gluttony**, bulimia, edacity, gluttonousness, sitomania

DESIRE *v* admire *(U.S.)*, be all for something, be hell-bent on, covet, crave, desiderate, hanker after, hunger after, hunger for, long for, wish for, yearn for; **seek**, court, make eyes at, make sheep's eyes at, moon over, solicit, woo; **wish**, be inclined towards, care for, fancy, feel like, have a heart to, have a mind to, incline towards, intend, like, list *(Archaic)*, need, require, take a fancy to, take to, want, will, would be glad to; **languish**, ache for, pant, pine for, sigh for, starve for, thirst for; **have high ambitions**, aim high, ambition *(Obs.)*, aspire, raise one's sights, set one's cap at, want the earth; **run after**, die for, do one's balls on, gasp after, gasp for, give one's eyeteeth for, have eyes only for, itch for, lust after, pant after, run mad after, scream for, set one's hat at, set one's heart on, slaver over, yen for; **flame**, burn, fire, rage; **offer oneself**, be in for, throw one's hat in the ring

DESIRER *n* coveter, hankerer, mammonist, mammonite, thirster, votary, wanter, wisher; **lover**, admirer, buff, devotee, enthusiast, votary; **languisher**, sigher; **glutton**, greedy-guts, trencherman; **social climber**, arriviste, careerist, company man, company woman, go-getter, pothunter; **aspirer**, aspirant, candidate, intender, seeker

DESIROUS *adj* desiderative, disposed, fain, inclined, partial, solicitous, volitional, volitionary, volitive, willing, wishful, would-be; **eager**, agog, all agog, breathless, impatient, keen; **ardent**, athirst, avid, fervent, libidinal, on fire, passionate; **mad for**, dying to, fixated on, keen on, longing for, nuts, nutty over, partial to, queer for, set on; **aspiring**, ambitious, aspirant *(Rare)*; **longing**, languishing, nostalgic, sentimental, wistful, yearning; **lustful**, aroused, concupiscent, libidinous, lickerish, lusty *(Archaic)*, on heat, randy, ruttish *(Obs.)*, toey; **votive**

DESIROUSLY *adv* achingly, longingly, nostalgically, yearningly; **aspiringly**, acquisitively, ambitiously, avariciously, covetously, cravingly, gluttonously, graspingly, greedily, insatiably, insatiately, rapaciously; **eagerly**, agog, ardently, avidly, hungrily, thirstily; **willingly**, fain, gladly, with good will

DESK *n* bureau, davenport, escritoire, roll-top desk, secretaire, secretary, worktable, writing desk, writing table. *See also* TABLE

DESOLATE *v* cast down, chill, demoralise, drive to despair, leave no hope

DESPAIR *n* demoralisation, desolateness, desolation, desperateness, desperation, hopelessness, inconsolability, inconsolableness; **pessimism**, defeatism; **melancholy**, depression, despond *(Archaic)*, despondency, oppression. *See also* HOPELESSNESS

DESPAIR *v* buckle under, despond, drop one's bundle, give it away, give up, give up the ghost, go to the pack, lose heart, lose hope; **be pessimistic**, look on the worst side; **write off**, hope for nothing more from

DESPAIRING *adj* broken-down, desolate, desperate, inconsolable, past hope or caring; **pessimistic**, dyspeptic; **melancholy**, byronic, depressed, melancholic, world-weary

DESPAIRINGLY *adv* desperately, pessimistically; **without hope**, bleakly, defeatedly, hopelessly

DESTINATION *n* bourn, goal, haven; **harbour**, airport, airstrip, anchorage, bus station, bus-stop, landing ground, landing strip, port, railway station, stop, terminal, terminus, train halt

DESTROY *v* annihilate, decimate, demolish, destruct, finish off, hit for six, make mincemeat of, make short work of, pull down, pulverise, ride down, slay *(Archaic)*, smash, smite, spiflicate, take out, tear down, wipe out, wipe the floor with, zap; **ravage**, desolate, devastate, eat, lay waste to, rape, waste; **eradicate**, deracinate, exterminate, extirpate, get rid of, outroot, root up; **erase**, blot out, efface, expunge; **abolish**, do away with, liquidate, make away with, unmake; **overthrow**, bring down, do for, fordo *(Archaic)*, subvert, undo; **deface**, depredate, undermine, vandalise; **consume**, gut, incinerate, put to the torch, raze; **poison**, blight, canker. *See also* RUIN

DESTROYER *n* abolisher, annihilationist, annihilator, decimator, demolisher, exterminator, extirpator, juggernaut, pulveriser, razer, unmaker; **desolator**, barbarian, depredator, havocker, Hun, ravager, ruiner, Visigoth, waster, wrecker; **scourge**, destructor, poison, the sword, thunderbolt; **bane**, blight, cancer, canker, devil, mould, must; **defacer**, hoodlum, vandal; **arsonist**, fire-raiser, firebug, incendiary, pyromaniac; **destructive agent**, acid, autolysin *(Biochem.)*, caustic, cautery, corrosive; **eraser**, effacer, eradicator, expunger; **nihilist**, anarchist, assassin, iconoclast, subversive, subverter

DESTRUCTION *n* abolishment, abolition, annihilation, consumption, death, decimation, decomposition, demolition, dissimilation *(Biol.)*, extinction, liquidation, pulverisation; **desolation**, depredation, devastation, havoc, ravage, ruin; **disintegration**, breakdown, dissipation, dissolution; **eradication**, deracination, extermination, extirpation; **erasure**, defacement, effacement, erasion, expunction, obliteration; **chemical breakdown**, autolysis, biodegradation, biolysis, catabolism, electrolysis, lysis, radiolysis; **destructiveness**, destructivity; **perniciousness**, fatalness, fellness; **vandalism**, hoodlumism. *See also* RUIN

DESTRUCTIVE *adj* depredatory, despoiling, devastating, ruinous, vandal, vandalic, wasting; **annihilative**, abolitionary, eradicative, exterminatory, extirpative, obliterative; **catabolic**, biodegradable, biolytic; **apocalyptic**, black, holocaustic; **pernicious**, baneful, cancerous, cankerous, consumptive, gnawing, pestiferous, poisonous

DESTRUCTIVELY *adv* devastatingly, ruinously, wastefully; **perniciously**, banefully, pestiferously, poisonously

DETERIORATE *v* decline, degenerate, dilapidate, disintegrate, get worse, go backwards, go downhill, go from bad to worse, go to pot, go to seed, go to the pack, pejorate, retrograde, retrogress, sicken, sink, slide, slip, wear out, worsen; **wear**, eat, erode, fray, frazzle, fret, ravel, scab, scuff, weather; **decay**, age, atrophy, caseate, shrivel, wither; **rot**, decompose, fes-

deteriorate

ter, go bad, go off, perish, putrefy, turn; **rust,** corrode, oxidise

DETERIORATED *adj* atrophic, atrophied, decadent, decayed, degenerate, degenerative, retrograde, retrogressive, wasted; **rotten,** acetified, adulterate, bad, cankerous, carrion, corrupt, decadent, high, off, pricked, putrescent, putrid, putrilaginous, spoiled, tainted, vitiated; **flyblown,** blown, flystruck, maggoty, vermiculate, worm-eaten, wormy; **rusty,** corroded, eroded, worn away; **decayed,** carious

DETERIORATING *adj* declining, failing, flagging, getting worse, in decline, no better, on the decline, on the downward path, sinking, slipping, wilting, worse

DETERIORATION *n* debasement, declension, declination *(U.S.),* decline, degeneracy, degenerateness, degeneration, impair *(Archaic),* impairment, involution, pejoration, retrogradation, retrogression; **contamination,** adulteration, bastardisation, contagion, corruption, rancidity, sophistication, spoilage, taint, tarnish, vitiation; **rottenness,** corruptness, putrefaction, putrescence, putridity, putridness, putrilage, rot; **decay,** atrophy, decadence, decomposition, disintegration, waste, wasting; **rustiness,** corrosion, corrosion fatigue, erosion; **rot,** blight, canker, dry rot, pest, wet rot; **rust,** corrosion; **bottle sickness,** casse

DETERIORATIVE *adj* contaminative, corrosive, corruptive, degenerative

DETERMINE *v* adjudge, appoint, arbitrate, award, bring in a verdict, conclude, decide, dispose, find *(Law),* judge, pass judgment on, resolve, rule, sentence, will

diagram

DEVIL *n* Antichrist, Beast, Beelzebub, cloven hoof, deuce, dragon, fiend, Lucifer, mischief *(Obs.),* Old Nick, Prince of Darkness, Satan, serpent, the Adversary, the evil one, the Tempter; **demon,** archenemy, belial, cacodaemon, daemon, Davy Jones, debil-debil *(Aborig.),* deil *(Scot.),* fiend, Flibbertigibbet, ghoul, hell-hound; **vampire,** ghoul, incubus, mare *(Obs.),* nightmare, succubus, therianthrope; **werewolf,** loup-garou, lycanthrope; **devilishness,** Death, diabolicalness, diabolism, fiendishness, ghoulishness, lycanthropy, vampirism

DEVILISH *adj* cloven-footed, cloven-hoofed, daemonic, demiurgeous, demiurgic, demoniac, demonian, demonic, diabolic, diabolical, evil-eyed, fiendish, satanic

DEVISE *v* cogitate, conceit *(Obs.),* conceive, dream up, glimpse, ideate, image, imagine, reckon, suppose, think, visualise; **occur to one,** come to one, cross one's mind, dawn on, dawn upon, pop into one's mind

DIAGRAM *n* atlas, carte *(Obs.),* chart, delineation, figure, graph, histogram, map, plat *(U.S.),* plot *(U.S.),* schema, schematic, spectrum; **blueprint,** cross-section, delineator *(Sewing),* design, draft, draught, drawing, elevation, green paper *(Brit.),* ground plan, illustration, layout, lines, outline, pattern, plan, profile, rough draft, section, skeleton, sketch; **formula,** prescription, receipt, recipe, scrip; **map projection,** azimuthal projection, conic projection, conical projection, cylindrical projection, Mercator's projection, trimetric projection, zenithal projection

diagrammatic — different

DIAGRAMMATIC *adj* cosmographic, cosmographical, delineative, graphic, nomographic, nomographical, photogrammetric, spectrographic; **architectonic**, architectonical; **in draft form**, on paper

DIARRHOEA *n* Bali belly, dysentery, Edgar Britts, incontinence, Jimmy Brits, Montezuma's revenge, runs, scouring, scours, shits, squitters, tomtits, trots

DIARY *n* black book, casebook, commonplace book, daybook, diurnal *(Archaic)*, flightlog, journal, log, tickler *(U.S.)*, workbook; **album**, scrapbook, skitebook. *See also* RECORD

DIDACTICALLY *adv* exponentially, pedagogically, preachingly, preceptively

DIE *v* be carried out feet first, be gathered to one's fathers, breathe one's last, buy it, cark, cark it, cash in, cash in one's chips, cease *(Obs.)*, conk out, croak, deaden, decease, depart, die off, die on someone, do a perish, exit, expire, finish *(Obs.)*, flit *(Obs.)*, give up the ghost, go, go the way of all flesh, go to one's account, go west, kick off *(U.S. Colloq.)*, kick the bucket, part, pass, pass away, pass in one's marble, pass on, peg out, perish, pop off, predecease, snuff it, starve *(Obs.)*, succumb, throw a seven, toss in the alley, turn up one's toes; **fall**, bite the dust, drop, kiss the dust, lick the dust; **asphyxiate**, catch one's death, drown, famish *(Archaic)*, feed the fishes, freeze, starve, suffocate, swing, walk the plank; **commit suicide**, die a martyr's death, die for the cause, kill oneself; **die down**, die back, die off, fade, fade away, fade out, fall away, miff *(Bot.)*, wither, wither away; **receive one's death warrant**, die the death; **have had it**, be a goner, be as good as dead, be at death's door, be written off; **be dead**, be dead and buried, be dead and gone, be history, be no more, lie six feet under, push up daisies; **sleep**, lie in state, repose, rest

DIFFER *v* bear no resemblance, disagree, diverge, divide, go different ways, speak a different language, vary; **contrast**, foil, mismatch; **discriminate**, separate the men from the boys, separate the sheep from the goats, sort, tell one from the other; **cause to differ**, modify, rearrange

DIFFERENCE *n* antithesis, diff, discord, dissemblance *(Archaic)*, dissimilarity, dissimilitude, dissonance, distinctness, inequality, shade of difference; **contrast**, distodistinction, foil; **disparity**, a fine distinction, a nice distinction, deviation, discrepancy, distance between, distinction, divergence, error, gap, generation gap, interval, variance; **spectrum**, cline, range; **heterogeneity**, diverseness, diversity, variety, variousness; **disparateness**, incommensurability, incommensurableness, incomparability, incomparableness, incompatibility, nonconformity, otherness, unlikeness, variation, variedness; **asymmetry**, dissymmetry

DIFFERENT *adj* aliunde, as like as chalk and cheese, cast in a different mould, contradistinctive, discrepant, disparate, dissimilar, divergent, foreign, heterologous, incommensurable, incomparable, other, otherwise, poles apart, removed, unequal, unlike; **heterogeneous**, all kinds of, all manner of, diverse, diversified, manifold, of all kinds, polytypic, varied, various; **distinct**, disjointed, disjunct, distinctive, separate, unconnected, unrelated; **asymmetric**, asymmetrical, dissymetric, dissymmetrical; **contrastive**, contrastable, contrasting, contrasty, distinguishable; **modified**, altered, varied; **mismatching**, clashing, discordant, dissociable, dissonant, incongruous, inconsistent, noncongruent

DIFFERENTLY *adv* disparately, dissimilarly, incommensurably, incomparably, inconsistently, otherwise; **diversely**, manifoldly, variously; **asymmetrically**, dissymmetrically

DIFFICULT *adj* awkward, complicated, cow of a, crook, crucial, curly, devil of a, diabolic, diabolical, dilemmatic, fiddly, hard, hell of a, helluva, intricate, knotty, nodal, tough; **painful**, distressful, distressing, trying; **arduous**, backbreaking, formidable, herculean, laborious, stiff, uphill; **burdensome**, bothersome, cumbersome, cumbrous, dear *(Archaic)*, grievous, heavy, onerous, oppressive, troublesome, weighty; **harsh**, rugged, scabrous, severe; **hairy**, dicky, dodgy, icky, kittle, spooky *(Surfing)*, sticky, ticklish, tight; **challenging**, demanding, formidable, graunchy *(N.Z.)*; **prickly**, spiny, thorny

DIFFICULTY *n* awkwardness, complexity, perplexity, thorniness; **arduousness**, onerousness, painfulness, toughness; **refractoriness**, bloodymindedness, intractability, intractableness, prickliness; **a difficulty**, catch, coil, complication, entanglement, fun and games, matter, nigger in the woodpile, node, rub, stick *(Obs.)*, trouble; **problem**, bugger, crux, facer, fair cow, headache, knot, stymie, the devil to pay, tickler; **task**, an uphill battle, backbreaker, challenge, chore, hard nut to crack, job, long haul, murder, snorter, stinker, struggle, tall order, the devil's own job; **burden**, care, cumber *(Archaic)*, weight; **teething troubles**, growing pains; **hardship**, asperity, rigour.
See also DILEMMA

DIFFUSIVENESS *n* contagiousness, diffusibility, pervasiveness, solubility, solubleness; **diffuseness**, dissipatedness

DIG *v* delve *(Archaic)*, ditch, dredge, fossick out, gouge, plough, shovel, spade, spud, unearth; **mine**, cut, drive, excavate, open-cut, pan, quarry, sink, stope, surface; **tunnel**, channel, sap; **root up**, bandicoot, burrow, grub, scratch out, undermine; **crater**, cave in, dibble, dish, hole, pit, scoop

DIGGER *n* bogger, boodler, burrower, fossicker, harrower, shoveller; **miner**, alluvial miner, black-sander *(N.Z.)*, coalminer, collier, Cousin Jack, golddigger, goldfielder, goldminer, gouger, grass captain, grave-digger, gumdigger, mineworker, opal miner, pitman, pitworker, reefer, sand miner, tributer; **excavator**, bore sinker, ditcher, navvy, sapper, tank sinker, tunneller

DIGGING *n* banjoing, shovelling; **mining**, blacksanding, coalmining, drift mining, fossicking, longwall mining; **excavation**, shallow sinking, stoping, wet sinking; **gold-digging**, goldmining; **gum-digging**

DIGGING *adj* burrowing, fossorial; **mining**, coalmining

DIGGING IMPLEMENT *n* banjo *(Colloq.)*, bogger, digging stick *(Aborig.)*, mattock, pick, pickaxe, scoop, shovel, spade, spud, trowel; **hoe**, dutch hoe, grub hoe, rotary hoe; **mechanical shovel**, steam shovel, tractor shovel; **dredge**, dredger, dredging machine; **grader**, bulldozer, calfdozer, dozer; **plough**, chain harrow, chisel-plough, disc harrow, disc plough, gang plough, harrow, rotary plough, seed drill, stump-jump plough; **excavator**, backhoe, drott; **jackhammer**, posthole digger

DIGGINGS *n* coalface, workings; **mine**, chalkpit, coal pit, open cut, pit, quarry; **reef**, alluvial, lode, mullocky reef, vein; **face**, prospect, workface; **trench**, cross-drive, crosscut, entrenchment, retrenchment, sap, tunnel; **pit**, downcast, downcast shaft, mineshaft, stope, well; **dump**, leavings, mullock, slagheap, spoil, tailings

DILAPIDATED *adj* attrite *(Obs.)*, beat-up, broken-down, dog-eared, down at heel, flea-bitten, hairy *(N.Z.)*, moth-eaten, old, out at elbows, ragged, ramshackle, ratty, rusty, scrubby, second-hand, seedy, shabby, shopsoiled, tacky, the worse for wear, third-hand, timeworn, toilworn, tumbledown, used, weather-beaten, weathered, weatherworn, well-worn, worn. *See also* DAMAGED

DILEMMA *n* blind alley, catch 22, double bind, impasse, nonplus, predicament, quandary, vicious circle; **fix**, corner, hole, hot water, pickle, quagmire, spot, squeeze, straits; **sticky wicket**, death seat *(Horseracing)*, hot seat, tight corner, tight spot; **mess**, can of worms, fine kettle of fish, hobble, hot potato, how-do-you-do, nodus, pretty kettle of fish, rat-trap, scrape. *See also* DIFFICULTY

DIRECT *v* aim, channel, cox, helm, lay, level, luff, steer, up *(Naut. Colloq.)*; **guide**, beacon, beckon, home, lead, motion, pilot, point, sign *(Obs.)*, talk down; **orientate**, point towards, range, redirect, set, sight, train, traverse; **lie**, face, give on to, look out on, present, tail

DIRECT *adj* on the beam, one-way, point-blank, rectilinear, straight, straightaway *(U.S.)*, straightforward, true, unerring

DIRECTION *n* aim, alignment, azimuth, bearing, beat, beeline, course, current, drift, eye *(Naut.)*, fly *(U.S.)*, heading, line, line of sight, loxodromic curve, magnetic bearing, orbit, orientation, path, rhumb, rhumb line, set, stream, streamline, streamline flow, stretch, sweep, tack, track, trajectory, trend, way; **aspect**, bearings, kiblah *(Islam)*, lie, sense *(Maths)*

DIRECTIONAL *adj* omnidirectional, omnirange, unidirectional, vaned; **steerable**, dirigible; **geotropic**, apogeotropic, chemotropic, heliotropic, negatively geotropic, positively geotropic, transversely geotropic

DIRECTION FINDER *n* alidade, astrocompass, automatic direction finder, compass, gyrocompass, gyroscope, gyroscopic compass, gyrostat, magnetic compass, navaid, radio direction-finder, telltale compass; **compass card**, compass rose, lubber line, magnetic needle, needle, pointer, quarter, rose; **point of the compass**, cardinal point, rhumb

DIRECTLY *adv* point-blank, straight, unerringly

DIRECTNESS *n* pointedness, straightness, sureness, unerringness

DIRT *n* filth, grime, grot, mess, soil, toe jam; **smudge**, blot, blotch, greasespot, pick, smirch, smut, smutch, stain, sully *(Obs.)*; **dust**, cinders, cobwebs, fallout, soot; **waste**, putrilage, sewage, sullage; **swill**, bilge, drainage, effluent, rinsings, slops, slush, wash; **muck**, cack, grease, scum, scunge, skim *(Obs.)*, slime, slush; **dandruff**, scurf; **mould**, fungus, mildew, must, rot; **sweepings**, garbage, refuse; **dag**, daglock, dagwool; **flytrap**, Afghan flytrap, Australian flytrap, Bedourie flytrap, Boulia flytrap

DIRTILY *adv* dingily, dustily, grimily, smudgily; **filthily**, foully, hoggishly, nastily, piggishly; **greasily**, muddily, slimily, sloppily; **impurely**, stagnantly, uncleanly; **squalidly**, frowzily, grubbily, sleazily, sordidly; **sootily**, smokily

DIRTINESS *n* feculence, filthiness, foulness, nastiness; **grubbiness**, griminess, miriness, muckiness, muddiness, sliminess, sloppiness; **impurity**, impureness, insanitariness, insanitation, uncleanliness, verminousness; **dustiness**, sootiness; **smeariness**, greasiness, smudginess, stickiness; **mouldiness**, mucidness, mustiness; **pollution**, carrion, contamination, corruption, defilement, putrefaction, putrescence, putridity, putridness, stagnancy, stagnation; **squalor**, dinginess, sleaziness, sordidness, squalidity, squalidness; **messiness**, frowziness, lousiness, manginess, scruffiness, slovenliness, untidiness; **piggishness**, hoggishness, piggery

DIRTY *v* befoul, begrime, besmirch, defile, foul, grime, smirch, soil; **smear**, bedaub, besmear, blur, clart *(Scot.)*, daub, slime, slur *(Obs.)*, smudge, smut, smutch, spot, thumb; **contaminate**, corrupt, desterilise, flyblow, infect, maculate, pollute, sully, taint; **mire**, bemire, bespatter, muddy, puddle, splash; **mess up**, muck, untidy

DIRTY *adj* black, dingy, dusty, grimy, grotty, scungy, smoky, smutty, sooty, thick with dust, unswept; **unclean**, impure, insalubrious, insanitary, maculate, polluted, uncleanly; **smeary**, cacky, clarty, greasy, miry, muddy, smudgy, smutchy; **grubby**, shopsoiled; **messy**, trashy *(U.S.)*, untidy; **foul**, feculent, filthy, mucky, nasty, offensive; **stagnant**, festering, septic; **rotting**, maggoty, tainted, verminous; **slimy**, mucid, sloppy, slushy. *See also* UNKEMPT

DIRTY PERSON *n* chat *(Colloq.)*, dag, draggletail, mucker, scruff, scunge, sloven, slut, warb; **polluter**, corrupter, defiler, pollutant; **guttersnipe**, mudlark, street Arab; **pig**, beast, hog, wallower; **litterbug**, litterer

DISAGREE *v* conflict, differ, diverge; **argue**, argue the toss, argufy, argy-bargy, bicker, contest, cook up a storm, disagree, dispute, fall out, have words, pettifog, stickle, wrangle; **object to**, buck at, cavil at, confound, contradict, controvert, disagree with, except against, pay out, protest against, reluct to *(Archaic)*, remonstrate, take exception to, take issue with; **dissent**, demur, shake one's head, stir the possum

DISAGREEMENT *n* argument, argy-bargy, bicker, bust-up, conflict, contention, contest, controversy, difference, ding, disputation, dispute, dissension, distance *(Obs.)*, division, set-to, strife, unpleasantness, upset, variance, words, wrangle; **objection**, cavil, contradiction, contrasuggestion, demur, demurral, difficulty, point of order; **denial**, denegation, disallowance, nay, negative, no; **dissent**, dissentience, dissidence; **protest**, remonstrance, remonstration

DISAPPEAR *v* dematerialise, disperse, dissolve, drop *(Naut.)*, evanesce, evanish *(Archaic)*, evaporate, fade, fleet *(Archaic)*, immerge *(Rare)*, leave no trace, melt, peter out, vanish; **melt into thin air**, become lost to sight, become lost to view, do a vanishing trick, go into smoke, pass out of sight, take a powder

DISAPPEARANCE *n* blackout, dematerialisation, departure, dispersion, evanescence, evaporation, fade-out, fading, passing, vanishing; **eclipse**, occultation, total eclipse; **vanishing point**

DISAPPEARING *adj* evanescent, evaporating, fading, vanishing; **dispersive**, evaporative

DISAPPROVAL *n* disapprobation, discountenance, disfavour, dislike, odium; **censure**, abuse, blame, commination, condemnation, criticism, denunciation, detraction, flak, invective, obloquy, rebuff, vitriol, vituperation; **remonstration**, admonition, execration, expostulation, protestation, remonstrance; **chastisement**, castigation, objurgation, reprehension, reprobation, reproval; **denunciation**, condemnation, crimination, damnation, denouncement, fulmination; **criticism**, animadversion, depreciation, dispraise, reflection, stricture; **contempt**, contumely, disparagement, scorn; **fault-finding**, captiousness, censoriousness, nitpicking, quibbling; **self-criticism**, self-abuse, self-reproach. *See also* REPRIMAND; BOO

DISAPPROVE OF *v* be unimpressed, deprecate, discommend, discountenance, frown on, frown upon, look down on, object to, take a dim view of, take exception to; **censure**, animadvert on, blame, condemn, criminate, damn, fault, pick to pieces, tax; **criticise**, bag, canvass *(Obs.)*, knock, monster, pan, pooh-pooh, roast, scarify, scathe, scorch, score *(U.S.)*, slam, slate, tear strips off, vituperate; **boo**, burl, catcall, hiss, slow clap. *See also* SCOLD

DISAPPROVER *n* booer, deprecator, hisser; **censurer**, carper, caviller, censor, complainer, critic, criticiser, cynic, Dutch uncle, fault-finder, hypercritic, knocker, niggler, nitpicker, quibbler, whingeing Pom *(Derog.)*, whinger; **denouncer**, condemner, denunciator, jeremiah, vituperator; **scolder**, admonisher, chider, rebuker, reproacher, reprover, scold, upbraider; **chastiser**, castigator, chastener; **protester**, expostulator, objector, remonstrant, remonstrator

DISAPPROVING *adj* admonitory, monitory, remonstrant, remonstrative, reproving, scolding; **censorial**, censorious, critical, hypercritical, overcritical; **fault-finding**, captious, derogatory, nitpicking, picky, quibbling, snide; **deprecatory**, contemptuous, contumelious, despiteous

(*Archaic*), insinuating, pejorative, sarcastic; **denunciatory,** comminatory; **disapprobative,** disapprobatory, dyslogistic, opprobrious; **condemnatory,** damnatory, damning, objurgatory, reprehensive, reprobative, uncharitable, upbraiding, vituperative; **scathing,** biting, blistering, blistery, scorching, slashing, withering

DISAPPROVINGLY *adv* askance, deprecatingly, deprecatorily, discouragingly, pejoratively; **chidingly,** admonishingly, reproachfully, reprobatively, reprovingly, scoldingly, upbraidingly; **censoriously,** captiously, carpingly, condemningly, contemptuously, critically, damningly, despiteously, dyslogistically, hypercritically, reprehensively, vituperatively; **scathingly,** ad hominem, bitingly, scorchingly, scornfully, sneeringly, uncharitably, witheringly

DISCARD *n* cast-off, jetsam, jettison, slough; **reject,** rejectamenta, throw-out, throwaway; **has-been,** heap, hulk, junk; **retired list,** scrap heap, slab-heap *(N.Z. Colloq.)*; **leftover,** cotton waste, dead letter, discontinued line, remainders, remnant, scrap, scrap iron, scrap metal, waste; **hand-me-down,** reach-me-down

DISCHARGE *v* bleed, drain, draw, drip, effuse, emanate, emit, exhaust, exude, flow out, froth, give off, issue, leak, let out, ooze, outflow, outpour, run, seep, spill, spout, teem, vent, weep, well

DISCONTENT *v* annoy, bite, chagrin, discomfort, disgruntle, dissatisfy, irritate, nag, nark, put out, put out of countenance, roil, worry

DISCONTENTED *adj* aggrieved, browned off, cast down, discontent, disgruntled, dissatisfied, fretful, fretting and fuming, ill-conditioned, malcontent, moody, never satisfied, not happy, out of humour, pissed-off, querulous, restless, seething, shitty, shitty-livered, sore, soured, troubled, uneasy, ungruntled *(Joc.)*, weary, wry; **grouchy,** bleating, carping, griping, grumbling, grumpy, moaning, murmuring, murmurous, narky, sulky, whingeing

DISCONTENTEDLY *adv* carpingly, complainingly, dissatisfiedly, fretfully, grouchily, grumblingly, grumpily, murmurously, querulously, wryly; **in the sulks,** in a mood, in high dudgeon, with one's face tied in a knot

DISCONTENTEDNESS *n* cold comfort, disappointment, discontent, discontentment, dissatisfaction, distemper, ennui, hatred, heartburning, moods, restlessness, seven-year itch *(Colloq.)*, unrest, verjuice; **grumpiness,** bitchery, disgruntlement, fretfulness, grouchiness, grumbles, murmuring, querulousness, s.o.l., shit on liver, sourness

DISCOURAGE *v* beat the stuffing out of, daunt, demoralise, disenchant, dishearten, disillusion, get someone down, knock the stuffing out of, slap down; **dissuade,** advise against, block, check, chill, damp, dampen, demotivate, deter, put a damper on, put off, quench someone's enthusiasm, restrain, talk out of, throw cold water on, wet-blanket; **remonstrate,** expostulate, protest; **stop,** frustrate, thwart

DISCOURAGEMENT *n* demoralisation, determent, deterrence, disenchantment, disheartenment, dispiritedness, dissuasion; **remonstrance**, expostulation, protest, warning

DISCOURAGER *n* block, check, damp, dampener, damper, dash, demoraliser, deterrent, disincentive, dissuader, obstacle, restraint, stop; **remonstrant**, expostulator, protestor; **killjoy**, spoilsport, wet blanket, wowser

DISCOURAGING *adj* deterrent, dispiriting, dissuasive, off-putting, soul-destroying; **remonstrative**, expostulatory, warning; **forbidding**, prohibitive

DISCOURAGINGLY *adv* dishearteningly, dispiritingly, dissuasively; **remonstratively**, expostulatingly

DISCOURSE *v* canvass, comment, criticise, descant, discuss, dissert *(Obs.)*, dissertate, lucubrate, pamphleteer, review, treat, write about, write up

DISCOURTEOUS *adj* badly behaved, disobliging, hoyden, hoydenish, ignorant *(Colloq.)*, ill-bred, ill-mannered, impolite, inurbane, mannerless, rude, tactless, uncivil, uncourtly, ungentlemanly, ungracious, unhandsome, unknightly, unladylike, unmannered, unmannerly; **brusque**, abrupt, bluff, blunt, brief, curt, short, short-spoken, terse; **insolent**, abusive, bold, bold-faced, brash, brassy, brazen, brazen-faced, cheeky, forward, fresh, impertinent, impudent, insulting, pert, sassy, saucy; **coarse**, coarse-grained, common as muck, crude, dead common, foul-mouthed, improper, rough, uncivilised, uncouth, unmannerly, unpolished, vulgar; **haughty**, cavalier, contemptuous, contumelious, disdainful, inconsiderate, off-hand, overbearing, presumptuous, snubby, supercilious; **surly**, bearish, boorish, churlish, crusty, gruff, ill-conditioned, immodest

DISCOURTEOUSLY *adv* disobligingly, ill-manneredly, impolitely, inurbanely, rudely, tactlessly, ungraciously, unhandsomely, with bad grace; **brusquely**, abruptly, bearishly, bluffly, bluntly, boorishly, briefly, churlishly, crustily, curtly, shortly, surlily, tersely; **impudently**, brassily, brazenly, forwardly, freshly, impertinently, insultingly, saucily; **coarsely**, crudely, immodestly, improperly; **haughtily**, cavalierly

DISCOURTEOUS PERSON *n* bastard, blackguard, boor, bull in a china shop, churl, Goth, gremmie, ocker, roughie, vulgarian, yahoo; **minx**, fishwife, hoyden, quean, tactless Tilly; **insulter**, knocker, snubber

DISCOURTESY *n* bad form, bad manners, conduct unbecoming, discourteousness, disobligingness, disrespect, ill-breeding, impoliteness, incivility, inurbanity, rudeness, solecism, tactlessness, ungraciousness, unhandsomeness, unknightliness, unmannerliness; **brusqueness**, abruptness, bluffness, bluntness, briefness, brusquerie, curtness, shortness, terseness; **impudence**, arse, brassiness, brazenness, cheek, chutzpah, crust, dumb insolence, forwardness, freshness, gall, hide, impertinence, sauce, sauciness, temerity; **coarseness**, bastardry, boorishness, crudeness, crudity, immodesty, improperness, impropriety, savageness, vulgarity; **surliness**, bearishness, churl-

discourtesy   **disenchantment**

ishness, crustiness, grouchiness, moroseness

DISCRIMINATE *v* have an ear for, have an eye for, know, know chalk from cheese, know the difference; **discern**, contradistinguish, difference, differentiate, distinguish, distinguish between, distinguish from, pick out, resolve *(Optics.)*, secern, separate the sheep from the goats, tell, winnow; **split hairs**, fine-draw, refine

DISCRIMINATING *adj* clear-eyed, clear-headed, clear-sighted, discriminate, discriminative, penetrating, perspicacious, sagacious; **subtle**, fine, fine-drawn, fine-spun, hairsplitting, nice, overcritical; **discerning**, cultured, delicate, fastidious, nice, refined, selective; **discreet**, judicious, tactful; **discretional**, discretionary, judicial

DISCRIMINATINGLY *adv* clear-sightedly, discerningly, discriminately, discriminatively, penetratingly, perspicaciously, sagaciously; **subtly**, delicately, finely

DISCRIMINATION *n* difference, differentiation, distinction, hairsplitting, selectivity; **discernment**, culture, delicateness, discretion, finesse, refinement, tact, taste; **perspicacity**, clear-headedness, clear-sightedness, insight, penetration, sagaciousness, sagacity

DISCRIMINATOR *n* differentiator, discerner, distinguisher, hairsplitter; **connoisseur**, aesthete, cognoscente

DISCURSIVE *adj* critical, disquisitional, dissertational, dissertative, expository

DISCUSSION *n* argumentation, consultation, controversy, cross-fire, cross-talk, debate, dialogism, disputation *(Obs.)*, korero *(N.Z.)*; **argument**, argy-bargy, bicker, polemic, words; **conference**, colloquium, colloquy, congress, gabfest, negotiation, palaver, parlance *(Archaic)*, parley, pourparler, powwow, seminar, symposiac, symposium, teach-in, workshop. See also TALK

DISDAINER *n* contemnor, despiser, scorner, sneerer, snubber, spurner; **dishonourer**, profaner, violator; **insolent**, baggage, minx, missy

DISDAINFUL *adj* coy *(Obs.)*, cynic, cynical, scornful, sneering; **derogatory**, derogative, disparaging, slighting, snide; **contemptuous**, contumelious, supercilious; **pejorative**, depreciative; **disrespectful**, impious, irreverent

DISEASE *v* disorder, distemper, fever, infect, inflame; **blast**, blight; **paralyse**, palsy

DISENCHANT *v* betray, betray one's hopes, dash one's hopes, disappoint, disillusion, dismay, mock one's hopes; **frustrate**, foil, tantalise, thwart; **be a disappointment to**, be less than one's hopes, fall short of the goal, not come up to expectations, not come up to scratch

DISENCHANTED *adj* baffled, disappointed, foiled, frustrated, let down, rooted *(Colloq.)*, stuffed *(Colloq.)*, thwarted

DISENCHANTMENT *n* disillusion, disillusionment, dismay, frustration, tantalisation; **anticlimax**, bathos, baulk, blow, bummer, comedown, disappointment, fizzer, foozle, hitch, letdown, mare's-nest, sell *(Colloq.)*, setback, swiz

DISFIGURE *v* deface, deform, mar, misshape, mutilate; **blemish**, blotch, discolour, distain, ensanguine, imbrue, imbue, splotch, stain; **scar**, pit, scratch; **freckle**, maculate, speckle, spot

DISFIGURED *adj* crooked, deformed, misshapen; **bruised**, black-and-blue, blebby, blistery, blue, ecchymosed, ecchymotic; **bloody**, blood-spattered, bloodstained, gory, sanguinary; **splotchy**, blotchy, blurry, patchy, scabby, smeary; **freckled**, freckly, macular, maculate, naevoid, spotted; **pimply**, acned, pimpled, spotty; **scarred**, cheloidal, cicatrised, keloidal, pockmarked, pocky, scarified

DISFIGUREMENT *n* beauty spot, birthmark, blemish, defect, deformity, fault, flaw, imperfection, lentigo, macula, mole, mutilation, naevus, stigma, strawberry mark, tarnish; **discolouration**, imbruement, imbueness; patchiness, scratchiness, spottiness; **pimple**, acne, blackhead, comedo, hick *(U.S.)*, milium, zit; **sore**, bleb *(Rare)*, blister, blood blister, bloodstain, bruise, ecchymosis, granulation, granulation tissue, phlyctena, proud flesh; **scar**, cheloid, cicatrix, keloid, pit, pock, pockmark, scratch; **wart**, boil, carbuncle, corn, cyst, furuncle, sty, verruca, wen; **wale**, weal, welt; **freckle**, blotch, dot, fleck, maculation, speckle, spot

DISGRACE *v* attaint, bring shame upon, degrade, dishonour; **shame**, derogate from, expose, humiliate, pillory, reproach, show up; **defame**, brand, discredit, disparage, drag through the mire, stigmatise, vilify; **defile**, blot, cloud, denigrate, foul, smear, smirch, stain, sully, taint, tarnish; **detract from**, cast a slur on, censure, cut down to size, debunk, put to shame, throw dishonour upon; **have a low opinion of**, see in a bad light, view unfavourably

DISGUISE *n* cache-sexe, cloak, domino, false face, fig leaf, G-string, incognito, loup, mask, veil, visor; **camouflage**, cover, disguise, ink *(Ichthyol)*, protective colouring; **masquerade**, fancy dress party, masked ball; **alias**, alter ego, nom de plume, penname, persona, pseudonym; **pretext**, dissemblance *(Archaic)*, dissimulation, double bluff, stalking-horse; **enigma**, riddle; **cryptography**, cipher, code, cryptochannel, cryptogram, cryptograph, cryptology, invisible ink, microdot, palimpsest

DISHONEST *adj* ambidextrous *(Archaic)*, cronk, crooked, cross, double-dealing, knavish, lurky, pettifogging, racketeering, rascally, roguish, rorty, shady, shifty, shonkie, slippery, two-faced, unjust *(Archaic)*; **corrupt**, available, bent, in it up to the hilt, open to bribery, Tammany-Hall, venal; **fraudulent**, fixed, set-up

DISHONESTLY *adv* cheatingly, corruptly, crookedly, fraudulently, knavishly, on the cross, on the fiddle, shadily, shiftily

DISHONESTY *n* crookedness, fraudulence, fraudulency, improbity, knavery, knavishness, rascality, roguery, shiftiness, trickery; **insincerity**, faithlessness, prevarication, unjustness *(Archaic)*; **corruption**, corruptibility, corruptibleness, corruptness, graft, jobbery, jobs for the boys, kick back, malversation, nepotism, payola, pork-barrelling, racketeering, venality; **cheating**, ambidexterity *(Archaic)*,

dishonesty

barratry, cardsharping, champerty *(Law)*, chicane, chicanery, double-dealing, double dipping, jiggery-pokery, pettifoggery, rookery, sharp practice, shifty business, skin game; **swindle**, bilk, cheat, dodge, fix, fraud, funny business, gerrymander, gyp, lurk, medifraud, racket, ramp, skulduggery, subreption, tax lurk, wangle, wile; **crime**, foul play, lawlessness, theft

DISINFECT *v* antisepticise, chlorinate, dip *(Agric.)*, fog, fumigate, sanitise, smoke, sterilise; **depurate**, deterge, douche, physic. *See also* CLEAN

DISLIKE *n* abhorrence, abomination, antipathy, averseness, aversion, detestation, disrelish, distaste, hatred, loathing, odium, repugnance, scunner; **opposition,** animosity, recalcitration, resistance

DISLIKE *v* abhor, abominate, detest, distaste *(Archaic)*, hate, have had, have no stomach for, have no use for, loathe, mind, object to, take a dislike to; **frown,** curl one's lip, make a face, pout, scowl; **fret and fume,** be on pins and needles, be put out, have a bad time of it; **put up with,** bear with, endure, hack, suffer

DISMISS *v* amove *(Law)*, arsehole, axe, boot, bounce, can *(U.S.)*, cavil *(Mining)*, chop, disbar, disbench, displace, drop, eject, fire, give someone notice, hunt, kick out, lay off, put out to grass, recall, relieve, remove, retrench, sack, shelve, stand down, strike off, unmake; **discharge,** demob, demobilise, drum out, muster out *(U.S.)*, pay off, pension off; **defrock,** deprive, disfrock, disordain, disrobe, unfrock; **suspend,** stand off; **depose,**

154

disobedience

deplume, dethrone, disseat, oust, overthrow, put the skids under, uncrown, unseat

DISMISSAL *n* cavil-out *(Mining)*, discharge, lay-off, lockout, loss of employment, retrenchment, standdown; **the axe,** bounce *(U.S. Colloq.)*, bullet, bum's rush, can *(U.S. Colloq.)*, chop, D.C.M., demission *(Rare)*, heave-ho, marching orders, notice, order of the boot, push, spear, the chuck, the sack, walking papers, walking ticket; **deposal,** comedown, deplumation, deposition, dethronement, disrobement, downfall, overthrow, removal; **resignation,** abdication, demission, retirement, spill *(Politics)*

DISMISSED *adj* axed, retrenched, sacked, time-expired, unemployed; **raddle-marked,** for the chop, on the skids

DISMISSER *n* axeman, deposer, dethroner, executioner, hatchet man, ouster, unmaker

DISMOUNT *v* get down, get off; **alight,** disembark, land, light, perch, settle

DISOBEDIENCE *n* civil disobedience, contempt, disturbance, filibusterism, non-compliance, non-cooperation, non-observance, passive resistance, rebeldom, transgression, violation; **delinquency,** contumaciousness, contumacy, disrespect, fractiousness, mutinousness, naughtiness, unruliness; **rebelliousness,** incompliancy, insubordination, recalcitrance, recalcitrancy, recalcitration, recreance, recreancy; **incorrigibleness,** frowardness, incorrigibility, indocility, perverseness, perversity, refractoriness, ungovernableness

DISOBEDIENT *adj* incompliant, non-compliant, transgressive; **disorderly**, anarchistic, insurgent, lawless, riotous; **rebellious**, contrary, contumacious, froward, indocile, insubordinate, mutinous, perverse, recalcitrant, recreant, seditious; treasonable, treasonous, violative *(U.S.)*, wilful; **delinquent**, naughty, rebel, urchin; **incorrigible**, fractious, rambunctious *(U.S.)*, refractory, unbroken, undisciplined, ungovernable, unmanageable, unruly; **illegal**, foul *(Sport)*

DISOBEDIENTLY *adv* incompliantly, insubordinately, naughtily; **incorrigibly**, ungovernably, unmanageably; **rebelliously**, contumaciously, delinquently, fractiously, frowardly, mutinously, perversely, recreantly, refractorily, transgressively, treasonably, treasonously

DISOBEY *v* drag one's feet, foul *(Sport)*, infringe, mutiny, rebel, recalcitrate, transgress, violate; **take the law into one's own hands**, go under someone's neck, kick over the traces, run riot

DISOBEYER *n* infringer, insubordinate, looter, non-complier, outlaw, rioter, traitor, violator; **rebel**, anarchist, dissenter, dissident, diversionist, insurgent, mutineer, recalcitrant, recreant, transgressor, urban guerilla; **delinquent**, hellion, juvenile delinquent, spiv, tear-arse, tearaway, urchin, wide boy *(Brit.)*

DISORDER *n* anarchy, bedlam, boulversement, chaos, confusion, discord, distemper, fuddle, moil, snafu *(U.S.)*, turmoil; **untidiness**, confusedness, derangement, disarrangement, disarray, dislocation, disorderliness, disorganisation, entanglement, labyrinth, messiness, misarrangement, sprawl, tangle, topsy-turviness, twine; **riotousness**, rampageousness, rowdiness, rowdyism, tumultuousness, uproariousness. *See also* COMMOTION

DISORDER *v* addle, balls up, box up, disjoint, dislocate, disorganise, disrupt, disturb, foul up, frig up, make a box of, mess up, mix up, muss up *(U.S.)*, scamp, snafu *(U.S.)*, tumble, upset; **raise Cain**, create, cry blue murder, make a song and dance about, rabble, raise hell, raise the dust, scream blue murder, whoop it up, whoop things up

DISORDERLY *adj* chaotic, deranged, disordered, haywire, higgledy-piggledy, hugger-mugger, messy, out of joint, snafu *(U.S.)*, sprawly, topsy-turvy, upside down; **unorganised**, desultory, immethodical, random, unbusinesslike, unclassified, undisciplined, unjustified *(Print.)*, unmethodical, unstructured, unsystematic; **disorganised**, disjointed, dislocated, fragmented, incoherent; **unsettled**, disturbed, troublous *(Archaic)*; **riotous**, harum-scarum, pandemoniac, pandemonic, rampageous, rowdy, rowdyish, tumultuary, tumultuous, turbulent, uproarious, wild

DISPENSARY *n* pharmacy; **pharmacopeia**, materia medica, open list; **medicine chest**, first-aid kit; **prescription**, scrip

DISPERSAL *n* deployment, diffusion, dissipation, scattering; **atomisation**, aeration, gaseous diffusion; **sprinkle**, spray, sprinkling; **dispersion**, decentralisation, diaspora, interspersion; **dissemination**, apportionment, circularisation, circulation, contagion,

dispersal   156   **displayed**

distribution, pervasion, semination; **branching,** divarication, flare, radiation, ramification, spread; **break-up,** demob, demobilisation, dissolution; **break-out,** escape, rout, stampede

DISPERSE *v* put to flight, rout, scatter, scatter to the winds, stampede; **deploy,** decentralise, diversify, farm out; **demobilise,** cast adrift, cast out, disband; **dissipate,** dispel, dissolve; **fan out,** branch, divaricate, radiate, ramify, spread, spread like wildfire, straggle; **diffuse,** circumfuse, effuse, pervade, thin; **strew,** bestrew, intersperse, sift, spill, string out; **disseminate,** apportion, broadcast, circularise, circulate, deal out, distribute, dole out, pass out, retail, seed, sow; **spread out,** make hay, ted; **sprinkle,** bespatter, besprinkle, dot, patter, sparge *(Rare),* spot, spray; **atomise,** aerate, nebulise, spray; **dust,** powder, sand; **spatter,** flash *(Obs.),* slosh, splash; **sputter,** spit, splutter

DISPERSED *adj* broadcast, cosmopolitan, diffuse, dissipated, far-flung, pervasive, scattered, widespread; **besprinkled,** besprent *(Poetic),* bestrewn; **sparse,** isolated, sporadic; **diffused,** branching, extended, ramiform

DISPERSEDLY *adv* abroad, around, broadcast, diffusely, diffusively, dissipatedly, flaringly, here and there, passim, sporadically; **scatteringly,** spatteringly; **pervasively,** contagiously

DISPERSER *n* stampeder, tedder; **scatterer,** diffuser, disseminator, dotter, duster, sifter; **dispeller,** nebuliser; **distributor,** broadcaster, circulariser; **sprinkler,** aerator, aerosol, aspergillum, aspersorium, atomiser, knapsack spray, scent spray, sparge pipe, sparger *(Rare)*

DISPERSIVE *adj* contagious, diffusive, disseminative, dissipative, dissolutive, flaring, scattering

DISPLAY *n* array, demo, demonstration, exhibition, expo, exposition, fair, panoply, show; **presentation,** exposure, manifestation, presentment, production, re-presentation, rendition, showing, unfoldment; **spectacle,** pageantry, phantasmagoria, pomp and circumstance, riot, splash, splurge, sunburst; **preview,** sneak preview, view; **ostentation,** bluff, bravura, colouring, exhibitionism, pyrotechnics, showmanship, trim *(U.S.),* window-dressing

DISPLAY *v* approve *(Obs.),* bring forward, demonstrate, exhibit, present, troop; **expose,** argue, bear, betray, bring to light, evidence, evince, lay bare, point up, release, reveal, uncover; **spotlight,** highlight, illuminate; **manifest,** act out, express, indicate, turn on, vent; **lay out,** hang out, hold up, produce, spread out, trot out, unfold, unroll; **parade,** make perform, put through one's paces, show off to its best advantage; **show,** blazon, brandish, dangle, flaunt, flourish, maintain a high profile, parade, shew *(Archaic),* sport, wear; **show off,** make a spectacle, promenade, steal the limelight

DISPLAY CASE *n* display window, gallery, goldfish-bowl, museum, open book, shopwindow, showcase, showroom

DISPLAYED *adj* arrayed, open, public; **exhibitive,** demonstrational, demonstrative, exhibitory, presentational

DISPLAYER *n* demonstrationist, demonstrator, exhibitor, manifestant, presenter, unfolder, window-dresser; **showman,** blazoner, exhibitionist, limelighter, pyrotechnist

DISPLEASE *v* bug, cause pain, cause trouble, chagrin, cut, displeasure *(Archaic),* dissatisfy, hurt, make life unpleasant, open Pandora's box, stir up a hornet's nest, upset, vex, wound; **sicken,** disgust, nauseate, offend, rankle, repel, revolt, set the teeth on edge, turn off, turn the stomach; **horrify,** appal, chill the spine, freeze the blood, frighten, give the heebie-jeebies, make one's hair stand on end, make the flesh creep; **grate,** be no picnic, chafe, jar, rub up the wrong way, sadden, trouble

DISPLEASED *adj* angry, black-browed, browned off, cut up, dissatisfied, ill-at-ease, indignant, jack of, miffed, narked, offended, out of humour, pissed-off, put out, resentful, sore, umbrageous *(Rare),* vexed, whingeing, wry; **hard to please,** cantankerous, discontented, perverse

DISPLEASURE *n* anger, chagrin, disfavour, dissatisfaction, indignation, miff, umbrage, vexation, vexedness; **discomposure,** discomfort, embarrassment, inquietude, malaise, mortification, uneasiness; **an awkward moment,** a bad patch, a moment's uneasiness, a sticky moment, a trouble spot, mauvais quart d'heure

DISPROOF *n* confutation, counter-evidence, disproval, elenchus *(Logic),* falsification, ignoratio elenchi *(Logic),* invalidation, rebuttal *(Law),* refutation

DISPROVE *v* confound, confute, cut the ground from under someone's feet, demolish, give the lie to, invalidate, knock the bottom out of, make a liar of, prove wrong, rebut, refute, reprove *(Obs.);* **tell another story**

DISPROVER *n* confounder, confuter, devil's advocate, falsifier, rebutter, refuter, reprover *(Obs.)*

DISPROVING *adj* confutative, elenctic; **disprovable,** rebuttable, refutable, unwarrantable

DISPUTANT *n* arguer, bickerer, contester, controversialist, disputer, eristic, pettifogger, stirrer, wrangler; **dissenter,** anti, contradictor, controverter, demurrer, denier, dissentient, dissident, maverick, objector, protestant, protester, remonstrant, remonstrator

DISREPUTABLE *adj* disrespectable, doubtful, odious, questionable, shady; **disgraceful,** damnable, dishonourable, illaudable, opprobrious; **discreditable,** compromising, damaging, invidious; **degrading,** demeaning, lowering; **ignoble,** ignominious, inglorious, shameful; **scandalous,** arrant, famous *(Obs.),* flagrant, glaring, ill-famed, infamous, notorious, outrageous; **blameworthy,** exceptionable, inexcusable, inexpiable; **reproachable,** censurable, criticisable, rebukeable; **of doubtful reputation,** questionable, suspect, suspicious, suss; **disgraced,** discredited, fallen, honourless; **humbled,** cut down to size, debunked; **nameless,** characterless, obscure; **unsung**

DISREPUTABLENESS *n* disreputability, doubtfulness, raffishness, seediness, shadiness, wretchedness; **disgracefulness,** damnableness, degradingness,

disreputableness 158 **dissipater**

despicability, despicableness, dishonourableness, ignominiousness, reproachfulness *(Obs.)*; **shamefulness,** abjection, abjectness, ignobility, ignobleness, ingloriousness, invidiousness, opprobriousness, pitiableness, pitifulness, unworthiness; **inexcusableness,** exceptionableness, inexcusability, inexpiableness; **reproachableness,** censurableness

DISREPUTE *n* attainder *(Obs.),* bad odour, contempt, disesteem, disfavour, disreputability, disreputation *(Archaic),* disrespect, disrespectability; **bad reputation,** bad name, doubtful character, past, shady reputation; **dishonour,** discredit, humiliation, indignity, insult; **disgrace,** crying shame, ignominy, obloquy, odium, opprobrium, shame; **scandal,** stink, watergate; **notoriety,** ill fame, infamy, notoriousness; **anonymity,** obscurity

DISSEMINATION *n* circularisation, communication, conveyance, notification, transmission; **briefing,** direction, exposition, instruction, showing; **debriefing,** feedback, interrogation; **propagandism,** indoctrination, proselytism

DISSIDENCE *n* conflict, confliction, contention, dissension, disunion, disunity, division; **resistance,** adverseness, antagonism, confrontation, contrariness, defiance, obstruction, obstructiveness, opponency, opposition, oppugnancy, rebelliousness, resistivity; **insurgence,** direct action, insurgency, insurrection, insurrectionism, sabotage, sedition; **passivism,** civil disobedience, non-cooperation, passive resistance; **recalcitrance,** obstructionism, recusancy, renitency, stand; **counterinsurgency,** backlash, counterplot

DISSIDENT *n* irreconcilable, non-cooperator, objector, obstructer, obstructionist, opposer, oppositionist, oppugner, protester, resistant, resister, thwarter, withstander, Young Turk; **rebel,** guerilla, hostile, insurgent, insurrectionary, insurrectionist, maquis, opposite *(Rare),* saboteur, terrorist, underground, urban guerilla; **challenger,** darer, defier, pebble *(Colloq.),* taunter; **antagonist,** adversary, assailant, assailer, combatant, combater, confrontationist, confronter, contender, enemy, foe, opponent, quarreller, splinter group; **arguer,** anti, con, contravener, controversialist, devil's advocate, disputer, eristic, gainsayer, rebutter

DISSIDENT *adj* antagonistic, anti, defiant, offside, opponent, opposing, oppositional, oppugnant, rival; **resistant,** averse, combative, defiant, defying, insolent, insurgent, insurrectional, insurrectionary, militant, non-cooperative, rebellious, reluctant *(Rare),* resistive, up in arms; **argumentative,** altercative, cantankerous, conflictive, confrontational, contentious, contrary, cross-grained, disputatious, disputative, dissentious, incompliant, peevish *(Obs.),* perverse, quarrelsome, stroppy; **obstructive,** aversive, obscurant, obscurantist; **incompatible,** alien, at loggerheads, at odds, irreconcilable, opposed; **unyielding,** adamant, firm of purpose, implacable, indomitable, persistent, recalcitrant, renitent, unshrinking

DISSIPATER *n* bacchanal, bacchant, Corinthian, goliard, good timer, indulger, profligate, rioter, rip, surfeit-

dissipater   159   **distortion**

er, wallower; **rake**, debauchee, debaucher, libertine, rakehell, roué, swinger *(Obs.)*

DISSONANCE *n* atonalism, atonality, cacophony, discord, discordance, inharmoniousness, wolf, wolf note; **cross-relation**, consecutive fifths, false relation, suspension; **unmusicalness**, tonelessness; **harshness**, roughness; **hoarseness**, frog in the throat, graininess, gutturalness, raggedness; **raucousness**, brassiness, raucity, stridency; **clang**, clash, jangle; **blare**, bray, stridor; **croak**, crack, goose, guttural, roup, snore; **groan**, creak; **rasp**, grate, gride, grind, jar, scraping, scratch, scroop, skirr

DISSONANT *adj* cacophonous, discordant, inharmonious; **atonal**, ajar, anharmonic, inharmonic, nonharmonic; **out of tune**, blue, bum, flat, off key, off pitch, sharp; **unmusical**, tuneless; **harsh**, grating, grinding, rasping, rough, rude, rugged; **hoarse**, cracked, croaky, grainy, gravelly, gritty, ragged, roupy; **creaky**, scrannel *(Archaic)*, squeaky; **raucous**, brassy, strident

DISSONANTLY *adv* atonally, discordantly

DISSYMETRIC *adj* dissymmetrical; **pinnate**, distichous, imparipinnate, pinnatifid, pinnatilobate, pinnatisect

DISTANT *adj* advanced, deep, far, far-off, faraway, farther, further, high, long *(Cricket)*, offshore; **away**, aloof *(Archaic)*, cold *(Games)*, distal, removed, terminal, wide; **furthermost**, apogean, endmost, extreme, farthermost, farthest, outermost, solstitial, ultimate, utmost, uttermost; **long-distance**, cross-country, langlauf, long-range, marathon; **yonder**, thither, yon *(Archaic)*, yond *(Archaic)*. *See also* REMOTE

DISTIL *v* boil down, chastise *(Archaic)*, decoct, distill, isolate, smelt, still *(Obs.)*

DISTILLED *adj* alembicated, distillable, distillatory

DISTILLERY *n* alembic, distillation column, pot still, smelter, smeltery

DISTINCTION *n* nicety, nuance, quiddity, quillet *(Archaic)*, subtlety

DISTORT *v* deform, misshape, put out of shape; **contort**, bend, buckle, cast, convolute, overdraw, strain, torture, twist, warp, wrench, wrest, wrick, wring, writhe

DISTORTED *adj* anamorphic, anamorphous, axonometric, bent, buckled, contorted, convoluted, convulsed, perverted; **deformed**, crooked, diastrophic *(Geol.)*, disfigured, epeirogenic, grotesque, miscreate *(Archaic)*, miscreated, misshapen; **warped**, kinky, twisted, wry

DISTORTEDLY *adv* convolutely, crookedly, deformedly, misshapenly, pervertedly; **askew**, awry, out of shape, skew-whiff

DISTORTER *n* contortionist, deformer, twister, warper, wrester, writher

DISTORTION *n* abnormity, crookedness, deformity, disfigurement, distortedness, malformation, misshapenness; **warp**, bend, bias, buckle, convolution, kink, knar *(Bot.)*, screw, strain, stress, twist, wrench, wrest, writhe; **deformation**, anamorphosis, antic *(Archaic)*, creep *(Engineering)*, diastrophism, set, shear strain, upheaval, uplift, upthrust; **facial distortion**, grimace, grin, snarl; **contortion**, convulsion, rictus, spasm

distortional

DISTORTIONAL *adj* contortional, convulsionary, convulsive

DISTRESSING *adj* bitter, grievous, harrowing, heartbreaking, hurtful, lamentable, pathetic, poignant, pungent, ruthful *(Archaic)*, upsetting; **dismal**, cheerless, chill, cloudy, dark, depressive, dreary, gloomy, joyless, murky, oppressive, sepulchral, sunless; **mournful**, elegiac, epicedial, epicedian, funereal, lugubrious, plaintive, sorrowful, tragic

DISUSE *n* desuetude, dispensation; **boycott**, discontinuance, discontinuation, rejection; **obsolescence**, defunctness, retirement, supersedure, supersession; **planned obsolescence**, throwaway society; **lack of use**, suspension, virginity; **lack of practice**, rustiness

DISUSE *v* decommission, de-emphasise, lay aside, mothball, retire, set aside; **discard**, can, condemn, ditch, dump, give the sword, have no use for, reject, scrap, throw away, throw out; **jettison**, throw overboard; **dispense with**, boycott, discontinue, leave off, pension off, put out to grass, superannuate; **outgrow**, cast off, doff, shed; **leave unused**, do without, hold, hold in abeyance, reserve, save, shepherd, spare

DISUSED *adj* derelict, scrap, waste; **obsolete**, antiquated, archaic, dead, discredited, extinct, obsolescent, out-of-date; **discarded**, cast-off, outgrown, outworn; **out of use**, defunct, in mothballs, laid up, out of commission; **superannuated**, on the shelf, retired, written off; **rusty**, out of practice, out of the habit

DIVE *n* bellybuster, bellyflop, bellywhacker *(Vic.)*, gainer, header, immersion, jackknife dive, plunge,

diversity

swallow dive, tuck; **dip**, duck, souse; **swoop**, pounce, stoop; **power-dive**, crash dive *(Aeron.)*, tail spin; **skydiving**, freefalling

DIVE *v* bellyflop, bomb, dive-bomb, go down like a stone, honey-pot, plummet, plunge, sound, submerge, take a header; **dip**, duck, dunk, immerse, souse; **swoop**, pounce, stoop; **bail out**, free-fall, jump; **nosedive**, crash-dive, power-dive, skydive

DIVER *n* frogman, skindiver; **dipper**, ducker, dunker; **skydiver**, freefaller

DIVERGE *v* bifurcate, branch, divaricate, divide, fork, furcate, gape, move apart, ramify, splay, trifurcate; **divert**, avert, detour, fly off, fly off at a tangent, haul off; **radiate**, branch out, branch out in all directions, eradiate, scatter, spread; **abduce**, abduct

DIVERGENCE *n* arborisation, bifurcation, branching, divarication, embranchment, furcation, moving apart, radiation, ramification, separation, trifurcation. *See also* BRANCH

DIVERGENT *adj* bifurcate, crotched, divaricate, furcate, splay, trifurcate; **radial**, abducent, averse, centrifugal, radiate; **branching**, arterial, brachiate, branchy, enate, ramiform, ramose, ramous, ramulose

DIVERGENTLY *adv* divaricately; **radially**, centrifugally

DIVERSELY *adv* diffusely, heterogeneously, miscellaneously, multifariously; **pell-mell**, indiscriminately

DIVERSITY *n* diverseness, diversification, miscellaneousness, variation; **heterogeneity**, eclecticism, heterogeneousness, many-sidedness, multifariousness, pluralism, promiscuity, promiscuousness

DIVERT *v* canalise, flume *(U.S.)*, head off, inflect, switch

DIVORCE *n* annulment, divorcement, family break-up, legal separation, separation; **maintenance**, alimony, support, visiting rights; **nullity of marriage**, discretion statement

DO *v* chuck, cut, effect, engineer, execute, exercise, follow out, fulfil, get round to, perform, perpetrate, transact, wreak; **act**, do one's stuff, do one's thing, function, functionalise, run; **proceed**, go on, keep one's hand in, practise, take steps; **engage in**, deal with, play, wage; **get stuck into**, get one's teeth into, whale into; **take the bull by the horns**, have the courage of one's convictions, put one's shoulder to the wheel, rush one's fences, sail in, take the plunge

DO EASILY *v* breeze through, do on one's ear, drive a coach and four through, glide through, iron out, lope through, make nothing of, make short work of, rest, romp, romp in, skate, step into, walk over, waltz; **win hands down**, romp home, shit it in, walk the course, win at a canter; **have it easy**, be on a soda, cop it sweet, have it made, live the life of Riley

DOER *n* actor, engager, executant, executioner, executor, executrix, exerciser, performer, perpetrator, practitioner, transactor; **initiator**, activist, actuator, animator, arouser, initiatress, initiatrix, provocative, provoker, stirrer, wakener; **agent**, agency, applier, fulfiller, wreaker; **pragmatist**

DOG *n* barker, bitch, bow-wow, canine, canis, cur, doggie, hound, mutt, pooch, pup, puppy, tripehound *(Joc.)*, tyke; **dog breeds**, Afghan, Airedale, Alsatian, Australian cattle dog, Australian silky terrier, Australian terrier, barb, basenji, basset hound, beagle, beardie, bird dog *(U.S.)*, bloodhound, blue cattle dog, blue heeler, boarhound, border collie, borzoi, Boston terrier, boxer, brach *(Obs.)*, brachet, buckhound, bullmastiff, bull-terrier, bulldog, cairn terrier, camp-dog, cardigan, cattle dog, chihuahua, chow, chow-chow, clumber, coachdog, cocker, cocker spaniel, corgi, dachshund, Dalmatian, Dandie Dinmont, deerhound, Doberman pinscher, draghound, elkhound, English setter, English springer spaniel, Eskimo dog, eye dog, forcing dog, fox terrier, foxhound, foxie, gazehound, German shepherd, golden retriever, Gordon setter, Great Dane, greyhound, gun dog, harrier, heeler, heeling dog *(N.Z.)*, housedog, husky, Irish setter, Irish terrier, Irish water-spaniel, Irish wolfhound, kangaroo dog, keeshond, kelpie, Kerry blue, King Charles spaniel, kuri *(N.Z.)*, Labrador, lakeland terrier, lap-dog, Lhasa apso, lurcher, Maltese dog, Manchester terrier, mastiff, Mexican hairless, newfoundland, Norwegian elkhound, Norwich terrier, Old English sheepdog, otterhound, papillon, peke, Pekingese, Pembroke, pig-dog, pointer, police dog, Pom, Pomeranian, poodle, pug, pye-dog, Queensland Blue Heeler, raccoon dog, red setter, retriever, Rhodesian ridgeback, Rottweiler, Russian wolfhound, Saint Bernard, saluki, Samoyed, sausage dog, schipperke, schnauzer, Scottish terrier, scotty, Sealyham, setter, sheepdog, Shih tzu, Skye terrier, slut, spaniel, spitz, spotted dog, springer, springer spaniel, Staffordshire terrier, staghound, Sussex spaniel, Sydney silky, terrier, toy dog, tumbler, wire-haired terrier, watchdog, waterdog, water-spaniel, Welsh corgi, Welsh springer spaniel, Welsh terrier, whippet, wire-haired terrier, wolfdog *(U.S.)*, wolfhound, Yorkshire terrier

DOING *n* engagement, execution, exercise, initiative, perpetration, play, pursuance

DOMAIN *n* demesne, estate, grounds, realm; **kingdom**, archduchy, archdukedom, barony, duchy, dukedom, empery, grand duchy, margravate, marquisate, palatinate, princedom, regency, vicegerency, viceroyalty, viscounty; **emirate**, khanate, sheikhdom, sultanate; **district**, arrondissement, barrio, borough *(U.S.)*, canton, county *(Brit.)*, deme, department, division, eparchy, hundred, local government area, municipal district *(Tas.)*, municipality, nomarchy, nome, precinct *(U.S.)*, prefecture, province, riding, shire, state, territory, ward; **electorate**, constituency *(Brit.)*; **jurisdiction**, judicature, magistracy, verge; **church land**, glebe, glebe land, prebend; **parish**, mission, vicariate; **diocese**, archbishopric, archdeaconry, archdiocese, bishopric, eparchy, see

DOMED *adj* arched, arcuate, arcuated, beehive, round, testudinate, vaulted, vaultlike, wagon-headed; **hemispherical**, hemispheroidal

DOMESTIC *adj* domiciliary, home, house, household; **residential**, tenemental, tenementary; **homey**, domestic, homely; **manorial**, seignorial *(Archaic)*

DOMESTICITY *n* domestication, domiciliation, homeliness; **domestic life**, domesticities, home life

DONE *adj* accomplished, all over bar the shouting, finished, in the can, over the hump, well-done, wrapped up

DO ONE'S DUTY *v* acquit oneself well, act honourably, answer the call of duty, avenge someone's honour, be at one's post, comport oneself well, discharge a duty, fulfil an obligation, pay off a score, perform a duty, satisfy, serve, settle a score, supererogate; **be responsible**, carry the can, have broad shoulders, have the ball in one's court, have the matter rest on one's shoulders, take it upon oneself

DOOR *n* back door, bulkhead, deadlight, Dutch door, fly, folding doors, French doors, French window, jib door, louvre, paddle, port, portal, portcullis, postern, screen door, shutter, stable door, stern door, stop door, storm door *(U.S.)*, swing door, trap, trapdoor, wing; **gate**, Bogan gate, boom gate, drafting gate, droprail, floodgate, headgate, hurdle gate, lock-gate, swing gate, taranaki gate *(N.Z.)*, tollgate, water-gate, wicket

DOUBLE *v* duplicate, geminate, redouble; **couple**, bracket, match, pair, twin

DOUBLENESS *n* biformity, dimerism, dimorphism, dualism, duality, duplicity; **double-sidedness**, bilateralism, bilateralness; **duplication**, doubling, gemination, twinning

DOUBT *n* credibility gap, distrust, distrustfulness, misdoubt, misgiving, mistrust, mistrustfulness, scepticalness, suspicion, uncertainty; **disbelief,** denial, discredit, incredility, incredulousness, unbelief, unbelievingness; **scepticism,** agnosticism, nihilism, pyrrhonism

DOUBT *v* call into question, deny, disbelieve, entertain doubts, harbour suspicions, have one's doubts, question, smell a rat, suspect, take with a grain of salt; **disbelieve,** discredit, distrust, misbelieve *(Obs.),* mistrust; **bring into question,** cause uncertainty, challenge, query, raise doubts

DOUBTER *n* agnostic, denier, disbeliever, distruster, doubting Thomas, infidel, mistruster, nihilist, nullifidian, sceptic, unbeliever

DOUBTING *adj* agnostic, diffident *(Rare),* disbelieving, distrustful, doubtful, inconvinceable, incredulous, mistrustful, sceptical, suspicious of, unbelieving

DOUBTINGLY *adv* agnostically, disbelievingly, distrustfully, inconvincibly, incredulously, mistrustfully, mistrustingly, sceptically, unbelievingly

DOWN *adv* adown *(Poetic),* below, downstairs, over, overboard, overside; **downwards,** downgrade, downhill, downward, downwardly

DRAIN *n* culvert, ditch, downcomer, downpipe, drainpipe, gutter, ponding board, sewer, spitter, spreader, watertable; **wastepipe,** gully trap, S-trap, soil pipe, stench trap; **spout,** gargoyle, spile *(U.S.),* waterspout

DRAMA *n* closet drama, conversation piece, costume drama, costume piece, epic, experimental theatre, Grand Guignol, history, kitchen-sink drama, mask, masque, melodrama, miracle play, monodrama, morality play, music drama, mystery play, panto *(Colloq.),* pantomime, passion play, piece, play, playlet, poetic drama, problem play, Punch and Judy show, puppet play, sequel, shadow play, tetralogy *(Class. Antiq.),* trilogy, work; **No,** kabuki, Noh, tamasha, wayang; **tragedy,** buskin, tragicomedy; **comedy,** bedroom comedy, black comedy, burlesque, camp, comedy of ideas, comedy of manners, commedia dell'arte, farce, high camp, high comedy, interlude, low comedy, musical comedy, sitcom, situation comedy, slapstick, theatre of the absurd, tragicomedy

DRAMATIC *adj* dramaturgic, dramaturgical, Grand Guignol, heavy, Thespian, tragic, tragicomic; **comic,** burlesque, clownish, comical *(Obs.),* custard-pie, farcical, hammy, harlequinesque, pantomimic, slapstick, variety, vaudevillian; **didactic,** agitprop; **theatrical,** histrionic, make-believe, scenic, stagy; **choric,** stichomythic; **solo,** monologic, one-man, one-woman

DRAMATICALLY *adv* acrobatically, cinematically, clownishly, farcically, histrionically, scenically, stagily, theatrically, tragically; **backstage,** behind the scenes, downstage, in the limelight, in the spotlight, in the wings, offstage, on the boards, on the stage, onstage, upstage

DRAWING *n* drafting, sketching, technical drawing; **sketch,** line drawing, outline, perspective; **draft,** cartoon, graffiti, rough, sinopia, thumbnail sketch, vignette, visual; **caricature,**

drawing 164 **drink**

strip cartoon; **pattern**, blot drawing, design; **shading**, crosshatching, hachure, hatching, shadow

DREADFUL *adj* crushing, demoralising, frightening, horrible, horrid, terrifying, traumatic; **gruesome**, appalling, creepy, frightful, ghastly, ghoulish, grim, grisly, horrendous, horrific, macabre, monstrous, nightmarish, shocking. *See also* UNPLEASANT; UNBEARABLE; SICKENING; PESTERING

DREAM *n* chimera, hallucination, mirage, nightmare, phantasm, phantasmagoria; **daydream**, pipedream, romantics, stardust; **utopia**, cloud-cuckoo-land, fairyland, pie in the sky, hope, wonderland

DRESS *n* caftan, chemise, cheongsam, dirndl, Dolly Varden, evening gown, exclusive, frock, gown, halterneck, hostess gown, jumper *(U.S.)*, kimono, mantua, maternity dress, Mother Hubbard, muu-muu, pinafore frock, polonaise, Princess line, robe, sack, sheath, shift, shirtmaker, stole *(Archaic)*, suit, sundress, teagown, topless, tunic, wedding dress; **wraparound**, haik, ihram *(Islam)*, lava-lava, pareu, sari *(India)*, sarong *(S.E. Asia)*; **skirt**, culottes, filibeg *(Scot.)*, hobble skirt, hoop, hoop skirt, hula skirt, kilt, kirtle, maxi, maxi-skirt, midi, mini, miniskirt, overskirt, peg top, piupiu *(N.Z.)*, tutu; **tunic**, gym-tunic. *See also* OUTFIT

DRESSMAKING *n* corsetry, rag trade *(Colloq.)*, tailoring

DRIER *n* blow-drier, clothes drier, fugal, hair drier, mangle, spin-drier, tumble-drier, tumbler, whizzer, wringer; **clothes hoist**, clothes horse, clothes line; **dehumidifier**, air conditioner, evaporator, exsiccator; **desiccant**, desiccator, siccative; **drainer**, draining-board; **wiper**, squeegee, windscreen-wiper; **towel**, bath sheet, bath towel, beach towel, handtowel, paper towel, tea-cloth, tea-towel; **blotter**, pounce; **astringent**, antiperspirant

DRILY *adv* aridly, thirstily

DRINK *n* amrita, beverage, dishwater, draught, drench *(Obs.)*, drinkables, drinking water, eye-opener, heart-starter, nectar, potables, tap *(Archaic)*, wash; **tea**, billy tea, black tea, brew, bush tea, chai, char, cuppa, Darjeeling, green tea, gunpowder, hyson, Jack the Painter, oolong, orange pekoe, Paraguay tea, pekoe, post-and-rail tea, saloop, tisane; **coffee**, café au lait, cappuccino, coffee royal, congou, drip coffee, espresso, flat white, Irish coffee, long black, milk coffee, mocha, plunger coffee, short black, vienna; **soft drink**, barley water, chalybeate, cider, cider-cup, coke, cola, cordial, creaming soda, crush, dry, fizz, fruit cup, ginger ale, ginger beer, hydromel, ice-cream soda, julep, lemon squash, lemonade, lolly water, mead *(U.S.)*, mineral water, orangeade, orgeat, pop, ptisan, punch, root beer *(U.S.)*, sarsaparilla *(U.S.)*, seltzer, soda, soda-water, spa water, spider, squash, tonic, tonic water, vichy water; **milk**, buttermilk, colostrum, cow juice, malted milk, milkshake, polymilk, shake, skim milk, the bottle, thick shake, whey, whole milk; **eggflip**, flip, Murrumbidgee oyster, prairie oyster; **guarana**; **cocoa**, chocolate

DRINK *v* bend one's elbow, down, drain, imbibe, quaff, raise one's elbow, refresh oneself with, sip, slurp, suck, swallow, swig, swill, toss off

DRINK ALCOHOL *v* bib *(Obs.)*, get a drink across one's chest, imbibe, lush, soak up, sock away, stop one, swig, tip the little finger, tipple, wet one's whistle; **drink heavily**, bash the turps, be on the bottle, bend the elbow, booze, carouse, drink like a fish, get into it, give it a bash, go on the scoot, go on the squiff, go on the stun, go on the tank, grog on, hit the booze, hit the bottle, indulge, iron oneself out, lay into it, mix one's drinks, nudge the bottle, piss on, souse, tank up, tope, turn to drink, write oneself off; **shout**, be in the chair, carry the mail, sneeze, splice the mainbrace, stand one's hand; **toast**, bumper

DRINKING SESSION *n* bacchanalia, barney, bash, bat, beer-up, bender, binge, blind, blinder, boatrace, booze, booze-up, boozeroo *(N.Z.)*, compotation, grog-on, grog-up, happy hour, jag, jamberoo, lush, piss-up, pub crawl, rort, scatter, six o'clock swill, soak, spree; **cocktail party**, bowl, drinks, wine-tasting, winebibbing

DRINKING VESSEL *n* beaker, blackjack, calix, can, cannikin, chalice *(Poetic)*, ciborium, coffee cup, cup, cylix, demitasse, goblet, grace-cup, grail, kylix, loving-cup, mug, pannikin, pint-pot, pottle, quart pot, rhyton, rummer, scyphus, skin, stein, stoup *(Scot. Archaic)*, tallboy, tankard, taster, teacup, toby jug; **drinking glass**, balloon, beer glass, bobby *(W.A.)*, brandy balloon, butcher, champagne flute, cruiser, handle, Lady Blamey, lady's waist, long-sleever, middy, pony, pot, schooner, snifter, tumbler, vegemite jar, wineglass; **glassware**, stemware; **gourd**, calabash, horn, wineskin; **can**, ring-pull can, tin, tin can, tinnie, tinny, tube

DRIVE *v* corner, fang, guttercrawl, motor, ride, scramble *(Racing)*, tool, tootle; **taxi**, bus, jitney, post, stage, train, tram; **cycle**, bicycle, scooter; **sledge**, bobsled, bobsleigh, skibob, sled, sleigh; **chariot**, gig; **hitch**, bum a ride, hitchhike, jump the rattler, ringbolt *(N.Z. Colloq.)*, scale, stow away

DRIVER *n* cabbie, chauffeur, chauffeuse, defensive driver, hackie, motorist, road rider, road-hog, Sunday driver, syce, taxi-driver, wheelman; **motorcyclist**, biker, bikie, hell's angel, milk bar cowboy; **bicyclist**, cyclist, wheelman; **engine-driver**, engineer *(U.S.)*, engineman, gripman, shunter; **charioteer**, carter, coachman, wagoner, whip; **conductor**, busman, connie, motorman, ticket inspector, trammie

DRUG *n* addictive drug, Bob Hope, bomb, dope, drug of dependence, gear; **narcotic**, hard stuff, junk; **tranquilliser**, stopper, stupefacient, stupefier; **hallucinogen**, mind-altering drug, psychedelic, psychoactive drug, psychochemical; **deal**, bag, deck, packet. *See also* NARCOTIC; MARIJUANA; STIMULANT; HALLUCINOGEN

DRUG ADDICTION *n* habit, monkey on one's back; **narcotism**, cocainism, morphinism, opiumism; **withdrawal**, cold-turkey, drying-out, methadone treatment

DRUG DEALER *n* dealer, dope-pedlar, doper, greengrocer, pusher, trafficker; **opium den**

DRUG EQUIPMENT *n* bong, chillum, hookah, hubble-bubble, water pipe; **hypodermic**, fit, hype, outfit, pick, works

DRUGGED *adj* blocked, bombed, dopey, loaded, mandied, off one's face, poppied, ripped, smacked-out, smashed, stoked, stoned; **high**, high as a kite, on a high, spaced, spaced-out, spacey

DRUG USE *n* bang, fix, hit, skinpop, trip; **high**, buzz; **overdose**, narcosis, OD, stupor

DRUG USER *n* acidhead, dope fiend, doper, glue-sniffer, head, hophead, hound *(U.S.)*, hype, mainliner, pothead, shithead, snowbird; **addict**, druggie, junkie, smackhead

DRUNK *adj* all-overish *(Obs.)*, blasted, blind, blithered, blotto, blued, canned, cast *(N.Z.)*, chocker, cock-eyed, corked, cut, drunken, full, groggy, half-seas-over, high, high as a kite, in one's cups, inebriated, inked, intoxicated, jagged, lit, lit up, lushy, molo, pickled, pie-eyed, pinko, pissed, pissy, plastered, potted, primed, ripe, rolling, screwed, shickered, slewed, sloshed, sozzled, spiflicated, spliced, stewed, stiff, stinking, stinko, stoked, stonkered, stung, tanked, the worse for wear, three sheets in the wind, tight, tired and emotional, under the weather, well-oiled, winy; **dead drunk**, dead to the world, drunk as a lord, drunk as a pissant, drunk as Chloe, far gone, flakers, fuddled, full as a boot, full as a bull, full as a fart, full as a goog, full as a state school, full as a tick, loaded, non compos, off one's face, out to it, paralytic, ripped, rotten, smashed, stoned, unable to scratch oneself, unconscious, under the table; **tipsy**, elevated, maudlin, merry, muzzy, squiffy, tiddly, woozy; **alcoholic**, bacchanalian, bacchic, beery, bibulous, boozy, dipso, dipsomaniacal, in the grip of the grape, sottish; **hung-over**, gone to Gowings, morning-after

DRUNKENLY *adv* bibulously, groggily, maudlinly, merrily, sottishly, tipsily, woozily; **intoxicatingly**, headily; **on the booze**, on the ran-tan, on the shicker, on the tank, on the turps

DRUNKENNESS *n* bacchanalianism, bibulousness, ebriety, fuddle, inebriation, inebriety, insobriety, intoxication, sottishness, tightness, tipsiness, wooziness; **alcoholism**, blue devils, d.t.'s, delirium tremens, dipsomania, heebie-jeebies, horrors, Joe Blakes, pink elephants *(Obs.)*, the dingbats, the shakes; **hangover**, a head, a terrible head, morning after

DRY *v* air-dry, blow-dry, drip-dry, kiln-dry, rough-dry, spin-dry, sunted, win *(Scot.)*; **wipe**, absorb, blot, mop, rub, sponge, squeegee, swab, towel; **drain**; **desiccate**, dehumidify, dehydrate, evaporate, exsiccate, mummify, season, torrefy, weather; **parch**, sear, shrivel, wither, wizen

DRY *adj* bone-dry, dry as a bird's arse, dry as a sunstruck bone, dry as the Nullarbor, fair, fine, high and dry, rough-dry, thirsty, tinderlike; **desiccated**, anhydrous, dried; **arid**, cloudless, dewless, droughty, floodless, fountainless, hazed-off, rainless, semiarid, subarid, sun-dried, sunbaked, torrid, waterless, xeric;

dry   167   **dutifulness**

withered, marcescent, sapless, sere, wizened; **waterproof,** coated, damp-proof, showerproof, staunch, water-repellent, water-resistant, watertight; **xerophilous,** xerophytic

DRYING *n* airing, dehumidification, dehydration, desiccation, evaporation, exsiccation, torrefaction, ustulation; **drainage,** dereliction *(Law);* marcescence

DRYING *adj* desiccant, desiccative, evaporative, exsiccative, parching, siccative, subastringent; **astringent,** styptic

DRYNESS *n* aridity, aridness, drought, semiaridity, the dry, torridity, torridness; **astringency,** stypticity; **watertightness; desert,** dead centre, dead heart, erg *(Geog.),* rain shadow

DULL *v* bedim *(Poetic),* faint *(Rare),* soften, take the shine out of; **matt,** deaden, fade, opaque; **tarnish,** discolour, muddy

DULL *adj* drab, dreary, faded, lacklustre, old, sad, toneless; **pale,** fishy, muted, soft, washed-out; **dingy,** dirty, gloomy, muddy, muggy, murky; **dim,** dusky, faint, obscure; **unreflecting,** antidazzle, antiglare, dead, dun, flat, glossless, leaden, lustreless, matt, matte, matted

DULLNESS *n* drabness, dreariness, lacklustre, paleness, softness; **dimness,** dusk, duskiness, faintness, gloom, obscurity; **murkiness,** dinginess, dirtiness, mugginess; **opacity,** opaqueness

DUNG *n* bullshit, coprolite, cow cake, cow pat, droppings, dunghill, manure, meadow cake, mess, muck, taranaki topdressing *(N.Z.).* See also DEFECATION

DURABILITY *n* durableness, serviceability, serviceableness; **fortitude,** backbone, doughtiness, hardiness, manliness, marrow, nerve, stalwartness, staunchness; **stamina,** inexhaustibility, relentlessness, staying power, tenacity, tirelessness; **indestructibility,** imperishability, impregnability, inexpugnability, inexpugnableness, invincibility, inviolability

DURABLE *adj* fortified, hard-wearing, heavy-duty, knockabout, serviceable, tough; **sturdy,** cast-iron, iron, steel, steely; **indestructible,** imperishable, impregnable, indomitable, inexpugnable, inextinguishable, invincible, inviolable; **tempered,** case-hardened, post-tensioned, pre-tensioned, thermotensile

DURATION *n* length, standing; **life span,** generation, life, lifetime, one's born days, run time, shelf life, short life, time limit; **aeon,** ages, donkey's years, eternity, yonks

DURING *prep* round, since, through, throughout, under

DUTIFUL *adj* civic-minded, conscientious, observant, religious, supererogatory

DUTIFULLY *adv* conscientiously, observantly, responsibly; **on duty,** on the spot; **by reason of obligation,** of necessity, perforce

DUTIFULNESS *n* religiousness, responsibleness; **conscientiousness,** conscience, morality, morals, sense of fitness, sense of right and wrong, still small voice within, voice of conscience; **loyalty,** allegiance, fealty; **propriety,** conduct becoming, decorum, discharge, fitness, fulfilment, observance, proper behaviour, seemliness, the proper thing, the right thing

DWELLING *n* abode, accommodation, address, domicile, dwelling house, dwelling place, establishment, habitation, hang-out, harbour, hermitage, home, home away from home, joint, kipsie, mansion *(Archaic)*, pad, pied-à-terre, place, residence, roof over one's head, shelter, shovel, squat, tabernacle *(Archaic)*, tenement; **habitat**, element, home ground, home range, medium, microhabitat, province, purlieu, range, sphere, zone; **residency**, consulate, Government house, prefecture; **fireside**, hearth, roof; **settlement**, colony, commune, plantation *(Hist.)*; **reservation**, Aboriginal reserve, Indian reservation, pa *(N.Z.)*, reserve; **retirement village**, halfway house, receiving home, rest home, sheltered housing; **foster home**, orphanage; **out-station**, country camp, outpost. *See also* BARRACKS; FLATS; HOUSE; CABIN; CARAVAN; CAMP; HOTEL

DYE *n* azo dye, chromogen, colorant, colour fast, dyestuff, ink, lake, mordant, natural dye, opaque, pigment, reactive dye, rinse, tincture *(Obs.)*, vat dye, wash; **counterstain**, stain; **paint**, acrylic colour, body colour, colourwash, distemper, gouache, oil colour, oils, polymer colour, primer, scumble, tempera, undercoat, underglaze, watercolour; **make-up**, blusher, eyeliner, eye shadow, greasepaint, lipgloss, lipstick, mascara, rouge, war paint; **pencil**, chalk, crayon, felt pen, texta. *See also* COLOUR

DYEING *n* chrome tanning, imbuement, impasto, painting, staining; **colour reproduction,** chromolithography, colour photography, four-colour process, photochromy, process printing, technicolour, three-colour process; **colour print**, aquatint, chromo, chromolithograph, colour proof, duotone, halftone, monochrome

Ee

EACH *adv* a pop, apiece, individually, one at a time, one by one, per capita, respectively, singly

EAR *n* cauliflower ear, lug, shell-like *(Joc.)*; **ear lobe**, earlap, lappet; **external ear**, auricle, concha, ear canal, outer ear, pavilion, pinna; **middle ear**, anvil, ear bone, eardrum, Eustachian tube, hammer, incus, malleus, ossicle, oval window, round window, stapes, stirrup bone, tympanum; **internal ear**, basilar membrane, ear stone, inner ear, labyrinth, organ of Corti, otolith, saccule, semicircular canal, utricle

EARLINESS *n* seasonableness; **prematurity**, precociousness, precocity; **early days**, early hour; **early mark**, early minutes; **false start**, break, breakaway; **pre-ignition**; **abortion**, miscarriage; **untimeliness**, unripeness; **early bird**, early riser

EARLY *adj* earliest, first, premier; **earlier**, elder, former, olden, youthful; **premature**, abortive, immature, premmie, previous, rathe, slink, unripe, untimely; **forward**, precocious, **seasonable**, timely *(Rare)*

EARLY *adv* at crack of dawn, at first crack, at sparrow fart, before time, bright and early, first thing, in the wee small hours; **earlier**, before, sooner; **beforehand**, ahead of time, in advance; **timely**, betimes, in good season, in time; **prematurely**, precociously, rathe *(Archaic)*

EASE *v* alleviate, comfort, console, cushion, facilitate *(Archaic)*, lighten, mitigate, relieve, soften, soothe, spare, sugar the pill, temper

EASILY *adv* comfortably, conveniently, easy, effortlessly, facilely, familiarly, flowingly, fluently, freely, hand over fist, home on the pig's back, lightly, like a bird, painlessly, readily, smooth, smoothly, well; **snugly**, cheaply, comfortably, comfortingly, glidingly, on a plate, on a platter, on easy street, snug, soothingly

EASINESS *n* comfort, comfortableness, ease, effortlessness, freedom, freeness, painlessness, snuggery, snugness; **life of Riley**, bed of roses, easy wicket, silk department; **facility**, ease, fluency, glibness, readiness, **manageableness**, facileness, handiness, manageability, smoothness

EASY *adj* cinchy, comfortable, easy as falling off a log, easy as pie, effortless, facile, familiar, fatty, jammy, light, like shooting fish in a barrel, like taking candy from a baby, painless, right, sweet, undemanding, unexacting; **simple**, cheap, convenient, fair, flat *(Racing)*, foolproof, free, intelligible, knotless, runaway, smooth, uncomplicated; **manageable**, do-it-yourself, manoeuvrable, tractable, wieldy; **convenient**, handy, ready; **facile**, flowing, fluent, glib, light

EASY THING *n* a sweet cop, armchair ride, breeze, child's play, cinch, fat *(Print.)*, gift, loaf, picnic, piece of cake, piece of piss, pushover, sitter, sitting duck, snack, snap, walkaway, walkover; **plain sailing**, highroad, line of least resistance, primrose path, romp, set-up, soda; **head start**, walk-up start

EAT *v* bog in, demolish, dig in, down, eat like a horse, engorge, get into, get outside of, get stuck into, gobble, gollop, gorge, grub, gulp, hoe in, hoe into, ingest, ingurgitate, knock back, knock off, live on, nosh, overeat, pick, pick at, put away, refresh oneself with, scoff, sink, slurp, stodge, swallow, take, taste, toss off, tuck in, wash down, wolf; **chew**, bite, champ, chomp, masticate, mumble, munch, nibble; **diet**, be on a diet; **dine**, banquet, break bread, breakfast, dine out, eat out, feast, junket, lunch, mess, put on the feedbag, sup, tiffin *(India)*, wine and dine; **flash one's dover;** **digest**, absorb *(Obs.)*, assimilate, keep down, stomach; **predigest**, peptonise

EATER *n* banqueter, breakfaster, carboholic, carnivore, crammer, deipnosophist, dietarian, dieter, digester, diner, epicure, feaster, feeder, flesh-eater, fruitarian, gastronome, gastronomist, geophagist, gobbler, gorger, gourmand, gourmet, gulper, junketer, masticator, muncher, nibbler, omnivore, omophagist, swallower, turophile, vegan, vegetarian; **cannibal**, anthropophagite, anthropophagus, man-eater; **drinker**, quaffer, swiller

EATING *n* assimilation, deglutition, digestion, engorgement, eupepsia, feasting, gastronomy, ingestion, ingurgitation, mastication, monophagia, monophagy, omnivorousness, omophagia, polyphagia; **cannibalism**, anthropophagy; **geophagy**, geophagism; **swallow**, bolus, gulp

ECCLESIASTIC *n* Amen snorter, beneficiary, bush brother, chaplain, churchman, clergyman, cleric, clerical, clerk, confessor, curate *(Archaic)*, curé, dominie, ecclesiast *(Archaic)*, incumbent, josser, kirkman *(Scot.)*, man of God, man of the cloth, minister, Monsignor, padre, parish priest, parson, pastor, prebendary, presbyter, priest, priestess, rector, residentiary, Reverence, reverend, shepherd, sin-shifter, sky pilot, vicar, vicar-general; **divine**, Doctor of the Church, evangelist, father, lawyer, rabbi, rabbin, rabbinate, seminarian, seminarist; **sanctifier**, anointer, baptiser, celebrant, consecrator, insufflator, mystagogue, officiant, officiator, ordainer, seculariser; **dean**, archpriest, canon, capitular, capitulary, chapter, prebendary, subdean, vicar forane; **bishop**, diocesan, patriarch, pontiff, prelate, suffragan; **Chief Rabbi**, high priest, rabbi, rabbin, rabbinate; **ayatollah**, high priest, imam, imaum, mullah; **archbishop**, Abba, archdeacon, eparch *(Greek Orthodox)*, Evangelist *(Mormon)*, exarch *(Eastern)*, ordinary, primate, provincial, vicar apostolic; **cardinal**, cardinalate, ecclesiarch, Eminence, hat, prince, red hat; **pope,** ecumenical patriarch, Holy Father, patriarch, Patriarch of Rome, pontiff, primate, vicar; **the clergy,** the cloth, the pulpit. *See also* PREACHER; RELIGIOUS DIGNITARY; MONASTIC

ECCLESIASTIC *adj* ecclesiastical, hierarchal, priest-ridden *(Derog.)*; **missionary**, evangelical, evangelistic, revivalist; **clerical,** Aaronic, churchmanly, cleric, hieratic, ministerial, pastoral, presbyteral, priestly, rabbinical, rectorial, reverend, sacerdotal, secular, vicarial, vicarly; **synodal**, capitular, capitulary, consistorial, consistorian; **diaconal**, archidiaconal, decanal, neophytic, proctorial, subdiaconal; **episcopal**, archiepiscopal, metropolitan, prelatic, primatial, suffragan; **papal**, apostolic, curial, legatine, pontifical, primatial, suburbicarian

ECCLESIASTICALLY *adv* clerically, clerkly, decanally, hieratically, ministerially, monastically, monkishly, sacerdotally; **evangelically**, evangelistically; **pontifically**, apostolically, ex cathedra, ministerially

ECONOMIC *adj* econometric, econometrical, economical, Keynesian, macro-economic, Marxist, micro-economic, socioeconomic

ECONOMICS *n* classical economics, demand-side economics, econometrics, macro-economics, micro-economics, monetarism, motivational research, political economy, supply-side economics; **economist**, cambist, chartist, dry, econometrician, free-trader, Keynesian, Marxist, monetarist, physiocrat, wet

ECONOMY *n* cash economy, demand economy, market economy; **free trade**, free enterprise, mercantile system; **monopoly**, corner, duopsony, monopsony, oligopoly, oligopsony; **private enterprise**, capitalism; **planned economy**, communism, socialism; **mixed economy**, welfare state

EDGE *n* brim, brink, brow, limbus; **outline**, contour, profile; **border**, board, fringe, headland *(Agric.)*, margin, rand, skirt, verge; **ambit**, bounds, bourn, circuit, circumscription, compass, confines, girdle; **rim**, chime, collar, flange, gunwale, lip, rail *(Surfing)*; **ledge**, eave; **hem**, apron, basque, flounce, frill, fringe, furbelow, orphrey, ruffle, selvedge, thrum, valance; **frontier**, borderline, bounds, coast *(Obs.)*, march, outskirts, precincts. *See also* LIMIT; KERBING; COASTLINE; FRAME

EDGE *v* engrail, fringe, mill, rim; **bind**, braid, hem, list, twine; **frame**, cordon, hedge in, margin, marginate, mat; **outline**, circumscribe, contour

EDGED *adj* bordered, marginate; **fringelike**, fringy

EDUCATED *adj* academic, antiquarian, book-learned, cultivated, cultured, erudite, learned, lettered, literate, owlish, pedantic, pseudo-learned, scholarly, scholastic, self-educated, self-taught, studied *(Rare)*, studious, well-educated; **practised**, full-fledged, schooled, well-grounded, well-versed; **informed**, abreast of, au courant, briefed, enlightened, posted, primed, up on, up-to-date

EDUCATION *n* adult education, coeducation, continuing education, day classes, evening classes, further education, higher education, physical education, physical training, primary education, re-education, schooling, secondary education, self-education, sex education, special education, technical education, tertiary education, three R's, vocational training. *See also* TEACHING

EDUCATIONAL *adj* edifying, educative, educatory, instructive

EDUCATIONAL OFFICE *n* chair, deanship, headmastership, lectureship, position, proctorship, professoriate, professorship; **tutorship**, instructorship, supervisorship

EFFORT n diligence, exertion, industriousness, industry, labour, lucubration, work; **drive**, conatus, endeavour, nisus, push, striving; **strain**, overexertion, overwork, stress *(Rare)*, travail, trouble; **muscle**, elbow grease, sweat of one's brow

EFFORTFUL adj arduous, backbreaking, burdensome, exertive, hard, heavy, herculean, laborious, labour-intensive, laboured, operose, strenuous, sweaty, toilful, toilsome, uphill, wearisome, weary; **industrious**, energetic, hard at it, hard-working, notable *(Archaic)*; **thorough**, diligent, painstaking, sedulous

EIGHT n eighth, octad, octameter, octarchy, octave, octet, octuplet, ogdoad; **octagon**, octahedron

EIGHT adj eightfold, eighth, octadic, octagonal, octahedral, octal, octamerous, octan, octonary, octuple

EJECT v avoid *(Obs.)*, boot out, bounce, chuck out, clean out, clear out, defenestrate, ding, fling out, jettison, kick out, oust, out, reject, rout, shoo, show one the door, throw out, turf out; **evict**, displace, turn out, turn out of house and home; **banish**, deport, exile, extradite, transport; **disbar**, black-list, dismiss, drum out, exclude, send down, strike off. *See also* EXPEL

ELASTIC n elastic band, lacker band, rubber band; **spring**, cee-spring, leaf spring, mainspring, spring-loading, springboard, torsion bar, valve spring

ELASTICISE v jell, jellify, jelly, plasticise

ELECT v put in, return, vote into office; **vote**, ballot, blackball, cast a vote, coopt, divide *(Parl. Proc.)*, go to the polls; **appoint**, adopt, affect, ordain *(Obs.)*, preselect. *See also* CHOOSE

ELECTION n by-election, general election, hustings, plebiscite, poll, presidential primary *(U.S.)*, primary *(U.S.)*, referendum, tanistry *(Hist.)*; **vote**, acclaim, ballot, blackball, division *(Parl. Proc.)*, show of hands, voice; **kind of vote**, absence vote, card-vote, casting vote, compulsory voting, conscience vote, cumulative voting, deliberative vote, donkey vote, exhaustive ballot, first-past-the-post voting, free vote, free vote, postal vote, preferential voting, second ballot, secret ballot; **suffrage**, franchise; **polling booth**, ballot-box, ballot-paper, booth, voting machine *(U.S.)*, voting paper; **psephology**, psephologist

ELECTIONEER v barnstorm, campaign, canvass, crusade, go on the stump *(U.S.)*, meet the people, press flesh, stump *(U.S.)*; **run for parliament**, stand; **hold an election**, dissolve parliament, go to the country, go to the people, go to the polls, prorogue parliament

ELECTIONEERING n agitprop, canvass, crusade, party political broadcast, party political speech, stump oratory, television debate, whistlestop *(U.S.)*; **dirty tricks**, gerrymander, pork-barrelling, smear campaign; **redistribution**

ELECTORATE n borough *(Brit.)*, congressional district *(U.S.)*, constituency *(Brit.)*, country seat, rotten borough *(Brit. Hist.)*, seat, swinging seat;

voter, abstainer, constituent, elector, electoral college, floating vote, floating voter, mandator, swinging voter; **right to vote,** franchise, isonomy, suffrage, universal suffrage

ELECTRIC *adj* galvanic, plug-in, supply, voltaic; **electronic,** microelectronic, solid-state, transistor; **ac-dc,** diphase, quarter-phase, single-phase, split-phase, three-phase, two-phase; **live,** alive, high-tension, high-voltage, low-tension; **electromotive,** electrodynamic, electrokinetic; **electrochemical,** electromagnetic, electrometallurgical, ferroelectric, hydro-electric, magneto-electric, photoelectric, piezoelectric, thermoelectric

ELECTRICAL DEVICE *n* black box; **photoelectric cell,** photocell, phototube, photovoltaic cell; **valve,** cathode-ray tube, electron gun, electron tube, heptode, magic eye, pentagrid, radio valve, thermionic valve, triode, tube, vacuum tube; **rectifier,** converter, crystal detector, half-wave rectifier, inverter, junction rectifier, rotary convertor, silicon-controlled rectifier, synchronous converter, thyristor; **resistor,** bleeder, resistance, rheostat; **capacitor,** air-condenser, condenser, grid condenser, trimmer, trimmer condenser, varactor; **solid-state device,** charge-coupled device, FET, field effect transistor, integrated circuit, junction transistor, MOS, p-n junction, phototransistor, semiconductor diode, transistor, tunnel diode, unijunction transistor, Zener diode; **klystron,** buncher resonator, catcher resonator; **crystal,** crystal oscillator, liquid crystal display, quartz plate

ELECTRIC CIRCUIT *n* circuit, circuitry, closed circuit, microcircuit, network, open circuit, printed circuit, stage, wiring; **short circuit,** short; **contact,** brush, busbar, commutator, slipring; **switch,** air-switch, button, contact-breaker, contactor, dimmer, dip switch, double-throw switch, interrupter, knife switch, make and break, point, push-button, stepping switch, switchgear, tumbler switch; **current collector,** pantograph, plough, skate, third rail, trolley; **power cable,** catenary, conduit, feeder, grid, jumper leads, power line, power wire, transmission line; **conductor,** amorphous semiconductor, dialectric, electrolyte, extrinsic semiconductor, insulator, intrinsic semiconductor, n-type semiconductor, p-type semiconductor, semiconductor, superconductor, thermistor, thermocouple, thermopile, winding; **solenoid,** coil, differential, field coil, field winding; **armature,** rotor, stator; **switchboard,** fuse box, junction box, switchbox; **fuse,** breaker, circuit-breaker, fuse link, fuse wire; **earth,** buzz bar, earth loop, earth return, ground plate, lightning conductor; **wire,** filament; **power point,** bayonet holder, double adapter, general-purpose outlet, receptacle *(U.S.),* socket, valve base, valve socket; **plug,** balun, connection, jack; **patch board; terminal,** anode, cathode, electrode, emitter, grid, plate

ELECTRIC GENERATOR *n* accumulator, battery, cadmium cell, cell, Daniell cell, dry battery, dry cell, Edison accumulator, electric cell, fuel cell, galvanic battery, gravity cell, mercury cell, Ni-Fe accumulator, primary cell, secondary cell, selenium cell, so-

electric generator — lar battery, standard cell, storage battery, voltaic battery, Weston cell, wet cell; **spark generator,** ignition coil, plug, spark coil, spark plug, sparker, tesla coil; **transformer,** booster, induction coil, isolating transformer, step-down transformer, step-up transformer, trannie; **power station,** generating station, power reactor, powerhouse, substation; **generator,** alternator, magneto, turbogenerator; **dynamo,** charger, electrostatic generator, power pack, static machine, Van de Graaff generator, Wimshurst machine

ELECTRICIAN n auto-electrician, electrical engineer, sparks, wirer

ELECTRICITY n juice, power, supply; **faradism,** galvanism, hydroelectricity, magneto-electricity, piezoelectricity, pyroelectricity, static electricity, thermoelectricity, triboelectricity, voltaism; **electric current,** alternating current, amperage, charge, current density, direct current, eddy current, Foucault current, grid current, impulse, ripple current, thermionic current; **spark,** arc, carbon arc; **voltage,** electric potential, electromotive force, grid bias, potential, potential difference, tension; **capacitance,** absolute permittivity, admittance, capacity, commutation, conductance, dielectric strength, elastance, electric field strength, flux, impedance, inductance, induction, load, power factor, reactance, relative permittivity, resistance, resistivity, superconductivity, susceptance, susceptibility, wattage; **static,** atmospherics, interference; **discharge,** brush discharge, corona, disruptive discharge, drain, flashover, gas discharge, glow discharge, leakage current, shot noise

ELECTRIC UNIT n ampere, ampere hour, ampere-turn, biot, coulomb, electromagnetic unit, farad, gigaelectron volt, gilbert, mho *(Obs.)*, ohm, siemens, volt, volt-ampere, watt

ELECTRIFY v charge, electrolyse, excite, galvanise, power, shock; **transistorise;** **earth,** ground, neutralise; **spark,** arc, discharge, flashover, strike an arc; **conduct,** commutate, convert; **connect,** patch

ELECTRONIC INSTRUMENT n clavinet, moog, rhythm machine, synthesiser, theremin, timbron; **barrel organ,** hand organ, harmonicon, hurdy-gurdy, musical box, nyckelharpa, orchestrion; **pianola,** player piano; **effects pedal,** chorus, phaser, phlanger, wah wah pedal

ELECTRONICS n avionics, electrical engineering, electrochemistry, electrodynamics, electrokinetics, electrostatics; **microelectronics,** microcircuitry, microminiaturisation

ELEVATOR n dumb waiter, escalator, heightener, lift

ELOQUENCE n articulateness, fluency, gift of the gab, good speaking, oratory; **rhetoric,** floridness, floweriness, grandiloquence, loftiness, magniloquence, orotundity, picturesqueness, word-painting; **wit,** Atticism, esprit, pungency, repartee, spice

ELOQUENT adj articulate, epideictic, epidictic, magniloquent, picturesque, silver, silver-tongued, slick, smart, smooth, smooth-spoken; **rhetorical,** apostrophic, cadenced, declamatory, florid, flowery, flowing, grandiloquent, grandiose, heroic, high-flown,

eloquent

high-sounding, homiletic, Johnsonian, lofty, oratorical, polemic, polemical, purple, recitative, sermonic, sonorous, swelling

ELOQUENTLY *adv* articulately, in a nutshell, picturesquely, slickly; **rhetorically**, loftily, magniloquently, oratorically

ELUDE *v* get away from, shake, shake off; **flee**, abscond, bilk, blow through, bolt, do a bunk, escape, flit, fly, run, take flight, take to flight, turn tail

ELUSIVE *adj* escapist, evasive, slippery; **fugitive**, fly-by-night, runaway; **aloof**, non-committal, unforthcoming; **oblique**, equivocal, equivocating, prevaricating, quibbling

EMBANKMENT *n* baulk, dyke, floodbank, floodgate *(N.Z.)*, levee, mound, retaining wall, revetment; **rampart**, barricade, berm, bulwark, parapet, stockade, vallation

EMBEZZLEMENT *n* defalcation, misappropriation, peculation; **fraud**, blackmail, bubble, cheat *(Law)*, clip, confidence trick, do, false pretences, fraudulent speculation, licence to print money, plant, rip-off, set-up, skin game, swindle; **plagiarism**, cribbing

EMBLEM *n* caduceus, image, status symbol, symbol, totem; **badge**, armband, brassard, button, chevron, cluster *(U.S. Army)*, cockade, cockleshell *(Hist.)*, cognisance *(Her.)*, collar, cordon, cordon bleu, facings, favour, flash, gong, gorget, hatband, love knot, medal, medallion, patch, pip, plaque, ribbon, shoulder-flash, spur, star, stripe, truelove knot, weeper; **seal**, broad seal, bull, bulla, cachet, chop *(India)*, colophon, common seal, great seal, hallmark, impress,

emotion

imprint, seal of office, seal of state, sigil, signet, trademark; **insignia**, badges of honour, badges of office, colours, racing stripes, seals of office, the seals

EMBLEMATIC *adj* armorial, heraldic, sigillary, sphragistic; **emblazoned**, blazoned, crested, escutcheoned; **in regalia**, cockaded, coronate, liveried, sceptred

EMBLEMATICALLY *adv* heraldically, symbolically

EMBLEMATISE *v* hallmark, seal, signet; **blazen**, blaze, charge, emblazon, marshal, quarter, unpale

EMBLEMATIST *n* armorist, blazoner

EMBLEM OF OFFICE *n* ; **crown** coronal, coronet, diadem; **badge of sovereignty**, globe *(Hist.)*, orb, sceptre, sword of state; **badge of authority**, baton, Black Rod, crosier, gavel, mace, mark of office, pastoral, rod, staff, truncheon, verge, wand, warder; **regalia**, hood *(Educ.)*, livery, pontificals, regimentals, robes of office, trappings of power, uniform, vestments

EMBOLDEN *v* buoy, encourage, hearten, inspire, inspirit, nerve, psych up

EMERGENT *adj* effluent, effusive, emanating, emanative, emanatory, emerging, excurrent, exoreic, forthcoming, issuant *(Rare)*, issuing, jessant *(Heraldry)*, outflowing, outgoing, outpouring; **eruptive**, effusive, expulsive

EMOTION *n* affect *(Psychol.)*, affection, feeling, feelings, mood, pulse, sensation, sentiment, thing, tune *(Obs.)*, vibes, vibrations; **spirits**, cheer, courage *(Obs.)*, morale, temper; **heart**, being, bosom, breast, heart of hearts,

emotion

heartstrings, mind, soul, spirit; **fervour,** ardency, ardour, elan, enthusiasm, fervency, ferventness, fervidness, fieriness, fire, flame, franticness, glow, heat, histrionics, impassionedness, melodrama, passion, passionateness, perfervour, rage, tear, torridity, torridness, vehemence, warmth; **ecstasy,** paroxysm, spasm, throe, transport

EMOTIONAL *adj* affective, feeling, passional, temperamental; **fervent,** ardent, churned up, enthusiastic, fervid, feverish, fiery, flaming, high-pitched, hot, impassionate *(Rare),* impassioned, intense, passionate, perfervid, torrid, vehement, warm-blooded; **heartfelt,** close to one's heart, deep, earnest, gut, heart-whole, infelt, profound, sincere; **effusive,** demonstrative, gushy; **ecstatic,** beside oneself, lyrical, rapt, rhapsodical; **sensitive,** delicate, hypersensitive, miffy, moody, passible, prickly, sensible *(Obs.),* sentient, supersensitive, susceptible, susceptive, thin-skinned, touchy; **sympathetic,** empathetic, empathic, responsive, understanding, warm; **sentimental,** bathetic, corny, gooey, icky, maudlin, mawkish, Mills-and-Boon, mushy, novelettish, romantic, rosewater, sloppy, soppy, soulful, soupy, syrupy; **theatrical,** histrionic, melodramatic

EMOTIONALISE *v* charge, get up a feeling, supercharge; **affect,** get to, move, stir; **impassion,** fire, inflame, kindle, set fire to, set on fire; **ravish,** rock, smite, transport

EMOTIONALIST *n* drama queen, dramatiser, prima donna, sob-sister, tinderbox; **romantic,** sentimentalist

EMOTIONALITY *n* demonstrativeness, effusiveness, emotionalism, emotiveness, emotivity, gushiness, lyricalness, lyricism, moodiness, romanticism; **sensitivity,** affectivity, delicacy, delicateness, hypersensitivity, passibility, refinement, sensibility, sensitiveness, sentience, susceptibility, susceptibleness, susceptiveness, susceptivity, touchiness, warmness, warmth; **sympathy,** empathy, fellow feeling, involvement; **sentimentality,** bathos, gooiness, hearts-and-flowers *(U.S.),* maudlinness, mawkishness, mush, sentimentalism, slobber, slush, soppiness, soulfulness, syrup; **melodrama,** love story, novelette, tearjerker

EMOTIONALLY *adv* affetuoso, animato, con anima, con espressione, demonstratively, effusively, feelingly, sympathetically, sympathisingly, warmly; **emotively,** affectingly, affectively, movingly, poignantly, pungently, touchingly; **fervently,** appassionato, ardently, con fuoco, enthusiastically, fervidly, fierily, glowingly, impassionedly, passionately, torridly, vehemently; **sensitively,** delicately; **deeply,** earnestly, from the bottom of one's heart, heart and soul, inly *(Archaic),* intensely, sincerely, with all one's heart; **sentimentally,** languishingly, mawkishly, melodramatically, sloppily, soppily, soulfully; **ecstatically,** rhapsodically

EMOTIVE *adj* affecting, heart-warming, moving, pathetic, poignant, pungent, rousing, stirring, touching

EMPHASISE *v* accent *(U.S.),* accentuate, boot home, labour, make a point of, make a thing of, press, stress, underline; **bring to the fore,** enhance, give weight to, highlight, put on the map; **magnify,** fete, glorify, lift

EMPIRICAL *adj* a posteriori, empiric, experimental, hypothetical, provisional; **tentative,** speculative

EMPIRICISM *n* empirical formula, experimentalism, experimentation, tentation, trial and error, verification

EMPLOY *v* accredit, appoint, assign, commission, constitute, empanel, engage, entrust, give power of attorney, hire, make, name, nominate, panel, place, postulate *(Eccles.),* seat, set in place over, slate, take on; **invest,** crown, enthrone, incardinate, mitre, ordain; **install,** inaugurate, induct, institute; **assign,** attach, depute, detail, tell off; **dob in for,** nobble with, put in; **reinstate,** revest

EMPLOYED *adj* actively employed, appointed, designate, elect, in a job, investitive, nominative, working

EMPLOYER *n* appointer, appointor *(Law),* assigner, commissioning editor, constituent, constitutor, designator, nominator, ordainer

EMPLOYMENT *n* admission, appointment, assignation, assignment, body hire, designation, empanelment, entrustment, nomination, placement, reinstatement, secondment; **overemployment,** featherbedding; **investiture,** coronation, enthronement, incardination, investment, ordainment, ordination, provision *(Eccles.);* **commission,** berth, billet, booking, brevet, detail *(Mil.),* errand, hat, incumbency, office, place, post, vacancy; **delegation,** deputation, procuration; **divine appointment,** the call, vocation

EMPLOYMENT OFFICE *n* employment service, labour exchange

EMPTINESS *n* inanition, inanity, vacancy, vacuity, vacuousness; **emptying,** evacuation, vacation; **vacuum,** inane, void; **blank,** blank space, clean slate, tabula rasa, white, white line, white space; **empty bottle,** dead marine, empty

EMPTY *v* avoid *(Obs.),* evacuate, turn out, vacate, void; **drain,** exhaust, use up

EMPTY *adj* a skinner, dead, exhausted, finished, inane, vacuous, vacuum, void; **vacant,** deserted, devoid, uninhabited, unoccupied; **blank,** clear, white; **unladen,** empty-handed

ENCHANT *v* appeal to, appetise, arouse, bewitch, bowl someone over, create desire, engage, enrapture, enthral, excite desire, fetch *(Colloq.),* have a way with one, knock one's eye out, knock sideways, make one's mouth water, ravish, stimulate, take one's fancy, tempt, turn one's head

ENCLOSE *v* box in, brick up, cabin, close, close in, conclude *(Obs.),* coop up, kernel, pinch, shut in, smother, surround; **envelop,** do up, enswathe, enwrap, wrap up; **encase,** bag, box, cage, case, casket *(Obs.),* crate, enshrine, mew, pocket, sack, saggar, shrine; **sheathe,** insheathe; **encircle,** belt, circumscribe, embay, gird, girdle, orb *(Poetic),* ring, surround; **wall in,** bower, chamber, closet, confine, embank, embower, enwall, fence in, hedge, immure, impale *(Rare),* imprison, incarcerate, lock off, pale; **pen,** corral, fold, impark, impound, paddock, pinfold, pound, sty

ENCLOSED *adj* boxed in, circumscribed, cleidoic, cloistered, close, confined, encased, enveloped, fenced-in, included, landlocked, shut-in, snowbound; **encircled**, ringed, succinct *(Archaic)*, surrounded; **close**, claustrophobic, smothery, without room to swing a cat

ENCLOSURE *n* approvement *(Law)*, circumscription, closure *(Obs.)*, encirclement, encompassment, entrapment, inning, purpresture, subdivision, surrounding; **envelopment**, boxing, encapsulation, encasement, enshrinement, enswathement, packaging; **incarceration**, confinement, immurement, impoundage, impoundment, poundage; **surround**, frame, gobo

ENCOURAGE *v* abet, entice, excite, heart, hype up, impel, importune *(Obs.)*, induce, motivate, motive, move, press, provide an example, put someone up to, set an example, stimulate, urge, work up; **inspire**, animate, awake, inform; **influence**, impress, lead by the nose, persuade, play upon another's feelings, prevail upon, sway, talk over, turn someone's head, weigh heavily with; **seduce**, bewitch, enchant, entrance, lead astray; **cheer**, barrack for, egg on, spirit, whoop; **promote**, advertise, drum up trade, sell, spiel, spruik; **recommend**, advocate, suggest; **nurture**, foster, nourish; **back up**, assure, support

ENCOURAGEMENT *n* abetment, exhortation, moral support; **motivation**, actuation, impulsion, incitation, incitement, inducement, induction *(Physiol.)*, influence, provocation, provocativeness, stimulation; **inspiration**, afflatus, awakening, soul; **enticement**, bewitchment, enchantment, seduction, temptation; **agitation**, activism, barratry, consciousness raising, incendiarism, inflammation, revolutionary activity, sedition, seditiousness, stirring

ENCOURAGER *n* abetter, patron, supporter; **motivator**, ampster, lobbyist, promoter, ring leader, urger; **inspirer**, actuator, animator, impeller; **barracker**, cheer squad, cheerer, cheerleader, flagwaver, rooter; **agitator**, actionist, activist, agent provocateur, enkindler, firebrand, incendiary, inciter, inflamer, provoker, rouser, seditionary, shit-stirrer, spurrer, stirrer, Yarra banker *(Vic.)*; **promoter**, advertiser, advertising agency, commercial traveller, drummer, salesperson, spruiker; **fosterer**, kindler, nourisher; **enticer**, blandisher, coaxer, enchantress, seducer, siren, tempter, wheedler

ENCOURAGING *adj* hortatory, incentive, inductive, motivational, motive, moving, stimulant, stimulative, tonic, touching; **inviting**, appetising, entrancing, inspirational, irresistible, piquant, provocative, provoking, rousing, seductive, stimulating, stirring, tempting, titillative; **impellent**, impulsive; **incendiary**, barratrous, inflammatory, seditionary, seditious

ENCOURAGINGLY *adv* hortatively, inspirationally; **appetisingly**, enticingly; **incitingly**, barratrously, inflamingly, inflammatorily, provocatively, seditiously; **movingly**, piquantly, provokingly, rousingly, stirringly, touchingly

ENDANGER *v* compromise, entrap, expose, imperil, jeopardise, peril, put the skids under; **menace**, bode ill, threaten

ENDEARMENTS *n* addresses, assiduities, attentions, blandishments, compliments; **amorous glances**, ogle, sheep's eyes; **kiss**, buss, osculation, pash, peck, smack, smacker; **embrace**, caress, clasp, clinch, clip *(Archaic)*, cuddle, hug, snuggle, squeeze, stroke; **petting**, fondling, necking, smooching, smoodging, spooning; **hanky-panky**, fun and games, slap-and-tickle, sport *(Obs.)*

ENDMAN *n* lanterne rouge, tail ender; **bell sheep**, cut-out

ENDMOST *adj* distal, furthermost, hindmost, rearmost

ENDURINGNESS *n* durability, durableness, endurance, everlastingness, lastingness, perpetuality, survival, unfailingness; **assiduity**, assiduousness, persistence, persistency, steadiness

ENEMY *n* adversary, archenemy, foe, ill-wisher, public enemy; **antagonist**, opponent, opposite side, rival, the other side; **firebrand**, fighting cock, troublemaker; **snake**, snake in the grass, traitor; **snubber**, xenophobe; **persona non grata**, bête noir

ENERGETIC *adj* aggressive, driving, dynamic, forceful, high-powered, high-pressure, impetuous, intense, motivated; **tireless**, unwearied, weariless; **vigorous**, active, athletic, quick *(Rare)*, sinewy, spirited, virile; **lively**, bouncing, ebullient, effervescent, flush, fresh, live, lusty, oomphy, peppy, proud *(Poetic)*, rompish, sappy, spritely, swinging, vibrant, vital, vivacious, vivid; **alive**, alive and kicking, full of beans, full of piss and vinegar; **spirited**, animated, dingdong, rousing, spanking, warm; **jazzy**, jazzed up, racy, souped-up; **invigorating**, bracing, brisk, crisp, invigorative

ENERGETICALLY *adv* aggressively, briskly, bustlingly, strenuously, tirelessly, unweariedly, vigorously; **full pelt**, amain *(Archaic)*, animatedly, forcefully, impetuously, impulsively, like billyo, madly, violently, with a vengeance; **spiritedly**, con forza, forzando, sforzando, sforzato; **vibrantly**, ebulliently, effervescently, invigoratingly, lively, vivaciously, warmly

ENERGISE *v* activate, animate, boost, brisk up, enliven, exhilarate, flush, ginger up, innerve, invigorate, jazz up, pep up, quicken, sauce, soup up, stimulate, vitalise, vivify, zest

ENERGISER *n* activator, booster, exhilarator, impeller, invigorator, prime mover, stimulant, stimulator, stimulus, sustainer, vivifier; **striver**, ginger group, hustler, laster, livewire, pusher

ENERGY *n* action, conatus, effort, force, impetus, impulse, motive power, motivity, power, stress, thrust, torque, vis viva; **atomic energy**, atomic power, binding energy, electric power, enthalpy, entropy, fusion energy, hydraulic power, hydro-electric power, internal energy, kinetic energy, momentum, nuclear energy, potential energy, shear stress, sunpower, waterpower, wattage, windpower, zero point energy; **quantum**, phonon, photon; **force**, centrifugal force, centripetal force, electrokinetic potential, electromotive force, magnetomotive force, solar energy, zeta-

energy

potential; **erg**, British thermal unit, calorie, joule, kilojoule, kilowatt-hour; **dyne**, newton, pound-force, poundal; **energetics**, biodynamics, dynamics, geodynamics, hydrodynamics, hydromechanics, physics; **watt**, horsepower, joules per second. *See also* VITALITY

ENERVATING *adj* castrating, enervative, exhausting, exhaustive, gorgonian

ENGRAVE *v* cut, grave, incise, scrimshaw; **print**, aquatint, lithograph, mezzotint, photolithograph, silk-screen print; **emboss**, boss, snarl; **etch**, bite; **impress**, stamp

ENGRAVER *n* burinist, cerographist, chalcographer, chaser, embosser, graver *(Archaic)*, pyrographer, tattooer, wood engraver, woodcutter, xylographer; **etcher**, lithographer, printer, tinter. *See also* ARTIST; CRAFTSMAN

ENGRAVING *n* cerography, chalcography, glyptography, pyrography, toreutics, woodcutting, xylography; **print**, aquatint, block print, cerograph, chromolithograph, halftone, line engraving, linocut, lithograph, mezzotint, oleograph, photolithograph, rubbing, silk-screen print, woodcut, wood engraving, xylograph; **printing**, die-sinking, die-stamping, etching, intaglio, lithography, metallography, oleography, photolithography; **plate**, remarque; **artist's proof**, proof

ENGROSS *v* absorb, amuse *(Obs.)*, consume, devour, enwrap, fascinate, grip, hold the stage, interest, intrigue, involve, occupy, spellbind

enormous

ENGROSSINGLY *adv* absorbingly, devouringly, fascinatingly, grippingly, interestingly, intriguingly, juicily, remarkably; **noticeably**, conspicuously, showily, strikingly

ENJOY *v* admire, appreciate, fancy, relish, savour, taste *(Archaic)*; **like**, care for, delight in, dig, get a kick out of, have a soft spot for something, love, take a fancy to, take pleasure in, take to, welcome; **revel in**, feast on, groove on; **go into ecstasies**, be crazy about, be mad about, blow one's mind, drool over, rave, swoon, trip

ENJOYER *n* delighter, reveller; **indulger**, feaster, sybarite, voluptuary; **bon vivant**, bon viveur, epicure, epicurean, gourmand, hedonist, high-stepper, jetsetter, worldling; **jet set**, beau monde, beautiful people; **admirer**, appreciator, fancier, lover

ENLARGEMENT *n* dilation, elongation, erection, excrescence, growth, hypertrophy, stretch, swell, swelling, tumidity; **inflatedness**, dilatancy, erectility, excrescency, pulse, swollenness

ENLIGHTENER *n* civiliser, demonstrator, initiator, refiner, torchbearer; **apostle**, evangelist, missionary, preacher, prophet; **adviser**, careers adviser, counsellor; **guru**, maharishi, sage, swami; **indoctrinator**, implanter, inculcator, promulgator, propagandist, publicist. *See also* TEACHER

ENLIVEN *v* animate, breathe life into, inspire, inspirit, jazz, jazz up, liven, liven up, pep, pep up, put new life into, vitalise, vivify, zap up

ENORMOUS *adj* astronomical, colossal, cyclopean, elephantine, giant, gigantean, gigantesque, gigantic, herculean, huge, immense, mammoth,

enormous mountain, mountainous, overblown, overgrown, prodigious, titanic, towering, tremendous, vast, vasty (*Poetic*); **bulky**, ample, full, massive, massy, monumental, portly, solid, voluminous; **grandiose**, august, distinguished, eminent, grand, great, Homeric, lordly, majestic, noble, princely, proud, regal; **awesome**, awe-inspiring, awful, fabulous, ineffable, mind-boggling, overwhelming, phenomenal, portentous, stupendous, terrible

ENORMOUSLY *adv* astronomically, colossally, gigantically, hugely, immensely, mountainously, tremendously, vastly

ENTER *v* bounce into, come in, get in, get inside, get into, go into, hop in, immigrate, jump in, re-enter, set foot in, step in; **board**, embark, embus, emplane, enplane, entrain; **encroach**, barge in, break in, break into, bust, butt in, crash, gatecrash, infiltrate, invade, push in, trespass

ENTERER *n* arrival, comer, entrant, immigrant, import, incomer, invitee; **invader**, encroacher, forcer, gatecrasher, interloper, intruder, trespasser; **doorkeeper**, commissionaire, concierge, doorman

ENTERING *adj* immigrant, incoming, ingoing, ingressive, inpouring, inrushing, invasive, inward; **embarking**, embussing

ENTERPRISING *adj* adventurous, venturesome

ENTERTAINER *n* busker, geisha, hoofer, jongleur, minstrel, mountebank, performer, play-actor, player, puppeteer, reciter, showgirl, showman, song-and-dance man, stroller, strolling player; **amuser**, blackface, comedian, comedienne, comic, farceur, farceuse, feed, humorist, slapstick comedian, stand-up comic, straight man, vaudevillian, vaudevillist; **clown**, buffoon, fool, jester, Pantaloon, Pierrette, Pierrot; **Columbine**, Harlequin, Scaramouche; **announcer**, anchorman, commentator, compere, deejay, disc jockey, diseur, DJ, epilogue, front man, linkman, presenter, prologue, quizmaster, race caller, ringmaster, talking head; **impersonator**, female impersonator, improvisator, improviser, masker, mime, mimer, mimic, mummer, mute, pantomime, pantomimist, personator; **multi-media personality**. *See also* ACTOR; CIRCUS PERFORMER; THEATRICAL COMPANY

ENTERTAINING *adj* absorbing, amusing, engrossing, riveting

ENTERTAINMENT *n* attraction, divertissement, night-life, performing arts, regalement, show business, vaudeville; **an evening out**, a night on the town, blow-out, rage; **show**, antic, blockbuster, circus, cirque, exhibition, extravaganza, fantoccini, festival, fluxus, follies, happening, harlequinade, ice show, lightshow, pageant, phantasmagoria, pyrotechnics, son et lumière, spectacle, spectacular, street theatre, three-ring circus, variety show, vaudeville; **cinema**, bioscope (*S. African*), celluloid, circuit, the cinema, the movies, the pictures, the silver screen; **cabaret**, floor show, revue; **road show**, sideshow; **benefit**, barrel, bespeak (*Obs.*)

ENTHUSE *v* fanaticise, fire, pique, switch on, warm, whet; **be eager**, be pie in (*N.Z.*), be sold on, be spoiling for, beat the gun, champ at the bit, fall over oneself, go to town about, jump the gun, rave, take fire, warm to, wax lyrical

ENTHUSIASM *n* anxiety, anxiousness, ardency, ardour, avidity, eagerness, ebullience, ebulliency, fire, flame, forwardness, furore, get-up-and-go, greediness, gusto, heart, heartiness, keenness, party spirit, pizzazz, rage, second wind, sharpness, vehemence, warmness, warmth, zeal, zealousness, zest, zestfulness, zing, zip; **devotion**, craze, dedication, devotedness, devotement, passion; **fanaticism**, chauvinism, desperation *(Colloq.)*, monomania, rabidity, rabidness, radicalness, voraciousness, voracity, zealotry

ENTHUSIAST *n* a beggar for, a nut about, afficionado, a glutton for, a great one for, boffin, devotee, eager beaver, fan, fancier, freak, high-flier, votaress, votary; **fanatic**, chauvinist, energumen, lunatic fringe, mad mullah, radical, tub-thumper, zealot

ENTHUSIASTIC *adj* ablaze, afire, aflame, agog, anxious, ardent, athirst, avid, eager, ebullient, fain *(Archaic)*, forward, greedy, hearty, hipped *(U.S. Colloq.)*, keen, on fire, raring, red-hot, sharp, sharp-set, toey, vehement, vital, warm, willing, wrapped, young-eyed, zealous, zestful, zesty, zingy; **extravagant**, gung ho, high-flown, high-flying, keen as mustard, on edge, voracious, wild *(Colloq.)*; **fanatical**, chauvinist, chauvinistic, fanatic, mad, overzealous, rabid

ENTHUSIASTICALLY *adv* agog, anxiously, ardently, avidly, eagerly, ebulliently, greedily, hard, heartily, keenly, sharply, urgently, vehemently, warmly, with all one's heart, zealously, zestfully; **fanatically**, chauvinistically, overzealously, rabidly, voraciously

ENTITLEMENT *n* capacity, colour, competence, droit, jus, majority, power, right, title

ENTRANCE *n* adit, aperture, archway, avenue *(Brit.)*, conning tower, doorway, entry, entryway, foyer, gateway, gorge, hall, hallway, hatchway, ingress, inlet, intake, introitus, loading bay, opening, passage, passageway, platform, porch, port, port of entry, porte-cochère, portico, vestibule; **door**, cat door, gate, hatch, lichgate, pearly gates, portal, postern, revolving door, stable door, stile, tollgate, trapdoor, turnstile, wicket; **access**, admission, admittance, embarkation, entrée, open door, re-entrance, reentry; **encroachment**, break-in, breaking and entering, bust, inflow, influx, inroad, invasion, trespass

ENTREAT *v* adjure, ask a boon, assail, beseech, impetrate, implore, importune, intreat *(Archaic)*, obsecrate, obtest, plead, pray, supplicate; **petition**, address, appeal to, apply to, go cap in hand to, go on bended knees to, have recourse to, re-petition, recur to *(Rare)*, turn to; **apply for**, bid for, make a bid, make an approach, move for, put in for; **desire**, crave *(Obs.)*, cry for, whistle for; **request**, ask, court, invite, pop the question, solicit, woo; **invoke**, call on, command, conjure, imprecate, require; **intercede**, interpellate, intervene; **bespeak**, book, commission; **lobby**, besiege, dun, ply, press, urge; **canvass**, ask around, consult, enquire of

ENTREATY *n* adjuration, assailment, begging, canvass, conjuration *(Archaic)*, impetration *(Rare)*, imploration, obsecration, pleading, solicitation, suppliance, treaty *(Obs.)*, urging; **plea**, appeal, epiclesis *(Liturgy)*, importunities, imprecation, invocation, prayer, supplication; **petition**, application, bid, claim, motion, postulate, postulation, proposal, round robin, suggestion, suit; **intercession**, interpellation; **invitation**, invite *(Colloq.)*, solicitation

EPHEMERAL *n* ephemera, ephemeron; **nine day wonder**, flash in the pan, one-hit wonder, puppy love; **flash**, flicker, pulse, spurt, vapour *(Archaic)*

EPISTEMOLOGICAL *adj* encyclopaedic, epistemic, pantologic, pantological, philosophical, polyhistoric; **scientific**, polytechnic, technical, technological

EQUAL *n* coequal, compeer, equivalent, fellow, match, parallel, peer, vis-a-vis; **dead heat**, barrage, deuce, draw, Mexican stand-off, tie; **break-even**, margin *(Econ.)*

EQUAL *v* compeer *(Archaic)*; **be evens**, balance, draw, poise, tie; **amount to**, add up to, come up to; **democratise**, level; **match**, be up with, get the measure of someone, go all the way with, measure up to, rival, run abreast, see *(Cards)*; **compare**, amount to the same thing, parallel

EQUAL *adj* equational, level; **even**, commeasurable, commensurate, fifty-fifty, half-and-half, isometric, par, proportionate; **equivalent**, enharmonic, equipollent, fellow, like, matchable, one-to-one, same; **level-pegging**, drawn, equalised, level, quits, tied; **ambidextrous**, two-handed; **coequal**, assessorial, comparable, concurrent, coordinate; **democratic**, egalitarian, equalitarian, isonomic; **as good as**, tantamount; **equidistant**, coextensive; **equipotent**, equimolecular, equinoctial, equipollent, equiponderant, equipotential; **symmetric**, balanced, bisymmetrical, isodiametric, isogonic, spheral, symmetrical; **equilateral**, equiangular, isosceles, square; **isostatic**, isenthalpic, isentropic, isoclinal, isodimorphous, isodynamic, isomerous, isotropic

EQUALISE *v* balance, bracket, equate, equilibrate, even out, level out, match, symmetrise; **break even**, break square; **coextend**, commeasure; **counterbalance**, counterpoise, counterweigh

EQUALITY *n* balance, commensuration, comparableness, evenness, levelness, parity, sameness; **symmetry**, bisymmetry, conformation, evenness, parallelism, regularity, symmetricalness; **equilibrium**, equilibration, equipoise, equiponderance, isostasy, poise; **counterweight**, balance, counterpoise; **egalitarianism**, democracy, equalitarianism, isonomy; **equalisation**, equation, equivalence, closeness, coextension, correspondence, equidistance, equipollence, equipollency, isometry, par; **coequality**, coordinateness, coordination, parity; **isomorphism**, isodimorphism

EQUALLY *adv* alike, both, correspondingly, identically, level, levelly, proportionately; **democratically**; **fifty-fifty**, ana *(Med.)*, close, commensurately, evenly, evens, half-and-half, isometrically; **abreast**, even stevens, neck and neck, nip and tuck *(U.S.)*,

equally / **err**

pari passu; **equivalently,** enharmonically; **equidistantly,** coextensively; **equilaterally,** bisymmetrically, isostatically, symmetrically; **comparably,** coequally, comparatively, coordinately

EQUIP v accommodate, accoutre, appoint, arm, dight *(Archaic)*, fit, fit out, fit up, fix, fix up, furnish, gear, grubstake, implement, kit *(Mil.)*, outfit, refit, rig out *(Naut.)*, rig up, set up, turn out; **endow,** keep in, maintain, support, sustain

EQUIPMENT n accessories, accessory, accoutrements, apparatus, appointments, appurtenances, baggage *(Mil.)*, equipage, gear, kit, manavelins *(Naut.)*, munitions, necessaries, outfit, paraphernalia, tackle, tackling, the necessary, turnout; **personal effects,** dunnage, luggage, stuff, swag, things; **fittings,** caparison, covering, dress, garnish, garnishment, garniture, harness, ornament *(Eccles.)*, rig, rigging, trappings, trim *(Motor Vehicles)*; **replacement part,** doover, spare, thingummybob, thingummyjig

EQUIPPED adj fitted, fitted out, full-rigged, good for, ready, rigged out, right, supplied, trim *(Obs.)*, well appointed, well-found

EQUIVALENT n actinomere, antimere, coequal, compeer, correspondent, fellow, homograph, homologue, homonym, homophone, isologue, isomer, match, parallel, peer, synonym

EQUIVOCATOR n prevaricator, procrastinator, temporiser; **waverer,** weathercock, wobbler; **abstainer,** fence-sitter, trimmer

ERECT v pitch, plumb, raise, raise up, right, set up, up-end, upraise, uprear; **cock up,** prick up, prickle, rear, rear up, sit up, uprise *(Archaic)*; **stand,** hold up, keep one's feet, stand up; **arise,** get to one's feet, rise, rise up

ERECT adj columnar, columned, rampant, ramping, stand-up, standing, standing up, steady, straight, straight up, tower-like, up, upright, upstanding; **vertical,** bluff, normal *(Maths)*, orthogonal, perpendicular, plumb, square

ERECTLY adv at right angles, bolt upright, on end, on hind legs, topside up, up, upright, uprightly; **perpendicularly,** plumb, vertically

ERECTNESS n straightness, uprightness; **perpendicularity,** aplomb, orthogonality, plumbness, right-angledness, verticality, verticalness; **perpendicular,** altitude, apothem, plumb, vertical; **plumbline,** plumb-bob, plumb-rule, plummet

EROTICISE v arouse, bring off, bring on, excite, feel someone up, finger up, fumble, go the grope, grope, pet, play stink finger, titillate, turn on; **have an erection,** crack a fat, get a hard on, put lead in one's pencil; **orgasm,** blow, come, cream one's jeans, ejaculate, shoot one's bolt, toss off; **practise coitus interruptus,** get off at Redfern; **masturbate,** flip oneself off, frig, jerk off, pull oneself off, toss off, wank, whack off. *See also* HAVE SEX

ERR v back the wrong horse, bark up the wrong tree, blunder, boob, contaminate, fall in, fault, get one's lines crossed, get the wrong end of the stick, goof, lapse, make a boo-boo, misapply, miscount, misdo, mismeasure, misplace, mispronounce, misstate, slip, stumble, trip up; **misconceive**, get someone wrong, misconstrue, mistake

ERROR *n* bad idea, balls-up, baulk, bloomer, blooper, blue, blunder, boner, boo-boo, boob, boss-shot, bug, clanger, fault, faux paus, fluff, foot-fault, Freudian slip, fuck-up, gaffe, GIGO, howler, inaccuracy, lapse, malapropism, misapplication, misapprehension, miscalculation, misconception, miscount, misjudgment, mismeasurement, mismove, misplacement, mispronunciation, mistake, oversight, parapraxis, slip, slip of the tongue, slip-up, solecism, stumble, trip, wrong foot; **comedy of errors**, farce; **clerical error**, author's error, contamination, corrigendum, erratum, haplography, literal *(Print.)*, misprint, offset, out *(Print.)*, printer's error, set-off, strike-through, typo; **false alarm.** *See also* FALSITY

ESCAPE *n* elusion, escapade, escapement *(Archaic)*, evasion, lam *(U.S.)*, runaway, scape *(Archaic)*; **moonlight flit**, disappearing trick, elopement, flit, slip, truancy; **break-out**, gaolbreak, getaway; **breakaway**, bolt, break, gambado, stampede; **close shave**, close call, close thing, narrow escape, near miss, near thing, squeak. *See also* MEANS OF ESCAPE

ESCAPE *v* break out, cut, cut and run, do a get, do a getaway, extricate oneself, flee, hit the toe *(Prison)*, lam *(U.S.)*, make a getaway, show a clean pair of heels, take it on the lam, turn tail; **bolt**, break away, stampede; **skip**, abscond, do a moonlight flit, elope, flit, fly the gap, get away, jump, run away, shoot the moon; **give someone the slip**, bilk, elude, shake, shake off, throw off; **slip through one's fingers**, get away, slip the collar; **scrape through**, get away with it, save one's bacon, save one's skin, survive; **get out from under**, do a fade, fade out; **get off**, secure an acquittal

ESCAPED *adj* at large, free, off the hook, on the lam, on the run, runaway; **fugitive**, truant; **elusive**, slippery; **breakaway**, ladino

ESCAPEE *n* absconder from public labour, absconder into the woods, absentee, absentee into the woods, absentee without leave, escaper, fleer, prison-breaker; **runaway**, bolter, breakaway, ladino, stampeder; **truant**, eloper; **dodger**, absconder, bilker, eluder; **fugitive**, boat people, reffo, refugee; **escapologist**, Houdini

ESSAY *n* apercu, composition, descant, discourse, disquisition, dissertation, exposition, lucubration, piece, quodlibet, theme, thesis, tract *(Relig.)*, tractate, treatise; **study**, analysis, examination, memoir, monograph, sketch, survey; **summary**, abstract, compendium, conspectus, digest, epitome, pandect, précis, resumé, synopsis; **dialogue**, colloquy; **introduction**, preface, prolegomenon, prologue, prolusion; **criticism**, appreciation, commentary, discussion, excursus, Midrash, textual criticism; **almagest**, botany, dispensatory, flora, formulary, herbal, pastoral, pharmacopoeia, poetics, zoology; **pamphlet**, blurb, booklet, broadsheet, screed; **article**, causerie, column, contribution, editorial, feature, feature story, leader, report, write-up; **critique**, comment, notice,

essay

review; **paper**, address, lecture, speech, symposium; **homily**, sermon

ESSAYIST *n* belletrist, editor, expositor, leader writer, monographer, pamphleteer; **critic**, commentator, editorialist, reviewer, scholiast

ESSENCE *n* basic, deep structure, fundamental, hypostasis, point, quick, the name of the game; **basis**, accidence, base, bottom, elements, first principle, root; **skeleton**, alphabet, constitution, construction, contexture, grammar, matrix; **grassroots**, brass tacks, nuts and bolts; **nittygritty**, crux, gist, juice, marrow, nub, pith, point, stuff; **spirit**, ABC, flavour, gist, meaning, sum, the long and the short of; **substance**, content, hard core, meat, substratum; **epitome**, abstract, being, dharma, elixir, entity, form, inscape, quiddity, quintessence, soul, type, vitals; **nature**, aroma, character, inbeing, inside, noumenon, principle, quality; **soul**, ambience, personality; **attribute**, property, quality; **extract**, boil-down, decoction, distillation, distillment, spirit

ESSENTIAL *adj* constitutional, constitutive, crucial, formal, intimate, intrinsic, qualitative, quintessential, resident, substantial, substantival, substantive, true, veritable, very; **epitomic**, epitomical; **typical**, characteristic

ESSENTIALLY *adv* constitutively, in substance, intimately, intrinsically, per se, qualitatively, subjectively, substantially, substantively; **veritably**, vitally; **inherently**, congenitally, connately, connaturally, immanently, innately, radically; **naturally**, by nature, in rerum natura, indigenously; **typically**, characteristically; **basically**, at bottom, at heart, basally, fundamentally, in essence, originally, primarily, ultimately; **elementarily**, elementally, hypostatically

ESSENTIALNESS *n* elementariness, essentiality, intrinsicality, inwardness, radicalness, substantiveness, vitalness; **fundamentality**, immanence, immanency, inherence, inherency; **innateness**, connation, indigenousness, intimateness

ETERNAL *adj* aeonian, coeternal, cosmic, eterne *(Archaic)*, sempiternal *(Archaic)*; **endless**, ceaseless, chronic, constant, incessant, interminable, lasting, never-ending, perpetual, unending; **permanent**, amaranthine, everlasting, imperishable, perdurable, perennial, unfading; **immortal**, ageless, dateless, deathless, elect *(Theol.)*, evergreen, timeless, undying

ETERNALISE *v* eternise, perpetuate; **immortalise**, elect *(Theol.)*; **last**, endure, go on and on, have no end, outlast

ETERNALLY *adv* coeternally, everlastingly, immortally, lastingly, perdurably, perennially, perpetually, unfailingly; **endlessly**, ceaselessly, constantly, interminably, timelessly, undyingly, week in week out, without cease; **permanently**, alway *(Archaic)*, always, aye, e'er, evermore, for ever, for ever and a day, for good, for good and all, for the duration, forever, forevermore, from age to age, from go to whoa, in perpetuity, in perpetuum, till the cows come home, till the end of time, without term, world without end

ETERNITY n coeternity, everlasting, sempiternity *(Archaic)*, time immemorial, time out of mind; **immortality,** amrita, athanasia, deathlessness; **immortal,** elect *(Theol.)*; **everlasting,** amaranth, eternal, perpetual motion, perpetuity, perpetuo moto; **permanence,** endlessness, eternalness, everlastingness, lastingness, perpetuality, timelessness; **perpetuation,** election *(Theol.)*, immortalisation, perpetuance

ETHEREAL adj aerial, airy, airy-fairy, astral, nebulous, shadowy, shady, vaporous; **evanescent,** fleeting, fugitive, transient, transitory; **ghostly,** spectral, wraithlike; **flimsy,** cardboard, insubstantial, paper, slight, tenuous, thin; **delicate,** gossamer. See also INTANGIBLE

ETHEREALISE v dematerialise, immaterialise, spiritualise, thin, vaporise; **idealise,** abstract, internalise, transcend

ETHNIC n aboriginal, autochthon, bushwhacker, Indian, indigine, native, tribesman; **black person,** black, blackamoor *(Archaic)*, brown brother, buck *(U.S.)*, chocolate drop *(Brit.)*, coloured, coon, darkie, fuzzy wuzzy, Jim Crow *(U.S.)*, jungle bunny, maroon, Negro, nig, nig-nog, nigger, sambo, savage, spade; **Aboriginal,** Abo, Aborigine, binghi, blackfellow, boong, burry, koori, myall, myrnonger, noongar *(W.A.)*; **gaucho,** wetback; **gipsy,** gippo, Romany; **islander,** hori *(N.Z.)*, kanaka, maori; **black woman,** bitumen blonde, gin, lubra, mary, Negress, Wahini; **white person,** albino, blond, buckra, gub *(Aborig.)*, gubba, honky *(U.S.)*, memsahib, pakeha *(N.Z.)*, paleface, wanda, wandoo, WASP *(U.S.)*, wonk; **full blood,** half-blood, halfcaste; **Semite,** Ikey Mo, Jew, kike; **Asian,** Asiatic, nog, slant-eye, slantyeyes, slopehead. See also PERSON

EVASIVELY adv avertedly, equivocatingly, evadingly, prevaricatingly, shrinkingly; **obliquely,** elusively, equivocally, temporisingly; **on the run,** in flight, on the lam *(U.S.)*

EVENING n curfew, e'en *(Poetic)*, eve *(Archaic)*, even *(Archaic)*, eventide, vesper; **sunset,** dark, decline, evenfall *(Archaic)*, fall of evening, nightfall, sundown; **twilight,** candlelight, dusk, gloaming *(Poetic)*, night, shades, shadows; **dinnertime,** bedtime, suppertime, teatime; **Evensong,** vespers *(Eccles.)*, vigil *(Eccles.)*. See also NIGHT

EVIDENCE n ammunition *(Colloq.)*, backup, circumstantial evidence, clue, corroborant, corroboration, cumulative evidence, direct evidence, documentation, goods *(Colloq.)*, indirect evidence, king's evidence, matter *(Law)*, prima-facie evidence, probable cause, proof, queen's evidence, state's evidence *(U.S.)*, title; **testimony,** alibi, appearances, attest *(Archaic)*, attestation, citation, deposition, statement, testimonial, witness; **conclusive evidence,** apodixis; **argument,** allegation, case, con, construction *(Geom.)*, demonstration, presumption, pro, proof, substantiation, the proof of the pudding; **swearing on oath,** affidavit, affirmation, avouchment, sustainment, sworn statement, testification *(Law)*, verification, vouch *(Obs.)*

EVIDENCE v evince, go to show, show, speak for itself, speak volumes, tell its own tale

EVIDENTIALLY adv a posteriori, corroboratively, demonstratively, in evidence; **for example**, e.g., for instance

EVILDOING n abomination, atrocity, crime, evil, infamous conduct, malefaction, seduction, villainy; **sin,** cardinal sin, deadly sin, debt, ill, original sin, trespass, wrong, wrongdoing; **fault,** demerit, foible, peccadillo, venial sin; **fall,** lapse; **debauchment,** depravation. See also IMMORALITY

EVOLUTION n coevolution, development, emergent evolution, evolvement, intergradation, natural selection, phylogeny, progress *(Biol.)*, sexual selection, speciation, survival of the fittest; **convergent evolution,** adaptation, convergence, naturalisation; **accommodation,** acculturation; **anthropogenesis,** cainogenesis, cytogenesis, monogenesis, orthogenesis, palingenesis, phytogenesis *(Bot.)*; **genetics,** cytogenetics, physical anthropology; **Darwinism,** Lamarckism, Neo-Darwinism, Neo-Lamarckism, transformism; **adaptiveness,** accommodativeness, struggle for existence

EVOLUTIONAL adj adaptational, formative; **adaptive,** accommodative, acculturative, intergradient

EVOLUTIONARY adj anthropogenic, cainogenetic, monogenetic, orthogenetic, palingenetic, phylogenetic, phylogenic, phytogenetic, phytogenetical; **mutant,** mutational, mutative; **evolutionistic,** Darwinian, Darwinist

EVOLUTIONIST n Darwinian, Darwinist, transformist

EVOLVE v coevolve, develop, intergrade; **adapt,** accord, acculturate, naturalise

EXAGGERATE v amplify, bull, bulldust, distend, embroider, hyperbolise, magnify, make a mountain out of a molehill, melodramatise, out-Herod Herod, puff up, sound off, stack it on, theatricalise, wiredraw; **overstate,** lay it on, lay it on thick, overwrite, pile on the agony, turn on the agony; **make a good story,** draw a long bow, imagine, pitch a tale, pull a long bow, romance, spin a yarn, tell stories; **overplay,** make too much of, overact, overcharge, overdo, overdraw, overkill, overshoot the mark

EXAGGERATED adj exaggerative, extravagant, high-flown, high-flying, highly coloured, histrionic, hyperbolic, magniloquent, outré, overdone, overstated, strained, tall

EXAGGERATION n embroidery *(Colloq.)*, enlargement, extravagance, hyperbole, hyperbolism, overkill, overstatement, puff, wiredrawing; **much ado about nothing,** all piss and wind, storm in a teacup; **tall story,** flight of fancy, lulu, purple passage, traveller's tale; **caricature,** parody; **theatricality,** heroics, histrionics, melodrama, melodramatics, playacting, theatricalism, theatricalness

EXAGGERATOR n boomerang bender, bull artist, bullshit artist, embroiderer, romancer, storyteller, wiredrawer

EXAMINATION n audition, baccalaureate, eleven-plus *(Brit.)*, exam, examen *(Eccles.)*, finals, matriculation, open-book examination, oral examination, paper, post, supplementary, test, test paper, tripos, viva, viva voce; **trial,** tryout; **driving test,** road test; **audit,** means test. *See also* INVESTIGATION: INSPECTION

EXAMINE *v* analyse, canvass, explore; **test,** ascertain, assay, prove, put to the proof, re-examine, take, try, try out, verify; **study,** audit, monitor, scan, scrutineer, scrutinise, vet; **inspect,** appraise, evaluate, overhaul, review; **diagnose,** auscultate, palpate, sound, X-ray. *See also* INVESTIGATE

EXAMPLE *n* etymon, exemplification, exemplum, instance, paradigm, pattern, praxis, precedent; **specimen,** piece, sample, sort, type, type genus, type specimen; **pacesetter,** fugleman, pacemaker; **paragon,** classic, exemplar, mirror; **ideal,** beau ideal, dream, ego ideal, idea, picture, the abstract; **standard,** canon, classic, measure, norm

EXCAVATION *n* bal, coal pit, cutting, goaf, gob, gullet, gum-hole *(N.Z.),* gunny, mine, mineshaft, pit, quarry, salt mine, saltpit, sawpit, stope, trench; **well,** oilwell, step-out well; **shaft,** drive, moulin, winze. *See also* HOLLOW; CAVE

EXCEL *v* be good value, be great at, be no slouch at, be pie on *(N.Z.),* be worth one's salt, come into one's own, have a way with, have the game sewn up, have the knack, have what it takes, know a thing or two, know how many beans make five, know one's onions, know what's what, make a good fist of, not put a foot wrong, pull off a hat-trick, rise to the occasion, shine at, sparkle; **master,** get on top of, learn, perfect; **be one's** **strong suit,** be in one's bailiwick, be up one's alley

EXCEPT *prep* apart from, bar, barring, bating *(Archaic),* beside, besides, but, ex *(Finance),* excepting, outside, save, with the exception of

EXCESSIVE *adj* dear, exceeding, exorbitant, overmuch, stiff; **immoderate,** all-fired *(U.S.),* deadly, devilish, extravagant, extreme, fearful, inordinate, obsessive, over-the-top, overweening, overwhelming, radical, unconscionable, undue; **too much,** cloying, de trop, satiating, syrupy, too-too

EXCESSIVELY *adv* a fair treat, beyond measure, deadly, devilish, devilishly, exceedingly, exorbitantly, extravagantly, fearfully, immoderately, inordinately, overly, overweeningly, overwhelmingly, unconscionably, unduly, unnecessarily; **superfluously,** redundantly, superabundantly; **extra,** by half, over, over and above; **too much,** a bit thick, ad nauseam, over the fence, over the odds, overmuch, tanto, to a fault, to the skies, too, troppo

EXCESSIVENESS *n* exorbitance, extremism, immoderateness, immoderation, inordinacy, inordinateness, intemperance, lavishness, unconscionableness; **extravagance,** conspicuous consumption, costliness *(Archaic),* extravagancy, extravagantness, prodigality, profligacy, recklessness; **overabundance,** ebullience, ebulliency, embarrassment, luxuriousness, overmuchness, overproduction, superabundance; **superfluousness,** redundancy; **congestion,** engorgement, fullness, overcrowding, overpopulation

EXCHANGE *n* barter, commutation, interchange, intermigration, metathesis, passage, reciprocation, traffic, transposition; **substitution**, grafting, metasomatism, novation, shift, subrogation, succession *(Ecol.)*, surrogation, transformation; **swap**, dicker, fungible, quid pro quo, trade, trade-in, valuable consideration. *See also* SUBSTITUTE

EXCHANGE *v* change, counterchange, swap, switch, trade, transpose; **interchange**, alternate, change places, compare notes, pass, reciprocate; **barter**, chop *(Obs.)*, dicker, trade. *See also* SUBSTITUTE

EXCHANGEABILITY *n* commutability, interchangeability, interchangeableness, reciprocity, synonymity, synonymy, transponibility

EXCHANGEABLE *adj* commutable, commutative, convertible, fungible, interchangeable, reciprocal, synonymic, synonymical, trade-in, transponible, transposable

EXCITABILITY *n* combustibility, combustibleness, excitableness, inflammability

EXCITABLE *adj* feisty *(U.S.)*, nervous, skittish, volitant; **restless**, excited, exhaustless, unquiet, unresting; **hyperactive**, always on the go, overactive

EXCITE *v* agitate, electrify, exhilarate, thrill; **overexcite**, frenzy, hype up, whip up, wind up, work up; **turn on**, intoxicate, send; **sensationalise**, dramatise

EXCITED *adj* above oneself, agog, ebullient, exalted, feverish, feverous, frisky, gone *(Colloq.)*, hectic, hyped-up, intoxicated, keyed up, on tenterhooks, red-hot; **agitated**, dithering, dithery, fluttery, jumpy, overwrought, tremulous, twittery, uncool, wrought-up; **frenzied**, crazy, delirious, hysterical, mad, maenadic, off one's head, phrenetic, wild; **hotblooded**, passionate, rackety; **excitable**, combustible, combustive, feisty *(U.S.)*, inflammable, nervy, overexcitable, toey

EXCITEDLY *adv* agitatedly, agog, breathlessly, feverishly, feverously, hectically, phrenetically, wildly

EXCITEMENT *n* agitation, ecstasy, excitation, exhilaration, fever, feverishness, orgasm, tension, thrillingness, wildness; **frenzy**, agony, conniptions, delirium, hysteria, hysterics, nympholepsy, overexcitement, pink fit, spin, state, stir; **fluster**, ado, dither, flurry, flustration, flutter, fuss, twitter; **sensationalism**, luridness, sensusism, titillation; **thrill**, bang, buzz, charge, frisson, kick; **furore**, boil-up, combustion, ferment, scene, sensation, three-day night; **much ado about nothing**, a storm in a teacup; **boiling point**, fever pitch, white heat

EXCITING *adj* awe-inspiring, breathtaking, evocative, exhilarating, exhilarative, hairy *(Colloq.)*, heady, intoxicative, lively, mind-bending, mind-blowing, nail-biting, thrilling, vibrant; **sensational**, lurid

EXCITINGLY *adv* ebulliently, exhilaratingly, headily, intoxicatingly, luridly, sensationally, thrillingly, vibrantly

EXCLUDE *v* except, include out, leave off, leave out, omit, overleap, preclude, skip; **eliminate**, cancel, cut, dele, delete, drop, rule out, sink; **get rid of**, cull, cut out, give the boot, off-

exclude / exercise

load, weed out, winnow. *See also* ISOLATE; BOYCOTT

EXCLUDED *adj* apart, beyond the pale, fringe, inadmissable, not included, out of court; culled, cast for age *(Agric.)*, separated; **exiled,** expatriate, in exile, ostracised, outcast

EXCLUDER *n* alienator, banisher, black-baller, forbidder, isolator, ostraciser, ouster; **segregator,** exclusionist, exclusivist, segregationist

EXCLUSION *n* elimination, exception, omission, ostracism, reservation, shut-out; **segregation,** apartheid, colour-bar, exclusionism, white Australia policy; **disqualification,** ban, debarment, disenfranchisement, disinheritance, excommunication, forbiddance, preclusion, reprobation; **bar,** barrier, no-go area, taboo; **exile,** banishment, estrangement, riddance, sequestration; **isolation,** aloneness; **deletion,** cancel *(Print.)*, cancellation, cut, dele, delenda, elision, ellipsis

EXCLUSIVE *adj* exclusory, preclusive, segregated, segregative; **restricted,** off-limits; **eliminative,** elimination, eliminatory, exceptive, knockout, omissive

EXCREMENTAL *adj* cacky, excrementitious, faecal, scatologic, stercoraceous, stercorous, stercoral; **excretal,** emunctory, evacuative, excretive, excretory, waste; **urinary,** cloacal, genitourinary, urinative, uriniferous, urinous, urogenous; **perspiratory,** sudoral, sudoriferous, sudorific, sudoriparous, sweaty, transpiratory; **menstrual,** catamenial, menstruous. *See also* SECRETORY

EXCRETE *v* exude; **perspire,** feel like a greasespot, foam, lather, sweat, swelter, transpire; **slaver,** drivel, expectorate, gob, golly, hawk, hoick, salivate, slag, slobber, snivel, spit, water; **ejaculate,** come, drop a load, dump a load, get one's rocks off, shoot one's bolt, toss off; **discharge,** matter, maturate, run, suppurate, weep; **menstruate,** be on the rags, flood, have the flags out, have the painters in, see the flowers, see the roses, see the visitors; **purge,** go through like a dose of salts, physic, scour; **secrete; lactate,** express milk, give milk. *See also* DEFECATE; URINATE

EXECRATORY *adj* abusive, anathematic, blasphemous, damnatory, execrative, foul, foul-mouthed, hard-mouthed, imprecatory, maledictory; **coarse,** bad, foul, strong, unparliamentary

EXECUTE *v* lynch, point the bone at; **electrocute,** gas; **hang,** gibbet, halter, stretch, string up, suspercollate, turn off *(Obs.)*; **garrotte,** bow-string, strangle; **crucify,** impale; **behead,** guillotine, send to the scaffold; **hang draw and quarter,** flay, quarter

EXERCISE *n* constitutional, daily dozen, exercitation, pacework, practice, sweat, work-out; **physical education,** acrobatics, aerobics, athletics, body building, callisthenics, exercises, gymnastics, isometrics, P.E., P.T., phys. ed., physical jerks, physical training, sport, weightlifting, yoga; **knee-bend,** forward roll, half lever, handspring, handstand, hang, heave, lunge, neck roll, press-up, push-up, scissors, somersault, split, turn

exercise restraint

EXERCISE RESTRAINT *v* back-pedal, be moderate, mince one's words, soft-pedal, take the middle road, trim

EXHUMATION *n* body-snatching, disentombment, disinterment

EXHUME *v* disentomb, disinter

EXIT *n* débouché, debouch *(Fort.)*, egress, mouth *(Phys. Geog.)*, outfall, outlet, solfatara, way out; **emergence**, appearance, coming out, debouchment, surfacing; **outflow**, burst, discharge, drainage, effluent, efflux, effluxion, effusion, emanation, emission, eruption, exudation, flash, issuance, issue, leak, leakage, outbreak, outburst, outpour, runoff, seep, seepage; **emigration**, brain drain, exile; **vent**, channel, chimney, chimneystack, chute, drain, exhaust, exhaust pipe, nozzle, opening, orifice, snout, spout, stovepipe, tap, taphole, venturi *(Naut.)*, vomitory, zoomie; **egression**, departure, escape, escapement *(Archaic)*, exodus, outgo, outgoing; **sally**, sortie

EXIT *v* clear *(Shipping)*, depart, emigrate, export, go forth, go out, hop it, issue forth, outfly *(Poetic)*, sally, sortie *(Mil.)*, spring forth, spring out; **emerge**, come forth, come out, debouch; **erupt**, break out, burst forth, burst out, escape

EXPECT *v* anticipate, ask, bargain for, contemplate, count upon, envision, foresee, have in store, look for, look to, prepare for, suppose, think, think likely; **plan against**, forestall, prevent *(Obs.)*, take precautions; **await**, attend, cool one's heels, drool, hold one's breath, kick one's heels, lie in wait, listen for, mark time, tarry *(Archaic)*, wait for, watch for, watch out for; **apprehend**, bide one's time,

192

expedience

contemplate, sweat on; **hope for**, look forward to, look to, pitch one's hopes at, promise oneself

EXPECTANT *adj* anticipant of, hopeful, tiptoe, tiptoe with excitement; **clockwatching**, anticipating, looking forward to; **anticipatory**, anticipative, expectative, prevenient; **apprehensive**, fearful, threatened

EXPECTANTLY *adv* agog, anticipatively, anticipatorily, apprehensively, in expectation of, on tenterhooks, on tiptoe, prospectively; **on the horizon**, almost upon us, in the pipeline, in view, just around the corner

EXPECTATION *n* anticipation, breathless expectation, clockwatching, eager anticipation, expectance, expectancy, foresight, wait, waiting; **hope**, belief, good faith, optimism; **apprehension**, apprehensiveness, curiosity, suspense; **prevenience**, prevenance

EXPECTED *adj* anticipated, future, imminent, impending, pending, prospective; **foreseen**, long expected, Messianic, prophesised; **favourite**, deemed most likely to succeed, fancied, kindly *(Mining)*

EXPECTED THING *n* consummation greatly to be desired, contingency, destiny, future, presumption, prospect, sanguine hope, the goods *(Colloq.)*; **dream**, thought, view; **foretaste**, prelibation; **time bomb**, pregnant situation; **expected person**, comer *(Colloq.)*, great white hope, hopeful, Messiah; **fancy**, favourite *(Sport)*

EXPEDIENCE *n* advantageousness, advisability, appropriateness, desirability, expediency, suitability; **resourcefulness**, extemporaneousness, extemporariness, extemporisation, pragmatism, utilitarianism; **fitness**, commodiousness, judiciousness, propriety, towardliness, towardness

EXPEDIENT *n* ad hoc decision, cards to play, gambit, means, means to an end, method, nostrum, plan, plot, policy, recourse, remedy, resort, resource, scheme, stepping stone, stock-in-trade, strategem, strings to one's bow, wherewithal; **convenience,** accommodation, advantage; **contrivance,** artifice, connivance, design, dodge, fiddle, gimmick, knack, loophole, shift, trick, waiting game, wangle; **makeshift,** bandaid solution, improvisation, jury mast, jury rig, locum tenens, remount, stopgap, substitute, temporary expedience; **last resort,** insurance, sheet anchor

EXPEDIENT *adj* advantageous, advisable, conducive to advantage, desirable, expediential, handy, opportune, profitable, timely, worth one's while; **appropriate,** applicable, befitting, fit, meet *(Archaic)*, proper, ripe, suitable, towardly *(Archaic)*; **politic,** deliberative, judicious; **workable,** practical, useful, utilitarian, utility; **convenient,** commodious, satisfactory; **improvised,** ad hoc, extemporal *(Archaic)*, extemporaneous, extemporary, extempore, improvisatory, jury *(Naut.)*, makeshift, stopgap

EXPEDIENTLY *adv* advantageously, advisably, desirably; **by means of,** through the means of, with the aid of; **conveniently,** appropriately, at the last moment, commodiously, in the nick of time; **to advantage,** just as well; **extemporarily,** extemporaneously, resourcefully; **in cold blood,** deliberately, politically, with an eye to the main chance

EXPEL *v* disgorge, dump, egest, ejaculate, eliminate, evacuate, express, extrude, pump out, spout, vent, void; **emit,** give off, give out, radiate, reek, send off, send out, spit, sputter, utter *(Rare)*; **deflate,** degas, degasify; **erupt,** burst, effuse, extravasate, regorge; **discharge,** excrete, exude, flux *(Obs.)*, pour out, suppurate. *See also* EJECT

EXPELLER *n* eliminator, evacuator, vomiter; **expellant,** aperient, cathartic, emetic; **ejector,** banisher, bouncer, chucker-out, evictor

EXPENSIVE *adj* a bit hot, dear, high-priced, pricey; **prohibitive,** beyond one's means; **extravagant,** big, excessive, exorbitant, extortionate, high, inflated, inflationary, steep; **valuable,** costly, precious, rich; **priceless,** beyond price, invaluable, unpriced *(Poetic)*, unvalued *(Obs.)*; **sumptuous,** plush, plushy, ritzy, swanky

EXPENSIVENESS *n* costliness, dearness; **valuableness,** preciousness, sumptuousness; **overvaluation,** inflatedness; **extortion,** daylight robbery, excessiveness, exorbitance, highway robbery

EXPERT *n* dab, dab hand, dead hand, gun, hot-shot, jack-of-all-trades, old chum, old hand, old stager, right-hand man, ringer; **master,** adept, artist, authority, craftsman, doctor *(Colloq.)*, engineer, master hand, master workman, master-craftsman, past master, professional, proficient, rattler *(Colloq.)*, specialist; **virtuoso,** ace, crack, giant, hepcat, high priest, king, maestro, old master, the greatest, thoroughbred, whiz, wizard; **talent,** enfant terrible, good material,

expert

prodigy, whiz kid, wunderkind; **allrounder**, ambidexter, renaissance man, universal genius

EXPLAIN *v* clarify, define, elucidate, explicate, expound, shed light on, throw light on, unfold; **interpret**, construe, deconstruct, make of, read, read between the lines, take, understand; **comment**, commentate, editorialise; **illustrate**, exemplify; **annotate**, edit, gloss, margin, pave

EXPLANATION *n* anagoge, clarification, eisegesis, elucidation, exegesis, explication, illumination, interpretation; **illustration**, exemplification; **exegetics**, deconstruction, diagnostics, euhemerism, hermeneutics, higher criticism, oneirocriticism, oneirology, semiotics, solarism, symbology; **key**, clue, crib, solution

EXPLANATORY *adj* declarative, declaratory, elucidative, elucidatory, explicative, exponential, expository, illuminating, illuminative, illustrational, illustrative, interpretational, interpretive; **annotative**, commentarial, epexegetic, exegetic, glossarial, scholiastic

EXPLODE *v* backfire, burst asunder, burst on the ear, fly off, fulminate, go off, implode, pop, selfdestruct; **set off**, blast, blow up, bomb, destruct *(Mil.)*, detonate, discharge, dynamite, fire, let off, shoot *(Mining)*, spring, squib, torpedo *(U.S.)*; **bang**, bark, boom, clap, crack, crash, peal, pound, slam, thump, thunder

EXPLOSION *n* blast, blow-out, blow-up, destruct, dissilience, eruption, fulmination, implosion; **report**, air-burst, backfire, burst, fire, gunfire; **discharge**, detonation, salvo, volley; **outburst**, storm, tornado; **explosive**

194

expulsion

power, brisance, explosiveness, ground-shock effect, megaton; **bang**, boom, clap, crack, crash, crump, peal, pop, pound, slam, slap, smash, thump, thunder, whiz-bang

EXPLOSIVE *n* charge, destruct system, shot *(Mining)*; **detonator**, cap, gunlock, igniter, matchlock, percussion cap, primer, selfdestruct, squib; **explosive device**, bomb, infernal machine, mine, shell, smokebomb, star shell, time bomb; **high explosive**, amatol, ammonal, atomic explosives, cheddite, cordite, cyclonite, cydonite, dynamite, gelignite, guncotton, gunpowder, hexogen, jelly, lycopodium, lyddite, maximite, melinite, mercury fulminate, nitro, nitroglycerine, nuclear explosives, picric acid, plastic, plastic explosive, smokeless powder, T.N.T., tonite, trinitrotoluene; **low explosive**, fulminating compound, fulminating powder, propellant; **wick**, fuse, touchpaper, train, tripwire

EXPLOSIVE *adj* dissilient, dynamitic, fulminatory, live, pyrotechnic, selfdestruct *(Mil.)*

EXPULSION *n* clearance, dehiscence, disgorgement, ejaculation, elimination, evacuation, extrusion, voidance; **eruption**, drainage, effusion, excretion, extravasation, flux, precipitation, suppuration; **discharge**, emission, eradiation, radiation; **regurgitation**, emesis, hurl, hyperemesis, vomiturition; **deflation**, degasification; **ejection**, defenestration, displacement, ejectment, eviction; **banishment**, deportation, exile, extradition, transportation; **disbarment**, dismissal, disqualification, exclusion, ouster

EXPULSIVE *adj* deflationary, ejective, eliminative, eliminatory, eruptive, expellant, extrusive *(Geol.)*; **effusive**, emissive, suppurative: **egestive**, carminative, cathartic, emetic, purgative, regurgitant, vomitive, vomitory

EXTEND *v* coextend, continue, cross, go, reach, run, span, spread, track *(U.S. Railways)*; **stretch out**, crane, outstretch; **lengthen**, draw out, drop the hem of, elongate, stretch, wiredraw

EXTINGUISH *v* bank down, blow out, damp down, douse, puff out, quench, rake out, smother, snuff out; **butt, stub out**; **put out**, defuse, switch off, turn out; **black out**, brown out

EXTINGUISHED *adj* dead, extinct, quenched, spent

EXTINGUISHER *n* douser, quencher; **sprinkler system**, fire hydrant, fireengine, fireplug *(U.S.)*; **fireextinguisher**, BCF, carbon dioxide, carbon tetrachloride, carbonic acid gas, foam, sand, sand, soda-acid, water

EXTINGUISHING *n* eclipse, extinction, extinguishment; **blackout**, brownout, darkness, lights out

EXTORT *v* blackmail, exact, force, garnish *(Brit.)*; **bludge off**, bite, bleed, bleed dry, cadge from, eat out of house and home, put the nips in, put the screws on, rack-rent, screw, shake, sweat

EXTORTIONIST *n* blackmailer, extorter, extortioner, grafter *(U.S.)*, rackrenter, Shylock, usurer; **swindler**, card sharp, card sharper, carpetbagger, hawk, kite, Ned Kelly, profiteer, sharper, thief; **vulture**, bloodsucker, vampire, wolf; **parasite**, bludger, leech, sponge, ten-per-center

EXTRACT *n* core, crush, decoction, educt, essence, extractive, infusion

EXTRACT *v* draw, draw out, epilate, eradicate, exhaust, extricate, pluck, pluck out, pull out, remove, root out, take out, weed out, withdraw; **cut out**, core, excise, exsect, rip out, tear out; **dig out**, dredge, mine, pull up, root up, unroot; **drain**, bleed, crush, decoct, exhaust, express, filter, filtrate, juice, milk, press, press out, pump, pump out, sluice, squeeze, squeeze out, start, suck, tap, wring from; **derive**, aspirate, render *(Cookery)*, seethe *(Obs.)*, soak, sublimate, sublime

EXTRACTION *n* epilation, eradication, exsection, extrication, removal, taking out, withdrawal; **pull**, tug, wrench; **drainage**, bleeding, decoction, draught, evulsion, expression, filtration, sublimation, suction, tapping

EXTRACTIVE *adj* abstractive, aspiratory, efferent; **obliterative**

EXTRACTOR *n* drawer *(Archaic)*, gouger, sucker; **auger**, corer, corkscrew, deriver, pigs'-feet *(Railways)*, wimble; **forceps**, pincers, pliers, tweezers; **pump**, stomach pump, vacuum pump, worm pump; **drainer**, crusher, filter, filterer, juicer, milker, milking machine, mill, squeezer, sweatbox, tapper, trocar *(Surg.)*; **bloodsucker**, leech, phlebotomist

EXTRAVAGANCE *n* a taste for luxury, champagne taste, conspicuous consumption, extravagant desire, extravagantness; **prodigality**, excess, profuseness, profusion, superfluity; **wastefulness**, dissipation, profligacy, profligateness, squander, thriftlessness, unthriftiness, wantonness, waste; **splurge**, bean, beanfeast, blow-out, jag, midnight feast, spree

EXTRAVAGANT *adj* costly *(Archaic)*, dissipative, lavish, prodigal, profuse, superfluous *(Obs.)*; **wasteful**, improvident, pound-foolish, profligate, thriftless, uneconomical, wanton

EXTREMITY *n* butt, club, end, finial, foot, heelpiece, pole, tag, tail, tail end, tailpiece, termination, tip, toe

EYE *n* eyeball, lamps, orb *(Poetic)*, peepers, white, winker; **eyelid**, lid; **pupil**, apple of the eye, iris, retina, yellow spot; **lash**, brow, eyebrow; **eye socket**, eyehole, orbit

EYE-CATCHER *n* centre of attraction, concern, cynosure, fascinator, focal point, focus of attention, lodestar, spellbinder

Ff

FACE *n* aspect, countenance, dial, features, metope, moosh, mug, pan, phiz, physiognomy, puss, visage; **jowl**, cheek, dewlap; **jaw**, chin, chops, point *(Boxing)*, underjaw. *See also* HEAD: EYE: NOSE: EAR: MOUTH

FACILITATE *v* cater, disencumber, ease, enable, frank, grease, make way for, speed

FACILITATION *n* convenience, easement, easer, simplification, stepping stone

FACTORY *n* assembly line, establishment, hong, industrial estate, industrial park, manufactory *(Archaic)*, sheltered workshop, shop, stable, trading estate, workshop; **foundry**, grindery, ironworks, machine shop, smelter, smeltery, steelworks, wireworks, works; **smithery**, blacksmith's shop, forge, smithy, stithy; **yard**, brickfield, brickyard, dockyard, freight terminal, goods yard, shipyard; **saltworks**, salina, saltern; **plant**, gasworks, installation, pilot plant, refinery, station; **sweatshop**, female factory *(Convict)*, salt mines, workhouse; **meatworks**, boiling-down works, freezing works, knackery, slaughterhouse; **mine**, colliery, pithead, stall

FAIL *v* bomb, die, die in the hole, die standing up, die the death, fall flat, fall short, fall through, give way, lapse, melt *(Archaic)*, miss the boat, miss the bus, not come up to scratch, not make the grade, not suffice, slump, wither on the vine; **collapse**, backfire, break down, clap out, come undone, crack, crack up, crash, end up in smoke, fall down, fizzle, flop, fold, fold up, go down like a lead balloon, go up in smoke, miscarry, misfire, nosedive; **come unstuck**, bomb, bomb out, come a buster, come a cropper, come a gutser, come to grief, do no good, draw a blank, fall flat on one's face, get nowhere, go to the devil, go to the wall, go under, have had it, have had one's chips, lay an egg, lose out on, not be able to take a trick, not get to first base; **miss**, go wide; **bungle**, abort, arse up, balls up, blow, botch, butcher, cock up, dig one's own grave, dud up, foozle, foul up, mess about, muck up, muff, mull, scupper *(Brit. Colloq.)*, trip up; **make a blue**, flunk, make a false step, strike out; **underachieve**, run dead *(Horse-racing)*; **lose**, be among the also-rans, be bested, bite the dust, come off second best, get left behind, lose out, take a beating; **give in**, admit defeat, cop out, crap out, default, dip out, give best, give way, go back on, let someone down, mess someone about, put up the shutters

FAILED *adj* done like a dinner, gone to Gowings, manqué, ruined, washed-up; **unsuccessful**, ineffective, ineffectual, lost, stickit *(Scot.)*, unplaced; **losing**, no-win, self-defeating; **unaccomplished**, abortive, stillborn

FAIL TO PAY *v* break an agreement, default, dishonour a cheque, do a moonlight flit, freeload, nullify an agreement, scarper, shoot through, welsh; **defraud**, bilk, cheat, swindle

FAILURE *n* abort, abortion, bomb, calamity, damp squib, disaster, fiasco, fizz, fizzle, fizzler, flop, forlorn hope, frost, lemon, misfire, muff, squib, turkey, wash-out, wipe-out, write-off; **fail**, flunk, plough *(Brit. Colloq.)*; **fall**, cropper, downfall, failing, lapse, nose-dive; **collapse**, bust-up, crack-up, crash, slump, smash; **loss**, a dead loss, blue duck *(Mil.)*, bottom, bummer, bust, naught, no-no; **bungle**, balls-up, blunder, botch, cock-up, error, foozle, hash, miscarriage, muck-up, muddle, slip, slip-up, stuff-up; **miss**, break *(Tenpin Bowling)*, fault, near miss, rabbit *(Cricket)*, strike *(Baseball)*; **unsuccessfulness**, abortiveness

FAIR *adj* candid, disinterested, dispassionate, fair-minded, impartial, objective, uninterested; **egalitarian**, democratic, equalitarian; **even-handed**, equable, equal *(Archaic)*, equitable, even, fair and square; **sporting**, sportsmanlike; **just**, conscionable, honest, morally right, reasonable, right, rightful, square; **deserved**, as it should be, fit, fitting, justifiable, lawful, legitimate, well-earned

FAIR GO *n* fair buck *(N.Z.)*, fair do *(N.Z.)*; **fair play**, cricket, good sportsmanship, Marquis of Queensbury rules, square deal

FAIR GO *interj* fair buck *(N.Z.)*, fair crack of the whip, fair do *(N.Z.)*, fair shake of the sauce bottle, fair suck of the sav, fair's fair

FAIRLY *adv* candidly, fair, fair and square, justly, on the square, sportingly, square; **impartially**, dispassionately, equably, equitably, even, objectively, without fear or favour, without prejudice, without regard to person; **rightfully**, by rights, in justice

FAIRNESS *n* candidness, candour, dispassionateness, fair-mindedness, impartiality, impartialness, objectiveness, objectivity; **justice**, justness, natural justice, poetic justice, propriety, right, rightfulness, rightness; **even-handedness**, egalitarianism, equability, equableness, equalitarianism, equitableness, equity, measure for measure; **karma**, inevitable consequence, retributive justice, scales of justice, sword of justice; **just reward**, desert, merit, merit money *(Indust. Law)*

FAIR PERSON *n* nature's gentleman, real sportsman, square-shooter

FAIRY *n* banshee *(Scot. Irish)*, brownie, elf, elfin, faerie *(Archaic)*, leprechaun, little people, pixie, pixy, sandman, sprite, tooth fairy, urchin *(Archaic)*; **imp**, bug, devilkin, eudemon, gremlin, hob, hobgoblin, kobold *(German)*, puck, siren, sprite, sylph, sylphid; **ogre**, dwarf, hag, monopode, pygmy, troll, witch; **bogyman**, boggle, bogle, bogy, boogieman, bugaboo, bugbear *(Obs.)*, Jack Frost; **Santa Claus**, Father Christmas, Kris Kringle, Saint Nicholas, Saint Nick, Santa. *See also* MYTHICAL BEING

FAITHFUL *adj* leal *(Scot. Archaic)*, liege, loyal, single-hearted, true, true-blue, true-hearted, white *(Brit. Colloq.)*; **honourable**, as good as one's word, good, straight, trustworthy; **dutiful**, allegiant, duteous, wedded; **reliable**, dedicated, dependable, devoted, trusty, unfailing; **resolute**, certain, constant, fixed, set, staunch,

faithful steadfast, strong, sure, unwavering; **authentic,** genuine

FAITHFULLY *adv* devotedly, leally, loyally, staunchly, steadfastly; **dutifully,** duteously; **resolutely,** stubbornly; **authentically,** straightly, truly *(Archaic)*

FAITHFULNESS *n* allegiance, devotedness, fealty *(Archaic)*, fidelity, loyalism, loyalty, troth *(Archaic)*, truth *(Archaic)*; **integrity,** bona fides, dependability, good faith, honour, probity, sincerity, true-heartedness, trustworthiness; **authenticity,** certainty, genuineness; **dutifulness,** devotion, duteousness, sense of responsibility, supererogation; **reliability,** adherence, adhesion, constancy, resolution, staunchness, steadfastness, strength

FAITHLESSLY *adv* falsely, recreantly, untruly; **treacherously,** felinely, perfidiously, traitorously, treasonably, treasonously

FAKE *n* act, bluff, cheat, deceit, deception, dissimulation, fraud, impersonation, imposture, pretence, sham; **frame-up,** put-up job, verbal; **hypocrisy,** cant, humbug, tokenism; **cupboard love,** crocodile tears, Judas kiss

FAKE *v* cook, doctor, falsify, fiddle, juggle, rig, trump up, twist; **frame,** bear false witness against, dolly, set up, verbal

FAKE *adj* bastard, bastardly *(Obs.)*, bodgie, bogus, counterfeit, done with mirrors, dummy, persuado, phoney, pinchbeck, pseudo, sham, simular, simulate *(Archaic)*, suppositious, suppositious, suppositive, unauthentic; **artificial,** celluloid, cheesy, ersatz, imitation, plastic; **pretended,** assumed, feigned, imposturous, ostensible, ostensive, professed, so-called, soi-disant, would-be; **meretricious,** flash, painted; **false,** adulterine, adulterous *(Obs.)*, fictitious, made out of whole cloth *(U.S.)*, spurious, untrue; **apocryphal,** fabulous, fairytale, mythical

FAKER *n* bodgie, cheat, dissembler, dissimulator, four-flusher, fraud, front man, impersonator, impostor, malingerer, persuado, phoney, pretender, pseud, pseudo, ringer, shammer, whited sepulchre, wolf in sheep's clothing; **charlatan,** empiric *(Obs.)*, mountebank, quack, quacksalver *(Archaic)*; **hypocrite,** boggler, equivocator, humbug, prevaricator

FAKERY *n* artificiality, artificialness, delusiveness, falseness, falsity, spuriousness, supposititiousness, untrueness; **fraudulence,** barney, charlatanism, deceitfulness, disingenuousness, fraudulency, humbuggery; **untruthfulness,** double-dealing, duplicity, insincerity, inveracity, lying, mendaciousness, mendacity, mountebankery, mythomania, quackery, twofacedness; **deviousness,** craftiness, cunningness, guile, insidiousness, tortuousness

FALL *n* crash, cropper, dive, flop, flump, plop, plump, plumper, pratfall *(U.S.)*, precipitation, prostration, purler, slip *(Geol.)*, slump, stumble, trip, tumble, whop, wipe-out *(Surfing)*; **pounce,** downrush, swoop; **free fall,** flat spin, jump, nosedive, sideslip, skydiving

FALL *v* bite the dust, come a cropper, come a gutser, crash-land, fall off, flop, flump, go for a sixer, go for six, hit the deck, keel over, knuckle over, lose one's balance, measure one's length, overbalance, pitch, slip, stumble, take a toss, take a trip, trip, tumble; **plump**, plunk, whop; **collapse**, avalanche, cave in, subside; **slump**, droop, prolapse, sag; **sink**, bog, founder, settle, swamp, touch bottom; **scuttle**, send to the bottom, sink, torpedo

FALLEN *adj* bowed, cast *(Agric.)*, downcast, droopy, sunken; **descending**, cataclinal, declivitous, descendent, downgrade, downhill, downward, katabatic; **deciduous**, caducous

FALLER *n* autumn leaf, flopper, stumbler; **windfall**, sailer *(N.Z.)*

FALL INTO DISUSE *v* antiquate, archaise, be superseded, give place, lapse, not catch on, rust; **go by the board**, go begging, go to waste, waste

FALL SHORT *v* fail, run short, ullage; **lack**, need, want; **be lacking**, be badly off for, be light on, be short of

FALSE *adj* apocryphal, erroneous, fallacious, inaccurate, incorrect, misleading, mistaken, off the beam, out, unfactual, unhistorical, untrue, wide of the mark, wrong; **astray**, awry, misapprehensive, off to billyo, on the wrong tack, up a gumtree, up the booay, up the pole; **deceptive**, hallucinatory, illusory; **fallible**, careless, erring; **misguided**, perverse, wrongheaded; **subjective**

FALSELY *adv* amiss, blunderingly, confusedly, erroneously, fallaciously, fallibly, inaccurately, incorrectly, misapprehensively, mistakenly, wrong, wrongly

FALSITY *n* fallacy, falseness; **erroneousness**, incorrectness, wrongness; **inaccurateness**, carelessness, casualness, confusedness, misapprehensiveness; **unreality**, untruth; **subjectivity**, personal equation, self-deception; **fallibility**, fallibleness. *See also* ERROR

FAMOUS *adj* epic, front-line, mentionable, notable, noted, noteworthy, of note, notorious, renowned; **well-known**, fashionable, hit, popular, well-established; **legendary**, deathless, fabled, fabulous, immortal, imperishable, never-fading, proverbial; **classic**, classical, historic, time-honoured

FAMOUS PERSON *n* celebrity, face, figure, first fiddle, heavy, heavyweight, hero, household name, identity, leading light, lion, luminary, magnate, notable, personage, personality, public figure, somebody, star, talk of the town, tall poppy, toast of the town, V.I.P., visiting fireman, worthy

FANCIFULLY *adv* fantastically, imaginatively, ingeniously; **imaginarily**, ideally, ideationally, notionally

FANTASISE *v* be away with the fairies, build castles in the air, daydream, dream, dream dreams, goof off, have visions, hear voices, live in a fantasy land, romance, romanticise, stargaze, tilt at windmills; **pretend**, make-believe; **imagine**, conjure up, ideate, invent; **envision**, image, picture, project, visualise; **concoct**, coin, fabricate, hatch, improvise

FANTASISER *n* daydreamer, Don Quixote, dreamer, fabler, fabulist, idealist, imaginer, improviser, poet, romancer, stargazer, storyteller, surrealist, Walter Mitty, wool-gatherer

FANTASTIC *adj* apocryphal, chimerical, fabled, fabulous, fancied; fictional, fictitious, ideational, imagin-

FANTASTIC ary, imaginational, legendary, made-up, metaphysical *(Archaic)*, mythic, mythological, poetic, storybook; **surreal**, phantasmal, phantom, surrealist, surrealistic, transcendental; **imaginative**, daedal *(Poetic)*, fancy, improvisatorial, improvisatory, ingenious

FANTASY *n* fancifulness, fancy, imagery *(Psychol.)*, imagination, imaginativeness, improvisation, ingeniousness, ingenuity, mind's eye; **imaginariness**, apocryphalness, fabulousness, fictitiousness, idealness, unreality, vaporosity, vaporousness; **idealism**, escapism, romanticism, surrealism, vision, visionariness; **stargazing**, wool-gathering, autism, introversion, schizophrenia, withdrawal *(Psychol.)*

FAREWELL *n* adieu, godspeed, goodbye, goodnight, send-off, valedictory; **parting**, leave, leave-taking, parting of the ways, valediction

FAREWELL *v* bundle off, ring out, see off, see out, see to the door, send off

FARM *n* bush farm *(N.Z.)*, croft *(Scot.)*, estate, free selection, hobby farm, homestead selection, plantation, property, selection, smallholding, stud-farm, vinery, vineyard; **farmhouse**, farmstead, grange, hacienda, homestead; **collective farm**, co-operative farm, kibbutz, kolkhoz; **station**, back-station, cattle-run, dude ranch *(U.S.)*, estancia, out-station, ranch, rancho, sheep station, sheep-run, spread *(U.S.)*, stock farm; **dairy farm**, creamery, dairy, herringbone dairy; **oyster-farm**, trout-farm, turtle-farm

FARM *v* be on the land, cocky, cowbang, cowspank, ranch; **drove**, drift, herd, hoozle, hunt away, jackeroo, muster, stockkeep, tail, wrangle *(U.S.)*; **graze**, agist, block-graze, crash-graze, creep-graze, fatten, feed, open-graze, pasture, range, run; **breed**, grow, lamb down, overstock, stock; **milk**, strip; **cultivate**, bring in *(N.Z.)*, grow, husband *(Obs.)*, improve, subdue; **plough**, chip, chisel-plough, delve, dibble, dig, disc, grub, harrow, hoe, labour *(Archaic or Poetic)*, rake, scarify, stub, stump, till; **fallow**, rest; **plant**, bed, heel in, implant, pot, prick out, slip, transplant, vernalise; **sow**, broadcast, checkrow *(U.S.)*, seed, sod-seed, stratify; **afforest**, forest. *See also* HARVEST

FARMABLE *adj* arable, cultivable, cultivatable, improvable, pasturable, tillable; **fallow**, uncultivated, unseeded

FARMER *n* boss cocky, husbandman, landsman, pastoralist, primary producer, ruralist, the man on the land; **small farmer**, agistor, blocker, blockie, bush-farmer, cockatoo, cocky, cove, crofter *(Scot.)*, dungaree settler, free selector, selector, stringy-bark cockatoo, wheat-cocky; **stockbreeder**, breeder, cutter-out, stirpiculturist, stock farmer, stock raiser; **dairy farmer**, cow-cocky, cowbanger, cowspanker, herd tester; **grazier**, cattleman, rancher, ranchero, run-holder, sheepman, station-owner, stockholder, stockkeeper, stockman *(U.S.)*, woolgrower; **apiarist**, apiculturist, beekeeper, sericulturist; **planter**, cane-cocky, canefarmer, canegrower, sugar farmer, tea planter; **winegrower**, blocker *(S.A.)*, oenologist, vigneron, vinedresser, vineyardist, viniculturist, viticulturer, viticulturist; **orchardist**, fruit-grower, fruiter, pomiculturist, pomologist; **hobby farmer**, Collins Street cocky, Piccadilly bushman *(Brit.)*, Pitt Street farmer, Queen Street bushie; **tenant farmer**, cropper, sharecropper *(U.S.)*, sharefarmer, sharemilker *(N.Z.)*; **farm manager**, overseer, station manager; **peasant**, bucolic, bushie, carl *(Archaic)*, churl, cottager, cottar, cottier, hick, redneck *(U.S.)*, ryot; **stock and station agent**, stock agent; **agriculturalist**, agriculturist, agrobiologist, agronomist, forester

FARMHAND *n* blue-tongue, help, jackeroo, jillaroo, knockabout, leatherneck, loppy, narangy, rouseabout, rouser, station hand, wood-and-water joey; **stockman**, buckaroo, cow hand, cowboy, cowgirl, cowpuncher *(U.S.)*, drover, gaucho, musterer, nutter, ringer, stock-driver *(N.Z.)*, stockrider, tailer, tailer-up, vaquero *(U.S.)*; **boundary rider**, jerker, lizard; **shepherd**, cowherd, crawler, dog driver, goatherd, gooseherd, herder, herdsman, monkey dodger, motherer, shepherdess, snail, swanherd, swineherd, wrangler *(U.S.)*; **dairyman**, cowman, dairymaid *(Archaic)*, dairywoman, milkmaid; **tiller**, ploughboy, plougher, ploughman; **reaper**, canecutter, cocksfooter *(N.Z.)*, emu-bobber, gleaner, harvester, harvestman, thresher; **haymaker**, crow *(N.Z.)*, tedder, windrower; **picker**, hop-picker, vintager

FARMING *n* agrarianism, agribusiness, agriculture, cultivation, husbandry, pastoralism, primary industry, ruralism; **agronomy**, agrobiology, agrology, agronomics, chemurgy, geoponics, pedology, soil mechanics, soil science; **mixed farming**, bush-farming, market gardening, subsistence farming; **stock farming**, agistment, animal husbandry, breeding, custom feeding, stock raising, wool-growing; **dairy farming**, cow-cockying, dairying, herd testing, sharemilking; **forestry**, afforestation, arboriculture, forestation, reforestation, silviculture; **viticulture**, oenology, viniculture, winegrowing; **apiculture**, sericulture; **marine farming**, aquiculture, mariculture; **organic farming**, biological control, companion planting, hydroponics, permaculture, tank farming; **ploughing**, contour ploughing, culture; **clean cultivation**, crop rotation, dry farming, extensive cultivation, intensive cultivation, ley farming, monoculture, multiple cropping, strip cropping; **harvesting**, cocksfooting *(N.Z.)*, harvest home, haymaking, inning, mowing, reaping; **grazing**, crash-grazing, intensive stocking, rotational grazing, set stocking, strategic grazing, strip grazing, zero grazing; **muster**, bangtail muster, round-up, yarding; **drenching**, dipping, mulesing

FARMING *adj* agrarian, agrestic, bucolic, country, georgic, pastoral, peasant, rural, rustic, villatic; **agricultural**, agrobiologic, agrologic, agrological, agronomic, agronomical, geoponic, hydroponic; **farmyard**, free-range, open-range, organic; **arboricultural**, silvicultural; **vinicultural**, oenological, viticultural; **apicultural**, apiarian, sericultural

FARMLAND n baulk, downland, fallow, field, glebe (Poetic), infield, lea (Archaic), ley, mead (Poetic), meadow (Brit.), paddock, swidden, turbary, water-meadow; **back paddock**, back country, back run, outfield; **tillage**, cornfield, cultivation paddock, hayfield, paddy, plough, tilth; **wheat-belt**, rice bowl; **pasture**, artificial grass, grass, improved pasture, pasturage, run-off (N.Z.); **grazing land**, long paddock, sheepwalk (Brit.), springer paddock, stock run; **farmyard**, barnyard, feedlot, home paddock, resting paddock, stockyard

FARM MACHINERY n aerator, chain harrow, combine harvester, cultivator, disc plough, harrow, harvester, plough, scarifier, stump-jump plough, tractor

FASHION n craze, cult, fad, fangle (Obs.), rage, the going thing, the last word, the latest, the new look, the thing, vogue, **style**, cut, guise, tone, trend; **haute couture**, bon ton; **fashionableness**, chic, coolness, dressiness, exclusiveness, faddishness, height of fashion, modishness, smartness, stylishness, trendiness, up-to-dateness; **dapperness**, jauntiness, nattiness, rakishness, sauciness, snappiness, sportiness, spruceness, swank, swankiness; **cultism**, dandyism, faddism, trendyism; **titivation**, dandification

FASHIONABLE adj all the go, all the rage, in, in vogue, up-to-date, up-to-the-minute, with-it; **dapper**, all gussied up, dandy, dandyish, dressed to the nines, snappy, spiffy, sporty, spruce, swanky; **chic**, cool, dashing, dashy, exclusive, faddish, faddy, fashion, gear (Brit.), high-stepping, hot, jaunty, mod, modish, natty, newfangled, rakish, saucy, smart, snazzy, stylish, supercool, swell, swish, swishy; **trendy**, ultrafashionable

FASHIONABLE PERSON n cultist, faddist, teeny-bopper, trendsetter, trendy; **beau monde**, grand monde, haut monde, the scene; **high society**, beautiful people, glitterati, jet set, smart set; **socialite**, jetsetter; **dandy**, ball of style, fop, gallant, gilded youth, high-stepper, jack-a-dandy, prinker, swell, titivator

FASHIONABLY adv à la mode, exclusively, modishly, on the scene, stylishly, stylistically; **dapperly**, dashingly, jauntily, nattily, rakishly, saucily, snappily, sprucely, swankily

FAST n hunger strike; **diet**, bread and water, iron rations, short commons, starvation diet; **fast day**, Advent, Asalahabuja, Friday, Lent, Ramadan, Yom Kippur. See also ABSTINENCE

FASTEN v affix, attach, fix, lace, secure, stick; **infix**, engage (Archaic), house, joggle, mortice, seat; **hang**, hook up, suspend; **bind**, bend, bight, colligate, knot, strap, tie, withe, wrap, wrap up; **do up**, belt up, button up, zip up; **lash**, bowse, cable, cord, frap, gammon (Naut.), gripe (Naut.), lace, reeve, rope, seize (Naut.); **nail**, bolt, rivet, screw, skew (Carp.); tack; **clamp**, clasp, clinch, grasp, grip; **stitch**, side-stitch, staple; **make fast**, anchor, moor, tie up; **tether**, enchain, hobble, hopple, leash, picket, shackle, stake; **lock**, bar, double-lock

FASTENED adj engaged, fast, firm, fixed, iron, secure; **bound**, bandaged, corded, fasciate, lashed, tied; **at anchor**, girt

FASTENER n bonder, locker, securer; **binder**, bracer, lasher, tier, trusser; **nailer**, pinner, riveter; **grasper**, clasper, clincher, gripper, hooker; **hitcher**, hobbler, shackler

FASTENING n affixture, attachment, fixation, infixion; **binding**, colligation, coupling, hitching, lashing, seizing *(Naut.)*, tying; **connexion**, engagement; **fixedness**, firmness, fixity, secureness

FAT n adipose, animal fat, blubber, cellulite, sebum, suet, tallow, yolk; **edible oil**, blown oil, butter, butterfat, castor oil, cooking oil, cottonseed oil, dripping, fat, ghee, gingili, grease, lard, marg, margarine, nut oil, oleo oil, olive oil, palm oil, safflower oil, sesame oil, soya bean oil, sweet oil *(U.S.)*, vegetable butter, vegetable oil; **fuel oil**, black gold, derv *(Brit.)*, diesel oil, dieseline, distillate, gas oil, mineral oil, petroleum, rock-oil, shale oil, train oil; **ointment**, anointment, balsam, lanolin, petrolatum, petroleum jelly, retinol, salve, unction, unguent, vaseline, wool fat; **essential oil**, bergamot, cajuput oil, cineol, eucalyptol, eucalyptus oil, eugenol, neroli oil, peppermint, sassafras oil, wintergreen, ylang-ylang; **cosmetic oil**, almond oil, brilliantine, coconut oil, face cream, hair oil, hand cream, hand lotion, lotion, Macassar oil; **lubricant**, antifriction, axle-grease, coolant, cyclopentane, grease; **wax**, cerumen, earwax, spermaceti; **miscellaneous oil**, bone oil, chrism, drying oil, fish oil, linseed oil, mustard oil, neat's-foot oil, rapeseed oil, sperm oil, stand oil, tung-oil, turpentine, vegetable tallow, wood pitch, wood tar; **lubrication**, force-feed, lube

FAT adj adipose, beefy, bloated, burly, chubby, corpulent, fleshy, gross, hulking, meaty, obese, overweight, plump, portly, pursy, roly-poly, rotund, stout, tubby; **potbellied**, abdominous, paunchy; **buxom**, bosomy, busty, chesty, deep-bosomed, junoesque, pneumatic, stacked, Wagnerian, well-stacked, well-upholstered; **squat**, bullocky, dumpty, dumpy, endomorphic, hefty, hippy, hunky, pudgy, pyknic, squab, squabby, squatty, stocky, thickset, well-built; **steatopygous**, steatopygic; **outsize**, overgrown, oversize, oversized

FATE n chance, destiny, Fates, Fortune, karma, kismet, luck, providence, the inevitable, Weird Sisters, wheel of Fortune; **destiny**, appanage, dole *(Archaic)*, doom, fatality, foredoom, fortune, fortunes, lot, star, sticky end; **predestination**, foreordainment, foreordination, predetermination, preordainment, preordination. *See also* INEVITABILITY

FATEFUL adj karmic, providential, weird *(Archaic)*; **predestinarian**, fatalistic, predeterminative. *See also* INEVITABLE

FAULTY SIGHT n ametropia, aniseikonia, anisometropia, astigmatism, cataracts, detached retina, diplopia, double image, eye defect, miosis, muscae volitantes, mydriasis, nebula, nystagmus, presbyopia, retinitis, scleritis, sclerotitis, scotoma; **short-sightedness**, myopia, nearsightedness; **long-sightedness**, hypermetropia, hyperopia; **dimness**, amblyopia, blear, dimness of vision, purblindness, tunnel vision; **night blindness**, nyctalopia; **ophthalmia**, con-

FAULTY SPEECH *n* alalia, alogia, anarthria, aphasia, aphonia, denasality, dyslalia, dysphonia, glossolalia, inarticulateness, infantilism, lallation, lambdacism, paralalia, rhinolalia, rhotacism, tachyphemia; **logopaedics; mutism,** dumbness, speechlessness; **speech impediment,** speech defect; **stammer,** disconnectedness, disjointedness, fumble, fumbling, splutter, sputter, stutter; **mispronunciation,** clip, falter, hesitation, ineloquence, lisp, mumble, mutter, quaver, slur; **gibberish, gibber; accent,** brogue, burr, drawl, nasalisation, twang

FAUNA *n* animal kingdom, animality; **wild animal,** wilding, wildlife, wildling; **vermin,** varmint; **game,** big game; **pet; mammal,** artiodactyl, carnivore, cetacean, chiropter, edentate, elephant, hyracoidean, insectivore, lagomorph, marsupial, monotreme, perissodactyl, pholidote, pinniped, primate, rodent, sirenian; **bird,** amphibian, crustacean, fish, insect, reptile, worm; **crossbred,** bitser, cross, grade, half-blood, hybrid, mong, mongrel; **microfauna,** animalcule *(Rare),* mite; **stable,** stud; **livestock,** farm animals; **zoo,** deer-park, insectarium, menagerie, vivarium

FAVOURABLE *adj* auspicious, bright, encouraging, fair, favonian, golden, hopeful, likely, promising, propitious, roseate, rosy, toward *(Obs.),* towardly *(Archaic)*

FAVOURABLENESS *n* rosiness, towardliness, towardness; **promise,** favourable auspices, good omen, likelihood *(Archaic);* **prospects,** expectations

FEARFULLY *adv* affrightedly, anxiously, apprehensively, shyly, timidly, timorously, tremblingly, tremulously, with knees knocking

FEASIBILITY *n* conceivability, conceivableness, feasibleness, practicability, practicalness, viability, workability, workableness; **possibility,** chance, contingency, eventuality, fighting chance, gamble, half chance, happenstance, liability, likelihood, off-chance; **accessibility,** attainability

FEASIBLE *adj* accessible, accomplishable, achievable, actable, executable, performable, practicable, superable, sustainable, viable, within reach, within the bounds of possibility, workable; **possible,** believable, conceivable, contingent, credible, imaginable, liable, on the cards, open, open-ended, potential

FEATHER *n* aftershaft, alula, auricular, axillary, coverts, filoplume, flight feather, hackle, penna, pin-feather, pinion, pinna, plume, plumelet, plumule, primary, rectrix, remex, secondary, sickle feather, tertial, tertiary, vibrissa; **quill,** barb *(Obs.),* barbicel, barbule, barrel, calamus, flue, herl, pinnula, rachis, shaft; **marabou,** osprey, ostrich feather, peacock feather; **plumage,** feathering; **contour feathers,** aigrette, barb, crest, crissum, ducktail, egret, flag, hackle, moustache, muff, topknot, torques, web, wing-coverts; **down,** eiderdown, floc-

feather   206   **fertile**

cus, swan's-down; **plume**, fletching, flight, panache, wing

FEATHER v fledge, fluff, plume, preen, ruffle; **fletch**, flight, tuft

FEATHERINESS n downiness, plumosity

FEATHERY adj downy, fledgy *(Rare)*, plumy; **plumate**, crested, cristate, plumose; **feathered**, pennate; **featherlike**, pinnal, pinnate, plumelike

FEED v bottle-feed, breastfeed, dripfeed *(Med.)*, foster *(Obs.)*, grub, nourish, nurse, nurture, regale, spoonfeed, suckle, victual *(Archaic)*; **keep a good table**; **serve**, dish up

FEEL EMOTION v be overcome, care, cheer *(Obs.)*, experience, mind, take to heart; **sympathise**, feel for, know what it is to, respond; **sentimentalise**, gush, slobber, slop over; **theatricalise**, bung it on, emote, ham it up, melodramatise, stack it on; **burn**, boil, fire, flame, glow, rage, seethe, smoulder, tear one's hair out; **thrill**, throb, vibrate

FEELER n antenna, finger, hand, palp, paw, tentacle

FEEL PAIN v agonise, anguish, burn one's fingers, suffer; **travail**, be on the rack, do a perish, have a bad time of it, have got 'em bad; **flinch**, start, twitch, wince; **writhe**, squirm

FEMALE adj gynaecomorphous, negative, yin; **feminine**, distaff, gentlewomanly, lady, ladylike, muliebral *(Rare)*, petticoat, spindle *(U.S.)*, womanlike, womanly; **matronly**, housewifely, matronal; **old-womanish**, anile, spinsterish; **girlish**, girly-girly, maidenly; **amazonian**, butch, mannish, viraginous; **tomboyish**, hoydenish; **effeminate**, emasculate, female *(Obs.)*, old-womanish, pooncey, queeny, sawney, unmanly, womanish

FEMINISE v effeminise, emasculate, emolliate, woman *(Obs.)*, womanise; **camp it up**, camp, pansy, ponce, queen it up

FENCE n barbwire fence, boundary, chock-and-log fence, cyclone fence, deadwood fence, dog fence, dog net, doglegged fence, dry-stone wall, electrified fence, ha-ha, hedge, hedgerow, kangaroo fence, pale, palisade, pest fence, picket fence, post-and-rail fence, rabbit fence, shark fence, shark net, snake fence *(U.S.)*, sunk fence, wire, wire entanglement, worm fence *(U.S.)*; **netting**, bird netting, flyscreen, flywire; **gate**, grate, grating, grille, starting gate; **bar**, bail, balustrade, barrier, rail, railing, the paint *(Horseracing)*, tollbar, traverse; **fencing materials**, cyclone wire, fencing panel, fencing wire, mesh, palings, weldmesh.   See also WALL

FEROCIOUS adj aggressive, aggro, bellicose, savage, truculent; **maenadic**, shrewish, termagant; **fierce**, furious, grim, hot, mad, rabid, rampant, red-hot, vehement; **bloodthirsty**, sanguinary, sanguine; **berserk**, paroxysmal.   See also VIOLENT

FERTILE adj eutrophic, fat, fecund, fructuous, fruitful, hearty, lush, luxuriant, pinguid, productive, rich; **abundant**, copious, generous, over-abundant, plenteous, polycarpic *(Bot.)*, pregnant, prodigal, profuse, prolific, rampant, superabundant, teeming, wealthy; **arable**, farmable; **profitable**, beneficial, useful, worthwhile

FERTILE LAND *n* arable, farmland, kindly ground, land of milk and honey, oasis, water-meadow; **topsoil,** humus, leaf mould, litter, potting mixture

FERTILELY *adv* fructuously, fruitfully, luxuriantly, productively, richly; **abundantly,** prodigally, prolifically, rampantly; **profitably,** effectively, effectually, usefully

FERTILISATION *n* enrichment, fecundation, green revolution, impregnation; **fruition,** emblements, fructification, fruitage, output, pullulation, vintage

FERTILISE *v* enrich, fatten, fructify, improve; **manure,** fatten, compost, dress, inoculate, lime, marl, mulch, nitrify, side-dress, super, top, top-dress

FERTILITY *n* arability, fatness, fecundity, fructuousness, fruitfulness, heartiness, luxuriance, pinguidity, productivity; **lushness,** richness, verdancy, verdure; **abundance,** cornucopia, foison *(Archaic),* overabundance, plenty, prolificacy, prolificness, rampancy, superabundance; **teeming womb, teeming loins; profitableness,** benefit, usefulness, utility

FESTIVAL *n* bangtail muster, carnival, fair, festa, festivity, fete, fete day, fiesta, gala, holiday, kermis, mardi gras, pageant, potlatch, Royal Show, saturnalia, show, Venetian carnival; **jubilee,** birthday, commemoration, commemorative, encaenia, feast, name-day, red-letter day, wedding anniversary; **holy day,** feast-day, high day; **harvest festival,** harvest home. *See also* JOY: CELEBRATION

FESTIVE *adj* carnie, festal, festival, holiday, merrymaking

FEVER *n* ague, calenture, febricity, febricula, feverishness, fire, flush, hectic, hyperpyrexia, pyrexia; **shaking,** algor, rigour

FEVERISH *adj* agued, aguish, febriferous, febrific, febrile, feverous; **delirious; faint,** giddy, gone, swimming; **unconscious,** comatose

FEW *adj* hardly any, infrequent, not many, rare, rare as hen's teeth, scarce as hen's teeth, several; **scant,** exiguous, light, little, low-density, scanty, scattered, skimpy, small, sparse, thin; **scarce,** diminished, reduced, tight

FIELD *n* approvement, back run, close, common *(Brit.),* cornfield, granary, gumfield, mead *(Poetic),* meadow, outfield, outland *(Obs.),* paddock, sheepwalk *(Brit.),* stock run; **saddling paddock,** birdcage, enclosure, home paddock, paddock; **farmyard,** barnyard; **schoolyard,** campus, playground, quad, quadrangle; **park,** parkland, pleasance, preserve, reserve; **meeting place,** agora, forum; **square,** esplanade, piazza, place, plaza, walk; **courtyard,** atrium, backyard, cloister, cloister-garth, close, cortile, court, forecourt *(Brit.),* frontage, garden, garth *(Archaic),* lawn *(Archaic),* parvis, yard; **patio,** terrace

FIERY *adj* alight, conflagrant, flagrant *(Rare),* flaming, flamy, flaring, on fire; **fireable,** combustible, combustive, flammable, ignescent, ignitable, inflammable, piceous, touchy; **incendiary,** calcinatory, caustic, igneous, inflammatory; **burnt,** ashen, ashy, charred, charry, sooty

FIGHT *n* barney, battle, blue, boil-up, bout, box-on, broil, brush, chance-medley, close, combat, ding, ding-

fight

dong, dogfight, domestic *(Colloq.)*, dust-up, encounter, go-in, grapple, lash *(Obs.)*, mayhem, mix-up, passage, pillow-fight, punch-up, rencounter, rough-house, rough-up, rumble, running battle, scrape, scrimmage, scuffle, set-to, skirmish, spat, tug, tug of war, turn-in, turn-up, tussle, wrestle, yike; **dispute,** altercation, argy-bargy, cut and thrust, debate, disagreement, discord, friction, fuss, high words, jangle, jar, kafuffle, logomachy, Mexican stand-off, misunderstanding, quarrel, ruckus, run-in, slanging match, splutter, squabble, war of nerves, words, wrangle; **free fight,** affray, battle royal, boilover, brawl, donny *(N.Z.)*, donnybrook, fray, free-for-all, gang-fight, melee, pitched battle, shebang *(N.Z.)*; **feud,** blood feud, gang warfare, vendetta; **duel,** affaire d'honneur, gunfight *(U.S.)*, shoot-out *(U.S.)*. *See also* CONTEST

FIGHT *v* barney, blue, box on, brawl, broil, buffet, come to blows, fight like Kilkenny cats, fisticuff, go the knuckle, mix it, rough-house, rumble, scrap, skirmish, spar, spat, thump; **wrestle,** buckle, grapple, scuffle, struggle, tussle; **set to,** assay, close with, combat, cross swords, draw first blood, encounter, join, meet, take arms, take on; **duel,** have someone on, joust, tilt, tourney *(Archaic),* undertake *(Obs.)*. *See also* CONTEST; **campaign,** battle, conflict, feud, fight it out, wage war

FIGHTER *n* battler, combatant, combater, contender, contestant, striver, struggler, tussler; **aggressor,** assailant, belligerent, feudist, fire-eater, swashbuckler; **knight,** banneret, cavalier, chevalier, jouster, knight-errant, paladin, samurai, shogun *(Jap.)*, tilter, younker *(Obs.)*; **warrior,** amazon, baresark, berserker, brave, champion, ghazi *(Islam.)*, hero, Hun, valkyrie; **fighting drunk, fighting cock; bullfighter,** matador, picador, toreador, torero; **swordsman,** backswordsman, duellist, épéeist, fencer, foilsman, gladiator, sabreur, sword; **gunfighter,** firelock, firer, franc-tireur, gun, gunman, gunner, gunslinger *(U.S.)*, marksman, markswoman, sharpshooter, shooter, sniper; **militarist,** chauvinist, hawk, jingoist, militant, war lord, warmonger; **mercenary,** auxiliaries, condottiere, foreign legion, freelance, hired gun, hireling, landsknecht, lansquenet, legionnaire, professional soldier, soldier of fortune; **adventurer,** buccaneer, filibuster, freebooter. *See also* PUGILIST; ARMED FORCES; SERVICEMAN; SOLDIER; HIGH COMMAND; COMBAT TROOPS

FIGURATIVE *adj* allusive *(Obs.)*, figural, figured, metaphoric, metaphorical, tropical, tropologic; **allegorical,** allegoristic, anagogical, archetypal, symbolic; **rhetoric,** euphuistic, hyperbolic; **idiomatic,** clichéd, colloquial; **ironic,** sardonic; **punning,** paronomastic; **antithetic,** climactic, inverted; **euphemistic,** hypocoristic, pantagruelian; **alliterative,** assonant, metrical, onomatapoeic, rhyming, rhythmic, rhythmical; **metonymical,** syneddochic

FIGURATIVELY *adv* allegorically, allusively, hyperbolically, hypocoristically, idiomatically, ironically, metaphorically, metonymically, tropologically; **so to speak,** as it were

FIGURATIVENESS *n* alliterativeness, allusiveness, idiomaticalness, ironicalness, tropology; **classicalism**, classicism

FIGURE OF SPEECH *n* allusion *(Obs.)*, asyndeton, calque, enallage, figuration, figure, hendiadys, kenning, metaphor, mixed metaphor, onomatopoeia, polysyndeton, rhetorical device, rhetorical question, simile, syllepsis, tmesis, trope, zeugma; **allegory**, anagoge, apologia, apologue, cautionary tale, exemplum, fable, old wives' tale, parable, proverb, satire, sermon; **idiom**, Americanism, Australianism, colloquialism, expression, idiotism *(Obs.)*, mot juste, phrase; **conceit**, catachresis, circumlocution, cliché, crank, malapropism, pleonasm, solecism, tautology; **imagery**, image, symbolism; **irony**, antiphrasis, bathos, dramatic irony; **play on words**, double entendre, equivoque, paronomasia, pun, quibble *(Archaic)*, riddle; **alliteration**, acrostic, anadiplosis, assonance, balance, gemination, hypallage, metanalysis, metathesis, metre, palindrome, parallelism, parenthesis, poetry, repetition, rhyme, rhythm, spoonerism; **antithesis**, anacoluthon, chiasmus, climax, euphuism, hysteron proteron, inversion, litotes, oxymoron; **allusion**, dysphemism, epexegesis, euphemism, hyperbole, hyperbolism, hypocorism, paralipsis; **metonymy**, metonym, synecdoche; **personification**, antonomasia, apostrophe, prosopopoeia

FILL *v* brim, bumper, charge, draw, fill up, run; **refill**, replenish, top up; **pack**, freight, lade, load, stow, supply; **occupy**, preoccupy; **fill in**, backfill, caulk *(Naut.)*, chink *(U.S.)*, chinse *(Naut.)*, grout, loam, pad, plaster, point *(Building)*, pug, shim, silt; **plug**, stop, stopper, tamp, wedge; **overfill**, drown, saturate, swamp; **cram**, choke, engorge, glut, jam, line, pack, stuff; **overrun**, crowd, throng

FILLER *n* packer, padder; **filling**, backfill, grout, packing, padding, sand fill, shim, washer; **occupant**, occupier, preoccupant, preoccupier

FILM *n* art film, B-grade film, bioscope *(Obs.)*, blue movie, cinéma-vérité, cinefilm, doco, documentary, double bill, double-feature, feature, films, flicks, footage, horror film, magazine, motion picture, movie, moving picture *(U.S.)*, mute negative, mute print, new wave, newsreel, nouvelle vague, peepshow, photoplay *(Obs.)*, picture, picture show, porno movie, reduction print, remake, rough cut, semidocumentary, silent film, skin flick, talkie, talking picture *(Obs.)*, telemovie, underground movie, video, video clip; **horse opera**, meat-pie western, spaghetti western; **short**, trailer, travelogue; **cartoon**, animated cartoon; **cinemascope**, cinematography, cinerama, computer animation, technicolour, vista-vision

FILM CREW *n* best boy, camera crew, cameraman, cinematographer, clapper loader, clapper preparer, continuity girl, floor manager, focus puller, gaffer, gofer, sound mixer

FILMIC *adj* celluloid, cinematic, cinematographic, filmable; **all-star**, star-studded; **movie-minded**, star struck; **slow-motion**, split-screen, wide-screen

FILTER *n* classifier, colander, cupel, riddle, riffle, ripple, screen, sieve, sifter, sluice, strainer, strake, tamis, tam-

filter

my, ultrafilter, wirecloth; **dialyser,** deioniser, dialysis machine, electrolyser, electrolytic cell, fractionator, insulator, macerater, precipitant, quicksilver cradle, scorifier; **cradle,** buddle, jig, puddling machine, puddling tub; **creamer,** elutriator, separator; **chemical separator,** cracker unit; **centrifuge,** centrifugal, microcentrifuge; **husker,** brake, cotton gin, gin, scutch, winnow, winnowing machine

FINAL *adj* back-end, climactic, eventual, extreme, last, lattermost, near, nth, supreme, terminal, ultimate; **latter,** afternoon, last-minute

FINALLY *adv* at last, at long last, eventually, in the long run, terminally, ultimately; **terminably,** definitively, once and for all, terminatively; **right through,** al fine, to the bitter end; **last,** lastly, latterly

FINANCE *v* back, bankroll, capitalise, fund, overcapitalise, put money into, underwrite; **float,** circulate, utter; **freeze,** tie up

FINANCIER *n* angel, backer, banker, gnome, merchant banker; **speculator,** arbitrager, bear, bull, investor, operator, piker, plunger, stag; **broker,** bucket shop, cambist, discount broker, jobber, kerb broker, sharepusher, sharebroker, stockbroker, stockjobber; **shareholder,** bondholder, stockholder

FIND *v* detect, discover, locate, trace, track down; **perceive,** descry, recognise, see, see through, spot; **light on,** alight on, alight upon, come by, come on, come upon, fall on, hit on, lob onto, pick up, stumble on; **strike,** be on a streak, hit upon; **unearth,** bring to light, dig out, dig up, elicit, ferret

finery

out, nose into, rummage out, rummage up, smell out, turn up, unkennel, worm out; **scent,** follow one's nose, get wind of, nose about, smell a rat

FINDABLE *adj* ascertainable, detectable, discoverable; **on the right track,** getting warm, on the scent, warm

FINDER *n* descrier, detector, discoverer, diviner, explorer, perceiver, spotter

FINDING *n* detection, discovery, exploration; **accidental discovery,** serendipity; **detective instinct,** nose; **find,** strike *(Mining),* treasure-trove, turn-up; **exposure,** a fair cop, revelation

FIND OUT *v* get on to, glean, realize, tumble to; **catch,** catch out, expose, find someone out, rumble, show up, spring, surprise, take by surprise

FINE ARTS *n* art, graphic arts, plastic arts, visual arts; **depiction,** abstraction, illustration, representation, scenography *(Obs.);* **artistry,** brushwork, craft, craftsmanship, draughtsmanship, feeling, touch; **art form,** calligraphy, ceramics, commercial art, computer art, embroidery, enamelling, engraving, folk art, graphics, illumination, intarsia, marquetry, mosaic, ordonnance, origami, painting, primitive art, printing, sculpture, serigraphy, tapestry, tessellation, weaving; **style,** breadth, form, idiom, tonality, tone; **technography,** art history. *See also* WORK OF ART: PAINTING: SCULPTURE: CERAMICS: DRAWING

FINERY *n* best, best bib and tucker, creation, evening dress, fallal, fallalery, formal dress, formals, frippery, full dress, gala outfit, glad rags,

finery   211   **fire**

going-away outfit, Sunday best, tails, white tie

FINIS *interj* all in the whippy's taken, that's that, the jig is up

FINISH *n* anticlimax, bitter end, catastrophe, climax, close, conclusion, consummation, dead finish, denouement, end, end point, ending, eventuation, expiry, finale, finals, grandstand finish, omega; **coda,** cadence, codetta, fine, stretta, tag; **epilogue,** amen, desinence, envoy, finis, punch line, ultimatum; **coup de grâce,** burn out, death knell, death-knock, expiration, quietus, tag end, the last straw; **last,** dernier cri, extreme *(Obs.)*, final, last word, point *(Obs.)*, term *(Archaic)*; **ending,** endgame, wind-up; **termination,** abruption, closure, closure motion, cut-off, discontinuance, finalisation, winding-up; **finality,** definitiveness, terminability, terminableness, ultimateness; **goal,** tape, ultimate, winning post, wire; **home straight,** home stretch, run-in; **terminus,** cul-de-sac, dead-end, railhead; **terminal,** destination; **closing time,** afternoon, curtain, evening, full-time, knock-off time, muck-up day, no-side, period, stumps, sunset, time; **settlement,** settling, upshot

FINISH *v* abolish, be in at the death, be on the home straight, be on the home stretch, close, complete, conclude, consummate, end, finalise, have done with, muddle through, perfect, play out, polish off, put the lid on, see the back of, settle, sew up, wind up, wrap up; **terminate,** break off, chop off, dissolve, draw stumps, drop, phase out, ring down the curtain on, rule off; **be ancient history,** be a closed book, be done with; **climax,**
come, eventuate; **expire,** be all over with, be all up with, be curtains for, come to a sticky end, decline, die, drop, end, pass away, surcease *(Archaic),* wane; **give out,** go out

FINISHED *adj* all over, all over bar the shouting, complete, completed, completive, done, made-up, over, washed up, winding-up, wound up; **moribund,** ante-mortem, dead-end, dying, extinguishable, extirpative, terminational, terminative

FINISHED PRODUCT *n* build, construct, construction, contrivance, fabrication, facture, form, handiwork, invention, job, make, making, manufacture, output, outturn, production, stuff, throughput, work; **creation,** baby, brainchild; **by-product,** breakdown product, catabolite, daughter product, end product, spin-off; **yield,** crop, culture, first fruits, fructification, fruit, fruitage, growth, harvest, produce, product; **derivate,** derivation, derivative; **discharge,** emanation, emission

FINISHER *n* concluder, consummator, destroyer, ender, terminator

FINITENESS *n* definability, definiteness, delimitation, finitude; **margination,** engrailment

FIRE *n* blaze, conflagration, deflagration, flames, flare-up, phlegethon; **open fire,** balefire *(Archaic),* bonfire, camp fire, pyre, watch-fire; **bushfire,** back-burn, blazer, burn-back, bushburn *(N.Z.),* grassfire, red steer, regeneration burn; **volcano,** fumarole, hellfire, hot spot, mantle plume, sulfatara; **flare,** flash, gleam, glint, glow, sparkle; **ember,** coal *(Obs.),* spark; **ash,** ashes, charcoal, cinder, soot;

smoke, belch, smother, smoulder; **fieriness,** inflammation

FIRE *v* emblaze *(Archaic),* enkindle, ignite, kindle, light, set fire to, set on fire; **incinerate,** burn in effigy, cremate, gut; **burn,** calcinate, carbonise, char; **roast,** scald, scorch, sear, singe, sizzle, toast; **cauterise,** brand, burn in; **burn off,** back-burn; **burn at the stake,** self-immolate

FIREFIGHTER *n* bush brigade, fire brigade, fireman; **fire station,** firehouse *(U.S.)*

FIRE ON *v* open up, pepper, shoot, snipe at; **bomb,** bombard, lay an egg, plaster, prang, saturate; **strafe,** pelt, shell, storm; **fusillade,** cannonade, enfilade, feint, demonstrate *(Mil.)*; **raid,** air-raid, blitz. *See also* ATTACK

FIREPLACE *n* chimney, chimney corner, grate, hearth; **incinerator,** crematorium, crematory, furnace

FIRER *n* enkindler, igniter, inflamer, kindler; **burner,** crematorist, cremator; **firebug,** arsonist, fire-raiser, incendiary

FIREWORKS *n* bonfire night, cracker night, fireworks display, Guy Fawkes Day, pyrotechnics; **firework,** banger, bunger, cascade, Catherine wheel, cracker, double bunger, double happy *(N.Z.),* firecracker, fizgig, girandole, jumping jack, maroon, petard, rocket, Roman candle, serpent, skyrocket, squib, sunburst, throwdown, tourbillion, wheel, whizbang; **bonbon,** table cracker

FIRING *n* auto-ignition, ignition, kindling, lighting; **combustion,** afterburning, detonation, explosion, flashback, spontaneous combustion; burning, auto-da-fé, cremation, incineration, the stake; **carbonization,** calcination; **arson,** black lightning, fire-raising, incendiarism, jewish lightning, pyromania

FIRST *adv* ahead, ahead of time, first-up, firstly, foremost, in advance, primarily, up front; **introductorily,** prefatorily, preliminarily, prelusively

FIRSTLY *adv* basically, first, for starters, fundamentally, imprimis, initially, to begin with; **originally,** ab initio, ab origine, ab ovo, anew, at first, at the first, da capo, de novo, first-up, from scratch, from the first, from the top, from the word go, in limine, in the bud, in the egg; **primevally,** primitively, primordially

FISCALLY *adv* in kind, in specie, monetarily, pecuniarily

FISH *n* food fish, free-swimmer, freshwater fish, ichthyoid, mouthbreeder, Pisces, saltwater fish; **benthos,** groundling, nekton, plankton; **tiddler,** fingerling; **shoal,** school

FISH *v* angle, bob, cast, dap, dib, fly-fish, gaff, gig, guddle, land, leister, net, play, rock-hop, seine, skitter, spin, spoon, strike, trawl, troll, whale, whip; **crab,** prawn, seal, shrimp, turtle

FISHERMAN *n* angler, crabber, fisher, fly-fisher, prawner, prawnie, rock-hopper, sealer, shrimper, spearfisherman, striker, trammeller, trawler, troller, whaleman, whaler

FISHING *n* angling, bay whaling, fly-fishing, ledger-baiting, ledgering, sealery *(Archaic),* shark meshing, shore whaling, spinning, whaling. *See also* PURSUIT

FISHING TACKLE *n* angle *(Archaic)*, bob, bobber, boulter, bunt, catching pole, clapnet, coop, creel, dropline, fish spear, fishing line, fishing rod, fizgig, float, gaff, gaughook, gig, grains, handline, herl, iron, lance, ledger line, ledger tackle, leister, long-line, net, purse seine *(U.S.)*, rod, scoop net, seine, sinker, spin rod, striker, trammel net, trawl line, trawl net, troll, witch's hat; **fishing lure**, bait, craypot, fly, ground bait, hackle, hackle fly, pot, pound net, spinner, spoon, spoonbait, trap, troll, wobbler; **fishhook**, Aberdeen hook, barbless hook, Carlisle hook, hook, Kendal sneck bent hook, kirby hook, Limerick hook, sproat hook

FISH OUT OF WATER *n* erratic, horse marine *(U.S.)*, misfit, square peg in a round hole

FISH PART *n* branchiae, gill; **fin**, anal fin, dorsal fin, finlet, pelvic fin, pinnule, ventral fin; **flipper**, paddle

FISHY *adj* elasmobranch, finned, finny, fishlike, ichthyic, ichthyoid, piscine

FIT *v* assort, comport with, consist with, get along, go with *(Colloq.)*, interlock, intermesh, match, mate, satisfy, suit; **agree**, answer, check, coincide, concur, conform, match, parallel; **add up**, cohere, commeasure, hang together *(Colloq.)*, square, tally; **apply**, pertain; **correspond**, accord, chime, concur, consort, dovetail, go hand in hand, go with, harmonise, key in, live up to, match, sympathise, tone in; **befit**, be cut out for, be one's cup of tea *(Colloq.)*, belong to, beseem, fit the bill, suit

FIVE *n* cinque *(Cards)*, fifth, fiver, lustrum, pentad, pentameter, pentarchy, quin, quinary, quinquennium, quintet, quintuplet; **pentagon**, pentagram, pentahedron, pentalpha, pentangle, quincunx

FIVE *adj* fifth, fivefold, pentagonal, pentahedral, pentamerous, quinary, quincuncial, quintuple

FIXATIVE *adj* ligamentary, ligamentous; **lockup**, self-locking

FLAG *n* banderol, banner, bannerette, burgee, dogvane, ensign, fanion, gonfalon, guidon, hoist, jack, labarum, pennant, pennon, standard, streamer, vexillum; **colours**, bunting, flying colours, racing colours; **flogger**

FLAKY *adj* exfoliative, flocculent, foliaceous, foliated, imbricate, imbricated, imbricative, lamellar, lamellate, laminable, laminar, scalelike

FLANK *v* come alongside, crab *(Aeron.)*, go alongside, juxtapose, lap *(Obs.)*, outflank, outskirt, sidle, skirt

FLAT *n* apartment, bachelor flat, bedsitter *(Brit.)*, bed-sitting room, condominium, diggings, digs, flatette, flatlet, home unit, lodgings, maisonette, own-your-own, penthouse, quarters, rooms, serviced flat, unit; **garden flat**, chalet *(Tas.)*, granny flat; **apartments**, apartment house *(U.S.)*, mansions *(Brit.)*; **block**, high-rise, tenement, tenement house, walk-up

FLATTER *v* brown-nose, buddy-buddy, butter, butter up, carney, eulogise, fawn, flannel up *(Brit.)*, lay it on thick, make much of, oil, overpraise, praise to the skies, puff, smarm, smoodge, speak someone fair, throw a bouquet; **behave sycophantically**, chum up to, dag *(Horse-*

flatter / **flirt**

racing), get gravel rash, jolly along, lick another's arse, make up to, pander to, pee in someone's pocket, play up to, slime, suck up to, toady; **cajole**, blandish, blarney, get round, palaver, sweet-talk, wheedle; **hero-worship**, adulate, conceit (Obs.); **curry favour**, duchess, make one's alley good, soap up, soft-soap; **be up each other**, be up one another

FLATTERER n adulater, arse-licker, bootlicker, brown-nose, courtier, crawler, encomiast, eulogist, fawner, flunkey, greaser, greasespot, member of a claque, pickthank, reptile, respecter of persons, satellite, smoodger, sycophant, toady; **wheedler**, blandisher, cajoler, carney, smooth talker, soft-soaper, sweet-talker; **self-flatterer**, mutual-admiration society

FLATTERING adj adulatory, complimentary, courtly, ingratiating, mealy-mouthed, obsequious; **sycophantic**, buddy-buddy, fawning, flunkeyish, fulsome, reptilean, servile, smarmy, smooth-faced, smooth-tongued, subservient, toadyish; **unctuous**, buttery, candied, honeyed, oily, soapy, soft

FLATTERINGLY adv complimentarily; **sycophantically**, fawningly, oilily, oily, subserviently

FLATTERY n adulation, blandishment, blandishments, compliment, flummery, gloze (Rare), oil; **sweet talk**, blarney, flannel (Brit.), honeyed words, jolly, palaver, soft soap, syrup; **panegyric**, encomium, eulogy, paean of praise; **ingratiation**, cajolement, cajolery, insinuation; **sycophancy**, fawning, flunkeydom, flunkeyism, obsequiousness, oiliness, puffery, smarm, smoodging, toady-ism, unctuousness; **hero-worship**, personality cult

FLESH n adipose tissue, fat, flab, lean, tissue; **gristle**, cartilage; **marrow**; **muscle**, Achilles tendon, brawn, hamstring, ligament, sinew, tendon, thew; **connective tissue**, aponeurosis, fascia, isthmus, membrane, peritoneum, pons, stroma, tunic

FLIGHT n air alert (Mil.), air cover, air picket, airflight, charter flight, contact flight, flip, fly, hop (Colloq.), joyflight, milk run, overflight, paradrop, solo, sortie; **fly-past**, flying circus; **formation**, escadrille (U.S. Mil.), flight, flying squad, squadron, stack, wing

FLIRT n beau, dallier, Don Juan, flirter, ladies' man, masher, ogler, philanderer, rake, seducer; **coquette**, cock-teaser, light o' love, minx, seductress, tease, teaser; **toy**, plaything; **caresser**, dandler, fondler, kisser, smoocher, smoodger; **wooer**, admirer, gallant, lover, serenader, suer, suitor, swain

FLIRT v coquet, dally, fool around, gallivant, play footsies, play the field, play tootsy, tease; **flirt with**, do a line with, do a mash with (Obs.), lead on, mash (Obs.), throw oneself at, toy with, vamp; **give someone the glad eye**, bat one's eyelids at, make a pass at, make eyes at, ogle, perv on; **proposition**, chat up, crack onto, do a line for, get off with, put the hard word on, seduce; **take out**, date, go steady, see, walk out with; **have an affair**, philander, play around, play up; **court**, address, pay court to, pursue, set one's cap at, spark (Archaic), sue (Archaic), woo; **love**, be in love with, care for, cherish, conceive a passion for, develop feelings for, die for, fall

flirt   215   **floral**

in love with, have a crush on, have eyes only for, look sweetly on; **have an understanding with**, plight one's troth to

FLIRTATION *n* amour, billing and cooing, coquetry, dalliance, seduction; **courtship**, courting, courtly attention, courtly love, gallantry, lovemaking *(Archaic)*, serenading, suit, wooing; **affair**, love affair, romance

FLIRTATIOUS *adj* coquet, coquettish; **romantic**, gallant, swainish; **amorous**, amatory, love-sick, lovelorn, sighing, sighing like a furnace, smitten, smitten by another's charms, spoony; **kissable**, embraceable, lovable, osculant

FLIRTATIOUSLY *adv* coquettishly, dallyingly, flirtingly

FLOAT *n* bob *(Angling)*, bobber, buoy, buoyage, floater, rubber ring, torpedo tube; **raft**, floating island, flotsam, pontoon, spar buoy

FLOAT *v* bob, hover, levitate, swim, waft

FLOOD *n* deluge, inundation; **overflow**, overgrowth, overrun, profusion, smother; **spread**, pervasion, suffusion; **pervasiveness**; **epidemic**, eruption, outbreak, plague; **infestation**, invasion

FLOOD *v* deluge, drown, engulf, inundate, overwhelm, poop *(Naut.)*, swamp, whelm *(Archaic)*; **overflow**, boil over, brim over, pour out, pour over, run over, spill, spill out, spill over, well over; **overrun**, cover, overgrow, overspread, run riot, smother; **spread**, ramble, run on, sprawl, spread out, swarm, trail; **pervade**, spread like wildfire, spread through, suffuse; **permeate**, metastasise, perfuse; **infest**, plague, swarm

FLOODED *adj* awash, inundated, overrun

FLOODER *n* inundator; **infester**, pervader

FLOODING *adj* diluvial, torrential; **diffused**, outspread, widespread; **rambling**, sprawling, trailing; **pervasive**, suffusive; **epidemic**, epidemical, rife

FLOOR *n* deck, decking, flooring, promenade deck; **landing**, fly gallery *(Theat.)*, fly-floor *(Theat.)*

FLOORING *n* decking, duckboard, floor covering, lino, linoleum, linotile, malthoid, planking, stringboard, vinyl, vinyl tile; **mat**, bath mat, beach mat; **carpet**, Aubusson carpet, Axminster carpet, body carpet, broadloom carpet, brussels carpet, carpet tile, carpeting, Persian carpet, red carpet, shagpile, stair-carpet, velvet carpet, wall-to-wall carpet; **rug**, footcloth *(Archaic)*, hearthrug, Kashmir rug, kazak, Kirman, oriental rug, prayer rug, runner, scatter rug, tapis; **seagrass matting**, coconut matting, matting, rush, Vietnamese matting

FLORA *n* botany, greenery, plant kingdom, plant life, plants, vegetable kingdom, vegetation, verdure

FLORAL *adj* flowery; **botanical**, vegetable, vegetal, vegetational, vegetative; **abloom**, blooming, bloomy, blossomy, efflorescent, florescent, florid *(Archaic)*, flowered, full-blown; **green**, grassy, lush, turfy, verdant, verdurous; **leafy**, foliaceous, foliaged, foliar, foliate, foliated, foliose, frondescent, in leaf, leaved; **viny**, ivied, twining; **tufty**, caespitose, stub-

floral   216   **flutter**

bled, stubbly; **herbaceous,** herbal, herby; **shrubby,** broomy, scrubby, shrub-like, stumpy; **ferny,** rushy; **brambly,** branchy, brushy, furzy; **bushy,** arboreous, bosky, forest-like, forested, wooded, woodsy, woody; **frutescent,** fruticose

FLOW n eruption, flowage, fluency, flux, fluxion *(Obs.)*, gurgitation, primary flow, run-off, turbulent flow, wash; **torrent,** debacle, flush, gush, gust, jet, onrush, spate, spurt, staunch, surge, uprush, upsurge, upsurgeance; **effluence,** efflux, exosmosis, issue; **influx,** affluence, afflux, endosmosis, incursion, inflow, inrush, inrushing, inset; **circulation,** capillarity, capillary action, convection, osmosis; **dribble,** drip, dripping, dropping, seep *(U.S.)*, spray, sprinkle, trickle; **pour,** decantation, *ash* **flow,** coulee, earthflow, lava flow, mudflow.   *See also* CURRENT; STREAM; SPRING

FLOW v course, eddy, fleet *(Archaic)*, flux, gutter, run, stream, swirl; **swell,** issue, run a banker, upsurge, well; **wash,** lap, lave, splash, swash; **flood,** deluge, inundate, overflow, overspill; **spurt,** gush, jet, spout, squirt; **flush,** disembogue, sluice, wash out; **ooze,** meander, wind; **set,** ebb, make; **dribble,** drip, seep, trickle; **strain,** drain, percolate, perk; **pour,** decant, spill

FLOWER n bud, floret, ray; *flower organ,* androecium, anther, bud, calycle, calyptra, calyx, carpel, carpogonium, carpophore, claw, connective, corolla, corona, disc, endothecium, filament, floral envelope, flower bud, footstalk, foramen, galea, gynoecium, gynophore, hypanthium, integument, labellum, labium, limb, lip, lodicule, nectary, operculum, ovary, ovule, palea, pedicel, perianth, petal, phalanx, pistil, pistillode, placenta, podium, pollen, pollen tube, receptacle, rictus, rostellum, sepal, spur, stamen, staminode, standard, stigma, stipe, style, stylopodium, tepal, torus, tube, unguis, valve, wing; **inflorescence,** anthodium, capitulum, catkin, cincinnus, corymb, cupule, dichasium, head, locusta, monochasium, panicle, raceme, spike, thyrsus, umbel, umbellule

FLOWER v bloom, blossom, bud, burgeon, foliate, fungate, gemmate, ratoon, spindle *(U.S. Obs.)*, tassel; **bear,** fruit; **germinate,** rise, root, shoot, spring, sprout, stool, strike, strike root, take, take root, tiller; **breed,** multiply, proliferate, pullulate, reproduce, teem; **cultivate,** fertilise, force, revegetate, scarify; **ripen,** flourish, hay off, run riot, thrive, wax; **climb,** creep, ramble, run, spindle *(U.S. Obs.)*, twine.   *See also* GROW

FLOWING adj affluent, fluent, fluxional, fluxionary, inrushing, mobile, osmotic, profluent; **effluent,** exosmic, exosmotic, **influent,** endoreic, endosmotic, incurrent

FLUCTUATE v break, flutter, intermit, stutter; **jerk,** break step, joggle, jolt, snatch *(Rowing)*

FLUFF n film, floss, foam, fuzz, gauze, thistledown

FLUTTER n flicker, fluctuation, nutation, seesaw, shake, sway, swing, teeter, totter, undulation, waddle, wag, waggle, wave, wiggle.   *See also* VIBRATION

FLUTTER v bat, beat, flick, flicker, flitter, quiver; **vibrate,** fluctuate, hunt *(Mach.)*, librate, oscillate, reciprocate, shuttle, shuttlecock, vacillate, waver; **roll**, seesaw, sway, swing, teeter, toss, totter, waddle, waggle, weave, wriggle; **wave**, brandish, flap, flourish, wag, wigwag

FLUTTERINGLY *adv* atremble, pantingly, tremulously, waveringly; **resonantly**, thrillingly, throbbingly; **shakily**, totteringly, waddlingly, wobblingly; **swayingly**, back and forth, backwards and forwards, flip-flop, pendulously, to and fro

FLUTTERY *adj* aflutter, asp *(Archaic)*, aspen, fly-away, palpitant, pulsatile, quavery, quivering, quivery, shivery, trembly, tremulant, tremulous, vibrant, vibratile, vibrative, vibratory, wavering; **resonant**, thrilling

FLY *v* be wafted, flit, flutter, hover, swarm, wing, wing one's way, winnow; **take off**, lift off, take wing; **glide**, hang-glide, plane, sailplane, soar, volplane; **parachute**, balloon, hot-air balloon; **pilot**, navigate; **loop**, buzz, crab, dive, fishtail, flatten, hedgehop, loop the loop, power-dive, pull out, roll, sideslip, trim, undershoot, whipstall; **swoop**, souse

FLYING *n* aviation, volitation; **gliding**, aerodonetics, aerostation, ballooning, hang-gliding, parachuting, paraflying, soaring; **aerobatics**, hedgehopping, skywriting; **take-off**, landing, lift-off, souse, stoop; **aero tow**, auto tow; **navigation**, area navigation, instrument flying, instrument landing; **aeronautics**, aerostatics; **airmanship**, airmindedness; **space travel**, astronautics, bioastronautics, cosmonautics, moonshot, walk in space

FLYING *adj* aerial, airborne, airworthy, volant *(Heraldry)*, volitant, volitational, winged; **aerobatic**, hedgehopping; **aerostatic**, heavier-than-air, lighter-than-air; **aeronautic**, aero, aeromarine; **astronautic**, aerospace, cosmonautic

FOLD *n* buckle, cockle, crease, crimp, crumple, dog-ear, press *(Obs.)*, ruga, rumple; **wrinkle**, crinkle, crow's-foot, laugh-line, laughter-line, line, pucker, rugosity; **pleat**, box pleat, knife pleat, pintuck, plait, ruche, tuck; **turn-up**, cuff, hem, lap, lapel, lappet; **frill**, flounce, gathering, gathers, ruff, ruffle, shirr, shirring

FOLD *v* crease, crumple, dog-ear; **wrinkle**, crinkle, furrow, knit, line, pucker, purse, shrivel; **corrugate**, concertina, knurl, ridge, rumple; **buckle**, double up, jackknife; **pleat**, kilt, pintuck, tuck; **lap**, enfold, hem, imply *(Obs.)*, interfold, reflex, turn back, turn down, turn up, wrap; **frill**, crimp, crimple, drape, gather, gauge, goffer, ruck, shirr

FOLDED *adj* complicate *(Bot.)*, conduplicate, dog-eared, double, replicate, turn-up, turndown; **crinkly**, rugate, rugged, rugose, wrinkly; **frilly**, crimpy, puckery, ruffed; **pleated**, accordion-pleated, box-pleated, kilted, plicate

FOLDING *n* enfoldment, invagination, plication; **paper folding**, origami

FOLLOW *v* come after, ensue, result, succeed, supervene, supervene on; **supersede**, supplant; **follow in someone's footsteps**, copy, follow suit

FOLLOWING *adj* in tow, incoming, proximate; **next**, immediate, junior, second, second-best; **consecutive**, alternate, continued, progressive,

FOOD n aliment, ambrosia *(Class Mythol.)*, blotting paper *(Colloq.)*, board, bush tucker, cate *(Archaic)*, cheer, chow, chow-chow, comestible, commons *(Brit.)*, compo rations *(Mil.)*, consumable, convenience food, dainty, delicacy, dodger, drip-feed *(Med.)*, eatables, eats, edibles, esculent, fare, fast food, finger food, foodstuff, forage, good cheer, goodies, grub, hangi *(N.Z.)*, health food, junk food, kosher, lazy ration *(Convict)*, macronutrient, manna, meat *(Archaic)*, mess, munga *(Mil. Colloq.)*, num-num, num-nums, nutrient, nutriment, nyum-nyum, pabulum, pigswill *(Colloq.)*, pig-tucker *(N.Z. Colloq.)*, potluck, provender, provisions, roughage, scoff, scouse *(Naut.)*, scran, slipslop, slops, solids, staple diet, stodge, sustenance, table, tack, trencher *(Archaic)*, tuck *(Brit.)*, tucker, viand, viands, victual *(Archaic)*, victuals, wholefood; **nourishment**, alimentation, diet, food value, nutrition, nutritiveness, survival level feeding, sustentation; **dietetics**. *See also* MEAL

FOOL n ass, automaton, bat, berk, Billy Muggins, blob, blockhead, boob, boofhead, buffer, bull head, bullet head, bunny, charlie, chinless wonder, chook, chucklehead, chump, clod, clodpate, clodpoll, clot, coot, cough drop, cretin, cuckoo, cully, dag, deadshit, dick, dickhead, dill, dillpot, ding-a-ling, dodo, dolt, donkey, dope, drip, driveller, drongo, drube, dullard, dumb Dora, dumb-bell, dumbcluck, dumdum, dummy, dunderhead, fart, fathead, flathead, foolish virgin, Fred Nerk, galah, galoot, gawk, gazob, gig, gimp, git *(Brit.)*, goat, goof, goon, goose, great ape, gup *(Aborig.)*, half-axe, hen, hoon, idiot, imbecile, imbo, jackass, jay, jerk, jerk-off, joe, juggins, knucklehead, lamebrain, lardhead, lemon, log, log of wood, loggerhead, loghead, lolly, loop, lunkhead *(U.S.)*, meat-head, melon, melonhead, muddle-head, mug, mug alec, muggins, mutton-head, nerd, nig-nog, nincompoop, ning-nong, ninny, nit, nitwit, noddy, nong, noodle, numbskull, nut, nut case, nutter, old woman, pea eater, pinhead, poon, popinjay, possum, pudding, pudding head, quoit, rabbit, sap, saphead, schmuck, shlemiel, shmo, silly, silly-billy, simple, simpleton, spoony, thickhead, tomfool, tonk, turkey, twaddler, twerp, twit, wally *(Brit.)*, whacker, wild goose, woodenhead; **birdbrain**, featherbrain, featherhead, flibbertigibbet, rattlebrain, scatterbrain, whirligig

FOOLERY n apery, baboonery, bêtise, buffoonery, carryings-on, chenanigans, fandangle, folly, funny business, stuff and nonsense, three-ring circus, tomfoolery

FOOLISH *adj* anserine, apish, baboonish, buffoonish, childish, clottish, empty, fatuous, footling, frivolous, idiotic, inane, light, light-headed, mad, moony, puerile, senseless, shallow, silly, Uncle Willy, vain *(Archaic)*, witless; **featherbrained,**

foolish   219   **forced**

batty, chuckleheaded, cuckoo, daffy, daft, dilly, dippy, dizzy, empty-headed, featherheaded, flighty, giddy, giggly, goofy, headless, hoity-toity, insipient, loony, luny, mad as a two-bob watch, mental, mug, nitty, nutty, nutty as a fruitcake, off one's nut, old-womanish, potty, sapheaded, sappy, scatterbrained, scatty, silly as a two-bob watch, silly as a wet hen, sonky, spoony, twitty, wacky; **ludicrous**, absurd, bathetic, farcical, imbecile, imbecilic, impertinent, nonsensical, preposterous, ridiculous, tomfool, unearthly, zany; **imprudent**, ill-advised, impolitic, unguarded, unwary, wild; **infatuated**, fond (Archaic), infatuate, sloppy, spoony

FOOLISHLY adv childishly, daftly, dotingly, fatuously, idiotically, ill-advisedly, imbecilely, impoliticly, imprudently, inanely, infatuatedly, pratingly, puerilely, sillily, unguardedly, unwarily, witlessly; **ludicrously**, absurdly, farcically, nonsensically, preposterously; **light-headedly**, dizzily, flightily, frivolously, goofily, madly, senselessly, shallowly

FOOLISHNESS n asininity, childishness, chuckleheadedness, daftness, dizziness, fatuity, fatuousness, flightiness, folly, frivolousness, goofiness, idiocy, imbecility, juvenileness, light-headedness, looniness, lunacy, madness, midsummer madness, nonsense, preposterousness, puerility, senselessness, silliness, stupidness, unwariness, witlessness; **ludicrousness**, absurdity, absurdness, bathos, ridiculousness; **infatuation**, dotage, sloppiness

FOOTGEAR n footwear; **shoe**, balmoral, block, blocked shoe, boot, brogan, brogue, brothel creepers, chopin, clodhopper, court shoe, desert boot, flat, flattie, gillie, kadaicha shoes, loafers, moccasin, Oxford, point shoe, pump, winklepicker; **clog**, patten, sabot, wooden shoe; **spats**, puttee, spatterdashes; **shoe part**, bootleg (U.S.), counter, half-sole, heel, heelpiece, heeltap, insole, platform, rand, sole, stiletto heel, tongue, upper, vamp, wedge heel; **sandshoe**, plimsoll (Brit.), runner, sneaker, tennis shoe; **spikes**, running spikes, sprigs, track shoe; **roller skate**, ice skate; **snowshoe**, racquet. See also BOOT: SANDAL: SOCK

FORCE n brute force, muscle, power, pressure, strength, the sword; **force majeure**, vis major; **threat**, blackmail, Hobson's choice; **enforcement**, exaction, penalty, sanction

FORCE v coerce, compel, constrain, distress (Archaic), dragoon, drive, frogmarch, juggernaut, lead by the nose, make, press, railroad (U.S.), screw; **intimidate**, give the third degree, lean on, put the heat on, put the screws on, slap down, terrorise; **bully**, blackjack, bludgeon, browbeat, bulldoze, bullyrag, squeeze (Colloq.), steamroll, steamroller, throw one's weight around, tyrannise; **conscript**, conscribe, draft, impress; **enforce**, exact; **force someone's hand**, rush; **insist on**, not take no for an answer, ram down someone's throat; **override**, pull rank on

FORCED adj coerced, compelled, constrained, enforced, hard-pressed; **compulsory**, necessary, required; **coercible**, compellable, constrainable,

forced   220   **forget**

exactable; **conscript**, conscripted, press-ganged

FORCEFUL *adj* driving, forcible, powerful, punchy, strong, strong-willed, swingeing *(Colloq.)*; **sledge-hammer**, steamroller; **tyrannical**, arbitrary, despotic, dictatorial, Nazi; **intimidating**, bullying, coactive, coercive, compulsive, heavy, impellent, jack-booted, overbearing, terrorist

FORCEFULLY *adv* forcibly, overpoweringly, powerfully, strong, strongly; **tyrannically**, arbitrarily, despotically, dictatorially, tyrannisingly; **coercively**, compulsively, compulsorily

FORCEFULNESS *n* powerfulness; **compulsion**, coaction, coercion, constraint, duress, rape; **conscription**, draft, impress *(Obs.)*, impressment, press; **tyranny**, arbitrariness, despotism, Nazism, tyrannicalness; **intimidation**, bullying, terrorisation; **forcedness**, compulsoriness

FORCER *n* coercer, compeller, constrainer, enforcer, exacter, impeller; **drafter**, press-gang; **tyrant**, despot, dictator, dictatrix, tyranniser; **bully**, bludgeoner, brave *(Obs.)*, browbeater, bruiser, bulldozer *(Colloq.)*, hector, intimidator, Nazi, standover man, steamroller, terroriser

FOREIGN *adj* alien, imported, irregular, non-resident, outlandish *(Archaic)*, strange *(Archaic)*, unacclimatised, unassimilated; **ethnic**, extraterritorial, peregrine; **gentile**, barbarous, pagan, paganish, tramontane, uncircumcised; **exotic**, adventive, unfamiliar; **extraneous**, adventitious, stray; **external**, ecdemic, heterogenous, outside; **uninvited**, excluded, intrusive

FOREIGNER *n* alien, denizen, non-resident, outlander, foreigner *(Archaic)*, unco *(Scot. Obs.)*; **stranger** *(Archaic)*, unco *(Scot. Obs.)*; **gentile**, barbarian, pagan, tramontane, uncircumcision *(Rare)*; **ethnic**, Arab, bohunk *(U.S.)*, continental, Creole *(U.S.)*, dago, ethno, gook *(U.S.)*, gringo, hollow log, hunky *(U.S.)*, spic, wog, wop; **refugee**, boat people, D.P., displaced person, reffo; **foreign population**, minority, out-group; **diaspora**, exodus; **stray**, adventive, cuckoo, irregular, straggler *(Agric.)*; **curiosity**, exotic; **foreign body**, inclusion, xenolith; **intruder**, a grape on the business, gatecrasher, interloper, stowaway, trespasser, uninvited guest

FOREIGNNESS *n* adventitiousness, alienage, alienism, exoticism, extraneousness, foreignism *(U.S.)*, outlandishness, strangeness; **alienation**, estrangement, exclusion; **migration**, emigration, immigration, transportation; **non-residency**

FORERUNNER *n* anticipator, apostle, early bird, forefather, foregoer, harbinger, herald, introducer, leader, outrider, outrunner, pioneer, precursor, predecessor, prophet, spearhead, trailblazer, usher *(Archaic)*, van, vanguard. *See also* ANTECEDENT

FOREST *n* greenwood, jungle, rainforest, sclerophyll forest, taiga, woodland, woods; **scrub**, boscage, bosket, brush, brushwood, canebrake *(U.S.)*, chaparral *(U.S.)*, coppice, copse, grove, hurst, spinney *(Brit.)*, thicket, wallum; **undergrowth**, underbrush, understorey, underwood

FORGET *v* clean forget, disremember, have no recollection of, let in one ear and out the other, misremember; **consign to oblivion**, blot out, bury, live

forget 221 **formality**

down, repress, unlearn; **be on the tip of one's tongue**, be almost there; **go out of one's head**, fly out of one's mind, slip one's mind

FORGETFUL *adj* absent, absent-minded, irretentive, oblivious, preoccupied, woolly-minded; **amnesic**, amnesiac, amnestic, forgetful-making *(Poetic)*, nepenthean; **forgotten**, out of mind, sunk in oblivion

FORGETFULLY *adv* absent-mindedly, obliviously

FORGETFULNESS *n* lotus land, oblivion, silence; **omission**, oversight, slip of the memory, slip of the mind

FORGETTER *n* absent-minded professor, amnesiac, lotus-eater; **nepenthe**, lotus

FORGETTING *n* blackout, memory lapse, mental block, overlooking, total blank; **absent-mindedness**, absence of mind, absentness, forgetfulness, irretentiveness, obliviousness, obliviscence, preoccupation; **amnesia**, anomia, fugue

FORGIVABLE *adj* absolvable, atonable, excusable, expiable, pardonable, remittable, venial

FORGIVABLY *adv* excusably, venially

FORGIVE *v* condone, discount, dismiss, disregard, extenuate, let bygones be bygones, overlook, pass over, think no more of; **pardon**, absolve, amnesty, assoil *(Law Archaic)*, excuse, justify, shrive; **spare**, acquit, clear, exculpate, exonerate, have a heart, release, remit, reprieve

FORGIVER *n* absolvent, condoner, excuser, pardoner, redeemer, sparer

FORGIVING *n* absolute pardon, amnesty, conditional pardon, exemption, indemnity, pardon, reprieve; exoneration, acquittal, condonation, exculpation, excusal, justification, vindication; **forgiveness**, grace; **absolution**, jubilee *(Rom. Cath. Ch.)*, plenary indulgence *(Rom. Cath. Ch.)*, remission *(Law)*, shrift *(Archaic)*

FORGIVING *adj* absolutory; **magnanimous**, graceful, placable

FORGIVINGLY *adv* gracefully, magnanimously, placably

FORGIVINGNESS *n* forbearance, forgiveness, magnanimity, magnanimousness, placability, placableness

FORMAL *adj* ceremonial, ceremonious, courtly, dignified, official, public, ritual, ritualistic, solemn, state, stately; **precise**, correct, starchy, stickling; **reserved**, frigid, icy, perfunctory, stiff, stilted, undemonstrative, uneasy; **dress**, full-dress, Sunday-go-to-meeting *(U.S.)*

FORMAL DRESS *n* academic dress, academicals, ball dress, best bib and tucker, black tie, class A's *(U.S.)*, court dress, dinner jacket, dinner suit, dress, dress coat, dress suit, evening dress, formals, number ones *(Navy)*, regalia, Sunday best, tails, uniform, white tie

FORMALISE *v* ceremonialise, officialise, solemnify, solemnise; **stand on ceremony**, observe protocol

FORMALITY *n* ceremoniousness, ceremony, dignity, pomp and circumstance, solemnness, state, stateliness; **etiquette**, form, protocol; **spit and polish**, drill; **preciseness**, correctness, gentility, precision, punctilio, punctiliousness, savoir-faire, savoir-vivre; **refinement**, niceness; **reservedness**, frigidity, frigidness, ice, iciness, perfunctoriness, reserve; **stiffness**, starch, starchiness, stiltedness, undemonstrativeness

FORMALLY *adv* ceremonially, ceremoniously, courtly, precisely, reservedly, solemnly, starchily, stiffly, stiltedly, with colours, with colours flying; **perfunctorily**, by the book, frigidly, icily, pro forma, undemonstratively

FORMAL OCCASION *n* formal function, observance, rite, ritual, solemnities, solemnity; **formalisation,** solemnification, solemnisation

FORSAKENLY *adv* desolately, forlornly

FORTHRIGHT *adj* aboveboard, bluff, blunt, candid, direct, downright, extroverted, foursquare, frank, genuine, guileless, honest, literal, matter-of-fact, open, open as the day, plain, plain-dealing, plain-spoken, sincere, straightforward, up-front

FORTHRIGHTLY *adv* bluffly, bluntly, candidly, downrightly, foursquare, foursquarely, genuinely, plainly

FORTHRIGHTNESS *n* bluffness, bluntness, candidness, candour, directness, downrightness, foursquareness, frankness, genuineness, singlemindedness, straightforwardness

FORTIFICATION *n* fieldwork, flanker, flèche, gabionade, lunette, muniment; **parapet,** bailey (Archaic), barbican, bulwark, rampart, redan, walls; **barricade,** parallel, salient, traverse; **battlement,** battery, blockhouse, crenellation, embrasure, emplacement, pillbox; **stockade,** abatis, air base, base, fastness, fraise, palisade; **stake,** barbwire, caltrop, gabion, spike; **movable shelter,** manta, mantelet, testudo, tortoise; **earthwork,** breastwork, contravallation, counterscarp, embankment, entrenchment, entrenchments, escarp, escarpment, glacis, mound, outwork, parados, ravelin, redoubt, retrenchment, scarp, sconce, vallum, works; **trench,** ditch, dug-out, dyke, enfilade, fosse, foxhole, moat, trenches; **trap,** booby trap. *See also* FORTRESS

FORTRESS *n* acropolis, bastille, castle, citadel, donjon, fastness, fort, fortalice, fortifications, garrison, hold (Archaic), keep, kremlin, Martello tower, peel, presidio, quadrilateral, stronghold, tower; **blockhouse,** gatehouse, watch-house, watchtower; **garrison town,** burg; **defensive position,** anchor, approaches, bastion, bridgehead, outpost. *See also* FORTIFICATION

FORTUNATE *adj* gracious (Obs.), happy, heaven-sent, lucky, providential; **prosperous,** blooming, booming, flourishing, made, palmy, roseate, rosy, Saturnian, thriving, up-and-coming; **auspicious,** benign, benignant, blessed, blest, bright, promising, propitious

FORTUNATELY *adv* auspiciously, beneficially, blessedly, for the best, happily, luckily, propitiously, providentially, rosily; **prosperously,** flourishingly, swimmingly, thrivingly

FORTUNE-TELLER *n* astrologer, ballgazer, chiromancer, crystal-gazer, futurologist, numerologist, palmist, rhabdomantist, stargazer, water diviner. *See also* PREDICTOR

FORTUNE-TELLING *n* astrology, augurship, augury, ballgazing, chirognomy, crystal-gazing, divination, divining, foretelling, futurology, hand-reading, metagnomy,

fortune-telling / **freak**

palmistry, prefiguration, prefigurement, prognostication, soothsaying, vaticination; **crystal ball,** crystal, fortune cookie; **horoscope,** ascendant, aspect, constellation, cusp, house, midheaven, planet, sign, star; **signs of the zodiac,** Aquarius *(water-bearer),* Aries *(Ram),* Cancer *(Crab),* Capricorn *(Goat),* Gemini *(Twins),* Leo *(Lion),* Libra *(Scales),* Pisces *(Fish),* Sagittarius *(Archer),* Scorpio *(Scorpion),* Taurus *(Bull),* Virgo *(Virgin);* **palmistry,** fate line, head line, heart line, lifeline, line of happiness, line of health, line of wealth, mount, mount of the moon, mount of Venus, rascette, simian line; **tarot cards,** Judgment, lesser arcanum, major arcanum, minor arcanum, the Fool, the Hanged Man, the Moon, the wheel of Fortune, triumph card, trump; **tarot suits,** cups, pentacles, swords, wands. *See also* PREDICTION

FORWARD *adv* ahead, forwards, in advance, in the forefront, in the lead, on, on ahead; **onward,** along, en route, forth, onwards

FOSSIL *n* eolith, neolith, petrified forest, relics, reliquiae, remains, ruins, stone-lily, vestige

FOUNDATION *n* base, basics, basis, first principles, groundwork, principle, rudiments; **spadework,** preparation; **initiative,** lead; **root,** grassroots, radix *(Maths);* **baseline,** datum level, datum plane, datum point, focus

FOUR *n* quartet, quaternary, quaternion, tetrad, tetralogy; **quadruplet,** quad, quadruplicate; **quadruple,** quadrivalency, quadruplication; **quarter,** fourth, quartering, quartern *(Obs.)*

FOURFOLD *adj* foursome, quadruple, quadruplex, quadruplicate, quaternary; **quadripartite,** quadrifid, quadrinomial *(Alg.),* quadrivalent *(Chem.),* quadrivial, quadruped, quartered, tetramerous; **fourth,** quarter

FRAGRANCE *n* aromaticity, balminess, deliciousness, odoriferousness, odorousness, perfumery, redolence, savour, savouriness, spice *(Poetic),* spicery, spiciness, sweet, sweetness, tang; **perfume,** aromatic, balm, bath cube, bath salts, essence, essential oil, incense, joss stick, scent; **cologne,** bay rum, eau de Cologne, lavender water, pomade, rosewater, toilet water; **pomander,** lavender bag, potpourri, pouncet box, sachet; **buttonhole,** nosegay, spray; **censer,** thurible; **breath-sweetener,** pastille

FRAGRANT *adj* aromatic, balmy, dulcet *(Archaic),* odoriferous, redolent, sweet, sweet-scented; **savoury,** ambrosial, ambrosian, delicious, flavorous; **spicy,** aloetic, balsamaceous, balsamic, moschate, musky; **strong,** fruity, heady, rich; **garlicky,** alliaceous

FRAME *n* annulet, architrave, archivolt, cased frame, epistyle, framing, lipping, moulding, ovolo, reeding, skirting board, washboard; **edging,** beading, bias binding, binding, braiding, gimp, list, piping, purfling, skirting, welting; **surround,** back, gutter *(Print),* mat, passe-partout; **circumference,** boundary, cordon, cushion *(Billiards),* perimeter, periphery, railing, ropes; **end,** beam-ends, head. *See also* EDGE

FREAK *n* chimera, grotesquerie, irregularity, monstrosity, neither fish flesh fowl nor good red herring, one

freak / **friendly**

of a kind, quip, rogue (*Biol.*), sport (*Biol.*), tertium quid, vagary, wonder; **rarity**, bastard, exotica, irregular, lusus naturae, odd, oncer, sight, unco (*Scot.*). *See also* STRANGENESS

FREEDMAN *n* clean potato, emancipated convict, emancipist, expiree, freedwoman, old hand, parolee, ticket-of-leaver; **free settler**, franklin, free agent, freeman, pure Merino

FREELY *adv* free, imprescriptibly, liberally, like water, open-handedly, **unconditionally**, by the run (*Naut.*), unboundedly, unlimitedly; **unreservedly**, anarchically, boisterously, incontinently, inordinately, intemperately, outright, outspokenly, spontaneously, unashamedly, unbiasedly, unconventionally, wantonly, wildly

FREIGHT *n* airfreight, carriage, cartage, expressage, freightage, haulage, pipage, portage, porterage, postage, towage, trackage (*U.S.*), truckage, wagonage (*Archaic*), waterage; **storage**, cellarage, poundage, stowage, tankage, yardage; **dockage**, anchorage, average, demurrage, dock-dues, ground, groundage, keelage, metage, pilotage, tonnage, wharfage. *See also* COST

FREQUENCY *n* commonness, continuity, relative frequency; **hertz**, cps, cycles per second, Hz, kHz, kilohertz, megahertz, MHz

FREQUENT *adj* common, continual, ever-recurring, habitual, incessant, non-stop, often (*Archaic*), recurrent, recurring, repeated, repetitional, rife; **repetitive**, cyclic, harping, iterative, nagging, stuck in a groove, tautological; **worn-out**, cliché-ridden, clichéd, old, stale, well-worn; **monotonous**, singsong; **multitudinous**, a dime a dozen, all over the place, thick on the ground; **regular**, drumming, rhythmical

FREQUENTLY *adv* continually, many a time, oft (*Poetic*), often, oftentimes (*Archaic*), recurrently, regularly, time after time

FRICTION *n* bite, traction; **drag**, pressure drag, profile drag, skin friction drag, windage; **aerodynamics**, tribology

FRIEND *n* ally, amigo, buddy, buddy-buddy, bully (*Obs.*), butty (*Brit.*), china, chum, cobber, comate, companion, comrade, crony, digger, ehoa (*N.Z.*), fellow, gossip (*Archaic*), hearty, hetaerist, mate, mucker (*Brit.*), neighbour, pal, pard (*U.S.*), pardner (*U.S.*), partner, sidekick, sparring partner, yokefellow; **acquaintance**, associate, contact, contact man, familiar, fraterniser, penfriend; **intimate**, best friend, blood brother, bosom friend, cater-cousin (*Archaic*), close friend, confidant, kith and kin, soul mate; **favourite**, minion, pet; **inseparables**, alter ego, birds of a feather, shadow; **sweetheart**, darling, love, lover; **girlfriend**, bovver boot (*Brit. Colloq.*), clinah (*Obs.*), moll, sheila; **boyfriend**, man

FRIENDLINESS *n* affability, affableness, amiability, amiableness, amicability, amicableness, amity; **cordiality**, approachability, approachableness, heartiness, hospitality; **warmth**, soft spot, warm-heartedness

FRIENDLY *adj* affable, amiable, amicable; **chummy**, brotherly, fraternal, matey, neighbourly, on good terms, pally; **warm-hearted**, approachable, folksy (*U.S.*), homey, open-hearted, outgoing; **welcoming**, cordial, genial,

friendly hospitable, warm; **hail-fellow-well-met**, backslapping, bluff, hearty; **acquainted**, familiar; **intimate**, bosom, close, incestuous, inseparable, involved, thick, thick as thieves, well in with; **devoted**, assiduous, devout, staunch; **compatible**, after one's own heart, hetaeristic, platonic, simpatico, sympathetic

FRIENDLY *adv* affably, amiably, amicably, friendlily, heartily, warm-heartedly, warmly, with open arms; **devotedly**, assiduously, devoutly; **intimately**, familiarly, fraternally, hetaeristically

FRIENDSHIP *n* backslapping, brotherhood, brotherliness, camaraderie, companionship, comradeship, fellowship, fraternalism, fraternity, hetaerism, mateship, mateyness, neighbourhood *(Archaic)*, neighbourliness, sodality; **goodwill**, fellow feeling, regard, solidarity, sympathy; **intimacy**, closeness, devotion, familiarisation, familiarity, intimateness, involvement, togetherness; **understanding**, entente; **fraternisation**, acquaintance, acquaintanceship, association, consociation, conversation, society; **greetings**, ingratiation, open arms, welcome; **attentions**, assiduities, embrace, endearment, handclasp, handshake, hug, kiss, squeeze

FRIGHT *n* affright *(Archaic)*, alarm, amazement *(Obs.)*, awe, blue funk, boggle, consternation, dismay, doubt *(Obs.)*, fear, fray *(Archaic)*, funk, heebie-jeebies, horror, horrors, jumpiness, panic, phobia *(Psychol.)*, scare, superstition, terror, the creeps, the jitters, willies; **apprehension**, alarm, alarum *(Archaic)*, angst, anxiety, anxiousness, apprehensiveness, care, concern, concernment, dis-ease, disquiet, disquietude, dread, misgiving, nervousness, qualm, trepidation, worriment; **timidity**, diffidence, shyness, timidness, timorousness, tremulousness; **tremble**, cold shivers, cold sweat, horripilation, shudder, start, tremor, turn *(Colloq.)*

FRIGHTEN *v* affray *(Archaic)*, affright *(Archaic)*, alarm, appal, awe, blanch, consternate, curdle the blood, fear *(Archaic)*, freak, fright *(Poetic)*, horrify, make one's flesh creep, make one's hair stand on end, petrify, put the breeze up, put the wind up, scare, scare the living daylights out of, strike fear into, terrify, terrorise, turn one's bowels to water; **daunt**, chill, demoralise, discourage, dishearten, dismay, dispirit

FRIGHTENED *adj* afraid, aghast, alarmed, awe-struck, green at the gills, horror-stricken, horror-struck, out of one's wits, panic, panic-stricken, panicky, petrified, scared, scared stiff, shit-scared, spooked, terror-stricken, terror-struck, trembly, tremulant, tremulous, white, white at the gills; **timorous**, afeard *(Archaic)*, anxious, apprehensive, dispirited, fearful, gun-shy, haunted, jittery, jumpy, nervous, pavid, phobic, shy, superstitious, timid, toey, windy, worried, worrisome

FRIGHTENED PERSON *n* blencher, milquetoast *(U.S.)*, panic merchant, shyer

FRIGHTENER *n* alarmist, boggle, bogle, bogy, bogyman, boogieman, bugaboo, bugbear, chamber of horrors, demoraliser, discourager, gorgon, gorgonian, hair-raiser, hobgoblin, holy terror, horror, intimidator, scarecrow, scaremonger, scarer, spinechiller, startler, taipo *(N.Z.)*, terrifier, terror, terrorister, thunderbolt

FRIGHTENING *adj* appalling, awe-inspiring, awesome, awful, bloodcurdling, crawly, creepy, creepy-crawly, Dantean, Dantesque, dire, direful, dread, dreadful, eerie, fearful, fearsome, forbidding, formidable, frightful, grim, grisly, hair-raising, hairy *(Colloq.)*, horrendous, horrible, horrid, horrific, nerve-racking, nightmarish, redoubtable, redoubted, scary, spinechilling, terrible, terrific

FRIGHTENINGLY *adv* alarmingly, appallingly, awesomely, awfully, chillingly, direfully, dreadfully, eerily, fearsomely, forbiddingly, formidably, grimly, hauntingly, horrendously, horribly, horridly, redoubtably, scaringly, terribly, terrifically

FRIGHTFULNESS *n* awe *(Obs.)*, awesomeness, awfulness, creepiness, direfulness, dreadfulness, eeriness, fearfulness, fearsomeness, forbiddingness, formidableness, grimness, grisliness, horribleness, horridness, terribleness, uncanniness; **terrorisation,** alarmism, demoralisation, discouragement, disheartenment, horrification, intimidation, terrorism

FRONT *n* A-side, face, fore edge, obverse; **head,** lead, top; **forefront,** firing line, fore, foreside; **anteriority,** forwardness; **facade,** facing, front, frontage, frontispiece *(Archit.)*, heading; **bow,** bowsprit, cutwater, forecastle, hawse, head, prow

FRONT *v* affront *(Archaic)*, face

FRONT *adj* anterior, frontal; **forward,** fore; **head,** head-on, headmost; obverse, facing-out, right

FRONTALLY *adv* anteriorly, forwardly; **forward,** afore, ahead, before, fore, forwards, frontwards, in advance, to the fore; **headfirst,** down by the head, head-on, headlong

FRUIT *n* apocarp, berry, boll, burr, capsule, caryopsis, cob, cone, cypsela, drupe, ear, follicle, hesperidium, hip, legume, loment, lomentum, mutt-eye, mutti, nut, nutlet, pepo, pod, pome, pseudocarp, pyxidium, regma, samara, sarcocarp, schizocarp, seed capsule, simple fruit, sorosis, strobilus, syncarp, tryma, xylocarp; **fruit part,** achene, acinus, acorn, awn, beak, beard, calyptra, coccus, down, drupelet, egret, endocarp, epicarp, exocarp, fructification, gumnut, kernel, loculus, mericarp, operculum, pappus, pericarp, pit, pulp, putamen, pyrene, rag, sarcocarp, septum, shell, stone, suture, sycarp, umbo, valve, wing

FUEL *n* combustible, feed, juice; **fueling,** bunkering, fuel-injection, priming; **woodheap,** pyre, woodpile; **firewood,** billet, brushwood, faggot, greasebush, greasewood, log, mallee roots, ovenwood, torchwood, yarran; **kindling,** briquette, firelighter, firing, morning sticks, mornings wood, tinder; **wick,** mantle, touchpaper; **coal,** anthracite, brown coal, coking coal, culm, lignite, wood coal; **coke,** char, charcoal; **peat,** turf; **gas,** bottled gas, coal gas, liquefied petroleum gas (L.P.G.), producer gas, town gas; **fossil fuel,** benzine *(U.S.)*, carburant, derv *(Brit.)*, diesel, diesel oil, dieseline, gas *(U.S.)*, gasoline *(U.S.)*, naphtha *(Obs.)*, oil, petrol, petroleum, standard, super; **kerosene,** avgas, kero, paraffin *(Brit.)*; **propellant,**

acetylene, borane, butane, carbinol, ethine, ethyl, grain *(Aerospace)*, heptane, isobutane, lead tetraethyl, liquid oxygen, lox, pentaborane, propane, solid propellant; **incendiary**, fireball, Greek fire, napalm, wildfire; **nuclear fuel**, pile, rod, uranium

FUEL *v* bunker, coal, coke, refuel, tank up; **fire**, feed the flames, lay a fire, prime, stoke, underfeed

FULL *adj* chock-a-block, chock-full, chocker, choke-full, cram-full, crammed, full up, jam-packed, jammed, replete, stopped; **brimful**, brimming, topped up, well filled; **loaded**, charged, fraught, laden; **bulging**, big with, pregnant with; **occupied**, preoccupied; **overfull**, at saturation point, drowned, overflowing, rolling in, saturate *(Poetic)*, saturated, slopping, swamped; **crowded**, packed, plethoric, solid, tight; **bursting at the seams**, gorged, sated

FULLNESS *n* capacity, impletion, maximum, one's fill, plenitude, satiety, saturation; **plenty**, abundance, full and plenty, plentifulness; **tightness**, cram, engorgement, saturation point; **replenishment**, completion, fill-up, refill; **occupancy**, occupation, preoccupancy; **cupful**, bumper

FULLY *adv* even, quite; **plenty**, solidly

FUNDAMENTAL *adj* au fond, basal, base, basic, basilar, bottom, deep down, essential, key, material, original, radical, ultimate, underlying, vital; **primary**, prime; **elementary**, elemental, hypostatic, raw, simple, skeleton; **substantial**, meaty

FUNDS *n* assets, bread and butter, capital, credit, cunning kick, exchequer, fast buck, finances, float, fund, income, liquid assets, liquidity, money in hand, petty cash, pocket, purse, quick assets, resources, revenue, royalty, savings, slush fund, slush money, supplies *(Govt.)*; **kitty**, jackpot, pool, stakes; **bond**, bond money; **funny money**, mickey mouse money. *See also* ALLOWANCE; TREASURY

FUNERAL RITES *n* exequies, funeral, obsequies, office *(Eccles.)*; **burial**, committal, entombment, immurement, inhumation, interment, intombment, inurnment, sepulture; **cremation**, incineration; **embalment**, mummification; **requiem**, dead march, dirge, knell, last post, requiem mass, resquiescat, resquiescent in pace, taps, threnody; **obituary**, elegy, epitaph, funeral oration, in memoriam, R.I.P.; **lamentation**, vigil, wake; **mourning**, crepe, widow's weeds; **funeral pyre**, balefire *(Archaic)*, pile; **shroud**, cerecloth, cerements, graveclothes, winding sheet. *See also* GRAVE; CEMETERY

FUNEREAL *adj* funerary; **obituary**, elegiac, obsequial, threnodial, threnodic; **sepulchral**, cinerary, crematory, cryptal, mausolean, mortuary, tomb-like

FURNITURE *n* accoutrements, appointments, appurtenances, fittings, fixtures, furnishings, furnishments *(Archaic)*

FURROW *n* cannelure, channel, chase, check *(Masonry)*, croze, dap, drill, fillister, flute *(Archit.)*, glyph, gouge, groove, nick, notch, rabbet, rebate, recess, rifle, rut, scarf, seam, sulcus, vallecula, wrinkle; **ditch**, canal, costean, coulisse, cut, dyke, entrenchments, gutter, keyway, moat, rill *(Astron.)*, rubble drain, sap *(Fortifications)*, slit trench, slot, sondage,

furrow trench, trough; **scratch**, microgroove, run-in groove, scarification, score; **milling**, broom finish, chatter marks, fluting, rifling, ruttiness, striation, sulcation

FURROW *v* chamfer, channel, flute, groove, mill, nick, rabbet, rebate, rifle, rout, rut, striate, trepan; **crease**, cockle, crumple, ripple, seam, wrinkle; **ditch**, costean, dyke, sap *(Fortifications)*, trench; **engrave**, chase, etch; **plough**, till; **scratch**, overscore, scarify, score

FURROWED *adj* fluted, glyphic, grooved, milled, ripply, rutty, scrobiculate, seamed, striate, sulcate, vallecular, valleculate, wrinkly

FURROWER *n* ditcher, gang plough, plough, trencher; **gouge**, burin, chisel, cold chisel, fuller, pressing board *(Bookbinding)*, router, trepan; **engraver**, chaser, etcher, fluter

FUTURE *n* afterlife, coming ages, futurity, hereafter, time to come; **tomorrow**, morrow *(Archaic)*, tonight; **mañana**, doomsday, judgment day, millenium, Pancake Day, the by and by, the sweet by and by; **imminence**, impendence, impendency

FUTURE *adj* after, eventual, to-be, unborn; **forward**, long-range, prospective; **futuristic**, space-age, twenty-first century; **imminent**, close at hand, impendent, impending, in the offing, in view, near, nearly upon one, nigh, pendent, pending, toward *(Obs.)*

Gg

GAIN *v* achieve, acquire, acquisition, annex, appointee, attain, bring home, catch, clear, collect, fetch, gather, get, get hold of, land, lay one's hands on, obtain, procure, realise, receive, recover *(Law)*, secure, take out, take over, win, wrest; **reach**, accede to, attain to, get to; **earn**, gross, net

GAINER *n* abandonee, accepter, alienee, appointee, assignee, concessionaire, concessionary, conferee, consignee, dole bludger, doley, donee, earner, endorsee, grantee, presentee, receiver, recipient; **heir**, assigns *(Law)*, beneficiary, coheir, coheiress, coinheritor, devisee, distaff, heir apparent, heir-at-law, heiress, heres, heritor *(Archaic)*, inheritor, inheritress, inheritrix, jointress, legatee; **insured,** assured *(Insurance)*, cestui que trust

GAMBLE *n* a pig in a poke, act of faith, adventure, bid, burl, flutter, leap in the dark, punt, Russian roulette, spec, speculation, venture; **bet,** aleatory contract, all-in bet, collect, daily double, double, double or quits, doubles, each-way bet, forecast quinella, jackpot tote, martingale, overround system, parlay, parimutuel *(U.S.)*, quadrella, quinella, saver, side bet, skinner, stakes, straight-out bet, triella, trifecta, wager; **bid,** call, calling, contract, declaration, jump bid, psychic bid; **record of bets,** book; **the luck of the draw,** the toss of the coin

GAMBLE *v* ballot, chance it, chance one's arm, dice, game, have a flutter, play, play the market, speculate, take a punt on, take risks, throw dice, try one's luck; **bet, gage** *(Archaic)*, get set, hazard, lay, plunge, punt, put, roll, stake; **play two-up,** head 'em; **take bets,** field a book, frame a book, make a book, run a book, tout; **bid,** call, go, outbid, overbid; **raise,** fatten *(Poker)*, jump *(Contract Bridge)*, sweeten *(Poker)*; **bid on,** back; **hedge,** lay off; **stake,** ante, vie *(Obs.)*, wage *(Obs.)*, wager; **bet each way,** be on the grouter, bet all-up, bet double or quits, bet evens, come in on the grouter, crush the price, go for broke, go for the doctor, parlay, play for dibs, put one's shirt on, stay; **toss,** come in, head them, mick, ned them, nut them, one them, skull them; **win,** be in the black, be on a good thing, be on a winning streak, whipsaw; **be at stake,** be in hazard

GAMBLER *n* better, bettor, bidder, crapshooter *(U.S.)*, dicer, gamester, hazarder, hippomaniac, player, punter, side-better, sport, stool pigeon, wagerer; **bookmaker,** bagman, bagswinger, balancer, bester, bookie, commission agent *(Brit.)*, fielder, geno *(Horseracing Colloq.)*, Ikey Mo, rails bookmaker, SP bookmaker, tick-tack man, turf accountant *(Brit.)*; **banker,** monte, ombre; **backer,** plunger, turfman; **alley loafer,** welsher; **bagboy,** bookie's runner, boxer, croupier, crusher *(Horseracing)*, ringkeeper, stakeholder; **two-up player,** alley clerk, boxer, centre, centreman, cockatoo, headie, ringie, spinner, tailie, tosser; **adventurer,** adventuress, gentleman of fortune, land shark, landjobber, speculator

GAMBLING *n* bookmaking, fan-tan, gaming, hippomania; **bingo**, housie-housie, hoy, lotto, tombola; **card game**, baccarat, blackjack, chemin de fer, chemmy, cooncan, cribbage, faro, poker, pontoon, rouge et noir, rummy, stud game, stud poker, trente et quarante, twenty-one, vingt-et-un; **dice**, craps, dicing, hazard, poker dice, thimblerig; **two-up**, swy, toss, toss-up; **chocolate wheel**, roulette; **lottery**, art union, ballot, Calcutta, consultation *(Colloq.)*, football pools, grab bag, lot, lucky dip, pakapoo, policy *(U.S.)*, pools, raffle, sweep, sweepstake, Tambaroora muster, the casket, the Golden casket; **odds**, even money, evens, long odds, long shot, pot, quotation, short odds, starting price, toss-up; **ambs-ace**, butterfly, crabs, doublets, floater, showdown, sixer, tern

GAMBLING *adj* hippomanic, sporting, turfy *(Horseracing)*

GAMBLING EQUIPMENT *n* parimutuel; **dice**, astragals, bones, die, ivories, poker dice; **poker machine**, fruit machine *(U.S. and Brit.)*, one-armed bandit, pokies, slot machine *(U.S.)*; **kylie**, bat, kip, stick; **chip**, blue chip, prize money, razoo, velvet; **stake**, ante, guts, jackpot, kitty, pool, pot

GAMBLING HALL *n* casino, disorderly house, gaming house, hell *(Brit.)*, poolroom; **two-up school**, alley, betting ring, lucky shop, pub TAB, ring, TAB, the machine *(N.Z. Horseracing)*, totalisator, Totalisator Agency Board

GAMESMAN *n* player; **enjoyer**, dabbler, dilettante; **frolicker**, larker, reveller; **cardplayer**, banker, dealer, discarder, dummy, elder hand, hand, lone hand, maker, pairs, pone

GAOLER *n* cerberus, deathwatch, four-by-two, guard, guarder, guardsman, kangaroo, mod squad, provost *(Obs.)*, screw, trump, turnkey, warden, warder, wardress; **incarcerator**, confiner, detainer, securer; **trusty**, farm constable; **apprehender**, captor, capturer

GAP *n* areola, blank, break, clearance, gape, hiatus, interspace, interstice, interval, lacuna, opening, space, vacancy, void; **split**, rent, slit, tear, vent; **air-gap**, crenel, intercolumniation, shake, spirket; **crack**, breach, chap, chimney, chink, cleavage, cleft, craze, crevice, cut, fissure, fracture, gash, mofette, rift, sand-crack; **chasm**, abysm *(Poetic)*, abyss, breakaway, canyon, chaos *(Obs.)*, chine *(Brit.)*, coomb, crevasse, dale, defile, dell, depth, dingle, gate, glen, gorge, graben, grike, gulch, gulf, gully, gut, hanging valley, pass, profundity, ravine, vale, valley, water-gap, wind-gap, yawn

GAPE *v* open, yawn; **space**, gap, interspace, separate, set apart, space out, spread out; **split**, cleave, crack, part

GAPING *adj* agape, ajar, broken, dehiscent, open, yawning; **spaced**, areolar, areolate, effuse, gappy, hiatal; **cleft**, cloven, cracked, dissected, parted, rent, slit, split; **interspatial**, interstitial

GARBAGE DUMP *n* dump, junk-heap, junkyard, midden, slagheap, tip; **rubbish tin**, ash can *(U.S.)*, dirt box, dustbin, garbage tin, kitchen tidy, litter

garbage dump

bin, trash can *(U.S.)*, w.p.b., w.p.b. file, wastebasket, wastepaper basket; cesspit, cess, cesspool, grease trap

GARDEN *n* garth *(Archaic)*, knot garden, roof garden, rooftop garden; **bed**, border, flowerbed, hotbed, rockery, seedbed; **plot**, patch, plat; **market garden**, allotment, kitchen garden, vegetable garden; **nursery**, bush house, conservatory, fernery, garden centre, glasshouse, grapery, greenery, greenhouse, hothouse, rosary, shrubbery; **green**, lawn, nature strip; **orchard**, arboretum, arbour *(Obs.)*, orangery, pinery; **park**, botanical garden, parterre, wilderness, wintergarden

GARDENER *n* arborist, landscape gardener, nurseryman, rosarian, topiarist; **market gardener**, cabbage-gardener, trucker *(U.S.)*; **groundsman**, greenkeeper, hedger

GARDENING *n* carpet bedding, espalier, horticulture, landscape gardening, pomiculture, pomology, topiary, trucking *(U.S.)*

GAS *n* ablative, aerosol, coal gas, detonating gas, electrolytic gas, flue gas, fluid, marsh gas, methane, natural gas, plasma, sewer gas, tear gas, town gas, water gas; **vapour**, breath *(Obs.)*, fumes, live steam, saturated vapour, steam, water-vapour; **smoke**, reek; **air**, atmosphere, exhalation, wind; **damp**, afterdamp, blackdamp, choke damp, firedamp, whitedamp; **effluvium**, eduction, emanon, exhaust, mofette; choof, chuff, huff, puff; **inert gas**, noble gas, rare gas; **ideal gas**, perfect gas, permanent gas; **fireball**, chromosphere, photosphere, prominence; **vapour trail**, condensation trail

gatherer

GASBAG *n* bag of wind, bull artist, bush-lawyer, expatiator, gusher, maunderer, windbag

GASEOUS *adj* effluvial, fluid, fluidal, fluidic, gasiform, pneumatic; **evaporative**, volatile; **vaporescent**, vaporific; **gassy**, fumelike, steamy, vaporous, vapoury

GASEOUSNESS *n* fluidity, fluidness, gaseity, gassiness, steaminess, vaporousness; **vaporisation**, atomisation, evaporation, evolution, fluidisation, gasification, vaporescence, volatilisation; **gassing**, aeration, fumigation, sulphurisation; **evaporability**, vapourability; **volatility**, volatileness; **pneumatics**, eudiometry, gas laws, pneumatology *(Obs.)*, pneumodynamics

GASTRIC *adj* anal, appendic, caecal, colonic, digestive, duodenal, excretory, ileac, intestinal, oesophageal, pyloric, rectal, stomachic

GATEWAY *n* archway, débouché *(Fort.)*, doorway, French door, torii

GATHER *v* amass, centralise, collect, congest *(Obs.)*, glean, ingather, rake, scramble up, throw together, whip in; **accumulate**, agglomerate, aggregate, conglomerate, cumulate, run; **hoard**, bank up, scavenge, sock away, stack away, stockpile; **cluster**, bale, bunch, bundle, clump, constellate; **heap**, lumber, pile, stack; **congregate**, assemble, band, forgather, group, mass, meet, regroup, sit, turn out; **crowd**, flock, herd, horde, huddle, pack, press, serry, throng; **convene**, call, convoke, muster, muster up, raise, rally, summon

GATHERER *n* bundler, gleaner, heaper, herder, ingatherer, mobber, musterer, stacker; **assembler**, congregator, convoker; **collector**, amasser, raiser; **hoarder**, bowerbird, magpie, stockpiler; **scavenger**, beachcomber, emu *(Colloq.)*; **discophil**, epidopterist, ex-librist, philatelist, phillumenist, stamp-collector

GATHERING *n* association, bee, get-together, meet, muster, roll-up, turn-out; **assembly**, assemblage, body, confluence, conflux, congregation, constellation, convocation; **meeting**, hui *(N.Z.)*, indaba *(S. African)*, witan, witenagemot; **group**, band, cohort, company, outfit, party, phalanx; **gang**, crew, emu parade, mob, pack, rabble, ruck, shower; **crowd**, crush, huddle, multitude, press, sea of faces, throng; **jam**, bunfight, squeeze; **corroboree**; **grouping**, class, college, school; **stable**, string; **pack**, pride; **bevy**, covey, flight, flock, gaggle; **herd**, drove, horde, troop; **shoal**, school; **association**, biome, climax community, colony, community, society; **congregativeness**, gregariousness, herd instinct, sociality; **centralisation**, centralism

GEIGER COUNTER *n* cloud chamber, counter, counter tube, dosimeter, scintillation counter, scintillometer

GENERAL *adj* all, all-round, any, broad, catholic, ecumenical, every, universal, universalistic; **comprehensive**, across-the-board, all-embracing, blanket, broad-spectrum, collective, inclusive, omnibus, panoptic, panoramic, plenary, sweeping; **cosmopolitan**, azonic, global, worldwide; **exoteric**, broadcast, encyclical; **prevalent**, common, current, pandemic, prevailing, regnant, rife, ruling, ubiquitous, widespread

GENERALISATION *n* abstraction, generality, universalisation; **conspectus**, bird's-eye view, broad spectrum, overview, panorama

GENERALISE *v* abstract, catholicise, universalise; **broadcast**, spread; **depersonalise**, impersonalise; **prevail**, be everywhere, obtain, rule

GENERALIST *n* all-rounder, jack-of-all-trades, one-man band, universalist

GENERALITY *n* catholicity, commonness, generalness, omnifariousness, prevailingness, prevalence, regnancy, ubiquitousness, ubiquity, universalism, universality, universalness; **cosmopolitanism**, cosmopolitism

GENERALLY *adv* across the board, everywhere, globally, high and low, sweepingly, ubiquitously, universally; **in general**, broadly, by and large, catholically, ecumenically, in the abstract, largely, on the whole, prevailingly, prevalently

GENEROSITY *n* bounteousness, bountifulness, charitableness, free-handedness, freeness, generousness, goodness, handsomeness, kindness, large-heartedness, largess, lavishness, liberality, liberalness, munificence, open-handedness, open-heartedness, princeliness, prodigality, soft-heartedness, unsparingness; **benefaction**, almsgiving, beneficence, bounty, charity, hospitality, philanthropy; **contribution**, act of charity, Christmas box, donation, favour, gift, good deed, good turn, largess, salvo, widow's mite; **open house**, liberty hall; **shout**, treat

GENEROUS *adj* beneficent, big, big-hearted, bounteous, bountiful, charitable, eleemosynary, free, free-

generous

handed, generous-spirited, grudgeless, handsome, hospitable, kindly, large, large-hearted, lavish, liberal, magnificent, munificent, open, open-handed, open-hearted, princely, prodigal, ungrudging, unsparing, unstinting; **touchable**, soft-hearted, susceptible

GENEROUSLY *adv* a fair treat, a treat, beneficently, bounteously, bountifully, charitably, freely, handsomely, lavishly, liberally, magnanimously, magnificently, munificently, open-handedly, open-heartedly, prodigally, profusely, unsparingly, unstintingly, with open hand, without stint

GENETIC *adj* genic, genotypic, idioplasmic, Mendelian; **hereditary**, descendible, hereditable, heritable, inheritable, inherited; **phyletic**, monophyletic, polyphyletic; **lineal**, direct, unilateral; **collateral**, indirect; **pedigreed**, blooded, well-bred; **purebred**, full-blooded, inbred, true, true-born, true-bred; **half-blooded**, half-breed, half-caste, miscegenetic; **hybrid**, crossbred, interbred, mongrel; **atavistic**, reversionary

GENETICS *n* hereditarianism, Mendel's laws, Mendelism; **eugenics**, A.I., A.I.D., artificial insemination, crossbreeding, genetic engineering, in-vitro fertilisation, inbreeding, miscegenation, mongrelism, outcrossing; **heritability**, hereditability; **reversion**, atavism, recapitulation; **gene**, allele, DNA, factor, gemmule, genetic code, genome, genotype, germ plasm, idioplasm, unit, unit factor.
See also ANCESTRY

GEOLOGY *n* astrogeology, crystallography, gemmology, lithology, mineralogy, palaeomagnetism, petrography, petrology, photogeology, tectonics, X-ray crystallography

GESTURE *n* beau geste, business *(Theat.)*, gesticulation, motion, shrug, wave; **nod**, beck, beckon, eyewink, nictation, nictitation, wink; **mime**, charade, mouth, mow *(Archaic)*, mug *(Brit.)*, smack

GESTURE *v* beckon, gesticulate, motion, point, recognise, shrug, wave; **mime**, pantomime, talk with one's hands; **cue**, peter *(Whist)*, telegraph one's punches, tick-tack *(Horseracing)*; **nod**, bob, give the nod, nictitate, shake one's head, wink; **grimace**, mouth, mow *(Archaic)*, mug *(Brit.)*, raise one's eyebrows

GET *v* accept, accrue, acquire, adopt, be in receipt of, collect, come by, cop, gain, gather, have, obtain, pocket, receive, take off one's hands, win; **come to hand**, fall into one's hands, fall to one's lot; **inherit**, become heir to, come into, come into one's own, heir, step into a fortune, succeed; **receipt**, sign for; **be on the dole**, go on the dole, live on handouts

GET DIRTY *v* collect dust, foul up; **mildew**, moulder, stagnate, putrefy, rot; **draggle**, drabble, pig it, live in a pig sty; **wallow**, roll in the mud

GETTING *n* acceptance, acquirement, acquisition, attainment, collection, earning, gathering, landing, obtainment, procuration, procurement, purchase, receipt, receival, reception, recipience; **inheritance**, appanage, bequest, coinheritance, devise, entail, gift, heritage, heritance *(Archaic)*, jointure, legacy

GHOSTLY *adj* ghoulish, phantasmal, spectral, spirit, spiritual, supernatural; **angelic**, archangelic, celestial, cherubic, godly *(Archaic)*, heavenly, seraphic, spiritual; **nymphal**, chthonian *(Gk. Myth.)*, nymphean, satyric, sylphic; **impish**, elfin, faerie *(Archaic)*, fairy

GIANT *n* behemoth, biggie, boomer, bouncer, bumper, colossus, giantess, Goliath, hulk, husky *(U.S.)*, jumbo, Juno, leviathan, monster, monstrosity, snorter, the daddy of them all, the father and mother of a, titan, whopper

GIFT *n* alms, bounty, Christmas hamper, Christmas stocking, compliment, contribution, donative, favour, grant, handout, handsel, keepsake, largess, manna from heaven, mortuary *(Archaic)*, present, presentation, pressie, prezzie, remembrance, subscription; **offering**, oblation, offertory *(Rom. Cath. Ch.)*, peace-offering, sacrifice; **tip**, baksheesh, beer money, Christmas box, consideration, cumshaw, douceur, gratification *(Archaic)*, gratuity, pourboire; **prize**, award, reward; **bequest**, devise *(Law)*, dowry, endowment, foundation, grant, legacy, subsidy, subvention; **bonus issue**, bonus, capital distribution, capital issue, premium; **give-away**, free sample, handout

GIVE *v* accord, administer, assign, award, bestow, confer, cough up *(Colloq.)*, dedicate, donate, extend, gift, hand out, heap, make a present of, oblige with, portion, present, provide, sacrifice, shower, spare, tender; **contribute**, chip in, dob in, fork out, kick in, subscribe; **tip**, baksheesh, remember; **consign**, commit, delegate, deliver, dispense, dispose of, entrust, give into someone's keeping, hand in, hand over, make over, part with, pass into someone's charge, put into someone's hands, sign away, surrender, turn over to; **grant**, allow, concede, seise *(Law)*, vouchsafe, yield; **bequeath**, devise *(Law)*, dower, endow, leave, settle *(Law)*, vest, will; **sacrifice**, give up, offer, spend

GIVE BIRTH *v* bear, bring forth, bring into the world, deliver, drop a bundle *(Colloq.)*, have, produce, pullulate, teem *(Obs.)*; **lie in**, be confined; **labour**, travail; **abort**, cast, miscarry; **fruit**, berry, germinate, set; **drop**, calve, farrow, fawn, foal, kid, kitten, lamb, litter, pig, pup, spawn, throw, twin, whelp, yean; **slink**, slip; **brood**, clutch, cover *(Obs.)*, hatch, nest

GIVER *n* almoner *(Hist.)*, angel *(Colloq.)*, benefactor, benefactress, bestower, conferrer, contributor, dedicator, deviser, dispenser, donator, donor, endower, fairy godmother, fat cat *(Politics)*, grantor, imparter *(Archaic)*, legator, philanthropist, presenter, Santa Claus, testator, testatrix, tipper

GIVING *n* accommodation, bequeathal, bestowal, commitment, conferment, conferral, consignment, dedication, dispensation, disposal, disposure *(Rare)*, impartation *(Archaic)*, impartment *(Archaic)*, investiture, presentation, presentment, provision, testation *(Law)*, vouchsafement

GLASSES *n* bifocals, eyeglasses, goggles, half-frames, lorgnette, pince-nez, specs, spectacles; **contact lenses**, hydrophilic contact lenses; **sun-**

glasses, dark glasses, polaroids, shades, sunnies; **goggles,** safety glasses; **monocle,** lorgnon. *See also* LENS

GLAZE *n* bloom, crust, finish, glost, laitance, lamella, patina, rust, salt glaze, scale, verdigris; **film,** filminess

GLIDE *v* coast, free-fall, freewheel, glissade, run, skate, slide, slip, slur

GLORIFICATION *n* celebration, emblazonment, extolment, immortalisation; **exaltation,** aggrandisement, lionisation, uplift

GLORIFY *v* aggrandise, chair, dignify, distinguish, emblaze *(Archaic),* emblazon, exalt, extol, fame, honour, illuminate, illumine, lionise, put on the map, translate, uplift, upraise, venerate; **immortalise,** classicise

GLOVE *n* boxing glove, doeskins, gauntlet, kid gloves, mitt, mitten, muff, wristlet; **cuff,** finger, palm, thumb

GLOWING *adj* ardent, candescent, flagrant *(Rare),* incandescent

GLUTTON *n* beast, cormorant, garbage-guts, gorger, gormandiser, greedy-guts, gulper, guts, gutser, guzzle-guts, guzzler, hog, pig, trencherman; **epicure,** epicurean, gastronome, gourmand

GO BACK *v* back, back-pedal, backwater, countermarch, ebb, recede, reflux, regorge, regress, regurgitate, retrocede, retrogress, reverse, track out *(Film);* **return,** boomerang, do a Melba, get back, home, make a comeback, return to the fold, turn back; **backtrack,** retrace one's footsteps; **retreat,** back down, back off, back out, back-pedal, draw one's horns in, flinch, pull one's horns in, pull out, retire, retract, shrink, withdraw; **relapse,** backslide, degenerate; **revert,** hark back

GOD *n* atua *(N.Z.),* daemon *(Greek Myth.),* deity, demigod, demigoddess, demiurge, earthmother, goddess, lares, manes, mimen, penates, presence, snake-god, sun-god; **incarnation,** avatar, embodiment; **false god,** Baal, idol; **pantheon,** powers, thearchy; **godship,** blessedness, divineness, divinity, glory, godhead, godhood, godliness, grace, sacredness, sacrosanctity, sanctimony *(Obs.),* sanctity, theomorphism

GOD *interj* à bas, begorrah *(Irish),* by jingo, by Jove, Christ, Christ almighty, egad, gadzooks *(Archaic),* gosh, Jeez, Jesus, Jesus Christ, Od *(Archaic),* perdie *(Archaic),* zounds *(Archaic);* **curses,** arse holes, blast, bloody hell, bugger, confound it, damn, damnation, darn, dash, drat, hell, hell's bells, hell's teeth, phut, pigs, the blazes, the hell with it, what the shit; **shit,** bugger me, bugger me dead, I'll be buggered, I'll be damned, I'll be hanged, I'll be jiggered, shit a brick; **bloody oath,** my colonial oath, my oath; **bull,** balls, bullshit, bullswool, crap; curse you, bash it, bore it up you, bugger you, get knotted, get shagged, go jump in the lake, go to blazes, go to buggery, go to hell, go to the devil, piss off, plague upon you *(Archaic),* shove it, sod it, stick it, stick that for a lark, take a running jump, up cook's arse *(N.Z.),* up you, upya, you can stick that for a joke; **may your chooks turn to emus and kick your dunny down**

GODLIKE *adj* deific, deiform, divine, godly, numinous, Olympian, theomorphic; **holy,** all-knowing, all-powerful, all-seeing, almighty, celestial, hallowed, heavenly, Messianic, omnipresent, omniscient, sacred, sacrosanct, sanctimonious *(Obs.);* **demiurgic,** demiurgeous; **tripersonal,** hypostatic, triune

GOING BACKWARDS *n* reaction, recession, regress, regression, rein back *(Equestrian),* retiral, retreat, retrocession, retrogradation, retrogression, retroversion, return, reversal, sternway *(Naut.),* withdrawal; **return,** countermarch, homecoming, round trip, U-turn; **reflux,** ebb, ebb tide, refluence; **flashback,** cutback *(U.S.);* **flinch,** retractation, retraction, shrink

GOOD *n* advantage, benefit, boon, silver lining, virtue; **blessing,** benediction, benefaction, favour, mercy; **the common good,** commonweal, commonwealth *(Obs.),* summum bonum, the public good, welfare

GOOD *adj* amazing, bang-up, bonny *(Scot.),* bonzer, bosker, brave *(Archaic),* braw *(Scot.),* budgeree, capital, castor, copasetic *(U.S.),* corking, crackerjack, cracking, crash-hot, daisy, dandy, decent, desirable, excellent, extra, extra grouse, extraordinaire, fabulous, famous, fantastic, fine, gas, gorgeous, grand, great, grouse, immense, kapai *(N.Z.),* keen, magnificent, marvellous, nice, nobby, not bad, peachy, pie *(N.Z.),* pretty *(Obs.),* proper *(Archaic),* ribuck *(Obs.),* ripping, royal *(Obs.),* rubydazzler, sensational, shining, slap-up, slashing, smashing, snifter, snodger *(Obs.),* sollicking, spiffing *(Brit.),* splendid, splendiferous, super, super-duper, superb, superfine, swell, swinging, terrif, terrific, tickety-boo *(Brit.),* top, topping *(Brit.),* trim *(Obs.),* wizard *(Brit.),* wonderful, you-beaut; **rare,** recherché, select, uncommon; **first-class,** A-1, ace, at one's best, best, champion, first-rate, five-star *(Brit.),* front rank, front ranking, high-class, high-grade, in the first flight, in the front rank, of the first water, optimum, purler, supreme, tip-top, top-flight, top-hole *(Brit.),* top-notch, unbeatable, up to par, up to scratch, up to standard, up to the knocker, up to the mark, world-class; **better,** superior; **ideal,** perfect; **premium,** bijou, blue-chip, choice, deluxe, elect, elegant, exquisite, finished, gilt-edged, goodly, hand-picked, polished, prime, select; **matchless,** especial, exceptional, irreplaceable, outstanding, peerless, prize; **sound,** A-OK *(U.S.),* healthful, healthy, trim; **beneficial,** aidful, salutary; **hunky-dory,** all cush *(Obs.),* all right, all serene, all Sir Garnet, fine and dandy, hunky, jake, jakerloo, okay, right, satisfactory; **sublime,** divine, dreamy, heavenly, insane, out of this world, unreal; **class,** golden, plummy, silk department, sterling, vintage; **helluva,** beaut, bully, hell of a, rum *(Archaic);* **neat,** cool, nifty; **benevolent; virtuous**

GOODBYE *interj* adieu, adios, aloha, arrivederci, au revoir, auf Wiedersehen, bon voyage, bonsoir, bye-bye, ciao, farewell, godspeed, good afternoon, good day, good evening, good morning, good night, hooroo, night-night, see you later, so

goodbye

long, ta-ta, vale, yickadee *(N.T.)*; **all aboard**, all ashore that's going ashore

GOOD FORTUNE *n* devil's own luck *(Brit.)*, happiness, luck, propitiousness, prosperity, rosiness, speed *(Archaic)*; **bonanza**, blessing, godsend, piece of good luck, snap, stroke of fortune, treasure-trove; **prosperousness**, blessedness, boom times, estate, flowering, fortunateness, luckiness, run of luck, serendipity, thriving, winning streak; **well-being**, weal *(Archaic)*, wealth *(Archaic)*, welfare; **break**, lucky streak

GOODNESS *n* choiceness, desirability, fineness, niceness; **excellence**, exceptionalness, exquisiteness, fabulousness, ideality, idealness, marvellousness, peerlessness, perfection, rareness, rarity, splendidness, supremeness, uncommonness, wonderfulness; **refinement**, class, elegance, finesse, finish, polish, selectness; **quality**, merit, preciousness, value, worth; **wholesomeness**, healthiness

GOOD PERSON *n* a bit of all right, a good sort, angel, beaut bloke, beaut sheila, bobby-dazzler, brick, card, cherub, Christian, cynosure of all eyes, demigod, dove, Galahad, goddess, good egg, good Joe *(U.S.)*, goodie, goody-goody, honey, impeccable, jewel, lion, model, one in a thousand, one of the best, perfection, rattler, ripsnorter, ruby-dazzler, saint, squarehead *(Prison)*, the pick of the bunch, the tops; **salt of the earth**, a good sport, ocker, one of nature's gentlemen, rough diamond, sportsman; **benefactor**, good and faithful servant, good master, just man, just woman, kind master, philanthropist, pillar of society, Robin Hood, worthy citizen; **hero**, amazon, champion, daredevil, great, hearty, heroine, one of the elite

GOODS *n* artefact, article, cargo, commodity, freight, merchandise, staple, stock, stock-in-trade, wares

GOOD TASTE *n* breeding, civilisation, civility *(Archaic)*, class, cultivation, culture, finesse, finish, genteelness, gentility, gentleness, politeness, refinement, seemliness, sensitivity; **taste**, appreciation, fancy, gusto, likes, liking, palate, penchant; **elegance**, bon ton, chic, choiceness, dapperness, dressiness, finery *(Rare)*, manners, poshness, savoir-faire, smartness, sophistication, style, tastefulness, tone, urbaneness, urbanity; **daintiness**, delicateness, fineness, rarefaction; **artistry**, virtuosity; **aesthetics**, delicacy, delicateness, discrimination, judgment, sensibility

GOOD THING *n* a bit of all right, beaut, beauty, bobby-dazzler, bottler, corker, cracker, crackerjack, daisy, dandy, dilly, dinkum, dinky, dinnyhayser, front-ranker, gas, gasser, honey, hot stuff, humdinger, just what the doctor ordered, knockout, miracle, peach, plum, purler, rube *(N.Z.)*, ruby-dazzler, sensation, sollicker, swan, topper, treasure, trimmer; **showpiece**, aristocrat, beauty, choice, flower, gem, jewel, masterpiece, masterwork, pearl, pink, pride, Rolls Royce; **beau ideal**, idea, ideal; **bijou**, titbit; **better**, superior; **the best**, acme, cap, climax, culmination, high point, high spot, ne plus ultra, the full two bob, the most, the mostest, tiptop, ultimate; **one in a million**, one in a thousand, the ant's pants, the bee's knees, the cat's pyjamas, the cat's

good thing   238   **gratefulness**

whiskers, the glassy, the greatest, the icing on the cake, the oil *(N.Z.)*

GORGE *v* be like vultures, bog in, cram, eat fit to bust, eat like a horse, gluttonise, gormandise, guts, have hollow legs, like one's food, make a pig of oneself, overeat, raven *(Obs.)*, stodge, stuff; **devour**, bolt, gobble, gulp, guzzle, ingurgitate, weigh into, wolf. *See also* EAT

GO SLOWLY *v* amble, coast, crawl, drag, inch, plod, run like a hairy goat, stalk, trundle; **lag**, compound *(Horseracing)*, fall behind, run dead *(Horseracing)*, straggle, trail; **tarry**, be slow off the mark, dally, dawdle, delay, demur *(Obs.)*, hang fire, hesitate, linger, loiter, lounge about, potter, saunter, stall for time, stay, stroll, take one's time; **work to rule**, drag the chain

GOSSIP *n* gossipmonger, newsmonger, quidnunc, scandalmonger, whisperer; **tale-bearer**, dobber, informer, sneak, taleteller, tattler, tattletale, telltale, tittle-tattle, tittle-tattler

GRADATION *n* shading; **step**, degree, notch, peg, pitch, point, remove, stage, strain *(Rare)*; **graduation**, calibration, scale; **measurement system**, Celsius scale, centimetre-gram-second system, Fahrenheit scale, foot-pound-second system, imperial system, International System of Units, metric system; **unit**, denomination, fundamental unit, indication, measure, size

GRADATIONAL *adj* calibrated, first-degree, graduated, hierarchical, second-degree, third-degree; **gradual**, fading, shading

GRADE *n* class, Dan, Kyu, level, order, rank, year; **level**, plane; **ranking**, footing, rate, standing, station, status; **shade**, nuance, shadow

GRADUALLY *adv* a little at a time, bit by bit, by degrees, inch by inch, little by little, step by step; **to some degree**, a bit, in some measure, somewhat, to some extent

GRADUATE *v* calibrate, divide, measure, scale; **grade**, class, rank, rate; **shade**, fade, melt into

GRAMMATICAL ERROR *n* abusage, barbarism, error, illiteracy *(Rare)*, impropriety, lapsus linguae, malapropism, misusage, mixed metaphor, slip, solecism, unfelicity; **faulty language**, anacoluthia, anacoluthon, bad grammar, lack of concord, mispunctuation, misspelling, slipslop

GRASPINGLY *adv* clingingly, tenaciously

GRASSLAND *n* down, heath, meadow, moor, pampas, prairie, savanna, steppe, tundra

GRATEFUL *adj* appreciative, appreciatory, thankful; **thankyou**, recognitive, recognitory; **obliged**, beholden, indebted, much obliged; **thankworthy**

GRATEFULLY *adv* appreciatively, appreciatorily, thankfully

GRATEFULNESS *n* appreciation, appreciativeness, gratitude, hearty thanks, thankfulness, thanks; **thanksgiving**, celebration, eucharist, grace, grace before meals, praises; **acknowledgement**, bow, bread-and-butter letter, credit, credit line, recognition, sense of obligation, thankyou, tribute, vote of thanks; **requital**, recognition of one's services, return, return

GRAVE *n* Davy Jones's locker, resting place; **tomb**, burial chamber, catacomb, confession *(Eccles.)*, crypt, cubiculum, dolmen, hypogeum, mastaba *(Egyptian Architecture)*, mausoleum, monument *(Obs.)*, sepulchre, sepulture *(Archaic)*, vault; **burial mound**, barrow, kurgan, tumulus; **headstone**, cairn, gravestone, ledger, stele, stone, tombstone; **cenotaph**, memorial, war memorial. *See also* CEMETERY

GRAVECLOTHES *n* cerements, winding sheet; **mourning clothes**, half-mourning, mourning, sables, weeds

GRAVIMETRY *n* avoirdupois weight, troy weight; **weight**, burden, charge, cumbrance, dead weight, encumbrance, lift, load, log, millstone, overburden, overcharge, overload, overweight, surcharge; **ballast**, burden, cargo, cumber, loading; **tare**, balance, bias, counterpoise, counterweight, makeweight, overbalance; **pack**, pikau *(N.Z.)*, shiralee, swag, tote; **paperweight**, barbell, dumbbell, plummet, sandbag, sinker; **weigh-in**

GREAT *adj* appreciable, big, biggish, considerable, extended, full-scale, good, good-sized, goodly, hearty, high, horse, king-size, large, large-scale, largish, mickle *(Scot.)*, mighty, much, muckle *(Scot.)*, oldman, respectable, sensible, sizeable, spacious, substantial, tidy; **abundant**, ample, considerable, copious, goodly, handsome, luxuriant, plenteous, plentiful, pretty, princely, rich, round, square, substantial, tall, tidy

favour, reward, thankyou present, tip, token of one's gratitude

GREATLY *adv* appreciably, considerably, in a big way, mightily, on a large scale, widely; **mostly**, for the most part, generally, in the main, largely, mainly, maximally, most, principally, substantially, to a degree; **much**, a lot, far, far and away, lots; **galore**, as all get-out, like anything, like buggery, like hell, like the devil, till it hurts, to the skies; **abundantly**, amply, by a long chalk, by far, by half, considerably, copiously, hand over fist, handsomely, in bulk, largely, luxuriantly, no end, opulently, richly, substantially, substantively, thickly, widely; **and how**, a half, and then some; **absolutely**, downright, exceedingly, extremely, far and away, fully, hollow, ineffably, insuperably, invincibly, monumentally, out and away, out and out, overwhelmingly, perfectly, plain, plumb, quite, spaciously, stark, supremely, surpassing *(Obs. Poetic)*, surpassingly, toweringly, unutterably, utterly; **awesomely**, devastatingly, extra-specially, fabulously, fantastically, frighteningly, frightfully, horribly, impossibly, phenomenally, portentously, prodigiously, shockingly, stupendously; **grandiosely**, big, grandly, regally; **massively**, bulkily, solidly

GREATNESS *n* ampleness, amplitude, bigness, bulk, bulkiness, enormity, enormousness, fullness, giganticness, hugeness, immenseness, immensity, largeness, magnitude, massiness, massiveness, mightiness, spaciousness, substantiality, tremendousness, vastitude, vastness; **intensity**, blaze, deep, deepness, denseness, depth, fierceness, grievousness, heat, in-

greatness   **grieve**

tenseness, intension, keenness, peak, perfervidity, perfervidness, perfervour, poignancy, severeness, severity, sharpness, violence, vividness; **stupendousness**, awesomeness, awfulness, fabulousness, fearfulness, frightfulness, ineffability, portentousness, prodigiousness, terribleness; **grandeur**, consequence, grandiosity, grandness, lordliness, majesty, might, nobility, nobleness, princeliness

GREED n avarice, avidity, concupiscence, cupidity, lust, rapacity; **greediness**, esurience, esuriency, gluttonousness, gluttony, hoggishness, overeating, piggery, piggishness, swinishness; **voracity**, insatiability, ravening *(Obs.)*, ravenousness, voraciousness, wolfishness; **epicureanism**, gourmandise. See also OVERINDULGENCE

GREEDY adj devouring, insatiable, rapacious, ravening *(Obs.)*, ravenous, voracious; **gluttonous**, gutsy, hoggish, hoglike, open-mouthed, piggish, swinish; **esurient**, epicurean, gastronomic, lickerish *(Archaic)*. See also OVERINDULGENT

GREEN n emerald, grass-green, jade green, leek green, vert *(Heraldry)*; **sea green**, aqua, aquamarine, beryl, Nile green, turquoise; **yellow-green**, chartreuse, lime-green, pea green, pistachio; **apple green**, almond green, celadon; **khaki**, bottle green, jungle green, olive, olive green; **grey-green**, mignonette, reseda, sage-green

GREEN adj glaucous, greenish, prasine, virescent, viridescent; **verdant**, grassy, green, leafy, verdurous

GREENNESS n verdancy, verdure, verdurousness, virescence, viridescence, viridity; **greenery**, verdure; **verdigris**; **green pigment**, bice, chlorophyll, chrome green, green verditer, Paris green, terre-verte, verditer, viridian

GREETING n beck *(Scot.)*, bow, cheerio call, hongi *(N.Z.)*, salaam, salutation, the glad hand; **regards**, compliment, remembrances; **introduction**, debut, knockdown, presentation, presentment

GREGARIOUSLY adv chummily, companionably, convivially, cordially, expansively, heartily, hospitably, sociably, socially, with open arms

GREY n ash-grey, iron-grey; **charcoal-grey**, gunmetal, slate; **dove colour**; **drab**, beige, dun, fuscous, isabel, mouse-dun, putty, stone, taupe; **merle**; **pearl**, off-white, oyster white, pearl blue, pearl grey; **French grey**, sage-green; **grey-blue**, Copenhagen blue, steel blue, steel grey; **grizzle**; **grisaille**; **greyness**, hoariness, leadenness, lividness; **silver**, argent, frostiness, silveriness

GREY adj ash-grey, ashen, ashy, cinereous, greyish, grizzly; **blue-grey**, livid, slaty; **dove-coloured**, columbine; **dapple-grey**, merle; **leaden**, dusty, frosty, leady; **smoky**, fuliginous; **drab**, beige, dun, fulvous, isabel, putty; **pearl-grey**, griseous, off-white, pearl, pearly; **sage-green**; **silver**, argent, iron, penumbral, silvern *(Archaic)*, silvery, steel

GREY-HAIRED adj canescent, grey, grey-headed, greying, grizzled, grizzly, hoar *(Archaic)*, hoary, pepper-and-salt, silver-haired, white-haired

GRIEVE v anguish, bleed for, deplore, grieve over, lament, pine *(Archaic)*, regret; **bemoan**, bewail, elegise, threnodise, weep over; **cry**, bawl, blub, blubber, boohoo, cry one's heart out, pipe one's eye, shed tears, snivel, snuffle, sob, tune one's pipes, weep; **moan**, croon *(Scot. Irish)*, groan, keen, sigh, ululate, wail; **whine**, howl, whimper; **mourn**, give someone a good send-off, hold a wake for, tangi *(N.Z.)*; **wear black**, don widows's weeds, go into mourning, wear sackcloth and ashes; **wring one's hands**, beat one's breast, rend one's garments; **half-mast the flag**

GRIEVER *n* lamenter, mourner, sorrower; **weeper**, bawler, blubberer, cry-baby, sniveller, snuffler, wailer; **keener**, crooner *(Scot. Irish)*, monodist, threnodist; **groaner**, sigher; **pietà**

GRIEVING *n* broken heart, dole *(Archaic)*, dolour, grief, lamentation, misery, moan *(Archaic)*, mournfulness, sadness, sorrow, woe; **lament**, cri de coeur, plaint *(Archaic)*, elegy, coronach, dead march, dirge, epicedium, jeremiad, monody, taps *(U.S. Mil.)*, threnody; **wake**, exequies, tangi *(N.Z.)*, vigil; **mourning**, armband, black, half-mourning, hatband, sables, weeds. *See also* CRY

GRIEVING *adj* cut up, desolate, grief-stricken, heartbroken, lamenting, mourning, sorrowful, sorrowing; **mournful**, dolorous, lugubrious, plaintive, woebegone, woeful; **crying**, blubbering, snivelly, sobbing, tearful, watery, weeping; **groaning**, ululant, wailful, wailsome; **elegiac**, epicedial, epicedian, exequial, threnodial, threnodic

GROIN *n* brush, crotch, mons pubis, mons veneris, mount of Venus, muff, pubes, pubic hair; **genitals**, genitalia, meat, nasties *(Brit.)*, perineum, private parts, privates, privy parts, pudenda; **female genitalia**, cervix, cherry, clitoris, Fallopian tubes, hymen, labia, maidenhead, nympha, ovary, tubes, uterus, womb, yoni; **vulva**, box, crack, cunt, date, dot, fanny, fork, furburger, gash, gear, growl, hole, honey pot, michael, mick, pudendum, pussy, quim, slit, snatch, tail, twat, vagina; **male genitalia**, cod, epididymis, foreskin, glans, linga, manhood, prepuce, prostate gland, scrotum, sporting equipment, vas deferens; **testicles**, aggots, balls, bollocks, cobblers, fun bags, gonads, goolies, knackers, Niagara falls, nuts, spermaries, stones *(Obs.)*, testes; **penis**, cock, dick, dickie, ding, dong, donger, dragon, fang, ferret, John, John Thomas, knob, mutton, old boy, old fellow, old man, one-eyed trouser snake, Percy, pizzle, prick, roger, short arm, tassel, the virile member, tonk, tool, wick, willie; **erection**, beef bayonet, beef bugle, fat, hard on, horn, phallus, pork sword, rod, shaft, stiff, stiffy, the bishop

GROVEL *v* be at another's beck and call, bend before, bow and scrape, bow to, chum up to, eat crow *(U.S.)*, eat humble pie, eat one's words, eat out of someone's hand, fawn, get gravel rash, kneel to, kowtow to, lick the dust, piss in someone's pocket, pocket one's pride, prostrate oneself, slaver, smarm, stoop *(Rare)*, toady, truckle

GROW *v* bloom, develop, rise, unfold; **accumulate**, accrete, accrue; **branch**, branch out, bush, extend, spread; **distend**, aggrandise, amplify, balloon, enlarge, expand, hypertrophy; **outgrow**, outreach; **overgrow**, dispread *(Archaic)*, grow like Topsy *(Colloq.)*, mushroom, outspread, out-

GROW stretch, overreach, overrun, overspread, run wild; **advance**, progress, snowball. See also FLOWER

GROWING adj anabolic, crescent, developing, going, proliferous, regenerative, rising; **accumulative**, accretive, cumulative; **developmental**, evolutional, evolutionary; **excrescent**, fungoid, gallic, intumescent, scirrhoid, scirrhous; **distensible**, distensile, enlargeable; **flourishing**, fulminant, hypertrophic, luxuriant, overgrown, rank, sturdy, wanton *(Poetic)*; **germinant**, germinative

GROWTH n anabolism, concrescence, development, evolution, evolvement, increase, intergrowth, upgrowth; **accumulation**, accretion, accrual, accruement, increment; **distension**, aggrandisement, amplification, enlargement, expansion, spread; **proliferation**, reproduction; **excrescence**, callus, cancer, desmoid, excrescency, fungus *(Pathol.)*, fusee, gall, growth, neoplasm, neurofibroma, neuroma, outgrowth, scirrhus, tumour; **intumescence**, ingrowth; **advance**, outreach, outspread, progress; **rebirth**, regeneration, revegetation; **overgrowth**, hypertrophy, overdevelopment; **ripeness**, vigour; **teething troubles**, growing pains

GUIDANCE n direction, guideline, recommendation, suasion; **consultation**, reference, referral; **advice**, briefing, counsel, counsel of perfection, words of wisdom; **hint**, piece of advice, pointer, points, suggestion, tip, word of advice; **exhortation**, charge, injunction, instruction, moralising; **criticism**, constructive criticism, correction, corrective; **admonition**, admonishment, earful, expostulation, protestation, warning

GUIDE n assessor, consulter, director, exhorter, mentor; **adviser**, advocate, advocator, amicus curiae, consigliore, consultant, councillor, counsellor; **authority**, advisory body, brains trust, oracle, sage; **careers adviser**, extension worker *(N.Z.)*, family doctor, farm consultant *(Agric.)*, marriage guidance counsellor; **confidant**, confessor, father confessor; **admoniser**, corrector, expostulator, monitor, warner; **back-seat driver**, kibitzer *(U.S.)*

GUIDE v advise, advocate, commend, counsel, give advice, kibitz *(U.S.)*, prescribe, recommend; **suggest**, move, propose, submit; **exhort**, charge, urge; **admonish**, advise against, expostulate, put someone straight, remonstrate, set someone straight, warn

GUIDE adj advisory, assessorial, consultative, consulting, deliberative; **exhortative**, hortative, recommendatory, suasive, suasory; **admonitory**, correctional, corrective, directive, expostulatory, moralising, warning

GUILT n blood guilt, blood-guiltiness, complicity, fault, guilt by association, guiltiness; **blameworthiness**, censurableness, criminality, damnableness, delinquency; **shame**, ashamedness, contriteness, contrition, embarrassment, peccavi, qualms

GUILTILY adv damningly, in flagrante delicto, red-handed; **ashamedly**, contritely, repentantly

GUILTY adj at fault, blood-guilty, bloodstained, double-dyed, faulty *(Obs.)*, in fault, in the wrong, nocent, to blame; **damned**, impure, unaneled;

GUITAR n axe, balalaika, banjo, banjolele, bass guitar, chitarra, cittern, easy rider *(U.S.)*, electric guitar, Hawaiian guitar, lead guitar, pedal steel guitar, resonator guitar, rhythm guitar, samisen, slide guitar, steel guitar, twelve-string guitar, ukulele; **lute**, archlute, bandore, biwa, bouzouki, chitarrone, domra, mandolin, ramkie, sitar, tamboura, theorbo, ud, vina; **harp**, cithara, crowd, crwth, Irish harp, kithara, lyre, rote, sackbut, sambuca; **zither**, autoharp, cither, cittern, dulcimer *(U.S.)*, koto, psaltery; **dulcimer**, cembalo, cimbalom, cymbalo, santir; **plectrum**, fingerpick, pick; **capo**, bottleneck, slide; **aeolian harp**, aeolian lyre, wind chimes, wind harp

GUN n automatic, equaliser *(Colloq.)*, firearm, firelock, firer, flintlock, gat, ironmongery, joint, matchlock, muzzle-loader, over-under, piece, pump action, rapid-firer, repeater, roscoe, semiautomatic, shooter, shooting iron, side-arms, small arms, smoothbore; **pistol**, automatic pistol, bulldog, Colt, derringer, hand gun, heater *(U.S. Colloq.)*, horse pistol, iron *(Brit. Colloq.)*, revolver, rod, six-shooter; **rifle**, armalite, automatic rifle, breech-loader, carabin, carbine, chassepot, elephant gun, Enfield, Mauser, Winchester rifle; **shotgun**, chokebore, double *(Colloq.)*, fowling-piece, petronel, pump gun, sawn-off shotgun, side by side *(Colloq.)*; **machine-gun**, Bofors gun, Bren gun, Gatling gun, Lewis gun, Owen gun, pompom, pounder, sten gun, Thomson machine gun, Tommy gun *(Colloq.)*; **cannon**, basilisk, Big Bertha, bombard, chase-gun, chaser, culverin, falconet, field-gun, field-piece, heavy metal, howitzer, mortar, sternchaser, trench mortar; **musket**, arquebus, blunderbuss, fusil, hackbut, harquebus; **blowgun**, blowpipe; **airgun**, air-rifle, BB gun, daisy gun, peashooter; **ray gun**; **spear gun**; **swivel gun**; **toy gun**, pop gun, water-pistol

GUNFIRE n firepower, flak; **gunshot**, penetration, snapshot; **bombardment**, barrage, blitz, broadside, burst, dispersion, fusillade, round, salvo, whip

GUN PART n barrel, bolt, breech, breechblock, butt, chamber, chase, chassis, chokebore, cock, cylinder, ejector, foresight, guncarriage, gunflint, gunstock, hair-trigger, half-cock, hammer, muzzle, muzzle brake, pull-through, ramrod, rib, safety catch, sear, sight, stock, touch-hole, trail, trigger, tumbler; **gunlock**, firelock, flintlock, matchlock, percussion lock, wheel-lock; **fuse**, boresafe fuse, proximity fuse

Hh

HABITATION *n* domicile, dwelling, residence; **inhabitancy,** abidance, cohabitation, inhabitation; **quartering,** baching, boarding, hostelling; **lodgment,** encampment, establishment, installation, location; **occupancy,** cotenancy, occupation, possession, tenancy

HABITUATE *v* acclimatise, accustom, condition, familiarise, harden, inure, naturalise, season

HABITUATION *n* acclimatisation, conditioning, hardening, inurement, naturalisation, seasoning, training

HAIL *interj* all hail, good on you, here's to, long life to, long live, viva

HAIR *n* flue, fluff, fuzz, lanugo, pile, shag; **filament,** penicil, whisker, wire; **bristle,** arista, chaeta, gare, seta, setula, vibrissa, villus; **hair of the head,** bush, combings, dreadlocks, frizz, head, locks, mane, mat, mop, thatch, tousle *(Rare)*; **grizzle,** snow; **curl,** kiss-curl, lock, pin-curl, quiff, ringlet, strand, tag, tress *(Archaic)*; **elflock,** cowlick, feather, forelock, foretop *(Obs.)*, lovelock, topknot, tourbillion, widow's peak; **bang,** bob, braid, bun, bunches, chignon, cue, ducktail, fringe, horse tail, lovelock, pigtail, plait, plat, pompadour, ponytail, puff, queue, tail, topknot, tress *(Archaic)*; **eyebrow,** cilia, eyelash, falsies; **pubes,** short and curlies, short hairs; **blonde,** ash-blond, coppernob, coppertop, fair head, goldilocks, lemonhead, peroxide blonde, platinum blonde, redhead, strawberry blonde, towhead; **brunette;** **whitebeard,** greybeard; **hairy-legs; fungus face; croppy,** curlyhead, long-hair

HAIRDRESSER *n* barber, coiffeur, comber, hairstylist, Sydney Harbour, wigmaker; **hairdresser's salon,** barber shop, beauty shop, wiggery

HAIRDRESSING *n* setting; **haircut,** afro, bob, clip *(Wool)*, crew cut, crop, cut, Eton crop, frizz, nana, pageboy, razor cut, shingle, trim; **hairstyle,** coiffure, hairdo, headdress *(Obs.)*, pouf, tire *(Archaic)*, tonsure; **wave,** blow-wave, cold wave, finger-wave, perm, permanent wave, root perm, water-wave

HAIRINESS *n* curliness, fuzziness, hirsuteness, hispidity, stubbiness; **fluffiness,** downiness, pilosity, pubescence, tomentum; **fleeciness,** furriness; **penicillation,** fimbriation, villosity

HAIRLIKE *adj* capillaceous, capillary, pileous, piliform, pilous; **bristlelike,** barbellate, penicillate, setaceous, setiform

HAIRPIECE *n* crepe hair, fall, postiche, switch, toupee; **wig,** bobwig, buzzwig, periwig, peruke, spencer, transformation *(Obs.)*

HAIRY *adj* bristly, brushy, chaetophorous, comate, comose, crinite, furred, furry, hirsute, hispid, maned, pileous, piliferous, pilose, rough, setaceous, setigerous, setose, setulose, shaggy, stubby, ulotrichous, whiskery, wire-haired; **fleecy,** downy, fluey, fluffy, fuzzy, lanuginose, tomentose; **flocculent,** bunchy, floccose, flocky, tufted, tufty; **arachnoid,** fimbrial, fimbriate, fimbriatte, pubescent, silky, villiform, villous; **long-haired,** be-

hairy   245   **happily**

wigged, ringleted, shockheaded, tressed, wigged; **ash-blond,** blonde, brunette, carroty, fair-haired, peroxide blonde, red-headed, strawberry blonde, towheaded; **bearded,** barbate, barbed, black-browed, sidewhiskered, whiskered; **grey,** grizzled, grizzly, hoary, white-haired, whiteheaded

HALF *n* equal part, fifty per cent, moiety; **halving,** bipartition, bisection, dichotomisation, dimidiation, division

HALL *n* antechamber, anteroom, corridor, foyer, galilee, hallway, lobby, loggia, narthex, parvis, porch *(U.S.),* propylaeum, vestibule; **auditorium,** ballroom, chamber; concert-hall, council chamber, dance hall, divan, durbar, hall, lecture theatre, reception room, rotunda, saloon, stateroom, theatre, theatrette

HALLUCINOGEN *n* angel dust, DET, dimethyltryptamine, DMT, PCP, phencyclidine, STP; **magic mushroom,** gold cap, gold top, psylocibin; **mescaline,** mesc, mescaline buttons, peyote; **LSD,** acid, lysergic acid, lysergic acid diethylamide, microdot, mike, ticket, trip. *See also* DRUG

HALVE *v* divide by two; **bisect,** cut in two, dichotomise, dimidiate, divide into halves, split in two; **go halves,** go fifty-fifty, share equally

HALVED *adj* bisected, cleft, cloven, divided, half; **in two parts,** bifid, bipartite, bisectional, dichotomous, dimerous, dimidiate

HANDLE *n* handgrip, handhold, helve, starting handle, winch, withe; **handlebars,** ape hangers; **haft,** grip, hilt, pistol-grip, snath, stock, whipstock

HANG *v* dangle, depend, pend, poise, swing; **overhang,** hang over, impend; **flow,** float, fly, stream; **hang down,** bag, blouse, droop, fall, flag, loll, lop, nod, sag, slouch; **drag,** draggle, sweep, trail; **suspend,** append, hang out, hang up, sling, string, string up

HANGER *n* billyhook, hook, peg, suspender

HANGING *n* impendence, impendency, pendency, pendulousness, pensileness, pensility, suspense, suspension, suspensiveness; **bagginess,** flabbiness, flaccidity, flaccidness, slouchiness; **hang,** dangle, drape, droop, fall, sag, set, slouch, sweep

HANGING *adj* dangling, dependent, overhung, pendent, pending, pendulous, pensile, poised, suspended, suspensive; **overhanging,** imminent, impendent, impending, projecting; **drooping,** cernuous, deflexed, epinastic, flagging, nodding, sagging; **baggy,** droopy, flabby, flaccid, flaggy, slouchy; **flowing,** floating, flying, streaming

HAPPILY *adv* beamingly, breezily, brightly, buoyantly, cheerfully, cheerily, chirpily, effervescently, giocoso *(Music),* gladly, gladsomely, gleefully, gleesomely, good-humouredly, good-naturedly, jocundly, jollily, joyfully, joyously, merrily, mirthfully, riantly, smilingly, spiritoso *(Music),* sunnily; **debonairly,** airily, blithely, blithesomely, exhilaratingly, gaily, jauntily, lightly, lightsomely, vivaciously; **frivolously,** flippantly, kittenishly, lightheartedly, light-mindedly; **genially,** convivially, heartily, jovially, mellowly, merrily, pleasantly; **hilarious-**

happily   246   **hard**

ly, boyishly, exuberantly, frolicsomely, playfully, sportively, tricksily

HAPPINESS *n* blithesomeness, cheer, cheerfulness, cheeriness, enlivenment, exhilaration, festiveness, festivity, gladness, gladsomeness, glee, gleefulness, gleesomeness, good cheer, good humour, good nature, good-humouredness, good-naturedness, jolliness, joy, lightsomeness, merriness, sunniness, sunny side, sunshine; **liveliness,** airiness, animal spirits, animation, boyishness, breeziness, brightness, debonairness, exuberance, frolicsomeness, gaiety, high spirits, hilariousness, hilarity, insouciance, jauntiness, jocundity, joie de vivre, jollity, merriment, mirth, playfulness, sparkle, sportfulness, sportiveness, sprightliness, vivacity; **joviality,** cordiality, geniality, genialness, goodwill, mellowness, pleasantness; **buoyancy,** alacrity, bounce, elasticity, resilience, uplift; **levity,** flippancy, flippantness, frivolousness, kittenishness, light-heartedness, light-mindedness, lightness, tricksiness

HAPPY *adj* beaming, blithe, blithesome, buoyant, carefree, careless *(Archaic),* cheerful, cheery, comfortable *(Obs.),* elate, elated, full of beans, gay, glad, gladsome, happy as a sandboy, happy as Larry, hilarious, insouciant, jocund, joyful, joyous, light, lightsome, mirthful, pleasant, riant, rident; **genial,** backslapping, boon, bully, convivial, cordial, forward, good-humoured, good-natured, jolly, jovial, mellow, merry, rollicking; **lively,** airy, boyish, breezy, bright, bright-eyed and bushytailed, carefree, chipper, chirpy, chirrupy, debonair, effervescent, exuberant, galliard *(Archaic),* giocoso *(Music),* jaunty, peart, perky, pert, radiant, spiritoso *(Music),* spiritous *(Obs.),* sprightly, vivacious; **hilarious,** bouncy, frolic, frolicsome, gamesome, tricksy, wanton *(Poetic);* **sanguine,** irrepressible, rose-coloured, sunny, sunshine, up-beat; **frivolous,** flip, flippant, giggly, kittenish, light, light-hearted, light-minded, lightsome, playful, sportive; **exhilarating,** exhilarant, exhilarative

HARANGUE *n* diatribe, exhortation, lecture, philippic, screed, sermon, tirade

HARANGUER *n* demagogue, phrasemonger, rabble-rouser, ranter, raver, rhetorician, soapbox orator, tub-thumper, word-monger

HARBOUR *n* anchorage, harbour of refuge, harbourage, haven, mole, moorage, moorings, roads, roadstead; **port,** free port, outport, seaport; **basin,** marina, tidal basin, wet dock; **quay,** dock, jetty, pier, slip *(U.S.),* staithe, wharf; **quayage,** wharfage. *See also* REFUGE; SHELTER

HARD *adj* adamant, adamantine, bricklike, concrete, concretionary, flinty, glass, glasslike, glassy, granitic, gritty, iron, ironbound, marble, marbly, pebbly, petrous, rocklike, rocky, semivitreous, steel, steely, stone, stonelike, stony, vitreous, vitriform, wooden, woody; **bony,** bonelike, chitinous, corneous, horny, osseous, ossiferous, osteoid, scaley, scleritic, sclerodermatous, scleroid, sclerosal, sclerotic, sclerous, testaceous; **rigid,** erect, erectile, indurate, inflexible, springless, starched, starchy, stark, stiff, stiff as a poker, taut, unbending, uncrushable, wiry; **tough,** chewie, chewy, leathery; **solid,** compacted, consistent *(Obs.),* dense, firm, imperviable, impervious, infusible, inpermeable, stout, stubborn, sturdy; **hardened,** high-speed *(Metall.),* ironbound, prestressed, sealed, strain-hardened, tempered, weather-beaten, weathered, weatherworn; **hardening,** calcifying, indurative, ossifying, petrifactive, sclerosed

HARD *adv* inflexibly, rigidly, starkly, stiff, tautly, tight, tightly, unbendingly, woodenly; **solidly,** sturdily; **stonily,** flintily; **glassily,** vitreously

HARDEN *v* fix, set, solidify, stiffen, tauten, toughen; **consolidate,** bind, compact, concrete, condense, firm; **petrify,** bake, calcify, callus, carburise, case-harden, chill *(Metall.),* cornify, crust, crystallise, encrust, fossilise, freeze, indurate, lignify, ossify, season, steel, temper, vitrify; **starch,** clear-starch

HARDENING *n* calcification, carburisation, concretion, crystallisation, cyanide hardening, ectostosis, encrustation, induration, lignification, nitriding, ossification, petrifaction, rigor mortis, sclerosis, set, setting, solidification, strain-hardening, vitrification, work-hardening; **hardener,** carburiser, clear-starcher, fixer, stiffener, toughener

HARDNESS *n* boniness, flintiness, horniness, infusibility, infusibleness, rockiness, solidity, solidness, steeliness, stoniness, stubbornness, temper, toughness, vitreosity, vitreousness, woodenness, woodiness; **rigidity,** erectility, firmness, inflexibility, inflexibleness, rigidness, rigour, stiffness, tautness; **Mohs scale,** Brinell number, Knoop hardness; **sclerometer,** indentor

HARM *n* bale *(Archaic),* damage, hurt, ill, injury, mayhem, offence *(Obs.),* trespass; **detriment,** a kick in the teeth, disadvantage, disservice, evil, mischief, prejudice; **ruin,** havoc, ravage, scathe *(Archaic),* waste; **bomb damage,** blast effect, cratering, ground-shock effect. *See also* DAMAGE; INJURY

HARMFUL *adj* cariogenic, corrosive, damaging, deleterious, detrimental, evil, hurtful, injurious, mischievous, mutilative, nocent, nocuous, noxious, pernicious, ruinous, scorching, wearing; **bruising,** contusive; **pestilent,** pestiferous, pestilential, putrefactive, saprogenic

HARMFULLY *adv* damagingly, hurtfully, injuriously, nocuously, noxiously, pestiferously, pestilently, ruinously; **detrimentally,** corrosively, deleteriously, for the worse

HARMFULNESS *n* corrosiveness, deleteriousness, hurtfulness, injuriousness, nocuousness, noxiousness

HARNESS *n* bellyband, bridle, britchen, halter, martingale, rein, surcingle, trace, tug. *See also* CORD

HARSHNESS *n* grimness, rigour, ruggedness, sternness; **strictness,** firmness, infrangibility, infrangibleness, iron hand, iron hand in a velvet glove, martinetism, rigidity, tight hand, tight rein, tyranny; **exactingness,** formalism, rigorism, rigorousness, severeness, severity, stringency, tender mercies *(Ironic);* **intransigence,** inclemency, iron, mercilessness, obduracy, obdurateness, relentlessness, unmercifulness, unrelentingness; **as-**

harshness   248   **have a job**

tringency, acerbity, asperity, sharpness; **puritanicalness**, asceticism, austereness, austerity, dourness, orthodoxy, puritanism

HARVEST *v* crop, cut, gather, glean, head, ingather, mow, pick, reap, scythe, strip; **thresh**, fan, flail, willow, winnow; **bale**, bind, ensile, rick, stook, windrow. *See also* FARM

HAT *n* barrel, bell-topper, billycock, boater, bowler, boxer, broadbrim, bun hat *(N.Z.)*, busby, cabbage-tree hat, cady, chapeau, chimneypot, cocked hat, deerstalker, derby *(U.S.)*, digger hat, Dolly Varden, fedora, hard-knocker, hard-hitter *(N.Z.)*, high hat, homburg, lemon squeezer *(N.Z. Colloq.)*, lid, mitre, mortarboard, opera hat, Panama, petasus, picture hat, pillbox, plug *(U.S. Colloq.)*, pork-pie hat, red hat *(Rom. Cath. Ch.)*, shovel hat, slouch hat, snap-brim, sombrero, stetson, stovepipe, taj *(Islam)*, tall hat, tarpaulin, ten-gallon hat, titfer, top hat, topper, toque, trencher, trilby, turban, wideawake; **sunhat**, sun-helmet, sunbonnet. *See also* HEADGEAR; CAP; HELMET

HATE *n* abhorrence, allergy, despite *(Archaic)*, disgust, dislike, hatred, loathing, malice, nausea, odium, rancour, revolt, revulsion; **detestation**, abomination, animosity, embitterment, execration, nauseation, repugnance; **enmity**, alienation, bad blood, bad feeling, bitterness, combativeness, estrangement, hostility, ill feeling, implacability; **misanthropy**, misandry, misogyny, race-hatred, racism, xenophobia; **the creeps**, the heebie-jeebies, the willies

HATE *v* abhor, abominate, be unable to abide, bear a grudge against, detest, execrate, hate someone's guts, have a hate on, loathe, recoil from, shrink from, view with horror, view with loathing; **be disgusted**, keck, revolt against, revolt from; **burn in effigy**, hang in effigy, stick pins into

HATEFUL *adj* abhorrent, abominable, accursed, contemptible, damnable, damned, despiteful *(Archaic)*, despiteous *(Archaic)*, detestable, disgustful *(Archaic)*, disgusting, dislikeable, execrable, hateable, hated, heinous, invidious, loathsome, nauseous, odious, rancorous, repugnant, revolting; **love-hate**, ambivalent

HATEFULLY *adv* abhorrently, abominably, accursedly, damnably, disgustfully, disgustingly, invidiously, nauseously, odiously, revoltingly

HATEFULNESS *n* abominableness, accursedness, contemptibility, damnableness, heinousness, invidiousness, loathsomeness, nauseousness, odiousness, rancorousness

HATER *n* abhorrer, detester, execrator, misanthrope, misogynist, racist, witch-hunter, xenophobe; **embitterer**, activist, stirrer; **enemy**, combatant

HATING *adj* antipathetic, bitter, combative, easily disgusted, embittered, execrative, hostile, inimical, misanthropic, misogynous, xenophobic; **spiteful**, execratory, malicious, viperish, viperous

HAUNT *v* bedevil, ghost, possess, spook; **communicate from the dead**, rap out

HAVE A JOB *v* carry a cut-lunch, fill, hold a chair, hold a portfolio, hold an office, hold down a job, join the workforce, occupy a position, take up a position; **earn a living**, bring home the bacon, keep body and soul together, keep the wolf from the door, make a living, produce, support oneself, turn an honest penny, turn out; **practise**, be in, carry on, concern oneself with, do, follow, have to do with, occupy oneself with, ply, profess, pursue, serve time as, spend one's time on, work as

HAVE DIFFICULTY *v* buy into trouble, catch a Tartar, fall foul, have one's work cut out; **make it difficult**, do it the hard way, flounder on, go through the mill, make heavy weather of, rub along, scratch along, wade through

HAVE GOOD TASTE *v* have a nose for, have an ear for, have an eye for

HAVE NO HOPE *v* be doomed to failure, have a fat chance, have Buckley's, have Buckley's chance, have no chance, have one's fate sealed

HAVE SEX *v* consummate a marriage, copulate, couple, fornicate, go all the way, have it away, have it off, have relations, make love, play tootsy, roll in the hay, root, swive *(Archaic)*, tread; **sleep with**, feature with, get off with, get with, have, hop into bed with, lay, lie with, make, pull, race, root, screw; **bed**, ball, bang, bull, do, do over, enjoy *(Archaic)*, get up someone, hump, knock off, mount, poke, possess, punch one through, roger, scrape, shag, slip it to, stuff, take; **get any**, crack it, get a bit, get into someone's pants, get one's end in, perform, score; **come across**; **commit adultery**, cuckold; **cohabit**, live together, live with, shack up with; **proposition**, crack onto, make a pass at, put the hard word on; **swing**, intrigue, sleep around; **captain; camp**, come out. *See also* EROTICISE

HAVE THE RIGHT *v* demand one's rights, stand on one's rights; **confer a right**, allow, entitle, ordain, sanction

HAVING FAULTY SIGHT *adj* ametropic, astigmatic, bespectacled, isometropic, miotic, mydriatic, nystagmic, one-eyed, presbyopic, sclerotitic; **near-sighted**, myopic, short-sighted; **long-sighted**, hypermetropic, hyperopic; **dim-sighted**, amblyopic, blear, bleary, bleary-eyed, dim, gravel-blind, purblind, sand-blind *(Archaic)*; **cross-eyed**, boss-eyed, cockeyed, squint, squint-eyed, strabismal, strabismic, strabismical, wall-eyed; **colour-blind**, dichromatic

HAZARDER *n* brinkman, dice man, equilibrist, perdu *(Obs.)*, shark bait *(Colloq.)*, soldier of fortune, stuntman; **brinkmanship**

HEAD *n* bean, belfry, block, chump, cobbra *(Obs.)*, crown, cruet, crumpet, dome, loaf, lolly, melon, nob, noddle, noggin, noodle, nut, onion, pate, sconce, scone, top; **skull**, brainpan, calvaria, cranium, inion, pan; **scalp**, poll, vertex; **brow**, forehead, temple; **brain**, encephalon, grey matter, little grey cells, white matter; **forebrain**, cerebral hemisphere, cerebrum, corpus callosum, cortex, end brain, hippocampus, infundibulum, prosencephalon, sensorium, telencephalon; **midbrain**, corpora quadrigemina, diencephalon, hypothalamus, interbrain, mesencephalon, optic thalamus, peduncle, thalamencephalon, thalamus; **afterbrain**, cerebellum, epencephalon, hindbrain, medulla oblongata, metencephalon, myelencephalon, pons; **convolution**, fissure, gyrus, lobe, sulcus, ventricle; **fontanelle**, foramen magnum; **craniology**, bumpology, cephalometry, craniometry, phrenology. *See also* FACE; EYE; NOSE; EAR; MOUTH

HEADBAND *n* bandeau, chaplet, fillet, snood, sweat-rag, sweatband; **veil**, fly-net, flyveil, loup, mask, veiling; **earflap**, earlap, earmuff, lug; **hairnet**, net. *See also* HEADGEAR; HAT

HEAD FOR *v* bear down on, carry on, course, fetch, fetch about, make for, strike out towards; **ply a course**, pursue a course, run a course, stand a course, track a course, wend one's way; **follow**, fly the beam, go by, ride the beam

HEADGEAR *n* millinery; **headdress**, commode, cornet, crown, pinner, pouf, puggaree, tiara, tire *(Archaic)*, turban; **hood**, amice, balaclava, calash, capuche, capuchin, cowl, wimple. *See also* HAT; CAP; HELMET; HEADBAND

HEADLAND *n* cape, foreland, head, naze, point, promontory; **isthmus**, landbridge, neck, strait *(Rare)*, tombolo; **peninsula**, tied island, tongue

HEAD OVER HEELS *adv* arse about face, arse over apex, arse over kettle, arse over tit, arse over turkey, arsyversy, backwards, base over apex, on one's head, topsy-turvily, topsyturvy, upside down; **inside out**, inversely, reversely; **contrariwise**, vice versa

HEALER *n* cupper, curer, leech *(Archaic)*, therapeutist, therapist, treater; **doctor**, apothecary *(Archaic)*, barefoot doctor, bio-technologist, clinician, doc, doctoress *(Rare)*, doctress *(Rare)*, family doctor, flying doctor, G.P., general practitioner, hakim, medic *(U.S.)*, medico, physician, quack, radio doctor; **specialist**, Collins Street doctor, consultant, ENT specialist, firm, Harley Street doctor, honorary, Macquarie Street doctor, neurologist, orthotist, paediatrician, podiatrist, prosthetist, urologist, visiting medical officer; **resident**, intern, registrar; **surgeon**, chirurgeon *(Archaic)*, orthopaedic surgeon, orthopod, plastic surgeon, sawbones; **diagnostician**, aetiologist, pathologist; **gynaecologist**, accoucheur, accoucheuse, midwife, obstetrician; **anaesthetist**; **pharmacologist**, chemist, druggist *(U.S.)*, pharmacist; **physiotherapist**, massager, massageuse, massagist, masseur, masseuse, physio; **paramedic**, ambo, ambulanceman, hospital orderly, medical orderly, nursing aide, orderly, stretcher-bearer, zambuck; **nurse**, amah, bush nurse, charge nurse, district nurse, dresser, health visitor *(Brit.)*, hospitaller, Karitane nurse, matron, Plunket nurse, registered nurse, sister, Tresillian nurse, wardsman; **naturopath**, acupuncturist, bonesetter, chiropractor, herbalist, homoeopathist, hygienist, iridologist, naprapath, osteopath; **faith-healer**; **mountebank**; **dentist**, dental technician, endodontist, exodontist, gumdigger, orthodontist, prosthodontist;

HEALING n folk medicine, internal medicine, medical science, medicine, physic *(Archaic)*, preventive medicine, therapeutics; **diagnostics**, aetiology, pathology, symptomatology; **acupuncture**, acupressure, chiropractic, herbalism, homeopathy, iridology, naprapathy, naturopathy, osteopathy, radionics, shiatsu; **allopathy**, dosology, homeopathy, iatrochemistry, pharmaceutics, pharmacology, pharmacy, posology; **psychosomatic medicine**, faith healing, mental healing; **surgery**, anaplasty, microsurgery, plastic surgery; **gynaecology**, gyniatrics, midwifery, obstetrics, tocology; **physiotherapy**, orthotics, physical therapy *(U.S.)*, physio, prosthetics; **dentistry**, bridgework, exodontia, odontology, orthodontics, periodontics, prosthodontics; **forensic medicine**, medical jurisprudence; **veterinary science**

HEALTH n bloom, clean bill of health, fitness, flourish *(Rare)*, good health, haleness, healthiness, normality, soundness, welfare, well-being; **robustness**, bonniness, buckishness, buxomness, freshness, go, heartiness, lustiness, red-bloodedness, strength, vigour; **condition**, constitution, form, tone, tonicity; **wholesomeness**, healthfulness, hygiene, salubriousness, salubrity, salutariness, sanitariness; **resilience**, recuperativeness

HEALTH CENTRE n health camp, health farm, hydro, quarantine, sanatorium, spa, watering-place

HEALTHILY adv buckishly, buxomly, lustily, robustly, soundly; **flourishingly**, freshly, glowingly, thrivingly; wholesomely, healthfully, hygienically, salubriously, salutarily, sanitarily

HEALTHY adj fine, fit as a fiddle, hale, hale and hearty, normal, resilient, right, right as rain, sane *(Obs.)*, sound, sound as a bell, well, whole; **flourishing**, blooming, bonny, bouncing, bright-eyed and bushytailed, buxom, fresh, full of beans, glowing, thriving; **fit**, buckish, fighting fit, hearty, in fine feather, in full feather, in high feather, in training, lusty, red-blooded, robust, strong, valid *(Archaic)*, vigorous; **tolerable**, all right, middling; **convalescent**, better, on the improve, on the mend, up and about

HEALTHY PERSON n ball of muscle, flourisher, thriver

HEAR v catch, get, hark, hearken; **listen**, be all ears, get a load of, hear out, list, prick up one's ears; **sound**, auscultate; **lip-read**, interpret; **give ear**, give audience, interview, lend an ear *(Archaic)*; **overhear**, bug, eavesdrop, listen in, tap

HEARER n audience, audient, audile, auditor, hearkener, listener; **eavesdropper**, earwig, overhearer; **audiologist**, acoustician

HEARING n audience, audition, listening; **audibility**, earshot; **perception**, diplacusis, hyperacusis, monophony, quadrophony, stereophony; **audiology**, acoustics, audiometry; **auscultation**, stethoscopy

HEARING adj attentive, audient, listening; **auditory**, acoustic, audile, audiovisual, aural, auricular; **audible**, heard; **audiological**, audiometric; **monophonic**, quadraphonic, stereophonic

HEARING AID *n* acoustic, audiphone, deaf-aid, dentiphone, ear trumpet, trumpet; **sign language**, dactylology, deaf-and-dumb language

HEARING DEVICE *n* headphone, headpiece, headset; **stethoscope**, audiometer, otoscope

HEART *n* pump, ticker; **aortic valve**, atrium, auricle, endocardium, epicardium, mitral valve, myocardium, pacemaker, pulmonary valve, semilunar valve, tricuspid valve, ventricle

HEART DISEASE *n* cardiac arrest, coronary occlusion, coronary thrombosis, heart attack, heart block, heart failure, myocardial infarction; **arrhythmia**, bradycardia, flutter heart, tachycardia, ventricular fibrillation; **hole in the heart**, blue baby; **thrombosis**, arteriosclerosis, atherosclerosis, phlebitis, phlebosclerosis, varicosis, varix; **embolus**, atheroma, embolism, plaque, thrombus; **hypertension**, hyperpiesia; **oedema**, dropsy, hypostasis, milk leg, white leg

HEAT *n* caloric, caloricity, enthalpy, phlogiston, solar energy, temp, temperament *(Obs.)*, temperature, total heat; **warmth**, lukewarmness, tepidity, tepidness, warmness; **intense heat**, ardour, burning heat, causticity, ferventness, fervidness, fervour, fever heat, perfervidity, perfervidness, perfervour, torridity, torridness; **red heat**, afterheat, overheat, steam heat, superheat, white heat; **incandescence**, calefaction, decalescence, recalescence

HEAT *v* heat through, heat up, hot up, incubate, irradiate, preheat, tepefy, warm, warm through, warm up; **thaw**, de-ice, defrost, melt, sweal; **overheat**, seethe *(Obs.)*, stew, superheat, sweat; **bake**, broil, chafe *(Obs.)*, cook, decrepitate, grill, roast; **parch**, burn, calcine, carbonise, torrefy; **heat-treat**, anneal, cupel, cure, recalesce, reverberate, vulcanise; **stove**, fire, kiln, kiln-dry, underburn *(Pottery)*; **cast**, found, smelt; **steam**, autoclave, sterilise; **boil**, decoct, kier, simmer

HEATED *adj* pyrogenous, roast, roasted; **gas-fired**, external-combustion, oil-fired, open-hearth

HEATER *n* incubator, superheater, warmer; **fireplace**, hearth, ingle; **room-heater**, convector, gas fire, heat reservoir, hypocaust, kerosene heater, open fire, radiator, space heater, storage heater, strip heater; **direct heating**, central heating, ducted heating, panel heating; **boiler**, califont *(N.Z.)*, chip heater, donkey, fire-tube boiler, geyser, hot-water service, immersion heater, water-back, water-tube boiler; **heat exchanger**, heat pipe, heat pump, heat sink, intercooler, recuperator; demister, de-icer; **water bath**, bain-marie, bath; **furnace**, afterburner, bosh, combustion chamber, combustion tube, converter, cupola, electric furnace, glass tank, muffle furnace, open-hearth furnace, regenerative furnace, regenerator, reverberatory furnace, solar furnace, tank furnace; **kiln**, brick-kiln, lehr, oast, oast-house, roaster; **brazier**, chauffer, cockle, devil; **blowtorch**, acetylene lamp, blowlamp, Bunsen burner, fantail, loggerhead, oxyacetylene burner, oxyhydrogen burner, pilot, pilot burner, pilot lamp, soldering iron; **sunglass**, argon laserphotocoagulator, burning-glass

HEATING *n* calefaction, incubation, insulation, tepefaction, thaw, warming; **calescence**, decalescence, incalescence; **boiling**, cooking, decoction, sterilisation; **incubation**, aluminothermy, eddy current heating, greenhouse effect, induction heating, open-hearth process, radiofrequency heating, reverberation; **heat therapy**, fomentation, insolation; **pyrolysis**, cupellation, destructive distillation, dry distillation, thermal cracking, torrefaction; **case-hardening**, cyanide hardening, vulcanisation; **steam treating**, crabbing; **sunbaking**, insolation, sunbathing

HEATING *adj* calefacient, calefactory, inflammatory, pyretic, pyrogenic, sudatory, warming; **incubatory**, incubational, slow; **burning**, calcinatory, caustic, pyrolytic; **calescent**, incalescent, recalescent

HEAT TRANSFER *n* advection, conduction, convection, radiation; **thermogenesis**, thermaesthesia, thermanaesthesia, thermolysis; **thermotropism**, thermotaxis, xerophily

HEAVEN *n* Canaan, paradise; **Elysium**, Asgard, Avalon, Elysian fields, Elysian plains, empyrean, Happy Hunting Grounds, Hesperides, Islands of the Blessed, Olympus, Valhalla; **Zion**, kingdom come, New Jerusalem, Pearly Gates, the sky *(Obs.)*; **heavenliness**, bliss, divineness, glory. *See also* AFTERWORLD

HEAVENLY *adj* blissful, celestial, divine, Elysian, empyreal, empyrean, paradisiacal, supernal, superterrestrial; **ultramundane**, otherworldly

HEAVENLY BODY *n* ball, celestial body, globe, luminary, moon, orb *(Poetic)*, planet, planetoid, sphere; **the earth**, lower world, terrene, the globe, world; **minor planet**, asteroid, planetoid; **planets**, Earth, Jupiter, Mars, Mercury, Neptune, Pluto, Saturn, Uranus, Venus; **asteroids**, Adonis, Apollo, Eros, Hermes, Icarus. *See also* STAR; SUN; MOON; METEOR

HEAVILY *adv* heavy, leadenly, lumberingly, ponderously, stodgily; **weightily**, heftily, solidly; **burdensomely**, cumbersomely, cumbrously, overwhelmingly

HEAVINESS *n* avoirdupois, displacement, mass, poundage, solidity, solidness, tare, weight, weightiness; **cumbrousness**, burdensomeness, cumbersomeness, leadenness, ponderability, ponderosity, ponderousness, preponderance, preponderation; **heftiness**, beef, beefiness, heft *(Obs.)*, lumpiness, stodginess

HEAVY *adj* heavier-than-air, leaden, leady, massive, ponderable, ponderous, preponderant, preponderating, stodgy, weighty; **hefty**, beefy, elephantine, hulking, lumbering, lumpy, overweight, solid; **burdensome**, cumbersome, cumbrous, oppressive, overburdensome; **heavy-laden**, burdened, loaded; **counterweighted**, equiponderant

HEAVY DRINKER *n* alcoholic, alkie, bacchanal, bacchant, bacchante, bar fly, beer swiper, bibber, booze artist, booze hound, boozer, boozician, boozington, cheap drunk, compotator, dipso, dipsomaniac, drinking school, drunk, drunkard, grog artist, guzzle-guts, guzzler, hard case, hard drinker, hophead, imbiber, indulger, inebriate, Jimmy Woodser, juice-freak, lolly legs, lush, lushington, metho, pissfreak, pisspot, plonko, pot walloper, shicker, soak, sot, souse, stiff, swigger, taverner *(Brit. Obs.)*, tippler, toper, tosspot, two-pot screamer, winebibber, winedot, wineskin, wino

HEIGHT *n* dizzy height; **loftiness,** domination, eminence, grandness, hilliness, sublimity *(Poetic)*; **steepness,** precipitousness; **altitude,** almucantar, elevation; **stature,** hand *(Horses)*, tallness; **rise,** loft, pitch.
See also APEX; MOUNTAIN; TOWER

HELL *n* Gehenna, hellfire, inferno, Pandemonium, purgatory, sheol, Tartarus; **damnation,** perdition, tarnation; **abyss,** pit, the bottomless pit. *See also* AFTERWORLD

HELLO *interj* aloha, ave, bonjour, g'day, good afternoon, good day, good evening, good morning, greetings, haeremai *(N.Z.)*, heil, hi, how ya goin' (mate), how're the bots biting *(N.Z.)*, how're you going, how's things, how's tricks, how-de-do, how-do-you-do, howdy, tenakoe *(N.Z.)*, yickadee *(N.T.)*; **bon appétit,** all the best, cheers, chin-chin, good health, skol, to your health; **goodbye,** bon voyage, cheerio, ciao

HELMET *n* bash hat, basinet, bearskin, bump cap, burgonet, busby, casque, crash hat, crash-helmet, hard hat, headpiece, helm *(Archaic)*, morion, pith helmet, safety helmet, sallet, skidlid, tin hat, topee

HELP *n* aid, assistance; **backing,** advocacy, boost, championship, encouragement, promotion; **patronage,** auspices, favour, recourse, sponsorship; **support,** aliment, alimentation, fosterage, nurture, protection, sustainment, sustenance, sustention; **comfort,** charity, cheer, favourableness, moral support; **relief,** deliverance, succour, visitation; **service,** good turn, yeoman service; **altruism,** almsgiving, benefaction, beneficence, mercy, philanthropy, subvention, voluntaryism; **solicitude,** attendance, attention, ministration, ministry; **facilitation,** accommodation; **helpfulness,** cooperativeness, obligingness, preferential treatment, responsiveness; **favouritism,** abetment, complicity, partisanship; **resource,** facility; **helping hand,** a leg up, boost, crutch, hand, lift, springboard, stepping stone

HELP *v* aid, bestead *(Archaic)*, oblige; **sustain,** carry through, comfort *(Obs.)*, succour, support, tide over; **administer to,** attend, care for, fix someone up, minister, nurse, spoon-feed, visit; **strengthen,** buoy, carry, prop up, stay; **nurture,** aliment, provide for; **further,** accelerate, boost, cultivate, facilitate, feed, foment, foster, pilot, promote, prompt; **favour,** patronise, shine on, shine upon, smile on, smile upon; **champion,** befriend, defend, go all the way for, push someone's barrow, root for *(U.S.)*, side with, stick up for, take sides, take someone's part, throw in one's lot with; **serve,** be at someone's service, be of service, be useful, hold someone's hand, make oneself useful, stand by, stand with; **abet,** collaborate; **assist,** bear a hand, come forward, give a hand, help out, lend a hand, rally, second; **cheer,** encourage, heart *(Archaic)*; **sponsor,** back, back up, bankroll, finance, put some-

help   **heresy**

one on his feet, set someone on his feet, subsidise; **chip in**, come to the party, pass round the hat, put money in the tin, whip round

HELPER *n* abetter, adjuvant, aider, ally, facilitator, help, obliger; **assistant**, adjutant, aide, aide-de-camp, assessor, assister, assistor *(Law)*, associate, best boy *(Films)*, bottle-holder *(Wrestling)*, coadjutor, coadjutress, croupier, deputy, handler, right hand, right-hand man, second, sidekick, yeoman *(Archaic)*; **auxiliary**, reinforcement, stand-by; **attendant**, acolyte, pursuivant; **servant**, domestic help, girl Friday, gopher, server, shitkicker, tweeny *(Obs.)*, yardman; **secretary**, private secretary, receptionist; **groomsman**, best man, bridesmaid, flower girl, matron of honour, pageboy, trainbearer; **benefactor**, angel, deliverer, easy touch, fairy godmother, favourer, intercessor, Lady Bountiful, paraclete, patron, patroness, provider, ready giver, Robin Hood, Santa Claus, soft touch, softie, subsidiser, sugar daddy; **supporter**, activist, advocate, backer, champion, fan, promoter, rooter; **nurturer**, administrator, carer, fosterer, fuzzy wuzzy angel, ministrant, nurse, succourer; **helpmate**, booster, companion, friend, friend in need, helpmeet *(Archaic)*, pal, vade mecum; **tower of strength**, Atlas, bastion, cheerer, comforter, moral support, pillar, prop, soldier, strengthener, support; **counsellor**, adviser, almoner, almsgiver, altruist, case worker, do-gooder, philanthropist, probation officer, settlement worker, social worker, voluntaryist

HELPFUL *adj* accommodating, cooperative, helping, obliging, responsive, well-disposed; **altruistic**, generous, patronal; **charitable**, eleemosynary, subventionary; **ministrative**, ministrant, visitational; **sustaining**, alimental, comfortable, nutrient, supporting; **auxiliary**, adjuvant, ancillary, assistant, subsidiary, supernumerary; **useful**, necessary *(Archaic)*, of service; **favourable**, advantageous, auspicial, beneficial, conducive to, propitious; **subsidised**, aided, backed; **contributary**, facilitatory, tributary

HELPFULLY *adv* altruistically, comfortingly, constructively, cooperatively, helpingly, obligingly, responsively; **on behalf of**, for the sake of, on someone's account; **by the aid of**, on the strength of, thanks to; **favourably**, favouringly

HERALDRY *n* armory, blazonry, emblazonry; **armorial bearings**, arms, blazon, coat of arms, crest, escutcheon, hatchment, lozenge, quarterings, shield; **device**, bearing, charge, ordinary; **sphragistics**, vexillology

HERE *adv* herein, inside, out here; **there**, ad loc, o'er *(Poetic)*, over there, thereabouts, thereat, thereby, yon *(Archaic)*, yond *(Archaic)*, yonder; **at hand**, herein, in, on board, on hand, on the scene, on the spot, round, to hand; **locally**, in loc. cit., in loco, in one's tracks, in situ, on the spot; **op. cit.**, opere citato; **suo loco**

HERESY *n* anathema, false doctrine, misbelief, miscreance *(Archaic)*; **unorthodoxy**, dissent, heterodoxy, schism, superstition *(Derog.)*, unconformity

heretic   256   **hiding**

HERETIC *n* anathema, heresiarch, miscreant *(Archaic)*, pervert, perverter; **dissenter**, nonconformist

HERETICAL *adj* excommunicate, heretic, miscreant *(Archaic)*, perverted, profane; **unorthodox**, heterodox, schismatic

HERO *n* champion, daredevil, dreadnought, heroine, lion, Spartan, stalwart, the brave, the good guys, tiger; **darer**, blood, gallant *(Archaic)*, sportsman, venturer

HEROIC STORY *n* epic, epos, gest, saga

HEY *interj* ahem, ahoy, cooee, cop this, halloo, hallow, hello, hey, there, hi, hist, I say, look here, N.B., nota bene, there, yack-ai, yoo-hoo; **look out**, fore, timber, watch that last step

HIDDEN *adj* blind, concealed, dark, dead *(Mil.)*, delitescent, perdu; **camouflaged**, apatetic, sugar-coated; **covered over**, blacked out, gilded, veiled; **private**, backstage, confidential, offstage, privy *(Archaic)*; **unadmitted**, ulterior; **unnoticed**, unmarked, unremarked, unwitnessed; **undercover**, deep-laid, gone to ground, hidden away, secluded, submerged, subterranean, underground; **covert**, anonymous, incognita, incognito, pseudonymous, secret; **obscure**, abstruse *(Obs.)*, arcane, occult, recondite, uniluminating; **cryptic**, cryptogrammic, cryptographic, enigmatical, shrouded in mystery, veiled in mystery

HIDE *n* cowhide, crop, fell, fur, greenhide, kid, pelt, peltry, woolfell *(Obs.)*; **animal skin**, bearskin, broadtail, buckskin, buff, calf, calfskin, cowskin, deerskin, doeskin, goatskin, horsehide, lambskin, pigskin, sealskin, snakeskin, swanskin; **leather**, grain, levant, mocha, morocco, morocco leather, ooze leather, shagreen, suede; **bootlace**, moult, pie piece, scarf, slough. *See also* SKIN

HIDE *v* blot, conceal, cover one's tracks, dissemble, dissimulate, hoodwink *(Obs.)*, hugger-mugger, hush up, mew up, obscure, occult, snooker *(Colloq.)*; **keep secret**, give nothing away, hold back, keep back, keep dark, keep one's own counsel, keep to oneself, let go no further, not breathe a syllable, not breathe a word; **envelop**, adumbrate, becloud, befog, blanket, cloak, clothe, draw the veil, enshroud, mantle, shade, shroud, smother, swallow up, veil; **cache**, bury, harbour, lock up, plant *(Colloq.)*, put out of sight, salt away, salt down, seclude, secrete, shut away, sink, stash, stow away, treasure; **cover**, curtain, cushion, ensconce, mask, screen, screen off; **erase**, efface, obliterate; **disguise**, camouflage, guise *(Scot.)*, mask, masquerade; **cover up**, black out, gild, paper over, whitewash; **watergate**, rort; **bamboozle**, snow; **censor**, suppress. *See also* LIE LOW

HIDER *n* concealer, disguiser, effacer, enveloper, harbourer, secretor; **dissembler**, crypto *(Colloq.)*, dissimulator, double agent, front, hoodwinker, incognita, incognito, masker, masquerader, mole, operative *(U.S.)*, secret agent, sleeper, snake in the grass, spy; **secret organisation**, underground; **cryptographer**, cryptographist

HIDING *n* adumbration, concealment, covering, coverture, deliteseence, effacement, retirement, screening, the dark; **anonymity**, pseudonymity; **secrecy**, covertness, darkness, hugger-mugger *(Archaic)*, retreat, secret, secretness, shade; **cover-up**, double blind, mystification, smokescreen, white lie, whitewash; **smokescreen**, blackout, brownout, dim-out *(U.S.)*, white-out

HIDING PLACE *n* covert, den, hide-out, hideaway, hidy-hole, lurk, mai mai *(N.Z.)*, mew, retreat; **cache**, plant *(Colloq.)*, stash; **concealed drawer**, false bottom; **hide**, priest-hole, snooker *(Colloq.)*; **ambush**, ambuscade, blind, suprise attack

HIGH *adj* aerial, aery *(Poetic)*, airy, aloft, apogeal, apogean, high-flying, high-level, midair, sky-high, skyey *(Poetic)*; **altitudinal**, hypsometric; **elevated**, highblocked, highest; **top**, topmost, upper, uppermost; **overhead**, hanging; **uphill**, upstairs. *See also* TALL

HIGH *adv* aerially, midair, overhead, uppishly, upwards; **on high**, aloft, o'er *(Poetic)*, on tiptoe; **loftily**, eminently, grandly, majestically; **mountainously**, precipitously, toweringly

HIGH COMMAND *n* generalissimo, supreme commander *(U.S.)*; **officer**, brass, brass hat, commandant, commissioned officer, constable *(Hist.)*, duty officer, ranker, red hat, staff officer, underofficer; **non-commissioned officer**, N.C.O., non-com. *See also* SOLDIER; SERVICEMAN; ARMED FORCES

HIGH FINANCE *n* big business, capitalisation, finance, funding, overcapitalisation, recapitalisation, wheeling and dealing; **banking**, clearing, merchant banking; **stockbroking**, brokerage, jobbing, stockbrokerage; **speculation**, agiotage, arbitrage, bondholding, bubble, hedge, investment; **dealings**, electronic funds transfer, kerbs, over-the-counter trading; **readjustment**, shake-out

HIGHLY REGARDED *adj* dear, esteemed, good, in high esteem, in high regard, respected, revered, reverend; **respectable**, ancient *(Archaic)*, decent, decorous, estimable, time-honoured, venerable, worthy; **commendable**, commendatory, laudable; **awesome**, awe-inspiring, awful, compelling, dread, dreadful, fearful, impressive, redoubtable, redoubted

HIGH REGARD *n* devotion, esteem, estimation, honour, regard, respect, veneration; **respectfulness**, civility, comity, consideration, courtesy, good manners, regardfulness; **adoration**, hero-worship, homage, idolatry, idolisation, idolism, obsequiousness, piety, piousness, worshipfulness; **awe**, dread, fear, reverence

HINDER *v* disturb, drag the chain, filibuster, forestall, hold up, impede, incommode, inconvenience, let *(Archaic)*, put a spoke in someone's wheel, queer someone's pitch, retard, set back, spike someone's guns, stonewall; **hamper**, cumber, encumber, lumber, weigh; **handicap**, cramp, penalise, pinch; **thwart**, baffle, bilk, counterwork, cross, dash, dish, dish up, foil, frustrate, interfere, put paid to, snooker, spite, stymie, traverse; **prevent**, forbid, foreclose, interdict, oppose, preclude, prohibit, stop; **trip**, booby trap, cripple, disenable, hogtie *(U.S.)*, lame, mask, snag, tie down, tie someone's hands, trip up; **discourage**, damp, take the wind out of one's sails; **cramp one's style**, discomfit, embarrass. *See also* OBSTRUCT

HINDERER *n* backstop, baffler, impeder, interceptor, interferer, interposer; **obstructer**, blocker, defeater, dog in the manger, filibusterer, obstructionist, stonewaller; **handicapper**, cumberer, lumberer; **preventer**, counterworker, forbidder, forestaller, opposer, thwarter; **discourager**, damper, heckler, killjoy, spoilsport, wet blanket

HINDERING *adj* cumbersome, cumbrous, impedient, impedimental, impedimentary, impeditive, obstruent, retardative, retardatory; **obstructive**, bloody-minded, difficult, filibusterous; **interceptive**, counteractive, interferential, preclusive, preventive, prohibitive; **in the way**, discouraging, inconvenient, obvious *(Obs.)*

HINDERINGLY *adv* discouragingly, impedingly, insurmountably, interferingly, obstructively, preclusively, prohibitively

HINDRANCE *n* difficulty, impedient, impediment, let *(Archaic)*, obstruction, rub *(Archaic)*; **encumbrance**, clog, cumber, cumbrance, dead weight, deadwood, fardel, hamper, impedimenta, incubus, lumber, remora *(Archaic)*, weight; **burden**, dead hand, drag; **preventive**, counter measure, countercheck, defeat, penalty; **bar**, conclusion *(Law)*, estoppel; **handicap**, discommodity, embarrassment, inconvenience; **hitch**, embugerance, fly in the ointment, glitch, nigger in the woodpile, snag, spanner in the works, stick *(Obs.)*; **setback**, check, damp, dash, drawback, facer, throwback; **delaying tactic**, filibuster, stall; **impasse**, brick wall, catch 22, deadlock, stalemate, sticking point, stumbling block, stymie, vicious circle; **bottleneck**, blockage, congestion, jam, shackle, trammels; **blind alley**, cul-de-sac, dead end; **bodycheck**, hand-off, intercept, stiff-arm tackle. *See also* OBSTACLE

HISS *n* sigh, sough, whisper; **rush of air**, swish, whish, whistle, whiz, whoosh, zip; **sibilant**, affricative, aspirate, fricative; **puff**, chuff, chug; **fizz**, bubble, bubbling, fizzing, fizzle, hubble-bubble; **rustle**, crinkle, froufrou; **snuffle**, sneeze, sniffle, snore, snort, sob, soufflé; **sizzle**, spatter, sputter; **suck**, slurp

HISS *v* affricate, aspirate, assibilate, blow, sibilate, whistle; **rustle**, crinkle, sigh, sough, swish, whisper; **whoosh**, whish, whiz, zip; **sniffle**, sneeze, sniff, snivel, snore, snuffle; **fizz**, effervesce, fizzle, frizzle, sizzle; **spit**, spatter, splutter, sputter; **hiss a performer**, give someone the bird

HISSER *n* fizzler, sizzler, sputterer; **snuffler**, sneezer, snorer, snorter

HISSING *n* affrication, assibilation, audible friction, frication, sibilance, sibilancy; **effervescence**, effervescency

HISSING *adj* affricated, aspirated, crinkly, fricative, rushing, rustling, sibilant, wheezy; **fizzy**, effervescent, effervescible, fizzling

HISTORIAN *n* annalist, chronicler; **archaeologist**, Egyptologist, Etruscologist; **antiquarian**, antiquary

HISTORICAL *adj* annalistic, archival, biographical, hierogrammatic, philologic

HISTORY *n* ancient history, annals, chronicles, modern history, story *(Obs.)*; **archaeology**, Egyptology, Etruscology, palaeogeography, palaeogeology, prehistory, protohis-

history   259   **hold**

tory, scatology; **antiquarianism,** medievalism, retrospection

HIT *n* bash, bat, belt, blow, bong, clap, crack, dint *(Obs.)*, drub, knock, swipe; **punch,** biff, box, buff, buffet, clip, clock, clonk, clout, clump, conk, cuff, dong, facer, fisticuff, flea in someone's ear, floorer, job, knuckle sandwich, plug; **pound,** packet, pile-driver, slog, slosh, slug, smash, smasher, sock, wallop, wham, whop; **body blow,** backhander, bolo punch, combination, cross, flick, haymaker, hook, left, pivot punch, rabbit punch, rabbit-killer, rally *(Boxing)*, right, sideswipe, sidewinder *(U.S.)*, sucker punch, uppercut; **king hit,** chop, coup de grâce, death-blow, flattener, knockout, stunner, woodener; **smack,** flap, paddywhack, slap, spank, spat, swat, thwack, whack; **whip,** cut, lash, pandy *(Scot.)*, slash, stripe, swish, switch, thrash, welt; **loft,** flier. *See also* STROKE; TAP

HIT *v* bat, bong, chop, connect with, crease, crown, ding, dob, sideswipe, smite, strike, swat, sweep, swing at, swipe, zot; **tap,** bob, dab, dub, fillip, flap, flick, pat, peck, rap, spat, tip, touch; **drum,** percuss, thrum; **bang,** knock, rap, slam, slap *(Obs.)*, thud, thump, wham, whang; **smack,** clap, paddle *(U.S.)*, slap, slipper, snap, spank, thwack, whack; **bash,** belt, dash, pound, ram, slog, sock, thump, wallop, whop; **punch,** biff, bop, box, buffet, clip, clock, clonk, clout, clump, conk, cuff, dong, dot, fist, fisticuff, hang one on someone, job, mug, plug, roof, scone, slug, take a poke at, uppercut; **hammer,** beetle, gavel, knap, tamp. *See also* BEAT; CUDGEL

HITTER *n* batsman, batter, pinch-hitter, striker; **beater,** larruper, smacker, smiter, striker, thrasher, walloper; **bludgeoner,** cudgeler, fustigator *(Archaic)*, hammerer, pounder, slogger, smasher, thumper; **flogger,** flagellant, lasher; **puncher,** boxer, fighter, fisticuffer, plugger, pugilist, pusher, shover, slugger

HITTING *n* bashing, buffeting, pounding; **beating,** bastinado, belting, drubbing, hammering, hiding, lacing *(Brit.)*, larruping, milling *(Brit.)*, pasting, plastering, spanking, tanning, thrashing, towelling, trimming, walloping; **assault,** battery, corporal punishment, once-over, the works; **whipping,** bob, bull, canary, flagellation, flogging, fustigation *(Archaic)*, lashing, tester; **stoning,** lapidation, pelting. *See also* IMPACT

HOLD *n* clench, clinch, close, grab, grapple, wrestle; **wrestling hold,** arm lock, body scissors, collar-and-elbow, grapevine, hammer lock, headlock, lock, maginnis, octopus clamp, scissors, toehold, wristlock; **grip,** bite, clutch, grasp, gripe, purchase; **eastern grip,** handshake grip; **hug,** bear hug, clasp, cuddle, embrace

HOLD *v* bite, clench, grip, gripe, handle, hold the road, nip; **hold down,** guy, immobolise; **grasp,** catch, catch at, clasp, clutch, clutch at, lay hold of, seize, strain; **clinch,** grapple, hang on, pin; **cling,** cleave, hold fast; **clamp,** cramp, vice; **reserve,** book, put aside; **detain,** buttonhole, collar; **withold,** deforce; **keep,** have, retain; **hug,** bosom, cuddle, embosom, embrace, fold, press; **nurse,** cradle, inarm

HOLDABLE *adj* graspable, retainable; **handled**, ansate, hilted; **held**, hand-held, unmounted

HOLDER *n* billy tongs, clams, forceps, lazy tongs, nippers, pincers, pliers, sugar tongs, tongs, tweezers; **clamp**, bitstock, bootjack, brace, bracing, clam, cramp, face-plate, head, jig, oarlock, tailstock, vice; **clasp**, catch, clip, split ring, tiepin, woggle; **clipboard**, copyholder, folder; **hook**, anchor, grapnel, grappling hook, grappling iron, jaw; **climbing irons**, chock-stone, clinker, piton

HOLDING *n* deforcement *(Law)*, retention, retentiveness, retentivity, tenaciousness, tenacity, tenure; **reservation**, booking, withholding; **prehension**, grasping, prehensility, retainment

HOLDING *adj* cheliform, grasping, griping, prehensile, raptorial; **tenacious**, clingy, retentive

HOLD IN LOW REGARD *v* belittle, depreciate, misesteem, misprise, underrate, underestimate, undervalue; **despise**, contemn *(Archaic)*, curl one's lip, disdain, disesteem, disprize *(Archaic)*, disvalue *(Rare)*, give someone the glassy eye, give someone the greasy eyeball, look down on, look down one's nose at, revile, scorn, snap one's fingers at, sneer at, sneeze at, sniff at, snuff at *(Obs.)*, thumb one's nose, turn one's nose up; **disrespect**, disregard, flout, make free with, profane, violate

HOLIDAY *n* bank holiday, day of rest, dies non, festa, fete, fete day, flexday, flexiday, half-day, half-holiday, half-term *(Brit.)*, lay day *(Sport)*, long weekend, Lord's day, Picnic Day, public holiday, Sabbath, weekend; leave, bush week, Christmas holidays, Easter holidays, furlough, holidays, hollies, hols, leave of absence, long service leave, long vacation, maternity leave, R and R *(U.S. Mil.)*, rec leave, shore leave, time off, vac, vacation; **study leave**, sabbatical, stu vac, swot vac

HOLINESS *n* godliness, sacredness, sacrosanctity, sanctification, sanctity, state of grace; **enlightenment**, conversion, initiation, regeneration; **sainthood**, beatification, canonisation, hallowedness, mahatmaism, martyrdom, saintliness, saintship

HOLLOW *n* calyx, cavity, cup, funnel; **hole**, kettle hole, pitfall, pot *(Scot.)*, pothole, tomo *(N.Z.)*; amygdale, druse, geode, vugh; **dish**, depression, scoop; **basin**, amphitheatre, bolson, bunker, caldera, cirque, coomb, corrie, crater, devil's punchbowl, doline, lap, pan, polje, retarding basin, river basin, saddle, salt flat, saltpan, shott, volcanic neck, walled plain; **valley**, dale, dell, dip, glen, gully, vale; **waterhole**, artesian basin, claypan, melon hole, namma hole, soak, soak hole, wallow, watering hole; **sink**, sinkhole, soakage pit, sump; **hollowness**, concaveness, concavity, curvature, sag. *See also* ORGANIC CAVITY; NICHE; CAVE; EXCAVATION; INDENTATION

HOLLOW *v* concave, dig out, dish, gouge, hollow out, scoop; **excavate**, burrow, drive, mine, open-cut, sink, tunnel, undermine; **pit**, crater, dimple; **drill**, dibble, rout; **dent**, depress, indent; **stamp**, impress, press in

HOLLOW *adj* cavernous, concave *(Obs.)*, cryptal, spelaean, tomblike; **sunken**, basined, dished, shallow;

concave, amphicoelous, bicordave, concavo-concave, concavo-convex, plano-concave; **pitted**, craterous, dented, dimpled, dimply, foveal, foveate, foveolate, pockmarked, rimose, variolous; **crannied**, nooky; **cup-shaped**, arytenoid, cotyloid, cuplike, cupped, cyathiform, glenoid, infundibular; **bottle-shaped**, ampullaceal; **bladder-like**, bladdery, pouchy, vesicular, vesiculate; **navel-like**, umbilicate, umbiliform

HOLY *adj* blessed, Christly, hallowed, sainted, saintly, supernal; **sacred**, sacrosanct; taboo, tapu *(N.Z.)*

HOLY DAY *n* feast-day, festival, fete, fete day, harvest festival, holiday, jubilee, movable feast, vigil; **fast day**, Day of Atonement, fast, Lent, Ramadan, rogations; **Holy Week**, Christmas, Easter, Eastertide, epiphany, Lent, Passion Week, Passover, Pentecost, Pesach, Ramadan, Shrovetide, tide

HOLY PERSON *n* arhat, bodhisattva, hafiz, maharishi, mahatma, man of God, saint; **martyr**, Job, patron saint, stigmatic; **icon**, Madonna, Mater dolorosa, noli-me-tangere, pietà; **halo**, aureole, gloriole, glory, nimbus, stigma

HOMOGENEITY *n* homogeneousness; **uniformity**, agreement, conformation, uniformness, unity; **sameness**, identicalness, indistinguishableness, selfsameness; **constancy**, evenness, monotony, steadiness

HOMOGENEOUS *adj* diffused, even, uniform; **solid**, monolithic, monomorphic, of a piece, unstratified; **constant**, monotonous, regular, steady; **monotone**, fleckless, immaculate *(Zool. Bot.)*, orthotropous *(Bot.)*, self-coloured; **identical**, identic *(Obs.)*, indistinguishable, same, selfsame

HOMOGENEOUSLY *adv* indistinguishably, solidly, uniformly; **constantly**, steadily, steady; **alike**, ibid, ibidem, identically

HOMOGENISE *v* gauge, identify, uniformalise *(Rare)*

HONEST *adj* aboveboard, all wool and a yard wide, authentic, bona fide, clean, downright, flat, legit, on the up and up *(U.S.)*, plain, scrupulous, square, straight, straight-out, straight-up, unfeigned, upright; **genuine**, dinkum, dinky, dinky-di, fair dinkum, true-hearted, truthful, veracious, veridical; **straightforward**, blunt, candid, earnest, frank, free-spoken, guileless, jonick, manly, open, outspoken, plain-spoken, round, simple-hearted, sincere, single, single-minded, unreserved, up-front; **reliable**, as good as one's word, sound, steadfast, true *(Archaic)*, trustworthy, trusty, upstanding; **fair**, disinterested, even-handed, honourable, virtuous

HONESTLY *adv* aboveboard, by fair means, fair and square, fairly, on the level, plainly, square, straight from the shoulder, unfeignedly; **straightforwardly**, candidly, frankly, from the bottom of one's heart, heart-to-heart, openly, outspokenly, sincerely, single-mindedly, straightly; **genuinely**, in all conscience, truthfully, veraciously, veridically, verily *(Archaic)*; **reliably**, trustily, trustworthily; **honourably**, virtuously, without fear or favour

HONESTLY *interj* blood oath, dicken, dinkum, fair dinkum, honest to God, honour bright, in truth, on my word

HONEST PERSON *n* flat *(Obs.)*, man of his word, man of honour, plain-dealer, square-shooter, straight talker, straightshooter, white man *(Brit.)*, woman of her word, woman of honour

HONESTY *n* incorruptness, integrity, plain dealing, plainness, probity, scrupulosity, sincerity, straightness; **straightforwardness**, candidness, candour, frankness, free-spokenness, openness, outspokenness, sincereness, single-mindedness, unreserve, unreservedness; **genuineness**, fact, reality, sooth *(Archaic)*, truth, truthfulness, unfeignedness, veraciousness, veracity, veridicality; **reliability**, bona fides, reliableness, soundness, trueness, trustiness, trustworthiness; **good faith**, uberrima fidei; **the genuine article**, the dinkum article, the drum, the full two bob, the good guts, the good oil, the griff, the real thing, the straight wire; **fairness**, honour, impartiality, manliness, virtue, virtuousness; **point of honour**, matter of principle

HOORAY *interj* alleluia, eureka, Glory be, heaven be praised, heyday *(Archaic)*, hosanna, hurrah, huzza, rah, saints be praised, whoopee

HOPE *n* aspiration, belief, confidence, esperance *(Obs.)*, faith, hopefulness, trust; **optimism**, buoyancy, enterprise, insouciance, overconfidence, positivism; **anticipation**, contemplation, expectation, foresight, foretaste; **wishful thinking**, false optimism, micawberism; **dream**, pie in the sky, pious hope, pipedream, velleity, vision; **favourite**, comer, fancy *(Horseracing)*, hope, white hope; **silver lining**, relief, uplift

HOPE *v* aspire after, aspire to, believe, have faith, trust; **be hopeful**, catch at straws, gamble, hope against hope, keep one's fingers crossed, look on the bright side, look through rose-coloured glasses, optimise, rally; **expect**, anticipate, believe in, contemplate, count on, count one's chickens before they are hatched, count upon, hope for, hope in, lean on, lick one's chops, lick one's lips, pin one's hopes on, place one's trust in, put confidence in, trust in; **dream**, build castles in the air, fantasise, live in a fool's paradise

HOPEFUL *adj* bullish, buoyant, optimistic, overconfident, positive, positivist, positivistic, rose-coloured, upbeat; **confident**, happy-go-lucky, insouciant, radiant, sanguine, starry-eyed; **aspiring**, aspirant *(Rare)*, would-be

HOPEFULLY *adv* hopingly, optimistically

HOPELESS *adj* beyond remedy, fatal *(Obs.)*, immediable, incurable, inoperable, irrecoverable, irredeemable, irremeable, irremediable, irreparable, irretrievable, irreversible; **desperate**, dead-end, futureless; **inevitable**, defeated, gone, unavoidable; **bleak**, black, comfortless, depressive, desolate, feral *(Archaic)*, funereal, unbearable

HOPELESSNESS *n* irrecoverableness, irredeemableness, irremediableness, irreparability, irreparableness, irretrievability, irretrievableness; **bleakness**, blackness, comfortlessness, dismalness, oppressiveness, unbearableness; **hopeless situation**, hell, living death; **vain hope**, chimera, illusion, mirage; **Murphy's Law.** *See also* DESPAIR

HORSE *n* Appaloosa, apple sauce, bay, bronco *(U.S.)*, brumby, chestnut, cob, cocktail, colt, cuddy, dobbin, dun, equine, fencer *(Equestrian)*, filly, foal, garron, gee-gee, gelding, hayburner, hinny, hound, jade, mare, mount, mustang, nag, nanto *(Aborig.)*, neddy, night-horse, Nubian, padnag, palfrey *(Archaic)*, palomino, Palouse pony, Percheron, piebald, pinto *(U.S.)*, pit pony, pony, prad, ridgeling, Shetland pony, shire horse, sorrel, speeler, stallion, steed, thoroughbred, Turk, Waler, Welsh pony, yarraman; **workhorse,** bloodstock, buckjumper, carthorse, charger, Clydesdale, courser, draughthorse, dray-horse, hack, hackney *(Obs.)*, high horse, hunter, moke, pacer, plug, pole horse, post-horse, quarter horse, rip, saddle-horse, screw, stockhorse, warhorse; **beast of burden,** ass, burro, dicky, donkey, llama, mule, packhorse, packtrain, workhorse; **team,** four-in-hand, span

HOSPITAL *n* base hospital, community hospital, cottage hospital, district hospital, general hospital, infirmary, institution, maternity hospital, pavilion, polyclinic *(Brit.)*, private hospital, public hospital, spital *(Obs.)*, teaching hospital; **field hospital,** clearing hospital, clearing station, dressing station; **clinic,** baby health centre, fertility clinic, health centre, prenatal clinic, STD clinic, the house that Jack built, V.D. clinic; **nursing home,** convalescent home, Home, hospice; **sanatorium,** isolation hospital, lazaretto, leprosarium; **sick room,** san, sanatorium, sick bay, solarium; **ward,** casualty, intensive care unit, labour ward, nursery, outpatients' department, private ward, public ward

HOSTILELY *adv* adversely, defiantly, quarrelsomely, rancorously, unfriendly *(Rare)*; **sullenly,** bearishly, spitefully, splenetically, sulkily, surlily; **reservedly,** remotely, reticently, stand-offishly, uncommunicatively, undemonstratively; **unsociably,** antisocially, inhospitably, insociably, unapproachably; **coldly,** chillingly, chilly, coolly, frostily, frozenly

HOT *adj* baking, blazing, blistering, furnace-like, hot as Hades, hot as Hay Hell and Booligal, roasting, scalding, scorching, sweltering; **fervent,** afire, aflame, ardent, fervid, fiery, perfervid; **incandescent,** candent, igneous; **burning,** glowing, live, living; **heated,** caustic, overheated, piping hot, red-hot, superheated, white-hot; **fiery,** angry, inflammatory; **fevered,** febrile, feverish, hectic, pyrexial, pyrexic, subfebrile; **warm,** lukewarm, tepid, warmish; **summery,** summer, summer-like, sun-drenched; **fine,** balmy, fair, genial, mild, sunny, sunshiny, temperate; **humid,** close, muggy, oppressive, stifling, suffocating, sultry, sweltering; **tropical,** equatorial, semitropical, torrid, tropic, ultratropical

HOTEL *n* convention centre, halfway house, hostel *(Archaic)*, hostelry *(Archaic)*, house, inn, lodge, motel, pub, public house, roadhouse, tavern; **hostel,** youth hostel; **boarding house,** guesthouse, hydro, lodging house, pension, resort, rooming house *(U.S.)*, spa; **bunkhouse,** charnel-house, dosshouse, flophouse;

hotel   **human**

poorhouse, almshouse, beadhouse *(Brit.)*, hospice; **creche**, baby-farm; **accommodation**, bed, bed and board, bed and breakfast, billet, board, full board, housing, lodging, lodgment *(Rare)*, pension

HOTHEAD *n* bull at a gate, harum-scarum, hotspur, madcap, rusher; **daredevil**, adventurer, adventuress, fire-eater, gambler, Icarus, Promethean, scapegrace; **desperado**, bravo, destructo

HOTLY *adv* fervently, fervidly, fierily, hot, perfervidly; **scorchingly**, sultrily, sunnily, torridly, tropically; **warmly**, tepidly; **incandescently**

HOUSE *n* home; **terrace house**, semi, town house, villa *(Chiefly Brit.)*, villa home, villa unit; **cottage**, bungalow, dower house, project house, tied cottage *(Brit.)*; **housing commission house**, council house *(Brit.)*, glebe house, state house *(N.Z.)*; **block**, duplex, mews, row, terrace); **housing estate**, cluster housing, council estate *(Brit.)*, estate, housing development; **homestead**, Government house *(Colloq.)*, grange, hacienda, hall, head station, ranch house, rancho, station house, the house; **country house**, chateau, court, dacha, manor, manor house, seat, villa; **bure**, donga *(Papua New Guinea)*, igloo, rondavel; **beehive house**; **adobe**, wattle and daub; **rectory**, manse, parsonage, presbytery, vicarage; **farmhouse**, farm; **bower**, bush house; **maisonette**, doll's house; **premises**, messuage; **lodge**, gatehouse, schoolhouse, tollhouse; **split-level house**, blockhouse, garrison, lake-dwelling, pile-dwelling; **palace**, castle, palazzo, seigneury, seigniory, seraglio. See also CABIN

HOUSE *v* accommodate, domicile, domiciliate; **lodge**, billet, board, put up, quarter, take in; **bed down**, sleep, stay at; **keep house**, run an establishment

HOW *adv* what *(Obs.)*, whereby; **however**, howsoever, howsomever; **any way**, by hook or by crook; **so**, thus; **hereby**, herewith; **in a manner**, after a fashion, in a fashion, in a manner of speaking

HOW ABOUT THAT *interj* can you beat that, fancy, garn, hush my mouth, I declare *(U.S.)*, I'll be a son of a gun *(U.S.)*, indeed, my hat, my sainted aunt, my word, well I never, will wonders never cease, you wouldn't read about it; **goodness**, ah, bless me, blimey, blow me down, bugger me, bugger me dead, by gum *(Brit.)*, fuck me, fuck me dead, goodness gracious, gorblimey, heavens, heigh-ho, heyday *(Archaic)*, la *(Archaic)*, O, oh, shiver my timbers, starve the bardies, starve the crows, stiffen the crows, stone the crows, strike me dead, strike me lucky, strike me pink, strike-a-light, struth; **hell's bells**, for crying out loud, good grief, hell's teeth, holy cow, holy mackerel, holy Moses, I ask you, Jesus, Jesus Christ, lawks *(Archaic)*, the devil, what, what on earth; **far out**, fuck, gee, gee whiz, Glory be, golly, lo and behold, oh boy, phew, shit, whew, wow

HUMAN *adj* carnal, earthborn, mortal; **incarnate**, impersonate; **humanoid**, anthropoid, anthropomorphous, australopithecine, hominoid, pithecanthropoid; **racial**, ethnic, interracial, intertribal, phyletic, phylogenic

humanisation / humour

HUMANISATION *n* anthropomorphosis; **personification**, anthropomorphism, pathetic fallacy, prosopopoeia; **humanism**, anthropocentricism, personalism

HUMANISE *v* anthropomorphise, incarnate, personalise, personify

HUMANITY *n* generations of man, human family, human race, human society, human species, humankind, man, mankind, microcosm, the living; **the world**, the earth, the universe; **people**, brothers, fellow creatures, fellow man, folk, neighbours; **race**, ethnic group; **earthling**, earthman, postdiluvian, tellurian; **humanness**, carnality, flesh, flesh and blood, human nature, manhood, subsistence (*Philos.*)

HUMBLE *v* abase, abash, bastardise, bring down, chagrin, confound *(Archaic)*, confuse, crush, cut down to size, dash, flatten, give someone the arse, give someone the big A, give someone the bum's rush, humiliate, lower, mortify, put someone in his place, put out of countenance, put someone down, send away with a flea in one's ear, snub, take down, take down a peg, wipe the floor with

HUMORIST *n* amuser, cap and bells, clown, comedian, comedienne, comic, farceur, jester, mimic, stand-up comic; **joker**, card, dag, doer, hard case, hard doer, monkey, scream, wag; **practical joker**, buffoon, gagger, imp, japer, pantagruelist, prankster, Rabelaisian; **banterer**, josher, kidder, sporter; **wit**, punster, quipster, wisecracker, witling; **satirist**, lampooner, lampoonist

HUMOROUS *adj* amusing, Chaplinesque, comic, comical, droll, fun, funny, humoristic, laughable, risible; **hilarious**, killing, priceless, screaming, side-splitting, uproarious; **Rabelaisian**, pantagruelian; **seriocomic**, tragicomical; **farcical**, absurd, Gilbertian, ludicrous, zany; **slapstick**, custard-pie, prankish; **witty**, Attic, bright, clever, salty, scintillating; **ironic**, caustic, dry, facete *(Archaic)*, mordant, sarcastic, wry; **quizzical**, daggish, whimsical; **bantering**, facetious, playful, sly, sportful, tongue-in-cheek; **jesting**, jocose, jocular, merry, mirthful, pleasant, waggish

HUMOROUSLY *adv* amusingly, comically; **hilariously**, killingly, screamingly, side-splittingly, uproariously; **wittily**, caustically, dryly, ironically, mordantly, saltily, sarcastically, satirically, with one's tongue in one's cheek, wryly; **quizzically**, amusedly, funnily, whimsically; **farcically**, absurdly, ludicrously

HUMOUR *n* Attic salt, Attic wit, comedy, drollery, fun, salt, whimsy, wit; **humorousness**, amusingness, drollness, funniness, hilariousness, jocoseness, jocosity, jocularity, risibility, uproariousness; **merriness**, clownishness, funny bone, impishness, mirthfulness, playfulness, scintillation, sense of humour, sportfulness, waggery, waggishness; **absurdity**, absurdness, comicality, comicalness, ludicrousness, whimsicality, whimsicalness, zanyism; **wittiness**, dryness, epigramatism, facetiousness, saltiness, wryness. *See also* COMEDY: MIRTH:JOKE

HUNCHBACKED *adj* gibbous, humpbacked, roach-backed, round-shouldered

HUNDRED *n* century, hundredth, ton

HUNDRED *adj* centesimal, centuple, hundredfold, hundredth

HUNGER *n* edaciousness, edacity, hungriness, pecker, stomach, turophilia, voraciousness, voracity

HUNGER *v* have hollow legs, have the munchies; **thirst**

HUNGRY *adj* edacious, empty, famished, hollow, hungry as a hunter, peckish, ravening, ravenous, sharp-set, starveling, starving, voracious; **gluttonous**, bulimic, greedy

HUNT *v* course, drive, follow the hounds, gun, prey, raven *(Obs.)*, ride to hounds, stalk, still-hunt *(U.S.)*; **ferret**, beagle, flight, hark back, hawk, run, scent; **trap**, ensnare, entrap, run to earth, run to ground, snare, springe, tree, wire; **rabbit**, beat, bird, fowl, frog, mouse, pigstick, rat, snipe, wolf

HUNTER *n* batfowler, beater, birder *(Colloq.)*, birdman, bounty hunter *(U.S.)*, chaser, chasseur, deerculler *(N.Z.)*, deerstalker, dog catcher, falconer, ferreter, field, fowler, fox-hunter, gun, harrier, hunt, huntress, huntsman, huntswoman, jaeger, mutton-birder, Nimrod, pigsticker, pink, pothunter, rabbiter, ranger, rat-catcher, shikari *(India)*, snarer, sportsman, sportswoman, stalker, trapper, trepanner, venerer *(Archaic)*, wildfowler, wirer, wolver, woodcraftsman *(U.S.)*, woodman *(Obs.)*, woodsman; **courser**, beagle, bloodhound, cry, gun dog, kangaroo dog, mouser, otterhound, pig-dog, preyer, ratter, retriever, sleuth, sleuthhound

HUNTING *n* bloodsport, course, coursing, deerstalking, dogging, falconry, flight shooting, fowling, fox-hunting, gunning, mutton-birding, pigsticking, sport, spotlighting, stalk, venery *(Archaic)*, wildfowling, woodcraft *(U.S.)*

HURRIEDLY *adv* cursorily, hastily, hectically, helter-skelter, hurriedly, hurry-scurry, hurryingly, in haste, on the fly *(U.S.)*, precipitantly, precipitately, summarily; **all at once**, pop, sharp, short, slam-bang, slap, slap-bang, smack; **promptly**, anon *(Archaic)*, directly, forthright *(Archaic)*, forthwith, in short order, presently *(Archaic)*, pronto, quick smart, smartly, soon, yarely; **express**, expeditiously, post, posthaste

HURRY *v* be quick off the mark, bicker, bust a gut, chase, come along, come on, dash, dispatch *(Archaic)*, get a move on, get a wriggle on, get the hell out of, haste *(Archaic)*, hasten, hie, hop to it, hurry-scurry, jump to it, lash, make haste, make it snappy, put one's best foot forward, rush, shake a leg, shoot, swash; **expedite**, express *(U.S.)*; **spur**, boot home *(Horseracing)*, brisk up, buck up, gee up, hustle, press, prick *(Archaic)*. *See also* SPEED

HURRY UP *interj* chop chop, get your arse into gear, giddy-up, jump to it, look alive, look lively, look sharp, mush, pull your finger out, rattle your dags, tantivy

HYBRID *n* creamie, cross, Eurasian, half-blood, half-breed, half-caste, heterozygote, mestizo, mongrel, mosaic *(Genetics)*, mulatto, mule, octoroon, quadroon; **bitser,** Heinz, melting pot, ten best breeds in town

HYBRID *adj* cross, half-blooded, half-caste, heterozygous, interbred, miscegenetic, mongrel, multi-racial

HYBRIDISE *v* cross, interbreed, mongrelise

Ii

ICE *n* brash *(Naut.)*, cornice, dry ice, floe, frazil, glacier, icecap, icefall, icefield, icefloe, icepack, icesheet, iceshelf, water-ice; **anchor-ice**, dead ice, drift ice, glaze, glaze ice, glazed frost, ground ice, icefoot, icefront, pack-ice, pancake ice; **ice needles**, frost flower, graupel, hail, hailstone, sleet, soft hail; **icicle**, bollard, serac; **iceberg**, berg; **ice-cube**, iceblock, party ice; **icerink**, rink; **glaciology**

IDEA *n* abstract, abstraction, apprehension, conceit, concept, conception, construct, form, generalisation, image, intellection, notion, recept, theory, thought; **fixed idea**, conceit, idée fixe, kink, obsession, vagary; **brainwave**, brainstorm, suggestion, tip, wrinkle *(Colloq.)*; **intuition**, feeling, gut feeling, gut reaction, hunch, inspiration, instinct, presentiment, sixth sense; **inkling**, glimmer, glimmering, glimpse, impression

IDEAL *adj* Platonic, Platonist, speculative, supposed, visionary

IDEALISM *n* ideology, Platonism; **metaphysics**, metempirics; **subjectivity**, internality, immaterialism, spiritualisation, spiritualism, spiritualness, transcendentalism, transcendentness, unworldliness

IDEALIST *n* ideologist, Platonist; **metaphysician**, immaterialist, metempiricist

IDLE *v* bludge, bum, coast along, donga, drowse, laze, lie, lie in, lie up, loaf, loll, lounge, moon about, not pull one's weight, rest, shirk, skulk, slack, sponge, swing the lead; **dawdle**, dally, delay, drag the chain, loiter, mooch, tarry, trail, wait; **bugger around**, arse about, arse around, boondoggle, bugger about, buggerise about, buggerise around, fart-arse, goof off, play silly buggers, trifle, twiddle. See also BE INACTIVE

IDLE *adj* bone-idle, faineant, indolent, lazy, oscitant, shiftless, slack, slothful, vacuous; **sluggardly**, dronish, effortless, inert, otiose, remiss, sluggard, sluggish, snail-like, workshy. See also INACTIVE

IDLENESS *n* accidie, acedia, effortlessness, faineance, indolence, inexertion, laziness, Mondayitis, oscitance, oscitancy, otiosity, shiftlessness, slackness, sloth, slothfulness, vacuousness; **lethargy**, anergy, languishment, languor, listlessness, sleepiness, sluggishness, spiritlessness, torpidity, torpidness, torpor. See also INACTION; PERIOD OF INACTION

IDLER *n* beat, bludger, bum, crawler, deadbeat, dole bludger, drone, faineant, layabout, loafer, lotus-eater, passenger, poler, shirk, shirker, skulk, skulker, slacker, sponger, trifler, waster, wastrel; **sluggard**, good-for-nothing, lazybones, log, log of wood, loller, recumbent, sleepyhead, snail, sooner; **dawdler**, dallier, delayer, lizard, loiterer, lounge lizard, lounger, tarrier; **paralytic**, catatonic, cot case

IDLY *adv* at a loose end, dallyingly, loiteringly, recumbently; **lazily**, indolently, languorously, otiosely, shift-

idly   269   **ill-bred**

lessly, slack, slackly, slothfully; **lethargically,** listlessly, mustily, passively, phlegmatically, spiritlessly, vacuously. *See also* INACTIVELY

IDOL *n* graven image, tin god; **zombie,** entellus, hanuman, uraeus; **fetish,** fertility symbol, juju, son-dei; **betyl,** circle *(Archaeol.)*, henge; **churinga,** bullroarer, tchuringa, thunder stick

IGNORAMUS *n* dogberry, doob, illiterate, lowbrow, nescient, simple; **boor,** alf, backwoodsman *(U.S.)*, barbarian, bog-Irish, clod, clodhopper, country bumpkin, country cousin, hayseed *(U.S.)*, hick, lout, ocker, ockerina, philistine, redneck, rube *(U.S.)*, troglodyte, yokel; **greenhorn,** amateur, babe, Johnny Raw, new chum, novice, parcel-post man, raw material, raw recruit, red-arse *(N.Z. Mil.)*, rookie, shlemiel, tabula rasa, tenderfoot, tyro, youngling; **outsider,** mushroom

IGNORANCE *n* blind spot, blindness, darkness, dogberryism, illiteracy, illiterateness, innumeracy, nescience, paralexia, simpleness; **unknowingness,** incognizance, unconsciousness, unwittingness; **inexperience,** artlessness, callowness, greenness, innocence, unadvisedness, unfamiliarity, unworldliness, verdancy, viridity; **boorishness,** barbarianism, barbarism, barbarity, illiberality, illiberalness, loutishness, ockerdom

IGNORANT *adj* backward, benighted, dark, dooby, natural, nescient, profane, simple, uneducated, unenlightened, unformed, uninformed, unlearned, unread, unscholarly, unschooled, unstudied, untaught, untutored; **unknowing,** in the dark, incognizant, insensible, unaware, unconscious, unwitting; **illiterate,** analphabetic, dyslectic, innumerate, paralexic, unlettered; **boorish,** backwoods, barbarian, barbarous, hick, illiberal, lowbrow, ocker, ockerish, philistine, redneck, troglodytic; **inexperienced,** amateur, armchair, artless, callow, clueless, fresh, freshwater, green, guiltless, home-town, inexpert, new-laid, raw, unexperienced, unseasoned, untravelled, unworldly, verdant, wet behind the ears, young

IGNORANTLY *adv* artlessly, illiterately, inexpertly, simple-mindedly, unlearnedly; **boorishly,** barbarically, illiberally; **unknowingly,** blindly, unawares, unconsciously, unsuspectedly, unwittingly

ILL *adj* ailing, bad, crook, dicky, down, in the miseries, indisposed, lousy, not so hot, off, off-colour, out of sorts, poorly, R.S., ratshit, sick, sick as a dog, unwell, wonky; **invalid,** bedridden, feeble, infirm, laid up, senile; **sickly,** adynamic, asthemic, debilitated, malnourished, peaky, pimping, sickish, wan, weakly, weedy, white-livered

ILL-BRED *adj* base, baseborn, ill-conditioned, illiberal, low, low-minded, lowbred, philistine, pleb, plebeian, underbred; **indecorous,** unbecoming, uncivil, uncivilised; **parvenu,** non-U, nouveau-riche; **uncouth,** Maori *(N.Z.)*, raw, rough, rough-and-ready, rough-spoken, rude, tramontane, troglodytic, unkempt; **loutish,** lairy, oafish, rowdy, rowdyish; **rustic,** awkward, backwoods, barnyard, buffoonish, bush, clodhopping, country, gauche, gorblimey; **brutish,** barbarian, barbaric, barbarous, beast-

ill-bred

like, boarish, brutal, harsh, heathenish, sensual, swinish. *See also* VULGAR

ILL HEALTH *n* delicacy, infirmity, infirmness, invalidism, peakiness, poor health, senility, sickliness, unhealthiness, unsoundness; **weakness,** adynamia, atrophy, cachexia, carphology, consumption, decay *(Obs.)*, marasmus, myasthenia, phthisis, tabes, tabescence. *See also* ILLNESS

ILLNESS *n* affection, affliction, ailment, complaint, discomfort, disease, disorder, distemper, idiopathy, indisposition, malady, malaise, morbidity, pip, sickness, trouble, upset; **breakdown,** atony, decay, dysfunction, shock; **symptom,** syndrome; **attack,** dose, paroxysm, touch, turn; **relapse**; **complication,** epiphenomenon, sequela; **infection,** auto-infection, Black Death, contagion, epidemic, exogenesis, murrain *(Archaic)*, pandemic, pest, pestilence, plague, zoonosis; **infectiousness,** contagiousness, deleteriousness, unwholesomeness; **infectious disease,** evil, felon, infection, sepsis, virus, zymosis; **wog,** bug, lurgi, lurgy, the dreaded lurgi. *See also* COLD: FEVER: NAUSEA: CRAMP; HEART DISEASE: MALNUTRITION VENEREAL DISEASE; TOOTHACHE: CANCER:

ILLOGICAL *adj* alogical, arbitrary, blind, capricious, discretionary, random; **irrational,** erroneous, fallacious, false, flimsy, gratuitous, groundless, ill-founded, incorrect, loose, post hoc, subreptitious, unaccountable, unreasonable, unreasoned, unscientific, unsound, weak, wrong; **groundless,** causeless, fond, implausible, reasonless, untenable;

illogicality

contradictory, antilogous, Irish, paradoxical, self-contradictory; **incompatible,** inconsistent, mutually exclusive; **absurd,** frivolous, harebrained, inept, insane, intuitive, nonsensical, scatterbrained; **fanciful,** emotional, fantastic, unreasoning; **incoherent,** disconnected, disjointed, lacking cohesion, rambling, unconnected, uncoordinated, wandering

ILLOGICALITY *n* ad hoc argument, false dilemma, false reasoning, illogicalness, inconsistency, irrationalness, misology, reasonlessness, unreason, unreasonableness; **fallaciousness,** error, groundlessness, illegitimacy, inconsequence, sophisticalness, ungroundedness, unsoundness; **arbitrariness,** blindness, capriciousness, randomness, speciousness, unaccountability, unaccountableness; **absurdity,** absurdness, bull, claptrap, garbage, ineptitude, ineptness, mere words, nonsense, rubbish, solecism; **inconsistency,** antilogy, contradiction, contradiction in terms, contradictoriness, incompatability, incompatibles, self-contradiction; **fallacy,** elenchus, equivocation, false premise, flaw, ignoratio elenchi, non sequitur, paralogism, quibble, quillet *(Archaic)*, quirk, sophism, sophistication, sophistry, weak argument, weak case; **vicious circle,** begging the question, hysteron proteron, petitio principii; **casuistry,** chicanery, equivocation, hairsplitting, Jesuitism, mystification, quibbling, quiddity, sophistry, special pleading, subterfuge

ILLOGICALLY *adv* illegitimately, inconsequently, inconsistently, irrationally, reasonlessly, unreasonably, unreasoningly, unsoundly; **intuitively**, brutally, brutishly, by intuition, like an animal; **arbitrarily**, alogically, blindly, groundlessly; **casuistically**, fallaciously, Jesuitically, sophistically; **fancifully**, emotionally, fantastically; **absurdly**, ineptly; **on the wrong tack**, awry

ILL-TREAT *v* ill-use, kick about, kick around, knock about, knock around, maltreat, maul, mishandle, mistreat, put the boot into, rough up; **pervert**, corrupt, profane, prostitute; **misuse**, abuse, fool around with, misapply, misappropriate, misemploy, overuse, overwear, squandor, tamper with, violate, waste; **mismanage**, misgovern, misrule

ILLUMINATE *v* emblaze *(Archaic)*, floodlight, illume, illumine, light, relume, spotlight; **irradiate**, insolate, roentgenise, solarise, sun; **kindle**, ignite, inflame; **gloss**, burnish, lustre, polish, schillerise, shine, varnish, wax

ILLUMINATOR *n* brightener, illuminant, inflamer, irradiator, kindler, lightener, lighter, scintillator; **torchbearer**, lamplighter, linkboy, linkman

ILLUSION *n* false perspective, FX, hocus-pocus, hokey-pokey, legerdemain, sleight of hand, special effects, trickery, trompe l'oeil; **trick**, gimmick *(U.S.)*, have *(Colloq.)*, spoof; **trick of the light**, aberration, distortion, reflection, refraction, virtual image. *See also* DELUSION

ILL WILL *n* animosity, enmity, malevolence; **malice**, despite *(Archaic)*, ill-naturedness, maliciousness, malignity, poisonousness, Schadenfreude, spite, venom, venomousness, virulence

IMAGE *n* conceit, crotchet, fiction, flight of fancy, idea *(Obs.)*, ideation, imagery, imago, notion, projection, representation, romance, vagary, vision, whimsy; **phantom**, eidolon, idol, little green men

IMITATE *v* ape, copy, do a *(Colloq.)*, duplicate, echo, emulate, follow, follow in someone's footsteps, follow suit, make like, mirror, take a leaf out of someone's book; **plagiarise**, counterfeit, forge; **mimic**, impersonate; **caricature**, burlesque, mock, monkey, parody, send up, spoof, take off, travesty; **feign**, affect, come the (something or someone) with, counterfeit, play at; **simulate**, represent, reproduce

IMITATION *n* apery, apishness, duplication, echo, emulation, emulousness, foreignism *(U.S.)*, imitativeness, impersonation, impression, mimesis, mimicry, representation, rivalry, simulation; **plagiarism**, plagiary, stealing; **copying**, duplicating, photocopying, reproducing, xeroxing; **onomatopoeia**, echoism; **copy**, a chip off the old block, duplicate, effigy, facsimile, likeness, photocopy, record, recording, replication, representation, reproduction, semblance, transcript, xerox; **forgery**, counterfeit, sham; **caricature**, burlesque, cartoon, mockery, parody, pastiche, postiche, send-up, skit, spoof, take-off, travesty

IMITATIVE *adj* apish, echoic, echolike, emulative, emulous, imitational, plagiaristic, pseudo, sequacious *(Archaic)*, simulative; **artificial**, counterfeit, dummy, ersatz, imita-

imitative

tion, mock, simulant; **mimic,** mimetic, pantomimic

IMITATIVELY *adv* apishly, emulously, literally, reproductively, word for word; **à la,** after, in the manner of

IMITATOR *n* ape, copier, copycat, echoer, emulator, epigone, follower, following, kook *(Surfing),* reproducer; **plagiariser,** magpie, plagiarist; **mimer,** caricaturist, impersonator, mimic, monkey, parodist, parrot; **feigner,** affecter, counterfeiter, simulant, simular, simulator; **forger,** short-story writer *(Prison Colloq.)*

IMMORAL *adj* corrupt, debauched, decadent, degenerate, degraded, depraved, ruined, unprincipled, vitiated; **disreputable,** knavish, louche, scoundrel *(Rare),* scoundrelly, scrofulous, villainous, worthless; **indecent,** base, loose, profligate, wanton; **frail,** only human, weak; **reprobate,** abandoned, incorrigible, irredeemable, lost, naught *(Obs.),* recidivous; **sinful,** Babylonian, black, black-hearted, dark, erring, evil, evil-minded, naughty *(Obs.),* nefarious, peccant, pernicious, sinister, vicious, wicked; **godless,** impious, irreligious, profane, unblessed, ungodly, unhallowed, unholy, unrighteous; **devilish,** accursed, cloven-footed, cloven-hoofed, demoniac, demonian, demonic, diabolic, diabolical, fiendish, hellish, infernal, satanic; **foul,** abominable, filthy, nasty, polluted, putrid, rank, rotten, ulcerous, unclean, unhealthy, vile; **atrocious,** enormous, gross, heinous, inexpiable, iniquitous, unforgivable, unpardonable; **corruptive,** seductive

impact

IMMORALITY *n* corruption, debauch *(Obs.),* debauchery, degeneracy, degeneration, degradedness, depravity, loose morals, moral turpitude, perversion, transgression, turpitude, vice; **foulness,** filthiness, nastiness, odiousness, rottenness, scrofulousness, uncleanliness, unhealthiness, vileness; **human frailty,** feet of clay, infirmity, looseness, the old Adam, wantonness, weakness, weakness of the flesh; **wickedness,** belial, blackness, corruptiveness, darkness, enormity, enormousness *(Archaic),* evilness, heinousness, ill *(Archaic),* illness *(Obs.),* iniquitousness, iniquity, maleficence, nefariousness, perniciousness, sinfulness, sinisterness, ungodliness, unholiness, unrighteousness, viciousness; **damnation,** depths, perdition. *See also* EVILDOING

IMMORALLY *adv* corruptly, decadently, degradedly, vilely, wantonly; **filthily,** nastily, rottenly, unhealthily; **evilly,** enormously, iniquitously, malignly, nefariously, perniciously, viciously, villainously, wickedly; **sinfully,** erringly, unrighteously; **diabolically,** hellishly, satanically

IMMORAL PERSON *n* blood, decadent, miscreant, profligate, reprobate, wretch; **backslider,** recidivist; **wrongdoer,** evildoer, malefactor, malefactress, sinner; **devil,** cloven foot, cloven hoof, demon, Mammon, Satan; **corrupter,** depraver, pander, polluter, seducer

IMPACT *n* concussion, impingement, impulse, jar, percussion, shock; **collision,** bang, bump, clash, conflict, confliction, crack-up, crash, elastic collision, hurtle *(Poetic),* knock, slam, smash, stack, thud, thump, whang;

smash-up, concertina crash, head-on, pile-up, stack-up; **prang**, ding, foul; **tackle**, bonecrusher, flying tackle, smother tackle; **rebound**, croquet, ricochet, roquet *(Croquet)*; **bounce**, dribble. *See also* HITTING

IMPEND *v* approach, be imminent, be near at hand, draw near

IMPENITENCE *n* brassiness, brazenness, impenitency, impenitentness, obduracy, obdurateness, obstinacy, recusancy, shamelessness, unblushingness

IMPENITENT *adj* remorseless, shameless, unashamed, unblushing, unreformed, unregenerate, unrepentant, unshriven; **obstinate**, brassy, brazen, brazen-faced, hardened, indurate, obdurate, recusant; **incorrigible**, irreclaimable, irredeemable

IMPENITENTLY *adv* brassily, brazenly, obdurately, shamelessly, unashamedly, unblushingly

IMPENITENT PERSON *n* constant offender, habitual criminal, hardened criminal, recidivist, recusant, self-confessed sinner

IMPERFECT *adj* incomplete, unideal; **defective**, bad, deficient, faulty, sketchy, unsound, vicious; **underdone**, immature, underdeveloped, unripe; **impure**, adulterated

IMPERFECTION *n* defectiveness, faultiness, imperfectness, sketchiness, weakness; **underdevelopment**, immatureness, immaturity, unripeness; **contamination**, adulteration, impureness, impurity; **defect**, bug, failing, fault, fly in the ointment, shortcoming, vice; **weak point**, Achilles heel, chink in one's armour, faultiness, feet of clay, weak link in the chain, weakness; **impurity**, blemish, flaw

IMPERFECTLY *adv* defectively, faultily, ill, sketchily

IMPERMANENT *adj* casual, deciduous, lapsable, movable, semipermanent; **temporary**, acting, commendatory, de bene esse, fill-in, interim, make-do, makeshift, pro tem, pro tempore, provisional, provisory, temporal, working; **transitory**, cursory, ephemeral, evanescent, fleeting, fugacious, fugitive, here to-day and gone tomorrow, in transit, like a dream, passing, shifting, summary, transient, volatile; **instant**, ad hoc, instantaneous, momentary; **short-lived**, mortal, perishable, primitive, short-life, spasmodic; **brief**, acute, brisk, meteoric, quick

IMPERMEABLY *adv* closely, hermetically, impenetrably, imperviously

IMPERSONAL *adj* anonymous, faceless, indefinite, indeterminate, of sorts, omnifarious, open, overhead, unmarked, unnamed, unspecified

IMPERSONALITY *n* depersonalisation, facelessness

IMPLICATIONALLY *adv* connotatively, implicatively, impliedly, predicatively; **allusively**, insinuatingly, obliquely, suggestively; **implicitly**, tacitly

IMPLY *v* allude to, get at *(Colloq.)*, hint at, infer *(Colloq.)*, insinuate, suggest; **implicate**, connote, involve, predicate

IMPORTANCE *n* account, concern, concernment, consequence, consequentiality, consideration, greatness, import, interest, magnitude, matter, moment, notability, notableness, noteworthiness, pith, significance, significancy, size, substance; **seriousness,** earnestness, eventfulness, fatefulness, graveness, gravity, momentousness, portentousness, solemnity, weight, weightiness; **essentiality,** essentialness, vitalness; **urgency,** acuteness, criticalness, pressure, primacy, priority; **profoundness,** deepness, profundity; **emphasis,** accent, accentuation, force, stress; **value,** goodness, worth; **eminence,** altitude *(Obs.),* distinction, egregiousness *(Obs.),* grandeur, grandiosity, grandness, mark, note, pre-eminence, prominence, stature, supremeness

IMPORTANT *adj* all-important, consequential, considerable, significant; **signal,** impressive, memorable, notable, noted, noteworthy, unforgettable; **emphasised,** pointed; **serious,** earnest, grave, heavy, weighty; **momentous,** climacteric, critical, eventful, fatal, fated, portentous; **earth-shattering,** breathtaking, colossal, earth-shaking, epoch-making, shattering, stirring, world-shaking; **newsworthy,** big-time, front-page; **essential,** material, pivotal, to the point; **basic,** fundamental, indispensable, irreplaceable, key, necessary, primary; **vital,** acute, high-priority, insistent, pressing, top-priority, urgent; **major,** arch, capital, cardinal, chief, first, foremost, leading, main, paramount, pet, primal, prime, principal, staple; **prominent,** big, conspicuous, distingué, distinguished, egregious *(Obs.),* eminent, grand, great, noble, pre-eminent; **exalted,** august, high, high-level, high-up, lofty, senior, top-level; **dominant,** number one, supreme, top, top-line, uppermost

IMPORTANTLY *adv* above all, uppermost; **significantly,** materially, notably, notedly, noteworthily; **seriously,** earnestly, for dear life, gravely; **momentously,** eventfully, fatefully, portentously, weightily; **vitally,** acutely, critically, pressingly, urgently; **basically,** fundamentally; **eminently,** dominantly, egregiously *(Obs.),* pre-eminently, prominently, supremely

IMPORTANT PERSON *n* arch *(Obs.),* bashaw *(Obs.),* big gun, big noise, big shot, big wheel, bigwig, brass, buzzwig, chief, dignitary, everybody who is anybody, giant, great, high-up, his nibs, magnate, magnifico, mogul, Mr Big, number one, numero uno, personage, pot, prince, principal, sire *(Obs.),* tall poppy, top brass, top dog, top-liner, V.I.P., visiting fireman, wheel, who's who; **star,** first fiddle, lead, leading light, prima donna; **key person,** anchorman, mainstay; **panjandrum,** boiled shirt, stuffed shirt

IMPORTANT THING *n* cardinal point, heart of the matter, issue, point, sixty-four dollar question, the thing; **climax,** climacteric, crisis, great divide, juncture, moment of truth, red-letter day, turning point; **key word,** punch line; **a matter of life and death,** a big deal, be-all and end-all, everything, importance *(Obs.),* no joke, no laughing matter, vital concern; **gist,** heart, substance, vitals, yolk; **basics,** bedrock, essentials, fundamentals, nitty-gritty, sine qua non; **cornerstone,** keynote, kingpin *(Colloq.),* linchpin; **pride of place,** face, front, head and front, spearhead; **notabilia,** notable *(Obs.),* rubric, something; **master-

important thing / **imprecision**

piece, centrepiece, chef-d'oeuvre, magnum opus, pièce de résistance

IMPORTUNACY *n* earnestness, imploringness, importunateness, importunity, prayerfulness, suppliantness; **beggary,** mendicancy, mendicity; **pressure,** insistence, instance *(Archaic),* urgency

IMPOSE *v* administer, agist, distrain, encroach, exact, inflict, lay a burden on, prescribe, put a responsibility on, require, wreak; **foist on,** land with, lumber, palm off on, saddle with, wish on; **requisition,** commandeer, levy, tax; **domineer,** command, demand, force, tyrannise

IMPOSER *n* administrant, agistor, distrainer, enforcer, exactor, inflictor, tasker, wreaker

IMPOSING *adj* domineering, exacting, overbearing

IMPOSITION *n* administration, distrainment, distraint, enactment, enforcement, exaction, infliction; **demand,** burden, edict, impost, order, order of the day, ordination, requirement, requisition, tax, ukase

IMPOSSIBILITY *n* hopelessness, inconceivability, insuperability, unimaginableness; **preclusion,** exclusion, incompatibleness; **paradox,** paradoxicalness; **impasse,** deadlock, no go, no-no; **infeasibility,** impassability, impracticability, impracticalness, inaccessibility, unworkability

IMPOSSIBLE *adj* beyond the bounds of reason, contrary to reason, hopeless, no-go, not to be thought of, out of court, out of the question, uncome-at-able; **infeasible,** absurd, impracticable, inexecutable, out of reach, quixotic, unaccomplishable, unachievable, unattainable, unfeasible, unobtainable, unworkable; **inconceivable,** incredible, unimaginable, unthinkable; **insuperable,** impassable, inextricable, insurmountable

IMPOVERISH *v* bankrupt, beggar, bleed white, clean out, pauperise, ruin, skin, take to the cleaners

IMPRECISE *adj* approximate, inaccurate, inexact, proximate, wide of the mark; **vague,** amorphous, aoristic, blurred, blurry, dim, dreamy, faint, faraway, hazy, indefinable, indefinite, indeterminate, indistinct, intangible, loose, misty, muddy, mysterious, mystic, nebulous, nubilous, obscure, tenuous, uncertain, undefined, vaporous, vapoury, veiled; **shadowy,** airy, bleary, blurry, ghostlike, ill-defined, phantom, wraithlike; **inexplicit,** ambiguous, confused, cryptic, enigmatic, equivocal, woolly

IMPRECISELY *adv* dreamily, inaccurately, indefinitely, indeterminately, inexactly, loosely, tenuously, vaguely; **ambiguously,** inexplicitly, woollily; **indistinctly,** faintly, hazily, mistily, nebulously, obscurely, vaporously; **approximately,** about, in some sort, like, more or less, or so, proximately, roughly, sort of; **upwards of,** off the ballpark

IMPRECISION *n* approximation, bush reckoning, impreciseness, inaccuracy, inaccurateness, inexactitude, inexactness, inexplicitness, looseness, rule of thumb; **vagueness,** grey area, indefinableness, indefiniteness, indeterminacy, indeterminateness, indetermination, intangibility, intangibleness, tenuousness; **shapelessness,** amorphism, amorphousness; **in-**

imprecision   **improver**

distinctness, bleariness, blur, blurriness, dimness, faintness, fog, haze, haziness, mistiness, nebulousness, shadow, vaporousness; **uncertainty**, ambiguity, ambiguousness, incomprehensibility, obscureness, obscurity, open question, pig in a poke, waffle, woolliness

IMPRINT *n* impression, print, stamp, touch *(Metall.)*

IMPRISON *v* gaol, immure, incarcerate, jug, lag, pound, put away, send down, send up, shut in, shut up, tuck away; **detain**, guard, hold, keep, keep in, remand, remit *(Obs.)*; **confine**, cabin, cloister, coop, cordon off, cramp, immure, lock in, lock up, pocket, restrain, secure, shut away, shut in, shut up; **intern**, gate; **slot**, slough up; **limit**, circumscribe; **cage**, corner, encage, hedge in, hem in, pound; **pen**, kraal *(S. African)*, paddock, stall; **fetter**, handcuff, manacle. *See also* ARREST

IMPRISONED *adj* captive, incarcerate; **secured**, confined, fast, pent, pent-up; **cramped**, claustrophobic, close, limitative, limited, poky, strait *(Archaic)*; **penal**, custodial, institutional, non-parole, penitentiary; **maximum-security**, minimum-security

IMPRISONMENT *n* false imprisonment, immurement, incarceration, internment, lockup, prison; **arrest**, apprehension, arrestment, attachment, capture, cop, pinch; **order**, capias, capias ad satisfaciendum, commitment, mittimus, writ; **captivity**, confinement, constraint, durance, durance vile, duress, solitary; **custody**, detainment, detention, house arrest, keeping, protective custody, remand, restraint, safety *(Obs.)*, surveillance, ward; **commitment**, committal; **time**, bed and breakfast, bird, brick, clock, drag, lag, lagging, lost weekend, porridge, rest, sleep, snooze, spin, stretch, swy, zack; **life imprisonment**, the lot, the twist

IMPROVE *v* ameliorate, amend, better, elaborate, enrich, fair *(Shipbuilding)*, fine, meliorate, perfect, refine on, transfigure, update, upgrade, uplift; **smarten**, brush up, chamfer up, detail, enhance, polish up, refurbish, touch up; **mend**, remodel, repair, retouch; **civilise**, cultivate, edify; **benefit**, facilitate, help; **advance**, be none the worse for, better oneself, climb, evolve, gain ground, make headway, progress, pull ahead, pull up; **reform**, go straight, mend one's ways, turn over a new leaf; **come good**, brighten, look up, pick up, rally, recover, recuperate, regenerate, take a turn for the better; **mellow**, develop, ripen

IMPROVED *adj* better, enhanced, enriched, on the improve, on the mend, on the up and up, on the upgrade, reformed, regenerate, up-and-coming, upwardly mobile

IMPROVEMENT *n* amelioration, amendment, betterment, enhancement, melioration, pick-up, recovery, uplift; **reform**, counter-reformation, reformation, regenaracy, regeneration, self-improvement; **progress**, advancement, development, enrichment, preferment, progression, promotion; **change for the better**, transfiguration, transformation; **advance**, a leap forward, stride; **repair**, mend, renovation, retouch

IMPROVER *n* ameliorant, ameliorator, developer, meliorator, meliorist, perfecter, uplifter; **mender**, detailer, re-

improver / **inactive**

pairer, retoucher; **reformer,** amender, progressionist, progressive, redresser, reformist; **conditioner,** civilising influence; **social climber,** advancer, upward mobile

IMPROVING *adj* ameliorative, amendatory *(U.S.),* beneficial, civilising, corrective, edificatory, edifying, meliorative, reformational, reforming, remedial; **progressive,** Fabian, reformist; **improvable,** ameliorative, amendable, developable, mendable, perfectible, reformable

IMPROVINGLY *adv* beneficially, edifyingly, progressively

IMPULSIVE PERSON *n* creature of impulse, goodtimer, tear-arse, tearaway

IMPUTABLE *adj* ascribable, assignable, attributable, due, **blamable,** accountable, answerable, blameful, chargeable, culpable, guilty, responsible, to blame

IMPUTATION *n* accreditation, arrogation, ascription, assignation, assignment, attribution, buck-passing, projection, witch-hunting; **blame,** censure motion, head-hunting, rap, reproach

IMPUTATIVELY *adv* assignably, attributably; **blamefully,** accountably, blamably, culpably; **accordingly,** in as much as, in that, in view of, now that, on account of, owing to, seeing that, thanks to, therefore

IMPUTE *v* affix, arrogate, ascribe, assign, attach, attribute, chalk up to, lay, lay at the door of, object *(Obs.),* put down, put on, put to, sheet home, source; **charge,** accredit with, accuse, attack, blame, bring to account, call to account, challenge, pick on; **pass the buck,** sling the hook

INACTION *n* cataplexy, inactivation, inactivity, inertness, inoperativeness, motionlessness, quiescence, repose, rest, spectator sport *(joc.),* stagnancy, stagnation, stoniness, supineness; **abstention,** arrest, default, delay, forbearance; **sedentariness,** vegetation; **quietness,** calmness, depression *(Econ.),* drowsiness, languidness, languor, quietude, stillness; **dawdling,** dalliance, tarriance *(Archaic);* **recumbency,** disengagement, Edwardianism, inoccupation, vacancy *(Rare);* **passiveness,** Fabianism, inactiveness, laissez faire, passion *(Rare),* passivity. *See also* IDLENESS: PERIOD OF INACTION

INACTIVATE *v* becalm, calm, easy *(Rowing),* put on the back burner, quiet, quieten, sedate; **paralyse,** palsy, petrify

INACTIVE *adj* abeyant, actionless, at a loose end, dummy, idle, in abeyance, inert, inoperative, noble *(Chem.),* passive, quiescent, recumbent, silent, supine; **sedentary,** chairborne; **lethargic,** catatonic, coasty, indolent *(Pathol.),* listless, musty, palsied, paralytic, phlegmatic, phlegmy, poppied, remiss, sleepy, slow, stonkered, thick, torpid; **dormant,** asleep, comatose, hibernating; **off-peak,** dead, dead-and-alive, drowsy, dull, dullish, easy, flat, inertial, languid, languishing, languorous, off-season, quiet, slack, sleepy, slow, sluggish, slumberous, stagnant; **out of action,** hors de combat, laid low, on the back burner, on the sidelines, run-down, u/s, unserviceable; **calm,** breathless, down, motionless, still, stock-still, stony,

inactive unmoving; **fogbound,** closed, icebound. *See also* IDLE

INACTIVELY *adv* down, inertly, on the back burner, quiescently, sedentarily, supinely; **sluggishly,** drowsily, languidly, languishingly, on ice, quietly, sleepily, torpidly; **at rest,** motionlessly, stagnantly, still, stonily. *See also* IDLY

IN AGREEMENT *adj* accordant, according, ad idem *(Law),* agreeable, agreed nem. con., agreeing, closeknit, compatible, concordant, congenial, consensual, consentaneous, consentient, empathetic, empathic, en rapport, harmonious, in accord, in tune, like-minded, of one accord, of one mind, simpatico, sympathetic, unanimous; **allied,** in cahoots, in league. *See also* ASSENTING

IN A LOUD VOICE *adv* at the top of one's lungs, at the top of one's voice, screamingly, vociferously; **clamorously,** clangourously, noisily

INAPPROPRIATE *adj* inadmissible, inapposite, inapt, ineligible, inopportune, out of place, unfit, unqualified, unsuitable, unsuited; **unwise,** crazy, ill-advised, impolitic, inadvisable; **inapplicable,** futile, impossible, impracticable, ineffective, infeasible, unpractical, vain

INAPPROPRIATELY *adv* awkwardly, impoliticly, inadvisably, inaptly, infelicitously, unqualifiedly, unsatisfactorily, unsuitably, untowardly; **inapplicably,** impossibly, impracticably, unpractically; **unwisely,** crazily, impoliticly, needlessly, uselessly

INAPPROPRIATENESS *n* impropriety, inadvisability, inappositeness, inaptitude, inaptness, unfitness, unqualifiedness, unsatisfactoriness; **inapplicability,** futility, impracticability, impracticableness, inapplicableness, infeasibility, unpracticality, unpracticalness, vainness; **uselessness,** needlessness, unsuitability, unsuitableness; **unwiseness,** craziness, impoliticness

INARTICULATE *adj* aphasic, disconnected, disjointed, dysphonic, fumbling, hesitant, ineloquent, quavery; **mute,** aphonic, dumb, silent, speechless, tongue-tied

INARTICULATELY *adv* disconnectedly, disjointedly, ineloquently, lispingly, mutteringly; **stammeringly,** falteringly, fumblingly, hesitantly, hesitatingly, mumblingly, stutteringly; **dumbly,** mutely, speechlessly

IN ASTONISHMENT *adv* agape, amazedly, with open mouth, wonderingly

INATTENTIVE *adj* half asleep, inobservant, oscitant; **abstracted,** absent-minded, bemused, distracted, distrait, dreamy, lost in thought, moony, preoccupied; **unheeding,** disregardful, inadvertent, regardless; **thoughtless,** mindless, not switched on, on auto, scatty, unmindful, unthinking; **careless,** casual, cursory, neglectful, remiss, rough, scatterbrained, slaphappy, slipshod, superficial

INATTENTIVELY *adv* absently, abstractedly, abstractly, cursorily, distractedly, in a dream, in the clouds; **unheedingly,** inadvertently, mindlessly, thoughtlessly, unmindfully, unthinkingly

INATTENTIVENESS *n* absence of mind, absent-mindedness, disregard, inadvertence, inattention, inobservance, mindlessness, thoughtlessness, unmindfulness, unthinkingness; **abstractedness,** abstraction, brown study, daydreaming, doodling, dreaminess, oscitance, oscitancy, reverie, wool-gathering; **carelessness**, neglect, neglectfulness, oversight, remissness

INBORN *adj* born, congenital, connate, connatural, inbred, indigenous, ingenerate *(Archaic)*, innate; **inherent**, built-in, constitutional, immanent, in-built, indigenous, inward, natural, radical; **personal**, complexional, specific, subjective, subjectivistic

INCENTIVE *n* appetiser, carrot, prompt, spiff; **stimulus**, fillip, hurry-up, impellent, impulse, inducer, pep talk, prodder, prompter, provocative, recommender, stimulant *(Rare)*, stimulative, stimulator, urge; **spur**, ankus *(India)*, battery stick, cattle prod, goad, gully-raker, paroo dog *(Agric.)*, prick *(Archaic)*, prod, riding crop, sting, stockwhip, whip; **shout of encouragement**, cheer, hype, war dance; **promotion**, advertisement, advertising campaign, commercial, film clip *(T.V.)*, hard sell, loss leader, plug, promo, recommendation, sell, soft sell, teaser, trailer *(Film)*; **inducement**, bribery, consideration, reward; **cajolery**, blandishment, flattery

INCLUDE *v* comprehend, count in, cover, embrace, entail, incorporate, number, subsume, take in; **comprise**, consist of, contain, have, hold; **be included**, be in it, have a finger in the pie

INCLUSION *n* comprehension, comprisal, coverage, embracement, entailment, incorporation; **inclusiveness**, comprehensiveness, generality

INCLUSIVE *adj* across the board, all-embracing, comprehensive, general, incorporative, overall, sweeping, total, umbrella, wholesale; **all told**, all found, all-in, all-included, all-inclusive, all-up, in all

INCLUSIVE OF *prep* cum, including, through *(U.S.)*; **amongst**, among, mongst *(Poetic)*, of, together with, with

INCOME *n* annuity, bread and butter, crust, disposable income, earnings, emolument, establishment *(Archaic)*, independent means, livelihood, meal ticket, money wages, nominal wages, pay, pay-packet, real wages, remuneration, revenue, salary, screw, secondary wage, sturt *(Mining)*, susso *(Obs.)*, take-home pay, total wage, truck, wage; **living**, benefice, fellowship, scholarship; **stipend**, bounty system *(Hist.)*, gratification *(Archaic)*, gratuity, pourboire, prebend *(Eccles.)*, recompense, reward; **basic wage**, award wage, industry award, living wage, minimum wage, ordinary pay; **penalty rate**, back pay, double time, half-pay, margin, overtime, piece rate, severance pay, sick pay, strike pay, time-and-a-half, triple time, weekend penalty rate; **blood money**, danger money; **allowance**, attraction money, climatic allowance, dirt money, district allowance, field allowance, heat money, height money, living allowance, loading, locality allowance, lost time allowance, meal allowance, mess allowance, mileage, per diem, percentage, separation allowance *(Mil.)*, shift allowance, subsistence allowance, tea money, tool allowance, war loading, weighting, zone allowance; **bonus**, bounty, cost-of-living bonus, perk, perquisite, premium; **advance**, sub *(Brit.)*; **royalty**, douceur, enfeoffment,

income   280   **incompetent**

farm, fee, levy, public lending right, retainer, retaining fee, retainment; **rent,** fair rent, farm *(English Hist.),* hire, peppercorn rent, quitrent, rental; **pension,** child allowance, child endowment, disability allowance, super, superannuation, welfare; **unemployment benefit,** dole, sickness benefit, sit-down money, suss

INCOMMODE *v* be inexpedient, disadvantage, discommode, disoblige, embarrass, gum up the works, hinder, indispose, never do, not do, put out

IN COMMON *adv* jointly, respectively

IN COMPANY WITH *adv* arm in arm, hand in hand, in convoy, side by side; **together,** jointly, unitedly; **in waiting,** in attendance

INCOMPATIBLE *adj* inconsistent, insolvable, irresolvable, mutually exclusive, paradoxical, preclusive, self-contradictory

INCOMPETENCE *n* fumbling, ignorance, inaptness, ineffectuality, inefficiency, ineptitude, inexperience, inexpertness, maladministration, mismanagement; **Peter principle; incapacity,** apraxia *(Pathol.),* disability, disablement, impotence, inaptitude, incapability, incapableness, incapacitation, unfitness; **artlessness,** amateurishness, amateurism, cubbishness, gaucheness, gaucherie, lubberliness, naivete, otherworldliness; **awkwardness,** angularness, bearishness, clumsiness, flat-footedness, gawkiness, heavy-handedness, left-handedness, lumpiness, lumpishness, maladdress, maladroitness, stiffness, ungainliness, ungracefulness, unhandiness, unskilfulness; **unprofessionalism,** lack of expertise, quackery; **hopelessness,** badness, poorness; **imbecility,** clownishness, folly, foolishness, goofiness; **uncouthness,** slovenliness, ungraciousness

INCOMPETENT *n* boggler, botcher, bungler, fumbler, incapable, misdoer, mismanager, mucker-up, muddler; **duffer,** bad shot, billygoat, clown, deadhead, dill, dunce, fart, fool, galoot, great ape, imbecile, lame dog, lame duck, palooka, rabbit *(Cricket),* spastic, unco; **clumsy person,** blunderbuss, blunderer, bull in a china shop, bumpkin, butter-fingers, clodhopper, gawk, gazob, hobbledehoy, hulk, lubber, lummox, lump, mullocker, slab, the awkward squad; **bad workman,** backyarder, blackjack merchant *(Plumbing),* bush carpenter, cobbler, cub, quack, snagger *(Shearing),* wood butcher; **sloven,** slob, slouch; **dead loss,** hopeless case, no-hoper, the end, the living end, write-off; **dogberry,** bureaucrat, flunkey, lackey, seatwarmer

INCOMPETENT *adj* ineffectual, inefficient, inept; **incapable,** impotent, inapt, unfit; **unpractised,** backyard, fumbling, inexpert, ungifted, unskilful, unskilled, untalented; **amateurish,** artless, cubbish, cut-lunch, half-baked, home-made, landlubberly, lubberly, unprofessional; **untrained,** callow, green, inexperienced, raw, semi-skilled; **slovenly,** bearish, gauche, offhand, uncouth, ungracious *(Obs.),* unhandy, unmechanical; **imbecile,** clownish, foolish, goofy, imbecilic, spastic, unco, uncool; **clumsy,** accident-prone, all thumbs, awkward, bumble footed, cack-handed, cacky-handed, clod-hopping, elephantine, flat-footed, footless *(U.S. Colloq.),* gawky, ham-fisted, heavy, heavy-handed, hipshot, hulking, left-handed, lumpish, lumpy, maladroit, ungainly, ungraceful, unwieldy. *See also* BADLY-DONE

INCOMPETENTLY *adv* amateurishly, artlessly, inaptly, incapably, lubberly, unfitly, unhandily, unprofessionally, unskilfully; **awkwardly,** angularly, bearishly, clumsily, flat-footedly, fumblingly, gawkily, left-handedly, lumpishly, maladroitly, uncouthly, ungainly, ungracefully, unwieldily; **imbecilely,** clownishly; **inefficiently,** arse-up, blunderingly, bunglingly, ill, ineptly, poorly, slovenly

INCOMPREHENSION *n* inapprehension, incoherence, incomprehensiveness; **puzzlement,** bafflement, bamboozlement, bewilderment, confusion, mystification, perplexity

INCONGRUITY *n* anomalousness, incongruence, oddness, unnaturalness; **unaptness,** improperness, impropriety, infelicity, unbecomingness, unfitness, unseemliness, unsuitability, unsuitableness; **disagreement,** antinomy, disaccord, nonconformity, repugnance; **discord,** contention, discordance, disharmony, inconsonance; **irreconcilability,** incompatibleness; **antibiosis,** disoperation

INCONGRUOUS *adj* absonant, anomalistic, anomalous, incongruent, odd, unnatural; **discrepant,** contradictory, inconsistent, repugnant; **incompatible,** ill-assorted, incoherent, irreconcilable, off, unbecoming, uncomformable, unfortunate, unhappy, unseemly; **inappropriate,** misplaced, out of character, out of keeping, out of place; **at variance,** at issue, at odds, contentious, controversial, in question; **unapt,** impertinent, improper, inept, infelicitous, irrelevant, unfit, unsuitable, unsuited, wrong; **dissonant,** discordant, disharmonious, inconsonant, out of phase, parataxic

INCONGRUOUSLY *adv* anomalously, incongruently, oddly; **unaptly,** improperly, inappropriately, incoherently, incompatibly, infelicitous, unfitly, unhappily, unsatisfactorily, unseemly, unsuitably; **discordantly,** discrepantly, dissonantly, inconsistently, inconsonantly, irreconcilably, out of step

IN CONTRAST *adv* by way of contrast, contrarily, on the contrary, on the other hand, vice versa

INCONVENIENCE *n* disadvantageousness, discommodity, incommodiousness, incommodity, inexpedience, inexpediency, unprofitability, unprofitableness, untowardness; **disadvantage,** disutility, drawback, ill effect, ill fortune, infelicity, liability, misfortune, penalty, slug; **awkwardness,** clumsiness, ineptitude, ineptness, infelicity; **unhelpfulness,** disobligingness, impertinence, inimicality, uncooperativeness

INCONVENIENT *adj* incommodious, inexpedient; **disadvantageous,** bad, cross, improper, infelicitous, needless, nugatory, objectionable, undesirable, unfortunate, unprofitable, unsatisfactory, unseemly, untoward, useless, worthless; **awkward,** clumsy, de trop, inept, infelicitous, unmanageable; **unhelpful,** disobliging, impertinent, inimical, uncooperative

INCONVENIENTLY *adv* disadvantageously, in a bad light, inappositely, incommodiously, ineptly, inexpediently, unprofitably; **unhelpfully,** disobligingly, inimically, uncooperatively

INCORRECT *adj* amiss, fallacious, faulty, wrong; **unworthy,** irregular, unchristian, unprofessional; **improper,** close to the wind, naughty, offensive, out-of-the-way, spicy, unacceptable, unbecoming, uncalled-for; **questionable,** censurable, reproachable; **unjustified,** undue. *See also* WRONG

INCREASE *n* accession, accretion, accumulation, addition, aggrandisement, amplification, appreciation, augmentation, bank-up, build-up, cumulation, enhancement, exacerbation, expansion, extension, gain, heterosis, increment, inflation, overfall, reinforcement; **intensification,** aggravation, concentration, crescendo, enrichment, escalation, exaggeration, intension, magnification, maximisation, regeneration, rise, swell; **proliferation,** elaboration, escalation, multiplication, propagation, pullulation, rash; **acceleration,** speed-up; **boom,** rally, revaluation, rise, upswing, upturn

INCREASE *v* accumulate, amplify, augment, boost, cumulate, double, enhance, enlarge, enrich, expand, redouble, reinforce, soup up, work up; **exaggerate,** add fuel to the fire, exacerbate, lay it on; **aggrandise,** beef up, blow up, broach, build up, bump up, clap on, deepen, develop, double, eke *(Archaic),* escalate, extend, flash, flesh out, gross up, heighten, hot up, increment, lengthen, let out, magnify, maximise, multiply, pad out, piece out, propagate, space out, spin out, step up, thicken, turn up, up; **accelerate,** gather, pick up, speed, speed up; **revalue,** approve *(Law),* bull, enhance, hike up, jump, load, mark up, pyramid, raise, raise the ante, rise, up the ante

INCREASED *adj* blown, blubber, blubbery, enlarged, erect, expanded, inflated, swollen, tumescent, tumid, tympanitic; **intensified,** concentrate, concentrated, crash, intensive; **more,** other, plus; **exaggerated,** extended, souped-up

INCREASER *n* accumulator, aggrandiser, augmenter, concentrator, empire builder, enhancer, expander, grower, maximiser; **amplifier,** enlarger, exagerator, heightener, magnifier; **inflator,** dilator, stretcher; **multiplier,** propagator; **expansionist,** inflationist; **accelerator,** booster

INCREASING *adj* crescendo, crescent, dilatant, dilative, expansive, growing, increscent, monotonic, multiplying, waxing; **enhancive,** concentrative, exaggerative, intensifying; **accelerative,** acceleratory, progressive; **augmentative,** accretive, accumulative, cumulative, exponential, multiplicative

INCREASINGLY *adv* accumulatively, crescendo, cumulatively, exponentially, multiplicatively; **more,** out of all proportion

IN DEBT *adj* encumbered, head over heels in debt, in arrears, in beyond one's depth, in difficulties, in financial difficulties, in the red, indebted, liable; **overdrawn,** behindhand, embarrassed, O/D, out of pocket; **bankrupt,** bust, insolvent, ruined

INDEBTEDNESS *n* embarrassment, judgment, obligation, tribute; **arrears,** arrearage, default, nonpayment; **account,** reckoning, score;

bankruptcy, bust, bust-up, commercial failure, financial collapse, financial crash, insolvency, receivership

INDECISION *n* aboulia, ambivalence, double-mindedness, doubtfulness, indecisiveness, tentativeness, uncertainness, undecidedness; **irresoluteness,** haltingness, inconsistency, infirmness, limpness, shakiness, unstableness, unsteadiness; **aimlessness,** unsettledness, unsettlement; **second thoughts,** pause, pendency, pendulousness, quandary, vacillation; **procrastination,** hesitation, temporisation; **evasion,** equivocation, prevarication, run-around; **capriciousness,** caprice, flightiness, skittishness, whimsicality

INDECISIVE *adj* aboulic, ambivalent, double-minded, doubtful, halting, inconsistent, inconstant, pendulous, shaky, tentative, vacillating, vacillatory; **unsure,** open, piss-weak, uncertain, uncommitted, undecided, unsettled, weak, weak-willed; **perplexed,** at a loss, at one's wit's end, in a sweat, on the horns of a dilemma; **irresolute,** aimless, capricious, errant, fickle, flighty, objectless, skittish, unstable, unsteady, whimsical; **evasive,** non-committal

INDENTATION *n* bingle, dent, depression, ding, dint, furrow, indent, puncture; **dimple,** pock, **pore,** crypt, domatium, fossa, fovea, foveola; **impression,** footprint, imprint, incision, print, toehold; **intaglio,** champlevé, cloisonné.   *See also* HOLLOW

INDEPENDENCE *n* autarchy, autocephaly, autonomy, home-rule, republicanism, self-determination, self-government, self-rule, separatism; **freedom,** discretion, free will, freedom of action, freedom of choice, liberty; **anarchy,** anarchism, libertarianism; **individualism,** individuality, self-expression; **self-sufficiency,** autarky, independent means, inner-direction, private means, self-reliance, toughness; **self-support,** private practice, self-employment, self-help

INDEPENDENT *adj* acephalous, autocephalous, autonomic, autonomous, free, hermetic, incoercible, indomitable, substantive; **self-determining,** self-governed, self-governing, self-regulating, self-ruling; **separatist,** isolationist, separate; **uncommitted,** detached, non-partisan, unattached, uninvolved; **anarchic,** anarchistic, libertarian; **single-handed,** sole, unconnected, undirected, unsupported.   *See also* SELF-SUFFICIENT

INDEPENDENTLY *adv* autonomically, autonomously, separately; **by oneself,** off one's own bat, on one's own, on one's own initiative, on one's own responsibility, on one's own undertaking, single-handedly, singly; **anarchically**

INDEPENDENT PERSON *n* autarkist, crossbencher, feme sole, free agent, free spirit, independent, individualist, lone hand, loner, mugwump *(U.S.),* one's own person, rugged individualist, self-made man, separatist; **breakaway,** splinter group; **anarchist,** libertarian; **independent contractor,** freelance, freelancer, private practitioner, self-starter

INDICATIVE *adj* connotative, denotative, evincive, gesticulatory, indexical, indicant, significant, significative, suggestive; **symbolic,** emblematic, figurative, pantomimic, repre-

INDICATIVE sentative, symbolical, symbolist, typical; **symptomatic**, prodromal, semiotic, stigmatic

INDICATOR n barometer, guide, index, indicant; **marker**, benchmark, cairn, checkpoint, cue dot *(Films)*, guidemark, landmark, mile post, milestone, post *(Horseracing)*, surface indication, target *(Survey)*, terminus, tidemark, vigia, witness mark *(Survey)*; **pointer**, arrow, cock, fingerpost, guidepost, hand, signpost; **buoy**, anchor buoy, bell buoy, cork; **buoyage**, balisage; **weathercock**, weathervane; **traffic sign**, fried egg, give-way sign, silent cop, stop sign, witch's hat; **traffic light**, amber light, green light, red light; **indicator light**, blinker, brakelight, hand signal, hazard lights, light, trafficator, turning-indicator, winker.   *See also* SIGNAL; SIGN

IN DIFFICULTIES adv behind the eight ball, hard put, hard put to it, in a jam, in deep water, in dire straits, in hot water, in the cactus, in the cart, in the shit, in the soup, in trouble, on one's beam ends, on the hook, on the spot, over a barrel, up against it, up shit creek, up shit creek in a barbwire canoe, up shit creek without a paddle, up the booay, up the creek, up the pole, with one's back to the wall; **between wind and water**, between Scylla and Charybdis, between the devil and the deep blue sea, in a cleft stick, on the horns of a dilemma

INDIRECTNESS n aberrance, anfractuosity, circuitousness, circuity, circularity, deviousness, obliqueness, obliquity, refractiveness, tortuosity, tortuousness, wryness

INDUSTRIAL ACTION n ban, bans and limitations, black ban, boycott, demarcation dispute, general strike, go-slow, green ban, lockout, picket, picket line, rolling ban, rolling strike, shutout, sit-down, sit-down strike, stop-work meeting, strike, sympathy strike, walkout, wildcat strike, work-to-rule; **collective bargaining**, collective agreement

INDUSTRY n cottage industry, primary industry, secondary industry; **technology**, high tech, high technology, industrialisation, industrialism, sunrise industry

INEFFECTUAL adj adiaphorous, brummy, cardboard cutout, helpless, imperfect *(Law)*, in chancery, ineffective, inefficacious, inept, non-effective, nugatory, null, null and void, unarmed, unmanned, void

INEFFECTUALLY adv helplessly, incapably, ineffectively, inefficaciously

INEFFECTUALNESS n ineffectiveness, ineffectuality, inefficaciousness, inefficacity, inefficacy, inefficiency, nullity, uselessness, voidness

INEFFECTUAL PERSON n alf, dead duck, deadhead, milksop, nine day wonder, old woman, paper tiger, sissy, spado, wimp; **has-been**, disso, non-effective, retread; **dud**, brummie, fizzer

INEQUALITY n asymmetry, disequilibrium, disparity, disproportion, disproportionateness, dissymmetry, imbalance, imparity, irregularity, overbalance, unbalance, unequalness, unevenness; **lopsidedness**, bias, list; **unequals**, mismatch, odds

INEVITABILITY n fatality, ineluctability, inevitableness, predetermination, sureness, unavoidability, unavoidableness; **fatalism,** karma, predestinarianism; **fatefulness,** feyness. See also FATE

INEVITABLE adj fatal, fated, ineluctable, ineludible, inescapable, predestinate, predetermined, predetermined, sure, unavoidable; **doomed,** fatal (Obs.), fey, starred. See also FATEFUL

INEVITABLY adv fatally, fatefully, ineluctably, ineludibly, providentially, surely, unavoidably

IN EXCHANGE FOR adv in lieu of, in loco parentis, instead of

IN FACT adv actually, certainly, certes (Archaic), definitely, for a fact, forsooth (Archaic), in faith (Archaic), in reality, in truth, indeed, just, quite, really, soothly, too (Colloq.), truly, verily (Archaic); **factually,** accurately, aright, correctly, justly, literally; **genuinely,** authentically, legitimately, veritably; **in effect,** de facto, effectively, essentially, in substance, realistically, to all intents and purposes; **validly,** logically, rigorously, soundly, tenably; **self-evidently,** axiomatically, undeniably

INFERIOR n adjunct, assistant, cog, junior, minor, number one, number two, second, second class, second tenor, secondary, sub, subaltern, subordinate, subsidiary, underling, yeoman (Archaic); **supporting artist,** backing group, ensemble, session musician, studio musician; **stand-in,** replacement, substitute, understudy

INFERIOR adj junior, minor, of lesser importance, puisne, puny (Obs.), secondary, thrown in the shade, under, yeoman, young, younger; **subordinate,** assistant, associate, attendant, auxiliary, subaltern, subordinative, subservient, subsidiary; **lowly,** base, below the salt, common, degrading, ignoble, infra dig, low, mean, non-U, of low caste, ordinary, peasant, poor, simple, vassal, vile, worse off; **less,** last, least (Archaic), lesser, littler, minimal, smaller, worse, worst; **second-class,** not the full quid, second-best, second-rate, secondary, sub, subnormal, substandard, third-rate; **adulterated,** adulterate, broken-down, watery; **of less height,** inferior, lower, subjacent

INFERIORITY n baseness, coarseness, ignobility, ignobleness, imperfection, lowness, meanness, mediocrity, vileness; **debasement,** adulteration, minimisation, subordination; **lowliness,** lack of position, lack of rank, lack of standing, poorness; **ordinariness,** scrubbiness, shoddiness; **subnormality,** bottom, low tide; **minimum,** least, less, lesser, worse, worst; **inferiority complex,** cultural cringe, feeling of inadequacy, sense of inadequacy

INFERIORLY adv lowly, secondarily, subordinately; **on the wrong side of the tracks,** in a humble station, in a low station, in lowly circumstances, in poor circumstances

INFERNAL adj chthonian, nether, stygian; **hellish,** purgatorial; **Dantean,** Dantesque, pandemoniac, pandemonic, sulphurous

INFERTILE adj barren, fruitless, sterile, unfruitful, unproductive; **arid,** desert, desolate, dried up, dry, exhausted, hungry, poor, sheep-sick (Agric.), sick, stony, submarginal, waste; **uncultivated,** fallow, unseeded, untilled, unused; **unprofitable,** abortive, academic, dead, dead-end, effete, ineffective, non-productive, Sisyphean, useless, vain; **counterproductive,** inefficient, uneconomic; **childless,** non-parous, nulliparous, without issue; **impotent,** castrated, neuter, sexless, spayed; **not reproducing,** acarpous *(Bot.)*, anovulatory, celibate, farrow, seedless, shy, unjoined, virgin, virginal; **contraceptive,** abortifacient

INFERTILITY *n* aridity, aridness, barrenness, desolateness, dryness, sterility; **unproductiveness,** fruitlessness, impotence, malfunction, non-productiveness, non-productivity, unprofitability, uselessness, vainness; **unfruitfulness,** childlessness; **menopause,** anovulation, change of life, climacteric

INFINITE *adj* immense, immoderate *(Obs.)*; **boundless,** endless, illimitable, indefinite, limitless, never-ending, perpetual, shoreless, spaceless, termless, unbounded, uncounted, unlimited, unmeasured, untold; **immeasurable,** countless, incalculable, incomputable, inestimable, inexhaustible, innumerable, interminable, myriad, numberless, transfinite, umpteen, uncountable, unfathomable, unmeasurable, without end, without measure, without number

INFINITELY *adv* ad infinitum, immeasurably, immensely, incalculably, inestimably, till the end of time, unmeasurably; **boundlessly,** endlessly, illimitably, unboundedly, unlimitedly. *See also* FOREVER

INFINITY *n* endlessness, eternity, immenseness, immensity, infiniteness, infinitude, perpetuity; **boundlessness,** illimitability, illimitableness, immeasurability, immeasurableness, unboundedness, unlimitedness; **infinite,** eternal, omnipotent; **abyss,** bottomless deep, bottomless pit. *See also* ETERNITY

INFLATION *n* cost-push inflation, credit squeeze, demand economy, demand-pull inflation, inflationary spiral, price spiral, stagflation; **appreciation,** capital appreciation, revaluation, upvaluation; **rise,** advance, hike, jump, mark-up; **surcharge,** extra, overcharge, rip-off, slug

INFLUENCE *n* affection, atmosphere, charisma, force, hold, imposingness, impression, imprint, leverage, mana, operation, penetration, potency, potentness, power, powerfulness, pressure, push, spell, sway, weight, whammy; **impact,** effect, impingement, incidence; **predominance,** ascendancy, predomination, prevailingness, regnancy; **patronage,** auspices, dominion, good offices, interest *(Obs.)*; **nepotism,** pull, stringpulling, wire-pulling. *See also* PERSUASION

INFLUENCE *v* act on, act upon, affect, bear on, decide, determine, impinge on, militate, move, move to, operate on, work on; **predominate,** hold the balance of power, hold the reins, preponderate, prevail, surmount; **pull rank,** pull strings *(Colloq.)*, pull the braid, pull wires *(U.S.)*, throw one's weight about, throw one's weight around; **be influential,** carry weight, grab, have a drag *(U.S. Colloq.)*, have pull, impress, make an impact on, strike, tell with, tip the scales, touch. *See also* PERSUADE

INFLUENCED *adj* affected, coloured, interested; **responsive**, exorable, impressible, impressionable, other-directed, pervious, plastic, sensitive, soft, susceptible, susceptive; **amenable**, adaptable, compliant, convincible, easy, facile, flexile, open, persuadable, persuasible, pliable, pliant, suggestible, tractable

INFLUENCER *n* affecter, assurer, catalyst, convincer, inspirer, reasoner; **persuader**, arguer, blandisher, cajoler, coaxer, pleader, swayer, sweet-talker, urger, wheedler; **brainwasher**, conditioner, hypnotiser, manipulator, mesmeriser, mesmerist; **lobbyist**, operator, string-puller, wire-puller; **lobby**, connections, pressure group; **influential person**, backer, backroom boy, big wheel, éminence grise, genius, high priest, patron, power, power behind the throne; **determinative**, determinant, organiser *(Embryol.)*

INFLUENTIAL *adj* active, decisive, far-reaching, impingent, imposing, intervenient, seminal, strong, weighty; **predominant**, ascendant, preponderant, preponderating, prepotent, prevailing, regnant; **charismatic**, infectious, manipulative, manipulatory, mesmeric; **convincing**, coaxing, luculent, persuasive, silver-tongued

INFLUENTIALLY *adv* catalytically, inspiringly, seminally; **predominantly**, decisively, imposingly, predominatingly, preponderantly, preponderatingly, prepotently, prevailingly, tellingly; **persuasively**, coaxingly, convincingly, luculently, mesmerically, tendentiously

INFORM *v* acquaint, apprise, circumstance *(Obs.)*, convey, drum up, fill in, give to understand, oil up, put in the picture, put wise; **brief**, communicate, direct, elaborate on, enlighten, impart, instruct, make known, show; **advertise**, propagandise, publicise; **notify**, advise, circularise, keep posted, notice *(U.S.)*, warn; **hint**, insinuate, intimate

INFORMAL *adj* unceremonious, unofficial; **casual**, easy, easygoing, free and easy, nonconformist, offhand, offhanded, relaxed, unbuttoned, unconcerned, unconventional; **uninhibited**, bohemian, permissive, unembarrassed; **colloquial**, conversational; **casually dressed**, déshabillé, in dishabille

INFORMALITY *n* approachability, approachableness, intimacy, intimateness, lack of ceremony; **casualness**, bohemianism, ease, easiness, lack of inhibition, offhandedness, permissiveness, unconventionality; **anomie**, social vacuum; **casual dress**, dishabille, fatigues, mufti, undress

INFORMALLY *adv* casually, unceremoniously, unembarrassedly, unofficially

INFORMANT *n* conveyor, informer, intelligencer *(Archaic)*, notifier, promoter *(Obs.)*, teller; **source**, adviser, authority, consultant, referral; **guide**, cicerone, courier; **grapevine**, channel; **tipster**, a little bird, urger; **pimp**, blabber, chocolate frog, copper's nark, dobber, dog, golliwog, grass, grasser, nark, shelf, silvertail, snitch, squealer, stool pigeon *(U.S.)*, supergrass, telltale, welsher; **spy**, eavesdropper, plant, scout, security police, sleeper, spook, wire-tapper *(U.S.)*

INFORMATION *n* change, dope, drum, gen, good guts, griff *(N.Z.)*, griffin *(N.Z.)*, hot tip, info, inside informa-

information   288   **injure**

tion, intelligence, lowdown, news, run-down, the dinkum oil, the facts, the good oil, the goods; **advice**, lead, tip, tip-off, warning, word, word in the ear; **hint**, clue, inkling, intimation, sidelight, suggestion, suspicion; **propaganda**, agitprop, PR, public relations; **report**, brief, case history, document, follow-up, praecipe, statement, story, summary, white paper; **bulletin**, circular, communiqué, memorandum, newsletter, notice; **message**, dispatch, dispatch note *(Brit.)*, line, note; **databank**, card file, card index, catalogue, clipping service, database, dossier, file, reference library, teletext; **data**, block *(Computers)*, datum, details *(Archaic)*, material, source material; **bit**, byte, field, word *(Computers)*; **baud**

INFORMATION AGENCY *n* bureau, clearing house, credit agency, mercantile agency, office, trade reference; **band**

INFORMATIVE *adj* directive, directory, documentary, encyclopaedic, informational, instructional, instructive, intelligential; **communicative**, chatty, communicatory, newsy

INFORMED *adj* abreast of, au courant, clued-up, cluey, enlightened, in on, in the know, in the picture, up, up-to-date, well-informed; **advised**, briefed, instructed, posted, primed, told

INFORMINGLY *adv* advisedly, communicatively, instructively

INGROWING *adj* accrete, ingrown; **geophilous**, epigenous, epigeous

INHABIT *v* affect, domicile at, habit *(Obs.)*, indwell, live in, occupy, reside in, squat, tenant; **move in**, settle in; **stay**, lie *(Archaic)*, sojourn, visit; **lodge**, board, quarter, room; **flat**, bach, bachelorise, pad down; **live out**, sleep out; **live together**, cohabit, live with, muck in, shack up with; **camp**, bivouac, bivvy, encamp, tent; **kennel**, nest, stable, stall, sty; **cabin**, barrack, hut; **caravan**, campervan; **dwell**, abide, bide *(Archaic)*, hang out, live, reside, stay, use *(Archaic)*, won *(Archaic)*; **come from**, belong to, hail from; **colonise**, people, plant, populate; **settle**, anchor, pitch *(Rare)*, swallow the anchor

INHABITABLE *adj* habitable, livable, tenantable

INHABITANT *n* abider, denizen, dweller, habitant, indweller, outlier, parishioner, resident, residentiary; **neighbour**, local; **frontiersman**, borderer, marcher; **inlander**, bogtrotter, highlander, islander, isthmian, lowlander, mainlander, mountaineer, sylvan, ultramontane, woodlander; **cave-dweller**, caveman, troglodyte; **terrestrial**, earthling, earthman, tellurian.   *See also* OCCUPANT: POPULATION

INHABITED *adj* lived-in, occupied, populated; **well-populated**, populous

INITIATE *v* auspicate *(Obs. Rare)*, bring in, bring into use, create, float, give birth to, give rise to, handsel, hatch, inaugurate, initialise *(Computers)*, innovate, instigate, introduce, launch, phase in, pioneer, premiere, set on foot, trigger, turn on; **establish**, found, ground, institute, set up; **baptise**, blood, christen; **prime**, clutch-start, crank, fetch, kick-start, set going, turn over.   *See also* START

INJURE *v* harm, hurt, traumatise; **wound**, beat up, concuss, disfeature, draw first blood, give someone a facial, run over, shatter, sprain, strain, wing; **maim**, bemaul, deface, deform, disfigure, make mincemeat of, mangle, mutilate; **bruise**, contuse, jam; **stab**, bayonet, bite, carve up, feather, pike, prick, run-through, spur, tusk; **cripple**, disable, hamstring, incapacitate, lame, nobble, scotch. *See also* DAMAGE

INJURED *adj* battle-scarred, bruised, corked, maimed, winged, wounded; **frozen**, frostbitten; **handicapped**, crippled, developmentally disabled, disabled, flat-footed, game, gammy, halt *(Archaic)*, hipshot, incapacitated, lame

INJURY *n* Blighty *(Brit.)*, breach *(Obs.)*, flesh wound, lesion, maim *(Rare)*, microtrauma, trauma, traumatism, wound; **specific injury**, bite, bruise, burn, contusion, fracture, march fracture, scratch, shiner, sprain, stab, strain, welt; **grievous bodily harm**, G.B.H.; **disability**, handicap, impediment; **limp**, cork knee, cork leg, flatfoot, halt *(Archaic)*. *See also* DAMAGE; HARM

INLAY *n* buhl, cross-banding, damascene, intarsia, marquetry, mosaic, niello, parquetry, purfle, tarsia

INNOCENCE *n* blamelessness, guiltlessness; **purity**, candour, immaculacy, immaculateness, maidenhead, maidenhood, maidenliness, pureness, sinlessness, state of grace, virginity, virtue, whiteness; **artlessness**, dupability, guilelessness, inexperience, simpleness, simplicity

INNOCENT *n* child, child of nature, cleanskin, dove, ingenue, lamb, newborn babe

INNOCENT *adj* blameless, clean, clean-handed, clear, guiltless, inculpable, irreproachable, not guilty, offenceless, reproachless, white-handed; **pure**, dovelike, immaculate, incorruptible, lamblike, lilywhite, maidenly, sinless, unsullied, untouched, virginal, virtuous, white; **artless**, dupable, green, inexperienced, simple, uncalculating, unworldly

INNOCENTLY *adv* blamelessly, inculpably; **purely**, immaculately, incorruptibly, virtuously

INNOVATE *v* break new ground, initiate, inspirit, originate, turn over a new leaf; **swing**, be with it; **modernise**, bring up to date, freshen, furbish up, refurbish, revamp, revive, update

INNOVATION *n* bright idea, innovativeness, modernity, neologism, neology, newie, note *(Colloq.)*, novation *(Rare)*, novelty, originality, wrinkle; **renovation**, re-creation, rebirth, recast, renaissance, renewal, revival, reviviscence, update; **modernisation**, aggiornamento, revivification, updating; **latest fashion**, the last word, the latest

INNOVATIVE *adj* innovational, innovatory, newfangled, novel, original, state-of-the-art, unconventional, unprecedented; **futuristic**, avant-garde, high-tech, sunrise, ultra-modern; **modern**, contemporary, current, fashionable, fresh as a daisy, just out, late-model, latest, live, mod, modernist, modernistic, neological, neoteric, new-fashioned, recent, redbrick, swinging, trendy, ultrafashionable, up-to-date, up-to-the-minute, with-it

INNOVATOR *n* innovationist, neologist, original, original thinker, originator, trailblazer; **moderniser,** freshener, refurbisher, restorer, reviver, revolutionary, Young Turk; **modern,** bright young thing, junior, modernist, swinger, trendy; **nouveau riche,** parvenu, upstart; **new wave,** a breath of fresh air, avant-garde, ginger group, nouvelle vague, young blood; **youth,** infancy, spring, springtime

IN ONE'S POSSESSION *adv* at call, in hand, in one's clutches, in one's own hands, on hand, to hand, to one's credit, to one's name, to the good

IN PURSUIT *adv* hot on the trail, in full cry, on the scent

IN QUESTION *adv* at issue, under discussion; **arguably,** disputably

INQUIRE INTO *v* examine, investigate, probe, review, scrutinise, study; **analyse,** anatomise, appraise, assay, assess, break down, catalogue, classify, codify, derive, digest, file, group, interpret, list, order, pull apart, pull to pieces, rank, reduce to order, sift, sort, unravel, winnow; **dissect,** prosect, randomise, segment

INQUISITIVELY *adv* agog, curiously, nosily, pryingly, questioningly

IN RETALIATION *adv* revengefully, vengefully, vindictively

IN RETURN *adv* back, in compensation

IN SECRET *adv* backstage, behind someone's back, behind the scenes, by the back door, cagily, clandestinely, close, closely, furtively, invisibly, on the q.t., on the quiet, on the side, secretly, sneakily, sneakingly, stealthily, surreptitiously, through the back door, under one's hat, under the table, underhand, up one's sleeve; **covertly,** clandestinely, collusively, under cover, underground; **confidentially,** between ourselves, between you and me, entre nous; **privately,** in camera, in confidence, in private, intimately, sub rosa, under the rose

INSECT *n* bitie, bloodsucker, borer, bug, creepy-crawly, daddy-long-legs, grub, hexapod, imago; **larva,** instar; **insect colony,** hive, termitarium, vespiary; **invertebrate,** arthropod, articulate *(Rare)*, segmented invertebrate; **cicada,** black prince, double drummer, floury baker, green Monday, greengrocer, red-eye, Union Jack, yellow Monday; **worm,** annelid, earthworm, helminth, leech, tube worm, vermicule

INSECT-LIKE *adj* entomic, hexapodous; **apian,** coleopterous *(beetles),* culicid *(mosquitoes),* muscid *(flies),* vespine *(wasps)*

INSECT PART *n* aculeus, austellum, sting, stinger; **feeler,** antenna, palpus; **compound eye,** ommateum, ommatidium; **segment,** abdomen, head, mesothorax, metathorax, thorax; **insect wing,** elytron, forewing, hemelytron

INSENSIBILITY *n* blockishness, dullness, impassiveness, impassivity, imperception, imperceptiveness, imperceptivity, impercipience, insensateness, insensitiveness, insensitivity, insentience, insusceptibility, obtuseness, unawareness; **senselessness,** anosmia, hypaesthesia, numbness, paralysis, sensory deprivation. *See also* UNCONSCIOUSNESS; ANAESTHESIA

INSENSIBLE *adj* hypaesthesic, imperceptive, impercipient, insensate, insensitive, insentient, insusceptible, lost to, obtuse, unaware; **numb**, dead, inert, lifeless, paralysed; **blockish**, blocked, dull, dullish, thick-skinned, unalive; **senseless**, anosmatic, tasteless *(Rare)*

INSERT *n* Dutchman *(Carp.)*, embolism, enclosure, fold-out, gusset, infiltrate, infusion, inlay, inlay graft, input, inset, interlining, noddy *(T.V. Colloq.)*, peg, stuffing, suppository, tibby; **injection**, enema, fuel-injection, infiltration, infusion, instillation, instilment, intrusion, jab, shot, skinpop

INSERT *v* catheterise, ease in, infix, inlet, inset, intercalate, interleaf, interleave, interlineate, introduce, intromit, jug, margin, overstuff, package, peg, pile, plug, pocket, pot, pouch, put in, rowel *(Vet. Science)*, sandwich, sheathe, slip in, slot in, stuff, tabernacle, thrum, tip in *(Print.)*, trench *(Obs.)*, tuck, whack in, work in; **interpolate**, insinuate, interject; **enclose**, bag, barrel, bottle, box, encapsulate; **embed**, bury; **enter**, enrol, file, fill in; **implant**, bed, embed, engraft, enroot, graft, heel in *(Bot.)*, impregnate, infix, inlay, inoculate, inseminate, plant, root, tub, vaccinate, variolate; **inject**, instil, intrude *(Geol.)*, mainline, shoot, skinpop, syringe

INSERTED *adj* embolismic, epenthetic, immersed, inlaid, interlineal, interlinear; **intercalative**, introducible, intrusive, intussusceptive, irruptive; **penetrating**, infiltrative, infusive, inoculative, interpenetrative, intervenient, penetrative

INSERTER *n* bottler, canner, enroller, grafter, implanter, infuser, inoculator, introducer, packer, stinger, vaccinator; **injector**, fuel-injector, hype, hypo, hypodermic, hypodermic needle, infiltrator, needle, spike, vaccine gun; **drill**, diamond drill, perforator

INSERTION *n* embolism, epenthesis, grafting, infixion, insinuation, intercalation, interpolation, introduction, intromission, putting in; **implantation**, embedding, embedment, embosty, engraftation, engraftment, graft, grafting, impregnation, inoculation, insemination, vaccination, vaccinisation, variolation

INSIDE *n* belly, bottom, bowels, contents, entrails, guts, innards, insides, interior, internal organs, interns *(Archaic)*, intestines, pith, viscera, vitals, within; **innermost**, core, endocrine, heart, kernel, marrow, penetralia; **inland**, dead heart, heartland, outback, red centre, up-country; **inwardness**, innerness, inscape, interiority, internality; **inset**, chine, concavity, fissure, insert, interstice, recess

INSIDE *adj* deep-seated, enclosed, inmost, inner, innermost, interior, intern *(Archaic)*, internal, interstitial, intestine, intestine, subcutaneous, visceral; **inland**, up-country; **inward**, endoreic, incurrent, ingrowing, re-entrant; **indoor**, domestic, in-house, inboard *(Naut.)*, ingrown, intimate, intramural; **inlying**, endogenous, intratelluric

INSIDE *adv* aboard, herein, in, inboard, indoors, therein, within, withindoors *(Obs.)*, inward, centripetally, hereinto, inly *(Archaic)*, inwards; **internally**, endogenously, interiorly, in-

inside   292   **insufficiency**

wardly; **inland**, up-country; **at home**, in the bosom of one's family, in the family

INSIPID *adj* flavourless, floury, milk-and-water, savourless, tasteless, undistinguished, unseasoned, vapid; **watery**, diluted, washy, wishy-washy; **flat**, dead, plastic; **mild**, bland, plain, unflavoured, unspiced

INSIPIDITY *n* blandness, insipidness, mildness, plainness, tastelessness, vapidity, washiness, weak flavour; **milk and water**, pap

INSISTENCE *n* clamorousness, clamour, hue and cry, importunity, insistency, public outcry; **demand**, call, claim, counterclaim, exaction, request, requisition, ultimatum; **order**, behest, command, decree, fiat, imperative, injunction, stipulation, ukase; **writ**, quo warranto, warrant; **levy**, burden, imposition, requirement, strain, tax; **bill**, dun, final demand, invoice, notice

INSISTENT *adj* demanding, exacting, exigent, imperative, stipulatory, urgent

INSISTER *n* asker, demander, exacter, stickler, stipulator; **claimant**, claimer, counterclaimant

INSIST ON *v* ask, call for, deliver an ultimatum, demand, order, require, stipulate; **claim**, counterclaim, postulate; **exact**, impose on, levy, make heavy demands on, requisition, tax; **bill**, dun, exact payment, foreclose, invoice

INSPECTION *n* field day, field trip, recce, reconnaissance, review *(Mil.)*, snoop, visit, visitation; **search**, dig, digging, exploration, hunt, potholing, quest, treasure hunt; **body-search**, frisk, house-search, ramp *(Prison)*; **legal search**, requisitions on title. See also INVESTIGATION; TEST

INSTITUTE *n* academy, college, faculty, institution; **guild**, chapel, confraternity, craft, livery company, lodge, mystery *(Archaic)*, trades union; **fellowship**, brotherhood, fraternity *(U.S.)*, sisterhood, sodality, sorority; **friendly society**, benevolent association, benevolent society, cooperative society, housing association, service club

INSTRUMENTALIST *n* bandsman, player, sideman; **fiddler**, bower, cellist, contrabassist, violin, violinist, violist, violoncellist; **strummer**, banjoist, bass guitar, bassist, guitarist, harper, harpist, lutenist, lyrist, mandolinist, plucker, sitarist, theorbist, thrummer, zitherist; **piper**, bagpiper, clarinettist, fagottist, fifer, flautist, flute, fluter *(Obs.)*, flutist *(U.S.)*, oboist; **blower**, bugler, cornet, horn-player, saxophonist, tailgater, tooter, trombonist, trumpet, trumpeter; **percussionist**, bones, cymbalist, drummer, kettledrummer, taborer, tambourinist, tympanist; **keyboardist**, accordionist, cembalist, harpsichordist, organist, pianist, virginalist; **vibist**, vibraphonist, xylophonist; **organ-grinder**, hurdy-gurdy man; **bellringer**, carillonist, carillonneur, ringer

INSUFFICIENCY *n* dearth, defect, deficiency, half-measure, lack, meagreness, pitifulness, scantiness, scarceness, scarcity, scrimpiness, shortage, want; **inadequacy**, inadequateness, incommensurateness, jejuneness, scragginess; **deficit**, deficiency, short-

insufficiency   293   **intellectual**

age, shortfall, ullage; **scarcity**, privation; **need**, penury, poorness, poverty

INSUFFICIENT *adj* deficient, inadequate, jejune, lean, light on (*Colloq.*), measly, scant, scanty, scarce, scrimp, scrimpy, short, slim, wanting; **poor**, incommensurate, meagre, piss-weak, scraggy, unequal to, weak

INSUFFICIENTLY *adv* deficiently, leanly, scantily, scantly, scrimpily; **inadequately**, incommensurately, jejunely, meagrely, poorly, scraggily

INSULT *n* affront, disparagement, flout, humiliation, hurt, indignity, outrage, put-down, revilement, slight, smack in the eye, snub, spurn, violation; **gibe**, taunt; **hiss**, boo, catcall; V-sign, thumbs up; **leer**, smirk

INSULT *v* blister, call names, humiliate, jeer at, slight, taunt, trample on, twit; **ridicule**, cheek, laugh at, put down, sauce, slang, tell someone a thing or two; **snub**, cut dead, disoblige, give someone the cold shoulder, set down, turn one's back on; **affront**, mortify; **be rude**, be lacking in courtesy, show disrespect; **snigger**, laugh, leer, sneer, snort; **gesture rudely**, cock a snoot at, look cross-eyed at, make a face at, poke out one's tongue at, thumb one's nose at

INSULTING *adj* abusive, injurious, scurrile, scurrilous; **cheeky**, airy, breezy, cavalier, flip, flippant, impertinent, off-hand, saucy; **impolite**, discourteous, familiar, rude, unceremonious, uncivil; **insolent**, audacious, impudent, presumptuous

IN SUPPLY *adv* in hand, in reserve, in stock, in the pipeline, on tap, on the menu

INSURANCE *n* assurance, coinsurance, consequential loss insurance, coverage, endowment insurance, fire insurance, protection, protective trust, public liability insurance, reinsurance, tontine, valued policy; **indemnity**, counterindemnity, guarantee, indemnification, security; **policy**, cover note, floating policy; **superannuation**, annuity, provident fund

INTANGIBILITY *n* abstractness, disembodiment, immateriality, immaterialness, impalpability, imponderability, imponderableness, incorporeity, inessentiality, intangibleness, invisibility, unreality; **ethereality**, airiness, etherealness, vaporosity, vaporousness; **evanescence**, fugitiveness, transience; **insubstantiality**, flimsiness, tenuousness, thinness

INTANGIBLE *adj* bodiless, disembodied, ectoplasmic, immaterial, impalpable, imperceptible, inappreciable, incorporate, incorporeal, insubstantial, invisible, unreal, untouchable; **supersensory**, imponderable, inconceivable, inessential, supersensible, supersensual, unessential, unknowable; **internal**, mental, subjective; **abstract**, conceptual, metaphysical, metempiric, metempirical, theoretical. *See also* ETHEREAL

INTANGIBLY *adv* impalpably, imponderably, unreally; **abstractly**, metaphysically, supersensibly, transcendentally, transcendently; **incorporeally**, immaterially, unsubstantially; **flimsily**, delicately, tenuously, thin, thinly; **ethereally**, aerially, fugitively, vaporously

INTELLECTUAL *n* academic, academician, blue, bluestocking, bookman, bookworm, Brahman, classicalist, classicist, diplomate, doctor, don *(Brit.)*, fellow, graduate, humanist, licentiate, pandit *(India)*, postgraduate, professor, rabbi, rabbin, researcher, sage, scholar, scholastic, schoolman, sophist; **highbrow**, connoisseur, Dryasdust, egghead, pedant; **bohemian**, long-hair

INTELLECTUAL *adj* academic, cerebral, learned, scholarly, scholastic; **highbrow**, bluestocking, bohemian, bookish, heavy, ivory tower, long-haired, pedantic

INTELLECTUALISM *n* bohemianism, bookishness, intellectuality, intellectualness, scholarliness, scholarship, scholasticism; **pedantry**, donnishness; **academia**, Academe, ivory tower, the academy; **intelligentsia**, clerisy, cognoscenti, literati

INTELLECTUALLY *adv* academically, bookishly, scholarly, scholastically

INTELLECTUAL PROPERTY *n* copyright, patent, petty patent, public lending right, trademark

INTELLIGENCE *n* ambidexterity, braininess, brains, brightness, brilliance, brilliantness, capacity, cleverness, genius, luminousness, smartness, strong-mindedness, understanding, wit; **sharp-wittedness**, acumen, aptitude, esprit, keenness, knowingness, penetration, penetrativeness, perspicacity, sharp-sightedness, sharpness; **nimbleness**, precociousness, precocity. See also WISDOM

INTELLIGENT *adj* able, brainy, bright, brilliant, capable, clever, cleverish, conceited *(Obs.)*, ingenious, intellective, intellectual, intelligential, knowledgeable, luminous, neat, smart, understanding; **quick on the uptake**, apprehensive, apt, nimble, precocious, quick, ready, ready-witted, receptive; **sharp-witted**, acuminous, acute, Attic, fly *(Colloq.)*, gnomic, keen, knowing, parlous *(Obs.)*, penetrating, perspicacious, quick-witted, sharp, sharp-sighted, wide-awake. See also WISE

INTELLIGENTLY *adv* brightly, brilliantly, capably, cleverly, intellectively, luminously, smartly; **shrewdly**, astutely, cannily, penetratingly, perspicaciously, politicly, sharply, subtly

INTEND *v* calculate, choose, destine, mean to, plan, vow; **have a good mind to**, have a great mind to, have half a mind to, think fit; **consider**, contemplate, meditate, think about; **desire**, list *(Archaic)*, long for, will, wish, yearn for

INTENDER *n* premeditator, voluntarist, voluntary

INTENSE *adj* bad, dense, exquisite, frightful, grievous, heavy, high, keen, particular, perfervid, poignant, profound, severe, sharp, special, terrible, terrific, violent, vivid

INTENSELY *adv* amain *(Archaic)*, dearly, deeply, grievously, highly, intensively, keenly, perfervidly, poignantly, resoundingly, severely, sharply, so, violently, vividly, with a vengeance

INTERACT *v* alternate, be a function of, be proportional to, come together, correlate, correspond, cut across one another, give and take, intercross, interflow, interlock, intermarry, intermingle, interplay, interrelate, intersect, intertwine, interweave, marry, mutualise, reciprocate; **exchange**, come and go between, commute, interchange, intercommuni-

interact cate, interconnect; **cause to interact,** interface

INTERACTION *n* alternation, bilateralism, bilateralness, exchange, interchange, interconnection, intercourse, interdependence, interplay, interrelation, mutuality, reciprocality, reciprocation, reciprocity, relationship; **mutualism,** biocenology, communion, symbiosis; **direct ratio,** correlation, correspondence, direct relation, functional relationship, inverse ratio, inverse relation; **barter,** trade; **toing and froing,** coming and going, commutation *(U.S.),* commuting; **exchange of ideas,** cross fertilisation, cultural exchange

INTERACTIVE *adj* bilateral, commutative, interfacial, internecine, mutual, reciprocal, reciprocative; **interdependent,** alternate, interchangeable, interconnected; **international,** interdominion, inter-island, intercollegiate, interdepartmental, intermundane, interpersonal, interracial, interstate, intertribal

INTERACTIVELY *adv* bilaterally, mutually, reciprocally, together

INTERESTING *adj* absorbing, arresting, conspicuous, engrossing, eye-catching, fascinating, gripping, juicy, newsworthy, noteworthy, noticeable, readable, remarkable, showy, striking

INTERESTINGNESS *n* conspicuousness, deepness, fascination, juiciness, newsworthiness, readability, readableness, remarkableness, savour, showiness, spice, zest

INTERIM *adj* intercurrent, intermediate, intermissive, interregnal, interspatial, intervenient, intervening

INTERIORISE *v* embed, internalise, put inside; **introvert,** withdraw into oneself

INTERJECTIONAL *adj* butting in, caesural, interjectory, interruptive, intrusive, parenthetic, parenthetical

INTERLACE *v* braid, enlace, entangle, intercross, intertwine, intervolve, interweave, plait, plash, pleach, reticulate, weave; **mat, mesh; trellis,** wattle

INTERLACEMENT *n* enlacement, entanglement, intertwinement, interweavement, matting, mesh, meshes, meshwork, netting, network, reseau, reticulation, wattling, webbing; **net,** bird netting, chain mesh, chain wire, drag-net, fishnet, mosquito net, purse seine, screen, seine, wire gauze, wire netting, wirecloth; **grid,** gauntlet *(Railways),* grating, gridiron, grillage, grille, reticle; **latticing,** latticework, treillage, wickerwork; **trellis,** trelliswork, wattle; **plait,** braid, wreath; skein, cat's cradle; **crisscross,** crackle, craze, frostwork; **shutter,** jalousie, wicket; **crosshair,** crosswire

INTERPRETATIVELY *adv* editorially, explanatorily, interpretively

INTERPRETER *n* constructionist, construer, deconstructionist, exegete, explainer, exponent, expounder, glossator *(Old Eng. Law);* **semiotician,** hermeneutist, hierophant, oneirocritic, solarist, symbolist; **paraphrast,** paraphraser, renderer; **commentator,** critic, editorialist, reviewer; **annotator,** glosser, scholiast

INTERPRETIVE *adj* explanatory, explicative, exponential, expository, illustrative, interpretational, interpretative; **paraphrastic,** transcriptive; **exegetic,** anagogic, anagogical, her-

interpretive

INTERRUPT v break into, bust up, cut, disconnect, disturb, punctuate, stop; **pause, hold it; interfere,** barge in, break in, burst in, butt in, chime in, chip in, cut in, horn in, intrude, irrupt; **interject,** cut someone short, get a word in edgeways, interpose, intervene

INTERRUPTED adj broken, desultory, disconnected, discontinuous, discrete, disjunctive, episodic, few and far between, fitful, intermittent, spasmodic, striated; **unconformable,** faulty

INTERRUPTEDLY adv at intervals, by snatches, desultorily, discontinuously, falteringly, fitfully, in fits and starts, spasmodically

INTERRUPTER n disturber, embuggerist, interjector, interposer, intruder, show stopper

INTERRUPTION n anacoluthon, discontinuation, discontinuity, disjunction, disturbance, embuggerance, embuggery, interposition, intrusion; **unconformity,** chasm, fault (Geol.); **pause,** abeyance, break, caesura, gap, hiatus, interlude, intermission, interregnum, interval, lacuna, rest, spell; **interjection,** digression, episode, exclamation, interposal, irrelevance, parenthesis; **commercial break,** station break

INTERVAL n gap, hiatus, interim, interruption, interspace, meantime, parenthesis, space, time; **interlude,** antimasque, entr'acte, episode, intermission, wait; **moratorium,** abeyance, cease-fire, grace (Law), interregnum, prorogation, suspension, truce; **lull,** break, breather, breathing space, dwell (Mach.), let-up, pause, recess, remission (Med.), respite, rest, shoot (Rowing), smoko, spell, tea-break; **lag,** dead time (Elect.), headway (Railways), hysteresis (Physics), lead (Engineering), response time, saros (Astron.), time-lag

INTERVENIENT adj interjacent, intermediate, interposed, intervening, interventional, irruptive, mesne, middle, sandwiched; **meddlesome,** busy, curious, interfering, nosy, obstructive, officious, stickybeaking

IN THE FRESH AIR adv alfresco, in the open air, out of doors, under the stars

IN THE FUTURE adv at length, eventually, finally, in the fullness of time, one of these days, sooner or later, ultimately; **imminently,** at any moment, before long, by and by, momentarily (U.S.), pendently, presently, shortly, soon; **onwards,** afterwards, forth, forwards, from this time on, hence (Archaic), henceforth, off, onwards in time, thence, thenceforth, thenceforward, thereafter; **some day,** mañana, one day, sometime, tomorrow, tonight; **next,** near, nigh; **in waiting,** a day off, a week off, in store, in the offing, in the wind, some time off; **yet,** still; **then,** thereon, thereupon, therewith, with that

IN THE PAST adv ago, already (U.S.), back, before now, beforetime (Archaic), by, erenow (Archaic), formerly, hitherto, since, sometime, sometimes (Obs.), then, whilom (Archaic); **before that time,** theretofore, thitherto (Rare); **yesterday,** last century, last week, last year, lately, latterly, recently, the other day, the other night, yesteryear (Poetic); **long ago,** at one time, early, erst (Archaic),

in the past   **in two**

in the past erstwhile *(Archaic)*, historically, immemorially, in the year dot, langsyne *(Scot.)*, late, once, once upon a time, sometime, wayback

INTOLERANCE *n* blindness, bumbledom, impenetrability, impenetrableness, narrow-mindedness, opinionativeness; **bigotry**, anti-Semitism, apartheid, colour-bar, colour prejudice, commie bashing, Jew-baiting, Jim Crowism, McCarthyism, poofter-bashing, racialism, racism, segregation, union bashing; **chauvinism**, ageism, jingoism, misoneism, sexism; **pettiness**, illiberality, illiberalness, littleness, small-mindedness, smallness; **parochialism**, clannishness, insularism, insularity, micrology, provincialism, sectionalism; **puritanism**, bowdlerism, Grundyism; **prejudice**, bias, preconception, prenotion, slant, warp; **deep north**, cracker-barrel, deep south, parish pump

INTOLERANT *adj* blind, blinkered, impenetrable, narrow, narrow-minded, unenlightened; **small-minded**, black-and-white, dogmatic, illiberal, Lilliputian, little, one-eyed, one-track, opinionated, opinionative, petty, picky, small; **parochial**, blue-rinse, conservative, fogram, hidebound, mealy-mouthed, old-line, puritan, puritanical, straitlaced; **insular**, clannish, home-town, jingoistic, parochial, provincial, parish-pump, poky; **bigoted**, anti-Semitic, chauvinist, chauvinistic, fascist, misoneist, sexist; **biased**, affectionate *(Obs.)*, ex parte, one-sided, partial, prejudiced, unfair, unilateral, warped

INTOLERANTLY *adv* blindly, ex parte, illiberally, impenetrably, narrow-mindedly, pettily; **parochially**, clannishly, insularly, provincially; **bigotedly**, anti-Semitically, chauvinistically

INTOLERANT PERSON *n* anti-Semite, bigot, closed mind, fascist, Jew-baiter, racialist, racist, segregationist; **chauvinist**, alf, male chauvinist, male chauvinist pig, ocker, poofterbasher; **wowser**, bible-basher, bowdleriser, jingoist, puritan; **fogy**, blimp *(Brit.)*, doctrinaire, fogram, fuddy-duddy, mossback, ramrod, stick-in-the-mud; **provincial**, Lilliputian, suburbanite

INTOXICATE *v* befuddle, besot, fox *(Obs.)*, fuddle, go to one's head, inebriate, liquor up, souse, wine

INTOXICATING *adj* alcoholic, hard, inebriant, intoxicant, intoxicative, spiritous *(Obs.)*, spirituous; **strong**, gutsy, heady, high-proof, nappy *(Brit.)*, neat, overproof, short, stiff; **winy**, beery, vinaceous, vinic, vinous; **proof**, single *(Archaic)*, underproof

INTRODUCE *v* herald, preface, prelude, premise, usher in; **pioneer**, blaze a trail, go ahead, guide, head, lead the way

INTRODUCTION *n* exordium, foreword, frontispiece, intro, lead-up, preamble, preface, preliminary, prelims, proem, prolegomena, prologue, prolusion, proposition *(Archaic)*, protasis, recitals *(Law)*; **prelude**, overture, voluntary; **curtain-raiser**, prerelease, teaser

IN TWO *adv* atwain; **half**, halfway, midway

IN TWOS *adv* à deux, in pairs, tete-a-tete; **dually**, bilaterally, binately, bipartitely, doubly, geminately; **double**, as much again, bis, in duplicate, twice, twofold

IN USE *adj* live, living; **occupied**, busy *(U.S.)*, engaged

INVERSION *n* chiasmus *(Ling.)*, hysteron proteron, palindrome, reversion; **inverse**, mirror image

INVERT *v* contrapose, oppose, polarise; **confront**, face, subtend

INVEST *v* average down, average up, bear, bull, buy in, close out, embark, hedge, hive off, job, operate, overbuy, play the market, play the stock market, scalp, speculate

INVESTIGATE *v* anatomise, delve into, dig, dissect, experiment, explore, fossick out, hunt up, look into, look up, plumb, pull apart, pull to pieces, reconnoitre, research, see how the land lies, see into; **check**, countercheck, go over, go through, road-test, sample, screen, snuff, swab *(Horseracing)*, vet; **survey**, case, have a good look around, hunt about, hunt around, look over, nose around, observe, overlook, oversee *(Obs.)*, peruse *(Archaic)*, review, see over, shop around, sweep *(Naut.)*, traverse, view. *See also* EXAMINE

INVESTIGATION *n* check, inquiry; **examination**, probe, review, reviewal, scrutiny, survey; **research**, experiment, R and D, research and development; **analysis**, anatomisation, appraisal, assay, criticism, diagnosis, dissection, evaluation, form criticism *(Theol.)*, overhaul, qualitative analysis, quantitative analysis, spectrum analysis; **screening**, airing, gallup poll, market research, mass observation, opinion poll, poll, questionnaire, random sampling, straw vote; **field study**, case study, field work, sampling; **cost-benefit analysis**, environmental impact study, feasibility study, systems analysis, time and motion study; **spot check**, countercheck, fatigue test, going-over, look, look-over, looksee, quality control, rummage, shakedown *(U.S.)*, trip-check, view; **self-examination**, soul-searching; **identification parade**, police line-up; **spying**, cloak-and-dagger stuff, counterespionage, counterintelligence, espionage, intelligence, wire-tapping. *See also* QUESTIONING; INSPECTION; TEST

INVISIBILITY *n* imperceptibleness, inconspicuousness, latency, latescence, obscureness, obscurity, smoke; **indistinctness**, blurriness, dimness, fogginess, shadowiness, umbrage *(Rare)*; **obscuration**, eclipse, immergence, immersion *(Astron.)*; **invisible ink**, sympathetic ink

INVISIBLE *adj* imperceptible, inconspicuous, insidious, latent, latescent, obscure, out of sight, sightless, viewless; **unseen**, unsighted; **obscured**, dead *(Mil.)*, fogbound, occult *(Obs.)*; **indistinct**, blurry, darkling *(Poetic)*, dim, faint, foggy, shadowy; **asymptomatic**

INVISIBLY *adv* behind the scenes, imperceptibly, inconspicuously, latently, viewlessly; **indistinctly**, blurrily, darkly *(Archaic)*, dimly, foggily, obscurely; **asymptomatically**

INVOLVE *v* catch up, commit, compromise, concern, condemn, entangle, entrap, implicate, incur, intervolve, overcommit, put up to, rope in; **interest**, intrigue

IN WRITING *adv* in black and white, on paper

IRREGULAR *adj* acyclic, agogic, aperiodic, arrhythmic, broken, catchy, desultory, discontinuous, fitful, fluttery, on-off, stop-go, uncertain, unequal, uneven, unrhythmical, unsteady, variable; **sporadic**, casual, erratic, flickering, fulgurating, infrequent, intermissive, intermittent, odd, periodic, remittent, snatchy, spasmodic, sporadical, unsystematic; **jerky**, abrupt, jolty, rickety, rough, unequal; **ragged**, patchy, scraggly, scraggy

IRREGULARITY *n* abruptness, aperiodicity, arrhythmia, casualness, desultoriness, fitfulness, fluctuation, inconstancy, jerkiness, patchiness, raggedness, randomness, uncertainness, unequalness, unevenness, unsteadiness, variability; **intermittence**, intermission, jump, remittence, remittency, surge

IRREGULARLY *adv* brokenly, by fits and starts, desultorily, fitfully, flutteringly, in fits and starts, infrequently, now and then, on and off, patchily, raggedly, uncertainly, unequally, unevenly, unsteadily; **intermittently**, at intervals, intermittingly, now and again, now and then, periodically, remittently, spasmodically, sporadically, whiles *(Archaic)*; **jerkily**, abruptly, roughly, unequally

IRRESOLUTELY *adv* indecisively, shakily, unstably, unsteadily, vacillatingly, waveringly; **uncertainly**, doubtfully, dubiously, haltingly, hesitatingly, hoveringly, pausingly, pendently, pendulously, uncommittedly, undecidedly; **aimlessly**, at random, errantly, flightily, skittishly; **evasively**, noncommittally; **inconclusively**, maybe, perhaps

IRREVERENCE *n* impiety, impiousness, irreligion; **profanity**, blasphemousness, blasphemy, desecration, iconoclasm, pollution, profanation, profaneness, sacrilege, simony, violation; **godlessness**, fall from grace, unblessedness, ungodliness, unholiness; **faithlessness**, agnosticism, atheism, free thought, indifferentism, irreligion, lack of faith, nescience, nihilism, scepticism, secularisation; **paganism**, heathendom, heathenism, heathenry, infidelity, pagandom; **secularism**, secularity, worldliness

IRREVERENT *adj* blasphemous, iconoclastic, impious, profanatory, sacrilegious, unregenerate, violative *(U.S.)*; **profane**, ungodly, unhallowed, unholy, unsanctified; **apostate**, accursed, churchless, creedless, faithless, godforsaken, godless, unredeemed; **unreligious**, agnostic, antichurch, anti-religious, antichristian, anticlerical, atheist, freethinking, irreligious, nescient, sceptic, sceptical, unbelieving, unchristian, uncircumcised, undevout; **heathen**, gentile *(Obs.)*, heathenish, infidel, pagan, paganish; **secular**, carnal, mundane, secularistic, unspiritual, worldly

IRREVERENTLY *adv* blasphemously, iconoclastically, irreligiously, profanely, sacrilegiously, unholily, unregenerately; **faithlessly**, heathenishly, sceptically, secularly, unbelievingly, unchristianly, worldly

IRREVERENT PERSON *n* blasphemer, desecrater, freethinker, iconoclast, polluter, profaner, simoniac, simonist, the ungodly, the unrighteous, violator; **unbeliever**, agnostic, atheist, irreligionist, materialist, nescient, nullifidian, sceptic, secular humanist *(Derog.)*, seculariser, secularist; **pagan**, gentile, heathen, infidel; **antichristian**, antichrist

IRRITABLE *adj* aggravated, apoplectic, atrabilious, bad-tempered, bilious, brittle, cantankerous, captious, crabbed, crabby, cranky, cross, cross-grained, crotchety, crusty, fiery, fractious, fretful, grumpy, hot-tempered, huffish, huffy, ill-humoured, ill-natured, ill-tempered, impatient, lemony, like a bear with a sore head, on edge, out of humour, peevish, peppery, pettish, petulant, quarrelsome, querulous, ratty, scotty, shirty, shitty, shitty-livered, short-tempered, snappish, snappy, snarly, snitchy, snuffy, sore, sour, spiky, spleenful, spleenish, splenetic, temperamental, terse, uptight, verjuice, vexed, vinegary, viraginous, virago-like, vixenish, waspish, waspy; **moody**, broody, glowering, ill-conditioned, lowering, morose, saturnine, sullen, surly; **irascible**, hasty, prickly, scratchy, testy, tetchy, touchy

IRRITABLENESS *n* atrabiliousness, bile, biliousness, cantankerousness, captiousness, crabbiness, crankiness, crossness, crotchetiness, crustiness, distemper, edginess, exasperation, fieriness, fractiousness, fretfulness, grouchiness, grumpiness, huffiness, ill humour, ill nature, ill temper, ill-naturedness, ill-temperedness, impatience, irritability, moodiness, moroseness, peevishness, perverseness, perversity, pettishness, petulance, prickliness, querulousness, shit on liver, snappishness, sourness, spleen, sulkiness, sullenness, surliness, terseness, vexedness, vinegar, vixenishness, waspishness; **irascibility**, hastiness, irascibleness, pepperiness, testiness, tetchiness, touchiness

IRRITABLE PERSON *n* bat, cow, crabstick, crosspatch, curmudgeon, grouch, iron maiden, scowler, sourpuss, virago, vixen, wasp, xanthippe

IRRITABLY *adv* apoplectically, biliously, cantankerously, captiously, crossly, exasperatedly, fierily, fractiously, fretfully, grumpily, hastily, huffily, huffishly, ill-humouredly, ill-naturedly, ill-temperedly, impatiently, peevishly, pettishly, petulantly, snappishly, splenetically, testily, tetchily, touchily, vexedly, vixenishly, waspishly; **moodily**, loweringly, morosely, scowlingly, sourly, surlily

IRRITATE *v* aggravate, bug, chafe, chagrin, crap someone off, drive someone up the wall, fret, gall, get on someone's nerves, get on someone's quince, get under someone's skin, get up someone's nose *(Brit.)*, give someone the irrits, give someone the shits, goad, jangle, nark, peeve, pique, provoke, rankle, rasp, rile, roil, tease, vex; **nag**, air-raid, grouch, scold, snap someone's head off

IRRITATING *adj* aggravating, infuriating, irritative, narky, provoking, vexatious *(Law)*

IRRITATINGLY *adv* aggravatingly, provokingly, vexingly

IRRITATION *n* aggravation, annoyance, chafe, fret, gall *(Archaic)*, provocation, rub, vexation; **fit of pique**, act, blow-up, cob *(N.Z.)*, pet, sulk, tantrum, temper, the hump, tiff

IRRITATOR *n* aggravator, hazer *(U.S.)*, provoker, teaser, vexer

ISLAND *n* atoll, cay, coral island, holm *(Brit.)*, inch *(Scot.)*, isle, islet, key; **archipelago; reef,** barrier reef, bombora, coral reef; **sandbank,** bar, barrier, sandbar, shoal, spit, swash

ISOLATE *v* alienate, cold-shoulder, freeze out, give the cold shoulder, ostracise, reject, send to Coventry, shut out, spurn; **banish,** excommunicate, exile, expatriate, send away, send packing, unchurch; **disinherit,** cut off without a penny, cut off without a shilling, foreclose. *See also* EXCLUDE: BOYCOTT

IT'S TRUE *interj* by jingo, fair dinkum, honestly, my oath, perdie *(Archaic)*, so help me, straight up, struth, too right

Jj

JACKET *n* banian, bedjacket, blazer, blouse, bumfreezer *(Brit. Colloq.)*, camisole, cassock, coat, doublet, Eton jacket, jerkin, jupon, kirtle *(Archaic)*, loafer *(Brit.)*, monkey-jacket, Norfolk jacket, sack, sack coat, sacque, slop, smoking-jacket, soutane, spencer, sports jacket, tunic, waistcoat, weskit; **heavy jacket**, anorak, battle jacket, donkey jacket *(Brit.)*, duffle coat, lumber-jacket, parka, pea jacket, reefer, tabard; **dress coat**, claw-hammer coat, coattails, dinner jacket, hacking jacket, mess jacket, morning coat, swallow-tailed coat, tail coat, tails; **cardigan**, cardie, twin-set; **bodice**, basque, bolero, vest, waistcoat; **straitjacket**; **life jacket**, Mae West. See also OVERCOAT

JEALOUS *adj* covetous, envious, green with envy, green-eyed

JEALOUSLY *adv* enviously, envyingly

JEALOUSY *n* covetousness, enviousness, envy, green-eyed monster, grudgingness, heartburn, heartburning, jaundice, jealousness, penis envy *(Psychol.)*, rivalry, sour grapes, yellows *(Obs.)*; **apple of discord**, bone of contention

JEWEL *n* bijou, cameo, doublet, gem, gemstone, girandole, precious stone, stone, toadstone; **cut jewel**, baguette, brilliant, briolette, cabochon, chip, rose, star, table, triplet; **diamond**, adamant, brilliant, ice, rough diamond, solitaire, sparkler; **opal**, black opal, cleanskin, colour, fire opal, flash, girasol, harlequin, hydrophane, nobby, solid, streak; **mother-of-opal**, Andamooka matrix, matrix

JEWELLERY *n* bijouterie, costume jewellery, paste, tomfoolery; **jewel**, brilliant, gem, pearl, precious stone, rock *(Colloq.)*, scarab, scarabaeus, solitaire, sparkler; **brooch**, anaglyph, breastpin, breastplate *(Judaism)*, cameo, fibula, ouch *(Archaic)*, pin, scatter pin, stickpin *(U.S.)*, tiepin; **bracelet**, anklet, armlet, bangle, wristlet; **ring**, circle, circus *(Obs.)*, engagement ring, eternity ring, nose-ring; **necklace**, beads, chain, chaplet, choker, collar, collarett, dog-collar, locket, peag, rivière, rope, strand, string, torque, wampum; **bead**, bugle bead, charm, drop, girandole, pear drop, pendant; **earring**, eardrop, labret, sleeper; **crown**, circlet, coronal, coronet, diadem, tiara; **parure**, equipage; **filigree**, engrailment, gadroon; **enamelwork**, champlevé, cloisonné, enamel, enamelling, Fabergé, japan, japanning, lacquer, tole, varnish

JOB *n* avocation, business, calling, career, craft, follow-the-job occupation, game, gig, grip, lurk, metier, mystery *(Archaic)*, occupation, practice, private practice, profession, pursuit, racket *(Colloq.)*, trade, vocation, walk of life, work; **position**, a sweet cop, appointment, billet, engagement, incumbency, office, place, post, posting, province, rank, role, sinecure, situation, station, vacancy; **field**, area of expertise, bailiwick, beat, department, domain, line of work, orbit, specialty, sphere, sphere of activity; **duty**, care, charge, chore, commission, concern, errand, obligation, responsibility, task; **the press of business**, the demands of one's job

JOIN *n* bond, close, connection, coupling, junction, juncture, nexus; **link**, connective, copula, interlink; **confluence**, abutment, concurrence, meeting point; **intersection**, cloverleaf, cusp, spinode; **attachment**, affix, appendage, appendant, appendicle; **chemical bond**, closed chain, conjugated bond, coordinate bond, coordinate covalent bond, covalent bond, dative bond, semipolar bond, triple bond, triplet, valency bond

JOIN *v* catenate, compact, concatenate, conjoin, connect, contact, couple, interconnect, interlink, link, match, mate, partner, unite; **bridge**, span; **bracket**, hyphenate; **interlock**, engage, fit, mesh; **fuse**, ankylose, intercommunicate, knit, marry; **merge**, ally, federalise, incorporate, integrate, lump together, roll into one; **couple**, conjugate *(Obs.)*, copulate, kiss, osculate, pair; **attach**, affix, annex, append, apply, fasten; **tie**, lace, seam, sew, string; **splice**, graft, hook up with, inarch, inosculate; **hinge**, articulate; **joint**, butt, dovetail, fay, mortise, tenon

JOINED *adj* conjunct, copular, copulate *(Obs.)*, osculatory; **united**, conjugate, conjugational, inseparable, partnered, rolled into one, Siamese, wedded; **joint**, allied, combined, conjoint, conjunctive, incorporated; **cohesive**, adhesive, loose-knit, well-knit; **adjacent**, common, conterminous, contiguous, neighbouring, setenant, semidetached, touching; **connected**, on-line; **seamed**, commissural, connectional, seamy, sutural; linked, concatenate; **attached**, appendant; **secure**, basifixed, firm, sessile; **inextricable**, ingrown, jammed, wedged

JOINER *n* affixer, carpenter *(U.S.)*, conjoiner, connecter, jointer, scarfer, seamer, uniter, welder

JOINING *n* conjunction, conjuncture *(Obs.)*, joinder; **union**, conjugation, copulation; **linkage**, catenation, concatenation, hyphenation, linkwork; **annexation**, affixture, appendance; **contact**, communication, hook-up, intercommunication, interconnection, networking, tie-up; **fusion**, combination, polymerisation; **splicing**, contingence, grafting, inarching, inosculation; **connectedness**, connectivity, inseparability, inseparableness, unitedness

JOINT *n* articulation, ball-and-socket joint, connector, knuckle joint, universal coupling, universal joint; **butt joint**, dovetail, lap joint, mitre-joint, mortice and tenon joint, rebate, scarf-joint, tongue-and-groove joint; **hinge**, butt, swivel; **fishplate**, fishjoint, gang nail; **tie**, bar, bridle *(Sewing)*, faggoting; **sleeve**, connecting rod, cross, nipple, reducer, turnbuckle; **plug**, crocodile clip, jack; **splice**, graft, karabiner, carabiner; **sprocket**, cog, tooth; **weld**, capillary fitting, cold shut, shut, spot-weld; **seam**, commissure, suture; **mortaring**, jointing, perpend, tuck pointing; **cornerstone**, keystone

JOINTLY *adv* conjointly, conjunctively, conjunctly, connectedly, connectively, syndetically; **close**, closely, inseparably, unitedly; **arm in arm**, hand in hand

JOIN UP *v* enlist, join, join the colours, take the king's shilling, volunteer

JOKE *n* funny, gag, jape, jest, jocularism, laugh, one-liner, punch line, shaggy dog story, wheeze; **prank**, antic, apery, apple-pie bed, berley, caper, capriccio, hotfoot *(U.S.)*, jig *(Obs.)*, leg-pulling, monkey tricks, monkeyshine *(U.S.)*, play, practical joke, short sheet, sport; **pun**, equivoque, paranomasia, play on words, quibble, word play; **witticism**, bon mot, boutade, crack, epigram, facetiae, in-joke, jeu d'esprit, nifty *(U.S.)*, quip, sally, wisecrack; **malapropism**, blooper, spoonerism; **banter**, badinage, chaff, gibe, josh *(U.S.)*, kid, persiflage, pleasantry, raillery, repartee, riposte; **dirty joke**, blue story, double entendre; **stale joke**, chestnut; **comics**, comic strip, funnies, strip cartoon. *See also* HUMOUR; COMEDY

JOKE *v* farce *(Obs.)*, fun, gag, jape *(Archaic)*, jest, pun, quip, repartee *(Obs.)*, wisecrack; **play the wag**, antic *(Obs.)*, fool, play; **amuse**, make someone laugh, slay; **banter**, chaff, josh *(U.S.)*, kid, pull someone's leg, rag; **satirise**, epigrammatise, lampoon

JOURNALIST *n* correspondent, cub reporter, newshawk, newshound, newsman, paparazzo, photojournalist, pressman, reporter, roundsman, special correspondent, stringer, war correspondent; **newsreader**, newscaster; **columnist**, editor, feature writer, gossip columnist, sob-sister; **newsagent**, newsdealer, newsstand, newsvendor; **news desk**, city desk *(Brit.)*, newsroom; **press agent**, flack *(U.S.)*, P.R.O., press officer, press secretary, public relations officer, publicity agent

JOURNEY *n* expedition, odyssey, travels; **trip**, drive, daytrip, excursion, fang, jaunt, joy-ride, junket, outing, round trip, sally, spin; **tour**, grand tour, lecture tour, mystery tour, package tour; **pilgrimage**, hajj *(Islam.)*; **lift**, hitch, pick-up; **patrol**, round; **swim**, bathe, skinny-dip, wade; **ski**, skate

JOY *n* exaltation *(Obs.)*, felicity, festiveness, gaiety, glee, gleefulness, gleesomeness, gratulation *(Archaic)*, joyfulness, joyousness, mirth, paradise, ravishment, rejoicing; **joie de vivre**, charivari, excess of spirits, exuberance; **elation**, elatedness, rapture, rapturousness; **triumph**, exultation, jubilance, jubilation; **revelry**, carousal, good cheer, jollification, merrymaking. *See also* CELEBRATION; FESTIVAL

JOYFUL *adj* blithe, cock-a-hoop, elate, elated, elevated, enrapt, exuberant, gleeful, gleesome, glowing, happy, high, high as a kite, in raptures, jolly, joyous, mirthful, on top of the world, overjoyed, rapturous, rejoicing

JOYFULLY *adv* blithely, elatedly, exuberantly, gleefully, gleesomely, glowingly, happily, joyously, jubilantly, rapturously, rejoicingly; **festively**, commemoratively, festally; **triumphantly**, exultantly, exultingly, gloatingly

JUDGE *n* adjudicator, arbiter, awarder, beak, justice, magistrate, referee, sentencer; **judiciary**, bench, court, Full Bench, judicature, syndicate; **wise judge**, a Daniel, a Daniel come to judgment, Solomon; **alcalde**, archon *(Greek Hist.)*, bailie *(Scot.)*, burgomaster, cadi *(Islam)*, chancellor, Chief Justice, circuit judge, coroner, Family Court judge, Federal Court judge, High Court judge, J.P., judge advocate, judge advocate general, Justice of the Peace, master, prefect *(Rom. Cath. Ch.)*, puisne judge, registrar, seneschal *(Archaic)*, squire *(U.S.)*, stipendiary magistrate, Supreme Court judge, syndic. See also JURY

JUDGESHIP n archonship, bench, chair, chancellorship, coronership, judicature, justiceship, magistracy, woolsack *(Brit.)*; **wig**, black cap

JUDGMENT n account, adjudgment, adjudication, arbitrament, arbitration *(Law)*, conclusion, condemnation, deliverance, diagnosis, discrimination, reckoning, resolution, umpirage; **ruling**, decision, determination, doom, mark, order, pronouncement; **verdict**, award, class resolution, declaration, decree, decretal, finding, non prosequitur, nonsuit, ratio decidendi, sentence; **justice**, judicature, jurisprudence

JUMBLE n clutter, dog's breakfast, dog's dinner, hash, huddle, huggermugger, litter, mess, mix, muddle, muss *(U.S.)*, tumble, upset; **mess-up**, a fine kettle of fish, a pretty kettle of fish, balls-up, boggle, cock-up, foul-up, frig-up, fuck-up, mix-up; **hotch-potch**, gallimaufry, mishmash; **bustle**, bun rush, helter-skelter, hurry-scurry, scramble

JUMP n bounce, bound, flier, flying jump, hop, hop skip and jump, leap, pounce, spring, take-off; **caper**, frisk, gambol, prance, skip; **buck**, capriole, croupade, curvet, gambado, tittup; **jumping**, buckjumping, hurdling, leapfrogging, leaping, saltation, transilience, vaulting; **long jump**, broad jump, Fosbury flop, high jump, hop step and jump, polevault, straddle, triple jump, vault, western roll; **ski-jump**, axel; **volte**, demivolt *(Horseriding)*

JUMP v bound, galumph, leap, lollop, ramp about, start, tumble, vault; **caper**, bob around, bob up and down, cavort, dance, exult *(Obs.)*, frisk, gambol, hop, prance, skip; **pounce**, spring; **buck**, buckjump, capriole, curvet, fence, jackknife, kangaroo, rear, tittup; **trampoline**, bounce; **jump over**, clear, hurdle, leapfrog, over *(Rare)*, overleap, top, vault

JUMPER n jersey, pullover, skinny rib, skivvy, sloppy joe, sweater, windcheater, windjammer, woolly

JUMPING adj salient, saltant, saltatorial, saltatory, saltigrade, transilient, vaulting; **buckish**, bouncing, bounding, capering, curvetting, frisky, hopping, leaping

JURY n grand jury *(U.S.)*, hung jury, inquest, panel, petty jury, quest, tales; **juror**, ambidexter *(Archaic)*, foreman, jurat, juryman, petty juror, talesman. See also JUDGE

JUST A SEC interj half a mo, hang on, hang on a bit, just a second, just a tick, wait a sec

JUSTIFIABILITY n defensibility, defensibleness; **veniality**, excusableness, venialness

JUSTIFIABLE adj defensible, pleadable, warrantable; **excusable**, pardonable, venial

JUSTIFICATION *n* allegation *(Law)*, apologia, apology, authority, burden of proof, defence, plea, pleading, reply, self-defence *(Law)*, self-justification, theodicy *(Theol.)*, title, vindication, warrant; **excuse**, alibi *(Colloq.)*, colour *(Law)*, denial, extenuating circumstance, pretext, salvo *(Rare)*, sob-story; **extenuation,** alleviation, cover-up, mitigation, palliation, snow job, white-washing

JUSTIFICATORY *adj* plausible, self-justifying, theodicean, vindicative, vindicatory, well-founded, well-grounded; **extenuative,** excusatory, exulptory

JUSTIFIER *n* accused, accuser, alleger, apologiser, apologist, defendant, excuser, extenuator, theodicean, vindicator

JUSTIFY *v* authorise, be a reason for, be an excuse for, explain, give the devil his due, plead ignorance, rationalise, set right, set the score right, vindicate, warrant; **excuse,** acquit, clear, exculpate, exonerate; **extenuate,** gloss over, make allowances, palliate, put a good face on, put in a good word for, speak up for, varnish over, whitewash

JUT *v* basset, beetle, exsert, flange, jut out, outcrop, outgrow, point out, poke out, thrust out; **protrude,** pout, project, shoot out; **stand out,** start, stick out, stick up; **protract,** extend; **bunch,** calk, clump, spike. *See also* BULGE

Kk

KANGAROO *n* big red, blue flier, boomer, joey, kanga, old man, roo

KEEP SECRET *v* black out, classify, hide, hush up, sit on, smother, withhold; **keep a secret**, clam up, hold one's tongue, keep one's mouth shut, keep one's own counsel, let it go no further, not breathe a word; **be secretive**, cabal, collude, huggermugger, intrigue, manoeuvre, plot, tick-tack

KEEP SINGLE *v* live alone; **divorce**, live separately, separate, split up

KERBING *n* capstone, coaming, coping, kerb, kerbstone; **roadside**, nature strip, shoulder, wayside; **building alignment**, alignment, building line

KICK *n* balloon, banana kick, boot, crosskick, drop kick, garryowen, hack, header, place kick, punt, rainmaker, scissors kick, spiral punt, spurn *(Obs.)*, stab, stab kick, tap-kick, torp, torpedo punt, up-and-under

KICK *v* crosskick, foot *(Obs.)*, hack, knee, put in the boot, put the boot into someone, spurn *(Obs.)*, toe; **stamp**, stomp

KILL *v* account for, bag, be in for the kill, do away with, do for, fordo *(Archaic)*, halal, kill off, make away with, shed blood, slay, smite, spiflicate *(Joc.)*, transport *(Obs.)*, zot; **murder**, assassinate, blow away, bump off, burke, croak, do in, get, knock off, liquidate, remove, rub out, take for a ride, waste *(U.S.)*; **execute**, condemn to death, dispatch, do to death, put to death, sign the death warrant of; **asphyxiate**, axe, bayonet, behead, blow the brains out, bone, brain, burn, choke, club, cut the throat of, dangle, decapitate, decollate, drown, electrocute, garrotte, gibbet, guillotine, hang, harpoon, impale, jugulate, knife, lapidate, lynch, neck, overlie, pick off, pike, pith, point the bone at, poison, poleaxe, pot *(Hunting)*, sabre, scalp, scrag, shoot, shoot down, sing, slaughter, smother, spear, spike, stick, stifle, stiletto, stone, strangle, strangulate, string up, suffocate, suspercollate, tomahawk, turn off *(Obs.)*, wring the neck of; **suicide**, blow one's brains out, commit harakiri, do oneself in, fall on one's sword, go off the bars, go off the tub, jump overboard, jump the Gap, kill oneself, o.d., put one's head in the oven, self-immolate, slit one's wrists, take poison; **sacrifice**, immolate; **put down**, destroy, put away, put out of misery, put to sleep. *See also* MASSACRE

KILLER *n* assassin, assassinator, bravo, butcher, Cain, cutthroat, decapitator, decimator, decollator, depopulator, dispatcher, gangster, gunman, hatchet man, head-hunter, hired killer, hit man, hit squad, manslaughterer, manslayer, massacrer, murderer, murderess, poisoner, purger, scalper, slaughterer, slayer, strangler, thug; **executioner**, deathsman *(Archaic)*, firing party, firing squad, garrotter, guillotiner, hangman, headsman; **sacrificer**, immolator; **butcher**, chainman *(N.Z.)*, gun-chain *(N.Z.)*, harpooner, knacker, slaughterman; **toreador**, bullfighter, matador, torero

KILLING *n* blood-letting, bloodshed, the kill; **murder**, assassination, chance-medley *(Law)*, dispatch, first-degree murder, foul play, manslaughter, manslaying, second-degree murder, violent death; **strangulation**, asphyxiation, jugulation, suffocation, thuggee; **homicide**, aborticide, exposure of infants, filicide, foeticide, fratricide, infanticide, matricide, parricide, patricide, regicide, sororicide, tyrannicide, uxoricide; **suicide**, bushido, felo-de-se, harakiri, Russian roulette, self-destruction, self-murder; **sacrifice**, hecatomb, immolation, ritual killing, suttee; **execution**, beheading, capital punishment, crucifixion, decapitation, decollation, electrocution, garrotte, halter, hanging, lapidation, lynching, stoning; **deicide**; **euthanasia**, mercy killing. *See also* MASSACRE; MEANS OF KILLING; PLACE OF KILLING

KILLING *adj* asphyxiant, deadly, death-dealing, fatal, lethal, manslaying, mortiferous, poisonous, suffocative, toxic; **germicidal**, bactericidal, insecticidal. *See also* MURDEROUS

KIND *adj* considerate, kindly, nice, open-hearted, regardful, solicitous, sweet, sweet-tempered, tactful, tender-hearted, thoughtful, warm-hearted, well-meaning; **benevolent**, beneficent, benignant, big-hearted, gracious, kind-hearted, mild *(Obs.)*, well-disposed, well-wishing; **sympathetic**, caring, consolatory, involved; **gentle**, benign, compassionate, forgiving, humane, lenient, mild, propitious, soft; **amiable**, decent, friendly, genial, good-hearted, grandfatherly, warm; **altruistic**, charitable, Christianly, humanitarian, philanthropic; **overkind**, paternalistic, smothery, well-meaning

KINDLY *adv* considerately, gently, humanely, mildly, nicely, solicitously, sweetly, thoughtfully; **benevolently**, beneficently, benignantly, graciously, kind-heartedly; **sympathetically**, comfortingly, warm-heartedly; **amiably**, decently, good-heartedly, warmly; **altruistically**, philanthropically; **paternalistically**

KINDNESS *n* considerateness, consideration, goodness, kind-heartedness, loving-kindness, niceness, regardfulness, solicitousness, solicitude, sweetness, tender-heartedness, thoughtfulness, warm-heartedness; **goodwill**, benevolence, grace, kindliness; **altruism**, charitableness, generosity, humanitarianism, philanthropy, unselfishness; **friendliness**, amiability, amiableness, geniality, good-heartedness, warmness, warmth; **gentleness**, benignancy, benignity, candour *(Obs.)*, graciosity, graciousness, humaneness, humanity, leniency, mildness, propitiousness, softness; **paternalism**, patronage

KINDRED *adj* kin, near, of kin, once removed, related, twice removed; **consanguine**, adoptive, agnate, agnatic, cognate, collateral, consanguineous, enate, german, half-blooded; **familial**, familiar *(Rare)*, family; **nepotic**, clannish, incestuous; **tribal**, tribalist, tribalistical

KINSHIP *n* agnation, clanship, cognation, consanguinity, filiation, nick *(Horse breeding)*, relation; **familial relationship**, brotherhood, fatherhood, fraternalism, fraternity, maternity, motherhood, parenthood, paternity, sisterhood; **cousinhood**, cosinage *(Law)*, cousinship; **kinship system**, matriarchy, patriarchy; **tribalism**, clannishness, nepotism

KISS *v* bill, blow a kiss, buss, lip *(Obs.)*, osculate, pash off, peck, smack; **embrace**, bosom, clasp, clip *(Archaic)*, cuddle, enfold, fold in one's arms, hug, lap, nestle, nuzzle, snuggle, squeeze; **caress**, chuck, chuck under the chin, coax *(Obs.)*, dandle, fondle, pat, stroke; **coo**, honey *(U.S. or Archaic)*, murmur sweet nothings; **make love**, bill and coo, bundle, canoodle, neck, pash, pet, smooch, smoodge, spoon

KITCHEN *n* bakehouse, bakery, butlery, caboose *(Naut.)*, cook-shop *(N.Z.)*, cookhouse, cuisine, dairy, gallery, galley, grill, grillroom, kitchenette, scullery, servery; **dining room**, breakfast room, cenacle, dinette, fraterhall, morning room; **dining hall**, bar, butlery, cocktail bar, cocktail lounge, dive, grillroom, lounge, mess, public bar, refectory, saloon bar, soup kitchen, swill, tearoom, wardroom

KNIFE *n* breadknife, carver, carving knife, case-knife, clicking knife, drawknife, drawshave, French knife, hunting knife, paperknife, pigsticker, sheath-knife, shiv *(Brit.)*, steel; **dagger**, kris, kukri, poniard, skean; **clasp-knife**, dover, flick-knife, jackknife, penknife, pocket-knife, switchblade; **heavy knife**, cradle, cradlescythe, froe, machete, panga, pruning hook, pruning knife, scythe, sickle, swingle; **scalpel**, bistoury, lance, lancet; **razor**, cutthroat, safety razor, shaver; **blade**, edge, edge tool, knife edge, runner, slice bar, tool

KNOB *n* bunch, head, knobble, knop, nub, nubbin, nubble, pinhead, prominence, stub, umbo; **burl**, bump, burr, emergence, gallnut, gnarl, knot, knur, node, nodule, nut-gall, trabecula, whelp; **process**, ala, apophysis, berry, bosset, calcar, calk, caruncle, condyle, cornu, coronoid process, hyperostosis, nose, osteophyte, wing; **jut**, cog, dent, dentation, denticle, denticulation, fang, finger, flange, joggle, languet, pallet, ratchet, serration, serrulation, tappet, tongue, tooth; **projection**, gargoyle, jag, limb, lip, peak, point, snag, spade, spout, thorn, toe; **saddle bow**, horn, pommel, pummel. *See also* BULGE

KNOBBY *adj* bony, bossy, burled, condylar, condyloid, gangliate, gangliated, ganglionic, gnarled, jointed, knobbed, knobbly, knurled, knurly, moniliform, nodal, nodose, nodular, nodulous, nubbly, osteophytic, ridged, torose, umbonate, umbonic, warty; **cusped**, bicorn, bicuspid, calcariferous, corniculate, cornuted, cuspidal, cuspidate, tricorn, tricuspid; **goosepimply**, goosy; **bumpy**, hummocky, lumpy, pebbly, snaggy; **jagged**, dentate, denticulate, dentirostral, jaggy, peaked, pointed, sawtoothed, serrated, toothed; **clumpy**, clumpish, lobate, lobular, multilobular, stubbed, stubby, tussocky. *See also* PROTUBERANT; SWOLLEN

KNOT *n* belay, bend, bow, bowline, carrick bend, cat's-paw, clench, clinch, clove hitch, figure of eight, fisherman's bend, granny, half-hitch, hawser bend, hitch, overhand knot, reef knot, rolling hitch, running knot, sheepshank, sheet bend, slipknot, square knot, surgeon's knot, timber hitch, turle knot, weaver's knot; **splice**, eye splice, snell *(Fishing)*

KNOW *v* can *(Obs.)*, cognise, intuit, ken *(Archaic)*, remember, savvy, wis *(Archaic)*, wit *(Archaic)*; **be familiar with**, have at one's finger tips; **grasp**, accept, apperceive, appreciate, apprehend, comprehend, digest, know by sight, perceive, read, recognise, see, sense, take; **know the score**, awake, be in the picture, have an ear to the ground, know how many beans make five, know the ropes, not have come down in the last shower; **be informed**, get wind of, get word of, hear of. *See also* UNDERSTAND

KNOWING *adj* apperceptive, cognitive, enlightened, insightful, perceptive, percipient, switched-on, understanding; **in the know**, au courant, cluey, hep, hip, not born yesterday, on the ball, on the beam, up on, with-it; **aware**, apprised, cognisant, informed, intelligent *(Rare)*, sensible, witting *(Archaic)*; **self-aware**, self-conscious

KNOWINGLY *adv* comprehendingly, consciously, perceptively, with one's eyes open, wittingly; **omnisciently**; **eruditely**, learnedly, philosophically, scientifically, technically, technologically, wisely; **urbanely**, sophisticatedly

KNOWLEDGE *n* cognition *(Obs.)*, enlightenment, illumination, information, ken, knowingness, light, science, technology, wisdom; **omniscience**, encyclopaedism, pansophy; **mastery**, apprehension, comprehension, experience, expertise, expertness, grasp, mastership, realisation, uptake; **rudimentary knowledge**, equipment, grounding, propaedeutics, rudiments; **smattering**, sciolism, smatter; **esotery**, privity, specialty, technicality; **common knowledge**, a household word, ancient history, open secret; **folklore**, folk memory, lore; **sophistication**, savoir-faire, savoir-vivre, urbaneness, urbanity, worldliness; **familiarity**, acquaintance, conversance, conversancy, intimateness; **study of knowledge**, architectonics, epistemology, exact science, pantology, science. *See also* UNDERSTANDING

KNOWLEDGEABLE *adj* Alexandrian *(Class. Antiq.)*, cultivated, educated, enlightened, highbrow, illuminate *(Obs.)*, informed, learned, lettered, read, skilled, versed, well-informed, well-read; **erudite**, classical, clerkly *(Archaic)*, humanistic, virtuoso, wise; **omniscient**, all-knowing, pansophic; **experienced**, able, expert, knowing, proficient, salted, savvy, sciential, versed in; **worldly-wise**, not born yesterday, sophisticated, urbane; **awake up to**, on to, privy to; **familiar**, acquainted, at home, au fait, big on, conversant, intimate with, no stranger to

KNOWLEDGEABLENESS *n* anthroposophy, clerkliness *(Archaic)*, education, eruditeness, erudition, learnedness, learning, reading, scholarship, wisdom

KNOWN *adj* given *(Maths)*, unspoken; **well-known**, familiar, famous, noted, notorious, old, proverbial; **perceptual**, identifiable, objective, perceptional, supraliminal; **esoteric**, gnostic

Ll

LABEL *n* car sticker, sticker, tab, tag; **hallmark,** countermark, frank, impress, imprint *(Bibliog.),* plate-mark, postmark, remarque *(Engraving),* seal, stamp, surcharge *(Philately),* touch *(Metall.),* touchmark, watermark; **brand,** blaze, chop *(India),* crop, earmark, fryingpan brand, logo, logotype, moko *(N.Z.),* raddle, rubber stamp, tattoo, trademark; **inscription,** legend, rubric; **identification,** badge, calling card, credentials, dead meat ticket, dog tag, ID, ID card, identity disc *(Mil.),* marking tape, meat tag, meat (ticket), name tag, OK card, papers, place-card, ration-card, register *(Comm.),* union card, visiting card; **nameplate,** bookplate, doorplate, escutcheon *(Naut.),* numberplate, shingle; **serial number,** call number, Dewey number, flight number *(Aeron.),* IBN, postcode, pressmark *(Bibliog.),* shelf mark; **station identification,** call sign *(Naut.),* signature tune; **ticket,** check *(U.S.),* docket *(U.S.),* excursion ticket, firemark, jetton *(Brit.),* meal ticket, platform ticket, price-tag, season ticket, transfer, transfer-ticket, voucher; **stamp,** health stamp *(N.Z.),* postage stamp, precancel, provisional; **notice,** clapperboard, clappers *(Films),* facia, noticeboard, signboard; **tombstone,** headstone

LABEL *v* identify, mark, personalise, tab, tag, ticket; **brand,** blaze, designate, earmark, fingerprint, notch, raddle, sear, stigmatise, tattoo; **stamp,** frank, hallmark, impress, imprint, postmark, print, roulette, rubricate, seal, surcharge *(Philately).* watermark; **sign,** autograph, consign *(Obs.),* initial, put one's mark on, resign, signature; **countersign,** countermark, ratify, undersign, underwrite

LABELLER *n* brander, dotter, franker, impresser, stamper, stigmatiser, tattooer; **brand,** branding iron, die, iron, stamp

LABOURER *n* blue-collar worker, bohunk *(U.S.),* coolie, day labourer, fellah, hand, hunky *(U.S.),* manual labourer, offsider, unskilled worker; **handyman,** blue-tongue, bogtrotter, factotum, fix-it man, jack-of-all-trades, odd-job man, rouseabout; **artisan,** artificer, artist *(Obs.),* craftsman, fabricant, master-craftsman; **fettler,** hairy-legs, jobber, permanent-way man, platelayer, sleeper cutter, snake-charmer, trackman *(U.S.),* trackwalker *(U.S.),* woollynose; **wharfie,** disso, dock labourer, docker, longshoreman *(U.S.),* lumper, seagull *(N.Z.),* stevedore, waterside worker, wharf labourer; **housekeeper,** hausfrau, home-maker, housemaid, housewife; **plumber,** blackjack merchant, drainer, turd strangler. *See also* WORKER

LACE *n* Alençon lace, binche lace, bobbin lace, bobbinet, brussels lace, cascade, Chantilly, cluny lace, drawn-thread work, duchesse lace, filet lace, gauze, guipure, lacework, macramé, Mechlin lace, mesh, needle-point lace, net, orris, pillow

lace

lace, point, reseau, tatting, tiffany, torchon lace, valenciennes; **embossment**, enlacement, moiré, morrie; **trimmings**, appliqué, bias binding, elastic, flouncing, goffer, lastings, piping, rickrack, ruche, ruching, ruffle, soutache, stripe, tape, tinsel *(Obs.)*

LACK COURAGE *v* be unable to say boo to a goose; **chicken out**, dingo, funk, go to water, have cold feet, pike out, show the white feather, skulk; **quail**, boggle, cower, flinch, shrink, waver

LACK OF CLARITY *n* abstruseness, ambiguity, ambiguousness, deepness, double meaning, reconditeness; **mysteriousness**, anagrammatism, elusiveness, inscrutability, vagueness; **incomprehensibility**, impalpability, impenetrability, impenetrableness, incomprehensibleness, inexplicability, inexplicableness, unaccountability, unaccountableness, unfathomableness, unintelligibility, unintelligibleness; **obscurity**, encryption, obscureness, opacity; **insolubility**, indecipherability, insolubleness, insolvability; **illegibility**, crabbedness, illegibleness, unreadability, unreadableness

LACK OF SAVOUR *n* unpalatability, unpalatableness, unsavouriness; **nastiness**, noisomeness, offensiveness, rankness, unwholesomeness; **rancidity**, brackishness, gaminess, tinniness; **pig-swill**, guk, gunk, pig-tucker *(N.Z.)*, slops; **bread and water**, prison fare, stodge

LAIC *adj* churchmanly, impropriate, laical, lay, secular, temporal, tertiary

LAKE *n* inland sea, lagoon, landlocked water, loch *(Scot.)*, lough, mere, overflow lake; **salt lake**, broad *(Brit.)*, drowned valley, playa, shott; **basin**, anabranch, confluence, conflux; **dam**, arched dam, gravity dam, lock, milldam, reservoir, sluice, tank, turkey's-nest tank; **billabong**, backwater, bayou *(U.S.)*, lunette, plunge *(U.S.)*; **waterhole**, bogeyhole, bogie, wallow, watering hole; **pool**, dike *(Brit.)*, linn *(Scot.)*, millpond, oxbow, pond, tarn, tidal pool; **swimming pool**, baths, pool; **fish pond**, fish ladder; **puddle**, plash, sump; **standing water**, dead water, mickery country, stagnant water, still water

LAKY *adj* lacustrine, lagoonal, pondlike, pondy

LAME *adj* hipshot; **arthritic**, gouty, rheumatic, rheumatoid, stiff; **paralysed**, paraplegic, quadriplegic; **dislocated**, out of joint

LAND *n* earth, real estate, terra, terra firma; **continent**, country, landmass, main, mainland; **terrain**, country; **ground**, floor *(Colloq.)*; **inland**, heartland, hinterland, interior, midland; **lithosphere**, asthenosphere, barysphere, centrosphere, crust, sial; **delta**, bird's-foot delta, fan delta; **flood plain**, doab, holm *(Brit.)*, warpland; **lowland**, innings, polder. *See also* SOIL

LAND *adj* earthy, geophilous, telluric, terraqueous, terrene, terrestrial; **ground**, ashore, shore, surface; **continental**, inland, landlocked; **coastal**, littoral, longshore, onshore, seaside; **insular**, archipelagic; **peninsular**, isthmian; **riverside**, deltaic, riparian, riverine

LANDDWELLER *n* landlubber, landsman, mainlander; **islander**, isthmian

LANDSLIDE *n* ash fall, ash flow, avalanche, cave-in, earthflow, landslip, mudslide, rock-fall, slide, snowslip, soil creep, subsidence; **sinkage**, settlement, settling

LANGUAGE *n* acrolect, basilect, code, competence, creole, dialect, idiolect, idiom, langue, lect, lingua franca, matrilect, mother tongue, parlance, parole, patois, performance, pidgin, regional dialect, register, social dialect, sociolect, speech, speech variety, tongue; **standard English**, formal English, good English, good grammar, literary language, prestige dialect, prestige form, the King's English, the Queen's English; **jargon**, argot, baby talk, back slang, cant, colloquialism, expletive, flash *(Obs.)*, hobson-jobson, informal language, jive, lingo, patter, rhyming slang, slang, swear word, taboo term, vernacular, vulgar; **gobbledegook**, cablese, commercialese, euphuism, jabberwocky, journalese, legalese, officialese, technical language, telegraphese, trade name; **terminology**, nomenclature, technology, trade description; **code**, clear, cypher, microdot, scrambled message; **language family**, family, group of languages, stock, subfamily; **language type**, agglutinating language, analytic language, artificial language, interlanguage, isolating language, metalanguage, object language, protolanguage, synthetic language, target language, tone language, universal language

LAST DAY *n* Armageddon, crack of doom, Day of Judgment, day of reckoning, Götterdämmerung, Judgment, Judgment Day, Last Day, millenary, millennium

LATE *adj* belated, latish, serotine *(Rare)*; **dilatory**, backward, behindhand, slow, tardif, tardy; **overdue**, belated, in retard *(Obs.)*; **last-minute**, eleventh-hour; **last**, latest, lattermost; **later**, latter, Upper *(Geol.)*

LATE *adv* belatedly, tardily; **latterly**; last

LATECOMER *n* Johnny-come-lately; **night owl**, stopout

LATENESS *n* backwardness, belatedness, tardiness; **last minute**, eleventh hour; **delay**, demurrage, detainment, hold-up, procrastination, retard, retardation, tarriance *(Archaic)*, wait

LAUGH *v* chortle, chuckle, guffaw, haw-haw; **giggle**, laugh in one's sleeve, laugh up one's sleeve, snicker, snigger, teehee, titter; **shriek**, cackle, hoot, roar, scream, shout, snort; **fall about**, break up, cachinnate, convulse, kill oneself, laugh fit to kill, laugh like a drain, laugh one's socks off, piss oneself, split one's sides; **smile**, grin

LAUGHINGLY *adv* merrily, mirthfully; **banteringly**, playfully, sportfully; **jocularly**, facetiously, jestingly, jocosely, jokingly, pleasantly

LAW *n* Aboriginal law, case law, civil law, commercial law, common law, consumer protection, criminal law, crown law, equity, family law, international law, Islamic law, law merchant, law of nations, law of the jungle, legislation, lex, maritime law, martial law, military law, natural law, organic law, penal code, Roman law, statute law, sumptuary law, unwritten law; **code**, canon, capitularies

(Frankish), Code Napoléon, corpus juris, Decalogue, judicature system, pandect, Ten Commandments, the Digest; **act**, act of Parliament, assize *(Archaic)*, bill, by-law, caption, charter, consolidation, dead letter, decree, edict, enactment, ex post facto law, measure, ordinance, ordonnance, private act, private bill, private member's bill, public bill, regulation, rescript, rider *(Parl. Proc.)*, standing order, statute, statutory instrument, ways and means *(Govt)*; **amendment**, novel *(Civil Law)*; **precedent**, authority, nice point, precept, ruling; **jurisprudence**, codification, jurimetrics, medical jurisprudence, nomography, nomology, rule of law

LAWFUL *adj* according to the law, allowable, authorised, chartered, constitutional, legal, legit, legitimate, licit, permitted, statutory, unalienable, valid, very *(Archaic)*; **paralegal**, quasi-judicial; **judicial**, forensic, jural, juridical, juristic, justiciary; **jurisprudential**, jurisprudent, nomographic, nomographical, nomological

LAWFULLY *adv* legally, legitimately, validly; **in the eye of the law**, de jure, jurally, juristically

LAWFULNESS *n* allowableness, constitutionality, legality, legitimacy, legitimateness, validity, validness; **legalisation**, legitimation, legitimisation, validation

LAWYER *n* articled clerk, jurisconsult, jurisprudent, jurist, legal adviser, legal eagle, legist, limb of the law, nomographer, nomologist, proctor *(Archaic)*, procurator, publicist, trial lawyer; **crooked lawyer**, ambidexter *(Archaic)*, pettifogger, shyster; **barrister**, advocate *(Scot. Law)*, barrister-at-law, bencher *(Brit.)*, counsel, counsellor *(U.S.)*, junior, K.C., King's Counsel, leader, mouthpiece, pleader, Q.C., Queen's Counsel, senior, silk, utter barrister; **prosecutor**, crown prosecutor, district attorney *(U.S.)*, fiscal, police prosecutor, public prosecutor; **solicitor**, attorney *(U.S.)*, attorney at law *(U.S.)*, chamber magistrate, clerk of the peace, commissioner for oaths, conveyancer, duty solicitor, notary, notary public, scrivener *(Archaic)*, shopfront lawyer; **attorney-general**, prothonotary, solicitor-general. *See also* LEGAL PROFESSION

LAY CHARGES *v* appeal *(Obs.)*, arraign, article, attaint *(Archaic)*, book, bring to book, carpet, charge, do for, hang something on, have up, impeach, implead, impute, incriminate, inculpate, indict, lag, lay a complaint, place on the mat, precondemn, prefer charges, press charges, swear out, throw the book at; **countercharge**, recriminate. *See also* ACCUSE

LAYER *n* flake, folium, interleaf, lamina, slice, thickness, tier; **band**, course, cross reef, flookan, flucan, frieze, friezing, line, lode, panel, reef, rib, schlieren, seam, stage, streak, string, string-course; **stratum**, bar, bone bed, cap rock, colluvium, counter, disconformity, floor, hardpan, horizon, killas, lamella, lithosphere, litter, mantle, mantle rock, pan, roadbed, sial, sill, sima, subsoil, substrate, substratum, superstratum, unconformity, underlay, varve, watertable; **strata**, coal measures, cross-course, measures, series

LAYERED *adj* cross-bedded, laminated, multilaminate, stratiform, tegular, three-ply; **split-level**, decked, double-deck, double-decker, storeyed; **stratal**, crustal, crusty, desmoid, substrative, superincumbent, superjacent, supernatant; **laminate**, clinker, flaggy, laminose; **striped**, sliced, vittate; **filmy**, membranous

LEADER *n* captain, cheerleader *(U.S.)*, driver, guide, helmsman, pilot, standard-bearer, trailblazer, wheelman; **mastermind**, brains, éminence grise, father, power behind the throne, wheeler-dealer; **leading light**, cock, prime mover, protagonist, ringleader, ruling spirit, top dog; **chairperson**, chair, chairman, chairwoman, master of ceremonies, moderator, prolocutor, symposiarch, toastmaster, toastmistress, whip; **principal**, chancellor, dean, headmaster, headmistress, provost, rector, rectorate, regent, scholarch, vice-chancellor, warden; **orchestra leader**, bandmaster, concertmaster, conductor, coryphaeus, first violin, kapellmeister; **pioneer**, pathfinder, scout; **bellwether**, Judas goat, Judas sheep; **scout leader**, akela, brown owl, group leader, guider, scouter, scoutmaster, tawny owl, troop leader. *See also* MANAGER

LEAF *n* cataphyll, frond, needle, pine needle, quatrefoil, scale, sclerophyll; **leaf organ**, arista, articulation, auricle, awn, axil, blade, cirrus, costa, footstalk, hair, lamina, leaf bud, leaflet, leafstalk, lobe, lobule, midrib, ocrea, petiole, phyllode, phyllome, pinna, pinnule, pulvinus, rachilla, rachis, rib, scale, sheath, stipel, stipule, stoma, tendril, tomentum, tooth, tunic, umbo, vagina, vein

LEAPER *n* caperer, frisker, hopper, hurdler, jumper, prancer, springer, tumbler, vaulter; **bucker**, buckjumper

LEARN *v* absorb, audit, compass, digest, experience, get down pat, get the hang of, get the knack of, imbibe, infix, ingest, know by heart, learn by rote, learn the ropes, master, memorise, pick up, take in; **get wise**, cut one's eyeteeth, cut one's teeth, get one's feet wet, live and learn, pick someone's brains, serve one's apprenticeship. *See also* STUDY

LEARNER *n* greenhorn, improver, kid, novice, probationer, raw recruit, rookie, tenderfoot, tyro; **beginner**, abecedarian, abecedary, cadet, fresher, freshette, freshman, underclassman *(U.S.)*; **trainee**, apprentice, articled clerk, prentice *(Archaic)*; **neophyte**, catechumen, disciple, follower, proselyte; **catechist**, chela *(India)*, ritualist, scholastic, seminarian, seminarist, theolog *(Colloq.)*. *See also* PUPIL

LEARNING *n* book-learning, bookishness, culture, erudition, latent learning *(Psychol.)*, lore, scholarship, studiousness; **comprehension**, absorption, assimilation, digestion, infixion, ingestion, insight, mastery, taking-in, understanding; **study**, boning up, brainwork, conning, cram, grind, homework, lucubration, memorisation, overstudy, prep, preparation, swotting, training. *See also* LESSON; COURSE

LEAVER *n* émigré, emigrant, migrant, valedict, voider; **absconder**, runaway

LEFT *n* left wing, verso; **left-hander,** cackyhander, left-footer, leftie, mollydooker, southpaw; **port,** larboard *(Naut. Obs.),* nearside, on *(Cricket),* on side, prompt-side *(Theat.);* **rule of the road**

LEFT *adj* left-hand, left-wing, leftward, sinister, sinistral, sinistrous; **left-handed,** cack-handed, cackyhanded, southpaw; **port,** larboard *(Naut. Obs.),* near, nearside, nigh *(Archaic),* on *(Cricket),* onside

LEFT *adv* aport, leftward, leftwards, on the left, sinisterwise, sinistrally

LEG *n* calf, crus, gam, lap, pins, props, shank, shin, stumps, thigh; **knee,** genu, kneecap, kneepan, marrowbones, pan, patella; **foot,** ankle, dogs *(Colloq.),* heel, hoof, instep, mundowie, pettitoes, podium, sole, tarsus; **toe,** big toe, hallux, little toe, minimus, pinkie, tootsy

LEGAL CENTRE *n* community justice centre

LEGALISE *v* authorise, decriminalise, enact, legitimate, legitimatise, legitimise, ordain, validate; **formulate,** codify

LEGAL ORDER *n* bench warrant, blister *(Colloq.),* blue *(Colloq.),* bluey *(Colloq.),* breve, call-up, capias, capias ad satisfaciendum, certiorari, citation, commitment, court order, death warrant, decree absolute, decree nisi, default summons, duces tecum, enactment, execution, garnishment, habeas corpus, mandamus, mittimus, monition *(Obs.),* originating summons, prerogative order, process, rule nisi, scire facias, subpoena, summons, supersedeas, ticket, warrant, writ, writ of execution, writ of prohibition, writ of right. *See also* COMMAND

LEGAL PROFESSION *n* bar, inner bar, law, outer bar; **legal advice,** legal aid. *See also* LAWYER

LEGISLATE *v* administer, govern, hold office, hold power, judge *(Jewish Hist.)*

LEGISLATION *n* government, law-making, lawgiving, policy *(Rare),* polity; **administration,** bureaucracy, civil service, commissariat, officialism, public service, quango, semigovernment authority, statutory authority; **regime,** ancien régime, Canberra, junta, kiap *(Papua New Guinea),* Kremlin, ministry, politburo, Quirinal, raj, regimen, the government, White House, Whitehall

LEGISLATIVE *adj* cabinet, comitial, congressional, curial, law-making, legislatorial, parliamentary, Quirinal; **unicameral,** bicameral; **governmental,** county, federal, municipal, state; **bureaucratic,** administrative

LEGISLATIVE BODY *n* assembly, congress, cowards' castle, legislature, moot *(Old Eng. Law),* parliament, soviet, talking shop *(Colloq.);* **administrative committee,** agora *(Greek Hist.),* board, caucus, comitia *(Roman Hist.),* commission, conclave, convocation, curia *(Roman Hist.),* duma *(Russian Hist.),* executive, executive council, meeting, presidium *(Russia),* senate, standing committee, subcommittee, synod; **municipal council,** borough council *(U.K.),* corporation *(U.K.),* county council, local authority, local government, municipality, shire, shire council, town council;

place of assembly, chamber, house, parliament house

LEND *v* advance, loan; **rent,** demise, hire out, lease out, let, re-lease, rent out, sublease, sublet, underlet; **mortgage,** bond; **fund,** accommodate, finance, re-finance, refund; **pawn,** hock, pledge, pop

LENDER *n* advancer, creditor, discounter, Ikey Mo, kulak, loan shark, loaner, moneylender, mortgagee, pawnbroker, uncle, usurer; **lessor,** landlady, landlord, rack-renter, sublessor; **credit union,** building society, permanent building society; **pawnshop,** hockshop, mont-de-piété, popshop

LENGTH *n* distance, expanse, extent, fetch, piece *(U.S.)*, range, reach, scope, space, spacing, span, straddle; **extension,** coextension, elongation, expansion, lankiness, lankness, lengthiness, linearity; **linear measure,** altitude, angular distance, chainage, easting, footage, latitude, long measure, longitude, mileage, northing, southing, surveyor's measure, westing; **trajectory,** arrowshot, bowshot, cannon shot, carry, cast, flight, gunshot, outreach, shot, throw; **hand's-breadth,** canvas, digit, finger, footstep, hank, head, march, neck, nose, pace, palm, step, stride; **yarn length,** bundle, hank, lea, spindle; **calibre,** bore, gauge; **miscellaneous length,** clearance, draw *(Mining)*, drift, drop, epoch *(Astron.)*, focal length, focus, freeboard, frontage, gap *(Aeron.)*, headway *(Railways)*, lap, overhang, overlap, pitch, recoil, setback, slippage, travel, turnaround, wheelbase; **unit of length,** air mile, angstrom, astronomical unit, barleycorn, centimetre, chain, cubit, degree, ell, em, fathom, foot, furlong, inch, international nautical mile, kilometre, league, light-year, meridional part, metre, micro-inch, micrometre, micron, mil, mile, millimetre, minute, module, nail, nautical mile, parsec, perch, pole, rod, sea mile, thou, verst, yard

LENGTHILY *adv* extendedly, lankily, lankly, long

LENGTH-MEASURER *n* cyclometer, fathomer, fathometer, foot rule, Gunter's chain, interferometer, log *(Naut.)*, micrometer, mileometer, odometer, rangefinder, ranger, rule, ruler, scale, stadiometer, surveyor's chain, tacheometer, tripmeter, ultra-micrometer

LENGTHWAYS *adv* along, at length, axially, fore-and-aft, from end to end, from stem to stem, in extenso, lengthwise, longitudinally, meridionally, out, tandem

LENIENCE *n* gentleness, leniency, lenity, mildness, moderation, temperance, toleration; **charitableness,** clemency, compassion, fellow feeling, forbearance, mercifulness, mercy, quarter; **relaxation,** unbending, laxness, elasticity, indiscipline, indulgence, laxity, liberalness, looseness, permissive society, Rafferty's rules; **dispensation,** days of grace, moratorium, reprieve

LENIENT *adj* agreeable, charitable, clement, complaisant, easy, easygoing, forgiving, gentle, humane, indulgent, kindly, liberal, merciful, mild, obliging, soft, soft-hearted, tolerant, uncritical, unexacting; **lax,** elastic, free and easy, loose, permissive, slack, unbuttoned, wide-open *(U.S. Law)*

LENIENTLY *adv* charitably, clemently, liberally, mercifully; **laxly**, elastically, indulgently, loosely

LENIENT PERSON *n* a good sport, indulger, liberaliser, loosener, mollycoddler, wittol *(Obs.)*

LENS *n* burning-glass, eyepiece, hand glass, magnifier, magnifying glass, meniscus, sunglass; **prism**, Wollaston prism; **microscope**, compound microscope, dark microscope, dark-field microscope, electron microscope, phase contrast microscope, polarising microscope, simple microscope, ultramicroscope, ultraviolet microscope; **telescope**, comet-finder, Gregorian telescope, Newtonian telescope, reflecting telescope, refracting telescope, spyglass, zenith tube; **binoculars**, field-glasses, opera glasses, telestereoscope; **periscope**, camera lucida, camera obscura; **projector**, magic lantern, planetarium, stereopticon, wheel of life, zoetrope; **hydroscope**, waterglass; **gastroscope**, pharyngoscope, proctoscope, urethroscope. *See also* GLASSES

LENT *n* Day of Atonement, jubilee

LESS *prep* bar, except, excluding, failing, minus, save, wanting, without

LESSON *n* class, lecture, module, object lesson, practical, section *(N.Z.)*, seminar, sermon, session, teach-in, tute, tutorial; **drill**, boat drill, dismounted drill, exercise, exercitation, fire drill, haute école *(Equestrian)*, pack drill, practice, rehearsal, rifle drill, rote learning, skeleton exercise, square bashing *(Mil.)*. *See also* LEARNING: COURSE

LET ONESELF GO *v* do as one pleases, do what one likes, find one's feet, freewheel, have one's fling, have one's own way, let it all hang out, let off steam, let one's hair down, play, run about, run riot, run wild, wanton; **deliver oneself from**, break free, break loose, cast off the trammels, get rid of, shake off the yoke, slip, slip the collar, throw off

LETTER *n* character, grapheme, hieroglyphic, homophone, ideogram, ideograph, numeral, pictogram, rune, sign, sphenogram, stenograph; **alphabet**, ABC, abecedary, futhorc, International Phonetic Alphabet, phonetic alphabet, Roman alphabet; **charactery**, alphabetisation, kana, notation, syllabary, transliteration; **cipher**, cuneiform, lettering, monogram, ogham, script, stencil, stenotype; **cardinal vowel**, consonant, continuant, digraph, diphthong, polyphone, trigraph, vowel; **capital letter**, block capital, block letter, capital, caps, print, upper case; **character face**, blockletter, bold, Gothic, italic, roman, small capitals, uncial; **small letter**, lower case, majuscule, minuscule; **superscript**, subindex, superior; **letter part**, ascender, cock-up, descender, initial

LEVEL *n* flat, plane, stratum, table; **horizontal**, artificial horizon, false horizon, geoid, horizon, mean sea-level, sea-level, true level

LEVEL *v* barrel, bed, cut, cut down, fell, flatten, floor, hew, hew down, knock end wise, knock endways, landplane, lay, lay down, mow down, raze, shake down; **even**, float, flush, garden, grade, pat, plane, planish, plaster, roll, smooth, square

LEVEL *adj* equal, even, flat, flattish, flush *(Print.)*, horizontal, invariable, plane, regular, smooth, square,

level   319   **liberator**

straight, table-top, tabular, uniplanar; **levelled,** compressed, flattened, pitch-faced *(Bldg Trades)*; **recumbent,** accumbent, fallen, horizontal, lolling, lolling about, lying down, procumbent, prone, prostrate, reclining, sprawling, supine

LEVELLER *n* evener, flattener, flatter, float, garden roller, grader, heavy roller, plane, planer, planisher, road roller, roll, roller, steamroller; **surveyor's level,** alidade bubble, chalkline, gimbals, plumb-rule, stringline, wye level

LEVELLY *adv* even, evenly, flat, flush, horizontally, level; **recumbently,** asprawl, flat out, flat out like a lizard drinking, on one's back, pronely, supinely

LEVELNESS *n* evenness, flatness, planeness, straightness; **recumbency,** accumbency, proneness, prostration, reclination, recumbent, supineness; **loll,** lounge

LIAR *n* belier, fabricator, falsifier, fibber, fibster, forswearer, misinformant, misreporter, mythomaniac, pathological liar, perjurer, storyteller

LIBERALISM *n* broad-mindedness, existentialism, informality, laissez faire, liberality, liberalness, non-intervention, non-restraint, toleration, tolerationism, unbiasedness

LIBERATE *v* deliver, emancipate, extricate, free, manumit, rescue, spring; **acquit,** absolve, affranchise, clear, discharge, disengage, disentail, dispense with, exempt, exonerate, frank, free, parole, ransom, release, unburden, vindicate *(Obs.)*; **let be,** leave alone, let alone, let go, remit *(Obs.)*; **unleash,** decontrol, give someone his head, loose, release, unbind, unbridle, uncage, unchain, unhand, unloose, unmuzzle, unscrew, unshackle, untie

LIBERATED *adj* emancipated, exonerated, free, free of the country *(Convict),* free on the ground *(Convict),* freeborn, released, scot-free; **freehold,** allodial; **liberal,** liberalist, liberalistic, non-restrictive, open-handed; **unbridled,** abandoned, all-in, anarchic, anarchistic, boisterous, facile, incoercible, incontinent, inordinate, intemperate, irrepressible, loose, outspoken, unbent, unbidden, unbitted, unbowed, unbroken, uncrossed, wanton, wild, wild and woolly; **uninhibited,** expansive, free, spontaneous, unashamed, unconventional, unembarrassed, unfettered, unreserved; **unlimited,** arbitrary, broad, common, laissez-faire, open, rampant, unbounded, unchartered, unclassified, unconditional, undetermined, unstructured, untrammelled

LIBERATION *n* affranchisement, deliverance, delivery, emancipation, enfranchisement, manumission, ransom, release; **acquittal,** absolution, exoneration, redemption; **discharge,** bail, bailment, dismissal, parole, remission; **disengagement,** decontrol, extrication; **freedom from conditions,** acquittance, disentailment, exemption, quittance; **unboundedness,** unaccountability, unbrokenness, unconditionality, unconditionalness, unlimitedness

LIBERATOR *n* emancipationist, emancipator, emancipist, libber, liberationist; **deliverer,** absolvent, acquitter, discharger, exonerator, manumitter, Messiah, ransomer, redeemer

libertarian 320 **lifter**

LIBERTARIAN *n* civil libertarian, existentialist, liberal, liberaliser, liberalist, non-interventionist, tolerationist

LIBERTY *n* autonomy, freedom, freeness, independence, self-determination; **licence**, familiarity, outspokenness, spontaneity, spontaneousness, unrestraint; **abandon**, anarchism, anarchy, incontinence, incontinency, indiscipline, inordinacy, intemperateness, irrepressibility, irrepressibleness, libertarianism, looseness, open-handedness, wantonness, wildness; **latitude**, breadth, elbow room, leg room, margin, option, play, poetic licence, tolerance; **leave**, exequatur, permission; **free hand**, blank cheque, fling, free rein, free swing, licence, open go, open slather, public domain; **immunity**, academic freedom, free speech, freedom of the seas; **sanctuary**, diplomatic immunity, franchise; **open door**, egress, entrance, entree, entry; **parole**, bail, cartel, force majeure, out, ransom, release, remission, ticket-of-leave; **the outside**, open *(Prison)*, rules *(Brit.)*, the outer *(Prison)*

LIBRARY *n* bibliotheca, book club, bookmobile, circulating library, lending library, lyceum, mobile library, morgue, public library, reference library, research library, stack, subscription library

LICENSED *adj* B.Y.O.(G.), honky-tonk, wet

LIE *n* alias, canard, disinformation, distortion, equivocation, evasion, exaggeration, fable, fabrication, factoid, fairytale, falsehood, fib, fiction, half-truth, invention, legal fiction, misinformation, misreport, misrepresentation, misstatement, perjury, pretext, prevarication, story, tale, tarradiddle, untruth, white lie, whopper

LIE *v* cant, dud up, fable, fabricate, fib, forswear oneself, lie like a trooper, perjure oneself; **equivocate**, not give a straight answer, palter, prevaricate, quibble; **exaggerate**, overstate, strain the truth, understate; **distort**, bend the truth, garble, misreport, pervert, tell a white lie

LIE LOW *v* burrow, go to ground, hole up, lie doggo, make oneself scarce, retire, retreat, take to the hills; **ambush**, couch, lie in wait, lurk. *See also* HIDE

LIFESAVER *n* beach inspector, beltman, lifeguard, reelman, surf-lifesaver

LIFT *n* elevator, fork hoist, fork lift, goods lift, grain elevator, hoist, noria, service lift; **pulley**, block and tackle, capstan, cat, winch, windlass; **crane**, derrick, goliath crane, luffing crane, tower crane; **lever**, jack, screwjack, wallaby jack, well sweep

LIFT *v* elevate, lever, prise, raise, upend, upheave, uplift, upraise; **hoist**, advance *(Archaic)*, exalt *(Archaic)*, fly *(Theat.)*, masthead, run up, sway up, up; **erect**, build, set up; **boost**, heighten, prop, stilt, underlay; **heave**, heft, hoick, pick up; **toss**, fork, lob, loft, sky, throw; **hitch up**, kilt, perk up, take up, tuck up; **wind up**, dredge up, fish up, haul up, jack up, pull up, winch, windlass; **trip anchor**, weigh anchor

LIFTER *n* booster, exalter *(Archaic)*, heaver, hoister, levitator, raiser, uplifter; **wincher**, jacker

lifting

LIFTING *n* Assumption, cranage, elevation, erection, exaltation *(Archaic)*, leverage, levitation, take-up, upheaval, uplift, upliftment, uptake; **boost**, a leg up, raise; **lift**, dead lift, deep knees bend, heave, jerk, press, snatch

LIGHT *n* illuminance, illumination, luminance; **lamplight**, candlelight, firelight, gaslight, torchlight; **limelight**, Bengal light, calcium light, magnesium light, red fire; **beam**, irradiation, moonbeam, pencil, phlegethon, ray, shaft, sunbeam, sunray; **glow**, candescence, gleam, incandescence, lustre, radiance, refulgence; **flash**, arc, blaze, flare, flare-up, fulguration; **sparkle**, blink, coruscation, flicker, gleam, glimmer, glimmering, glimpse *(Archaic)*, glint, glisten, glister *(Archaic)*, glitter, scintillation, shimmer, spark, twinkle, twinkling, wink; **daylight**, broad day, day, daytime, sun, sunburst, sunlight, sunniness, sunshine; **dawn**, daybreak, false dawn, first light, sunrise; **aurora**, aurora australis, aurora borealis, northern lights, polar lights; **airglow**, afterglow, alpenglow, blink *(Meteorol.)*, gegenschein, green flash, iceblink, rainbow, snowblink, sunbow, sundog, white-out; **moonlight**, earthlight, earthshine, moonshine, starlight, zodiacal light; **will-o'-the-wisp**, friar's lantern, ignis fatuus, jack-o'-lantern, marsh light, wildfire; **parhelion**, mock moon, mock sun, paraselene, photosphere; **halo**, aureole, circle, corona. *See also* BRIGHTNESS

LIGHT *adj* airy-fairy, delicate, feathery, filmy, fine, flimsy, floaty, flossy, fluffy, fuzzy, gauzy, gossamer, papery, papyraceous; **airy**, aerial, aery,

lighting

ethereal, rare, rarefied, spiritual, spirituel, spirituelle, tenuous, thin; **unsubstantial**, imponderable, lightweight, weightless

LIGHTER *n* anarchist, friction match, fusee, light, lucifer, match, safety match, slow match, vesta; **flint**, steel; **taper**, fuse, proximity fuse, spill, touchpaper, touchwood, train, wick; **torch**, firebrand, firestick; **firebox**, tinderbox; **detonator**, primer; **tinder**, amadou, combustible, ignescent, inflammable, punk *(U.S.)*

LIGHT-FOOTED *adj* agile, alacritous, alert, lambent, lightsome, nimble, tripping, volant, volante

LIGHTING *n* illumination, irradiation; **electric light**, arc lamp, arc light, bulb, city lights, fluorescent tube, gas lamp, gaslight, glow lamp, harbour lights, incandescent lamp, mercury-vapour lamp, neon lamp, port light, port lights, quartz-iodine lamp, starboard light, tungsten lamp; **chandelier**, corona, cresset, lustre, pendant; **concealed lighting**, indirect lighting, panel lighting, strip lighting, strobe lighting; **lamp**, Aldis lamp, dark lantern, droplight, flashlight, hurricane, hurricane lamp, lampion, lantern, night-light, slush lamp, standard lamp, storm-lantern *(Brit.)*, Tilley lamp, torch, wall-washer; **safety lamp**, Davy lamp; **Chinese lantern**, fairy lights, jack-o'-lantern; **streetlight**, lamp standard, lamppost, pavement light; **footlights**, floats, floodlight, foots, klieg light, limelight, spot, spotlight, sunlamp; **headlight**, courtesy light, flasher, flickers, fog lamp, headlamp, indicator light, sidelight, stoplight, tail-light; **searchlight**, star shell, Very light; **lighthouse**,

lighting

leads *(Naut.)*, pharos; **flashbulb**, electronic flash, flash, flashcube, flashgun, flashlight, photoflash lamp, photoflood lamp, strobe; **safelight; floodlight projector**, up-lighter

LIGHTLY *adv* filmily, flimsily, fluffily, fuzzily, light; **airily**, ethereally, tenuously, thinly; **agilely**, lambently, light-footedly, lightly, lightsomely, volante

LIGHTNESS *n* filminess, fineness, flimsiness, fluffiness, fuzziness, gauziness; **airiness**, ethereality, etherealness, rarefaction, rareness, rarity, tenuousness, thinness; **weightlessness**, imponderability, imponderableness, levity, zero gravity; **buoyancy**, floatability, flotage, flotation, hover, poise, wafture; **agility**, lambency, light-footedness, lightsomeness, nimbleness

LIGHTNING *n* ball lightning, chain lightning, fire *(Archaic)*, fireball, glance, heat lightning, sheet lightning, summer lightning, thunderbolt, wildfire; **St Elmo's fire**, corpasant

LIKELIHOOD *n* every chance, good chance, good prospect, likeliness, probability, promise, reason to hope, reasonable chance, well-founded view; **credibility**, plausibility, verisimilitude; **expectation**, conditional probability, normal curve, presumption, probability curve, reasonable hope; **favourite**, best bet, goer, great white hope, the one most likely to succeed

LIKELY *adj* apparent, like *(Archaic)*, odds-on, on the cards, presumable, probable, promising, to be expected; **liable to**, apt to, in line, incident to, incidental to, like to *(Archaic)*, likely to, ready to; **credible**, easy to believe, ostensible, plausible, verisimilar

LIKELY *adv* apparently, belike *(Archaic)*, doubtless, doubtlessly, easily, in all likelihood, in all probability, like as not, London to a brick, no doubt, ostensibly, presumably, probably, seemingly, ten to one, to all appearances

LIMB *n* appendage, extremity, manus, member. *See also* ARM; LEG

LIMBER *v* limber up, stretch, tenter

LIMIT *n* measure, mete, pale, precincts, riverside; **demarcation**, delimitation, partition, Rubicon; **boundary**, by-line, dead-ball line, ditch, goal line, line, score, sideline, tramlines; **deadline**, cut-off, term *(Archaic)*, time limit; **terminus**, farthest reaches, termination, the ends of the earth, ultima Thule; **horizon**, equator, skyline; **upper limit**, ceiling, high-water mark, limitations, strings; **lower limit**, dead finish, low water mark, the end of one's tether, threshold. *See also* EDGE

LIMIT *v* circumscribe, conscribe, contain, define, delimit, draw the line, terminate; **demarcate**, beat the bounds, mark out, peg, zone; **bound**, bank, kerb

LIMITING *adj* borderline, cut-off, delimitative, extreme, limitary, limitative, restrictive, terminational, terminative; **limited**, definite, finite, restricted

LIMPLY *adv* droopingly, flabbily, flaccidly, flaggingly, flimsily, loosely, slack, slackly, tenuously; **shakily**, groggily, totteringly, tremulously

LINE *n* axis, band, bar, canal *(Astron.)*, crossbar, dash, guideline, hatch, outline, ray, ribbon, rule, straight, streak, stria, strip, stroke, swath, tail, thread, track, trail, vein, veinlet; **row**, file, hedgerow, Indian file, orthostichy, procession, queue, rank, single file, train, windrow; **geometric line**, asymptote, chord, circumference, curve, diameter, directrix, median, perimeter, radius, secant, tangent; **equator**, great circle, meridian, parallel; **lineation**, crosshatching, grain, hatching, ruling, striation, veining; **specific line**, baseline, buttock line, condensation trail, contour, contour line, em rule, fall line *(Geog.)*, International Date Line, load line, magistral *(Fort.)*, magistral line *(Fort.)*, pinstripe, pitch line, Plimsoll line, ridge, service line, sideline, taw *(Marbles)*, thalweg, touchline, vapour trail, waterline

LINE *v* band, crosshatch, hatch, ray, rule, rule off, streak, striate, strip, stripe, vein; **align**, collimate, lay out, range, rank, rectify, windrow; **line up**, defile, queue, string, string out, trail

LINEALLY *adv* collinearly, linearly, rectilinearly

LINEAR *adj* bilinear, collinear, lineal, one-dimensional, rectilinear, running; **meridian,** diametral, diametrical, meridional, perimetric, perimetrical, tangential; **line-like,** flagelliform, stringlike, threadlike, vermiform, vinelike, wiredrawn; **lined,** lineate, liny, streaky, striate, veined

LINER *n* colourer, sheather, stuccoer, surfacer, waxer

LINGUIST *n* dialectician, dialectologist, etymologist, field linguist, generativist, glottologist *(Obs.)*, grammarian, lexicographer, morphologist, parser, philologer, philologist, phonetician, psychologist, semanticist, semasiologist, sociolinguist, vernacularist; **archaist,** archaiser, euphuist

LINGUISTIC *adj* etymological, glottologic *(Obs.)*, grammatical, morphemic, morphological, paralinguistic, philological, phonemic, phonetic, psycholinguistic, semantic, sociolinguistic, syntactic, syntactical; **agglutinate,** agglutinative, analytic, centum, inflective, isolating, satem, synthetic

LINGUISTICS *n* applied linguistics, comparative linguistics, comparative philology, computational linguistics, descriptive grammar, dialectology, etymology, generative grammar, generative semantics, glossology *(Obs.)*, glottology *(Obs.)*, grammar, language acquisition studies, lexicography, lexicology, metalinguistics, morphemics, morphology, morphophonemics, onomastics, paralinguistics, philology, phonemics, phonetics, phonology, pragmatics, prescriptive grammar, psycholinguistics, semantics, semasiology, sentential calculus, sociolinguistics, structuralism, stylistics, syntax, tagmemics, transformational grammar; **grammaticality,** acceptability, correctness, grammaticism, well-formedness; **deep structure,** base component, generation, rewrite rules, surface structure, transform, transformation, word order

LINGUISTIC UNIT *n* lexeme, archiphoneme, distinctive feature, immediate constituent, morpheme, phoneme, semantic component, syntactic unit, syntagm, tagmeme, taxeme; **root**, radical, stem, theme; **inflection**, accidence, accident, conjugation, conversion, declension, flection, internal change, metaplasm, paradigm, suppletion; **involution**, abbreviation, anacoluthon, enallage, gemination, reduplication, syllepsis, syncope, syncretism; **clause**, adverbial clause, apodisis (conclusion), coordinate clause, dependent clause, descriptive clause, hypotaxis, independent clause, main clause, noun clause, principal clause, protasis (condition), relative clause, restrictive clause, subordinate clause

LIQUEFACTION *n* deliquescence, dispersion, dissolution, emulsification, fluidisation, fusion; **leaching**, lixiviation, percolation, washing away

LIQUEFIABLE *adj* eutectic, eutectoid, fusible, thixotropic; **soluble**, dissoluble, dissolvable, dissolvent, solvable, water-soluble; **deliquescent**, liquescent, **hydrophilic**, hydrophobic, hydrotropic; **solvent**, anticoagulant

LIQUEFIER *n* fluidiser, fluidifacient; **solvent**, alkahest, anticoagulant, antifreeze, dispersion medium, dissolvent, dissolver, emulsifier, menstruum

LIQUEFY *v* deliquesce, melt, run, sweal, thaw; **dissolve**, disintegrate, disperse; **liquidise**, fluidise, flux, fuse, render, smelt, try; **soak**, infuse, leach, lixiviate, percolate, steep

LIQUID *n* aqua, condensate, dew, effusion *(Pathol.)*, emulsion, fluid, grume, juice, liquor, moisture, sap, wet; **solution**, colloidal solution, decoction, distillate, emulsion, emulsoid, hydrosol, infusion, lixivium, lye; **bath**, dip, soak, souse, steep, wash; **drop**, bead, blob, dewdrop, drip, droplet; **melt**, metal *(Glassmaking)*, thaw; **spillage**, spill, splash; **percolate**, leachate, seepage, soakage; **water-divining**, dowsing, rhabdomancy. *See also* WATER

LIQUID *adj* emulsive, fluctuant *(Med.)*, fluent *(Rare)*, fluid, fluidal, fluidic, molten, run, running, runny; **watery**, aqueous, hydrogenous, hydrous, hygric, juicy, sappy, serous, succulent, water, waterish, waterlike, wishy-washy; **dissolved**, in solution, liquefied, solute, uncongealed; **hydraulic**, hydrodynamic, hydrokinetic, hydrologic, hydromechanical, hydrostatic

LIQUIDITY *n* fluidity, fluidness, flux, liquidness, serosity, wateriness; **solubility**, dissolubility, dissolubleness, dissolvableness, solubleness, solvability, solvableness; **fusibility**, fusibleness, thixotropy; **hydrology**, fluid mechanics, hydraulics, hydrodynamics, hydrokinetics, hydromechanics, hydrostatics

LIQUIDLY *adv* fluidly

LIST *n* beadroll, catalogue, inventory, listing, record, register, scroll, tally; **table**, chart, scale; **calendar**, almanac, atlas, gazette, gazetteer, yearbook; **word list**, concordance, dictionary, glossary, lexicon, syllabary, synonymy, thesaurus, vocabulary; **contents**, bibliography, bibliotheca, corrigenda, errata, index, sigla, syllabus, synposis; **account**, invoice, ledger, receipt; **waybill**, basket *(Econ.)*, bill of lading, bill of quantities, check list, manifest, price-list, stocktaking; **roll**, accession list, active list, army list, book *(Racing)*, cartulary, census, class list, class roll, electoral roll, empanelment, enrolment, file, law list, mailing list, muster roll, necrology, panel, payroll, peerage, poll, racecard, roster, rota, short list, sick list, slate, studbook, ticket *(Politics)*, transfer list, waiting list, waitlist; **credits**, directory, list of contributors; **roll of honour**, honour board, honour scroll; **list of saints**, canon, hagiology, martyrology; **telephone directory**, pink pages *(Obs.)*, teledex, yellow pages; **black list**, black book, Index *(R.C. Church)*; **conduct sheet**, charge sheet *(Law)*, crime sheet *(Mil.)*

LIST *v* accession, book, catalogue, index, inventory, table, tabularise, tabulate, take stock; **enrol**, empanel, inscribe, matriculate, poll, register; **black-list**, short-list, waitlist; **enumerate**, docket *(Law)*, itemise, recount, run through; **schedule**, bill, calendar, gazette

LISTER *n* bibliographer, cataloguer, cataloguist, enroller, indexer, itemiser, tabulator

LISTING *n* analysis, assay, breakdown, citation, enumeration, itemisation, recountal, tabularisation, tabulation

LITIGANT *n* alleger, appellant, complainant, libellant, party, plaintiff, privy, suer, suitor; **accused**, co-defendant, defendant, libellee, respondent; **witness**, crown witness, defence witness, interested party

LITIGATE *v* bring an action against, bring to justice, bring to trial, file a suit against, fit, go to law, implead, proceed against, process, prosecute, put on trial, replevy, settle out of court, sue, take to court; **arraign**, accuse, bring in, charge, cite, convene, give in charge, impeach, indict, libel, plead *(Obs.)*, serve with a writ, subpoena, summon

LITIGATION *n* action, audit *(Archaic)*, case, cause, dispute, hearing, instance, law, lawsuit, legal proceeding, petition, plea, proceeding, process, question *(Obs.)*, reference, suit; **legal action**, assumpsit, cattle trespass, class action, commercial cause, cross-action, fender case *(Colloq.)*, interpleader, praemunire *(Brit.)*, remand, remanet, repetition, replevin, test case, trover, wager of law *(Old Eng.)*; **summons**, arraignment, citation, compurgation *(Obs.)*, detainer, habeas corpus, impeachment, subpoena, writ

LITIGIOUS *adj* quarrelsome; **litigant**, trial; **summonsed to appear**, due in court, for the high jump, subpoenaed; **actionable**, appealable, committable, issuable, judicable, justiciable, reviewable, suable, triable

LIVE *v* be, breathe, endure, exist, keep body and soul together, persist, subsist, survive; **come to life**, be born, light up, lighten; **revive**, awaken, come to, quicken, resurge, resurrect, rise

LIVELINESS *n* animation, ebullience, ebulliency, effervescence, effervescency, friskiness, ginger *(Colloq.)*, life, vibrancy

LIVING *n* existence, modus vivendi, struggle for existence, subsistence, survival, sustentation; **life**, being, creation, nature; **course of life**, days, expectation of life, life cycle, life-expectancy, race *(Archaic)*; **longevity**, long life, survivorship, viability; **animation**, a new lease of life, quickening, reanimation, resurgence, resurrection, revival, reviviscence, vitalisation, vivification; **vital force**, anima, animus, atman, ghost *(Obs.)*, libido, life force, pneuma, prana, psyche, soul, spirit, vital fluid, vital spark, zombie; **lifeblood**, blood, breath, heart, heart's blood, heart-blood, marrow, pith, pulse

LIVING *adj* above ground, animate, breathing, existent, in the flesh, in the land of the living, live, on deck, quick *(Archaic)*, surviving, to the fore; **alive**, alive and kicking, red-blooded, vital; **long-lived**, longeval, vivacious *(Archaic)*; **viable**, capable of life; **resurgent**, renascent, resurrectional, resurrectionary, reviviscent; **vital**, animated, full of life, jazzy, peppy, pert, proud, snappy, spirited, vivacious, vivid, zingy, zippy; **green**, blooming, fresh, juicy, sappy, verdant; **life-giving**, animating, animative, quickening, vivifying

LIVING ROOM *n* calefactory, club, clubroom, common room, drawing room, green room, hall, lounge, lounge room, megaron, mess, misericord, parlour, rest room, salon, sitting room, solar, staffroom; **sunroom**, snuggery, solarium, sunlounge; **smoking room**, divan, smokeroom; **nursery**, playroom, rumpus room; **conservatory**, gallery, saloon

LIVING THING *n* biota, nature, organic matter; **chromatin**, chromosome, DNA, double helix, gene, genetic material, plasmagene, spireme; **biotype**, genotype, phenotype

LO *interj* behold, look, watch

LOAN *n* accommodation, advance, boomerang *(Colloq.)*, bridging finance, imprest, permanent loan, soft loan, terminating loan, touch *(Colloq.)*; **lease,** lease-back, leveraged lease, let, location *(Civil Law)*, sublease, under-lease; **rent**, bond money, Duke of Kent *(Colloq.)*, farm *(English Hist.)*, ground rent, hire, rack-rent; **mortgage**, encumbrance, equitable mortgage, first mortgage, home loan, monkey *(N.Z. Colloq.)*, poultice *(Colloq.)*; **tenancy**, lessee-ship, under-tenancy; **charter**, hire; **hire-purchase**, credit foncier, H.P., never-never *(Orig. Brit.)*; **usury**, pawnbroking, usance *(Obs.)*

LOGIC *n* cogency, coherence, equipollence, equipollency, legitimacy, legitimateness, logicality, modality, rationalisation, rationality, reasonableness, syllogisation, unanswerableness, undeniability, validation, validity, validness; **the Enlightenment**; **sense**, common sense, pragmatism, reason. *See also* REASONING

LOGICAL *adj* cogent, coherent, consequent, consequential, deductive, dianoetic, discursive, illative, inferential, legitimate, ratiocinative, rational, reasonable, reasoned, skilful *(Obs.)*, sound, tenable, valid; **deducible**, extractable, inferable

LOGICALLY *adv* cogently, coherently, deductively, discursively, illatively, legitimately, rationally, reasonably, validly

LOINCLOTH *n* breechcloth, breechclout, dhoti *(India)*, futah, G-string, lap-lap, loin-clout, lungi *(India)*

LONG *adj* elongate, elongated, expanded, expansive, extended, farthest, lengthy; **lengthwise**, axial, endlong *(Arch.)*, fore-and-aft, full-length, longitudinal, overall, whole-length; **extendable**, expansible, expansile, ex-

long

tensible, extensile; **metric,** kilometric, kilometrical, milliary, sesquipedalian, uncial; **lank,** gangling, gangly, lanky, rangy

LOOK *n* bo-peep, butchers, Captain, Captain Cook, cook, dek, dekko, eye, eyeful, gander, gaze, geek, geez, gig, gink, optic, regard, screw, shooftee, squiz, view; **glimpse,** sight; **peek,** peep, pry, squint; **glance,** aspect *(Archaic),* blink, eyebeam, eyeshot, eyewink; **stare,** gape, glare, goggle; **leer,** ogle; **look of disdain,** greasy eyeball, hairy eyeball, the glassy eye; **inspection,** look-over, once-over, recce, reconnaissance, reconnoitre, review, scan, survey; **sheep's eyes.** See also SEEING

LOOK *v* embrace, eye, get a load of, gig, have an optic at, lamp, look, look after, look at, look on, observe, preview, regard, rubberneck, sit in on, spy on, tout, twig, watch; **ogle,** leer at, perv on; **inspect,** case, eyeball, look over, rake, reconnoitre, study, survey, sweep; **keep watch,** invigilate, keep a weather eye open, keep one's eyes open, keep one's eyes peeled, keep one's eyes skinned, oversee, overwatch, sentinel, wake *(Archaic),* watch, watch over; **glance at,** glimpse at, run one's eye over, scan, skew, skim, squiz; **peek,** have a dekko, have a sticky beak, peep, peer, pry, squint; **stare,** gape, gawk, gawp, glare, goggle, have eyes only for, quiz *(Obs.);* **have a view of,** command, overlook; **gaze,** contemplate, pore; **see through,** pierce, see into; **look for,** keep an eye out for, look out for, watch out for. *See also* SEE

lose

LOOKER *n* argus, audience, beholder, bystander, contemplator, eyewitness, gazer, gig, invigilator *(Obs.),* looker-on, observer, onlooker, sightseer, spectator, spier, viewer, watcher, witness, witnesser; **starer,** gaper, rubberneck, sticky beak; **descrier,** espier, seer *(Rare);* **peeping Tom,** gubba, leerer, ogler, peeper, spy, voyeur; **spotter,** birdwatcher, racegoer, televiewer, supertwitcher, theatregoer, twitcher; **lookout,** watch

LOOKOUT *n* captive balloon, conning tower, crow's-nest, observation post, observatory, outlook, viewpoint

LOOPHOLE *n* bypass, conscience clause, doubletalk, escape clause, escape mechanism, sidestep; **tax lurk,** tax haven, tax shelter; **quibble,** chicanery, equivocation, fencing, hedge, prevarication, procrastination, quibbling, quillet *(Archaic),* quip, quirk, salvo *(Rare),* temporisation

LOOT *n* boodle *(U.S.),* booty, earn *(Prison),* pickings, plunder, spoils, stolen goods, swag

LOSE *v* be all up, bite the dust, come off second best, come off worst, get the worst of it, go down, go under, lose out, meet one's match, meet one's Waterloo, overreach, take a tumble; **give in,** break down, drop one's bundle, say uncle, sky the towel, throw in one's hand, throw in the sponge, throw in the towel, throw it in, yield; **fail,** be among the also-rans, bomb, bomb out, collapse, get the thumbs down, get the wooden spoon, give up the ghost, give way, go down, go to the wall, have had it, win the wooden spoon

LOSE COLOUR *v* blanch, blench, change colour, discolour, etiolate, fade, go green at the gills, go white, go white at the gills, sallow, tarnish, turn pale, wan *(Poetic)*; **dull**, dilute, pale, subdue; **decolour**, achromatise, bleach, decolourise

LOSER *n* also-ran, defeatist, has-been, non-starter, underdog, victim, wooden spooner

LOSING *n* annihilation, confusion *(Obs.)*, conquest, defeat, discomfiture, downfall, downthrow, overthrow, overturn, pulverisation, rout, subdual, subjection, subjugation; **drubbing**, beating, checkmate, confutation, hiding, licking, punishment, shellacking, sui, suimate, thrashing, towelling, trimming *(U.S.)*, walloping; **reversal**, check, foil *(Archaic)*, repulse, reverse, upset; **whitewash**

LOSING *adj* beat, beaten, bested, creamed, defeated, dished, dished up, done like a dinner, down, down-and-out, downfallen, euchred, gone a million, lost, outclassed, outmanoeuvred, pipped at the post, subdued

LOST *adj* bereft, bushed, cast, forfeit, gone, in limbo, irreclaimable, irrecoverable, irredeemable, lost to, slewed

LOUD *adj* big, deafening, deep, forte, fortissimo, full, sonorous, strong, voiceful; **audible**, distinct; **crescendo**, rising; **resounding**, echoing, reboant, resonant; **shrill**, piercing, strident, ululant; **powerful**, deep-throated, stentorian; **vociferous**, loudmouthed, vociferant; **howling**, roaring; **thunderous**, clamorous, clangourous, fulminant, fulminatory, fulminous, strepitous, sulphurous, thundering

LOUDEN *v* lift, raise, rise, swell

LOUDLY *adv* aloud, forte, fortissimo, loud

LOUDMOUTH *n* blusterer, boyo, clamourer, noise maker, raver, roarer, roisterer, stentor, vociferant, vociferator, yammerer, yawper

LOUDNESS *n* audibility, distinctness, forte, volume; **crescendo**, rise, swell; **noisiness**, boisterousness, clamorousness, obstreperousness, riotousness, tumultuousness, unquietness, uproariousness, vociferousness

LOUD SOUND *n* babel, ballyhoo, bedlam, bluster, brawl, broil, brouhaha, bruit *(Archaic)*, bust-up, clamour, clangour, din, hubbub, hullabaloo, hurly, hurly-burly, melee, noise, outcry, pandemonium, pother, racket, rough-house, rout, row, ruckus, rumpus, shemozzle, tumult, turmoil, uproar; **bang**, blast, clap, clash, crash, explosion, report; **clang**, beep, blare, clarion call, peal; **thunder**, roar, roaring, roll, sonic boom, thunderclap, thunderpeal; **slurp**, snore, snort, stridor; **howl**, shriek, ululation; **vociferance**, vociferation, yammer, yap, yawp; **cachinnation**, belly laugh; **noisy place**, bear garden, pandemonium

LOVE *n* adoration, affection, attachment, calf love, devotion, fondness, love at first sight, passion, puppy love; **infatuation**, crush, dotage, pash; **spiritual love**, agape, caritas, charity, courtly love, platonic love, platonism; **Venus**, eros; **cupid**, amoretto, amorino

LOVE *v* be enamoured of, be smitten with, be soft on someone, care for, carry a torch for; **fall in love**, adore, be nuts on, be nuts over, do one's balls on, do one's nuts over, dote on, fall for, have got it bad for, idolise, lose one's heart to, take a shine to; **lust after**, have the hots for; **embrace**, caress, cuddle, embosom, fondle, hug; **infatuate**, besot, smite

LOVE AFFAIR *n* affair, affaire de coeur, amour, eternal triangle, flirtation, intrigue, liaison, romance; **date**, assignation, tryst

LOVER *n* admirer, adorer, beloved, captive, darling, doter, fair *(Archaic)*, favourite, flame, idoliser, light-o'-love, mash *(Obs. Colloq.)*, paramour, spoony, steady, sweetheart, sweeting *(Archaic)*, truelove, valentine; **lovebirds**, couple, pair; **boyfriend**, beau, boy, bully *(Obs.)*, follower *(Obs.)*, gallant *(Archaic)*, guy, inamorato, spark, swain *(Poetic)*; **amorist**, casanova, Don Juan, fancy man, gay Lothario, gigolo, ladies' man, lady-killer, philanderer, rake, Romeo, sugar daddy, womaniser; **de facto**, tallyman; **catamite**, cat, minion; **girlfriend**, babe *(U.S.)*, baby *(U.S.)*, donah, dulcinea, girl, inamorata, ladylove, lass, leman *(Archaic)*, potato peeler, sheila; **mistress**, fancy woman, gun-moll, kept woman, moll, tallywoman, woman; **ex**, lost love; **love-object**, apple of the eye, dreamboat, goddess, heartthrob, idol; **honey**, chérie, chuck *(Archaic)*, darl, dear, duck, ducky, luv, mavourneen, pet, precious, snooks, snookums, sugar, sweet, sweetie, tootsy

LOVING *adj* adoring, affectionate, amoroso, amorous, devoted, fond, kind *(Archaic)*, loving, tender; **amatory**, amorous, erotic, passionate, romantic, sportive *(Obs.)*; **infatuated**, at someone's feet, besotted, captive, doting, gaga, gone on, in love, lovelorn, lovesick, lovey-dovey, shook on, smitten, struck on, stuck on, sweet on, uxorious; **love-hate**, ambivalent

LOVINGLY *adv* affectionately, amoroso, con amore, dearly, fondly, tenderly; **adoringly**, amorously, passionately

LOVINGNESS *n* affectionateness, amorousness, lovesickness, passionateness, tenderness; **dearness**, adorableness

LOWER *v* abase *(Archaic)*, bring down, douse *(Naut.)*, let down, pull down, strike *(Naut.)*, take down; **set down**, drop off; **knock down**, bring down, deck, down, drop, fell, grass *(Football)*, lay, level, overthrow, run down, sling *(Football)*, throw, topple, tumble, wooden; **dump**, deposit, ditch, plonk, precipitate, throw down; **bow**, bob, crouch, curtsy, dip, duck, nod, stoop

LOW REGARD *n* disesteem, dishonour, disregard, disrespect; **disdain**, contempt *(Law)*, contumely, cynicism, despite, misprision, ridicule, scorn; **disrespectfulness**, contemptuousness, contumeliousness, derisiveness, flippancy, flippantness, impiety, impiousness, irreverence, scurrility, scurrilousness, superciliousness; **insolence**, audacity, cheek, cheekiness, effrontery, gall, impudence, presumption; **impoliteness**, discourtesy, unceremoniousness, uncivility

LUBRICATOR *n* grease gun, oilcan, oiler; **oilman**, spudder

LUCK *n* cess *(Irish)*, Chinaman's luck, fortune, the luck of the Irish; **chance**, fortune, half a chance, hap, potluck, lot, plight, potluck, **fluke**, accident, act of God, coincidence, fortuity, haphazard, happenstance, incidental, stroke of fortune, the luck of the draw; **pot shot**, break, chance, look-in, risk, show *(U.S.)*, spin, throw; **a run of good luck**, a good trot; **bonanza**, pianola *(Cards)*, windfall; **bad luck**, ambs-ace, misadventure, mischance, misfortune, the deuce, the devil; **jinx**, hex, hoodoo, jonah, mozzle, schlemiel

LUCKINESS *n* fortuitism, fortuitousness, fortuity, fortunateness, serendipity; **haphazardness**, accidentalness, adventitiousness, arbitrariness, casualness, flukiness, hazardousness, indeterminacy, promiscuousness, ticklishness

LUCKY *adj* arsy, tinny; **happy-go-lucky**, adventurous, careless; **fortunate**, providential; **chance**, accidental, adventitious, aleatory, arbitrary, casual, chanceful, chancy, circumstantial, fortuitous, indeterminate, promiscuous, scratch, unmeant; **haphazard**, arbitrary, coincidental, desultory, fluky, hit-and-miss, hit-or-miss, random, sporting

LUCKY CHARM *n* birthstone, four-leaf clover, good luck charm, good omen, horseshoe, mascot, merrythought, rabbit's foot, talisman, wishbone

LUCKY PERSON *n* child of fortune, lucky dog, rising man, tin-arse

LUNAR *adj* circumlunar, lunarian, moony, sublunary, superlunary, translunary

LUXURY *n* a bed of roses, a place in the sun, easy street, good living, life of Riley, plenty, the fat of the land, the good life; **heyday**, golden age, good old days, good times, halcyon days, happy days, summer, sunshine

Mm

MACHINE *n* apparatus, appliance, attachment, bitser, contraption, contrivance, device, engine, mechanical device, unit; **mechanism**, action, appurtenances, assembly, clockwork, movement, parts, rig, subassembly, works; **motor**, motor drive, prime mover, servo, servomechanism, servomotor; **plant**, assembly line, enginery, equipment, machinery, tooling; **simple machine**, inclined plane, screw, wedge, wheel and axle; **lever**, crow, crowbar, jemmy, pinch-bar; **winch**, block and tackle, burton, capstan, cat *(Naut.)*, coffee grinder *(Naut.)*, deadeye *(Naut.)*, garnet, headgear *(Mining)*, jeer, luff tackle, parbuckle, pulley, sheave, sheaveblock *(Naut.)*, snatch block, wharve, whim, whip, winder, windlass; **waterwheel**, water-motor, watermill, windmill; **automaton**, auto, automatic, humanoid, robot

MAD *adj* barmy, barmy as a bandicoot, bats, batty, bonkers, certifiable, certified, crackbrained, cracked, crackers, crackpot, crazed, crazy, cuckoo, daffy, daft, demented, deranged, dilly, dingbats, dotty, far gone, frantic *(Archaic)*, gaga, gonzo, insane, kinky, loco *(U.S.)*, loony, loopy, lunatic, luny, mad as a cut snake, mad as a gumtree full of galahs, mad as a hatter, mad as a March hare, mad as a meataxe, madding, maniac, maniacal, manic, mental, moonstruck, non compos, nuts, nutty, nutty as a fruitcake, odd, off one's block, off one's face, off one's head, off one's nut, off one's onion, off one's pannikin, off one's rocker, off one's saucer, off one's scone, off one's tile, off one's trolley, off the air, off the beam, off the rails, off the wall, off-centre, original, out of one's head, out of one's mind, out of one's tree, over the edge, peculiar, porangi *(N.Z.)*, potty, psycho, queer, round the bend, round the twist, schizo, screwed up, soft in the head, starkers, strange, troppo, unbalanced, unhinged, up the pole, wrong in the head, yarra; **frenzied**, beresk, berko, berserk, beside oneself, distraught, frantic, frenetic, maddened, maddening, possessed, rabid, uncontrollable, violent

MADDEN *v* craze, dement, derange, frenzy, loco *(U.S.)*, overthrow *(Obs.)*, turn someone's mind, unbalance

MADE *adj* compact, factitious, wrought; **ready-made**, prefabricated; **made-to-order**, bespoke, custom-built, custom-made *(U.S.)*

MADNESS *n* craziness, daftness, derangement, franticness *(Archaic)*, insaneness, insanity, looniness, lunacy, queerness, rage *(Obs.)*, strangeness, unbalance, unreason, unsoundness of mind, wildness; **nervous breakdown**, mental illness, mental instability; **delirium**, deliration, deliriousness, hallucination, morbidity, morbidness, raving; **mental flaw**, aberration, crack; **brainstorm**, fit, frenzy, pink fit; **craze**, mania, obsession

MAD PERSON *n* basket case, bedlamite *(Archaic)*, crackbrain, crackpot, demoniac, dingbat, energumen, fruit cake, loco *(U.S.)*, loony, lunatic, luny, madman, madwoman, maenad, maniac, nut, nutter, odd bod, phrenetic, psycho, schizo, schizoid, schizophrenic

MAGAZINE *n* annals, annual, bi-monthly, bulletin, dreadful, fanzine, fashion journal, fashion magazine, fortnightly, girlie magazine, glossy, house journal, house magazine, illustrated, journal, monthly, periodical, pictorial, publication, quarterly, review, semimonthly, semiyearly, slick *(U.S.)*, trade journal, trade magazine, weekly; **issue**, back number, backrun, number; **serial**, continuation, instalment, part, sequel

MAGIC *n* alchemy, bewitchery, bewitchment, black art, black magic, conjuration, diablerie, diabolism, enchantment, fetishism, glamour, hoodoo, kadaicha magic *(Aborig.)*, sorcery, sortilege, sympathetic magic, thaumaturgy, theurgy, voodoo, white magic, witchcraft, witchery, witching, wizardry; **prestidigitation**, legerdemain, pass, sleight of hand

MAGIC *adj* magical, mystic, sorcerous, thaumaturgic, theurgic, theurgical, witching, wizard, wizardly; **alchemical,** alchemic, alchemistic, alchemistical; **voodooistic**, fetishistic, talismanic

MAGIC SPELL *n* hex, mozz, spell; **incantation**, abracadabra, hocus-pocus, hokey-pokey, mumbo jumbo; **charm**, amulet, fetish, grigri, juju, obeah, obi, phylactery *(Archaic)*, talisman; **wand**, Aladdin's lamp, black cat, broomstick, kadaicha shoes *(Aborig.)*, kurdaitcha shoes *(Aborig.)*, magic carpet, philosopher's stone, witch's cauldron; **magic potion**, philtre, potion;

make

crystal ball, mirror *(Archaic)*; **pentagram**, magic circle, magic square

MAGNETISM *n* archaeomagnetism, earth magnetism, electromagnetism, palaeomagnetism, terrestrial magnetism; **ferromagnetism**, diamagnetism, ferrimagnetism, paramagnetism; **magnetisation,** magnetic moment, magnetic permeability, magnetic susceptibility, remanence, retentivity; **magnetic potential,** coercive force, electrovalent bond, flux, flux density, ionic bond, magnetic field strength, magnetic flux, magnetic induction, magnetomotive force; **magnetic field,** electromagnetic field, electromagnetic wave, gravitational field; **magnetic pole**, magnetic dipole, magnetic element, magnetic monopole, unit pole; **magnetic bottle,** magnetic mirror. *See also* ATTRACTION

MAGNETOMETRY *n* magnetochemistry, magnetohydrodynamics; **electromagnetic unit**, gamma, gauss, magneton; **unified field theory,** general theory of relativity, Newton's law of gravitation; **magnetometer,** fluxgate, fluxmeter, magnetograph, variometer

MAIL *n* airmail, certified mail, consignment, express, parcel post, post, priority-paid mail, registered mail, registered post, registered publications post, S.A.L., surface mail; **fan mail**, junk mail; **delivery**, first post, last post; **mailbag**, post-bag; **post office**, Australia post, dead-letter office, G.P.O., letterbox, locked bag, postbox, post-office box, poste restante. *See also* MESSAGE

MAKE *v* compound, do, effect, effectuate, fashion, form, generate, mould, prepare, produce, set, shape, synthesise, work; **construct**, build, erect, fabricate, forge, frame, knock together, knock up, make up, manufacture, mock up, prefabricate, raise, turn out, whip up; **constitute**, compose, form, make up. *See also* CREATE

MAKE AN EFFORT *v* bend the bow, exert oneself, keep at it, pull one's weight, put one's shoulder to the wheel, roll up one's sleeves, take the labouring oar, tax oneself; **spare no effort**, bend over backwards, burst one's boiler, bust a gut, bust one's boiler, do all in one's power, do all one can, do one's darnedest, do one's utmost, do or die, do the best one can, fall over backwards, go all out, go eyes out, go out of one's way, go to great lengths, lean over backwards, leave no stone unturned, move heaven and earth, pull out all the stops, sink or swim; **work at**, beaver away at, belabour *(Obs.)*, buckle down to, buckle into, bullock at, cope with, elaborate, get stuck into, grapple with, have the bit between one's teeth, hoe into, hop into, knuckle down to, lay out to, pitch into, plough into, put one's back into, stick to, take to, turn to, wade into; **toil**, burn the midnight oil, do double duty, drudge, graft, grind, grub, keep one's nose to the grindstone, labour, lucubrate, moil, outwork, plod, plug, slave, slog, sweat blood, tiger, tug, work, work day and night, work like a dog, work like a galley slave, work like a horse, work like a Trojan, work like Jacky, work one's guts out, work one's slot out; **take pains**, agonise over; **battle**, scrabble, scramble, scrimmage, scuffle, strive, struggle; **get moving**, bestir oneself, get cracking, pull one's finger out, pull one's socks up, set to, strike a blow

MAKE DO *v* adapt, extemporise, improvise, shift, think on one's feet; **take advantage of**, be in the right place at the right time, benefit, clean up, fall back on, find a loophole, fish in troubled waters, get mileage out of, jockey, make a good thing out of, make the best of, make the most of, profit, resort to, seize an opportunity, strike while the iron is hot, turn to one's advantage; **make every post a winning post**, climb on the bandwagon, get with the strength; **play a waiting game**, bide one's time, trim; **connive**, arrange, contrive, intrigue, plot, wangle, wriggle

MAKEFAST *n* anchorage, dolphin, moorage, moorings; **bollard**, bitt, post, timberhead

MAKE HAPPY *v* elate, elevate, enliven, exhilarate, glad *(Archaic)*, gladden, hearten, jollify, revive

MAKE HISTORY *v* go down in history, hit the headlines, make a noise in the world, make one's mark, raise one's head, set the world on fire; **star**, blaze, resound, shine

MAKE INFERTILE *v* exhaust, impoverish, overcrop; **sterilise**, castrate, fix, geld, neuter, spay

MAKE MUSIC *v* busk, execute, interpret, melodise, perform, play, render, sound; **strike up**, begin to play; **accompany**, vamp; **trill**, flourish, shake; **slur**, glide; **jazz**, jam, swing, syncopate; **sight-read**; **play by ear**, lug; **fiddle**, bow, double-stop, scrape, stop; **pluck**, harp *(Poetic)*, lute, pick, plunk, strum, thrum, twang; **sweep the strings**; **strike**, beat, drum, roll, tabor; **play the piano**, soft-pedal, tickle the ivories, touch; **play the organ**, register, unstop; **ring**, carillon, chime, knell, peal, toll; **blow**, break, bugle, fife, flute, overblow, pipe, skirl *(Scot.)*, trump *(Archaic)*, trumpet, whistle; **tongue**, double-tongue; **conduct**, beat time, keep time, lead; **compose**, arrange, double, harmonise, improvise, note, orchestrate, realise, score, set, transpose; **figure**, finger

MAKE PEACE *v* bury the hatchet, come to terms with, compromise, hold out the olive branch, make it up, make up, negotiate terms, patch up a quarrel, shake hands, turn swords into ploughshares; **pacify**, bring peace, bring to terms, bring to the table, demilitarise, denuclearise, disarm, offer the hand of peace, pacificate, quiet, quieten, reconcile, restore harmony, temper *(Obs.)*; **appease**, assuage, becalm, defuse, gentle *(Rare)*, mollify, pour oil on troubled waters, subdue, tranquillise; **retreat**, turn the other cheek, withdraw; **be at peace**, keep the peace, live in harmony

MAKE PLEASANT *v* dulcify, please, sauce, sweeten, zest

MAKE POSSIBLE *v* afford, allow, capacitate, enable, permit

MAKE UNHAPPY *v* break the heart of, distress, grieve, harrow, hurt, rend the heart of, upset; **depress**, dash, deject, get someone down, sadden; **darken**, cloud, dampen, gloom, oppress

MAKE WHOLE *v* complement, fill, fill a gap, fill in, fill out, make good, round off, supplement; **integrate**, piece together, synthesise, synthetise, totalise; **complete**, accomplish, consummate, finish, perfect, perform *(Obs.)*,

put the finishing touches; **follow through**, carry through, explore every avenue, follow up, go the whole hog, go through with, tie up the loose ends; **finalise**, clench, clinch, close, come full circle, settle; **mature**, flower, fulfil

MAKING *n* building, construction, contrivance, crystallisation, development, elaboration, erection, fabrication, facture, fashion *(Obs.)*, formation, manufacture, manufacturing, output, prefabrication, preparation, production, synthesis, synthesisation, turning, turnout, twinning *(Crystall.)*, working; **structure**, composition, constitution, construction, make-up, reconstruction. *See also* CREATION

MALE *adj* gentlemanly, he, positive, yang; **masculine**, macho, manlike, manly, potent, virile; **bull**, buck, hunky, stag, well-endowed, well-hung; **mannish**, amazonian, butch, unfeminine, unwomanly; **boyish**, coltish; **homosexual**, camp, effeminate, gay, high-camp

MALNUTRITION *n* avitaminosis, beriberi, chlorosis, deficiency disease, kwashiorkor, marasmus, milk fever, pellagra, rickets, scurvy

MAN *n* brave, he, husband, male; **mankind**, menfolk; **bloke**, bastard, bugger, chap, chappie, codger, coot, cove, cully *(Archaic)*, dandy, dog, dude *(U.S.)*, feller, fellow, geezer, guy, hombre, jack, johnny, joker, scout, skate *(U.S.)*, snoozer *(Obs.)*, tomcat, wallah, whoreson *(Obs.)*; **heman**, alf, apeman, bronzed Aussie, bull, butch, caveman, jock, macho man, male chauvinist, male chauvinist pig, MCP, ocker, rugger-bugger; **buck**, blade, blood, bodgie, homo, lair, lout, son of a gun, stag, Teddy Bear; **a good sort**, hunk, spunk, stud; **gentleman**, gent, rye, squire; **lad**, boy, bucko, colt, cub, gossoon *(Irish)*, jackanapes, nipper, urchin, youth; **sissy**, aunty, dude *(U.S.)*, eunuch, gussie, lily, little Lord Fauntleroy, milksop, nancy boy, old woman, pansy, ponce, wimp; **homosexual**, camp, faggot, gay, poonce, pork 'n bean, queen

MANAGE *v* administer, administrate, be in charge of, carry on, conduct, direct, handle, keep in order, overlook, oversee, run, see to, steward, superintend, supervise; **control**, be in the chair, govern, guide, head, head a team, lead, preside over, steer, take over, take the reins; **domineer**, boss *(Colloq.)*; **sweat**, drive; **organise**, get up, mastermind, package *(Finance)*; **manage one's resources**, economise, husband

MANAGEMENT *n* admin, administration, dispensation *(Theol.)*, economy, government, organisation; **supervision**, conduct, direction, handling, intendance, intendancy, oversight, running, superintendence, superintendency, surveillance; **managership**, chairmanship, chairpersonship, commission, superintendentship, supervisorship; **housekeeping**, economy *(Archaic)*, housewifery, husbandry, ménage; **bureaucracy**, apparatus, board, body corporate, bureau, directorate, umbrella organisation *(Comm.)*

MANAGER *n* administrator, adminstratrix, bureaucrat, burgrave, commissar, commissary, commissioner, comptroller, controller, curator, director, director-general, directress, directrix, dispensator, engineer, entrepreneur, executive, executor, functionary, governor, Grand Master, head, inspector, inspector-general, intendant, manageress, master, monitor, office-bearer, officer, president, principal, procurator, secretary-general, super, superintendent, supervisor, surveillant, taskmaster, taskmistress; **boss**, boss cocky, chief, employer, gaffer, pannikin boss, slavedriver, sweater *(Colloq.)*, two-bob boss; **overseer**, charge hand, forelady, foreman, foreperson, forewoman, headman, supervisor; **official**, agent, dignitary, silvertail, vizier; **master**, lord, matriarch, mistress, padrone *(U.S.)*, patriarch, patron; **housekeeper**, bailiff, castellan, chamberlain, chatelaine, factor, housewife, land agent *(Brit.)*, majordomo, manciple *(Brit.)*, matron, park ranger, ranger, reeve *(Hist.)*, seneschal, steward; **hotelier**, innkeeper, motelier, publican, restauranteur, restauratrix. *See also* LEADER

MANAGERIAL *adj* administrative, bureaucratic, directorial, dispensational, entrepreneurial, executive, governmental, hegemonic, organisational, superintendent, supervisory, surveillant

MANAGERIALLY *adv* administratively, bureaucratically, executively, governmentally

MANCHESTER *n* dry goods, lingerie *(Archaic)*, mercery, napery, piece goods, soft goods; **drape**, arras, curtain, drapery, runner, tapestry; **soft furnishings**, curtains, drapes, hangings, upholstery; **upholstery fabric**, chintz, frisé, madras muslin, tabaret;

carpet, Aubusson carpet, Axminster carpet, hooked rug, Wilton carpet

MANLINESS *n* animus, gentlemanliness, machismo, maleness, manhood, mannishness, masculineness, masculinity, unfeminineness, virtue *(Obs.)*; **virility**, manly vigour, potency, virileness; **male chauvinism**, male supremacy, masculism, paternalism; **boyishness**, coltishness

MANY *n* a big mob, a good few, a good many, a great many, a hatful, a heap, loads, lot, lots *(Colloq.)*, mass, more than one can poke a stick at, more than one can shake a stick at, myriad, pile, quite a few, some few, stacks, tons; **crowd**, army, array, battalion, bevy, cloud, fleet, flock, forest, hive, horde, host, legion, mob, multitude, power *(Colloq.)*, ruck, swarm, throng, tribe, troop; **numbers**, billions, dozens, hundreds, millions, quintillions, scores, thousands, zillions

MANY *adj* any number of, biggest mobs of *(Colloq.)*, bulk, considerable, countless, innumerable, multiple, multiplex, multiplicate, numerous, plural, pluralist, umpteen, uncounted, untold, various; **multifarious**, all-round, manifold, many-sided; **abounding**, abundant, affluent, ample, aplenty, copious, easy *(Comm.)*, plenteous, plentiful, profuse, prolific, rife, superabundant; **teeming**, alive with, aswarm, crawling with, crowded, legion, multitudinous *(Poetic)*, populous, stiff with, thick with

MAP *v* blueprint, chart, contour, diagram, diagrammatise, draft, outline, plat *(U.S.)*, plot, protract, represent, schematise, trace. *See also* DIAGRAM

MARBLE *n* acker *(S.A.)*, agate, aggie, alley, bottler, bottley, connie, doog, fat, glassy, peewee, taw

MARGINALLY *adv* perimetrically, peripherally, submarginally; **finitely**, definably, restrictively, terminatively

MARIJUANA *n* bhang, cannabis, dope, ganja, grass, hemp, Indian hemp, kef, kif, Mary Jane, pot, shit, tea, the herb, the weed; **hash**, hashish; **hash oil**, THC; **joint**, jay, log, number, reefer, roach, scoob, stick. *See also* DRUG

MARINER *n* boatie, hearty, jack, lascar, matelot, raftsman, sailor, salt, sea-dog, seafarer, shellback, shipman *(Archaic)*, shipmate, submariner, tar, tarpaulin *(Rare)*; **ship's crew**, company, complement, crew, ship; **navy**, mercantile marine, merchant marine, merchant navy, senior service; **yachtsman**, rock-hopper, sailor, windsurfer, yachtswoman, yachty, yottie; **windjammer**, reefer, sheethand; **ferryman**, bargee, boatman, bumboatman, gondolier, lighterman, wherryman; **oarsman**, bow, bow oar, bowhand, bowman, canoeist, galley slave, oar, paddler, punter, rower, sculler, stroke, waterman; **rowing crew**, bank, eight, four. *See also* SEAMAN

MARITAL *adj* concubinary, conjugal, connubial, matrimonial; **nuptial**, bridal, epithalamic, hymeneal, postnuptial, spousal; **wifely**, matronly, uxorial; **bigamous**, digamous, endogamous, exogamic, exogamous, leviratic, leviratical, monandrous, monogamistic, monogamous, polyandrous, polygamous, polygynous

maritally   337   **mathematical operation**

MARITALLY *adv* conjugally, connubially, matrimonially; **bigamously**, polygamously

MARK *v* chalk, chalk up, direct, dot, hatch, mark up, overscore, pencil, red-pencil, rule, score, touch, underline, underscore, write; **check**, check off, cross, cross off, record, tally, tick, tick off; **punctuate**, accent, accentuate, dagger, hyphenate, hyphenise, lemmatise, obelise, point, star, subscribe, superscribe

MARRIAGE *n* conjugal bliss, conjugality, connubiality, matrimony, unitedness, wedded bliss, wedlock; **wifehood**, matronage, wifedom, wifeliness; **match**, alliance, union; **mismatch**, mésalliance, misalliance, mismarriage; **type of marriage**, endogamy, exogamy, group marriage, levirate, sororate; **arranged marriage**, mariage de convenance, marriage of convenience, morganatic marriage; **de facto marriage**, cohabitation, common-law marriage, companionate marriage, concubinage, living in sin, trial marriage; **mixed marriage**, intermarriage, miscegenation; **remarriage**, deuterogamy; **love match**; **bigamy**, digamy, monandry, monogamy, monogyny, polyandry, polygamy, polygyny. *See also* WEDDING

MARRIAGEABILITY *n* eligibility, marriageableness, nubility

MARRIED *adj* hitched, hooked, one, spliced, united, wedded

MARRY *v* espouse, make an honest woman of, take to wife, wed, wive *(Rare.)*; **get married**, become one, go off, settle down; **elope**, run away; **pair off**, ally with, cohabit, match, mate, set up housekeeping; **intermarry**, miscegenate; **remarry**, commit bigamy; propose, offer, pop the question; **betroth**, affiance, contract matrimony, engage, hook, lead to the altar, precontract, promise, win; **join in marriage**, conjugate *(Obs.)*, declare man and wife, hitch, join, splice, tie, tie the knot, unite; **give in marriage**, give away, marry off

MARTIAL *adj* amazonian, combatant, combative, filibusterous, pugilistic, pugnacious, warlike; **soldierly**, soldierlike

MASCULINELY *adv* manly *(Archaic)*, mannishly; **boyishly**, coltishly

MASSACRE *n* battue, bloodbath, butchery, carnage, holocaust, shambles, slaughter; **genocide**, ethnocide, race murder; **purge**, decimation, depopulation, pogrom. *See also* KILLING

MASSACRE *v* butcher, cut down, cut to pieces, mow down, put to the sword, slaughter; **purge**, annihilate, commit genocide, decimate, depopulate, exterminate, liquidate, wipe out. *See also* KILL

MATERIALISE *v* body forth, embody, incarnate, objectify, substantialise; **crystallise**, degrade, fix, fractionate, neutralise

MATHEMATICAL *adj* algebraic, arithmetic, geometric, geometrical, trigonometric, trigonometrical; **statistical**, demographic; **computable**, calculable, countable, enumerable, integrable, numerable

MATHEMATICAL OPERATION *n* addition, combination, derivation, division, enumeration, evolution, factorisation, integration, involution, long division, multiplication, permutation, quadrature, rationalisation,

mathematical operation 338 meal

short division, subtraction, times, transform, transposition, variation; **algorithm,** algorism; **equation,** binomial theorem, differential equation, identity, quadratic, simultaneous equations, wave equation; **formula,** empirical formula, golden rule, rule, rule of three; **statistical distribution,** binomial distribution, decile, mathematical expectation, Maxwell-Boltzmann distribution, normal distribution, ogive, ordinate, pentile, percentile, Poisson distribution, probability curve, quartile, range, relative frequency, standard deviation, standard error, variance; **matrix,** array, Latin square, magic square

MATHEMATICIAN n algebraist, arithmetician, geometrician; **statistician,** actuary, demographer, demographist; **counter,** computer, estimator, figurer, integrator, numerator, scorer, tallier, teller

MATHEMATICS n algebra, analytical geometry, analytics, arithmetic, binary arithmetic, calculus, combinatorial analysis, coordinate geometry, differentiation, Euclidean geometry, floating point arithmetic, geometry, higher mathematics, infinitesimal calculus, integral calculus, maths, number theory, quadratics, quaternions, relaxation, set theory, theoretical arithmetic, trigonometry; **applied mathematics,** biometrics, biometry, Boolean algebra, computational linguistics, critical-path analysis, dead reckoning, factor analysis, Fourier analysis, mathematical logic, mensuration, Monte Carlo method, numerical analysis, statistics

MATTER n antimatter, material, stuff, substance; **mass,** block, body, concrete; **grain,** crystal, granule, micron, particle, sand, seed crystal; **thing,** anything, article, doodackie (N.Z.), doodah, doofer, doohickie, doover, dooverlackie, object, phenomenon, something, thingummybob, thingummyjig, wigwam for a goose's bridle; **the tangible,** being, concreteness, corporality, corporeality, corporealness, corporeity, earthliness, embodiment, existence, fleshliness, materialisation, materiality, materialness, naturalness, palpability, substantiality, substantiation, tangibility; **cosmos,** creation, macrocosm, nature, plenum, universe, world

MEAL n agape, banquet, barbecue, barby, blow-out, buffet, chew-'n'-spew, clambake, collation, cookout (U.S.), feast, feed, gorge, hangi (N.Z.), junket, kai, love feast, luau, mess, midnight feast, nosh-up, picnic, refection, regale, repast, short order (U.S.), smorgasbord, spread, table d'hôte, tuck-in, TV dinner; **snack,** afternoon tea, bite, coffee break, continental breakfast, crib, Devonshire tea, elevenses (Brit. Colloq.), little lunch, morning piece (W.A.), morning tea, munchies, nibble, nosh, playlunch, refreshment, scroggin; **breakfast,** brekkie, brunch, bush breakfast, déjeuner, wedding breakfast; **lunch,** big lunch, counter lunch, cut-lunch, fork luncheon, luncheon, oslo lunch, packed lunch, ploughman's lunch (Brit.), pub lunch, tiffin (India); **dinner,** din-din, din-dins, dinnies, fork dinner, high tea (Brit.), progressive dinner, supper, tea; **course,** afters, antipasto, dessert, dish, entree, entremets, fork dish, hors d'oeuvre, pièce de résistance, plat du jour, pudding, savoury, side-dish, soupe du jour, starters, sweets. *See also* FOOD

MEAN *v* betoken, connote, denote, designate, express, imply, import, indicate, purport, represent, signify, stand for

MEAN *adj* careful, cheeseparing, churlish, close, close-fisted, mangy, mingy, miserly, near, niggard, niggardly, nigh *(Archaic)*, parsimonious, penny-ante, penny-pinching, penurious, pinchpenny, skimpy, small, stingy, tight, tight-arsed, tight-fisted; **avaricious**, greedy, hard-fisted, hungry, Ikey Mo, iron-fisted, money-grubbing, sordid; **ungenerous**, grudging, illiberal *(Rare)*, shabby, uncharitable, unhandsome. *See also* MISER; BE MISERLY

MEANING *n* content, drift, effect, force, gist, hang, import, importance *(Obs.)*, intendment *(Law)*, intent, matter, message, point, purport, sense, significance, signification, substance, tenor, the strong of, value; **connotation**, implication, nuance, polysemy; **denotation**, acceptation, application, definition, designation, extension *(Logic)*, indication, signification, usage; **synonymousness**, equivalence, synonymity, synonymy; **ambiguity**, double meaning

MEANINGFUL *adj* pithy, pointed, portentous, pregnant, profound, significant; **connotative**, allusive, evocative, suggestive; **denotative**, designative, explicit, expressive, indicative, meaning, notional, presentive, significative; **synonymous**, equivalent, synonymic, synonymical; **ambiguous**, polysemous; **semantic**, semasiological

MEANINGFULLY *adv* pointedly, portentously, pregnantly, profoundly, significantly

MEANINGLESSNESS *n* absurdness, gassiness, inconsequence, inconsequentiality, pointlessness, ridiculousness, senselessness, trashiness, unmeaningness

MEANLY *adv* churlishly, mangily, parsimoniously, penuriously, stingily, tightly; **avariciously**, hungrily; **ungenerously**, shabbily, uncharitably, unhandsomely, with a sparing hand

MEANNESS *n* cheeseparing, churlishness, closeness, manginess, miserliness, niggardliness, parsimony, penuriousness, stinginess, tightness; **avarice**, avariciousness, greediness, hungriness, sordidness; **ungenerosity**, illiberality, shabbiness, smallness, uncharitableness, ungenerousness, unhandsomeness

MEANS OF ESCAPE *n* back door, bolthole, Davis apparatus, escape hatch, escape lock, fire-escape, ladder; **loophole**, cop-out, let-out; **vent**, safetyvalve. *See also* ESCAPE

MEANS OF KILLING *n* coup de grâce, deathblow, dispatch, quietus; **death warrant**, auto-da-fé, death penalty; **gallows**, bough *(Archaic)*, drop, gibbet, high jump, long drop, rope, rope's end; **guillotine**; **gas chamber**, Auschwitz, Belsen, Dachau, gas oven; **electric chair**, chair, hot seat; **poison**, arsenic, asphyxiant, cyanide, hemlock, poison cart

MEANWHILE *adv* betweenwhiles, intermediately, meantime, whiles *(Obs.)*

measurable *adj* assessable, gaugeable, mensurable, quantifiable, rateable, surveyable

MEASURE *v* dial, gauge, mete *(Archaic)*, meter, quantify; **rate**, assess, evaluate, grade, revalue, score; **calibrate; pace**, calliper, cube, fathom, sound, span, step, tape, titrate, walk; **survey**, shoot, triangulate; **scale**, plot, prick off

MEASURED *adj* assayed, gauged, known by measurement, paced

MEASUREMENT *n* admeasurement, measure, mensuration, quantification; **exact science**, metrology; **evaluation**, analysis, rating; **calibration; dimensions**, size, vital statistics; **gauge**, dial, digital readout, instrument, LCD, measure, meter, recording instrument, VU meter

MEASURING *adj* dimensional, mensural, mensurative, metrical, quantitative

MECHANICAL *adj* mechanistic, motor, motored, powered; **robotic**, bionic, robotistic; **automatic**, self-acting, self-adjusting, semiautomatic, servo-assisted, servomechanical

MECHANISATION *n* automation, automatism, engineering, industrialisation, motorisation, robotism

MECHANISE *v* automate, motorise; **tool up**, gear up

MEDDLE *v* have a finger in the pie, interfere, intermeddle, mess in, nose about, nose into, poach *(Tennis)*, poke one's nose into, put in, put one's bib in, stick one's bib in, stick one's nose in, sticky-nose, stickybeak, weigh in with; **interrupt**, barge in, bib in, butt in, get a word in edgeways, put one's oar in

MEDIATE *v* arbitrate, conciliate, decide, go between, intercede, interpose, intervene, negotiate, umpire; **appease**, compromise *(Obs.)*, propitiate, temporise; **settle**, arrange, bring together, bury the hatchet, compose, heal, make up, pacify, patch things up, pour oil on troubled waters, smooth things over

MEDIATION *n* arbitrament, arbitration, compromise, conciliation, diplomacy, good offices, healing, intercession, intermediacy, intermediation, interposal, interposition, intervention, negotiation, pacification, propitiation, reconcilement, temporisation, treaty *(Rare)*, troubleshooting; **peace-making ceremony**, armistice, makarrata, parley, treaty, truce; **peace-pipe**, calumet, flag of truce, olive branch, white flag

MEDIATOR *n* arbiter, arbitrator, arbitress, conciliation committee, conciliator, diplomat, diplomatist, firefighter, interceder, intercessor, intermediator, intervener, interventionist, negotiator, propitiator, referee, troubleshooter, ump, umpie, umpire; **reconciler**, healer, paraclete; **compromiser**, temporiser; **intermediary**, go-between, mouthpiece, next friend, proxy

MEDIATORY *adj* arbitral, arbitrational, arbitrative, conciliatory, diplomatic, intercessional, intercessory, intervenient, interventional, mediate, mediative, propitiative, propitiatory, reconciliatory

MEDICAL *adj* biomedical, clinical, doctoral, iatric, paramedic, paramedical, premedical, prosthetic; **Aesculapian**, Galenic, Hippocratic; **allopathic**, homeopathic; **diagnostic**, diacritic; **surgical,** chirurgic, chirurgical, operating, operative, postoperative; **dental,** orthodontic; **medicable,** curable, operable

MEDICAL TREATMENT n first aid, intervention, spontaneous cure, therapy, treatment; **nursing,** after-care, care, intensive care, rest cure; **physiotherapy,** manipulation, massage, massotherapy, mechanotherapy, orthoptic exercises, physio; **occupational therapy,** diversionary therapy, O.T.; **speech therapy,** speech pathology; **heat therapy,** diathermy, heliotherapy, insolation, phototherapy, radiothermy, thermotherapy; **hydrotherapy,** hydropathy, pneumatotherapy, water cure; **lavage,** irrigation, toilet, wash-out; **artificial respiration,** kiss of life, mouth-to-mouth resuscitation, resuscitation; **surgery,** ablation, excision; **radiotherapy,** irradiation, X-ray therapy; **immunisation,** auto-immunisation, auto-inoculation, immunotherapy, inoculation, mithridation, pasteurism, prophylaxis, take, tuberculisation, vaccination, vaccinisation, variolation; **transfusion,** blood transfusion, exchange; **blood-letting,** cupping, phlebotomy, venesection, venipuncture; **transplantation,** grafting, implantation, plastic surgery, skin graft; **dialysis,** haemodialysis; **chemotherapy,** chelation therapy, organotherapy; **electrotherapy,** cardioversion, cataphoresis, defibrillation, faradism, fulguration, galvanism; **hypnotherapy; cauterisation,** cautery, cryocautery, cryosurgery, cryotherapy, electrodessication, electrolysis, hypothermia

MEDICATE v dispense, dose, physic, prescribe, treat; **cure,** doctor, heal, nurse, rehabilitate, remedy, restore; **resuscitate,** revive, revivify; **operate,** ablate, amputate, curette, cut, debride, decerebrate, excise, operate on, resect, set, spay; **inoculate,** mithridatise, pasteurise, tuberculise, vaccinate, variolate; **drench,** fog, footrot, spray; **massage,** manipulate, percuss

MEDICATION n alterant, alterative (Obs.), curative, drug, medicament, medicine, physic, prescription, specific; **dose,** dosage, draught, drench; **botanical,** herb, simple (Archaic); **adjuvant,** synergist; **materia medica,** pharmacopoeia; **pharmacy,** pharmaceutics, pharmacognosy, pharmacology; **dispensary,** chemist, drug store; **cure,** arcanum, boot (Obs.), bush cure, catholicon, cup, cure-all, faith cure, folk remedy, mithridate (Obs.), nostrum, panacea, placebo, proprietary; **prophylactic,** antiserum, antivenene, preventive, remedy, serum, vaccine; **antidote,** alexipharmic, bezoar (Obs.), counterpoison, theriac, treacle (Obs.); **application,** bath, cold pack, compress, corn plaster, eyewash, fomentation, hot pack, icepack, icebag, mud bath, mustard plaster, poultice, stupe, wash, wet pack; **dressing,** bandage, bandaid, blister plaster, court plaster, diachylon, dossil, elastoplast, frog plaster, lint, plaster, pledget, shin plaster (U.S. Obs.), sticking plaster, swab; **suture,** stitch; **ointment,** abirritant, balm, balsam, cerate, counterirritant, demulcent, emollient, hand cream, inunction, liniment, lotion, magma, salve, unction, unguent; **powder,** fuller's earth, pomander, triturate; **pes-**

medication / **member**

medication (cont.) sary, bougie, implantation, suppository; **pill**, bolus, cap, capsule, durule, football, pilule, tab, tablet, tabloid, time-release capsule, troche, wafer; **lozenge**, cachou, confection, excipient, masticatory, pastille; **elixir**, decoction, drops, electuary, philtre, potion, ptisan, tincture, tisane; **inhalation**, errhine, vaporisation; **injection**, booster, hypodermic, jab, needle, shot; **sling**, plaster, plaster cast, spica, suspensor, tourniquet; **surgical appliance**, caliper, crutch, orthosis, peg leg, prosthesis, truss, wooden leg; **filling**, bridge, cap, crown, inlay

MEDICINAL *adj* curative, healing, panacean, remedial, sanatory, sanitive, therapeutic, **active**, alterant, alterative *(Obs.);* **antidotal**, alexipharmic, antitoxic, prophylactic, theriacal; **adjuvant**, synergetic, synergic, synergistic; **nervine**, tetanic; **tonic**, roborant; **calmative**, sedative, tranquilising; **endermic**, hypodermic, intravenous, parenteral, topical; **ethical**, magistral, officinal

MEDIOCRE *adj* half-pie, indifferent, mean, middling, nothing to boast of, nothing to write home about, undistinguished; **so-so**, average, fifty-fifty, much of a muchness; **tolerable**, fair, fair to middling, goodish, moderate, not bad, not so dusty, passable, unobjectionable; **no great shakes**, minor, not so hot, not too hot, nothing out of the box, of sorts, second-best, second-class, second-rate; **commonplace**, colourless, conventional, millrun, mundane, nondescript, ordinary, pedestrian, run-of-the-mill; **hackneyed**, common, deja vu, hack, tired, trite; **bourgeois**, middle-of-the-road, middlebrow

MEDIOCRITY *n* averageness, mundaneness, ordinariness, pedestrianism, triteness; **passableness**, fairness, indifference, tolerableness

MEEK *adj* abashed, ashamed, browbeaten, cheap, crestfallen, guidable, humbled, lowly, mean, out of countenance, shamefaced, sheepish, small, struck all of a heap; **humble**, abject, flunkeyish, intropunitive, self-critical, self-effacing, servile, submissive, supple, wormlike; **obsequious**, sycophantic, toadyish

MEEKLY *adv* abjectly, cap in hand, crawlingly, humbly, on bended knee, servilely; **crestfallenly**, ashamedly, ignominiously, shamefacedly, sheepishly, with one's tail between one's legs

MEEKNESS *n* abasement, humbleness, lowliness, resignation, self-abasement, self-effacement, sense of shame, worm's eye view; **humility**, abashment, abjectness, chagrin, cheapness, confusion, crestfallenness, modesty; **servility**, flattery, flunkeyism, obsequiousness, servileness, suppleness, sycophancy, toadyism

MEET AN OBSTACLE *v* back up, baulk at, come up against, refuse, seize, seize up, stick at, stop at

MEETING PLACE *n* casino, chapterhouse, community centre, community hall

MELTING POT *n* crucible, cupel, retort

MEMBER *n* charter member, clubman, clubwoman, committeeman, committeewoman, communitarian; new member, entrant, initiate; **federator**, federalist, internationalist, leaguer, uniter; **Mason**, Apexian, billy goat rider, communicant, conventicler, Freemason, guildsman, Jaycee, Lion, liveryman *(Brit.)*, Oddfellow, Rechabite, Rosicrucian, Rotarian, Soroptimist

MEMBER OF PARLIAMENT *n* backbencher, congressman, congresswoman, deputy, honourable member, law-maker, legislator, legislatress, magnate, Member of the House of Representatives, MHR, MP, oncer, parliamentarian, representative, senator; **alderman**, bailie *(Scot.)*, burgess *(Hist.)*, burgomaster, city father, councillor, lord mayor, mayor, mayoress, provost *(Scot.)*, town councillor; **independent**, crossbencher, freelance, mugwump *(U.S.)*; **minister**, administrator, attorney-general, cabinet minister, foreign secretary *(Brit.)*, frontbencher, member of cabinet, minister without portfolio, postmaster general, secretary, secretary of state *(U.S.)*, shadow minister, speaker, state secretary, statesman, stateswoman, statist *(Obs.)*, treasurer; **prime minister**, P.M., premier; **power behind the throne**, éminence grise, grey eminence; **party whip**, numbers man. See also POLITICIAN

MEMENTO *n* keepsake, relic, remembrance, remembrancer, souvenir, token, trophy; **commemoration**, auld lang syne, commemorative, testimonial; **memorial**, cenotaph, chantry, cornerstone, epitaph, foundation stone, pantheon, Tomb of the Unknown Soldier, tombstone, tope, war memorial

MEMORABLE *adj* catchy, eidetic, haunting, recallable, recognisable, retainable; **unforgotten**, fresh, graven, green, unforgettable

MEMORABLY *adv* unforgettably; **reminiscently**, nostalgically; **in memoriam**, commemoratively, memorially, pro memoria

MEMORISE *v* commit to memory, embalm, etch in one's memory, fix in one's mind, learn; **revise**, refresh one's memory, rub up on; **note**, item, jot, minute; **know by ear**, know by heart, know by rote

MEMORY *n* collective memory, long-term memory, memory span, recall, retainment, retention, retentiveness, retentivity, short-term memory; **remembrance**, engram, impression, memory, trace *(Psychol.)*; **flashback**, association of ideas, recapture, recurrence; **memoirs**, anecdotes, autobiography, biography, history, memorabilia, reminiscences. See also REMEMBERING

MENACE *n* commination, sword of Damocles, threat; **menaces**, intimidation, standover tactics, strongarm methods; **bluster**, defiance, fulmination; **blackmail**, embracery; **gunboat diplomacy**, mailed fist; **war cloud**, dark clouds, gathering clouds, thunder; **fearsomeness**, minaciousness, minacity, ominousness, sinisterness, ugliness

MENACE *v* intimidate, look daggers, look daggers at, overhang, shake the fist at, threaten; **bully**, badger, blackjack, blackmail, bludgeon, bullyrag, do a heavy, heavy, hector, put pressure on, stand over; **bark**, growl, snarl; **bluster**, fulminate, talk big, tell someone what for, thunder; **overawe**,

menace 344 **metal**

concuss, cow, have under threat; **have hanging over one**

MENACER *n* bludgeoner, blusterer, bucko, bully, standover man, standover merchant, threatener; **blackmailer**, embraceor

MENACING *adj* baleful, black, comminatory, intimidating, minacious, minatory, Tammany-Hall, threatening, ugly; **foreboding**, boding ill, ominous; **sinister**, slinky, stealthy

MENACINGLY *adv* darkly, minaciously, minatorily, threateningly; **sinisterly**, balefully, uglily; **forebodingly**, bodingly, ominously

MENTAL *adj* cerebral, intellectual, intelligential, noetic, phrenic, psychic, psychobiological, psychological, psychophysiological; **conscious**, apprehensive, cognitive, perceptional, perceptive, percipient, sensible; **intelligent**, clever, intellective, rational, reasonable, sane; **psychogenetic**

MENTALLY *adv* intellectively, intellectually, psychically, psychologically; **consciously**, perceptively; **intelligently**, reasonably, sanely

MESSAGE *n* communication, notification, piece of information, word; **correspondence**, exchange of letters; **letter**, aerogram, air letter, billet-doux, brief *(Obs.)*, communication, covering letter, dead letter, dispatch, encyclical, epistle, express letter, favour *(Obs.)*, love letter, missive, note, writing; **bread-and-butter letter**, follow-up, reply; **card**, lettercard, notelet, postal *(U.S.)*, postal card *(U.S.)*, postcard, Valentine; **circular**, advertisement, bulletin, dodger, form letter, junk mail, open letter, pamphlet, petition, round robin; **telegram**, cable, cablegram, express, gorillagram, heliogram, phonogram, radiotelegram, strippergram, telex, wire; **postal order**, bank draft, money order, postal note; **postal chess**, correspondence chess, postal shoot, postal vote. *See also* MAIL

MESSENGER *n* herald, mercury, officer at arms, orderly, peon, pursuivant; **envoy**, ambassador, legate; **bellboy**, bellhop, callboy, devil, errand boy, gopher, leg man, messenger boy, pageboy *(Brit.)*; **doorman**, commissionaire; **courier**, dispatch bearer, dispatch rider, express, runner; **carrier pigeon**, homing pigeon; **postman**, mail sorter, mailman, postboy, postie *(Colloq.)*, postmaster, postmaster general, postmistress, postrider, telegraph boy; **telegraphist**, telegrapher, wirer

METAL *n* alloy, amalgam; **iron**, alpha iron, cast iron, delta iron, ferrite, flan, gal, galvanised iron, galvo, gamma iron, grey cast iron, grey iron, hot metal, ingot iron, ingot steel, iron pyrites, mitis, pig-iron, pig-lead, spelter, spiegeleisen, white cast iron, wrought iron; **fusible metal**, cast iron, eutectic, eutectoid, malleable iron; **ingot**, bar, bead, billet, bullion, cast, pig, sinter, sow; **bell metal**, gunmetal, mischmetal, pot metal, silvering, speculum metal, tinwork, tool steel, type metal; **foil**, black plate, expanded metal, latten, leaf, nickel plate, plate, rolled steel, taggers, tin plate, tinfoil; **gold foil**, Dutch foil, Dutch gold, Dutch leaf, Dutch metal, gilding, gilt, gold leaf, gold plate, mosaic gold, ormolu, rolled gold; **dross**, regulus, scoria, slag, speiss, sprue; **mould**, ingot mould, pig, sow; **steel**, carbon steel, cast steel, chrome steel, chromium steel, Damascus steel, damask, hard steel, heat-resisting steel, high steel, killed steel, low steel, martensite, medium steel, mild steel, soft steel, stainless steel, tool steel, tungsten steel, vanadium steel; **zinc,** spelter; **blank,** burr, coin, compact, faggot, planchet; **lodestone,** magnet, permanent magnet; **metalwork,** ironwork, metal goods, metalware, tinsel, tole, trifles, vermeil

METALLIC *adj* bimetallic, metalline, mineral; **golden,** aureate, auric, aurous, gilded, gilt, gold; **brass,** brassy, brazen; **bronzy; copper,** coppery, cupreous, cupric, cuprous; **iron,** ferric, ferritic, ferrous; **lead,** leaden, plumbeous, plumbic, plumbous; **silver,** argent, argental, argentic, argentine, argentous, lunar, lunarian, silvery; **platinum,** platinic, platinoid; **steel,** steely; **tinny,** stannic, stannous; **zinc,** zincic, zincky, zincous

METALLIFEROUS *adj* aluminiferous, argentiferous, auriferous, cupriferous, ferriferous, ferruginous, nickeliferous, plumbiferous, quick, stanniferous, yttriferous, zinciferous

METALLURGIC *adj* metallurgical, mineralogical, vulcanian; **ductile,** eutectic, eutectoid, forgeable, mitis, self-annealing, self-hardened, self-hardening, weldable

METALLURGY *n* alchemy, cyanide process, electrometallurgy, electrowinning, hydrometallurgy, metallography, metallurgical engineering, Mond process, pyrometallurgy; **mineralogy,** petrology; **smithing,** drop-forging, flame-hardening, heat treatment; **pouring,** die-casting, metal spinning, metal spraying, rolling; **welding**

METALWORKER *n* coiner, gilder, metal fabricator, pewterer; **smith,** blacksmith, founder, galvaniser, goldbeater, goldsmith, ironmaster, ironsmith, ironworker, plumber, silversmith, smelter, steelworker, tinman, tinner, tinsmith, welder, whitesmith; **metallurgist,** alchemist, mineralogist

METALWORKS *n* foundry, ironworks, rolling mill, smelter, smithery, smithy, stannary, steelworks, strip mill, tinworks, wireworks; **furnace,** blast furnace, finery, hearth

METEOR *n* bolide, falling star, fireball, shooting star; **meteorite,** meteoroid, siderite, siderolite; **comet,** Halley's comet; **nucleus,** coma, tail, train. *See also* STAR; HEAVENLY BODY

METEOROLOGIST *n* climatologist, skywonkie, weather forecaster, weatherman

METHOD *n* guise, manner, mode, procedure, sort, technics, technique, way, wise *(Archaic);* **line,** approach, tack; **avenue,** channel, course, highroad, path, road, stepping stone, track; **means,** agent, how, implement, instrument, medium, tool, vehicle, way, ways and means, wherewithal; **process,** mechanics, mechanism, modus operandi, operation; **expedient,** device, gimmick, nostrum; **customary method,** custom, practice, routine, usual way

MICROPHONE *n* bug, hydrophone, mike, radiophone, thermophone; **resonator,** reverberator, sound post, sounding-board; **public-address system,** bullhorn, loudhailer, loudspeaker, megaphone, PA, speaking trumpet, tannoy *(Brit.)*

MIDDLE CLASS n bourgeoisie, equites, lower middle class, petite bourgeoisie, professional class, upper middle class; **member of the middle class**, bourgeois, businessman, capitalist, employer, petit bourgeois, professional, rentier, yeoman; **upstart**, nouveau riche, parvenu, social climber

MIDDLE-CLASS adj comfortably well-off, non-U, petit-bourgeois, risen from the ranks, untitled, upwardly mobile

MIDWIFE n accoucheur, accoucheuse, deliverer, gynaecologist, obstetrician

MILITARISE v activate (U.S.), arm, crusade, embattle, mobilise, put on a war footing; **recruit**, call up, conscript; **enlist**, join up; **soldier**, bear arms, campaign, go on active service; **prepare for action**, clear the decks

MILITARY SERVICE n active service, hitch (U.S. Colloq.), soldiering; **recruitment**, call-up, conscription, draft, national service, selective service. See also WAR

MILL n chip-mill, flour mill, ginnery, rolling mill, sawmill

MILLION n millionth; **billion**, billionth; **trillion**, nonillion, octillion, quadrillion, quintillion, septillion, septillionth, sextillion, sextillionth, trillionth; **milliard**; **googol**, gogoogol, googolplex

MILLION adj billion, billionth, millionth, nonillion, nonillionth, octillion, septillion, septillionth, sextillion, sextillionth, trillion, trillionth

MIND n belfry, breast, consciousness, head, headpiece, loaf, psyche, sconce, sentient, skull, upper storey; **intellect**, brains, capacity, faculties, genius, grey matter, intelligence, judgment, lights, mentality, percipience, powers, psychology, rationality, reason, saneness, sanity, sense, thought, understanding, wit, wits

MINDER n attendant, ayah, babysitter, carer, childminder, fosterer, guardian, housefather, housemother, houseparent, keeper, nanny, nurse, parent; **ministrant**, cherisher, mollycoddler; **fusser**, fusspot, old woman

MINER n burrower, quarrier, sapper, tunneller; **potholer**, caver, speleologist

MINERAL n ore; **reef**, bloom, bushoo, deep ground, deposit, jeweller's shop, ledge, lens, lode, mother lode, ore body, ore shoot, outcrop, pipe, pocket, quartz reef, surface reef, underset, vein, winning; **gold-bearing soil**, alluvial, alluvial cone, alluvial fan, alluvial ground, bar, pay-dirt, placer, wash, washing; **colour**, glance, opacite; **metal dust**, dust, gold dust, platinum black, sponge; **nugget**, floater, slug; **gold**, fool's gold, iron pyrites, yellow metal

MIRROR n cheval glass, distorting mirror, glass, hand glass, looking glass, magic mirror, pier glass, rear-vision mirror, reflector, speculum, wing mirror

MIRTH n laughing, laughter, merriment; **smile**, grin; **giggle**, snicker, snigger, teehee, the giggles, titter; **laugh**, belly laugh, cachinnation, convulsion, guffaw, haw-haw, horse laugh, roar; **shriek**, cackle, chortle, hoot, howl, shout. See also HUMOUR

MISBEHAVE v act up, be up to no good, blackguard, commit transgressions, corrupt others, cut up nasty, cut up rough, deviate from the straight and narrow, forget oneself, go astray, lapse, misconduct oneself, muck up, play up, roque, sell oneself short, sow wild oats, trespass; **cheat,** duckshove, indulge in sharp practice, swindle; **make mischief,** be up to monkey business, be up to monkey tricks, make trouble, mess about, mess around, play hob; **riot,** brutalise, destroy property, rough-house, run riot, smash property, vandalise; **overstep the mark,** ask for it, ask for trouble, go too far; **lose one's temper,** carry on, glower, sulk

MISBEHAVIOUR *n* bad behaviour, bad manners, delinquency, dereliction, improperness, impropriety, malfeasance, malpractice, malversation, misconduct, misdoing, naughtiness, pertness; **rascality,** bastardry, caddishness, cruelty, devilment, doggery, knavishness, malefaction, obstreperousness, waywardness; **disrespect,** discourtesy, impudence, incivility, insolence, lese-majesty *(Joc.)*, tactlessness; **mischievousness,** devilment, elfishness, impishness, mischief, mischief-making, roguery, roguishness; **slyness,** archness, kittenishness, tricksiness; **bad temper,** acerbity, acrimony, asperity, bad language, bad looks, harsh words, tartness, unparliamentary language, virulence; **sullenness,** moroseness, rudeness, stubbornness; **hooliganism,** criminality, irresponsibility, irresponsibleness, juvenile delinquency, larrikinism, restiveness, rowdyism, ruffianism, vulgarity; **infamous conduct,** bestiality, blackguardism, brutality, brutishness, conduct unbecoming, infamy

MISCHIEF-MAKER *n* elf, gremlin, imp, jackanapes, monkey, muck-up, pickle, prankster, rogue, scallywag, scamp; **enfant terrible,** perisher, tyke, Young Turk; **gamin,** gamine, guttersnipe, mudlark *(Brit. Colloq.)*; **bastard,** bear, blackguard, bugger, whoreson; **hooligan,** bovver boy *(Brit. Colloq.),* disorderly person, goon, hellion, hoodlum, hoon, irresponsible, juvenile delinquent, larrikin, rugger-bugger, scourer *(Brit. Hist.)*; **wrongdoer,** delinquent, duckshover, hard case, incorrigible, recidivist, wrong 'un

MISCONCEIVER *n* extenuator, perverter, prejudger

MISDEMEANOUR *n* evil deeds, peccadillo, slip, transgression, trip, wrongdoing; **escapade,** caper, capriccio, caprice, monkey tricks, monkeyshine, prank, trick; **disorder,** disorderliness, disorderly conduct, riot, roughhouse, rumble

MISER *n* cheapskate, churl, codger, curmudgeon, death adder, dog in the manger, Ikey Mo, jew *(Derog.)*, meanie, money-grubber, niggard, penny pincher, pinchpenny, screw, scrooge, Shylock, skinflint, tightwad; **piker,** last of the big spenders

MISFORTUNE *n* accident, ambs-ace, bale *(Archaic),* clap *(Obs.),* contretemps, evil, evil chance *(Archaic),* hard lines, hard luck story, ill, infortune *(Obs.),* misadventure, mischance, raw deal, setback; **mishap,** mess-up, slip; **calamity,** blight, catastrophe, debacle, disaster, plague, tragedy, visitation; **blow,** body blow, kick in the arse, king hit, peripeteia, reversal, reverse, slump, smack in the eye, turnabout; **hard lines,** hard ched-

misfortune

dar, hard cheese, hard luck, just one's luck, stiff cheddar, stiff cheese, stiff luck, the deuce, the devil, tough luck; **mixed blessing; run of bad luck,** bad trot, chapter of accidents, hard times, night, rainy day; **evil star,** bad fairy, cross, curse, fire, hex, mozz, scourge; **black-letter day,** Black Friday; **disaster area,** Pandora's box; **adversity,** asperity, hard life, hardship, rough end of the pineapple, sorrow, trouble, worriment; **ruination,** kiss of death, the worst; **fate worse than death**

MISGUIDANCE *n* bum steer, furphy, misdirection, wrong advice; **debauchment,** debauchery *(Obs.),* depravation, perversion

MISGUIDE *v* give a false impression, give someone a bum steer, lead astray, lead into error, misadvise, miscounsel, misdirect, misinform, mislead, misrepresent, misteach; **deprave,** debauch, deceive, demoralise, empoison, lead astray, pervert, subvert; **confuse,** bewilder, mystify, throw someone off the scent; **fool,** give someone the wrong idea, lead a merry dance, lead by the nose, lead someone up the garden path

MISGUIDED *adj* misdirected, misled, pseudolearned; **debauched,** confusing, deceptive, fallacious, illusory, perverted; **misleading**

MISINTERPRET *v* belie, caricature, distort, falsify, flatter, garble, libel, miscolour, misdescribe, misquote, misreport, misrepresent, parody, portray falsely, put a false construction on, skew, slant, travesty, twist

MISJUDGE *v* be unable to see the wood for the trees, fly in the face of facts, go off half-cocked, have a bias, jump to the wrong conclusion, misapprehend, miscalculate, misconceive, misconstrue, misestimate, misreckon, mistake, misvalue, not see beyond one's nose, overestimate, overplay one's hand, overrate, overvalue, prejudge, presume, presumise, reckon without, underestimate, underrate

MISJUDGED *adj* based on false premises, exaggerated, ill-judged, injudicious, misunderstood, overestimated, overrated, overvalued, superficial, underestimated, underrated, undervalued, unsound, wrong, wrong-headed

MISJUDGMENT *n* error, hasty conclusion, jaundiced view, misapprehension, miscalculation, misconception, miscue, misestimate, misestimation, mistake, misunderstanding, overestimate, overestimation, underestimate, underestimation, warped judgment

MISLEADER *n* false prophet, will-o'-the-wisp; **debaucher,** depraver; **debauchee,** pervert

MISPLACE *v* misarrange, misdeliver, misfile; **displace,** antevert, buck, dislodge, disseat, heave *(Geol.),* unbalance, unhorse, unsaddle, unseat; **dislocate,** disjoint, luxate; **decentre,** unbalance

MISPLACED *adj* ectopic *(Pathol.),* erratic *(Geol.),* heterotopic, parallactic; **displaced,** adventitious *(Bot. Zool.),* astray, dislocated, unbalanced; **homeless,** houseless, stateless, unaccommodated; **eccentric,** off-centre, skew-whiff, wonky

MISPLACEMENT *n* disturbance, ectopia, epeirogenesis, epeirogeny, heave *(Geol.),* heterotopia, malposition, prolapse, spill, spillage, version; **dis-**

placement, adventitiousness *(Bot. Zool.),* dislocation, dislodgment, driftage, eluviation, luxation; **homelessness,** no-man's-land, statelessness, vagrancy

MISPRONOUNCE *v* clip, lisp, nasalise, slur; **stammer,** falter, fumble, haw, hem, hesitate, hum and haw, mumble, mutter, quaver, stutter; **splutter,** clutter, gabble, sputter, swallow one's words

MISREPRESENTATION *n* distortedness, distortion, exaggeration, false portrayal, falsehood, falsification, garble, libel, misdescription, misinterpretation, misquotation, misquote, misreport, perversion, violence; **bad likeness,** anamorphosis, burlesque, caricature, parody, travesty

MISREPRESENTED *adj* distorted, misrepresentative

MISREPRESENTER *n* belier, distorter, falsifier, garbler, misreporter

MISTER *n* bung, Esq., esquire, goodman *(Archaic),* herr, m'sieur, monsieur, Mr, Mynheer, sahib, san, señor, signor, signore, sir; **sir,** aga, Alhaji, Dan *(Archaic),* dignity, Doctor, dom, Don, effendi, emir, Grace, honour, imperator, landgrave, Lord, maestro, maharaja, milord, mirza, monseigneur, nawab, pasha, seignior *(Archaic),* Serenity, swami, Tunku, tycoon, worship, your lordship; **Grace,** dom, Holiness, Lord, Monsignor, Reverence; **mate,** blue, bluey, boss, cobber, comrade, dig, digger, Mack *(U.S.),* man, matey, old fruit *(Brit.),* sirrah, skeeter, snow, snowy, son, sonny, uncle; **so-and-so,** what's-his-face, what's-his-name

MISTIME *v* go off at half-cock, go off half-cocked, miscue, miss, overtime *(Photog.),* shoot one's bolt; **lose an opportunity,** blow it, let a chance slip through one's fingers, miss the boat, miss the bus; **misdate,** antedate, postdate, predate

MISUNDERSTAND *v* be all at sea, be at cross purposes, have one's wires crossed, make little of, make neither head nor tail of, make nothing of, misinterpret, miss the point, see through a glass darkly

MISUSE *n* abusage, abuse, improper use, maladministration, misapplication, misappropriation, misdirection, misemployment, mismanagement, misusage, overuse, waste; **malpractice,** barbarism, corruption, malversation, perversion, prostitution, simony, violation; **maltreatment,** ill usage, ill use, ill-treatment, mishandling, mistreatment, misuse *(Obs.)*

MISUSER *n* abuser, lurk man, mauler; **perverter,** corrupter, pervert, subverter

MIX *v* blunge, dash, mash, paddle, puddle *(Mining),* roil, shake, shake up, stir; **blend,** admix, emulsify, fold, homogenise, impregnate, interblend, interlard; **compound,** brew, prepare; **amalgamate,** alloy, conglomerate, fuse, merge; **diversify,** assort; **shuffle,** jumble, scramble; **mingle,** commix, immingle, immix, interfuse, interlace, interlard, intermingle, intermix, intersperse; **adulterate,** contaminate, debase, sophisticate, vitiate; **temper,** attemper, doctor, season, tincture, water, water down

MIXED *adj* assorted, kaleidoscopic, mingled, miscellaneous, motley, multifarious; **jumbled,** diversiform,

mixed / **mockery**

farraginous, hotch-potch, macaronic *(Obs.)*, medley, muddled, scrappy, unclassified, unsorted; **diverse**, daedal *(Poetic)*, diversified, many-sided, multi-racial, multicultural, pluralist, pluralistic; **heterogeneous**, eclectic, heteromerous, multilingual, polyglot, promiscuous; **fifty-fifty**, half-and-half, Jekyll-and-Hyde, pepper-and-salt; **conglomerate**, complex, composite, conglomeritic; **adulterated**, commercial, cut, sophisticated; **impure**, foul, tainted, vitiated

MIXER *n* amalgamator, blender, food processor, jumbler, mingler, shuffler, vitamiser; **paddle**, blunger *(Pottery)*, egg whisk, egg-beater, larry *(Bldg Trades)*, palette knife, puddling machine, rabble; **adulterater**, adulterant, vitiator

MIXTURE *n* assortment, medley, melange, miscellany, mix; **jumble**, bag of tricks, catch-all, fantasia, farrago, flotsam and jetsam, gallimaufry, grab bag, hodgepodge, hotchpotch, medley, mixed bag, motley, odds and ends, olio, omnium gatherum, paraphernalia, patchwork, pell-mell, polyglot, potpourri, rummage, salmagundi, shandygaff, smorgasbord; **assemblage**, album, assembly, box, bundle, collection, congeries, group; **pastiche**, cento *(Archaic)*, collage, infusion, pasticcio, patchwork, tincture; **musical medley**, macaronic verse; **mingling**, admixture, amalgamation, blending, commixture, conglomeration, diffusion, fusion, immixture, integration, interfusion, interlarding, interpolation, junction, marriage, merger, mixing, stirring, transfusion; **intermixture**, entanglement, interlacement, intermingle-ment, interspersion, lacing; **synaeresis**, crasis, synaesthesia, synaloepha *(Phonet.)*; **miscibility**; **adulteration**, admixture, contamination, corruption, debasement, sophistication, vitiation; **hybridisation**, hybridism, interbreeding, miscegenation, mixed marriage, mongrelisation, mongrelism, mosaicism *(Genetics)*

MOCK *v* chuck off at, debunk, deride, fleer at, flout, gibe, gig, have a shot at, heckle, jeer, jest, monkey, scoff, take the micky out of; **ridicule**, laugh at, make a fool of, make a monkey of, make fun of, poke borak at, poke fun at, poke mullock at, rib, sport; **taunt**, barrack, burl, gird at, guy, howl down, joe, laugh out of court, rubbish; **banter**, chaff, chiack, get a rise out of, josh, pull someone's leg, quiz *(Obs.)*, rag, rally, take a rise out of, tease, twit; **hoot**, howl; **satirise**, befool, burlesque, lampoon, send up, squib, travesty; **pillory**, blister, gibbet, pasquinade, razz, roast

MOCKER *n* cynic, derider, flouter, jeerer, ridiculer, scoffer, sneerer; **taunter**, barracker, giber, heckler, twitter; **banterer**, chaffer, leg-puller, teaser; **satirist**, caricaturist, lampooner, parodist, pasquinader, satiriser

MOCKERY *n* borak *(Aborig.)*, derision, derisiveness, name-calling, razz, ridicule; **sarcasm**, irony, satiricalness; **taunting**, heckling, heehaw, ribaldry; **chaff**, chiack, chiacking, teasing; **banter**, badinage, persiflage, raillery; **satire**, burlesque, caricature, cartoon, iambic *(Gk Lit.)*, lampoon, parody, pasquil, pasquinade, send-up, skit, squib, travesty; **rogue's march**; **mock**, crack, dig, flout, gibe, gird *(Archaic)*,

mockery

hit, knock, rub, scoff, witticism; **taunt**, fleer, jeer, twit; **jest**, joke, leg-pull; **howl of derision**, hoot

MOCKING *adj* deriding, derisive, fleering, Hudibrastic, jeering, nipping, quizzical, sarcastic, sardonic, sarky, scoffing; **bantering**, sportful, teasing; **satiric**, burlesque, satirical

MODEL *n* copy *(Archaic)*, dummy, exemplar, mock-up, mount, pattern, pilot, working model; **template**, form, guide, mitre box, shape; **mould**, cast, casting, core, dariole, deckle, die, matrix, roughcast; **stamp**, engraving, pig, pig-bed, plate, seal, stamper, woodblock, woodcut; **design**, cartoon, sinopia; **block**, last; **original**, archetype, manuscript, master, parent, protocol, prototype, stock, the copy

MODEL *adj* classic, classical, ideal; **standard**, formulaic, normal, normative, sample, typical; **original**, archetypal, archetypical, prototypal; **exemplary**, citatory, copybook, exemplificative, paradigmatic, paradigmatical, precedential

MODERATE *v* attemper, milden, mitigate, modify, modulate, palliate, qualify, season, soften, temper, tone down, turn down; **restrain**, allay, appease, assuage, lay, mollify, slake, soothe, staunch *(Archaic)*; **calm**, cool down, cool off, defuse, pacify, quell, quiet, quieten, stay, still, tranquillise; **abate**, attenuate, bate, relax, relent, remit, slack, slacken, wane; **dull**, blunt, buff, cushion, deaden, tame

MODERATE *adj* judicious, middle-of-the-road, modest, non-extreme, reasonable, restrained, temperate; **mild**, balmy, gentle, kindly, lenient, smooth, soft, tempered; **calm**, cool,

modestly

even, peaceful, quiet, stormless, tranquil; **soothing**, assuasive, attenuant, lenitive, mitigative, mitigatory, modulative, palliative; **dull**, dullish, innocuous, insipid, tame

MODERATELY *adv* in moderation, modestly, restrainedly, temperately, to a degree; **calmly**, coolly, evenly, quietly; **mildly**, balmily, gently, leniently; **dully**, innocuously, tamely

MODERATION *n* golden mean, judiciousness, moderateness, modesty, reasonableness, restraint, self-control, temperance, temperateness; **mildness**, balminess, gentleness; **calmness**, coolness, quietness, subduedness; **dullness**, innocuousness, insipidity, tameness

MODERATOR *n* damper, deadener, restrainer, seasoner, temperer; **assuager**, allayer, lenitive *(Rare)*, mitigator, modulator, mollifier, palliative, palliator, queller, quieter, relaxer, soother, tranquilliser; **middle-of-the-roader**, Menshevik, moderate, non-extremist; **neutraliser**, buffer, cushion, dashpot *(Mach.)*

MODEST *adj* backward, backward in coming forward, bashful, blushful, blushing, coy, demure, diffident, nice *(Obs.)*, reserved, restrained, retiring, sheepish, shy, skittish, verecund *(Rare)*, withdrawn; **self-effacing**, self-deprecating, unassuming, unobtrusive, unostentatious, unpretending, unpretentious; **decent**, chaste, missish, prim and proper, prudish, pure, virtuous

MODESTLY *adv* backwardly, bashfully, blushingly, coyly, demurely, sheepishly, shyly; **self-effacingly**, self-deprecatingly, unassumingly, unostentatiously, unpretendingly, unpre-

modesty

tentiously, with no fuss or bother, without ceremony

MODEST PERSON *n* blusher, effacer, shrinking violet, wallflower

MODESTY *n* backwardness, bashfulness, constraint, coyness, demureness, diffidence, humility, pudency, reserve, shamefacedness, sheepishness, shyness, timidity; **self-effacement,** effacement, self-deprecation, unassumingness, unobtrusiveness, unpretentiousness; **decency,** chastity, decorum, purity

MOMENT *n* a brace of shakes, breath, crack, flash, instant, jiffy, minute, mo, sec, second, shake, split second, tick, trice, twinkle, twinkling, whipstitch *(U.S.)*, wink; **point,** article *(Archaic)*, epoch *(Astron.)*, juncture, point of time, time

MOMENTARILY *adv* for a moment, momently; **soon,** after a bit, anon *(Archaic)*, awhile, before long, erelong *(Archaic)*, in a bit; **in a moment,** all at once, in a brace of shakes, in half a mo, in less than no time, in no time, in no time at all, in two shakes of a dog's tail, in two ticks, quickly, readily; **instantly,** at once, at sight, forthright *(Archaic)*, forthwith, here and now, immediately, instantaneously, on sight, on the spot, shortly, with this; **suddenly,** abruptly, all at once, at the drop of a hat, extempore, impromptu, impulsively, on the spot, on the spur of the moment, out of hand, without notice

MOMENTARINESS *n* abruptness, suddenness, transience; **instantaneity,** immediacy, immediateness, instancy *(Rare)*, instantaneousness, quickness

moon

MOMENTARY *adj* passing, transient; **instantaneous,** immediate, instant, overnight, present *(Obs.)*, quick, split-second; **minute,** ready-made; **sudden,** abrupt, ad hoc, impromptu, impulsive, snap

MONASTIC *n* ascetic, bodhisattva, bonze, brother, caloyer, canon regular, canoness, coenobite, enthusiast, fakir, Flagellant, flagellator, Fra, frère, friar, holy Joe, incluse, lama, lay brother, maharishi, mendicant, monk, nun, out sister, recluse, regular, religious, shaveling *(Archaic)*, sister, stylite, vestal, vower; **novice,** canon, canonry, neophyte, ordinand, postulant, scholastic, seminarian, seminarist, tertiary, regular tertiary, secular tertiary; **provost,** abbé, abbess, abbot, hegumen *(Greek Orthodox)*, monk, mother, mother superior, prior, prioress, rector, Reverend Mother, right reverend, superior, votaress, votary, votress; **dervish,** Calender, dancing dervish, fakir, howling dervish, sheikh, spinning dervish, whirling dervish; **dalai lama.** *See also* ECCLESIASTIC

MONASTIC *adj* ascetic, ascetical, claustral, cloistral, institutionary, monachal, monasterial, professed, regular, religious, tonsured; **conventual,** abbatial, coenobitic, coenobitical, monkish, rectorial, succursal

MONASTICISM *n* coenobitism, monachism; **religious order,** congregation, discipline, lamasery *(Buddhism)*, major order, minor order, monkery, monkhood, observance, rule, veil

MONUMENT *n* foundation stone

MOON *n* earth satellite, lamp *(Poetic)*, Paddy's lantern *(N.Z.)*, Phoebe; **paraselene,** mock moon; **phase,** first quarter, interlunation, last quarter, mansion, quadrature, quarter; **crater**, mare, mascon, ray, rill, sea, walled plain; **crescent**, full moon, gibbous moon, half-moon, harvest moon, moonrise, new moon, old moon, waning moon, waxing moon; **moons**, Amalthea *(Jup.)*, Callisto *(Jup.)*, Charon *(Pluto)*, Deimos *(Mars)*, Europa *(Jup.)*, Galilean satellites *(Jup.)*, Ganymede *(Jup.)*, Io *(Jup.)*, Phoebus *(Mars)*, Titan *(Sat.)*, Triton *(Nep.)*

MORAL *adj* axiological, casuistic, ethic; **moralistic**, carping, conscience-stricken, puritan, sermonising, wowserish; **ethical**, clean, decent, honourable, snowy

MORALISER *n* moralist, nag, puritan, wowser

MORALITY *n* cardinal virtues, ethics, moral philosophy, morals, natural law, professional ethics, right, rightness; **ethic**, moral, moral code, moralism, standard

MORALLY *adv* ethically, on principle

MORAL SENSE *n* categorical imperative, conscience, mens rea *(Law)*, superego

MORBID CURIOSITY *n* prurience, voyeurism; **curio**, conversation piece, peepshow; **curious person**, buttinski, earwig, eavesdropper, inquisitive, nosy parker, peeping Tom, prier, pry, quidnunc, rubberneck, stickybeak, voyeur; **thirst for knowledge**, inquiring mind

MORE *n* a bit on the side, allowance, another, anotherie, gash, margin, over, seconds; **extra**, etceteras, plus, supernumerary, supplement, supplementary. *See also* ADDITION; POSTSCRIPT

MORNING *n* a.m., dayspring *(Poetic)*, forenoon, midmorning, morn *(Poetic)*, morrow *(Archaic)*; **dawn**, break of day, cockcrow, dawning, daybreak, light, sparrow fart, spring *(Archaic)*, sun-up, sunrise; **small hours**, matins, prime; **breakfast-time**, brunch, elevenses *(Brit.)*, playtime

MORNING SONG *n* aubade, dawn serenade

MOST *adj* best, consummate, extreme, maximal, maximum, maximus, supreme, top, utmost, uttermost, veriest; **majority**, dominant, main, ruling; **all-time**, absolute, almighty, arrant, awful, bally, blank, bleeding, bloody, blooming, bumper, downright, effing, fantastic, father and mother of a, flagrant, flaming, flipping, flopping, frigging, fucking, hang of a, howling, humming, mortal, out-and-out, passing, plain, plumb, positive, rank, rattling, resounding, smacking, sollicking, some, spanking, stark, stinking, surpassing, swingeing, tearing, thoroughgoing, thumping, thundering, uncommon, unmitigated, unqualified, utter, walloping, whacking

MOTIVE *n* arrière-pensée, drive, impetus, incentive, interest, raison d'être, reason, the why and the wherefore, ulterior motive, what makes one tick

MOTOR VESSEL *n* flyboat, hot-water boat, motor boat, oil-burner, powerboat, rubber duckie, runabout, speedboat; **steamship**, paddle-steamer, paddleboat, side-wheeler, steamboat, steamer, stern-wheeler; **cabin cruiser**, cruiser, houseboat; hy-

motor vessel 354 **move**

drofoil, hydroplane, seaplane *(U.S.)*; **ferry,** car ferry, ferryboat, punt, wherry *(Brit.)*; **wetbike; submarine,** bathyscaphe, bathysphere, minisub, sub, submersible, U-boat

MOULDING *n* Aaron's-rod, astragal, baguette, beading, beadwork, bed moulding, bolection; **cable moulding,** cabling, cavetto, chain-moulding, chainwork, chaplet, chevron, congé, cordon, dogtooth, egg and anchor, egg and dart, egg and tongue, fillet, gadroon, necking, quad, quadrant moulding, reed, reglet, scotia, surbase, torus; **boss,** crocket, knob, pellet, **stud; spur,** cusp, finial, goffer, poppyhead, terminal; **frieze,** cornice, dancette, guilloche, string-course; **crest,** antefix, brattishing, cresting; **fluting,** glyph, strigil, triglyph; **table,** banderol, cartouche, medallion, metope, plaque; **facing,** panelling; **architrave,** archivolt, epistyle; **roundel,** bezant, ovum, rose; **tracery,** fan tracery

MOUND *n* ant heap, ant hill, barrow, burial mound, dene, effigy-mound, embankment, hummock, hump, kurgan, midden, mogul, molehill, monticule, moraine, niggerhead, salt dome, seif-dune, stage, tell, tope *(Buddhism)*, tumulus, upthrow *(Geol.)*; **rampart,** bulwark, dike, mole; **hill,** barchan, bill, butte *(U.S. Canada)*, down, drumlin, dune, foothill, gentle Annie *(N.Z.)*, headland, hen-cackle *(N.Z.)*, hill site, hillock, hilltop, holt *(Poetic)*, hurst, incline, island, knob, knoll, kop *(S. African)*, kopje *(S. African)*, mesa, monadnock, outcrop, promontory, rise, sand dune, sand hill, skillion, swell, tor, wold. *See also* MOUNTAIN; APEX; HEIGHT

MOUNTAIN *n* alp, ben *(Scot.)*, bluff, cliff, cone, crag, crag-and-tail, escarpment, fjeld, massif, mount, nunatak, peak, pinnacle, plateau, precipice, prominence, table, tableland, volcano, wall *(Mountaineering)*; **mountain range,** alps, chain, continental divide, cordillera, ghats *(India)*, interfluve, palisades *(U.S.)*, sierra, slopes, the tops, tiers *(Tas.)*; **ridge,** esker, horseback, offset, os, rand *(S. African)*, sideling *(N.Z.)*, siding *(N.Z.)*, spur, watershed; **high country,** highland, paramo, the heights, uplands. *See also* MOUND; APEX; HEIGHT

MOUNTAINOUS *adj* alpine, cordilleran, high-country, highland, montane, mountain, rangy, subalpine *(Phys. Geog.)*, upland, volcanic, vulcanian; **precipitous,** cliffy, cragged, ridgy, steep; **hilly,** hillocky, hummocky. *See also* HIGH; TALL

MOUTH *n* cakehole, chook's bum, gob, hole, kisser, maw, moosh, mug, north and south, puss, rattletrap, trap; **lip,** labium, labrum; **tooth,** choppers, clackers, denticle, dentition, fang, pearly gates, snag, snaggle-tooth, tusk; **eyetooth,** baby tooth, bicuspid, canine, carnassial, cheektooth, grinder, incisor, laniary, microdont, milk tooth, molar, premolar, wisdom tooth; **false teeth,** denture, falsies, plate, tatters, tatts; **tongue,** clapper, glossa, lingua; **gum,** faucal pillars, fauces, gingiva, hard palate, palate, alveolus, soft palate, tooth ridge, velum, uvula

MOVE *n* action, business *(Theat.)*, gesture, motion, movement; **gait,** footfall, footwork, locomotion, pace, step, stride, walk; **bounce,** bob, dip, gurgitation, nod, nutation, prance, shrug; **jerk**, cant, jolt, snatch, stamp, start, stroke, whip; **slide**, fishtail, flap, glide, skid, slip, slither, stroke, swim; **wriggle**, squirm, writhe; **course**, drift, march, run, sweep, tack, way *(Naut.)*; **circuit**, circle, circulation, orbit, traverse

MOVE *v* go, heave *(Naut.)*, make one's way, run, stir, surge, walk *(Obs.)*; **ply**, plough, truck; **bounce**, bob, dap, hop, jump, nod, noddle, prance, surge; **jerk**, flitter, flutter, play, skitter, squib, waver, winnow *(Archaic)*; **slide**, aquaplane, plane, skid, skim, slip, slither; **glide**, bowl, coast, cruise, kite, ride, roll, roll along, sail, skim, spank, sweep; **wriggle**, squirm, writhe; **mobilise**, agitate, animate; **budge**, give way, shift, work; **start**, clutch-start *(Motor Vehicles)*, flip, launch, let rip, rev up, turn over

MOVEMENT *n* action, Brownian motion, evolution, motion; perpetual motion, perpetuo moto; **mobility**, agility, degree of freedom *(Mech. Engineering)*, manoeuvrability, motility, movability; **tropism**, galvanotropism, geotropism, heliotaxis, heliotropism, negative geotropism, nyctitropism, photokinesis, phototaxis, phototropism, positive geotropism, sleepmovement, thermotaxis, thigmotaxis; **mobilisation**, dislocation *(Geol.)*; **dynamics**, hydrokinetics, kinematics, kinesiology, kinetics, mechanics; **Newton's laws**, Einstein's general theory of relativity, Einstein's special theory of relativity

MOVING *adj* automobile, automotive, locomotive, locomotor, motile, self-moving; **in motion**, astir, away, live, off, running, shifting, volitant; **motor**, psychomotor, sensorimotor; **circula**tory, ambient, circulative; **tropic**, geotropic, heliotactic, heliotropic, nutational, photokinetic, phototropic, thermotaxic, thigmotactic; **mobile**, dynamic, kinematic, kinematical, kinetic, manoeuvrable, motive

MS *n* dame, Donna, frau, fraulein, goodwife, goody, lady, ma'am, madam, Madame, mademoiselle, Madonna, Miss, missus, mistress, Mrs, señora, señorita, signora, Tengku, your ladyship

MUCH *n* abundance, copiousness, flood, heap, lot, mass, mountain, muchness, ocean, peck, pile, plenty, power, profusion, quantity, quiverful, raft, rain, sea, sight, store, torrent, volume, wealth, world; **a great deal**, acres, any amount, bags, big mobs, biggest mobs, lashings, mint, neckful, no end, oodles, reams, scads, stacks, tons, whips; **most**, best part, bulk, majority, the lion's share; **maximum**, peak, the full bore; **extreme**, extremeness, extremity, the nth degree, the nth power, utmost, uttermost

MUDDLE *n* balls-up, kettle of fish, mess, mess-up, no-man's-land, shambles, shemozzle; **disturbance**, babel, bouleversement, furore, hullabaloo, jungle, madhouse, maelstrom, melee, picnic, pother, riot, shindig, shindy, song and dance, tumult, turmoil, uproar, upset; **disorder**, clutter, confusedness, messiness, pandemonium, tumultuousness, turbidity, turbulence; **entanglement**, embranglement, embroilment, enravelment, ravelment, tangle; **maze**, labyrinth

MUDDLE *v* ball up *(U.S. Brit.)*, balls-up, embrangle, embroil, entangle, fuck up, jumble, make a mess of, mix up, overset, ravel, screw up

MUDDLED *adj* at sixes and sevens, in a mess, in a muddle, in disorder, indiscriminate, messy; **riotous**, hectic, pandemonic, tumultary, tumultuous, turbid, turbulent, wild; **snafu**, situation normal all fucked up

MULTICOLOUR *n* dichroism, dichromatism, opalescence, polychromatism, polychromy, trichroism, trichromatism, variedness, variegation; **rainbow**, bow, prism, spectrum; **mosaic**, kaleidoscope, motley, patchwork, tessellation; **veining**, cloudiness, dicing, fasciation, imbrication, marbling, marking, ocellation, streakiness; **blotch**, blaze, fleck, maculation, ocellus, speck, splash, spot, stain; **mottle**, dapple, speckle; **brindle**, merle; **stripe**, candy stripe, fascia, pinstripe, streak, vein; **plaid**, argyle, check, checker, hound's tooth check, polka dot, tartan, tattersall

MULTICOLOURED *adj* bicolour, dichroic, dichromatic, dichromic, particoloured, pavonine, polychromatic, polychrome, prismatic, psychedelic, rainbow, trichroic, trichromatic, tricolour, tricoloured, two-tone, varicoloured, varied, variegated; **versicolour**, changeable *(Archaic)*, chatoyant, cloudy, moiré, mother-of-pearl, nacreous, opalescent, opaline, shot, watered; **motley**, harlequin, heather-mixture, heterochromatic, heterochromous, mealy, pepper-and-salt; **brindled**, black-and-blue, calico *(U.S.)*, dapple-bay, dapple-grey, dappled, flea-bitten, merle, mickey mouse, mottled, piebald, pied, pinto *(U.S.)*, roan, skewbald, tabby, tortoiseshell; **spotted**, blotchy, dotted, speckled, splashy, spotty, stippled, variolitic; **barred**, banded, candy-striped, fasciate, paly *(Heraldry)*, ring-streaked, ringed, striped; **veined**, marbled, streaky; **check**, checked, chequered, company *(Heraldry)*, tessellate; **ocellated**, bird's-eye, eyed; **plaid**, argyle, plaided, tattersall

MUM'S THE WORD *phr* it must go no further, keep it under your hat, no-one will be the wiser

MURDEROUS *adj* bloodthirsty, butcherly, cutthroat, homicidal, slaughterous, thuggish; **sanguinary**, bloodguilty, bloodstained, bloody, crimson, internecine, red-handed; **fratricidal**, deicidal, filicidal, foeticidal, genocidal, matricidal, parricidal, patricidal, regicidal, sororicidal, tyrannicidal, uxoricidal; **suicidal**, banzai, kamikaze, self-destructive; **sacrificial**, capital, immolatory. *See also* KILLING

MURDEROUSLY *adv* bloodthirstily, homicidally, sanguinarily; **sacrificially**, capitally, suicidally

MURDEROUSNESS *n* bloodthirstiness, perniciousness, sanguinariness

MUSIC *n* accord, consonance, ensemble, harmony, unison; **melody**, air, chime, klangfarbenmelodie, lilt, sonance *(Obs.)*, strain, theme, tune; **subject**, countersubject, idea, principal, subsidiary; **musicality**, canorousness, harmoniousness, lyricalness, lyricism, mellifluousness, melodiousness, sweetness, tunefulness; **accompaniment**, alberti bass, backing, bass, basso continuo, basso ostinato, boogie bass, bourdon, burden, continuo, drone, figured bass, ground bass, obbligato, stride piano, thoroughbass, tutti, vamp, walking bass. *See also* SINGING

MUSICAL *adj* consonant, harmonic, perfect; **melodious**, canorous, harmonious, Lydian, lyrical, mellifluous, mellow, Orphean, songful, sweet, tunable *(Archaic)*, tuneful; **melodic**, diapasonic, homophonic, monodic, monophonic; **instrumental**, grand, orchestral, symphonic; **unaccompanied**, secco, solo; **vocal**, choral, choric, lyric, melic, operatic; **treble**, falsetto, piping, reedy; **bass**, continuo; **classical**, baroque, romantic; **jazz**, bottleneck, cool, hep *(U.S.)*, hip *(U.S.)*, honky-tonk; **pop**, calypso; **threnodic**, epicedial, epicedian, threnodial; **rhapsodical**, quodlibetical; **figurate**, florid; **through-composed**, strophic

MUSICAL BAND *n* band, big band, brass band, bush band, combo, concert band, dance band, gumleaf band, jazz band, jug band, military band, one-man band, steel band, string band, troupe, wind band; **group**, beat group, pop group, rock group, super group; **orchestra**, chamber orchestra, palm court orchestra, string orchestra, symphony orchestra; **ensemble**, concertino, duo, nonet, octet, quartet, quintet, septet, sextet, string quartet, trio; **section**, back line, brass, front line, kitchen section, lead guitar, percussion, rhythm guitar, strings, woodwind; **tutti**, ripieno

MUSICAL INSTRUMENT *n* piece, stick; **tuning device**, diapason, fork, monochord, phonoscope, pitchpipe, tonometer, tuning fork. *See also* WIND INSTRUMENT; BRASS INSTRUMENT; STRING INSTRUMENT; PIANO; GUITAR; PERCUSSION INSTRUMENT; ELECTRONIC INSTRUMENT

MUSICALLY *adv* canorously, harmoniously, lyrically, mellifluously, melodiously, rhapsodically, rhythmically, sweetly, tunefully; **polyphonically**, contrapuntally, fugally; **vocally**, chorally, operatically; **tonally**, achromatically, diatonically, harmonically; **atonally**, chromatically, enharmonically

MUSICAL PHRASE *n* figure, phrase, repetend, riff; **passage**, break, episode, fill, middle eight, period; **cadence**, buzz bar, close, feminine cadence, half-cadence, imperfect cadence, interrupted cadence, perfect cadence, plagal cadence; **tone row**, retrograde inversion, row, series; **coda**, codetta, stretta, tag; **slur**, ligature, melisma

MUSICAL PIECE *n* composition, cycle, morceau, movement, opus, opuscule, potboiler, standard, work; **study**, étude, five-finger exercise, gradus; **arrangement**, realisation, rifacimento, setting, transcription, transposition; **fanfare**, bravura, fanfaron, flourish, tucket; **overture**, concert-overture, praeludium, prelude; **interlude**, entr'acte, intermezzo, ritornello, verset *(Archaic)*; **finale**, postlude; **refrain**, chorus, derry, falderal, ritornello, tag; **character piece**, arabesque, bagatelle, ballade, capriccio, caprice, fantasia, humoresque, idyll, impromptu, invention, legende, nocturne, novelette, pastorale, perpetual motion, perpetuo moto, pibroch, potpourri, quodlibet, reverie, rhapsody, romance, scherzo, sketch, toccata. *See also* SONG; OPERA

MUSICAL SCORE *n* charts, chord chart, full score, gradual, head, music, part, prick-song *(Hist.)*, sheet music, short score, top lines, vocal score; **libretto,** book, wordbook; **stave,** bar, double bar, leger line, line, measure *(U.S.),* space, staff; **note,** bind, dot, hook, stem, tail, tie; **direction,** expression mark, fermata, ligature, presa, rest, segno, signature, slur, time signature; **notation,** neumes, solfa, solfège, solfeggio, solmisation, staff notation, tablature, tonic sol-fa

MUSICIAN *n* artiste, concert artist, duettist, executant, muso, performer, sessionman, soloist, studio musician, virtuoso; **jazz player,** bebopper, cat, hepcat, swinger; **rhythmist,** syncopator; **accompanist,** répétiteur, vamper; **tuner,** temperer; **composer,** arranger, contrapuntist, dodecaphonist, harmonist, madrigalist, melodiser, melodist, monodist, scorer, singer-songwriter, songwriter, symphonist, transposer, writer; **hymnologist,** hymnist, hymnodist, psalmist, psalmodist, threnodist; **musicologist; tin-pan alley.** See also INSTRUMENTALIST; SINGER; CONDUCTOR

MUSICIANSHIP *n* articulation, ensemble, execution, feeling, music appreciation, musicality, touch, virtuosity; **musicology,** doctrine of affection, ethnomusicology, harmonics, hymnology, melodics, rhythmics

MUSIC-LOVER *n* audience, concertgoer, listener

MUTINY *n* act of defiance, insurrection, outbreak, rebellion, resistance, revolt, revolution, sedition, unauthorised march, unauthorised stoppage, uprising, violation of the law, wildcat strike

MYTHICAL BEAST *n* androsphinx, basilisk, bunyip, centaur, Cerberus, Charybdis, chimaera, cockatrice, criosphinx, Cyclops, dragon, dragoness, easter bunny, Echidna, Gorgon, Grendel, griffin, gryphon, harpy, hippocampus, hippogriff, Hydra, Kraken, Loch Ness monster, Medusa, Minotaur, monster, monstrosity, Nessie, Pegasus, phoenix, Python, roc, salamander, Scylla, sea-monster, sea-serpent, seahorse, snark, sphinx, unicorn, wampus, wyvern; **abominable snowman,** alma, big-foot *(North America),* sasquatch *(North America),* yeti

MYTHICAL BEING *n* baresark, berserker, hero, superman; **mermaid,** merman, naiad, nereid, nix, nixie, seamaid, undine, water nymph; **Grace,** Aglaia, Euphrosyne, Thalia; **nymph,** dryad, hamadryad, numen, nymphette, oread, satyr, silvan, sylvan, wood nymph, wood spirit; **genie,** djinn, genii, genius, jinn, jinnee; **giant,** Aegir, Argus, Atlas, Brobdingnagian, Cyclops, Fafnir, Fasolt, Gog, Goliath, Heracles, Hercules, Magog, Pantagruel, Polyphemus, Titan. See also FAIRY; PHANTOM

Nn

NAIL *n* brad, ceiling dog, clasp-nail, clout nail, dog nail, dog spike, doornail, drawing-pin, panel pin, skewnail, sparable, spike, sprig, stub nail, tack, tintack; **screw**, dowel screw, grubscrew, Phillips screw, screw-eye, self-tapping screw, setscrew, thumbscrew, woodscrew; **pin**, belaying pin, bodkin, cotter, dowel, forelock, hatpin, headpin, key, kingpin, nog, pintle, safety pin, split pin, stickpin *(U.S.)*, stud, swivel pin, tap-bolt, tiepin, treenail, trunnel, wedge, wristpin; **rivet**, explosive rivet

NAKEDLY *adv* au naturel, en déshabillé, in one's birthday suit, in the altogether, in the bollock, in the bollocky, in the bols, in the buff, in the nick, in the nuddy, in the nude, in the raw, nudely, starkers, starkly

NAME *n* appellation, compellation, courtesy title, handle, honorific, hypocorism, moniker, style, title; **common name**, binomial, homonym *(Biol.)*, polynomial *(Zool. Bot.)*, synonym, tautonym, vernacular, vox barbara; **denomination**, designation, homonym, proper name, tag; **given name**, Christian name, family name, first name, forename, middle name, namesake, pet name, praenomen; **surname**, byname, cognomen, family name, maiden name, metronymic, patronymic; **eponym**, patrial, titular; **nickname**, addition *(Obs.)*, agnomen *(Class. Antiq.)*, byname, cognomen, epithet, sobriquet; **alias**, anonym, bodgie *(Colloq.)*; **pseudonym**, allonym, codename, cryptonym, nom de guerre, nom de plume, pen-name, stage-name; **trade name**, business name, style; **placename**, toponym; **byword**, synonym; **misnomer**; **brand**, label, trade name, trademark

NAME *v* baptise, call, christen, clepe *(Archaic)*, entitle, hypocorise, surname, title; **designate**, codename, denominate, denote, dub, hail, mention, nominate, style, tag, term; **sign**, autograph, endorse, subscribe

NAMED *adj* hight *(Archaic)*, nee, nominate, y-clept *(Archaic)*

NAMER *n* baptiser, denominator, designator, nomenclator; **signer**, endorser

NAMING *n* appellation, baptism, designation; **eponymy**, antonomasia, **onomastics**, toponymy; **nomenclature**, Geneva System, terminology, toponymy *(Anat. Rare)*

NAPPY *n* diaper *(U.S.)*, pilchers, swaddle, swaddling clothes

NARCOTIC *n* ; **heroin** H, hammer, horse, junk, shit, skag, smack, snow; **opium**, laudanum, meconium, opiate, poppy, twang; **morphine**, diacetylmorphine, diamorphine, M, Miss Emma, morph, Morphia; **mandrax**, mandy; **downers**, amytal, barbiturate, codeine, nebbie, nembutal, phenobarb, phenobarbitone, seconal, yellow, yellow jacket. *See also* DRUG

NARRATE *v* chronicle, fable, recite, recount, relate, report, set forth, story *(Rare)*, tell, write; **describe**, delineate, depict, depicture, outline, paint, picture, represent, sketch; **fictional-**

NARRATE ... ise, mythologise, novelise, romance, spin a yarn, yarn

NARRATIVE *n* account, annals, chronicle, history, record, report, statement; **plot**, action, argument, continuity *(Broadcasting)*, counterplot, fable *(Archaic)*, intrigue, scenario, story-line, subplot, synopsis, underplot; **narration**, delineation, depiction, description, picture, portrayal, profile, recital, relation, representation, sketch, voice-over *(Films)*, word-painting. *See also* STORY

NARRATIVE *adj* delineative, depictive, descriptive; **fictional**, anecdotal, anecdotic, legendary, mythical, mythopoeic, romantic

NATION *n* buffer state, city, city-state, commonweal *(Archaic)*, commonwealth, democracy, nation-state, polity, republic, respublica, sovereignty, state; **kingdom**, monarchy, princedom, principality, realm, royalty; **dictatorship**, autocracy, despotism, police state, tyranny; **plutocracy**, pentarchy, tetrarchy, theocracy; **superpower**, atomic power, land power, nuclear power, power, sea-power, superstate, suzerain, world power; **third world country**, banana republic, developing country; **confederation**, bloc, Commonwealth, federation; **empire**, colony, dominion, empery *(Poetic)*, lebensraum; **territory**, condominium, independency, mandate, protectorate, trust territory; **country**, fatherland, land, shore, soil; **homeland**, home, home country, motherland, native land, old country

NATIONAL *n* citizen, compatriot, countryman, patrial; **patriot**, nationalist, stalwart; **jingoist**, chauvinist, mafficker *(Brit.)*, minute man *(U.S.)*, supernationalist

NATIONAL *adj* country, patrial, state, territorial; **supranational**, imperial, metropolitan, supernational; **domestic**, civil, home, inland, interior, internal, intestine; **nationwide**, transnational

NATIONALISM *n* love of country, nationality, patriotism, public spirit, supernationalism; **regionalism**, parochialism, provincialism; **symbol of nationhood**, Anzac, Australia Day, national flag, national song, slouch hat; **jingoism**, chauvinism, flag-wagging, flag-waving; **imperialism**, colonialism, expansionism

NATIONALIST *adj* patriotic, public-spirited; **jingoistic**, chauvinistic, chauvinistic, flag-wagging, flag-waving

NATIONALITY *n* aboriginality, citizenship, compatriotism; **nationhood**, statehood, territoriality

NATIONALLY *adv* domestically, internally, territorially; **patriotically**, chauvinistically, nationalistically, pro patria

NATURAL *adj* innate, instinctive, normal, unformed, unschooled; **primitive**, in a state of nature, native, savage, uncivilised, unlearned; **wild**, feral, ladino, tameless, warrigal, wilding *(Archaic)*, wildish; **undeveloped**, rough, trackless, unimproved, untouched, waste

NATURALIST *n* bionomist, ecologist, physiographer; **nature lover**, conservationist, greenie

NATURALLY *adv* wild; **primitively**, savagely, wildly; **instinctively**, by birth, innately

NATURE *n* the great outdoors, the wild, tiger country, waste, wilderness, wilderness area; **balance of nature**, ecosystem; **ecology**, autecology, bionomics, natural history, natural science, nature study, physic *(Obs.)*, physiography, synecology

NATURE RESERVE *n* chase, flora and fauna reserve, game reserve, national park, sanctuary

NAUSEA *n* airsickness, altitude sickness, Barcoo spews, biliousness, carsickness, jet lag, mal de mer, mawkishness, morning sickness, mountain sickness, nauseousness, regurgitation, seasickness, trainsickness; **indigestion**, dyspepsia, dysphagia, heartburn, hyperacidity, hypoacidity, waterbrash; **stomach-ache**, colic, collywobbles, gripes, painter's colic; **diarrhoea**, amoebic dysentery, bloody flux, dysentery, food poisoning, gastro, gastroenteritis, Jimmy Brits, the runs, the shits, tomtits, trots

NAUSEOUS *adj* airsick, bilious, green at the gills, mawkish, seasick, squeamish, trainsick, upset, warby, white at the gills; **constipated**, costive; **incontinent**; **jacked-up**

NAUTICAL *adj* marine, naval, shipboard; **floating**, afloat, sailing, waterborne; **seaworthy**, A1 at Lloyd's, fit for sea, shipshape and Bristol fashion, watertight; **ocean-going**

NAVIGATION *n* astronavigation, celestial navigation, contact flight, teleran

NEAR *prep* about, around, beside, by, nigh, on, round, towards

NECESSARILY *adv* crucially, indispensably, obligatorily, perforce, requisitely

NECESSARY *adj* indispensable, necessitative, needful, requisite; **essential**, all-important, apodictic, crucial, exigent, imperative, mandatory, obbligato *(Music)*, obligate *(U.S.)*, pressing, urgent, vital; **obligatory**, de rigueur, prerequisite

NECESSITATE *v* ask, call for, claim, demand, need, oblige, require, take, want; **must**, have to, need to, needs must, should; **need**, can do with, could do with, crave

NECESSITIES *n* bare necessities, estovers, necessaries, occasions *(Obs.)*; **need**, call, use, want; **requirement**, essential, exigency, hinge, imperative, must, necessary, postulate, prerequisite, requisite, requisition, sine qua non

NECESSITY *n* compulsion, indispensability, indispensableness, matter of life and death, needfulness, requisiteness, urgency

NECK *n* nape, nucha, scrag, scruff; **throat**, gorge, gullet, little red lane, maw, pharynx; **air passage**, bronchial tubes, bronchiole, bronchus, lung, pipes, trachea, tube, windpipe; **larynx**, Adam's apple, epiglottis, glottis, vocal cords, voice box

NECKWEAR *n* boa, comforter, fichu, fraise, muffler, neckband, neckcloth, neckerchief, neckpiece, ruff; **collar**, bertha, chitterling *(Obs.)*, choker, collaret, collet, dicky, Eton collar, facings, front, guimpe, jabot, lapel, mandarin collar, peter pan collar, revers, roll-collar, stock, Vandyke collar, wing collar; **tie**, black tie, bow tie, choker, cravat, necktie, old school tie, white tie, Windsor tie; **clerical collar**, bands, dog-collar, Geneva bands; **scarf**, babushka, bandanna, barb, fascinator, four-in-hand, kerchief, madras, mantilla, nubia, tippet, victorine; **neckline**, décolletage, halter, halter-neck, polo-neck, scoop neck, turtleneck, V-neck

NEGLECT v default, disregard, evade, forget, forgo *(Archaic)*, leave out, let slide, let slip, not do, omit, overlook, pigeonhole, pretermit, scamp, shut one's eyes to, turn one's back on; **treat neglectfully**, mismother *(Agric.)*; **skim**, cut corners, huddle up, skimp

NEGLECTED adj derelict, in limbo, ragged, run-down, undone *(Archaic)*

NEGLECTED PERSON n cinderella, gamin, grass widow, gutter-snipe, latchkey child, mudlark *(Brit.)*, street Arab, street urchin, urchin

NEGLECTFUL adj careless, casual, disregardful, dizzy, forgetful, heedless, lax, mindless, negligent, omissive, regardless, slack, slipshod, thoughtless; **irresponsible**, delinquent, derelict, reckless, remiss

NEGLECTFULLY adv delinquently, forgetfully, heedlessly, laxly, mindlessly, negligently, thoughtlessly; **carelessly**, any way, anyhow, casually, hastily, raggedly, recklessly, slack, slackly

NEGLECTFULNESS n carelessness, casualness, forgetfulness, hastiness, heedlessness, irresponsibility, irresponsibleness, laxness, mindlessness, recklessness, remissness, slackness, thoughtlessness; **negligence**, delinquency, disregard, evasion, mismothering *(Agric.)*, preterition, pretermission, waste *(Law)*; **neglect**, conduct conducing, default, dereliction, lapse, laxity, miss *(Colloq.)*, nonfeasance, omission; **laches**, res ipsa loquitur

NEGLIGIBLY adv inconsiderably, infinitesimally, microscopically, vestigially; **scantily**, exiguously, skimpily, slightly, sparingly, sparsely; **merely**, alone, only, simply; **at least**, in the least; **just**, by degrees, by inches, by the skin of one's teeth, hardly; **in a nutshell**, in miniature

NERVOUS SYSTEM n autonomic nervous system, central nervous system, parasympathetic nervous system, peripheral nervous system, sympathetic nervous system; **nerve**, axon, dendrite, funiculus, ganglion, nerve fibre, pathway, reflex arc, synapse, tract

NEUTRAL n abstainer, civilian, fence-sitter, isolationist, moderate, mugwump, neuter *(Archaic)*, neutralist, non-belligerent, non-combatant

NEUTRAL adj apathetic, apolitical, detached, disinterested, even-handed, impartial, indifferent, neuter *(Archaic)*, non-aligned, non-committal, non-involved, non-partisan, uncommitted

NEUTRALITY n abstention, apathy, detachment, disinterestedness, even-handedness, impartiality, indifference, isolation, isolationism, lack of involvement, neutralism, nonaggression, non-alignment, non-involvement; **neutral country**, neutral territory, no-man's-land, open city

NEUTRALLY adv disinterestedly, impartially

NEVERTHELESS adv all the same, anyhow, anyway, howbeit, however, just the same, non obstante, nonetheless, notwithstanding, regardless, still, though, withal *(Archaic)*, yet

NEW *adj* brand-new, fresh, green, hot, mint, new-laid, piping hot, red-hot, spick-and-span, unworn, virgin, virginal; **emergent**, nascent, newly-formed, promising, raw, renascent, revivescent, up-and-coming; **first**, initial, maiden, pioneer; **young**, fledgling, immature, junior, newish, redbrick *(Brit.)*, untried, youngish; **inventive**, creative, enactory *(Law)*, initiatory

NEWLY *adv* emergently, fresh, freshly, new, virginally; **modernly**, neoterically, not long ago, recently, swingingly; **innovatively**, for the first time, inspiritingly, novelly, originally, unprecedentedly

NEWNESS *n* change, curiousness, freshness, new look, novelty; **modernity**, modernism, modernness, recency, recentness, up-to-dateness

NEWS *n* information, intelligence, sound *(Obs.)*, tidings; **rumour**, ana, blue duck, bruit *(Archaic)*, buzz, dirt, gossip, hearsay, noise *(Archaic)*, renown *(Obs.)*, tale, talk, tattle, whisper; **bulletin**, announcement, communiqué, dispatch, handout, press conference, press release; **the latest**, stop press, the score; **gossiping**, tale-bearing, taletelling

NEWS ITEM *n* a good spread, beat-up, cover story, exclusive, feature story, flash, item, leading article, personal *(U.S.)*, report, scoop, sensation, story, write-up; **newscast**, newsreel; **column**, editorial, gossip column, leader; **advertisement**, headline, banner, caption, head, side heading, streamer

NEWSPAPER *n* biweekly, blatt, broadsheet, buster *(N.Z. Obs.)*, daily, extra, final, gazette, journal, kite *(Colloq.)*, local, mouthpiece, news-sheet, newsletter, organ, paper, print, publication, rag, semiweekly, sheet, softcover, supplement, tabloid, triweekly, weekly; **comic**, feuilleton, funnies, horror comic, strip; **fourth estate**, press, print media, print press, the daily blatts, yellow press

NICHE *n* alcove, ambry, angle, apse, apsis, bay window, cockpit, columbarium, conch, inglenook, nook, pigeonhole, recess, set-off, setback, tabernacle; **socket**, caisson, groove, mortice, rebate. See also HOLLOW

NIGHT *n* weeknight; **night-time**, dead of night, graveyard shift *(Mining Colloq.)*, midnight, moonrise, overnight, the witching hour; **the small hours**, piccaninny daylight. See also EVENING

NIGHTLY *adj* acronychal, all-night, nightlong, noctivagant, nocturnal, overnight, owl-like, owlish; **midnight**, midnightly; **evening**, goodnight, vesper, vespertine; **twilight**, crepuscular, duskish, moonlight

NIGHTLY *adv* all night, midnightly, nightlong, nights, nocturnally, overnight, under the stars

NIGHT OWL *n* all-nighter, night-bird, nighthawk, nightwalker, owl

NIGHTWEAR *n* nightclothes; **dressing-gown**, bathrobe, beach robe, brunch coat, negligee, nightrobe, peignoir, robe, shave coat, shaving coat, shaving jacket; **pyjamas**, jamas, jamies, nightdress, nightgown, nightrobe, nightshirt, P.J.s

NINE *n* ennead, ninth, nonet; **nonagon**, enneagon

NINE *adj* enneadic, ninefold, ninth, nonagonal

no

NO *interj* like hell, nae *(Scot.)*, nary *(U.S. Brit.)*, nay, never, nix, no such luck, no way, nope, not a bit of it, not by a long sight, not for quids, not on your life, noway, nowise, scarcely; **pigs,** baal *(Aborig.)*, balls, like fun, not on your nelly, nuts, phooey, speak for yourself, up you, upya

NOISE ABROAD *v* bruit, herald, noise, retail; **gossip,** chew the fat, fly a kite, rumour; **tattle,** inform on, pimp, tell tales

NOISY *adj* blustery, boisterous, bouncing, hurly-burly, obstreperous, pandemoniac, pandemonic, pell-mell, rackety, rambunctious *(U.S. Colloq.)*, riotous, rip-roaring, roisterous, rumbustious, tumultuary, tumultuous, unquiet, uproarious

NONACHIEVER *n* cipher, disaster area, failure, gutless wonder, no-hoper, nonentity, underachiever; **dud,** crookie, dead duck, debacle, disaster, lost cause; **loser,** also-ran, autumn leaf *(Horseracing Colloq.)*, bad shot, booby, easybeats, ferret *(Cricket)*, flop, hairy goat, lapser, non-starter, stiff *(Horseracing)*

NON-BEING *n* inexistence, inexistency, non-existence, nonentity, nullity; **nothingness,** absence, blank, blankness, negation, nihility, nowhere, vacuum, void, voidness; **insubstantiality,** abstractness, intangibility, intangibleness, invisibility, nebulousness, the intangible; **annihilation,** abolition, abrogation, annulment, defeasance, dematerialisation, destruction, disannulment, elimination, erasure, expunction, extermination, extinction, genocide, obliteration, removal. *See also* NOTHING

nonconformity

NONCONFORMIST *n* beat, beatnik, bodgie, bohemian, drop-out, flower-child, hippie, hipster, long-hair, Promethean, sharpie; **eccentric,** a one, bird, card, case, caution, character, crank, dag, ding-a-ling, dingbat, enfant terrible, erratic, freak, fruit cake, geezer, half-axe, hangman *(N.Z.)*, kook, nut, nut case, odd bod, odd-ball, original, poon, queer fish, rat-bag, screwball, wack, weirdo; **deviant,** bent, deviate *(U.S.)*, pervert; **radical,** angry young man, Bolshevik *(Derog.)*, dissenter, extremist, iconoclast, rebel, Red, reformist; **misfit,** fish out of water, no-hoper, square peg in a round hole; **exception,** curiosity, freak, heteroclite, irregular, odd one out, oddity, rarity; **bohemia,** beat generation, beautiful people, cafe society, demimonde, hip-hop culture, the Push

NONCONFORMIST *adj* anomalous, heteroclite, heterodox, informal, irregular, non-standard, nonconforming, unconformable, uncustomary, unorthodox, unusual; **exceptional,** extraordinary, tremendous, unexampled, unheard-of, unique; **aberrant,** aberational, abnormal, bent, deviant, freakish, kinky, perverted, quirky, unnatural; **eccentric,** bizarre, crank, cranky, crazy, daggish, daggy, erratic, kooky, mad as a meataxe, maggoty, odd, odd-bod, oddball, off-beat, pixilated, queer, ratbaggy, ratty, screwy, singular, wacky, way-out; **unconventional,** alternative, beat, bohemian, unfashionable; **radical,** bold, iconoclastic, reformist

NONCONFORMITY *n* bohemianism, disconformity, inconformity, informality, irregularity, licence, nonconformance, unconventionality, unfashionability, unfashionableness; **eccentricity**, craziness, oddness, queerness, singularity, singularness; **aberrance**, aberrancy, abnormality, deviance, deviancy, deviation, kinkiness, unnaturalness; **radicalness**, boldness, dissent, heresy, heterodoxy, iconoclasm, progressiveness, rebellion, unorthodoxy; **exceptionalness**, extraordinariness, tremendousness, uniqueness

NONEXISTENT *adj* absent, blank, extinct, inexistent, missing, napoo, unhistorical; **intangible**, abstract, insubstantial, invisible, metempiric, theoretical, unessential, virtual; **no**, none *(Archaic)*, null

NONFLAMMABILITY *n* athermancy, fire-resistance, incombustibility; **fireproof clothing**, asbestos suit, fire blanket

NONFLAMMABLE *adj* athermanous, fireproof, fire-resistant, flame-proof, incombustible, thermoduric

NON-PAYING *adj* bankrupt, behind, behindhand, broken, gazetted, in arrears, insolvent, ruined, unable to make both ends meet, unable to pay

NON-PAYMENT *n* avoidance, default, dishonour, evasion, moonlight flit, repudiation; **tax avoidance**, bottom-of-the-harbour scheme, dry Slutzkin, tax dodge, tax evasion, tax evasion scheme, tax haven, tax lurk, tax shelter, underground economy, wet Slutzkin; **bankruptcy**, bust, failure, insolvency, insufficiency of funds, overdrawn account, receivership

NONSENSE *n* abracadabra, babble, bizzo, blah, blather, chatter, double-dutch, fable, fandangle, fiddle-faddle, fiddlesticks, flapdoodle, flim-flam, flummery, footle, froth and bubble, fustian, gaff *(Rare)*, gas, Greek, guff, gunk, guyver, hocus pocus, hokum *(U.S.)*, hooey, jabber, jabberwocky, jargon, kid-stakes, macaroni, malarky, mere words, moonshine, mumbo jumbo, pack of nonsense, palaver, pap, patter, persiflage, rant, rave, rhubarb, rigmarole, slipslop, sound and fury, stuff and nonsense, tarraddiddle, tongue, tosh, trash, tripe, trumpery, twaddle, verbiage, waffle, yak, yawp; **absurdity**, amphigory, bagatelle, contradiction, exaggeration, imbecility, inanity, inconsistency, paradox, platitude, quibble, sophism, triviality, vagueness, verbalism; **nonsense verse**, derry; **tomfoolery**, jiggery-pokery, monkey tricks, mummery, practical joke, shenanigans; **bullshit**, a load of old cobblers, balderdash, balls, baloney, bilge, bollocks, bosh, bull, bulldust, bullo, bullswool, bumf, bunk, bunkum, claptrap, cock-and-bull, codswallop, crap, drivel, eyewash, farmyard confetti, Flemington confetti, fudge, gammon, gammon and spinach, garbage, gibberish, heifer dust, hogwash, horseshit *(U.S.)*, hot cock, kybosh, piffle, poppycock, rot, rubbish, shit, tommyrot

NONSENSICAL *adj* absurd, cockeyed, crappy, extravagant, fantastic, foolish, inconsistent, jumbled, macaronic *(Obs.)*, paradoxical, piffling, preposterous, rich, ridiculous, sophistical, too-too; **meaningless**, amphigoric, insignificant, moonshiny, pointless, senseless, unmeaning, without rhyme or reason; **inconsequential**, babbly, farcical, flim-flam, futile, gassy, incoherent, inconsequent, quibbling, raving, rubbishy, windy

NONSENSICALLY *adv* absurdly, incoherently, inconsequentially, inconsequently, jabberingly, meaninglessly, paradoxically, pointlessly, ridiculously, senselessly, unmeaningly

NON-USER *n* boycotter, discarder, rejecter, shepherd, sparer

NOON *n* lunchtime, mean noon, midday, midnoon, noonday, noontide, noontime

NOSE *n* beak, boko, bracket, bugle, button, conk, hooter, nozzle, proboscis, schnozzle, smeller, snoot, snout, snoz; **nostrils**, nares, olfactories

NOSTALGIA *n* **retrospectivity** retroactivity, retrospect, retrospection, review; **flashback**, repeat, replay; **time machine**

NOTCHED *adj* biserrate, crenate, crenulated, deckle-edged, dentate, denticulate, double serrate, fringed, knurled, ridged, scalloped, serrate, serrated, serriform, serrulate, toothed, warded; **indented**, broken, erose, etched, gnawed away, gorgy, grooved, gullied, incised, valleyed

NOTHING *n* aught *(Obs.)*, bugger all, damn-all, F.A., fuck-all, naught *(Archaic)*, nihil, nil, nix, no-one, not a sausage, not hide nor hair, nought, nowt, s.f.a., sweet F.A., zilch; **zero**, duck *(Cricket)*, duck's egg *(Cricket)*, love *(Tennis)*. *See also* NON-BEING

NOTIONAL *adj* conceptual, ideal, ideate, ideational, inspirational, intellective

NOTIONALLY *adv* conceptually, ideally, ideationally

NOTWITHSTANDING *prep* after all, despite, for all, in despite of, in spite of, in the face of

NOVICE *n* beginner, greenhorn, raw recruit; **amateur**, calf, dabbler, dilettante, dilutee, landlubber *(Naut.)*, landsman, lilywhite *(Sport)*, lubber, potterer, tinkerer

NOW *adv* at present, at the present moment, at this point in time, before one's very eyes, currently, here and now, just now, nowadays, presently, still, under one's very eyes; **as of now**, for the nonce, for the time being, in the short run; **directly**, outright, right, straight; **today**, nowadays, tonight; **to date**, as yet; **already**, yet; **immediately**, anon *(Archaic)*, at once, on the spur of the moment, right away, straightaway, straightway

NO WORRIES *interj* no problem, no probs, no sweat

NUCLEAR ENERGY *n* atomic energy, atomic power, nuclear power; **nuclear reactor**, atomic pile, boiling-water reactor, breeder, breeder reactor, converter, fast breeder reactor, fast reactor, fusion reactor, nuke *(U.S. Colloq.)*, pile, power reactor, pressurised water reactor, production reactor, propulsion reactor, reactor, thermal reactor, ZETA; **nuclear core**, absorber, lattice, moderator, reflector; **particle accelerator**, accelerator, atom-smasher, betatron, cosmotron, cyclotron, doughnut, electronuclear machine, stellarator, storage ring, synchrotron, tokomak. *See also* ATOMIC RADIATION; RADIOACTIVATION; ATOMIC BOMB

NUDIST *n* artiste, disrober, jaybird, naturist, skinny-dipper, streaker, stripper; **nude**, beefcake, centrefold, cheesecake, full-frontal, pin-up

NUMBER *n* digit, figure, value; **numeral**, chapter *(Horol.)*, cipher, lining figure *(Print.)*, modern figure *(Print.)*; **integer**, binary digit, binary number, natural number, perfect number, whole number; **cardinal number,** ordinal number; **decimal number,** compound number, decimal fraction, floating point number, half-integer, mixed number, real number, recurring decimal, repeating decimal, transcendental; **imaginary number,** complex number, composite number; **prime number,** square number; **surd,** irrational number; **variable,** dependent variable, independent variable, unknown, X; **constant,** invariable, invariant; **absolute value,** magnitude, modulus; **factor,** common factor, divisor, submultiple; **coefficient,** regression coefficient; **square,** cube, exponential, factorial, root mean square; **square root,** cube root, root; **mathematical function,** binomial, expression, form, formula, integral, polynomial, potential, quadratic, quadrinomial, quantic, quintic, step function, trinomial; **mathematical series,** arithmetic progression, geometric progression, harmonic progression, time series; **continuum,** domain, field; **number element,** characteristic, decimal place, decimal point, exponent, mantissa, repetend, significant figures; **fraction,** common fraction, complex fraction, compound fraction, continued fraction, improper fraction, proper fraction, recurring fraction, simple fraction, vulgar fraction; **denominator,** common denominator, lowest common denominator; **numerator**

NUMBER *v* numerate; **paginate,** foliate, folio, page

NUMBERING *n* foliation, numeration, pagination

NUMBER SYSTEM *n* binary notation, binary number system, binary scale, decimal system, duodecimal system, hexadecimal system, octal system; **Arabic numerals,** aleph-nought, aleph-null, aleph-zero, algorism, cipher, Roman numerals; **numerical set,** network, sequence, subordinate set, subsequence, subset, system, tree; **arithmetic scale,** reflexive relation, relation, sliding scale; **numerology;** **numeracy**

NUMERATE *adj* good at figure-work

NUMERICAL *adj* alphanumeric, numeral, numerary, numeric; **integral,** digital, prime, round, whole; **real;** **fractional,** half-integral, rational; **imaginary,** even, odd; **negative,** positive, subtractive; **exponential,** differential, irrational, logarithmic, logometric; **cardinal,** ordinal; **decimal,** binary, duodecimal, duodenary, hexadecimal, octal, quinary, sexagesimal, uncial, undecimal; **submultiple,** aliquant *(Obs.)*, aliquot *(Obs.)*; **reciprocal,** complementary

NUMERICALLY *adv* by numbers, in numbers; **alphanumerically,** in numbers and letters

NUMEROUSNESS *n* innumerability, innumerableness, multiplicity, pluralism, plurality; **abundance,** affluence, ampleness, amplitude, copiousness, plenteousness, plentifulness, profusion, thickness; **multitudinousness,** manifoldness, many-sidedness, multifariousness

NURSERY *n* creche, day nursery, kindergarten

NUTRITIONALLY *adv* alimentally, dietetically, gastronomically, nutritively, tropically

NUTRITIVE *adj* alible, alimental, alimentative, nutrient, nutritional, sustentative, trophic

Oo

OBEDIENCE *n* compliance, deference, non-resistance, observance, observation *(Obs.)*, passiveness, passivity, subjection, submission; **dutifulness**, ductility, duteousness, duty, fealty, homage, loyalty, obsequiousness, orderliness, servility, submissiveness, towardliness *(Archaic)*, tractability, yieldingness; **compulsion**, domination, enforcement

OBEDIENT *adj* compliant, devoted, obsequious *(Rare)*, puppet, servile, yielding; **dutiful**, duteous, faithful, law-abiding, leal *(Archaic)*, loyal, observant, orderly; **tractable**, controllable, docile, guidable, henpecked, non-resistant, passive, pliant, subservient, towardly *(Archaic)*, under control

OBEDIENTLY *adv* compliantly, observantly; **dutifully**, duteously, loyally; **tractably**, yieldingly; **in compliance with**, at one's beck and call

OBEY *v* do someone's bidding, do what one is told, follow, follow someone's lead, grovel, jump through hoops, play second fiddle, serve, submit, toe the line; **comply**, answer the helm, carry out, carry out orders, clear *(Naut.)*, comply with, defer to, fulfil, heed, keep, mind, observe, shape up or ship out

OBEYER *n* clean potato, complier, follower, non-resistant, observant, observer; **yes-man**, arse-licker, brown-nose, lackey, puppet, slave, stooge, teacher's pet

OBLIGATE *v* astrict, bind, oblige, tie; **be one's duty to**, be incumbent on, be up to, befit, behove, devolve, fall to one's lot, import, rest in, rest on, rest upon, rest with; **be obligated**, had better, have got to, ought, should

OBLIGATED *adj* beholden, bound, duty-bound, fain *(Archaic)*, in duty bound, obligate *(U.S.)*, obliged, under a compliment to someone, under an obligation to someone; **liable**, accountable, amenable, answerable, charged, responsible, saddled with

OBLIGATION *n* bounden duty, charge, devoir *(Archaic)*, duty, incumbency, onus, ought, responsibility; **bond**, agreement, astriction, band, call of duty, categorical imperative, contract, faith, personal responsibility, tie, trust, white man's burden; **liability**, burden *(Comm.)*, judgment *(Law)*, levy, service due, tax, tithe, tribute, vassalage; **job**, assignment, calling, commission, function, mission, office, part, role, task, undertaking, vocation; **quota**, darg, production target

OBLIGATORILY *adv* bindingly, incumbently, irremissibly; **on one's own responsibility**, at one's own risk, on one's hands, upon one's own head

OBLIGATORY *adj* binding, bounden, de rigueur, imperative, incumbent, irremissible, necessary, obliging, peremptory *(Law)*, required

OBSCENE *adj* blue, filthy, foul, ithyphallic, lascivious, lewd, licentious, pornographic, rank, ripe, salacious, scabrous, scatalogical, thersitical, vile; **vulgar**, bawdy, broad, Corinthian, Cyprian, dirty, earthy,

Fescennine, fruity, Rabelaisian, racy, raffish, rakish, randy, ribald, salty, smutty; **suggestive,** borderline, close to the bone, close to the knuckle, daring, juicy, naughty, near the bone, near the knuckle, risqué, spicy, titillating; **erotic,** hot, phallic, priapic, sexy; **indecent,** coarse, curious, indecorous, off-colour; **unprintable,** unrepeatable, unspeakable; **foul-minded,** foul-mouthed, prurient, voyeuristic; **immodest,** flaunting, revealing, scarlet, shameless

OBSCENITY *n* bawdiness, filthiness, foulness, lasciviousness, lewdness, obsceneness, profanity, rankness, salaciousness, scabrousness, vileness; **indecency,** bawdry, coarseness, dirtiness, ribaldry, vulgarness, wantonness; **foul-mindedness,** prurience, scopophilia, skeptophilia, voyeurism; **suggestiveness,** earthiness, raciness, raffishness, smuttiness; **immodesty,** impudicity, indecorousness, shamelessness; **impureness,** impurity, unchasteness; **dirty word,** four-letter word, vulgarism. *See also* PORNOGRAPHY

OBSCURE *v* black out, blot, darken, darkle, fog, hide

OBSEQUIOUS *adj* menial, parasitic, servile, slavish, slimy, smarmy, sycophantic, toadyish, wormlike, wormy; **submissive,** acquiescent, amenable, compliant, concessionary, concessive, corrigible, deferent, deferential, ductile, easily managed, flexible, manageable, obedient, pliant, tractable, yielding; **bowed,** broken, browbeaten, cowed, crushed, downtrodden, henpecked, humbled, prostrate, subjective *(Obs.)*

OBSEQUIOUSLY *adv* cap in hand, deferentially, in obedience to, meekly, menially, slavishly, slimily, subserviently, tamely, trucklingly; **submissively,** acquiescingly, amenably, compliably, compliantly, corrigibly, flexibly, in compliance with, on bended knee, resignedly, yieldingly

OBSEQUIOUSNESS *n* humbleness, self-abasement, servility, slavishness, sliminess, submissiveness, subservience, subserviency, suppleness; **deference,** genuflection, homage, kowtow, obeisance, prostration, salaam, slime, smarm; **sycophancy,** toadyism

OBSERVATORY *n* tracking station; **celestial globe,** orrery, planetarium, planisphere, zodiac

OBSTACLE *n* barrier, baulk, block, hurdle, stop, traverse; **barricade,** abatis, balloon barrage, barbed wire, barrage, blockade, booby trap, caltrop, cheval-de-frise, concertina wire, fence, gabionade, trou-de-loup, wire entanglement; **gate,** cattle ramp, cattlegrid, cattlestop *(N.Z.)*, portcullis, turnpike, turnstile; **roadblock,** boom gate, humps, judder bar *(N.Z.)*, speed bumps, speed-trap, tollbar; **crash barrier,** bollard, guardrail; **dam,** boom, breakwater, dyke, embankment, sandbank, sandbar, sudd, weir; **chock,** doorstop, floor stop, trig, wedge; **deflector,** baffle, baffle plates, breakweather, breakwind, stopping *(Mining)*, windbreak; **airlock,** airtrap, P trap, vapour lock; **bunker,** hazard, sandtrap; **jump,** crossbar, fence *(Showjumping)*, oxer, waterjump; **obstacle race,** debil-debil country, obstacle course. *See also* HINDRANCE

OBSTRUCT v intercept, interpose, obtrude; **block**, arrest, bar, barricade, blockade, close, dam, embank, hedge in, snow in, stop; **choke**, clog, congest, foul, gorge, gum up, jam, occlude, oppilate, stop up; **chock**, trig, wedge; **bunker**, trap; **bodycheck**, backstop, box in, hem in. *See also* HINDER

OBSTRUCTED *adj* air-bound, choked, clogged, congested, fitchered, icebound, impassable, insurmountable, snowbound; **blocked off**, barricaded, dead-end; **frustrated**, confounded, dished, stopped

OBSTRUCTIVENESS *n* bloody-mindedness, obstructionism; **interference**, forestalment, interception, interposal, interposition, interruption, mental block; **prevention**, forbiddance *(Rare)*, limitation, preclusion, restriction; **discouragement**, crossing, frustration, oppilation, thwarting; **cumbrousness**, awkwardness, unwieldiness

OBVIOUS *adj* apparent, appreciable, black-and-white, broad, clean-cut, clear, clear as day, clear-cut, distinct, evident, in the foreground, manifest, notable, noticeable, palpable, pellucid, plain, plain as a pikestaff, plain as the nose on your face, unmistakable, vivid; **conspicuous**, outstanding, prominent, pronounced, salient, splendent, striking, under one's nose; **glaring**, flagrant, notorious, shroudless, unshaded; **self-evident**, axiomatic, incontestable, self-explanatory, truistic

OBVIOUSLY *adv* appreciably, clear, clearly, evidently, in evidence, manifestly, noticeably, palpably, plainly; **conspicuously**, prominently, pronouncedly; **self-evidently**, axiomatically

OBVIOUSNESS *n* apparentness, clearness, conspicuousness, manifestness, palpability, prominence; **truism**, axiom, self-evidence

OCCULTIST *n* cabbalist, demonologist, occulter, pythoness, Rosicrucian, shaman, sibyl, sorcerer, sorceress, spiritist, spiritualist, supernaturalist, warlock, witch, wizard; **mind-reader**, telepath, telepathist, thought-reader; **medium**, clairaudient, clairsentient, clairvoyant, evocator, necromancer, oracle, psychic, seer, spirit-rapper, spiritist; **demoniac**, energumen, zombie

OCCUPANT *n* cotenant, homesteader, householder, leaseholder, occupier, tenant; **home-maker**, homebody; **household**, family, ménage; **cohabitant**, cohabitator, flatmate, inmate *(Archaic)*; **lodger**, boarder, hosteller, paying guest, roomer *(U.S.)*; **guest**, commensal, sojourner, visitor. *See also* INHABITANT; POPULATION

OCCUR *v* arise, arrive *(Obs.)*, be, break out, brew, come about, come one's way, come to pass, come up, fall, give, hap *(Archaic)*, happen, offer, pop up, rise, see the light of day, take place, transpire, turn up; **bechance**, befall, betide, come over, worth *(Archaic)*; **turn out**, come off, fall out, fare, go off, go on, pass off, prove

OCCURRENCE *n* circumstance, contingency, contingent, episode, event, experience, hap *(Archaic)*, happening, incident, occasion, passage *(Archaic)*, phenomenon; **incidence**, advent, incurrence, occasion. *See also* AFFAIR; SITUATION

OCCURRENT *adj* actual, afoot, emergent, going, happening, in progress, incidental, occasional, occurring, on, passing, up; **phenomenal**, empirical, experiential, experimental, practical

OCEANOGRAPHER *n* aquarist, hydrographer, oceanaut, thalassographer

OCEANOGRAPHIC *adj* oceanographical, thalassographic

OCEANOGRAPHY *n* aquiculture, bathometry, hydrography, marine biology, oceanics, thalassography

ODOURLESS *adj* inodorous, scentless; **deodorant; anosmatic**

ODOURLESSNESS *n* freshness, inodourousness, lack of smell, ring of confidence, scentlessness; **deodorisation; deodoriser**, activated charcoal, deodorant; **anosmia**, inability to smell

OFFER *n* bid, overbid, proffer, proposal, proposition, psychic bid *(Bridge)*, tender, underbid; **recommendation**, suggestion; **approach**, feeler, opener, overture; **formal proposal**, motion; **last offer**, ultimatum

OFFER *v* bargain, bid, extend, give, hold out, overbid, tender, underbid; **propose**, advance, hawk an idea, initiate, lay a plan before, make a suggestion, move a motion, present, project, proposition, propound, put forward, put up, raise a matter, sponsor, submit, suggest; **make an overture**, approach, launch, make oneself available, offer oneself, overture, put oneself at another's disposal, sound out, stand for, volunteer; **proposition**, crack onto, put the hard word on *(Colloq.)*; **advocate**, recommend, stand for; **toast**

OFFERER *n* bidder, presenter, tenderer; **proposer**, proponent, propounder, sponsor; **bargainer**, underbidder

OFFERING *n* candidature, presentation, presentment; **launching**, sponsorship; **bidding**, calling; **oblation**, propitiation, sacrifice

OFFICE *n* boardroom, chamber, chancellery, composing room, confined space, consulting room, counting room, headquarters, operations room, orderly room, registry, registry office, salesroom, studio, surgery, tally-room

OFFICIALLY *adv* authoritatively, ex cathedra, from the horse's mouth; **in the name of**, by the authority of, in virtue of

OFF ONE'S GUARD *adv* on the hop, unawares, with one's pants down

OFFSPRING *n* family, fruit of the womb, generation, increase, issue, posterity, progeny, seed, team *(Obs.)*, young; **scion**, cadet, clone, daughter, descendant, firstborn, firstling, hybrid, mongrel, offshoot, pigeon pair, son, sprig, sprout; **twin**, quad, quadruplet, quintuplet, sextuplet, triplet; **illegitimate**, basket *(Euph.)*, bastard, by-blow, git, love child, whoreson *(Obs.)*; **orphan**, orphanage *(Archaic)*; **baby**, a little stranger, baba, bairn, blue baby, bottle baby, bub, infant, neonate, nursling, papoose, premmie, test-tube baby, the little stranger, war baby; **toddler**, mite, tot. *See also* CHILD; ANIMAL OFFSPRING

OH *interj* bejesus, blimey, boy, by George, by gum *(Brit.)*, coo *(Brit.)*, cor, crikey, cripes, dear, egad, God almighty, gorblimey, gosh, gracious, gramercy *(Archaic)*, Great Scott, ha-ha, hello, heyday *(Archaic)*, ho, hot dog *(U.S.)*, I say, jeepers creepers *(U.S.)*, Jesus, jiminy, jingaloes, lord, marry *(Archaic)*, my, my word, oops, struth, the dickens, well, what, whoops, why, woops, yikes, yow. See also HOW ABOUT THAT

OIL *n* aromatic oil, fixed oil, oleoresin, volatile oil

OIL *v* grease, lubricate; **butter,** lard; **anoint,** baste

OILILY *adv* greasily, oily, soapily

OILINESS *n* greasiness, lubricity, oleaginousness, pinguidity, unctuosity, unctuousness; **fattiness,** adiposeness, adiposity, fatness

OILWELL *n* gusher, step-out, step-out well; **grasspay sandstone**

OILY *adj* greasy, lubricous, slick, slippery, soapy; **unctuous,** balsamic, chrismal, oleaginous, unguinous; **lubricant,** antifriction, lubricative; **fatty,** buttery, butyraceous, fat, lardaceous, lardlike, lardy, pinguescent, pinguid, stearic; **mono-unsaturated,** polyunsaturated; **adipose,** blubbery; **sebaceous,** waxy

OLD *adj* aboriginal, age-old, ancient, antediluvian, antemundane, antique, as old as Adam, as old as Methuselah, as old as the hills, fossil, fossil-like, original, out of the ark, preadamite, preglacial, prehistoric, primitive, primordial, pristine; **immemorial,** long-gone, of yore, olden *(Archaic)*; **outmoded,** antiquated, archaic, archaistic, behind the times, dated, demoded, discontinued, extinct, moss-grown, obsolescent, obsolete, out of date, out of fashion, outdated, passé, slow, square, steam *(Colloq.)*; **vintage,** antique, classic, classical, dateless, former, rancio, ripe, veteran; **timeworn,** crumbling, decayed, decrepit, moth-eaten, threadbare; **burnt out,** beat-up, clapped-out; **stale,** fusty, mouldy, mucid, musty, rancid; **second-hand,** hand-me-down, preloved, pre-owned, third-hand

OLDNESS *n* agedness, anecdotage, antiqueness, elderliness, hoariness, old age; **great age,** ancientness, antiquarianism, antiquity, archaism, classicality, classicism, medievalism; **ageing,** fossilisation; **decrepitude,** obsolescence, primitiveness, ruin; **staleness,** fustiness, mouldiness, mucidness, mustiness, rancidity, rancidness

OLD PEOPLE *n* Dad's army, old guard, older generation, the aged, the ageing, the old; **old person,** ancient, antediluvian, dotard, fogram, fossil, geri, geriatric, has-been, methuselah, museum piece, old bird, old crock, old fogy, old identity, old stager, old thing, oldie, oldster, relic, senior, senior citizen, wrinklie; **old man,** colonel blimp, father, gaffer *(Brit.)*, grandsire, grey beard, old boy, old codger, old fellow, old-timer, whitebeard; **old woman,** beldam, biddy, carline *(Scot.)*, crone, dame, gammer *(Brit. Archaic)*, grandam, granny, grimalkin, hag, harpy, mother, old boiler, old chook, old girl, old maid; **elder,** doyen, elder statesman, grand old man, matriarch, Nestor, patriarch; **centenarian,** nonagenarian, octogenarian, quinquagenarian, septuagenarian, sexagenarian

OMEN *n* augury, auspice, boding, foreboding, forerunner, forewarning, harbinger, herald, portent, presage, prodigy *(Rare)*, sign, signifier, type, writing on the wall; **harbinger of evil,**

death knell, premonition of death, time bomb; **destiny,** fate, fortune

ON BEHALF OF *prep* for, in the name of; **by,** of *(Archaic)*

ON BENDED KNEE *adv* on all fours, on hands and knees, on one's haunches

ON CONDITION THAT *conj* and *(Archaic),* as, as long as, if, on the understanding that, provided, provided that, providing, so as, so long as, so that *(Obs.),* sobeit *(Archaic),* though; **unless,** except *(Archaic),* excepting *(Archaic),* lest, nisi, save *(Archaic),* without *(Brit. Colloq.);* **if and only if,** iff *(Logic)*

ON CREDIT *adv* on account, on H.P., on hire-purchase, on lay-by, on the never-never, on the nod, on tick

ON DISPLAY *adv* demonstratively, for all to see, from the housetops, in the open, on show, on view, open to the public, openly, publicly; **manifestly,** blatantly, obviously, patently

ONE *n* ace, ane *(Scot.);* **single item,** monad, none other than, odd, odd one, one-off, singleton, solo, the one and only, unicum *(Rare),* unit; **individual,** one, one-man band, one-man show, soloist; **loner,** crusoe, hatter, Jimmy Woodser, lone wolf, odd man out

ONE *adj* a, an, ane *(Scot.),* any, unit, unitarian, unitary; **single,** exclusive, individual, mere *(Law),* only, only-begotten, singular, sole, unique; **unilateral,** azygous, haploid, unipolar; **unifying,** unific; **lone,** insular, one-out, single-handed, solitary, solo, unaccompanied, unattended

ONE *pron* ane *(Scot.),* any, each

ONENESS *n* conjugation, conjunction, ecumenicalism, identicalness, identity, indivisibility, indivisibleness, solidarity, unification, unity; **singleness,** aloneness, exclusiveness, individuality, oddness, solitariness, unicity, uniqueness; **loneliness,** isolation, seclusion, solitude

ON FOOT *adv* afoot, on footback, on shanks's pony

ONLY *adv* solely; **once,** for the nonce

ON THE MOVE *adv* on the go, on the wing, under way, under weigh *(Naut.),* up and about; **to and fro,** back and forth, hither and thither

ON THE WING *adv* on the fly *(U.S.);* **aerially,** aeronautically, astronautically, cosmonautically

OPACITY *n* denseness, density, opaqueness, solidity, thickness; **turbidity,** cloudiness, muddiness

OPAQUE *adj* dense, intense, thick; **turbid,** cloudy, muddy, roily

OPEN *v* reopen, throw open, unbar, unbolt, unclench, unclose, uncork, undo, unglue, unhook, unlatch, unlock, unplug, unseal, unstop, unwrap, unzip; **pierce,** bore, breach, broach, buttonhole, drawbore, drill, eat into, eye, eyelet, gimlet, hole, loophole, peck, perforate, pin-prick, pink, prick, prickle, prong, rebore, roulette, scuttle *(Naut.),* stab, stave, tunnel, wimble, window; **tear,** gap, slash, slit; **force,** jemmy, pick

OPEN *adj* agape, ajar, dehiscent, expanded, overt *(Her.),* undone, unsealed, wide-open; **gaping,** expanded, oscitant, patulous, rictal, ringent, wide; **perforated,** cancellate, holey, porous

OPEN *adv* ajar; **wide**, gapingly, patulously, yawningly

OPEN-AIR *adj* alfresco, exposed, plein air

OPENER *n* key, latchkey, latchstring, ripcord *(Aeron.)*, skeleton key, tin-opener, undoer; **drill**, borer, broach, cardpunch *(Computers)*, driller, hole puncher, perforator, piercer, trepan, wimble

OPENING *n* aperture, chink, cranny, gap, gape, hole, interstice, ostiole, perforation, pinhole, pinprick, pit, prick, slit, slot, yawn; **orifice**, blastopore, blowhole, fistula, foramen, foramen magnum, jaws, meatus, micropyle, mouth, os, osculum, pore, stoma; **breach**, break, crack, fissure, leak, puncture, rent, rift, wash-out; **bore**, blowhole, borehole, mofette, Mohole, quarry, winning; **manhole**, drop, hatch, hatchway *(Naut.)*, stokehole, trap, trapdoor, vampire *(Theat.)*; **scupper**, hawse, hawsehole, lubber's hole, scuttle; **escape lock**, David apparatus; **peephole**, hagioscope, judas hole, peep, spy-hole, squint; **miscellaneous opening**, airbrick, airhole, core, core hole, embrasure, grille *(Royal Tennis)*, gunport, hazard *(Royal Tennis)*, loop *(Archaic)*, loophole, machicolation, port *(Mil.)*, service hatch, sleeve, weephole

OPENNESS *n* gape, oscitance, oscitancy, patulousness, rictus

OPEN UP *v* become open, bilge *(Naut.)*, break, crevasse, dehisce, fissure, leak, pop, reopen, rift; **gape**, expand, loosen, open out, run, spread, undouble, unfold, unfurl, yawn

OPERA *n* ballad opera, comic opera, extravaganza, grand opera, light opera, music drama, music theatre, musical, musical comedy, opéra bouffe, opéra comique, opera seria, operetta, oratorio, pastorale, rock opera, singspiel, zarzuela

OPERATE *v* be operative, function, go, play, run, serve; **work**, act, be in operation, be in working order, be under way, take effect, tell; **actuate**, act on, erect, float, functionalise, gear up, ignite, make work, move, ply, run in, summon up, switch on, wind up; **administer**, administrate, apply, command, drive, hold, manage; **drive**, force *(Obs.)*, operate, power; **apply**, exercise; **implement**, bring to bear, institute

OPERATING *adj* effectual, in effect, operant, operational; **going**, acting, afloat, alive, at work, effective, efficient, go, in force, in motion, in play, in the pipeline, in the system, live, on, on deck, on stream, operational, operative, up, working; **running**, A-OK, going strong, good; **functional**, applied, economic, expedient, practical, useful

OPERATION *n* action, activity, application; **function**, affair, cycle, exercise, procedure, process; **actuation**, effectuation, implementation, making; **governance**, administration, control, management, treatment; **machinery**, order

OPERATOR *n* actuator, administrant, agent, applier, commission, effecter, force, operant; **headquarters**, command, management, operations branch

OPINION *n* conception, conclusion, conviction, editorial, estimate, idea, impression, mind, notion, preconception, prejudice, prenotion, prepossession, rooted opinion, sentence

opinion

(Obs.), sentiment, surmise, theory, thinking, thought; **public opinion,** ground swell, vox pop, vox populi; **viewpoint,** position, school of thought, stance, standpoint, view, Weltanschauung, world view. *See also* BELIEF

OPPORTUNISM *n* craftiness, cunning, gamesmanship, political skill, shiftiness, timeserving; **back scratching,** flattery, sycophancy

OPPORTUNIST *n* carpetbagger, self-seeker, timeserver, trimmer *(Politics)*; **flatterer,** back scratcher, gamesman, sycophant; **wangler,** conniver, Machiavellian, wriggler; **improviser,** adaptor, extemporiser, improvisator

OPPORTUNIST *adj* artful, crafty, cunning, devious, resourceful, shifty; **self-seeking,** fawning, flattering, servile, sycophant, timeserving; **scheming,** astute, calculating, deceitful, deliberate, Machiavellian, manipulative, ruthless

OPPORTUNITY *n* chance, occasion, open, open go, opening, potency *(Obs.)*, potential, potentiality, resource, room, scope; **psychological moment,** high time, right moment, right time

OPPOSE *v* answer back, be set against, contend against, counter, fall foul of, make a stand against, object to, obstruct, rebut, recalcitrate, repugn *(Obs.)*, resist, set one's face against, side against, stand against, stand out against, strive against, take on, talk back to, tangle with, withstand; **defy,** beard, brave, brave it out, brazen out, breast, champion *(Obs.)*, check, face, hold out against, kick against the pricks, persist, reluct *(Archaic)*, stand one's ground, stand

oppositely

up to, stick up to; **outface,** call someone's bluff, dare, fly in the face of, heavy, hurl defiance at, laugh to scorn, outstare, put it on someone, set at naught, thumb one's nose; **challenge,** bare one's teeth, bluster, call in question, show fight, threaten, throw down the gauntlet; **rebel,** buck, find fault, kick

OPPOSING *adj* antagonistic, antithetic, antithetical, conflicting, contradictory, contrary, contrasted, ditheistic, inconsistent, like chalk and cheese, mutually exclusive, opposed, opposite, oppositional, paradoxical, the other, tother *(Archaic)*; **antonymic,** opposite in meaning; **inverse,** arsyversy, back-to-front, converse, inversive, reverse; **on opposite sides,** antipodean, at cross purposes, at opposite poles, like oil and water; **ambivalent,** ac-dc, bisexual, hermaphrodite, hermaphroditic, hermaphroditical, two-edged

OPPOSITE *adj* diametrically opposite, face to face, vis-a-vis; **opposed,** contrary, counter, cross, foul, opposable, polarised; **adverse,** contrapositive, opponent; **polar,** bipolar; **antipodal,** antipodean

OPPOSITE *adv* dos-à-dos, oppositely, overleaf, vis-a-vis; **contrarily,** adversely, contrariwise, counter, per contra; **bilaterally,** distichously

OPPOSITE *prep* against *(Obs.)*, anent *(Archaic)*, face to face with, facing, vis-a-vis; **against,** over against

OPPOSITELY *adv* adversatively, antithetically, conversely, opposite, paradoxically, poles apart; **contrarily,** au contraire, but then, contrariwise, contrary, on the contrary, on the other hand, rather, thereagainst

oppositely   377   **orator**

(Archaic), to the contrary; **inversely,** reversely, topsy-turvy, vice versa; **ambivalently**

OPPOSITE MEANING *n* antipode *(U.S.)*, antipodes, antithesis, contraposition, contrary, converse, the other extreme; **inverse,** contrary, counter, reverse; **antonym; enantiosis,** a contradiction in terms, adversative, irony, paradox, sarcasm; **hermaphrodite**

OPPOSITENESS *n* antagonism, contrariety, contrariness, contrast, opposability, opposition, paradoxicalness; **ambivalence,** ambitendency, bisexuality, hermaphroditism

OPPOSITE POSITION *n* antithesis, inverse, reverse; **contraposition,** adverseness, confrontment, contrariness, opposition; **polarity,** bilateralism, bilateralness, bipolarity, dissymetry, polarisation; **pole,** antipode *(U.S.);* **opposite number,** flip side, verso, vis-a-vis

OPTIC *adj* catoptric, dioptric, fibreoptic, optical; **reflecting,** reflectional, reflective

OPTICAL *adj* ocular, ophthalmic, optic, photopic, visual; **binocular,** emmetropic, orthoptic, orthoscopic, stereoscopic, stereoscopical; **audiovisual**

OPTICS *n* dioptrics, geometrical optics; **fibre optics,** catoptrics

OPTIMIST *n* bull, positivist, truster; **aspirant,** aspirer, young hopeful

OPTIONAL *adj* alternative, discretional, elective, facultative, permissive, selective, volitional, volitionary, voluntary, votive *(Rom. Cath. Ch.);* **multiple-choice,** either-or, two-way; **eclectic**

OPTIONALLY *adv* ad libitum, alternatively, at one's discretion, discretionally, electively, volitionally; **eclectically,** preferentially, selectively; **rather,** by choice, first, preferably, sooner, voluntarily

ORANGE *n* amber, cadmium orange, tangerine; **orange-red,** ginger, henna, poppy, rust, scarlet; **orange-brown,** terracotta; **peach,** apricot, coral, yellow-pink; **brass,** copper, old gold

ORANGE *adj* amber, carroty, scarlet, tangerine, terracotta; **ginger,** rusty; **peach,** apricot, coralline, luteous. *See also* YELLOW

ORATION *n* address, address-in-reply *(Parl. Proc.),* allocution, declamation, defence, discourse, effusion, homily, inaugural, King's speech, lecture, maiden speech, monologue, narration, panegyric, Queen's speech, sermon, soliloquy, speech, spiel; **recitation,** reading, recital, set speech; **prologue,** exordium, peroration; **funeral oration,** valediction, valedictory; **eulogy,** encomium; **speechifying,** homiletics, sermonising

ORATOR *n* declaimer, demagogue, elecutionist, haranguer, homilist, lecturer, mouthpiece, narrator, oratress, oratrix, polemicist, rabblerouser, ranter, reader, rhapsodist, rhetor, rhetorician, soap-box orator, speaker, spokesperson, stump orator, stylist, tub-thumper, valedictorian *(U.S.),* word-spinner, Yarra banker; **spieler,** amster, deipnosophist, poet, smart talker, spruiker; **public speaker,** after-dinner speaker, toastmaster, toastmistress; **preacher,** Amen snorter, bible-basher, gospeller, holy Joe, hot-gospeller, pulpiteer, sermoniser

ordain

ORDAIN *v* foreordain, order, predestinate, predestine, predetermine, preordain; **doom**, destine, foredoom

ORDER *n* combination, configuration, conformation, form, geometry, Gestalt *(Psychol.)*, matrix, method, shape, structure, syntax *(Obs.)*, system, taxis; **arrangement**, arrayal, calibre, cast, collation, collocation, composition, dispensation, disposal, disposition, disposure *(Rare)*, distribution, layout, line-up, make-up, ordination, permutation, placement; **battle formation,** battleline, close-order, echelon, flight formation; **brick arrangement,** bond, colonial-bond, English bond, Flemish bond, four-and-a-half bond, garden-wall bond, half bond, hit-and-miss brickwork, stack bond, stretcher bond, toothing; **floral formation,** aestivation, anthotaxy, phyllotaxis, vernation

ORDER *v* compose, fix, form, gather *(Bookbinding)*, make *(Print.)*, permute, range, rank, set, settle; **arrange**, coordinate, orchestrate, permute, program *(Computers)*, rotate, seed *(Sport)*, set to rights, structure, tabularise, tabulate, timetable; **rearrange**, re-format, re-sort, readjust, recast, recompose, redeploy, reorder; **systematise**, alphabetise, codify, coordinate, methodise, organise, rationalise, regularise, systemise

ORDERED *adj* architectonic, structured; **orderly**, businesslike, methodical, scientific, streamlined, systematic, tight-knit, well-regulated; **harmonious**, cosmic, organic; **sequential**, chronological, seriate, synchronistic, tabular

ordinary

ORDERER *n* aligner, collator, composer, disposer, distributor, marshaller; **organiser**, alphabetiser, filer, methodiser, rationaliser, schematiser, systematiser, systematist, systemiser

ORDERING *n* alphabetisation, orchestration, organisation, rationalisation, recomposition, redeployment, schematisation, systematisation, systemisation; **coordination**, imposition *(Print.)*, regimentation, regularisation, subjunction; **systematics**, architectonics, methodology, systematology

ORDERLY *adv* harmoniously, harmonistically, regularly, systematically, systemically; **sequentially**, in order, just so, seriately, step by step, stepwise

ORDINARILY *adv* averagely, indifferently, middling, middlingly, moderately, on the average; **commonly**, exoterically, medially, mundanely, prosaically, tritely, usually

ORDINARINESS *n* commonness, commonplaceness, exotericism, mediocrity, pedestrianism, prosaicness, triteness, triviality, trivialness; **average**, medium, middle, norm, normality, par, standard; **commonplace**, banality, cliché, platitude, prosaism, trivialism, triviality; **standardisation**

ORDINARY *adj* average, fair to middling, indifferent, mediocre, medium, middling, moderate, normal, par, par for the course, standard; **mean**, medial; **common**, banal, common-or-garden, commonplace, day-to-day, everyday, exoteric, middle-of-the-road, middlebrow, mill-run, moderate, mundane, pedestrian, prosaic,

ordinary   **outside**

run-of-the-mill, tired, tolerable, trite, trivial, vulgar

ORDINARY PERSON *n* middle-of-the-roader, middlebrow; **everyman,** Aussie battler, Joe *(U.S.),* Joe Bloggs, Joe Blow, John Citizen, the man in the street

ORGANIC CAVITY *n* alveolus, antrum, atrium, bladder, caecum, cell, cellule, cul-de-sac, follicle, lacuna, reservoir, sac, sinus, venter, ventricle, vesicle, vestibule, womb; **bodily hollow,** armpit, axilla, fontanelle, infundibulum, saltcellar, snuffbox; **navel,** omphalos, umbilication, umbilicus. *See also* HOLLOW

ORGANISM *n* animalcule, individual, zooid; **micro-organism,** aerobe, anaerobe, anaerobiont, coenocyte, infusorian, intestinal flora, microbe, microfauna, microparasite, monad, nanoplankton, protist, protistan, protozoan; **pathogen,** bacillus, bacteria, bacteriophage, bacterium, bug, germ, parvovirus, PPLO, rickettsia, virus, wog; **cell,** corpuscle, protoplast; **culture,** plate, pure culture, subculture; **colony,** clump, coenobium, plasmodium, zoogloea

ORIGINAL *adj* conceptive, exordial, first, fontal, front-end, inaugural, inceptive, incipient, initial, initiative, initiatory, instigative, institutive, primary, radical, unprecedented; **germinal,** elementary, embryo, embryonic, nascent, seminal; **rudimentary,** abecedarian, basic, foundation, fundamental, introductory; **primeval,** early, inchoate, inchoative *(Rare),* primigenial, primitive, primordial, pristine, protomorphic; **cosmogonic,** cosmogonical, cosmological

OUTBURST *n* blaze, burst, ebullition, flaw *(Obs.),* gust, outbreak, outrage *(Obs.),* riot, start *(Archaic),* tornado, torrent, whiff, willy; **flush,** swell, wave

OUTFIT *n* change, ensemble, layette, separates, trousseau, turnout; **suit,** bag of fruit, dinner suit, dress suit, evening suit, lounge suit, monkey suit, morning dress, pants-suit, safari suit, slacks suit, three-piece, tuxedo, two-piece; **overalls,** boilersuit, coogans, dungarees, ovaries *(Colloq.). See also* UNIFORM; FINERY; DRESS

OUTLAW *v* illegalise, illegitimise, put outside the law

OUT OF PLACE *adv* adventitiously *(Bot. Zool.),* astray, in no-man's-land, on the streets, out, out of joint

OUTSIDE *n* exterior, external, outward, superficies, surface, top; **face,** facade, facia, front; **covering,** crust, epidermis, rind, shell, skin, superstratum; **outline,** boundary, circumference, periphery, profile, silhouette

OUTSIDE *adj* exoteric, exterior, external, extrinsic, out, outer, outward; **surface,** covering, crustal, crusty, epidermal, epidermic, epigene, epigenic, superficial, top; **out-of-doors,** alfresco, extramural, field, open-air, outdoor; **peripheral,** boundary, circumjacent, surrounding; **extraneous,** outlying

OUTSIDE *adv* out, outward, outwards, thereout *(Archaic),* without; **on the outside,** externally, extrinsicly, on the face of it, on the surface, outwardly, superficially; **out of doors,** abroad, alfresco, en plein air, in the open air, out the back, outdoors, withoutdoors *(Obs.)*

OUTSIDE *prep* beyond, out, round, without *(Archaic)*

OUTSIDER *n* fringe dweller, harijan *(India)*, Ishmael, lost soul, marginal man, outcast, outlander, pariah, reprobate, social leper; **exile**, alien, expatriate, refugee

OUTWARDNESS *n* exteriority, externality, extrinsicality, superficiality, superficialness

OVAL *n* ellipse, ellipsoid, geoid; **ovoid**, almond, amygdala *(Anat.)*, cartouche *(Archit.)*, egg, ovum *(Archit.)*

OVAL *adj* ecliptic, egg-shaped, ellipsoid, ellipsoidal, elliptical, obovate, obovoid, olivary, ovate, oviform, ovoid, pear-shaped, pineal, piriform, spatulate *(Bot.)*, testiculate, vesical

OVERCHARGE *v* charge like a wounded bull, gazump, overprice, overvalue, surcharge

OVERCOAT *n* balmacaan, box coat, buff, cutaway, dreadnought, frockcoat, gaberdine, greatcoat, jubbah, matinee coat, pelisse, peplos, petersham, Prince Albert, raglan, redingote, surcoat, topcoat, ulster; **overgarment**, frock, outer garments, overclothes, overdress, paletot, tabard, toga, vestment, wrapper; **coverall**, cover-up, dustcoat, duster *(U.S.)*, housecoat, overall; **apron**, bib, feeder, pinafore, pinny, smock. *See also* CLOAK; RAINCOAT; JACKET

OVERINDULGE *v* burn the candle at both ends, carouse, debauch, dissipate, go on the tiles, go round the traps, go to town, indulge, live fast, live hard, live high on the hog, luxuriate, paint the town red, racket, riot, run riot, sow one's wild oats, surfeit, wallow, wanton; **give oneself up to**, give free rein to

OVERINDULGENCE *n* bacchanalianism, crapulousness, debauchery, dissipatedness, dissipation, dissoluteness, excess, immoderacy, intemperance, intemperateness, profligacy, profligateness, rakishness, riotousness, self-indulgence, unrestraint, wantonness, wildness. *See also* GREED

OVERINDULGENT *adj* abandoned, crapulous, dionysian, immoderate, incontinent, orgiastic, profligate, rakehelly *(Archaic)*, saturnalian, unbridled, uncontrolled, unmeasured, unrestrained; **dissipated**, Corinthian, debauched, dissolute, gay, goliardic, licentious, rakish, riotous, wanton; **self-indulgent**, compulsive, indulgent, intemperate. *See also* GREEDY

OVERSEAS *adv* abroad, in foreign parts; **exotically**, outlandishly, strange, strangely

OVERSUPPLY *v* cloy, congest, cram, drug, engorge, fill to overflowing, glut, OD, overdose, overfill, sate, satiate, stuff, surfeit; **deluge**, flood, glut the market, load, overwhelm, plaster, riddle, smother, swamp; **overproduce**, overstock, pile up

OVERTAKE *v* catch up with, forereach, gain upon, lap, overhaul, ride down; **leave behind**, beat, forerun *(Obs.)*, leave at the post, leave standing, outdistance, outpace, outrun, outstrip, shoot ahead; **pass**, go beyond, go past, move past, shoot by, shoot past, whistle by, whistle past, whizz by, whizz past; **skirt**, slide past, slip past; **overshoot**, go further, move ahead, override, overrun, overshoot the

overtake

mark, overstand *(Naut.)*, overstep, overstride

OVERTAKING *n* overlapping, overstepping, passing; **passing lane**, fast lane, outside lane

OVERTURN *n* bouleversement, careen *(Naut.)*, overset, overspill, overthrow, tip, turnover, upset; **headstand**, cartwheel, somersault, topsy-turvy; **topsy-turviness**, topsy-turvydom

OVERTURN *v* overset *(Rare)*, overthrow, skittle, tip, tip over, tip up, turn over, upset, upturn; **invert**, inverse *(Rare)*, put the cart before the horse; **overbalance**, capsize, careen *(Naut.)*, keel over, loop *(Canoeing)*, overspill, pitch pole, somersault, stand on one's head, tumble, turn cartwheels, turn turtle

OVERTURNED *adj* arse-up, arsy-versy, back-to-front, topsy-turvy, upset, upside down, upturned, wrong side up; **inverted**, awkward *(Obs.)*, backward, inversive, reversionary; **converse**, inverse

OWING *adj* chargeable, due, floating, outstanding, payable, undischarged, unpaid

OWN *v* be worth, bear, command, enjoy, enjoy the use of, have, have all to oneself, have in hand, hold, hold in fee, possess; **gain possession of**, enfeoff, get one's hands on, occupy, overrun, squat in; **corner**, engross, monopolise, privatise

ownership

OWN *adj* ain *(Scot.)*, appropriative, belonging, inalienable; **of one's own**, exclusive, personal, private, privy, proper; **claimed**, bespoke, previously claimed, spoken for; **of the house**, maison; **pre-owned**, pre-loved, second-hand, used

OWNER *n* capitalist, franklin, joint owner, monopolist, occupant, possessor, proprietary, proprietor, proprietress, riparian, tenant, tenant in common; **holder**, claimholder, coparcener, copyholder, freeholder, impropriator, squatter; **landlord**, absentee landlord, body corporate, landholder, landlady, landowner; **lord**, lady, laird, master, mistress, seignior; **alienee**, cestui que vie

OWNERSHIP *n* demesne, domain, easement, estate, grasp, holding, interest, occupancy, possession, proprietary, proprietorship, stake, tenure, vested interest; **lordship**, lairdship, landownership, landowning, seigniority; **monopoly**, corner *(Finance)*, monopolisation, monopolism; **use**, coparcenary, copyhold, exclusive right, freehold, gavelkind, impropriation *(Eccles. Law)*, leasehold, mortmain, seigniorage, seisin, socage *(Archaic)*, tenancy, vacant possession, villeinage *(Archaic)*; **title**, company title, copyright, fee, fee simple, fee tail, feoff, feud, patent, reversion, title deed, Torrens title, trust instrument

Pp

PACIFICATION *n* appeasement, assuagement, conciliation, détente, frank and free discussion, meaningful exchange, mediation, mollification, negotiation, peacekeeping, reconciliation, tranquillisation; **peace-offering**, calumet, compromise, dove, olive, olive branch, overtures, peacepipe, pipe of peace; **white flag**, flag of truce; **demilitarisation**, nonproliferation

PACIFISM *n* ahimsa, disarmament, peace march, peace movement; **peaceableness**, amicability, amicableness, anti-militarism, friendship

PAIN *n* affliction, discomfort, hurt, injury, malaise; **irritation**, thorn in one's flesh, trouble; **suffering**, passion *(Archaic)*, pathos *(Obs.)*, travail; **agony**, anguish, distress, excruciation, hell, slow death, torment, torture, tortures; **ordeal**, baptism of fire, gethsemane, Golgotha, trial; **martyrdom**, crucifixion; **algolagnia**, masochism, sadism, sadomasochism; **algometry**, algometer. *See also* ACHE

PAIN *v* ache, anger *(Obs.)*, give one gip, gripe, hurt, jump, play hell, play merry hell, smart, throb, tingle, trouble, twinge; **sting**, urticate; **chafe**, fret, gall, pinch, rub; **fester**, rankle; **cause pain**, afflict, anguish, cut up, distress, excruciate, harrow, hurt, rack, torment, vex *(Archaic)*, wring; **wound**, bite, lacerate, nip, prick, stab, sting, tear; **torture**, crucify, excruciate; **prolong the agony**, kill by inches

PAINFUL *adj* afflictive, distressful, distressing, harrowing, heart-rending, piquant *(Archaic)*, poignant; **excruciating**, torturous; **biting**, bitter, burning, cruel, nipping, piercing, shooting, stabbing, throbbing; **griping**, colicky, fulgurating; **sore**, exposed, raw, tender; **achy**, footsore, footworn, headachy, saddle-sore; **suffering**, aching, racked with pain

PAINFULNESS *n* bitterness, distressfulness, hurtfulness, malignancy, poignancy, severeness, severity; **soreness**, anger *(Obs.)*, irritancy, sensitiveness, tenderness; **qualmishness**, queasiness, queerness, seediness, wooziness; **pain threshold**

PAINT *n* acrylic paint, antifouling, clobber, colourwash, couch, daub, distemper, dope, duco, emulsion paint, estapol, gesso, glair, glaze, glazing, graining, ground colour, impastation, japan, kalsomine, lacquer, luminous paint, lustre *(Pottery)*, metalflake duco, oil-paint, overglaze, paintwork, plastic paint, poster colour, poster paint, primer, sealant, size, slip *(Pottery)*, spirit varnish, splash coat, thixotropic paint, tiger's-eye, varnish, wash, water-paint, whitewash; **undercoat**, undercoating, underseal

PAINTING *n* bark painting, batik, cave painting, daubery, drip painting, portraiture; **picture**, diptych, icon, lunette, panel, pastiche, polyptych, predella, triptych; **portrait**, figure, half-face, half-length, nude, profile, self-portrait, silhouette, torso; **study**, landscape, marine, moonscape, nocturne, pastoral, scene, seascape, still life, tableau, townscape, view, waterscape; kakemono, tanka; **fresco**, frieze, mural; **painting technique,** alla prima, chiaroscuro, direct painting, encaustic, gouache, grisaille, sfumato, sgraffito, stipple; **painting medium,** acrylics, aquarelle, monochrome, oils, poster colour, stereochrome, tempera, wash, watercolour; **canvas,** easel, picture plane, support; **palette,** oils, paintbox, paints

PARENT n oldie, olds, parents, the olds; **foster-parent,** godparent, gossip *(Archaic),* step-parent; **mother,** mama, mamma, mammy, mater, mater dolorosa, materfamilias, mom, mum, mummy, old girl, old lady, old woman; **foster-mother,** godmother, mother-in-law, stepdame *(Archaic),* stepmother; **father,** begetter, dad, daddy, gaffer *(Brit. Colloq.),* genitor, governor, old boy, old man, pa, papa, pappy, pater, paterfamilias, patriarch, père, pop, poppa; **foster-father,** father-in-law, godfather, stepfather; **grandparent,** great-grandfather, great-grandmother, great-grandparent; **grandmother,** beldam *(Archaic),* gran, grandam, grande dame, grandma, grandmamma, granny, nanna, nanny; **grandfather,** grampers, gramps, grampus, grandad, grandpa, grandpapa, grandsire *(Archaic),* pop, poppa

PARENTAGE n parenthood, parenting; **paternity,** fatherhood, fatherliness; **maternity,** mothercraft, motherhood, mothering, motherliness

PARENTAL adj parent-like; **maternal,** grandmotherly, novercal; **paternal,** grandfatherly, patriarchal; **avuncular; daughterly,** filial

PARLIAMENTARY adj congressional, senatorial; **consistorial,** convocational, synodal

PARLIAMENTARY PROCEDURE n standing orders; **motion,** ay, no, urgency motion, vote of confidence, vote of no confidence; **division,** absolute majority, majority, minority; **question time,** budget speech, dorothy dixer, maiden speech, reply; **sitting,** assembly, opening, recall, recall of parliament; **dissolution,** dismissal, double dissolution, prorogation

PART n canton, fraction, moiety, percentage, portion, proportion; **constituent,** component, detail, element, ingredient, integral, integrant, member, module, particular; **section,** compartment, department, desk, division, panel, partition, segment, subdivision, subsection; **cross-section,** example; **allotment,** allocation, allowance, contingent, cut, dividend, helping, length, lot, parcel, quantum, quota, rake-off, share, whack; **chunk,** dollop, hunk, lump; **slice,** cantle, finger, shive *(Archaic),* wedge; **greater part,** body, bulk, majority, mass; **particle,** bite, crumb, driblet, morceau, morsel, nibble, nubbin *(U.S.),* nubble; **fragment,** bit, catch, chip, flake, flinders, fritter, piece, scrap, shiver, shrapnel, shred, sliver, snatch, spill, splinter, split, whittling; **bits and pieces,** fragmentation, odds and ends, smithereens

PARTIAL adj halfway, imperfect, incomplete, part; **fragmentary,** bitty, disjointed, fragmental, piecemeal, scrap, scrappy, splintery; **partite,** bipartite, compartmentalised, departmentalised, divided, dividual *(Archaic),* divisional, divisionary,

partial

multipartite, sectional, segmental, segmentary, segmented, volumed; **articulated,** modular

PARTIALLY *adv* fractionally, in part, parcel *(Archaic),* part, partly; **piecemeal,** bit by bit, part by part, piece by piece, scrappily

PARTICIPANT *n* accessory, contributor, member, participator, party, sympathiser

PARTICIPATE *v* be up to one's neck in, become committed, buy in, buy into, enter, enter into, get into, get involved, get up to, go the whole hog, have a hand in, have an interest in, join, join in, make a stand, mix up in, partake in, share, stand up, step in, take a stand, take part, take sides

PARTICIPATING *adj* concerned with, hands-on, implicated, in the same boat, in the thick of, involved; **interested,** concerned, engaged, for, full of, rapt in, wrapped up in

PARTICIPATION *n* accessoriness, affiliation, commitment, complicity, concernment, engagement, entanglement, immixture, implication, interest, interestedness, involvution, involvement, stake, sympathy

PARTICULAR *adj* certain, circumstantial, definite, deictic, especial, one, peculiar, precise, special, specific, such, such and such, that, this, what, which; **for a particular occasion,** ad hoc, magistral *(Pharm.);* **bespoke,** custom-built, custom-made, customised, made-to-measure, made-to-order, specially made, tailor-made; **respective,** appropriate, different, distributive, dividual *(Archaic),* each, ilka *(Scot.),* proper, separate, several; **of one's own,** one's, own, personal, private, unipersonal; **specifiable,** assignable, circumscriptive, definable, differentiable, identifiable, isolable

partner

PARTICULARISE *v* characterise, customise, define, determine, distinguish, have someone tabbed, identify, individualise, mark, specialise, type; **circumstantiate,** circumstance *(Obs.),* detail, differentiate, elaborate, itemise; **specify,** assign, designate

PARTICULARITY *n* categoricalness, circumscription, circumstantiality, definability, definiteness, definitiveness, distinctness, inimitableness, separateness, specificity, specificness, typicalness, uniqueness

PARTICULARLY *adv* ad hoc, ad hominem, circumstantially, e.g., especially, in detail, in particular, namely, peculiarly, specially, specifically, to wit, videlicet, viz.; **for my part,** as far as I am concerned, in my opinion, on all counts, speaking for myself; **there,** here, locally, where; **respectively,** apart, apiece, bit by bit, each, individually, separately, severally; **differentially,** diacritically, dividually *(Archaic)*

PARTICULARS *n* article, circumstance, detail, element, fine print, item, minutiae, nitty-gritty, note, parameter, part, piece, point, portion, property, small print

PARTNER *n* associate, bedfellow, colleague, compeer, confrère, copartner, duumvir, fellow, mate *(Archaic),* offsider, peer; **silent partner,** sleeping partner; **assistant,** acolyte, adjunct, adjutant, aide, attaché, attendant, chaperone, right hand, second, secondary; **helpmate,** helping hand, helpmeet *(Archaic);* **comrade,** brethren, brother, frère, sister; **workfellow,** messmate, shipmate, team-mate,

partner

workmate, yokefellow; **compatriot,** countryman, countrywoman, townsman, townswoman. *See also* ACCOMPLICE

PARTNER *v* accompany, associate, assort *(Archaic)*, chaperone, company *(Archaic),* consociate, consort, mate, squire; **ally with,** go into business with, hang around with, hang with, keep company with, latch on to, mess with, pal up with, string along with, take up with, tie up with; **haunt,** follow, shadow; **assist,** attend, have a hand in, help, participate, take a hand in

PARTY *n* après-ski, at-home, bottle party, celebration, conversazione, cracker night, festivity, get-together, house-warming, potlatch, reunion, revel, revelry, rout, send-off, shivoo, singsong, social, social occasion, soiree, tea-party, third half, turn, turnout, twenty-first, wayzgoose; **dance,** ball, barn-dance, dinner-dance, fancy-dress ball, fandango *(U.S.),* hoedown *(U.S.),* hop, mask, masked ball, masquerade, ridotto; **house party,** blanket party, pyjama party, slumber party; **barbecue,** barby, clambake *(U.S.),* cookout *(U.S.),* fry *(U.S.),* luau, picnic, picnic races; **rort,** bust-up, destroy party, destructo, ding, hooley, hui *(N.Z.);* **booze-up,** beer-up, boozeroo *(N.Z.),* bowl, carousal, carouse, cocktail party, drinks, grog-on, wassail; **wedding breakfast,** bridal *(Archaic),* reception; **bucks' party,** bucks' night, girls' night out, hen's party, hens' night, kitchen tea, shower tea, stag party

PASSABLY *adv* after a fashion, averagely, fairly, in a fashion, indifferently, mundanely, so-so, tolerably

past

PASSAGEWAY *n* adit, draft tube, drift, heading, lateral, tunnel; **airway,** airdrive, air-duct, airshaft, breezeway, port, porting, shaft, slot, snorkel, upcast, uptake, ventiduct, windsail; **furrow,** crevice, flue, flute, fulgurite, groove; **chimney,** chimneypot, flue, funnel, smokestack, stack, tallboy

PASSENGER *n* back-seat driver, cabbie's jockey, fare, hitcher, pillion, swinger; **hitchhiker,** stowaway

PASS THROUGH *v* pass, pick one's way, plough through, ply, thread one's way, transit; **percolate,** perfuse, perk *(Colloq.),* permeate, soak in, soak through

PAST *n* antiquity, auld lang syne, bygone, days of old, days of yore, Dreamtime *(Aborig.),* foretime, history, horse-and-buggy age, langsyne, the good old days, time immemorial, time out of mind, yesterday, yore *(Archaic);* **earliness,** antiqueness, historicity

PAST *adj* back, bygone, dead-and-buried, departed, erstwhile, foregone, former, historical, late, lost, of yore, old-time, olden, one-time, other, over, quondam, sometime, whilom *(Archaic),* yesterday; **nostalgic; retrospective,** memorial, retroactive; **perfect,** perfective, pluperfect, preterite; **primeval,** atavistic, primal, pristine; **early,** mythical, old, olden *(Archaic);* **ancient,** classical, immemorial, preadamite, premillennial, venerable; **prehistoric,** antediluvian, Archaean, archaeological, Archaeozoic, azoic, eolithic, Neanderthal, palaeogeographical, palaeogeological, Palaeolithic, preglacial, prehuman, primeval, primitive, primordial, protolithic; **fossil,** fossil-like, fossiliferous;

postdiluvian, postclassical, postwar; **recent**, latter-day, low, of late

PASTE *n* clobber, dope, goo; **clag**, mess; **gore**, clot; **syrup**, tear-arse, treacle; **semifluid**, colloid, semisolid; **gel**, gelatinoid, glair, jelly.   *See also* SLUDGE

PAT *n* bob, dab, fillip, flick, flip, peck, rap, tap, tip, touch; **stamp**, appel *(Fencing)*, tamp; **prod**, attaint *(Obs.)*, bunt, butt, dig, goose, jab, jerk, poke, stab; **push**, jog, jolt, jostle, nudge, stir; **accolade**, dubbing.   *See also* HIT: STROKE

PATH *n* bikeway, bridle-track, bridle-path, cycleway, pack-track, pathway, ride, towpath; **footpath**, banquette *(U.S.)*, causeway, flagging, flags, flagstones, footway, pavement, paving, roadside, side path, sidewalk *(U.S.)*, walk, walkway, wayside; **lane**, alley, alleyway, pall-mall, passage, passageway; **aisle**, ambulatory, bay, corridor, hall; **arcade**, cloister, colonnade, gallery, loggia, ropewalk, slype; **arch**, archway; **subway**, tunnel, underpass; **manway**, catwalk, duckboard, gangboard, gangway, logway, ridgeway; **bridge**, aerobridge, drawbridge, floating bridge, footbridge, pontoon, span, viaduct, walkway; **track**, bush track, fire trail, nature trail, snigging track, trail, walking track; **course**, cinder track, dirt track, drag strip, dromos, gallop, home straight, home stretch, racecourse, racetrack, sandtrack, straight, straightaway *(U.S.)*, the turf, track; **ramp**, cattle ramp, cattlepit, cattlestop *(N.Z.)*; **chute**, crush, drafting race, race; **walk**, pad, sheepwalk.   *See also* ROUTE: ROAD: ACCESS

PATIENCE *n* endurance, enduringness, forbearance, fortitude, long-suffering, longanimity, meekness, resignation, stoicalness, sufferance, sustainment, tolerance, toleration

PATIENT *n* case, day-patient, inpatient, invalid, lame duck, outpatient, private patient, public patient, subject, T.P.I., valetudinarian, victim, wreck; **sufferer from specific complaint**, arthritic, asthmatic, bleeder, diabetic, haemophiliac, lazar *(Archaic)*, leper, paraplegic, quadriplegic, spastic; **convalescent**, recuperator

PATIENT *adj* enduring, forbearing, long-suffering, meek, stoical, tolerant; **persevering**, diligent, persistent

PATIENT PERSON *n* Griselda, Job, long-sufferer, Stoic

PATRIARCHAL *adj* patriclinous, patrilineal; **matriarchal**, distaff, matriclinous, matrilineal, spindle *(U.S.)*; **legitimate**, lawful, well-born; **illegitimate**, base, baseborn, bastard, bastardly *(Obs.)*, misbegotten, on the wrong side of the blanket, unfathered, unlawful

PAVING *n* clinker, cobble, cobblestone, pavement, paviour, quarry tile, tile, tiling; **bitumen**, asphalt, blacktop, macadam, seal, surface dressing, tarmac, tarmacadam, tarseal; **concrete**, cement, Leichhardt grass, Leichhardt lawn

PAY *v* advance, defray, disburse, dispend *(Archaic)*, expend, invest, lay out, outlay, overpay, prepay, refund, remit, render payment, spend; **pay up**, alley up, ante up, cash up *(Obs.)*, dip into one's pocket, fork out, loosen the purse strings, part up, pay one's way, pony up *(U.S.)*, shell, shell

pay   387   **peaceful**

out, stump up, subscribe, untie the purse strings; **settle,** acquit, adjust, amortise, clear, compound, discharge, extinguish *(Law),* liquidate, pay off, redeem, satisfy, square, square up; **pay the bill,** bear the costs, foot the bill, pay the costs, pay the piper, pick up the tab, stand the costs, stand treat; **contribute,** club in, tithe *(Obs.);* **make payable,** declare; **remunerate,** cross someone's palm with silver, gratify *(Obs.),* grease someone's palm, recompense, recoup, reimburse, reward, tickle someone's palm; **yield,** return; **deposit,** plank down, put down

PAYABLE *adj* collect, defrayable, disbursable, dischargeable, due, expendable, penal, prepayable, redeemable, remittable, renderable; **taxable,** customable, declarable, dutiable, excisable, leviable

PAYER *n* defrayer, disburser, discharger, expender, ratepayer, remitter, subscriber; **contributor,** contributory, tributary, tributer; **taxpayer,** taxable *(U.S.)*

PAY HOMAGE *v* abase oneself, bend the knee, bow, bow and scrape, congratulate *(Obs.),* dip one's lid, fall down before, fire a twenty-one gun salute, genuflect, humble oneself, kiss the hem of another's garment *(Archaic),* kneel, kowtow, present arms, prostrate oneself, pull one's forelock, remove one's hat, salaam, salute, touch one's forelock, tug one's forelock, uncap, uncover; **defer to,** keep one's distance, make up to, make way for, stand aside for, stand back for

PAYMENT *n* aid *(Europ. Hist.),* amortisation, amortisement, claim, commission, composition, cop, defrayal, disbursement, discharge, down payment, drawback, foregift, handsel, hansel, imprest, key money, maintenance, overpayment, perpetuity, prepayment, quarterage, redundancy, remittance, satisfaction, soft dollars, spot cash, time payment, token payment, valuable consideration; **expenditure,** capital expenditure, cost, current expenses, expense, expenses, incidentals, outgo, outgoings, outlay, pump priming; **contribution,** benevolence *(Eng. Hist.),* indemnity, Peter's pence, subscription, subsidy, tribute; **settlement,** extinguishment, recoup, recoupment, redemption, requital, return, settling; **pay-off,** baksheesh, blackmail, kickback, touch; **refund,** drawback, recompense

PEACE *n* agreement, amnesty, bloodlessness, compromise, concord, harmony, neutrality, non-belligerency, non-resistance, non-violence, nonaggression, peaceful coexistence; **peacefulness,** quiet, quietness, sereneness, serenity, tranquillity, tranquilness; **peacetime,** halcyon days, nirvana; **armistice,** cease-fire, moratorium, rest, retirement, retreat, suspension of hostilities, truce, withdrawal; **demilitarised zone,** no-man's-land

PEACEFUL *adj* amicable, bloodless, eirenic, harmonious, irenic, non-violent, nonaggression, pacific, subdued; **peaceable,** calm, halcyon, pacific, peacetime, quiet, retired, serene, tranquil; **anti-war,** antimilitarist, dovish, neutral, non-combatant, non-proliferation, paci-

peaceful   **perceptive**

fist; **peacekeeping**, pacificatory; **appeaseable**, mollifiable, subduable

PEACEFULLY *adv* amicably, mollifyingly, pacifically, peaceably, quietly, serenely, subduedly, tranquilly; **nonviolently**, bloodlessly

PEACEMAKER *n* appeaser, arbitrator, assuager, compromiser, conciliator, dove, make-peace *(Rare)*, mediator, mollifier, non-resistant, pacificator, pacifier, quieter; **pacifist**, conch, conchie, conscientious objector, flowerchild, non-belligerent, noncombatant, peacenik

PEACETIME *adj* post-bellum, postwar, prewar

PEN *n* bullpen, byre, cattlepen, compound, corral, fold, holding paddock, kraal, mews, paddock, piggery, pigsty, pinfold, pound, sheepcote, sheepfold, stable, stall, stockade, stockyard, sty, walk; **holding pen**, catching pen, counting-out pen, creep feeder, crush, crush-pen, dip, drafting yard, draining pen, farrowing house, forcing pen, sheep dip; **barrier stall**, starting box, starting grid, swabbing stall

PENDANT *n* drop, hanging ornament; **swing**, cuddle seat, hammock, trapeze; **pendulum**, bob, bobber, lead; **tassel**, bobble, dangle, fandangle; **hanging**, curtains, drapery, drapes, tapestry, wall-hanging; **skirt**, tail, tippet *(Hist.)*, train; **flap**, flapper, lappet

PENITENCE *n* attrition, contriteness, contrition, guilt, mortification, repentance, self-reproach, soul-searching; **remorse**, abashment, grief, remorsefulness, shame, sorrow, sorrowfulness; **regret**, compunction, regretfulness, rue *(Archaic)*, sorriness;

apology, beg-pardon, by-your-leave; **regrets**, apologies, excuse

PENITENT *n* a sadder and a wiser man, magdalen, penitential, prodigal son

PENITENT *adj* abashed, ashamed, contrite, repentant, self-accusing, shamefaced; **regretful**, afraid, bad, compunctious, guilty, remorseful, rueful, ruthful *(Archaic)*, sorry; **apologetic**, deprecatory

PERCEIVE *v* apperceive, appreciate, become aware of, become conscious of, cognise, drink in, experience, feel, observe, savour, sense, suffer, taste *(Archaic)*; **regain consciousness**, come back to one's senses, come to

PERCEPTION *n* affect *(Obs.)*, apperception, appreciation, aura *(Pathol.)*, experience, impression, mental impulse, observation, percept, sensation, sense, sense datum, undersense; **perceptiveness**, aesthesia, anabiosis, awareness, conscience *(Obs.)*, consciousness, feeling, mind, passibility, sense, sensuousness, sentience, wits; **feeling**, feel, feelings, ferment, flutter, frisson, hot flush, inner glow, irritation, pain, prick, quiver, reaction, stir, thrill, tingle, tingling, tremor; **five senses**, five wits, sensorium

PERCEPTIONAL *adj* observational, perceptual, sensate; **perceptible**, appreciable, cognisable, phenomenal, sensible, vivid; **perceived**, appreciated, sensed; **sensory**, organoleptic, sensorial, sensorimotor *(Physiol.)*, sensual, sensuous

PERCEPTIVE *adj* affected, alive to, anabiotic, apperceptive, aware, cognisant, conscious, feeling, passible, protopathic, sensate, sensible, sentient, touched, ware *(Archaic)*; **per-**

cipient, observant, paraesthetic, sensitive; **supersensitive,** acute, exquisite, hyperaesthetic, hypersensitive, intense, irritable, keen, miffy, prickly, thin-skinned, ticklish, touchy

PERCEPTIVELY *adv* consciously, observantly, observingly, sensitively, sentiently; **acutely,** on the raw, to the quick, vividly

PERCEPTIVITY *n* coenaesthesia, immediacy *(Philos.)*, impressibility, impressionability, irritability, paraesthesia, percipience, sensibilities, sensibility, sensitisation, sensitiveness, sensitivity, susceptibility, synaesthesia, telaesthesia, tone; **hypersensitivity,** acuteness, hyperaesthesia, keenness, supersensitiveness, touchiness

PERCUSSION INSTRUMENT *n* idiophone, membranophone, metallophone, percussion; **percussion section,** battery, kitchen section; **drum,** atabal, bass drum, baya, bongo, conga, cuica, friction drum, gran cassa, kettledrum, quica, side-drum, snare-drum, tabla, tabor, taboret, taborin, tabret, tambour, tambourine, timbal, timbales, timbrel, timpani, tom-tom, tympanum; **drum kit,** skins, traps; **cymbal,** crash cymbal, high hat, ride cymbal, splash cymbal; **maraca,** calabash, castanet, Chinese block, cowbell, guiro, jew's-harp, sistrum, washboard, woodblock; **rhythm sticks,** clapping sticks, claves, music sticks, songsticks; **triangle,** anvil; **lagerphone,** crescent *(U.S.);* **bullroarer,** churinga, thunder stick; **noisemaker,** bones, clapper, hooter, rattle, whip, whistle, wobble board; **gong, tamtam; bell,** carillon, handbell, tintinabulum; **glockenspiel,** carillon, celesta, chime, harmonica, peal, tubular bells; **xylophone,** gamelan, gender, marimba, vibes *(Collog.),* vibraharp, vibraphone; **glass harmonica**

PERFECT *v* bring to perfection, complete, consummate, idealise, leave nothing to be desired, redintegrate, round off; **purify,** polish; **ripen,** mature

PERFECT *adj* absolute, consummate, hundred-per-cent, infinite, quintessential; **whole,** complete, entire, finished, intact; **sublime,** beautiful, heavenly, ideal, superb; **unparalleled,** inimitable; **flawless,** blotless, clean, clear, copperplate, fair, faultless, fine, good, immaculate, impeccable, incorrupt, inviolate, pure, spotless, stainless, unblemished, unimpaired, unscratched, unspoilt, unsullied, unworn, white; **infallible,** indefectible, inerrable, sound, watertight

PERFECTION *n* absoluteness, completeness, entireness, ideality, idealness, infiniteness, infinitude; **prime,** bloom, matureness, maturity; **consummation,** completion, redintegration; **purity,** cleanness, faultlessness, flawlessness, immaculacy, immaculateness, impeccability, incorruptness, pureness; **infallibility,** indefectibility, inerrability, inerrableness, infallibleness, watertightness

PERFECTIONIST *n* purist; **perfecter,** finisher, polisher, purifier

PERFECTIONIST *adj* idealist, idealistic, puristic, utopian

PERFECTIVE *adj* purificatory, redintegrative

PERFECTLY *adv* consummately, ideally, superbly; **flawlessly,** faultlessly, immaculately, impeccably; **infallibly,**

perfectly — permit

perfectly indefectibly, inerrably; **to a turn**, to perfection

PERFECT THING *n* acme, apotheosis, beau ideal, culmination, idea *(Philos.)*, ideal, ideal type, quintessence, summit, the Absolute, the abstract, top; **classic**, model, standard; **utopia**

PERFORATE *v* bite, crack, dub, gore, impale, javelin, penetrate, pierce, pike, prick, prickle, prong, reach, rowel, run through, stab, stick, sting, thrust, transfix, work into

PERFORATION *n* impalement, inburst *(Rare)*, penetration, prick, stab, sting, transfixion

PERFORM *v* act, appear in, clown, improvise, mime, mum, outact, play, play-act, show, tread the boards, ventriloquise, walk a slackwire, walk a tightrope, wing; **portray**, come *(Colloq.)*, emote *(Colloq.)*, impersonate, personate, represent; **recite**, busk, do a number, put across, regale with; **support**, co-star, compere, second; **go on the stage**, go on the road, have one's name in lights, make one's bow, star, tour; **overact**, ham it up, rant

PERFORMANCE *n* command performance, flop, sell-out; **premiere**, debut, first night, matinee, one-night stand; **crowd-pleaser**, potboiler, smash, smash-hit, tear-jerker, weepie; **preview**, off-Broadway run, tryout; **rehearsal**, clambake *(U.S.)*, run-through

PERIOD *n* season, space, span, term, time, tract; **period of duty**, hours, session, stint, stretch; **reign**, diaconate, dictatorship, papacy, regency, sitting, tenancy, tenure; **bout**, go, innings, round, shift, turn; **run**, patch, spell, streak; **era**, age, culture, cycle, day, epoch, generation, siècle, times, Yuga *(Hinduism)*; **episode**, page, stage; **academic year**, Lent term, Michaelmas term, semester, term, trimester, Trinity term; **prison sentence**, bird, clock, dream, hitch, jolt, Kath, lag, life, stretch, time; **prison term**, a brick, a clock, a drag, a sleep, a spin, a swy, a zack, the lot

PERIOD OF INACTION *n* abeyance, cold storage, latent period, laying-off season, low season, off-season, sit-down strike, strike, vacation, waiting; **calm**, Irishman's hurricane, peace, slack, slumber, slump; **dormancy**, aestivation, diapause, hibernation, sleep, suspended animation, torpor; **loaf**, laze, loll *(Archaic)*, lounge, slack, wait; **paralysis**, atropism, catatonia, diplegia, hemiplegia, palsy, panplegia, paralysation, paraplegia

PERMISSIBILITY *n* admissibility, admissibleness, allowableness, sufferableness

PERMISSIBLY *adv* admissibly, allowably, allowedly

PERMISSION *n* dispensation, go-ahead, green light, imprimatur, leave, passport, planning permission, release, sanction, thumbs up, vouchsafement; **licence**, authorisation, clearance *(Football)*, empowerment, faculty *(Eccles.)*, indult, nihil obstat, permit, pratique, the call, warrant; **free hand**, blank cheque, carte blanche, liberty; **consent**, acquiescence, appro, approbation, approval, courtesy

PERMIT *v* admit, allow, consent to, countenance, give one's permission, give the nod to, have, let, sanction, suffer, tolerate, vouchsafe; **license**,

permit

authorise, clear, empower, legitimate, privilege, warrant

PERMITTED *adj* allowed, authorised, granted, sanctioned; **permissible**, admissible, allowable, lawful

PERMITTER *n* approver, authoriser, consenter, licenser

PERSEVERANCE *n* diligence, persistence, stamina, staying power

PERSEVERE *v* bear with, crack hardy, crack hearty, endure, forbear, hang in, have patience with, hold the line, last the distance, persist, ride out, see through, sit tight, stay with, stick at, stick it out, stick to one's guns, sustain, weather the storm; **bear up**, bite one's lip, cool one's heels, grin and bear it, grit one's teeth, hold one's tongue, keep one's cool, keep one's temper, kick one's heels, put on a brave front, roll with the punches, take it on the chin, take the rough with the smooth; **bear**, abide, accept, bide *(Archaic)*, brook, cop, digest, hack it, lump it, put up with, stomach it, suffer, support, swallow, take, take it, tolerate

PERSEVERING *adj* assiduous, consistent, diligent, dogged, perseverant, sedulous, single-minded, strong-willed, tenacious, uncompromising; **steadfast**, enduring, firm, hardy, heart of oak, indefatigable, inexorable, staunch, stout, stout-hearted, sturdy, tough; **persistent**, determined, high-pressure, important *(Obs.)*, importunate, importune, pertinacious, unflagging, unremitting

PERSEVERINGLY *adv* firm, firmly, like grim death, manfully, pertinaciously, sedulously, staunchly, stout-heartedly, stoutly, tenaciously, through thick and thin, uncompromi-

personal property

singly; **assiduously**, diligently; **persistently**, doggedly, inexorably

PERSIST *v* box on, hang in, hang in there, keep at it, keep on, keep up, lay in, lay in there, persevere, plod on, plug on, push, rub along, rub on, rub through, see through, soldier on, stay, stick it out, stick out for; **apply oneself**, dig in, grind, peg away at, plough through, toil, work at; **endure**, bear up, hang on, hold on, not take no for an answer, sit pat, stand one's ground, stick to one's guns, worry along, worry through

PERSISTENCE *n* doggedness, firmness, grit, inexorability, inexorableness, perseverance, pertinaciousness, pertinacity, resoluteness, resolution, resolve, tenaciousness, tenacity; **assiduity**, application, assiduousness, diligence, industry, push, sedulity, sedulousness, single-mindedness; **indefatigability**, endurance, indefatigableness, persistence, stamina, stay *(U.S.)*, staying power, steadfastness, stoutness, tirelessness

PERSON *n* individual, lot, one, party, persona, personage, personality, presence, wight *(Archaic)*; **human being**, being, hominoid, Homo, Homo sapiens, human, mortal; **head**, hand, nose; **character**, bird, bleeder *(Brit.)*, blighter, bod, body, card, cookie, creature, cuss *(U.S.)*, customer, element, fellow, gink, kiddo, stick, type; **worthy**, Christian, soul. *See also* ETHNIC

PERSONAL PROPERTY *n* belongings, collectibles, effects, equipment, gear, goods, goods and chattels, household goods, lares and penates, moveables, paraphernalia, personal effects, personalty, stock-in-trade, tangibles,

personal property   392   **photographer**

things; **article of personal property**, chattel, chattel personal, chose *(Law)*, fixture *(Law)*, moveable *(Law)*. *See also* PROPERTY

PERSUADE *v* bounce, convince, handrush, induce, lead, lead someone on, lobby, overpersuade, put up to, talk around, talk into, wrangle; **urge**, blandish, blarney, cajole, carry away, coax, importune, solicit, sweet-talk, wheedle; **manipulate**, bias, brainwash, condition, impose on, manage, mesmerise, pervert, prejudice, prepossess, psych, seed, sway, swing, tamper with, twist round one's little finger; **argue**, assure, plead, reason, talk. *See also* INFLUENCE

PERSUASION *n* agitation, agitprop, brainwashing, cajolery, conditioning, convincement, emotional blackmail, hypnotisation, lobbyism, manipulation, mesmerisation, mesmerism, psychological warfare, salesmanship, suggestion; **argument**, hard sell, persuasive, pitch, propaganda, sales talk, soft sell, spiel. *See also* INFLUENCE

PESSIMIST *n* bear, counsel of despair, demoraliser, melancholiac; **doomwatcher**, doomsdayman

PESTERING *adj* bothersome, importunate, onerous, oppressive, teasing, tormenting; **bloody-minded**, bad-tempered, bitchy, cantankerous, doggish, icky, ill-natured, impossible, liverish, mean, ornery. *See also* UNPLEASANT

PHANTOM *n* apparition, appearance, astral, astral body, embodiment, Intelligence, invisible, materialisation, phantasm, presence, spectre, supernatural, wight *(Archaic)*, wraith; **ghost**, poltergeist, revenant, spook, wandoo, zombie; **soul**, manes, psyche, shade, shades, spirit; **attendant spirit**, familiar, familiar spirit, genius

PHOTOACTIVE *adj* heliotactic, heliotropic, photophilous, photosensitive, phototonic, phototropic

PHOTOGRAPH *n* bromide, contact print, drop-out, facsimile, frame, glossy, photo, pickie, picture, positive, print, proof, shooter, shot, snap, snapshot, still, visual, wirephoto; **slide**, lantern slide, microfiche, trannie *(Colloq.)*, transparency; **black-and-white**, colour photo, monochrome, sepia, vignette; **negative**; **composite photograph**, double exposure; **portrait**, candid, mug shot; **close-up**, blow-up, enlargement, long shot, reduction; **photomural**, panel, photomontage; **ambrotype**, anaglyph, autoradiograph, autotype, blueprint, calotype, cyanotype, daguerreotype, ferrotype, gravure, heliotype, hologram, macrograph, microdot, microform, micrograph, microphotograph, photochronograph, photogram, photomicrograph, platinotype, radiograph, roentgenogram, schlieren photograph, shadowgraph, stereophotograph, telephotograph, tintype, tomogram, X-ray photograph

PHOTOGRAPH *v* film, mug *(U.S.)*, shoot, snap; **develop**, enlarge, fix, print, reduce; **tone**, fog, intensify, sensitise, solarise, tint; **expose**, overexpose, underdevelop, underexpose

PHOTOGRAPHER *n* cameraman, cinematographer, daguerreotyper, daguerreotypist, photojournalist, shutterbug, snapshotter; **photoresearcher**

PHOTOGRAPHIC *adj* photogenic; **overexposed**, contrasty, foggy, grainy, in focus, out of focus, underdeveloped, underexposed

PHOTOGRAPHY *n* aerial photography, astrophotography, colour photography, flash photography, four-colour photography, halftone photography, heliography, infra-red photography, microphotography, nephography, photochromy, photojournalism, photoresearch, spark photography, spectroheliography, subtractive photography, synchroflash photography, three-colour photography, time-lapse photography; **photogravure**, photo-offset, photolithography

PHYSICAL EXAMINATION *n* amniocentesis, antenatal, Apgar score, auscultation, Binet test, biopsy, bioscopy, blood test, cancer smear, checkup, electrocardiograph, fluoroscopy, follow-up, Guthrie test, medical, P.K.U. test, palpation, Pap smear, postnatal, radiology, radioscopy, rhinoscopy, Rorschach test, short-arm parade, smear test, tracheoscopy, Wassermann reaction, X-ray; **post-mortem examination**, autopsy, forensic examination, inquest, necropsy, necrotomy, post-mortem

PHYSICALLY DEFORMED *adj* acromegalic, bandy-legged, bow-legged, club-footed, crookbacked, gibbous, hare-lipped, humpbacked, humped, hunchbacked, knock-kneed, pigeon-toed, sway-backed, taliped, valgus

PHYSICS *n* astrophysics, classical physics, macrophysics, natural philosophy, physical science, quantum electrodynamics, quantum mechanics

PIANO *n* concert grand piano, cottage piano, digitorium, dumb piano, fortepiano, goanna *(Colloq.)*, grand, grand piano, pianoforte *(U.S.)*, prepared piano, spinet, square piano, upright, upright piano; **clavier**, cembalo, clavecina, clavicembalo, clavichord, harpsichord, spinet, virginal; **organ**, American organ, calliope, choir organ, electric organ, electronic organ, harmonium, pipe organ, portative, portative organ, positive organ, reed organ, regal, seraphine, unit organ, wurlitzer; **accordion**, concertina, piano accordion, squeezebox

PIERCER *n* aiguille, antler, awl, brochette, caltrop, claw, cock, eyeleteer, fork, glover's needle, hayfork, horn, knitting needle, marlinespike, nail, pigsticker, point, prick *(Obs.)*, rapier, skewer, stiletto, stylet, tooth; **spur**, goad, prick *(Archaic)*, prod, rowel, sting; **hypodermic needle**, hype, hypo, spike, vaccine point; **spear**, arrow, arrowhead, assegai, grains, harpoon, lance, pile, shaft, spearhead; **needle**, acicula, aciculum, pin, point, ram, rostellum, rostrum, spicula, spicule, spiculum, spine, spinule; **spike**, crampon, creeper, grapnel, grappling iron, pike, piton, pricket, prong, spit, sticker, tenaculum, tine; **sting**, aculeus, emergence, stinger; **pick**, ice-axe, icepick, pick-axe, yam stick; **bit**, borer, brace and bit, bradawl, burin, centre-bit, diamond point, drill, gimlet, jackhammer, mattock, miser, pneumatic drill, post-hole digger, power drill, sticker, stopper, twist drill, wimble; **punch**, centre-punch, pirri point, puncheon; **barb**, barbule, beard, flue,

piercer   394   **pity**

fluke, pinnula, pinnule; **thorn**, aculeus, prickle, snag, spica

PIG *n* Berkshire, gilt, landrace, piggie, porker, razorback, shoat, sow, swine, Wessex saddleback

PIGSTY *n* Augean stables, pigpen, sty; **fleapit**, plague-spot; **rubbish heap**, dunghill, garbage bin; **cesspool**, cloaca, gutter, sewer, slough

PILOT *n* ace, aircrew, airman, airwoman, aviator, aviatrix, aviatrix, birdman, bush-pilot, captain, copilot, crew, flier, flight engineer, high-flier, navigator, observer, paraflier, sky pilot *(U.S.)*, skyman, test pilot; **cabin crew**, air hostess, flight attendant, steward, stewardess; **aeronaut**, balloonist, parachutist; **glider**, hang-glider, soarer; **astronaut**, cosmonaut, spaceman, spacewoman; **aeroplane passenger**, pax

PIPING *n* blowpipe, gas main, gas pipe, main, pipe, pipeline, service pipe, steampipe, umbilical cord *(Aerospace)*, water main, waterworks; **agricultural pipe**, boom spray, sprinkler system; **stinkpipe**, exhaust pipe, tailpipe; **navel pipe**, spurling pipe; **hose**, hosepipe; **siphon**; **tube**, straw, sucker, tubulure

PIRATE *n* buccaneer, corsair, freebooter, picaroon, rover *(Archaic)*, sea-robber, sea-rover, Viking

PISS OFF *interj* aroint thee *(Archaic)*, arsehole off, avaunt *(Obs.)*, away, away with you, be off, beat it, begone, bugger off, buzz off, fuck off, get fucked, get knotted, get lost, get nicked, get rooted, get stuffed, go jump in the lake, go to blazes, go to buggery, hence *(Archaic)*, hop it, nick off, rack off, rack off hairy legs, scat, scram, shove it, skedaddle, vamoose; **exeunt**, exeunt omnes, exit

PITCH *n* absolute pitch, concert A, concert pitch, relative pitch; **key**, home key, key signature, major, major key, minor, minor key; **register**, chest register, compass, diapason, head register, head voice, range, tessitura; **intonation**, sharpness, tuning; **tonality**, bitonality, key, polytonality; **timbre**, brilliance, croon, intensity, quality, tone, tone colour, voice; **dynamics**, swell; **modulation**, transition; **glissando**, portamento, slide

PITIABLE *adj* miserable, pathetic, piteous, pitiful, poor, rueful, ruthful *(Archaic)*, sorry, wretched

PITIABLY *adv* pathetically, piteously, pitifully, ruefully, ruthfully, wretchedly

PITIER *n* bleeding heart, condoler, softie, sympathiser; **humanitarian**, philanthropist

PITIFULNESS *n* miserableness, piteousness, pitiableness, wretchedness; **pathos**, touchingness

PITY *n* feeling, fellow feeling, graciosity, heart, humaneness, humanity, ruefulness, ruthfulness, softheartedness, sorriness, tenderheartedness, tenderness; **compassion**, bowels of compassion *(Archaic)*, charity, clemency, compassionateness, grace, mercifulness, mercy, misericordia, quarter, remorse *(Obs.)*, rue *(Archaic)*, ruth *(Archaic)*; **sympathy**, commiseration, condolence, consolation, empathy; **compassionate leave**

PITY *v* be cruel to be kind, be moved, compassion, compassionate, enter into, feel for, feel with, have a heart,

pity

soften, sympathise with, take pity on; **bleed for,** bemoan, feel sorry for; **condole,** commiserate, send one's condolences; **humanise**

PITYING *adj* bleeding, feeling, humane, humanitarian, rueful, ruthful *(Archaic),* sorry; **compassionate,** clement, gracious, merciful, piteous *(Archaic),* sparing; **sympathising,** commiserative, condolatory; **softhearted,** lenient, sympathetic, tenderhearted

PITYINGLY *adv* humanely, ruthfully, **compassionately,** clemently, graciously, mercifully; **sympathisingly,** commiseratively, condolingly, sympathetically

PLACE *v* lay, locate, lodge, perch, position, post, put, set, station, stick; **deposit,** bank, put down, set down; **table,** prefer, present, put forward; **put on,** apply, paint, slap on, slather, slosh, superpose, trowel; **store,** bestow, load, pigeonhole, stack, stow, truck

PLACED *adj* positioned, settled, stationed

PLACEMENT *n* emplacement, location, lodgment, placing, positioning, postposition, reposition, setting, settlement, settling, stationing; **putting down,** deposit, deposition; **tabling,** preferment, presentation; **putting on,** application, superposition; **storage,** bestowal, bestowment, loading, packing, stowage

PLACE OF KILLING *n* abattoirs, butchery, knackery, shamble, slaughterhouse; **arena,** bullring, mort *(Hunting);* **death cell,** death row; **battlefield,** battleground

plane figure

PLACE OF WORSHIP *n* bora *(Aborig.),* high place, holy, sacred place, sacred site, sanctuary, stupa; **Holy City,** Fatima, Holy Land, Jerusalem, Lourdes, Mecca, Medina, Varanasi, Vatican City. *See also* CHURCH; ABBEY; SHRINE

PLAN *n* counsel, design, device, idea, intent, intention, project, proposal, proposition, scheme; **suggestion,** cogitation, conception, contemplation, imagination *(Archaic),* motion, thought; **program,** agenda, arrangements, book, budget, démarche, format, nostrum, outline, regime, regimen, schedule, schema, schematism, syllabus, system, timetable; **policy,** ideology, line, platform; **tactics,** card, commander's concept, concept of operations, dart, healy *(Prison Colloq.),* pitch, ploy, stratagem, strategic plan, strategy, tactic. *See also* CONSPIRACY

PLAN *v* arrange, engineer, forecast, frame, jack *(N.Z.),* mastermind, organise, tee up; **schedule,** bill, budget, slate, timetable; **map out,** chalk out, chart, lay out, set out; **devise,** cast, cast about for, cogitate, compass, concert, concoct, contrive, design, hatch, imagine *(Archaic),* project, propose; **systemise,** systematise. *See also* CONSPIRE

PLANE FIGURE *n* decagon, dodecagon, enneagon, heptagon, hexagon, isogon, nonagon, octagon, pentagon, polygon, quindecagon, re-entrant polygon, undecagon; **triangle,** equilateral triangle, isosceles triangle, right-angled triangle, scalene triangle, spherical triangle; **quadrilateral,** diamond, lozenge, oblong, parallelogram, quadrangle, rectangle, rhom-

plane figure   396   **pleasant**

boid, rhombus, square, trapeze, trapezium, trapezoid; **curve,** cardioid, circle, ellipse, parabola, quadrant; **star,** asterisk, hexagram, pentacle, pentagram, pentalpha, pentangle

PLANETARY *adj* global, planetoidal, sublunary, tellurian, telluric, terrene, terrestrial, translunary; **meteoric,** cometic, meteoritic; **planetesimal**

PLANNED *adj* concerted, devised, prearranged, projected, put-up; **systematic,** schedular, schematic; **strategic,** tactical; **teleological,** destined, telic

PLANNER *n* architect, delineator, designer, draughtsman, plotter; **cartographer,** map-maker, mapper, surveyor

PLANT *n* amphibian, annual, anthouse plant, biennial, bine, broom, bulb, bush, carnivore, climber, corm, creeper, cushion plant, endophyte, ephemeral, epiphyll, epiphyte, ericoid, evergreen, fan palm, forb, geophyte, halophyte, herb, liana, liane, mallee, microphyte, monocarp, palm, parasite, perennial, rambler, rosette, runner, sand-binder, saprophyte, sedge, shrub, succulent, trailer, tree, tumbleweed, tussock, twiner, vine, whipstick, winder; **ornamental plant,** bouquet, boutonniere, cacoon, calabash, corsage, gourd, gum tips, jequirity, job's-tears, nosegay, posy, wreath; **plant classification,** acotyledon, acrogen, alga, angiosperm, bacteria, blue-green algae, brown algae, bryophyte, club moss, conifer, cormophyte, cryptogam, cyanobacterium, cyanophyte, cycad, dicotyledon, endogen, eukaryote, exogen, fern, fungus, green algae, gymnosperm, hepatic, lichen, liverwort, monocotyledon, moss, phanerogam, prokaryote, protist, pteridophyte, red algae, schizophyte, seed plant, spermatophyte, thallophyte, vascular plant; **flowering-plant family,** amaryllid, araliad, aroid, asclepiad, bromeliad, cactus, chenopod, composite, crucifer, cucurbit, daisy, dipterocarp, epacrid, goosefoot, grass, labiate, legume, lily, orchid, palm, sedge, umbellifer

PLASTER *n* cement render, drummy, facing, gyprock, parget, plastering, pricking coat, render, revetment, roughcast, setting coat, skimming coat, wattle; **veneer,** brick veneer, burlwood veneer, panelling, wainscot; **wallpaper,** dado, flock paper, lining paper, paper

PLATFORM *n* apron *(Theat.)*, bandstand, barbette, bema *(Greek Antiq.)*, bridge, pageant *(Hist.)*, stage; **podium,** dais, footpace, hustings *(Politics)*, pace, pulpit, rostrum, soapbox, tribune; **docking,** boatswain's chair, bosun's chair, cradle, jiggerboard, springboard *(Timber Industry)*; **pallet,** hack, skidway *(Timber Industry)*, staddle

PLATING *n* case *(Metall.)*, casing, electroplating, enamel, enamelling, enamelwork, foliation, galvanisation, gilding, gold plate, leading, nickel plate, overlay, oxidation, oxidisation, patina, plate, rolled gold, silvering, silverplate, tarnish, vitreous enamel

PLAYFULLY *adv* friskily, frolicsomely, gamesomely, sportively; **for fun,** for kicks, in fun; **amusingly,** enjoyably

PLEASANT *adj* acceptable, agreeable, bland, compatible, enjoyable, inoffensive, nice, offenceless, palatable, piacevole, pleasing, sapid, simpatico, to one's taste, welcome; **amiable,**

pleasant **pleasure**

adorable, benign, courteous, genial, good-natured, good-tempered, kindly, likeable, lovable, sweet-tempered; **charming,** attractive, becoming, comely, cute, easy on the eyes, engaging, glam, glamorous, graceful, piquant, pretty, taking, winning, winsome; **cheerful,** cosy, jolly, merry *(Archaic);* **delightful,** delectable, delicious, delightsome *(Archaic),* fragrant, gladsome, glorious, goluptious, gorgeous *(Colloq.),* heavenly, lovely *(Colloq.),* luscious; **sweet,** bittersweet, dulcet, mellifluous

PLEASANTLY *adv* acceptably, agreeably, amiably, inoffensively, nicely, piacevole, pleasingly; **charmingly,** attractively, becomingly, delectably, deliciously, delightfully, delightsomely *(Archaic),* engagingly, piquantly, sweetly

PLEASANTNESS *n* acceptability, acceptableness, agreeableness, amenity, blandness, inoffensiveness, likeability, likeableness, niceness, palatability, palatableness, pleasingness; **amiability,** amiableness, lovability, lovableness; **charm,** attractiveness, comeliness, cuteness, douceur, glam *(Colloq.),* glamour, grace, gracefulness, loveliness; **cheerfulness,** cosiness; **delightfulness,** delectability, delectableness, deliciousness, delightsomeness *(Archaic),* gloriousness, gorgeousness, heavenliness, lusciousness, luxuriousness, mellifluousness, sweetness; **pleasant place,** Eden, Elysium, heaven, millennium, paradise

PLEASE *v* divert, elicit a positive response, gratify, grow on, list *(Archaic),* pleasure, rub up the right way, tickle; **enchant,** beguile, charm,

delectate, enrapture, entrance; **gladden,** beatify, delight, glad *(Archaic),* imparadise, joy *(Obs.),* thrill to bits, transport

PLEASE *interj* for God's sake, for goodness sake, for heaven's sake, I beg of you, pray, prithee *(Archaic)*

PLEASED *adj* glad, happy, happy as a bastard on Father's Day, happy as Larry, joyful, joyous; **enchanted,** charmed; **delighted,** chuffed, enrapt, overjoyed, pleased as Punch, rapt, stoked, thrilled, tickled pink, tickled to bits, tickled to death; **euphoric,** beatific, blissful, ecstatic, enraptured, high, high as a kite, in raptures, on a high, rapturous, raving; **enjoying oneself,** in the groove, turned on

PLEASURABLE *adj* appealing, enjoyable, funky, groovy, likeable, mild-mannered, pleasant; **pleasing,** entertaining, gratifying, satisfying; **idyllic,** Edenic, Elysian, halcyon, paradisiacal

PLEASURABLY *adv* enjoyably; **gratifyingly,** satisfyingly; **hedonistically,** hedonically, indulgently, sybaritically, voluptuously; **delightedly,** happily, zestfully; **ecstatically,** blissfully, idyllically, paradisiacally, rapturously

PLEASURE *n* delight, delightedness, gladness, gladsomeness, happiness, joy, joyfulness, joyousness, lust *(Obs.),* pleasance *(Archaic);* **enjoyment,** delectation, recreation, refreshment; **gratification,** fulfilment, satisfaction, sensuality, voluptuosity, voluptuousness; **indulgence,** epicureanism, feasting, festivity, hedonics, hedonism, luxuriation, luxuriousness, luxury, pleasure principle; **pleasurableness,** enjoyableness, pleasantness, thrillingness; **creature comforts,**

cakes and ale, comfort, cosiness, ease, snugness, well-being; **liking**, fancy, palate, partiality, predilection, propensity *(Obs.)*, relish, taste; **appreciation**, admiration, love; joie de vivre, gusto, zest, zestfulness; **rapture**, abandonment, bliss, ecstasy, exaltation, rapturousness, transport; **seventh heaven**, beatification, beatitude, blessedness, blissfulness; **enchantment**, beguilement, bewitchment, ravishment, titillation; **euphoria**, ecstatics, raptures, transports; **thrill**, buzz, charge, kick; **high**, trip, upper

PLEASURE-LOVING *adj* high-stepping, indulgent, luxurious, pleasure-seeking, sybaritic, voluptuary, voluptuous; **hedonistic**, epicurean, hedonic

PLEBEIANISM *n* humbleness, ignobility, ignobleness, low birth; **popularisation**, vulgarisation

PLIABILITY *n* flexibility, flexibleness, limberness, lissomness, litheness, pliableness, pliancy, pliantness, suppleness, tone, twistability; **resilience**, bounce, bounciness, buoyancy, rebound, renitency, spring, springiness, temper, tension, tonicity, torsibility; **elasticity**, aero-elasticity, give, plasticity, sponginess; **stretchability**, ductility, stretchiness, tensility, tractility, Young's modulus; **elasticisation**, jellification, plasticisation

PLIABLE *adj* bendable, bendy, double-jointed, flexible, flexile, flippant *(Obs.)*, limber, lissom, lithe, pliant, springy, supple, twistable, twisty, whippy, willowy, wristy; **resilient**, bouncy, buoyant, inflated, renitent, spring, spring-loaded, tonic; **elastic**, aero-elastic, al dente, boneless, elastomeric, gelatinous, indiarubber, jellied, rubbery; **mouldable**, fictile, plastic, thermoplastic; **stretchable**, ductile, stretch, stretchy, tensible, tensile, tractile

PLIANTLY *adv* flexibly, limberly, lithely, pliably, springily, supply; **resiliently**, elastically, plastically

PLUG *n* bathplug, bung, cork, fipple, gasket, jackass *(Naut.)*, shive, spigot, spile, spill, stop, stopper, stopple *(Archaic)*, stuffing box, tap; **cap**, bottle top, crown cap, crown seal, screwtop; **sealing wax**, cachet, cane, seal; **sealing strip**, weather strip *(Bldg. Trades)*, weather-stripping; **wad**, tampion *(Gunnery)*, tampon

PLUMB THE DEPTHS *v* go deep; **plumb**, fathom, heave the lead, sound, take soundings

POCKET *n* bin *(Colloq.)*, fob, hip-pocket, poke *(Archaic)*, pouch *(Scot.)*, sporran

POET *n* ballad-monger, bard, dithyrambist, elegist, hymnist, hymnodist, idyllist, imagist, jongleur, laureate, lyricist, lyrist, maker *(Archaic)*, metrician, metrifier, metrist, minnesinger, minstrel, monodist, poet laureate, poetaster, poetess, prosodist, rhymer, rhymester, scop, singer, skald, songster, songwriter, sonneteer, troubadour, trouvère, vers librist, versifier

POETIC *adj* bardic, Parnassian; **lyric**, elegiac, idyllic, lyrical, melic, odic; **heroic**, Dantesque, epic, Homeric; **bucolic**, pastoral; **satiric**, mock-heroic; **metric**, measured, metrical, prosodic, prosodical, quantitative, rhythmical, scannable; **versicular**, stanzaic, stichic, strophic, systolic

POETICALLY *adv* epically, lyrically, prosodically; **rhythmically**, metrically

POETIC RHYTHM *n* metre, metrics, movement, numbers, rhythmics, scansion, sprung rhythm, versification; stress, accent, beat, ictus; **systole; enjambment**

POETRY *n* poesy, verse; **balladry**, concrete poetry, goliardery, hymnody, hymnology, minstrelsy, namby-pamby, nonsense verse, satire; **poetic art**, ars poetica, poetics, prosody, the Muse; **poem**, lines, monostrophe, piece, prose poem, rhyme, rime, song, strain; **book of poetry**, anthology, chapbook, divan *(Obs.)*, Parnassus; **lyric**, ballade, canzone, cento, Cowleian ode, dithyramb, ditty, eclogue, epode, erotic, Horatian ode, idyll, irregular ode, ithyphallic, madrigal, monody, ode, pantun, Pindaric ode, Pseudo-Pindaric ode, regular ode, rondeau, rondel, roundel, rune, Sapphic ode, sestina, sextain, sonnet, tanka, villanelle, virelay; **ballad**, broadsheet, bush ballad, doggerel, fit, jingle, macaronic, nursery rhyme, singsong; **epic**, chanson de geste, épopée, epopoeia, epos, heroic verse, heroics, rhapsody; **romance**, ballad, fabliau, geste *(Archaic)*, lay, roman, romaunt; **georgic**, bucolic, pastoral; **elegy**, dirge, lament; **epithalamium**, prothalamion; **hymn**, psalm; **epigram**, acrostic, charm, clerihew, gnomic verse, haiku, limerick

POINTED *adj* acuate, aculeate, acuminate, acute, bicorn, cornuted, cultrate, cusped, cuspidal, cuspidate, ericoid, fastigiate, obeliscal, oxy, subacute, superacute; **barbed**, pinnular, pinnulate, pinnulated; **beaked**, beaky, lipped; **spearlike**, lanceolate, oblanceolate; **arrowy**, harpoonlike, sagittal, sagittate; **cone-shaped**, coniform. *See also* SHARP; SPINY

POINT OF CONVERGENCE *n* crunode, cusp, focus, hub, node, vanishing point; **line of convergence**, asymptote, confluent, spoke

POINT OF VIEW *n* attitude, opinion, outlook, pose, position, stance, stand, thing, view, viewpoint; **inclination**, bent, bias, cast, impulse, lean, leaning, penchant, ply, prejudice, set, slant, tenor, turn; **predisposition**, amenability, diathesis, disposition, exposure, habit, liability, liableness, susceptibility, susceptibleness, susceptiveness, susceptivity, tendency, weakness; **affinity**, affect *(Obs.)*, affection *(Obs.)*, appetence, aptitude, liking, partiality, predilection, proclivity, proneness, propensity, readiness, talent *(Obs.)*; **trend**, climate, course, current, direction, drift, gravitation, motion, movement, stream, tide, undercurrent, wave, wind

POISON *n* autotoxin, bait, bane, endotoxin, exotoxin, intoxicant, potion, toxicant, toxin, toxoid; **venom**, snakebite, sting, venin, zootoxin; **germ**, infection, virus; **biocide**, agent orange, agent purple, agent white, anticrop agent, defoliant, fungicide, herbicide, picloran, weedicide, weedkiller; **chemical agent**, biological weapon, nerve agent, phosgene, sternutator, yellow rain; **radiation**, fallout, strontium-90; **poison gas**, adamsite, arsine, asphyxiant, damp, diphosgene, effluvium, gas, mephitis, miasma, mofette, mustard gas, vapours; **pesticide**, acaricide, arsenicals, chlordane, DDT, dichlorodiphenyltrichloroethane, dieldrin, insecticide, malathion, metaldehyde, miticide, Paris green, pyrethrum, rotenone; **dichlorophenoxyacetic acid**, 2, 4-D; **trichlorophenoxyacetic acid**, 2, 4, 5-T, dioxin, toxaphene; **poisonousness**, nocuousness, noisomeness, noxiousness, toxicity, venomousness, virulence

POISON v drug, empoison, envenom, hocus, venom *(Archaic)*; **bait**, cyanide *(N.Z.)*, loco *(U.S.)*; **sting**, urticate; **contaminate**, denature, denaturise, infect; **biomagnify**

POISONER n baiter, contaminator, stinger; **poison cart**, gas chamber, gas oven

POISONING n alcoholism, autointoxication, autotoxaemia, bromism, ciguatera, cinchonism, gassing, intoxication, lead poisoning, urtication; **contamination**, biomagnification, denaturation, toxication; **biological warfare**, aerial spraying

POISONOUS adj baited, baneful, contaminative, germ-laden, mephitic, miasmal, miasmatic, miasmatical, miasmic, nocuous, noisome, noxious, pestilent, pestilential, poison, venenose *(Rare)*, venomous, vicious *(Obs.)*, virulent; **toxic**, autotoxic, carcinogenic, cyanic, epipastic, escharotic, fungicidal, strychnic, toxicant, toxicogenic, zootoxic

POISONOUSLY adv banefully, nocuously, noisomely, venomously; **noxiously**, mephitically, pestilently

POLE n barber's pole, beanpole, caber, flagpole, jackstaff, maypole, totem pole; **telegraph pole**, breakaway, frangible, Stobie pole, utility pole; **barge pole**, catching pole, roping pole; **mast**, jigger, jiggermast, jury mast, mizzenmast, royal mast, samson post, topmast; **boom**, bowsprit, bumpkin, dolphin striker, gaff, jackyard, jib boom, jockey pole, martingale, spar, sprit, steeve, traveller, yard

POLICE n armed constabulary, CIB, CID, coastguard, commissary, consorting squad, constabulary, customs, dog squad, drug squad, ducks and geese, FBI *(U.S.)*, filth *(Brit.)*, flying squad, force, fuzz, gendarmerie, military police, Scotland Yard, secret police, the boys in blue, the law, the long arm of the law, vice squad, water police

POLICEMAN n bobby, bull, constable, convict constable, cop, copper, customs officer, demon, detective, farm constable *(Convict)*, flat, flatfoot, gendarme, heavy, inspector, jack, Joe, john, jonnop, lawman *(U.S.)*, Mickey, mountie *(Canada)*, narc, operative *(U.S.)*, patrolman, peeler *(Obs.)*, pig *(Colloq.)*, pointsman *(N.Z.)*, police constable, police officer, policewoman, provost marshal, ranger, roundsman *(U.S.)*, rozzer, screw, sergeant, speed-cop, super, superintendent, trap, trooper, walloper; **proctor**, attendance officer, bulldog, prison officer, provost, screw, truant officer, warden *(U.S. Prison)*, warder; **parking policeman**, brown bomber, grey ghost, meter maid *(Brit. Colloq.)*, traffic warden *(Brit.)*; **posse**, posse comitatus, vigilance committee *(U.S.)*, vigilance man *(U.S.)*, vigilante *(U.S.)*; **peace officer**, marshal *(U.S.)*, sheriff, special, special constable

POLICE STATION n cop shop *(Colloq.)*, gendarmerie

POLISH n bull *(Mil.)*, glare, glaze, shine, shoeshine

POLISH v beeswax, buff, burnish, dub, furbish, lustre, planish, rub up, shine, wax

POLITICAL adj party, sociopolitical; **electioneering**, agitprop, barnstorming, whistlestop

POLITICAL IDEOLOGY n centrist, coalitionist, democrat, federalist, fusionist, liberal, liberalist, moderate, ochlocrat, reformist, small-l liberal, technocrat, unicameralist; **left-winger**, bolshevik, bolshevist, bolshie, collectivist, com, commie, commo, communalist, communist, comrade, leftie, leftist, Leninist, Maoist, Marxist, nationaliser, parlour pink *(Colloq.)*, pink, pinkie, pinko *(U.S.)*, progressive, radical, red, republican, socialist, sovietist, syndicalist, Trotskyite, weekend revolutionary *(Derog.)*; **revolutionary**, Jacobin, terrorist, urban guerilla; **nationalist**, free-stater *(Brit.)*, home-ruler, Little Englander, separatist; **feminist**, radical feminist, suffragette, suffragist, women's libber; **conservationist**, environmentalist, greenie; **right-winger**, capitalist, capitalist roader *(Derog.)*, conservative, counter-revolutionary, fundamentalist, grouper, legitimist, mossback *(U.S.)*, reactionary, revisionist, right-to-lifer, tory, true blue; **fascist**, absolutist, Caesarist, czarist, elitist, feudalist, imperialist, monarchist, monocrat, neo-fascist, royalist, stratocrat, territorialist, theocrat, totalitarian, tsarist; **hawk**, cold warrior

POLITICAL SPECTRUM n centre, faction, left, left wing, right, right wing, wing; **pressure group**, big business, business, labour, lobbyist, management, the bosses

POLITICIAN n agitprop, agro-politician, barnstormer, candidate, canvasser, crusader, crypto, favourite son *(U.S.)*, fellow traveller, king maker *(U.S.)*, lobbyist, political activist, political enthusiast, politico, pollie, strategist, stump orator, tub-thumper. See also MEMBER OF PARLIAMENT

POLITICISE v agitate, propagandise, raise consciousness; **lobby**, pressure; **redistribute**, gerrymander

POLITICS n class warfare, lobbyism, mugwumpery, party politics, political football, power structure, statecraft, statesmanship, statism *(Obs.)*, war conducted by other means; **diplomacy**, balance of power, brinkmanship, cold war, domino theory, escalation, gunboat diplomacy, irredentism, power politics, Realpolitik, shuttle diplomacy, summitry, ultimatum; **political science**, geopolitics

POOR adj badly off, depressed, disadvantaged, dowerless, down at heel, down on one's arse, down on one's luck, down to the bottom dollar, down to the last crust, fortuneless, gone to Gowings, hard up, indigent, landless, miserable, miserable as a bandicoot, needful, needy, on one's beam-ends, on one's uppers, out at elbows, poor as a bandicoot, poor as a church mouse, underprivileged, without; **destitute**, beggarly, done for, down and out, impoverished, living on queer street, mendicant, on skid row, on the streets, penurious, poverty-stricken, slummy, starveling, vagrant, wretched; **broke**, bled white, broke to the wide, dead motherless broke, flat broke, impecunious, on the beach, on the outer, on the strap, out of pocket, penniless, skint, skun, stiff, stiff as a crutch, stony, stony-broke, strapped, stumped up; **bankrupt**, broken, stumered

POORHOUSE *n* almshouse; **slums**, dump, shantytown; **depressed area**, distressed area

POORLY *adv* comfortlessly, impecuniously, indigently, miserably, on the wrong side of the tracks, penuriously, wretchedly; **from hand to mouth**, at subsistence level, on a shoestring, on the breadline, on the downgrade

POOR PERSON *n* beadsman, beadswoman, cracker *(U.S.)*, derelict, dero, down-and-out, garreteer, have-not, needer, pauper, poor white *(U.S.)*; **beggar**, almsman, almswoman, beggarman, hobo, mendicant, starveling, tatterdemalion, vag, vagabond; **ragamuffin**, Arab, cinderella, guttersnipe, street Arab; **the poor**, poor white trash *(Derog.)*, the have-nots, the other half

POPULAR *adj* best-selling, chartbound, commercial *(Music)*, hitbound, pop

POPULARITY *n* mass appeal; **popular success**, gorilla *(U.S.)*, rage, smash, smash-hit, top of the pops

POPULATION *n* citizenry; **towndweller**, burgess, burgher, citizen, city dweller, fringe dweller, metropolitan, slummer, townie, townsman, townswoman; **suburbanite**, commuter, exurbanite; **townspeople**, suburbia, townsfolk, township *(Brit. Hist.)*, village; **countrydweller**, backcountryman, backblocker, backwoodsman, bushie, bushman, bushwhacker *(U.S.)*, cottager, cottar *(Scot.)*, cottier, countryman, countryside, countrywoman, hatter, peasant, provincial, ryot, villager; **settler**, colonist, currency lad, currency lass, illegitimate, overstraiter *(Hist.)*, soldier settler, squatter; **migrant**, alien, black hat, ethnic, ethno, immigrant, New Australian, new chum, reffo; **native**, aborigine, autochthon, indigene. *See also* INHABITANT; OCCUPANT

PORNOGRAPHY *n* blue movie, child pornography, dirty postcard, filth, hard porn, hot stuff, obscenity, skinflick, smut, soft porn; **pornographic writing**, banned book, curiosa *(U.S.)*, erotica, ithyphallic, yellowback; **bawdy yarn**, double entendre, limerick; **indecent exposure**, hambone, poppy show, strip, striptease. *See also* OBSCENITY

PORTRAIT *n* copy, counterfeit *(Obs.)*, delineation, depiction, drawing, engraving, etching, facsimile, half-face, half-length, idea *(Obs.)*, identikit, image, likeness, painting, photograph, picture, presentment, projection, representation, semblance, silhouette, sketch, speaking likeness, study; **caricature**, cartoon, comic, comic strip; **statue**, antic *(Archaic)*, bronze, bust, effigy, gargoyle, glyph, head, herm, sculptured figure; **effigy**, automaton, doll, dummy, figurine, guy, jackstraw, manikin, mannequin, marionette, model, puppet, robot, waxwork; **totem**, churinga, idol, tiki, totem pole; **mask**, character, disguise, person, persona

PORTRAY v catch a likeness, delineate, depict, depicture, draw, engrave, etch, hold the mirror up to nature, just hit off, line, paint, picture, write; **caricature,** cartoon; **photograph,** X-ray; **carve,** cast, sculpt

POSE n antic, attitude, position, posture; **bearing,** carriage, deportment, manner, outward, port, set; **stance,** stand; **accumbency,** couching, decumbence, decumbency, prostration, recumbency; **sitting,** seat, seating, sedentariness, straddle; **bending,** bow, curtsy, kneeling, kowtow, squat, stoop; **slouch,** droop, sprawl

POSE v imitate, position oneself, posture, posturise, square off *(Boxing),* square one's shoulders, stand up properly, stand up straight, strike a pose; **bear oneself,** carry oneself; **stand erect,** be upstanding, draw oneself up, stand up

POSER n attitudinarian, croucher, kneeler, posturer, saluter, sitter, sprawler, squatter, straddler

POSITION n line *(Mil.),* locus, pitch, place, plot, point, possie, set, set-up, site, situation, situs, spot, station; **location,** address, whereabouts; **locale,** haunt, locality, post, setting, stamping ground; **rendezvous,** tryst, trysting place, venue

POSITION v allocate, bung, determine, draw, emplace, establish, install, instate, localise, locate, park, pinpoint, pitch, place, plank down, plant, pose *(Archaic),* posit, re-position, site, situate, stage, station; **deploy,** collocate, dispose, line, range; **lie,** rest, sit, stand, take one's place; **lay,** plank down, plonk down, whack down

POSITIONED adj bestead *(Archaic),* disposed, located, placed, sited, situate *(Archaic),* situated

POSITIONING n collocation, configuration, deployment, deposition, distribution, emplacement, establishment, installation, instatement, localisation, orientation, pitch, placement; **echolocation,** echo ranging, fix *(Colloq.),* radiolocation; **radar,** asdic, Doppler radar, loran, magnetron, minitrack *(Aerospace),* radar scanner, radio beacon, radio-compass, sonobuoy

POSSIBLY adv by chance, haply *(Archaic),* happen *(Brit. Colloq.),* maybe, mayhap *(Archaic),* peradventure *(Archaic),* perchance *(Archaic),* perhaps, potentially, practicably

POST n bedpost; **pile,** block *(Qld.),* piling, stilt; **gatepost,** gradient post, heelpost, hitching post, quintain, strainer, strainer post, winning post; **bollard,** barrel, bitt, loggerhead; **column,** anta, atlantes, gnomon, monolith, obelisk, pilaster, pillar, pylon, shaft, verge; **dado,** die, scape, trunk

POSTSCRIPT n allonge, annex, annexure, appendix, codicil, embolism, endorsement, rider, schedule, subjunction, subscription; **epilogue,** addendum, corollary, envoy, excursus, follow-up; **footnote,** end note, note, protocol, scholium.   *See also* ADDITION

POSTURAL adj attitudinal; **accumbent,** decumbent, face downwards, flat out, lying dowm, procumbent, prone, prostrate, reclining, recumbent, spread-eagled, supine; **kneeling,** crouching, drooping, stooped; **standing,** erect, upright

POVERTY *n* destitution, distress, impecuniosity, impecuniousness, indigence, miserableness, misery, necessity, need, neediness, pauperism, penuriousness, penury, poorness, privation, starvation, want, wretchedness; **impoverishment**, deprivation, pauperisation; **beggardom**, beggarhood, beggarliness, beggary, hoboism, mendicancy, mendicity; **poverty line**

POWDER *n* bulldust *(Colloq.)*, coaldust, cosmic dust, crocus, diamond dust, dust, flowers of sulphur *(Chem.)*, glacial meal, grit, ground glass, gum *(Coal Mining)*, icing sugar, platinum black *(Chem.)*, pounce, powdered chalk, powdered charcoal, pumice, rock-flour, sawdust, slack *(Coal Mining)*, streak *(Mineral.)*, triturate; **ash**, ash fall, cinder, fly-ash, volcanic ash; **sand**, black sand, greensand, shingle; **flour**, bran, grist, grits, meal; **plaster**, cement, flock, petuntse *(Geol.)*; terra alba *(Geol.)*; **ochre**, kamala *(Bot.)*, kohl, mascara, rouge; **talcum powder**, face powder, sachet; **bloom**, efflorescence; **speck**, corn, detritus, filing, fine *(Mining)*, fines, grain, mote, particle, seed, spore, sporule

POWDER *v* abrade, bray, bruise, comminute, crumble, crunch, crush, levigate, pound, pulverise, rasp, triturate; **dolly**, pestle, puddle; **grind**, file, grate, kibble, mill; **granulate**, corn, grain; **effloresce**, come to dust, disintegrate, fall to dust, moulder, reduce to powder

POWDERED *adj* attrite *(Obs.)*, desiccated, ground, kibble, milled, pulverised, sifted, stoneground; **fine**, crumby, impalpable, light, pulverisable

POWDERER *n* file, grater, grinder, pouncer, pulveriser, rasp; **pestle**, dolly, posser; **millstone**, ball mill, grindstone, mortar, muller, puddling box, puddling tub, spider; **mill**, flour mill, gristmill, hand mill, quern; **konometer**

POWDERINESS *n* friability, friableness, mealiness; **grittiness**, sabulosity, sandiness

POWDERING *n* abrasion, comminution, detrition, filing, granulation, grind, grinding, levigation, pulverisation, triturate, trituration; **milling**, dollying *(Mining)*, quartz-crushing, rock-crushing

POWDERY *adj* branlike, efflorescent, flocculent, furfuraceous, granular, pruinose, pulverulent; **floury**, farinaceous, flourlike, mealy; **ashy**, ashen; **sandy**, arenaceous, dusty, gritty, sabulous

POWER *n* authority, force, forcefulness, might, mightiness, potence, potency, potentness, powerfulness, puissance *(Archaic)*, strength; **dominion**, danger *(Obs.)*, domain, empire, jurisdiction, rule, sovereignty, sway; **force**, action, activity, clout, effect, energy, leverage, teeth, thrust, vigorousness, vigour, virtue, wallop *(Colloq.)*

POWERFUL *adj* all-powerful, almighty, armipotent, elemental, mighty, omnipotent, plenipotent, plenipotentiary, potent, potential *(Rare)*, puissant *(Archaic)*, strong; **authoritative**, commanding, magisterial, masterful; **domineering**, autocratic, dictatorial, imperious, overruling, tyrannical; **energetic**, emphatic, exertive, high-performance, high-powered, knockdown, knockdown

powerful drag-out, lively, punchy, raunchy, sledge-hammer, spunky, telling, vigorous

POWERFULLY *adv* almightily, mightily, omnipotently, potently, puissantly *(Archaic)*, strong, strongly, with might and main; **authoritatively,** commandingly, masterfully; **domineeringly,** autocratically, dictatorially, imperiously, tyrannically; **energetically,** emphatically, raunchily, spunkily, vigorously

POWERFUL PERSON *n* autocrat, baron, big brother, boss cocky, cock of the walk, crowner of kings, dictator, dynamo, éminence grise, force majeure, grey eminence, head sherang, high priest, high-flier, Mr Big, operator, oppressor, plenipotentiary, predominator, prime mover, robber baron, strong man, top dog, tycoon, tyrant; **the Establishment,** vested interests

POWERLESS *adj* emptied, feeble, impotent, impuissant, incapable, unable, void, weak; **incapacitated,** buggered, castrated, crippled, debilitated, enervate, enervated, fucked, neutralised, paralysed, screwed up, shot, washed-out, washed-up; **ataxic,** asthenic, atactic, avirulent; **decrepit,** obsolete, over the hill, past it, senile, superannuated; **good-for-nothing,** gutless, milky, milquetoast, pathetic, prostrate, sissy, useless

POWERLESSLY *adv* impotently, ineffectually

POWERLESSNESS *n* asthenia *(Path.),* brewer's droop, debility, decrepitude, exhaustion, helplessness, impotence, impuissance, inability, inanition, incapability, incapableness, incapacity, incompetence, ineptitude, milkiness, senility, weakness; **enervation,** ataxia, caducity, debilitation, decay, enfeeblement, impalement, impoverishment, incapacitation, paralysis, slough, wane

POWER TO ACT *n* charter, empowerment, licence, permit, power of attorney; **appointment,** installation, nomination, ordination

PRACTISE LAW *v* advise, assist, brief, defend, do conveyancing, plead cases, prepare briefs, prosecute, represent; **take silk,** be called to the bar

PRACTISE MEDICINE *v* cure, doctor, heal, medicine, treat; **nurse,** special; **have a good bedside manner; diagnose,** auscultate, sound, success

PRAM *n* bathchair, crash cart, jinrikisha, perambulator, pushchair, pusher *(Brit.),* rickshaw, stroller, wheelchair

PRAYER *n* angelus, chaplet, collect, commination, confiteor, devotions, divine office, exercise, litanies, Hail Mary, invocation, Kol Nidre, Kyrie eleison, litany, little office, mission, novena, ordinance, orison, pater, paternoster, petition, placebo, praise, proper, requiescat, requiescat in pace, rosary, suffrage, vigil; **liturgy,** antiphonary, breviary, common prayer, hours, lectionary, mahzor, missal, office, ordinal, ordo, pontifical, processional, psalmody, rubric, siddhur, Tantra; **prayer formula,** Eastern Rite, formalism, Greek Rite, Liturgical Latin, liturgics, ordinance, religions *(Obs.),* Roman rite, Russian Rite, sacramentality; **creed,** Apostles' Creed, Athanasian Creed, credo, Nicene Creed; **mantra,** mandala, om, omphaloskepsis, prayer wheel *(Buddhism);* **church service,** chapel, church, complin, conventicle, divine service, Evensong, folk mass, High

Mass, lection, low mass, meeting, ordinary, pleasant Sunday afternoon, prayer meeting, preaching, requiem, ritual, sacrifice, synagogue, thanksgiving, the Lord's Supper, vespers, watchnight service, worship; **hymn**, Agnus Dei, alleluia, anthem, antiphon, antiphony, ascription, Ave, Ave Maria, blessing, cantata, canticle, cantus, carol, chant, credo, creed, doxology, gloria, greater doxology, hallelujah, introit, lesser doxology, mass, metrical psalm, Miserere, Nunc Dimittis, offertory, praise, processional, prose, psalm, psalmody, recessional hymn, respond, response, responsory, Sanctus, service, spiritual, Te Deum, Tersanctus, tract, versicle; **passion play**, mystery play, pageant; **canonical hours**, complin, laudes, lauds, little hours, matin, nones, preparation, prime, sext, tierce, vespers

PREACHER *n* evangel, evangelist, hot-gospeller, missioner, missionary, predicant *(Obs.)*, pulpiteer *(Derog.)*, revivalist, Sal, Sallie, Salvation Army, Salvationist, Salvo; **acolyte**, deacon, deaconess, diaconate, exorcist; **catechist**, catechiser. *See also* ECCLESIASTIC

PRECEDE *v* antecede, antedate, beat, come before, foredate, forego, forerun, predate; **anticipate**, predict, prevent *(Obs.)*, prophecy

PRECEDENCE *n* ascendancy, predominance, predomination, prerogative *(Obs.)*, pride of place, priority, seniority; **primacy**, headship, hegemony, leadership, lordship, overlordship, paramountcy, sovereignty, supereminence, supremacy; **preponderance, preponderation, prevailingness, prevalence**

PRECEDING *adj* antecedent, anterior, early, former, precedent, precessional, precursive, prevenient, previous, prior, yester *(Archaic)*; **aforesaid**, above, aforementioned, foregoing, said, which; **prefixal**, preposed, prepositive

PRECISE *adj* accurate, bang-on, exact, in focus, on the beam, pat, perfect, point-device *(Archaic)*, right on, sharp, sharp-cut, spot-on; **unambiguous**, definite, univocal, unmistakable; **minute**, fine, particular; **measured**, calculated, determinate, mathematical, nicely calculated, strict, unerring, well-defined; **explicit**, elaborate, elaborative, express, identical, very; **true**, even, flush, level; **made-to-measure**, made-to-order, precut, ready-made; **punctilious**, fastidious, meticulous, punctual, rigorous, scrupulous, severe; **pedantic**, donnish, pedantical; **refined**, correct, nice, proper, pukka, right; **literal**, letter-perfect, technical, verbal, verbatim *(Rare)*, verbatim, word perfect

PRECISELY *adv* accurately, minutely, squarely, strictly, to a nicety, to a T, unerringly, with clockwork precision; **exactly**, dead, dead-centre, even, flat, full, giusto *(Music)*, just, plonk, plumb, slap-bang, square; **measuredly**, mathematically, scientifically; **flush**, even, true; **punctiliously**, punctually, scrupulously; **pedantically**, donnishly; **verbatim**, ad litteram, ad verbum, explicitly, literally, literatim, off pat, pat, sic, to the letter, word for word

PRECISION n accuracy, accurateness, correctness, niceness, nicety, preciseness, squareness, unerringness; **exactness,** definiteness, exactitude, fidelity, punctiliousness, truth, veracity; **alignment,** face edge, face side, register *(Print.)*, tram *(Mach.)*, true, trueness, working edge, working face; **sharpness,** definition *(Optics)*; **regulation,** adjustment, calibration, sensedation; **formulation,** formularisation, formulisation; **literality,** explicitness, literalism, literalness, the letter of the law; **strictness,** pedantry, scrupulosity, severeness, severity; **punctilio,** technicality

PRECISIONIST n elaborator, formulator, formuliser, literaliser, literalist, pedagogue, pedant, perfectionist, refiner

PREDATORY adj bloodsucking, confiscatory, dispossessory, predacious, prehensile, privative, raptorial, ravening; **extortionary,** extortive, grasping, greedy, leechlike, on the make, on the take, parasitic, rapacious, vampirish, vulture-like

PREDICT v cast, divine, forecast, foresee, foretell, harbinger, herald, presignify, prognosticate, prophesy, read, see, shadow forth, soothsay, vaticinate; **promise,** augur, auspicate *(Archaic)*, bid fair to, point to, raise expectations, raise hopes; **signify,** indicate, suggest; **tell someone's fortune,** cast a horoscope; **cross someone's palm with silver,** have one's fortune told; **warn,** bode, forebode, omen, portend, presage; **prefigure,** pretypify; **tip,** nap *(Horseracing)*; **estimate,** cost, guess, judge, take a stab at

PREDICTION n bodement, prophecy, self-fulfilling prophecy; **forecast,** cast, prognosis, prognostic; **estimate,** approximation, cost estimate, cost-benefit analysis, guesstimate, judgment, predicted cost, quantity survey; **tip,** nap *(Horseracing)*; **promise,** reason to hope, something to look forward to. *See also* FORTUNE-TELLING

PREDICTIVE adj prefigurative, prognosticative, prophetic, significative; **prophetic,** all-seeing, augural, auspicial, divinatory, fatal *(Obs.)*, mantic, oracular, prognostic, vatic, vaticinal, weatherwise; **auspicious,** promising; **ominous,** boding, disastrous *(Archaic)*, fateful, foreboding, ill-boding, sinister

PREDICTIVELY adv mantically, oracularly, prophetically; **ominously,** bodingly, forebodingly, sinisterly

PREDICTOR n augur, Chaldean, diviner, foreboder, foreteller, geomancer, haruspex, oneiromancer, oracle, presager, prognosticator, prophesier, prophet, seer, soothsayer, vaticinator; **prophet of doom,** Cassandra, jeremiah. *See also* FORTUNE-TELLER

PREDISPOSED adj apt to, capable of, disposed, given to, in a fair way to, inclined, partial, prone, ready, tending; **biased,** affectionate *(Obs.)*, appetent, partisan, prejudiced, tendentious; **tempered,** minded, spirited; **susceptible,** accessible, amenable, diathetic, exposed, liable, open, subject, susceptive, vulnerable; **inclinational,** inclinatory

PREDOMINANCE n almightiness, ascendancy, omnipotence, predomination, preponderance, preponderation, superhumanity, supremacy,

predominance supremeness; **autocracy**, dictatorship, lordship, tyranny

PREDOMINANT *adj* absolute, ascendant, eminent, high-flying, master, paramount, pre-eminent, preponderant, preponderating, prepotent, sovereign, supreme

PREDOMINANTLY *adv* eminently, pre-eminently, predominatingly, preponderantly, preponderatingly, prepotently, sovereignly, supremely

PREDOMINATE *v* command, have carte blanche, hold in fee, hold sway over, hold the balance of power, put the maginnis on, ride, rule; **preponderate**, outman, outvote, outweigh; **surmount**, be in the ascendant, have one's day, triumph

PREGNANCY *n* foetation, gestation, gravidity, interesting condition, sitting; **parity**, multiparity, oviparity, ovoviviparity, polycyesis, primiparity, viviparity; **unwanted pregnancy**, mistake, unplanned pregnancy.
See also CONCEPTION; BIRTH; REPRODUCTION

PREGNANT *adj* banged-up, big, enceinte, expectant, gone, gravid, heavy, impregnate, in pod, in the family way, in the pudding club, in trouble, knocked-up, preggers, up the duff, with child, with young; **brood**, stud; **natal**, congenital, parturient, peri-natal, post-partum, postnatal, prenatal, puerperal; **lying-in**, maternity, obstetric; **broody**, clucky, in season, oestrous, on heat, philoprogenitive; **biparous**, fissiparous, livebearing, multiparous, oviparous, ovoviviparous, primiparous, pupiparous, uniparous, viviparous; **ecbolic**, oxytocic

prepare

PREHISTORIC MAN *n* Australopithecine, cavedweller, caveman, Cro-Magnon man, Heidelberg man, Java man, lakedweller, Neanderthal man, Neanderthaloid, Palaeolithic man, Peking man, Pithocanthropus

PREJUDICE *n* bias, fixed idea, idée fixe, partisanship, predilection, predisposition, prepossession; **preconception**, prejudgment, prenotion, presumption, presupposal, presupposition, presurmise; **wrong-headedness**, blind spot, doublethink, injudiciousness, jaundice, self-deception

PREJUDICED *adj* doctrinaire, intolerant, one-eyed, one-sided, partial, predisposed, self-opiniated, stupid, unbalanced, unreasonable; **insensate**, blind, boss-eyed, purblind, self-deceptive, short-sighted

PREPARATION *n* alertness, anticipation, concert pitch, preparedness, readiness; **preparations**, address *(Obs.)*, arrangements, hedge, make-ready *(Print.)*, plan, precaution, preparative, provision, scramble *(Mil.)*; **groundwork**, foundation, training; **rehearsal**, dress rehearsal, drill, knock-up, practice, run-through, trial run, warm-up; **stand-by**, red alert; **countdown**, lead time

PREPARATORY *adj* introductory, preliminary, preparative

PREPARE *v* address *(Obs.)*, arm, dight *(Archaic)*, equip, fit, fit out, furbish, furnish, gear, gear up, get into working order, get ready, kit, make ready, make up, overhaul, prep *(Med.)*, prime, refit, win *(Mining)*; **prime**, cock, unlimber; **dress**, curry, forward *(Bookbinding)*, gather *(Bookbinding)*, lick into shape, taw; **bring to readiness**, brew, concoct, gestate, hatch,

prepare 409 **press**

incubate, mature, ripen; **rehearse,** bring up to form, bring up to scratch, drill, groom, run through, teach, train, warm up; **make preparations,** address oneself to, arrange, close ranks, cook up a plan, do one's homework, draw up, gather together, get up, lead up to, make provision, take steps, tee up; **prepare oneself,** buckle down, clear the decks, get into harness, gird up one's loins, go into training, roll up one's sleeves, serve an apprenticeship, set one's house in order; **anticipate,** foresee, keep one's powder dry, lay in stores, look ahead, provide against a rainy day, provide for the future

PREPARED *adj* bound *(Archaic)*, expedite *(Obs.)*, fit, in readiness, in working order, on one's toes, on tap, operational *(Mil.)*, raring to go, ready, set, yare *(Archaic)*; **forearmed,** armed to the teeth, booted and spurred, in battle array, in battle-readiness, prep, prompt, sword in hand; **in best bib and tucker,** dressed to the nines, dresses to kill, with one's warpaint on; **previously prepared,** already prepared, canned *(U.S.)*, forthcoming, prerecorded, ready-made

PREPAREDLY *adv* at hand, at the ready, in hand, in the wings, on call, on ice, on stand-by, on the qui vive; **ready and waiting,** in the pipeline, in the press, under consideration, up one's sleeve; **in preparation,** afoot, in embryo, in train, on the drawing board, on the stocks

PRESENCE *n* appearance, immanence, immanency, occupancy, occupation; **attendance,** audience, durbar *(India Hist.)*, turn-up; **omnipresence,** incidence, ubiquitousness, ubiquity

PRESENT *adj* as large as life, attendant; **immanent; omnipresent,** ubiquitous

PRESERVE *v* salvage, salve, save; **save one's bacon,** bear a charmed life

PRESERVED *adj* alcoholic, canned, corned, cured, frozen, pickled, potted, salt, salted, sun-cured, tinned, vacuum-packed; **coated,** rainproof, showerproof, waterproof; **fireproof,** fire-resistant, flame-resistant, flameproof; **stuffed,** taxidermal, taxidermic

PRESS *n* ball mill, box iron, calender, clothes press, cylinder, cylinder press, garbage compactor, mangle, mill, monkey, oil-press, pestle, ram, road-roller, roll, rolling mill, rolling pin, stamp mill, stamp-head, steam-roller, supercalender, wine press, wool press; **iron,** cramp, cramp iron, flatiron, fluting iron, hot-press, steam iron; **stamp,** clicking press, imprinter, puncheon, stamper; **presser,** ironer, trampler, treader; **compressor,** pump, supercharger; **extruder,** crush, crusher, squasher, squeezer, squelcher, wringer; **tourniquet; clamp,** clench, clip, nipper, pincher

PRESS *v* beat out, calender, iron, iron out, mangle, mill, pestle, steamroller, supercalender, pressurise, squelch, supercharge *(Mach.)*, trample, tread; **compress,** affix, astringe, clamp, clench, clip, constrict, depress, detrude, impact, jam, knead, nip, pack, pinch, pug *(Agric.)*, scrunch, squash, squeeze, strangulate, vice; **squeeze out,** crush, express, extrude, wring off, wring out; **impress,** imprint, incuse, print, stamp, touch *(Metall.)*, trace

PRESSED *adj* addressed, compressed, dense, extrusive *(Geol.)*, impacted, incuse, milled, superdense

PRESSING *n* constriction, detrusion, expression, extrusion, impaction, ironing, jam, milling, nip, pinch, press, scrunch, squash, squeeze, strangulation *(Pathol. Surg.)*, trample, vellication

PRESSURE *n* air-pressure, critical pressure, fluid pressure, gauge pressure, nip *(Naut.)*, osmotic pressure, pressure head, shock wave, superdensity, trigger pressure, vapour pressure; **strain,** stress, tension

PRESSURE GAUGE *n* altimeter, aneroid barometer, barometer, Bourdon gauge, Fortin's barometer, gravimeter, indicator *(Motor Vehicles)*, mercury barometer, piezometer, static-pressure tube, statoscope, thermobarometer, vacuum gauge

PRESSURE UNIT *n* bar, barye, foot of water, inch of mercury, inch of water, kilopascal, millibar, millimetre of mercury, pascal, standard atmosphere, torr; **isobar,** isopiestic; **piezometry,** hydrostatics

PRESUMPTUOUS *adj* assuming, assumptive, audacious, blushless, brazen, humptious, familiar, forward, hubristic, shameless; **high-handed,** bossy, dictatorial, dogmatic, domineering, imperious, magisterial, magistral *(Rare)*, officious, overbearing, pushy, self-assertive, swashbuckling; **dismissive,** dismissory

PRETEND *v* boggle, cry wolf, dissemble, dissimulate, feign, fudge, keep up appearances, lead a double life, masquerade, pay lip-service to, play a part, put on an act, sham; **impersonate,** pass oneself off as, personate; **malinger,** swing the lead

PRICE CONTROL *n* fair trade *(U.S.)*, orderly marketing, price-fixing, resale price maintenance *(U.S.)*, valorisation; **price index,** basket, consumer price index, cost of living, cost-of-living index, tax indexation; **price war,** price discrimination, price-cutting

PRIDE *n* amour-propre, crest, high spirit, mettle, self-respect, stomach *(Obs.)*; **self-esteem,** conceit, immodesty, narcissism, self-conceit, self-congratulation, self-importance, self-love, self-opinion, self-regard, self-satisfaction, vanity, wind; **conceitedness,** boastfulness, vainness; **condescension,** inflatedness, loftiness, lordliness, malapertness, overconfidence

PRIDE ONESELF *v* claim, credit to oneself; **have a good opinion of oneself,** be above oneself, be too big for one's boots, be up oneself, boast, fancy oneself, fish for compliments, have a swelled head, have tickets on oneself, think oneself Christmas; **talk down to,** condescend, lord it over, patronise; **lord it,** pontificate, put on dog, put on side, stand on one's dignity; **preen,** bloat, huff *(Archaic)*, inflate, plume oneself, primp, put on airs, put on airs and graces, swell with pride

PRINT *v* print out, pull, run off, type; **go to press,** put to bed; **lithograph,** engrave, italicise, linotype, offset, overlay, photoengrave, photolithograph; **set,** compose, filmset, handset, impose, typeset; **justify,** lead, overrun, overset, white

PRINTER *n* chromolithographer, clicker, compositor, copyeditor, engraver, filmsetter, lithographer, photoengraver, pressman, printer's devil, proofreader, stereotyper, stonehand, typefounder, typesetter, typographer, zincographer; **printery**, composing room, press, printers

PRINTING *n* engraving, letterpress, lithography, print, screen-printing, silk-screening, typography; **typesetting**, composition, computer typesetting, filmsetting, photocomposition, phototypesetting

PRINTING PRESS *n* addressograph, composing machine, cylinder press, electrograph, flat-bed cylinder press, intertype, line printer, linotype, perfector, platen, press, rotary press, stopcylinder press; **typeface**, face, fixed type, font, fount, matrix, movable type, pie, type

PRINTWORK *n* edition, impression, issue, offprint, one-off, preprint, print run, printing, publication, revision; **imprint**, colophon; **page**, bleed, column, crosshead, crossheading, foldout, fore edge, gatefold, guard, insert, lift-out, measure, overmatter, runaround, run-in, sheet, signature, spill, tibby, wrapround; **folio**, duodecimo, quarto, sexto, sixteenmo, trigesimosecundo, twelvemo; **copy**, artwork, body matter, fudge, letterpress, matter, overprint, typescript; **presswork**, imposition, make-ready, overlay, register; **format**, dummy, mock-up, paste-up

PRISON *n* bagnio, bin, bird, birdcage, boob, booby hatch *(U.S.)*, caboose, cage, calaboose *(U.S.)*, choky, clink, college, cooler, coop, factory *(Hist.)*, female factory *(Convict)*, gaol, hole, hoosegow *(U.S.)*, jail, jailhouse *(U.S.)*, jug, limbo, nick, pen, penitentiary, pokey, quad, quod, rock college, roundhouse *(Obs.)*, salt mines, slammer, state prison *(U.S.)*, stir, the can, the logs *(Convict)*, tower; **compound**, concentration camp, internment camp, labour camp, penal settlement, prison farm, prison-camp, rules *(Brit.)*, stalag, stockade *(U.S.)*; **Botany Bay**, Bastille, Devil's Island, Fort Denison, Moreton Bay, Norfolk Island, Pinchgut, Port Arthur, the establishment, the Ocean Hell, the Tench, the Tower *(Brit.)*; **lockup**, brig, bullpen *(U.S.)*, detention centre *(Brit.)*, dock, watchhouse; **reform school**, Borstal *(Brit.)*, reformatory, training school; **prison ship**, hulks. *See also* CELL

PRISONER *n* boobhead, crim, criminal, gaolbird, gaolie, graduate *(Colloq.)*, jailbird, keyman, lag, lifer, prisoner of the crown, probation pass-holder, state prisoner *(U.S.)*, trusty; **convict**, canary, canary bird, cockatoo, Cockatoo Islander, con, croppy, demon, Derwent duck, emancipist, expiree, government man, Hawkesbury duck, inmate, legitimate, old hand, prisoner servant, ticket-of-leaver, transportee, vandemonian; **inmate**, intern *(U.S.)*, internee; **prisoner of war**, POW; **periodic detainee**, shitkicker, short-timer, toeragger, weekender; **chain-gang**, gaol gang, iron gang; **captive**, detainee

PROCREATOR *n* breeder, broodbitch, brooder, engenderer, fertiliser, generator, impregnator, propagator, sitter, springer, stud, venter; **mother**, mother-to-be, multipara, primigravida, primipara

procurer *n* arranger, bawd, fixer, go-between, maquereau, pander, panderer, pimp, procuress

profane *v* defile, deflower, desecrate, dishallow, pollute, violate; **blaspheme**, swear; **deconsecrate**, excommunicate, secularise

profit *n* advantage, fruit of one's labours, gain, remuneration; **financial profit**, bunce, capital gains, clean-up, clearings, commission, dibs, dividend, divvies, earnings, earnings per share *(Stock Exchange)*, earnings yield *(Stock Exchange)*, gains, graft, gravy, grist for the mill, gross profit *(Comm.)*, increase, interest, issue *(Law)*, money, net profit *(Comm.)*, percentage, plus, proceeds, rake-off, return, revenue *(Econ.)*, share, take, takings, the main chance, use *(Obs.)*, velvet, yield; **spoils**, a fast buck, booty, filthy lucre, lucre, something that fell off the back of a truck, theft, unjust enrichment; **money-spinner**, a sprat to catch a mackerel

profit *v* advantage, cash in on, clean up, make capital of, make money, profiteer, reap great reward

profitable *adj* advantageous, engrossing, gainful, lucrative, productive, remunerative, worthwhile; **making a profit**, ahead, better off, in pocket, running at a profit, showing a profit, to the good

program *n* chat show, docu-drama, game show, live broadcast, mini-series, quiz show, radio play, radio program, serial, series, soap, soap opera, soapie, talent quest, talk show, talk-back program, telefilm, telethon

progressivism *n* Fabianism, meliorism, progressionism, progressiveness, reformism

prohibit *v* ban, blue-pencil, bowdlerise, censor, clip the wings of, enjoin, forbid, forfend, inhibit, interdict, prevent, proclaim, proscribe; **debar**, banish, bar, disbar, disqualify, exclude, expel, ground, interdict, rule out, send down, shield *(Obs.)*; shut, shut out, unchurch, unfrock, warn off; **disallow**, black-list, forbid the banns, kill, make taboo, outlaw, repress, veto; **disqualify**, disable, incapacitate; **blackban**, blackball, boycott, declare black, embargo, ostracise, send to Coventry

prohibited *adj* black, forbidden, impermissible, inadmissible, ineffable, not to be countenanced, not to be thought of, off-limits, out of bounds, verboten; **contraband**, banned, illegal, illicit, unauthorised, unlicensed; **taboo**, unclean; **ineligible**, incapable, incompetent *(Law)*; **closed**, close *(Sport)*

prohibiter *n* blackball, dry *(U.S. Colloq.)*, forbidder, inhibiter, jeremiah, prohibitionist, proscriber, teetotaller, vetoer, wowser; **censor**, bowdleriser, Lord Chamberlain

prohibition *n* ban, charging order *(Law)*, enjoiner *(Law)*, enjoinment, injunction, interdict, writ of prohibition; **debarment**, bar, inhibition, interdict, veto; **black ban**, black list, boycott, embargo, Expurgatory Index, Index, Index of Prohibited Books; **prohibited item**, contraband, forbidden fruit, ineligible, no-no, outlaw, restricted exhibition; **taboo**, juju; **disqualification**, disability, impediment, impedimenta, incapability, incapableness, incapacity; **censorship**, bowdlerisation, bowdlerism; **repression**, extinction, hindrance, interdiction, proscription, restriction, suppression; **disablement,** exclusiveness, inadmissibility, incapacitation, ineligibility; **impermissibility,** forbiddance *(Rare)*

PROHIBITIVE *adj* censorial, exclusive, injunctive, interdictory, proscriptive

PROHIBITIVELY *adv* proscriptively; **in no way,** on no account; **inadmissibly,** exclusively, ineligibly

PROMISCUITY *n* licence, looseness, promiscuousness, unchasteness, unchastity; **profligacy,** profligateness, raffishness, rakishness; **lechery,** goatishness, lecherousness, libertinage, libertinism

PROMISCUOUS *adj* easy, fast, free, free-living, immoral, libertine, licentious, lickerish, light, loose, nice *(Obs.)*, slack, unchaste, unvirtuous, vicious; **harlot,** fallen, sluttish, whorish; **lecherous,** goatish, profligate, raffish, rakehelly *(Archaic)*, rakish, satyric

PROMISCUOUS PERSON *n* bike, Cyprian, easy lay, floozy, goodtime girl, harlot, jezebel, man-eater, prostitute, scarlet woman, scrubber *(Brit.)*, slack, slut, town bike, tramp, wanton, whore *(Archaic)*, working girl; **lecher,** Don Juan, goat, lad, libertine, Lothario, philanderer, profligate, rake, rakehell *(Archaic)*, satyr, wencher, wolf, womaniser

PROMISE *v* agree, give one's word, mortgage, pledge, plight, swear, vow, wager *(Hist.)*; **contract,** arrange, bind, commit, engage, lend-lease, oblige, pre-engage, precontract, subcontract, tie, undertake; **article,** bind out, indent, indenture; **bargain,** come to terms, covenant, dicker *(Politics)*, do a deal, go in with, settle, strike a bargain, tut; **stipulate,** give terms, make conditions; **league,** accede, ally

PROMOTE *v* advance, brevet, kick upstairs, prefer, upgrade; **exalt,** elevate, raise

PROMOTION *n* advance, advancement, brevet, preferment; **Peter principle**

PROPELLANT *n* boost, impellent, reaction propulsion; **catapult,** dinger, ging, shanghai, sling, slingshot, trap; **launch complex,** cosmodrome, launching pad, pad *(Aerospace)*, silo *(Mil.)*, slips *(Shipbuilding)*, ways; **paddle,** float, oar, scull, sweep; **spur,** ankus *(India)*, crop, gad, goad, stick, whip; **propeller,** bow thruster *(Naut.)*, paddlewheel, prop, rotor, screw, screw-propeller, tail rotor

PROPELLENT *adj* impellent, impulsive, propulsive; **self-propelled,** automobile, automotive, self-propelling

PROPERTIED *adj* land-holding, landed, landowning, tenurial; **possessed of,** long *(Comm.)*, possessory, proprietary, proprietorial

PROPERTY *n* appanage, assets, capital, endowment, holdings, one's all, peculium, possessions, principal, proprietary, resources, salvage, settlement *(Law)*, substance, temporalities, temporals, thirds *(Law)*; **dowry,** dot, dower, dower house, jointure, marriage portion, marriage settlement, portion; **estate,** deceased estate, heirloom, hereditament, heritage, legacy, patrimony, reversion; **after-acquired property,** escheat; **fixed assets,** capital assets, capital goods; **liquid assets,** current assets, floating assets, liquidity; **stocks and shares,** blue chip, capital stock, gilt-edged

property   **prototypal**

investment. *See also* PERSONAL PROPERTY; REAL ESTATE

PROPOSITIONAL *adj* problematic, quodlibetical, thematic, theorematic

PROSPER *v* be on to a good thing, cotton *(Obs.)*, do a roaring trade, go from rags to riches, have never had it so good, have the Midas touch, live high, live on milk and honey, make one's pile, soar, speed *(Archaic)*, strike it lucky, strike it rich, strike oil, succeed, thrive; **boom**, be on the crest of the wave, be on the make, be on the up and up, bloom, blossom, flourish, rise in the world, thrive; **be in luck**, be born under a lucky star, be born with a silver spoon in one's mouth, be in clover, be in the silk, be in velvet, be on a good wicket, be sitting pretty, bear a charmed life, cop it sweet, fall on one's feet, have it made, have the ball at one's feet, live off the fat of the land

PROSTITUTE *n* aspro, bagswinger, battler, callgirl, chromo, cocotte, courtesan, Cyprian *(Obs.)*, doxy *(Archaic)*, drab, fallen woman, fancy woman, gun-moll, harlot, hooker, hustler *(U.S.)*, kelly, kewpie, light o' love *(Brit. U.S.)*, lowheel, model, moll, painted lady, painted woman, pro, prossie, quean, scarlet woman, second-hand Sue, streetwalker, strumpet, tart, town bike, trollop, wench, white slave, whore, worker, working girl; **gigolo**; **procuress**, bawd, madam; **pimp**, bludger, bully, fancy man, hoon, pander, ponce, poofter-rorter, procurer, whiteslaver; **whoremonger**, crack, whoremaster

PROSTITUTE ONESELF *v* crack it, walk the streets, whore; **solicit**, accost, hustle; **procure**, bludge, live on immoral earnings, pander, pimp, ponce; **whore**, wench *(Archaic)*

PROSTITUTION *n* business, harlotry, solicitation, streetwalking, the game, whoredom; **procuration**, procurement

PROTECT *v* bulwark, defend, forfend *(U.S.)*, guard, keep, ward *(Archaic)*, watch over; **patrol**, picket *(Mil.)*; **immunise**, inoculate, vaccinate; **bless**, charm, sain *(Archaic)*

PROTECTED *adj* guarded, immune, secure, under one's wing

PROTECTION *n* backstop, bulwark, defence, screen, umbrella; **safe-conduct**, air cover, convoy, escort, protective custody; **custody**, aegis, auspices, care, cover, coverture, fatherly eye, safekeeping, tutelage, ward, wardship; **guardianship**, custodianship, wardenry, wardenship

PROTECTIVE *adj* alimentary *(Law)*, custodial, guardian, tutelary

PROTECTOR *n* committee *(Law Obs.)*, father, genius loci, guardian, patron *(Roman Hist.)*, patroness, protectress, tutelary, tutor *(Archaic)*; **guard**, air-raid warden, coast-watcher, coastguard, concierge, conservator, curator, custodian, fire warden, firewatcher, janitor, watch, watchman, patrolman, security guard, security officer, sentinel, sentry; **bodyguard**, convoy, escort, patrol, safeguard; **defender**, harbourer, keeper, shelterer, shielder

PROTOTYPAL *adj* archetypal, archetypical, embryo, first, primary, prime, protoplastic, introductory, inaugural, isagogic, precursory, prefatory, pre-

prototypal   415   **psyche**

liminary, prelusive, prelusory, preparatory, proemial, prolegomenous, prolusory, propaedeutic; **advance,** ahead of one's time, fore, forehand, headmost, leading, up-front; **anticipatory,** anticipative

PROTRACT v prolong, prolongate *(Rare),* string out; **maintain,** keep, preserve, retain, sustain; **resume,** renew, take up; **outlast,** outlive, survive

PROTRACTOR n clinometer, declinometer, gradiogragh, gradiometer, inclinometer, set square, sextant, square, transit *(U.S.),* transit theodolite, triangle *(U.S.),* try square, variometer

PROTUBERANT adj beetle, beetling, exserted, extant *(Archaic),* extrusive, imminent, obtrusive, overhanging, pendent, prognathous, projectile, projecting, prominent, protractile, protrudent, protrusile, protrusive, rostral, salient, tumular; **raised up,** eminent, erect, proud; **spined,** calcarate, horned, horny, muricate, spurred, thorny; **popeyed,** bug-eyed, exophthalmic; **tentacled,** tentacular, vibracular, villiform. *See also* SWOLLEN; KNOBBY

PROUD adj bloated, conceited, condescending, consequential, inflated, jumped-up, lofty, lordly, malapert, narcissistic, overblown, overproud, patronising, pragmatic, puffed-up, self-conceited, self-important, self-loving, self-opinionated, self-satisfied, smug, snubby, stuck-up, tight-arsed, vain; **boastful,** immodest, prideful, self-congratulatory; **purse-proud,** house-proud; **ostentatious,** pretentious; **high-spirited,** mettlesome

PROUDLY adv conceitedly, immodestly, inflatedly, loftily, malapertly, smugly, vainly; **boastfully,** lordly *(Archaic),* pridefully

PROVERB n adage, byword, dictum, saying, truth, word *(Obs.);* **maxim,** aphorism, apophthegm, epigram, gnome, logion, notabilia, saw, sentence *(Obs.);* **axiom,** postulate, principle, theorem; **apologue,** moralism, parable; **device,** catchword, motto, poesy *(Obs.),* slogan, tag; **platitude,** banality, bromide, cliche, commonplace, prosaism, truism

PROVERB v aphorise, apophthegmatise, epigrammatise

PROVERBIAL adj aphorismatic, aphorismic, aphoristic, axiomatic, epigrammatic, gnomic, parabolic, sententious; **platitudinous,** moralising, stock, trite

PROVERBIALLY adv aphoristically, parabolically

PROVINCIAL adj boorish, churlish, cloddish, clodhopping, hayseed, hick, hillbilly, peasant, rube, yeoman, yokel, yokelish; **country-born,** country-bred, Dad'n'Dave, folksy, swainish. *See also* RURAL

PROVOKE HATRED v alienate, cause bad blood, disaffect, embitter, estrange, incur enmity, incur wrath, make another see red, raise someone's ire, set by the ears, sow dissension, stir up bad blood; **be anathema to,** disgust, go against the grain, make someone's flesh creep, nauseate, revolt, stink in one's nostrils, turn someone's stomach

PSYCHE n libido, motive force, pneuma, self, soul, vital impulse; **ego,** id, superego; **the unconscious,** collective

psyche   416   **psychologist**

unconscious, inner space, preconscious, subconscious; **preconsciousness**, coconsciousness, subconsciousness; **engram**, memory, trace; **motivation**, drive

PSYCHIATRICALLY *adv* psychoanalytically, psychogenetically, psychologically, psychotherapeutically

PSYCHIC DISORDER *n* alienation, anomie, craze, deliration, dementia, derangement, insanity, maladjustment, mania, neuropsychosis, neurosis, psychopathy, psychosis, schizothymia; **dementia praecox**, hebephrenia; **nervous breakdown**, breakdown, collapse; **paranoia**, hallucinosis; **dissimulation**, simulation; **amnesia**, fugue; **masochism**, sadism, sadomasochism; **psychosomatic disorder**, hysterical fever, hysterical pregnancy, phantom pregnancy; **specific learning difficulty**, agraphia, alexia, alogia, amentia, aphasia, dysarthria, dysgraphia, dyslexia, dysphasia, dysphemia, glossolalia, paralexia, strephosymbolia, stuttering, word blindness; **mental deficiency**, autism, cretinism, Down's syndrome, idiocy, imbecility, mental retardation, Mongolism, moronity

PSYCHIC DISTURBANCE *n* complex, fetish, fixation, fixed idea, hang-up *(Colloq.)*, obsession, phobia; **mania**, cacoethes, compulsion, craze; **hallucination**, delusion, illusion; **inhibition**, censor, censorship, repression, suppression; **Freudian slip**, parapraxis; **regression**, reversion; **schizophrenia**, battle fatigue, culture shock, identity crisis, multiple personality, shell shock, split personality; **shock**, trauma; **hysteria**, frenzy, hysterics

PSYCHOANALYSE *v* condition, depersonalise, hypnotise; **fixate**, introspect, overcompensate, rationalise, repress, sublimate; **psychologise**, be an amateur psychologist; **certify**, stultify

PSYCHOLOGICAL *adj* nomological, psychobiological, psychogenetic, psychophysical, psychophysiological; **idiographic**, nomothetic; **psychoanalytic**, Freudian, Jungian, psychoanalytical, psychographic, psychometric; **psychiatric**, mental, neuropsychiatric, psychiatrical, psychopathological, psychotherapeutic

PSYCHOLOGICALLY DISTURBED *adj* fixated, maladjusted; **insane**, deranged, disordered, lunatic, maniac, maniacal, unbalanced; **compulsive**, manic, obsessional; **manic-depressive**, cycloid, cycloidal, cyclothymic; **depressive**, atrabilious, hypochondriac, melancholiac, melancholic, morbid, phobic; **neurotic**, hung-up *(Colloq.)*, hysteric, hysterical, neuropathic, psychasthenic; **psychotic**, paranoid, psycho *(Colloq.)*, psychopathic, schizo *(Colloq.)*, schizoid, schizophrenic; **delusional**, expansive; **shell-shocked**; **boob happy**, stir-crazy; **mentally deficient**, autistic, cretinous, mentally handicapped, mongoloid, retarded, subnormal

PSYCHOLOGIST *n* analyst, behaviourist, Freudian, Jungian, nomologist, psychoanalyser, psychoanalyst, psychobiologist, psychopathologist, sensationist; **third force**; **hypnotist**, hypnotiser; **psychiatrist**, alienist *(Obs.)*, headshrinker, orthopsychiatrist, psychotherapist, shrink, trick cyclist

PSYCHOLOGY *n* nomology, pneumatology *(Archaic)*, psychogenesis, psychometry; **psychology discipline,** abnormal psychology, aesthetics, behavioural psychology, behaviourism, existential psychology, Gestalt psychology, hedonics, introspection, metapsychology, occupational psychology, parapsychology, psychoanalysis, psychophysics, sensationism; **psychologism; psychiatry,** alienism, orthopsychiatry, psychopathology, psychopathy

PSYCHOTHERAPY *n* aversion therapy, behaviour therapy, catharsis, E.C.T., electroconvulsive therapy, narcosynthesis, psychotherapeutics, shock treatment, therapy, treatment; **counselling,** child guidance; **group therapy,** encounter group, T-group; **psychodrama,** acting out; **psychoanalysis,** analysis, hypnoanalysis, psychognosis; **psychograph,** psychometer; **personality test,** Binet test, free association test, ink-blot test, Rorschach test; **hypnosis,** hypnotisation, hypnotism; **certification,** stultification; **mental hospital,** bedlam, booby hatch, funny farm, giggle factory, loony bin, lunatic asylum, madhouse, nut factory, nuthouse, psychiatric hospital, rat factory *(N.Z. Colloq.)*, retreat

PSYCHOTIC *n* cyclothymiac, hypochondriac, lycanthrope, manic-depressive, mattoid, melancholiac, paranoiac, psycho *(Colloq.)*, psychopath, schizo *(Colloq.)*, schizoid, schizophrenic; **neurotic,** hysteric, neuropath, wreck; **ambivert,** extrovert, introvert; **masochist,** sadist, sadomasochist; **erotomaniac,** d.o.m., dirty old man, exhibitionist, fetishist, flasher, narcissist, nymphomaniac, pervert, satyr, sex maniac, voyeur; **maniac,** bedlamite *(Archaic)*, lunatic, madman; **mental deficient,** ament, cretin, idiot, moron

PUB *n* beer-hall *(S. African)*, boozer, boozeroo *(N.Z.)*, bunny club, drinking-house, free house, grog shop, hotel, inn, local, off-licence *(Brit.)*, opera house, pisser, porterhouse *(Archaic)*, public house, rubbidy, rubbidy-dub, shypoo joint *(W.A.)*, tap *(Brit.)*, taphouse, tavern, tied house, watering hole, wateringplace; **shanty,** bloodhouse, gin palace, joint; **wineshop,** bottle department, bottle shop, cellars; **sly-grog shop,** honky-tonk, shebeen *(Irish Scot.)*, speak-easy; **bar,** beer garden, bistro, bodega, clipjoint, cocktail bar, groggery, hot spot, ladies' lounge, ladies' parlour, lounge, lounge bar, nightclub, nineteenth hole, private bar, public bar, saloon, saloon bar, taproom *(Brit.)*, wine bar; **brewery,** distillery, mill, still, winery

PUBLIC *adj* common, communal, demotic, mob, popular, vernacular, vulgar; **folk,** grassroots, parish-pump, parochial

PUBLICAN *n* innkeeper, lamber-down, licensee, shanty-keeper, taverner *(Brit.)*, vintner; **barman,** barkeeper, barmaid, bartender, cellarmaster, wine waiter

PUBLICISE *v* advertise, ballyhoo, bark, bawl, bill, build up, cry up, pamphleteer, promote, puff, tout; **announce,** annunciate, celebrate, declare, enounce, enunciate, intimate, preconise, proclaim, report; **decree,** adjudge, expedite, gazette, pronounce; **publish,** ask *(Archaic)*, blaze, blazon, broadcast, circulate, divulgate, give out, go the rounds, hawk about, herald, issue, promulgate, propagate, voice; **trumpet,** blare, call, count, knell, knoll *(Archaic),* resound, ring, ring in, ring out, sound, tick, toll, trump; **tell,** out with, rap out, speak, utter; **notify,** apprise of, post, stir *(Rare)*

PUBLICIST *n* adman, advertiser, billposter, bullsticker, copywriter, pamphleteer, placarder, plugger; **announcer,** declarer, divulgater, enunciator, notifier, proclaimer, promulgater, warner; **herald,** barker, bawler, bellman, crier, officer at arms, sandwich man, spieler, town crier, trumpeter, vaunt-courier *(Archaic);* **toastmaster,** toastmistress

PUBLICITY *n* build-up, daylight, notice, promotion; **advertising,** ballyhoo, billing, hype; **publication,** broadcast, divulgation, gazettal, issuance, issue, notification, promulgation, propaganda

PUBLIC NOTICE *n* announcement, annunciation *(Rare),* banns, celebration, cry *(Obs.),* declaration, enouncement, enunciation, hue and cry, intimation, proclamation, protest, report; **notice,** bill, bulletin, green paper, notice paper; **advertisement,** ad, advert, blurb, classified ad, classifieds, commercial, plug, promo, teaser ad, trailer, want ad; **personal column,** obit, obituary, personal *(U.S.);* **poster,** banner, placard, wanted poster; **handbill,** broadsheet, broadside, brochure, circular, flier, flyer, handout, leaflet, literature, pamphlet, playbill, prospectus, showbill, throwaway, ticket *(Rare);* **sticker,** bumper sticker, car sticker; **billboard,** bulletin board *(U.S.),* corkboard, hoarding, noticeboard, Ritchie board, sandwich board; **edict,** ban, decree, deliverance, dictum, diktat, manifest, manifesto, platform, pronouncement, rescript

PUBLISH *v* feature, issue, lay before the public, print, run; **report,** report, reveal, write up; **broadcast,** radio, relay, telecast, televise; **scoop; edit,** prepare copy, put to bed, sub, subedit

PUGILIST *n* boxer, bruiser, ex-pug, fisticuffer, infighter, palooka, prizefighter, pug, slugger, sparring partner; **bantamweight,** featherweight, flyweight, heavyweight, middleweight, welterweight; **bludgeoner,** buffeter, cudgeller, **wrestler,** grappler, junior; **judoist,** ju-jitsuist, judoka. *See also* FIGHTER

PULL *n* drag, draw, haul, heave *(Naut.),* lug, tow, tug; **wrench,** tear, twist, wrest; **hitch,** jerk, pluck, tweak, twitch, yank

PULL *v* bowse *(Naut.),* brail *(Naut.),* clew *(Naut.),* drag, draw, hale, haul, heave, lug, rouse away *(Naut.),* snig, trice; **tow,** kedge, tug, warp; **trail,** daggle *(Obs.),* **wrench,** tear, wrest; **strain at,** tear at; **jerk,** pluck, twitch, yank; **hitch,** hike up; **winch,** purchase, wind up, windlass

PULLER *n* haler, hauler, tugger; **towrope,** hawser, messenger, towline; **winch,** capstan, coffee-grinder winch, davit, parbuckle, whim *(Mining),* windlass; **pulley,** block and tackle, crab, garnet, halyard, jeer, shearlegs; **prime mover,** bank engine *(Railways),* banker *(Railways),* caterpillar, locomotive, tow truck, towboat, towie, traction engine, tractor, tug, tugboat

pulling   419   **punishment**

PULLING *n* draught, drawing, haulage, pull, stress, towage, traction, tractive power *(Railways)*

PULP *n* chyme, mash, pap, pomace, slops, sop, squash, squelch; **dough**, magma *(Chem.)*, paste, sponge

PULP *v* knead, mash, masticate, sodden, sop, squash, squish

PULPINESS *n* pastiness, soddenness, sogginess, sponginess, squashiness; **pulping**, mashing, mastication

PULPY *adj* doughy, pappy, pasty, sodden, soggy, sopping, spongy, squashy, squishy

PUNGENCY *n* acridity, acridness, gaminess, piquancy, poignancy, raciness, saltiness, spicery, spiciness; **bite**, edge, race, sting, strength, tang; **pepperiness**, fieriness, sharpness; **roughness**, harshness

PUNGENT *adj* acrid, ammoniacal, penetrating, sharp, strong; **piquant**, fiery, hot, poignant, racy, savoury; **spicy**, alliaceous, garlicky, gingery, peppery, salty, tangy; **gamy**, earthy, high, rank

PUNGENTLY *adv* acridly, fierily, piquantly, poignantly, saltily, spicily

PUNISH *v* afflict, condemn, gruel, penalise, visit *(Obs.)*; **discipline**, bring to book, castigate, chasten, chastise, come down on, correct, give someone a lesson, have a rod in pickle, lay it on, scold, strafe, throw the book at, vindicate *(Obs.)*; **sentence**, blanket, imprison, lag, pillory, stock *(Obs.)*; **fine**, amerce, estreat, mulct; **keelhaul**, duck, masthead; **persecute**, have heads over, have someone's head, make an example of, tar and feather, victimise; **excommunicate**, attaint, damn, interdict, rusticate; **torture**, break on the wheel, excruciate, give the third degree, grill, rack, thumbscrew

PUNISHABLE *adj* statutable, statutory; **visitational**, amerceable, excommunicable, excommunicative, excommunicatory

PUNISHED *adj* disenfranchised, excommunicate, infamous *(Law)*, penalised; **convicted**, damned, for it, for the high jump, in for it, off tap

PUNISHER *n* amercer, condemner, sentencer; **discipliner**, castigator, chastener, chastiser, corrector, excommunicator, persecutor; **caner**, flogger, fustigator *(Archaic)*, lasher, scourger, swinger, thrasher, walloper, whipper; **executioner**, bow-stringer, crucifier, deathsman *(Archaic)*, firing squad, garrotter, hangman, headsman, lynch mob, lyncher, lynching party; **torturer**, inquisitor; **avenger**, vindicator

PUNISHING *adj* castigatory, corrective, disciplinary, penal, penitentiary, penological, punitive; **correctional**, baculine, fire-and-brimstone, flagellant; **amercing**, confiscatory, expropriatory, mulctuary *(Obs.)*; **retributive**, persecutional, persecutive, persecutory, vindicatory *(Obs.)*, vindictive; **comminatory**, damning, interdictory

PUNISHMENT *n* condemnation, disciplinary action, penalisation, penalty; **forfeiture**, amercement, attainder, attaint, praemunire; **chastisement**, castigation, chastening, correction, discipline, dressing-down, the treatment, what-for; **retribution**, nemesis, poetic justice; **retaliation**, comeuppance, reprisal, requital, vengeance, wrath; **judgment**, day of judgment,

punishment   420   **pursuit**

day of reckoning, doom, visitation; **banishment**, anathema, commination, excommunication, exile, interdict, monition, outlawing, proscription, transportation; **hellfire**, Gehenna, purgatory; **persecution**, victimisation; **fine**, forfeit, lesson, mulct, parking ticket, penalty, sanction; **imposition**, impost, infliction, lines, task

PUPIL *n* boarder, child, day pupil, dayboy, daygirl, high-schooler, junior, kindergartener, schoolboy, schoolgirl, schoolkid; **student**, autodidact, bursar, co-ed, collegian, day student, evening student, exhibitioner *(Archaic)*, external student, imbiber, learner, mature age student, part-time student, postgraduate student, practiser, scholar, scholarship holder, sophomore *(U.S.)*, undergrad *(U.S.)*, undergraduate; **bookworm**, grind, swot; **slow-learner; prefect**, head boy, head girl, school captain, senior; **graduate**, diplomate, fellow, graduand, licentiate, matriculant, matriculate, postgraduate; **classmate**, alumna, alumnus, fellow student, former student, old boy, old girl. *See also* LEARNER

PUPPET *n* finger puppet, glove puppet, hand puppet, marionette, Punch and Judy, shadow puppet

PURGATIVE *n* cathartic, diuretic, eccritic, laxative, loosener, physic, purge, purger; **enema**, clyster *(Obs.)*; **sudorific**, diaphoretic; **snuff**, errhine

PURGATIVE *adj* cathartic, diuretic, eccritic, errhine, evacuant; **sudorific**, diaphoretic, hidrotic

PURPLE *n* burgundy, magenta, orchid, petunia, plum, purpure *(Heraldry)*, raspberry; **lilac**, lavender, mauve, violet; **amethyst**, heliotrope; cerise, carmine, grape, solferino; **indigo**, indigo blue, raisin, royal purple

PURPLE *adj* aubergine, magenta, purpure *(Heraldry)*; **purplish**, amaranthine, amethystine, vinaceous, violescent; **lilac**, lavender, lilaceous, mauve, violet; **cerise**, carmine, vinous; **indigo**, perse

PURPLE DYE *n* amaranth *(U.S.)*, carmine, crystal violet, cudbear, gentian violet, mauve, orchil, purple of Cassius, solferino, Tyrian purple

PURPOSELESS *adj* aimless, collar-proud, idle, lazy, perfunctory, tardy, unambitious, unenterprising, workshy; **unwitting**, unconscious, unintentional, unpremeditated, unwilled

PURSUE *v* chase, chivvy *(Brit.)*, course, dog, follow up, halloo, hallow, hound, hunt, hunt down, lie in wait, shadow, take after *(U.S.)*, tree; **track**, dog, lodge, nose after, nose out, pug, sleuth, spoor, trail, wind; **search**, explore *(Obs.)*, forage, foray, fossick, mouse, noodle *(Mining)*, pearl, prospect, prowl, quest, rake, scout, scrimmage, seek

PURSUER *n* blacktracker, bounty hunter *(U.S.)*, chaser, hunter, prowler, spoorer, tracer, tracker; **searcher**, fossicker, noodler, pearler, prospector, rummager, seeker

PURSUING *adj* hunting, piscatorial, piscatory, predatory, preying, pursuant, raptorial, venatic

PURSUIT *n* chasings, derry, hide-and-seek, hidings, hue and cry, man-hunt, prowl, stern chase, tiggy touchwood, wild-goose chase; **hunt**, battue, beat, chase, chivvy, drag hunt, kangaroo drive, safari, still hunt *(U.S.)*. *See also* HUNTING

PUT TO SLEEP *v* bed down, hushaby, lull, lullaby, sedate, sing to sleep

PUZZLE *n* conundrum, headache, mystery, paradox, pons asinorum, poser, problem, puzzler, sealed book, sticker, stickler, stumper, teaser, tickler; **crossword**, acrostic, anagram, cryptic crossword, cryptonym, logogriph, rebus, Rubik's cube, tangram

PUZZLE *v* amuse *(Obs.)*, anagrammatise, baffle, bamboozle, confuse, elude, mystify, perplex, riddle, stick, throw off the scent

PYROGEN *n* calefacient, febrifacient, inflamer, rubefacient

Qq

QUALIFICATION *n* but, condition, if, limitation, modification, provision, proviso, qualifier, rider, strings; **precondition**, hinge, hypothesis, premise, prerequisite; **reservation**, afterthought, arrière-pensée, reserve; **conditional clause**, article, codicil, condition precedent, condition subsequent, fine print, in terrorem clause, small print, stipulation, tail

QUALIFY *v* condition, limit, provide, stipulate

QUANTIFY *v* amass, measure, number, preponderate, reach, take stock

QUANTITATIVELY *adv* volumetrically; **so much**, a bit of, as far as, better than, that, upwards of

QUESTION *n* a good question, awkward question, challenge, demand, dorothy dixer, feeler, inquiry, interrogatory, leading question, moot point, poser, query, question on notice, question without notice

QUESTION *v* ask, challenge, demand, enquire, inquire, query, seek an answer, survey; **interview**, audition, examine; **interrogate**, catechise, cross-examine, cross-question, debrief, give the third degree, grill, hammer, pick someone's brains, pose, probe, pump, put to the question, quiz, re-examine (*Law*), sift the evidence, sweat

QUESTIONER *n* asker, catechiser, demander, enquirer, inquirer, inquisitor, interrogator, interviewer, querist, question-master, quizzer, re-examiner, seeker; **investigator**, field worker, researcher, scout; **pollster**, canvasser, sampler; **examiner**, analyst, appraiser, assayer, checker, critic, dissector, examinant, observer, prober, scanner, scrutiniser, surveyor; **auditor**, datary (*Rom. Cath. Ch.*), head-hunter, health inspector, inspector, reviewer, scrutator, scrutineer, systems analyst, talent scout; **committee**, court of inquiry, Royal Commission, standing committee, working party; **examinee**, catechumen, interviewee

QUESTIONING *n* catechisation, catechism, debriefing, interrogation, interview; **cross-examination**, cross-questioning, quiz, re-examination, trial; **inquisition**, dialectic, dialogue, discussion, post-mortem, socratic method. *See also* INVESTIGATION; INSPECTION; TEST

QUESTIONING *adj* inquisitional, inquisitorial, interrogational, interrogative, interrogatory, searching; **inquiring**, curious, snoopy; **investigative**, analytic, appraising, diagnostic, exploratory, fact-finding, heuristic, laboratorial, observational, research, scientific, scrutinising; **inspectional**, check, inspective

QUIET *adj* dreamy, gentle, sedate, soft-spoken; **whispering**, murmuring, murmurous, susurrant; **husky**, croaky, groaning, gruff, hoarse, hollow, roupy, thick, throaty; **tinkling**, humming, ripply, twittery; **soft**, dim, low, low-pitched, small, still, stilly; **faint**, distant, inaudible, indistinct, inward, muffled, muted; **unstressed**, unaccented, unemphasised, weak;

quiet

whispered, stealthy; **dull**, dead, tinny, tubby; **deadening**, dulling, tempering

QUIETEN *v* lower, quiet, shush, soften; **temper**, damp, deaden, drown, dull, overdamp, pug, soft-pedal; **devocalise**, devoice; **become quieter**, die away, drop, fade

QUIETENER *n* damper, deadener, muffle, mute, overdamper, silencer, soft pedal, softener, sordino, sourdine, temperer; **deadening**, acoustic tile, insulation

QUIETLY *adv* dimly, inwardly, low, small, soft, softly, stilly; **sotto voce**, under one's breath, with bated breath; **piano**, calando, decrescendo, diminuendo, pianissimo; **gently**, dreamily, sedately; **murmuringly**, cooingly, groaningly, moaningly, murmurously; **huskily**, gruffly, hollowly, thickly, throatily, tinnily

QUIETNESS *n* faintness, inaudibility, indistinctness, softness; **gentleness**, dimness, dreaminess, sedateness; **dullness**, deadness, tinniness; **huskiness**, frog, gruffness, hoarseness, hollowness, lowness, roup, throatiness; **devocalisation**, ecthlipsis

QUIET SOUND *n* burble, burr, croon, hum, murmur, murmuration, murmuring; **whisper**, aside, susurration, susurrus, undertone; **sigh**, breath, hiss, sniff, swish, waft; **moan**, groan, grumble, grunt, whine; **babble**, prattle, twitter; **lap**, gurgle, plash, purl, ripple; **rustle**, ruffle, scroop, stir; **scratch**, scuff, squeak; **click**, tick; **tinkle**, clink, tinkling; **pitter-patter**, pat, patter, pitapat

Rr

RACE n course *(Archaic)*, trial; **footrace**, Bay to Breakers, city to surf, cross-country, dash, egg-and-spoon race, fun run, hare and hounds, marathon, obstacle race, relay, running race, sack-race, scurry, sprint, three-legged race, walking race, wheelbarrow race; **slalom**, dauerlauf, downhill, rallycross, stock-car race; **swimming race**, iron-man race, medley relay, relay, surf race; **boat race**, bumping race *(Brit.)*, head of the river, regatta, repechage, sculls; **car race**, drag, drag race, Grand Prix, hill climb, motocross, motorkhana, MX, rally; **cycle race**, devil take the hindmost, madison, prime, pursuit, roller race, scramble, stage race, tour, Tour de France; **soapbox derby**, billycart race

RACECOURSE n birdcage, collecting ring, flat, ring, stretch, track

RACEHORSE n approved, approved horse, boom galloper, creeker, donk, encourage horse, improver horse, intermediate horse, maiden, maiden horse, progressive horse, running mate, steeplechaser

RACING n dogs, flat racing, greyhound racing, horseracing, point-to-point, races, red hots, the gallops, the turf, trots; **horserace**, advanced handicap, approved handicap, barrier trial, boilover, chase, classic, derby, encourage handicap, feature double, flying handicap, futurity, graduation stakes, Grand Prix, improver handicap, intermediate handicap, juvenile handicap, maiden handicap, morning glory, novice handicap, nursery handicap, picnic races, plate, produce stakes, progressive handicap, race meeting, steeplechase, sweepstake, transition, transition handicap, trial, trial handicap, welter

RACK n hack; **stand**, inkstand, penholder, tantalus, umbrella stand, whatnot; **grate**, brazier, chauffer, firebox, hay oven, haybox, hearth

RADIATION n actinic rays, alpha radiation, beta radiation, black light, cosmic rays, infra-red, luminous energy, near infra-red, photon, radio wave, red light, roentgen ray, sunrays, thermal radiation, travelling wave, ultra violet, visible light, wave, wave train, white light, X-ray

RADIO n crystal set, earphone, gibson girl, pedal wireless, radio receiver, radio set, receiver, receiving set, steam radio, trannie, transceiver, transistor, walkie-talkie, wireless, wireless set; **transmitter**, racon, radio beacon, radio transmitter, transmitting set; **modulator**, tuner; **microphone**, cans *(Colloq.)*, carbon microphone, dial, pick-up; **valve**, beam tube, dynatron, pentode, tickler coil, triode; **airplay**, air, airshift; **interference**, hash, jitter, noise, whistler; **modulation**, demodulation, diplexer, duplexer, heterodyne method, phase modulation, pulse-time modulation, superheterodyne method, synchrodyne method; **amplitude modulation**, AM, FM, frequency modulation

RADIOACTIVATION *n* activation, breeding, capture, conversion, excitation, induction, initiation, ionisation, multiplication, spallation, transformation, transition; **fission,** binary fission, photofission; **fusion,** fusion reaction, nuclear fusion, thermonuclear reaction; **reaction,** chain-reaction, nuclear reaction, pair production; **meltdown,** China syndrome, critical mass. *See also* ATOMIC RADIATION; NUCLEAR ENERGY; ATOMIC BOMB

RAFT *n* balsa, cat, catamaran, float, kon-tiki *(N.Z. Angling)*, life raft, scow; **floating bridge,** bateau, pontoon, stakeboat; **buoy,** lifebuoy

RAILWAY *n* branch line, feeder, hump, line, loop, main line, permanent way, plate rail, rack-railway, rail, railway line, road *(U.S.)*, scenic railway, section, sidetrack *(U.S.)*, siding, switchback, third rail, track, trackage, trunk, trunk line; **tramline,** tram, tramway; **underground,** metro, tube *(Brit.)*, underground railway; **cableway,** teleferic; **cable railway,** cable tramway, funicular, funicular railway; **points,** gauntlet, switch *(U.S.)*

RAIN *v* precipitate; **drizzle,** spit, sprinkle; **pour,** bucket, shower, deluge, pelt, piss down, rain cats and dogs, storm *(U.S.)*, teem

RAINCOAT *n* burberry, camlet, Drizabone, mac, mackintosh, oiler *(U.S.)*, oilskins, rubbers *(U.S.)*, slicker, trench coat, waterproof. *See also* CLOAK; OVERCOAT

RAINFALL *n* hydrometeor, meteor *(Obs.)*, precipitation, water cycle; **rain,** blood rain, convectional rain, drizzle, precipitate, serein, virga, water, wet; **raindrop; shower,** flurry, spit, sprinkle; **downpour,** cloudburst, cockeye bob, deluge, equinoctial, pour, rainstorm, spate, storm, the Deluge *(Bible)*, thundershower, thunderstorm, torrent, waterspout; **rainy season,** bogaduck weather, monsoon, the wet

RAINFALL MEASUREMENT *n* hydrometeorology, udometry; **rain gauge,** hyetograph, ombrometer, pluviometer, udometer; **unit of rainfall,** inch, millimetre, point

RAINY *adj* drizzly, pluvious, showery, wet; **teeming,** soppy, torrential

RAISE UP *v* elevate, erect, heighten, uplift, upraise, uprear

RAPE *n* defilement, fate worse than death, pack-rape, ravishment, statutory rape *(U.S.)*, violation; **indecent assault,** assault, interference; **incest; seduction,** ruin *(Archaic)*

RAPE *v* defile, outrage, ravish, violate; **pack-rape,** stir the porridge; **seduce,** deflower, ruin, wrong; **assault,** interfere with

RAPIST *n* defiler, deflowerer, ravisher, violater

RARE *adj* few, few and far between, rare as hen's teeth, scarce, uncommon, unheard-of; **rarefactive; infrequent,** seldom *(Obs.)*; **sporadic,** intermittent, occasional; **unusual,** almost unheard-of, unprecedented

RARELY *adv* hardly ever, infrequently, little, once, once in a blue moon, scarcely, scarcely ever, seldom; **at times,** every now and again, every now and then, every once in a while, every so often, from time to time, now and again, now and then, occasionally, on occasion, once in a blue moon, once in a month of Sundays,

rarely

once in a while, sometime *(Rare)*, sometimes; **never**, nevermore

RARENESS *n* fewness, rarity, scarceness, scarcity, uncommonness; **rarefaction**; **infrequency**, seldomness; **rarity**, bibelot, collector's item, rara avis, rare bird, rare book; **intermittence**, discontinuity

RASH *adj* brash, foolhardy, hardy, harum-scarum, headlong, ill-advised, ill-judged, imprudent, irrational, unadvised, unconsidered, unwise; **headstrong**, ardent, harebrained, heady, heedless, hot-blooded, hot-headed, impatient, impetuous, incautious, indiscreet, mad, madcap, passionate, warm-blooded; **overconfident**, confident, overbold, presumptuous; **hasty**, improvident, impulsive, precipitant, precipitate, precipitative, precipitous, premature; **audacious**, bold, cavalier, daredevil, devil-may-care, free-and-easy, reckless, temerarious, wildcat; **unreasonable**, crazy, triggerhappy, wanton, wild; **blind**, blindfold, desperate; **suicidal**, banzai, kamikaze

RASHLY *adv* audaciously, foolhardily, harum-scarum, heedlessly, ill-advisedly, improvidently, imprudently, incautiously, indiscreetly, recklessly, temerariously, unadvisedly; **adventurously**, for the hell of it; **headstrongly**, head over heels, headfirst, headily, headlong, hotheadedly; **overconfidently**, boldly, confidently; **hastily**, impetuously, impulsively, precipitantly, precipitately, precipitously, prematurely; **unreasonably**, crazily, wantonly, wildly; **pell-mell**, at full fling, neck or nothing, to the hilt; **blindly**, blind, desperately

react

RASHNESS *n* foolhardiness, headiness, heedlessness, hot-headedness, improvidence, imprudence, incaution, incautiousness, indiscreetness, indiscretion, lack of caution, thoughtlessness, unadvisedness; **haste**, hastiness, impetuosity, impetuousness, precipitancy, precipitateness, precipitation, precipitousness, prematurity, rush; **audacity**, audaciousness, boldness, overconfidence, presumption, recklessness, temerariousness, temerity, wildcatting; **adventurousness**, adventurism, daredevilry; **unreasonableness**, craziness, madness, unreason, wantonness; **blindness**, desperateness, desperation; **rash act**, leap in the dark

RATE *n* cadence *(Mil.)*, pace, tempo, time; **quick time**, double time, quick march; **rush**, career, tantivy, whirl; **scamper**, dart, scoot, scud, scurry, scutter, whisk; **gallop**, canter, clip, lope, romp, sprint; **run**, burn, fang, hit-out, schuss, spin; **walking pace**, footpace. *See also* SPEED; VELOCITY

RAW *adj* crude, green, in the rough, incomplete, premature, rough, rude; **untreated**, en déshabille, in a state of nature, natural, undressed, unlaid, untilled. *See also* UNREADY

RAW MATERIALS *n* producer goods, raw stock, resources, staple, stuff, substance; **raw material**, bone, clay, fibre, glass, metal, mineral, ore, paper, plastics, timber, wax. *See also* TIMBER; BUILDING MATERIALS; PAPER

REACT *v* answer, reply, respond, take it; **shy**, curl *(Colloq.)*, jerk, prop, start, wince; **over-react**, freak out; **recoil**, cannon, kick, ricochet; **rebound**,

react   427   **rear**

boomerang, come home to roost, rebound, spring back

REACTION *n* answer, echo, feedback, reply, response, return; **reflex**, knee jerk, shy, start, wince; **recoil**, backlash, boomerang, kick, kickback, rebound, repercussion, reverberation; **backstroke**, cannon, carom, ricochet

REACTIVE *adj* corresponsive, responsive, sensitive, tropistic; **reflex**, boomerang, feedback, repercussive; **hyperreactive**, supersensitive

READ *v* bury oneself in, go over, peruse, pore over, study, wade through; **scan**, browse, dip into, leaf through, look at, run through, skim, speed read, taste, thumb through

READABLE *adj* decipherable, legible, perusable, written

READER *n* bibliophile, bookworm, browser, peruser; **readership**, readers, subscribers; **proofreader**, copyreader, proofer, taster

READING *n* perusal, read; **literacy**, reading ability; **readableness**, decipherability, legibility, legibleness, readability; **machine reading**, bar coding, MICR encoding, OCR, optical character reading

REAL *adj* actual, concrete, de facto, factual, incarnate, objective, positive, solid, substantial, substantive; **existent**, contemporary, current, extant, going, ingenerate, living, original, pre-existent, self-existent, surviving, uncaused

REAL ESTATE *n* country seat, demesne, domain, dominant estate, dominant tenement, entail, fee simple, fee tail, fief, freehold, immoveables *(Law)*, land *(Law)*, lordship *(Hist.)*, manor, mesnalty, real property, realty, seigneury, seigniory, servient tenement, tenement, thanage

REALISM *n* commonsense, earthiness, factualism, factualness, sense, soberness; **reality**, hardpan, the facts of life, the harsh reality, the truth of the matter, tintacks; **worldliness**, hardheadedness, pragmatism, worldly-mindedness; **naturalism**, cinéma-vérité, mimesis, social realism, verism

REALIST *n* factualist, hardhead, nuts-and-bolts man, pragmatist, utilitarian, verist

REALISTIC *adj* banausic, bread-and-butter, commonsensical, down-to-earth, fanciless, matter-of-fact, no-nonsense, pragmatic, sober, utilitarian, worldly, worldly-minded; **naturalistic**, factual, lifelike, living, mimetic, photographic, real, three-dimensional, true to life, truthful; **earthy**, kitchen-sink, raw, verist, veristic, warts-and-all

REALISTICALLY *adv* factually, soberly

REAR *n* arrear *(Archaic)*, background, backside, gorge, stern; **back**, B-side, reverse, smooth *(Tennis)*, tail, verso; **backside**, behind, breech, butt, buttocks, dorsum, hindquarter, posterior, rump, tail, tail end; **posteriority**, postposition; **rearguard**; **retroflexion**, resupination, retroversion

REAR *v* breed, bring up, discipline, house-train, nurture, teach manners to, toilet-train

REAR *adj* aft, after *(Naut.)*, epaxial, hind, hinder, posterior, tail; **hindmost**, aftermost, backmost, rearmost, sternmost; **background**; **backstage**, upstage; **back**, reverse, tail; **backward**, hindward, rearward; **retroflex**,

rear   **recorder**

resupinate, **retrorse**, **retroussé**, **revolute**

REASON *v* argue, chop logic, contend, debate, moot *(Obs.)*, ratiocinate, refine on, refine upon, subtilise; **deduce**, collect *(Rare)*, conclude, derive, figure, gather, induce

REASONER *n* arguer, debater, logician, philosophiser, polemicist, ratiocinator, refiner, syllogiser, synthesist

REASONING *n* argument, argumentation, assumption, consecution, debate, dialectic, discursion, discursiveness, discussion, disputation, exercise, illation, philosophism, polemic, proof, ratiocination, rationale, reason, refinement, subtilisation, syllogism, synthesis; **logic**, apologetics, Aristotelian logic, Aristotelianism, dialectics, formal logic, mathematical logic, methodology, polemics, propositional calculus, symbolic logic, syntax. *See also* LOGIC

RECEIVABLE *adj* adoptable, collectable, heritable, inheritable, obtainable; **receptive**, acceptant, recipient; **hereditary**, inherited, patrimonial, testamentary

RECLINE *v* lie, lie down, loll, loll about, lounge, measure one's length, prostrate oneself, repose, shake, spinebash, sprawl, stretch out

RECONCILABLE *adj* accordable, compliant, compoundable, conformable

RECORD *n* account, annal, autobiography, bio, biography, chronicle, commentary, curriculum vitae, document, history, life, track record, travels; **annals**, archives, commentaries, oral history, reminiscences, transactions; **notes**, adversaria, brief, cahier, case history, case record, detail *(Archaic)*, dictation, minutes; **note**, billet, chit, chitty, entry, memorandum, notation, observation, registration, sidenote; **file**, card catalogue, card file, card index, fiche, field book, filing card, form, microfiche, notebook, pocket-book, scribble block, scribble pad, slip, stub, table-book, tablet, work sheet; **parish register**, family Bible, vestry book; **register**, cartulary, logbook, manifest, plod, service rdcord, visitors' book; **scorebook**, scoreboard, scorecard, scoresheet; **score**, notch, return; **quipu**, pictograph; **legal record**, act, breve, cadastre, charter, corpus, court roll, discharge, docket, gazette, grant of probate, Hansard, law report, memorandum, muniments, patent, power of attorney, praecipe, presents, probate, provenance, statute, statute book, terrar, terrier, title deed, transcript, transumpt, will, writ; **electoral register**, census *(Class. Antiq.)*, electoral roll. *See also* DIARY; CERTIFICATE

RECORD *v* book, calendar, card, catalogue, chronicle, diarise, enrol, enter, inscribe, item, journalise, keep tabs on, keep track of, log, manifest, minute, notate, note, protocol, put down, register; **file**, archive; **tally**, mark up, nick, notch up, put on the slate, rack, score

RECORDER *n* amanuensis, annalist, biographer, chaser, chronicler, clerk, diarist, filer, hagiographer, historian, jerquer, rapporteur, registrar, scorer, secretary, tallyclerk, tallyman; **personnel**, office, secretariat; **recording instrument**, black box, flight recorder

RECORDING *n* album, disc, pressing, record, soundtrack, take; **LP**, A-side, black disc, B-side, CD, compact disc, digital disc, EP, extended play, flip side, forty-five, laser disc, mono, quadradisc, seventy-eight, single, thirty-three; **track**, cut, groove, microgroove, run-in groove; **smash-hit**, bullet, chart-buster, gold, gold record, gorilla *(U.S.)*, number one, platinum record, top forty, top ten; **sound library**, discography

RECOVERY *n* amends *(Obs.)*, convalescence, cure, rally, recruitment, recuperation, rehabilitation, sanation

RECTIFIABLE *adj* amendable, emendable, reformable

RED *n* blood red, carnation, Chinese red, chrome red, cinnabar, Congo red, crimson, flame colour, ginger, Indian red, pompadour, Pompeian red, poppy, ruby, rust, titian, Turkey red, Venetian red; **maroon**, grape, murex, murrey; **pink**, flesh, flesh colour, hot pink, peachblow, rose, shocking pink

RED *adj* cardinal, cherry, laky, ruddy, stammel *(Obs.)*; **crimson**, carmine, cerise, claret, cramoisy *(Obs.)*, garnet, incarnadine, incarnate, ruby; **scarlet**, vermeil, vermilion; **blood-red**, bloodied, bloodlike, bloodstained, bloody, ensanguined, gory, sanguine, sanguineous, sanguinolent; **magenta**, murex, port, vinous, wine; **pink**, blush, carnation, damask; **rose**, rosaceous, rose-coloured, roseate, roselike, rosy; **salmon**, apricot, coral, coralline, peach, salmon pink, sandy; **pinkish**, flamingo, flesh-coloured; **carroty**, flame-coloured, gingery, orange; **russet**, brick red, lateritious, mahogany, maroon, rubiginous, rusty, testaceous

REDDEN *v* bloody, crimson, ensanguine, gild *(Obs.)*, raddle, rubricate; **rouge**, henna; **flush**, blush, change colour, colour, colour up, have the blood rush to one's cheeks, inflame, mantle, rose

REDDENING *n* blushing, erubescence, rubefaction, rubescence, rubrication, rufescence; **rubricator**

REDDISH *adj* erubescent, rubicund, rubrical *(Obs.)*, ruddy, rufescent, rufous, rutilant *(Rare)*, strawberry, warm; **inflamed**, angry *(Med.)*, bloodshot, erythematous, erythrismal, inflammatory, injected, rubefacient; **red-faced**, blowzy, blushing, florid, flushed, high-coloured, raddled, rosy-cheeked, rouged, rubescent, rubicund; **red-headed**, carroty, sandy

RED DYE *n* alkanet, anchusin, annatto, brazil, cochineal, henna, keel *(Brit.)*, kermes, lake, madder, orcein, puccoon, purpurin, raddle, red ochre, redwood, rhodamine, rosaniline, ruddle, safranine, sappanwood; **rouge**, blusher, lip salve *(Archaic)*, lipstick

REDHEAD *n* blue, carrot top, strawberry blonde

REDLY *adv* bloodily, sanguinely, rosily, roseately; **red-facedly**, floridly

REDNESS *n* colour, floridity, floridness, gules, reddishness, rubicundity, ruddiness; **rosiness**, pinkness; **bloodiness**, angriness, erythema *(Pathol.)*, erythrism, erythroderma, erythrophobia, flush, hectic flush, inflammation, sanguineness

REFERENCE BOOK *n* atlas, calendar, dictionary, digest, directory, encyclopaedia, fauna, gazetteer, gradus, key, lapidary, lexicon, source book, thesaurus, wordbook, yearbook; **guidebook**, guide, itinerary, roadbook; **handbook**, companion, enchiridion, manual, phrasebook, stylebook, vade mecum, writer *(Obs.)*; **bibliography**, catalogue, reading list

REFLECTION *n* total internal reflection; **refraction**, birefringence, diffraction, interference, refringence; **polarisation**, coma, fringe; **aberration**, achromatism, aplanatism, chromatic aberration, spherical aberration, stigmatism; **angle of incidence**, angle of reflection, angle of refraction, cardinal points, centre of curvature, focal plane, focal point, focus, image, mirror image, nodal point, principal axis, principal focus, principal points; **focal length**, critical angle, depth of field, depth of focus, dioptre, magnification, numerical aperture, power, resolution, resolving power

REFUGE *n* asylum, bolthole, cot, cover, covert, coverture, funk-hole, hide-out, hideaway, place of safety, sanctuary; **hospice**, home, hospitium, imaret, retreat, spital *(Obs.)*; **traffic island**. See also SHELTER; HARBOUR

REFUSAL *n* declension, declination *(Obs.)*, declinature, denial, first refusal, negation, no, non-compliance, point-blank refusal, rebuff; **negativity**, disapproval, discountenance, negativeness, negativism; **veto**, disallowance, pocket veto *(U.S.)*, thumbs down

REFUSE *v* abnegate, begrudge, deny, not come at, not hear of, reject, repel, repulse, slam the door in someone's face; **baulk at**, beg off, chicken out, jack up, kick, kick against, veto, decline, disallow, negative, send back, withhold consent from; **give up**, kick the habit, pass up, renounce; **deprive**, dispossess, divest, strip; **rebuff**, disapprove, discountenance, knock back, not have a bar of it, not have any of it, repudiate, stick in one's throat, throw out, turn away, turn down; **draw the line at**, have nothing to do with, have second thoughts, not be in it, send away with a flea in the ear, set one's face against, turn a deaf ear to, turn one's back on, wash one's hands of; **reject**, cast away, cast off, discard, disown, forswear, junk

REFUSER *n* abnegator, denier, depriver, rejecter, repeller, repulser; **decliner**, baulker, disclaimer, dissenter, dissident, negativist, protestant, rebel, recusant

REGARDFUL *adj* bareheaded, cap in hand, deferent, deferential, humble, obeisant, obsequious, pious, respectful, reverential, suppliant, tributary; **awe-struck**, adoring, worshipful

REGION *n* area, corner, country, district, extent, land, limit *(Obs.)*, locale, locality, location, natural region, neck of the woods, pale, parts, precinct, province, purlieu, quarter, redevelopment area, restricted area, scope, stretch, swath, time zone, tract, tract of land, zone, zonule; **subdistrict**, subregion *(Geog.)*; **neighbourhood**, precincts, purlieus, vicinage, vicinity; **territory**, beat, range, terrain; **quarter**, colony, ghetto, pocket; **borderland**, border, bounds, corridor,

region   431   **rejoice**

enclave, exclave, frontier *(U.S.)*, hook, march, no-man's-land; **lowland**, mickery country, surge area, surge line, tideland, warpland; **top end**, upstate *(U.S.)*; **Eastern States**, northland, southland, west; **inland**, heartland, hinterland, interior, midland, up-country

REGIONAL *adj* areal, subregional, territorial, topographic, topographical, zonal; **local**, municipal, parochial, topical; **provincial**, cantonal, county, departmental, diocesan, divisional, eparchal, prefectural; **interstate**, intrastate, upstate *(U.S.)*; **neighbouring**, vicinal

REGIONALLY *adv* topographically; **locally**, provincially, territorially, topically

REGRESSER *n* flincher, retractor, reverser, shrinker; **relapser**, atavist, backslider, degenerate

REGRESSIVE *adj* backward, recessional *(Eccles.)*, recurrent *(Anat.)*, refluent, retroactive, retrograde, retrogressive, reverse; **reversional**, atavistic, retrospective

REGULAR *adj* equinoctial, even, isochronal, isochronous, measured, menstrual, oscillating, periodic, periodical, pulsating, recurrent, rhythmic, rhythmical, seasonal, sequential, serial, synchronous, systolic, throbbing, tidal, tidelike; **alternate**, alternant, bicyclic, cyclic, every other, peristaltic, reciprocal, revolving, rotary, rotatable, rotational, rotative, rotatory, successive

REGULARISATION *n* justification, normalisation, regimentation, self-justification *(Print.)*, social control, socialisation; **conventionalisation**, ordering, stylisation

REGULARISE *v* gauge, normalise, right, socialise, standardise, uniformalise *(Rare)*; **stylise**, classicise, reduce to order, stereotype, style; **adjust**, align, bowdlerise, bring into line, expurgate, fit, regiment, regulate, set, set to rights

REGULARITY *n* frequency, isochronism, natural frequency, periodicity, rhythm, rhythmics, rotation, sequacity, synchronisation, synchronousness, timing, uniformity; **biorhythms**, alternation of generations, circadian rhythms, course, courses, life cycle, menses, menstrual cycle, monthly, oestrus cycle, period

REGULARLY *adv* in phase, isochronally, isochronously, like clockwork, measuredly, periodically, rhythmically, sequaciously, serially, steadily, steady, synchronously; **alternately**, about, at intervals, by rote, by turns, every other day, in rotation, in turn, seasonally, to-and-fro, turn and turn about; **round**, through

REJECTION *n* dismissal, heave-ho, knock-back, repudiation, repulse, the big A, unrequitedness; **cast-off**, abnegation, discard, reject, throw-out, throwaway

REJOICE *v* clap hands, exult, fling one's cap in the air, have one's heart leap for joy, hug oneself, jollify, joy, jubilate, jump for joy, make merry, thank one's lucky stars, tread on air, walk on air; **celebrate**, commemorate, jubilate, maffick *(Brit.)*; **fete**, shivaree *(U.S.)*; **triumph**, crow, exalt *(Obs.)*, gloat, glory; **carol**, gratulate *(Archaic)*, hail, hymn, sing for joy; **congratulate**, pledge, toast; **go wild**, be on the tiles, carouse, dance the night away, go to town, jollify, paint the town red, revel, roister, whoop it up; **banquet,** feast, junket, kill the fatted calf

REJOICER *n* caroller, celebrant, celebrator, exalter *(Obs.)*, mafficker, merrymaker, reveller, roisterer, wassailer; **feaster,** bacchant, banqueter, junketer

RELATE *v* ally, associate, connect, mutualise, tie in; **concern,** appertain to, apply to, be in respect of, have regard to, have to do with, pertain to, refer to, touch; **interrelate,** cohere, correlate; **reciprocate,** mutualise *(U.S.)*

RELATED *adj* affined, affinitive, akin, analogous, appendant, associated, connected, connectional, correspondent, incident, interrelated, relational, relative; **proportional,** commensurate, correlative, pro rata, proportionate; **common,** joint, shared; **correlative,** correlate *(Rare)*, interrelated, mutual, mutually related, reciprocal, reciprocative; **relevant,** applicable, apposite, appurtenant, apropos, in point, pertinent, suitable, to the point

RELATEDLY *adv* associatively, coherently, connatedly; **appositively,** appositionally, connectedly, near, nearly; **analogously,** analogically, correspondently

RELATION *n* affinity, alliance, apposition, association, cognation, coherence, communality, connation, connection, correlation, correspondence, marriage, nearness, propinquity, proportionality, rapport, relativity, respondence; **compatibility,** analogousness, appositeness, compatibleness, correlativeness, relativeness; **interrelation,** intercommunion, interrelationship, reciprocality, reciprocation

RELATIONSHIP *n* affiliation, alliance, ascription, association, connection, filiation, habitude *(Obs.)*, liaison, relation, tie, tie-up; **transitive relation,** class inclusion; **something in common,** common denominator; **ratio,** correlation, perspective, proportion, scale; **commensuration,** percentage

RELATIVE *n* clansman, clanswoman, enate, in-law, kinsman, kinswoman, next of kin, relation, tribesman; **kin,** clan, flesh, flesh and blood, gens *(Anthrop.)*, horde, kindred, kinsfolk, kith and kin, name, parentage, people, sept, tribe *(Joc.)*; **family,** blended family, extended family, family circle, folks, gens *(Roman Hist.)*, ilk, nuclear family; **tribalist,** nepotist; **blood relation,** agnate, cognate, collateral, connection, connexion; **aunt,** aunty, great-aunt; **uncle,** grand-uncle, great-uncle; **niece,** grand-niece, great-niece; **nephew,** grand-nephew, great-nephew; **cousin,** country cousin, cousin-german, first cousin, first cousin once removed, full cousin, second cousin.   *See also* PARENT; SIBLING; KINSHIP

RELATIVELY *adv* according as, commensurately, in proportion, pro rata, proportionally; **reciprocally,** answerably, appositely, correlatively, in common, mutually, together

RELIGION *n* belief, church, connection, covenant, denomination, discipleship, faith, inspiration, persuasion, rule; **state religion,** established church, establishment; **theology,** divinity, ecclesiology, eschatology, hagiography, hagiology, ontology, soteriology, theodicy

RELIGIOUS *adj* deistic, deistical, ditheistic, monolatrous, monotheistic, pantheistic, polytheistic, spiritual, supernaturalistic, theandric, theanthropic, theist, theistic, theocentric, tritheistic; **evangelical**, born-again, charismatic, evangelistic, gospel, kerugmatik, mystic, Pentecostal, perseverant, redemptive, redemptory; **fundamentalist**, fire-and-brimstone; **theological**, ecclesiastical, eschatological, hagiographic, ontological; **canonical**, credal, creedal, divine, ecclesiologic, ecclesiological, orthodox, patristic, subscriptive; **denominational**, schismatic, sectarian; **interdenominational**, catholic, reunionistic, subjectivistic

RELIGIOUS CEREMONY *n* celebration, ceremonial, common; procession, recession, rite, ritual, solemnities, thanksgiving; **consecration**, Alleluia, canon, celebration, collect, Communion, confiteor, epiclesis, Epistle, Eucharist, eulogia, fraction, introit, Kyrie eleison, lavabo, mystery, oblation, offertory, ordinary, preface, sacrifice, sanctification, Secret, the Lord's Supper; **initiation**, anabaptism, aspersion, baptism, christening, circumcision, confirmation, dedication, immersion, initiation ceremony, insufflation, lustrum, paedobaptism, palingenesis, simple vow, vow; **offering**, donary, flagellation, holocaust, immolation, libation, offertory, sacrifice, thank-offering, victim; **benediction**, benison *(Archaic)*, blessing, love; **last sacraments**, anointment, extreme unction, viaticum; **love feast**, agape, Chaburah, Seder; **corroboree**, bora, ceremony, tabi song *(Aborig.)*

RELIGIOUS DIGNITARY *n* beadle, church commissioner, churchwarden, elder, moderator, presbyter, proctor, sexton, sidesman, verger, vestryman, warden; **elders**, classis, colloquy, parish council, presbytery; **deputy**, acolyte, curate, impropriator, oblate, ostiary, porter, surrogate; **papal envoy**, ablegate, apostolic delegate, friary, legate, nuncio; **vicar choral**, cantor, chanter, chazzan, precentor, succentor; **pardoner**, simoniac, simonist. *See also* ECCLESIASTIC

RELIGIOUS FOLLOWER *n* believer, biblicist, churchgoer, disciple, elect, evangelical, evangelist, follower, fundamentalist, saint, sectary, subjectivist; **neophyte**, catechumen; **congregation**, flock, fold, the faithful; **layperson**, charge, churchman, churchwoman, civilian, diocesan, laic, layman, laywoman, papal knight, parishioner, secular; **lay preacher**, acolyte, lay reader; **server**, altar boy, parish clerk, sacristan; **laity**, brother, brotherhood, confraternity, regular tertiaries, secular tertiaries, sidesman, sodality, tertiary

RELIGIOUS MINISTRY *n* clerkship, cloth, curacy, cure, deaconate, deaconry, deaconship, diaconate, eldership, officiation, orders, presbyterate, priestcraft, priesthood, priestliness, rabbinate, rectorate, sacerdotalism, subdiaconate, vicariate, vicarship; **benefice**, cure, incumbency, living, parish, pastorate, pastorship, sinecure, title; **abbotship**, abbacy, deanship, priorate, priorship, rectorate, subdeanery; **archdeaconate**, archdeaconry, archidiaconate, archpriesthood, canonicate, canonry, canonship, chapter, precentorship; **bishopric**, episcopacy, episcopate, episcope, lawn sleeves, mitre, patriarchate, pontificate, prelacy, prelateship, prelatism, prelatist, prelature, see, suffragan, surrogateship, throne; **archbishopric**, archiepiscopacy, archiepiscopate, bench, eparchy *(Greek Orthodox)*, primacy, primateship; **cardinalship**, cardinalate, purple, red hat; **papacy**, apostolate, apostolic succession, Curia, Curia Romana, patriarchate, Pontifical College, pontificate, popedom, primacy, primateship, tiara

RELIGIOUS PERSON *n* believer, churchgoer, the faithful; **dogmatist**, apologist, dogmatiser; **crusader**, bible-banger, bible-basher, biblicist, bibliolater, evangelical, evangeliser, evangelist, fundamentalist, hot-gospeller, Sal, Sallie, Salvo

REMEMBER *v* be mindful of, bethink oneself of *(Archaic)*, conjure up, live in the past, relive, retrace, revive, think of; **retain**, hold in mind, keep in mind, mind *(Archaic)*; **recollect**, place, recall, recognise; **reminisce**, flashback, hark back to, rake up the past; **haunt**, obsess, possess; **have a good memory**, have a memory like an elephant

REMEMBERING *n* anamnesis, hindsight, nostalgia, recognition, recollection, reminiscence, retrospection, review; **memorisation**, learning, mnemonics, mnemotechnics, rote learning. *See also* MEMORY

REMIND *v* admonish, jog someone's memory, refresh someone's memory, remember *(Archaic)*; **prompt**, cue, hint, jog; **be on the tip of one's tongue**, come back, recur; **evoke**, be reminiscent of, breathe of, bring back, call to mind, call up, put in mind of, recall, remind of, ring a bell, strike a chord

REMINDER *n* admonishment, admonition; **prompt**, autocue, cue card, prompter, teleprompter; **cue**, dorothy dixer, leading question; **aide-mémoire**, hurry-up, jotting, memento mori, memo, memorandum, memory-jogger, minute, mnemonic, monitor, note, phylactery *(Archaic)*, record, round robin

REMINISCENT *adj* anecdotal, narrative, nostalgic; **evocative**, redolent of, remindful; **recollective**, mnemonic, recognitive, recognitory

REMNANT *n* bob, butt, counterfoil, end, fag, fag-end, frazzle, rump, shred, stub, stump, tail; **remains**, flotsam and jetsam, oddment, odds and ends, relics, relicts, residue; **remainder**, balance, carryover, hangover, holdover *(U.S.)*, leaving, margin, odd, remanet, residual, residuum, rest, surplus; **leftovers**, orts, scrag end, scraps; **vestige**, relic, scrap, skeleton, trace; **leavings**, dross, foot, foots, grounds, heeltap, sediment, sludge, snuff, waste; **debris**, flotsam, jetsam, shipwreck, wreck, wreckage; **dregs**, alluvium, crust, deposit, dottle, draff, fur, geest, lee, lees, marc, scum, spent grains; **clippings**, borings, filings, grass clippings, paring, peelings, sawdust, scrapings, scraps, swarf; **tailings**, dump, mullock, spoil; **tartar**, wine stone; **off-cut**, cutting, docking, off-cuts; **pomace**, chum, rape, trash; **ash**, bone ash, bone earth, boneblack, calx, cinders, dust; **scruff**, salamander, scale, scoria, sow, sprue, tap-cinder; **weapon debris**; **cotton waste**, lint, strass; **tree stump**,

remnant   435   **remove**

stool, stub, stump; **sewage**, sewage farm, sewerage, sullage, sullage pit, waste product; **bombsite**, rubble, ruins; **earthly remains**, ashes, clay, dust, earth, mortal remains

REMNANT *adj* last, left, left behind, left over, net, odd, other, remainder, remaining, remnant, surviving; **vestigial**, residual, residuary, rudimentary

REMOTE *adj* devious, godforsaken, lonely, out, out-of-the-way, outlandish, outlying, wayback; **outback**, back-country, backblock, backwoods; **inaccessible**, unapproachable, unreachable, untouchable; **overseas**, o.s., transalpine, transoceanic, transpacific, ultramontane; **ultramundane**, beyond the universe, out of this world. *See also* DISTANT

REMOTELY *adv* deviously, outlandishly; **far**, a long way away, a long way off, afar, afield, deeply, distantly, far and near, far and wide, far away, in the distance, not within cooee, off to billyo, off to buggery, offshore, on the horizon; **away**, awa *(Scot.)*, distally, forth, hence *(Archaic)*, off, out, outward, recessively; **outback**, back of beyond, beyond the black stump, up the booay; **aloof**, aloofly, at arm's length, wide; **too far**, out of range, out of reach; **yonder**, over there, thither, yon *(Archaic)*, yond *(Archaic)*

REMOTENESS *n* aloofness, deviousness, farness, loneliness, outlandishness; **distance**, length, range: **a long way**, a fair way, a good way, a light-year, a long chalk, a long haul, light-years, miles; **remotest point**, aphelion, apocynthion, apogee, apolune, outer, solstice

REMOTE PLACE *n* back of beyond, back of Bourke, back of the black stump, Bandywallop, Bullamakanka, jumping-off place *(U.S.)*, never-never, Outer Mongolia, Timbuktu, wayback, Woop Woop, wop-wops *(N.Z.)*; **end**, antipodes, ends of the earth, infinity, outer limits, Thule, ultima Thule, utmost, uttermost; **back country**, backblocks, backwoods, booay, boondocks *(U.S.)*, goat country, mallee, outback, the waybacks *(N.Z.)*, tiger country; **outpost**, back-station, out-station; **back run**, back paddock, outrun, run-off *(N.Z.)*; **offing**, outing

REMOVAL *n* abstraction, avulsion, deracination, dislodgment, eradication, exsection, extirpation, extraction, purge, remotion, remove, ripping out, shift, stripping, uprooting, withdrawal; **disinterment**, disentombment, exhumation; **obliteration**, erasure, rubbing out, wiping out; **clearance**, clean sweep, clearing, sweep; **brushing away**, Australian salute, Barcoo salute; **emptying**, drainage, unfouling, venting; **unloading**, deconsolidation, offloading, unpacking; **clear-felling**, back-burning, burning-off, bush bashing, bush-burning *(N.Z.)*, bush-falling *(N.Z.)*, cabling, chaining-off, clear-cutting, double-logging, frilling, logging, mullenising, ring-barking, scrub-cutting, scrub-rolling, scrub bashing, sucker-bashing

REMOVE *v* grub out, root out, scrub, strike, strip, take away, take down, take off, thin out, uproot; **take out**, abstract, aspirate, bale out, prescind, withdraw; **disinter**, disentomb, exhume; **obliterate**, blank, blank out, erase, rub off, rub out, wipe off, wipe out; **cut out**, excide, excise, extirpate; **pull off**, nip, pick, pick out, prise, pull up, put off; **unload**, debark, deconsolidate, off-load, unpack; **get rid of**, brush aside, clear, clear away, get shot of, make a clean sweep, make away with, see the back of, ship, shuffle off, shunt, sweep away, swish off, swoop up, whisk away; **clear of**, free from, purge of, rid of; **clear-fell**, back-burn, cable, chain off, clear-cut, frill, log, mullenise, ringbark

RENEGADE *adj* apostate, tergiversant, traitorous; **born-again**, converted, reborn, redeemed, reformed, regenerate; **naturalised**

REPAIR *n* darn, mend, patch; **overhaul**, careenage, checkup, drop test *(Joc.)*, refit, service; **restoration**, cannibalisation, renovation, reparation, vamp; **reclamation**, innings, land reclamation, reafforestation, reclaim, rescue, retrieval, revegetation, salvage; **replenishment**, recruitment, reinforcement; **redemption**, postliminy, ransom, restitution

REPAIR *v* cannibalise, careen, cicatrise, clobber *(Obs.)*, doctor, fix, make whole, overhaul, reassemble, redintegrate, refit, restore, service, tinker; **cobble**, fox, half-sole, resole, vamp; **renovate**, bodgie up, do over, do up, fix up, freshen up, jack up *(N.Z.)*, lift, make over, reface, refurbish, revamp, touch up, vamp up; **mend**, darn, patch, piece up, reduce *(Surg.)*, sew; **reclaim**, reafforest, reforest, retrieve; **replenish**, recruit; **redeem**, ransom; **rehabilitate**, put someone on his feet, recondition, regenerate, reinstate; **revive**, bring to life, reanimate, recall *(Poetic)*, recreate, resurrect, resuscitate, revitalize, revivify

REPAIRER *n* fix-it man, fixer, handyman, renovator, repairman, restorer, service man; **mender**, careener, cobbler, darner, patcher, piecer, spiderman, steeplejack, tailor, tinker, vamper; **rejuvenator**, reclaimant, reclaimer, recoverer, resurrectionist, salvager; **restorative**, febrifuge, freshener, lifesaver, pick-me-up, pick-up, refresher, shot in the arm, tonic

REPEALABLE *adj* rescindable, rescissible, revocable

REPEAT *v* encore, parrot, replay, retake, run through again; **echo**, re-echo, resound, reverberate; **ding**, drum; **do to death**, beat into the ground, cuckoo, hammer, harp upon, thrash out; **come again**, ditto, go over, go over the same ground, quote, re-word; **practise**, re-act, re-enact, reconstruct, redraft, reduplicate, rehearse, remake, reproduce; **recommence**, reappear, repair, restore; **renew**, reopen, resume; **iterate**, circulate *(Maths Obs.)*, come back to, ingeminate, recapitulate, recapture, recur, redouble, reiterate, return to, revert to, run, tautologise

REPEATEDLY *adv* again and again, cyclically, day by day, day in day out, in-and-in, morning noon and night, over and over, perennially, till doomsday, time and time again, without end, year after year; **afresh**, again, anew, bis, da capo, dal segno, ditto, once more, over *(Brit.)*, over again; **repetitiously**, constantly, pleonastically, tautologically

REPEL *v* avert, beat off, chase away, dispel, drive away, drive back, drive off, fight off, force away, force back,

repel force off, frighten away, frighten off, hand off, parry, put the frighteners on (*Brit.*), repulse, scare away, scare off, send away, stave off, stink out, ward off; **rebuff**, arsehole, cut, give the arse, give the big A, give the bum's rush, keep at a distance, keep at arm's length, see someone about his business, snub, spurn, turn away, turn down, turn one's back on; **dismiss**, bundle off, bundle out, cast away, cast off, cast out, exile, fling aside, pack off, put off, reject; **shed**, burke, ditch, doff, get rid of, give the flick, hunt, piss off, wipe

REPELLENT *adj* dismissive, dismissory, off-putting, repelling, repulsive

REPETITION *n* ingemination, iterance, iteration, recurrence, recursion, reiteration, renewal, resumption, return, series, succession; **repeat**, action replay, duplication, encore, re-enactment, re-run, reappearance, recapitulation, reconstruction, redraft, reduplication, remake, repeat performance, retake, return season; **reprise**, burden, canon, chorus, fugue, imitation, ostinato, passacaglia, recapitulation, refrain, repeat, retend, ritornells, rondo, round; **practice**, rehearsal, rote learning, training; **twin**, clone, copy, duplicate, Xerox; **anaphora**, anadiplosis, dittography, emphasis, gemination, pleonasm, redundancy, tautology, twinning; **repetitiousness**, periodicity; **repetend**, circulating decimal (*Obs.*), recurring decimal, repeating decimal; **ditto**, ditto marks, quotation, quote

REPETITIVE *adj* ding-dong, dittographic, iterant, iterative, monotonous, pleonastic, redundant, reiterant, reiterative, repetitious, resumptive, tautological, tick tock; **repeated**, continual, habitual, incessant, invariant, perennial, reconstructive, recurrent, recurring, recursive, reduplicate, reduplicative, reiterated, return, twicetold, unvarying, usual; **echolike**, recapitulative, recapitulatory, repercussive, reverberative, reverberatory; **anaphoric**, abovementioned, aforementioned, aforesaid, cataphoric, exophoric

REPORT ON *v* blow the whistle on, delate, dob in, dob on, drop, drop in, give up, grass, nark, peach (*Brit.*), put in, put someone's weights up, put the finger on, rat on, shelf, shelve, shop, sing, squeak, squeal, tell on, tip off, tip someone the wink, top off, welsh; **expose**, blow, drop a bundle

REPOSE *v* couch, lie down, prostrate, spread-eagle, stretch out; **sit**, sit up; **straddle**, sit astride, spraddle, sprawl; **kneel**, bow, curtsy, genuflect, have one's knees fold beneath one, knee (*Obs. Poetic*), kowtow, sink; **squat**, crouch, kangaroo (*Colloq.*); **slouch**, stoop

REPRESENT *v* allegorise, emblematise, emblemise, express, figure, illustrate, image, prefigure, stand for, symbol, symbolise, type, typify; **personify**, assume a character, characterise, imitate, impersonate, incarnate, mimic, personate, play charades, pose

REPRESENTATION *n* expression, symbolisation, symbolism, symbology, typology; **impersonation**, characterisation, enactment, mimesis, personation, personification; **allegory**, fable, imagery, parable; **typification**, prefiguration, prefigurement; **por-**

trayal, art, iconography, iconology, imagery, photography, portraiture, sculpture; **graphics**, design work, ichnography, photocopying, tracing; **cartography**, cosmography, hypsography, hypsometry; **model**, diorama, pageant, panorama, tableau, tableau vivant; **planetarium**, georama, globe

REPRESENTATIONAL *adj* iconic, iconographic, iconological; **symbolical**, allegorical, emblematic, figurative, ilustrative, symbolic, symbolistic; **representative**, prefigurative, typical, typological

REPRESS *v* crush, put down, quash, quell, smother, squash, squelch, stifle, tame; **persecute**, burden, grieve *(Obs.)*, grind under, lade, oppress, trample on, tyrannise; **enslave**, enfeoff, enthral, feudalise, imperialise, mediatise, slave, thrall *(Archaic)*, yoke *(Obs.)*; **subdue**, beat down, bring down, bring someone to his knees, bring to heel, bring to terms, bring under, compel, down, kneel on, overcome, overpower, prostrate, reduce, stoop *(Archaic)*, strangle, strangulate, vanquish; **keep down**, have at one's beck and call, have by the balls, have by the short and curlies, have by the short hairs, keep on a string, keep under, put the maginnis on; **domineer**, browbeat, henpeck, overbear, overlord, override, tread on, treat like dirt, walk all over

REPRESSED *adj* at one's beck and call, at one's feet, downtrodden, henpecked, under the thumb; **enslaved**, aggrieved, subject to, thrall *(Archaic)*; **servile**, controllable, hierodulic, prostrate, slavish, subduable, submissive, wormlike

REPRESSER *n* authoritarian, despot, oppressor, overrider, persecutor, queller, subjugator, trampler, tyranniser, tyrant; **conqueror**, coloniser, enthraller, vanquisher; **slaveholder**, enslaver, slave-trader, slaver

REPRESSION *n* subjection, subjugation; **oppression**, persecution, pressure; **subdual**, colonisation, conquest, quelling; **feudal system**, assignment system, colonialism, feudalisation, helotism, helotry, heteronomy, peonage, serfdom, serfhood, vassalage, villeinage; **slavery**, bondage, chains, enslavement, enthralment, servitude, thraldom, thrall; **slave trade**, blackbirding, corvée, forced labour, slave-trading

REPRESSIVE *adj* domineering, on top, overbearing, overpowering, possessive; **oppressive**, burdensome, despotic, grievous *(Archaic)*, persecutional, persecutive, persecutory, tyrannic, tyrannical, tyrannous; **authoritarian**, hard-handed, heavy-handed

REPRESSIVELY *adv* burdensomely, despotically, oppressively, overpoweringly, tyrannically, tyrannisingly, with a heavy hand

REPRESSIVENESS *n* authoritarianism, burdensomeness, oppressiveness

REPRIMAND *n* admonishment, lecture, rebuke, reproach, reproof, reproval, schooling *(Archaic)*, scolding, upbraiding; **tongue-lashing**, a flea in one's ear, a kick in the pants, a piece of one's mind, bagging, blast, chip, counterblast, dressing-down, earful, jaw, lashing, pasting, rating, razz, roast, roasting, rocket, rub, scorcher, serve, slam, slap, talking-to, the rounds of the kitchen, the treatment, trimmings, wigging *(Brit.)*; **tirade**, diatribe, jeremiad, philippic; **attack**, broadside, onslaught. *See also* DISAPPROVAL: BOO

REPRODUCE *v* breed, procreate, propagate; **beget**, bring forth, engender, father, generate, get, mother, sire; **lay**, oviposit, ovulate, spawn, spore; **fertilise**, cross-fertilise, cross-pollinate, fecundate, pollen, pollinate, superfetate; **breed**, backcross, clone, crossbreed, duplicate, grade, grow, hybridise, inbreed, interbreed, intercross, milt, mongrelise, multiply, nick, outbreed, propagate; **graft**, engraft, inarch, layer; **implant**, nidate. *See also* CONCEIVE: GIVE BIRTH

REPRODUCTION *n* bearing, engenderment, generation, increase, procreation, propagation, pullulation; **sexual reproduction**, allogamy, amphimixis, autogamy, cleistogamy, entomophily, exogamy, gamogenesis, hydrophily, isogamy, karyogamy, oogamy, syngamy, syngenesis, xenogamy, zoogamy; **biogenesis**, cainogenesis, palingenesis *(Obs.)*; neoteny, paedogenesis; **asexual reproduction**, agamogenesis, apogamy, apomixis, blastogenesis, duplication, fission, gemmation, parthenogenesis, schizogenesis, vegetativeness, virgin birth; **maturation**, abstriction *(Bot.)*, gametogenesis, heterospory, oogenesis, ovulation, spermatogenesis, sporogenesis, sporogony; **digenesis**, metagenesis; **epigenesis**, germ theory, pangenesis, preformation; **cell-division**, crossing over, crossover, cytogenesis, cytogenetics, cytokinesis, haplosis, meiosis, metaphase, mitosis, phase, prophase, synapsis; **oestrous cycle**, heat, rut. *See also* CONCEPTION: PREGNANCY: BIRTH

REPRODUCTIVE *adj* conceptive, fecund, fertile, fertilisable, generative, procreant, procreative, progenitive, propagable, propagative, virile; **genital**, genito-urinary, sexual; **seminal**, embryonic, germinal, seminiferous; **sporiferous**, sporogenous; **eugenic**, dysgenic, eugenical, stirpicultural; **inbred**, heterozygous; **amitotic**, meiotic, mitotic; **allopolyploid**, aneuploid, diploid, euploid, haploid, polyploid, triploid

REPRODUCTIVE AGENT *n* come *(Colloq.)*, semen, seminal fluid, spunk *(Colloq.)*; **seed**, basidiospore, cyst, endospore, gamete, gametocyte, gemma, gemmule, germ, germ cell, germen, grain, heterogamete, isogamete, oosperm *(Obs.)*, oospore, ovule, planogamete, prothallium, sperm, spermatocyte, spermatozoon, spore, sporule, swarm spore, swarmer; **egg**, egg cell, oocyte, oogonium, oosphere, ovule, ovum; **spawn**, berry, coral, hen fruit *(Colloq.)*, milt, roe; **pollen**, pollinium; **chromosome**, chromatid, chromatin, deoxyribonucleic acid, heterochromatin, X chromosome, Y chromosome; **gametophore**, antheridium, basidium, gametangium, hymenium, ovisac, sporophore; **blastocyst**, blastoderm, blastodisc, centromere, centrosome, centrosphere, chalaza, egg cell, endoblast, endoderm, endosperm, endothecium, entoblast, germ layer, germ plasm, germinal disc, germinal vesicle, hypoblast, idioplasm, morula, proembryo, pronucleus, trophoblast, yolk

REPRODUCTIVE ORGANS *n* genitalia, genitals, loins *(Bible Poetic)*, private parts, privates, pudenda; **uterus,** clitoris, Fallopian tubes, ovary, vagina, vulva, womb; **testicles,** epidydimus, penis, prostate gland, scrotum, testis, vas deferens; **sex gland,** gonad; **hormones,** chorionic gonadotrophin, oestrogen, progesterone, progestogen; **amniotic fluid,** afterbirth, amnion, amniotic membrane, caul, chorion, Graafian follicle, placenta, umbilical cord, waters

REPTILE *n* reptilian; **snake,** Joe Blake; **lizard,** saurian

REPTILIAN *adj* reptile; **snake-like,** anguine, colubrine, ophidian, serpentine, snaky, viperine, viperish; **coldblooded,** poikilothermal; **lizard-like,** lacertilian, lizard, saurian

REPULSION *n* antipathy, aversion *(Obs.),* dislike, distaste, repellence; **dismissal,** brush-off, cold shoulder, cut, rebuff, repulse, snub, spurning

REPUTABILITY *n* creditableness, respectability, respectableness, worthiness; **exaltedness,** augustness, illustration *(Rare),* illustriousness, venerability, venerableness; **majesty,** dignity, gloriousness, grandeur, impressiveness, splendidness, splendour, stateliness; **brilliance,** dazzle, halo, lustre, radiance

REPUTABLE *adj* admirable, considerable, estimable, honourable, of good reputation, respectable, respected, valued, well-thought-of; **eminent,** celebrated, distingué, distinguished, exalted, great, illustrious, important, pre-eminent, prestigious, prominent, splendid, splendorous, star, venerable, worthy; **special,** premium, prestige; **noble,** august, dignified, glorious, grand, great, haughty *(Archaic),* impressive, lofty, lordly, majestic, Olympian, princely, proud, stately, sublime, uplifted

REPUTABLY *adv* admirably, creditably, exaltedly, illustriously, respectably, worthily; **famously,** eminently, in the public eye, notedly, notoriously, pre-eminently, prominently; **splendidly,** augustly, gloriously, impressively, stately

REPUTATION *n* account, attribute *(Obs.),* character, conceit *(Archaic),* esteem, estimation, memory, name, odour, regard, report, repute, score, value, worth; **rank,** footing, form, position, standing, station, status, stock; **good reputation,** credit, distinction, good name, good report, good repute, high repute, honour, worship *(Archaic);* **renown,** fame, famousness, mark, note, notedness, noteworthiness, notoriety; **importance,** altitude, consequence, consideration, distinction, eminence, pre-eminence, superiority; **prestige,** cachet, eclat, face, kudos; **glory,** exaltation, stardom

REQUEST *n* claim, demand, requisition, ultimatum; **cadge,** bite, hum, sting, touch; **begging letter,** agony column, classified ad, personal column, want ad

REQUITER *n* indemnifier, redresser, restorer, satisfier; **penitent,** atoner, expiator, mourner *(U.S.),* purger

RESIDENT *adj* indwelling, quartered, residentiary; **native,** aboriginal, autochthonous, indigenous; **firstgeneration,** currency, native-born; **home,** domestic, local; **migrant,** alien, ethnic, naturalised; **parasitic,** entophytic, entozoan, entozoic, epizoic, inquiline, inquilinous; **commensal**, symbiotic; **aerial**, arboreal, arenicolous, epigeal, fenny, geophilous, marine, riparian, terrestrial, terricolous

RESIGN *v* bow out, chuck it in, give the tube away *(Shearing)*, go into retirement, leave, quit, retire, roll over *(Politics)*, sign off, snatch one's time, step down, take off, tender one's resignation, vacate a position; **abdicate**, give up the throne, lay down the burden of office

RESONANCE *n* fullness, fullness of tone, hollowness, resonation, reverberation, rotundity, rotundness; **echo**, re-echo, repercussion, replication; **plangency**, sonority, sonorousness, vibrancy

RESONANT *adj* echoic, echolike, repercussive, resounding, reverberant, reverberative, reverberatory; **sonorous**, fruity, gonglike, plummy, rotund, round, sounding, vibrant, voiceful; **plangent**, loud, reboant, wiry; **hollow**, cavernous, sepulchral; **rumbly**, rolling, stertorous, thundering, thunderous

RESONANTLY *adv* loud, loudly, resoundingly, smack, sonorously, soundingly, vibrantly

RESONATE *v* resound, reverberate, ring out; **echo**, re-echo, re-sound, redouble, repeat *(Horol.)*, reply, revoice

RESONATOR *n* cavity resonator, echo chamber, echo unit, reverberation unit, reverberator, rhumbatron; **clacker**, chimer, clicker, honker, hummer, rattler, thrummer; **bell**, carillon, chime, cowbell, sacring bell, shark bell, sleighbell, tenor, tom, treble; **clapper**, tongue; **alarum**, buzzer

RESPECT *v* consider highly, esteem, have a high opinion of, hold in high esteem, hold in high regard, honour, regard, revere, reverence, think highly of, think much of, think well of, weigh *(Obs.)*; **idolise**, adore, hallow, hero-worship, look up to, venerate, worship; **prize**, cherish, love, take to one's bosom, treasure; **fear**, dread *(Obs.)*, hold in awe

RESPECTABILITY *n* admirableness, respectableness, venerability, venerableness; **awesomeness**, dreadfulness, fearfulness, redoubtableness; **estimableness**, value, worth, worthiness

RESPECTABLY *adv* venerably; **awesomely**, awfully, dreadfully, fearfully, impressively, redoubtably

RESPECTER *n* commemorator, honourer, observer, tributary, tributer, valuer, venerator; **honourer**, adorer, fan club, genuflector, hero-worshipper, idoliser, kowtower, saluter

RESPECTFULLY *adv* deferentially, regardfully; **in deference to**, with all respect, with respect; **adoringly**, piously, worshipfully

RESPIRATORY *adj* bronchial, glottal, laryngeal, pharyngeal, tracheal

REST *n* bange, camp, ease, leisure, loaf, Maori P.T. *(N.Z. Colloq.)*, relaxation, spinebash, spinebashing, vacancy *(Obs.)*; **lull**, abeyance, cessation, fallow, interlude, pause, recess, respite, spell; **break**, blow, boil-up, breath, breather, breathing space, half-time, nick *(Archaic)*, pit stop, pull-in, sit-down, time-out; **calm**, equilibrium, peace, quiet, quietude, reposal, repose; **calmness**, composedness, composure, downiness, easefulness, heart's ease, leisureliness, poise, quietness, reposefulness, restfulness; **sick leave**, m.d.o. *(N.Z. Colloq.)*, sickie; **meal break**, brew-up, coffee break, dinnertime, lemons *(Sport)*, lunch hour, lunchtime, orange time, playlunch, playtime, smoko, tea-break

REST *v* compose oneself, fallow, lull, quiet, quieten, settle, sit; **have a rest**, bange, breathe, camp, curl up, die down, have a break, have a spell, lie down, lie fallow, pause, put one's feet up, recess, settle down, sit down, spell, take a seat; **relax**, ease, unbend, unbrace, wind down; **take it easy**, coast along, hang loose, lie at ease, linger, live on one's fat, rest on one's laurels, rest on one's oars; **lie at rest**, couch, lair, loll, perch, recline, repose, roost, spinebash; **pause**, boil the billy, take five; **holiday**, camp, flex, flex off, get away from it all, shut up shop, vacation

RESTAURANT *n* B.Y.O., bevery, bistro, brasserie, buffet, buffet car *(Railways)*, caf, cafe, cafeteria, canteen, chophouse *(Brit. U.S.)*, coffee bar, coffee house, coffee shop, diner, dining car *(Railways)*, dining hall, dining room, eatery, eating house, el cheapo, greasy spoon, grillroom, hash house, inn *(Brit.)*, joint, luncheonette, meals on wheels, pizzeria, pull-in *(Brit.)*, refectory, restaurant car, road house, self-service, snack bar, soda fountain *(U.S.)*, soup kitchen, steakhouse, takeaway, tavern, tearoom, teashop *(Brit.)*, trattatoria

RESTER *n* camper, holiday-maker, lady of leisure, lingerer, loller, lotus eater, relaxer, spinebasher

RESTFULLY *adv* at ease *(Mil.)*, at rest, easefully, reposefully; **calmly**, composedly, leisurely, quietly, soothingly; **at leisure**, at one's leisure, off, off duty

RESTING *adj* still; **fallow**, off, off-duty; **restful**, leisured, leisurely; **calm**, composed, poised, possessed; **sabbatical**, ferial, holiday

RESTORATIVE *adj* recreational, redintegrative, refreshing, regenerative, rejuvenescent, reparative; **plastic**, anaplastic *(Surg.)*

RESTRAIN *v* bate, button down, chastise *(Archaic)*, check, circumscribe, clip someone's wings, constrain, control, curb, detain, enjoin *(Law)*, hinder, hobble, hopple, stop, tether; **repress**, bite back, bottle up, keep back, put down, sit on, stifle, strangle, suppress; **hold back**, choke, contain, hold in, keep down, rein back, rein in; **silence**, burke, gag, guillotine *(Parl. Proc.)*, muzzle; **chain**, collar, enchain, enfetter, fetter, gyve, handcuff, jess *(Falconry)*, leg-rope, manacle, put in irons, shackle, trammel; **bail**, bail up, crib, pillory, stock *(Obs.)*; **bit**, bridle, curb, halter; **tie up**, astrict, bind, cord, gird, hogtie, pinion, rope, swaddle, truss, wire; **anchor**, cast anchor, skid, stay

RESTRAINEDLY *adv* discreetly, measuredly; **restrictedly**, constrainedly, in check, on the bit

RESTRAINER *n* binder, inhibiter, retainer; **controller**, constrainer, limiter, obstructionist, stinter, withholder

RESTRAINING *adj* binding, inhibitory, limitative, restrictive; **repressive**, inhibiting, suppressive

RESTRAINING ORDER *n* covenant, D-notice, embargo, injunction *(Law)*, patent, prohibition, tail, writ; **gag**, guillotine *(Parl. Proc.)*

RESTRAIN ONESELF *v* bite one's lip, get a hold on oneself, hold one's horses, let sleeping dogs lie, pull one's punches, refrain; **play gooseberry**

RESTRAINT *n* astriction, censorship, comstockery *(U.S.)*, containment, control, inhibition, repression, restriction, suppression; **limitation**, clampdown, rationing, squeeze, stint, stranglehold; **self-control**, moderation; **bondage**, binding, enchainment; **curfew**, custody, detainment, detention, tuition *(Archaic)*

RESTRAINTS *n* ball and chain, bands, bilbo, bracelet, chains, darbies *(Prison Colloq.)*, fetters, gyves, handcuffs, hobble, hobblechain, manacle, nippers, shackle, tether, trammel; **pillory**, bail, crib, stocks, trave; **restraint**, bind, bond, brake, chain, check, constraint, cramp, curb, dead hand, stop; **keeper**, keeping, key, sprag, sprig, tie; **doorstop**, chock, skid; **roofguard**, snowguard; **rail**, fiddle *(Naut.)*, throatlatch, tug

RESTRICT *v* confine, constrict, contain, cramp, embargo, ground, inhibit, stop, withhold; **limit**, peg, ration, stint, straiten

RESTRICTED *adj* constrained, limited; **repressed**, hidebound, pent-up; **bound**, affined *(Obs.)*, confined, corded, detained, earthbound, fast, fenced-in, housebound, icebound, imprisoned, jessed, stormbound; **restrained**, discreet, low-key, low-profile, measured, reserved

RESULT *n* effect, ensemble, resultant, turnout; **consequence**, apodosis, attendant, consequent, bottom line, fallout, flowthrough, issue, legacy, outcome, outgrowth, pay-off, repercussion, side-effect; **conclusion**, crystallisation, end, event, foregone conclusion, realisation, redound, termination; **sequel**, after-effect, aftermath, aftertaste, sequence, sequent, train; **development**, elaboration, evolution

RESULT *v* end, pan out, terminate in, turn out; **follow**, attend, ensue, proceed from; **emanate**, issue from

RESULTANT *adj* appendant, attendant, consecutive, consequent, consequential, flowthrough, sequent, sequential, terminational, terminative; **derivative**, derivate, secondary; **emanative**, emanatory

RETALIATE *v* fight back, give as good as one gets, make payment, pay off, pay out, reciprocate, retort, return enemy fire, return the compliment, riposte, take the law into one's own hands, turn on; **get even with**, call it quits, fix someone, get back at, get one's own back, have someone's guts for garters, pay back, pay back in the same coin, pay off a score, pay off old scores, settle a debt, settle a score, square off with, turn the tables on; **revenge**, avenge, have revenge, pay a debt, venge *(Archaic)*, vindicate *(Archaic)*

RETALIATION *n* avengement, paying back, quid pro quo, reciprocation, reciprocity, reprisal, retorsion, retortion, retribution, return, revenge, utu *(N.Z.)*, vendetta; **vengefulness**, revanchism, revengefulness, vengeance, vindictiveness, wrath; **counter-terrorism**, counterblast; re-

ply, response, retort, riposte; **tit for tat,** a dose of one's own medicine, a game that two can play, a kick in the arse, a Roland for an Oliver, a taste of one's own medicine, an eye for an eye, blow for blow, give-and-take, talion, the biter bit; **unwritten law,** lex talionis

RETALIATORY *adj* reciprocal, recriminatory, retributive, revengeful, vengeful; **returnable,** requitable

RETICENCE *n* aloofness, low profile, undemonstrativeness, understatement; **speechlessness,** dumbness, silence, taciturnity, unexpressiveness; **reserve,** backwardness, bashfulness, shyness; **secrecy,** closeness, incommunicativeness, secretiveness

RETICENT *adj* aloof, low-key, low-profile, quiet, self-contained, undemonstrative, underplayed, unexpressive; **shy,** backward, bashful, in the wings; **tight-lipped,** close, close-lipped, dark, incommunicative, noncommittal, secret, secretive; **taciturn,** incommunicative, laconic, monosyllabic, of few words; **silent,** dumb, inarticulate, speechless, tongue-tied

RETICENTLY *adv* aloofly, undemonstratively, unexpressively; **shyly,** backwardly, bashfully; **incommunicatively,** dumbly, speechlessly; **secretively,** close, closely, secretly

RETURN TO NORMAL *n* recovery, reestablishment, regression, rehabilitation, reinstatement, remitter, return to normal; **revival,** reanimation, rebirth, recreation, renaissance, resurgence, resurrection, resuscitation; **renewal,** Indian summer, instauration, redintegration, refreshment, regeneracy, regeneration, rejuvenation, rejuvenescence, second youth, urban renewal

REVEAL *v* come out with, disclose, discover *(Archaic),* display, enucleate, impart, shew *(Archaic),* show, unfold, unroll; **expose,** bare, bring out, bring to light, disinter, flush out, give air to, make public, mark, open, publish, rake up, root up, show up, smoke out, take the lid off, turn up, unbrick, uncase, uncloak, unclothe, uncover, unlock; **release,** compromise *(Mil.),* declassify; **enlighten,** undeceive; **unmask,** give the lie to, nail, reveal in true colours, strip off a disguise, unveil; **blurt out,** blow the gaff, blunder, drop a bundle, let on, let out, let slip, let the cat out of the bag, noise off, shoot off one's mouth, spill the beans, tell; **blab,** babble, blabber, give away, sneak, spill, split on, tattle, tell on, tell tales, tell tales out of school, tittle-tattle. *See also* CONFESS

REVEALED *adj* bare, exposed, full-frontal, unconcealed; **current,** known, reported; **professed,** confessed, ostensible, ostensive, self-confessed; **public,** open, semipublic

REVEALER *n* betrayer, discloser, displayer, divulger, enlightener, expresser, imparter, oracle, revelationist, revelator, undeceiver, unmasker; **confessor,** admitter, unbosomer; **telltale,** blabber, blabbermouth, blower, blunderer, grass, ratter, sieve, stool pigeon, supergrass, tattler, tittle-tattler

REVEALING *n* communication, disclosure, divulgement, divulgence, enucleation, impartation, impartment, intimation; **exposure,** disinterment, overexposure, unfoldment, unveil-

revealing   445   **rhyme**

ing; **revelation**, apocalypse, discovery, enlightenment, epiphany; **confession**, admission, shrift *(Archaic)*; **revealment**, daylight, publicity; **exposedness**, bareness, openness

REVEALING *adj* indicative, telltale; **revelatory**, apocalyptic, explanatory, oracular; **confessional**, confessionary *(Eccles.)*; **indiscreet**, gossipy, leaky, tattletale

REVELATION *n* a foot in the mouth, betrayal, Freudian slip, give-away, indiscretion, telltale sign; **eye-opener**, bibful, exposé, startling disclosure; **leak**, blab, leakage, tattle, verbal; **whole truth**, clean breast

REVERE *v* adore, reverence, venerate, worship; **fear God**, keep the faith

REVERENCE *n* adoration, dedication, devotedness, devotement, devotion, devoutness, faith, honour, love, respect, trust, veneration; **piety**, cardinal virtues, godliness, good life, goodness, pietism, piousness, religiousness, righteousness, services, virtue; **prayerfulness**, communion, contemplation, meditation, mysticism, religion *(Obs.)*, religiosity; **religious frenzy**, beatitude, ecstasy, enthusiasm, gift of tongues, jerks *(U.S.)*, theopathy, zealotry; **pilgrimage**, hajj; **ecclesiasticism**, bibliolatry, churchmanship, fundamentalism, orthodoxy; **crusading spirit**, missionary zeal; **spirituality**, earnestness, inwardness, otherworldliness, spiritualism

REVERENT *adj* believing, devoted, devotional, devout, faithful, godfearing, godly, pious, prayerful, religious; **spiritual**, contemplative, meditative, spiritualist, spiritualistic, supermundane, vatic

REVERSION *n* atavism, backsliding, degeneration, devolution *(Biol.)*, relapse

REVIVE *v* be restored, come to life, get one's second wind, make a comeback, pick up, recover, rejuvenate, renew, return to life, return to normal

REVOLT *v* agitate, mutiny, rebel, rise up, rise up in arms, storm the barricades

REVOLUTION *n* blood in the streets, counter-revolution, coup d'état, insurgence, insurgency, insurrection, mutiny, palace revolution, rebellion, revolt, riot, rising, subversion, upheaval, uprising

REVOLUTIONARY *n* activist, agent provocateur, agitator, counter-revolutionary, dynamiter, insurrectionary, insurrectionist, malcontent, rebel, rioter, subversive, subverter

REVOLUTIONARY *adj* counter-revolutionary, subversive; **rebellious**, insurgent, insurrectional, insurrectionary, malcontent, rebel, revolting

RHETORICAL DEVICE *n* alliteration, anaphora, anastrophe, antithesis, apostrophe, assonance, asyndeton, balance, ellipsis, epigram, euphemism, euphuism, flourish, flower of rhetoric, inversion, ornament, parallelism, period, prolepsis, rhetorical question, syncope; **bon mot**, mot juste, Parthian shot, pass *(Archaic)*, sally

RHYME *n* alliteration, alliterativeness, assonance, clink, crambo *(Derog.)*, eye rhyme, female rhyme, feminine rhyme, half rhyme, internal rhyme, masculine rhyme, onomatopoeia, perfect rhyme, rhyme scheme

RHYTHM n beat, lilt, number *(Obs.)*, swing, tempo, time; **rhythm type**, cross rhythm, hemiola, isorhythm, polyrhythm, singsong, syncopation; **common time**, common measure, duple rhythm, measure, quadruple time, simple time, triple measure, triple rhythm, triple time, triplex; **up-beat**, anacrusis, arsis; **down-beat**, thesis; **syncopator**, timekeeper; **metronome**

RHYTHMICAL adj driving, eurythmic, measured, rhythmic, singsong, uptempo; **metronomic**; **iambic**, anapaestic, dactylic, ithyphallic, spondaic, tribrachic, trochaic

RIDE v canter, gallop, hack, jogtrot, pace, prance, rack, single-foot, trot

RIDER n buckjumper, cavalier, cavalry, equestrian, horseman, horsewoman, jockey, post, postboy, postilion, postrider

RIDGE n anticline, arris, bank, carina, costa, embankment, isocline, knurl, razorback, ripple, ripple-mark, stopridge, striation, strix; **corrugation**, carination; **corrugated iron**, corrugated board, corrugated paper; **corduroy road**

RIDING n canter, equitation, gallop, hacking, jogtrot, single-foot

RIGHT n starboard bowside, off side; **recto**; **forehand**; **off**; **dexterity**, dextrality, righthandedness; **righthander**

RIGHT adj dexter, dextral, righthand; **right-handed**, dexterous, dextral; **forehand**, forehanded; **off**; **starboard**, offside, right-ward

RIGHT adv dextrally, on the right, on the starboard bow, rightwards, starboard

RIGHTFUL adj entitled, just, prerogative, titled, true, welcome; **jural**, prescriptible, prescriptive, usufructuary

RIGHT OF WAY n access, appurtenance *(Law)*, easement, ingress, ingression

RIGHTS n claim, droit, entitlement, jus, lien, prescription *(Law)*, say, title, toll *(Obs.)*; **authority**, parliamentary privilege, power of appointment, precedence, prerogative, privilege; **charter**, bill of rights, muniments; **civil rights**, civil liberty, freedom, human rights, individualism; **franchise**, ballot, secret ballot, suffragetism, universal suffrage; **birthright**, heirship, inheritance *(Obs.)*, primogeniture, ultimogeniture; **royal prerogative**, droit de seigneur, escheatage, preference, regalia, regality; **state rights**, land rights; **specific claim**, ancient light, angary, beach claim *(Mining)*, cabotage, crop lien, fishery, profit a prendre, reef claim, right of search, servitude, trackage *(U.S. Railways)*, turbary, uti possidetis, water right; **title deed**, strata title, Torrens title, user *(Law)*, usufruct

RING n annulet, annulus, areola, areole, circle; **band**, belt, collar, girdle, headband, ruff, torques *(Zool.)*; **garland**, daisy-chain, wreath; **bracelet**, bangle, chaplet, circlet, circus *(Obs.)*, cirque *(Poetic)*, coronet, crown, earring, garland *(Naut.)*, keeper, ringlet, wristlet; **hoop**, quoit *(Games)*, rubber ring; **loop**, noose, piston ring, terry *(Textiles)*, washer; **grummet**, gudgeon, terret, traveller *(Naut.)*; **corona**, halo, nimbus *(Art)*, photosphere. *See also* CIRCLE; WHEEL

RING *v* carillon, chime, dong, knell, knoll *(Archaic)*, ring the changes, toll; **jingle**, chink, clank, clink, jangle, tinkle; **clang**, clangour, ding; **twang**, ping, plunk, sing, thrum; **trumpet**, blare, honk, trump; **trill**, vibrate

RINGER *n* bellman, bellringer, campanologer, campanologist

RINGING *n* clang, clangour, ding, ding-dong, knell, peal, ring, stroke, ting, tintinnabulation, toll, whang; **jingle**, ting-a-ling, tinkle, tinkling, trill; **bellringing**, campanology, change-ringing; **peal**, bob, change, dodge, hunt, ring, rounds, touch

RINGING *adj* amphoric, bell-like, jingly, silvery, tinkling, tintinnabular; **twangy**, clangourous, zingy; **rattly**, abuzz; **clumpy**, clumpish, wooden

RISEN *adj* emersed, uplifted; **erect**, issuant, jessant, rampant; **erectile**, erective; **scansorial**

RISK *v* be in the running, chance, chance one's arm, do on the off-chance, gamble, give it a go, have a go, run a risk, sail close to the wind, take a pot shot, venture; **hit the jackpot**, be one's lucky day, fall on one's feet, land on one's feet, live a charmed life; **jinx**, hoodoo, jonah, kill a Chinaman, put the mocker(s) on

RISK *v* chance, hazard; **dare**, court disaster, enter the lion's den, gamble, live dangerously, run the gauntlet, tempt fate, tempt providence, venture, walk into the dragon's mouth; **play with fire**, be between Scylla and Charybdis, be in dire straits, be on the brink, be on the precipice, be out on a limb, bell the cat, dice with death, hang by a thread, play chicken, ride for a fall, run the gauntlet, run the risk of, sail too near the wind, skate on thin ice, take one's life in one's hands, walk a slackwire, walk a tightrope

RITUALISTIC *adj* canonical, cruciferous, ember, formalistic, haggadic *(Judaism)*, haggadical, Lenten, liturgical, paschal, ritual, rubrical, sabbatical, vesper; **benedictional**, benedictory, dedicative, dedicatory; **sacramental**, Eucharistic, Eucharistical, oblatory; **hymnal**, doxological; **sacrificial**, flagellant, holocaustic

RITUALLY *adv* ceremonially, ceremoniously, ritualistically, traditionally

ROAD *n* carriageway, drag, frog and toad, roadway, street, thoroughfare; **the bitumen**, blacktop, macadam, metal road, sumpbuster, tarmac; **highway**, arterial road, distributor, divided road, dual carriageway, highroad, postroad, priority road, ringroad, trunk road, turnpike *(U.S.)*; **expressway**, autobahn, fast road, freeway, motorway; **beefroad**; **avenue**, boulevard, mall, parkway, place, row, terrace; **promenade**, alameda *(U.S.)*, esplanade, front, parade, seafront; **back road**, backtrack, bypass, byroad, cart track, detour, line, side road; **backstreet**, alley, bypath, bystreet, byway, side street, sideway; **dead end**, blind alley, cul-de-sac; **dirt road**, gravel road, unmade road, unsealed road, unsurfaced road; **access road**, feeder, service road, turn-off; **cross-street**, crossroad, crossway, slip-road *(Brit.)*; **junction**, bottleneck, intersection, roundabout, **crossover**, overbridge, overpass; **causeway**, dyke, stepping stones; **zigzag**, switchback; **tollway**, turnpike; **stock-route**, drove, lane, long paddock; **lane**, fast

ROB *v* bail up, clean out, hold up, mug, reave *(Archaic)*, roll, stick up, strongarm *(U.S.)*, waylay; **burgle**, barber *(Prison)*, blind-stab *(Prison)*, burglarise *(U.S.)*, bust; **steal**, abstract, acquire, annex, appropriate, bag, bone, clout on, convey *(Obs.)*, cop, filch, finger, flog, frisk, get down on, ginger, grab, half-inch, heist, hoist, hook, knock off, liberate, lift, make away with, make off with, milk the till, mooch, nick, nim *(Archaic)*, nip, nonch *(Prison)*, oozle, palm, pick, pick pockets, pilfer, pinch, purloin, race off with, rat *(Mining)*, reef off, rifle, run off with, shake, shanghai, shoplift, snaffle, sneak, snitch, snowdrop, souvenir, spirit away, swipe, take, tea-leaf, thieve, thump, walk off with, whip off; **plunder**, carry off, depredate, despoil, gut, loot, maraud, pill *(Archaic)*, pillage, prey upon, ransack, rape, rifle, sack, spoil *(Archaic)*, spoliate, strip, strip bare; **freeboot**, buccaneer, picaroon, pirate, run, smuggle, take to the road *(Obs.)*; **kidnap**, abduct, hijack, shanghai, skyjack; **impress**, crimp, press; **duff**, gully-rake, lift cattle, poach, rustle

ROBBERY *n* appropriation, rapacity, sacrilege, stealing, subreption, theft, thievery, thievishness; **larceny**, crib, fingering, five-finger discount, kleptomania, nonch *(Prison)*, petty larceny, pilferage, pilfering, pinch, pony *(U.S.)*, shoplifting; **burglary**, bust, crack, heist, hoist, housebreaking, job; **cattle stealing**, cattleduffing, horse-duffing, poddy-dodging, rustling; **body-snatching**, resurrectionism *(Hist.)*; **banditry**, bushranging, highway robbery, hold-up, robbery under arms, smash-and-grab, snatch, stick-up, thuggee, thuggery; **piracy**, buccaneering, hijack, kidnapping, privateering, skyjack; **pillage**, brigandage, brigandry, depredation, despoilment, despoliation, maraud, mosstrooping, plunder, plunderage, rapine, raven *(Obs.)*, sack, spoliation

ROCK *n* igneous rock, metamorphic rock, mylonite, sedimentary rock, siliceous rock, ultrabasic rock, ultramafic rock, volcanic rock; **boulder**, bomb, erratic, eruptive, floater, gibber; **stone**, billy boulder, boondy *(W.A.)*, brinnie, chinaman, cobble, cobblestone, drake stone, goolie, niggerhead, pebble, yonnie; **standing stone**, betyl, cairn, cromlech, dolmen, headstone, menhir, orthostat, tombstone; **fossil**, belemnite, thunder egg, thunderbolt, thunderstone; **meteorite**, aerolite; **gravel**, brash, debris, lapilli, rubble, scree, shingle

ROCKINESS *n* chalkiness, schistosity, stoniness; **petrifaction**, petrogenesis, silicification

ROCK OUTCROP *n* basset, blow, boss, inlier, roche moutonnée; **concretion**, dogger, septarium, spherulite; **rock stack**, aiguille, dyke, needle, yardang, zeuge; **stalactite**, column, stalagmite, stylolite; **megalith**, monolith; **batholith**, laccolith, xenolith; **stratum**, aquifer, basement, basement complex, bed, bedding, bedrock, bone bed, cap rock, combined aquifer, footwall, ledge, lens, lode, shelf, sill, vein; **moraine**, glacial meal, rock flour, till; **rock formation**, series, shield

ROCKY *adj* lithic, lithoid, marmoreal, petrous, stone, stony; **fragmental**, clastic, conglomerate, crystalloid, crystalloidal, pyroclastic, secondary; **crystalline**, asteriated, crystalliferous, idiomorphic, microcrystalline; **volcanic**, tuffaceous; **stratiform**, stratigraphic; **sedimentary**, aqueous, arenaceous; **intrusive**, hypabyssal, irruptive; **acid**, acidic, basic, felsic, intermediate, mafic; **precious**, diamantine, sapphirine, semiprecious

ROD *n* connecting rod, piston rod, pitman *(U.S.)*, reach, tie rod; **shaft**, countershaft, crankshaft, jackshaft, prop shaft, propellor shaft, quill, quill shaft, rockshaft, shafting, tail shaft; **axle**, arbor, axis, axletree, mandrel, pinion, pintle, spindle; **pin**, break pin, broach, fid, hob, linchpin, peg, pivot, shear pin, stem, toggle, tongue; **skewer**, brochette

ROLL *n* backflip, cartwheel, eskimo roll *(Canoeing)*, esquimautage *(Canoeing)*, flick-roll *(Aeronautics)*, flip, neckroll, snap-roll, somersault, tumble

ROLL *v* somersault, troll, tumble; **wallow**, labour; **bowl**, burl, devolve *(Archaic)*, rim *(Sport)*, roll along (down); **wheel**, trundle

ROLL UP *v* belay, clew, marl, reel, rewind, scroll, spool; **entwine**, entwist, enwind, twine, twirl, wisp *(Rare)*; **convolve**, circumflex, fold, gnarl

ROOF *n* cupola, curb roof, dome, drop ceiling, gambrel roof, hip roof, hipped roof, mansard roof, northlight roof, pop-top, roofing, rooftree, saddle roof, sawtooth roof, shell, skillion roof, southlight roof, span roof; **pergola**, marquise, penthouse; **canopy**, baldachin *(Relig.)*, ciborium, tester; **tarpaulin**, dustcover, dustsheet, fly, oilcloth, pool blanket, tarp, throwover, tilt, tonneau

ROOM *n* apartment, atrium, attic, basement, chamber, cockloft, compartment, garret, pad, shovel *(Colloq.)*, solar, suite; **veranda**, piazza *(U.S.)*, porch *(U.S.)*, sleep-out; **gallery**, box, choir loft, clerestory, dedans, floor, gazebo, jube, lantern, loft, loge, loggia, parvis, traverse, tribune; **bathroom**, bath, caldarium, comfort station, en suite, laundry, lav, lavatory, lavvy, powder room, public convenience, rest room, sauna, steam room, washroom; **clinic**, cas *(Colloq.)*, sick room, solarium, surgery, theatre, ward; **dressing-room**, change room, fitting room, tiring room *(Archaic)*; **darkroom**, biobox, booth, projection room; **cell**, black hole, black peter, dummy *(N.Z.)*, fleapit, guardroom, oubliette, slot, slough; **booth**, bower, cabin, carport, crib, den, skillion, stall; **capsule**, airlock, caisson, cockpit, cofferdam, command module, cuddy *(Naut.)*, engine-room, recompression chamber, stank; **compartment**, carrel, cubicle, phone box, polling booth, signal box, telephone booth, waiting room, well; **cellar**, basement, coal cellar, coal hole, crypt, subbasement, subcellar, undercroft, vault; **strongroom**, vault; **gunroom**, casemate; **schoolroom**, classroom, study; **crypt**, mastaba, morgue, vault; **chapel**, ante choir, antechapel, athenaeum, bema, cella, chancel, choir, naos, sacristy, vestry. *See also* LIVING ROOM; KITCHEN; BEDROOM; HALL

ROOT n buttress root, monopodium, prop root, taproot, tuberous root; **root organ**, calyptra, pneumatophore, radicel, root cap, root hair, root nodule, rootlet, tuber, velamen

ROTATE v brace *(Naut.)*, circumrotate, circumvolve, revolve, turn, windmill *(Aeron. Colloq.)*; **circle**, circuit, circulate, circumnavigate, encircle, orb, orbit, ring, transit; **spiral**, corkscrew; **turn**, about-face, about-turn, caracole, pirouette, turn around, wheel; **jibe**, slew around, swing, yaw; **turn over**, flip, pronate, supinate. *See also* SPIN

ROTATION n autorotation, circulation, circumrotation, circumvolution, free rotation, precession, revolution, rolling, turning; **pronation**, supination; **turning power**, torque; **circuit**, circle, compass, cycle, equatorial, gyre, orb *(Rare)*, orbit. *See also* SPIN; ROLL

ROUGH n sumpbuster, tiger country; **white water**, chop, haystack *(Canoeing)*, overfall, turbulence; **crag**, peak

ROUGH adj bitty, bullate, bumpy, gnarled, knaggy, knotty, lumpy, nodular, pebbly, roughish, rubbly, rugose, spotty, stubbed, uneven, wrinkled; **jagged**, chopping, choppy, hackly, irregular, jaggy, muricate, rafferty *(N.Z.)*, ragged, scraggy, squarrose, tattered, turbulent; **craggy**, cragged, ironbound, rocky, rugged, savage; **jolty**, bumpy, rough, uneven; **coarse**, coarse-grained, cross-grained, grainy, ground, harsh, matted, rough-hewn, rude, shaggy, shagreen, shagreened, unfinished, unpolished; **scaly**, furfuraceous, scabrous, scurfy; **bristly**, bushy, ciliate, fimbriate, hispid, prickly, spiniferous, spinous, spiny, thorny, tufted

ROUGHEN v coarsen, grain, hack, rasp, rough, rough up, shag; **key**, knurl, scabble, stab; **rumple**, rub the wrong way, ruffle; **chap**, rub

ROUGHLY adv irregularly, rough, rudely, unevenly; **bumpily**, spottily; **craggily**, ruggedly; **jaggedly**, raggedly, scraggily; **dentately**, crenately, denticulately; **coarsely**, harshly, scabrously, shaggily

ROUGHNESS n asperity, brokenness, rudeness, rugosity; **bumpiness**, inequality, irregularity, key *(Bldg Trades)*, lumpiness, nodosity, spottiness, stubbedness, unevenness; **cragginess**, jaggedness, ruggedness, savageness, scragginess; **crenulation**, corrugation, dentation, denticulation, ripple, serration, serrulation; **coarseness**, bite, grain, graininess, granulation, harshness, scratchiness, texture; **shagginess**, hispidity, raggedness, scabrousness, scaliness

ROUND v ball, conglobate, globe, orb, sphere; **roll up**, clew, coil up; **granulate**, pellet, pelletise, pill *(Textiles)*

ROUND adj conglobate, conglomerate, conglomeratic, coniform, cylindric, cylindrical, globate, globoid, globose, globular, moony, orbicular, orbiculate, orby *(Rare)*, spheral, spheric, spherical, spheroid, spheroidal, spherular, sphery; **capitate**, clavate, claviform, club-shaped, mooned; **beady**, gibbous, granular, pea-like, pilular, pisiform; **buttony**, discal, disclike, discoid, discoidal, platelike, scutate

ROUNDNESS n globosity, globularity, granularity, orbicularity, ovalness, sphericality, sphericity; **conglobation**, lobation; **circularity**, annularity

ROUTE *n* beat, channel, course, highway, lane, line, march, path, tack, track, wake; **itinerary**; **short cut**, crosscut, cut-off, direttissimo; **trade route**, lifeline; **air-route**, air structure, air-corridor, airlane, airline, airway, flight path, glide path, great circle route, kangaroo route; **trajectory**, orbit; **sea lane**, shipping lane.   *See also* PATH; ROAD; RAILWAY; ACCESS

ROWING BOAT *n* bateau, caique, coble, dinghy, dinky, double scull, eight, felucca, flattie, gig, gun, longboat, outrigger, pair, rowboat, scull, shell, skiff, surfboat, toothpick, wherry *(U.S.)*, whiff; **canoe**, dugout, faltboat, foldboat, kayak, piragua, pirogue, surf ski; **coracle**, bidarka, umiak; **punt**, gondola, sampan; **galley**, bireme, galleass, galliot, longship, quinquereme, trireme

RUB *v* embrocate, flannel, rub down, stroke, towel; **rub away**, abrade, degrade, denude, erode, fret, sculpture *(Phys. Geog.)*; **sandpaper**, fray, glasspaper, grate, graze, grind, paper, rasp, sand, sandblast, scuff, shave, stone, strop, whet; **chafe**, rub together; **scrabble**, claw, scrape, scratch

RUBBER *n* amadou, buna, butyl rubber, caoutchouc, crepe rubber, elastic bitumen, elastomer, elaterite, foam rubber, gum, gutta-percha, indiarubber, jelly, mineral caoutchouc, nitrile rubber, Pará rubber, quayule, sponge rubber, stereo-regular rubber, two-way stretch

RUBBING *n* effleurage, embrocation, frottage, massage, rub, rub-down; **rubbing away**, abrasion, attrition, denudation, erosion, fret, scraping, wearing away; **graze**, abrasion, scrape, scratch, scuff

RUBBISH BIN *n* ash can *(U.S.)*, ashtray, car tidy, dustbin *(Brit.)*, dustpan, garbage bin, hell, hell box, kitchen tidy, litter-bin, pedal bin, pig-bucket, rubbish tin, tidy, w.p.b., wastebasket, wastepaper basket; **catchpit**, catchbasin, silt pit; **spittoon**, cesspit, cuspidor, grease trap, slop-basin, slopbucket, sullage pit

RUIN *n* belial *(Eccles.)*, comedown, defeat, doom, downfall, fall, fate, labefaction, perdition, ruination, ruinousness, undoing, watergate, Waterloo; **collapse**, crash, crunch; **smash**, destruct *(Mil.)*, prang, shipwreck; **conflagration**, holocaust, incineration; **blast effect**, ground-shock effect, scorched earth *(Mil.)*; **ruins**, ashes, rack, wrack, wreck, wreckage; **disaster**, avalanche, calamity, catastrophe, debacle, fatality; **the end**, the beginning of the end, the crunch, the finish, the last straw, the living end, the moment of truth, the road to ruin.   *See also* DESTRUCTION

RUIN *v* bugger up, bust up, cook someone's goose, do in, frig up, fuck up, jigger, play havoc with, put paid to, root; **break**, break down, graunch *(N.Z.)*, shatter, wreck; **scuttle**, scupper, shipwreck, sink, torpedo.   *See also* DESTROY

RUINED *adj* buggered, bust, busted, done for, done up, downfallen, fallen, fucked, gone to Gundy, had it, jiggered up, kaput, lost, naught *(Archaic)*, no good to Gundy, rooted, stonkered, stuffed, undone, up the spout

RULE n axiom, canon, convention, custom, dictate, formula, generality, golden rule, ground rule, hard and fast rule, hinge, institute, institution, law, maxim, model, motto, natural order, observance *(Rom. Cath. Ch.)*, order, ordinance, precept, prescript, principle, procrustean bed, regulation, routine, rule of thumb, standing order, sutra *(Sanskrit)*, theorem; **discipline**, bushido *(Jap. Hist.)*, dos and don'ts, ethics, protocol, ritual; **tenets**, articles, articles of association, code, constitution, elements, organon *(Philos.)*, ruling, teaching; **standard**, criterion, determinant, double standard, gauge, yardstick

RULER n administrator, arch *(Obs.)*, archon, ataman, begum, cacique, caliph, caudillo, chief, chieftain, dame *(Archaic)*, dato, elder, elector, eponym, ethnarch, gerent, hero *(Gk. Antiq.)*, hetman, jarl *(Scand. Hist.)*, judge *(Jewish Hist.)*, lady, laird, liege, lord (of the manor), lord temporal, matriarch, overlord, pendragon, plutocrat, potentate, primate *(Rare)*, principal, seignior *(Archaic)*, sire *(Obs.)*, suzerain, tribal elder; **bureaucrat**, apparatchiki, aristocrat, hierocrat, panjandrum *(Colloq.)*, Pooh-Bah *(Colloq.)*, technocrat; **civilian official**, alcalde, director, politician, provost, syndic; **governor**, area commander, bashaw, bey, captain, commissar, constable *(Brit.)*, department head, eparch, exarch, gauleiter, grand vizier *(Islam)*, legate *(Rom. Hist.)*, mandarin, minister, pasha, prefect, proconsul, satrap, stadtholder, tetrarch; **military commander**, admiral, general, leader; **church ruler**, archbishop, imam, lama, pope; **the authorities**, officialdom, the government, the powers that be; **head of government**, chancellor, consul *(Rom. Hist.)*, doge, duumvir, P.M., premier, president, president-elect, prime minister, protector, triumvir; **emperor**, Caesar, czar, czarina, empress, imperator, imperial, Kaiser, Mikado, Negus, Padishah, Pharaoh, tsar, tsarina; **autocrat**, absolute monarch, ayatollah *(Colloq.)*, Big Brother, despot, dictator, dictatress, dictatrix, Duce, feudal lord, Führer, oligarch, paramount, robber baron, shogun, supremo, tyrant, war lord

RURAL adj agrarian, agricultural, country, exurban, rustic, village, villatic; **outback**, back-country, backwoods, high, hinterland, up-country; **country-style**, countrified, country-fashion; **pastoral**, Arcadian, bucolic, sylvan, woodland. *See also* PROVINCIAL

RURALISE v go bush, rusticate; **bushwhack**

RURALISM n agrarianism, bucolicism, pastoralism; **rusticity**, provincialism, provinciality, rurality, swainishness; **ruralisation**, bushwhacking, countrification, pastoralisation, rustication. *See also* THE BUSH

RURALLY adv bucolically, pastorally, provincially, rustically; **beyond the black stump**, back of beyond, from the sticks, in the mulga, up the booay, up the mulga

Ss

SADDLERY *n* harness, tack; **bridle**, barnacles, bearing rein, bit, cannon bit, check rein, curb, drop noseband, girth, hackamore *(U.S.)*, halter, headgear, headstall, martingale, muzzle, noseband, overcheck, rein, ribbons, snaffle, surcingle, twitch, withy; **yoke**, oxbow; **tether**, creance *(Falconry)*, dog run, jess *(Falconry)*, lead, leg rope, obstruction, slip

SAFE *adj* all right, cocksure *(Obs.)*, fail-safe, inviolate, right as rain, safe and sound, safe as houses, secure, shockproof, sure *(Archaic)*; **harmless**, innocuous, innoxious; **low-toxicity**, hypo-allergenic; **protective**, childproof, flameproof, shark-proof, waterproof; **armoured**, armourplated, bulletproof, ironclad, loricate, mailed, panoplied, shellproof

SAFELY *adv* in good hands, in safe hands, out of harm's way, securely

SAFETY *n* safeness, secureness, security; **harmlessness**, innocence, innocuousness, innoxiousness; **safety margin**, factor of safety; **safeguard**, guard, precaution, protection; **immunity**, active immunity

SAFETY HARNESS *n* lunger belt *(Gymnastics)*, monkey rope, safety belt, seat belt; **lifeline**, breeches buoy; **lifebelt**, air-jacket, float, life jacket, life vest, life-preserver *(U.S.)*, lifebuoy, Mae West

SAILING SHIP *n* barque, barquentine, brig, brigantine, caravel, carvel, catboat, clipper, cutter, dandy, dogger, fore-and-after, galleon, hermaphrodite brig, hoy, ketch, lugger, polacca, schooner, sloop, smack, tartan, three-decker, three-master, topsail schooner, two-master, yawl, xebec; **sailing boat**, auxiliary, carrack, dhow, dory, drogher, dromond, felucca, junk, keel, keelboat, knockabout, pinnace, proa, sabot, sail, sailboard, sailboat, sailer, sharpie, windjammer, windsurfer, yacht; **catamaran**, cat, trimaran

SALEABLE *adj* marketable, on sale, resaleable, vendible; **commercial**, retail, wholesale; **marked down**, remaindered

SANDAL *n* espadrille, flip-flop, jandal *(N.Z.)*, rubber *(Colloq.)*, slaps, thong, zori; **slipper**, carpet slipper, mule, pantofle, scuff. *See also* FOOTGEAR

SANE *adj* all there, clear-headed, compos mentis, lucid, normal, present, rational, reasonable, sound of mind; **sober**, responsible, self-possessed, well-balanced

SANELY *adv* lucidly, rationally; **in one's right mind**, in possession of one's faculties, responsibly, soberly

SANITY *n* lucidity, lucidness, normalcy, normality, rationality, reason, saneness, soundness of mind; **soberness**, responsibleness, sobriety

SATIABLE *adj* appeaseable, quenchable

SATISFACTION *n* fulfilment, gratification, implementation *(Archaic)*; **satisfactoriness**, suitability, suitableness; **contentment**, comfort, content, contentedness; **appeasement**, assuage-

satisfaction

ment; **fullness,** impletion *(Obs.),* repleteness, repletion; **satiation,** jadedness, satiety; **sufficiency,** bellyful, fill, glut

SATISFACTORILY *adv* all cush, all right, okay, very well, well; **satisfyingly,** gratifyingly; **comfortably,** contentedly

SATISFACTORY *adj* all right, fair enough, good enough, jake, jakerloo, nominal *(U.S.),* okay; **up to scratch,** good, right, well-done; **satisfying,** gratifying, rewarding; **square,** hearty

SATISFIED *adj* comfortable, content, contented, thirstless; **satiated,** full as a butcher's pup, full as a goog, full up, replete, sated; **jaded,** blasé

SATISFIER *n* a natural, fulfiller, gratifier, sufficer; **quencher,** thirst-quencher; **appeaser,** assuager

SATISFY *v* deliver the goods, fill the bill, fulfil, hit the nail on the head, hit the spot, implement *(Archaic),* rise to the occasion, serve, suffice, suit; **appease,** assuage, content, gratify, pacify; **pander to,** pamper, please; **satiate,** feed, fill, glut, quench, sate, slake, stay; **pall,** cloy, jade

SAVE *v* go easy on, husband, make every penny work, put it all down south, scrape by on, squirrel; **skimp on,** stint on; **be sparing,** cut one's coat according to one's cloth, economise, keep costs down, keep within one's budget, make both ends meet

SAVER *n* economiser, hoarder, squirrel; **sparer,** stinter

SAVOUR *n* deliciousness, lusciousness, mellowness, niceness, palatability, palatableness, sapidity, savouriness, tastiness, toothsomeness; **relish,** life, tang, zest

school

SAVOUR *v* lap up, lick one's fingers, smack the lips; **taste good,** tickle the palate

SAW *n* back-saw, bandsaw, bowsaw, breakdown saw, bucksaw, bushman's saw, buzz-saw, chainsaw, circular saw, cold saw, compass saw, coping saw, crosscut saw, crown saw, diamond saw, docking saw, framesaw, fretsaw, gangmill, gangsaw, goose saw, grubsaw, hacksaw, handsaw, hargan, jigsaw, muley saw *(U.S.),* panel saw, pitsaw, planer saw, ripsaw, scroll-saw, tenon saw, trephine, whipsaw

SAY WHAT ONE THINKS *v* be without guile, call a spade a spade, have nothing to hide, let it all hang out, wear one's heart on one's sleeve

SCALES *n* balance, jockey scales, microbalance, spring balance, steelyard, weighbridge

SCHEMER *n* complotter, conspirator, conspiratress, contriver, designer, framer, hatcher, intriguer, machinator, plotter; **planner,** arranger, deviser, strategist, systematiser, systematist, systemiser, tactician, teleologist

SCHOOL *n* area school, blackboard jungle, bush school, central school, comprehensive school, consolidated school, dame school, demonstration school, district school, educational institution, feeder school, hospital school, one-teacher school, rural school, secondary modern school *(Brit.),* state school; **independent school,** charity school *(Brit.),* G.P.S., non-government school, non-state school, parish school, pension, private school, public school, ragged school *(Brit.);* **opportunity school,** special school; **boarding school,** day

school; **open school**, alternative school, open classroom, open planning, progressive school; **correspondence school**, school of the air; **summer school**, finishing school; **girls' school**, heifer paddock; **alma mater**, old school; **convent**, seminary; **Sunday school**, Sabbath school; **kindergarten**, creche, day care, infants' school, nursery, nursery school, preschool; **primary school**, grade school *(U.S.)*, junior school, prep, prepatory school; **secondary school**, grammar school, high, high school, junior college *(U.S.)*, junior high school, lycée, selective high school, technical school. *See also* COLLEGE

SCISSORS *n* clippers, nail scissors; **shears**, b-bows, bog-eye, bogghi, bows, clips, daggers, grass-clippers, hand shears, handpiece, jingling Johnnies, lizard, pinking shears, pruning shears, secateurs, snips, swords, tinsnips, wire-cutter, wool-shears

SCOLD *v* admonish, chasten, chastise, chide, give someone a bad mark, go on at, name *(Parl. Proc.)*, rebuke, remonstrate with, reprehend, reprimand, reproach, reprobate, reprove, rouse at, rouse on, tick off, tongue, twit, wig *(Brit.)*; **lecture**, chat, jaw *(Colloq.)*, lesson, rag *(Colloq.)*, read someone a lecture, school *(Archaic)*, tutor; **scold severely**, attack, baste, bawl out, be on at, berate, blast, blast hell out of, blow up, bore up, carpet, castigate, denounce, denunciate, dress down, flay, fulminate against, give a pay, give beans, give gip, give heaps, give someone hell, give someone Larry Dooley, give someone what for, give the rough side of one's tongue, give the rounds of the kitchen, go crook at, go crook on, go to town on, haul over the coals, hoe into, keelhaul, lash, make mincemeat of, mat, objurgate, paste, pelt, play hell with, put on the mat, put the boot into, rail at, rap over the knuckles, rate, row *(Obs.)*, sally up *(N.Z.)*, take a piece out of, take to task, tongue-lash, upbraid, whip; **jump on**, jump down someone's throat, pull up. *See also* DISAPPROVE OF

SCORE *n* aggregate, circulation, count, head, raw score, strength, tally, total; **attendance**, enrolment; **majority**, quorum, quota

SCOWL *n* flounce, frown, lour, pout, snarl

SCREEN *n* sconce *(Obs.)*, windbreak; **awning**, brise-soleil, dodger *(Naut.)*, heat shield, shade, sunblind, sun-break; **fireguard**, cowl *(Railways)*, fire-curtain, firebreak, firescreen, firewall, safety curtain; **bar**, bollard, buffer, bull-bar, bumper, bumper bar, cowcatcher, crash barrier, fender, grate, grating, guardrail, handrail, kangaroo bar, sponson, stone shield

SCRIPTURAL *adj* biblical, canonical, gospel, legal, oracular, textuary; **apocryphal**, pseudepigraphic, pseudepigraphous; **Koranic**, Mosaic, Pentateuchal, Talmudic, Vedaic, Vedic, Vulgate

SCRIPTURALISM *n* bibliolatry, fundamentalism, textualism; **exegesis**, exegetics, form criticism, hermeneutics, higher criticism, isagogics, kerugma; **Talmud**, commentaries, Halakah, Midrash, Mishnah

SCRIPTURALIST *n* biblicist, exegete, fundamentalist, futurist, textualist, textuary; **Talmudist**, evangel, hag-

scripturalist   456   **seaman**

gadist, hierogrammat, hierogrammatist, synoptic, the Seventy

SCRIPTURALIST *adj* bibliolatrous, evangelical, evangelistic, exegetic, fundamentalist, kerugmatik; **haggadistic**, hierogrammatic

SCRIPTURE *n* canon, dharma, Holy Scripture, Holy Writ, oracles, patristics, patrology, revealed religion, revelation, sacred text, the Word of God, Word; **the Law,** beatitude, commandment, evangel, law, Mosaic Law, tables, Testament, text; **Bible,** Authorised Version, family Bible, Good Book, Holy Bible, the Book, Vulgate; **Gospel,** Acts, antilegomena, Apocalypse, Canticles, chapter, Epistle, Haggadah, harmony, Heptateuch, lesson, logion, New Testament, Old Testament, Pentateuch, Revelation, Septuagint, Song of Solomon, synoptic, Testament, Torah; **psalm,** anthem, metrical psalm, Miserere; **apocrypha,** legend, pseudepigrapha, tradition; **Koran,** Alkoran; **Veda,** Atharva-Veda, Rig-Veda, Sama-Veda, Upanishad, Yajur-Veda; **Avesta; the Book of Mormon**

SCULPTURAL *adj* sculpturesque, statuary; **carved,** engraved, glyptic, graven *(Archaic),* sculptured; **in relief,** anaglyptic, embossed, repoussé, toreutic

SCULPTURE *n* ceroplastics, modelling, statuary; **carving,** woodcarving, woodwork; **statue,** bronze, bust, figurine, marble, monument *(Obs.),* plaster cast, stabile, statuette; **relief,** alto-rilievo, bas-relief, basso-rilievo, demirelief, glyph, high relief, low relief, mezzo-rilievo, relievo, round; **petroglyph,** rock carving, rock engraving; **mobile,** kinetic art; **cameo,** miniature

SEA *n* brine, briny, Davy Jones's locker, ditch, Neptune, ocean, profound, the blue, the deep, the drink, wave *(Archaic);* **open sea,** blue water, main, open, seaway, seven seas, the high seas; **waters,** territorial waters, offing, outing, outside; **shallow,** low water, tidewater *(U.S.);* **sea-floor,** benthos, ooze; **marine habitat,** euphotic zone, water-column. *See also* BAY; SURF; LAKE

SEA *adj* aquatic, halophilous *(Zool. Bot.),* marine, Neptunian, oceanic, pelagic, seaborn, seawater, thalassic; **maritime,** deepwater, ocean-going, seaborne, seafaring, seagoing; **deep-sea,** abyssal, benthic, deepwater, demersal *(Zool.);* **underwater,** subaquatic, subaqueous, submarine, suboceanic, undersea; **surfy,** insurgent, surgy; **tidal,** lunitidal, neap; **neritic; littoral,** circumlittoral, inlying, inshore, seagirt *(Poetic);* **offshore,** off, outward-bound, seaward; **overseas,** surface, transmarine, transoceanic, transpacific, ultramarine

SEAMAN *n* a.b., able seaman, able-bodied seaman, artisan, bluejacket, bunting tosser, deckhand, Jack Tar *(Brit.),* leatherneck *(U.S.),* lime-juicer, limey, lower deck, marine, ordinary seaman, rating, topman; **ship's officer,** admiral, captain, captain, commander, commodore, deck officer, engine-room artificer, engineer officer, ensign *(U.S.),* first mate, first officer, flag captain, flag officer, lieutenant commander, master, master mariner, number one, officer of the watch, privateer, rear admiral, sea-captain, second mate, shipmaster, skipper, vice-admiral, wardroom; **petty officer,** bo's'n, boatswain, bosun, jaunty,

seaman master-at-arms, steward *(U.S.)*, yeoman; **helmsman**, cox, coxswain, leadsman, navigator, pilot, steersman, wheelman *(U.S.)*; **midshipman**, middy; **purser**, supercargo; **cabin boy**, powder monkey. *See also* MARINER

SEA NYMPH *n* bathing beauty, Lorelei, mermaid, nereid, sea witch, siren, undine, water-sprite; **Neptune**, merman, the old man of the sea, Triton

SEARCH *v* comb, leave no stone unturned, ransack, rat through, rummage; **cast about**, seek a clue; **look for**, cherchez la femme, keep an eye out for, nose after, nose for, seek, suss out; **frisk**, shake; **spy**, drag out, draw out, fish out, fly a kite, nose about, nose into, poke about, poke around, poke one's nose into, pry, smell out, sniff out, snoop, sound out; **explore**, fossick, geologise, wildcat

SEARCHER *n* ransacker, rummager; **detective**, bloodhound, dick, frisker, gumshoe *(U.S.)*, private eye, private investigator, shamus, sleuth, tec; **ticket inspector**, snapper, ticket snapper; **explorer**, fossicker, hunter, potholer, prospector, search party, sourdough *(U.S.)*, spelunker, wildcatter *(U.S.)*

SEASIDE *n* coast, seaboard, seacoast, seafront, waterfront, waterfrontage; **shore**, bank, beach, dene, dunes, foreshore, sands, seashore, shingle, shoreline, strand, strandline, wash, wharf *(Obs.)*; **seabed**, bed, bottom, wavecut platform

SEASON *n* equinox, quarter, seedtime, solstice, tide, time of the year; **spring**, blossom time, Maytide, Maytime, prime, springtime, vernal equinox, vernal point; **summer**, dog days, heat, heat wave, height of summer, Indian summer, midsummer, silly season, summer solstice, summeriness, summertime; **autumn**, autumnal equinox, autumnal point, fall *(U.S.)*, harvest, harvest home; **winter**, depth of winter, freeze, freeze-up, midwinter, winter solstice, wintertime, wintriness; **the wet**, monsoon; **the dry**

SEASONAL *adj* equinoctial, solsticial; **seasonable**, in, in season; **spring**, vernal; **summer**, aestival, estival *(U.S.)*, midsummer, summer-like, summery; **autumn**, autumnal; **winter**, brumal, hibernal, midwinter, wintry

SEASONALLY *adv* seasonably; **autumnally**, summerly, vernally, wintrily

SECLUDE *v* cloister, closet, insulate from, isolate, relegate, rusticate, sequester, sequestrate *(Archaic)*, shut away; **retreat**, go to ground, hibernate, hole up, pull one's head in, shut out the world, skulk; **repel**, hold off, insulate oneself from, keep a low profile, keep at arm's length, keep away, withdraw from; **be isolated**, be in a world of one's own, be off the beaten track; **be antisocial**, go it alone, keep one's distance, keep one's own counsel, keep oneself to oneself

SECLUDED *adj* claustral, cloister-like, cloistered, cloistral, monachal, monasterial, monastic, monkish, seclusive, sequestered; **secret**, closet, private, privy *(Archaic)*; **remote**, desolate, distant, isolated, obscure, unmanned; **unfrequented**, buried, godforsaken, lonesome, off the beaten track, out-of-the-way, tucked-away. *See also* SOLITARY

SECLUDEDLY *adv* ascetically, hermitically, monastically, monkishly, seclusively; **privately**, backstage, out of court, secretly

SECLUSION *n* isolation, privacy, privity *(Obs.)*, purdah, secrecy; **asylum**, a world of one's own, backwater, cloister, corner, hermitage, hideaway ivory tower, refuge, retreat, sanctuary, sanctum; **private place**, cloister, closet, convent, holy of holies, inner sanctum, mew, monastery, monkery, nook, nunnery, sanctum sanctorum; **the back of beyond**, desert island, dump, hole, shell, the end of the earth. *See also* SOLITUDE

SECOND *n* b, B, beta, number two, secondary, trail *(Racing)*

SECRECY *n* caginess, closeness, covertness, dark, hugger-mugger *(Archaic)*, privacy, privateness, privity *(Obs.)*, secretness; **confidentiality**, confidence, confidentialness; **clandestineness**, collusiveness, furtiveness, slyness, sneakiness, stealth, stealthiness, surreptitiousness; **conspiracy**, cabal, collusion, conjuration *(Obs.)*, intrigue, plot; **code**, argot, cant, cipher, tick-tack

SECRET *n* classified information, confidence, dark secret, official secrets; **skeleton in the cupboard**, family skeleton, skeleton in the closet; **silent number**

SECRET *adj* classified, close, confidential, intimate, irrevealable, personal, private, privy *(Archaic)*, snug *(Obs.)*, top-secret; **hush-hush**, backroom, cabinet, cameral, closet, in camera, inner, interior; **unlisted**, concealed, ex-directory, invisible, unadmitted, unnamed

SECRETION *n* endocrine, incretion, juice, recrement, sebum, serous fluid, serum, smegma, synovia; **bile**, gall, pancreatic juice; **semen**, come, cream, ejaculation, emission, lovejuice, seed, spoof, spunk; **hormone**, autacoid, enzyme, histamine, lymph, steroid; **mucus**, bogie, booboo, expectoration, phlegm, snivel, snot, sputum; **saliva**, salivation, slag, slaver, slobber, spit, spittle; **earwax**, cerumen; **tear**, sleep, teardrop; **lactation**, beestings, colostrum, milk; **animal secretion**, cast, castor, cuckoospit, flyspeck, manna, pheromone, royal jelly, toad spittle, trehala; **seborrhoea**, blennorrhoea

SECRETIVE *adj* cagey, cloak-and-dagger, collusive, furtive, hole-and-corner, hugger-mugger, obreptitious, sly, sneaking, sneaky, stealthy, surreptitious, tiptoe, underhand; **clandestine**, backdoor, backstairs, bootleg *(U.S.)*, undercover, under-the-counter, underground

SECRETLY *adv* cryptically, on the side, under the counter; **privately**, behind closed doors, behind the scenes, between ourselves, between you and me, confidentially, entre nous, in camera, in confidence, in secret, in the background, on the q.t., sub rosa, under the rose; **stealthily**, behind one's back, like a thief in the night

SECRETORY *adj* exudative, mucosal, recremental, runny, secernent, secrisionary, secretive, serous; **glandular**, biliary, bilious, endocrine, galactic, galactopoietic, hormonal, lacteal, lactiferous, salivary, sialoid; **watery**, ichorous, lochial. *See also* EXCREMENTAL

SECRET PLACE n conclave, conventicle, corner, hideaway, recesses; **closed court**, camera *(Law)*

SECRET SOCIETY n backroom boys, cabal, huddle, inner circle, inside; **Resistance**, maquis *(French Hist.)*, underground *(Europ. Hist.)*

SECURE v cocoon, cover, guard, pad, protect, safeguard, screen, shade, shadow, shield, wrap; **armour**, bard, cuirass, mail, visor; **defilade**, sconce

SEE v behold, observe, view, witness; **catch sight of**, clap eyes on, glance *(Obs.)*, glimpse, lay eyes on, set eyes on, sight, twig, view *(Hunting)*; **discern**, descry, detect, distinguish, espy, ken *(Archaic)*, notice, recognise, resolve, scry *(Archaic)*, spot, spy; **visualise**, envisage, vision; **vide**, vide ante, vide infra, vide post, vide supra.
See also LOOK

SEED n albumen, aril, arillode, caruncle, coma, cotyledon, endopleura, endosperm, funicle, funiculus, hilum, perisperm, plumule, radicle, raphe, suspensor, testa, umbilicus; **seedling**, coleoptile, coleorhiza, collar, cotyledon, epicotyl, hypocotyl, radicle, seed leaf

SEEING n eye, eyesight, light *(Archaic)*, sight, vision; **binocularity**, stereopsis, stereoscopy, stereovision; **sharp-sightedness**, far-sightedness, perspicacity *(Archaic)*; normal vision, trichromatopsia; **day vision**, photopia; **night vision**, scotopia; **optics**, ophthalmology. See also LOOK: **observation**, contemplation, espial, invigilation *(Obs.)*, lookout, notice, observance, scrutiny, surveillance, watch; **visualisation**, envisagement, vision; **voyeurism**, scopophilia

SEEK GUIDANCE v confide in, consult, refer to, seek advice; **be advised**, take advice, take counsel, take one's cue from

SELFISH adj asocial, egocentric, egoistic, egoistical, egotistic, egotistical, narcissistic, self-absorbed, self-aware, self-centred, self-loving, self-regarding; **self-indulgent**, incogitant, inconsiderate, possessive, self-pitying, spoilt; **mercenary**, base, calculating, hoggish, hoglike, self-interested, self-seeking, small, sordid, venal

SELFISHLY adv egoistically, egotistically, in one's own interest, self-indulgently; **mercenarily**, sordidly, venally

SELFISHNESS n egocentricity, egoism, egomania, egotism, narcissism, self-absorption, self-awareness, self-interest, self-love, self-regard, self-seeking; **self-indulgence**, hoggishness, inconsiderateness, inconsideration, possessiveness, self-pity, wank; **mercenariness**, baseness, careerism, cupboard love, opportunism, sordidness, venality

SELF-SEEKER n brute, egocentric, egoist, egomaniac, egotist, hog, roadhog; **wanker**, spoilt brat; **mercenary**, careerist, opportunist; **sponge**, bludger, fortune-hunter, gimme girl, gold-digger, sponger

SELF-SUFFICIENT adj autarkical, individualistic, inner-directed, self-contained, self-made, self-reliant, self-supported, self-supporting, self-sustaining; **freelance**, self-employed. See also INDEPENDENT

SELL v auction, dispose of, flog, hock, market, offer, outsell, oversell, realise, regrate, resell, retail, sell out,

sell

sell short, sell up, short, turn over, wholesale; **peddle,** hawk, offer for sale, put on the market, send to market, tout, vend; **push,** hard-sell, hustle *(U.S.)*; **sell off,** discount, dump, knock down, remainder, undersell, unload; **be sold,** go, go like hot cakes, go under the hammer, move

SELLER *n* broker, commission agent, commission merchant, dealer, discounter, flogger, merchant, middleman, regrater, reseller, retailer, stockist, tallyman, trader, trafficker, vendor, warehouseman, wholesaler; **travelling salesman,** agent, bagman, chapman *(Brit.),* cheapjack, colporteur, commercial traveller, drummer, faker *(U.S.),* Ghan, hawker, huckster, packman, pedlar, pitchman *(U.S.),* rep, representative, sutler, traveller; **shopkeeper,** bourgeois, cashier, chandler, checkout chick, checkout operator, clerk *(U.S.),* counterjumper, salesclerk *(U.S.),* salesgirl, saleslady, salesman, salesperson, saleswoman, shop assistant, shopgirl, shopman *(Rare),* storekeeper; **spieler,** barker, tout, touter; **auctioneer; dishonest trader,** black marketeer, blackbirder, bootlegger, dud-dropper, fence, short, slaver

SELLING *n* inertia selling, marketing, merchandising, pyramid selling, runout campaign, sales promotion, vendition; **auction,** crown auction, Dutch auction, public auction, vendue; **sale,** bazaar, clearance sale, clearing sale, closing-down sale, disposal, fete, fire sale, garage sale, jumble sale, reduction sale, resale, rummage sale, tie-in sale *(U.S.),* walk-in walk-out sale; **sales talk,** colportage, hard sell, patter, sales pitch, salesmanship, sell, soft sell, spiel

SEND A MESSAGE *v* leave word, pass information, send word; **correspond,** communicate with, correspond with, drop a line to, respond to, write; **circularise,** advise, file a report, notify; **mail,** consign, letterbox, post; **telegraph,** cable, telephone, telex, wire; **address,** direct, redirect

SENSUALISE *v* erotise; **animalise,** bestialise, debauch

SENTIENT *n* observer, receptor, sensor

SEPARATE *v* crumble, decompose, disintegrate, dissociate, explode, fall apart, fall to pieces, shatter, spall, splinter, spring, start; **disconnect,** break away, disarticulate, disassemble, disengage, disjoin, dismount, disunite, loose, loosen, overhaul, splay, unbind, unbuckle, unbutton, unclasp, uncouple, unfasten, unfix, ungird *(Archaic),* unglue, unhasp, unhinge, unhitch, unhook, unlay, unlimber, unlink, unpick, unplug, unravel, unsolder, unstick, untuck, unwind, unyoke; **sever,** abscind, cut, detach, disbranch, disbud, dissever; **part company,** break up, bust up, disband, divorce, opt out, part, sell dearly, split up; **break off,** calve, chip, cut off, destalk, hew off, sever, shear, slice, slice off, snip, strip, sunder; **rupture,** breach, break, cleave, crack, crash, crevasse, dash, disrupt, divide, divorce, fault, fissure, fracture, maul *(U.S.),* open, part, rift, rip, rive, slit, split, sunder, wedge; **dismember,** break up, carve up, cut up, decartelise, decollate, departmentalise, disaffiliate, disband, disperse, dissect, dissolve, disunite, factionalise, quarter, segment, segregate, trisect; **disjoint,**

separate

dismantle, dismember, dissect, dissever, divide, enucleate, joint, knock down, macerate, ravel, ribbon, riffle, separate; **cast loose**, cast off *(Naut.)*, slip, unbend, unloose, untie; **bisect**, bifurcate, dichotomise, divide, fork, furcate; **allot**, chapter, compartment, compartmentalise, cut, demarcate, divide, fence off, fraction, fractionise, hedge, lot, mark off, part, partition, screen, sector, separate, serialise, shut off, size, space, spread, subdivide, wall; **detach**, break away, cull, distinguish from, draft, extract, hive off, maroon, pair off, sequester, sequestrate *(Archaic)*, shut off; **disassociate**, atomise, blanch, centrifugalise, centrifuge, cream, decompound, demulsify, desorb, dialyse, dissociate, distil, electrolyse, flake, hydrolyse, liberate, precipitate, screen, segregate, sleave; **partition**, Balkanise, dismember, divide and rule; **shred**, fractionate, gad, knap, spall, tease, ultracentrifuge; **pull apart**, dilacerate, dynamite, fritter, lancinate, rend, rip, rip off, scrap, slit, sliver, stave, tear, tear to pieces, tear up; **flake**, cast, exfoliate, foliate, husk, laminate, shed, slough; **isolate**, exile, island; **double-declutch**, double-shuffle; **be divisible into**, fall into

SEPARATE *adj* apart, detached, disconnected, discrete, disjunct, distinct, dividual *(Archaic)*, segregate; **loose**, free, loose hair, unattached, unbolted, unbuttoned, unconnected, yokeless; **adrift**, castaway, cut loose; **divided**, cleft, compartmental, creviced, cut, diffractive, dipartite, disjointed, disrupt, dissected, episodic, multifid, parted, partite, ripped, riven, ruptured, split; **cleft in two**, bifid,

separation

bifurcate, bilobed, bilocular, bipartite, cloven, dichotomous, dimerous, forficate, forked, furcate, swallow-tailed; **trifurcate**, trifid, trifurcated, triparted, tripartite; **alienated**, disembodied, remote, removed, segregated; **cracked**, broken, crazed, fractural, fragmentary, fragmented, splintery; **clastic**, fragmental, green *(Metall.)*; **unmixible**, immiscible, incoherent; **freestanding**, outstanding, singular; **crumbly**, crumby, exfoliative, flaky, splitting; **parting**, ripping

SEPARATELY *adv* alone, apart, distantly, dividually, individually, loose, loosely, on the side, singly, singularly, unconnectedly; **disjunctively**, divisively, partitively; **disconnectedly**, discretely, episodically, incoherently; **asunder**, atwain *(Archaic)*, bifidly, bipartitely, dispersedly, in two

SEPARATION *n* cleavage, compartmentalisation, defibrillation, departmentalism, detachment, disassembly, disbandment, disconnection, disengagement, disjunction, disjunction, dismantlement, dismemberment, dispersion, dissolution, disunion, division, grade separation, nonunion, partition, partitionment, resolution, scission, section, segmentation, segregation, sequestration, severalty, severance, sporulation, subdivision, trifurcation, tripartition, trisection; **disconnectedness**, brokenness, decartelisation, discreteness, disembodiment, disjointedness, disjuncture, disseverance, dissevertion, disseverment, disunity, flakiness, fragmentariness, separateness, unconnectedness; **bifurcation**, bipartition, dichotomy, dualism, furcation; **disintegration**, dilaceration, disasso-

separation   462   **servant**

ciation, disruption, dissilience, dissociation, divulsion, nivation, shakeout, sunderance, unravelment; **breakage**, crash, crumble, dissolution; **dismemberment**, disarticulation, disjointedness, embryotomy; **political division**, Balkanisation, demarcation, partitionment, sectionalisation, zoning; **apartheid**, class barriers, class distinction, colour-bar, segregation; **filtration**, centrifugation, cupellation, elutriation, flotation, fragmentation, screening, segregation, vacuum filtration; **analysis**, resolution, sunderance; **chemical separation**, atmolysis, chromatography, column chromatography, cracking, debourbage, dehydrogenation, desorption, dialysis, diffraction, dissection, distillation, distilment, echelon, electrolysation, electrolysis, electrowinning, fractional distillation, fractionation, hydrolysis, ion exchange chromatography, partition, precipitation, scorification, synersis, thin layer chromatography; **chemical disintegration**, atomisation, breakdown, decomposition, deionisation, disassociation, dissociation, fission, photodisintegration, photofission, photolysis; **demodulation**, detection

SEPARATOR *n* breaker-down, detacher, disarticulator, dismemberer, disperser, divider, harrower, ripper, subdivider, sunderer, zootomist; **screener**, cutter-out, dry-blower, rippler, scutcher, thresher, winnower; **dag picker**, dagger; **splitter**, mauler *(U.S.)*, river

SEQUENCE *n* catena, chain, concatenation, consecution, continuation, continuity, course, cycle, prolongation, round, series, succession; following, cavalcade, column, cortege, procession, progression, retinue, string, suite, trail; train; **single file**, Indian file, tandem

SEQUENTIAL *adj* consecutive, on end, processional, progressional, running, sequent, serial, seriate, successive; **unbroken**, direct, entire, flowing, indiscrete, run-on, solid, steady, straight

SERIES *n* continuum, gradation, one thing after another, progression, sequence, succession; **line**, chain, column, file, Indian file, procession, queue, rank, run, stream, string, train; **arithmetical progression**, arithmetic series, geometric progression, geometric series

SERIOUS *adj* earnest; **decisive**, certain *(Obs.)*, constant, single-minded, stable, staunch, steadfast, steady, steady of purpose, stout, stout-hearted, sturdy; **resolute**, decided, determinate, determined, firm, resolved

SERVANT *n* menial, server, servitor, underservant, wallah; **domestic**, abigail, au pair, ayah, bedmaker, chambermaid, char, charlady, charwoman, cleaning lady, daily, domestic help, general *(Obs.)*, girl, handmaid, help, home aid, home help, houseboy, housekeeper, housemaid, lady's maid, maid, maidservant, old Dutch, parlourmaid, sadie, slavey, soubrette, tweeny *(Obs.)*, woman; **nursemaid**, amah, mammy *(U.S.)*, mother's help, nanny; **washerwoman**, dhobi, laundress, washerman; **lady-in-waiting**, gentlewoman *(Hist.)*; **bondservant**, assignee, blackbird, bondman, bondsman, bondwoman, carl *(Obs.)*, helot, Nubian, prisoner servant, serf, slave, thrall, vassal *(Archaic)*, villain, villein

servant *(Hist.)*; **concubine**, odalisque; **attendant**, bumboy, camp follower, follower, hatchet man, henchman *(Obs.)*, lackey, mercenary, roadie; **aide-de-camp**, ADC, aide, batman *(Mil.)*, orderly *(Mil.)*, squire; **armourbearer**, armiger, caddie, caddy, linkboy, mate; **beadle**, verger; **retainer**, liege, liegeman, man, samurai; **entourage**, attendance, cortege, retinue, varletry *(Archaic)*, villeinage. See also BUTLER

SERVICEMAN *n* effective, enlisted man *(U.S.)*, servicewoman; **conscript**, choco, chocolate soldier, draftee *(U.S.)*, nasho, selectee *(U.S.)*; **national service**, conscription, draft; **recruit**, rookie, sprog, substitute, volunteer; **militiaman**, armed constabulary *(N.Z. Obs.)*, Dad's army, Home Guard, militia, minute man *(U.S.)*, reserve, reservist, state trooper, territorial; **ex-serviceman**, campaigner, old soldier, returned soldier, RSL, vet *(U.S.)*, veteran, warhorse; **noncombatant**, base wallah, base walloper *(N.Z.)*, shiny-arse, tin soldier; **military policeman**, gendarme. See also SOLDIER; COMBAT TROOPS; ARMED FORCES

SET AN EXAMPLE *v* lead the way, provide a model, set the pace, show the way

SET SAIL *v* get under way, put to sea, sail, weigh anchor; **go to sea**, cruise, follow the sea, ship, voyage; **picaroon**, buccaneer; **make way**, beat, luff, make heavy weather, pinch, point, sail close to the wind, scud, thrash; **tack**, bear away, broach, ease off, go about, harden sheets, haul up, overlay, overstand; **shorten sail**, back and fill, blanket, fill away, jibe, reef; **make sail**, overhaul, sheet home; **dismast**, unrig

SEVEN *n* hebdomad, heptad, heptameter, heptarchy, septenary, septet, septuplet, seventh; **heptagon**, heptahedron

SEVEN *adj* heptagonal, heptahedral, heptamerous, septenary, septuple, sevenfold, seventh

SEW *v* darn, fine-draw, hem; **stitch**, buttonhole; **embroider**, appliqué, broider *(Archaic)*, crochet, enlace, hook, tat, work; **interface**, buckram, interline; **brocade**, damask, emboss, quilt; **pipe**, comb; **weave**, beetle, bolt, card, comb, garnet, loom *(Rare)*, pick, ripple, scribble, scutch, spin, spindle, tease, teasel, throw, twill, willow; **felt**, nap, tack; **knit**, purl, rib

SEWER *n* darner, dressmaker, hemmer, machinist, needlewoman, seamstress, tailor; **weaver**, knitter, spinster *(Obs.)*, tatter; **textile worker**, comber, flaxie *(N.Z. Colloq.)*, napper, rippler, teaseller

SEWING *n* appliqué, broderie anglaise, broidery *(Archaic)*, contexture, couching, crewelwork, crochet, cutwork, darning, dressmaking, embroidery, Florentine trapunto, invisible mending, knitting, needlepoint, needlework, overcasting, patchwork, petit point, quilt, quilting, sampler, smocking, tapestry, trapunto; **spinning**, beating-up, carding, combing, crabbing, felting, filature, intertwining, interweaving, picking, shedding; **lacing**, tatting; **weaving**

SEWING MACHINE *n* charka, knitting machine, napper, overlocker, scutch; **sewing aid**, bobbin, bodkin, buttonholer, card, clew, comb, crochet hook, darner, darning needle, distaff,

sewing machine   464   **sexuality**

dobbie, dobby, filature, godet, hemming foot, knitting needle, knitting wire, monkey, needle, pick, reed, ripple, rippler, sacking needle, spindle, tacking needle, temple, thimble, three-cornered needle, upholsterer's needle; **spinning wheel**, spinning jenny, throstle; **loom**, Jacquard loom, power loom, scribbler; **flax mill**, filature, willower

SEX *n* female, gender, male, opposite sex; **bisexualism**, androgyny, hermaphroditism, virilism; **sexlessness**, asexuality; **lust**, arousal, concupiscence, excitement, heat, horniness, hotpants, libido, oestrus, passion, pride *(Obs.)*

SEX AID *n* dildo, vibrator; **aphrodisiac**, cantharides, love philtre, love potion, love-juice, powdered blister beetles, Spanish fly; **sex shop**, porn shop; **sexploitation**, sex-sell; **pornography**, hard-core, hard-core pornography, porno, soft-core pornography

SEX OBJECT *n* arse, black velvet, crumpet, cunt, fuck, gash, lay, snatch, tail, talent, twat, yellow satin; **stud**, cunthook, hunk; **sex symbol**, cover girl, pin-up

SEXUAL *adj* female, gamic, male, sexed; **hermaphroditic**, androgynous, epicene, hermaphrodite, hermaphroditical, intersexual; **sexless**, asexual; **heterosexual**, unisexual; **bisexual**, ac-dc, bi; **homosexual**, camp, fruity, gay, high-camp, invert, lesbian, queer; **transsexual**; **paraphiliac**, algolagnic, anilingual, bestial, masochistic, onanistic, pederastic, sadist, sadistic, transvestite, voyeuristic; **incestuous**

SEXUAL INTERCOURSE *n* carnal knowledge, coition, coitus, commerce, congress, connection, consummation, copulation, favours, funny business, intercourse, intimacy, jigjig, knowledge *(Law Archaic)*, lovemaking, sex, twat; **act of sexual intercourse**, a tumble in the hay, bang, fuck, grind, jump, kneetrembler, lash, morning glory, naughty, nooky, poke, quickie, roll, root, screw, shag; **sexual behaviour**, facts of life, lovelife; **illicit sex**, a bit on the side, adultery, forbidden fruit, fornication; **love-play**, feel, foreplay, fumble, hanky-panky, slap-and-tickle; **oral sex**, anilingus, blow job, cunnilingus, fellatio, furburger, hair pie, sixty-nine, soixante-neuf; **missionary position**; **coitus interruptus**; **orgy**, gang bang, gang slash, gang splash, gangie, group grope, group stoop, team cream; **orgasm**, climax, ejaculation, nocturnal emission, the big O, wet dream

SEXUALITY *n* alloerotism, carnality, earthiness, eroticisation, eroticism, lewdness, sensuality, venery; **sexiness**, alluringness, bed-worthiness, bedroom eyes, cheesecake, erogeneity, it, oomph, seductiveness, sex appeal; **promiscuity**, amorism, bawdry, whorishness; **erotomania**, nymphomania, satyriasis; **frigidity**, coldness, frigidness; **heterosexuality**, unisexuality; **bisexuality**; **homosexuality**, inversion, pederasty, queerness; **lesbianism**, sapphism, tribadism; **transvestism**, eonism; **sodomy**, bestiality, buggery; **paraphilia**, necrophilia, perversion, scopophilia, voyeurism; **indecent exposure**, exhibitionism; **sadomasochism**, algolagnia, b. and d., bondage, discipline, masochism, sadism; **fetishism**; **masturbation**, autoerotism, jerk-off, onanism, self-abuse, wank

SEXUALLY *adv* carnally, intimately, sensually; **sexily,** alluringly, permissively; **sexlessly,** asexually

SEXUAL PARTNER *n* bedfellow, cohabitant, cohabiter, paramour, partner, pick-up, sleeping partner; **fornicator,** adulterer, adultress, amorist, cicisbeo, co-respondent, erotic, eroticist; **erotomaniac,** nympho, nymphomaniac, satyr; **swinger,** gang banger, onion; **lover,** fancy man, sugar daddy; **womaniser,** Bluebeard, easy rider (*U.S.*), goat, lecher, pants man, ruiner, seducer, sheikh; **premature ejaculator,** minute man; **cradle-snatcher,** baby snatcher; **mistress,** concubine, demimondaine, hetaera, leman (*Archaic*), woman; **seductress,** mantrap, teaser, vamp; **hussy,** bike, floozy, gunnie, scrubber (*Brit.*), wanton; **groupie,** band moll

SEXUAL RELATIONSHIP *n* affair, amour, intrigue, involvement, liaison, love affair, ménage à trois, one-night stand; **dirty weekend,** lost weekend, naughty forty-eight

SEXUAL TYPE *n* hetero, heterosexual, straight; **bisexual,** epicene, hermaphrodite, switch hitter; **homosexual,** arse bandit, aunty, bimbo, bronzer, cat, catamite, dung puncher, effeminate, fag, faggot, fairy, flit, fruit, Ganymede, gay, hock, homo, horse's hoof, minion, nancy boy, nut man, pansy, pederast, poof, poofter, poonce, poove, punk, quean (*Obs.*), queer, queer, quince, second-hand Sue, shirt-lifter, swish, tonk; **lesbian,** butch, dyke, femme, les, lezz, lezzy,

tribade; **transsexual; sodomite,** bugger, bummer, sod; **muff-diver; paraphiliac,** fetishist, necrophiliac, peeping tom, pervert, porno, secco, transvestite, voyeur; **exhibitionist,** flasher; **sadomasochist,** algolagnist, masochist, sadist; **masturbator,** jerk-off, rod-walloper, wanker

SEXY *adj* alluring, bed-worthy, beddable, erogenous, oomphy, seductive; **erotic,** alloerotic, anatomical, aphrodisiac, autoerotic, carnal, earthy, erotogenic, fruity, sensual; **aroused,** excited, horny, on heat, randy, raunchy, ruttish, toey; **lecherous,** evil-minded (*Joc.*), libidinous, on the make, oversexed, randy; **in like Flynn,** made; **permissive,** loose, promiscuous, swinging; **pornographic,** porno; **copulative,** intimate, orgastic, venereal

SHADE *n* penumbra, shadow, umbra, umbrage (*Obs.*); **cloud,** fog, lour, mist, murk, smog, smoke; **pall,** covering, shroud. *See also* DARKNESS

SHADOWY *adj* adumbral, bosky, bowery, darkened, penumbral, shaded, shady, tenebrific, tenebrous, umbrageous, umbrifericy; **twilight,** crepuscular, dusk, duskish; **dim,** caliginous (*Rare*), darkish, wan (*Archaic*); **dull,** bleary, cloudy, dingy, dirty, dismal, foggy, gloomy, hazy, lack-lustre, lowering, misty, murk (*Archaic*), murky, overcast, sad, smoky, sombre, subfusc, sunless. *See also* DARK

SHAFT *n* lath, pale, paling, palisade, picket, slat, slip, spline, stake, stave; **board,** chump, floorboard, skirt, skirting, skirting board; **plank,** deal, gangplank, gangway, skid, wale; **beam,** baulk, binder, couple, dead shore, flitch beam, girder, joist, rafter, rolled steel joist, RSJ, sleeper, stanchion, straining beam, timber; tree; **crossbeam**, collar tie, summer, tie beam, transom, traverse

SHAFTED *adj* beamed, trabeated, transomed; **columned**, dipteral, hypostyle, peristylar

SHALLOW *n* bank, bar, bombora, coral reef, flat, ford, low-water mark, reef, sandbank, sandbar, shallows, shelf, shoal; **shallowness**, superficiality, superficialness; **scratch**, pinprick; **thin coat**, gloss, skin, veneer

SHALLOW *v* flatten, shoal, silt up

SHALLOW *adj* flat, low, shoal, shoaly; **superficial**, ankle-deep, knee-deep, skin-deep, slight

SHAPE *n* fashion, figuration, figure, form, lines, mould, turn; **design**, pattern, schematism, scheme; **geometry**, spherics, topology; **multiformity**, dimorphism, heteromorphism, heteromorphy, metamorphosis, polymorphism, pseudomorphism, stereoisomerism, trimorphism; **polymorph**, dimorph, habit, trimorph; **cast**, die, formwork, matrix, swage block.
See also STRUCTURE

SHAPE *v* fashion, figure, form, model, pattern; **structure**, define, develop, formalise, formulate, frame, incubate; **design**, geometrise, round, square, style, tailor; **mould**, block, cast, found, ingot, tree; **sculpt**, carve, chisel, cut, rough-hew, trim, whittle; **forge**, beat out, dolly, hammer out, smith; **turn**, blow, spin, throw; **stamp**, die, swage, tool

SHAPED *adj* figurate, figured, formal; **multiform**, biform, dimorphous, heteromorphic, idiomorphic, morphologic, peloric, polymorphous, pseudomorphic, pseudomorphous, triform, trimorphic, trimorphous; **wrought**, blown, cast, chiselled, molten, plastic, repoussé

SHAPELESS *adj* amorphous, baggy, blobby, featureless, formless, inchoate, indefinite, indigested, nondescript; **unshaped**, rudimentary, uncut, unformed, unhewn

SHAPELESSNESS *n* amorphia, amorphism, amorphousness, formlessness; **lump**, agglomeration, aggregation, cloud, mass, smudge

SHAPER *n* chiseller, fashioner, former, founder, sculptor

SHARE *n* a slice of the action, a slice of the cake, allotment, allowance, bit, bunce, chop, cut, darg, deal *(Obs.)*, dividend, dole, fraction, helping, interest, lay *(Fishing)*, lot, portion, preallotment, proportion, quantum, quota, rake-off, ration, round, split, stint, whack

SHARED *adj* common, divided, dividual *(Archaic)*, joint, participable, split; **distributable**, apportionable, commonable, dividable, divisible; **distributive**, distributional, respective

SHARE OUT *v* admeasure, administer, allocate, allot, apportion, assign, assort, average out, carve up, deal, demark, detail, dish out, dispense, distribute, divide, divvy up, dole out, give out, hand out, issue, lot, mete out, morsel, parcel out, partition, portion, ration, redistribute, repartition, serve out, subdivide, unlock the land *(Hist.)*; **share**, divvy, go Dutch, go halves, go into, split, whack up; **participate**, get in for one's chop, get one's corner, get one's share, partake

SHARER *n* allottee, partaker, participant, participator, sharecropper *(U.S.)*, sharefarmer, sharemilker *(N.Z.)*; allotter, dealer *(Cards)*, dispensator, dispenser, partitioner, partitionist

SHARING OUT *n* cavil *(Mining)*, communalism, communism, Dutch shout, Dutch treat, job sharing, profit sharing, sharing, socialism, tontine; **distribution**, admeasurement, administration, allocation, allotment, apportionment, appropriation, assignation, assignment, assortment, carve-up, chop-up, deal, dispensation, divide, division, issue, participation, partition, partitionment, rationing, redistribution, repartition, share-out

SHARP *adj* acuate, acute, cultrate, fine, keen, sharp-edged, trenchant *(Poetic)*; **biting**, acid, acidulous, acrid, acrimonious, bitter, cutting, mordacious, penetrating, piercing, pointed, pungent, shrewd *(Archaic)*, shrill *(Poetic)*; **double-edged**, two-edged; **self-sharpening**. *See also* POINTED; SPINY

SHARPEN *v* acuminate, edge, point, put kinchella on *(Shearing)*, set, spike, strap *(Obs.)*, whet; **point**, barb, shag, Vandyke

SHARPENER *n* hone, pencil-sharpener, slip, strap, strickle, strop, whetstone

SHARP-EYED *adj* clear-eyed, clearsighted, eagle-eyed, far-seeing, far-sighted, hawk-eyed, lyncean, lynx-eyed, perspicacious *(Archaic)*, sharp-sighted; **watchful**, argus-eyed, observant, open-eyed, surveillant, wakeful; **voyeuristic**

SHARPLY *adv* acutely, finely, keenly, prickingly; **piercingly**, cuttingly, penetratingly, pointedly, shrewdly; **bitingly**, acridly, acrimoniously, bitterly

SHARPNESS *n* acumination, acuteness, keenness; **pointedness**, prickliness, spininess, spinosity, thorniness; **acuity**, acuteness, shrewdness, subtleness, subtlety

SHARP POINT *n* cusp, mucro, neb, nib, pike, pinpoint, point, prickle, tip; **spire**, flèche, minaret, steeple; **stylus**, needle, scribe, scriber, style, stylo pen

SHEAR *v* barber, barrow, chop, cut, pink, poke off, ring, tomahawk, undress; **dag**, belly, channel, crutch, ring, wig; **ring the board**, do a Jimmy Gibbs, ring the shed, swing the gate

SHEARER *n* bladeshearer, bladesman, brute, gouger, greasy, jingling Johnny, sheepshearer, stooper, stud, tiger, woolhawk; **ringer**, deuce artist, deucer, dreadnought, good iron, gun shearer, ryebuck shearer, shed-boss; **learner**, barrowman, Cunnamulla gun, drummer, snagger; **shedhand**, baler, board boy, broomie, bundle gorger, hummer, penner *(N.Z.)*, picker, picker-up, pony, sheepo, tarboy; **dagpicker**, dag boy, dagger; **fleecepicker**, fleece-oh, fleecie, fleecy, piece-picker, table hand; **roller**, fleeceroller, skirter, woolroller; **expert**, squirt; **wool classer**, con man, guesser, wool sorter, wool stapler

SHEARING *n* barrowing, sheepshearing; **Barcoo challenge**, throwing the belly wool; **wool classing**, bulk classing, core testing

SHEARS *n* b-bows, blades, bows, daggers, dover, handshears, snow comb, swords, tongs; **handpiece**, bogghi, hatbox, lizard, merry widows

SHEEP *n* barebelly, bellwether, carry-over lamb, cobbler, cosset, crock, ewe, fat lamb, flock ewe, flock ram, full-mouth, hogget, joe, jumbuck, prime lamb, ram, sandy cobbler, shearer, shornie, sound-mouth, spring lamb, teg, treble fleece, tup, wet sheep, woolly, yeo; **goat,** billy, billygoat, kid, nanny-goat, nubian goat

SHELF *n* bookrack, cupboard, étagère *(Furnit.),* gradin *(Eccles.),* hob, mantelpiece, mantelshelf, mantle, shelving, whatnot; **rack,** hack, hayfeeder *(Agric.)*

SHE'LL BE APPLES *interj* she'll be sweet, she's apples

SHELTER *n* air-raid shelter, Anderson shelter, bunker, fallout shelter, hardened site, storm cellar *(U.S.);* **hut,** beach hut, gunyah, humpy *(Aborig.),* mia-mia *(Aborig.),* Nissen hut, wurley *(Aborig.);* **shed,** booth, box, busshelter, picnic shelter, press-box, sentry-box, shelter-shed; **tent,** awning, bell tent, hutchie, marquee, pup tent, stock-camp, tarpaulin; **arbour,** bower, mai mai *(N.Z.),* pergola, summerhouse; **garage,** boathouse, boatshed, carport, coach-house, depot, hangar, hoverport, running shed *(Railways);* **den,** burrow, cote, earth, hutch, kennel, lodge, nest, sett. *See also* REFUGE: HARBOUR

SHELTER *v* ensconce, harbour, haven, house, lodge, shroud *(Obs.);* **garage,** embower, hive, kennel, shed

SHELVING *n* bookshelf, étagère, kitchen shelf, revolving shelf, vegetable racks, vegetable trays, vegetaire, whatnot

SHINE *v* beam, beat, effulge, glare, outshine *(Rare),* overshine; **glow,** halo *(Rare),* incandesce; **sparkle,** bicker, blink, coruscate, flicker, glance, gleam, glimmer, glint, glisten, glister *(Archaic),* glitter, scintillate, shimmer, spangle, spark, twinkle, wink; **flash,** fulgurate, lighten; **radiate,** diffract, ray, reflect, refract; **luminesce,** fluoresce, phosphoresce; **burn,** blaze, flame, flare

SHIRT *n* banian, body shirt, boiled shirt *(Colloq.),* byrnie, cilice, Crimean shirt, jac shirt, sark *(Scot. Archaic),* sports shirt, sweatshirt, T-shirt, tank top, tee-shirt; **top; blouse,** boob tube, chemisette, guimpe, overblouse, stomacher; **shirt-tail,** Australian flag *(Colloq.),* flag

SHOOT *v* blaze, bolt, discharge, fire, let fly, loose, throw, twang, volley; **gun,** bombard, cannon, cannonade, machine-gun, pistol, plunk, pot, snipe; **catapult,** bungy

SHOP *n* establishment, outlet, point of sale, p.o.s., store, tallyshop *(Brit.);* **market,** bazaar, exchange, flea market, marketplace, mart; **supermarket,** cash and carry, hypermarket *(Brit. U.S.),* superette; **shopping centre,** arcade, mall, shopping complex, shopping precinct *(Brit.),* shoppingtown; **stall,** barrow, booth, counter, stand; **salesroom,** floor space, shopwindow; **department store,** chain-store, emporium, retail store; **general store,** army surplus store, chaff-and-grain store, co-op, corner shop, disposal store, duty-free shop, prodgie, produce store, trading post; **food shop,** bakery, butchery, macellaria, charcuterie, dairy, deli, delicatessen, dellie, fair, grocery, ham-and-beef shop, pie-

shop   **shouting**

cart, rialto, sweetshop, tuckshop; **bookshop**, bookstall, bookstand, newsagency, newsstand, stationer; **clothes shop**, boutique, jeanery, slopshop; **haberdashery**, mercery; **hardware store**, ironmongery; **secondhand shop**, junk shop, op-shop, opportunity shop, thrift shop; **tobacconist; toyshop; pawnshop**, hockshop *(U.S.)*, Moscow, pop-shop; **bar**, bodega, bottle department, bottle shop, cellars, grog shop, speak-easy, wine bar, wineshop; **café**, bistro, coffee bar, coffee house, coffee shop, espresso bar, estaminet, gelataria, kiosk, milk bar, tea-garden, tea-house, tearoom, teashop; **saleyard** *(Brit.)*; **birdcage** *(N.Z.)*, caryard, timber yard; **booking office**, box office *(Theat.)*, office; **vending machine**, automat, slot machine

SHORT *adj* brief, cut-off, short and sweet, truncate, truncated; **little**, dwarfed, knee-high to a grasshopper, pint-size, snub, snubby, stunted, undersized; **stocky**, nuggetty, squat; **tubby**, fubsy, podgy, stodgy; **low-rise**

SHORTEN *v* abbreviate, curtail, cut, epitomise, telescope; **cut down**, crop, cut, detruncate, truncate; **cut across**, cut corners, cut off a corner

SHORTNESS *n* littleness, stockiness; **podginess**, stubbiness, tubbiness

SHORT PERSON *n* dwarf, little person, nugget *(Colloq.)*, pigmy, pudding, short arse, shortie, stodge

SHORT-WINDED *adj* asthmatic, chesty, wheezy; **catarrhal**, allergic, stuffed up, stuffy; **consumptive**, hectic, tubercular, wasting; **pneumonic**, pleuritic

SHOT *n* cannon shot, cannonry, discharge, gunshot, pot, pot shot, round, shoot, shooting, snipe; **volley**, blaze, bombardment, cannonade, fire, firing, fusillade, rapid fire

SHOUT *n* bawl, bellow, holler, whoop, yell; **howl**, cry, outcry, squall, squawk, wail, whimper, whine, yawp, yelp, yowl; **shriek**, scream, screech, squeal; **cheer**, encore, huzza; **call**, azan, clarion, hoot, muster, mustering, note, page, rollcall, summons; **hail**, cooee, oyez; **distress call**, alarm, alarum; **war cry**, battle cry, watchword

SHOUT *v* bell *(Obs.)*, bellow, clamour, clangour, hawk, holler, outcry, scream blue murder, sing out, sound off, vociferate, yell; **whoop**, crow, hoot, tally-ho, whistle; **scream**, screech, shriek, shrill, sing *(Convict)*, skirl *(Scot.)*, squall, squeal; **howl**, bark, bawl, bray, hoot, yawp, yelp, yowl; **pule**, mewl, waul, whimper; **call out**, cry out, exclaim, interject; **hail**, call, cooee, give a hoy, halloo, hallow, summon, yo-ho, yoo-hoo; **cheer**, encore, huzza

SHOUTER *n* bawler, bellower, brayer, clamourer, hooter, howler, vociferant, vociferator, yeller; **screamer**, screecher, shrieker, squaller, squealer, wailer, yawper, yelper; **exclaimer**, caller, caller-out, cheerer, ejaculator, interjector; **crier**, hailer, muezzin *(Islam)*, musterer, summoner, tipstaff

SHOUTING *n* calling, clamour, clangour, cry, hue, hue and cry, outcry, vociferance, vociferation; **exclamation**, ejaculation, interjection

SHOUTING *adj* clamant, clamorous, clangourous, noisy, uproarious, vociferant, vociferous; **exclamatory**, interjectional, interjectory

SHOW *n* demonstration, fanfare, fanfaron, gala performance, pageant, parade, razzle-dazzle, spectacle, spread; **pomp,** display, eclat, gimmickry, glitter, pageantry, pomp and circumstance, pomposity, razzamatazz, wallow; **flourish,** bravura, flash, flaunt; **style,** panache, pizzazz; **flamboyance,** flamboyancy, machismo; **finery,** best, frippery, full dress, gaudery, war paint

SHOWER *v* beat, cascade, hail, pelt, pepper, plop, rain, snow

SHOWILY *adv* flamboyantly, flashily, flauntingly, floridly, garishly, gaudily, loud, loudly, obtrusively, vulgarly; **ostentatiously,** overelaborately, pompously, pretentiously

SHOWINESS *n* beadledom, fineness, flashiness, obtrusiveness, ostentation, ostentatiousness, pomposity, pompousness, pretentiousness, sharpness; **garishness,** floridity, floridness, gaudiness, loudness, overelaborateness, sportiness, vulgarity, vulgarness

SHOW OFF *v* call attention to oneself, camp it up, cut a dash, flounce, glitter, grandstand, hog the limelight, keep a high profile, lair it up, maintain a high profile, make a figure, make a spectacle of oneself, strut; **flaunt,** display, flash, flourish, parade, play to the gallery, show off to the best advantage, sport; **dress up,** bedeck, doll up in, lair up, overdress, overelaborate, prank, primp, tart up, trick out in, trick up in; **sensationalise,** lairise

SHOW-OFF *n* actor, actress, duchess, exhibitionist, flaunter, macho, peacock, Pooh-Bah, poser, poseur, turkey cock, wallower, Woolloomooloo Yank; **silvertail,** glitterati, social climber

SHOWY *adj* done for effect, exhibitionistic, flash, flashy, flaunty, florid, frilly, garish, gaudy, gimmicky, glittering, lairy, loud, obtrusive, rich, sporty, tarted up, tinsel, tizzy, vulgar; **ostentatious,** chichi, extravagant, flamboyant, high-camp, high-flown, overelaborate, pompous, pretentious, up-market; **macho; dressed to the nines,** dressed fit to kill, dressed up like a sore toe, in one's glad rags

SHRILL *v* pipe, skirl *(Scot.)*; **screech,** caterwaul, shriek, squawk, squeal; **whine,** pule, sing, wail; **toot,** flute, stridulate, tootle; **whistle,** blow, wheeze, wolf-whistle; **squeak,** beep, bleep, creak, pip

SHRILL *adj* clarion, ear-piercing, ear-splitting, high, piercing, sharp, strident, stridulatory, stridulous; **screeching,** screaming, screechy, wailsome; **piping,** pipy, reedy; **squeaky,** creaky, scrannel *(Archaic),* thin, tinny; **whining,** puling; **high-pitched,** acute, alto, falsetto, high, high-frequency, high-toned, shrill, soprano, treble

SHRILLNESS *n* creakiness, flutiness, high frequency, reediness, sharpness, squeakiness, stridor, stridulation, stridulousness, thinness, tinniness, wheeziness

SHRILLY *adv* creakily, sharply, shrill, stridently, stridulously, wheezily; **squeakily,** thin, thinly

SHRINE *n* aedicule, chantry, chapel, feretory, Lady Chapel, martyry, oratory; **sanctuary,** adytum, ark of the covenant, cella, holy of holies, naos, oracle, presbytery, sacrarium, sanctum, sanctum sanctorum, tabernacle;

altar, bema, chancel, high altar, prothesis, the Lord's table; **altarpiece**, antependium, baldachin, ciborium, reredos; **ambry**, almery, credence, fenestella; **reliquary**, phylactery; **font**, baptistery, laver, stoup; **grail**, chalice, lune, lunette, monstrance, pyx; **thurible**, censer; **sacring bell**; **purificator**; **menorah**, paschal candle

SIBLING *n* cater-cousin *(Archaic)*, fraternal twin, half-blood, identical twin, Siamese twins, sib; twin; **littermate**; **brother**, binghi *(Aborig.)*, blood brother, brer *(U.S.)*, brother-german, brother-in-law, bud *(U.S.)*, fosterbrother, frater, frère, full brother, half-brother, stepbrother, whole brother; **sister**, blister, foster-sister, full sister, half-sister, sister-german, sister-in-law, skin and blister, stepsister, whole sister

SICKENING *adj* abominable, chunderous, daggy, deformed, foul, frowzy, gooey, icky, messy, nauseating, offensive, revolting, scungy, sticky, untouchable, yucky, yuk; **tasteless**, fulsome, gross, in bad taste, insincere; **poisonous**, insalubrious, noxious, pestilential, slimy, toxic; **rank**, dirty, evil smelling, filthy, frowsty, mephitic, noisome, on the nose, pissy, pooheyy, putrid, rancid, reeky, rotten, stinking, stinko. *See also* UNPLEASANT; UNBEARABLE; DREADFUL; PESTERING

SIDE *n* border, cheek, edge, flank, hand, jowl, temple, wing; **jamb**, haunch; **profile**, half-face, silhouette; **sidepiece**, edge *(Skiing)*; **winger**, flanker, outrider, postilion; **weatherside**, lee, leeside, leeward, sunny side; **starboard**, beam, bulwark, gunwale, larbord *(Obs.)*, port, quarter, saxboard, weatherboard; **closed side**, inside, open side *(Skating)*

SIDE *adj* by, collateral, flanking, lateral, sidelong, sidling, skirting, stoss; **sideways**, half-face, in silhouette, side-on; **costal**, parietal

SIDEWAYS *adv* askance, askew, beside, broadside on, collaterally, edgeways, half-face, laterally, to lee-ward, to wind-ward; **alongside**, abeam, aboard, abreast, aside, by, ex parte, on all sides, on beam-ends, on the left, on the right; **side by side**, cheek by jowl

SIGN *n* allegory *(Obs.)*, emblem, ensign, figure, manifestation, sacrament, symbol, taw, tessera, token, totem; **character**, colophon, hieroglyphic, hierogram, ideogram, ideograph, logogram, logograph, monogram, note *(Music)*; **mark**, black mark, block *(Cricket)*, chalk, check *(U.S.)*, cross, diacritic, dot, engram *(Biol.)*, erasure, fingermark, line, lineation, marking, note, point, print, tick, tittle, trace, underline, underscore; **signature**, autograph, countersignature, henry; **spoor**, fingerprint, footmark, footprint, footstep, ichnite *(Palaeontol.)*, pug, tracks, trail, vapour trail *(Aerospace)*; **trace**, hint, smell, soupçon, suggestion, suspicion, vestige, vestigium, waft *(Naut.)*, waif *(Naut.)*; **evidence**, appearances, face; **symptom**, attribute *(Fine Arts)*, characteristic, denotation, determinative, diagnostic, indication, prodrome *(Pathol.)*, show *(Pathol.)*, significant *(Archaic)*, signifier; **sign of the times**, straw in the wind; **stigma**, broad arrow, mark of Cain. *See also* SIGNAL; INDICATOR; GESTURE

signal / **silent**

SIGNAL *n* catchword, clew, clue, cue, hint, lead, message, selah *(Bible)*, sennet, the office; **password**, countersign, parole *(U.S. Mil.)*, secret sign, watchword, word; **warning signal**, cone, red flag; **alarm**, air alert, alarum *(Archaic)*, all clear, burglar alarm, fire alarm, fog signal, tocsin; **distress signal**, distress call, distress rocket, Mayday, pan, SOS; **railway signal**, distant signal, home signal; **light signal**, Aldis lamp, amber, anchor light, balefire *(Archaic)*, beacon, Belisha beacon, bonfire, flare, flash, heliograph, light, lighthouse, localiser beacon, magnesium light, maroon, pharos, pilot lamp, pilot light, red fire, riding light, rocket, storm signals *(Naut. Meteorol.)*, tracer, Very light, watch-fire; **radio beam**, beam, blip, localiser *(Aeron.)*; **telephone ring**, dial tone, engaged signal; **beep**, bleep, gating signal *(Elect.)*, pinger, pip, time signal; **military signal**, advance, assembly, boots and saddles *(U.S.)*, call, charge, havoc *(Archaic)*, last post, last trump, lights out, reveille, rollcall, rouse *(Obs.)*, taps *(U.S.)*, tattoo; **death knell**, muffled drum, passing bell. See also INDICATOR; SIGN

SIGNAL *v* beacon, beam *(Radio)*, flag, flag down, flare, semaphore, sign *(Obs.)*, wigwag *(Navy)*; **sound the alarm**, beat the drum, beat the gong, ring, whistle; **lower the flag**, dip the flag, half-mast, salute, strike *(Naut.)*; **show the way**, blaze a trail, buoy *(Naut.)*, demarcate, mark the way, point the way

SIGNALLER *n* flaggie, flagman, gesticulator, gesturer, heliographer, indicator, marker, switchman *(U.S.)*, waver, wigwagger

SIGNER *n* signatory, the undersigned; **graphologist**, hieroglyphist, hierogrammat, marksman *(Law)*, punctuator, rubricator, symbolist

SIGNIFY *v* bespeak, connote, denote, design *(Obs.)*, feature, index, indicate, involve, mean, point to, proclaim, signalise; **symbolise**, betoken, emblematise, emblemise, represent, symbol, typify

SIGNPOST *n* arrow, beacon, beam, beckon, landmark, lighthouse, lodestar, pharos, pylon, traffic sign, vane, weathercock

SILENCE *n* hush, lull, peace, quiescence, quiet, quietness, stillness; **period of silence**, pause, rest, tacet; **dead space**, anechoic chamber, cone of silence, soundproof box; **soundlessness**, inaudibility, noiselessness; **muteness**, dumbness, voicelessness; **speechlessness**, reticence, sullenness, tacitness, taciturnity

SILENCE *v* hush, lull, mum, quiet, quieten, shush, still; **suppress**, burke, play down, soft-pedal, squash, squelch, stifle, subdue; **mute**, drown the noise, gag, muffle, muzzle, tongue-tie; **soundproof**, deaden

SILENCE *interj* hist, hush, hum, mum's the word, sh, shush, shut up, shut your face, shut your mouth, shut your mouth there's a bus coming, soft *(Archaic)*, whist

SILENCER *n* deadener, muffle, muffler, quieter, squasher

SILENT *adj* hush *(Archaic)*, hushed, quiescent, quiet, quiet as the grave, still, stilly; **unsounded**, tacit, unsaid, unspoken, unuttered, unvoiced; **inaudible**, noiseless, soundless, subsonic, supersonic; **silenced**, muffled, sub-

silent / **simplification**

dued; **soundproof**, anechoic, echoless; **inarticulate**, coy *(Obs.)*, mousy, quiet as a mouse, tongue-tied; **speechless**, dumb, mute, mute, songless, tuneless, voiceless, wordless; **tight-lipped**, dark, po-faced, pokerfaced, reticent, sullen, taciturn

SILENTLY *adv* inaudibly, noiselessly, quiescently, quietly, soundlessly, still, stilly, subduedly; **speechlessly**, dumbly, mutely; **reticently**, sullenly, tacitly, taciturnly, voicelessly

SIMILAR *adj* akin, alike, all of a piece, analogical, cut from the same cloth, like, not unlike, reminiscent of, semblable, suggestive of, tarred with the same brush; **comparable**, conformable, correspondent, homothetic, parallel, suchlike; **assimilable**; **approximate**, approaching, bastard, close, much the same, near, pseudo, quasi; **congeneric**, cognate, congenerous, connatural, consanguineous; **isomorphic**, isologous

SIMILARITY *n* analogousness, analogy, closeness, comparableness, conformableness, conformance, correspondence, isomorphism, likeness, resemblance, semblance, similitude; **approximation**, affinity, approach, imitation *(Biol.)*, nearness, parallelism, propinquity; **rhyme**, alliteration, assonance, metaphor, pun, simile; **conformity**, equality, equivalence, identity, parity

SIMILARLY *adv* analogically, analogously, comparably, conformably, connaturally, correspondently, correspondingly, nearly, semblably; **likewise**, by the same token, in kind, item *(Obs.)*; **approximately**, in the neighbourhood of, nearly

SIMILAR THING *n* approximation, close match, match, parallel; **perfect match**, alter ego, another, chip off the old block, clone, dead spit, doppleganger, double, image, lookalike, mate, mirror image, second self, spit, spitting image, twin; **analogue**, counterpart, isomorph, opposite number; **class**, community, family, subset; **set**, birds of a feather, matching pair, matching set, pair, peas in a pod, pigeon pair, Siamese twins, twins, two of a kind; **peer**, equal, fellow, peer group

SIMPLE *adj* Attic, common-or-garden, commonplace, everyday, homespun, mere, obvious, ordinary, plain, sheer, simplex, single, very, workaday; **elementary**, back-to-basics, basic, elemental, fundamental, rudimentary; **no-frills**, bare, matter-of-fact, naked, prosaic, unadorned, undecorated, unfancy; **pure**, absolute, au naturel, entire *(Obs.)*, homogenous, native, natural, neat, perfect, stark, straight, unadulterated, unalloyed, uniform, unmixed, unsophisticated, virgin; **straightforward**, direct, resolvable, straight, uncomplicated; **simplistic**, oversimplified

SIMPLICITY *n* elementariness, ordinariness, resolvability, resolvableness, rudimentariness, simpleness; **purity**, homogeneity, homogeneousness, pureness, unsophisticatedness, unsophistication; **straightforwardness**, directness, plainness, straightness

SIMPLIFICATION *n* degradation *(Chem.)*, denouement, disembarrassment, disentanglement, resolution, solution, streamlining, unravelment;

simplism, over-simplification, reductionism

SIMPLIFY v clarify, clear, make plain, streamline; **disentangle,** disembarrass, disembroil, disentwine, ravel, sort out, uncoil, uncross, unknit, unlash, unloose, unmix, unplait, unravel, unscramble, unsnarl, untangle, untie, unwind; **comb,** brush, card; **resolve,** break down, degrade *(Chem.)*, disintegrate, dissociate; **oversimplify,** popularise

SIMPLY adv downright, merely, only, ordinarily, plainly, purely; **straightforwardly,** commonly, elementarily, naturally, rudimentarily, unmixedly, unsophisticatedly; **simplistically**

SIMULTANEITY n coeternity, coexistence, coincidence, concomitance, concurrence, concurrency, contemporaneousness, intercurrence, isochronism, sync, synchronisation, synchronism, synchronousness, timing, unison; **coevolution**

SIMULTANEOUS adj accompanying, coetanious, coeternal, coeval, coexisting, coextensive, coincident, coincidental, coinstantaneous, concomitant, concurrent, contemporaneous, contemporary, coseismal, inseparable, intercurrent, isochronal, isochronous, synchronic, synchronistic, synchronous; **twin,** twinborn

SIMULTANEOUSLY adv at once, at the same moment, at the same time, coevally, coincidentally, coincidently, concurrently, contemporaneously, ensemble *(Obs.)*, hand in hand, in concert, in step, in sync, in unison, isochronally, isochronously, neck and neck, synchronistically, synchronously, together

SIN-BIN n carnal car, frigmobile, fuck truck, shaggin' wagon

SING v anthem, carol, croon, descant, discourse, hum, hymn, lilt, outsing, precent, psalm, quaver, solfa, troll, vocalise, warble, yodel; **chorus,** chime in, choir, consort *(Obs.)*; **intone,** chant; **serenade,** shivaree *(U.S.)*

SINGER n cantatrice, chanter, chanteuse, choirboy, chorister, crooner, descanter, hummer, serenader, singer-songwriter, solfaist, songbird, songster, torch-singer, troller, vicar choral, vocaliser, vocalist, voice, warbler; **folk singer,** balladeer, bard, carol-singer, caroller, folkie, gleeman *(Archaic)*, jongleur, minnesinger, minstrel, troubadour, yodeller; **soprano,** coloratura, diva, dramatic soprano, prima donna; **contralto,** alto, mezzo, mezzosoprano, second; **tenor,** heldentenor, heroic tenor; **countertenor,** castrato, falsetto; **bass,** baritone, base *(Obs.)*, basso, basso profundo; **cantor,** chanter, chazzan, coryphaeus, precentor; **choir,** cantoris, chorale *(U.S.)*, chorus, consort, liedertafel, quire *(Archaic)*, waits

SINGING n Ambrosian chant, balladry, Bayreuth bark, bel canto, charm, dhrupad, minstrelsy, monotone, vocalisation, vocalism, vocality, vocalness, vocals; **part-singing,** close harmony, fauxbourdon, organum; **recitative,** recitativo secco, scena, Sprechgesang, Sprechstimme. *See also* OPERA

SINGLE adj celibate, chaste, lone, partnerless, unattached, unmarried, unwedded, virgin; **spinsterish,** old-maidish, on the shelf; **widowed,** vidual; **premarital**

SINGLE PERSON *n* bachelor, bachelor girl, back, feme sole, lonely heart, misogamist, old maid, spinster, tabby, virgin; **divorcee**, divorcer; **single parent; widow**, dowager, grass widow *(U.S.)*, grass widower *(U.S.)*, relict, widower; **widow's weeds**, black, mourning band; **singles bar**, dating service *(U.S)*, lonely hearts' club, marriage bureau, parents without partners club

SINGLE STATE *n* bachelorhood, bachelorship, celibacy, maidenhood, misogamy, single blessedness, singleness, spinsterhood, virginity

SIREN *n* beeper, bell, foghorn, hooter, horn, klaxon, whistle

SITUATION *n* circumstances, conjuncture, kettle of fish, juncture, scene, set-up, shebang, show, state of affairs. *See also* AFFAIR; OCCURRENCE

SIX *n* half-a-dozen, half-dozen, hexad, hexameter, hexarchy, sextet, sextuplet, sixth; **hexagon**, hexagram, hexahedron

SIX *adj* half-a-dozen, half-dozen, hexadic, hexagonal, hexahedral, hexamerous, senary, sexpartite, sextuple, sixfold, sixth

SIZE *n* capacity, dimensions, extent, magnitude, proportions, scale, scope, volume; **hugeness**, enormousness, giantism, giganticness, immenseness, immensity, mightiness, monstrousness, outsize, oversize, prodigiousness, sizeableness, vastitude, vastness, voluminousness; **amplitude**, ampleness, breadth, extensiveness, spaciousness, spread, sweepingness; **bulk**, beefiness, bulkiness, buxomness, corpulence, corpulency, dumpiness, embonpoint, fatness, flesh, fleshiness, grossness, heftiness, massiness, massiveness, obeseness, obesity, plumpness, rotundity, rotundness, squatness, steatopygia, tubbiness

SIZEABLY *adv* enormously, extensively, gigantically, hugely, immensely, massively, monstrously, prodigiously, sweepingly, vastly; **amply**, capaciously, spaciously, voluminously; **exceedingly**, ever so; **corpulently**, bulkily, grossly, obesely, rotundly, squabbily, squatly; **monumentally**, palatially; **wholesale**, in bulk

SKETCHBOOK *n* colouring-in book, sketchblock, sketchpad

SKIN *n* bark, buff *(Colloq.)*, epicarp, fur, hide, integument, peel, pericarp, rind, sheath, shell; **membrane**, caul, cortex, film, fraenulum, indusium, lamella, pellicle, scale, squama, tela, tunic, web, webbing; **corium**, cuticle, cuticula, cutis, derma, dermatome, epidermis, scarfskin; **hangnail**, agnail; **marsupium**, epicanthus; **peel**, husk, jacket, peeling, zest. *See also* HIDE

SKIN *adj* cutaneous, cuticular, dermal, dermatomic, dermic, epicanthic, epidermal, epidermic, membranaceous, membranous, subcutaneous; **dermatoid**, dermoid; **hypodermic**, endermic, percutaneous; **cortical**, corticate, lamellar, lamellate, pellicular, scutellate; **crustaceous**, crusty, scurfy; **leather**, cordovan, coriaceous, leathern *(Archaic)*, shagreen, shagreened

SKY *n* azure, canopy, celestial sphere, cope, ether, firmament, heavens, solar system, sphere, welkin *(Archaic)*; **stratosphere**, Appleton layer, atmosphere, chemosphere, E-layer, exosphere, Heaviside layer, inversion layer, ionosphere, Kenelly-Heaviside

sky   476   **sleep**

layer, lower atmosphere, magnetosphere, troposphere, upper atmosphere, Van Allen belt; **space**, aerospace, deep space, infinite, inner space, outer space, plenum; **cosmos**, creation, macrocosm, nature, universe, world

SLANDER *n* calumny, dirt, innuendo, insinuation, libel, malediction, personality, scandal; **invective**, attack, obloquy; **jeer**, backhander, barb, fling, flout, nip, put-down, rub; **smear-word**, byword, epithet, pejorative, slur, smear; **denigration**, aspersion, assassination, backbiting, calumniation, character assassination, decrial, defamation, objurgation, revilement, sledging *(Cricket)*, vilification; **disparagement**, abuse, assailment, criticism, detraction, excoriation, vituperation; **muckraking**, dirty tricks, smear campaign; **red-baiting**, poofter-bashing

SLANDER *v* asperse, backbite, badmouth, belie, calumniate, defame, denigrate, libel, malign, put the knife into, shitcan, squib, traduce, vilify, vilipend; **blacken**, besmirch, bespatter, empty the bucket on, muckrake, put shit on, scandal *(Archaic)*, sling mud at, smear, throw mud at, tip the bucket on; **revile**, abuse, assail, attack, be personal, belabour, blackguard, bullyrag, excoriate, fling out, fulminate against, get stuck into, lash, make mincemeat of, objurgate, slag *(U.S.)*, slag off at, slam, slate, sling off at, slur, snipe at, throw off at, vituperate; **disparage**, belittle, cry down, damn, decry, demean, depreciate, diminish, disprize, disvalue *(Rare)*, downgrade, lessen, make little of, pooh-pooh, riddle, slight, sneer at

SLANDERER *n* backbiter, backstabber, belier, calumniator, defamer, libeller, maligner, traducer; **scandalmonger**, blackener, muck-raker, mud-slinger, tabby; **disparager**, decrier, denigrator, depreciator, detractor, dispraiser, knocker, vilipender; **vilifier**, abuser, asperser, assailant, assailer, assassinator, attacker, railer, reviler, vituperator

SLANDEROUS *adj* calumnious, defamatory, libellous, scandalous; **abusive**, denunciatory, invective, maledictory, objurgatory, opprobrious, vituperative; **disparaging**, belittling, contemptuous, derogative, derogatory, detractive, pejorative, personal, slighting, snide

SLEDGE *n* bob, bobsled, bobsleigh, catamaran *(N.Z.)*, coaster *(U.S.)*, fart machine, hurdle, ice-yacht, iceboat, jumper, koneke *(N.Z.)*, skibob, skidboard, skidoo, sled, sleigh, toboggan, troika; **ski**, ice skate, skate; **land yacht**, land sailer, sandyacht

SLEEP *n* beauty sleep, camp, kip *(Brit.)*; **nap**, catnap, doze, forty winks, nod, siesta, snooze, zizz; **sleep-in**, lie-in

SLEEP *v* be dead to the world, dream, push up zeds, repose, sleep like a log, sleep like a top, slumber, stack zeds; **nap**, catnap, doze, drowse, rest, snooze, take a nap, take forty winks; **hibernate**, lie dormant; **go to sleep**, crash, die on someone, doss down, drop off, fall asleep, fall off, flake, flake out, go to the land of nod, nod off; **go to bed**, bed down, bunk, camp, get between the sheets, go to beddybyes, hit the hay, hit the sack, jump into bed, kip down, retire, roll in, roost, settle down for the night, turn in; **sleep in,** lie in, oversleep

SLEEPER *n* dosser, dreamer, slumberer, snorer; **sleepyhead,** dozer, napper; **sleepwalker,** somnambulant, somnambulator, somnambulist

SLEEPINESS *n* doziness, drowse, drowsiness, oscitance, yawn, yawning; **lethargy,** inertia; **snoring,** tossing and turning, zzz; **sleepwalking,** somnambulation, somnambulism, somniloquy; **sleeping sickness,** encephalitis lethargica, narcolepsy, narcosis

SLEEPING *n* bye-byes, shut-eye, somnolence; **rest,** lie-down, reposal, repose; **dormancy,** aestivation, coma, hibernation, sopor, torpor; **oblivion,** dream, hypnosis, trance; **land of nod,** dreamland, sandman; **lullaby,** berceuse, cradle song

SLEEPING-PILL *n* depressant, hypnotic, narcotic, opiate, sedative, sleeping-draught, soporific, stopper, torpedo

SLEEVE *n* arm, bat-wing sleeve, bishop sleeve, dolman sleeve, oversleeve

SLOPE *n* bank, banking, brae *(Scot.)*, cant, couloir, crag-and-tail, escarp, grade, gradient, hillside, icefront, oblique, obliquity, side, slant, steep, superelevation, tilt, ubac, versant; **ramp,** chamfer, chute, counter, counterscarp, escarp, gangway, glacis, nursery slope, raked floor, shaft, ski run, ski-jump, skidboard, skidway, slippery dip, slipway, stepped floor, talus, tambour; **pitch,** anhedral, attitude, bank, batter, camber, cant, chandelle, dihedral, dip, knockdown, lean, list, rake, skew, wane; **incline,** acclivity, ascent, inclination, jump-up, upgrade *(U.S.)*, uphill, upsweep;

declivity, anticline, declension, declination, descent, dip, downgrade, drop, drop-off, fall, geanticline, icefall, isocline, monoclinal, monocline, nappe, preponderation, syncline

SLOPE *v* bank, be at an angle, cant, lean, list, oblique, shelve, slant, splay, steeve, sway, tilt, tip, verge; **grade,** bank, batter, chamfer, decline, escarp, hade, heel, pitch, rake, weather; **climb,** incline, steepen, uprise *(Archaic),* uptilt; **fall,** delve, descend, dip, preponderate, sink

SLOPING *adj* cant, declivous, inclinatory, inclining, leaning, lopsided, on her beam ends, preponderating, skew, slanting, slantwise, weathered; **banking,** anhedral, dihedral; **anticlinal,** centroclinal, isoclinal, monoclinal, synclinal; **aslant,** aslope, atilt, declivitous, gradient, inclined, oblique, prone; **steep,** abrupt, critical, gorgy, headlong *(Archaic),* precipitous, sharp, sheer, uphill

SLOPINGLY *adv* preponderatingly, slantingly, slantwise; **aslope,** aslant, atilt; **steeply,** abruptly, obliquely, precipitously, pronely, sharply, sheer, sheerly

SLOPINGNESS *n* abruptness, inclination, obliqueness, precipitousness, proneness, sharpness, sheerness, steepness

SLOW *adj* deliberate, languid, languorous, lazy, leisured, leisurely, low-geared; **sluggish,** leaden, lymphatic, phlegmy *(Obs.),* retarded, slack, sullen *(Obs.),* torpid; **snail-like,** bumper-to-bumper, lumbering, slow-motion, snail-paced, tardigrade; **dilatory,** laggard, lagging, tardy, unready; **retardative,** retardatory

SLOWCOACH *n* ambler, crawler, dallier, dawdler, delayer, laggard, lingerer, plodder, potterer, slowpoke, slug, snail, straggler, Sunday driver, tarrier, tortoise

SLOWLY *adv* at one's leisure, bumper-to-bumper, deliberately, languidly, languorously, lazily; **gradually**, bit by bit, by degrees, by easy stages, by inches, inch by inch, inchmeal, little by little, piecemeal, poco a poco, step by step; **dilatorily**, dallyingly, laggardly, loiteringly, potteringly, tardily; **sluggishly**, leadenly, lumberingly, ploddingly, slackly, sullenly

SLOWNESS *n* deliberateness, deliberation, flat-footedness, lack of speed, laggardness, leadenness, phlegm *(Obs.)*, sluggishness; **delay**, dilatoriness, lag, latency *(Computers)*, retardation, tardiness, tarriance *(Archaic)*; **hesitation**, demur *(Obs.)*, hesitancy; **slackness**, languidness, languor, leisureliness; **go-slow**, work-to-rule; **deceleration**, brakeage, calando, moderation *(Physics)*, slowdown, slowup

SLUDGE *n* activated sludge, guck, heavy mud *(Geol.)*, mud, ooze, slime, slob *(Irish)*, slush; **bog**, marsh, mire, quicksand, slough, swamp; **magma**, eruption; **viscosity**, creaminess, gelatinousness, glairiness, glutinosity, glutinousness, gooiness, mucosity, ropiness, sloppiness, stringiness, thickness, threadiness, toughness, treacliness, viscidity, viscidness, viscousness; **gelatinisation**, gelation, impastation, thickening. *See also* PASTE

SLUDGY *adj* miry, muddy, slimy, sloppy, slushy; **viscous**, claggy, close *(Rare)*, clotted, colloidal, curdled, gelatinoid, gelatinous, glairy, glutinous, gooey, lyophilic *(Chem.)*, magmatic, melting, mucous, oozy, semifluid, semisolid, soupy, syruplike, thick, treacly, unset, viscid, viscoid; **stringy**, ropy, thready, tough; **boggy**, boggish

SMALL *adj* baby, diminutive, dinky, ickle, itsy-bitsy, little, microscopic, mini, miniature, minuscule, minute, pint-size, teeny, teeny-weeny, tiny, two-by-four *(U.S.)*, wee, weeny; **petite**, dainty, dapper, delicate, elfin, gamin, light, mignon, slender, slight, slim; **undersized**, puny, runty, short, stunted; **scant**, abbreviated, brief, exiguous, meagre, scanty, skimpy, spare, sparing, sparse, wisplike, wispy; **compact**, desktop, microcosmic, pocket size, small-scale; **Lilliputian**, dwarfish, gnomish, pygmaean; **squat**, squab, stumpy; **incommodious**, poky; **beady**, grainy, granular

SMALL AMOUNT *n* ambs-ace, least, minimum, minimus; **next to nothing**, a fat lot, bugger-all, cat's whisker, damn-all, fuck-all, s.f.a., sweet F.A.; **tinge**, lick, smack, strain, taste, tincture, touch; **trace**, cast, dab, dash, hint, shadow, show, sign, suspicion, thought, vestige; **skerrick**, inch, iota, jot, patch, pea, peppercorn, rag, rap, scrap, straw, tap, tittle, whit; **spark**, gleam, scintilla; **hair's-breadth**, ace, hair, hairbreadth, whisker; **sprinkling**, handful, sprinkle; **pittance**, mess of pottage, peanuts, starvation wages; **modicum**, bit, pennyworth, pinch, scantling, smidgin, snip, snippet, soupçon, stiver, tot, trifle; **drop**, dribble, driblet, gout *(Archaic)*, nip; **point**, dot, pinhead; **crumb**, break, chip, droob, morceau, morsel; **sliver**, paring, shaving, snippet; **grain**, granule, nubbin *(U.S.)*, nubble, pellet; **atom**, atomy *(Archaic)*, molecule, mote, particle; **speck**, fleck, flyspeck, spot; **ounce**, minim, pennyweight, scruple; **portion**, share, tithe; **mouthful**, spoonful, thimbleful

SMALLEST *adj* least, minim, minimum, slightest; **inconsiderable**, fractional, inappreciable, infinitesimal, insignificant, insubstantial, lightweight, marginal, minimal, minor, negligible, vestigial; **measly**, halfpenny, mere, paltry, pelting *(Archaic)*, petit, petty, potty, trifling; **mean**, niggardly, stingy; **slight**, certain; **cursory**, superficial, tenuous; **just**, bare, mere, no more than, only

SMALLGOODS *n* charcuterie; **ham**, bacon, flitch, gammon, ham-de-luxe, pastrami, prosciutto, rasher, speck; **sausage**, Aberdeen sausage, austral *(S.A. Obs.)*, bag of mystery, banger *(Brit. Colloq.)*, battered sav, Belgium sausage, black pudding, blood pudding, bologna sausage, boloney *(Colloq.)*, bratwurst, brawn, cabanossi, camp pie, cheerio, chipolata, chorizo, cocktail frankfurt, continental frankfurt, csabai, Devon, empire sausage, frankfurt, Fritz, garlic sausage, German sausage, haggis, kabana, knackwurst, liver sausage, liverwurst, luncheon meat, luncheon sausage, mortadella, peperoni, polony *(W.A.)*, pork fritz, provolone, rillettes, salami, sausage meat, sav, saveloy, snag, snarler *(N.Z. Colloq.)*, snorker, spam *(Brit.)*, vienna, wiener *(U.S.)*, Windsor sausage, wurst; pâté, foie gras, pâté de foie gras, terrine

SMALLNESS *n* diminutiveness, littleness, minuteness; **neatness**, dapperness; **shortness**, dwarfishness, squatness, stumpiness; **runtiness**, puniness, scrubbiness; **exiguity**, exiguousness, scantiness, skimpiness, slightness, spareness; **sparsity**, sparseness; **insubstantiality**, inconsiderableness, negligibility, triflingness; **pettiness**, meanness, niggardliness, sparingness, stinginess

SMALL PERSON *n* dwarf, fingerling, half-pint, hop-o'-my-thumb, manikin, midge, midget, mite, pipsqueak, pygmy, shrimp, squab, Tom Thumb; elf, elfin, gamine, minikin, wisp; **lightweight**, bantam, feather, featherweight, skeeter, titch; **runt**, squirt, stunt

SMALL THING *n* diminutive, miniature; **minutiae**, details; **splinters**, flinders, matchwood; **microcosm**, Lilliput

SMELL *n* aroma, bouquet, fume, odour; **waft**, breath *(Obs.)*, vapour, whiff; **scent**, drag *(Hunting)*, sniff, snuff, trace, trail; **sense of smell**, flair, hyperosmia, nose, olfaction. *See also* FRAGRANCE; STENCH

SMELL OUT *v* breathe, get wind of, savour, scent, sniff, snuff, whiff

SMELLY *adj* a bit on the nose, bilgy, cacodily, cheesy, fetid, funky *(U.S.)*, high, malodorous, mephitic, nasty, offensive, on the bugle, on the nose, pongo, pongy, putrid, rammish, rank, reeky, ripe, stinking, stinko, whiffy; **stuffy**, airless, frowsty, frowzy, fusty, musty; **effluvial**, miasmal, miasmatic, miasmatical, miasmic

SMILER *n* grinner; **giggler**, cackler, chortler, chuckler, screamer, shouter, shrieker, titterer

SMOKE *v* chain-smoke, do the drawback, draw, inhale, puff, pull, suck, whiff

SMOKING ROOM *n* divan, smoker, smokeroom, smoking car, smoking carriage

SMOOTH *v* even, face, fettle, planish, pumice, rub down, sleek, slick, smoothen, strike, worm *(Naut.)*; **sandpaper**, crop *(Textiles)*, drove, file, glasspaper, grind, plane, sand, scrape, trim *(Carp.)*; **comb**, rake; **coat**, glaze, lay, plate, surface; **pave**, macadamise, seal; **flatten**, bulldoze, float, grade, trowel; **press**, calender, iron, iron out, roll; **unwrinkle**, sironise

SMOOTH *adj* alabaster, soft, velvet, velvet-like, velvety; **sleek**, ganoid, glacé, polished, satin, satiny, sericeous, shiny, silken, silky, sleeky, slick, smug; **glassy**, glare, glazy, icy; **slippery**, greasy, slithery; **streamlined**, fastback, flowing, fluent, profluent; **glissando**, gliding, legato; **creamy**, lubricous; **even**, fair, flat, platelike, tabular, tabulate, unruffled; **bald**, baldish, bare, glabrate, glabrous, waterworn; **ratite**; **cold-rolled**, coated; **crease-resistant**, siroset

SMOOTHER *n* comber, filer, glazer, grinder, planer, planisher, surfacer, trimmer *(Carp.)*, troweller; **polisher**, furbisher, lapper, waxer; **putty powder**, polish, rottenstone; **file**, bastard file, block plane, compass plane, cropper, crosscut file, drove, emery board, emery cloth, emery paper, facer, facing tool, grinder, grinding wheel, grindstone, jack plane, land plane, nailfile, plane, rasp, riffler, rubber, sander, sanding machine, sandpaper, smoothing plane, stone, trimmer; **abrasive**, abradant, carborundum; **smoothing device**, battledore, bulldozer, calender, comb, float, grader, jointer *(Carp.)*, lap, rake, rolling pin, slicker *(Foundry)*, smoothing-iron

SMOOTHLY *adv* smooth; **silkily**, glassily, sleekly, slickly; **flowingly**, fluently, glidingly, legato; **evenly**, even

SMOOTHNESS *n* evenness; **sleekness**, glassiness, shininess, silkiness, slickness, slipperiness, velvetiness; **creaminess**, fluency, greasiness; **glissade**, glide, portamento, slide

SMOOTH OBJECT *n* alabaster, glass, ice, marble, plate, satin, silk, slickensides, smooth, velvet

SNOW *n* firn, névé, snow cap, snow country, snowdrift, snowfield, snowflake, snowline, virga; **sludge**, slush; **snowstorm**, avalanche, blizzard, flurry, hailstorm, snowfall; **snowball**, snowman; **frost**, black frost, freeze, hoar, hoarfrost, Jack Frost, permafrost, rime, silver frost, white frost; **absolute zero**, degrees of frost, freezing point, frost point

SOBERSIDES *n* boy scout, owl, straight man; **wowser**, damper, Job's comforter, killjoy, misery, party pooper, snufflebuster, sourpuss, streak of misery, wet blanket

SOCIABILITY *n* companionableness, conviviality, good fellowship, gregariousness, hospitableness, hospitality, party spirit, sociableness, sociality; **cordiality**, advances, approachability, approachableness, backslapping, bonhomie, cordialness, expansiveness, gladhanding, joviality, mellowness; **social relations**, commerce, companionship, company, comradeship, fellowship, routs and

sociability 481 **softness**

revels, social intercourse, socialness, society; **open house,** welcome

SOCIABLE *adj* approachable, chummy, clubbable, companionable, cordial, folksy *(U.S.)*, gregarious, hospitable, neighbourly, outgoing, social; **convivial,** Anacreontic, backslapping, boon, expansive, hail-fellow-well-met, jolly; **welcoming,** greeting, salutatory

SOCIETAL *adj* associational, associative, comitial, curial, institutional, institutionary, organisational; **communal,** collective, common, cooperative, mutual, social; **allied,** associated, coalition, joint; **federal,** confederative, federalist, fusionist, league, unitarian, united; **corporate,** corporative, incorporate, incorporated; **fraternal,** comradely, freemasonic, masonic; **intercommunity,** interclub, interdepartmental; **congregational,** tribal, tribalist, tribalistic; **cliquey,** clannish, cliquish, incestuous

SOCIETY *n* association, auxiliary, club, foundation, group, movement, sewing circle; **alliance,** affiliation, affinity group, alignment, axis, bloc, camp, coalition, combination, front, union, united front; **interest group,** lobby; **federation,** commonwealth, confederacy, confederation, consociation, league, umbrella organisation; **branch,** chapter, local *(U.S.)*. *See also* COMMUNITY; INSTITUTE; COMMITTEE; CLIQUE; CORPORATION

SOCK *n* alberts *(Colloq.),* almonds *(Colloq.),* ankle-sock, bobbysock *(U.S.),* bootee, gaiter, leggings, toe sock

SOFT *adj* cottony, downy, floccose, flocculent, flocky, flossy, piled, pillow-like, pillowy, silky, spongy, velutinous, velvet, velvet-like, velvety; **delicate,** lacerable, tender; **crumbly,** crumby, floury, friable, loose, mealy; **plastic,** ductile, flexible, flexile, floppy, lax, malleable, mouldable, pliable, pliant, pulvinar, semiplastic, supple, thermoplastic, tractable, tractile, waxen, whippy, willowy; **creamy,** smooth; **mushy,** dozy, fleshy, fluctuant, lush, marshy, pithy, pulpy, splashy, spongy, springy, unset; **doughy,** stodgy; **emollient,** mollescent, softening; **mellow,** mild

SOFTEN *v* emolliate, macerate, pulp, tenderise, thaw; **cushion,** ease, pad, pillow, upholster; **mellow,** milden; **relax,** supple, unbend, unbrace

SOFTENER *n* macerater, macerator, plasticiser, tenderiser

SOFTLY *adv* delicately, silkily, tenderly; **flexibly,** floppily, laxly; **pliably,** plastically, pliantly, supplely, supply, tractably; **mildly,** mellowly; **mushily,** lushly

SOFTNESS *n* downiness, flocculence, silkiness, velvetiness; **suppleness,** ductility, flexibility, flexibleness, floppiness, malleability, malleableness, plasticity, pliability, pliableness, pliancy, pliantness, tractability, tractableness, tractility; **delicateness,** tenderness; **laxness,** laxation, laxity, mellowness, mildness; **tenderness,** soft-heartedness; **friableness,** mealiness; **creaminess,** smooth texture; **mushiness,** doziness, fleshiness, pulpiness, rottenness, sectility, sponginess; **stodginess,** doughiness; **softening,** emollition, laxation, maceration, mollescence

SOIL *n* dirt, earth, loam, mould *(Poetic)*, rhizosphere, topsoil, zonal soil; **ochre**, chestnut soil, red earth, terra rossa, umber; **subsoil**, bind, hardpan, underclay, undersoil; **clay**, adobe, argil, bole, china clay, fuller's earth, kaolin, potter's clay; **marl**, black cotton soil, black earth, chernozem, malm, regur, rendzina, tropical black earth; **sand**, diatomaceous earth, kieselguhr, mineral sand; **deposit**, alluvium, eluvium, geest, loess, sediment, warp, wash; **humus**, black soil, brown forest soil, duff, mould, muck, muck soil, peat; **podsol**, gleisoil, gumbo *(U.S.)*; **drift**, apron, boulder clay, diluvium, moraine, till; **calcrete**, caliche, capstone; **acid soil**, alkali soil, azonal soil, intrazonal soil. *See also* LAND

SOLAR *adj* circumsolar, combust, heliacal, parheliacal, solarian, subsolar; **lunisolar**

SOLDIER *n* Anzac, blue-bonnet, crunchie, desert rat, digger, doughboy *(U.S.)*, Federal *(U.S.)*, G.I., galloglass, Hun, imperial, Jerry, Joe *(U.S.)*, lobster, man-at-arms, pongo *(N.Z.)*, rat, redcoat, regular, sepoy *(India)*, tommy, Tommy Atkins, trooper, Unknown Soldier, Yankee; **infantryman**, foot soldier, footman *(Obs.)*, footslogger, janissary, peon, pioneer; **artilleryman**, bazookaman, bombardier, bomber, cannoneer, gunner, powder monkey, spotter, strafer; **rifleman**, carabineer, fusilier, grenadier, harquebusier, musketeer, pistoleer; **swordsman**, halberdier, lance, paviser, pikeman, sabre, spear, spearman; **archer**, arbalester, bowman, crossbowman; **cavalryman**, bashibazouk, cameleer, carabin, carabineer, cavalier, cuirassier, demon, dragoon, guardsman *(Brit.)*, horse marine *(U.S.)*, horseman, hussar, lancer, light-horseman, trooper, uhlan; **centurion**, flanker, legionary, manipular, palatine; **standard-bearer**, colour company, colour party, colour sergeant, cornet, ensign, guidon, vexillary; **sentinel**, sentry; **bodyguard**, fugleman; **drill sergeant**, drillmaster, drum-major; **engineer**, miner *(Obs.)*, sapper, signalman, specialist *(U.S.)*. *See also* SERVICEMAN; COMBAT TROOPS; ARMED FORCES; HIGH COMMAND

SOLID *n* decahedron, dodecahedron, heptahedron, icosahedron, octahedron, pentahedron, polyhedron, prism, pyramid, trisoctahedron; **hexahedron**, cube, cuboid, dice, parallelpiped, rhombohedron, rhombus; **tesseract**, hypercube; **sphere**, cone, conoid, cylinder, oblate spheroid, prolate spheroid, solid of revolution, toroid, torus, tube, ungula; **helix**, spiral; **crystal**, baguette, brilliant, rose

SOLID *adj* bushy, caked, close, close-grained, concentrated, condensed, consolidate *(Archaic)*, dense, gross, massy, so thick you can cut it with a knife, stodgy, thick, thickish, thickset; **concretionary**, constringent; **impenetrable**, concrete, impermeable, impervious; **clotted**, clotty, coagulated, curdy, grumous; **condensable**, congealable

SOLID BODY *n* body *(Geom.)*, cake, cluster, concrete, concretion, condensate, conglomerate, conglomeration, grume, hard core, lump, mass; **clot**, blood clot, thrombosis; **curd**, coagulum, congelation

solidifier 483 **sombreness**

SOLIDIFIER n coagulant, coagulator, condenser, congealer, thickener, thickening; **densimeter,** hydrometer, pycnometer

SOLIDIFY v cluster, cohere, conglomerate, full; **clot,** coagulate; **curdle,** clabber, curd; **thicken,** cake, concentrate, concrete, condense, congeal, inspissate, silt, silt up

SOLIDITY n closeness, cohesion, compaction, concentration, condensation, congealment, congelation, constringency, denseness, density, grossness, relative density, solidness, specific gravity, stodginess, thick, thickness, tightness; **solidification,** concentration, eburnation, gelation, inspissation, thickening; **impenetrability,** impenetrableness, impermeability, impermeableness, imperviousness

SOLIDLY adv hard, impenetrably, impermeably, imperviously; **densely,** grossly, stodgily, thick, thickly

SOLITARILY adv alone, aloof, aloofly, distantly, lonelily, lonesomely, on one's pat, out on a limb, remotely; **antisocially,** insularly

SOLITARY n hatter (Colloq.), introvert, isolate, lone wolf, loner, maverick, skulker, troglodyte; **hermit,** anchoress, anchorite, ascetic, eremite, monk, recluse, seclusionist, solitary; **castaway,** maroon; **lonely heart,** a rose on the rubbish tip, wallflower; **isolationist,** little Englander

SOLITARY adj anchoritic, ascetic, ascetical, eremitic, eremitical, eremitish, hermitic, hermitical, monkish; **antisocial,** asocial, morose, troglodytic, unfriendly, withdrawn; **aloof,** friendless, incommunicado, lone, out of circulation, recluse, reclusive, singular (Obs.), stand-offish, strange, unapproachable; **lonely,** insular, introversive, introvert, isolative, like a shag on a rock, lone (Poetic), lonesome, lorn, misanthropic, shy, unfriended. See also SECLUDED

SOLITUDE n desolateness, desolation, friendlessness, isolation, loneliness, lonesomeness, obscureness, obscurity, reclusion, remoteness, secludedness, solitariness; **aloofness,** distance, insularity, introversion, reserve, secrecy; **withdrawal,** hibernation, relegation, retirement, rustication, segregation, sequestration (Archaic). See also SECLUSION

SOLUTION n conclusion, deduction, determination, explanation, generalisation, illation, key, proof, solvent. See also ANSWER

SOLVE v crack (Colloq.), deduce, explain, figure out, find the key to, get out, hammer out, puzzle out, thrash out, turn the scales, work out, zero in; **resolve,** clear up, conclude, extract, find; **answer a need,** meet a requirement, satisfy

SOMBRE adj black, bleak, cheerless, dismal, dispiriting, grey, melancholy, sour, wintry; **solemn,** awful, deep, grave, grim, heavy; **sedate,** demure, owl-like, owlish, serious, sober, soberminded, staid; **stern,** dour, frowning, humourless, mirthless

SOMBRELY adv gravemente (Music), heavy, seriously

SOMBRENESS n bleakness, dismalness, greyness, grimness, melancholy, sourness, wintriness; **austereness,** austerity, harshness, rigorousness, rigour, severeness, severity; **sternness,** dourness, mirthlessness; **soberness,** demureness, sedateness, sobermindedness, sobriety; **solemnity,**

sombreness 484 **sound system**

deepness, depth, graveness, gravity, seriousness, solemness, **solemnification**, solemnisation

SOMETHING DIFFERENT n a whole new ball game, horse of another colour, something else, something else again, this that or the other, variations on a theme; **another**, anotherie, change, choice, hybrid, modification, otherie, tertium quid, variety

SONG n anthem, ballad, barcarolle, calypso, cantata, cantilena, canto, cantus, canzone, canzonet, chanson, chant, comeallyers, descant, ditty, folk song, frottola, hit song, hymn, lay, lied, national anthem, nursery rhyme, patter song, penillion, shanty, song cycle, tabi song (Aborig.), torch song, vocal, vocalise, Volkslied, walata (N.Z.), warble; **part-song**, canon, glee, madrigal, villanella; **round**, catch, roundelay, troll; **aria**, arietta, cabaletta, cavatina, concert aria; **yodel**, styrienne; **lullaby**, berceuse, cradlesong; **drinking song**, brindisi, wassail (Obs.); **marriage song**, epithalamium, hymeneal, prothalamion; **dirge**, coronach, elegy, epicedium, lament, lamentation, monody, threnody; **theme song**, jingle, leitmotiv, signature, signature tune, theme tune; **part**, canto, canto fermo, cantus firmus, chart, descant, fundamental bass, line, organum, second, secondo, vocals, voice part

SOPORIFIC adj hypnotic, narcotic, somniferous, somnific, soporiferous, torporific

SORE n abscess, blain, boil, canker, carbuncle, cold sore, fester, furuncle, gathering, gumboil, scab, sinus, stigma, ulcer, weal, whitlow; **pustule**, blackhead, bulla, eruption, head, wen, whelk; **contusion**, haematoma; **rash**, barber's itch, barber's rash, gravel rash, prickly heat, shaving rash; **acne**, herpes, impetigo, pimples, school sores, zits; **dermatitis**, brigalow itch, cradle cap, eczema, hives, uredo, urticaria

SO THAT conj for to (Archaic), in order that, in order to, to

SOUL n atman, inner being, mind, monad, self, spirit, spiritual self; **life force**, breath of life, ectoplasm (Spiritualism), etheric body, etheric force, vital force; **phantom**, apparition, astral body, astral spirit, eidolon, ghost, image, spirit, vapour (Archaic), wraith

SOUND n audition (Rare), noise, note, sonance (Obs.), tone, tune (Obs.), vox; **complex sound**, chord, combination tone; **sonority**, consonance, euphonicalness, euphoniousness, euphony, harmonisation, harmony, sonorousness, symphony (Archaic), syntony; **assonance**, alliteration, onomatopoeia, rhyme, stave (Pros.)

SOUND v cipher, phonate, strike, strike up; **tune**, euphonise, pitch, syntonise, tone; **lower the pitch**, depress, sink; **raise the pitch**

SOUNDED adj atonic, close, closed, dark, fortis, free, hard, lenis, low, narrow, neutral, rough, rounded, stopped, unilateral, unrounded, weak

SOUND SYSTEM n audio system, hi-fi system, music system, playback, stack, stereo; **gramophone**, jukebox, nickelodeon, phonautograph, phonograph (U.S.), record-changer, record-player, stereogram, turntable; **stylus**, cartridge, crystal, pick-up; **radio**, radio-cassette, radiogram, tuner, wireless, wireless set; **amplifier**, amp, box, brick, preamp, preamplifier, preselector; **speaker**, horn, tweeter, woofer; **tone control**, Dolby system, fuzz box, graphic equaliser, mixer; **tape-recorder**, cassette deck, dictaphone, magnetic recorder, recorder, recording head, reel-to-reel, tape deck, wire recorder; **reel**, cartridge, cassette, spool, take-up spool; **electromagnetic tape**, magnetic tape, tape, tape loop

SOUR v acetify, acidify, acidulate, brine, pickle, salt

SOUR adj acetous, acid, acidic, aciduous, acidy, astringent, lemon, sharp, sourish, subacid, tart, tartish, vinegar-like, vinegarish, vinegary; **bitter**, acerbic, bitterish, bittersweet; **salty**, brackish, brinish, briny, salt, saltlike; **dry**, brut, demi-sec, flinty, sec, unsweetened; **rough**, austere, harsh; **unripe**, green

SOURNESS n acidity, astringency, austereness, sharpness, subacidity, subacidness, tartness; **bitterness**, acerbity, **saltiness**, brackishness, brininess, salinity; **acidulation**, acidification; **acid**, bitters, brine, gall, lemon, vinegar

SO WHAT interj big deal, che sarà sarà, do tell, for aught one cares, hard cheddar, hard cheese, it's all one to me, stiff cheddar, stiff cheese, that's the way the cookie crumbles, what of it, what the hell, who cares

SPACE n accommodation, air space, elbow-room, floor space, head room, houseroom, lebensraum, leg room, play, room, room to breathe, room to move, sea room, serene (Archaic), standing room; **scope**, ambit, compass, orb (Astrol.), range, verge; **expanse**, area, continuum, open; **storage**, roomage, stowage; **roominess**, commodiousness, spaciousness, wideness; **spatiality**, 3-D, three-dimensionality; **vacuum**, free space, vacuity, void; **space-time**, four-dimensional continuum, Minkowski world. *See also* AREA

SPACECRAFT n capsule, earth satellite, fixed satellite, launch vehicle, lunar module, module, posigrade rocket, probe, re-entry vehicle, satellite, sonde, space probe, space shuttle, space station, spaceship, sputnik, stage, step rocket, thruster, vehicle, vernier rocket

SPACIOUS adj commodious, expansive, open, roomy, wide; **spatial**, space, three-dimensional

SPACIOUSLY adv commodiously, expansively, roomily, widely; **spatially**, three-dimensionally

SPEAK v articulate, chin, emit, enounce, enunciate, give tongue to, give voice to, phonate, pronounce, pyalla, say, sound, syllable, tongue, utter, vent, vocalise, voice; **think aloud**, soliloquise; **recite**, intonate, intone; **dictate**, deliver, give out, read, trot out; **speak of**, mention, name, tell, tell of; **comment**, allow (U.S.), express, observe, outspeak, pass comment, pass comment on, pass comment upon, quote, remark, state, talk off the top of one's head, ventilate, weigh one's words; **quoth**; **talk**, bend someone's ear, blow down someone's lug, chew someone's ear, earbash, get on one's soapbox, get up on the stump, harangue, harp, jaw, jawbone, preach at, talk nineteen to the dozen; **exclaim**, ejaculate, gasp; **chatter**, babble, blab, blabber, blather, burble, clack, drivel, gab, gabble,

speak   486   **speed**

jabber, jaw, patter, smatter *(Obs.)*, twaddle, yap; **blurt**, come out with, drop, jerk out; **snap**, hurl, rasp, snarl, spit, spit it out, throw out; **whine**, bleat, blubber, cant, grumble, snivel, snuffle; **whisper**, breathe, lip, murmur, peep, sigh; **shout**, raise one's voice, yell; **slur**, burr, drawl, twang; **buzz**, croak, drone, thrum

SPEAKER *n* native speaker, sayer, talker, vocaliser, voicer; **exclaimer**, ejaculator, quipster; **reciter**, articulator, deliverer, elocutionist, enunciator; **drawler**, snuffler; **babbler**, blabber, blabbermouth, clacker, earbasher, gabber, gossip, patterer, twaddler, whisperer; **ranter**, blusterer, haranguer

SPEAKING *n* breath, language, locution, mouth, speech, tongue, utterance, vocalisation, voice; **expression**, cadence, delivery, intonation, reading, recital, tone; **talk**, pyalla, say, words; **comment**, ejaculation, exclamation, interjection, observation, phrase, quip; **babble**, blab, blather, burble, clack, doubletalk, drivel, gab, gabble, gibberish, humdrum, jabber, jaw, patter, spiel, twaddle, yap; **whisper**, aside, stage whisper; **somniloquy**; **emphasis**, accent, stress; **fluency**, articulateness, competence, loquacity, vocalism, vocality, vocalness; **pronunciation**, articulation, diction, enouncement, enunciation, phonation; **phonetics**, acoustic phonetics, articulatory phonetics, orthoepy, perceptual phonetics, phonemics, phonics, phonography, phonology, spelling pronunciation, syllabism

SPEAK WELL *v* have the gift of the gab; **declaim**, hold forth, mouth, orate, pour forth, pull out all the stops, reel off, smart talk, spiel, spout, spruik; **address**, apostrophise, call, have one's say, have the floor, hold forth, read, speak; **harangue**, give someone an earful, lecture, perorate, preach at, say a mouthful, sermonise

SPEAR *n* assegai, dart, eelspear, gaff, gidgee, gig, harpoon, javelin, leister, trident, woomera; **lance**, bill, gisarme, halberd, partisan, pike, shaft, spontoon, twibill, vouge; **boomerang**, kylie, throwing stick; **flail**, thunderbolt

SPECIALIST *n* authority, boffin, buff, consultant, crack, expert, hot dog *(U.S.)*, judge, old hand, sophisticate, stager, technician, veteran, virtuoso; **connoisseur**, appreciator, apprehender, cognoscente, maven, perceiver, percipient, recognisor; **generalist**, illuminate *(Archaic)*, illuminist, pansophist, pantologist, scientist, wake-up; **scholar**, clerk *(Archaic)*; **illuminati**, clerisy, faculty, literati

SPECTACULAR *adj* gala, panoplied, splendid; **showy**, blazing, dashing, dashy, eyecatching, for show, ornate, ostentatious, phantasmagorical, pyrotechnic, splashy, triumphal

SPEED *n* celerity, fastness, fleetness, quickness, rapidity, speediness, swiftness; **promptness**, dispatch, expedition, expeditiousness, immediateness, promptitude, smartness, summariness; **haste**, cursoriness, hastiness, helter-skelter, hurriedness, hurry, hurry-scurry, posthaste *(Archaic)*, precipitancy, precipitateness, precipitation, rush, stampede; **briskness**, activeness, agility, alacrity, lightness, mercurialness, nimbleness, sharpness, slippiness, snappiness. *See also* RATE; VELOCITY

SPEED *v* bat, bowl, clip, flash, fleet, fly, hightail it, hurtle, lope, pike, post, romp, scud, shift, skirr, skitter, slip, spank, spear, spear on, spin, tear, travel, whip, whirl, whiz, zap, zip, zoom; **drive fast,** barrel along, beetle along, belt, break the sound barrier, burl, burn, crack on sail, do a ton *(Obs.)*, fang, flat-chat, give it a rap, go like a bomb, go like a cut cat, go like a rocket, go through on the padre's bike, herb, hunt along, pelt, rip, rocket, scorch, streak; **dart,** dive, flit, glint, leap, play, pop, pounce, scoot; **scamper,** clatter, rattle, scramble, scurry, scutter, scuttle; **run,** chevy, chivvy, double *(Mil.)*, double-time, gallop, hare, hotfoot it, make the running, pace, race, run like a hairy goat, schuss, scour, sprint, step out; **stampede,** bolt, career, rampage. *See also* HURRY

SPEEDILY *adv* apace, at a fair bat, at a rate of knots, by leaps and bounds, fast, fleetly, hotfoot, like a bat out of hell, like a bird, like a house on fire, like a shot, like billyo, like mad, like one thing, meteorically, pell-mell, quickly, rathe *(Archaic)*, swiftly; **briskly,** actively, agilely, nimbly, sharp, snap, snappily; **flittingly,** dartingly, trippingly; **flat out,** amain *(Archaic)*, at full speed, flat chat, flat out like a lizard drinking, for the lick of one's life, full chat, full fling, full pelt, full sail, full tilt, headlong, hell for leather, in nothing flat, tantivy; **in double time,** at the double, doppio movimento, double-quick; **accelerando,** allegretto, allegro, mosso, prestissimo, presto, veloce, vivace

SPEEDOMETER *n* accelerometer, amphometer, dumaresq, log *(Naut.)*, logchip, logline, machmeter, Pitot tube, radar trap, speedo, tacho, tachograph, tachometer

SPEEDSTER *n* darter, dasher, fleer, flier, flitter, galloper, goer, Jehu, racer, rattler, rusher, scorcher *(Obs.)*, speed-merchant, speeder, speeler, sprinter; **pacesetter,** pacemaker, pacer; **express,** blue streak, clipper, flier, hot rod; **expediter,** hastener, rusher

SPEEDY *adj* arrowy, blistering, express, fast, flighty *(Rare)*, high-speed, jet-propelled, meteoric, nippy, quick, rapid, swift, tantivy, toey, ton-up *(Brit.)*, wingy; **spanking,** clipping, cracking, double-quick, furious, headlong, raking, tripping; **brisk,** alacritous, briskish, expeditious, prompt, sharp, smart, snappy, yare *(Archaic)*; **hurried,** hasty, helter-skelter, hurry-scurry, precipitant, precipitate, rush, sudden *(Archaic)*; **nimble,** active, agile, alert, fleet, fleet-footed, flitting, flying, light on one's feet, slippy, swift-footed, whippy, wing-footed *(Archaic)*, zippy; **rakish,** clipper-built, racing, streamlined; **transonic,** hypersonic, relativistic, subsonic, supersonic

SPIN *n* backspin, English *(U.S. Billiards)*, overspin, side *(Billiards)*, tail spin, top, top spin, twist *(Cricket Baseball)*, underspin; **twist,** twiddle, twirl, whirl, whirlabout; **spinning,** burling, centrifugation, gyration, hunting, twisting, whirling, winding; **swirl,** puddle *(Rowing)*, purl, ripple; **eddy,** maelstrom, vortex, whirlpool; **catherine-wheel,** girandole, pinwheel; **propeller,** impeller; **waterwheel,** flywheel, windmill; **spinner,** gyroscope,

spin   488   **sport**

peg top, teetotum, top, twirler; **cyclone,** tornado, tourbillion, twister, typhoon, whirlwind, willy-willy. See also ROTATION: ROLL

SPIN *v* gyrate, twirl, whirl, whirr; **eddy,** centrifugalise, centrifuge, swirl; **whip,** stir; **dizzy,** giddy. *See also* ROTATE

SPINNING *adj* circulative, circulatory, gyroscopic, gyrostatic, orbital, precessional, rotational, rotatory, trochal; **revolving,** gyratory, planetary *(Mach.)*, rolling, rotary, rotative, swirly, swivel-like, vortical, vorticose, vortiginous, whirlabout; **clockwise,** anticlockwise, counterclockwise, dextrorotatory, laevorotatory; **stem-winding,** paddle-wheel, screw, stern-wheel *(Naut.)*, twin-screw

SPINY *adj* acanthoid, acanthous, echinate, echinated, echinoid, spiculate, spined, spinescent, spiniferous, spinose, spinous; **prickly,** acanthaceous, brambly, burry, snaggy, spurred, thistlelike, thistly, thorny; **spiky,** apiculate, mucronate, spicate, spikelike, spinelike, spinulose, spiny, spurlike, thornlike; **needle-shaped,** acerose, acicular, aciculate, aciform, fanglike, needle-like, spiculate. *See also* SHARP: POINTED

SPIRAL *n* screw, thread, turbinate; **curl,** scroll, verticil, whorl; **convolution,** circination, involution *(Bot.)*, obvolution

SPIRAL *adj* circinate, curled, involute, involutional, obvolute, obvolutive, rolled, turbinate

SPIRITUAL *adj* extramundane, ghostly *(Archaic),* hyperphysical, interior, inward, otherworldly, spiritous *(Obs.),* supernatural, superphysical, transcendent, transcendental, translunary, transmundane, unworldly

SPIRITUALLY *adv* internally, inwards, Platonically, within

SPLASH *n* dash, drip, plop, spatter, splat, splatter, squash, squelch, squish, swash, wash

SPLASH *v* plash, plop, sputter, squash, squelch, squish

SPLASHY *adj* plashy, squishy

SPOIL *v* addle, befoul, blast, blight, canker, contaminate, deflower, empoison, sully, taint, tarnish, vitiate; **corrupt,** adulterate, bastardise, commercialise, prostitute; **wreck,** arse up, bitch, botch, break, bugger up, bungle, cook, crab, cruel, cruel one's pitch, foul up, frig, fuck up, graunch *(N.Z.),* gum up, gum up the works, louse up, make a hash of, make a muck of, muck, muck up, pakaru *(N.Z.),* puckeroo, queer, ruin, screw. *See also* DAMAGE

SPOKEN *adj* articulate, nuncupative, oral, parol, phonatory, speaking, verbal, viva-voce, vocal; **voiced,** accented, pronounced, sonant, sonantal, tonic; **speakable,** enunciable, pronounceable, utterable, vocable; **pronunciational,** orthoepic; **interjectory,** ejaculative, ejaculatory, exclamatory, interjectional; **phonal,** phonemic, phonetic, phonic, phonogrammatic, phonologic, vocalic; **homophonous,** dissimilative; **voiceless,** breathed, unvoiced

SPORT *n* spectator sport; **sporting match,** event, fixture, friendly, international, match, match-of-the-day, play-off, replay, test; **sports day,** bangtail muster, carnival, field day, meeting, rodeo, track meet; **games,**

sport 489 **spring**

Commonwealth games, Olympiad, Olympic games, the Olympics; **tournament**, championship, comp, competition, gymkhana, head of the river *(Rowing)*, rubber; **doubles**, four, foursome *(Golf)*, singles, threesome *(Golf)*, twosome

SPORTINGLY *adv* athletically, sportfully

SPORTS *adj* sportful; **sports grade**, amateur, friendly, international, league, national, Olympic, pro-am, professional, representative, state

SPORTSGROUND *n* arena, cockpit, pitch, playing field, sports complex, stadium; **playing area**, ballpark *(U.S.)*, bowling green, clay court *(Tennis)*, covered court, grass court *(Tennis)*, green *(Bowls)*, hard court *(Tennis)*, icerink, links *(Golf)*, net *(Cricket)*, paddock *(N.Z.)*, piste *(Fencing)*, practice range *(Golf)*, prize ring, ring *(Boxing)*, rink *(Bowling Curling)*, shooting gallery, squared ring (circle), tennis court, velodrome *(Cycling)*; **gymnasium**, gym; **pool**, lido *(Brit.)*, natatorium *(U.S.)*, spa; **test cricket ground**, Adelaide Oval, Brisbane Cricket Ground *(The Gabba)*, Edgbaston *(Birmingham)*, Headingley *(Leeds)*, Lord's *(London)*, Melbourne Cricket Ground *(M.C.G.)*, Old Trafford *(Manchester)*, Sydney Cricket Ground *(S.C.G.)*, The Oval *(London)*, Trent Bridge *(Nottingham)*, Western Australian Cricket Ground *(The WACA)*

SPORTSMAN *n* amateur, athlete, Corinthian, first string, gamesman, jock *(U.S.)*, junior, player, pothunter, reserve grade, senior, sporter, sportswoman, tourneyer; **international player**, cap, international, tourist;

team, eighteen *(Aus. Rules)*, eleven, fifteen *(Rugby Union)*, nine *(Baseball)*, side, squad

SPORTSMANLIKE *adj* sporting, sporty

SPORTSWEAR *n* all-in-one, casuals, creams, jogging suit, jumpsuit, playsuit, romper suit, rompers, slipsuit, sports uniform, strip, sunsuit, sweatsuit, tracksuit, trog suit, tunic, whites

SPOUSE *n* affinity, better half, consort, helpmate, helpmeet *(Archaic)*, mate, partner, yokefellow; **wife**, feme covert, goodwife *(Archaic)*, lady, missus, old Dutch, old lady, old woman, rib, the little woman, the old ball and chain, trouble and strife, woman; **husband**, goodman *(Archaic)*, his lordship, hubby, lord *(Archaic)*, lord and master, old man; **newlywed**, benedick, blushing bride, eloper, honeymooner, war bride; **de facto**, concubine, de facto husband, de facto wife, mistress; **marrier**, bigamist, deuterogamist, monogamist, polygamist; **couple**, Darby and Joan, husband and wife, man and wife, pair; **bridal pair**, bride, bridegroom, groom

SPRIGHTLINESS *n* alacrity, animation, briskness, dapperness, dash, enlivenment, fastness, go, hurriedness, liveliness, quickness, raciness, spryness, verve; **restlessness**, exhaustlessness, inquietude, nervous energy, pottering, skittishness, tinkering, unquietness; **vigour**, eagerness, energy, heartiness, life, red-bloodedness, spirit, spiritedness, vigorousness, vivacity; **hyperactivity**, overactivity

SPRING *n* fount, fountainhead, headspring, source, springhead, springlet, well, wellspring; **headwaters**, head, headstream, riverhead; **fountain**,

spring

conduit *(Archaic)*, font *(Archaic)*, fount; **bubbler,** drinking fountain; **geyser,** hot spring, thermae, thermal springs; **mineral spring,** salina, spa, waters; **waterfall,** cascade, cataract, chute, falls, Niagara, overflow, rapids, spout.   *See also* FLOW; CURRENT; STREAM

SPY *n* beagle, counterspy, double agent, informer, mole, secret agent, snoop, snooper, spier, undercover agent, wire-tapper; **secret service,** A.S.I.O., A.S.I.S., C.I.A., intelligence organisation, J.I.O., K.G.B., M.I.5, S.A.S.

SQUANDER *v* be prodigal, blow, blue, burn up one's capital, kill the goose that laid the golden eggs, knock down, lamb down, lash out, pay through the nose, run through, spend freely, spend money like water, splash, splurge; **waste,** confound *(Obs.)*, consume, dilapidate, fritter, fritter away, make ducks and drakes of, misspend, riot away, throw away; **gamble away,** game away, sport away; **dissipate,** burn the candle at both ends

SQUANDERER *n* big spender, dissipater, fritterer, jetsetter, misspender, playboy, prodigal, profligate, scattergood, spendthrift, two-bob millionaire, waster, wastrel

SQUARE *n* quadrate; **quadrilateral,** oblong, parallelogram, quad, quadrangle, rectangle, rhomboid, rhombus, tetragon, trapezium, trapezoid; **tetrahedron,** triangular pyramid

SQUARE *adj* foursquare, quadrangular, quadrate, quadratic, quadrilateral, squarish, tetragonal; **tetrahedral**

stairs

STABLE *n* bails, cowshed, offices *(Brit.)*; **shed,** board, depot shed, shearing shed, stand, woolshed; **barn,** granary, hayshed, hopper, pit silo *(U.S.)*, silage pit, silo

STAGE *n* boards, false stage, footlights, pageant, rostrum, scene *(Class. Antiq.)*; **apron,** coulisses, curtain, downstage, flies, fly gallery, fly-floor, fly-loft, forestage, gridiron, parterre *(U.S.)*, pit, proscenium, slips, stage left, stage right, tormentor, wing; **backdrop,** cyclorama, decor, flat, flown scenery, mise en scène, scenery, set, set piece, setting, special effects, stage effect; **machinery,** animation, effect, projection room, sound effects; **green room,** dressing room

STAGE *v* direct, mount, premiere, present, produce, put on, run, screen, serialise, stage-manage; **cast,** audition, typecast; **preview,** try out; **dramatise,** farcify, melodramatise, ring down the curtain, ring up the curtain, theatricalise

STAGEHAND *n* dresser, flyman, machinist *(Rare)*, projectionist, prompt, scene-shifter, technician; **property man,** propman; **designer,** choreographer, costume designer, make-up artist, set designer, wardrobe mistress

STAGING *n* adaptation, dramatisation, dramaturgy, improvisation, mounting, presentation, production, recitation, revival, screening, serialisation, stage-management; **stichomythia**

STAIRS *n* apples, companionway, escalator, flight, spiral staircase, staircase, stairway, steps; **stair,** curtail step, doorstep, footstep, gradin, horseblock, step; **tread,** going *(Building Trades)*, nosing, riser; **ladder,**

rope-ladder, scale *(Obs.)*, stepladder, turret *(Fort.)*, wall bars; **rung,** ratline, rundle

STAMMERER *n* fumbler, lisper, mumbler, mutterer, splutterer, sputterer, stutterer; **mute,** dummy

STAND *n* bipod, coaster, crutch, easel, hallstand, hatstand, high hat *(Films Television)*, music stand, spider, stretcher *(Painting)*, tank-stand *(Engineering)*, top hat, tripod, trivet *(Cookery)*, valet; **holder,** candelabra, candelabrum, candlestick, chandelier, flambeau, frog, gasolier, girandole, hold; **andiron,** barbecue, dog, firedog, pothook, toast-rack, trammel; **shipway,** chock *(Naut.)*, dogshore *(Naut.)*, rest, saddle *(Naut.)*; **frame,** chassis, clothes drier, clothes hanger, clothes horse, clothes prop, coathanger, fadge frame, hanger, headframe *(Mining)*, headgear *(Mining)*, horse *(Gymnastics)*, lath *(Bldg. Trades)*, lathing *(Bldg. Trades)*, sawhorse *(Carp.)*, skids, stocks, thorough brace *(U.S. Vehicles)*, trestle; **anvil,** armature, horse, stithy

STAND TO REASON *v* add up, cohere, make sense

STAR *n* dark star, fixed star, protostar, sun, X-ray star; **giant star,** red giant, supergiant; **dwarf star,** starlet, white dwarf; **nova,** supernova; **variable,** eclipsing variable; **constellation,** asterism, binary star, cluster, double star, globular cluster, multiple star, open cluster; **galaxy,** island universe, metagalaxy, Milky Way, radio galaxy, spiral galaxy; **Southern Cross,** Crater, the Cross; **morning star,** daystar, Lucifer, Venus; **evening star,** Hesperus, Venus, Vesper; **pole star,** lodestar; **nebula,** extra-galactic nebula, irregular nebula, Magellanic cloud, planetary nebula, stardust; **zodiacal light,** aurora, aurora australis, aurora borealis, Haidinger's brush; **star motion,** star drift, star stream; **black hole,** pulsar, quasar; **constellations,** Aquarius *(Water-bearer)*, Aries *(Ram)*, Cancer *(Crab)*, Capricorn *(Goat)*, Gemini *(Twins)*, Leo *(Lion)*, Libra *(Scales)*, Pisces *(Fish)*, Sagittarius *(Archer)*, Scorpio *(Scorpion)*, Taurus *(Bull)*, Virgo *(Virgin)*. *See also* SUN; METEOR

START *n* alpha, beginning, commencement, early days, epoch, exordium, inception, inchoation, incipience, lead-off, offset, onset, opening, origin, origination, outset, square one; **dawn,** dawning, morning, prime, spring, springtide, springtime, youth, zero hour; **Dreamtime,** alcheringa; **opening time; genesis,** birth, birthplace, derivation, nascence, nativity, provenance, provenience, womb; **source,** fount, fountain, fountainhead, head, headspring, headstream, rise, riverhead, seminary, spring, springhead, well, wellhead, wellspring; **germ,** bud, conception, embryo, primordium, protoplasm, seed; **primitiveness,** fundamentality; **first cause,** big bang theory, cosmogony, cosmology; **inauguration,** establishment, induction, initiation, instigation, institution, introduction; **debut,** coming out, inaugural, maiden speech, premiere, unveiling

START *v* bundy on, clock on, fall to, fire away, get away, get cracking, get going, get off on the right foot, get off on the wrong foot, get weaving, hit off, hoe in, kick off, lead off, pitch in, ring up the curtain, rip in, set to, set to work, set up shop, shove off, sign on, start the ball rolling, wade in; **begin**, belt into, commence, ease into, embark on, enter into, get stuck into, gin *(Archaic)*, open, rip into, set about, set on foot, wade into; **arise**, burst forth, come, come into the world, crop up, dawn, proceed, rise, set in, spring up, well up; **come out**, make one's debut; **start again**, make a fresh start, recommence, resume, take up. *See also* INITIATE

STARTER *n* commencer, instigator, launcher, opener, promoter; **beginner**, abecedarian, infant, initiate, neophyte, new chum, novice, novitiate, recruit, red-arse, rookie, tyro; **debutante**, deb; **spearhead**, apostle, pioneer, trendsetter, vanguard; **founder**, Adam, First Fleet, founding father, inaugurator, initiater, institutor, introducer, originator, patriarch, progenitor; **first**, aborigines *(Rare)*, firstling

STARTING LINE *n* grid, mobile barrier, scratch, starting gate, starting mark, tape; **flying start**, getaway, kick-off, Le Mans start, send-off, standing start; **jumping-off place**, springboard, threshold

STEADIER *n* balancer, bracer, entrencher, fixative, mordant, securer, stabiliser, tightener; **stabilising device**, air foil, aerofoil, aileron, antiroll bar, automatic gain control, brace, castor, cowcatcher, draganchor, drag-sheet, dragsail, drift anchor, drift sail, drogue, fiddle, guestrope, guy, gyroscope, gyrostabiliser, gyrostat, hygrostat, outrigger, pyrostat, sea-anchor, sponson, tailplane, thermostat; **ballast**, kentledge

STEADILY *adv* fixedly, indissolubly, irreducibly, steadfastly, unblinkingly; **stably**, firm, foursquarely, gyrostatically, securely, steady; **fast**, firm, firmly, hard and fast, tight, tightly; **even**, evenly, isostatically, on an even keel

STEADINESS *n* determinateness, entrenchment, firmness, foursquareness, secureness, sureness, tightness; **stability**, fastness, fixedness, fixity, indissolubility, indissolubleness, inexorability, inextensibility, irreducibility, irreducibleness, stableness, steadfastness, thermostability, unalterableness, viscosity; **fixture**, footing, rootage; **climax**, ground state, node; **statics**, aerostatics, thermostatics

STEADY *v* balance, ballast, brace, build on a rock, compact, firm, fix, guy, root, secure, settle, stabilise, tighten; **firm**, harden, set; **be steady**, have one's sea legs, hold the road, retain one's equilibrium

STEADY *adj* roadholding, secure, sure, sure-footed; **stable**, critical *(Physics)*, earthbound, foursquare, indissoluble, inextensible, irreducible, monostable, noble *(Metall.)*, stabile, thermostable, windless; **even**, balanced, homeostatic, isostatic, magnetostatic; **steadfast**, fixed, unblinking; **set**, consistent *(Obs.)*, fast, firm, fixed, hard-set, impacted, stiff, tight

STEADYING *n* fixation, impaction, stabilisation; **equilibrium**, balance, conservation of physical quantity, homeostasis, inertia, isostasy, plateau, poise, stable equilibrium, zero population growth

STEERER *n* aimer, cox, coxswain, driver, helmsman, leader, manoeuvrer, pilot, wheelman *(U.S.)*; **automatic pilot**, automatic flight control system, beam-riding, celestial guidance, command guidance, inertial guidance, inertial navigation, radio control, talkdown

STEERING WHEEL *n* accelerator, brake, choke, clutch, pedal; **joystick**, aileron, elevator, flaps, tab, throttle; **ship's wheel**, engine-room-controls, helm, rudder, ship's telegraph

STELLAR *adj* asteriated, astral, sidereal, star-studded, starred, starry, stelliferous *(Obs.)*; **Sothic**

STEM *n* cane, cladode, cladophyll, floccose stem, rhizome, sympodium, tiller, vimen; **stem part**, aculeus, ala, articulation, axis, bark, bole, bough, branch, bud, bulb, bulbil, caudex, caulicle, caulis, cladode, cladophyll, corm, crown, culm, gemma, gemmule, haulm, internode, joint, leafscar, lenticel, node, phylloclade, phyllotaxy, prickle, rootstock, runner, scar, shoot, stolon, sucker, tendril, thorn, tiller, tomentum, trunk, tuber, tunic, turion, twig, wing

STENCH *n* fetor, funk *(U.S.)*, niff, odour, pong, reek, smell, stink; **malodorousness**, cheesiness, fetidity, fetidness, nastiness, noisomeness, offensiveness, rancidity, rankness, ripeness; **miasma**, cacodyl, effluvium, exhalation, malodour, mephitis; **mustiness**, frowziness, fustiness, stuffiness; **body odour**, BO, halitosis; **stink bomb**; **stinker**, reeker, smeller, stinkpot

STERILISED ANIMAL *n* barrow, eunuch, mule, neuter, poulard, steer

STICK *n* broomstick, crab stick, hickory, rattan; **birch**, ferula, ferule, swish, switch; **rod**, cue, divining rod, perch, stave; **walking-stick**, alpenstock, cane, crutch, ski-pole, stilts, supplejack, sword cane, swordstick; **dolly**, copper stick, posser, washing dolly; **digging stick**, yam stick; **slapstick**, bauble; **bullroarer**, churinga, thunder stick; **yardstick**, tally; **staff**, baton, club, distaff, fescue *(Obs.)*, loom, mace, pikestaff, shaft, singlestick, swagger stick, tipstaff, truncheon *(Archaic)*, wand, warder; **ramrod**, pontil, probang, punty, toby

STICKILY *adv* clingingly, glutinously, tenaciously, viscidly, viscously; **tightly**, fast, intently, solidly; **cohesively**, adherently, adhesively, coherently, en bloc, indivisibly

STICKINESS *n* adhesiveness, glutinousness, glutinousness, tackiness, viscidity, viscidness, viscosity, viscousness; **cohesiveness**, glueyness, tack, tenaciousness, tenacity; **cohesion**, adherence, adhesion, agglutination, binding, cementation, coherence, colligation, concretion, conglutination, fixation, fusion, sizing, solidification

STICK TOGETHER *v* agglutinate, cement, conglutinate, glue, paste, size; **solder**, bind, bond, fix, frit, fuse, sweat, unite, wattle; **cohere**, adhere, cleave, clog, gum up, stick together, take; **cling**, hold, hold on

STICKY *adj* claggy, cloggy, gluey, gluggy, glutenous, glutinous, gummy, icky, mucilaginous, tacky, tenacious, viscid, viscoid, viscous; **cohesive**, adherent, adhesive, agglutinant, agglutinate, agglutinative, clingy, coherent, conglutinate, conglutinative,

sticky

consistent *(Obs.)*; **fast,** bonded, fixed, solid, tight

STILL *conj* e'en *(Poetic),* e'en so, even, for aught, no matter what, notwithstanding, yet; **although,** albeit, howbeit *(Obs.),* however; **at all events,** in any case, in any event, in spite of everything, on all counts, under any circumstances

STIMULANT *n* amphetamine, beans, benny, benzedrine, businessman's trip, caffeine, crystal, dexedrine, goof ball, jolly bean, meth, methedrine, pep pill, purple heart, speed, upper, yippee beans, zedoary; **cocaine,** angel, angie, coca, coke, snow, white lines. *See also* DRUG

STOCKS AND SHARES *n* block, blue chip, capital stock, common shares, contributing share, convertible note, cumulative preference share, debenture, deferred delivery share, deferred share, equities, founders' shares, funds, futures, futures contract, joint stock, long-term bond, marketable parcel, ordinary share, per cent, preference shares, preference stock, preferred stock *(U.S.),* rails, scrip, scrip issue, securities, stock unit, trading stock, tranche, vendor's shares; **all-ordinaries,** all-resources, chemicals, industrials, Kangaroos *(Brit.),* metals, miners, oils, steel, utilities *(U.S.);* **capital issue,** bonus, bonus issue, capital distribution, rights issue; **option,** call, double option, put, put option, right, stoploss order; **dividend,** interest, margin, turn, unearned increment; **share index,** all-ordinaries index, allords, Dow-Jones index *(U.S.);* **marriage,** crossing. *See also* CAPITAL

STOLEN *adj* hot

STOP *v* arrest, bail up, bait, baulk, becalm, blow up *(N.Z.),* bring up with a jolt, buttonhole, check, estop *(Law),* foil *(Archaic),* gag *(Parl. Proc.),* hinder, hold up, inhibit, intercept, interrupt, prevent, pull the plug on, pull up, pull up short, rise, snub, stunt, suppress; **staunch,** stay, stem; **discontinue,** abandon, abate *(Law),* abort, break, break off, break up, bug, choke, close, closure *(Parl. Proc.),* cut, cut short, do away with, end, estop, interrupt, knock on the head, kybosh, nip in the bud, prorogue *(Parl. Proc.),* put the kybosh on, scotch, sideline, silence, sit on, snub *(U.S.),* stint *(Archaic),* wind up; **cease,** bundy off, call it a day, call it off, call it quits, chuck it, chuck it in, chuck one's hand in, come to a full stop, come to a halt, come to a standstill, declare *(Cricket),* give it away, give it up as a bad job, give over, give up, pack it in, pack the game in, shut down, shut up shop; **desist,** abort, break *(Boxing),* cut it out, discontinue, draw up, drop, fetch up, freeze, halt, hang up, hesitate, hold it, hold on, intermit, lay off, leave it at that, leave off, let up, mark time, pause, prop, quit, raise, recess, respite, rest, rest on one's oars, sign off, snatch one's time, stagnate, stand, stay *(Archaic),* stint *(Archaic),* stop in one's tracks, stow it, surcease *(Archaic),* walk out, wind down; **knock off,** break off, down tools, knock it off; **deadlock,** be at a standstill, stalemate; **brake,** anchor, back and fill, hit the anchors; **switch off,** shut off, turn off; **cast anchor,** bring to, heave to, lay to, snub *(Naut.);* **stall,** feather *(Aeron.),* whipstall

STOP *interj* avast *(Naut.)*, belay, halt, whoa, wo; **enough,** barley *(Brit. Obs.)*, break it down, come off it, cut it out, enough's enough, hold it, knock it off, lay off, so, soft *(Archaic)*, steady on, stop it, stow it, turn it up

STOPPAGE *n* abatement, abruption, arrest, break-up, breakdown, cease *(Obs.)*, check, close, closure, desistence, freeze, shutdown, snarl-up, suspension, tie-up; **halt,** abscission, bait *(Archaic)*, break, catch, cessation, dead stop, deadlock, discontinuance, discontinuation, full stop, interhouse deadlock *(Parl. Proc.)*, prop, stalemate, stand, standstill, stint *(Obs.)*, stopping, stunt, suppression; **respite,** armistice, forbearance, intercept, interception, moratorium, pause, pretermission, prorogation; **interruption,** abeyance, interval, lapse, let-up, lull, remission, stay, stick *(Obs.)*, surcease, truce; **stall,** whipstall; **stagnation,** stagnancy; **prevention,** check, estoppage, inactivation, suspension; **preventive,** gag *(Parl. Proc.)*, kangaroo closure, snub, walkout; **notice to quit,** caveat *(Law)*, declaration *(Cricket)*

STOPPER *n* cork, estoppel, impediment, lock, staunch, sticking point, stop; **brake,** air-brake, bandbrake, brake drum, brake parachute, brakes, communication cord, disc brake, drum brake, footbrake, handbrake, hydraulic brake, pneumatic brake, retro-rocket, speed brake, vacuum brake; **tap,** cut-off, inhibitor, throttler; **anchor,** arrest *(Mach.)*, dogstick, mud hook, sprag

STORAGE *n* deposition, reposition, stowage, tankage, wharfage; **refill,** refit; **store,** bank, cache, clamp *(Brit.)*, depot, dump, fond *(Obs.)*, fund, library, pool, repertory, repository, reservoir, stack, stock; **reserve,** backlog, backup, bulk, hoard, nest egg, savings, spare parts, stockpile; **cornucopia,** harvest

STORE *v* bank, keep, put by, reposit, stow, tun; **stable,** barn, dump, garage, warehouse, wharf; **stock,** amass, get in, hoard, hutch, lay in, mount up, salt away, save, stack, stock up, stockpile

STOREHOUSE *n* bond store, godown, magazine, pantechnicon, thesaurus, treasure house, warehouse; **supply depot,** base *(Mil.)*, commissariat, commissary *(U.S.)*, logistics branch, public utility, quonset hut *(U.S. Mil.)*, railhead; **treasury,** bursary, exchequer; **granary,** elevator, silo; **coalbunker,** coal cellar, coalhole, coaling station

STOREMAN *n* caterer, chandler *(Obs.)*, provedore, provider, providore, purveyor, stockman *(U.S.)*, storekeeper, supplier, victualler; **quartermaster,** sutler

STOREY *n* basement, belvedere, cellar, clerestory, entresol, flat *(Obs.)*, floor, ground floor, hayloft, mezzanine, piano nobile, roof garden, rooftop garden, story *(U.S.)*, upstairs

STORY *n* anecdote, episode, fit, gest *(Archaic)*, idyll, nouvelle, novelette, novella, romance, short story, tale, yarn; **novel,** antinovel, fiction, roman, roman à clef, sci-fi, science fiction, shocker, stream-of-consciousness novel, thriller, western, whodunit; **allegory,** apologue, bestiary, exemplum, fable, parable; **legend,** fable, fairytale, folk story, folktale, myth, old wive's tale; **saga,** epic, romance, romaunt; **cycle,** legendary, legendry; **biography,** autobiography.   *See also* NARRATIVE

STORYTELLER *n* anecdotist, annalist, chronicler, fabler, fabulist, jongleur, magsman, narrator, raconteur, relater, reporter, romancer; teller; **fictionist,** mythologist, novelist, short-story writer

STOVE *n* cooker *(Brit.),* cook-top, fuel stove, gas cooker, gas range, gas ring, gas stove, kitchener, oilstove, pot-belly stove, range, spirit stove, stovette, wetback *(N.Z.),* wood stove; **oven,** charcoal-burner, colonial oven, Dutch oven, gas oven, hangi *(N.Z.),* hay oven, haybox, Maori oven *(N.Z.),* micro-oven, microwave oven, one-fire stove, two-fire stove, umu; **spit,** roasting spit, rotisserie; **griller,** broiler, grill, toaster; **camp fire,** barbecue, barby, hibachi, primus, salamander; **hotplate,** element; **burner,** combustor, gas burner, gas jet, gaslight, oil-burner

STRAIGHT *adj* agonic, direct, even, level, rectilinear, right, true, waveless; **rigid,** erect, inflexible, soldierlike, unbent, unbowed

STRAIGHT *adv* directly, due, right, slap, smack; **in line**

STRAIGHT EDGE *n* brace, rod, rule, ruler, T-square, truing plane, trying plane

STRAIGHTEN *v* extend, lock, set straight, unbend, uncross, uncurl, untwine, untwist, unwind; **align,** line up, range

STRAIGHTNESS *n* alignment, directness, rectitude *(Rare),* rightness; **straightening,** bracing, extension; **line,** in-line, rank, row; **beeline,** diret- tissimo, short cut; **straight,** back straight, home straight

STRANGE *adj* abnormal, absonant, anomalous, atypical, borderline, different, iffy, improper, odd, oddish, out of character, peculiar, queer, unclassifiable, unconformable; **unusual,** amazing, esoteric, exotic, extraordinary, freak, out-of-the-way, outlandish, outré, outsize, rare, raving, remarkable, singular, sui generis, thumping, thundering, unaccustomed, uncommon, unexampled, unheard-of, unique, unparalleled, unprecedented, unwonted *(Archaic),* way-out, without parallel; **eccentric,** antic *(Obs.),* bizarre, crazy, fanciful, fantastic, far-out, funny, gonzo, off the rails, outlandish, Pickwickian, quaint, quizzical, rum, rummy, screwy; **freakish,** bastard, freaky, grotesque, malformed, monstrous, preterhuman, prodigious, teratoid, unnatural; **erratic,** aberrant, irregular, variable; **perverted,** deviant, kinky, psychopathic, wayward; **uncanny,** eerie, eldritch *(Scot.),* fey, preternatural, supernatural, supernormal, transnormal, unco *(Scot.),* unearthly, weird; **teratological,** teratogenic

STRANGELY *adv* abnormally, amazingly, atypically, differently, exceptionally, extraordinarily, peculiarly, uncommonly, unusually, unwontedly; **unnaturally,** bizarrely, crazily, funnily, kookily, oddly, pathologically, pervertedly, queerly, wildly; **irregularly,** anomalously, erratically; **fantastically,** exotically, fancifully, freakishly, grotesquely, monstrously, outlandishly, quaintly; **supernaturally,** eerily, preternaturally, supernormally, uncannily, weirdly

strangeness

STRANGENESS *n* anomalousness, bizarreness, eccentricity, esotericism, exceptionalness, exoticism, extraordinariness, fancifulness, freakiness, freakishness, funniness, grotesqueness, incongruousness, kinkiness, oddness, outlandishness, quaintness, queerness, ratbaggery, singularness, uncommonness, unconformity, uncouthness, unusualness, unwontedness; **abnormality**, aberrance, aberrancy, aberration, abnormity, anomaly, exception, incongruity, irregularity, isolated instance, oddity, peculiarity, peloria, singularity, special case, supernormality; **monstrousness**, enormity, enormousness, grotesqueness, prodigiousness, **eeriness**, feyness, preternaturalism, uncanniness, unearthliness, unnaturalness, weirdness; **perversion**, deviation, kink, pica, twist; **teratology**, teratologist. *See also* FREAK

STRANGE PERSON *n* deviant, eccentric, grotesque, kook, misfit, monster, nonconformist, odd bod, oddball, original, pervert, prodigy, queer fish, ratbag

STRATAGEM *n* artifice, arts, catch, con, contrivance, craft, dodge, double, fake, fakement *(Obs.)*, game, gimmick, legerdemain, little game, manoeuvre, plot, roughie, ruse, shenanigan, shift, shrewdie, sleight of hand, trepan *(Archaic)*, trick, wangle, wheeze *(Brit. Colloq.)*, wrinkle; **bluff**, diversion, evasion, feint, ploy, rort, stew, subterfuge; **trap**, ambush, contrivance, mesh, net, pitfall, web

STRATIFICATION *n* bedding, delamination, interlamination, interstratification, lamination; **scaliness**, flakiness, foliation, imbrication, squamation, squamousness, superimposition, superincumbence, superincumbency, superposition

STREAM *n* arroyo, creek, englacial stream, flow, fresh, freshet, tail; **streamlet**, beck *(Brit.)*, brook, brooklet, burn *(Scot.)*, millstream, rill, rivulet, runlet, runnel; **river**, thoroughfare, torrent, trunk, watercourse; **tributary**, affluent, anabranch, arm, branch, confluent, distributary, effluent, feeder, influent, reach, wadi; **underground river**, sub-artesian water, underdrainage, vein; **gush**, flush, jet, spurt, surge, upsurge; **confluence**, conflux, estuary, mouth; **slack water**, backwater, fan delta, marsh, stagnant pool, swamp. *See also* CURRENT; FLOW; SPRING

STREAMY *adj* englacial, fluvial, fluviatile, fluvioglacial, potamic, riverine; **tributary**, estuarial, estuarine, upriver; **fountain-like**, fontal

STRENGTH *n* arm, force, main, might, mightiness, muscle, potence, potency, potentness, power, powerfulness; **muscularity**, beef, brawn, brawniness, heftiness, huskiness, robustness, stalwartness, steeliness, sthenia; **wiriness**, athleticism, stringiness; **vigour**, juice, nerve, pith, sinew; **machismo**, lustiness, manliness, robustness, rudeness, ruggedness, vigorousness; **sturdiness**, stockiness, stoutness

STRENGTHEN *v* fortify, harden, reinforce, sinew, steel, stiffen, tone up; **consolidate**, build up, confirm; **brace up**, fortify, man, nerve, rally; **reinforce**, brace, pile, rib, riprap, stay *(Archaic)*, support, sustain; **fortify**, arm, reinforce, sconce *(Obs.)*; **harden**, anneal, steel, temper; **proof**, weatherproof

strengthener

STRENGTHENER *n* brace, bracer, fortifier, reinforcement, stiffener

STRICT *adj* martinetish, no-nonsense, rigid, Spartan, tight, unswerving; **hard and fast**, binding, infrangible, ironclad, irrefragable, strictly enforced, unbreakable; **puritanical**, ascetic, ascetical, austere, Calvinistic, dour, hard on oneself, orthodox, prudish, puritan, straight-arrow, straitlaced; **harsh**, a bit much, a bit solid, demanding, draconian, draconic, exacting, exigent, fierce, gruelling, rigoristic, rigorous, searching, severe, strait *(Archaic)*, stringent; **unmerciful**, hard-baked, hard-headed, inflexible, intransigent, iron-handed, merciless, obdurate, relentless, unbending, uncompromising, unrelenting, unsparing, unyielding; **astringent**, cruel, cutting, sharp; **persecutory**, discriminatory, down on, persecutive, punitive, rough on; **firm**, grim, hard, hard as nails, iron, rugged, stark *(Archaic)*, stern, stiff

STRICTLY *adv* according to the book, literally, rigidly, strictly speaking, technically, to the letter, verbatim, word for word; **harshly**, cruelly, grimly, hard, intransigently, mercilessly, relentlessly, roundly, ruggedly, unmercifully, unrelentingly, unsparingly, with a heavy hand; **stringently**, severely, sharply, starkly, sternly; **exactingly**, draconically, rigorously, straitly; **firmly**, infrangibly, irrefragably, stiffly, unbendingly; **puritanically**, ascetically, astringently, austerely, dourly

STRICT PERSON *n* disciplinarian, Dutch uncle, formalist, hanging judge, hard master, hard taskmaster, martinet, slavedriver, tyrant; **intran-**

498

stroke

sigent, die-hard, rigorist, stickler; **puritan**, ascetic, Calvinist, Hole and Corner man *(Hist.)*, Spartan

STRIKE *n* ban, black ban, green ban, limitation, sit-down, sit-down strike, sit-in, walkout, wildcat strike

STRING *n* aglet, apron-strings, bootlace, bride, cordon, drawstring, fillet, lace, lacing, latchstring, petersham, point *(Archaic)*, shoelace, streamer, tie; **twine**, cordelier, purl, spun yarn, tatting, torsade, whipcord, whipping; **ornamental cord**, aiguillette, braid.
See also CORD; TAPE; THREAD

STRING INSTRUMENT *n* chest of viols, strings; **violin**, fiddle, kit, pouchette, rebec, sourdine; **viola**, alto, second, tenor; **cello**, violoncello; **double bass**, barytone, bull fiddle, contrabass, string bass, tea-chest bass; **viol**, bass viol, chordophone, double-bass viol, gamba, viola d'amore, viola da braccio, viola da gamba, violone; **bow**, fiddle bow, fiddlestick; **mute**, sordiao, sourdine; **nail violin**, nail harmonica, singing saw

STRIVER *n* conchie, doer, endeavourer, perfectionist; **battler**, grinder, lucubrator, plodder, plugger; **workhorse**, a beggar for punishment, a tiger for punishment, grafter, heaver, labourer, party hack, toiler

STRIVING *adj* conative, grasping, struggling; **last-ditch**, all-out, desperate; **effortful**, essayistic

STROKE *n* agricultural, backhand, backstroke, bunt, cover drive, drive, half-volley, lob, outstroke, pelt, rush, slash, smash, strike, swash, swipe, volley; **slice**, back cut, chop, chop stroke, cross-shot, cut, glance, late cut, leg glance, pitch shot, sweep; **hook**, edge, snick, top; **shot**, break

stroke *(Billiards)*, bricole, cannon, carom, follow, massé; **thrust**, bind, botte *(Fencing)*, home thrust, joust, lunge, tilt. *See also* HIT; TAP; KICK

STRONG *adj* barrel-chested, brawny, built like a brick, built like a brick shithouse, bull, bullish, bullocky, hefty, husky, mesomorphic *(Physiol.)*, muscly, muscular, nuggetty, powerful, staunch, sthenic, stocky, stout, strong as a mallee bull, strong as an ox, sturdy, well-built; **mighty**, armipotent, main *(Obs.)*, potent, potential *(Rare)*; **herculean**, Atlantean, titanic; **athletic**, able-bodied, amazonian, hard-fisted, sinewy, strapping, stringy, thewy, wiry; **robust**, bouncing, doughty, full-blooded, hardy, lustful *(Archaic)*, lusty, nervy, robustious, rude, rugged, stalwart, two-fisted *(U.S.)*, vigorous; **virile**, macho, manly, masculine; **inexhaustible**, fatigueless, relentless, staminal, tireless, unstoppable, untiring, unwearied

STRONGLY *adv* athletically, doughtily, heftily, lustily, mightily, muscularly, potently, powerfully, robustiously, robustly, rudely, ruggedly, stalwartly, stockily, stoutly, sturdily, vigorously, with might and main; **tirelessly**, inexhaustibly, relentlessly, unstoppably, unweariedly

STRONG PERSON *n* athlete, Atlas, ball of muscle, ball of strength, behemoth, bruiser, bull, butch, gangster *(N.Z. Colloq.)*, giant, Goliath, he-man, Hercules, husky *(U.S.)*, iron man, lion, macho, muscle man, Samson, stalwart, strapper, strongman, superman, Tarzan, titan; **nugget**, mesomorph; **giantess**, Amazon, Boadicea, virago

STRUCTURAL *adj* architectonic, architectural, constructional, constructive, tectonic; **skeletal**, anatomical, osteological, physiological; **prefabricated**, demountable, modular

STRUCTURE *n* composition, constitution, contexture, make, make-up, microstructure, morphology, ordonnance, workings; **build**, anatomy, frame, physique; **architecture**, mode, style; **crystal lattice**, macrostructure, space lattice; **formation**, crystallisation, figuration. *See also* SHAPE

STUBBORN *adj* adamant, diehard, dogged, impracticable, inexorable, inflexible, intractable, obdurate, obstinate, opinionated, opinionative, pertinacious, self-opinionated, self-willed, stiff, stiff-necked, tenacious, uncompromising, unshakeable, unswayed; **determined**, hard-bitten, hard-set, hardened, hell-bent, recusant, tough; **perverse**, bloody, bloody-minded, bolshie, contumacious, cross-grained, cussed, difficult, gnarled, gnarly, incorrigible, intransigent, peevish *(Obs.)*, refractory, restive, thwart *(Archaic)*, unmanageable, unreasonable, untoward *(Archaic)*, wilful, wrong-headed; **mulish**, asinine, boneheaded, bull-headed, bullet-headed, bullish, ornery *(U.S.)*, pigheaded, piggish

STUBBORNLY *adv* determinedly, doggedly, inexorably, inflexibly, intractably, obdurately, obstinately, pertinaciously, stiffly, tenaciously; **perversely**, cussedly, incorrigibly, refractorily, restively, unmanageably, unreasonably, untowardly *(Archaic)*, wilfully, wrong-headedly; **mulishly**, asininely, bull-headedly, piggishly

STUBBORNNESS *n* contumacy, doggedness, impracticability, inconvincibility, inexorableness, inexorability, intractability, intractableness, intransigence, intransigency, obduracy, obdurateness, obstinacy, obstinateness, recusancy, refractoriness, tenaciousness, tenacity; **self-will,** piggery, piggishness, pigheadedness, wilfulness; **bloody-mindedness,** cussedness, incompliancy, perverseness, perversity, restiveness, wrong-headedness; **asininity,** mulishness

STUBBORN PERSON *n* bolshie, hard nut to crack, hardliner, hardnose, incorrigible, intransigent, trac *(Prison Colloq.)*; **bonehead,** bullet-head, bullhead, donkey, mule, pig

STUDENTSHIP *n* discipleship, fellowship, undergraduateship; **apprenticeship,** cadetship, licentiateship

STUDY *v* burn the midnight oil, con, cram, gen up, grind away at, grub, ingrain, lucubrate, mug up, overstudy, swot, swot up; **revise,** bone up on, brush up on, read, restudy, review; **practise,** cultivate, drill, familiarise, knock up, rehearse, run through, train; **major in,** do honours in, minor in *(U.S.),* read, specialise in. *See also* LEARN

STUPID *adj* addlebrained, addlepated, anserine, asinine, barmy, blind, boneheaded, boobyish, bull-headed, bullet-headed, bullish, cloddish, clueless, crass, daggy, dead from the neck up, dense, dippy, dizzy, doltish, drippy, drooby, dumb, dunderheaded, empty, empty-headed, fat-witted, fatheaded, fatuous, foolish, fuckwitted, goofy, gormless, headless, insensate, irrational, lubberly, mindless, muddleheaded, mug, nutty, oafish, opaque, pudding-headed, punch-drunk, punchy, ridiculous, silly, silly as a hatful of worms, silly as a snake, silly as a two-bob watch, silly as a wet hen, silly as a wheel, sodden, soft in the head, soft-headed, soggy, spastic, thick, thickheaded, thick-skulled, thick-witted, troglodytic, unthinking, unwise, vacuous, wooden-headed; **slow-witted,** a brick short, a brick short of a load, backward, barren, blockish, blunt, brainless, dead-and-alive, dim, dimwitted, doltish, dopey, dull, dullish, half-witted, inapt, not the full quid, purblind, short a sheet of bark, slow, slow on the uptake, thick as two short planks, three bangers short of a barbie, unapt, unwitting, weak-minded, without enough brains to give oneself a headache, witless; **unintelligent,** a shingle short, anile, cretinous, defective, doddering, doting, feeble-minded, gaga, imbecile, imbecilic, in one's second childhood, ineducable, mentally deficient, mentally handicapped, moronic, retarded, senile, simple, simple-minded, subnormal, unteachable, weak in the upper storey; **superficial,** facile, fatuitous, fluffy, frivolous, shallow, shallow-minded, shortsighted; **stultifying,** retardative, retardatory

STUPIDITY *n* bêtise, blockishness, brainlessness, cloddishness, crassitude, crassness, denseness, density, doltishness, dullness, dumbness, gormlessness, half-wittedness, lubberliness, mindlessness, oafishness, opacity, silliness, simplicity, soft-headedness, sogginess, stupidness, thickheadedness, thickness, unintelligence, vacancy, vacuity, vacuousness, witlessness, woodenheadedness, woodenness; **low intelligence,** amentia, anility, defectiveness, dotage, feeble-mindedness, idiocy, idiotism, imbecility, insanity, madness, mental deficiency, moronism, retardation, senility, simple-mindedness, simpleness, subnormality, unreason, weak-mindedness; **foolishness,** dogberryism, folly, impoliticness, imprudence, insipience, madness, unreason, unwisdom, unwiseness; **superficiality,** fatuity, shallowness, short-sightedness, superficialness

STUPIDLY *adv* asininely, blankly, blockishly, crassly, densely, doltishly, dully, dumbly, glassily, half-wittedly, mindlessly, oafishly, sillily, simple-mindedly, simply, thickly, unintelligently, unthinkingly, unwisely, vacantly, vacuously, witlessly, woodenly

STUPID PERSON *n* ass, automaton, blockhead, blunderbuss, boob, booby, boofhead, bullet-head, bullhead, cement head, changeling *(Archaic),* clod, clodpate, clodpole, clot, cuckoo, cully *(Archaic),* deadshit, dick, dickhead, dill, dillpot, dimwit, dodo, dolt, donkey, dope, doter, doughie, drongo, droob, duffer, dullard, dumb Dora, dumbbell, dumbcluck, dumbo, dumdum, dummy, dunce, dunderhead, egg roll, fathead, flathead, fool, Fred Nerk, fuckwit, galah, gazob, git, goof, goon, goose, gup *(Aborig.),* imbo, innocent, jackass, jay, jerk, jerk-off, juggins, knucklehead, loggerhead, loghead, loon, lout, lowbrow, lubber, lunkhead *(U.S.),* meat-head *(U.S.),* melon, melonhead, moo *(Brit.),* mooncalf, mopoke, moron, mutt, mutton-head, nerd, nig-nog, nincompoop, ningnong, ninny, nit, nitwit, noddy, nong, noodle, numbskull, nutter, oaf, one-ten, parrot, peabrain, pinhead, poon, pudding, pudding head, pup, puppy, rock-ape, sap, saphead, schmuck, shithead, shmo, silly-billy, simpleton, slow-learner, slowcoach, slowpoke, spoony, stock, stupid, subman, thick, thickhead, tomfool, trog, troglodyte, twerp, twit, wally, woodenhead, zany; **imbecile,** ament, cretin, defective, halfwit, idiot, mental defective, moron, subnormal

SUBJECT *n* liegeman, man, serf, vassal; **servant,** assigned servant, dogsbody, flunkey, forced labourer, kanaka, lackey; **slave,** captive, chattel, galley slave, helot, hierodule, peon, serf, thrall, villein; **puppet,** creature, satellite, stooge

SUBJECT MATTER *n* controversy, flute, issue, subject, substance, talk of the town, talking point, topic, topic of the day; **theme,** burden, motif; **text,** article, tirade; **field,** area, domain, field of interest, major *(Educ.),* realm, specialty, territory; **quadrivium,** trivium; **person referred to,** party, subject; **thing referred to,** object, referent

SUBSTITUTE *n* a poor excuse for, alternate, ersatz, fudge, locum, ossia, pinch-hitter, relay, relief, replacement, ring-in, second string, stand-in, sub, surrogate; **changeling,** elfchild, oaf. *See also* EXCHANGE

SUBSTITUTE *v* dub, replace, ring in, subrogate, surrogate; **relieve,** pinch-hit, sit in for, spell, stand in, sub; **graft,** transplant. *See also* EXCHANGE

substitutive *adj* ersatz, false, substitutional, substitutionary; **transpositional**, metathetic, metathetical

SUBTRACT *v* abate, deduct, subduct *(Rare)*, take, take away; **decrease**, apocopate, bang, clip, curtail, cut, cut back, decimate *(Obs.)*, diminish, dock, lessen, lop, pare down, prune, reduce, retrench, snuff, trash, trim, truncate, whittle; **excise**, core, enucleate, exscind, exsect, extirpate, pit, remove; **discount**, allow, knock off, rebate, slash; **detract**, derogate. *See also* CUT OFF

SUCCEED *v* arrive, be in the box seat, bring home the bacon, carry all before one, carry the day, click, come through, crack it, curl the mo, do the trick, get a guernsey, get it together, have it made, make good, make the grade, pass, pull oneself up by the bootstraps, put it across, ride it out, set the world on fire, shine, steal the show, take the cake, triumph, win one's spurs; **win**, carry off, carve out, crack, gain, score, sew up, take; **go like a bomb**, clean up *(Sport)*, get it in one, go great guns, guess it in one, have it in one, romp home, romp in, shit it in, sweep the board, walk away with, walk off with, win at a canter, win by a neck; **land on one's feet**, be on to a good thing, hit the jackpot, strike pay-dirt; **have it both ways**, kill two birds with one stone; **outmatch**, come off best, get the better of, have the better of, have the last laugh on, one-up, outflank, outgo, outperform, outweigh, overmaster, overreach; **get ahead**, be ahead, be going places, distance, draw first blood, gain ground, get to first base, go far, go places, go to town, leave someone for dead, rise, soar, take off

SUCCESS *n* do *(N.Z.)*, go, hit, killing, sleeper *(Colloq.)*, winner, wow; **win**, conquest, game set and match, triumph, vanquishment, victory; **walkover**, landslide, snip, soda, walk-up start, walkaway; **Pyrrhic victory**

SUCCESSFUL *adj* first-past-the-post, fruitful, home and hosed, home on the pig's back, in like Flynn, made, on top, triumphal, triumphant, unbeaten, victorious; **winning**, premier, up

SUCCESSFULLY *adv* conqueringly, effectually, like a charm, swimmingly, with a bang; **triumphantly**, victoriously

SUCCESSFULNESS *n* favourable issue, flying colours, victoriousness, winning; **first place**, first, honours, line honours; **band wagon**

SUCCESSIVELY *adv* in array, in file, in line, in tandem, one by one, sequentially, seriation, successionally, tandem

SUCCESSOR *n* descendant, follower, heir, incomer, succeeder, superseder, supplanter

SUCH IS LIFE *phr* that's the way it goes, that's the way the cookie crumbles, them's the breaks

SUFFOCATE *v* asphyxiate, choke, drown, smother, stifle, strangle, strangulate

SUFFOCATION *n* apnoea, asphyxiation, breathlessness, choking, drowning, smothering

SUN *n* daystar *(Poetic)*, eye of the day *(Poetic)*, midnight sun, Phoebus *(Poetic)*, sun-disc; **aureole**, corona, halo, photosphere, rainband, sunglow;

parhelion, mock sun; **sunspot**, facula, flocculus, penumbra, solar flare, solar wind, umbra. *See also* STAR

SUNBAKE *v* bask *(Archaic)*, insolate, sun, sunbathe

SUPERFICIALLY *adv* on the surface, skin-deep, spread thin

SUPERIOR *adj* best, crack, crackerjack, cracking, excellent, first, first-rate, giant, good, great, greatest, maximal, of the first water, ripping, spiffing *(Brit.)*, super, super-duper, superfine, superlative, top, top-flight, topping *(Obs.)*; **above average**, a cut above, head and shoulders above, in a different class, in a different league, more than a match for, streets ahead; **incomparable**, beyond compare, inapproachable, inimitable, matchless, nonpareil, Olympian, out of this world, supereminent, superordinate, unapproachable, unbeatable, unequalled, unmatched, unparalleled, unrivalled, unsurpassed, untouchable, world-beating; **supreme**, divine, magnificent, sublime, supernal, surpassing, transcendent, transcendental; **classy**, blue-chip, blue-ribbon, classic, deluxe, export, high-toned, quality, silk department, up-market; **elect**, chosen; **prize**, prize-winning, record, record-breaking, winning

SUPERIORITY *n* distinction, eminence, excellence, excellency, first class, meliority, pre-eminence, prominence, superlativeness; **matchlessness**, divineness, divinity, inapproachability, incomparability, incomparableness, loftiness, sublimeness, sublimity, supremeness, surpassingness, transcendence, transcendentness, ultimateness, unapproachableness; **quality**, goodness, value, worth; **one-upmanship**

SUPERIORLY *adv* best, excellently, sublimely, supereminently, superlatively, supernally, supremely, surpassing *(Obs. Poetic)*, surpassingly, transcendentally, transcendently; **incomparably**, inapproachably, matchlessly, unapproachably; **above**, beyond, extra, far and away, head and shoulders above, out and away, over; **par excellence**, beyond compare; **in the ascendant**, one jump ahead

SUPERNATURAL *adj* hyperphysical, miraculous, mythical, paranormal, preternatural, psychic, superhuman, supernaturalist, supernaturalistic, supersensual, transcendental; **occult**, cabbalistic, cryptic, esoteric, hermetic, masonic, mystic, mystical, occultist, Rosicrucian, secret; **spiritistic**, spiritual, spiritualist, spiritualistic, unfleshly; **parapsychological**; **unearthly**, eerie, spooky, uncanny, weird; **clairvoyant**, canny *(Archaic)*, clairaudient, clairsentient, mediumistic, second-sighted, telepathic; **telekinetic**, psychokinetic; **shamanic**, sibylic, sibylline; **witching**, wizard, wizardly; **bedevilled**, bewitched, possessed, unlaid; **haunted**, ghost-ridden

SUPERNATURAL EVENT *n* materialisation, precipitation, psychography; **astral trip**, astral travel, exteriorisation; **bedevilment**, bewitching, entrancement, possession, trance; **psychokinesis**, planchette, telekinesis, teleportation; **table-lifting**, spirit-rapping, table-turning; **ouija**, ouija-board, psychograph; **miracle**, mirabilia, wonder; **augury**, divination, sortilege

SUPERNATURALLY *adv* mystically, superhumanly

SUPPLIER *n* accommodator, caterer, endower, equipper, fitter, furnisher, maintainer, organiser, outfitter, provider, provisioner, purveyor; **quartermaster**, camp follower, commissary, feeder, sutler, victualler, vivandière; **housekeeper**, butler, cellarman, manciple *(Brit.)*, servant, steward

SUPPLIES *n* allowance, ammunition *(Obs.)*, G.I. *(U.S. Army Colloq.)*, necessities, needs, resources, stores, viaticum, wherewithal; **commodity**, sideline, staple; **property**, matériel, merchandise, stock-in-trade, wares; **equipment**, baggage, gear, hardware, impedimenta; **provisions**, canteen, commons *(Brit.)*, groceries, grubstake, iron rations, provender, rations, victuals *(Archaic)*; **portion**, helping, serve; **trousseau**, layette, whites *(Brit.)*

SUPPLY *n* aid, endowment, fitment, furnishing, maintenance, provision, purveyance, service, subvention, suppliance, sustentation; **supply bill**, advance, civil list *(Brit.)*; **airdrop**, airlift, tanker service

SUPPLY *v* bring home the bacon, fill, make good, munition, plenish *(Scot.)*, prime, provision, ration, reinforce, replenish, restock, victual; **provide**, afford, come to light with, come up with, feed, find, furnish, lay on, line up, minister to *(Archaic)*, ply, present, purvey; **provide for**, allow for, cater for, do for, fend for, make provision for

SUPPLY VEHICLE *n* baggage train, cargo ship, container ship, container terminal, freight ship, freighter, lorry, road train, RORO, semitrailer, supply train

SUPPORT *n* brace, crutch, prop, rest, stay; **base**, basement, basis, bed, bedding, bedrock, box bed, drum, foundation, groundwork, hardcore, pigsty *(Railways)*, putlog, socle, step *(Naut.)*, stock, stylobate, substratum *(Biol.)*, substruction, substructure; **keystone**, cornerstone, foundation stone, monolith, raft, springer; **wall**, embankment, retaining wall; **float**, pontoon, raft; **fulcrum**, arbor *(Mach.)*, axis, axle, hinge, oarlock, pivot, racer *(Gunnery)*, rowlock, spindle, swivel *(Gunnery)*, thole *(Naut.)*, tholepin, trunnion *(Gunnery)*; **runner**, rocker, trundle, undercarriage *(Vehicles)*; **rest**, arm, armrest, back rest, cantle, chinrest *(Music)*, headrest, ladder back *(Furnit.)*; **bridge**, jigger, rest *(Billiards)*; **spider**; **footrest**, footboard, footing, footstool, hassock, horseblock, ottoman *(Furnit.)*, plank, pouf, rung, running board, scarcement, skid, step, stretcher *(Rowing)*, tread, tuffet

SUPPORT *v* base, bear, endure, prop, shoulder, stay, sustain, take the strain, upbear *(Rare)*, uphold; **bolster**, buttress, chock *(Naut.)*, corbel *(Archit.)*, jack up, pile, pillar, rail, reinforce, rib, shore, shore up, slab, spile, stanchion, steady, stick, strengthen, strut, timber, trig, truss, underlay, underpin, underprop, underset; **hold**, pin, stake; **brace**, bracket, clamp, cleat, gusset, traverse *(Naut.)*; **mount**, block, frame, set, step *(Naut.)*; **scaffold**, espalier, trellis; **crutch**, splint, **cushion**, pillow, seat; **pivot**, poise, stabilise

SUPPORTED *adj* backed, bolstered, mounted, ribbed, secured, transomed, trussed, walled; **highblocked**, highset; **suspended**, overhung, underhung

SUPPORTING *adj* sustentacular; **structural**, skeletal; **base**, foundation

SURETY *n* assurance, bond, cover, coverage, insurance, protection, security; **guarantee**, avouchment, guaranty, promise, warrant, warranty; **pledge**, bail, collateral, deposit, earnest, gage, hostage, pawn, plight *(Rare)*, wage *(Obs.)*; **trust**, discretionary trust, fixed trust, flexible trust, trust corporation; **mortgage**, equitable mortgage, hypothec *(Roman Law)*, hypothecation, legal mortgage, stock mortgage; **suretyship**, bailment, sponsion, sponsorship; **offsetting**, covering, crossholding, safeguarding

SURF *n* choppy water, comb, head sea, shoulder, tube; **wave**, billow, bore, eagre, surge, swell, tidal wave, tsunami; **breaker**, beach comber, beacher, hump, shore break, slop; **greenback**, close-out, comber, greenie; **whitecap**, haystack, white horse; **ripple**, beach break, set; **wake**, backwash. *See also* SEA

SURFBOARD *n* board, body board, boogie board, downrailer, elephant gun, hot dog, kickboard, kneeboard, malibu board, pin, pintail, pop-out, spear, stubby, surf mat, surfoplane

SURFER *n* aquanaut, boardie, clubbie, goofy-foot, hot-dogger, natural foot, seaweed, skindiver, surfie, water-baby, water-rat, wax-head

SURPASS *v* exceed, excel, head, rise to the occasion, surmount *(Obs.)*, top, tower over; **eclipse**, extinguish, overshadow, overshine, steal the show, transcend; **lead the way**, break the record, gain ground, go ahead, never miss a trick, not miss a trick, outpace, outrange, outrun, pull ahead, run; **show up**, cast in the shade, put in the shade, take the shine out of; **outclass**, knock spots off, lick, outdo, outrank, rank *(U.S.)*, ring the board, ring the shed, run rings round someone, wipe the floor with; **outact**, outbrave, outsing; **best**, beat, defeat, encompass *(Obs.)*, get the better of, have someone on the hip, have the laugh on, jump the gun, outmanoeuvre, outplay, outwit, score off, steal a march on; **better**, cap, euchre *(U.S.)*, improve on, increase, overtop, trump, up

SURPLUS *n* deluge, drug *(Comm.)*, excess, flood, nimiety, outpouring, overflow, overplus *(U.S.)*, overrun, overstock, oversupply, pile-up, plethora, superfluity, superflux, surplusage; **more than enough**, bellyful, glut, gutful, surfeit, too much, too much of a good thing; **overdose**, OD, overkill; **luxury**, fruit for the sideboard, luxury article, luxury item, milk and honey, more than is needed; **overlap**, allowance, margin, over; **something extra**, bonus, fringe benefit, gash; **extra person**, odd man out, super, supernumerary

SURPLUS *adj* excess, luxury, overabundant, redundant, superabundant, supererogatory, superfluous, supernumerary, uncalled-for, unnecessary, waste; **overfull**, bursting, congested, crammed, engorged, flown *(Archaic)*, flush, inflated, overcrowded, plethoric, rolling in, smothery, stuffed, turgid; **extra**, over, ultra

surprise / **swamp**

SURPRISE *n* amaze *(Archaic)*, amazement, astonishment, surprisal, wonder; **alarm,** shock, startle.   *See also* ASTONISHMENT

SURPRISE *v* amaze, astonish, astound, bowl over, make someone open his eyes; **shock,** alarm, appal, startle, take aback; **take by surprise,** ambush, bushwhack, catch, catch off-guard, catch out, catch unawares, get the jump on, king-hit, overtake.   *See also* ASTONISH

SURPRISED *adj* alarmed, like a stunned mullet, startled, taken aback; **astonished,** astounded, bushwhacked, thunderstruck.   *See also* ASTONISHED

SURPRISER *n* dumbfounder, eye-opener, shocker, startler; **bombshell,** bolt out of the blue, sucker punch *(Boxing),* thunderbolt; **bonus,** dark horse, godsend, manna from heaven; **irony,** bricole, note, sudden, surprise ending, turn-up, turn-up for the books

SURPRISING *adj* precipitant, precipitate, precipitative, precipitous, sudden, unpremeditated; **astonishing,** amazing, shock, shocking, spooky, startling; **surprise,** extemporary *(Obs.),* uncalculated, unexpected, unforeseen, unguessed, unheralded; **bonus,** too good to be true, unhoped-for, unlooked-for.   *See also* ASTONISHING

SURPRISINGLY *adv* amazingly, astonishingly, startlingly; **unexpectedly,** against all expectations, by surprise, contrary to all expectations, in an unguarded moment, like a thief in the night, out of the blue, unawares, without warning; **suddenly,** all at once, all of a sudden, amain *(Archaic),* precipitantly, precipitately, precipitously, sudden *(Poetic);* **strange to say,** marvellous to relate, mirabile dictu.   *See also* ASTONISHINGLY

SURROUND *v* box in, compass, encircle, enclose, hem in, stake out; **circle,** embrace, encompass, involve, round, wreathe; **engird,** encincture, enlace, girdle, hoop, loop, span; **enfold,** swathe, wrap

SURROUNDING *adj* all-round *(U.S.),* ambient, background, circum-ambient, circumfluent, circumfluous, circumjacent, outward

SURROUNDINGS *n* entourage, environs, geographic environment *(Sociol.),* precincts, purlieu, surrounds; **environment,** habitat, medium, milieu; **element,** sphere, world; **ecosphere,** ecosystem, macrocosm; **encirclement,** encincture, encompassment, enlacement; **aureole,** border, halo; **setting,** background, location *(Films),* mise en scène, scene, scenery, stage; **context,** frame of reference; **atmosphere,** aura, climate, vibes, vibrations; **ambience,** circumambience, circumfluence, circumfusion

SUSCEPTIBLENESS *n* exorability, impressibility, impressionability, impressionableness, persuasibility, pliability, pliancy, sensibility, sensitiveness, sensitivity, suggestibility, suggestiveness, susceptibility, susceptiveness, susceptivity, tractability, tractableness; **amenability,** amenableness, other-directedness, other-direction, perviousness

SWAMP *n* alluvion, bog, flat, flow *(Scot.),* gluepot, innings, marish *(Archaic),* marsh, mire, morass, mud-flat, quagmire, quicksand, slob

swamp 507 **swimmer**

(Irish), slough, wallow, wash; **fen,** bayou (U.S.), everglade (U.S.), salina, salt marsh, shott, wet ground; **swampland,** maremma, marshland, wetlands; **paddy field,** prairie (U.S.); **mud,** mire, ooze, slush

SWAMPINESS n marshiness, squashiness

SWAMPY adj boggy, fenny, marish (Archaic), marshy, paludal, plashy, quaggy, sloughy; **oozy,** slushy, splashy, squashy, squelchy; **muddy,** miry

SWEAR v abuse, anathematise, ban (Archaic), bitch and talk, blacken, blackguard, blaspheme, bugger, confound, curse, cuss (U.S.), damn, darn, drat, imprecate, let rip, mozz, swear, swear like a trooper, thunder against, use bad language, use foul language, vilify; **put a curse on someone,** beshrew (Archaic), curse, execrate, hex, imprecate, put the mozz on; **call down curses on,** curse up hill and down dale

SWEARER n abuser, blasphemer, curser, execrator, imprecator

SWEARING n abuse, abusiveness, billingsgate, bullocky, cursing, damnation, dirt, filth, foul language, invective, language, obloquy, unparliamentary language, vilification, vituperation; **blasphemy,** blasphemousness, profanity; **execration,** anathema, anathematisation, ban, excommunication, malediction, proscription; **curse,** commination, cuss (U.S.), dirty word, epithet, imprecation, oath, profanity, scurrility, swearword; **the great Australian adjective,** blankety blank, the big f.

SWEET adj ambrosial, dulcet (Archaic), luscious, nectareous; **syrupy,** cloying, saccharine, sickly, sugary, sweetish, syruplike; **sweetened,** candied, cream, glacé, honied

SWEETEN v candy, crystallize, ice, syrup

SWEETLY adv lusciously, sweet

SWEETNESS n lusciousness, saccharinity, sickliness, sugariness, sweetishness; **sweetener,** honey, sweetening, syrup, topping; **sugar,** cyclamate, dextrose, fructose, fruit sugar, glucose, saccharin; **sweets,** candy, confectionary, guk, gunk, junk food, lollies, toffies; **sweet tooth; sugar concentration,** brix

SWERVE v jink (Rugby), lurch, prop, skew, skid (Aeron.), slew, twist, wheel, whirl; **veer,** broach (Naut.), gripe (Naut.), hang in (Horseracing), hang out (Horseracing), haul, haul off (Naut.), jib, jibe, run off the track, run via the Cape (Horseracing), shy, stay (Naut.), tack, wear (Naut.), weathercock, yaw; **turn,** angle, bear away, bend, claw (Naut.), corner, face (Mil.), fade (Surfing), fall away (Naut.), fleet (Naut.), head, put about (Naut.), square, turn away, warp; **turn round,** about-face, back, back water, box, boxhaul, bring about, chuck a U-ie, go about (Naut.), reverse, stem (Skiing)

SWIM v bathe, body-shoot, body-surf, breast-stroke, drift, fleet (Obs.), float, skinny-dip, snorkel, strike out, tread water; **wade,** slop

SWIMMER n aquanaut, bather, skindiver, skinny-dipper, surfer, wader

SWIMMING *n* body-surfing, natation, skindiving; **swimming stroke,** Australian crawl, backstroke, butterfly, butterfly stroke, crawl, dog paddle, dolphin kick, overarm, scissors kick

SWIMMING *adj* natant, natatorial, pinnigrade

SWIMWEAR *n* bathers, bathing suit, bathing trunks, bikini, cossie, costume, cozzie, diving suit, maillot, monokini, neck-to-knees, string bikini, swimmers, swimming costume, swimming trunks, swimsuit, togs, trunks, waders, vees

SWINDLE *v* chicane, fleece, graft, gyp, hustle *(U.S.)*, job, lamb, make a fast buck, pettifog, racketeer, wangle; **feather one's own nest,** look after number one, look out for number one, take care of oneself; **cheat,** fix, play with marked cards, rig, tamper; **deceive,** deliberately mislead, speak with double tongue, speak with forked tongue, trick out of

SWOLLEN *adj* blubber, blubbery, puffy, strumose, strumous, tumefacient, tumescent, tumid, tumorous; **bulgy,** bulbaceous, bulbous, bunchy, busty, chubby, mushroom, round, turgent *(Obs.)*, turgescent, ventricose; **billowy,** balloon, bloused, blown, bursiform; **potbellied,** poddy *(Brit. Colloq.)*; **humped,** gibbous, humpbacked, humpy, hunchbacked; **blistery,** blebby, bullate, condylomatous, eruptive, scabby, scabrous, torose, vesicular, vesiculate; **crested,** caruncular, carunculate, carunculous, cristate; **tubercular,** polypoid, tuberculate, tuberculoid, tuberculose, tuberculous, tuberose, tuberous, verrucose. *See also* PROTUBERANT; KNOBBY

SWOLLENNESS *n* billowiness, rotundity, rotundness, tuberosity, tumefaction, tumescence, tumidity, turgor; **lumpiness,** bumpiness, gibbousness, nodality, nodosity, tuberculation, verrucosity, vesication, vesiculation; **convexity,** crenation, crenature, entasis, ventricosity; **protrusion,** evagination, exsertion, extrusion, herniation, protraction, salience, saliency

SWORD *n* backsword, bayonet, blade, brand, broadsword, claymore, cold steel, cutlass, épée, estoc, falchion, foil, glaive, hanger, pigsticker, prick *(Obs.)*, rapier, sabre, scimitar, simitar, smallsword, snickersnee, steel, sticker, sword bayonet, Toledo, tuck, yataghan; **sword part,** chape, crossguard, foible, forte, quillon, roundel; **knife,** anlace, barong, bowie knife, crease, creese, dagger, dirk, flickknife, kris, kukri, machete, misericord, panga, parang, poniard, sheath-knife, shiv *(Brit. Colloq.)*, skean, stiletto, stylet, ulu; **axe,** battle-axe, broadaxe, poleaxe, tomahawk, tommyaxe, tommyhawk, twibill *(Archaic)*

SYSTEMATISATION *n* architectonics, economy *(Theol.)*, systematics, systematism, systematology, systemisation, teleology; **town planning,** Radburn planning

Tt

TABLE *n* bedside cabinet, bedside table, butterfly table, coffee table, counter, desk, draw table, dressing-table, drop-end table, drop-leaf table, extension table, folding table, gate-leg table, kitchen table, lazy Susan, nest of tables, occasional table, pedestal table, round table, telephone table, trestle table, work-table, workbench; **dining table**, breakfast table, dinette, dining-nook, dining suite, dinner table, refectory table; **side table**, console, console table, pier table; **bar**, buffet, cocktail bar, counter. *See also* DESK

TABLEWARE *n* china, chinaware, crockery, dinner service, dinner set, ironware, tea-set; **bowl**, coupe, dariole, eggcup, epergne, fingerbowl, mortar, porringer, ramekin, rice bowl, soup plate, sugar basin, tazza; **saucer**, bonbonnière, coquille, scallop, shell; **tureen**, crater, monteith, punchbowl; **plate**, bombe, butterdish, dish, sizzle plate; **platter**, ashet *(Scot.)*, charger, paten, patina *(Rom. Antiq.)*; **tray**, salver; **cone**, cornet, cornucopia; **coolamon**, pitchi

TACTILE *adj* haptic, tactual, textural; **palpable**, tangible, touchable; **touching**, tangent; **handled**, felt, touched

TAKE *v* adopt, annex, arrogate, assume, borrow, enter *(Law)*, jump *(Mining)*, misappropriate, nim *(Archaic)*; **retake**, repossess, restore, resume; **appropriate**, commandeer, confiscate, convert *(Law)*, expropriate, impound, impress, impropriate, possess oneself of, sequester *(Law)*, sequestrate *(Law)*, usurp; **tax**, attach, distrain, garnishee, levy; **dispossess**, disseise, divest, divest *(Archaic)*, forjudge; **disinherit**, cut off without a cent; **deprive**, bankrupt, beggar, beguile of, bereave, divest *(Archaic)*, do out of *(Colloq.)*, fleece, impoverish, reave *(Archaic)*, steal, strip *(Archaic)*, take from; **crop**, cull, gather, reap, subtract

TAKEABLE *adj* adoptable, appropriable, assumable, attachable *(Obs.)*, confiscable, detachable, distrainable, escheatable, impoundable, pregnable, resumable; **deprivable**, divestible, fleeceable

TAKE ADVANTAGE *v* benefit, profit, work a point; **get the jump on**, gain ascendancy over, get someone's measure, get to the windward of, pull rank, pull the braid

TAKE ADVANTAGE OF *v* bludge on, come it a bit much, let in for, pole on, put in the fangs, put in the hooks, put in the nips, put in the screws, put on, put the acid on, put upon; **leave someone holding the baby**, die on someone, leave in the lurch, not play the game

TAKE DRUGS *v* drop *(Colloq.)*; **turn on**, blow one's mind, bomb out, drop acid, fly high, goof, smoke, snort, trip; **hit up**, hit, mainline, shoot, shoot up, skinpop; **OD**, overdose

TAKER *n* appropriator, enterer, grabber, harpy, Indian giver *(Colloq.)*, snatcher, wrester; **depriver**, confiscator, dispossessor, disseisor, distrainer, expropriator, impounder, sequestrator, usurper; **capturer**, abductor,

taker   510   **talker**

captor, catcher, conqueror, rapist, ravisher, seizer, seizor *(Law)*

TAKE REFUGE *v* go to ground, lay to *(Naut.)*, put in *(Naut.)*, take cover, take shelter

TAKE SHAPE *v* crystallise, jell, shape up

TAKE THE CLOTH *v* profess, serve, take the veil, take vows, vow; **ordain**, cloister, consecrate, cowl, episcopise, incardinate, institute, mitre, order, profess, secularise, tonsure

TAKING *n* annexation, appropriation, arrogation, attachment, confiscation, conversion, dispossession, distrainment, distraint, distress, entry *(Law)*, escheatment, expropriation, forcible entry, impoundage, impoundment, misappropriation, reprise *(Law)*, resumption, sequestration, usurpation; **tax**, deduction, impost; **extortion**, blackmail *(Law)*, Rachmanism, rapacity, shakedown, usury, vampirism; **deprivation**, bereavement, divestiture, divestment, divesture, privation

TAKINGS *n* boot, booty, catch, grab, haul *(Colloq.)*, prize, snatch, spoils, take

TALK *n* civilities, commerce *(Obs.)*, commune, communion, confab, confabulation, conversation, conversazione, converse, dialogue, discourse, give-and-take, intercourse, interlocution, repartee, shop talk, small talk, table talk, tale *(Obs.)*, yabber; **chat**, causerie, chinwag, coze *(Obs.)*, rap, wongi, yarn; **interview**, press conference; **heart-to-heart**, duologue, tete-a-tete; **telephone call**, call, galah session, person-to-person; **chatter**, cackle, chitchat, claver *(Scot.)*, gab, natter, palaver, persiflage, prate, prattle; **gossip**, dirt, furphy, gossiping, scandal, scuttlebutt, tattle. *See also* DISCUSSION

TALK *v* commune, confab, confabulate, confer, converse, dialogue, discourse, get together, have a word with, palaver, parley, pass the flute, pass the kip, powwow, speak, talk shop, wongi, yabber; **negotiate**, talk over; **chat**, bat the breeze, claver *(Scot.)*, coze *(Obs.)*, natter, palaver, pass the time of day, rap, visit *(U.S.)*, yarn; **gossip**, chew the fat, chew the rag, scandal *(Archaic)*, tattle; **gab**, gasbag, go on, jaw, jawbone; **chatter**, cackle, clatter, jabber, mag, prate, prattle, rattle; **discuss**, canvass, controvert, debate, have it out, kick about, kick around, korero *(N.Z.)*, thrash out; **argue**, argy-bargy, bicker

TALKATIVE *adj* chatty, communicative, garrulous, gassy, gossipy, loquacious, of many words, voluble; **conversational**, conferential, north-south interlocutory; **talkback**, open-line

TALKATIVENESS *n* chattiness, communicativeness, garrulity, garrulousness, gassiness, jaw, longwindedness, loquacity, volubility, volubleness

TALKER *n* collocutor, colloquist, conversationalist, converser, debater, dialogist, dialoguer, discourser, interlocutor, interlocutrice, interlocutrix; **windbag**, bag of wind, big mouth, buttonholer, fluter, gasbag, rattletrap, yabberer; **interviewer**, interviewee; **negotiator**, negotiant, **chatterbox**, cackler, chatterer, flibbertigibbet, gabber, magger, magpie, prater, prattler; **gossip**, gossiper, gossipmonger, newsmonger, scandalmonger, tattler

TALK NONSENSE *v* babble, blather, chatter, crap, crap on, fudge, gabble, gammon, garble, gas, gibber, jabber, jargon, jargonise, mag, maunder, patter, piffle, quibble, rabbit on, rant, rave, signify little, talk rubbish, talk through one's arse, talk through one's hat, talk through the back of one's neck, twaddle, waffle, yak, yawp

TALL *adj* lanky, rangy, strapping, tallish; **towering**, all-highest, beetling, colossal, dominating, dominative, eminent, exalted, giant, gigantic, grand, high, high-rise, lofty, majestic, overhanging, soaring, sublime *(Poetic)*, supernal, topless, towery, uplifted; **spired**, spirelike, spiry, towerlike, towery, turrical, turriculate. *See also* HIGH; MOUNTAINOUS

TALL PERSON *n* beanpole, beanstalk, colossus, giant, giraffe, lofty, lolly legs, long streak of misery, long streak of pelican shit, longshanks, six-footer, slab, strapper, streak, yard of drink water

TALLY-HO *interj* halloo, hallow, hoicks, yo-ho, yoicks

TANGIBLE *adj* bodily, concrete, concretive, corporal, corporeal, cosmic, external *(Metaphys.)*, fleshly, material, mechanical, natural, objective, palpable, phenomenal, physical, spatiotemporal, substantial

TANGIBLY *adv* concretely, concretively, corporally, corporeally, materially, physically, substantially

TANGLE *n* bob, can of worms, disorder, dog's breakfast, dog's dinner, knot, mat, mess, nodus, ravel, shakings *(Naut.)*, snarl, twine; **maze**, Chinese puzzle, labyrinth, wheels within wheels. *See also* COMPLEXITY; **imbroglio**, fracas, melee; **rigmarole**, ins and outs, involution; **complex**, composite, compound, network, structure, system, tissue

TANGLE *v* convolute, disorder, embrangle, enmesh, entangle, entrammel, fall foul of, foul, jumble, knot, mat, ravel, shuffle, snarl, wind

TANGLED *adj* afoul, cotted *(Wool)*, disordered, entangled, foul, implicit *(Obs.)*, inextricable, kaleidoscopic, knotted, knotty, matted, perplexed, tangly; **mazelike**, labyrinthine, mazy. *See also* COMPLEX

TAP *n* bung, faucet *(U.S.)*, plug, spigot, stop; **valve**, ball valve, butterfly valve, check valve, inlet valve, mixing valve, needle valve, piston *(Music)*, slide valve, throttle valve; **cock**, ballcock, bib cock, petcock, stopcock, turncock

TAPE *n* ferret, inkle, marking tape, masking tape, red tape, ribbon, strapping; **band**, sandal, sling, snood, strap, thong; **bandage**, brace, breeching, ligature, tourniquet; **belt**, belting, girdle, tie

TAPESTRY *n* altarpiece, arras, dossal, frontlet, hanging, reredos, wall-hanging

TASTE *n* aftertaste, degustation *(Obs.)*, finish; **flavour**, body, flavouring, race, sapor, savour; **tang**, nip, smack, soupçon, tinge; **tastiness**, delicateness, flavoursomeness, freshness, mellowness, palatability, richness, sapidity, savouriness; **palate**, relish, taste-buds, tooth; **acquired taste**, foretaste, prelibation; **gustation**, tea-tasting, wine-tasting

TASTE *v* eat, lick, relish, sample, savour, smack one's lips, try; **taste of**, smack of; **mellow**, age, mature, ripen; **flavour**, tinge

TASTEFUL *adj* choice, exquisite, fancy, fine; **chic**, dapper, dressy, elegant, nifty, nobby; **stylish**, smart, sophisticated, urbane; **up-market**, aristocratic, classy, deluxe, highbrow, posh, rich, silken, swell, toffy

TASTEFULLY *adv* aesthetically, civilly, delicately, genteelly, in good taste, politely, seemly; **elegantly**, dapperly, dressily, urbanely; **daintily**, delicately, finically, fussily, gently, squeamishly; **aristocratically**, poshly, richly

TASTER *n* savourer, tea-taster, wine-taster

TASTY *adj* agreeable, appetizing, delicate, delicious, flavorous, flavourful, flavoursome, fresh, sapid, yummy; **full-bodied**, big, foxy, fruity, generous, gutsy, rancio, rich, strong, vintage; **mellow**, creamy, smooth; **plain**, mild

TAX *n* cess *(Brit.)*, clawback *(Colloq.)*, dues, farm *(Obs.)*, geld, price *(Archaic)*, scot *(Archaic)*, ship money *(Hist.)*, tallage *(Hist.)*, taxation, tithe, tithing; **income tax**, capital gains tax, gift tax, indirect tax, supertax, surtax, wealth tax, withholding tax; **duty**, countervailing duty, death duty, droit, estate duty, reprise, stamp duty, valuation; **excise**, consumption tax, customs, customs duties, fair trade *(Brit.)*, primage, purchase tax *(Brit.)*, sales tax, tariff, V.A.T., value added tax; **levy**, contribution, custom, impost, task *(Obs.)*, toll, tribute; **poll tax**, capitation, head money

TAX *v* assess, excise, overtax, surtax, tariff, task *(Obs.)*

TAX COLLECTOR *n* assessor, farmer, inspector, publican *(Rom. Antiq.)*, taxman; **customs officer**, exciseman, gauger

TEACH *v* coach, cram, cultivate, drill, edify, educate, enlighten, ground, illumine, instruct, prepare, qualify, school, sophisticate, spoon-feed, team-teach, train, tutor; **induct**, apprentice, familiarise, implant, inculcate, indoctrinate in, initiate, introduce; **lecture**, harangue, preach, promulgate, proselytise, sermonise; **illustrate**, demonstrate, show, work at the chalkface; **examine**, assess, catechise; **re-educate**, rehabilitate

TEACHABLE *adj* docile, educable; **house-trained**, housebroken, toilet-trained

TEACHER *n* academic, educationalist, educationist, educator, guide, heurist, instructor, mentor, pedagogue, preceptor, scribe *(Jewish Hist.)*, seminarian, sophist *(Greek Antiq.)*; **school-teacher**, beak, boss, chalkie, crammer *(Brit.)*, dame, dominie, form master, form mistress, governess, guzinter, headmaster, headmistress, housemaster, housemistress, master, mistress, P.T. instructor, pedant *(Obs.)*, principal, relief teacher, remedial teacher, schoolie, schoolman, schoolmarm, schoolmaster, schoolmistress, sportsmaster, sportsmistress, subprincipal; **tutor**, supervisor, teacher aide, usher *(Brit. Archaic)*; **professor**, aspro, associate professor, chancellor, dean, don, emeritus, proctor, prof, provost, reader, rector, senior lecturer, vice-chancellor, visiting professor; **lecturer**, docent *(U.S.)*, senior tutor, teaching fellow; **rhetor**, rhetorician; **teaching staff**, cadre, department, faculty, school; **coach,** catechiser, catechist, drillmaster, riding master, trainer; **animal trainer,** breaker, horsebreaker, lion tamer; **disciplinarian,** discipliner. *See also* ENLIGHTENER

TEACHING *n* catechesis, direction, drilling, edification, exegesis, explanation, implantation, inculcation, indoctrination, initiation, instruction, manual training, preaching, promulgation, propaganda, proselytism, schooling, spoon-feeding, training, tuition, tutelage, tutorage; **guidance,** consciousness raising, edification, enlightenment; **rearing,** breeding, bringing-up, civilisation, cultivation, house-training, nurture, parenting, potty-training, toilet-training, upbringing; **didacticism,** didactics, doctrinism, pedagogics, pedagogy, scholasticism. *See also* EDUCATION

TEACHING *adj* catechetical, catechistic, consciousness-raising, didactic, edificatory, educational, exegetical, exponential, indoctrinatory, instructional, instructive, mind-expanding, pedagogic, pedagogical, preceptive, sermonic, tuitionary; **introductory,** preliminary, propaedeutic, simple; **advanced,** difficult

TEACHING METHOD *n* chalk and talk, direct method, heuristic method, hypnopaedia, Montessori method, Socratic method, team teaching; **teaching aid,** cuisenaire rods, epidiascope, language laboratory, overhead projector, teaching machine, visual aid

TEACHINGS *n* doctrine; **primer,** catechism, prescribed text, set book, textbook, workbook

TELECAST *v* beam *(Radio),* broadcast, colourcast, newscast, televise, transmit

TELECOMMUNICATIONS *n* communications, electronic media, media, telecine; **public broadcasting; community radio;** broadcast, colourcast, feature, newscast, outside broadcast, phone-in, satellite broadcast, simulcast, talkback, telecast, telefilm, teleplay, telethon, transcription, transmission; **telephone,** blower, extension, handpiece, handset, hot line, intercom, intercommunication system, interphone, party line, pay phone *(U.S.),* phone, processor, public telephone, receiver, red phone, tie line, videophone; **telephone call,** bell, buzz, international call, ISD call, person-to-person call, reverse-charge call, ring, STD call, tingle, tinkle, trunk call; **international subscriber dialling,** ISD code, STD code, subscriber trunk dialling; **exchange,** central *(U.S.),* PABX, PBX, Private Automatic Branch Exchange, private branch exchange, step-by-step, telephone exchange, trunks; **switchboard,** crossbar switch, switch; **telephone box,** callbox *(Brit.),* kiosk *(Brit.),* pay station *(U.S.);* **telegraphy,** telegraphics; **teleprinter,** teletype, teletypewriter, telex. *See also* TELEVISION; RADIO

TELECOMMUNICATIONS STATION *n* citizen band radio, earth station, pirate radio, radio station, relay station, station, studio, television station; **network,** hook-up, radio link, radio relay; **landline,** transmission line; **communication satellite,** comsat; **signal,** airwaves, carrier, carrier wave, continuous waves, direct ray, direct

telecommunications 514 **tester**

wave, ground wave, medium wave, radio signal, radio wave, sky wave; **crystal,** cat's whisker, crystal detector, crystal rectifier; **control room**

TELEPHONE v bell, buzz, call, dial, get through to, ring, ring up

TELEVISION n black-and-white, boob tube, cable television, closed-circuit television, colour television, idiot box, monitor, satellite television, set, small screen, tellie, the box, tube, TV, video *(U.S.);* **video cassette recorder,** teleplayer, VCR, video recorder; **phototelegraphy,** telephotography, teletext; **teleprompter,** autocue

TEMPERATURE n absolute temperature, critical temperature, curie point, fixed point, melting point, strike, sulphur point, transition temperature, triple point; **boiling point,** fire point, flashpoint, ignition temperature, steam point; **body temperature,** blood heat; **heat capacity,** calorific value, heat content, latent heat, water equivalent

TEMPORAL adj chronological, fourth-dimensional, space-time, time

TEMPORARILY adv ad hoc, for the moment, for the nonce, for the time being, in the interim, in the meantime, pro tempore, provisionally; **transitorily,** ephemerally, fleetingly, flickeringly, fugaciously, fugitively, transiently; **in passing,** by the way, casually, en passant; **briefly,** acutely, in the twinkling of an eye, meteorically

TEMPORARINESS n changeableness, currency, impermanence, impermanency, temporality; **transitoriness,** caducity, evanescence, fleetingness, fugacity, fugitiveness, transience, transientness, volatileness, volatility

TEMPORARY APPOINTMENT n commendam, interim council, interregnum, regency, temporals; **temporary,** ad hoc committee, casual, temp, transient; **temporary thing**

TEN n decade, decimal, decuple, dicker *(Hist.),* tenth; **decagon,** decahedron

TEN adj decagonal, decimal, decuman, decuple, denary, tenfold, tenth

TENDRIL n shaft, stem, thread

TEND TO v go, gravitate towards, have in the blood, incline, lean towards, look towards, stand, trend, verge towards

TEST n ascertainment, assay, bio-assay, check, crucible, drill stem test, flame test, herd testing, mantoux test, titration, touch; **experiment,** control experiment, inquiry, leap in the dark, probe; **trial,** field trial, pilot, pilot film, pilot study, run-through, test case, trial run, tryout, walk-through, war game, work-out; **trial by ordeal,** acid test, baptism of fire, ordeal

TEST v approve *(Obs.),* essay, put to the test, tempt *(Obs.),* trial, try out; **try,** discuss *(Rare),* sample, taste; **hypothesise,** explore every avenue, fly a kite, try out an idea; **experiment,** ascertain, assay, prove, titrate; **monitor,** control, evaluate

TEST adj pilot, probative, trial; **probational,** on appro, on approval, on probation, on trial, verificatory

TESTER n analyst, assayer, empiricist, essayist, experimentalist, experimenter, gauger, herd tester, researcher, sampler, scientist; **testing agent,** determinative, gauge, litmus paper, monitor, reagent, test paper, touchstone; **test group,** guineapig, pilot

tester

plant, subject; **control group**, criterion, standard, touchstone, yardstick; **laboratory**, insectary, proving ground, test tube, wind-tunnel

TESTIFIER n attestor, crown witness, deponent, deposer, earwitness, eyewitness, identifier, informant, swearer, voucher, witness, witnesser; **verifier**, affirmant, affirmer, authenticator, compurgator, corroborant, corroborator, establisher

TESTIFY v affirm, attest, bear witness, depone *(Archaic)*, depose, give evidence, jump the box, swear, witness; **argue**, adduce evidence, allege, exhibit, go on, lead evidence

TESTIMONIAL adj a posteriori, demonstrable, demonstrational, deposable, documentary, evidential, evidentiary, manifestable, probative, substantiative; **confirmatory**, corroborative, corroboratory, probate, verificative, verifying

TEXTBOOK n ABC, arithmetic, catechism, geography, grammar, hornbook, institutes, primer, reader, schoolbook, special, speller, spelling book, text; **workbook**, copybook

TEXTILES n cloth, contexture, fabric, homespun, material, stuff, texture, tissue; **knit**, knitting, stockinet; **cotton print**, batik, challis, chiné, futah, India print, persiennes, sarong; **rag**, bribe, fag-end, flock, lock, necks, tatter, thrum, waste; **lining**, buckram, fleece, interfacing, interlining, venetian; **padding**, bombast *(Obs.)*; **suiting**, blanketing, coating, sacking, shirting, skirting, towelling, vesting *(U.S.)*; **waterproof**, camlet, japara, mackintosh, nettlecloth, oilcloth, oiled silk, oilskin, tammy; **lint**, gauze, jaconet; **swatch**, bolt, length, piece,

the best

roll, web. *See also* WEAVE; LACE; SEWING; MANCHESTER

TEXTURE n fabric *(Textiles Geol.)*, finish, wale *(Textiles)*; **viscosity**, consistency; **unit of viscosity**, centipoise, centistokes, stoke, stokes

THANKS FOR NOTHING interj big deal, no thanks to you

THANKYOU interj gramercy *(Archaic)*, merci, merci beaucoup, ta, thanks, thanks a bunch, thanks a million; **Deo gratias**, praise be to God, thanks be to God

THEATRICAL COMPANY n circus, ensemble, rep, repertory, stock company *(U.S.)*, troop *(Rare)*, troupe; **cast**, characters, dramatis personae; **chorus**, duo, nonet, octet, quartet, quintet, septet, sextet, trio

THE AUTHORITIES n Big Brother, faceless men, officialdom, the administration, the elite, the establishment, the powers that be, the ruling classes, them

THE BEST n the acme, the cap, the crème de la crème, the cream, the fat, the first, the pick, the pink, the pride; **the ultimate**, the crest, the glassy, the height, the maximum, the noon, the noontide, the sublime of, the summit, the top, the tops; **first choice**, preference, primary; **nonpareil**, beauty, classic, clinker, clipper, collector's item, cracker, crackerjack, dilly, dinkum, dinky, doozey, dynamite, nonesuch, one out of the box, ringer, ripper, ripsnorter, something else, something else again, something extra *(U.S.)*, speciality, top-liner, topnotcher; **masterpiece**, chef d'oeuvre, magnum opus, masterwork

THE BUSH *n* city surroundings, countryside, meadows and pastures, the country, the land, the open, the provinces, the soil; **bush-country,** brush, bushland, the brigalow, the donga, the mallee, the mulga, the saltbush, the scrub, tiger country, weald *(Archaic),* woodlands, woods; **back country,** back of beyond, back of Bourke, back of the black stump, backblocks, backwoods, booay, boondocks *(U.S.),* cactus, goat country, hinterland, never-never, the outback, the sticks; **dead centre,** dead heart, the centre, the red centre. *See also* RURALISM

THE CHOSEN *n* seed *(Sport),* the elect, top seed; **nominee,** candidate

THE DEAD *n* dearly departed, ghosts, loved ones, shades, the deceased, the defunct, the departed, those who have gone before; **corpse,** ashes, body, cadaver, carcass, corps *(Obs.),* last remains, mummy, relics, stiff; **casualty,** fatality; **zombie,** walking dead; **death rate,** casualty list, death register, death toll, deathroll, mortality, mortality rate, necrology, road toll; **war dead,** the fallen, the slain

THE INTANGIBLE *n* the abstract, the imponderable, the unknowable; **abstraction,** concept, conception, idea, ideal, supposition; **figment,** bubble, idol, imagining, mirage, smoke; **straw company,** kite *(Comm.)*

THE MEDIA *n* electronic media, Fleet Street, fourth estate, print media, the press; **press gallery,** press-box; **journalism,** coverage, photojournalism, reportage; **publication,** syndication; **news agency,** news syndicate, press agency, press office; **newsiness,** newsworthiness

THEN *adv* at that time, there, with that; **during that time,** the while; **sometime,** far, long, somewhere

THEORISATION *n* abstractness, speculativeness, supposititiousness, theoretics

THEORISE *v* hypothesise, philosophise; **propound,** argue, move, move, offer, propose, put up a case, say, submit

THEORIST *n* armchair philosopher, armchair revolutionary, assumer, conjecturer, doctrinaire, doctrinarian, philosopher, philosophiser, presumer, supposer, surmiser, theoretician, theoriser

THE PRESENT *n* here and now, instant, now, nowadays, the present juncture, the present moment, the present time, the times, the twentieth century, today, tonight; **immediacy,** immediateness, instancy

THE PUBLIC *n* body politic, common *(Obs.),* commonality, commonweal *(Archaic),* commonwealth, community, community at large, country, democracy, general *(Archaic),* general public, people, people in general, state; **society,** age, everyone, world

THERMAL *adj* caloric, calorific, phlogistic *(Obs.),* thermic; **thermometric,** calorimetric, calorimetrical, pyrometric, pyrometrical, thermometrical, thermoscopic, thermoscopical; **thermodynamic,** geothermic, photothermic, thermodynamical, thermostatic; **adiabatic,** diathermanous, diathermic, isenthalpic, isocheimal, isothermal, isothermal; **radiant,** convectional, decalescent, endothermic, exothermic; **thermophilic,** thermotaxic, thermotropic

THERMOMETER n Beckmann thermometer, gas thermometer, maximum and minimum thermometer, micropyrometer, platinum thermometer, pyrheliometer, pyrometer, pyrophotometer, resistance thermometer, telethermometer, thermobarograph, thermograph, thermophile, thermoscope; **cryometer,** cryoscope; **thermostat,** calorimeter, pyrostat; **calorie,** British thermal unit, cal, small calorie, therm; **temperature scale,** Celsius scale, centigrade scale, Fahrenheit scale, international practical temperature scale, Kelvin scale, Rankine scale, Reaumur scale; **thermometry,** calorimetry, telethermometry; **thermodynamics,** thermionics, thermochemistry, thermoelectricity, thermostatics

THE SUPERNATURAL n cabbala, magic, the occult, the spiritism; **occultism,** animism, cabbalism, esotericism, esotery, spiritualism, supernaturalism; **witchcraft,** black magic, black mass, demonology, devilry, diablerie, sorcery, witchery, wizardry; **psychomancy,** demonomancy, mythology, necromancy, spirit-rapping; **ESP,** clairaudience, clairsentience, clairvoyance, extrasensory perception, psychometry, second sight, sixth sense; **telepathy,** mind-readng, thought transference, thought-reading; **psychic research,** parapsychology, psychokinetics, psychosophy; **unearthliness,** weirdness

THICK adj blocky, bold, bold-face, chunky, full-faced (Print.), thickish; **wide,** broad, deep, expansive, extensive, outspread, spacious, spread, widish; **spatular,** spatulate; **bloated,** blubbery, puffy; **full,** ample, baggy, generous; **broad,** beamy, broad across the beam, broadish, steatopygic, wide-hipped; **fat,** adipose, corpulent, crass, fatly, fatted, fattish, gross, obese, overweight, paunchy, plump, poddy (Brit.), podgy, porky, portly, pursy, stout, well-built, well-fed, well-rounded; **thickset,** bulky, bull-necked, fubsy, stocky, stubbed, stubby, stumpy; **solid,** dense, heavy, sodden, stodgy

THICKENING n callosity, callus, coagulation, dilatation, induration, varicosity; **chunk,** chump, clog, clot

THICKLY adv bulkily, crassly, fully, podgily, solidly, stockily, stodgily, stoutly, stumpily, thick; **widely,** broadly, extensively, spaciously, wide

THICKNESS n amplitude, beam, breadth, depth, latitude, third dimension, tread, wideness, width; **diameter,** bore, calibre, gauge, module (Archit.), radius; **extent,** expanse, extensiveness, spread; **bulk,** body, bulkiness; **fullness,** bagginess

THIEF n abstracter, acquirer, appropriator, boodler (U.S.), bumper, cribber, cutpurse, dip (Prison), filcher, fingerer, flogger, forty, frisker, head-puller, hoister, jumper (Mining), kleptomaniac, kway, light fingers, lurcher, peter thief (Prison), pickpocket, pilferer, purloiner, pussyfooter, ratter (Mining), robber, shoplifter, sneakthief, snowdropper, stealer, tea-leaf, water-rat (U.S.); **burglar,** cat-burglar, cracksman, housebreaker, picklock, yegg (U.S.); **safebreaker,** safeblower, tankman (Prison); **fence,** receiver of stolen goods; **bandit,** bravo, brigand, bushranger, dacoit, Dick Turpin, footpad, high-

thief   518   **thinking**

wayman, knight of the road, moss-trooper, Ned Kelly, pad, poofterrorter, Robin Hood, thug, waylayer; **pirate**, buccaneer, corsair, filibuster, freebooter, hijacker, marauder, picaroon, privateer, rover *(Archaic)*, sea-robber, sea-rover, skyjacker, viking, wrecker; **looter**, depredator, despoiler, forayer, harpy, marauder, pillager, plunderer, predator, ransacker, rifler, robber baron, sacker, spoiler, spoliator; **kidnapper**, baby snatcher; **body-snatcher**, ghoul, resurrectionist; **cattleduffer**, duffer, gully-raker, horse-duffer, poacher, poddydodger, rustler, tea-and-sugar bushranger

THIEVING *adj* burglarious, kleptomaniac, larcenous, light-fingered, stealing; **crooked**, bent; **piratical**, bushranging, predatory, rapacious, thuggish

THIN *v* attenuate, fall away, fine, finedraw, taper; **slim**, count calories, diet, lose weight, reduce, slenderise, take off weight; **emaciate**, extenuate *(Archaic)*, macerate, peak; **narrow**, confine, constrict, straiten

THIN *adj* angular, bony, cadaverous, gaunt, hatchet-faced, lank, meagre, peaked, peaky, poor, raw-boned, scraggy, scrannel *(Archaic)*, scrawny, skinny, thin as a lath, thin as a rail, thin as a rake; **slender**, attenuate, ectomorphic, gracile, lean, light, slight, slim, small, spare, spindly, wiry, wisplike, wispy, wraithlike; **svelte**, hourglass, slinky, waisted, waspwaisted, waspish, willowish, willowy; **stalky**, asthenic, gangling, gangly, lanky, rangy, spindle-legged, spindleshanked, spindling; **skeletal**, atrophied, marasmic, tabescent, wasted, weedy; **narrow**, close, cramped, strait *(Archaic)*; **wafer-thin**, eggshell, fine-drawn, paper, papery, papyraceous, wafery; **threadlike**, capreolate, spidery, tendrilous; **bladelike**, lathlike, lathy; **fine**, fine-spun, gossamer, hair's-breadth, hairbreadth, hairline, spiry, subtle, tenuous, terete

THINK *v* allow *(U.S.)*, bash one's brains out, be in a brown study, bethink oneself of *(Archaic)*, brood, cast about, cerebrate, chew over, chew the cud, cogitate, concentrate, conceptualise, consider, contemplate, cudgel one's brains, deliberate, dream of, envisage, free-associate, ideate, introspect, meditate, mull over, muse, opine, perpend *(Archaic)*, ponder, pore over, put on one's thinking cap, reckon, reflect on, reflect upon, revolve in one's mind, ruminate, run upon, speculate, suppose, take into consideration, take it into one's head, take to heart, think out, think over, think through, turn over in one's mind, use one's loaf, use one's noodle, ween *(Archaic)*, weigh up, wonder; **philosophise**, theologise; **rethink**, reconsider, review

THINKER *n* brooder, cogitator, concentrator, contemplator, deliberator, headworker, meditator, muser, philosophiser, puzzler, ruminator

THINKING *n* brown study, cerebration, cogitation, concentration, contemplation, deliberation, free association, headwork, ideation, intellectualisation, introspection, lateral thinking, meditation, musing, philosophism, preoccupation, reconsideration, reflection, rumination, stream of consciousness, thought, wool-gathering; **thoughtfulness**, contemplativeness, deliberativeness, introspectiveness, meditativeness, pensiveness, percept, profoundness, profundity, reflectiveness, transcendentalism

THINKING *adj* cerebral, cogitative, considerate *(Archaic)*, contemplative, deliberative, meditative, museful, musing, pensive, phrenic, preoccupied, reflective, ruminant, ruminative, speculative, thoughtful

THINLY *adv* lankily, leanly, slenderly, slimly, stalkily, taperingly, thin; **gauntly**, angularly, cadaverously, lankly, meagrely, peakily, scraggily; **narrowly**, close, closely, straitly

THINNESS *n* angularness, cadaverousness, emaciation, gauntness, gracility, lankness, lean and hungry look, marasmus, meagreness, peakiness, poorness, scragginess, scrawniness, skinniness, tabescence; **leanness**, lankiness, slenderness, slightness, slimness, spareness, stalkiness, wiriness; **fineness**, attenuation, foliation, maceration; **tenuousness**, subtleness, subtlety, tenuity; **slimming**, calorie-counting, reducing, slenderising, weight-watching; **narrowing**, intake; **narrowness**, bottleneck, choke, narrow, neck, strait *(Archaic)*; **hairbreadth**, hairline, hairstroke; **blade**, lath, shim, spline, taper, thong; **strip**, belt, fascia, fillet, ray, stripe

THIN PERSON *n* a mere shadow of one's former self, bag of bones, beanpole, beanstalk, Belsen horror, cornstalk, ectomorph, hatchet face, lolly legs, long streak of pelican shit, scarecrow, scrag, skeleton, skin and bones, snapper, spindlelegs, spindleshanks, spindling *(Rare)*, streak, sylph, weed, wisp, wraith; **slimmer**, calorie counter, reducer, weight watcher

THIRD *adj* ternary, tertiary, triennial; **antepenultimate**, third last; **three**, threefold, treble

THIRSTY *adj* droughty, drouthy, dry, dry as a pommy's towel, parched

THOROUGH *adj* all-out, all-up, boots-and-all, deep-dyed, dyed-in-the-wool, in-depth, out-and-out, outright, overall, regular *(Colloq.)*, thoroughgoing, thoroughpaced, wholesale; **utter**, arrant, crashing, extreme, grand, gross, proper, stark, unmitigated; **extensive**, broad, clean, clear, cross-country, house-to-house, macroscopic, sweeping, wall-to-wall; **comprehensive**, detailed, encyclopaedic, exhaustive, intensive; **completive**, complemental, complementary, consummative, suppletory. *See also* WHOLE

THOROUGHLY *adv* broadly, comprehensively, exhaustively, extensively, in depth, intensively, sweepingly; **throughout**, across the board, from A to Z, from arsehole to breakfast time, from beginning to end, from end to end, from head to foot, from top to bottom, from top to toe, over, through, through and through; **clear**, broad, clean, hands down, well, wide. *See also* WHOLLY

THOUGHTFULLY *adv* cogitatively, contemplatively, in a brown study, meditatively, musingly, pensively, reflectively, ruminatingly, speculatively

THOUSAND *n* chiliad, millenary, millennium, millesimal, thou

THOUSAND *adj* millenarian, millenary, millennial, millesimal, thousandfold, thousandth; **ten thousand,** myriad

THREAD *n* combed yarn, hank, noil, oakum, pack-thread, pick, pile, ply, rope yarn, rove, roving, sleave, sliver, slub, strand, thrum, tops, tram, yarn; **fibre,** fibril, filament, filum; **manmade fibre,** acetate fibre, carbon fibre, lurex, monofil, tinsel; **floss,** dental floss; **tendril,** byssus *(Zool.),* chalaza, chord, cobweb, crosshair, gossamer, neurofibril, promycelium *(Bot.),* tentacle, vegetable silk; **skein,** ball, clew, cop *(Textiles),* hank; **fishing line,** dropline, gut line, line, tackle, trawl line; **fibrillation.** *See also* CORD; STRING

THREATEN *v* wave a big stick

THREE *n* hat-trick, leash *(Sport),* tern, ternary, ternion, threesome, triad, trilogy, trine, trinity, trio, triple, triunity; **triarchy,** trimester, triumvirate, troika; **triplet,** triplicate; **triennium; three-piece,** triplex

THRIFT *n* abstemiousness, chariness, forehandedness *(U.S.),* frugality, frugalness, saving, spareness, sparingness, thriftiness; **economy,** carefulness, husbandry, providence, prudence; **economisation,** cost cutting, economies of scale, good housekeeping

THRIFTILY *adv* economically, frugally, providently, savingly; **abstemiously,** charily, sparingly, stintingly

THRIFTY *adj* economic, economical, frugal, money-conscious, notable *(Archaic),* penny-wise, provident, saving; **abstemious,** careful, chary, forehanded *(U.S.),* spare, sparing

THROW *n* cast, chuck, fling, flirt, heave, hurl, incurve *(Baseball),* put, shy, toss, upcast; **bowl,** bumper, chinaman, delivery, flier, flipper, floater, full pitch, full toss, gazunder, googly, half-volley, inswinger, leg break, leg spinner, leggie, lob, off break, off spinner, outswinger, pitch, topspinner, wrong 'un, yorker; **pass,** flick pass *(Aus. Rules),* flickback *(Rugby Football),* flip pass *(Ice Hockey)*

THROW *v* bung, cant, cast, chuck, dart, dash, detrude, fling, flip, heave, hoy, hurl, hurtle, jerk, launch, let fly, lob, pass, peg, pitch, pitchfork, shoot, shy, skim, sling, toss, whirl *(Obs.);* **bowl,** deliver, flight, pitch; **flop,** dump, flump, plunk, precipitate, whop

THROWER *n* caster, flinger, heaver, hurler, impeller, pitcher, precipitator, tosser; **bowler,** deliverer, pace bowler, paceman, spinner

THROW OUT *v* file in the w.p.b., put on the scrap-heap, remainder, scrap

THRUST *n* detrusion, jerk, jostle, push, ram, shove, upthrust; **impetus,** drift, drive, impulse, impulsion, jet propulsion, projection, propulsion, send *(Naut.),* sweep; **trundle,** roll

THRUST *v* boot home, crowd, jostle, push, ram, shoulder, shove; **propel,** drive, impel, launch, precipitate, project, send; **roll,** pedal, trundle, wheel; **edge,** elbow, nudge, poke; **flick,** fillip, flirt

TIDILY *adv* neatly, shipshape, snug, snugly, straight, to rights, trim

TIDINESS *n* apple-pie order, eutaxy, harmony, methodicalness, neatness, orderliness, regularity, snugness, systematism, tautness, trim, trimness

TIDY *v* do up, dress, fettle *(Archaic)*, groom, neaten, put one's house in order, set one's house in order, straighten, tidy up, trig; **array**, file, interfile, lay out, place, set out; **dispose**, align, collate, collocate, distribute, justify *(Print)*, right; **marshal**, draw up, dress, form up *(Mil.)*, rally, regiment, troop *(Mil.)*

TIDY *adj* feat *(Archaic)*, just so, neat, regular, smug, snug, tiddly *(Naut.)*, trig, trim, well-groomed; **well-ordered**, shipshape, spick-and-span, taut, trim; **disciplined**, obedient, well-behaved

TIGHTS *n* bodystocking, leg warmers, leotard, maillot; **stocking**, hose, nylons, pantihose. *See also* UNDERWEAR

TIMBER *n* bentwood, cabinet wood, driftwood, hardwood, matchwood, millwork, softwood, stumpage *(U.S.)*, veneer, wood, wrought timber; **woodchips**, wood flour, wood pulp, woodwool; **lumber**, clog, fascine, flitch, four-by-two, log, nog, plank, rollway *(U.S.)*, sawlog, scantling, shake, splint, stay, stick, stock, stud, two-by-four, yule log; **chipboard**, beaverboard *(U.S.)*, boxboard, cane-ite, corkboard, Gibraltar board *(N.Z.)*, particle board, pegboard, strawboard; **woods**, amboyna, bamboo, basswood, beech, birch, black locust, black pine, box, briar-root, briarwood, brushwood, calabash, calamander, calamus, camphorwood, candlewood, cedar, cypress, durmast, ebony, elm, fir, gopherwood, greenheart, guaiacum, gum, hazel, hickory, Huon pine, ironwood, kingwood, lancewood, larch, lignum vitae, loblolly, logwood, longleaf pine, mahogany, mallet, maple, Monterey pine, mulga, myall, oak, padauk, partridge-wood, pine, poon, poplar, red bean, red beech, red cedar, red fir, red oak, redwood, rosewood, saffronheart, sandalwood, santal, satinwood, shagbark, shittim wood, spruce, sumach, tamarack, teak, tupelo, wainscot, walnut, white birch, white cedar, white pine, white poplar, whitewood, wicopy *(U.S.)*, willow, yew, yiel-yiel, zebrawood

TIME *n* Father Time, fourth dimension, Kronos, race *(Archaic)*, sands of time, space-time, years; **fixed time**, chronogram, date, hour, obit, operative date *(Law)*, pull date, zero hour; **office hours**, flexitime, gliding time, overtime

TIME *v* clock, keep time, minute; **date; bundy on**, clock in, clock on, punch the bundy; **periodise**

TIMEKEEPER *n* chronologist, clocker *(Horseracing)*, timer; **clockmaker**, horologist, watchmaker

TIMELINESS *n* good timing, opportuneness, propitiousness, seasonableness; **punctuality**, promptitude, promptness, punctualness

TIMELY *adj* opportune, pat, ripe, seasonable, synchronised, well-timed; **punctual**, prompt; **crucial**, critical; **last-minute**, eleventh-hour

TIMELY *adv* critically, in due course, in season, opportunely; **punctually**, in good time, on cue, on the beat, on the dot, on the knocker, on the nail, on the tick, on time, promptly, sea-

timely   **tiredness**

sonably, sharp; **in the nick of time,** betimes, in time

TIME MEASUREMENT *n* carbon dating, chronology, chronometry, dendrochronology, dialling, fluorine dating, geochronology, horology, measurement, potassium-argon dating, radiocarbon dating, timing; **calendar,** almanac, ephemeris *(Obs.)*, Gregorian calendar, Jewish calendar, Julian calendar, Roman calendar; **date,** date line *(Journalism)*, date stamp, day, day of the month, year; **mean time,** Central Standard Time, daylight-saving, Eastern Standard Time, ephemeris time, Greenwich Mean Time, local time, mean solar time, standard time, summer time, true time, universal time, Western Standard Time, WST, zulu time *(Mil. Colloq.)*; **intercalation,** embolism

TIMEPIECE *n* clepsydra, horologe, sundial, timekeeper, water-clock; **clock,** alarm clock, astronomical clock, atomic clock, caesium clock, chronograph, chronometer, cuckoo clock, digital clock, grandfather clock, grandmother clock, photochronograph; **watch,** block, digital watch, hunter, hunting watch, repeater, stem-winder, ticker, wristwatch; **biological clock,** biological timeclock; **timer,** autotimer, bundy, chronopher, chronoscope, chronotron, eggtimer, hourglass, parking meter, sand-glass, stopwatch, time clock; **time signal;** curfew, last post, pips, retreat, reveille, taps *(U.S. Mil.)*, wait *(Obs.)*

TIME SHEET *n* cheat sheet, plod, schedule, timebook, timecard, timetable

TIMIDLY *adv* basely, cravenly, faint-heartedly, fearfully, fearsomely, in a blue funk, in a funk, nervelessly, pusillanimously, recreantly, spinelessly, tamely

TIRE *v* do in, exhaust, fag, fatigue, knock up, poop, prostrate, root, take it out of, tucker, use up, weary, whack; **jade,** frazzle, irk; **overwork,** drive, gruel, outwear, overwear, put through the mangle, shag, strain, task, tax, wear

TIRED *adj* bug-eyed, dull, fatigued, footsore, heavy-eyed, heavy-laden, jaded, jadish, on one's last legs, overweary, sleepy, toilworn, war-weary, wayworn, wearful, weary, worn, worn-out; **exhausted,** fordone *(Archaic)*, overwrought, prostrate, psychasthenic, run-down, spent, strained, stretched, wrung-out; **all in,** beat, beaten, blown, buggered, bushed, bushwhacked, clapped-out, dead, dog-tired, done for, done in, euchred, fagged, far gone, flat as a tack, flat out, fucked, jack, jiggered up, knackered, knocked-up, not for the count, pooped, R.S., ratshit, rooted, shagged, stonkered, washed-out, washed-up, wasted, whacked, wrecked, zapped, zonked; **like death,** green at the gills, half-dead, like death warmed up, white at the gills

TIREDLY *adv* jadedly, jadishly, wearifully, wearily

TIREDNESS *n* fatigue, lassitude, wearifulness, weariness; **jadedness,** jadishness, staleness; **over-tiredness,** frazzle, psychasthenia, strain; **exhaustion,** battle fatigue, collapse, combat fatigue, inanition, limit of endurance, prostration, wornness

TIRING *adj* exhaustive, gruelling, irksome, killing, tiresome, wearing, wearisome

TITLE *n* bastard title, caption, half-title, heading, masthead, rubric, subheading, subtitle, titlepage; **signature**, autograph, by-line, endorsement, henry, mark, subscription

TOBACCO *n* baccy, flat *(Prison)*, nicotine, snout, weed; **plug**, nailrod, niggerhead, pigtail, quid, twist; **broadleaf**, caporal, cavendish, perique, shag; **snuff**, maccaboy, rappee; **cigarette**, african, cancer stick, ciggie, coffin nail, dart, durry, fag, gasper *(Brit.)*, O.P., reefer, skag, smoke; **tailor-made**, filter, filter tip; **roll-your-own**, greyhound, racehorse, rollie; **the makings**, cigarette paper, filler, tissue, wrapper; **fag-end**, bumper, butt, dottle; **cigar**, cheroot, cigarillo, claro, panatela, perfecto, toby jug *(U.S.)*; **pipe**, briar, briar-root, briarwood, chibouk, churchwarden, clay pipe, corncob, doodie, dudeen *(Irish)*, matchbox, meerschaum; **water pipe**, bong, chillum, hookah, hubble-bubble, kalian, narghile; **peace-pipe**, calumet, pipe of peace; **pipestem**, bowl; **drag**, drawback, puff, pull, toke, whiff

TOGETHER *adv* at one blow, jointly; **collectively**, associatively, conjointly, conjunctionally, coordinately

TOIL *n* donkey work, drudgery, fag, graft, grind, moil, slavery, slog, sweat, swink *(Archaic)*; **laboriousness**, arduousness, burdensomeness, operoseness, strenuosity, strenuousness, sweatiness, toilsomeness; **burden**, backbreaker, chore, fatigue, load, task

TOILET *n* bathroom, bog, brasco, can *(U.S.)*, carzey *(Brit.)*, crapper, did, diddy, dumpty, dunny, dyke, euphemism, garderobe *(Archaic)*, head *(Naut.)*, jakes *(Archaic)*, jerry, john, la, la-di-da, latrine, lav, lavatory, little girls' room, loo, low-down suite, Mary's room, pan, pedestal, pisser, roundhouse, smallest room, the throne, toot, urinal, water-closet, WC; **outhouse**, backhouse *(U.S.)*, boghouse, cloaca, dunny, earth closet, pissahore, privy, shed, shithouse, shouse, stool, the little house; **public toilet**, amenities, convenience, gents, ladies, powder room, public convenience, rest room, toilet facilities; **sanitary can**, chemical toilet, dry pan, dunny can, honey pot, thunderbox; **bedpan**, bedroom mug, bottle, chamber, chamber-pot, commode, gozunder, jerry, pot, potty, thundermug, tub *(Prison)*; **cesspool**, cess, cesspit, sink *(Rare)*; **sewerage**, sep, septic, septic system, septic tank, sewage farm, sewer; **sanitary man**, Dan, sanny man; **night cart**, dunny cart, honey cart, seventeen door sedan; **kitty litter**, deep litter

TOLERANCE *n* broad-mindedness, cosmopolitanism, cosmopolitism, open-mindedness, receptiveness, receptivity, unbiasedness; **latitude**, toleration; **liberality**, breadth, catholicity, generosity, generousness, largemindedness, liberalness; **liberalism**, latitudinarianism, tolerationism

TOLERANT *adj* generous, open, open-minded, receptive, unbiased, unprejudiced; **broad-minded**, cosmopolitan, large-minded, latitudinous, permissive; **liberal**, catholic, free-

tolerant

thinking, latitudinarian, liberal-minded, liberalist, liberalistic

TOLERANTLY *adv* broad-mindedly, open-mindedly, receptively, unbiasedly; **liberally**, generously

TOMFOOL *v* act the angora, act the goat, antic *(Obs.)*, arse about, arsehole about, bugger around, fart about, fuck around, make a joe of oneself, mess around, muck around, play silly buggers, ponce

TOOL *n* artefact, implement, instrument, utensil; **gadget**, gismo, jigger; **stock-in-trade**, haberdashery, hardware, ironmongery, ironware, notions

TOOTHACHE *n* cavity, decay, dry socket, gingivitis, gumboil, malocclusion, odontalgia, odontoblast, periodontitis, plaque, pyorrhoea, Rigg's disease; **oral disease**, glossitis, monilia, noma, ptyalism, stomatitis, thrush, trench mouth

TOP *n* ace, apex, apogee, cap, crown, foreside, head, height, ne plus ultra, peak, pinnacle, summit, tip, tiptop, upper limit, vertex, zenith; **top layer**, ceiling, housetop, roof, rooftop, treetop, watertable; **topside**, bridge, upperdeck, upside; **topping**, coating, surfacing; **crownpiece**, abacus *(Archit.)*, capital, capitulum, capstone, chapiter, copestone, coping, crest, crown, crowner, head, headpiece, pediment, summer; **crest**, arête, cap, cop *(Obs.)*, cope, lip, ridge, watershed; **climax**, crest of the wave, culmination, high point, peak

TOP *v* cap, crest, crown, head, overlook, overshadow, overtop; **surmount**, bestraddle, bestride, mount, pinnacle, ride, scale, transcend; **climax**, culminate, peak

TOP *adj* apical, apogeal, apogean, ceiling *(Colloq.)*, climactic, culminant, head, meridian, supermedial, tiptop, topmost, zenithal; **overtopping**, overlooking, superincumbent, transcendent, transcending

TOPICAL *adj* apposite, bearing on the matter, germane, pertinent, relative, relevant

TORMENTOR *n* afflicter, crucifier, harmer, sadomasochist, torturer

TOSS *v* roll about, toss and turn, twist, welter *(Obs.)*, writhe; **seethe**, boil, churn, fret, heave; **flutter**, flitter, quake, ripple, ruffle; **convulse**, palpitate

TOUCH *n* contact, feel, handle; **stroke**, brush, chuck, flick, graze, pat, tap, trait *(Rare)*; **feeling**, fingering, handling, manipulation, palpation; **massage**, rub, rub-down, squeezing; **sense of touch**, palpability, tact, tactility; **touch sensation**, itchiness, pins-and-needles, ticklishness; **tickle**, itch, tingle. *See also* TEXTURE

TOUCH *v* feel, palp *(Obs.)*, palpate; **handle**, fiddle with, finger, manipulate, thumb, twiddle; **tickle**, kittle *(Brit.)*, prickle, scratch; **pat**, chuck, tap; **stroke**, brush, graze, knead, massage, paddle, pat, rub; **grope**, feel up, grabble, palm, paw, taste *(Obs.)*

TOUCHER *n* fingerer, fumbler, groper, handler, tickler, twiddler

TOWER *n* acropolis, beacon, belfry, belltower, belvedere, broach spire, campanile, column, conning tower, cooling tower, cupola, dome, elevator, helter-skelter *(Brit.)*, Martello tower, minaret, pagoda, peel *(Brit.)*,

tower 525 **train**

pile, pillar, pylon, pyramid, shot tower, silo, skyscraper, spire, steeple, transmission tower, turret, watchtower; **perch**, coign of vantage, crow's nest, eyrie, lookout, vantage point; **loft**, attic, garret, hayloft, mansard roof, upstairs.   *See also* APEX: HEIGHT

TOWER *v* bestride, command, crown, dominate, domineer, overhang, overlie, overlook, overshadow, overtop, rise above, stand over, surmount, tower above; **soar**, ascend, climb, mount, rise; **have a bird's-eye view**, be suspended, hang, hover, perch

TOWN *n* boom town, closed town, company town, exurb, fishing town, ghost town, growth centre, home town, market town, mining town, outport, port, rail town, satellite town, seaport, township; **country town**, Bandywallop, Bullamakanka, clachan, county town *(Brit.)*, hamlet, kainga *(N.Z.)*, kampong *(S.E. Asia)*, kraal *(Africa)*, one-horse town, pa *(N.Z.)*, settlement, subtopia *(Brit.)*, village, whistlestop *(U.S.)*; **main street**, outskirts, pedestrian plaza, shopping centre, shopping mall, shopping precinct *(Brit.)*.   *See also* CITY

TRACTIVE *adj* draught, tractional

TRADE *n* adventure, barter, big business, biz, business, buying and selling, concern, dealings, exchange, market, operation, trading, traffic, venture; **commerce**, brokerage, commercialism, marketing, mercantilism, merchandising; **export**, drop shipment, exportation, re-exportation, shipment, shipping; **importation**; **smuggling**, free trade *(Obs.)*, running

TRADE *v* barter, cheapen *(Archaic)*, deal, dicker *(U.S.)*, export, fair-trade, go offshore, handle, import, jew *(Derog.)*, market, merchandise, overtrade, re-export, recapitalise, smuggle, trade in, traffic, wheel and deal; **negotiate**, bargain, chaffer, haggle, higgle, huckster

TRADER *n* bourgeois, chandler, chapman *(Archaic)*, dealer, free-trader, kulak *(Russian Hist.)*, marketeer, merchant, merchant prince, middleman, monger; **tradespeople**, private sector, trade; **businessman**, adventurer, businesswoman, commercialist, entrepreneur, little man, mercantilist, merchandiser, small businessman, tycoon, wheeler-dealer; **broker**, agent, forwarding agent, ship-broker, syndic; **barterer**, bargainer, exchanger, stag; **smuggler**, courier, drug-runner, free-trader *(Obs.)*

TRADE UNION *n* artel, brotherhood, guild, industrial union, labour union, mystery *(Archaic)*; **chapel**, local *(U.S.)*; **shop committee**, works committee

TRADE UNIONIST *n* guildsman, labour, redfed *(Colloq.)*, syndicalist, unionist, Wobbly; **union delegate**, delegate, delo, organiser, rep, shop steward; **striker**, picketeer

TRADING *adj* commercial, commercialistic, entrepreneurial, mercantile, merchant

TRAIN *n* boat-train, cane train, container train, division, freight train, goods train, mail, metro, mixed train, picker-up, rattler *(U.S. Colloq.)*, special, sweeper, tube train *(Brit.)*, unit *(N.Z.)*; **locomotive**, bank engine, banker, chuff-chuff, chuffer, diesel, engine, iron horse *(Archaic)*, loci

train   526   **transport**

(N.Z.), loco, mogul, puffer; **rolling stock**, bogie cattle wagon, bogie sheep van, boxcar *(U.S.)*, brake van, buffet car, caboose *(U.S.)*, car, carriage, coach, corf, couchette, day coach *(U.S.)*, dining car, display van, dogbox carriage, flat-top, freight car *(U.S.)*, goods wagon, guard's van, hopper car, louvre van, luggage van, observation car, railcar, railcarriage, railcoach, railmotor, restaurant car, roomette *(U.S.)*, saloon car, skip, sleeper, sleeping car, smoker, tank wagon, tender, tin hare, truck, van, wagon, wagon-lit, water-carrier; **section car**, flivver, kalamazoo, quad, quadracycle, velocipede *(N.Z. Railways)*; **Chips**, Fish, Ghan, Indian Pacific, Newcastle Flier, Overlander, Prospector, Puffing Billy, Rocket, Silver Fern *(N.Z.)*, Southern Aurora, Spirit of Progress, Sunlander, The Alice, XPT

TRAM *n* buckjumper, cable car, cable tram, dreadnought, dummy, inclinator, streetcar *(U.S.)*, toast-rack, trailing tram, tramcar, trolley, trolley car *(U.S.)*, trolleybus; **cable car**, telpher

TRANSLATABLE *adj* decipherable, paraphrasable, renderable; **interpretable**, construable

TRANSLATE *v* render, transcribe, transliterate, turn, vernacularise; **decipher**, decode, demystify, solve, unravel; **rephrase**, metaphrase, paraphrase, reword, simplify, spell out; **lip-read**

TRANSLATION *n* transcript, transcription, transliteration, vernacularisation; **paraphrase**, abridgement, epitome, metaphrase, précis, resumé, rewording, simplification; **version**, lection, reading, rendering, rendition, varia lectio; **construction**, angle, construe, sense, slant, understanding

TRANSLATOR *n* dragoman, lip-reader, transcriber, vernacularist; **decoder**, decipherer

TRANSPARENCY *n* diaphaneity, diaphanousness, pellucidity, pellucidness, penetrability, sheerness, transparence; **clearness**, clarity, limpidity, limpidness, liquidness, lucence *(Archaic)*, lucency *(Archaic)*, lucidity, lucidness; **glassiness**, vitreosity, vitreousness; **semi-transparency**, translucence, translucency, translucidity

TRANSPARENT *adj* diaphanous, pellucid, see-through, sheer; **semitransparent**, semitranslucent, translucent, translucid; **clear**, bright, limpid, liquid, lucent *(Archaic)*, lucid; **glasslike**, crystal, crystalline, glassy, hyaline, hyaloid, vitreous

TRANSPARENTLY *adv* diaphanously, pellucidly, translucently; **clearly**, bright, brightly, limpidly, liquidly, lucidly; **glassily**, vitreously

TRANSPARENT SUBSTANCE *n* crystal, glass, hyaline; **gossamer**, gauze, sheer silk

TRANSPORT *n* airlift, cabotage, carriage, cartage, commissariat, conveyance, drayage, entrainment, express, expressage, ferriage, forwarding, handling, haulage, passage, piggyback, portage, traffic, transit, transportation, truckage, trucking, wagonage *(Archaic)*, waterage; **transfer**, move, removal, remove, shanghai *(Prison Colloq.)*, shift, shunt, transferal, transference, translation, translocation, transmittal, transmittance; **logistics**; **delivery**, collection, courier service, deliverance, dispatch, express delivery, paradrop, special delivery; **dink,** donkey *(S.A.),* double, double-bank

TRANSPORT *v* carry, convey, frank, freight, lift, move, relocate, remove, run, shanghai *(Prison Colloq.),* shift, take, traffic, transfer, translate, translocate, transmit, transpose *(Rare);* **send,** check *(U.S.),* consign, dispatch, forward, pass on, relay, remit, transmit; **express,** herb *(Colloq.),* rush; **deliver,** bail, discharge, drop, dump, land, off-load; **collect,** bring, fetch; **cart,** dray, jitney, rail, railroad *(U.S.),* team *(U.S.),* trolley, truck, wagon, wheelbarrow; **ship,** barge, boat, canoe, ferry, flume *(U.S.),* lighter, lock, punt, raft, row, wherry; **shunt,** reship, switch *(U.S.),* tranship; **airfreight,** airlift, fly, parachute; **manhandle,** bear, frogmarch *(Brit. U.S.),* hump, lump, pack, pikau *(N.Z.),* port, tote; **stevedore,** load, unload; **dink,** donkey *(S.A.),* double, double-bank, double-dink

TRANSPORT *adj* airborne, logistic *(Mil.),* overland, pack, portative, roll-on roll-off, windborne

TRANSPORTABILITY *n* moveability, moveableness, portability, transferability, transmissibility; **clearance capacity,** conductivity

TRANSPORTABLE *adj* consignable, conveyable, deliverable, dischargeable, movable, portable, portative, remissible, remittable, transferable, translatable, transmissible, transmittable

TRANSPORTER *n* consignor, dispatcher, remitter, sender, transmitter; **carrier,** carter, common carrier, conveyor, courier, deliverer, fetcher, forwarder, freighter, haulier, mover, packman *(N.Z.),* removalist, remover, shifter, shipper, track *(Prison Colloq.),* transferrer, transporter, trucker *(U.S.),* water-carrier; **porter,** bearer, bheesti, grip *(Films Television),* pallbearer, stretcher-bearer; **driver,** bullock-puncher, bullocker, bullocky, cameleer, Ghan; **stevedore,** loader, longshoreman *(U.S.),* seagull *(Colloq.),* wharf labourer, wharfie; **coalman,** coal-heaver, collier *(Obs.);* **beast of burden,** ass, burro, camel, donkey, moke, mule, packhorse, packtrain

TRAVEL *v* buzz about, do, fare *(Archaic),* gang *(Scot.),* get about, get around, go, go around, journey, make one's way, peregrinate, repair, run up (over) (round), see the world, slope *(Colloq.),* take oneself, tour, wade *(Obs.);* **migrate,** come out, emigrate, immigrate; **gallivant,** excurse, gad about, jaunt, joy-ride, junket, trip *(Rare);* **roam,** circumambulate, extravagate, go walkabout, have itchy feet, hump the bluey, knock about, knock around, meander, range, rove, swag, waltz Matilda, wander; **ply,** commute, itinerate, patrol, round, whistlestop; **hike,** bushwalk, ramble, tramp, trek

TRAVELLER *n* journeyer, peregrinator, voyager, wayfarer; **tourist,** excursionist, globetrotter, jetsetter, joy-rider, junketer, tourer, tripper; **migrant,** boat people, emigré, immigrant, Jimmy Grant, migrator, refugee, repatriate; **wanderer,** bedouin, Egyptian, gippo, gipsy, gypsy, peripatetic, rambler, ranger, roamer, Romany, rover, travelling labour, Wandering Jew; **hiker,** bushwalker; **itinerant,** bird of passage, bogtrotter, rolling stone; **pilgrim,** hajji, palmer, visitant;

traveller 528 **trick**

tramp, bagman, battler, beachcomber, bender, bum, coaster, coiler, deadbeat, drummer, hobo, Murrumbidgee whaler, outcast, overlander, rogue, street Arab, sundowner, swagger *(N.Z.)*, swaggie, swagman, swamper, toe-ragger, tramper, vag, vagabond, vagrant, whaler; **explorer**, trekker; **travelling salesman**, hawker, pedlar, rep, representative, roundsman; **commuter**, kiss-and-ride commuter, season ticket holder, straphanger; **drover**, Afghan, bullockpuncher, bullocker, bullocky, cameleer, Ghan, mahout, mule-skinner *(U.S.)*, muleteer, overlander, swamper *(U.S.)*; **skater**, ice-skater, langlaufer, skier, sleigher, snowshoer, tobogganer, tobogganist; **skateboarder**, roller-skater, skater; **rower**, sculler

TRAVELLING *n* itinerancy, itineration, passage, peregrination, staging, travel, wayfaring; **commuting**, commutation *(U.S.)*, straphanging; **tourism**, globetrotting; **migration**, immigration, nomadism, repatriation, transhumance; **vagabondism**, excursiveness, fugitiveness, vagabondage, vagrancy, vagrantness, walkabout; **wanderlust**

TRAVELLING *adj* globetrotting, seafaring, touring; **migratory**, anadromous, immigrant, migrant, migrational, nomadic, transhumant; **expeditionary**, odyssean; **peripatetic**, ambulant, arrant *(Obs.)*, deadbeat, Egyptian, errant, excursive, extravagant *(Obs.)*, gippo, gipsy, gipsy-like, itinerant, itinerary *(Rare)*, of no fixed address, rambling, romany, vagabond, vagarious, vagrant

TRAVERSE *v* cross, crosscut, cut across, cut through, ford, over *(Rare)*, pass over, voyage; **bridge**, span

TRAVERSING *n* crossing, perambulation, transit, traverse; **passage**, flow-through, passing

TRAY *n* autotray, dumb waiter, lapboard, tea-trolley, tea-tray, traymobile, wheeling tray

TREASURY *n* bank, chamber *(Obs.)*, coffers, exchequer, fisc, mint, thesaurus; **cash desk**, cash register, checkout, peter, point-of-sale terminal, p.o.s. terminal, till; **strongroom**, strongbox, vault; **moneybox**, piggy bank; **money market**, foreign exchange market; **treasurer**, bursar, cashier, collector

TRIAL *n* appeal, coronial inquiry, court martial, hearing, impeachment, inquest, inquiry, inquisition, mistrial, nisi prius, prosecution, retrial, show trial, state trial, trial by jury

TRIBUTE *n* approbation, attention, commendations, compliments, congratulations, toast; **respects**, court, deference, devoirs, duty, fealty, loyalty, obedience; **bow**, congé, curtsy, genuflection, kneeling, kowtow, obeisance, observance *(Archaic)*, presenting arms, prostration, reverence, salaam, salutation, salute. *See also* COMMEMORATION

TRICK *n* angle, bubble, caper, cheat, chizz *(Brit.)*, con, confidence trick, do, effect *(Theat.)*, fakement, fastie, feint, fetch, fiddle, finesse, flim-flam, frost, gyp, have, hype *(U.S.)*, juggle, line, plant, put-on, sell, set-up, shift, slanter, sleight *(Rare)*, smokescreen, snow job, stew, sting *(U.S.)*, swiftie, swindle, swiz, swizzle, take, takedown, trepan *(Archaic)*, wrinkle;

trick

hoax, berley, humbug, kid, kidstakes, leg-pull, practical joke, prank, prankery; **legerdemain,** sleight of hand

TRICK v abuse *(Archaic)*, baffle *(Obs.)*, bamboozle, befool, bluff, bull, catch, cheat on, cog the dice, come the double on, come the raw prawn, come the uncooked crustacean, deceive, delude, dupe, equivocate, fast-talk, foist in, foist into, foist on, fool, fox, gull, handle, have, have a lend of, have someone on, hocus-pocus, hoodwink, humbug, hype *(U.S.)*, impose on, lead up the garden path, load the dice, misinform, mislead, pull a fast one, pull a fastie, pull a swiftie, pull the wool over someone's eyes, put it across, put one over, put over a fast one, put shit on, seel *(Archaic)*, sell, sophisticate, string along, swift-talk, take for a ride, take in, throw dust in someone's eyes, two-time; **hoax,** gag, gammon, hocus, kid, make a fool of, mock, play a joke on, pull someone's leg, rag, send on a fool's errand, sport with, trifle with; **counterfeit, fake; sneak,** gumshoe *(U.S.)*, mooch, sidle, slink, steal, tiptoe; **feint,** pretend

TRICKERY n abuse *(Archaic)*, archness, bamboozlement, beguilement, bluff, chenanigan, cozenage, craft, cunning, deceit, deception, defraudation, delusion, dupery, equivocation, eyewash, fast-talking, forgery *(Archaic)*, four-flush, hocus-pocus, hokey-pokey, indirection, intrigue, irony, jiggery-pokery, jugglery, monkey business, pretext, sharp practice, shenanigan, stealth, subterfuge, wiles; **false pretences,** impersonation, personation; **deceitfulness,** duplicity, sneakiness, speciousness, stealthiness, surreptitiousness

TRICKSTER n adventurer, adventuress, bamboozler, beguiler, bluffer, cheat, cheater, cozener, defrauder, deluder, diddler, duper, feigner, fiddler, finagler, flim-flammer, front man, gyp, gypper, hoodwinker, hotpointer, impersonator, juggler, personator, slyboots, sneaker, swindler, swizzler, trepanner *(Archaic)*, tricker, twister, welsher; **deceiver,** gay deceiver, Mata Hari; **con man,** balancer, confidence man, dud-dropper, false-pretender, gypster, illywhacker, lurk man, mouthman, paperhanger, rorter, share-pusher, slicker, thimblerigger; **leg-puller,** kidder, ragger; **dissembler,** actor, hoaxer, gagger, joker, leg-puller, practical joker, prankster, spoofer

TRIGONOMETRICAL FUNCTION n cos., cosec, cosecant, cosine, haversine, secant, sin., sine, tan., tangent, vers., versed sine; **hyperbolic function,** cosech, cosh, cotanh, sech, sinh, tanh; **logarithm,** common logarithm, napierian logarithm, natural logarithm; **antilog,** antilogarithm; **pi, e**

TRIMMING n border, clock, edging, fixings, fringe, lace, orphrey, passementerie, piping, torsade, trim, whipping; **flounce,** caparison, falbala, frill, furbelow, valance; **braid,** binding, braiding, galloon, gimp; **loop,** picot, purl; **tassel,** bobble, fandangle, pompom, zizith; **spangle,** gilding, glitter, gold leaf, ormulu, paillette, pearly, sequin, tinsel; **gold braid,** aiguillette, bullion, cordon, epaulet, gimp, lace, sword knot; **plume,** aigrette, crest, panache

TRINKET *n* bauble, bibelot, bijou, bric-a-brac, doodad, fallal, garden gnome, gaud, gewgaw, gimcrack, gingerbread, knick-knack, ornament, pretties, scrimshaw, trumpery

TRIPARTITE *adj* ternate, three-piece, three-ply, threefold, threesome, triadic, trichotomic, trichotomous, trifid, triform, trilinear, trimerous, trinal, trinary, trine, trinomial, triparted, triple, triplex, triplicate; **triangular,** three-cornered, three-square, trigonal, trihedral, trilateral; **tripedal,** tripodal, tripodic

TRIPLE *v* cube, treble, triplicate; **trisect**

TRIPLICATION *n* triplicity; **triangularity; trisection,** trichotomy, tripartism, tripartition; **trisector**

TRIPLY *adv* threefold, thrice, trebly; **tripartitely,** ternately; **triangularly,** trilaterally

TROUSERS *n* applecatchers, baggies, bags, breeches, britches, buckskins *(U.S.),* chaps, cords, corduroys, crawlers, creepers, daks, denims, drainpipes, duds, flannels, flares, galligaskins, gauchos, hipsters, jeans, jodhpurs, knee breeches, knickerbockers, knickers, knicks, Levis, long'uns, Oxford bags, pantaloons, pants, peg tops, plus-fours, pyjamas, riding breeches, slacks, slop, strides, trews *(Scot.),* trunk hose, tweeds, velveteens; **shorts,** bermuda shorts, board shorts, Bombay bloomers, boxer shorts, hotpants, lederhosen, trunks *(Obs.)*

TRUCK *n* lorry, mini-van, pantechnicon, table-top, taxi truck, transit van, utility van, van; **semitrailer,** artic *(N.Z. Colloq.),* articulated lorry, low-loader, prime mover, rig, road train, semi, transport; **tip-truck,** dump truck, dumper, tip-cart; **convoy,** beef train, caravan, motorcade, wagon train *(U.S.);* **armoured car,** blitz buggy, jeep, panzer, tank, troop-carrier; **bus,** charabanc, coach, double-decker, green cart, minibus, motor coach, motorbus, omnibus, service car, single-decker

TRUE *adj* accurate, certain, correct, dead set, definite, dinkum, dinky-di, fair dinkum, for real, inerrant, ridge, ridgy-didge, right, sooth *(Archaic),* veritable *(Rare);* **genuine,** actual, authentic, factual, historical, legit, legitimate, literal, real, veritable, very; **verifiable,** affirmable, authenticable, certifiable, checkable; **realistic,** recognisable, true to life, true to nature; **valid,** just, logically true, rigorous, sound, straight, tenable; **verified,** authenticated, proved; **self-evident,** a priori, axiomatic, tautological, truistic, undeniable

TRUE BLUE *n* beaut, trouper, white man *(Brit. Colloq.);* **loyalist,** liegeman, the faithful

TRUNCATED *adj* castrated, couped, crop-eared, cut short, docked, lopped, poley, premorse, truncate

TRUNCATION *n* attrition, curtailment, decrement, deduction, dockage, enucleation, evisceration, excision, expurgation, exsection, extirpation, removal, subduction *(Rare),* subtraction; **castration,** elastration, emasculation, gelding, the unkindest cut of all; **circumcision,** clitoridectomy; **epilation,** depilation; **amputation,** mutilation

TRUNK *adj* abdominal, acetabular, costal, diaphragmic, dorsal, iliac, pectoral, pelvic, pubic, sacral, thoracic, umbilical

TRUTH *n* actuality, fact, reality, sooth *(Archaic)*, the Absolute *(Metaphys.)*, troth *(Archaic)*, what's what; **self-evident truth**, axiom, first principle, truism; **the truth**, gospel, griff, griffin *(N.Z.)*, the drum, the full two bob, the genuine article, the lowdown, the real McCoy, the real thing, the strong of it, the true, the whole truth and nothing but the truth; **factualness**, actualness, historicity, realness, trueness, verity; **correctness**, accuracy, accurateness, infallibility, rightness, rigorousness, soundness, tenableness, validity; **genuineness**, authenticity, legitimacy, legitimateness

TRUTHFUL *adj* honest, true *(Archaic)*, veracious, veridical; **sincere**, candid, downright, frank, genuine, plain-spoken, unfeigned

TRUTHFULLY *adv* dead set, honestly, true, veraciously, veridically; **sincerely**, candidly, frankly, genuinely, unfeignedly

TRUTHFULNESS *n* honesty, straightness, veracity; **sincerity**, genuineness, unfeignedness; **candour**, downrightness, frankness, plain-speaking

TRYST *n* assignation, lover's meeting; **love-letter**, billet-doux, love knot, valentine; **love potion**, aphrodisiac, philtre

TURBULENCE *n* agitation, convulsion, ferment, inquietude, tempest, torment, trouble, turmoil, unquietness, unrest, vexedness; **commotion**, ado, bobberie, cataclysm, catastrophe, disturbance, fuss, hubbub, hurly-burly, much ado about nothing, song and dance, tumult, volcanicity; **convulsion**, palpitation, paroxysm, spasm, throe, welter; **flurry**, jactation, jiggle, joggle, jounce, popple, shake, shaking, startle, succussion, tingle, toss; **excitement**, ebullience, ebulliency, tempestuousness; **boil**, churning, ebullition, seethe, vortex; **quake**, shudder; **the shakes**, delirium tremens

TURBULENT *adj* agitated, jittery, restless, rough, tempestuous, troublous *(Archaic)*, unquiet; **excited**, ebullient, palpitant; **vexed**, disturbed, unquiet; **fluttery**, jumpy, quaky, saltatory, shaky, tremulous; **convulsant**, convulsional, convulsive, paroxysmal

TURBULENTLY *adv* disturbingly, ebulliently, excitedly, vexedly; **flutteringly**, convulsively, shakily; **tempestuously**, unquietly

TURN *n* about-face, about-turn, caracole, christiania *(Skiing)*, facing *(U.S. Mil.)*, kick turn *(Skiing)*, left turn, pirouette, right turn, tack, three-point turn, volte *(Manège)*, volte-face, yaw

TURN *v* corner, quarter, tack; **zigzag**, Major-Mitchell, wind

TURNING INSIDE-OUT *n* evagination, eversion, extroversion

TURN INSIDE OUT *v* evaginate, evert

TWELVE *n* dozen, gross, twelfth; **dodecagon**, dodecahedron

TWENTY *adj* twentieth, vicenary, vigesimal

TWIST *n* crinkle, curl, curlicue, gyrus, slub, torsade, tortuosity, twirl, verticil, volute *(Zool.)*, whorl, wind; **convolution**, circumflex, roll, winding; **coil**, clew, flake, hank, service *(Naut.)*, skein; **helix**, double helix, right-handed helix, right-handed

twist

spiral, screw, screw thread, scroll, spiral, square thread, thread, volute, worm; **coil spring,** balance spring, hairspring

TWIST *v* circumnutate, coil, convolve, corkscrew, crinkle, intort, screw, serve *(Naut.)*, spiral, whip, wind, wrap, wrench, wring; **snake,** squiggle, vermiculate, weave, wriggle, writhe; **curl,** braid, crimp, crimple, crisp, frizz, frizzle, roll, wave

TWISTED *adj* cochleate, coiled, convolute, convoluted, snaily-horn, turreted, verticillate, whorled; **spiral,** corkscrew, dextral, helical, helicoid, helicoidal, screwed, sinistrorse, tortile, turbinate

TWISTING *adj* anfractuous, circuitous, circular, flexuose, flexuous, peristaltic, roundabout, serpentine, sinuate, sinuous, snaky, tortuous, voluminous *(Obs.)*, winding; **tendril-like,** capreolate, tendrillar, vinelike; **curly,** crimpy, crinkly, crisp, crispate, crispy, frizzy; **wriggly,** rolling, sigmate, squiggly, vermicular, vermiculate, volute, wiggly

TWISTINGLY *adv* circuitously, circularly, flexuously, round, sinuously, tortuously, vermicularly, windingly; **convolutely,** dextrally, helically, helicoidally, verticillately

TWO *n* binary, brace, couple, couplet, deuce *(Cards)*, doublet, duad, duumvirate, dyad, pair, pigeon pair, twa *(Scot.)*, twain *(Archaic)*, twosome, yoke; **twin,** fellow, match, pair; **twins,** Castor and Pollux, fraternal twins, Gemini, identical twins, Siamese twins, Tweedledum and Tweedledee

TWO *adj* binary, both, dual, dyad, dyadic; **twinned,** binate *(Bot.)*, conjugate, coupled, dizygotic *(Embryol.)*, geminate, paired, twin; **double,** biparous, diploid, duple, duplex, duplicate, duplicative, twofold; **two-sided,** amphibious, bicameral, biform, bilateral, binucleate, dimorphous, double-sided, two-handed, two-piece, twosome; **second,** alternate, every other, latter, secondary

Uu

UGLIFY *v* blemish, contort, deface, deform, disfigure, distort, marr, soil, spoil, vandalise

UGLILY *adv* dreadfully, grotesquely, hideously, ill-favouredly, **unattractively,** plainly, unhandsomely; **inelegantly,** gracelessly, stiffly; **dowdily,** frumpily, frumpishly

UGLINESS *n* dreadfulness, haggishness, hideousness, ill-favouredness, unsightliness; **unattractiveness,** plainness, unhandsomeness, unloveliness; **grotesqueness,** deformity, distortion, grotesquerie; **dowdiness,** frumpiness, frumpishness, homeliness, manginess; **uglification,** disfigurement; **inelegance,** gracelessness, horsiness, stiffness

UGLY *adj* dreadful, foul, frightful, grotesque, hideous, horrid, monstrous, not fit to be seen, odious, toadlike, ugly as sin, with a face like a bagful of arseholes, with a face like the back of a bus, with a face that would stop a clock; **unattractive,** beer-sodden, bloated, coarse, common, crooked, disfigured, distorted, favourless *(Archaic)*, gaunt, graceless, haggard, hard-favoured, hard-featured, ill-favoured, ill-looking, ill-proportioned, ill-shaped, inelegant, lumbering, misshapen, repellant, repulsive, shapeless, stiff, unbeauteous, unbeautiful, uncomely, uncouth, ungainly, ungraceful, unhandsome, unlovely, unprepossessing, unseemly *(Obs.)*, unshapely, unsightly; **mean,** clumsy, dingy, foul, mangy, rickety, rough, rude, scrubby, squalid; **ghastly,** cadaverous, Gothic *(Lit.)*, grim, grisly, gruesome, shocking; **plain,** blemished, homely, ordinary; **horsy,** horse-faced; **haggish,** haggy; **dowdy,** dowdyish, drack, dumpy, frumpish, frumpy, gawky, shabby, shapeless; **showy,** crude, garish, gaudy, gross, overdecorated, overdone, specious

UGLY PERSON *n* baboon, bag, beldam *(Archaic)*, cow, eyesore, face-ache, fright, gorgon, gorilla, hag, harpy, harridan, hellcat, horror, lemon, old bag, old cow, old trout, scarecrow, sight, toad, trout, ugly duckling, witch; **grotesque,** guy, monster, monstrosity, Punchinello; **frump,** dowdy, fleabag, hausfrau

UNAVAILABLE *adj* elusive, inaccessible, irretraceable, not to be had, unobtainable, unrealisable; **vain,** futile, unavailing, unlikely

UNBEARABLE *adj* enough to drive one mad, enough to try the patience of Job, insufferable, intolerable, more than flesh and blood can bear, not to be borne, not to be put up with, past bearing, unendurable, unsupportable; **distressing,** afflicting, comfortless, depressing, disheartening, harrowing, heartbreaking, heartrending. *See also* UNPLEASANT; SICKENING; DREADFUL; PESTERING

UNCERTAIN *adj* arguable, changeable, debatable, doubtable, doubtful, dubersome *(Brit. and U.S.)*, dubious, dubitable, facultative, fallible, in doubt, in the air, insecure, open, precarious, problematic, questionable, random, rocky, slippery, suspenseful, ticklish, unauthenticated, uncon-

uncertain

firmed, unpredictable, unreliable, unsourced, unstable, untrustworthy; **ambiguous,** amphibolic, amphibological, amphibolous, aoristic, apocryphal, cloudy, cryptic, enigmatic, equivocal, indefinite, indistinct, mysterious, obscure, oracular, paradoxical, undefined, vague, veiled; **marginal,** borderline, cliff-hanging; **conditional,** casual *(Obs.),* chancey, chancy, contingent, dependent on circumstances, provisional, subject to circumstances; **unknown,** hypothetical, uncounted, undetermined, unmeasured, unnumbered, unresolved, unsettled, unsure, untold, without number; **indeterminable,** incalculable, indemonstrable, indeterminate, indiscernible, inestimable, innumerable, unknowable, unmeasurable; **unsure,** aimless, ambivalent, at one's wit's end, dithering, dithery, halting, hesitant, hesitative, indecisive, nonplussed, perplexed, puzzled, suspensive, unassured, undecided, undetermined, unresolved, unsettled, vacillating; **doubtful,** agnostic, dubitative

UNCERTAINLY *adv* ambiguously, arguably, cloudily, contingently, dubitably, equivocally, haltingly, incalculably, indiscernibly, obscurely, precariously, problematically, unpredictably; **indeterminably,** indemonstrably, inestimably, unknowably, unmeasurably; **indecisively,** agnostically, doubtfully, dubiously, hesitantly, hesitatingly, hesitatively, in a state of uncertainty, indeterminately, on the horns of a dilemma, perplexedly, suspensefully, undecidedly, unresolvedly

UNCERTAIN THING *n* borderland, borderline, chance, cliff-hanger, conjecture, contingency, contingent, leap in the dark, lineball, neither fish nor fowl, pig in a poke, possibility, problem, rumour, the joker in the pack, unknowable, unknown, unknown factor, variable, x *(Maths);* **open question,** enigma, matter of opinion, moot point, mystery, obscureness, obscurity, query, question; **quandary,** dilemma

UNCERTAINTY *n* ambivalence, bewilderment, doubtfulness, haltingness, hesitancy, hesitation, indecision, indecisiveness, misgiving, pendency, perplexity, self-distrust, undecidedness, unresolvedness, unsettledness, unsureness, vacillation; **doubt,** agnosticism, dubiety, dubitation, incertitude; **indeterminancy,** incalculability, incalculableness, indemonstrability, indiscernibleness, unknowableness, unknowableness, unpredictability, unpredictableness, unreliability, untrustworthiness; **indeterminateness,** dependence, dubiousness, fallibility, fortuitousness, peradventure *(Archaic),* precariousness, suspense, uncertainness; **ambiguity,** ambiguousness, amphibology, amphiboly, cloudiness, double meaning, equivocalness, vagueness

UNCLEAR *adj* abstract, abstruse, confused, dark, deep, dim, equivocatory, esoteric, hazy, mystical *(Rare),* obscure, opaque, recondite; **puzzling,** baffling, bewildering, beyond comprehension, challenging, confusing, difficult, elusive, paradoxical, past comprehension, perplexing; **inapprehensive,** incomprehensive; **mysterious,** arcane, cryptic, enigmatic, inscrutable, mystic; **Delphic,** Delphian, oracular; **incomprehensible,** all Greek, beyond one's depth, clear as mud, fathomless, impalpable, impenetrable, inappreciable, unintelligible; **insoluble,** impenetrable, incalculable, inexplicable, insolvable, unaccountable, unexplainable, unfathomable, unknowable, unscrutable, unsearchable; **illegible,** crabbed, cramped, hieroglyphic, ill-defined, indecipherable, unreadable

UNCLEARLY *adv* abstrusely, ambiguously, bafflingly, bewilderingly, darkly, deeply, equivocatingly, obscurely, recondithely; **mysteriously,** cryptically, elusively, enigmatically, incomprehensively, inscrutably, **unintelligibly,** fathomlessly, impalpably, impenetrably, incomprehensibly, inexplicably, unaccountably, unfathomably; **over one's head,** beyond one's depth, out of one's depth; **insolubly,** insolvably; **illegibly,** crabbedly, unreadably

UNCOMPROMISING *adj* confirmed, immovable, insistent, iron-fisted, resolute, strong-willed, unbending, vocal; **wilful,** headstrong, self-willed, wanton; **intent,** bent on, bound to, hell-bent on, intent on, set on

UNCONDITIONAL *adj* clear, cool *(Colloq.),* round, straight, straight-out, termless, unqualified; **categorical,** definitive, unexceptional; **regardless,** independent, irrespective; **utter,** absolute, flat, implicit, out-and-out, outright, perfect, unmitigated; **total,** arrant, complete, downright, positive, pure, sheer, thorough

UNCONDITIONALITY *n* absoluteness, categoricalness, definitiveness, implicitness, law of excluded middle, the Absolute, unqualifiedness

UNCONDITIONALLY *adv* categorically, clear, clearly, come hell or high water, implicitly, unexceptionally, unmitigatedly, unqualifiedly, with no strings attached; **utterly,** absolutely, arrantly, completely, definitively, easily, flat, flatling *(Archaic),* flatly, purely, soever, totally; **independently,** irrespectively; **unequivocably,** explicitly, in so many words, unquestionably

UNCONSCIOUS *adj* asleep, comatose, oblivious, out cold, out like a light, syncopic; **dazed,** bleary, bleary-eyed, blurry, groggy, non compos, silly, stunned, stupid, stuporous; **punch-drunk,** concussed, like a stunned mullet, punchy; **drugged,** blind, dopey; **hypnotic,** autohypnotic, hypnagogic, hypnoid, hypnologic, hypnopompic, trancelike

UNCONSCIOUSLY *adv* blindly, comatosely, insensately, lifelessly, numbly, senselessly; **dazedly,** blearily, dully, groggily, stupidly; **blockishly,** impassively, obtusely

UNCONSCIOUSNESS *n* Lethe, lifelessness, nothingness, oblivion, sleep; **grogginess,** amazement *(Obs.),* bleariness, blindness, concussion, daze, stupefaction, stupidness, stupor, subconsciousness; **faint,** blackout, catalepsy, coma, epilepsy, fit, grand mal, petit mal, swoon, swound *(Archaic),* syncope, trance; **hypnotism,** animal magnetism *(Obs.),* autohypnosis, hypnogenesis, hypnosis. *See also* INSENSIBILITY: ANAESTHESIA

UNCONVENTIONALLY *adv* informally, irregularly, unfashionably; **eccentrically,** erratically, out of step, singularly, uniquely, unnaturally

UNCOUTHLY *adv* loutishly, oafishly, rowdily; **awkwardly**, broadly, rustically; **uncivilly**, illiberally, indecorously, low-mindedly; **brutishly**, barbarically, brutally, harshly, heathenishly, roughly, rudely, swinishly

UNDER *prep* beneath, neath *(Scot. Poetic)*, underneath

UNDER ATTACK *adv* between two fires, on the receiving end, under fire, under siege

UNDER CONTROL *adv* in check; **in control**, at the helm, at the wheel

UNDERGO *v* bechance, befall, come upon, encounter, endure, experience, fare, incur, meet, meet with, run across, run into, run up against, stumble on, stumble upon, walk into

UNDERLIE *v* base, bottom, found, underlay

UNDERSTAND *v* bottom, catch on, click, comprehend, cotton on, fathom, follow, get, get inside, get the message, get the picture, have someone taped, healy, jerry to, make head or tail of, penetrate, savvy, see, see the light, take a tumble to, take a wake-up, take in, the penny drops, trick to, tumble to, twig. *See also* KNOW

UNDERSTANDING *n* insight, sight *(Obs.)*, skill *(Obs.)*; **awareness**, apperception, cognisance, consciousness, initiation, recognisance, recognition, self-awareness, self-consciousness, self-knowledge, sense; **perception**, cognition, noesis, observation, percept, perceptiveness, perceptivity, percipience, sensibility. *See also* KNOWLEDGE

UNDERTAKE *v* assume, attempt, come to holts with, do, engage in, fix, go ahead with, have, launch, mind, purpose, set up, stage, stand, tackle, take on, take upon oneself, work; **break new ground**, cross the Rubicon, embark, enter on, launch forth, venture upon; **have irons in the fire**, have a lot on one's plate; **get on with the job**, do someone's dirty work, get a grip on, get one's teeth into, get stuck into, go to it, hop into, make bold to, put one's hand to the plough, put one's shoulder to the wheel, square up to, take in hand, take the bit between one's teeth, take upon one's shoulders, throw oneself into, turn one's hand to; **attempt the impossible**, square the circle

UNDERTAKER *n* burier, cremationist, embalmer, funeral director, gravedigger, mortician, sexton; **pallbearer**, mourner, mute

UNDERTAKING *n* affair, enterprise, operation, program, thing, venture, voyage *(Obs.)*; **assignment**, commission, engagement, job, plan, project, task, work; **campaign**, adventure, crusade, emprise *(Archaic)*, mission, quest, search; **forlorn hope**, leap in the dark, tall order; **embarkation**, assumption, candidature, commitment, espousal

UNDERWEAR *n* chiton, combinations, dishabille, flannels *(Obs.)*, lingerie, long johns, smalls *(Brit. Colloq.)*, underclothes, undergarment, underthings, undies, unmentionables; **camisole**, bodice *(Obs.)*, chemise, diaper shirt, hoop, hoop skirt, sark *(Scot. Archaic)*, spencer, undershirt *(U.S.)*, undersleeve; **petticoat**, balmoral, bustle, crinoline, farthingale, half-

underwear slip, pannier (Obs.), slip, underskirt; **foundation garment**, boob tube, bra, brassiere, busk, corset, corsetry, cup, easies (N.Z.), falsies, girdle, pasty, roll-ons, stays, step-ins; **singlet**, Jacky Howe, Jimmy Howe, undervest, vest; **panties**, bloomers, briefs, drawers, gorgeous gussies, grundies, gussies, knickers, pantalets, pants, scanties; **underpants**, boxer shorts, grundies, jockey shorts, jockeys, jocks, reginalds, underdaks, Y-fronts; **supporter**, athletic support, codpiece, jock, jockstrap, support; **figleaf**, cache-sexe. See also TIGHTS

UNDETERMINED adj in the air, inconclusive, open, pendent, pending, uncertain, undecided; **perplexing**, debatable, paradoxical, problematical, questionable, ticklish

UNDRESS v bare, debag, dishelm (Archaic), disrobe, divest, do a hambone, expose oneself, peel, pill (Archaic), strip, uncover, unhood; **go naked**, chuck a brown-eye, flash, jaybird, skinny-dip, streak

UNDRESSING n dismantlement, disrobement, divestiture, divestment, divesture, exposure, indecent exposure, poppy show, striptease

UNEQUAL adj anisotropic, asymmetrical, disparate, irregular, unbalanced, uneven; **disproportional**, disproportionate, out of proportion; **lopsided**, anisometric, dissymetric, dissymmetrical, oblique, one-sided, secund, unilateral; **perissodactyl**, perissodactylous; **scalene**

UNEQUALLY adv irregularly, unevenly; **lopsidedly**, askew, awry, disproportionately

UNFAIR adj a bit rough, bloody, hard, inofficious, invidious, loaded, on the cuff (N.Z.), raw, unjust, unjustified, unrighteous, wanton; **undeserved**, gratuitous, improper, uncalled-for, unearned, unexpected, unfitting; **discriminatory**, biased, nepotic, one-eyed, one-sided, partial, partisan; **unauthorized**, unconstitutional, unsanctioned, unwarrantable, unwarranted; **foul**, dirty, unsportsmanlike; **unpardonable**, inexcusable, objectionable, unjustifiable; **oppressive**, extortionate, inequitable, iniquitous, injurious

UNFAIRLY adv below the belt, dirtily, foul; **unjustly**, extortionately, gratuitously, iniquitously, injuriously, inofficiously, invidiously, oppressively, unrighteously, wantonly; **unworthily**, improperly, unfitly

UNFAIRNESS n gratuitousness, inequality, inequity, iniquitousness, iniquity, injury, invidiousness; **discrimination**, bias, cronyism, favouritism, leaning, nepotism, onesidedness, partiality, preferential treatment; **injustice**, dirtiness, inofficiousness, miscarriage of justice, misjudgment, rum go, unjustness, wrong; **oppression**, abuse, bloodiness, dirtiness, injuriousness, oppressiveness, tyranny, unrighteousness, wantonness; **headhunting**, kangaroo court, McCarthyism, Star Chamber, witchhunting

UNFAITHFUL adj disloyal, faithless, false, forsworn, recreant, slippery, unreliable, untrue; **treacherous**, apostate, double-dealing, false-hearted, feline, perfidious, renegade, snaky, traitorous, treasonable, treasonous; **adulterous**, adulterine

UNFAITHFULNESS n disloyalty, faithlessness, falseness, falsity, infidelity, untrueness; **treacherousness,** apostasy, doubleness, felineness, felinity, insidiousness, perfidiousness, recreance, recreancy, tergiversation, traitorousness, treasonableness. *See also* BETRAYAL

UNFASTEN v disyoke, unbrace, unfetter, unfix, unfreeze, unharness, unhasp, unhitch, unhook, unmoor, unpeg, unpin, unpin, unscrew, unsling, unsnap, unstick, unyoke

UNFORTUNATE n bad news, Job, lame duck, miser *(Obs.),* poor cow, poor fish, ruin, scapegoat, schlemiel *(U.S.),* underdog, victim, wreck, wretch; **deadbeat,** derelict, dero, down-and-out, toe-ragger, vagrant

UNFORTUNATE adj badly off, hapless, miserable, poor, stricken, underprivileged, unhappy, wretched; **luckless,** out of luck, star-crossed, starred, unlucky; **ill-fated,** accident-prone, accursed, cursed, curst; **hard-hit,** in a bad way, in deep water, in dire straits, in the poo, in the shit, in the wars, in trouble, smitten, up against it; **down-and-out,** deadbeat, down on one's arse, down on one's luck

UNFORTUNATELY adv from bad to worse, haplessly, ill, lucklessly, tragically, unfavourably, unhappily, unluckily

UNFORTUNATENESS n inauspiciousness, unfavourableness, unluckiness; **calamitousness,** disastrousness, ruggedness, ruinousness, tragicalness; **agony,** distress, misery, unhappiness, woe, wretchedness; **lucklessness,** haplessness

UNFRIENDLINESS n animosity, animus, bad feeling, enmity, hostility, ill feeling, ill will, inimicality, malevolence, rivalry, virulence; **antipathy,** adverseness, antagonism, defiantness, opposition, quarrelsomeness; **alienation,** disaffection, estrangement, incompatibility; **bitterness,** jealousy, rancorousness, rancour, resentment, spite, spitefulness, the sulks. *See also* UNSOCIABILITY

UNFRIENDLY adj adverse, antagonistic, hostile, inimical, malevolent, oppositional; **quarrelsome,** aggressive, belligerent, defiant, fighting drunk, pugnacious; **traitorous,** disloyal, snaky, treacherous; **bitter,** rancorous, resentful, spiteful, spleenful, splenetic. *See also* UNSOCIABLE

UNGRAMMATICAL adj anacoluthic, incorrect, slipshod, solecistic, unidiomatic, wrong

UNGRATEFUL adj incapable of gratitude, ingrate, insensible of benefits, unappreciative, unthankful, whingeing; **forgetful,** oblivious, unmindful; **thankless**

UNGRATEFULLY adv unappreciatively, unthankfully; **thanklessly**

UNGRATEFULNESS n indifference, ingratitude, thanklessness, unappreciativeness, unthankfulness; **grudging thanks,** a show of gratitude; **ingrate,** ungrateful wretch

UNHAPPINESS n cheerlessness, disconsolateness, disconsolation, downheartedness, dreariness *(Archaic),* dumpishness, sadness, wistfulness; **misery,** bale *(Archaic),* comfortlessness, crestfallenness, distress, dole *(Archaic),* dolefulness, dolorousness, dolour, mournfulness, plaintiveness, rue *(Archaic),* ruefulness, ruth

(Archaic), ruthfulness, sorrow, sorrowfulness, tearfulness, woe, woefulness, wretchedness; **depression**, blue devils, blues, damp, dejectedness, dejection, despondency, gloom, gloominess, glumness, leadenness, low-spiritedness, maudlinness, mopishness, pensiveness, pessimism, prostration, vapourishness *(Archaic)*, Weltschmerz; **midlife crisis**, male menopause, MLC; **melancholy**, atrabiliousness, Byronism, melancholia, moodiness, spleen *(Archaic)*; **sullenness; loneliness**, forlornness, homesickness, lonesomeness, lovelornness; **dismalness**, depressiveness, dreariness, gloominess, infelicity, joylessness, mirthlessness, miserableness, oppressiveness, sunlessness, unblessedness; **distressfulness**, pathos, poignancy; **heartache**, anguish, heartbreak, heartbrokenness, heartsickness

UNHAPPY *adj* blue, cheerless, comfortless, disconsolate, distressful, doleful, doloroso, dolorous, dreary *(Archaic)*, droopy, dumpish, dumpy, forlorn, gloomy, glum, grievous, happy as a bastard on father's day, heavy, heavy-hearted, heavy-laden, in the miseries, joyless, maudlin, miserable, miserable as a bandicoot, mournful, sad, sorrowful, sorry, upset; **dejected**, chapfallen, chopfallen, crestfallen, damp *(Archaic)*, depressed, despondent, down, down in the dumps, down in the mouth, downcast, downhearted, exanimate, hipped, hippish, leaden, low, low-spirited, melancholiac, melancholic, melancholy, mopey, mopish, prostrate, ratshit, run-down, vapourish *(Archaic)*, wistful; **lonely**, homesick, like a bandicoot on a burnt ridge, like a shag on a rock, lonesome, lorn *(Archaic)*; **broken-hearted**, broken up, grief-stricken, heart-stricken, heartbroken, heartsick, heartsore, lovelorn; **weepy**, in tears, lachrymal, lachrymose, tearful, teary; **moody**, atrabilious, broody, Byronic, morose, saturnine, splenetic *(Obs.)*, sullen; **humourless**, mirthless; **unfortunate**, baleful *(Archaic)*, rueful, unblessed, woebegone, woeful, wretched

UNHAPPY PERSON *n* languisher, lemon, lonely heart, long face, martyr, mater dolorosa, miser *(Obs.)*, misery, miseryguts, mope, moper, sad sack, streak of misery, wet blanket, wowser; **melancholiac**, brooder, depressive; **wretch**, object of compassion, poor unfortunate

UNIFORM *n* cap and gown, gown, habit, livery, silks, vestment; **military clothing**, battle fatigues, battledress, class A's *(U.S.)*, dress uniform, fatigue dress, fatigues, full dress, gigglesuit, mess kit, number ones, order, Regimentals, service dress, tropical dress, tropical whites, tunic, undress; **spacesuit**, G-suit, pressure suit; **religious clothing**, alb, canonicals, cassock, chasuble, chimar, chimer, clericals, cloth *(Obs.)*, cope, cotta, dalmatic, ephod *(Judaism)*, epitrachelion *(Greek Orthodox Ch.)*, fanon, frock, Geneva gown, mantelletta *(Rom. Cath. Ch.)*, omophorion *(Eastern Ch.)*, pluvial, pontificals, rochet, scapular, soutane, surplice, tunicle, vestments; **prison clothing**, gigglesuit *(Obs.)*, magpie clothing; **hairshirt**, sanbenito

UNIMPORTANCE *n* immateriality, immaterialness, inessentiality, insignificance, irrelevance, worthlessness; **triviality**, bathos, impertinence, inconsequentiality, irrelevance, puerility, triflingness, trivialism, trivialness; **frivolity**, frivolousness, frothiness, lightsomeness, yeastiness; **pettiness**, insignificance, littleness, nothingness, obscureness, obscurity, paltriness, puniness, tenuousness, venality, venialness; **minimisation**, trivialisation

UNIMPORTANT *adj* foolish (Archaic), forgettable, futile (Obs.), inappreciable, insignificant, light, obscure, pint-size, simple, small, small-time, tenuous, two-by-four (U.S.), unconsidered, uneventful; **unessential**, dispensable, expendable, inessential, non-essential, peripheral; **inconsequential**, immaterial, impertinent, irrelevant; **accidental**, circumstantial; **superficial**, shallow; **subordinate**, less, minor, paltry, petit (Law), venial; **secondary**, subsidiary; **fiddling**, farting, mickey mouse, picayune, piddling, piffling, pimping, potty (Brit.), tinhorn (U.S.); **frivolous**, fallal (Obs.), frothy, idle, jesting, light, lightsome, lightweight, slight, yeasty; **trivial**, footling, for the birds, frying pan, gewgaw, gimcrack, gingerbread, inconsiderable, nugatory, petty, puerile, puny, trifling, twopenny-halfpenny, worthless

UNIMPORTANTLY *adv* insignificantly, tenuously, uneventfully, venially, worthlessly; **irrelevantly**, circumstantially, immaterially, peripherally, unessentially; **frivolously**, dallyingly, frothily, jestingly, jokingly, lightsomely, yeastily; **inconsequentially**, inconsiderably, pettily, puerilely, punily, triflingly, trivially

UNIMPORTANT PERSON *n* also-ran, cipher, figurehead, insignificancy, insignificant, jackstraw, man of straw, nobody, non-person, nonentity, nothing, obscurity, trifler, amateur, dabbler, dallier, dilettante, piddler; **lightweight**, minnow, peanut, picayune, pipsqueak, pygmy, shitkicker, small fry, snippet, twerp, zed

UNIMPORTANT THING *n* inessential, minim, non-essential, non-event, nothing, unessential; **side issue**, accident, accidental, afterthought, bye, circumstance, immateriality, indifference, insignificant, irrelevance, red herring, sideshow; **trifle**, bêtise, breath, falderal, fiddle-faddle, frivolity, impertinence, joke, petty detail, pinpoint, triviality; **bagatelle**, bauble, bit of tinsel, chip (U.S.), fiddlestick, flummery, frippery, frivolity, gewgaw, gimcrack, gingerbread, kickshaw, knick-knack, peppercorn, picayune, straw, tinker's cuss, tinker's damn, toy, trinket, whatnot; **cavil**, fleabite, pinprick; **trivia**, minutiae; **chickenfeed**, kid-stakes, small beer, small change, small potatoes; **peccadillo**, venial sin; **insignificant place**, backstreet, byway, one-horse town, sideway, whistlestop (U.S.)

UNIONISM *n* compulsory unionism, restrictive practice, syndicalism, trade unionism, unionisation; **union movement**, organised labour

UNKEMPT *adj* bedraggled, daggy, draggletailed, frowzy, grubby, scrubby, sleazy, slovenly, sluttish, wretched; **scruffy**, scabby, scrofulous, scurfy, snotty, snotty-nosed, unwashed; **flea-bitten**, buggy, chatty,

unkempt   541   **unlawfully**

crawling, lousy, mangy, pediculous, sordid, squalid; **piggish,** beastlike, hoggish, hoglike. *See also* DIRTY

UNKIND *adj* cutting, disobliging, incogitant, inconsiderate, thoughtless, uncharitable, unchristian, ungenerous, ungentle, unkindly, unpitying; **ill-willed,** cattish, catty, despiteful *(Archaic),* ill-natured, malevolent, malicious, malignant, mean, misanthropic, nasty, poisonous, sharp-tongued, shrewd *(Archaic),* snaky, spiteful, venomous, viper-like, viperish, viperous, virulent; **cruel,** bloody-minded, cold-blooded, crool, cutthroat, dispiteous *(Archaic),* harsh, heartless, inhuman, inhumane, merciless, pitiless, remorseless, ruthless, sadistic, unmerciful, unrelenting, unsparing, unsympathetic; **brutal,** atrocious, beastly, brutish, butcherly, fell, fiendish, fierce, lupine, savage, tigerish, vicious, vulture-like

UNKINDLY *adv* soullessly, thoughtlessly, uncharitably, unfeelingly, ungently, unsympathetically; **maliciously,** cattily, despitefully *(Archaic),* ill-naturedly, malignantly, misanthropically, nastily, poisonously, venomously; **cruelly,** cold-bloodedly, cuttingly, heartlessly, inhumanly, inhumanely, mercilessly, remorselessly, ruthlessly, sadistically, unmercifully; **brutally,** brutishly, fiendishly, fiercely, savagely, tigerishly, viciously

UNKINDNESS *n* cattiness, cattishness, disobligingness, harshness, ill-treatment, maltreatment, meanness, misanthropy, nastiness, soullessness, uncharitableness, unfeelingness, unkindliness; **inconsiderateness,** insensitivity, thoughtlessness, unfeelingness; **cruelty,** bloody-mindedness, brutality, brutishness, cold-bloodedness, cruelness, flintiness, heartlessness, inhumanity, mental cruelty, mercilessness, pitilessness, remorselessness, ruthlessness, sadism, savageness, savagery, unmercifulness, unrelentingness, viciousness; **fiendishness,** atrociousness, fellness, tigerishness; **brutalisation,** dehumanisation

UNKIND PERSON *n* abuser, animal, brute, harmer, monster, sadist, savage, Turk, victimiser, vulture; **Job's comforter; cat,** tigress, viper

UNKNOWN *n* anon., anonymity, stranger; **closed book,** dark horse; **gamble,** pig in a poke

UNKNOWN *adj* strange, trackless, unbeknown *(Colloq.),* uncharted, unco *(Scot.),* unexplored, unfamiliar, unheard, unheard-of, unplumbed, unrecognised, unsounded, unsuspected; **unnamed,** anonymous, unbranded, unlisted

UNLAWFUL *adj* backstreet, backyard, illegal, illegitimate, illicit, non-legal, racketeering, unauthorized, wrongful; **contraband,** black, black-market; **law-breaking,** crim, criminal, criminological, crooked, felonious, malfeasant, recidivistic, recidivous; **indictable,** actionable, punishable, tortious; **lawless,** anarchic, chaotic; **above the law,** despotic, tyrannical; **outlawed,** out of bounds, outside the law; **fraudulent,** collusive, conspiratorial; **unconstitutional,** extrajudicial, irregular, unstatutory

UNLAWFULLY *adv* illegally, illegitimately, illicitly, lawlessly, unconstitutionally, wrongfully; **criminally,** crookedly, feloniously; **dead to**

UNLAWFULNESS *n* illegality, illegalness, illegitimacy, illicitness, lawbreaking, unconstitutionality, wrong side of the law, wrongfulness; **criminality**, banditry, crookedness, delinquency, feloniousness, felony, gangsterism, lawlessness, outlawry, racketeering, recidivism, standover tactics; **lynch law**, gang rule, kangaroo court, mob law, mob rule. *See also* CRIME

UNLIKELIHOOD *n* fishiness, improbability, unlikeliness; **an outside chance**, a hundred to one, a long chance, a poor chance, bare possibility, Buckley's chance, long shot, poor chance, remote possibility, small chance; **tall story**, exaggeration, shaggy dog story, the story about the one that got away

UNLIKELY *adj* at long odds, contrary to expectation, far-fetched, fishy, implausible, improbable, inconceivable

UNLIKELY *adv* hardly, improbably, scarcely, unlikely

UNMANAGEABLE *adj* hard-mouthed *(Equestrian)*, mean, uncontrollable; **refractory**, bloody, bloody-minded, hard-set, impossible, impracticable, intractable, restive

UNPAID *adj* due, not yet payable, outstanding, undischarged; **deferring payment**, moratory; **complimentary**, free, gratis, tax-deductible, tax-free, untaxed; **honorary**, uncustomed, unpaid, unremunerated, unrewarded, voluntary

UNPLEASANT *adj* awful, bad, beastly, bitter, dire, dislikeable, displeasing, forbidding, hard, hell of a, helluva, lousy, nasty, painful, perishing, rough, sharp, tough, ugly, unacceptable, uncomfortable, undesirable, unenviable, ungrateful, unpalatable, unpleasing, unsavoury, untoward; **disagreeable**, abhorrent, detestable, distasteful, execrable, hateful, loathly *(Archaic)*, loathsome, objectionable, obnoxious, odious, rebarbative, repellent, repugnant, repulsive, revolting, uninviting, vile, wicked *(Colloq.)*. *See also* UNBEARABLE; SICKENING; DREADFUL; PESTERING

UNPLEASANTLY *adv* abhorrently, appallingly, awfully, disagreeably, distastefully, dreadfully, forbiddingly, hatefully, insufferably, intolerably, lousily, objectionably, rottenly, uncomfortably; **gruesomely**, ghoulishly, horrendously, horribly, horridly, monstrously, obnoxiously, poisonously, vilely; **revoltingly**, repellently, repugnantly, repulsively, sickeningly; **filthily**, abominably, foully, frowzily, loathsomely; **noisomely**, mephitically, rankly, stinkingly; **bitchily**, cantankerously, doggishly, ill-naturedly

UNPLEASANTNESS *n* awfulness, badness, disagreeableness, distastefulness, dreadfulness, frightfulness, harshness, insufferableness, intolerability, intolerableness, irksomeness, lousiness, meanness, monstrousness, nastiness, poisonousness, unbearableness, uncomfortableness; **obnoxiousness**, fulsomeness, repellence, repellency, repulsiveness; **gruesomeness**, creepiness, ghastliness, ghoulishness, grimness, grisliness, horribleness; **bloody-mindedness**, bad temper, bitchiness, cantankerousness, doggishness; **discomfort**, irritation, pain; **filthiness**, abominableness, beastliness, foulness, goo, guck, gunk, insalubrity, loathsomeness, muck, rottenness, slime, sourness, vileness

UNPLEASANT PERSON *n* bag, bastard, bête noire, bugger, cunt, cunthook *(N.Z.)*, deadshit, ghoul, hazer, heavy, iron maiden, mother-fucker *(U.S.)*, pill, prick, repeller, reptile, shocker, stinker, twat, varmint *(Archaic)*

UNPLEASANT PLACE *n* hell, hellhole, purgatory, the dead end, the end, the living end, the pits

UNPLEASANT THING *n* a bad scene, a cow of a something, a fair cow, a taste of one's own medicine, bitter cup, bitter pill, blow, dose, four-letter word, horror, incubus, lemon, nightmare, pain, pain in the arse, pain in the behind, pain in the bum, pain in the neck, sorry sight, thorn in one's flesh, wormwood and gall; **chore**, dirty work, nuisance, taskwork; **abomination**, anathema, detestable action, shameful vice, wickedness

UNREADINESS *n* improvidence, lack of preparation, neglect, unpreparedness; **rawness**, crudeness, crudity, rudeness

UNREADY *adj* cold, flat-footed, ill-equipped, ill-prepared, out of order, unarmed, unarranged, unorganised, unprepared; **half-baked**, sketchy; **on the anvil**, on the drawing-board, under discussion; **improvident**, happy-go-lucky, shiftless, unthrifty. *See also* RAW

UNREALISTIC *adj* airy-fairy, capricious *(Obs.)*, escapist, fairytale, fanciful, far-out, idealist, idealistic, moonshiny, notional, romantic, starry-eyed, unreal, utopian, vaporous, visionary

UNRELATED *adj* dissociated, foreign, immaterial, impertinent, inconsequent, independent, irrelevant, unconnected; **absolute**, irrelative, positive, unique; **kinless; beside the point,** not to the purpose

UNRELATEDNESS *n* distance, foreignness, impertinence, inconsequence, independence, irrelativeness, irrelevance; **absoluteness**, uniqueness

UNSAVOURY *adj* ill-flavoured, indigestible, inedible, unappetizing, uneatable, unpalatable; **rough**, astringent, austere, coarse, strong; **off**, corked, corky, nasty, noisome, on the turn, tinny; **rank**, acrid, brackish, fetid, gamy, rammish, rancid

UNSELFISH *adj* altruistic, benevolent, disinterested, high-minded, non-profitmaking, public-spirited, self-devotional, self-effacing, self-forgetful, self-renunciatory, self-sacrificing, selfless; **generous**, big, big-hearted, chivalrous, magnanimous, noble, philanthropic

UNSELFISHLY *adv* altruistically, benevolently, chivalrously, disinterestedly, nobly

UNSELFISHNESS *n* altruism, disinterest, disinterestedness, self-devotion, self-renunciation, self-sacrifice; **generosity**, magnanimity, philanthropy

UNSELFISH PERSON *n* altruist, humanitarian, martyr, noble soul, philanthropist, saint

UNSOCIABILITY *n* exclusiveness, inhospitableness, inhospitality; **surliness**, bearishness, moroseness, spleen, sulkiness, sullenness; **coldness**, chill, chillness, coolness, frostiness; **uncommunicativeness**, retire-

ment, retreat, silence, undemonstrativeness, withdrawal; **reserve,** aloofness, distance, offishness, remoteness, reservedness, reticence, standoffishness, unapproachableness.
See also UNFRIENDLINESS

UNSOCIABLE *adj* antisocial, dissociable, dissocial, forbidding, ill-disposed, inhospitable, insociable, unwelcoming; **sullen,** bearish, farouche, morose, sulky, surly; **reserved,** in one's shell, indrawn, reticent, retiring, unforthcoming, withdrawn; **aloof,** distant, exclusive, inapproachable, offish, remote, standoff, stand-offish, unapproachable, uncommunicative, undemonstrative; **cold,** chill, chilly, coldish, cool, frigid, frosty, frozen, icy; **antipathetic,** disaffected, incompatible, intolerant, unsympathetic; **alienated,** estranged, irreconcilable, isolated. See also UNFRIENDLY

UNTIDILY *adv* frowzily, seedily, shabbily, sleazily, sloppily; **chaotically,** all over the shop, at random, at sixes and sevens, higgledy-piggledy, topsyturvy, willy-nilly; **helter-skelter,** hurly-burly, hurry-scurry, pell-mell; **confusedly,** confusingly, desultorily, discomposedly, immethodically; **riotously,** harum-scarum, rowdily, tempestuously, tumultuously, uproariously, wildly

UNTIDINESS *n* dishabille, dishevelment, dowdiness, frowziness, sleaze, sleaziness, sloppiness, slovenliness, tousle *(Rare),* unkemptness; **pigsty,** brothel, disaster area, dump, fleapit, shambles

UNTIDY *v* dishevel, ruffle, rumple, tousle; **jumble,** clutter, derange, disarrange, disarray, litter, shuffle; **sprawl,** knock about, slummock; **confuse,** anarchise, discompose, embroil, fuddle, gum up the works, make hay, make the feathers fly, make the fur fly, put the cart before the horse, rock the boat, throw a spanner in the works, upset the applecart

UNTIDY *adj* bedraggled, blowzy, dishevelled, down at heel, frowzy, mussy *(U.S.),* out at elbow, out at the elbow, raggle-taggle, scruffy, shaggy, slatternly, sleazy, slipshod, sloppy, slovenly, slummocky, sluttish, tatty, unkempt, warby, wild, wild and woolly, windblown, windswept

UNTIDY PERSON *n* chat, dag, derelict, dero, dowdy, ragamuffin, ragbag, scarecrow, scrubber, scruff, scunge, slattern, sleaze, sloven, slummock, slut, warb; **rowdy,** boyo, harum-scarum; **rabble,** mob; **disarranger,** disorganiser, disturber, jumbler, rifler

UNTIMELINESS *n* bad timing, inopportuneness, inopportunity, interruption, unseasonableness; **mistiming,** asynchronism; **false start,** miscue, wrong entry *(Music);* **anachronism,** archaism, prolepsis; **obsolescence,** fustiness, obsoleteness

UNTIMELY *adj* abortive, early, ill-timed, innopportune, interruptive, late, out of season, overhasty, premature, unseasonable; **mistimed,** asynchronous, fast, slow; **anachronous,** anachronistic, archaic, demoded, fusty, obsolescent, obsolete, old hat, old-fashioned, old-time, olde-worlde, out of fashion, out-of-date, outdated, outmoded, outworn

UNTIMELY *adv* inopportunely, out of turn; **out,** behind, out of season, out of time, unseasonably

UNUSED *adj* unbeaten, unfired, untapped, untouched, untravelled, virgin; **at a loose end,** at liberty, free, loose, standing, vacant

UNWHOLESOME *adj* insalubrious, morbid, morbific, unhealthy, unsound; **septic,** abscessed, cankerous, infect *(Archaic)*, mature, purulent, scorbutic, ulcerative, ulcerous, watery; **cancerous,** carcinomatous, tumorous; **wasted,** atrophied, degenerate, waxy; **anaemic,** exsanguine; **inflamed,** angry, bloodshot; **dropsical,** hydropic; **acute,** afflictive, progressive; **subclinical; chronic,** confirmed; **incurable,** immedicable, remediless; **infectious,** catching, endemic, epidemic, pandemic; **inflammatory,** phlogistic; **deleterious; pathogenetic,** bacterial, germinal, viral; **cryptogenic,** iatrogenic, idiopathic, psychosomatic

UNWILLING *adj* averse, difficult, disinclined, hesitant, indisposed, loath, negative, reluctant, reserved, scrupulous, uncooperative, unenthusiastic, uninclined; **involuntary,** automatic, autonomic, compulsive, matter-of-course, mechanical, mesmeric, reflex, semi-automatic; **backward,** bashful, shy, timid

UNWILLINGLY *adv* aversely, grudgingly, hesitatingly, loathly, reluctantly, **with a bad grace; involuntarily,** automatically, autonomically, by rote, compulsively, mechanically; **backwardly,** bashfully, shyly, timidly; **purposelessly,** idly, tardily; **unintentionally,** accidentally, in spite of oneself, unconsciously, unwittingly

UNWILLINGNESS *n* averseness, disinclination, indisposition, unenthusiasm; **reluctance,** hesitation, reservation, scrupulosity; **involuntariness,** automatism, mechanicalness; **automatic response,** compulsion, knee-jerk reaction; **idleness,** laziness, perfunctoriness, tardiness; **aimlessness,** purposelessness; **backwardness,** bashfulness, shyness, timidity; **obstacle,** difficulty, scruple; **unintentionality,** unconsciousness, unwittingness

UNWORTHINESS *n* indignity *(Obs.)*, unfitness; **presumption,** encroachment

UNWORTHY *adj* incompetent, undeserving, unfit, unqualified, would-be; **presumptuous,** assuming, self-styled, upstart

UP *adv* airwards, heavenward, skyward, sunward, upstairs, upwardly, upwards

URBAN *adj* burghal, citied, civic, cosmopolitan, intercity, interurban, megalopolitan, metropolitan; **citified,** townish; **suburban,** cross-town, downtown, slummy, uptown

URBANISATION *n* suburbanisation, urban renewal; **civics,** topography, town planning

URBANISE *v* citify, municipalise, suburbanise

URINATE *v* cross swords, drain the dragon, have a Japanese bladder, have a pee, leak, make water, micturate, pee, piddle, piss, point Percy at the porcelain, pot, powder one's nose, relieve oneself, shake hands with the wife's best friend, splash the boots, strain the potatoes, tinkle, wash one's hands, water the horse, wee-wee, wet

URINATION *n* hey-diddle-diddle, Jimmy Riddle, Johnny Bliss, leak, micturition, number one, pee, piddle, piss, slash, snake's, snake's hiss, twinkle, wee, wee-wee, werris; **call of nature**; **urine**, piss, stale, water; **diuresis**, bed-wetting, enuresis, frequency

URINO-GENITAL *adj* ejaculatory, genital, penile, prostate, scrotal, testicular, uretal, urethral, urinary, vaginal, vulvar

USE *n* appliance, application, employment, exercise, exertion, improvement, usage; **deployment**, exploitation, optimisation, telesis, utilisation; **consumption**, enjoyment, exhaustion, expenditure, usufruct *(Roman Law)*; **access**, break *(Radio)*, easement; **recovery**, reclamation, resurrection, revival; **wear**, wear and tear

USE *v* employ, make use of, ply, wield; **put to use**, bestow, dispose of, optimise, parlay, utilise; **bring into use**, deploy, find, mobilise, press into service; **apply**, bear, bring to bear, exercise, exert; **capitalise on**, get the best out of, improve, make the most of, turn to account, use to the full; **avail oneself of**, adopt, draw on, enjoy, seize, take up; **resort to**, fall back on, have recourse to, make do with, run to; **exploit**, milk, play, take advantage of, tap, trade on; **recycle**, recover, resurrect, revive

USEABLE *adj* applicative, applicatory, effective, exercisable, functional, practicable, practical, serviceable, subservient, utilisable, viable; **exploitable**, deployable, employable, tappable; **consumable**, enjoyable, expendable; **available**, disposable, ready, ready-made; **recoverable**, reclaimable, recyclable; **valid**, good, good for

USED UP *adj* exhausted, spent; **worn**, second-hand

USE FAULTY LANGUAGE *v* mispunctuate, misspeak, misspell, misword, miswrite

USEFUL *adj* handy, helpful, of use, serviceable; **all-purpose**, adaptable, convertible, flexible, general-purpose, multipurpose, purposive; **beneficial**, advantageous, available *(Archaic)*, profitable, valuable

USEFULLY *adv* serviceably; **advantageously**, profitably, valuably

USEFULNESS *n* advantageousness, profitableness, valuableness, value, worth; **function**, advantage, avail, good, purpose, service; **practicability**, instrumentality, practicality, viability; **useableness**, serviceability, serviceableness, useability, utility; **availability**, readiness

USELESS *adj* functionless, ineffective, ineffectual, inutile, naught (Obs.), non-effective, unemployable, unpractical; **worthless**, trashy, two-bob, valueless; **good-for-nothing**, fit for nothing, no-good, not worth a pinch of shit, not worth a whoop, not worth shucks (U.S.), not worth the candle; **rubbishy**, bodgie, brashy, draffy, dreggy, drossy, dud, grotty, jerry-built, pathetic, r.s., ratshit, trumpery, u$dp228]s, up to mud, up to putty, up to shit, warby, weak; **worn-out**, broken-down, clapped-out, condemnable, done, effete, inoperable, on the blink, on the scrap heap, on the way out, out of order, out of plumb, played-out, unfit, unserviceable; **obsolete**, obsolescent, otiose; **ne'er-do-well**, vagabond; **waste**, refuse, scrap; **futile**, abortive, bootless, empty, futilitarian, idle, no use, of no use, purposeless, Sisyphean, unavailing, vain; **invalid,** informal, inoperative; **redundant,** superfluous, unnecessary

USELESSLY *adv* effetely, otiosely, potteringly; **futilely,** bootlessly, emptily, idly, in vain, unavailingly, vainly

USELESSNESS *n* bootlessness, inutility, unemployability, unserviceability; **unsuitability,** inconvenience, inoperativeness, unfitness; **worthlessness,** drossiness, effeteness, inadequacy, inefficiency, trashiness, valuelessness; **futility,** futileness, idleness, otiosity, purposelessness, superfluousness, unnecessariness, vainness, vanity; **stultification,** crippling, thwarting; **impracticability,** impracticalness, unpracticality, unpracticableness, unworkability; **disservice,** disadvantage

USER *n* applier, exerciser, utiliser; **consumer,** enjoyer, exhauster, expender, spender; **exploiter,** urger

USE UP *v* consume, do, expend, go through, run through, spend; **exhaust,** clean out, finish up, work out

Vv

VACCINATION *n* antiserum, inoculant, inoculate, inoculation, inoculum, vaccinisation

VACILLATE *v* abstain, back and fill, balance, blow hot and cold, boggle, change one's tune, chop and change, dicker, fluctuate, halt, hang, have a bit both ways, hesitate, hover, oscillate, pause, sway, swing, tergiversate, um and ah, waver, whiffle, wobble; **agonise over**, be torn between, be up in the air; **shillyshally**, buggerise about, buggerise around, dillydally, frig around, give someone the run around, meander, pussyfoot, pussyfoot around; **prevaricate**, evade, procrastinate, temporise

VALUE *n* money's worth, the full two bob, worth; **face value**, book value, nominal value, par value; **assessment**, appraisal, appraisement, appreciation, duty, estimate, transvaluation; **quotation**, forward quotation, quote; **exchange rate**, cable rate, ratio

VALUER *n* appraiser, appreciator, estimator, valuator, valuer general

VAPORISE *v* ablate, atomise, fluidise, gasify, volatilise; **steam**, fume, fumigate, gas, vapour; **evaporate**, boil; **smoke**, reek

VAPORISER *n* atomiser, evaporator, fluidiser, generator, steamer, vaporimeter, volatiliser; **gasworks**, gasholder, gasometer

VARIABLE *adj* adjustable, alterable, amendable, changeable, convertible, deformable, flexible, flexile, malleable, modifiable, permutable, pervertible, rectifiable, temperable, transformable, transmutable; **variational**, adaptational, dissimilative, gradational, mutational, mutative, revisional, sportive *(Biol.)*; **conversionary**, conversional, diversified, metabolic, transmutational; **transformational**, alchemic, alchemical, alchemistic, alchemistical, metamorphic, transilient, transitional, transitionary, transitive

VARIABLY *adv* adaptively, adjustably, alterably, convertibly, flexibly, transitionally, transitively

VEHICLE *n* commercial vehicle, conveyance, motor vehicle, wheeler; **tracklaying vehicle**, bulldozer, caterpillar, caterpillar tractor, crawler, front-end loader, halftrack, tractor, tractor shovel, weasel; **amphibian**, duck *(Mil.),* hovercraft, hovertrain. *See also* CAR; CARRIAGE; WAGON; TRUCK; TRAM; TRAIN; BICYCLE; SLEDGE

VEHICULAR *adj* : **automotive** convertible, four-wheel drive, gran turismo, hardtop, motor, multicylinder, multimotored, pre-crumple, souped-up, tracked, trackless, veteran, vintage; **table-top**, flat-bed

VELOCITY *n* airspeed, angular velocity, burnout velocity, characteristic velocity, critical velocity, escape velocity, flap speed, geostrophic wind speed, gradient wind speed, ground speed, group velocity, muzzle velocity, orbital velocity, phase velocity, radial velocity, stall speed, terminal velocity, velocity of light; **mach,**

velocity   549   **vibrate**

mach number, sound barrier, speed of sound; **knot**, k.p.h., m.p.h., r.p.m. *See also* SPEED: RATE

VENEREAL DISEASE *n* French pox, gonorrhoea, great pox, herpes, herpes simplex, jack, load, lues, nonspecific urethritis, officer's pox *(Mil.)*, padre's pox, pox, S.T.D., Saigon rose, sexually transmitted disease, social disease, syphilis, tabes, tabes dorsalis, the clap, V.D.; **syphilitic lesion**, chancre, gumma

VERBOSE *adj* diffuse, diffusive, gabby, garrulous, lengthy, long-drawn out, longwinded, loquacious, overblown, profusive, prolix, rambling, tedious, voluble, wordy; **amplificatory**, circumlocutionary, overelaborated, periphrastic, pretentious; **digressive**, apostrophic, discursive, divergent, episodic, excursive, prolegomenous, roundabout; **redundant**, empty, pleonastic, tautological

VERBOSELY *adv* diffusely, diffusively, digressively, discursively, divergently, overelaborately, periphrastically; **garrulously**, at great length, in extenso, longwindedly, loquaciously, profusely, prolixly, wordily; **redundantly**, pleonastically

VERBOSITY *n* gabbiness, garrulity, garrulousness, gift of the gab, longwindedness, loquacity, overelaborateness, overelaboration, prolixity, surplusage, verboseness, volubility, volubleness, wordiness; **diffuseness**, diffusion, diffusivity; **digressiveness**, discursiveness, vagrancy

VERSIFY *v* berhyme, metrify, poetise, sing; **rhyme**, clink, jingle; scan

VERY *adv* almightily, almighty, awfully, badly, bleeding, bloody, blooming, damned, darned, decidedly, deuced, deucedly, devilish, devilishly, effing, ever so *(Brit.)*, extra, frigging, fucking, full *(Archaic)*, how, jolly, mighty *(U.S.)*, molto, not a little, not half, particularly, passing *(Archaic)*, perishing, perishingly, piss, plenty, precious, pretty, rattling, real, remarkably, ruddy, signally, stinking, terribly, terrifically, thumpingly, thunderingly, too, uncommon, uncommonly

VESSEL *n* amphora, ampulla, creamer, cruse, ewer, greybeard, hydria, jug, pitcher, potiche, toby jug, urn, vase; **jar**, Canopic vase, pipkin, pot; **crock**, pithos; **coffeepot**, teapot; **boat**, gravy boat, sauce boat; **bucket**, bale, baler, ice bucket, kibble, pail, piggin, pipkin *(U.S.)*, stoup *(Scot.)*, water-carrier, watering-can; **dipper**, clamshell; **jerry can**, carboy, kerosene tin, milk can; **chamber-pot**, bedpan, bedroom mug, bottle, dry pan, gazunder, Melbourne Cup *(N.Z.)*, po, sanitary can, thunder-mug, urinal; **rocker**, banjo, cradle *(Mining)*, puddling tub, rumble, tumbling box, V-box. *See also* BASIN: BOTTLE: BARREL: DRINKING VESSEL

VEXING *adj* inciting, invidious, irritating, odious, provocative, provoking

VIBRATE *v* beat, dandle, joggle, judder, pulsate, pulse, pump, shudder, thrill, throb; **shake**, dither, dodder, palpitate, pant, quake, quaver, shimmy, shiver, tremble, twitter, wobble; **go back and forth**, come and go, fishtail, go backwards and forwards, go to and fro, go up and down, rock, seesaw; **shake up**, bucket, concuss, jar, jig, jounce, welter; **buzz**, chatter, pound, quaver, rattle, resonate, twang, whirr

VIBRATING *adj* libratory, nutant, nutational, oscillating, oscillatory, pendulous, pulsatory, swinging, undulatory, up-and-down, vacillating, vacillatory; **shaky**, doddering, doddery, juddering, reeling, rocky, rolling, tottery, waggly, wobbling; **dithery**, agitated, all a-twitter, twittery; **earth-shaking**, seismic

VIBRATION *n* beat, drumming, judder, pulsation, pulse, throb, trepidation; **earthquake**, earth tremor, foreshock, microseism, moonquake, quake, seaquake, seiche, seism, shake, temblor; **shiver**, fremitus, shimmy, tremor, wobble; **quiver**, buzz, dither, palpitation, quaver, roll, shake, shiver, thrill, tremolo, twang, twitter, vibrato, whirr; **vibrancy**, shakiness, the shivers, tremulousness, vibratility, waviness; **buffeting**, concussion, jar, joggle, jounce, shake-up. *See also* FLUTTER

VIBRATOR *n* buzzer, diaphragm, pulsator, rattle, reciprocator; **shaker**, dodderer, flutterer, swayer, swinger, throbber, trembler, twitterer, waddler, waverer, wiggler, wobbler

VICTIM *n* downtrodden people, forfeiter, kill, martyr, oppressed people, prey, protomartyr, sacrifice, scapegoat, sin offering, sufferer, willing sacrifice; **dupe**, cat's paw, cully *(Archaic)*, greenhorn, gudgeon, gull, mug, new chum, pawn, pigeon, puppet, sucker, tool, whipping boy. *See also* BUTT

VICTIMISATION *n* discrimination, frame-up, harassment, racial discrimination, sexual discrimination, unfair treatment; **persecution**, genocide, holocaust, massacre, oppression, torment

VICTIMISE *v* come down heavily on, crack down on, deal hardly with, discriminate against, get tough with, punish selectively, single out; **persecute**, be a scourge, decimate, give no quarter, grind down, grind down the faces of the poor, harass, impose hardship upon, massacre, molest, oppress, spite, subdue, suppress

VICTIMISED *adj* discriminated against, hard done by, ill-treated, ill-used, persecuted, singled-out, stigmatised; **downtrodden**, crushed, ground-down, heavy-laden, oppressed, stricken, under the whip, under the yoke

VIEW *n* landscape, outlook, panorama, prospect, scene, vista; **range of vision**, command, eyeshot, ken, prospect *(Archaic)*, purview

VIOLENCE *n* bloodthirstiness, furiousness, rabidity, rabidness, rampancy, sanguinariness, sanguineness, vehemence; **boisterousness**, rampageousness, severeness, severity, storminess, turbulence, volcanicity; **aggression**, aggressiveness, aggro, bovver, hubris; **fierceness**, ferity, ferociousness, ferocity, forcibility, forcibleness, grimness, savageness, savagery, shrewishness, truculence; **barbarianism**, barbarity, loutishness, rudeness, wildness; **brutality**, bestiality, ruffianism, toughness

VIOLENT *adj* driving, forceful, forcible, strongarm, terrorist; **boisterous**, blustery, rampageous, riotous, rough-and-tumble, uproarious, wild; **foul**, dirty, furious, rough, rugged *(Obs.)*; **drastic**, severe, slashing; **sensational**, blood-and-thunder, violent; **cataclysmic**, catastrophic, earth-shaking, earth-shattering; **stormy**, cyclonic, tornadic, tornado-like, torrential, tur-

violent   551   **visualisation**

bulent, typhonic, volcanic, vulcanian. *See also* FEROCIOUS: BRUTAL

VIOLENTLY *adv* ferociously, savagely, truculently; **fiercely, furiously,** grimly, like fury, rabidly, rampantly, vehemently; **bloodthirstily,** sanguinarily, sanguinely; **brutally,** barbarically, bestially, ferociously, loutishly, rudely; **forcibly,** amain *(Archaic),* hammer and tongs, heavily, slam-bang, slap-bang, with a vengeance; **stormily,** turbulently; **wildly,** roughly, tooth and nail, wild; **blusteringly,** aggressively, boisterously, swashingly, uproariously

VIOLENT OUTBURST *n* bluster, fury, heat, rage; **force,** brunt *(Archaic),* main, shock; **cataclysm,** catastrophe; **storm,** blizzard, cloudburst, cyclone, dust squall, dust storm, gale, hailstorm, hurricane, maelstrom, sandstorm, snowstorm, squall, tempest, tornado, whirlwind, willy-willy; **paroxysm,** throes

VIOLENT PERSON *n* aggressor, assaulter, attacker, pirate, terrorist, trespasser, violator; **bully,** blusterer, brave *(Obs.),* bruiser, dragon, swashbuckler; **lout,** barbarian, hoon; **Turk,** tartar; **ruffian,** apache, brute, bull, chokeman, gorilla, muscle man, nightrider *(U.S.),* pug-ugly *(U.S.),* poofter-basher, poofter-rorter, rowdy, thug, tough; **shrew,** fury, harridan, hell-cat, maenad, scold, spitfire, termagant, virago

VISIBILITY *n* apparentness, perceptibility, visibleness; **conspicuousness,** boldness, clearness, obviousness, plainness, prominence; **focus,** eyeshot, range, resolution, view

VISIBLE *adj* macroscopic, objective, observable, overt; viewable; **perceivable,** apparent, discernible, evident, obvious, perceptible; **in focus,** clear, clear-cut, plain, unblurred, unclouded, undisguised, unmistakable; **conspicuous,** exposed, eye-catching, for all to see, in full view, in view, marked, on view, open, open to view, plain as day, uncovered, under one's nose, within range; **bold,** full-faced *(Print.),* in bold relief

VISIBLY *adv* apparently, before one's very eyes, evidently, observably; **conspicuously,** boldly, clear, clearly, obviously, plainly, under one's nose; **at sight,** on sight

VISIT *n* call, gam *(U.S. Naut.),* social call, visitation; **stopover,** abode, sojourn, stay, stop, tarry *(Archaic);* **tour,** tourism; **the rounds,** the traps; **visitors day,** open day

VISIT *v* blow in, call, call on, dance attendance, drop across, drop by, drop in, drop over, first-foot *(Scot.),* go and see, go over to, leave one's card, look in, look in on, look up, make a call, pay a call, pay a visit, pop in, pop over, run across to, run over to, run round to, see, stop by, wait on, wait upon; **return a visit,** pay back the visit; **do the rounds,** do the calls, keep in touch, tour, visit the traps; **stay,** sojourn, stay with, stop off at, stop over, tarry; **frequent,** haunt

VISITOR *n* caller, first foot *(Scot.),* guest, stranger, visitant; **frequenter,** habitué, haunter, roundsman; **tourer,** tourist

VISUALISATION *n* appearance, manifestation, materialisation, pentimento, reappearance

VITALITY *n* aliveness, animal spirits, animation, ardour, brio, ebullience, effervescence, exuberance, libido, liveliness, lustiness, spirit, spiritedness, sprightliness, vibrancy, vital force, vitalness, vivaciousness, vivacity; **invigoration,** energising, enlivenment, innervation, stimulation, vitalisation, vivification; **vigour, bang** *(U.S.),* dash, elan, kick, nerve, pep, peppiness, red-bloodedness, snap, sthenia, verve, vigorousness, vim, zap, zest, zing, zip; **dynamism,** athleticism, briskness, freshness, rompishness, tirelessness, unweariedness; **get-up-and-go,** bustle, ginger, go, gumption, herbs, hustle, oomph, pull, push, spunk, steam; **drive,** aggressiveness, ambition, enterprise. *See also* ENERGY

VOCABULARY *n* accents *(Poetic),* glossary, language, lexicon, lexis, text, vocab, wordage

VOLUNTARILY *adv* by choice, by one's own free will, volitionally; **at will,** as you like, when ready; **intentionally,** by design, consciously, deliberately, designingly, in cold blood, on purpose, premeditatedly, purposefully, purposely, purposively; **with a view to**

VOLUPTUARY *n* bacchant, bacchante, epicure, epicurean, erotic, eroticist, erotologist, hedonist, sensualist, sybarite; **lecher,** beast, brute, d.o.m., dirty old man, goat, swine; **earth-mother**

VOLUPTUOUS *adj* carnal, earthy, epicurean, erotic, erotogenic, erotological, fleshly, hedonistic, sensual, sensualistic, supersensual, sybaritic, voluptuary; **concupiscent,** hircine, hot, lascivious, lecherous, libidinous, lubricious, lustful, rampant, ruttish *(Obs.);* **bacchanalian,** bacchanal, bacchic, dionysian; **bestial,** beastly, boarish, brute, brutish, debauched, swinish

VOLUPTUOUSNESS *n* bacchanalianism, carnality, earthiness, erotism, erotology, fleshliness, hedonism, luxuriousness, luxury, pleasure, pleasure principle, sensualism, sensuality, volupté, voluptuosity; **concupiscence,** goatishness, lecherousness, lechery, lewdness, libidinousness, lubricity, lustfulness; **lust,** eros, libido, sexual desire; **bestiality,** animalism, beastliness, debauchery, swinishness; **orgy,** bacchanal, bacchanalia; **fleshpots**

VOMIT *n* barf, berley, big spit, chuck, chunder, pellet, puke, sick, technicolour yawn, vomitus, yellow yawn

VOMIT *v* barf *(U.S.),* bark, be sick, bring up, chuck, chunder, cry ruth, feed the fishes, fetch up, have a sale *(N.Z.),* herk, hurl, keck, make a sale *(N.Z.),* perk up, puke, regurgitate, reject, retch, sick up, throw up, spew

VULGAR *adj* banausic, broad, coarse, coarse-grained, crass, crude, gross, heavy, indelicate, inelegant, unpolished, unrefined; **bawdy,** burlesque, earthy, profane, Rabelaisian, raunchy, ribald, scurrilous, strong; **unmentionable,** unparliamentary, unprintable, unrepeatable; **tasteless,** atrocious, outlandish, unaesthetic; **unfashionable,** dowdy, nunty, tatty; **garish,** cheap, chocolate-box, clinquant, commercial, common, flashy, fulsome, gaudy, gingerbread, meretricious, raffish, tarty, tawdry, tinsel, tinsel-like, tinselly, tizzy; **loud,** blatant, blushless, obtrusive; **kitsch,** Gothic, rococo. *See also* ILL-BRED

VULGARIAN *n* bounder, cad, low-life; **philistine**, groundling, mucker *(Brit.)*, pleb, plebeian, rough diamond; **nouveau riche**, arriviste, parvenu, upstart; **peasant**, bushie, hayseed, yokel; **boor**, alf, buffoon, carl *(Archaic)*, churl, clown, ocker, rugger-bugger; **slob**, dick, dickhead, goon, oaf, swine, yob; **lair**, city slicker, masher *(Obs.)*, mug-lair, Teddy Bear, two-bob lair; **lout**, hector, hoon, rough, roughie, roughneck, rowdy, thug, yahoo, yegg *(U.S.)*; **barbarian**, apeman, beast, brute, caveman, savage, tramontane, trog, troglodyte; **vulgariser**, ribald, sensationalist

VULGARISE *v* cheapen, lower; **coarsen**, rusticate; **brutalise**, barbarise, brutify; **tart up**, commercialize, tinsel; **be vulgar**, lair it up, show bad taste

VULGARISM *n* burlesque, choice language, dirty word, ribaldry, slang; **kitsch**, gingerbread; **vulgarisation**, barbarisation, brutalisation, rustication

VULGARITY *n* commonness, grossness, low-mindedness, lowness, rudeness, rusticity, uncivility, uncouthness, vulgarism, vulgarness; **coarseness**, earthiness, ribaldry, sensuality, sensuism; **philistinism**, ill-breeding, illiberality, illiberalness, plebeianism; **bad taste**, no taste, tastelessness; **unmentionableness**, unparliamentariness, unrepeatability; **garishness**, blatancy, flashiness, fulsomeness, gaudiness, gothicism, loudness, outlandishness, sensationalism; **tawdriness**, dowdiness, frumpishness, unfashionableness, unkemptness; **indecorousness**, gaucherie, impropriety, indecorum, indelicacy, unbecomingness, unseemliness; **rowdiness**, bawdiness, boorishness, buffoonery, loutishness, oafishness, rowdyism, swinishness; **barbarism**, atrociousness, atrocity, barbarianism, barbarity, baseness, brutishness, harshness, heathenishness, heathenism, heathenry, life in the raw

VULGARLY *adv* basely, bawdily, coarsely, commonly, grossly; **tastelessly**, atrociously, indelicately, inelegantly, unaesthetically, unbecomingly; **unmentionably**, unparliamentarily, unrepeatably; **blatantly**, fulsomely, obtrusively, outlandishly; **garishly**, flashily, gaudily, loud, loudly, tawdrily

VULNERABILITY *n* indefensibility, indefensibleness, nakedness, susceptibility, unguardedness, unsafeness, unsafety, untenability, unwariness, vulnerableness

VULNERABLE *adj* derelict, insecure, naked, obnoxious, unarmed, unassured, unattended, uncovered, undefended, unguarded, unsecured, unwary; **indefensible**, untenable

Ww

WAFFLE *n* all piss and wind, empty words, gabber, garbage, gush, load of old rubbish, mere words, nonsense, padding, palaver, rigamarole, sermonising, sound and fury signifying nothing, twaddle, verbiage; **amplification**, expansion, expatiation; **digression**, apostrophe, discursion, divagation, divergence, episode, excursus; **redundancy**, pleonasm, redundance, tautology; **circumlocution**, periphrasis, roundabout language

WAFFLE *v* bullshit, gasbag, gush, maunder, rabbit on, rant, rant and rave, rap on, run on, talk nonsense, talk someone blind, talk the leg off an iron pot, verbalise, yack on; **expatiate**, amplify, descant, dilate on, enlarge upon, expand, harp on, sermonise; **overelaborate**, draw out, pad out, protract; **digress**, divagate, diverge, ramble, wander

WAGE WAR *v* attack, commit hostilities, declare war, dig up the hatchet, engage in hostilities, give battle, go to war, invade, join battle, make war, raise one's banner, resort to war, take the offensive, take up arms, take up the cudgels; **be at war**, battle, be on the warpath, combat, contest, fight, make a stand, stand, stoush *(Colloq.)*, strive, war; **pillage**, burn, lay waste, put to the sword, ravage, scorch, shed blood, slaughter; **besiege**, beleaguer, blockade, dig in, lay siege to, siege; **barrage**, blitz, bomb, strafe, torpedo; manoeuvre, brush, counter-march, march, operate, outflank, skirmish, sortie; **deploy**, change front, deraign *(Archaic)*, enfilade, marshal

WAGON *n* bullock dray, bullock wagon, camion, cart, dray, jinker, oxcart, telega, truck, tumbrel, wain *(Poetic)*; **sanitary cart**, dunny cart, night cart, sanny cart, seventeen door sedan, sullage tanker; **trailer**, band wagon *(U.S.)*, box-trailer, dog trailer, float, horse float, horsebox, tandem trailer; **barrow**, applecart, billycart, bogie, dolly, go-cart, golf buggy, handbarrow, handcart, noddy *(N.Z. Railways)*, pushcart, shopping buggy, shopping stroller, shopping trolley, soapbox, tea-trolley, tea-wagon, teacart *(U.S.)*, trolley, wheelbarrow. *See also* CARRIAGE

WAITER *n* Ganymede, garcon, server, waitress; **bartender**, bar useful, barkeep, barmaid, barman, drawer *(Archaic)*, drink waiter, tapster *(Archaic)*, useful, wine waiter; **kitchen hand**, bus boy *(U.S.)*, cupbearer, kitchener, kitchenmaid, scullion, tea lady; **flight attendant**, air hostess, hostess, hostie, steward, stewardess

WAKE UP *v* awake, awaken, rouse, rub the sleep from one's eyes, wake, waken; **rise**, get out of bed, get up, hit the deck, rise and shine, surface, turn out; **arouse**, call, knock up, raise *(Archaic)*

WAKE UP *interj* rise and shine, wakey-wakey

WAKING *n* arousal, awakening, rouse; **wakefulness**, insomnia, restlessness, sleeplessness; **reveille**, early-morning call

WALK *n* airing, blow *(Colloq.)*, constitutional, promenade, roam, saunter, stroll, turn, wander; **march**, anabasis, cakewalk, forced march, routemarch; **hike**, grind *(N.Z.)*, mush, rogaine, safari, tramp, trek, walkathon

WALK *v* amble, ambulate, defile, foot, foot it, footslog, goosestep, hoof it, leg it, march, mosey *(U.S. Colloq.)*, mush, pace, pad, parade, saunter, shamble, shank *(Scot.)*, slouch, somnambulate, step, stride, stroll, strut, swagger, swamp, sweep, toddle, tootle, tramp, tread, troop, truck, trundle, waddle; **promenade**, do the block, perambulate, stretch one's legs, take the air; **jaywalk**; **mince**, cakewalk, pansy, sashay, trip, waltz; **limp**, dot and carry one, hobble, hop, shuffle, stagger, stumble along, totter; **plod**, clamp, clump, lumber, pound, slog, thump, toil, traipse, tramp, trample, trudge; **run**, breeze along, chase, double-time, jog, lope, pat, scour; **scramble**, slither, wriggle; **brachiate**

WALKER *n* ambler, cakewalker, foot-passenger *(Archaic)*, footer, footslogger, marcher, passer-by, pedestrian, saunterer, stepper, strider, stroller, strutter, toddler, treader, trudger, waddler; **jaywalker**; **jogger**, galloper, loper, pacer, runner; **limper**, hobbler, shuffler, the walking wounded, totterer; **sleepwalker**, noctambulist, somnambulant, somnambulator, somnambulist

WALKING *n* ambulation, bushwalking, circumambulation, legwork, pedestrianism, perambulation; **sleepwalking**, somnambulation, somnambulism; **gait**, amble, dogtrot, double time, footing, goosestep, hobble, jog, lope, muddling pace, pace, plod, roll, saunter, shamble, shuffle, step, strut, stump, toddle, tread, waddle

WALKING *adj* ambulatory, heel-and-toe, high-stepping, pedestrian, perambulatory, strutting, unmounted; **sleepwalking**, noctivagant, somnambulant, somnambulistic; **gressorial**, digitigrade, gradient, plantigrade, unguligrade

WALL *n* ashlaring, brattice, bulkhead, cavity wall, firewall, partition, party wall, withe; **screen**, iconostasis, jube, reredos, transenna, veil; **curtain**, drop, drop curtain, drop scene, firecurtain, safety curtain, tormentor; **diaphragm**, dissepiment, interface, mediastinum, septum, velum; **buffer**, cushion, fender, pudding fender, shock absorber, stopping; **deflector**, baffle, baffle plates, starling; **air-curtain**, airlock; **shield**, biological shield, butt, stone shield, washboard; **buffer zone**, Bamboo Curtain, border, frontier, Iron Curtain, no-man's-land. *See also* FENCE

WANDERING *adj* itinerant, meandering, noctivagant, peripatetic, rambling, roving, vagarious, vagrant

WANDERINGLY *adv* errantly, excursively, from pillar to post, itinerantly, meanderingly, vagrantly; **on the road**, off, on the track, on the wallaby, on the wallaby track, on the wing; **aboard**

WANE *v* abate, fade out, fall, fall off, lag, peak, peak and pine, peter out, tail away, tail off, trail off; **depreciate**, break, drop, drop off, sag, slip, tumble; **decline**, crumble, decay, dwindle, ebb, fade away, subside, waste away, wear away. *See also* DECREASE

WAR *n* appeal to arms, civil war, hostilities, resort to arms, shooting war, total war, trench warfare, war of attrition, war of nerves, war to the knife, warfare, world war; **state of war,** state of siege; **biological warfare,** chemical warfare, germ warfare; **atomic warfare,** nuclear warfare; **unconventional warfare,** evasion, guerilla warfare, subversion, terrorism; **psychological warfare,** propaganda; **economic warfare,** attrition, blockade, scorched earth policy; **gigantomachia,** theomachy; **holy war,** crusade, jihad.   *See also* ACT OF WAR

WARLIKE *adj* armipotent, bellicose, belligerent, bloodthirsty, combatant, hawkish, martial, militant, pugnacious; **militaristic,** chauvinist, chauvinistic, jingoistic

WARMONGER *n* aggressor, campaigner, chauvinist, combater, crusader, fighter, hawk, militant, militarist

WARMONGERING *n* aggression, bellicosity, belligerence, combativeness, fight, hostility, militancy, pugnacity, warlikeness; **militarism; jingoism,** chauvinism, national prejudice

WARN *v* advertise *(Obs.),* caution, exhort, forewarn, garnish *(Law),* give someone a tip, premonish, previse, put wise, tip off; **alarm,** alert, gong; **patrol,** keep nit, keep watch

WARNER *n* cockatoo, exhorter, lookout, monitor, nit-keeper, patrol, sentinel, sentry, shark patrol, vedette, watchdog, watchman; **picket,** air picket *(Mil.),* outrider; **monitor,** airborne early warning system *(Mil.),* distant early warning system *(U.S. Mil.),* early warning system, indicator, radar, sonobuoy; **alarmist,** Cassandra

WARNING *n* alarm, alarum *(Archaic),* alert, appel *(Fencing),* caution, Mayday *(Radio),* red alert, red flag; **warning signal,** beacon, danger signal, distant signal *(Railways),* exclamation mark *(Brit.),* fog signal, hazard flasher, hazard lights, red light, seamark, skull and crossbones, stoplight, storm signals, storm warning; **alarm bell,** alarm clock, alarum, burglar alarm, curfew, foghorn *(Naut.),* gong, horn, klaxon, shark bell, shark siren, siren, tocsin; **forewarning,** foreboding, omen, premonition, presentiment, symptom, the writing on the wall; **admonition,** caution, caveat *(Law),* denunciation, exhortation, garnishment *(Law),* lecture, memento mori, monition, notice, notification, threat, tip-off, warning; **example,** deterrent, lesson, object lesson

WARNING *adj* exemplary, instructive, monitory, premonitory, sematic, telltale; **threatening,** ominous; **admonitory,** cautionary, exhortative

WASHER *n* face flannel, face washer, facecloth, flannel, loofah, washcloth, washrag; **toothbrush,** dental floss, dentifrice, tooth-stick, toothpaste, toothpick; **swab,** cotton bud; **napkin,** serviette, table napkin; **nappy,** diaper *(U.S.);* **handkerchief,** hanky, nose rag, snot rag; **toilet paper,** bum fodder, dunny paper, lavatory paper; **doormat,** foot-scraper; **dishcloth,** bottlebrush, dishrag, dishwasher, dolly mop, scourer, sponge, steel wool, washleather, wettex; **pull-through,** electric eel, four-by-two, pipe-cleaner, ramrod; **syringe,** syrette

WASTE *n* chaff, debris, dregs, dross, effluent, husks, junk, leavings, lumber, mullock, offscourings, scrap,

waste skimmings, slack *(Coal Mining)*, slag, slash *(N.Z.)*, tailings, waste matter, waste product, wastepaper; **garbage**, gunk, litter, muck, outcast, refuse, rubbish, trash; **encumbrance**, cumbrance, deadwood, snuff, white elephant; **dead stock**, cast-offs, delenda, rags, rejectamenta, rejects, remainders

WASTELAND *n* desert, desolation, dust bowl, gumland *(N.Z.)*, no-man's-land, waste, wilderness; **duffer**, shicer *(Mining)*

WASTE OF TIME *n* fun and games, waste of breath; **fool's errand**, labour in vain, wild-goose chase; **a dead loss**, dead duck, failure

WASTE ONE'S TIME *v* cry for the moon, flog a dead horse, labour in vain, labour the obvious, piss into the wind, whistle against the wind, whistle in the wind

WASTER *n* futilitarian, wastrel

WATER *n* Adam's ale, aqua, drinking water, tap-water, wave *(Archaic)*; **groundwater**, artesian water, bore water, connate water, floodwater, gravitational water, melt-water, mickery, pondage, rainwater, soakage, sub-artesian water, underground water, watertable; **salt water**, brine, sea water; **waterworks**, water board; **coordinated water**, heavy water, vadose circulation, water of constitution *(Obs.)*, water of crystallisation, water of hydration; **bilge**, dishwater, slops, sullage, swill

WATERCRAFT *n* boat, bottom, class boat, cockle, cockleshell, consort, craft, flatboat, flatiron, greyhound, hog, launch, monohull, pink, prow *(Poetic)*, shallop, ship, shipboard, skiff, vessel, whaleboat; **tub**, hulk, log, wreck; **jolly-boat**, cockboat, hoy, tender, yawl *(Obs.)*; **barge**, gondola *(U.S.)*, lighter, scow; **pirate ship**, corsair, rover *(Archaic)*, sea-rover; **training ship**, school ship, flagship, mother ship; **shipping**, flotage, marine, merchant navy, watercraft; **fleet**, argosy, armada, column, convoy, escadrille *(Obs.)*, fleet in being, flotilla, navy, screen, squadron; **warship**, aircraft-carrier, assault craft, battle cruiser, battleship, capital ship, caravel, carrier, corsair, cruiser, cutter, destroyer, destroyer escort, dreadnought, E-boat, fire ship, flag, flagship, flat-top, frigate, gunboat, H.M.A.S., H.M.S., ironclad, landing craft, man-o'-war, man-of-war, mine-layer, mine-sweeper, minisub, monitor, pocket battleship, privateer, PT boat, Q-ship, R.A.N., razee *(Obs.)*, ship of the line, submarine, superdreadnought, three-decker, torpedo-boat, torpedo-boat destroyer, troop-carrier, trooper, troopship, U-boat, vedette; **merchant vessel**, argosy, bilander, bulk carrier, cargo boat, coaster, collier, container ship, factory ship, freighter, fruiter, Indiaman, liner, merchantman, oil tanker, packet (boat), pearler, sealer, sixty-miler, slaver, supertanker, tanker, trader, tramp, tramp steamer, whaler; **water taxi**, aquacab; **fishing vessel**, crabber, drifter, fisherman, fishing smack, hooker, smack, trawler; **ark**, bumboat, dredger, fireboat, hospital ship, iceboat, icebreaker, lifeboat, lightship, revenue cutter *(Brit.)*, showboat, snagger, surf rescue boat, transport, tug, tugboat, victualler, weathership. *See also* MOTOR VESSEL; SAILING SHIP; ROWING BOAT; RAFT

WAVERER *n* acrobat, chameleon, erratic, flibbertigibbet, oscillator, tergiversator

WEAK *adj* adynamic, asthenic, atonic, atrophic, atrophied, effete, enervate, enervated, expugnable, fatigable, helpless, infirm, invalid, nerveless, on one's last legs, sinewless, subduable, weak as gin's piss, weak as water; **frail**, delicate, dicky, faint, feckless, feeble, hothouse, languishing, languorous, limp, little, low, mushy, pimping, puny, sickly, silly *(Obs.)*, slight, small, soft, tender, thewless, thready, weedy, wet, wishy-washy; **pale**, anaemic, colourless, peaky, wispy; **effeminate**, anile, doting, dotty, female *(Obs.)*, feminine, sawney, womanish; **wonky**, doddered, doddering, doddery, groggy, rocky, shaky, tottery, tremulant, tremulous; **broken**, broken-down, decrepit, droopy, gone, perished, prostrate, wrecked; **loose**, flabby, flaccid, flagging, languid, limp, loose-jointed, slack, tenuous; **debilitative**, enervative, exhaustive

WEAKEN *v* attenuate, blunt, deaden, debilitate, demoralise, devitalise, disable, enervate, enfeeble, prostrate, sap, slake *(Obs.)*, swamp, wilt; **collapse**, break down, conk out; **waste**, atrophy, die, die away, disintegrate, droop, fade, fail, faint *(Archaic)*, fall away, falter, flag, go soft, go to seed, languish, pass out, rot away, sink, subside, turn to jelly; **soften**, wilt; **loosen**, loose, open, relax, slack, slacken, unclasp, unlace, unlash, unloose, unstrap, unstring; **shake**, totter

WEAKENER *n* deadener, enervator, enfeebler, softener, underminer

WEAKLING *n* asthenic, broken reed, cream puff, cry-baby, dotard, gutless wonder, jellyfish, paper tiger, poofter *(Derog.)*, softie, sop, subman, wimp, wreck; **weak spot**, Achilles heel, breaking point, disability, failing, failure, foible, weak link

WEAKLY *adv* delicately, frailly, helplessly, impotently, infirmly; **faintly**, dotingly, effetely, fecklessly, feebly, languidly, languishingly, mushily, nervelessly; **palely**, bloodlessly, colourlessly, peakily, punily; **femininely**, languorously, tenderly, womanishly

WEAKNESS *n* adynamia, anaemia, anergy, asthenia, atony, debility, decay, decrepitude, delicateness, dotage, effeteness, faintness, fecklessness, feebleness, frailness, helplessness, infirmness, languor, lassitude, littleness, lowness, malaise, mushiness, nervelessness, powerlessness, prostration, puniness, tremulousness; **enfeeblement**, anility, atrophy, brokenness, debilitation, devitalisation, disablement, disintegration, enervation, intolerance; **frailty**, caducity, destructibility, destructibleness, infirmity, pregnability, shakiness, sickliness, unsubstantiality, vincibility, vincibleness, violability; **paleness**, colourlessness, peakiness; **looseness**, flabbiness, flaccidity, flaccidness, flimsiness, languidness, languishment, limpness, slackness, tenuousness; **droop**, languish, tremor, wilt; **fatigue**, corrosion fatigue

WEALTH *n* cash in hand, dollars, filthy lucre, gold, gumtree money, lucre, Mammon, means, money, pelf, petrodollars, riches, the ready, the readies, weal *(Obs.)*; **fortune**, a pretty penny, big bickies, king's ransom, megabucks, mint, motser, pile, tidy sum, wad; **resources,** land *(Econ.),* natural resources, resources boom; **treasure,** blue chip, bonanza, capital, goldmine, nest egg, private means, treasure-trove; **affluence,** forehandedness *(U.S.),* glory, prosperousness, solidity, soundness, substantiality; **richness,** abundance, opulence, sumptuousness; **enrichment,** aggrandisement, self-aggrandisement; **el dorado,** Babylon, Golconda, land of milk and honey

WEALTHILY *adv* affluently, fatly, richly, substantially; **opulently,** in the lap of luxury, luxuriously, palatially, sumptuously, sybaritically; **prosperously,** successfully, thrivingly

WEALTHY *adj* affluent, brownstone *(U.S.),* copper-bottomed, filthy rich, flush, forehanded *(U.S.),* in funds, in pocket, in the money, loaded, made of money, on easy street, opulent, prosperous, rich, rolling, solid, stinking, substantial, well-fixed, well-heeled, well-lined, well-off, well-to-do; **nouveau riche,** cashed-up, get-rich-quick, new-rich; **opulent,** Edwardian, palatial, palatine, ritzy, sumptuous, sybaritic; **capitalist,** capitalistic, chrematistic, mammonistic, nabobish, plutocratic

WEALTHY PERSON *n* billionaire, Croesus, dollar millionaire, fat cat, man of means, man of substance, Midas, millionaire, millionairess, moneybags, moneyed man, multi-millionaire, pound millionaire, sugar daddy; **nouveau-riche,** new-rich, parvenu; **tycoon,** aggrandiser, baron, capitalist, king, magnate, merchant prince, money-maker, nabob, plutocrat; **mammonist,** mammonite; **playboy,** gilded youth, jetsetter, silvertail, sybarite, toff; **the rich,** plutocracy, the haves, the idle rich, the other half, the ruling class; **high society,** beautiful people, jet set, society

WEAPON *n* atomic weapon, biological weapon, blast weapon, clean weapon, deadly weapon, death ray, deterrent, fragmentation weapon, kiloton weapon, megaton weapon, nominal weapon, nuclear weapon, nuke, salted weapon, secret weapon, thermonuclear weapon; **weaponry,** ack-ack, artillery, cannonry, enginery, field artillery, gunnery, musketry, rocketry; **arms,** armament, armoury, gear *(Archaic),* hardware, heavy metal, matériel, militaria, munitions, ordnance. *See also* GUN; AMMUNITION; BOMB; SWORD; SPEAR; ARSENAL

WEAR *v* dress in, have on, sport; **put on,** doll up, don, hop into, huddle on, invest *(Rare),* try on; **rug up,** bundle up, cover up, do up, enrobe, get up, muffle up, re-dress, wrap up; **change,** disarray, shift *(Archaic);* **overdress,** lair up, mocker up

WEATHER *n* elements, meteor *(Obs.);* **climate,** clime, microclimate, regime, seasonal pattern; **continental climate,** equatorial climate, insular climate, maritime climate, Mediterranean climate, polar climate, temperate climate, tropical climate; **fair weather,** balminess, fairness, halcyon days, shine; **calm weather,** doldrums; **rough weather,** inclemency, intemperateness, storm, storminess, sultriness, thunder, tornado, unsettledness, wintriness. *See also* ATMOSPHERIC PRESSURE; CLIMATOLOGY

WEATHER BUREAU *n* pilot balloon, sounding balloon, sounding rocket, weather station, weathership

WEATHER DEVICE *n* aerometer, barograph, barometer, baroscope, Fortin's barometer, glass, hygrograph, hygrometer, hygroscope, maximum and minimum thermometer, mercury, microbarograph, psychrometer, radiometeorograph, radiosonde, thermometer, weatherglass, wet-and-dry bulb hygrometer; **weathervane,** cyclonoscope, vane, weather eye, weathercock

WEAVE *n* feel, pattern, stitch, wale, watering; **weft,** pick, shoot, warp, woof; **nap,** float, pile; **plain weave,** basket weave, double cloth, double tabby, interlock, khaddar, locknit, satin, tabby, twill, two-way stretch, union, waffle-weave, warp-face weave, whipping; **yarn,** cabling, fibre, filament, fluff, rove, roving, thread, twist

WEDDING *n* bridal, espousal, nuptials, spousals; **church wedding,** civil marriage, double wedding, elopement, shotgun wedding, white wedding; **marriage rites,** nuptial mass, solemnisation, wedding service; **marriage celebrant,** celebrant, solemniser, uniter; **bridal party,** best man, bridesmaid, flowergirl, groomsman, maid of honour, matron of honour, paranymph; **banns,** lines *(Brit.)*, marriage certificate; **reception,** wedding breakfast; **wedding march,** charivari, epithalamium, nuptial song, prothalamion, wedding song; **honeymoon; proposal,** offer; **engagement,** affiance, betrothal, contract, precontract; **troth,** hand, promise; **dowry,** marriage portion, marriage settlement; **matchmaker,** go-between, marriage broker. *See also* MARRIAGE

WEIGH *v* bulk, tip the scales at, weigh a ton, weigh in at; **outweigh,** outbalance, overbalance, overweigh, preponderate; **balance,** poise *(Obs.)*, scale, tare; **burden,** break the back of, charge, cumber, encumber, load, lumber, overbear, overburden, overcharge, overlade, overload, overweight, overwhelm, pack, surcharge, tax

WELCOME *v* be sociable, entertain, receive; **keep in with,** be all over, cultivate, familiarise *(Rare)*, ingratiate, make one's marble good with, make up to, smother, smother with kindness; **heap coals of fire on someone's head**

WELD *v* braze, cement, solder

WELL *adv* amazingly, bonnily, capitally, excellently, fabulously, famously, finely, grandly, magnificently, marvellously, sensationally, soundly, splendidly, superbly, swingingly, tremendously, unreally, wizardly *(Brit.)*, wonderfully; **exquisitely,** choicely, divinely, elegantly; **uncommonly,** exceptionally, extremely, peerlessly, remarkably, supremely, ultra, unco *(Scot.)*, uncommon *(Archaic)*; **fine,** all cush, great, okay, right; **beneficially,** advantageously

WELL-BEHAVED *adj* as good as gold, good, good-mannered, law-abiding, pukka, respectable, seemly, straight-arrow *(Colloq.)*

WELL DONE *interj* attaboy, beaut, beauty, bewdy, bully, curl the mo, good egg, good for you, good iron, good on you, good show, that's the shot, your blood's worth bottling; **goodo,** good, great, hot dog *(U.S.)*;

well done / **wheel**

right on, hear hear, no risk, spot-on, touché; **hip hip hooray,** alleluia, hallelujah, hooray, huzza *(Archaic),* kapai *(N.Z.),* pie *(N.Z.),* three cheers, viva; **bravo,** encore

WET *v* baptise, water; **bedew,** dew; **moisten,** baste, damp, dampen, embrocate, foment, humidify, irrigate, moisturise, water down; **impregnate,** imbibe *(Obs.),* imbrue, imbue; **sweat,** reek, slobber, weep; **sprinkle,** asperse, drop *(Archaic),* hose, shower; **splash,** dabble, dash, plash, slop, spat, splatter, squirt; **drench,** ret, rot, sop, swamp, waterlog; **soak,** macerate, marinade, marinate, sodden, souse, steep, water-soak, welter *(Archaic);* **irrigate,** float, flood, inundate, subirrigate, water; **immerse,** bathe, douse, duck, immerge *(Rare),* submerge; **dip,** dap, puddle, sop; **bathe,** go for a swim, have a dip, swim

WET *adj* humorous *(Obs.),* hydric, moist, soggy, sticky, sweaty; **damp,** clammy, dampish, dank, humid, hygric, mesic; **dewy,** lachrymose, rainy, slobbery; **lush,** juicy, sappy, succulent; **boggy,** fenny *(Brit.),* marshy, muddy, oozy, plashy, sloppy, sloshy, splashy; **irrigational,** irrigative; **hygrophilous;** **sodden,** dozy *(N.Z.),* impregnate, soggy, sopping, soppy, waterlogged, wringing wet; **awash,** swimming, water-sick, watery; **immersed,** submerged, submersed

WETLY *adv* damply, dankly, humidly, moistly; **soggily,** sloppily; **soddenly,** soppily; **succulently,** lushly; **dewily,** sweatily

WETNESS *n* clamminess, dewiness, drench, moistness, ooziness, sloppiness, soddenness, sogginess, soppiness, stickiness, wet; **dampness,** dankness, humidness, sweatiness; **lushness,** succulence, succulency; **humidity,** regain *(Textiles),* relative humidity, vapour concentration; **moisture,** damp, rising damp; **bog,** fen *(Brit.),* wet ground; **seepage,** seep

WETTER *n* baptiser, bather, douser, drencher, ducker, inundator, splasher, steeper, waterer; **dampener,** damper, humidifier, macerater, moistener, moisturiser, rinser; **irrigator,** soaker

WETTING *n* drench, marinade, soak, soakage, souse, steep; **saturation,** calcification *(Geol.),* inundation, rinsing; **irrigation,** aspersion, drip irrigation, flood irrigation, subirrigation, watering, wild flooding; **immersion,** affusion, baptism, bath, bogie *(Colloq.),* duck, immergence, rinse, submergence, submersion; **fomentation,** embrocation, humidification, imbuement; **maceration,** marination; **splash,** dash, plash, splosh

WHEEL *n* cartwheel; **waterwheel,** millwheel, paddlewheel *(Naut.),* windmill; **spinning wheel,** charka, potter's wheel; **roulette,** chocolate wheel, wheel of fortune; **cogwheel,** epicycloidal wheel, flywheel, gearwheel, gipsy, pinion, pinwheel, planet wheel, ratchet wheel, rowel, sheave, sprocket wheel, spur wheel; **castor,** rundle, truck *(Gunnery),* trundle; **tyre,** inner tube, pneumatic tyre, radial, radial-ply tyre, slick *(Colloq.),* tubeless tyre, whitewall, widey; **catherine-wheel,** pinwheel; **gyroscope,** gyrostat. *See also* CIRCLE; RING

WHERE *adv* where'er *(Poetic)*, whereabout *(Rare)*, whereat, wherein, wheresoever, wherever, whither; **wherefrom**

WHERE *conj* where'er *(Poetic)*, wherein, **whence**, whencesoever, wherefrom; **whereto**, whither *(Archaic)*; **whereabouts**

WHILE *conj* as, whiles *(Archaic)*, whilst; **when**, once, whene'er *(Poetic)*, whenever, whensoever *(Archaic)*; **until**, till; **whereupon**, against *(Archaic)*

WHITE *n* alabaster, chalk, cream, flour, ivory, lily, milk, mother-of-pearl, nacre, off-white, pearl, snow; **silver**, argent; **albino**

WHITE *adj* blank, candid *(Obs.)*, floury, lilied, lily-white, pale, white as a ghost, white as a sheet; **snowy**, frosty, snow-white, snowlike; **creamy**, cream, cream-coloured; **ivory**, alabaster, chalky, eburnean; **milky**, lacteous, milk-white, opalescent, opaline; **off-white**, albescent, broken white, fair, light, oyster white, whitish; **foaming**, sudsy; **silver**, argent, silvern *(Archaic)*, silvery; **blond**, albino, ash-blond, bald *(Zool.)*, blonde, canescent *(Biol.)*, hoar *(Archaic)*, hoary, platinum blonde, towheaded, white-haired; **pearly**, nacreous

WHITEN *v* blanch, bleach, blench, etiolate; **chalk**, blanco, calcimine, do one's sandshoes, pipeclay, powder one's face, white *(Obs.)*, whitewash

WHITENER *n* blancher, bleach, bleacher, blue-bag, blueing, bluing, washing blue, whitening, whitewash; **white pigment**, Chinese white, flake white, pipeclay, Venetian white, white lead, whiting, zinc white

WHITENESS *n* blondness, blondness, creaminess, frostiness, hoariness, lactescence, milkiness, opalescence, pearliness, silveriness, snowiness, whitishness; **lightness,** brightness; **albinism**

WHITENING *n* albescence, blanching, etiolation

WHOLE *n* alpha and omega, entire, synthesis, synthesisation, tale *(Archaic)*, total, totality; **all**, the lot, the whole bang lot, the whole boodle, the whole box and dice, the whole caboodle, the whole hog, the whole kit and caboodle, the whole shooting match, the works; **whole amount,** aggregation, altogether, ensemble, full amount, sum, summation; **full set,** complement, corpus, full board *(Shearing)*, full house, series, system; **gamut,** circle, continuum, cycle, range

WHOLE *adj* all, compleat *(Archaic)*, complete, entire, full, livelong, plenary, total; **intact**, acatalectic, full-length, inedited, inviolate, unabbreviated, unabridged, unbroken, uncensored, uncut, undivided, unexpurgated, uninterrupted; **absolute**, consummate, dead, diametrical, living, perfect, plenipotentiary, unconditional, unconditioned, unqualified; **finished**, made-up, mature, rounded, well-rounded; **hundred-per-cent,** full on, full out, undamped; **inclusive,** integrated, integrative, round, sum, tutti, tutto; **self-contained**, self-sufficient, self-sufficing. *See also* THOROUGH

WHOLENESS *n* absoluteness, completeness, entireness, entirety; **intactness**, integrality, integration, integrity, perfection, soundness, unbrokenness, undividedness, un-

wholeness   **willingly**

interruptedness, unity; **completion**, continuity, finish, finishing touches, follow-through, follow-up, last touch, totalisation; **consummation**, fruition, fulfilment, matureness, maturity, ne plus ultra; **supplementation**, filling; **thoroughness**, clean sweep, exhaustiveness, extensiveness, sweepingness; **comprehensiveness**, circumstantiality, circumstantiation, inclusiveness

WHOLESOME *adj* clean, healthful, hygienic, macrobiotic, salubrious, salutary, salutiferous, sanatory, sanitary; **tonic**, analeptic, recuperative

WHOLLY *adv* absolutely, completely, consummately, entirely, every bit, every inch, first and last, grossly, heartily, hundred-per-cent, on the whole, perfectly, point-device *(Archaic)*, properly, thoroughly, totally, unconditionally, utterly; **unbrokenly**, undividedly, uninterruptedly; **altogether**, all, all told, as a whole, bodily, in all, in full, in sum, in the aggregate, in toto, inclusively, integrally *(Rare)*, overall, tout ensemble; **to the full**, bag and baggage, boots and all, cap-a-pie, down to the ground, from head to foot, holusbolus, lock stock and barrel, neck and crop, root and branch, to the backbone, to the bitter end, to the hilt, to the letter, to the teeth; **head over heels**, head over tail, head over turkey, heart and soul, hook line and sinker; **downright**, dead, deathly, fair, fairly, hard *(U.S.)*, outright, quite, simply, stark, starkly, straight, wholesale; **with a vengeance**, and then some, in full force; **radically**, diametrically.   See also THOROUGHLY

WHY *adv* forwhy *(Archaic or Joc.)*, how, how come *(Colloq.)*, what for, whence *(Archaic)*, whencesoever *(Archaic)*, wherefore

WIDTHWISE *adv* breadthways, broadside, broadways

WILFULNESS *n* an iron hand, iron will, resoluteness, resolution, singlemindedness, strength of purpose, strength of will, willpower; **decisiveness**, decidedness, decision, deliberateness, determinateness, determination, determinedness, earnestness, firmness, heart of oak, immovability, immovableness, intension, intentness, killer instinct, premeditation, purposefulness, purposiveness, seriousness, seriousness of purpose, stability, stableness, steadfastness, steadiness; **a will of one's own**, headstrongness

WILL *n* choice, craving, desire, inclination, pleasure, velleity, volition, want, wish, yen; **intention**, animus *(Law)*, frame of mind, gleam in one's eye, intent, purpose, tendency *(Lit.)*; **voluntarism**, conation *(Psychol.)*, free will, pleasure principle

WILLING *adj* desirous, longing; **voluntarist**, voluntaristic; **intended**, conative *(Psychol.)*, conscious, deliberate, intentional, intentioned, planned, premeditated, premeditative, prepense, purposeful, purposive; **voluntary**, free-will, self-determined, volitional, volitionary, volitive

WILLINGLY *adv* as lief, as soon, fain *(Archaic)*, gladly, readily, with a will, with open arms; **voluntarily**, of one's own accord, of one's own free will, ultroneously; **wholeheartedly**, con amore, heart and soul, ungrudgingly,

willingly   564   **windward**

unmurmuringly, with all one's heart, with good grace

WILLINGNESS *n* alacrity, desire, eagerness, enthusiasm, inclination, promptness, readiness, wholeheartedness; **agreeability,** a willing heart, complaisance; **free will,** ultroneousness, voluntariness

WIND *n* advection, air current, airflow, airstream, convection, crosswind, current, current of air, down draught, draught, headwind, overdraught, standing wave, tail wind, up draught, windage; **breeze,** air, breath, cat's-paw, doctor, fresh breeze, gale *(Archaic),* gentle breeze, land breeze, moderate breeze, sea-breeze, slight breeze, strong breeze, trade wind *(Archaic),* variable wind, zephyr; **strong wind,** blow, buster, gale, high wind, near gale, stiff wind, strong gale, whole gale, windstorm; **gust,** blast, flaw, flurry, puff, waft; **whirlwind,** dust devil, tornado, tourbillion, twister *(U.S.),* williwaw *(N.Z.),* willy-willy; **storm,** blizzard, buran, cyclone, dust squall, dust storm, hurricane, magnetic storm, monsoon, squall, tempest, typhoon, white squall; **seasonal winds,** equinoctial, etesian winds, north-easter, north-wester, sou'wester, south, south-easter, south-wester, southerly, southerly buster, westerly; **regional winds,** Albany doctor, barber *(N.Z.),* bora, brickfielder, Esperance doctor, Fremantle doctor, gregale, levanter; **mistral,** chili, föhn, north, samiel, simoom, sirocco; **trades,** antitrades, roaring forties; **easterly,** Zephyrus

WIND GAUGE *n* airsock, anemometer, anemoscope, wind cone, wind sleeve, windsock; **anemogram,** anemograph, wind rose; **wind speed,** geostrophic wind speed, gradient wind speed; **Beaufort scale,** wind scale

WINDINESS *n* breeziness, draughtiness, gustiness

WIND INSTRUMENT *n* aerophone, organ *(Obs.),* reed, wind, wood, woodwind; **flute,** comb and paper, didgeridoo, fife, fipple flute, fistula *(Obs.),* flageolet, gumleaf, ocarina, panpipe, penny whistle, piccolo, pipe, pipes, quill, recorder, shakuhachi, tin whistle, transverse flute; **clarinet,** basset horn, chalumeau, clarinet, hornpipe, sax, saxophone, tarogato; **oboe,** aulos *(Greek Hist.),* bassoon, contrabassoon, cor anglais, crumhorn, double bassoon, English horn, fagotto, hautboy, heckelphone, shawm; **bagpipes,** cornemuse, drone, musette, pipes; **harmonica,** harp, melodica, mouth organ, sho; **kazoo,** mirliton, swanee whistle, Tommy talker

WINDOW *n* ancient light *(Law),* bay, bay window, bow window, bullseye, casement, catherine-wheel, dormer window, drop window, fanlight, fenestella, fenestra, French window, gable window, hopper window, Jesse window, lancet window, light, louvre window, lunette, luthern, picture window, quarter-vent window, rose, rose window, sash-window, sidelight, skylight, transom; **porthole,** flipper window *(Colloq.),* port

WINDWARD *adv* aweather, downwind, upwind; **before the wind,** close to the wind, downwind, in the teeth of the wind, large, near, upwind, windrode; **onshore,** katabatic, offshore, quartering; **windily,** breezily

WINDY *adj* blowy, breezy, draughty, puffy; **blustery**, Aeolian, boreal, favonian, flawy, gusty, monsoonal, squally; **fair**, free, large *(Obs.)*; **stiff**, cyclonal, cyclonic, cyclonical, strong, tempestuous, tornadic, tornado-like, typhonic; **windswept**

WINE *n* bulk wine, plonk, quaffing wine, red wine, steam, the grape, vin bianco, vin ordinaire, vin rouge, vino, white wine; **champagne**, bubbly, champers, fizz. *See also* ALCOHOL

WINEMAKING *n* bottom fermentation, brewing, estufado system, fining, maderisation, malolactic fermentation, tirage, top fermentation, vinification, working; **oenology**, viniculture; **yeast**, dosage, finings, hops, John Barleycorn, oenocyanin, wort; **barm**, beeswing, bottle sickness, casse, crust, slops, suds, tartar, wash; **alcoholicity**, alcoholic strength, beeriness, kick, proof, spirituousness, vinosity; **vintage**, bin, bottle age, brew, tirage; **woodiness**, stalkiness, velvetiness

WINNER *n* ace, champ, champion, conqueror, giant-killer, knockout, master, scorer, vanquisher, victor, victress; **bolter**, boom galloper, goer, knocktaker, mudlark, skinner; **placegetter**; **winning hit**, boomer, bottler, score, trump card; **whiz-kid**, natural *(Colloq.)*, prodigy, wunderkind

WINY *adj* oenological, vinicultural, viniferous, winebibbing; **vintage**, auslese, beerenauslese, cru, estate, flor, oloroso, rancio, rounded, spätlese, velvety; **woody**, beeswinged, fat, malty, pricked, stalky; **dry**, brut, fini, petillant, spritzig

WIRE *n* cheese-cutter, crosshair, crosswire, haywire, piano wire, tie wire, wire rope; **electric cord**, cable, cablet, cabling, coaxial cable, cord, flex, fuse wire, lead, line, main, pigtail, wire, wiring; **chain**, chain cable, sling. *See also* CORD

WISDOM *n* counsel *(Archaic)*, farsightedness, judiciousness, long-headedness, prudence, sageness, sapience, sapiency; **shrewdness**, astuteness, canniness, policy, sagaciousness, sagacity, subtleness, subtlety, supersubtlety; **commonsense**, gumption, horse sense, levelheadedness, mother wit, nous, reason, savvy, sense, sensibleness; **profundity**, deepness, profoundness. *See also* INTELLIGENCE

WISE *adj* far-seeing, far-sighted, judicious, longheaded, old, prudent, quaint *(Archaic)*, sagacious, sage, sapient, sapiential, witty *(Obs.)*; **shrewd**, astute, canny, politic, statesmanlike, subtle, supersubtle; **commonsensical**, level-headed, reasonable, sensible; **profound**, deep. *See also* INTELLIGENT

WISE GUY *n* clever dick, know-all, smart alec, smart arse, smartie, smartypants, wiseacre, witling *(Archaic)*

WISELY *adv* deeply, far-sightedly, judiciously, profoundly, prudently, sagaciously, sagely, sapientially, sapiently; **commonsensically**, reasonably, sensibly

WISE PERSON *n* doctor, elder, greybeard, hakim *(Islam)*, intellectual, level-head, light, Nestor, owl, philosopher, sage, sapient, seer, Solon, tohunga *(N.Z.)*, wise virgin, wise woman, witch, wizard *(Archaic)*; **ge-**

wise person   566   **word**

nius, mastermind, prodigy, wit *(Archaic)*, wunderkind; **oracle**, brains trust, elder statesman, expert, guru, master, whiz; **intelligentsia**, illuminati

WITH DIFFICULTY *adv* awkwardly, cumbersomely, ill, painfully, stiffly, troublesomely

WITH EFFORT *adv* agonisingly, arduously, burdensomely, drudgingly, grindingly, heavily, heavy, laboriously, labouringly, strenuously, sweatily, toilfully, toilsomely; **industriously**, ably, enthusiastically, for all one's worth, for the life of one, hard, operosely, with might and main; **athletically**, agilely, gymnastically

WITHOUT *prep* minus, off, sans *(Archaic)*, senza, sine, wanting

WOMAN *n* donna, earthmother, fair *(Archaic)*, female, feme *(Law)*, femme, gentlewoman, lady, she, squaw, wife; **womankind**, distaff side, fair sex, feminie *(Archaic)*, femininity, gentle sex, weaker sex, womenfolk; **sheila**, babe, baby, bart *(Obs.)*, bint, bird, bit, bit of fluff, broad, brush, bush, charlie, Charlie Wheeler, chick, chook, clinah *(Obs.)*, dame, donah *(Obs.)*, filly, flapper, heifer, hen, j.t., jam tart, jane, judy, ockerina, petticoat, piece, potato peeler, puss, quean *(Scot.)*, skirt, sort, tabby, tabo, tart, wench, widgie; **black woman**, gin, lubra, mary, wahine *(N.Z.)*; **white woman**, albino, mem-sahib; **seductress**, carnie, corpus delicti, enchantress, femme fatale, foxy lady, hot stuff, houri, kitten, mantrap, minx, nymphette, popsy, sex kitten, sexpot, siren, temptress, vamp, vamper, vampire; **beauty**, a good sort, bathing beauty, bathing belle, beauty queen, belle, charmer, doll, goddess, Juno, nymph, sylph, Venus, witch; **amazon**, butch, dyke, Lesbian, virago; **feminist**, suffragette, suffragist, women's libber; **girl**, damsel *(Archaic)*, demoiselle, lass, lassie, mademoiselle, maid, maiden, missy, virgin; **tomboy**, hoyden, romp; **old woman**, beldam, biddy, boiler, carline *(Scot.)*, crone, dowager, granny, matron, old chook, old duck, old girl, old maid

WOMANLINESS *n* anima, femaleness, femineity, feminineness, femininity, gentlewomanliness, ladylikeness, matronliness, muliebrity, unmanliness, womanhood; **effeminacy**, effeminateness, womanishness; **feminisation**, emasculation, emollition

WONDER *v* gape, gawp, gaze, marvel

WONDERFULNESS *n* awesomeness, inexpressibleness, insaneness, marvellousness, miraculousness, prodigiousness, stupendousness, wondrousness; **superbness**, extraordinariness, remarkableness, sublimeness, sublimity

WOODCUTTER *n* axeman, bush-faller, bushman *(N.Z.)*, bushwhacker *(N.Z.)*, faller, feller, hewer, jarrah-jerker *(W.A.)*, logger, sleeper cutter, stumper, timber-getter; **sawyer**, breakerdown, crosscutter *(N.Z.)*, sawer

WORD *n* content word, element, expression, function word, lexeme, particle, substitute, term, vocable; **noun**, adjective, adverb, article, conjunction, gerund, participle, preposition, pronoun, substantive, verb; **monosyllable**, tetragram, triliteral; **polysyllable**, jaw-breaker, sesquipedalian, tonguetwister; **coinage**, back formation, ghost word, neologism, neology,

word / **working class**

non-word; **Australianism,** inkhorn term, Latinism; **euphemism,** genteelism; **blend,** contraction, haplography, portmanteau word; **malapropism,** catachresis, corruption, parapraxis; **archaism,** counterword, literalism; **colloquialism,** dialecticism, vernacularism, vulgarism; **expletive,** interjection, swearword; **catchcry,** battle cry, buzz word, catchphrase, catchword, cry, epithet, slogan, watchword; **byword,** household word; **qualifier,** attributive, complement, definitive, distributive, prepositive

WORD PART *n* affix, bound form, combining form, formative, formative element, syllable, word element; **prefix,** proclitic; **suffix,** postfix *(Rare)*

WORK *n* darg, employment, handiwork, industry, labour, legwork, piecework, workload, yakka; **bonus work,** dirty work, hackwork, mixed functions, overwork, taskwork; **task,** assignment, care, charge, chore, commission, duty, errand, job, job of work, mission, piece of work; **working bee,** corvée, fatigue *(Mil.)*, fatigue duty, working party; **working holiday,** busman's holiday

WORK *v* devil, do hackwork, labour, moil, outwork, sweat, toil, work off a dead horse; **be employed,** carry a cut-lunch, carry on a business, drive a trade, have a steady job, have an honest job, ply one's trade, turn an honest penny, turn an honest quid; **serve,** lackey; **freelance,** fag, job, moonlight, scab

WORKER *n* industrial, operative, tradesman, tradeswoman, working girl, workingman, workman; **employee,** breadwinner, jobholder, wage-earner; **casual,** day labourer, extra, floater, hobo, journeyman *(Obs.)*, supernumerary, temp, temporary; **hard worker,** a tiger for punishment, compulsive worker, glutton for punishment, grafter, wheel-horse *(U.S.)*, willing horse, workaholic, work-horse; **toiler,** battler, dogsbody, drudge, drudger, moiler, old soldier, slave, slogger; **bad worker,** clock-watcher, cobbler, dilutee, slopworker; **freelance,** backyarder, freelancer, independent contractor, moonlighter; **pieceworker,** jobber, outworker; **white-collar worker,** clerk, pen-pusher, shiny-arse; **professional,** career girl, career woman. *See also* LABOURER

WORKERS *n* labour, labour force, labour market, shop floor, workfolk, workpeople; **staff,** cadre, general staff, office, personnel; **shift,** day shift, night shift, quick shift; **gang,** assembly line, chain-gang, crew, learners' chain, squad, the chain, working party; **coworker,** colleague, fellow servant *(Law)*, fellow worker, offsider, partner

WORKING *adj* at work, busy, employed, engaged, in a job, in harness, labouring, occupied, on duty, on fatigue *(Mil.)*, on the job; **blue-collar,** factory-floor, flunkeyish, sweated; **white-collar,** clerical, managerial, professional

WORKING CLASS *n* humbler orders, lower class, lower orders, lumpenproletariat, proletariat, rank and file, the masses, third estate, white trash *(U.S.)*; **commonfolk,** all the world and his wife, common *(Obs.)*, commonage, commonalty, commons, crowd, demos, every man and his dog, every Tom Dick and Harry, folk, hoi polloi, mobile vulgus, multitude, plebs, populace, small fry, the many, the million, Tom Dick and Harry, vulgar *(Archaic)*; **rabble,** canaille, cattle, doggery, dregs of society, gutter, herd, mob, raff, ragtag and bobtail, rout, ruck, scum, tag *(Obs.)*, the great unwashed, varletry *(Archaic)*, vermin

WORKING-CLASS *adj* lower-class, lumpenproletarian, plebeian, proletarian, underprivileged; **lowborn,** base *(Archaic)*, baseborn, ceorlish *(Archaic)*, churlish, dunghill, ignoble, low, lowbred, obscure, of low birth, of low parentage, of mean birth, of mean parentage, peasant, simple, ungentle *(Archaic)*, unpolished

WORK METAL *v* cold-work, work; **plate,** foil, galvanise, gild, metal, platinise, silver-plate, steel, tin, zinc, zincify; **forge,** cast, drop-forge, found, heat-treat, sinter, stithy *(Archaic)*; **amalgamate,** alchemise, meld; **smelt,** reduce; **weld,** braze; **coin,** mint

WORK OF ART *n* chef-d'oeuvre, classic, creation, magnum opus, masterpiece, oeuvre, opus, production; **objet d'art,** antique, collectable, museum piece, old master, period piece, virtu; **set piece; found object,** ready-made; **collage,** assemblage, combine painting, montage, papier collé; **collection,** loan collection

WORKPLACE *n* work station, workhouse, workshop; **workroom,** atelier, studio, study; **office,** bureau, business, chambers, head office; **regional office,** branch, district office, local office; **laboratory,** lab, research laboratory

WORRIED *adj* anxious, apprehensive, drawn, exercised, overanxious; **trembly,** in a funk, shaky, tremulous, wobbly; **tense,** high-strung, highly strung, highly-wrought, on tenterhooks, overstrung, uptight; **nervous,** edgy, fidgety, fretful, hyper, hypersensitive, jittery, jumpy, like a cat on a hot tin-roof, like a cat on hot bricks, nappy *(Equestrian)*, nervy, scratchy, skittish, toey, twitchy, uneasy, unquiet; **fraught,** distressful, feverish, feverous, frantic, frenetic, frenzied, hag-ridden, het-up, like a blue-arsed fly, on the rack, overwrought, unstrung, upset; **agitated,** flustered, fluttery, hot and bothered, in a flap, in a tizz; **ill-at-ease,** uncomfortable; **self-conscious,** paranoid

WORRIEDLY *adv* anxiously, fretfully, nervously, overanxiously, self-consciously, uneasily; **in trepidation,** agitatedly, distressfully, feverishly, feverously, frantically, frenetically; **tensely,** disquietly, skittishly, uncomfortably

WORRIER *n* fidget, flutterer, fusser, jitterbug, worrywart; **panic merchant,** mouse; **nervous wreck,** basket case

WORRY *n* anxiety, anxiousness, disquiet, disquietude, franticness, fussing, jimjams, nervousness, overanxiety, overanxiousness; **trepidation,** agitation, consternation, distress, feverishness, perturbation, tremulousness; **nerves,** butterflies, flutter, gooseflesh, goosepimples, tremor; **the twitches,** creeps, fidgets, jitters, jumps, shakes, shivers, willies; **tenseness,** self-consciousness, tension, tensity; **jumpiness,** boggle, dysphoria, edginess, fidgetiness, restlessness, skittishness, twitchiness, uneasi-

worry ness; **fuss**, bother, flurry, fluster, flustration, needle, trouble, worriment; **flap**, dither, fever, funk, stew, sweat, tizz, tizzy, twit, twitter

WORRY v bother, come unstuck, flap, flurry, fluster, flutter, fret, fuss, get one's knickers in a knot, get one's knickers in a twist, lose sleep over, overreact, pother, stew, sweat; **have the jitters**, boggle, funk, go to pieces, have a willy, jump, shy, start, startle; **fidget**, have ants in one's pants, have got 'em bad, hop up and down; **jitter**, chatter, rattle; **sweat blood**, go hot and cold all over, tear one's hair out

WORRYING adj disquieting, distressing, disturbing, niggling, upsetting

WORSHIP n adoration, blessing, celebration, ceremonial, extolment, latria, love, prayer, worshipfulness; **veneration**, apotheosis, canonisation, dulia, ennoblement, enshrinement, enthronement, glorification, hierolatry, hyperdulia, iconolatry, idolatry, Mariolatry *(Derog.)*, piety, reverence, transfiguration; **prostration**, bow, genuflection, sacramental, sign of the cross

WORSHIP v adore, extol, glorify; **pray**, count one's beads, magnify *(Archaic)*, make a novena, praise, psalm, say one's beads, tell one's beads; **meditate**, contemplate, go on retreat, watch; **humble oneself**, bow, cross, fall on one's knees, genuflect, go down on one's knees, kneel, kowtow, prostrate oneself, sain *(Archaic)*; **exalt**, beatify, canonise, ennoble, enshrine, enthrone, hallow, honour, mysticise, revere, reverence, saint, transfigure, venerate, **deify**, apotheosise, divinise

WORSHIPFUL adj adoring, reverend, reverent, reverential; **prayerful**, churchgoing, dedicated, devotional, hierodulic *(Antiq.)*, practising; **hagiolatrous**, hierolatrous, Mariolatrous; **idolatrous**, fetishistic, haggy, pagan; **heliolatrous**, druidic, druidical, heliolithic, ophiolatrous

WORSHIPPER n adorer, consecrator, devotee, extoller, fanatic, genuflector, glorifier, kowtower, mystic, palmer, petitionary *(Archaic)*, pilgrim, praiser, votaress, votary, votress; **psalmist**, cantor *(Judaism)*, caroller, lauder, muezzin *(Islam)*, psalmodist, reader; **churchgoer**, celebrant, communicant, congregation, invoker, kirkman *(Scot.)*, watcher; **hierolater**, iconolater, Marian; **sacrificer**, flagellant, flagellator, immolator; **cultist**, coven, deifier, demonist, demonolater, diabolist, Druid, Druidess, fetishist, firewalker, hag, heliolater, Magi, Magus, pagan, paynim *(Archaic)*, phallicist, rainmaker, Rastafarian, Satanist, shaman, shamanist, sun-worshipper, tohunga *(N.Z.)*, votary, witch

WRAPPER n envelope, enveloper, folder, wrapping; **wrapping paper**, aluminium foil, cellophane, gift-wrapping, gladwrap, shrink-wrap, silver foil, silver paper, tinfoil; **book cover**, binder, binding, board, bookbinder, bookbinding, case, doublure, dust jacket, dustcover, dustsheet, full binding, headband, jacket, mull, self-cover, spine

WRITE v character *(Archaic)*, doodle, print, scratch, scrawl, scribble, scribe *(Rare)*, scrive, scroll, trace, write out; **pencil**, chalk, charcoal, pen; **type**, touch-type; **author**, co-author, com-

write   570   **written composition**

pose, contribute, ghost, indite, lucubrate, make, pen, rewrite, utter; **write down**, dash down, dash off, draft, jot down, knock off, minute, set down, take down, write up; **portray**, depict, express, limn *(Archaic)*

WRITER *n* annotator, author, authoress, co-author, columnist, composer, contributor, copywriter, essayist, inditer, littérateur, stylist, wordsmith; **portrayer**, depicter; **dialogist**, colloquist, librettist; **hack**, devil, garreteer, ghost, ghost writer, jotter, pamphleteer, paragrapher, penny-a-liner, scribbler; **scriptwriter**; **penman**, calligrapher, calligraphist, hieroglyphist; **scribe**, amanuensis, clerk, copy typist, copyist, court reporter, Hansard reporter, inscriber, pen-pusher, penciller *(Horseracing)*, scrivener *(Archaic)*, stenographer, stenographist, tachygrapher, tachygraphist, transcriber; **scrawler**, cacographer, scratcher, scribbler; **secretary**, private secretary; **typist**, typiste

WRITING *n* calligraphy, chirography, manuscript; **handwriting**, fist, hand; **penmanship**, clerkship, pencraft; **longhand**, copperplate, court hand, cursive, roundhand, running writing, script; **shorthand**, dictation, logography, phonography, stenography, stenotypy, tachygraphy; **typewriting**, typing; **scrawl**, cacography, scratch, scribble; **writing style**, character, expression, fluency, language, literariness, stylisation, stylistics; **literature**, belles-lettres, humanism, letters, prose, republic of letters; **philology**, diplomatics, palaeography

WRITING FORM *n* boustrophedon, cipher, cuneiform, demotic, graffiti *(Archaeol.)*, grammalogue, hieratic, hieroglyphics, idiography, kanji, mirror writing, notation, ogham *(Irish Hist.)*, palaeography, pictography, picture writing, stylography, syllabism; **braille**, point system

WRITING MATERIALS *n* jotter, letter paper, notepad, notepaper, onion skin, pad, papyrus, parchment, scribble block, scribble pad, scroll, stationery, table-book, vellum, writing pad, writing paper; **slate**, diptych, tablet, tablets, triptych; **blackboard**, chalkboard, whiteboard; **pen**, ballpoint pen, biro, dip-pen, felt pen, fountain pen, graphos, micrograph, quill, speedball nib, stylo pen, stylograph, stylus; **pencil**, lead pencil; **chalk**, charcoal, crayon

WRITTEN *adj* chirographic, handwritten, longhand, stylographic; **calligraphic**, copperplate, round, roundhand; **cursive**, flowing, running; **scrawly**, cacographic, scratchy, scrawled, scribbly; **italic**, engrossed, italicised; **inscriptional**, epigraphic, inscriptive, lapidary *(Masonry)*

WRITTEN COMPOSITION *n* cameo, holograph, inditement, opus, opuscule, sketch, text; **manuscript**, codex, document, draft, inedita, MS., schedule *(Obs.)*, script, treatise, typescript; **scroll**, palimpsest, parchment; **jottings**, adversaria, notes, screed; **extract**, analects, chapter, excerpt, gobbet, par, paragraph, passage, pericope, quotation, selection, tag, tirade; **annotation**, comment, cross-index, cross-reference, end note, footnote, gloss, induction, interlineation, interlining, note, preface, rubric, scholium, sidenote, subtitle, superscription; **rewrite**, adaptation, redaction, revision, rifacimento; **cap-

WRONG *n* aberration, error, fault, misdeed, misprision, misstep; **crime**, delict, felony, malefaction, outrage, tort, victimless crime; **transgression**, abuse, malpractice, offence, trespass; **minor transgression**, peccadillo, slip, stumble, trip; **misbehaviour**, misdemeanour; **sin**, actual sin, cardinal sin, mortal sin, seven deadly sins, venial sin; **vice**, besetting sin, weakness

WRONG *v* abuse, aggrieve, do the dirty on, grieve *(Obs.)*, harm, offend against; **offend**, sail close to the wind, scandalise; **debauch**, corrupt; **err**, go to the bad, misplay, sin, trespass, trip; **compound one's error,** add insult to injury

WRONG *adj* delinquent, erring, peccant; **immoral**, aberrant, aberrational, inofficious, unconscionable, unethical, unprincipled, unscrupulous; **criminal**, crim, illegal, lawless, unlawful, wrongful; **outrageous**, heinous, reprehensible; **villainous**, blackhearted, blackguardly, conscienceless; **vicious**, debauched, depraved, perverse, perverted, unclean, uncleanly; **unrepentant**, incorrigible, unreformed, unregenerate; **evil**, evildoing, harmful, wicked; **bad**, black, damnable, flagitious, foul, indefensible, obnoxious *(Obs.)*, piacular, putrid, shameful, unwarrantable; **base**, bastardly, caitiff, cheap, contemptible, currish, deadshit, ignominious, low, low-down, mean, scabby, scurvy, whoreson. *See also* INCORRECT

WRONGDOER *n* blackguard, evildoer, malpractitioner, villain; **transgressor**, sinner, trespasser; **criminal**, crim, first offender, malfeasor, tortfeasor

WRONGFULNESS *n* badness, blameworthiness, censurableness, depravity, peccancy, sinfulness, sordidness, uncleanliness, unregeneracy, wickedness; **evil**, evildoing, evilness, flagitiousness, foulness, heinousness, outrageousness, viciousness; **immorality**, aberrance, aberrancy, delinquency, disgracefulness, obliquity, perverseness, perversity, unconscionableness, unprincipledness, unscrupulousness; **baseness**, blackguardism, contemptibility, contemptibleness, currishness, damnableness, despicability, despicableness, villainousness, villainy; **criminality**, illegality, reprehensibility, suability; **mens rea**, cold-blooded murder, malice aforethought, premeditated murder; **frailty**, turpitude, weakness; **impropriety**, bad form, improperness, incorrectness, inexcusability, inexcusableness, irregularity, offensiveness, shabbiness, unacceptableness, unbecomingness

XYZ

YARD *n* allotment, battleaxe block, block, building block, curtilage, lot, plot, vacant allotment; **industrial estate**, industrial park, trading estate *(Brit.)*; **car park**, parking area, parking lot; **goods yard**, car yard, shipyard, stockyard, timber yard; **airfield**, flying field, pad *(Aeron.)*; **gas field**, goldfield, oilfield

YELLOW *adj* canary, chartreuse, citreous, citrine, lemon, quercetic, sulphurous, sulphury, xanthic, xanthous, yellowish; **ochre**, ochreous, ochroid, ochrous, ochry, rutilant *(Rare)*; **ash-blond**, blond, blonde; **buff**, corn-coloured, fallow, flaxen, flaxy, isabel, sandy, stramineous, straw-coloured, tawny, tow; **creamy**, champagne, cream, cream-coloured, eggshell; **yellowing**, flavescent; **sallow**, chlorotic, jaundiced, sallowish; **gold**, aureate, brass, brazen, coppery, gilt, golden. See also ORANGE

YELLOW *v* gild; **turn yellow**, jaundice, sallow

YES *interj* amen, ay, yair, yea, yeah; **certainly**, absolutely, all right, blood oath, by all manner of means, can do, dicken, exactly, fair enough, granted, my colonial oath, my oath, no sweat, not half, O.K., pardi *(Archaic)*, quite, quite so, rather *(Brit.)*, right on, so be it, sure thing *(U.S.)*, that's the stuff, to be sure, truly, verily, very well, you bet

YOUTH *n* boyhood, early years, girlhood, salad days, sweet sixteen, tender age, youthhood; **adolescence**, awkward age, puberty, pubescence; **infancy**, babyhood, childhood, infanthood, preadolescence, swaddling clothes, the cradle; **minority**, nonage

YOUTHFUL *adj* juvenescent, prentice, rejuvenescent, vernal, youngish, youngling; **ageless**, evergreen, fresh, young-eyed; **childish**, babyish, infantile, infantine, puerile; **urchin**, boyish, coltish, cubbish, girlish; **callow**, beardless, green, immature, undeveloped, unfledged, wet behind the ears; **infant**, baby, in arms, neonatal, newborn, preschool, yeanling; **preadolescent**, prepubescent, school-age; **adolescent**, hebetic, juvenile, kidult, pre-adult, pubescent, teen, teenage; **young**, small, tender; **younger**, baby, cadet, junior, kid, minor, puisne *(Law)*; **youngest**, minimus *(Brit.)*; **under-age**, minor *(Brit.)*

YOUTHFULLY *adv* boyishly, coltishly, girlishly; **childishly**, babyishly, immaturely, juvenilely, puerilely

YOUTHFULNESS *n* boyishness, coltishness, girlishness, juvenescence, tenderness, juvenility, rejuvenescence, youth; **childishness**, babyishness, cubbishness, juvenileness, puerilism, puerility; **callowness**, greenness, immatureness, immaturity, inexperience

ZOOLOGIST *n* birdman, birdwatcher, bug-hunter, entomologist, ethologist, ichthyologist, malacologist, myrmecologist, oologist, ornithologist, zoogeographer; **aquarist**, aviculturist, pisciculturist; **animal-lover**, ailurophile, bird-fancier, dog-fancier, hippomaniac, zoophile

Index

abandon $n \rightarrow$ 1 liberty v 2 depart 3 stop
abduct $v \rightarrow$ 1 capture 2 diverge 3 rob
ability $n \rightarrow$ 1 capability 2 competence
able $adj \rightarrow$ 1 capable 2 competent 3 intelligent 4 knowledgeable
abnormal $adj \rightarrow$ 1 nonconformist 2 strange
abolish $v \rightarrow$ 1 cancel 2 destroy 3 finish
about $adj \rightarrow$ 1 awake 2 almost 3 imprecisely 4 regularly *prep* 5 concerning 6 near
above $adj \rightarrow$ 1 preceding *adv* 2 before 3 superiorly
abrupt $adj \rightarrow$ 1 discourteous 2 irregular 3 momentary 4 sloping
absent $adj \rightarrow$ 1 forgetful 2 nonexistent
absolute $adj \rightarrow$ 1 certain 2 most 3 perfect 4 predominant 5 simple 6 unconditional 7 unrelated 8 whole
absorb $v \rightarrow$ 1 dry 2 eat 3 engross 4 learn
abuse $n \rightarrow$ 1 disapproval 2 misuse 3 slander 4 swearing 5 trickery 6 unfairness 7 wrong v 8 act unkindly 9 ill-treat 10 slander 11 swear 12 trick 13 wrong
accent $n \rightarrow$ 1 assertiveness 2 faulty speech 3 importance 4 poetic rhythm 5 speaking v 6 emphasise 7 mark
accept $v \rightarrow$ 1 approve 2 assent to 3 believe 4 get 5 know 6 persevere
access $n \rightarrow$ 1 bridge 2 entrance 3 right of way 4 use
accident $n \rightarrow$ 1 luck 2 misfortune 3 unimportant thing
accommodate $v \rightarrow$ 1 conform 2 equip 3 house 4 lend
accompany $v \rightarrow$ 1 make music 2 partner
account $n \rightarrow$ 1 importance 2 indebtedness 3 judgment 4 list 5 narrative 6 record 7 reputation
accurate $adj \rightarrow$ 1 precise 2 true
accuse $v \rightarrow$ 1 impute 2 litigate
achieve $v \rightarrow$ 1 accomplish 2 gain
acknowledge $v \rightarrow$ 1 answer 2 assent to 3 be grateful 4 confess
acquaintance $n \rightarrow$ 1 friend 2 friendship 3 knowledge
act $n \rightarrow$ 1 action 2 affectation 3 angry act 4 command 5 fake 6 irritation 7 law 8 record v 9 attitudinise 10 behave 11 do 12 operate 13 perform
active $adj \rightarrow$ 1 busy 2 energetic 3 influential 4 medicinal 5 speedy
add $v \rightarrow$ compute
addition $n \rightarrow$ 1 building 2 combination 3 increase 4 mathematical operation 5 name
adjacent $adj \rightarrow$ 1 close 2 joined
adjust $v \rightarrow$ 1 change 2 pay 3 regularise
administration $n \rightarrow$ 1 imposition 2 legislation 3 management 4 operation 5 sharing out
admire $v \rightarrow$ 1 approve 2 desire 3 enjoy
admission $n \rightarrow$ 1 assertion 2 charge 3 cost 4 employment 5 entrance 6 revealing
advantage $n \rightarrow$ 1 antecedence 2 expedient 3 good 4 profit 5 usefulness v 6 be expedient 7 profit
adventure $n \rightarrow$ 1 attempt 2 danger 3 gamble 4 trade 5 undertaking v 6 act rashly
advertise $v \rightarrow$ 1 encourage 2 inform 3 publicise 4 warn
advise $v \rightarrow$ 1 guide 2 inform 3 practise law 4 send a message
affect $n \rightarrow$ 1 emotion 2 perception 3 point of view v 4 aim at 5 attitudinise 6 be important 7 change 8 elect 9 emotionalise 10 imitate 11 influence 12 inhabit
afford $v \rightarrow$ 1 make possible 2 supply
afraid $adj \rightarrow$ 1 frightened 2 penitent
again $adv \rightarrow$ repeatedly
against *prep* $\rightarrow$ 1 opposite *conj* 2 while
age $n \rightarrow$ 1 period 2 the public v 3 be old 4 deteriorate 5 taste
agent $n \rightarrow$ 1 doer 2 manager 3 method 4 operator 5 seller 6 trader
agile $adj \rightarrow$ 1 athletic 2 busy 3 light-footed 4 speedy

agony *n* → 1 contest 2 excitement 3 pain 4 unfortunateness

agree *v* → 1 be similar 2 be willing 3 conform 4 fit 5 promise

aid *n* → 1 charity 2 help 3 payment 4 supply *v* 5 help

aim *n* → 1 conjecture 2 direction *v* 3 direct

air *n* → 1 appearance 2 behaviour 3 characteristics 4 gas 5 music 6 radio 7 wind

alarm *n* → 1 fright 2 shout 3 signal 4 surprise 5 warning *v* 6 frighten 7 surprise 8 warn

alert *n* → 1 warning *v* 2 warn *adj* 3 attentive 4 light-footed 5 speedy

alien *n* → 1 foreigner 2 outsider 3 population *adj* 4 dissident 5 foreign 6 resident

all *n* → 1 whole *adj* 2 general 3 whole *adv* 4 wholly

allow *v* → 1 give 2 have the right 3 make possible 4 permit 5 speak 6 subtract 7 think

all right *adj* → 1 approved 2 bribable 3 good 4 healthy 5 safe 6 satisfactory *adv* 7 certainly 8 satisfactorily *interj* 9 yes

ally *n* → 1 accomplice 2 cooperator 3 friend 4 helper *v* 5 associate 6 be friends 7 join 8 promise 9 relate

alone *adv* → 1 negligibly 2 separately 3 solitarily

aloof *adj* → 1 apathetic 2 distant 3 elusive 4 reticent 5 solitary 6 unsociable *adv* 7 remotely 8 solitarily

also *adv* → 1 additionally

alternative *n* → 1 choice *adj* 2 nonconformist 3 optional

always *adv* → 1 changelessly 2 continually 3 eternally

amateur *n* → 1 approver 2 ignoramus 3 novice 4 sportsman 5 unimportant person *adj* 6 ignorant 7 sports

ambition *n* → 1 aim 2 desideratum 3 desire 4 vitality *v* 5 desire

ammunition *n* → 1 evidence 2 supplies

among *prep* → 1 between 2 inclusive of

amuse *v* → 1 engross 2 joke 3 puzzle

analyse *v* → 1 examine 2 inquire into

anger *n* → 1 displeasure 2 painfulness *v* 3 pain

angry *adj* → 1 displeased 2 hot 3 reddish 4 unwholesome

announce *v* — publicise

annoy *n* 1 annoyance *v* 2 damage 3 discontent

answer *n* → 1 reaction *v* 2 be adequate 3 be expedient 4 fit 5 react

anxious *adj* → 1 enthusiastic 2 frightened 3 worried

any *adj* → 1 general 2 one *pron* 3 one

apologise *v* → 1 atone for 2 be penitent

apology *n* → 1 compensation 2 justification 3 penitence

appeal *n* → 1 accusation 2 allure 3 charity 4 entreaty 5 trial *v* 6 lay charges

appetite *n* → desire

applicant *n* → 1 asker 2 attempter

apply *v* → 1 attempt 2 contact 3 fit 4 join 5 operate 6 place 7 use

appoint *v* → 1 command 2 depute 3 determine 4 elect 5 employ 6 equip

appointment *n* → 1 assignation 2 command 3 employment 4 job 5 power to act

appreciate *v* → 1 approve 2 assess 3 become greater 4 be grateful 5 enjoy 6 know 7 perceive

appreciation *n* → 1 approval 2 assessment 3 essay 4 good taste 5 gratefulness 6 increase 7 inflation 8 perception 9 pleasure 10 value

appropriate *v* → 1 rob 2 take *adj* 3 apt 4 conventional 5 expedient 6 particular

approve *v* → 1 assent to 2 authenticate 3 display 4 increase 5 test

aptitude *n* → 1 aptness 2 competence 3 intelligence 4 point of view

area *n* → 1 course 2 region 3 space 4 subject matter

argue *v* → 1 assert 2 disagree 3 display 4 persuade 5 reason 6 talk 7 testify 8 theorise

argument *n* → 1 abridgment 2 disagreement 3 discussion 4 evidence 5 narrative 6 persuasion 7 reasoning

armour *n* → 1 defence 2 secure

army $n \rightarrow$ 1 armed forces 2 crowd 3 many

arrange $v \rightarrow$ 1 agree 2 change 3 make do 4 make music 5 mediate 6 order 7 plan 8 prepare 9 promise

arrest $n \rightarrow$ 1 capture 2 imprisonment 3 inaction 4 stoppage 5 stopper v 6 capture 7 obstruct 8 stop

art $n \rightarrow$ 1 artistry 2 cunning 3 fine arts 4 representation

artificial $adj \rightarrow$ 1 affected 2 cunning 3 fake 4 imitative

artist $n \rightarrow$ 1 actor 2 aesthete 3 expert 4 labourer

ashamed $adj \rightarrow$ 1 meek 2 penitent

ask $v \rightarrow$ 1 entreat 2 expect 3 insist on 4 necessitate 5 publicise 6 question

asleep $adj \rightarrow$ 1 dead 2 inactive 3 unconscious

assembly $n \rightarrow$ 1 combine 2 convergence 3 council 4 crowd 5 gathering 6 legislative body 7 machine 8 mixture 9 parliamentary procedure 10 signal

assess $v \rightarrow$ 1 appraise 2 inquire into 3 measure 4 tax 5 teach

assignment $n \rightarrow$ 1 agency 2 employment 3 imputation 4 obligation 5 sharing out 6 undertaking 7 work

assistant $n \rightarrow$ 1 helper 2 inferior 3 partner adj 4 helpful 5 inferior

assume $v \rightarrow$ 1 be arrogant 2 believe 3 conjecture 4 take 5 undertake

assurance $n \rightarrow$ 1 arrogance 2 assertion 3 certainty 4 contract 5 insurance 6 surety

atmosphere $n \rightarrow$ 1 characteristics 2 gas 3 influence 4 sky 5 surroundings

attach $v \rightarrow$ 1 add 2 capture 3 employ 4 fasten 5 impute 6 join 7 take

attack $n \rightarrow$ 1 accusation 2 illness 3 reprimand 4 slander v 5 attempt 6 be violent 7 impute 8 scold 9 slander 10 wage war

attend $v \rightarrow$ 1 be present 2 care for 3 expect 4 help 5 partner 6 result

attention $n \rightarrow$ 1 attentiveness 2 care 3 courtesy 4 help 5 tribute

attitude $n \rightarrow$ 1 affectation 2 angle 3 point of view 4 pose 5 slope

attract $v \rightarrow$ 1 allure 2 be pleasant

audience $n \rightarrow$ 1 crowd 2 hearer 3 hearing 4 looker 5 music-lover 6 presence

authorise $v \rightarrow$ 1 assent to 2 authenticate 3 depute 4 justify 5 legalise 6 permit

avenge $v \rightarrow$ retaliate

avoid $v \rightarrow$ 1 be neutral 2 cancel 3 deny 4 depart 5 eject 6 empty

awake $v \rightarrow$ 1 encourage 2 know 3 wake up adj 4 attentive

award $n \rightarrow$ 1 gift 2 judgment v 3 determine 4 give

aware $adj \rightarrow$ 1 attentive 2 knowing 3 perceptive

away $adj \rightarrow$ 1 absent 2 distant 3 moving adv 4 deflectively 5 remotely *interj* 6 piss off

back $n \rightarrow$ 1 frame 2 rear 3 single person v 4 ascend 5 finance 6 gamble 7 go back 8 help 9 swerve adj 10 past 11 rear adv 12 behind 13 in return 14 in the past

backwards $adv \rightarrow$ 1 behind 2 head over heels

bad $adj \rightarrow$ 1 badly-done 2 deteriorated 3 execratory 4 ill 5 imperfect 6 inconvenient 7 intense 8 penitent 9 unpleasant 10 wrong adv 11 badly

bait $n \rightarrow$ 1 allure 2 attractor 3 bribe 4 fishing tackle 5 poison 6 stoppage v 7 allure 8 annoy 9 poison 10 stop

balance $n \rightarrow$ 1 account 2 comparison 3 composure 4 congruity 5 equality 6 figure of speech 7 gravimetry 8 remnant 9 rhetorical device 10 scales 11 steadying v 12 account 13 compare 14 counteract 15 dance 16 equal 17 equalise 18 steady 19 vacillate 20 weigh

ball $n \rightarrow$ 1 a good time 2 ammunition 3 bulge 4 dance 5 human body 6 party 7 thread v 8 have sex 9 round

ban $n \rightarrow$ 1 exclusion 2 industrial action 3 prohibition 4 public notice 5 strike 6 swearing v 7 prohibit 8 swear

band $n \rightarrow$ 1 belt 2 crowd 3 gathering 4 information agency 5 layer 6 line 7 musical band 8 obligation 9 ring 10 tape v 11 gather 12 line

bang $n \to$ 1 boom 2 drug use 3 excitement 4 explosion 5 hair 6 impact 7 loud sound 8 sexual intercourse 9 vitality v 10 be loud 11 boom 12 cut 13 explode 14 have sex 15 hit 16 subtract

banish $v \to$ 1 eject 2 isolate 3 prohibit

bank $n \to$ 1 angle 2 coastline 3 mariner 4 ridge 5 seaside 6 shallow 7 slope 8 storage 9 treasury v 10 account 11 limit 12 place 13 slope 14 store

bar $n \to$ 1 award 2 beam 3 cancellation 4 court of law 5 exclusion 6 fence 7 hindrance 8 island 9 joint 10 kitchen 11 layer 12 legal profession 13 line 14 metal 15 mineral 16 musical score 17 pressure unit 18 prohibition 19 pub 20 screen 21 shallow 22 shop 23 table 24 boycott 25 come between 26 fasten 27 obstruct 28 prohibit *prep* 29 except 30 less

bare $v \to$ 1 reveal 2 undress *adj* 3 adequate 4 revealed 5 simple 6 smallest 7 smooth

base $n \to$ 1 battleground 2 bottom 3 buttocks 4 essence 5 fortification 6 foundation 7 singer 8 storehouse 9 support v 10 support 11 underlie *adj* 12 bad 13 bottom 14 cowardly 15 fundamental 16 ill-bred 17 immoral 18 inferior 19 patriarchal 20 selfish 21 supporting 22 working-class 23 wrong

basic *adj* $\to$ 1 essence 2 bottom 3 characteristic 4 fundamental 5 important 6 original 7 rocky 8 simple

bastard $n \to$ 1 bad person 2 bad thing 3 discourteous person 4 freak 5 man 6 mischief-maker 7 offspring 8 unpleasant person *adj* 9 fake 10 patriarchal 11 similar 12 strange

bead $n \to$ 1 arch 2 bubble 3 bubbling 4 jewellery 5 liquid 6 metal

beam $n \to$ 1 angle 2 buttocks 3 light 4 shaft 5 side 6 signal 7 signpost 8 thickness v 9 shine 10 signal 11 telecast

beat $n \to$ 1 boom 2 direction 3 idler 4 job 5 nonconformist 6 poetic rhythm 7 pursuit 8 region 9 rhythm 10 route 11 vibration v 12 agitate 13 boom 14 cheat 15 defeat 16 flutter 17 hunt 18 make music 19 overtake 20 precede 21 set sail 22 shine 23 shower 24 surpass 25 vibrate *adj* 26 losing 27 nonconformist 28 tired

before *adv* $\to$ 1 early 2 frontally *prep* 3 at

behind $n \to$ 1 buttocks 2 rear *adj* 3 non-paying *adv* 4 after 5 untimely

being $n \to$ 1 emotion 2 essence 3 living 4 matter 5 person

bell $n \to$ 1 animal call 2 animal part 3 percussion instrument 4 resonator 5 siren 6 telecommunications v 7 be loud 8 call (of animals) 9 shout 10 telephone

below *adv* $\to$ 1 after 2 down

bend $n \to$ 1 curve 2 distortion 3 knot v 4 curve 5 distort 6 fasten 7 swerve

benefit $n \to$ 1 advantage 2 charity 3 entertainment 4 fertility 5 good v 6 improve 7 make do 8 take advantage

best $n \to$ 1 finery 2 show v 3 defeat 4 surpass *adj* 5 competent 6 good 7 most 8 superior *adv* 9 superiorly

bet $n \to$ 1 gamble v 2 be uncertain 3 gamble

betray $v \to$ 1 disenchant 2 display

better $n \to$ 1 gambler 2 good thing v 3 defeat 4 improve 5 surpass *adj* 6 good 7 healthy 8 improved

bid $n \to$ 1 attempt 2 cost 3 entreaty 4 gamble 5 offer v 6 appraise 7 command 8 gamble 9 offer

big *adj* $\to$ 1 expensive 2 generous 3 great 4 important 5 loud 6 pregnant 7 tasty 8 unselfish *adv* 9 braggingly 10 greatly

bill $n \to$ 1 account 2 accusation 3 bill 4 bird part 5 capital 6 cash 7 insistence 8 law 9 mound 10 public notice 11 spear v 12 account 13 insist on 14 kiss 15 list 16 plan 17 publicise

bin $n \to$ 1 barrel 2 pocket 3 prison 4 winemaking

bind $v \to$ 1 adhesive 2 annoyance 3 bond 4 bore 5 musical score 6 restraints 7 soil 8 stroke 9 cover 10 edge 11 fasten 12 harden 13 harvest 14 obligate 15 promise 16 restrain 17 stick together

bird $n \to$ 1 aeroplane 2 aim 3 certain thing 4 fauna 5 imprisonment 6 non-

bird 577 **bomb**

conformist 7 period 8 person 9 prison 10 woman v 11 hunt

bistro n → 1 pub 2 restaurant 3 shop

bite n → 1 angle 2 answer 3 bit 4 complainer 5 friction 6 hold 7 injury 8 meal 9 part 10 pungency 11 request 12 roughness v 13 be angry 14 beg 15 be had 16 discontent 17 eat 18 engrave 19 extort 20 hold 21 injure 22 pain 23 perforate

bitter n → 1 beer adj 2 acrimonious 3 distressing 4 hating 5 painful 6 sharp 7 sour 8 unfriendly 9 unpleasant

blab n → 1 revelation 2 speaking v 3 reveal 4 speak

blame n → 1 accusation 2 disapproval 3 imputation v 4 disapprove of 5 impute

bland adj → 1 composed 2 insipid 3 pleasant

blank n → 1 absence 2 centre 3 emptiness 4 gap 5 metal 6 non-being v 7 annihilate 8 remove adj 9 absent 10 bare 11 boring 12 colourless 13 confused 14 cursed 15 deficient 16 empty 17 most 18 nonexistent 19 white

blanket n → 1 bedclothes 2 cloak v 3 cover 4 hide 5 punish 6 set sail adj 7 general

blaze n → 1 fire 2 greatness 3 label 4 light 5 multicolour 6 outburst 7 shot v 8 be hot 9 blow 10 catch fire 11 cut 12 emblematise 13 label 14 make history 15 publicise 16 shine 17 shoot

blazing adj → 1 angry 2 hot 3 spectacular

bleak adj → 1 bare 2 cold 3 hopeless 4 sombre

blend n → 1 abridgment 2 word v 3 combine 4 cook 5 mix

bless v → 1 approve 2 be grateful 3 protect

block n → 1 bit 2 callousness 3 discourager 4 flat 5 footgear 6 head 7 house 8 information 9 matter 10 model 11 obstacle 12 post 13 sign 14 stocks and shares 15 timepiece 16 yard v 17 discourage 18 obstruct 19 shape 20 support

bloke n → man

bloodthirsty adj → 1 ferocious 2 murderous 3 warlike

bloom n → 1 beauty 2 colour 3 glaze 4 health 5 mineral 6 perfection 7 powder v 8 be fertile 9 be healthy 10 flower 11 grow 12 prosper

blossom v → 1 be fertile 2 flower 3 prosper

blow n → 1 accomplishment 2 attack 3 bragging 4 breathing 5 concert 6 corporal punishment 7 disenchantment 8 hit 9 misfortune 10 rest 11 rock outcrop 12 unpleasant thing 13 walk 14 wind v 15 breathe 16 depart 17 eroticise 18 fail 19 hiss 20 make music 21 report on 22 shape 23 shrill 24 squander

bludge v → 1 avoid 2 beg 3 borrow 4 idle 5 prostitute oneself

bluff n → 1 bombast 2 display 3 fake 4 mountain 5 stratagem 6 trickery v 7 beguile 8 trick adj 9 discourteous 10 erect 11 forthright 12 friendly

blunder n → 1 bungle 2 error 3 failure v 4 become confused 5 bungle 6 err 7 reveal

board n → 1 book part 2 coating 3 council 4 court of law 5 edge 6 food 7 hotel 8 legislative body 9 management 10 shaft 11 stable 12 surfboard 13 wrapper v 14 contact 15 enter 16 house 17 inhabit

boast n → 1 bragging 2 challenge v 3 brag 4 pride oneself

boat n → 1 vessel 2 watercraft v 3 transport

bohemian n → 1 artist 2 intellectual 3 nonconformist adj 4 informal 5 intellectual 6 nonconformist

boil n → 1 bulge 2 disfigurement 3 sore 4 turbulence v 5 be angry 6 be hot 7 bubble 8 cook 9 feel emotion 10 heat 11 toss 12 vaporise

bold n → 1 letter adj 2 believing 3 courageous 4 discourteous 5 nonconformist 6 rash 7 thick 8 visible

bolt n → 1 escape 2 gun part 3 textiles v 4 back out 5 elude 6 escape 7 fasten 8 gorge 9 sew 10 shoot 11 speed

bomb n → 1 bang 2 car 3 casualty 4 drug 5 explosive 6 failure 7 rock v 8 dive 9 explode 10 fail 11 fire on 12 lose 13 wage war

bonus *n* → 1 addition 2 bribe 3 gift 4 income 5 stocks and shares 6 surplus 7 surprise *adj* 8 additional 9 surprising

booby trap *n* → 1 allure 2 bomb 3 fortification 4 obstacle *v* 5 hinder

boost *n* → 1 help 2 lifting 3 propellant *v* 4 energise 5 help 6 increase 7 lift

border *n* → 1 bookbinding 2 edge 3 garden 4 region 5 side 6 surroundings 7 trimming 8 wall *v* 9 be close

bossy *adj* → 1 knobby 2 presumptuous

botch *n* → 1 bad thing 2 bungle 3 failure *v* 4 bungle 5 fail 6 spoil

bother *n* → 1 annoyance 2 busyness 3 confusion 4 worry *v* 5 annoy 6 care for 7 confuse 8 worry

bounce *n* → 1 bragging 2 dismissal 3 happiness 4 impact 5 jump 6 move 7 pliability 8 arrest 9 brag 10 dismiss 11 eject 12 jump 13 move 14 persuade

bountiful *adj* → 1 abundant 2 generous

bouquet *n* → 1 applause 2 plant 3 smell

bowl *n* → 1 ball 2 drinking session 3 party 4 tableware 5 throw 6 tobacco *v* 7 move 8 roll 9 speed 10 throw

braid *n* → 1 curl 2 hair 3 interlacement 4 string 5 trimming *v* 6 edge 7 interlace 8 twist

brand *n* → 1 candle 2 denigration 3 label 4 labeller 5 name 6 sword *v* 7 disgrace 8 fire 9 label

brash *n* → 1 ice 2 rock *adj* 3 discourteous 4 rash

breach *n* → 1 crime 2 gap 3 injury 4 opening *v* 5 open 6 separate

breathtaking *adj* → 1 exciting 2 important

breed *n* → 1 ancestry 2 character 3 class *v* 4 cause 5 create 6 farm 7 flower 8 rear 9 reproduce

brilliant *n* → 1 jewel 2 jewellery 3 solid *adj* 4 beautiful 5 bright 6 colourful 7 intelligent

broad *n* → 1 lake 2 woman *adj* 3 big 4 general 5 liberated 6 obscene 7 obvious 8 thick 9 thorough 10 vulgar *adv* 11 thoroughly

broadcast *n* → 1 publicity 2 telecommunications *v* 3 communicate 4 disperse 5 farm 6 generalise 7 publicise 8 publish 9 telecast *adj* 10 dispersed 11 general *adv* 12 dispersedly

broad-minded *adj* → tolerant

broken *adj* → 1 damaged 2 gaping 3 interrupted 4 irregular 5 non-paying 6 notched 7 obsequious 8 poor 9 separate 10 weak

brood *n* → 1 animal offspring 2 class *v* 3 be unhappy 4 give birth 5 think *adj* 6 pregnant

brush *n* → 1 act of war 2 animal part 3 cleansing 4 contact 5 electric circuit 6 fight 7 forest 8 groin 9 the bush 10 touch 11 woman *v* 12 clean 13 contact 14 simplify 15 touch 16 wage war

brusque *adj* → discourteous

bud *n* → 1 adolescent 2 bulge 3 flower 4 sibling 5 start 6 stem *v* 7 start

budge *v* → move

buff *n* → 1 desirer 2 hide 3 hit 4 overcoat 5 skin 6 specialist 7 yellow *v* 8 clean 9 moderate 10 polish *adj* 11 brown 12 yellow

bug *n* → 1 belief 2 error 3 fairy 4 illness 5 imperfection 6 insect 7 microphone 8 organism *v* 9 annoy 10 displease 11 hear 12 irritate 13 stop

bulk *n* → 1 body 2 greatness 3 much 4 part 5 size 6 storage 7 thickness *v* 8 weigh *adj* 9 many

bulletin *n* → 1 information 2 magazine 3 message 4 news 5 public notice

bully *n* → 1 arrogant person 2 forcer 3 friend 4 lover 5 menacer 6 prostitute 7 violent person *v* 8 act unkindly 9 be arrogant 10 be violent 11 force 12 menace *adj* 13 good 14 happy *interj* 15 well done

bump *n* → 1 airflow 2 bulge 3 impact 4 knob *v* 5 collide 6 defeat

bunch *n* → 1 accumulation 2 clique 3 knob *v* 4 gather 5 jut

bundle *n* → 1 accumulation 2 length 3 mixture *v* 4 cover 5 gather 6 kiss

bunkum *n* → 1 bombast 2 nonsense

burden *n* → 1 cost 2 difficulty 3 gravimetry 4 hindrance 5 imposition 6 insistence 7 music 8 obligation 9 rep-

burden 579 **catch**

etition 10 subject matter 11 toil *v* 12 repress 13 weigh

burl *n* → 1 attempt 2 gamble 3 knob *v* 4 disapprove of 5 mock 6 roll 7 speed

burn *n* → 1 clearance 2 injury 3 rate 4 stream 5 be close 6 be hot 7 desire 8 feel emotion 9 fire 10 heat 11 kill 12 shine 13 speed 14 wage war

burnish *n* → 1 brightness *v* 2 illuminate 3 polish

burst *n* → 1 exit 2 explosion 3 gunfire 4 outburst *v* 5 break 6 expel

bushed *adj* → 1 confused 2 lost 3 tired

busy *adj* → 1 intervenient 2 in use 3 working

but *n* → 1 qualification *adv* 2 conditionally *prep* 3 except

buzz *n* → 1 animal call 2 click 3 drug use 4 excitement 5 news 6 pleasure 7 telecommunications 8 vibration 9 call (of animals) 10 click 11 fly 12 speak 13 telephone 14 vibrate

by *adj* → 1 side *adv* 2 closely 3 in the past 4 sideways *prep* 5 at 6 near 7 on behalf of

bygone *n* → 1 past *adj* 2 past

cackle *n* → 1 birdcall 2 mirth 3 talk *v* 4 chirp 5 laugh 6 talk

cagey *adj* → secretive

calamity *n* → 1 failure 2 misfortune 3 ruin

calculate *v* → intend

calm *n* → 1 composure 2 period of inaction 3 rest *v* 4 inactivate 5 moderate *adj* 6 climatic 7 composed 8 inactive 9 moderate 10 peaceful 11 resting

camouflage *n* → 1 colour 2 disguise *v* 3 hide

camp *n* → 1 battleground 2 drama 3 man 4 rest 5 sleep 6 society *v* 7 feminise 8 have sex 9 inhabit 10 rest 11 sleep *adj* 12 male 13 sexual

can *n* → 1 alcohol container 2 box 3 buttocks 4 dismissal 5 drinking vessel 6 toilet *v* 7 be able 8 be permitted to 9 conserve 10 dismiss 11 disuse 12 know

candid *n* → 1 photograph *adj* 2 clean 3 fair 4 forthright 5 honest 6 truthful 7 white

caper *n* → 1 caprice 2 dancing 3 joke 4 jump 5 misdemeanour 6 trick *v* 7 jump

capsize *v* → overturn

captive *n* → 1 lover 2 prisoner 3 subject *adj* 4 imprisoned 5 loving

card *n* → 1 good person 2 humorist 3 message 4 nonconformist 5 person 6 plan 7 sewing machine *v* 8 clean 9 compute 10 record 11 sew 12 simplify

career *n* → 1 attack 2 job 3 rate *v* 4 speed

careless *adj* → 1 apathetic 2 false 3 happy 4 inattentive 5 lucky 6 neglectful

carry *n* → 1 length *v* 2 be important 3 capture 4 compute 5 conceive 6 help 7 transport

cart *n* → 1 wagon *v* 2 transport

carve *v* → 1 cut 2 depict 3 portray 4 shape

case *n* → 1 condition 2 container 3 covering 4 evidence 5 litigation 6 nonconformist 7 patient 8 plating 9 wrapper *v* 10 enclose 11 investigate 12 look

cast *n* → 1 amount 2 appearance 3 character 4 colour 5 copy 6 corporation 7 depth 8 faulty sight 9 length 10 metal 11 model 12 order 13 point of view 14 prediction 15 secretion 16 shape 17 small amount 18 theatrical company 19 throw *v* 20 compute 21 depict 22 distort 23 fish 24 give birth 25 heat 26 plan 27 portray 28 predict 29 separate 30 shape 31 stage 32 throw 33 work metal *adj* 34 drunk 35 fallen 36 lost 37 shaped

casual *n* → 1 temporary appointment 2 worker *adj* 3 apathetic 4 impermanent 5 inattentive 6 informal 7 irregular 8 lucky 9 neglectful 10 uncertain

catastrophe *n* → 1 finish 2 misfortune 3 ruin 4 turbulence 5 violent outburst

catch *n* → 1 amount 2 bolt 3 difficulty 4 holder 5 part 6 song 7 stoppage 8 stratagem 9 takings *v* 10 allure 11 beguile 12 be timely 13 be timely 14 find out 15 gain 16 hear 17 hold 18 surprise 19 trick

caution *n* → 1 cautiousness 2 command 3 nonconformist 4 warning *v* 5 warn

cease *n* → 1 stoppage *v* 2 die 3 stop

celebrate *v* → 1 approve 2 command respect 3 publicise 4 rejoice

celebrity *n* → famous person

cement *n* → 1 adhesive 2 building materials 3 paving 4 powder *v* 5 coat 6 stick together 7 weld

censor *n* → 1 disapprover 2 prohibiter 3 psychic disturbance *v* 4 hide 5 prohibit

ceremonial *n* → 1 breviary 2 custom 3 religious ceremony 4 worship *adj* 5 formal

chain *n* → 1 jewellery 2 length 3 mountain 4 restraints 5 sequence 6 series 7 wire *v* 8 fasten

chair *n* → 1 authority 2 bicycle 3 educational office 4 judgeship 5 leader 6 means of killing *v* 7 glorify

chamber *n* → 1 bedroom 2 cave 3 committee 4 compartment 5 council 6 gun part 7 hall 8 legislative body 9 office 10 room 11 toilet 12 treasury *v* 13 enclose

champion *n* → 1 accomplice 2 defender 3 fighter 4 good person 5 helper 6 hero 7 winner *v* 8 help 9 oppose *adj* 10 good

chance *n* → 1 danger 2 fate 3 feasibility 4 luck 5 opportunity 6 uncertain thing *v* 7 risk *adj* 8 lucky

charcoal *n* → 1 fire 2 fuel 3 writing materials *v* 4 blacken 5 depict 6 write

charm *n* → 1 allure 2 amulet 3 atom 4 beauty 5 birdcall 6 jewellery 7 magic spell 8 pleasantness 9 poetry 10 singing *v* 11 allure 12 be pleasant 13 bewitch 14 please 15 protect

chase *n* → 1 aim 2 furrow 3 gun part 4 nature reserve 5 pursuit 6 racing *v* 7 cut 8 furrow 9 hurry 10 pursue 11 walk

chat *n* → 1 dirty person 2 talk 3 untidy person *v* 4 scold 5 talk

cheat *n* → 1 crook 2 cunning person 3 dishonesty 4 embezzlement 5 fake 6 faker 7 trick 8 trickster *v* 9 beguile 10 fail to pay 11 misbehave 12 swindle

check *n* → 1 counterbalance 2 discourager 3 furrow 4 hindrance 5 investigation 6 label 7 losing 8 multicolour 9 restraints 10 sign 11 stoppage 12 test *v* 13 correct 14 discourage 15 fit 16 investigate 17 mark 18 oppose 19 restrain 20 stop 21 transport *adj* 22 multicoloured 23 questioning

cheeky *adj* → 1 discourteous 2 insulting

cheer *n* → 1 appearance 2 applause 3 congratulation 4 emotion 5 food 6 happiness 7 help 8 incentive 9 shout *v* 10 approve 11 congratulate 12 encourage 13 feel emotion 14 help 15 shout

cheerful *adj* → 1 happy 2 pleasant

chew *n* → 1 bit *v* 2 eat

chief *n* → 1 cook 2 important person 3 manager 4 ruler *adj* 5 important

chill *n* → 1 brace 2 cold 3 coldness 4 unsociability *v* 5 be cold 6 cool 7 desolate 8 discourage 9 frighten 10 harden *adj* 11 cold 12 distressing 13 unsociable

chime *n* → 1 edge 2 music 3 percussion instrument 4 resonator *v* 5 fit 6 make music 7 ring

chip *n* → 1 cut 2 gambling equipment 3 jewel 4 part 5 reprimand 6 small amount 7 unimportant thing *v* 8 cook 9 cut 10 depict 11 farm 12 separate

choke *n* → 1 steering wheel 2 thinness *v* 3 fill 4 kill 5 obstruct 6 restrain 7 stop 8 suffocate

chop *n* → 1 dismissal 2 emblem 3 hit 4 label 5 rough 6 share 7 stroke *v* 8 contest 9 cook 10 cut 11 dismiss 12 exchange 13 hit 14 shear

chore *n* → 1 difficulty 2 job 3 toil 4 unpleasant thing 5 work

circle *n* → 1 auditorium 2 cell 3 idol 4 jewellery 5 light 6 move 7 plane figure 8 ring 9 rotation 10 whole *v* 11 rotate 12 surround

civic *adj* → urban

civilisation *n* → 1 good taste 2 teaching

claim *n* → 1 assertion 2 entreaty 3 insistence 4 payment 5 request 6 rights

claim *v* 7 assert 8 insist on 9 necessitate 10 pride oneself

clamp *n* → 1 clip 2 holder 3 press 4 storage *v* 5 fasten 6 hold 7 press 8 support 9 walk

clap *n* → 1 applause 2 click 3 explosion 4 hit 5 loud sound 6 misfortune *v* 7 approve 8 explode 9 hit

clarify *v* → 1 be transparent 2 explain 3 simplify

clash *n* → 1 act of war 2 argument 3 dissonance 4 impact 5 loud sound *v* 6 argue 7 be dissonant 8 collide

clasp *n* → 1 button 2 endearments 3 hold 4 holder *v* 5 capture 6 fasten 7 hold 8 kiss

class *n* → 1 class 2 community 3 gathering 4 goodness 5 good taste 6 grade 7 lesson 8 similar thing *v* 9 graduate *adj* 10 classificatory 11 good

classify *v* → 1 class 2 inquire into 3 keep secret

clay *n* → 1 ceramics 2 raw materials 3 remnant 4 soil *v* 5 coat

cleanse *v* → 1 clean

clear *n* → 1 language *v* 2 acquit 3 bare 4 be transparent 5 clarify 6 exit 7 forgive 8 gain 9 jump 10 justify 11 liberate 12 obey 13 pay 14 permit 15 remove 16 simplify *adj* 17 acoustic 18 acquitted 19 bright 20 composed 21 empty 22 innocent 23 obvious 24 perfect 25 thorough 26 transparent 27 unconditional 28 visible *adv* 29 brightly 30 clearly 31 obviously 32 thoroughly 33 unconditionally 34 visibly

clever *adj* → 1 competent 2 cunning 3 humorous 4 intelligent 5 mental

climb *n* → 1 ascent *v* 2 ascend 3 flower 4 improve 5 slope 6 tower

cling *v* → 1 hold 2 stick together

clock *n* → 1 hit 2 imprisonment 3 period 4 timepiece 5 trimming *v* 6 hit 7 time

clot *n* → 1 bit 2 fool 3 paste 4 solid body 5 stupid person 6 thickening *v* 7 solidify

cloth *n* → 1 religious ministry 2 textiles 3 uniform

clown *n* → 1 circus performer 2 country dweller 3 entertainer 4 humorist 5 incompetent 6 vulgarian *v* 7 bungle 8 perform

club *n* → 1 extremity 2 living room 3 society 4 stick *v* 5 associate 6 combine 7 cudgel 8 kill

clue *n* → 1 evidence 2 explanation 3 information 4 signal

clumsy *adj* → 1 callous 2 incompetent 3 inconvenient 4 ugly

clutch *n* → 1 accumulation 2 animal offspring 3 hold 4 steering wheel *v* 5 capture 6 give birth 7 hold

coach *n* → 1 teacher 2 train 3 truck *v* 4 teach

coarse *adj* → 1 discourteous 2 execratory 3 obscene 4 rough 5 ugly 6 unsavoury 7 vulgar

coast *n* → 1 coastline 2 edge 3 seaside *v* 4 descend 5 glide 6 go slowly 7 move

coat *n* → 1 animal's coat 2 coating 3 covering 4 jacket *v* 5 cook 6 smooth

coax *v* → 1 kiss 2 persuade

coherent *adj* → 1 apt 2 logical 3 sticky

coil *n* → 1 busyness 2 difficulty 3 electric circuit 4 twist *v* 5 twist

coin *n* → 1 circle 2 coinage 3 metal *v* 4 be wealthy 5 circulate 6 create 7 fantasise 8 work metal

collaborate *v* → 1 betray 2 cooperate 3 help

collar *n* → 1 animal's coat 2 bubbling 3 edge 4 emblem 5 jewellery 6 neckwear 7 ring 8 seed *v* 9 capture 10 control 11 cook 12 hold 13 restrain

colleague *n* → 1 companion 2 partner 3 workers

collect *v* → 1 gamble 2 prayer 3 religious ceremony *v* 4 cash 5 gain 6 gather 7 get 8 reason 9 transport *adj* 10 payable

colossal *adj* → 1 big 2 enormous 3 important 4 tall

combat *n* → 1 act of war 2 argument 3 fight *v* 4 fight 5 wage war

come *v* → 1 reproductive agent 2 secretion *v* 3 appear 4 arrive 5 eroticise 6 excrete 7 finish 8 perform 9 start

comfort *n* → 1 alleviation 2 aid 3 bedclothes 4 contentedness 5 easiness 6 help 7 pleasure 8 satisfaction *v* 9 alleviate 10 ease 11 help

comfortable $n \to$ 1 bedclothes *adj* 2 alleviant 3 content 4 easy 5 happy 6 helpful 7 satisfied

commend $v \to$ 1 approve 2 guide

comment $n \to$ 1 assessment 2 clarification 3 commentary 4 essay 5 speaking 6 written composition v 7 clarify 8 discourse 9 explain 10 speak

commercial $n \to$ 1 incentive 2 public notice *adj* 3 mixed 4 popular 5 saleable 6 trading 7 vulgar

commission $n \to$ 1 agency 2 authority 3 command 4 committee 5 cost 6 employment 7 job 8 legislative body 9 management 10 obligation 11 operator 12 payment 13 profit 14 undertaking 15 work v 16 command 17 depute 18 employ 19 entreat

commit $v \to$ 1 command 2 give 3 involve 4 promise

common $n \to$ 1 field 2 religious ceremony 3 the public 4 working class *adj* 5 boring 6 customary 7 frequent 8 general 9 inferior 10 joined 11 liberated 12 mediocre 13 ordinary 14 public 15 related 16 shared 17 societal 18 ugly 19 vulgar

compassion $n \to$ 1 lenience 2 pity v 3 pity

compel $v \to$ 1 force 2 repress

compete $v \to$ contest

competition $n \to$ 1 contest 2 sport

complain $v \to$ be ungrateful

complete $v \to$ 1 accomplish 2 finish 3 make whole 4 perfect *adj* 5 competent 6 finished 7 perfect 8 unconditional 9 whole

complicate $v \to$ 1 cause difficulties *adj* 2 complex 3 folded

compliment $n \to$ 1 applause 2 congratulation 3 flattery 4 gift 5 greeting v 6 approve 7 congratulate

comply $v \to$ 1 capitulate 2 conform 3 obey

compose $v \to$ 1 combine 2 create 3 make 4 make music 5 mediate 6 order 7 print 8 write

comprehend $v \to$ 1 include 2 know 3 understand

comprehensive *adj* $\to$ 1 general 2 inclusive 3 thorough

compress $n \to$ 1 medication v 2 press

comprise $v \to$ include

conceal $v \to$ hide

conceivable *adj* $\to$ feasible

concentrate $v \to$ 1 attend to 2 become greater 3 centralise 4 converge 5 solidify 6 think *adj* 7 increased

concept $n \to$ 1 idea 2 the intangible

concern $n \to$ 1 affair 2 company 3 eye-catcher 4 fright 5 importance 6 job 7 trade v 8 be important 9 involve 10 relate

conclude $v \to$ 1 accomplish 2 determine 3 enclose 4 finish 5 reason 6 solve

concoct $v \to$ 1 create 2 fantasise 3 plan 4 prepare

concrete $n \to$ 1 adhesive 2 building materials 3 matter 4 paving 5 solid body v 6 harden 7 solidify *adj* 8 hard 9 real 10 solid 11 tangible

condemn $v \to$ 1 disapprove of 2 disuse 3 involve 4 punish

condense $v \to$ 1 abbreviate 2 harden 3 solidify

condition $n \to$ 1 deed 2 health 3 qualification v 4 be healthy 5 habituate 6 persuade 7 psychoanalyse 8 qualify

conduct $n \to$ 1 behaviour 2 management v 3 accompany 4 electrify 5 make music 6 manage

confident *adj* $\to$ 1 believing 2 certain 3 hopeful 4 rash

confidential *adj* $\to$ 1 hidden 2 secret

confirm $v \to$ 1 assent to 2 authenticate 3 strengthen

confiscate $v \to$ take

conflict $n \to$ 1 contest 2 disagreement 3 dissidence 4 impact v 5 argue 6 disagree 7 fight

congeal $v \to$ 1 be prejudiced against 2 solidify

connect $v \to$ 1 collide 2 electrify 3 join 4 relate

conquer $v \to$ 1 capture 2 defeat

conscientious *adj* $\to$ dutiful

conscious *adj* $\to$ 1 mental 2 perceptive 3 willing

consent $n \to$ 1 affirmation 2 agreement 3 permission v 4 agree

consequence $n \to$ 1 coming after 2 greatness 3 importance 4 reputation 5 result

consider v → 1 attend to 2 intend 3 think

considerate adj → 1 kind 2 thinking

consistent adj → 1 apt 2 congruous 3 hard 4 persevering 5 steady 6 sticky

constant n → 1 number adj 2 changeless 3 continual 4 eternal 5 faithful 6 homogeneous 7 serious

consultant n → 1 guide 2 healer 3 informant 4 specialist

consume v → 1 absorb 2 destroy 3 engross 4 squander 5 use up

contain v → 1 include 2 limit 3 restrain 4 restrict

contaminate v → 1 dirty 2 err 3 mix 4 poison 5 spoil

contempt n → 1 disapproval 2 disobedience 3 disrepute 4 low regard

continuous adj → continual

contradict v → 1 answer 2 deny 3 disagree

contrary n → 1 contrast 2 opposite meaning adj 3 argumentative 4 bent 5 disobedient 6 dissident 7 opposing 8 opposite adv 9 oppositely

contribute v → 1 cooperate 2 give 3 pay 4 write

contrite adj → 1 ashamed 2 penitent

contrive v → 1 beguile 2 conspire 3 create 4 make do 5 plan

control n → 1 competence 2 composure 3 operation 4 restraint v 5 manage 6 restrain 7 test

controversy n → 1 disagreement 2 discussion 3 subject matter

convenient adj → 1 easy 2 expedient

conversation n → 1 behaviour 2 friendship 3 talk

converse n → 1 communication 2 opposite meaning 3 talk v 4 talk adj 5 opposing 6 overturned

convey v → 1 capture 2 communicate 3 inform 4 rob 5 transport

convict n → 1 criminal 2 prisoner

convince v → persuade

cool n → 1 composure adj 2 cold 3 composed 4 fashionable 5 good 6 moderate 7 musical 8 unconditional 9 unsociable

cope n → 1 cloak 2 sky 3 top 4 uniform v 5 cover

copy n → 1 imitation 2 model 3 portrait 4 printwork 5 repetition v 6 follow 7 imitate

core n → 1 centre 2 extract 3 inside 4 model 5 opening v 6 extract 7 subtract

corner n → 1 bend 2 crisis 3 economy 4 ownership 5 region 6 seclusion 7 secret place v 8 drive 9 imprison 10 own 11 swerve 12 turn

correct v → 1 adjust 2 punish adj 3 formal 4 precise 5 true

corrupt v → 1 convert 2 dirty 3 ill-treat 4 spoil 5 wrong adj 6 bribable 7 deteriorated 8 dishonest 9 immoral

count n → 1 accusation 2 aristocrat 3 computation 4 score v 5 compute 6 publicise

counter n → 1 computer record 2 counteraction 3 footgear 4 Geiger counter 5 layer 6 mathematician 7 opposite meaning 8 shop 9 slope 10 table v 11 counteract 12 oppose adj 13 opposite adv 14 opposite

counterfeit n → 1 copy 2 imitation 3 portrait v 4 circulate 5 imitate 6 trick adj 7 fake 8 imitative

country n → 1 land 2 nation 3 region 4 the public adj 5 farming 6 ill-bred 7 national 8 rural

couple n → 1 lover 2 shaft 3 spouse 4 two v 5 double 6 have sex 7 join

course n → 1 advance 2 attack 3 behaviour 4 bridge 5 direction 6 hunting 7 layer 8 meal 9 method 10 move 11 path 12 point of view 13 race 14 regularity 15 route 16 sequence v 17 flow 18 head for 19 hunt 20 pursue

court n → 1 committee 2 council 3 court of law 4 field 5 house 6 judge 7 tribute v 8 allure 9 desire 10 entreat 11 flirt

cove n → 1 bay 2 boss 3 cave 4 farmer 5 man

cover n → 1 book part 2 container 3 covering 4 disguise 5 protection 6 refuge 7 surety v 8 be adequate 9 compensate 10 darken 11 flood 12 give birth 13 hide 14 include 15 publish 16 secure

cower v → 1 be frightened 2 lack courage

coy *adj →* 1 affected 2 disdainful 3 modest 4 silent

crack *n →* 1 attempt 2 break 3 buttocks 4 click 5 dissonance 6 expert 7 explosion 8 gap 9 groin 10 hit 11 joke 12 madness 13 mockery 14 moment 15 opening 16 prostitute 17 robbery 18 specialist *v* 19 be dissonant 20 be mad 21 break 22 explode 23 fail 24 gape 25 perforate 26 separate 27 solve 28 succeed *adj* 29 superior

cradle *n →* 1 basket 2 bath 3 bed 4 beds 5 breeding ground 6 filter 7 knife 8 platform 9 vessel *v* 10 clean 11 hold

craft *n →* 1 aircraft 2 artistry 3 competence 4 cunning 5 fine arts 6 institute 7 job 8 stratagem 9 trickery 10 watercraft

crafty *adj →* 1 competent 2 cunning 3 deceitful 4 opportunist

cramp *n →* 1 clip 2 holder 3 press 4 restraints *v* 5 hinder 6 hold 7 imprison 8 restrict

cranky *adj →* 1 angry 2 irritable 3 nonconformist

crash *n →* 1 defecation 2 explosion 3 failure 4 fall 5 impact 6 loud sound 7 ruin 8 separation *v* 9 be in debt 10 be loud 11 break 12 collapse 13 collide 14 defecate 15 descend 16 enter 17 explode 18 fail 19 separate 20 sleep *adj* 21 increased

crave *v →* 1 be jealous of 2 desire 3 entreat 4 necessitate

crazy *adj →* 1 excited 2 inappropriate 3 mad 4 nonconformist 5 rash 6 strange

credible *adj →* 1 believable 2 feasible 3 likely

credit card *n →* capital

crest *n →* 1 animal's coat 2 apex 3 bird part 4 bookbinding 5 bulge 6 courage 7 feather 8 heraldry 9 moulding 10 pride 11 top 12 trimming *v* 13 top

crevice *n →* 1 break 2 gap 3 passageway

cripple *n →* 1 casualty *v* 2 hinder 3 injure

critical *adj →* 1 assessorial 2 dangerous 3 disapproving 4 discursive 5 important 6 sloping 7 steady 8 timely

criticise *v →* 1 assess 2 disapprove of 3 discourse

crooked *adj →* 1 bent 2 curved 3 disfigured 4 dishonest 5 distorted 6 thieving 7 ugly 8 unlawful

crop *n →* 1 accumulation 2 bag 3 bird part 4 cut 5 finished product 6 hairdressing 7 hide 8 label 9 propellant *v* 10 be fertile 11 cut 12 harvest 13 shorten 14 smooth 15 take

cross *n →* 1 fauna 2 hit 3 hybrid 4 joint 5 misfortune 6 sign *v* 7 cross 8 extend 9 hinder 10 hybridise 11 mark 12 traverse 13 worship *adj* 14 crossing 15 dishonest 16 hybrid 17 inconvenient 18 irritable 19 opposite

crow *n →* 1 black 2 farmhand 3 machine *v* 4 be loud 5 brag 6 chirp 7 rejoice 8 shout

crucial *adj →* 1 crossing 2 difficult 3 essential 4 necessary 5 timely

crude *adj →* 1 discourteous 2 raw 3 ugly 4 vulgar

cruel *v →* 1 spoil *adj* 2 callous 3 painful 4 strict 5 unkind

cruise *v →* 1 move 2 set sail

crumble *n →* 1 separation 2 be old 3 powder 4 separate 5 wane

crush *n →* 1 drink 2 extract 3 gathering 4 love 5 path 6 pen 7 press *v* 8 break 9 contract 10 extract 11 humble 12 powder 13 press 14 repress

crust *n →* 1 covering 2 discourtesy 3 glaze 4 income 5 land 6 outside 7 remnant 8 winemaking *v* 9 accuse 10 harden

cry *n →* 1 act of war 2 animal call 3 hunter 4 public notice 5 shout 6 shouting 7 word *v* 8 be unhappy 9 call (of animals) 10 grieve

cuddle *n →* 1 endearments 2 hold *v* 3 hold 4 kiss 5 love

culture *n →* 1 custom 2 discrimination 3 farming 4 finished product 5 good taste 6 learning 7 organism 8 period

curb *n →* 1 controlling device 2 restraints 3 saddlery *v* 4 control 5 restrain

cure n → 1 medication 2 recovery 3 religious ministry v 4 conserve 5 heat 6 medicate 7 practise medicine

curtail v → 1 cut 2 shorten 3 subtract

customer n → 1 buyer 2 person

cut n → 1 bit 2 break 3 capital punishment 4 chance 5 character 6 cost 7 decrease 8 exclusion 9 fashion 10 furrow 11 gap 12 hairdressing 13 hit 14 part 15 recording 16 repulsion 17 share 18 stroke v 19 abstain 20 act unkindly 21 cross 22 cudgel 23 cut 24 decrease 25 deflect 26 depart 27 dig 28 displease 29 do 30 engrave 31 escape 32 exclude 33 harvest 34 interrupt 35 level 36 medicate 37 repel 38 separate 39 shape 40 shear 41 shorten 42 stop 43 subtract adj 44 decorative 45 decreased 46 drunk 47 mixed 48 separate

cycle n → 1 bicycle 2 musical piece 3 operation 4 period 5 rotation 6 sequence 7 story 8 whole v 9 alternate 10 drive

damp n → 1 discourager 2 gas 3 hindrance 4 poison 5 unhappiness 6 wetness v 7 control 8 decrease 9 discourage 10 hinder 11 quieten 12 wet adj 13 unhappy 14 wet

dank adj → wet

dart n → 1 clothes 2 plan 3 rate 4 spear 5 tobacco v 6 speed 7 throw

dash n → 1 artistry 2 caprice 3 discourager 4 hindrance 5 line 6 race 7 small amount 8 splash 9 sprightliness 10 vitality 11 wetting v 12 hinder 13 hit 14 humble 15 hurry 16 make unhappy 17 mix 18 separate 19 throw 20 wet interj 21 God

date n → 1 assignation 2 buttocks 3 groin 4 love affair 5 time 6 time measurement v 7 arrange 8 be sociable 9 flirt 10 time

dawdle v → 1 bungle 2 go slowly 3 idle

daydream n → 1 delusion 2 dream v 3 be inattentive 4 delude oneself 5 fantasise

daze n → 1 confusion 2 unconsciousness v 3 anaesthetise 4 confuse

deadly adj → 1 excessive 2 killing adv 3 excessively

dear n → 1 lover adj 2 beloved 3 difficult 4 excessive 5 expensive 6 highly regarded interj 7 oh

debate n → 1 discussion 2 fight 3 reasoning v 4 contest 5 reason 6 talk

debris n → 1 remnant 2 rock 3 waste

decay n → 1 deterioration 2 ill health 3 illness 4 powerlessness 5 toothache 6 weakness v 7 be ill 8 deteriorate 9 wane

deceased adj → dead

deceit n → 1 fake 2 trickery

decent adj → 1 adequate 2 correct 3 courteous 4 good 5 highly regarded 6 kind 7 modest 8 moral

decide v → 1 choose 2 determine 3 influence 4 mediate

declare v → 1 assert 2 confess 3 pay 4 publicise 5 stop

decline n → 1 decrease 2 deterioration 3 evening v 4 age 5 deteriorate 6 finish 7 refuse 8 slope 9 wane

decompose v → 1 deteriorate 2 separate

decree n → 1 command 2 insistence 3 judgment 4 law 5 public notice v 6 command 7 determine 8 publicise

decrepit adj → 1 aged 2 old 3 powerless 4 weak

deduce v → 1 reason 2 solve

deduct v → subtract

defeat n → 1 hindrance 2 losing 3 ruin v 4 cancel 5 surpass

defect n → 1 deficiency 2 disfigurement 3 imperfection 4 insufficiency

defiance n → 1 dissidence 2 menace

deficit n → 1 debt 2 deficiency 3 insufficiency

definite adj → 1 certain 2 limiting 3 particular 4 precise 5 true

defraud v → 1 cheat 2 fail to pay

defy v → oppose

degrade v → 1 decrease 2 demote 3 disgrace 4 materialise 5 rub 6 simplify

degree n → 1 angle 2 astronomic point 3 class 4 gradation 5 length

delay n → 1 inaction 2 lateness 3 slowness v 4 be late 5 go slowly 6 idle

deliberate *v* → 1 think *adj* 2 cautious 3 composed 4 opportunist 5 slow 6 willing

delicate *adj* → 1 beautiful 2 colourless 3 cultivated 4 delicious 5 discriminating 6 emotional 7 ethereal 8 light 9 small 10 soft 11 tasty 12 weak

delight *n* → 1 pleasure *v* 2 be pleasant 3 please

delinquent *n* → 1 disobeyer 2 mischief-maker *adj* 3 disobedient 4 guilty 5 neglectful 6 wrong

deliver *v* → 1 give 2 give birth 3 liberate 4 speak 5 throw 6 transport

delude *v* → 1 beguile 2 trick

delve *v* → 1 dig 2 farm 3 slope

demand *n* → 1 bill 2 command 3 desire 4 imposition 5 insistence 6 question 7 request *v* 8 command 9 impose 10 insist on 11 necessitate 12 question

demolish *v* → 1 destroy 2 disprove 3 eat

demonstrate *v* → 1 authenticate 2 display 3 fire on 4 teach

den *n* → 1 animal dwelling 2 bedroom 3 cabin 4 hiding place 5 room 6 shelter

denounce *v* → 1 accuse 2 scold

dense *adj* → 1 hard 2 intense 3 opaque 4 pressed 5 solid 6 stupid 7 thick

deny *v* → 1 doubt 2 refuse

depend *v* → 1 be inferior 2 be uncertain 3 hang

deposit *n* → 1 accumulation 2 capital 3 coating 4 mineral 5 placement 6 remnant 7 soil 8 surety *v* 9 lower 10 pay 11 place

depress *v* → 1 cheapen 2 decrease 3 hollow 4 make unhappy 5 press 6 sound

depression *n* → 1 angle 2 apathy 3 atmospheric pressure 4 cheapness 5 decrease 6 despair 7 hollow 8 inaction 9 indentation 10 unhappiness

describe *v* → narrate

desert *n* → 1 dryness 2 fairness 3 wasteland *v* 4 abandon 5 depart *adj* 6 infertile

design *n* → 1 creation 2 diagram 3 drawing 4 expedient 5 model 6 plan 7 shape *v* 8 create 9 depict 10 plan 11 shape 12 signify

desperate *adj* → 1 dangerous 2 despairing 3 hopeless 4 rash 5 striving

despicable *adj* → bad

despise *v* → 1 be arrogant 2 hold in low regard

despite *n* → 1 hate 2 ill will 3 low regard *prep* 4 notwithstanding

destiny *n* → 1 expected thing 2 fate 3 omen

destitute *adj* → 1 abandoned 2 poor

detach *v* → separate

detail *n* → 1 armed forces 2 employment 3 part 4 particulars 5 record *v* 6 decorate 7 employ 8 improve 9 particularise 10 share out

detect *v* → 1 find 2 see

deter *v* → discourage

determined *adj* → 1 changeless 2 persevering 3 serious 4 stubborn

detest *v* → 1 dislike 2 hate

develop *v* → 1 become greater 2 complicate 3 create 4 evolve 5 grow 6 improve 7 increase 8 photograph 9 shape

devious *adj* → 1 cunning 2 deceitful 3 deflective 4 opportunist 5 remote

devotion *n* → 1 enthusiasm 2 faithfulness 3 friendship 4 high regard 5 love 6 reverence

digest *n* → 1 abridgment 2 classification 3 essay 4 reference book *v* 5 abbreviate 6 absorb 7 class 8 eat 9 inquire into 10 know 11 learn 12 persevere

digit *n* → 1 arm 2 length 3 number

dim *v* → 1 darken *adj* 2 dull 3 having faulty sight 4 imprecise 5 invisible 6 quiet 7 shadowy 8 stupid 9 unclear

diminish *v* → 1 be few and far between 2 decrease 3 slander 4 subtract

din *n* → loud sound

dip *n* → 1 angle 2 candle 3 dive 4 hollow 5 liquid 6 move 7 pen 8 slope 9 thief *v* 10 disinfect 11 dive 12 lower 13 slope 14 wet

disadvantage *n* → 1 harm 2 inconvenience 3 uselessness *v* 4 incommode

disappoint *v* → disenchant

disaster $n \rightarrow$ 1 failure 2 misfortune 3 nonachiever 4 ruin

discharge $n \rightarrow$ 1 accomplishment 2 acquittal 3 bodily discharge 4 denial 5 dismissal 6 dutifulness 7 electricity 8 exit 9 explosion 10 expulsion 11 finished product 12 liberation 13 payment 14 record 15 shot v 16 accomplish 17 acquit 18 dismiss 19 electrify 20 excrete 21 expel 22 explode 23 liberate 24 pay 25 shoot 26 transport

discipline $n \rightarrow$ 1 course 2 monasticism 3 punishment 4 rule 5 sexuality v 6 be strict 7 punish 8 rear

discontinue $v \rightarrow$ 1 abandon 2 disuse 3 stop

discover $v \rightarrow$ 1 find 2 reveal

discreet $adj \rightarrow$ 1 cautious 2 discriminating 3 restricted

disgust $n \rightarrow$ 1 hate v 2 displease 3 provoke hatred

dish $n \rightarrow$ 1 allurer 2 beautiful person 3 hollow 4 meal 5 tableware v 6 abandon 7 dig 8 hinder 9 hollow

dishevelled $adj \rightarrow$ untidy

disloyal $adj \rightarrow$ 1 unfaithful 2 unfriendly

dismal $adj \rightarrow$ 1 bad 2 distressing 3 shadowy 4 sombre

disorganise $v \rightarrow$ disorder

dispatch $n \rightarrow$ 1 accomplishment 2 information 3 killing 4 means of killing 5 message 6 news 7 speed 8 transport v 9 accomplish 10 hurry 11 kill 12 transport

dispute $n \rightarrow$ 1 argument 2 disagreement 3 fight 4 litigation v 5 argue 6 disagree

disrespect $n \rightarrow$ 1 discourtesy 2 disobedience 3 disrepute 4 low regard 5 misbehaviour v 6 hold in low regard

dissatisfy $v \rightarrow$ 1 discontent 2 displease

dissent $n \rightarrow$ 1 complaint 2 disagreement 3 heresy 4 nonconformity v 5 disagree

dissolve $v \rightarrow$ 1 cancel 2 cinematise 3 collapse 4 deny 5 disappear 6 disperse 7 finish 8 liquefy 9 separate

distinct $adj \rightarrow$ 1 acoustic 2 different 3 loud 4 obvious 5 separate

distinguish $v \rightarrow$ 1 award 2 class 3 discriminate 4 glorify 5 particularise 6 see

distract $v \rightarrow$ 1 amuse 2 confuse

distress $n \rightarrow$ 1 pain 2 poverty 3 taking 4 unfortunateness 5 unhappiness 6 worry v 7 alarm 8 be out of luck 9 force 10 make unhappy 11 pain

distribute $v \rightarrow$ 1 class 2 disperse 3 share out 4 tidy

distrust $n \rightarrow$ 1 doubt v 2 doubt

disturb $v \rightarrow$ 1 agitate 2 confuse 3 disorder 4 hinder 5 interrupt

ditch $n \rightarrow$ 1 channel 2 drain 3 fortification 4 furrow 5 limit 6 sea v 7 abandon 8 avoid 9 descend 10 dig 11 disuse 12 furrow 13 lower 14 repel

divide $v \rightarrow$ 1 break 2 sharing out v 3 class 4 compute 5 differ 6 diverge 7 elect 8 graduate 9 separate 10 share out

do $n \rightarrow$ 1 celebration 2 embezzlement 3 success 4 trick v 5 accomplish 6 arrest 7 be adequate 8 be expedient 9 behave 10 cause 11 cheat 12 cut off 13 have a job 14 have sex 15 make 16 travel 17 undertake 18 use up

dominate $v \rightarrow$ tower

donate $v \rightarrow$ give

doom $n \rightarrow$ 1 death 2 fate 3 judgment 4 punishment 5 ruin v 6 assess 7 ordain

double $n \rightarrow$ 1 actor 2 copy 3 gamble 4 gun 5 similar thing 6 stratagem 7 transport v 8 increase 9 make music 10 speed 11 transport 12 big 13 deceitful 14 folded 15 two adv 16 in twos

doubtful $adj \rightarrow$ 1 disreputable 2 doubting 3 indecisive 4 uncertain

down $n \rightarrow$ 1 beard 2 descent 3 feather 4 fruit 5 grassland 6 mound v 7 absorb 8 defeat 9 drink 10 eat 11 lower 12 repress adj 13 ill 14 inactive 15 losing 16 unhappy adv 17 below 18 decreasingly 19 inactively

drab $n \rightarrow$ 1 grey 2 prostitute adj 3 boring 4 brown 5 dull 6 grey

draft $n \rightarrow$ 1 diagram 2 drawing 3 forcefulness 4 military service 5 serviceman 6 written composition v 7 depict 8 force 9 map 10 separate 11 write

drag *n* → 1 bore 2 carriage 3 costume 4 friction 5 hindrance 6 imprisonment 7 pull 8 race 9 road 10 smell 11 tobacco *v* 12 go slowly 13 hang 14 pull

draw *n* → 1 allure 2 attraction 3 attractor 4 breathing 5 equal 6 length 7 pull *v* 8 cash 9 contest 10 cook 11 depict 12 discharge 13 equal 14 extract 15 fill 16 portray 17 position 18 pull 19 smoke

dream *n* → 1 beautiful person 2 delusion 3 example 4 expected thing 5 hope 6 period 7 sleeping *v* 8 be inattentive 9 be indifferent 10 delude oneself 11 fantasise 12 hope 13 sleep

dress *n* → 1 clothes 2 equipment 3 formal dress *v* 4 clothe 5 cook 6 fertilise 7 prepare 8 tidy *adj* 9 formal

drift *n* → 1 accumulation 2 current 3 direction 4 length 5 meaning 6 move 7 passageway 8 point of view 9 soil 10 thrust *v* 11 farm 12 swim

drill *n* → 1 formality 2 furrow 3 inserter 4 lesson 5 opener 6 piercer 7 preparation *v* 8 hollow 9 open 10 prepare 11 study 12 teach

drip *n* → 1 bad person 2 bore 3 flow 4 fool 5 liquid 6 splash *v* 7 discharge 8 flow

drive *n* → 1 access 2 attack 3 charity 4 effort 5 excavation 6 journey 7 motive 8 psyche 9 stroke 10 thrust 11 vitality *v* 12 dig 13 force 14 hollow 15 hunt 16 manage 17 operate 18 thrust 19 tire

droop *n* → 1 descent 2 hanging 3 pose 4 weakness *v* 5 be tired 6 be unhappy 7 fall 8 hang 9 weaken

drop *n* → 1 a drink 2 animal offspring 3 bead 4 bit 5 decrease 6 descent 7 jewellery 8 length 9 liquid 10 means of killing 11 opening 12 pendant 13 slope 14 small amount 15 wall *v* 16 abandon 17 be tired 18 descend 19 die 20 disappear 21 dismiss 22 exclude 23 finish 24 give birth 25 lower 26 quieten 27 report on 28 speak 29 stop 30 take drugs 31 transport 32 wane 33 wet

drum *n* → 1 barrel 2 brothel 3 information 4 percussion instrument 5 support *v* 6 click 7 hit 8 make music 9 repeat

duck *n* → 1 avoidance 2 dive 3 lover 4 nothing 5 vehicle 6 wetting *v* 7 avoid 8 dive 9 lower 10 punish 11 wet

dud *n* → 1 ineffectual person 2 nonachiever *adj* 3 useless

due *adj* → 1 apt 2 imputable 3 owing 4 payable 5 unpaid *adv* 6 adequately 7 straight

dumb *adj* → 1 absent 2 inarticulate 3 reticent 4 silent 5 stupid

dump *n* → 1 arsenal 2 cabin 3 diggings 4 garbage dump 5 poorhouse 6 remnant 7 seclusion 8 storage 9 untidiness *v* 10 disuse 11 expel 12 lower 13 sell 14 store 15 throw 16 transport

duplicate *n* → 1 copy 2 imitation 3 repetition *v* 4 copy 5 double 6 imitate 7 reproduce *adj* 8 copied 9 two

dust *n* → 1 cloud 2 commotion 3 dirt 4 mineral 5 powder 6 remnant *v* 7 clean 8 disperse

duty *n* → 1 job 2 obedience 3 obligation 4 tax 5 tribute 6 value 7 work

eager *adj* → 1 desirous 2 enthusiastic

early *adj* → 1 original 2 past 3 preceding 4 untimely *adv* 5 in the past

earth *n* → 1 animal dwelling 2 chemical element 3 electric circuit 4 land 5 remnant 6 shelter 7 soil *v* 8 electrify

economical *adj* → 1 cheap 2 economic 3 thrifty

effect *n* → 1 accomplishment 2 influence 3 meaning 4 power 5 result 6 stage 7 trick *v* 8 accomplish 9 do 10 make

elaborate *v* → 1 be precise 2 change 3 clarify 4 complicate 5 improve 6 make an effort 7 particularise *adj* 8 complex 9 decorative 10 precise

element *n* → 1 armed forces 2 chemical element 3 dwelling 4 part 5 particulars 6 person 7 stove 8 surroundings 9 word

embrace *n* → 1 endearments 2 friendship 3 hold *v* 4 absorb 5 assent to 6 hold 7 include 8 kiss 9 look 10 love 11 surround

encounter $n \rightarrow$ 1 argument 2 convergence 3 fight v 4 argue 5 converge 6 fight 7 undergo

end $n \rightarrow$ 1 aim 2 death 3 extremity 4 finish 5 frame 6 remnant 7 remote place 8 result v 9 finish 10 result 11 stop

endure $v \rightarrow$ 1 be 2 compose oneself 3 continue 4 dislike 5 eternalise 6 live 7 persevere 8 persist 9 support 10 undergo

engage $v \rightarrow$ 1 attract 2 call attention to 3 employ 4 enchant 5 fasten 6 join 7 marry 8 promise

engagement $n \rightarrow$ 1 act of war 2 allure 3 assignation 4 attentiveness 5 contest 6 contract 7 doing 8 fastening 9 job 10 participation 11 undertaking 12 wedding

enhance $v \rightarrow$ 1 emphasise 2 improve 3 increase

enigma $n \rightarrow$ 1 code 2 disguise 3 uncertain thing

enlarge $v \rightarrow$ 1 add 2 defer 3 grow 4 increase 5 photograph

enough $n \rightarrow$ 1 adequacy *adj* 2 adequate *adv* 3 adequately *interj* 4 stop

enterprise $n \rightarrow$ 1 competence 2 corporation 3 courage 4 hope 5 undertaking 6 vitality

entire $n \rightarrow$ 1 whole *adj* 2 perfect 3 sequential 4 simple 5 whole

entry $n \rightarrow$ 1 account 2 competitor 3 entrance 4 liberty 5 record 6 taking

envelop $v \rightarrow$ 1 enclose 2 hide

environment $n \rightarrow$ surroundings

epic $n \rightarrow$ 1 drama 2 heroic story 3 poetry 4 story *adj* 5 courageous 6 famous 7 poetic

episode $n \rightarrow$ 1 act 2 interruption 3 interval 4 musical phrase 5 occurrence 6 period 7 story 8 waffle

eradicate $v \rightarrow$ 1 destroy 2 extract

erase $v \rightarrow$ 1 destroy 2 hide 3 remove

errand $n \rightarrow$ 1 agency 2 aim 3 employment 4 job 5 work

erratic $n \rightarrow$ 1 fish out of water 2 nonconformist 3 rock 4 waverer *adj* 5 changeable 6 deflective 7 irregular 8 misplaced 9 nonconformist 10 strange

escort $n \rightarrow$ 1 protection 2 protector v 3 accompany

establishment $n \rightarrow$ 1 changelessness 2 corporation 3 creation 4 dwelling 5 factory 6 habitation 7 income 8 positioning 9 religion 10 shop 11 start

esteem $n \rightarrow$ 1 approval 2 assessment 3 high regard 4 reputation v 5 appraise 6 assess 7 respect

estimate $n \rightarrow$ 1 assessment 2 computation 3 opinion 4 prediction 5 value v 6 assess 7 compute 8 predict

eternity $n \rightarrow$ 1 duration 2 infinity

ethnic $n \rightarrow$ 1 foreigner 2 population *adj* 3 foreign 4 human 5 resident

evacuate $v \rightarrow$ 1 back out 2 defecate 3 depart 4 empty 5 expel

evade $v \rightarrow$ 1 avoid 2 neglect 3 vacillate

evaluate $v \rightarrow$ 1 assess 2 examine 3 measure 4 test

even $n \rightarrow$ 1 evening v 2 level 3 smooth *adj* 4 composed 5 equal 6 fair 7 homogeneous 8 level 9 moderate 10 numerical 11 precise 12 regular 13 smooth 14 steady 15 straight *adv* 16 additionally 17 fairly 18 fully 19 levelly 20 precisely 21 smoothly 22 steadily *conj* 23 still

ever *adv* $\rightarrow$ continually

every *adj* $\rightarrow$ general

evident *adj* $\rightarrow$ 1 obvious 2 visible

evil $n \rightarrow$ 1 evildoing 2 harm 3 illness 4 misfortune 5 wrongfulness *adj* 6 angry 7 bad 8 calamitous 9 harmful 10 immoral 11 wrong

exact $v \rightarrow$ 1 extort 2 force 3 impose 4 insist on *adj* 5 concise 6 correct 7 precise

example $n \rightarrow$ 1 part 2 warning

excellent *adj* $\rightarrow$ 1 good 2 superior

excite $v \rightarrow$ 1 activate 2 cause 3 electrify 4 encourage 5 eroticise

exclaim $v \rightarrow$ 1 shout 2 speak

excuse $n \rightarrow$ 1 justification 2 penitence v 3 acquit 4 atone for 5 forgive 6 justify

exhaust $n \rightarrow$ 1 exit 2 gas v 3 discharge 4 empty 5 extract 6 make infertile 7 tire 8 use up

exhibit $n \rightarrow$ 1 authentication v 2 display 3 testify

exist

exist $v \rightarrow$ 1 be 2 live
expand $v \rightarrow$ 1 grow 2 increase 3 open up 4 waffle
expedition $n \rightarrow$ 1 act of war 2 journey 3 speed
expense $n \rightarrow$ 1 cost 2 payment
experience $n \rightarrow$ 1 knowledge 2 occurrence 3 perception v 4 feel emotion 5 learn 6 perceive 7 undergo
experiment $n \rightarrow$ 1 attempt 2 investigation 3 test v 4 attempt 5 investigate 6 test
explain $v \rightarrow$ 1 clarify 2 justify 3 solve
explicit $adj \rightarrow$ 1 clear 2 meaningful 3 precise
exploit $n \rightarrow$ 1 accomplishment 2 action v 3 use
explore $v \rightarrow$ 1 examine 2 investigate 3 pursue 4 search
expose $v \rightarrow$ 1 abandon 2 air 3 bare 4 disgrace 5 display 6 endanger 7 find out 8 photograph 9 report on 10 reveal
express $n \rightarrow$ 1 mail 2 message 3 messenger 4 speedster 5 transport v 6 confess 7 display 8 expel 9 extract 10 hurry 11 mean 12 press 13 represent 14 speak 15 transport 16 write adj 17 precise 18 speedy adv 19 hurriedly
extent $n \rightarrow$ 1 area 2 length 3 region 4 size 5 thickness
exterior $n \rightarrow$ 1 outside adj 2 outside
extra $n \rightarrow$ 1 actor 2 inflation 3 more 4 newspaper 5 worker adj 6 additional 7 good 8 surplus adv 9 excessively 10 superiorly 11 very
extraordinary $adj \rightarrow$ 1 astonishing 2 nonconformist 3 strange
extreme $n \rightarrow$ 1 finish 2 much adj 3 distant 4 excessive 5 final 6 limiting 7 most 8 thorough

fabulous $adj \rightarrow$ 1 astonishing 2 enormous 3 fake 4 famous 5 fantastic 6 good
face $n \rightarrow$ 1 appearance 2 arrogance 3 cosmetics 4 diggings 5 famous person 6 front 7 important thing 8 outside 9 printing press 10 reputation 11 sign v 12 argue 13 cover 14 direct 15 front 16 invert 17 oppose 18 smooth 19 swerve

fast

fade $v \rightarrow$ 1 be old 2 cinematise 3 darken 4 die 5 disappear 6 dull 7 graduate 8 lose colour 9 quieten 10 swerve 11 weaken
faint $n \rightarrow$ 1 unconsciousness v 2 become unconscious 3 be ill 4 be tired 5 dull 6 weaken adj 7 cowardly 8 dull 9 feverish 10 imprecise 11 invisible 12 quiet 13 weak
fair $n \rightarrow$ 1 amusement park 2 display 3 festival 4 lover 5 shop 6 woman v 7 change 8 improve adj 9 adequate 10 beautiful 11 clear 12 climatic 13 courteous 14 dry 15 easy 16 favourable 17 honest 18 hot 19 mediocre 20 perfect 21 smooth 22 white 23 windy adv 24 fairly 25 wholly
faith $n \rightarrow$ 1 belief 2 hope 3 obligation 4 religion 5 reverence
fall $n \rightarrow$ 1 decrease 2 evildoing 3 failure 4 hairpiece 5 hanging 6 ruin 7 season 8 slope v 9 be dismissed 10 be immoral 11 be of no repute 12 capitulate 13 collapse 14 conceive 15 cost 16 die 17 hang 18 occur 19 slope 20 wane
false $adj \rightarrow$ 1 fake 2 illogical 3 substitutive 4 unfaithful
familiar $n \rightarrow$ 1 friend 2 phantom adj 3 easy 4 friendly 5 insulting 6 kindred 7 knowledgeable 8 known 9 presumptuous
family $n \rightarrow$ 1 ancestry 2 class 3 criminal 4 language 5 occupant 6 offspring 7 relative 8 similar thing adj 9 correct 10 kindred
fan $n \rightarrow$ 1 airway 2 approver 3 audience 4 cooler 5 enthusiast 6 helper v 7 arouse 8 cool 9 harvest
fancy $n \rightarrow$ 1 caprice 2 choice 3 conception 4 desire 5 expected thing 6 fantasy 7 good taste 8 hope 9 pleasure v 10 choose 11 desire 12 enjoy adj 13 decorative 14 fantastic 15 tasteful $interj$ 16 how about that
fascinate $v \rightarrow$ 1 allure 2 bewitch 3 engross
fast $n \rightarrow$ 1 holy day v 2 abstain adj 3 busy 4 closed 5 deceitful 6 fastened 7 imprisoned 8 promiscuous 9 restricted 10 speedy 11 steady 12 sticky 13

fast 591 **flat**

untimely *adv* 14 speedily 15 steadily 16 stickily

fatal *adj* → 1 deadly 2 hopeless 3 important 4 inevitable 5 killing 6 predictive

fatigue *n* → 1 tiredness 2 toil 3 weakness 4 work *v* 5 tire

fault *n* → 1 break 2 disfigurement 3 error 4 evildoing 5 failure 6 guilt 7 imperfection 8 interruption 9 wrong *v* 10 disapprove of 11 err 12 separate

favourite *n* → 1 choice 2 expected thing 3 friend 4 hope 5 likelihood 6 lover *adj* 7 approved 8 beloved 9 chosen 10 expected

fear *n* → 1 fright 2 high regard *v* 3 be frightened 4 frighten 5 respect

feast *n* → 1 a good time 2 celebration 3 festival 4 meal *v* 5 eat 6 rejoice

feeble *adj* → 1 ill 2 powerless 3 weak

feel *n* → 1 condition 2 perception 3 sexual intercourse 4 touch 5 weave *v* 6 perceive 7 touch

feeling *n* → 1 emotion 2 fine arts 3 idea 4 musicianship 5 perception 6 pity 7 touch *adj* 8 emotional 9 perceptive 10 pitying

fellow *n* → 1 equal 2 equivalent 3 friend 4 intellectual 5 man 6 partner 7 person 8 pupil 9 similar thing 10 two *adj* 11 equal

fetch *n* → 1 attempt 2 length 3 trick *v* 4 arrive 5 cost 6 enchant 7 gain 8 head for 9 initiate 10 transport

fetish *n* → 1 idol 2 magic spell 3 psychic disturbance

feud *n* → 1 fight 2 ownership *v* 3 fight

few *adj* → rare

fiddle *n* → 1 expedient 2 restraints 3 steadier 4 string instrument 5 trick *v* 6 be inattentive 7 fake 8 make music

fidget *n* → 1 worrier *v* 2 belt into 3 worry

fierce *adj* → 1 acrimonious 2 ferocious 3 strict 4 unkind

figure *n* → 1 appearance 2 decoration 3 diagram 4 famous person 5 figure of speech 6 musical phrase 7 number 8 painting 9 shape 10 sign *v* 11 appear 12 compute 13 decorate 14 make music 15 reason 16 represent 17 shape

file *n* → 1 computer record 2 information 3 line 4 list 5 powderer 6 record 7 series 8 smoother *v* 9 inquire into 10 insert 11 powder 12 record 13 smooth 14 tidy

filthy *adj* → 1 bad 2 dirty 3 immoral 4 obscene 5 sickening

fire *n* → 1 attack 2 brightness 3 candle 4 capital punishment 5 death 6 emotion 7 enthusiasm 8 explosion 9 fever 10 lightning 11 misfortune 12 shot *v* 13 arouse 14 desire 15 dismiss 16 emotionalise 17 enthuse 18 explode 19 feel emotion 20 fuel 21 heat 22 shoot

firm *n* → 1 company 2 corporation 3 healer *v* 4 harden 5 steady *adj* 6 fastened 7 hard 8 joined 9 persevering 10 serious 11 steady 12 strict *adv* 13 perseveringly 14 steadily

first *n* → 1 starter 2 successfulness *adj* 3 advanced 4 early 5 important 6 new 7 original 8 prototypal 9 superior *adv* 10 firstly 11 optionally

fit *n* → 1 congruity 2 drug equipment 3 madness 4 poetry 5 story 6 unconsciousness *v* 7 accuse 8 equip 9 join 10 litigate 11 prepare 12 regularise *adj* 13 apt 14 competent 15 expedient 16 fair 17 healthy 18 prepared

fix *n* → 1 bribe 2 dilemma 3 dishonesty 4 drug use 5 positioning *v* 6 arrange 7 conserve 8 cook 9 equip 10 fasten 11 harden 12 make infertile 13 materialise 14 order 15 photograph 16 repair 17 steady 18 stick together 19 swindle 20 undertake

flag *n* → 1 animal part 2 coating 3 feather 4 shirt 5 watercraft *v* 6 be inactive 7 communicate 8 decorate 9 hang 10 signal 11 weaken

flash *n* → 1 camera part 2 chute 3 emblem 4 ephemeral 5 exit 6 fire 7 jewel 8 language 9 light 10 lighting 11 moment 12 news item 13 show 14 signal *v* 15 be angry 16 catch fire 17 disperse 18 increase 19 shine 20 show off 21 speed 22 undress *adj* 23 fake 24 showy

flat *n* → 1 bar 2 footgear 3 honest person 4 level 5 policeman 6 racecourse 7 shallow 8 stage 9 storey 10 swamp

flat 592 **fugitive**

11 tobacco v 12 inhabit adj 13 blunt 14 boring 15 composed 16 dissonant 17 dull 18 easy 19 honest 20 inactive 21 insipid 22 level 23 shallow 24 smooth 25 unconditional adv 26 levelly 27 precisely 28 unconditionally

flimsy n → 1 copy adj 2 ethereal 3 illogical 4 light

fling n → 1 attempt 2 liberty 3 slander 4 throw v 5 throw

floor n → 1 bottom 2 land 3 layer 4 room 5 storey v 6 bowl over 7 confuse 8 defeat 9 level

flourish n → 1 decoration 2 health 3 musical piece 4 rhetorical device 5 show v 6 be fertile 7 be healthy 8 display 9 flower 10 flutter 11 make music 12 prosper 13 show off

fluent adj → 1 beautiful 2 changeable 3 easy 4 flowing 5 liquid 6 smooth

fluff n → 1 bungle 2 burp 3 error 4 hair 5 weave v 6 bungle 7 burp 8 feather

flush n → 1 fever 2 flow 3 outburst 4 redness 5 stream v 6 be hot 7 clean 8 coat 9 energise 10 flow 11 level 12 redden adj 13 energetic 14 level 15 precise 16 righteous 17 wealthy adv 18 levelly 19 precisely

fly n → 1 attempt 2 camp 3 carriage 4 clothes 5 direction 6 door 7 fishing tackle 8 flight 9 roof v 10 elude 11 hang 12 lift 13 speed 14 transport adj 15 cunning 16 intelligent

focus n → 1 centre 2 foundation 3 length 4 point of convergence 5 reflection 6 visibility v 7 attend to 8 centralise 9 converge

foil n → 1 actor 2 arch 3 coating 4 contrast 5 difference 6 losing 7 metal 8 sword v 9 coat 10 defeat 11 differ 12 disenchant 13 hinder 14 stop 15 work metal

follow v → 1 coming after 2 stroke v 3 accompany 4 advance 5 conform 6 have a job 7 head for 8 imitate 9 obey 10 partner 11 result 12 understand

fond adj → 1 storage adj 2 believing 3 foolish 4 illogical 5 loving

fool n → 1 entertainer 2 incompetent 3 stupid person v 4 joke 5 misguide 6 trick

forbid v → 1 boycott 2 hinder 3 prohibit

fork n → 1 bend 2 branch 3 break 4 groin 5 musical instrument 6 piercer v 7 diverge 8 lift 9 separate

fortune n → 1 fate 2 luck 3 omen 4 wealth

forward v → 1 prepare 2 transport adj 3 advanced 4 discourteous 5 early 6 enthusiastic 7 front 8 future 9 happy 10 presumptuous 11 frontal adv 11 frontally

foul n → 1 impact v 2 collide 3 dirty 4 disgrace 5 disobey 6 obstruct 7 tangle adj 8 bad 9 dirty 10 disobedient 11 excretory 12 immoral 13 mixed 14 obscene 15 opposite 16 sickening 17 tangled 18 ugly 19 unfair 20 violent 21 wrong adv 22 unfairly

fraction n → 1 chemical agent 2 number 3 part 4 religious ceremony 5 share v 6 separate

fragile adj → brittle

frail n → 1 amount 2 basket adj 3 brittle 4 immoral 5 weak

frame n → 1 bone 2 building 3 conspiracy 4 container 5 enclosure 6 photograph 7 stand 8 structure v 9 accuse 10 create 11 edge 12 fake 13 make 14 plan 15 shape 16 support

freak n → 1 enthusiast 2 nonconformist v 3 frighten adj 4 strange

free v → 1 alleviate 2 liberate adj 3 cheap 4 easy 5 escaped 6 generous 7 independent 8 liberated 9 promiscuous 10 separate 11 sounded 12 unpaid 13 unused 14 windy adv 15 freely

fresh n → 1 stream adj 2 additional 3 clean 4 cold 5 discourteous 6 energetic 7 healthy 8 ignorant 9 living 10 memorable 11 new 12 tasty 13 youthful adv 14 cleanly 15 coldly 16 newly

frontier n → 1 edge 2 region 3 wall adj 4 boundary

frugal adj → 1 abstinent 2 cheap 3 thrifty

frustrate v → 1 argue 2 counteract 3 discourage 4 disenchant 5 hinder

fugitive n → 1 avoider 2 escapee adj 3 elusive 4 escaped 5 ethereal 6 impermanent

fumble — grasping

fumble n → 1 bungle 2 faulty speech 3 sexual intercourse v 4 bungle 5 eroticise 6 mispronounce

funny n → 1 joke adj 2 humorous 3 strange

fuse n → 1 electric circuit 2 explosive 3 gun part 4 lighter v 5 combine 6 join 7 liquefy 8 mix 9 stick together

fuss n → 1 busyness 2 commotion 3 confusion 4 excitement 5 fight 6 turbulence 7 worry v 8 annoy 9 become confused 10 belt into 11 complain 12 worry

gag n → 1 joke 2 restraining order 3 stoppage v 4 close 5 joke 6 restrain 7 silence 8 stop 9 trick

game n → 1 amusement 2 contest 3 courage 4 fauna 5 job 6 stratagem v 7 gamble adj 8 courageous 9 injured

gang n → 1 committee 2 gathering 3 workers v 4 associate 5 travel

garbage n → 1 bad thing 2 dirt 3 illogicality 4 nonsense 5 waffle 6 waste

gasp n → 1 absorption 2 breathing v 3 absorb 4 breathe 5 speak

gate n → 1 access 2 camera part 3 cost 4 dam 5 door 6 entrance 7 fence 8 gap 9 obstacle v 10 imprison

gay n → 1 affected person 2 man 3 sexual type adj 4 colourful 5 happy 6 male 7 overindulgent 8 sexual

generation n → 1 age 2 ancestry 3 creation 4 duration 5 offspring 6 period 7 reproduction

genius n → 1 character 2 characteristic 3 competence 4 influencer 5 intelligence 6 mind 7 mythical being 8 phantom 9 wise person

gentle v → 1 make peace adj 2 courteous 3 kind 4 lenient 5 moderate 6 quiet

genuine adj → 1 correct 2 faithful 3 forthright 4 honest 5 true 6 truthful

ghost n → 1 living 2 phantom 3 soul 4 writer v 5 haunt 6 write

giant n → 1 expert 2 important person 3 mythical being 4 strong person 5 tall person adj 6 big 7 enormous 8 superior 9 tall

gig n → 1 carriage 2 concert 3 contract 4 fishing tackle 5 fool 6 job 7 look 8 looker 9 rowing boat 10 spear v 11 annoy 12 drive 13 fish 14 look 15 mock

globe n → 1 ball 2 emblem of office 3 heavenly body 4 representation v 5 round

gloomy adj → 1 distressing 2 dull 3 shadowy 4 unhappy

glory n → 1 approval 2 beauty 3 contentedness 4 god 5 heaven 6 holy person 7 prayer 8 reputation 9 wealth v 10 brag 11 rejoice

gloss n → 1 appearances 2 beauty 3 brightness 4 clarification 5 commentary 6 shallow 7 written composition v 8 explain 9 illuminate

glow n → 1 colourfulness 2 emotion 3 fire 4 light v 5 be hot 6 feel emotion 7 shine

go n → 1 attempt 2 bargain 3 health 4 period 5 sprightliness 6 success 7 vitality v 8 depart 9 die 10 extend 11 gamble 12 move 13 operate 14 sell 15 tend to 16 travel adj 17 operating

goad n → 1 incentive 2 piercer 3 propellant v 4 arouse 5 irritate

govern v → 1 control 2 legislate 3 manage

grace n → 1 artistry 2 beauty 3 forgiving 4 god 5 gratefulness 6 interval 7 kindness 8 pity 9 pleasantness

gradient n → 1 ascent 2 curve 3 slope adj 4 sloping 5 walking

graft n → 1 dishonesty 2 insertion 3 joint 4 profit 5 toil v 6 insert 7 join 8 make an effort 9 reproduce 10 substitute 11 swindle

grain n → 1 bead 2 break 3 character 4 colour 5 fuel 6 hide 7 line 8 matter 9 powder 10 reproductive agent 11 roughness 12 small amount v 13 bare 14 powder 15 roughen

grand n → 1 piano adj 2 affected 3 beautiful 4 enormous 5 good 6 important 7 musical 8 reputable 9 tall 10 thorough

grasp n → 1 competence 2 hold 3 knowledge 4 ownership v 5 attempt 6 fasten 7 hold 8 know

grasping n → 1 holding adj 2 avaricious 3 holding 4 predatory 5 striving

graze n → 1 contact 2 cut 3 rubbing 4 touch v 5 contact 6 cut 7 farm 8 rub 9 touch

grim adj → 1 dreadful 2 ferocious 3 frightening 4 sombre 5 strict 6 ugly

grind n → 1 battler 2 dissonance 3 learning 4 powdering 5 pupil 6 sexual intercourse 7 toil 8 walk v 9 be dissonant 10 make an effort 11 persist 12 powder 13 rub 14 smooth

grip n → 1 bag 2 competence 3 handle 4 hold 5 job 6 transporter v 7 capture 8 engross 9 fasten 10 hold

gripe n → 1 complaint 2 hold v 3 capture 4 complaint 5 fasten 6 hold 7 pain 8 swerve

grit n → 1 courage 2 persistence 3 powder v 4 be dissonant

groove n → 1 custom 2 furrow 3 niche 4 passageway 5 recording v 6 furrow

ground n → 1 cause 2 freight 3 land v 4 bowl over 5 electrify 6 initiate 7 prohibit 8 restrict 9 teach adj 10 bottom 11 land 12 powdered 13 rough

group n → 1 armed forces 2 class 3 company 4 gathering 5 mixture 6 musical band 7 society v 8 gather 9 inquire into

gush n → 1 bleeding 2 flow 3 stream 4 waffle v 5 feel emotion 6 flow 7 waffle

guts n → 1 abdomen 2 courage 3 gambling equipment 4 glutton 5 inside v 6 gorge

guy n → 1 butt 2 lover 3 man 4 portrait 5 steadier 6 ugly person v 7 hold 8 mock 9 steady

hack n → 1 axe 2 car 3 cut 4 horse 5 kick 6 platform 7 rack 8 shelf 9 writer v 10 cut 11 damage 12 dislike 13 kick 14 ride 15 roughen adj 16 mediocre

hallow v → 1 consecrate 2 pursue 3 respect 4 shout 5 worship interj 6 cooee 7 hey 8 tally-ho

hammer n → 1 club 2 ear 3 gun part 4 narcotic v 5 accuse 6 beat 7 decrease 8 hit 9 question 10 repeat

hand n → 1 applause 2 arm 3 feeler 4 gamesman 5 height 6 help 7 indicator 8 labourer 9 person 10 side 11 wedding 12 writing

handsome adj → 1 accomplished 2 beautiful 3 generous 4 great

handy adj → 1 competent 2 easy 3 expedient 4 useful

hardy n → 1 chisel adj 2 courageous 3 persevering 4 rash 5 strong

harrow n → 1 digging implement 2 farm machinery v 3 farm 4 make unhappy 5 pain

harsh adj → 1 callous 2 difficult 3 dissonant 4 ill-bred 5 rough 6 sour 7 strict 8 unkind

hatch n → 1 animal offspring 2 covering 3 entrance 4 line 5 opening v 6 darken 7 depict 8 fantasise 9 give birth 10 initiate 11 line 12 mark 13 plan 14 prepare

haughty adj → 1 arrogant 2 discourteous 3 reputable

haul n → 1 amount 2 pull 3 takings v 4 pull 5 swerve

have n → 1 illusion 2 trick v 3 buy 4 cause 5 get 6 give birth 7 have sex 8 hold 9 include 10 own 11 permit 12 trick 13 undertake

hawk n → 1 attacker 2 exhortionist 3 fighter 4 political ideologist 5 warmonger v 6 be loud 7 excrete 8 hunt 9 sell 10 shout

hazard n → 1 danger 2 gambling 3 obstacle 4 opening v 5 attempt 6 gamble 7 risk

headlong adj → 1 rash 2 sloping 3 speedy adv 4 frontally 5 rashly 6 speedily

hearty n → 1 friend 2 good person 3 mariner adj 4 abundant 5 busy 6 enthusiastic 7 fertile 8 friendly 9 great 10 healthy 11 satisfactory

heap n → 1 accumulation 2 discard 3 much v 4 add 5 gather 6 give

heave n → 1 exercise 2 lifting 3 misplacement 4 pull 5 throw v 6 bulge 7 lift 8 misplace 9 move 10 pull 11 throw 12 toss

hectic n → 1 fever 2 busy 3 excited 4 hot 5 muddled 6 short-winded

hedge n → 1 fence 2 high finance 3 loophole 4 preparation v 5 avoid 6 enclose 7 gamble 8 invest 9 separate

heel n → 1 bad person 2 bottom 3 curve 4 footgear 5 leg v 6 slope

herd $n \to$ 1 gathering 2 working class v 3 farm 4 gather

hermit $n \to$ 1 believer 2 solitary

hesitate $v \to$ 1 be uncertain 2 be unwilling 3 go slowly 4 mispronounce 5 stop 6 vacillate

highlight $v \to$ 1 colour 2 display 3 emphasise

hinge $n \to$ 1 bone 2 centre-line 3 joint 4 necessities 5 qualification 6 rule 7 support v 8 join

hint $n \to$ 1 allusion 2 guidance 3 information 4 sign 5 signal 6 small amount v 7 inform 8 remind

hitch $n \to$ 1 bond 2 disenchantment 3 hindrance 4 journey 5 knot 6 military service 7 period 8 pull v 9 drive 10 marry 11 pull

hoard $n \to$ 1 accumulation 2 storage v 3 gather 4 store

hoist $n \to$ 1 flag 2 lift 3 robbery v 4 lift 5 rob

hole $n \to$ 1 animal dwelling 2 bay 3 buttocks 4 cabin 5 dilemma 6 groin 7 hollow 8 mouth 9 opening 10 prison 11 seclusion v 12 break 13 dig 14 open

home $n \to$ 1 animal dwelling 2 dwelling 3 house 4 nation 5 refuge v 6 direct 7 go back adj 8 domestic 9 national 10 resident

honour $n \to$ 1 award 2 commemoration 3 faithfulness 4 high regard 5 honesty 6 mister 7 reputation 8 reverence v 9 congratulate 10 glorify 11 respect 12 worship

hook $n \to$ 1 allure 2 anchor 3 curve 4 fishing tackle 5 hanger 6 hit 7 holder 8 musical score 9 region 10 stroke v 11 beguile 12 capture 13 curve 14 deflect 15 marry 16 rob 17 sew

hop $n \to$ 1 dance 2 flight 3 jump 4 party v 5 dance 6 depart 7 jump 8 move 9 walk

hopeful $n \to$ 1 children 2 expected thing adj 3 expectant 4 favourable

horizontal $n \to$ 1 level adj 2 level

horrible $adj \to$ 1 dreadful 2 frightening

horrify $v \to$ 1 displease 2 frighten

hostile $n \to$ 1 dissident adj 2 hating 3 unfriendly

hound $n \to$ 1 bad person 2 dog 3 drug user 4 horse v 5 act unkindly 6 arouse 7 be unfriendly 8 pursue

hover $v \to$ 1 lightness v 2 float 3 fly 4 tower 5 vacillate

hug $n \to$ 1 endearments 2 friendship 3 hold 4 hold 5 kiss 6 love

huge $adj \to$ 1 big 2 enormous

humane $adj \to$ 1 kind 2 lenient 3 pitying

humid $adj \to$ 1 hot 2 wet

humiliate $v \to$ 1 disgrace 2 humble 3 insult

hunch $n \to$ 1 anticipation 2 bulge 3 caprice 4 conjecture 5 idea v 6 bulge

hunt $n \to$ 1 hunter 2 inspection 3 pursuit 4 ringing v 5 dismiss 6 flutter 7 pursue 8 repel

hurl $n \to$ 1 expulsion 2 throw v 3 speak 4 throw 5 vomit

hurt $n \to$ 1 harm 2 insult 3 pain v 4 act unkindly 5 displease 6 injure 7 make unhappy 8 pain adj 9 acrimonious

hurtle $n \to$ 1 impact v 2 collide 3 speed 4 throw

hygienic $adj \to$ 1 clean 2 wholesome

ice $n \to$ 1 formality 2 jewel 3 smooth object v 4 be cold 5 coat 6 cool 7 sweeten

ideal $n \to$ 1 aim 2 example 3 good thing 4 perfect thing 5 the intangible adj 6 good 7 model 8 notional 9 perfect

identical $adj \to$ 1 homogeneous 2 precise

identify $v \to$ 1 class 2 homogenise 3 label 4 particularise

idiot $n \to$ 1 fool 2 psychotic 3 stupid person

if $n \to$ 1 qualification $conj$ 2 on condition that

ignore $v \to$ 1 be unfriendly 2 defeat

illegal $adj \to$ 1 anarchic 2 disobedient 3 prohibited 4 unlawful 5 wrong

illustrate $v \to$ 1 clarify 2 depict 3 explain 4 represent 5 teach

imaginary $adj \to$ 1 delusive 2 fantastic 3 numerical

imagine $v \to$ 1 believe 2 conjecture 3 delude oneself 4 devise 5 exaggerate 6 fantasise 7 plan

imminent *adj* → 1 dangerous 2 expected 3 future 4 hanging 5 protuberant

immoral *adj* → 1 promiscuous 2 wrong

immortal *n* → 1 eternity *adj* 2 changeless 3 eternal 4 famous

impatient *adj* → 1 desirous 2 irritable 3 rash

imperative *n* → 1 command 2 insistence 3 necessities *adj* 4 commanding 5 insistent 6 necessary 7 obligatory

imperious *adj* → 1 autocratic 2 commanding 3 powerful 4 presumptuous

impersonate *v* → 1 imitate 2 perform 3 pretend 4 represent *adj* 5 human

implore *v* → entreat

imply *v* → 1 accuse 2 be likely 3 fold 4 mean

import *n* → 1 enterer 2 importance 3 meaning 4 absorb 5 be important 6 mean 7 obligate 8 trade

impotent *adj* → 1 incompetent 2 infertile 3 powerless

impracticable *adj* → 1 impossible 2 inappropriate 3 stubborn 4 unmanageable

impress *n* → 1 emblem 2 forcefulness 3 label *v* 4 be approved 5 command respect 6 encourage 7 engrave 8 force 9 hollow 10 influence 11 label 12 press 13 rob 14 take

impression *n* → 1 idea 2 imitation 3 imprint 4 indentation 5 influence 6 memory 7 opinion 8 perception 9 printwork

impromptu *n* → 1 caprice 2 musical piece *adj* 3 capricious 4 momentary *adv* 5 momentarily

improvise *v* → 1 be impulsive 2 create 3 fantasise 4 make do 5 make music 6 perform

impudent *adj* → 1 arrogant 2 discourteous 3 insulting

impulsive *adj* → 1 capricious 2 encouraging 3 momentary 4 propellent 5 rash

incapacitate *v* → 1 injure 2 prohibit

incessant *adj* → 1 continual 2 eternal 3 frequent 4 repetitive

incline *n* → 1 mound 2 slope *v* 3 bend 4 slope 5 tend to

inconsistent *adj* → 1 different 2 illogical 3 incompatible 4 incongruous 5 indecisive 6 nonsensical 7 opposing

incorporate *v* → 1 associate 2 combine 3 include 4 join *adj* 5 intangible 6 societal

incorrect *adj* → 1 false 2 illogical 3 ungrammatical

incredible *adj* → 1 astonishing 2 impossible

indefinite *adj* → 1 changeable 2 impersonal 3 imprecise 4 infinite 5 shapeless 6 uncertain

index *n* → 1 book part 2 classification 3 indicator 4 list *v* 5 list 6 signify *adj* 7 brachial

indifferent *adj* → 1 apathetic 2 bored 3 mediocre 4 neutral 5 ordinary

indignant *adj* → 1 acrimonious 2 angry 3 displeased

induce *v* → 1 cause 2 encourage 3 persuade 4 reason

inept *adj* → 1 illogical 2 incompetent 3 incongruous 4 inconvenient 5 ineffectual

inert *adj* → 1 apathetic 2 idle 3 inactive 4 insensible

infant *n* → 1 offspring 2 starter *adj* 3 youthful

infectious *adj* → 1 influential 2 unwholesome

infer *v* → imply

inflexible *adj* → 1 callous 2 changeless 3 hard 4 straight 5 strict 6 stubborn

infrequent *adj* → 1 few 2 irregular 3 rare

infringe *v* → 1 contravene 2 disobey

inherit *v* → get

inhibit *v* → 1 prohibit 2 restrict 3 stop

initial *n* → 1 bookbinding 2 letter *v* 3 assent to 4 label *adj* 5 new 6 original

inland *n* → 1 inside 2 land 3 region *adj* 4 inside 5 land 6 national *adv* 7 inside

inner *n* → 1 aim *adj* 2 characteristic 3 inside 4 secret

innovate *v* → 1 create 2 initiate

inquisitive *n* → 1 morbid curiosity *adj* 2 curious

insecure *adj* → 1 changeable 2 uncertain 3 vulnerable

insignificant *n* → 1 unimportant person 2 unimportant thing *adj* 3 nonsensical 4 smallest 5 unimportant

insinuate *v* → 1 accuse 2 beguile 3 imply 4 inform 5 insert

insist *v* → assert

insolent *n* → 1 disdainer *adj* 2 arrogant 3 discourteous 4 dissident 5 insulting

inspect *v* → 1 examine 2 look

inspire *v* → 1 breathe 2 cause 3 embolden 4 encourage 5 enliven

install *v* → 1 employ 2 position

instant *n* → 1 moment 2 the present *adj* 3 current 4 impermanent 5 momentary

instruct *v* → 1 command 2 inform 3 teach

insubordinate *n* → 1 disobeyer *adj* 2 disobedient

intact *adj* → 1 abstinent 2 perfect 3 whole

integrate *v* → 1 combine 2 compute 3 join 4 make whole

intensive *adj* → 1 increased 2 thorough

intent *n* → 1 meaning 2 plan 3 will *adj* 4 attentive 5 careful 6 uncompromising

intercede *v* → 1 entreat 2 mediate

interest *n* → 1 attentiveness 2 capital 3 company 4 debt 5 importance 6 influence 7 motive 8 ownership 9 participation 10 profit 11 share 12 stocks and shares *v* 13 be important 14 engross 15 involve

interfere *v* → 1 hinder 2 interrupt 3 meddle

interior *n* → 1 inside 2 land 3 region *adj* 4 inside 5 national 6 secret 7 spiritual

interjection *n* → 1 interruption 2 shouting 3 speaking 4 word

interminable *adj* → 1 changeless 2 continual 3 eternal 4 infinite

intermittent *adj* → 1 interrupted 2 irregular 3 rare

intervene *v* → 1 come between 2 entreat 3 interrupt 4 mediate

interview *n* → 1 assignation 2 questioning 3 talk *v* 4 hear 5 question

intimidate *v* → 1 force 2 menace

intricate *adj* → 1 complex 2 difficult

intrigue *n* → 1 conspiracy 2 cunning 3 love affair 4 narrative 5 secrecy 6 sexual relationship 7 trickery *v* 8 allure 9 beguile 10 conspire 11 engross 12 have sex 13 involve 14 keep secret 15 make do

intrude *v* → 1 insert 2 interrupt

invade *v* → 1 advance 2 attack 3 enter 4 wage war

invalid *n* → 1 patient *v* 2 be ill *adj* 3 ill 4 useless 5 weak

invent *v* → 1 create 2 fantasise

invite *v* → 1 entreaty *v* 2 allure 3 arrange 4 be sociable 5 entreat

inward *adj* → 1 entering 2 inborn 3 inside 4 quiet 5 spiritual *adv* 6 inside

iron *n* → 1 club 2 fishing tackle 3 gun 4 harshness 5 labeller 6 metal 7 press *v* 8 press 9 smooth *adj* 10 durable 11 fastened 12 grey 13 hard 14 metallic 15 strict

irrational *adj* → 1 illogical 2 numerical 3 rash 4 stupid

irregular *n* → 1 combat troops 2 foreigner 3 freak 4 nonconformist *adj* 5 foreign 6 incorrect 7 nonconformist 8 rough 9 strange 10 unequal 11 unlawful

irrelevant *adj* → 1 incongruous 2 unimportant 3 unrelated

irresponsible *n* → 1 anarchist 2 mischief-maker *adj* 3 anarchic 4 badly-behaved 5 neglectful

irrigate *v* → 1 channel 2 wet

issue *n* → 1 departure 2 exit 3 flow 4 important thing 5 magazine 6 offspring 7 printwork 8 profit 9 publicity 10 result 11 sharing out 12 subject matter *v* 13 circulate 14 discharge 15 flow 16 publicise 17 publish 18 share out

item *n* → 1 account 2 concert 3 news item 4 particulars *v* 5 memorise 6 record *adv* 7 additionally 8 similarly

jail *n* → prison

jam *n* → 1 concert 2 gathering 3 hindrance 4 pressing *v* 5 fill 6 injure 7 make music 8 obstruct 9 press

jar *n* → 1 alcohol container 2 dissonance 3 fight 4 impact 5 vessel 6 vi-

bration v 7 be dissonant 8 displease 9 vibrate

jargon n → 1 language 2 nonsense v 3 talk nonsense

jaunty n → 1 seaman adj 2 beautiful 3 fashionable 4 happy

jaw n → 1 face 2 holder 3 reprimand 4 speaking 5 talkativeness v 6 scold 7 speak 8 talk

jerk n → 1 bad person 2 fool 3 lifting 4 move 5 pat 6 pull 7 stupid person 8 thrust v 9 conserve 10 fluctuate 11 move 12 pull 13 related 14 throw

jet n → 1 aeroplane 2 black 3 flow 4 stream v 5 flow adj 6 black

jettison v → 1 discard v 2 abandon 3 disuse 4 eject

job n → 1 affair 2 difficulty 3 finished product 4 hit 5 obligation 6 robbery 7 undertaking **v** 8 hit 9 hit 10 invest 11 swindle 12 work

jog n → 1 pat 2 walking v 3 advance 4 remind 5 walk

joint n → 1 bone 2 break 3 dwelling 4 gun 5 marijuana 6 pub 7 restaurant 8 stem v 9 join 10 separate adj 11 combined 12 joined 13 related 14 shared 15 societal

jolly n → 1 flattery adj 2 happy 3 joyful 4 pleasant 5 sociable adv 6 very

journey v → travel

jumpy adj → 1 excited 2 frightened 3 turbulent 4 worried

junior n → 1 children 2 inferior 3 innovator 4 lawyer 5 pugilist 6 pupil 7 sportsman adj 8 following 9 inferior 10 new 11 youthful

junk n → 1 discard 2 drug 3 narcotic 4 sailing ship 5 waste v 6 refuse

just adj → 1 correct 2 fair 3 rightful 4 smallest 5 true adv 6 in fact 7 negligibly 8 precisely

juvenile n → 1 actor 2 adolescent 3 animal offspring adj 4 youthful

keen n → 1 cry v 2 grieve adj 3 bladed 4 desirous 5 enthusiastic 6 good 7 intelligent 8 intense 9 perceptive 10 sharp

keep n → 1 charity 2 fortress v 3 care for 4 conserve 5 hold 6 imprison 7 obey 8 protect 9 protract 10 store

key n → 1 clarification 2 classification 3 explanation 4 island 5 nail 6 opener 7 pitch 8 reference book 9 restraints 10 roughness 11 solution v 12 roughen adj 13 fundamental 14 important

kick n → 1 complaint 2 excitement 3 pleasure 4 reaction 5 vitality 6 winemaking v 7 oppose 8 react 9 refuse

kidnap v → 1 capture 2 rob

king n → 1 aristocrat 2 expert 3 wealthy person adj 4 big 5 great

knit v → 1 textiles v 2 fold 3 join 4 sew

knock n → 1 boom 2 hit 3 impact 4 mockery v 5 collide 6 disapprove of 7 hit

labour n → 1 birth 2 effort 3 political spectrum 4 trade unionist 5 work 6 workers v 7 emphasise 8 farm 9 give birth 10 make an effort 11 roll 12 work

lacerate v → 1 cut 2 pain adj 3 cutting

lack n → 1 absence 2 deficiency 3 insufficiency v 4 fall short

lad n → 1 adolescent 2 man 3 promiscuous person

lady n → 1 aesthete 2 courteous person 3 Ms 4 owner 5 ruler 6 spouse 7 woman adj 8 courteous 9 female

land n → 1 nation 2 real estate 3 region 4 wealth v 5 arrive 6 descend 7 dismount 8 fish 9 gain 10 transport

lap n → 1 circle 2 fold 3 hollow 4 leg 5 length 6 quiet sound 7 smoother v 8 absorb 9 care for 10 flank 11 flow 12 fold 13 kiss 14 overtake

lapse n → 1 descent 2 error 3 evildoing 4 failure 5 neglectfulness 6 stoppage v 7 be immoral 8 be neglected 9 descend 10 err 11 fail 12 fall into disuse 13 misbehave

large adj → 1 big 2 generous 3 great 4 windy adv 5 windward

lash n → 1 club 2 cord 3 eye 4 fight 5 hit 6 sexual intercourse v 7 cudgel 8 fasten 9 hurry 10 scold 11 slander

last n → 1 finish 2 model v 3 be 4 be adequate 5 continue 6 eternalise adj 7 final 8 inferior 9 late 10 remnant adv 11 finally 12 late

launch n → 1 watercraft v 2 initiate 3 move 4 offer 5 throw 6 thrust 7 undertake

lax adj → 1 lenient 2 neglectful 3 soft

lay n → 1 poetry 2 sex object 3 share 4 song v 5 direct 6 gamble 7 have sex 8 impute 9 level 10 lower 11 moderate 12 place 13 position 14 reproduce 15 smooth adj 16 laic

layout n → 1 diagram 2 order

lazy adj → 1 idle 2 purposeless 3 slow

lead n → 1 actor 2 advance 3 advantage 4 ammunition 5 antecedence 6 channel 7 cord 8 foundation 9 front 10 important person 11 information 12 interval 13 pendant 14 saddlery 15 signal 16 wire v 17 direct 18 make music 19 manage 20 persuade 21 print adj 22 metallic

league n → 1 alliance 2 class 3 contract 4 length 5 society v 6 associate 7 promise adj 8 societal 9 sports

lean n → 1 flesh 2 point of view 3 slope v 4 slope adj 5 insufficient 6 thin

leave n → 1 absence 2 farewell 3 holiday 4 liberty 5 permission v 6 avoid 7 depart 8 give 9 resign

lecture n → 1 essay 2 harangue 3 lesson 4 oration 5 reprimand 6 warning v 7 scold 8 speak well 9 teach

legacy n → 1 getting 2 gift 3 property 4 result

legitimate v → 1 prisoner v 2 legalise 3 permit adj 4 fair 5 lawful 6 logical 7 patriarchal 8 true

lemon n → 1 complainer 2 failure 3 fool 4 sourness 5 ugly person 6 unhappy person 7 unpleasant thing adj 8 sour 9 yellow

lessen v → 1 decrease 2 slander 3 subtract

let n → 1 hindrance 2 loan v 3 cause 4 hinder 5 lend 6 permit

levy n → 1 income 2 insistence 3 obligation 4 tax v 5 beg 6 charge 7 impose 8 insist on 9 take

liable adj → 1 feasible 2 in debt 3 obligated 4 predisposed

libel n → 1 misrepresentation 2 slander v 3 litigate 4 misinterpret 5 slander

liberal n → 1 libertarian 2 political ideologist adj 3 generous 4 lenient 5 liberated 6 tolerant

licence n → 1 certificate 2 liberty 3 nonconformity 4 permission 5 power to act 6 promiscuity

lick n → 1 small amount v 2 defeat 3 surpass 4 taste

life n → 1 being 2 bubbliness 3 duration 4 liveliness 5 living 6 period 7 record 8 savour 9 sprightliness

likeness n → 1 imitation 2 portrait 3 similarity

limp n → 1 injury v 2 walk adj 3 weak

link n → 1 bond 2 candle 3 join v 4 join

list n → 1 frame 2 inequality 3 slope v 4 desire 5 edge 6 hear 7 inquire into 8 intend 9 please 10 slope

listless adj → 1 apathetic 2 bored 3 inactive

little adj → 1 few 2 intolerant 3 short 4 small 5 weak adv 6 rarely

live v → 1 be 2 behave 3 be pleased 4 inhabit adj 5 busy 6 colourful 7 current 8 electric 9 energetic 10 explosive 11 hot 12 innovative 13 in use 14 living 15 moving 16 operating

lively adj → 1 bright 2 bubbly 3 busy 4 colourful 5 energetic 6 exciting 7 happy 8 powerful adv 9 busily 10 energetically

load n → 1 ammunition 2 amount 3 contents 4 electricity 5 gravimetry 6 toil 7 venereal disease v 8 fill 9 increase 10 oversupply 11 place 12 transport 13 weigh

loaf n → 1 easy thing 2 head 3 mind 4 period of inaction 5 rest v 6 idle

lobby n → 1 hall 2 influencer 3 society v 4 entreat 5 persuade 6 politicise

local n → 1 anaesthetic 2 inhabitant 3 newspaper 4 pub 5 society 6 trade union adj 7 regional 8 resident

location n → 1 computer record 2 habitation 3 loan 4 placement 5 position 6 region 7 surroundings

lock n → 1 bolt 2 chute 3 dam 4 hair 5 hold 6 lake 7 stopper 8 textiles v 9 fasten 10 straighten 11 transport

lodge n → 1 animal dwelling 2 cabin 3 hotel 4 house 5 institute 6 shelter v 7

lodge

house 8 inhabit 9 place 10 pursue 11 shelter

lofty *adj* → 1 tall person *adj* 2 arrogant 3 eloquent 4 important 5 proud 6 reputable 7 tall

log *n* → 1 diary 2 fool 3 fuel 4 gravimetry 5 idler 6 length-measurer 7 marijuana 8 speedometer 9 timber 10 watercraft *v* 11 account 12 cut 13 record 14 remove

loiter *v* → 1 go slowly 2 idle

loll *n* → 1 levelness 2 period of inaction 3 rest *v* 4 hang 5 idle 6 recline 7 rest

lonely *adj* → 1 remote 2 solitary 3 unhappy

loom *n* → 1 appearance 2 sewing machine 3 stick *v* 4 appear 5 sew

loop *n* → 1 circle 2 contraception 3 curve 4 fool 5 opening 6 railway 7 ring 8 trimming *v* 9 curve 10 fly 11 overturn 12 surround

loose *v* → 1 liberate 2 separate 3 shoot 4 weaken *adj* 5 illogical 6 immoral 7 imprecise 8 lenient 9 liberated 10 promiscuous 11 separate 12 sexy 13 soft 14 unused 15 weak *adv* 16 at liberty 17 separately

lot *n* → 1 accumulation 2 amount 3 condition 4 fate 5 gambling 6 luck 7 many 8 much 9 part 10 person 11 share 12 yard *v* 13 separate 14 share out

love *n* → 1 desire 2 friend 3 nothing 4 pleasure 5 religious ceremony 6 reverence 7 worship *v* 8 enjoy 9 flirt 10 respect

lovely *adj* → 1 beautiful 2 pleasant

low *n* → 1 animal call 2 atmospheric pressure 3 bottom *v* 4 call (of animals) *adj* 5 bad 6 bare 7 bottom 8 ill-bred 9 inferior 10 past 11 quiet 12 shallow 13 sounded 14 unhappy 15 weak 16 working-class 17 wrong *adv* 18 below 19 quietly

lowly *adj* → 1 bottom 2 inferior 3 meek *adv* 4 inferiorly

loyal *adj* → 1 conservative 2 faithful 3 obedient

luck *n* → 1 fate 2 good fortune

ludicrous *adj* → 1 foolish 2 humorous

manipulate

lug *n* → 1 ear 2 headband 3 pull *v* 4 make music 5 pull

lull *n* → 1 interval 2 rest 3 silence 4 stoppage *v* 5 put to sleep 6 rest 7 silence

lumber *n* → 1 hindrance 2 timber 3 waste *v* 4 arrest 5 cut 6 gather 7 hinder 8 impose 9 walk 10 weigh

luminous *adj* → 1 bright 2 clear 3 intelligent

lure *n* → 1 allure 2 attractor 3 desideratum 4 allure 5 attract

lyric *n* → 1 poetry *adj* 2 musical 3 poetic

mad *adj* → 1 angry 2 celebratory 3 enthusiastic 4 excited 5 ferocious 6 foolish 7 rash

magnate *n* → 1 famous person 2 important person 3 member of parliament 4 wealthy person

magnify *v* → 1 approve 2 emphasise 3 exaggerate 4 increase 5 worship

maiden *n* → 1 adolescent 2 racehorse 3 woman *adj* 4 new

main *n* → 1 contest 2 land 3 piping 4 sea 5 strength 6 violent outburst 7 wire *adj* 8 important 9 most 10 strong

maintain *v* → 1 assert 2 equip 3 protract

majesty *n* → 1 aristocracy 2 aristocrat 3 greatness 4 reputability

major *n* → 1 course 2 pitch 3 subject matter *adj* 4 aged 5 important

make *n* → 1 amount 2 character 3 finished product 4 structure *v* 5 accomplish 6 allure 7 arrive 8 be timely 9 build 10 cause 11 combine 12 compute 13 employ 14 flow 15 force 16 have sex 17 order 18 write

makeshift *n* → 1 expedient 2 expedient *adj* 3 impermanent

malignant *adj* → 1 dangerous 2 deadly 3 unkind

manifest *n* → 1 list 2 public notice 3 record *v* 4 authenticate 5 display 6 record *adj* 7 apparent 8 blatant 9 obvious

manipulate *v* → 1 arrange 2 beguile 3 change 4 medicate 5 persuade 6 touch

manner $n \to$ 1 affectation 2 behaviour 3 character 4 custom 5 method 6 pose

manoeuvre $n \to$ 1 action 2 stratagem v 3 keep secret 4 wage war

mantle $n \to$ 1 cloak 2 covering 3 fuel 4 layer 5 shelf v 6 bubble 7 cover 8 hide 9 redden

manual $n \to$ 1 car 2 reference book *adj* 3 brachial

manufacture $n \to$ 1 finished product 2 making v 3 make

march $n \to$ 1 advance 2 edge 3 length 4 move 5 region 6 route 7 walk v 8 wage war 9 walk

margin $n \to$ 1 edge 2 equal 3 income 4 liberty 5 more 6 remnant 7 stocks and shares 8 surplus v 9 edge 10 explain 11 insert

marine $n \to$ 1 armed forces 2 painting 3 seaman 4 watercraft *adj* 5 nautical 6 resident 7 sea

mark $n \to$ 1 abdomen 2 aim 3 characteristic 4 depth 5 importance 6 judgment 7 reputation 8 sign 9 title v 10 attend to 11 class 12 cut off 13 label 14 particularise 15 reveal

marked *adj* $\to$ visible

marketable *adj* $\to$ saleable

market research $n \to$ investigation

marksman $n \to$ 1 fighter 2 signer

mask $n \to$ 1 armour 2 disguise 3 drama 4 headband 5 party 6 portrait v 7 cover 8 hide 9 hinder

massive *adj* $\to$ 1 astonishing 2 big 3 enormous 4 heavy

master $n \to$ 1 boss 2 children 3 expert 4 judge 5 manager 6 model 7 owner 8 seaman 9 teacher 10 winner 11 wise person v 12 defeat 13 excel 14 learn *adj* 15 accomplished 16 authoritative 17 predominant

match $n \to$ 1 contest 2 copy 3 cord 4 equal 5 equivalent 6 lighter 7 marriage 8 similar thing 9 sport 10 two v 11 adjust 12 be similar 13 copy 14 counteract 15 double 16 equal 17 equalise 18 fit 19 join 20 marry

mate $n \to$ 1 friend 2 mister 3 partner 4 servant 5 similar thing 6 spouse v 7 defeat 8 fit 9 join 10 marry 11 partner

material $n \to$ 1 information 2 matter 3 textiles *adj* 4 fundamental 5 important 6 tangible

matter $n \to$ 1 accusation 2 affair 3 amount 4 bodily discharge 5 cause 6 difficulty 7 evidence 8 importance 9 meaning 10 printwork v 11 be important 12 excrete

matter-of-fact *adj* $\to$ 1 forthright 2 realistic 3 simple

mature $v \to$ 1 age 2 make whole 3 perfect 4 prepare 5 taste *adj* 6 aged 7 unwholesome 8 whole

meagre *adj* $\to$ 1 deficient 2 insufficient 3 small 4 thin

measure $n \to$ 1 amount 2 example 3 gradation 4 law 5 limit 6 measurement 7 musical score 8 printwork 9 rhythm v 10 graduate 11 quantify

median $n \to$ 1 average 2 centre 3 line *adj* 4 central

meditate $v \to$ 1 aim at 2 assess 3 intend 4 think 5 worship

meet $n \to$ 1 contest 2 gathering v 3 agree 4 argue 5 associate 6 be sociable 7 contact 8 converge 9 fight 10 gather 11 undergo *adj* 12 apt 13 expedient

meeting $n \to$ 1 assignation 2 contact 3 contest 4 convergence 5 crowd 6 gathering 7 legislative body 8 prayer 9 sport 10 contacting

melancholy $n \to$ 1 despair 2 sombreness 3 unhappiness *adj* 4 bored 5 despairing 6 sombre 7 unhappy

mellow $v \to$ 1 age 2 improve 3 soften 4 taste *adj* 5 happy 6 musical 7 soft 8 tasty

mend $n \to$ 1 improvement 2 repair v 3 improve 4 repair

mercy $n \to$ 1 good 2 help 3 lenience 4 pity

merge $v \to$ 1 associate 2 combine 3 join 4 mix

merry *adj* $\to$ 1 drunk 2 happy 3 humorous 4 pleasant

mesh $n \to$ 1 allure 2 fence 3 interlacement 4 lace 5 stratagem v 6 allure 7 contact 8 interlace 9 join *adj* 10 crossed

mess $n \to$ 1 barracks 2 dilemma 3 dirt 4 dung 5 food 6 jumble 7 kitchen 8

mess   602   **motion**

living room 9 meal 10 muddle 11 paste 12 tangle *v* 13 eat

middle *n* → 1 abdomen 2 centre 3 ordinariness *v* 4 centralise *adj* 5 central 6 intervenient

migrant *n* → 1 arriver 2 leaver 3 population 4 traveller *adj* 5 resident 6 travelling

mild *adj* → 1 beer *adj* 2 bright 3 composed 4 courteous 5 hot 6 insipid 7 kind 8 lenient 9 moderate 10 soft 11 tasty

militant *n* → 1 fighter 2 warmonger *adj* 3 aggressive 4 dissident 5 warlike

mill *n* → 1 extractor 2 powderer 3 press 4 pub *v* 5 agitate 6 edge 7 furrow 8 powder 9 press

mimic *n* → 1 entertainer 2 humorist 3 imitator *v* 4 imitate 5 represent *adj* 6 imitative

mind *n* → 1 character 2 desire 3 emotion 4 opinion 5 perception 6 soul *v* 7 attend 8 be cautious 9 care for 10 dislike 11 feel emotion 12 obey 13 remember 14 undertake

mine *n* → 1 bomb 2 diggings 3 excavation 4 explosive 5 factory *v* 6 dig 7 extract 8 hollow

miniature *n* → 1 sculpture 2 small thing *adj* 3 decreased 4 small

minister *n* → 1 ambassador 2 ecclesiastic 3 member of parliament 4 ruler *v* 5 help

minor *n* → 1 course 2 inferior 3 pitch *adj* 4 inferior 5 mediocre 6 smallest 7 unimportant 8 youthful

minute *n* → 1 account 2 angle 3 crucial moment 4 length 5 moment 6 reminder *v* 7 memorise 8 record 9 time 10 write *adj* 11 momentary 12 precise 13 small

mire *n* → 1 sludge 2 swamp *v* 3 cause difficulties 4 dirty

miscarry *v* → 1 be early 2 be infertile 3 fail 4 give birth

miserable *adj* → 1 bad 2 pitiable 3 poor 4 unfortunate 5 unhappy

misery *n* → 1 grieving 2 poverty 3 soberside 4 unfortunateness 5 unhappiness 6 unhappy person

mislead *v* → 1 beguile 2 misguide 3 trick

miss *n* → 1 children 2 failure 3 neglectfulness *v* 4 avoid 5 be inattentive 6 fail 7 mistime

mission *n* → 1 act of war 2 agency 3 aim 4 delegate 5 domain 6 obligation 7 prayer 8 undertaking 9 work

mistake *n* → 1 bungle 2 error 3 misjudgment 4 pregnancy *v* 5 err 6 misjudge

mix *n* → 1 combine 2 jumble 3 mixture *v* 4 be sociable 5 combine

mob *n* → 1 gathering 2 many 3 untidy person 4 working class *v* 5 attack *adj* 6 public

mobile *n* → 1 sculpture *adj* 2 changeable 3 flowing 4 moving

mock *n* → 1 mockery *v* 2 imitate 3 trick *adj* 4 imitative

model *n* → 1 antecedent 2 copy 3 good person 4 perfect thing 5 portrait 6 prostitute 7 representation 8 rule *v* 9 depict 10 shape

moderate *n* → 1 moderator 2 neutral 3 political ideologist *v* 4 decrease *adj* 5 mediocre 6 ordinary

moment *n* → 1 average 2 crucial moment 3 importance

monitor *n* → 1 controlling device 2 guide 3 manager 4 reminder 5 television 6 tester 7 warner 8 watercraft *v* 9 control 10 examine 11 test

monkey *n* → 1 animal's coat 2 humorist 3 imitator 4 loan 5 mischief-maker 6 press 7 sewing machine *v* 8 imitate 9 mock

monopolise *v* → 1 buy 2 control 3 own

monotonous *adj* → 1 boring 2 frequent 3 homogeneous 4 repetitive

moody *adj* → 1 discontented 2 emotional 3 irritable 4 unhappy

mop *n* → 1 absorber 2 brush 3 hair *v* 4 clean 5 dry

mope *n* → 1 apathetic person 2 unhappy person *v* 3 be indifferent 4 be unhappy

morose *adj* → 1 irritable 2 solitary 3 unhappy 4 unsociable

mortar *n* → 1 adhesive 2 building materials 3 gun 4 powderer

motion *n* → 1 defecation 2 entreaty 3 gesture 4 move 5 movement 6 offer 7 parliamentary procedure 8 plan 9 point of view v 10 direct 11 gesture

mould n → 1 character 2 copy 3 destroyer 4 dirt 5 metal 6 model 7 shape 8 soil v 9 copy 10 decorate 11 depict 12 make 13 shape

mount n → 1 ascent 2 fortune-telling 3 horse 4 model 5 mountain v 6 ascend 7 become greater 8 have sex 9 stage 10 support 11 top 12 tower

mouth n → 1 exit 2 gesture 3 opening 4 speaking 5 stream v 6 gesture 7 speak well

mow n → 1 gesture v 2 cut 3 gesture 4 harvest

muff n → 1 failure 2 feather 3 glove 4 groin v 5 bungle 6 fail

mug n → 1 face 2 fool 3 gesture 4 mouth 5 victim v 6 attack 7 gesture 8 hit 9 photograph 10 rob adj 11 foolish 12 stupid

multiply v → 1 become greater 2 compute 3 flower 4 increase 5 reproduce

murky adj → 1 cloudy 2 distressing 3 dull 4 shadowy

murmur n → 1 complaint 2 quiet sound v 3 complain 4 speak

muscle n → 1 effort 2 flesh 3 force 4 strength

mute n → 1 entertainer 2 quietener 3 stammerer 4 string instrument 5 undertaker v 6 silence adj 7 inarticulate 8 silent

mutilate v → 1 cut 2 cut off 3 disfigure 4 injure

mutter n → 1 faulty speech v 2 complain 3 mispronounce

mutual adj → 1 interactive 2 related 3 societal

mystify v → 1 confuse 2 misguide 3 puzzle

nag n → 1 horse 2 moraliser v 3 annoy 4 discontent 5 irritate

nail n → 1 animal part 2 arm 3 length 4 piercer v 5 capture 6 fasten 7 reveal

nap n → 1 bedclothes 2 prediction 3 sleep 4 weave v 5 be inattentive 6 predict 7 sew 8 sleep

narrow n → 1 thinness v 2 thin adj 3 intolerant 4 sounded 5 thin

native n → 1 ethnic 2 population adj 3 characteristic 4 natural 5 resident 6 simple

near v → 1 come close adj 2 close 3 future 4 kindred 5 left 6 mean 7 similar adv 8 closely 9 in the future 10 relatedly 11 windward

neat n → 1 cattle adj 2 competent 3 good 4 intelligent 5 intoxicating 6 simple 7 tidy

need n → 1 deficiency 2 desire 3 insufficiency 4 necessities 5 poverty v 6 desire 7 fall short 8 necessitate

needle n → 1 direction finder 2 inserter 3 leaf 4 medication 5 piercer 6 rock outcrop 7 sewing machine 8 sharp point 9 worry

negative n → 1 denial 2 disagreement 3 photograph 4 deny 5 refuse adj 6 denying 7 female 8 numerical 9 unwilling

neighbour n → 1 friend 2 inhabitant

nerve n → 1 arrogance 2 courage 3 durability 4 nervous system 5 strength 6 vitality v 7 embolden 8 strengthen

nervous adj → 1 excitable 2 frightened 3 worried

net n → 1 fishing tackle 2 headband 3 interlacement 4 lace 5 sportsground 6 stratagem v 7 fish 8 gain adj 9 crossed 10 final 11 remnant

next adj → 1 close 2 following adv 3 after 4 in the future

nice adj → 1 accomplished 2 delicious 3 discriminating 4 good 5 kind 6 modest 7 pleasant 8 precise 9 promiscuous

nick n → 1 departure 2 furrow 3 kinship 4 prison 5 rest 6 arrest 7 be precise 8 cheat 9 cut 10 furrow 11 record 12 reproduce 13 rob

nimble adj → 1 athletic 2 competent 3 cunning 4 intelligent 5 light-footed 6 speedy

nip n → 1 a drink 2 coldness 3 pressing 4 pressure 5 slander 6 small amount 7 taste v 8 depart 9 hold 10 pain 11 press 12 remove 13 rob

noble n → 1 aristocrat adj 2 aristocratic 3 enormous 4 important 5 inactive 6 reputable 7 steady 8 unselfish

non-committal *adj* → 1 elusive 2 indecisive 3 neutral 4 reticent

nonsense *n* → 1 foolishness 2 illogicality 3 waffle

normal *n* → 1 average 2 ordinariness *adj* 3 bent 4 conventional 5 customary 6 erect 7 healthy 8 model 9 natural 10 ordinary 11 sane

notable *n* → 1 famous person 2 important thing *adj* 3 accomplished 4 effortful 5 famous 6 important 7 obvious 8 thrifty

notch *n* → 1 access 2 bend 3 cut 4 furrow 5 gradation 6 record *v* 7 cut 8 label

note *n* → 1 account 2 attentiveness 3 birdcall 4 cash 5 clarification 6 importance 7 information 8 innovation 9 message 10 musical score 11 particulars 12 postscript 13 record 14 reminder 15 reputation 16 shout 17 sign 18 sound 19 surpriser 20 written composition *v* 21 account 22 add 23 attend to 24 make music 25 memorise 26 record

noted *adj* → 1 famous 2 important 3 known

notice *n* → 1 assessment 2 attentiveness 3 dismissal 4 essay 5 information 6 insistence 7 label 8 publicity 9 public notice 10 seeing 11 warning *v* 12 attend to 13 inform 14 see

nucleus *n* → 1 atom 2 centre 3 meteor

nurse *n* → 1 healer 2 helper 3 minder *v* 4 care for 5 feed 6 help 7 hold 8 medicate 9 practise medicine

nurture *n* → 1 help 2 teaching *v* 3 encourage 4 feed 5 help 6 rear

nut *n* → 1 bead 2 bolt 3 food 4 fruit 5 head 6 mad person 7 nonconformist

objective *adj* → 1 artistic 2 fair 3 known 4 real 5 tangible 6 visible

oblige *v* → 1 help 2 necessitate 3 obligate 4 promise

oblique *n* → 1 slope *v* 2 deflect 3 slope *adj* 4 allusive 5 bent 6 deflective 7 evasive 8 sloping 9 unequal

obscure *v* → 1 darken 2 hide *adj* 3 allusive 4 dark 5 disreputable 6 dull 7 hidden 8 imprecise 9 invisible 10 secluded 11 uncertain 12 unclear 13 unimportant 14 working-class

observant *adj* → 1 obeyer *adj* 2 attentive 3 dutiful 4 obedient 5 perceptive 6 sharp-eyed

obsession *n* → 1 certainty 2 desire 3 idea 4 madness 5 psychic disturbance

obsolete *adj* → 1 antique 2 disused 3 old 4 powerless 5 untimely 6 useless

occasional *adj* → 1 causal 2 occurrent 3 rare

occupation *n* → 1 capture fullness 3 habitation 4 job 5 presence

occupy *v* → 1 be present 2 engross 3 fill 4 inhabit 5 own

ocker *n* → 1 Australian 2 discourteous person 3 good person 4 ignoramus 5 intolerant person 6 man 7 vulgarian *adj* 8 ignorant

odd *n* → 1 freak 2 one 3 remnant *adj* 4 incongruous 5 irregular 6 mad 7 nonconformist 8 numerical 9 remnant 10 strange

odour *n* → 1 reputation 2 smell 3 stench

off *n* → 1 right *adj* 2 absent 3 deteriorated 4 ill 5 incongruous 6 moving 7 resting 8 right 9 sea 10 unsavoury *adv* 11 absently 12 away 13 decreasingly 14 deflectively 15 in the future 16 remotely 17 restfully 18 wanderingly *prep* 19 without

offend *v* → 1 act unkindly 2 annoy 3 be immoral 4 contravene 5 displease 6 wrong

offensive *n* → 1 attack *adj* 2 aggressive 3 annoying 4 dirty 5 incorrect 6 sickening 7 smelly

offer *n* → 1 assertion 2 attempt 3 cost 4 wedding *v* 5 appraise 6 give 7 marry 8 occur 9 sell 10 theorise

official *n* → 1 appointee 2 bureaucrat 3 manager *adj* 4 agential 5 authoritative 6 commanding 7 formal

offset *n* → 1 compensation 2 copy 3 counterbalance 4 curve 5 error 6 mountain 7 start *v* 8 be adequate 9 compensate 10 counteract 11 print *adj* 12 compensatory

offsider *n* → 1 labourer 2 partner 3 workers

old-fashioned *adj* → 1 antique 2 untimely

on *n* → 1 left *adj* 2 left 3 occurrent 4 operating *adv* 5 continually 6 forward *prep* 7 concerning 8 near

only *adj* → 1 one 2 smallest *adv* 3 negligibly 4 simply

ooze *n* → 1 sea 2 sludge 3 swamp *v* 4 discharge 5 flow

oppose *v* → 1 contrast 2 hinder 3 invert

oppress *v* → 1 be unfriendly 2 make unhappy 3 repress 4 victimise

option *n* → 1 choice 2 liberty 3 stocks and shares

opulent *adj* → wealthy

oracle *n* → 1 guide 2 occultist 3 predictor 4 revealer 5 shrine 6 wise person

orb *n* → 1 ball 2 emblem of office 3 eye 4 heavenly body 5 rotation 6 space *v* 7 enclose 8 rotate 9 round

orbit *n* → 1 astronomic point 2 circle 3 direction 4 eye 5 job 6 move 7 rotation 8 route *v* 9 rotate

orderly *n* → 1 healer 2 messenger 3 servant *adj* 4 obedient 5 ordered

organise *v* → 1 associate 2 combine 3 manage 4 order 5 plan

origin *n* → 1 ancestry 2 being 3 creation 4 start

out *n* → 1 error 2 liberty *v* 3 eject *adj* 4 false 5 outside 6 remote *adv* 7 absently 8 away 9 lengthways 10 out of place 11 outside 12 remotely 13 untimely *prep* 14 outside

outback *n* → 1 inside 2 remote place *adj* 3 remote 4 rural *adv* 5 remotely

outlaw *n* → 1 anarchist 2 criminal 3 disobeyer 4 prohibition *v* 5 boycott 6 prohibit

outlet *n* → 1 exit 2 shop

outline *n* → 1 abridgment 2 diagram 3 drawing 4 edge 5 line 6 outside 7 plan *v* 8 abbreviate 9 depict 10 edge 11 map 12 narrate

outspoken *adj* → 1 assertive 2 callous 3 honest 4 liberated

outstanding *adj* → 1 good 2 obvious 3 owing 4 separate 5 unpaid

over *n* → 1 more 2 surplus *v* 3 jump 4 traverse *adj* 5 additional 6 finished 7 past 8 surplus *adv* 9 above 10 across 11 down 12 excessively 13 repeatedly 14 superiorly 15 thoroughly *prep* 16 across

overbearing *adj* → 1 conservative 2 discourteous 3 forceful 4 imposing 5 presumptuous 6 repressive

overlook *v* → 1 be inattentive 2 bewitch 3 forgive 4 investigate 5 look 6 manage 7 neglect 8 top 9 tower

overpower *v* → repress

overtake *v* → 1 advance 2 come close 3 surprise

overthrow *n* → 1 dismissal 2 losing 3 overturn *v* 4 defeat 5 destroy 6 dismiss 7 lower 8 madden 9 overturn

pack *n* → 1 amount 2 bag 3 gathering 4 gravimetry 5 group 6 fill 7 gather 8 press 9 transport 10 weigh *adj* 11 transport

package *n* → 1 accumulation 2 bag *v* 3 cover 4 insert 5 manage

page *n* → 1 book part 2 butler 3 period 4 printwork 5 shout *v* 6 number

paint *n* → 1 dye *v* 2 coat 3 colour 4 depict 5 narrate 6 place 7 portray

pale *n* → 1 fence 2 limit 3 region 4 shaft *v* 5 enclose 6 lose colour *adj* 7 colourless 8 dull 9 weak 10 white

pan *n* → 1 cookware 2 face 3 head 4 hollow 5 layer 6 leg 7 signal 8 toilet *v* 9 cinematise 10 clean 11 cook 12 dig 13 disapprove of

panic *n* → 1 fright *v* 2 be frightened *adj* 3 frightened

parade *n* → 1 crowd 2 road 3 show *v* 4 display 5 show off 6 walk

parallel *n* → 1 comparison 2 equal 3 equivalent 4 fortification 5 line 6 similar thing *v* 7 be similar 8 equal 9 fit *adj* 10 comparable 11 congruous 12 similar

paralyse *v* → 1 disease 2 inactivate

parcel *n* → 1 accumulation 2 bag 3 part 4 cover *adv* 5 partially

pardon *n* → 1 acquittal 2 forgiving *v* 3 acquit 4 forgive

park *n* → 1 amusement park 2 field 3 garden *v* 4 position

part $n \to$ 1 break 2 magazine 3 musical score 4 obligation 5 particulars 6 song v 7 depart 8 die 9 gap 10 separate *adj* 11 partial *adv* 12 partially

pass $n \to$ 1 access 2 bridge 3 certificate 4 channel 5 condition 6 gap 7 magic 9 rhetorical device 9 throw v 10 advance 11 approve 12 be adequate 13 defecate 14 die 15 exchange 16 overtake 17 pass through 18 succeed 19 throw

passage $n \to$ 1 access 2 advance 3 bay 4 bridge 5 defecation 6 entrance 7 exchange 8 fight 9 musical phrase 10 occurrence 11 path 12 transport 13 travelling 14 traversing 15 written composition

paste $n \to$ 1 adhesive 2 jewellery 3 pulp v 4 beat 5 coat 6 scold 7 stick together

pat $n \to$ 1 quiet sound 2 touch v 3 hit 4 kiss 5 level 6 touch 7 walk *adj* 8 precise 9 timely *adv* 10 precisely

patch $n \to$ 1 emblem 2 garden 3 period 4 repair 5 small amount v 6 electrify 7 repair

pattern $n \to$ 1 decoration 2 diagram 3 drawing 4 example 5 model 6 shape 7 weave v 8 decorate 9 shape

pause $n \to$ 1 indecision 2 interruption 3 interval 4 rest 5 silence 6 stoppage v 7 interrupt 8 rest 9 stop 10 vacillate

peculiar *adj* $\to$ 1 mad 2 particular 3 strange

peep $n \to$ 1 look 2 opening v 3 appear 4 chirp 5 look 6 speak

peer $n \to$ 1 aristocrat 2 equal 3 equivalent 4 partner 5 similar thing v 6 appear 7 look

people $n \to$ 1 community 2 humanity 3 relative 4 the public v 5 inhabit

perhaps *adv* $\to$ 1 by chance 2 irresolutely 3 possibly

periodic *adj* $\to$ 1 astronomical 2 irregular 3 regular

perish $v \to$ 1 collapse 2 deteriorate 3 die

permanent *adj* $\to$ 1 changeless 2 eternal

perpetual *adj* $\to$ 1 continual 2 eternal 3 infinite

persecute $v \to$ 1 act unkindly 2 annoy 3 be unfriendly 4 punish 5 repress 6 victimise

personal $n \to$ 1 news item 2 public notice *adj* 3 anthropological 4 inborn 5 own 6 particular 7 secret 8 slanderous

pervert $n \to$ 1 heretic 2 misleader 3 misuser 4 nonconformist 5 psychotic 6 sexual type 7 strange person v 8 change 9 ill-treat 10 lie 11 misguide 12 persuade

perverted *adj* $\to$ 1 distorted 2 heretical 3 misguided 4 nonconformist 5 strange 6 wrong

pest $n \to$ 1 annoyance 2 deterioration 3 illness

pet $n \to$ 1 fauna 2 friend 3 irritation 4 lover v 5 eroticise 6 kiss *adj* 7 chosen 8 important

phase $n \to$ 1 appearance 2 condition 3 moon 4 reproduction

phenomenal *adj* $\to$ 1 astonishing 2 enormous 3 occurrent 4 perceptional 5 tangible

physical *adj* $\to$ 1 bodily 2 tangible

pick $n \to$ 1 anchor 2 choice 3 digging implement 4 dirt 5 drug equipment 6 guitar 7 piercer 8 sewing machine 9 thread 10 weave v 11 choose 12 cook 13 eat 14 harvest 15 make music 16 open 17 remove 18 rob 19 sew

picture $n \to$ 1 beautiful person 2 example 3 film 4 narrative 5 painting 6 photograph 7 portrait v 8 fantasise 9 narrate 10 portray

piece $n \to$ 1 affair 2 bit 3 drama 4 essay 5 example 6 gun 7 length 8 musical instrument 9 part 10 particulars 11 poetry 12 textiles 13 woman

pig-headed *adj* $\to$ stubborn

pile $n \to$ 1 accumulation 2 arsenal 3 building 4 fuel 5 funeral rites 6 hair 7 many 8 much 9 nuclear energy 10 piercer 11 post 12 thread 13 tower 14 wealth 15 weave v 16 gather 17 insert 18 strengthen 19 support

pilot $n \to$ 1 heater 2 leader 3 model 4 seaman 5 steerer 6 test v 7 direct 8 fly 9 help *adj* 10 test

pin n → 1 aim 2 jewellery 3 nail 4 piercer 5 rod 6 surfboard v 7 hold 8 support

pinch n → 1 bar 2 bit 3 imprisonment 4 pressing 5 railway 6 robbery 7 small amount v 8 arrest 9 be miserly 10 cut 11 damage 12 enclose 13 hinder 14 pain 15 press 16 rob 17 set sail

pioneer n → 1 forerunner 2 leader 3 soldier v 4 starter v 5 initiate 6 introduce adj 7 new

pious adj → 1 regardful 2 reverent

pirate n → 1 thief 2 violent person v 3 rob

pit n → 1 bank 2 danger 3 diggings 4 disfigurement 5 excavation 6 fruit 7 hell 8 opening 9 stage v 10 bury 11 dig 12 disfigure 13 hollow 14 subtract

pitch n → 1 amount 2 angle 3 gradation 4 height 5 length 6 persuasion 7 plan 8 position 9 positioning 10 slope 11 sportsground 12 throw v 13 erect 14 fall 15 inhabit 16 position 17 slope 18 sound 19 throw

pitiful adj → 1 bad 2 pitiable

place n → 1 class 2 condition 3 dwelling 4 employment 5 field 6 job 7 position 8 road v 9 employ 10 position 11 remember 12 tidy

placid adj → composed

plain v → 1 complain adj 2 acoustic 3 clear 4 forthright 5 honest 6 insipid 7 most 8 obvious 9 simple 10 tasty 11 ugly 12 visible adv 13 clearly 14 greatly

plane n → 1 aeroplane 2 condition 3 grade 4 level 5 leveller 6 smoother v 7 fly 8 level 9 move 10 smooth adj 11 level

plant n → 1 conspiracy 2 embezzlement 3 factory 4 hiding place 5 informant 6 machine 7 trick v 8 create 9 farm 10 hide 11 inhabit 12 insert 13 position

plaster n → 1 adhesive 2 building materials 3 medication 4 powder v 5 beat 6 coat 7 fill 8 fire on 9 level 10 oversupply

plate n → 1 armour 2 brace 3 camera film 4 circle 5 coating 6 copy 7 electric circuit 8 engraving 9 metal 10 model 11 mouth 12 organism 13 plating 14 racing 15 smooth object v 16 coat 17 conserve 18 smooth 19 work metal

play n → 1 amusement 2 behaviour 3 doing 4 drama 5 joke 6 liberty 7 space v 8 amuse oneself 9 contest 10 do 11 fish 12 gamble 13 joke 14 let oneself go 15 make music 16 move 17 operate 18 perform 19 speed 20 use

plead v → 1 entreat 2 litigate 3 persuade

plentiful adj → 1 abundant 2 great 3 many

plenty n → 1 abundance 2 fertility 3 fullness 4 luxury 5 much adv 6 fully 7 very

plot n → 1 conspiracy 2 diagram 3 expedient 4 garden 5 narrative 6 position 7 secrecy 8 stratagem 9 yard v 10 beat a path 11 beguile 12 conspire 13 cooperate 14 keep secret 15 make do 16 map 17 measure

plug n → 1 electric circuit 2 electric generator 3 hat 4 hit 5 horse 6 incentive 7 joint 8 public notice 9 tap 10 tobacco v 11 approve 12 close 13 fill 14 hit 15 insert 16 make an effort

plunder n → 1 loot 2 robbery v 3 attack 4 rob

plus n → 1 more 2 profit adj 3 additional 4 increased conj 5 and

poach v → 1 cook 2 meddle 3 rob

pocket n → 1 airflow 2 amount 3 funds 4 hollow 5 mineral 6 region v 7 be inactive 8 capture 9 enclose 10 get 11 imprison 12 insert

point n → 1 animal part 2 electric circuit 3 essence 4 face 5 finish 6 gradation 7 headland 8 important thing 9 knob 10 lace 11 meaning 12 moment 13 particulars 14 piercer 15 position 16 rainfall measurement 17 sharp point 18 sign 19 small amount 20 string v 21 bulge 22 cheat 23 direct 24 fill 25 gesture 26 mark 27 set sail 28 sharpen

poised adj → 1 hanging 2 hanging 3 resting

poke n → 1 bag 2 pat 3 pocket 4 sexual intercourse v 5 have sex 6 thrust

polite adj → 1 courteous 2 cultivated

pollute v → 1 dirty 2 profane

pompous *adj* → 1 bombastic 2 showy

poorly *adj* → 1 ill *adv* 2 incompetently 3 insufficiently

pop *n* → 1 attempt 2 drink 3 explosion 4 parent *v* 5 explode 6 lend 7 open up 8 speed *adj* 9 musical 10 popular *adv* 11 hurriedly

port *n* → 1 case 2 destination 3 door 4 entrance 5 harbour 6 left 7 opening 8 passageway 9 pose 10 side 11 town 12 window *v* 13 transport *adj* 14 left 15 red

positive *n* → 1 photograph *adj* 2 assertive 3 certain 4 hopeful 5 male 6 most 7 numerical 8 real 9 unconditional 10 unrelated

possess *v* → 1 capture 2 haunt 3 have sex 4 own 5 remember

possessive *adj* → 1 repressive 2 selfish

post *n* → 1 combat troops 2 employment 3 examination 4 indicator 5 job 6 mail 7 makefast 8 position 9 rider *v* 10 account 11 drive 12 place 13 publicise 14 send a message 15 speed *adv* 16 hurriedly

postpone *v* → defer

pot *n* → 1 abdomen 2 alcohol 3 alcohol container 4 award 5 cookware 6 fishing tackle 7 gambling 8 gambling equipment 9 hollow 10 important person 11 marijuana 12 shot 13 toilet 14 vessel *v* 15 conceive 16 conserve 17 cook 18 farm 19 insert 20 kill 21 shoot 22 urinate

potent *adj* → 1 male 2 powerful 3 strong

pounce *n* → 1 absorber 2 bird part 3 dive 4 drier 5 fall 6 jump 7 powder *v* 8 bulge 9 dive 10 jump 11 speed

pound *n* → 1 cash 2 cell 3 explosion 4 hit 5 pen *v* 6 be loud 7 enclose 8 explode 9 hit 10 imprison 11 powder 12 vibrate 13 walk

pour *n* → 1 amount 2 flow 3 rainfall *v* 4 flow 5 rain

power *n* → 1 artistry 2 authority 3 capability 4 electricity 5 energy 6 entitlement 7 force 8 influence 9 influencer 10 many 11 much 12 nation 13 reflection 14 strength *v* 15 electrify 16 operate

practical *n* → 1 lesson *adj* 2 busy 3 competent 4 expedient 5 occurrent 6 operating 7 useable

practice *n* → 1 action 2 custom 3 exercise 4 job 5 lesson 6 method 7 preparation 8 repetition

practise *v* → 1 be accustomed to 2 conspire 3 do 4 have a job 5 repeat 6 study

praise *n* → 1 approval 2 prayer *v* 3 approve 4 be grateful 5 worship

prance *n* → 1 jump 2 move *v* 3 attitudinise 4 dance 5 jump 6 move 7 ride

pray *v* → 1 atone for 2 entreat 3 worship *interj* 4 please

precaution *n* → 1 anticipation 2 preparation 3 safety

precede *v* → advance

predecessor *n* → forerunner

prefer *v* → 1 choose 2 place 3 promote

preference *n* → 1 choice 2 rights 3 the best

premature *adj* → 1 early 2 rash 3 raw 4 untimely

premier *n* → 1 member of parliament 2 ruler *adj* 3 early 4 successful

present *n* → 1 affair 2 gift *v* 3 appear 4 award 5 be sociable 6 direct 7 display 8 give 9 offer 10 place 11 stage 12 supply *adj* 13 current 14 momentary 15 sane

preserve *n* → 1 field *v* 2 commemorate 3 conserve 4 cook 5 protract

press *n* → 1 advance 2 commentary 3 container 4 cupboard 5 fold 6 forcefulness 7 gathering 8 lifting 9 newspaper 10 pressing 11 printer 12 printing press *v* 13 advance 14 attack 15 emphasise 16 encourage 17 entreat 18 extract 19 force 20 gather 21 hold 22 hurry 23 rob 24 smooth

presume *v* → 1 be arrogant 2 believe 3 be likely 4 conjecture 5 misjudge

pretentious *adj* → 1 affected 2 bombastic 3 proud 4 showy 5 verbose

pretty *v* → 1 beautify *adj* 2 beautiful 3 courageous 4 cultivated 5 good 6 great 7 pleasant *adv* 8 very

prevent *v* → 1 expect 2 hinder 3 precede 4 prohibit 5 stop

price *n* → 1 cost 2 tax *v* 3 appraise

primitive $n \to$ 1 artless person adj 2 impermanent 3 natural 4 old 5 original 6 past

principal $n \to$ 1 actor 2 beam 3 capital 4 competitor 5 conductor 6 criminal 7 important person 8 leader 9 manager 10 music 11 property 12 ruler 13 teacher adj 14 important

private $adj \to$ 1 hidden 2 own 3 particular 4 secluded 5 secret

prize $n \to$ 1 award 2 contest 3 gift 4 takings v 5 appraise 6 approve 7 respect adj 8 good 9 superior

probe $n \to$ 1 investigation 2 spacecraft 3 test v 4 inquire into 5 question

problem $n \to$ 1 annoyer 2 difficulty 3 puzzle 4 uncertain thing adj 5 badly-behaved

procedure $n \to$ 1 behaviour 2 custom 3 method 4 operation

produce $n \to$ 1 finished product v 2 accomplish 3 be fertile 4 cause 5 display 6 give birth 7 have a job 8 make 9 stage

professional $n \to$ 1 expert 2 middle class 3 worker adj 4 accomplished 5 sports 6 working

progress $n \to$ 1 action 2 advance 3 continuation 4 evolution 5 growth 6 improvement v 7 advance 8 grow 9 improve

project $n \to$ 1 plan 2 undertaking v 3 communicate 4 fantasise 5 jut 6 offer 7 plan 8 thrust

prolong $v \to$ protract

prominent $adj \to$ 1 important 2 obvious 3 protuberant 4 reputable

promising $adj \to$ 1 favourable 2 fortunate 3 likely 4 new 5 predictive

pronounce $v \to$ 1 assert 2 publicise 3 speak

propaganda $n \to$ 1 information 2 persuasion 3 teaching 4 war

propose $v \to$ 1 assert 2 guide 3 marry 4 offer 5 plan 6 theorise

prose $n \to$ 1 prayer 2 writing

prospective $adj \to$ 1 expected 2 future

protest $n \to$ 1 bad debt 2 challenge 3 disagreement 4 discouragement 5 public notice v 6 assert 7 be unable to pay 8 discourage

proud $adj \to$ 1 arrogant 2 courageous 3 energetic 4 enormous 5 living 6 protuberant 7 reputable

prove $v \to$ 1 authenticate 2 conserve 3 cook 4 examine 5 occur 6 test

proverb $n \to$ figure of speech

provoke $v \to$ 1 activate 2 anger 3 annoy 4 arouse 5 cause 6 irritate

public $adj \to$ 1 displayed 2 formal 3 revealed

publish $v \to$ 1 publicise 2 reveal

puff $n \to$ 1 absorption 2 bragging 3 breathing 4 bulge 5 cloud 6 exaggeration 7 gas 8 hair 9 hiss 10 tobacco 11 wind v 12 brag 13 breathe 14 flatter 15 publicise 16 smoke

pun $n \to$ 1 figure of speech 2 joke 3 similarity v 4 joke

punch $n \to$ 1 drink 2 hit 3 piercer v 4 hit

punctual $adj \to$ 1 precise 2 timely

puny $adj \to$ 1 inferior 2 small 3 unimportant 4 weak

pure $adj \to$ 1 abstinent 2 clean 3 innocent 4 modest 5 perfect 6 simple 7 unconditional

push $n \to$ 1 advance 2 attack 3 clique 4 dismissal 5 effort 6 influence 7 pat 8 persistence 9 thrust 10 vitality 11 arouse 12 collide 13 persist 14 sell 15 thrust

put $n \to$ 1 stocks and shares 2 throw v 3 gamble 4 place

puzzle $n \to$ 1 amusement v 2 confuse

quality $n \to$ 1 character 2 condition 3 essence 4 goodness 5 pitch 6 superiority adj 7 superior

quarrel $n \to$ 1 argument 2 chisel 3 fight v 4 argue 5 be unfriendly

quarter $n \to$ 1 direction finder 2 four 3 lenience 4 moon 5 pity 6 region 7 season 8 side v 9 emblematise 10 execute 11 house 12 inhabit 13 separate 14 turn adj 15 fourfold

queer $n \to$ 1 sexual type v 2 spoil adj 3 bad 4 mad 5 nonconformist 6 sexual 7 strange

query $n \to$ 1 question 2 uncertain thing v 3 doubt 4 question

quest $n \to$ 1 inspection 2 jury 3 undertaking v 4 pursue

questionable *adj* → 1 disreputable 2 incorrect 3 uncertain 4 undetermined

queue *n* → 1 hair 2 line 3 series *v* 4 line

quiet *n* → 1 peace 2 rest 3 silence *v* 4 inactivate 5 make peace 6 moderate 7 quieten 8 rest 9 silence *adj* 10 inactive 11 moderate 12 peaceful 13 reticent 14 silent

quit *v* → 1 back out 2 depart 3 resign 4 stop

quite *adv* → 1 fully 2 greatly 3 in fact 4 wholly *interj* 5 yes

quiz *n* → 1 contest 2 questioning *v* 3 look 4 mock 5 question

quote *n* → 1 repetition 2 value *v* 3 appraise 4 repeat 5 speak

race *n* → 1 advance 2 ancestry 3 chute 4 class 5 community 6 current 7 humanity 8 living 9 path 10 pungency 11 taste 12 time *v* 13 accelerate 14 contest 15 have sex 16 speed

racket *n* → 1 crime 2 dishonesty 3 job 4 loud sound *v* 5 be happy 6 be loud 7 be sociable 8 overindulge

rage *n* → 1 anger 2 angry act 3 celebration 4 desire 5 emotion 6 entertainment 7 enthusiasm 8 fashion 9 madness 10 popularity 11 violent outburst *v* 12 be angry 13 be pleased 14 be sociable 15 be violent 16 blow 17 desire 18 feel emotion

raid *n* → 1 act of war 2 attack *v* 3 attack 4 fire on

raise *n* → 1 lifting *v* 2 build 3 bulge 4 care for 5 communicate 6 compute 7 cook 8 erect 9 gamble 10 gather 11 increase 12 lift 13 louden 14 make 15 promote 16 stop 17 wake up

ram *n* → 1 club 2 piercer 3 press 4 sheep 5 thrust *v* 6 hit 7 thrust

random *adj* → 1 disorderly 2 illogical 3 lucky 4 uncertain

range *n* → 1 class 2 difference 3 dwelling 4 length 5 mathematical operation 6 pitch 7 region 8 remoteness 9 space 10 stove 11 visibility 12 wide *v* 13 change 14 class 15 direct 16 farm 17 line 18 order 19 position 20 straighten 21 travel

rate *n* → 1 cost 2 grade *v* 3 appraise 4 assess 5 class 6 deserve 7 graduate 8 measure 9 scold

rather *adv* → 1 oppositely 2 optionally *interj* 3 yes

ration *n* → 1 share *v* 2 restrict 3 share out 4 supply

rational *adj* → 1 logical 2 mental 3 numerical 4 sane

reach *n* → 1 channel 2 length 3 rod 4 stream *v* 5 arrive 6 come close 7 compute 8 extend 9 gain 10 perforate 11 quantify

read *v* → 1 reading 2 explain 3 know 4 predict 5 speak 6 speak well 7 study *adj* 8 knowledgeable

ready *adj* → 1 cash 2 conspiracy *adj* 3 agreeable 4 easy 5 equipped 6 intelligent 7 predisposed 8 prepared 9 useable

real *adj* → 1 correct 2 numerical 3 realistic 4 true *adv* 5 very

realise *v* → 1 accomplish 2 actualise 3 be realistic 4 cash 5 gain 6 make music 7 sell

reason *n* → 1 cause 2 logic 3 mind 4 motive 5 reasoning 6 sanity 7 wisdom *v* 8 persuade

reasonable *adj* → 1 adequate 2 fair 3 logical 4 mental 5 moderate 6 sane 7 wise

rebel *n* → 1 disobeyer 2 dissident 3 nonconformist 4 refuser 5 revolutionary *v* 6 anarchise 7 disobey 8 oppose 9 revolt *adj* 10 disobedient 11 revolutionary

recall *n* → 1 cancellation 2 command 3 memory 4 parliamentary procedure *v* 5 cancel 6 dismiss 7 remember 8 remind 9 repair

recede *v* → 1 cancel 2 go back

receive *v* → 1 absorb 2 be sociable 3 gain 4 get 5 welcome

reckless *adj* → 1 capricious 2 neglectful 3 rash

reckon *v* → 1 assess 2 compute 3 depend on 4 devise 5 think

recognise *v* → 1 approve 2 assent to 3 be sociable 4 heed 5 gesture 6 know 7 remember 8 see

recommend *v* → 1 approve 2 encourage 3 guide 4 offer

recover v → 1 be healthy 2 compensate 3 gain 4 improve 5 revive 6 use

redeem v → 1 buy 2 compensate 3 pay 4 repair

reduce v → 1 abstain 2 cheapen 3 compute 4 decrease 5 photograph 6 repair 7 repress 8 subtract 9 thin 10 work metal

refined adj → 1 beautiful 2 clean 3 courteous 4 cultivated 5 discriminating 6 precise

reflect v → 1 deflect 2 shine

reform n → 1 correction 2 improvement v 3 atone for 4 be penitent 5 convert 6 improve

refugee n → 1 arriver 2 escapee 3 foreigner 4 outsider 5 traveller

refund n → 1 compensation 2 payment v 3 lend 4 pay

refuse n → 1 dirt 2 waste v 3 be inactive 4 meet an obstacle adj 5 useless

regard n → 1 attentiveness 2 courtesy 3 friendship 4 high regard 5 look 6 reputation v 7 attend to 8 look 9 respect

regret n → 1 complaint 2 penitence v 3 be penitent 4 grieve

regular n → 1 monastic 2 soldier adj 3 changeless 4 customary 5 frequent 6 homogeneous 7 level 8 monastic 9 thorough 10 tidy

reign n → 1 authority 2 period

reinforce v → 1 increase 2 strengthen 3 supply 4 support

reject v → 1 discard 2 rejection v 3 abandon 4 disuse 5 eject 6 isolate 7 refuse 8 repel 9 vomit

relative adj → 1 comparable 2 related 3 topical

relax v → 1 be informal 2 be lenient 3 compose oneself 4 decrease 5 moderate 6 rest 7 soften 8 weaken

release n → 1 acquittal 2 death 3 liberation 4 liberty 5 permission v 6 display 7 forgive 8 liberate 9 reveal

reliable adj → 1 faithful 2 honest

relief n → 1 abatement 2 alleviation 3 charity 4 help 5 hope 6 sculpture 7 substitute

relieve v → 1 alleviate 2 dismiss 3 ease 4 substitute

remain v → 1 be 2 continue

remainder n → 1 remnant v 2 sell 3 throw out adj 4 remnant

remark n → 1 attentiveness v 2 attend to 3 speak

remarkable adj → 1 astonishing 2 interesting 3 strange

repay v → compensate

replace v → 1 compensate 2 substitute

reply n → 1 answer 2 justification 3 message 4 parliamentary procedure 5 reaction 6 retaliation v 7 answer 8 react 9 resonate

report n → 1 answer 2 assessment 3 essay 4 explosion 5 information 6 loud sound 7 narrative 8 news item 9 public notice 10 reputation v 11 appear 12 narrate 13 publicise 14 publish

require v → 1 command 2 desire 3 entreat 4 impose 5 insist on 6 necessitate

rescue n → 1 alleviation 2 repair v 3 alleviate 4 liberate

resent v → be angry with

resist v → 1 conservation v 2 abstain 3 be inactive 4 oppose

resolve v → 1 persistence v 2 choose 3 clarify 4 determine 5 discriminate 6 see 7 simplify 8 solve

respect n → 1 courtesy 2 high regard 3 reverence

respectable adj → 1 great 2 highly regarded 3 reputable 4 well-behaved

respond v → 1 prayer v 2 answer 3 behave 4 feel emotion 5 react

responsible adj → 1 imputable 2 obligated 3 sane

restore v → 1 compensate 2 medicate 3 repair 4 repeat 5 take

retire v → 1 depart 2 disuse 3 go back 4 lie low 5 resign 6 sleep

return n → 1 account 2 answer 3 compensation 4 going backwards 5 gratefulness 6 payment 7 profit 8 reaction 9 record 10 repetition 11 retaliation v 12 answer 13 compensate 14 elect 15 go back 16 pay adj 17 repetitive

revenge n → 1 retaliation v 2 retaliate

reverse n → 1 contrast 2 losing 3 misfortune 4 opposite meaning 5 opposite position 6 rear v 7 cancel 8 con-

reverse trast 9 go back 10 swerve *adj* 11 opposing 12 rear 13 regressive

revise *v* → 1 change 2 change 3 correct 4 memorise 5 study

revolting *adj* → 1 hateful 2 revolutionary 3 sickening 4 unpleasant

reward *n* → 1 compensation 2 gift 3 gratefulness 4 incentive 5 income *v* 6 award 7 compensate 8 pay

rich *adj* → 1 abundant 2 colourful 3 cooked 4 decorative 5 expensive 6 fertile 7 fragrant 8 great 9 nonsensical 10 showy 11 tasteful 12 tasty 13 wealthy

ridicule *n* → 1 low regard 2 mockery *v* 3 insult 4 mock

ridiculous *adj* → 1 foolish 2 nonsensical 3 stupid

riot *n* → 1 celebration 2 commotion 3 display 4 misdemeanour 5 muddle 6 outburst 7 revolution *v* 8 be violent 9 misbehave 10 overindulge

ripe *adj* → 1 drunk 2 expedient 3 obscene 4 old 5 smelly 6 timely

rise *n* → 1 ascent 2 astronomical point 3 height 4 increase 5 inflation 6 loudness 7 mound 8 start *v* 9 appear 10 ascend 11 become greater 12 be happy 13 come close 14 cost 15 erect 16 flower 17 grow 18 increase 19 live 20 louden 21 occur 22 start 23 stop 24 succeed 25 tower 26 wake up

ritual *n* → 1 custom 2 formal occasion 3 prayer 4 religious ceremony 5 rule *adj* 6 formal 7 ritualistic

rival *n* → 1 competitor 2 enemy *v* 3 contest 4 equal *adj* 5 dissident

river *n* → 1 channel 2 separator 3 stream

roam *n* → 1 walk *v* 2 travel

romance *n* → 1 flirtation 2 image 3 love affair 4 musical piece 5 poetry 6 story *v* 7 exaggerate 8 fantasise 9 narrate

romantic *n* → 1 emotionalist *adj* 2 emotional 3 flirtatious 4 loving 5 musical 6 narrative 7 unrealistic

rot *n* → 1 deterioration 2 dirt 3 nonsense *v* 4 deteriorate 5 get dirty 6 wet

rotten *adj* → 1 bad 2 deteriorated 3 drunk 4 immoral 5 sickening

rouse *n* → 1 signal 2 waking *v* 3 activate 4 anger 5 arouse 6 wake up

row *n* → 1 argument 2 house 3 line 4 loud sound 5 musical phrase 6 road 7 straightness *v* 8 argue 9 be loud 10 contest 11 scold 12 transport

royalty *n* → 1 aristocracy 2 funds 3 income 4 nation

rubbish *n* → 1 bad thing 2 illogicality 3 nonsense 4 waste *v* 5 mock

rude *adj* → 1 badly-behaved 2 brutal 3 discourteous 4 dissonant 5 ill-bred 6 insulting 7 raw 8 rough 9 strong 10 ugly

rumour *n* → 1 allusion 2 news 3 uncertain thing *v* 4 communicate 5 noise abroad

run *n* → 1 move 2 period 3 rate 4 series *v* 5 alternate 6 cash 7 contest 8 discharge 9 do 10 elude 11 excrete 12 extend 13 farm 14 fill 15 flow 16 flower 17 gather 18 glide 19 hunt 20 liquefy 21 manage 22 move 23 open up 24 operate 25 publish 26 repeat 27 rob 28 speed 29 stage 30 surpass 31 transport 32 walk *adj* 33 liquid

rush *n* → 1 advance 2 attack 3 busyness 4 flooring 5 rashness 6 rate 7 speed 8 stroke *v* 9 advance 10 attack 11 be busy 12 force 13 hurry 14 transport *adj* 15 speedy

rustle *n* → 1 hiss 2 quiet sound *v* 3 hiss 4 rob

rut *n* → 1 custom 2 furrow 3 reproduction *v* 4 conceive 5 furrow

ruthless *adj* → 1 callous 2 opportunist 3 unkind

sabotage *n* → 1 damage 2 dissidence *v* 3 damage

sacrifice *n* → 1 gift 2 killing 3 offering 4 prayer 5 religious ceremony 6 victim *v* 7 give 8 kill

sad *adj* → 1 bad 2 colourless 3 dull 4 shadowy 5 unhappy

sag *n* → 1 decrease 2 descent 3 hanging 4 hollow *v* 5 capitulate 6 curve 7 fall 8 hang 9 wane

sail *n* → 1 sailing ship *v* 2 depart 3 move 4 set sail

sailor *n* → mariner

saint *n* → 1 good person 2 holy person 3 religious follower 4 unselfish person *v* 5 consecrate 6 worship

salary *n* → income

sale *n* → 1 bargain 2 selling

salute *n* → 1 congratulation 2 courtesy 3 tribute *v* 4 pay homage 5 signal

sample *n* → 1 example *v* 2 investigate 3 taste 4 test *adj* 5 model

sand *n* → 1 extinguisher 2 matter 3 powder 4 soil *v* 5 disperse 6 rub 7 smooth

sarcasm *n* → 1 comedy 2 mockery 3 opposite meaning

satellite *n* → 1 accomplice 2 companion 3 dependant 4 flatterer 5 heavenly body 6 spacecraft 7 subject

savage *n* → 1 bad person 2 ethnic 3 unkind person 4 vulgarian *v* 5 attack *adj* 6 angry 7 ferocious 8 natural 9 rough 10 unkind

say *n* → 1 rights 2 speaking *v* 3 speak 4 theorise

saying *n* → proverb

scale *n* → 1 covering 2 glaze 3 gradation 4 leaf 5 length-measurer 6 list 7 relationship 8 remnant 9 size 10 skin 11 stairs *v* 12 ascend 13 drive 14 graduate 15 measure 16 top 17 weigh

scamper *n* → 1 rate *v* 2 speed

scandal *n* → 1 bad thing 2 disrepute 3 slander 4 talk *v* 5 slander 6 talk

scar *n* → 1 disfigurement 2 stem *v* 3 disfigure

scare *n* → 1 fright *v* 2 frighten

scatter *v* → 1 drinking session *v* 2 disperse 3 diverge

scene *n* → 1 act 2 excitement 3 painting 4 situation 5 stage 6 surroundings 7 view

school *n* → 1 fish 2 gathering 3 teacher *v* 4 scold 5 teach

science *n* → 1 competence 2 knowledge

scoff *n* → 1 food 2 mockery *v* 3 eat 4 mock

score *n* → 1 account 2 cost 3 cut 4 furrow 5 indebtedness 6 limit 7 record 8 winner *v* 9 cut 10 disapprove of 11 furrow 12 have sex 13 make music 14 mark 15 measure 16 record 17 succeed

scorn *n* → 1 arrogance 2 disapproval 3 low regard *v* 4 be arrogant 5 hold in low regard

scowl *n* → 1 boo *v* 2 become irritated 3 dislike

scramble *n* → 1 jumble 2 preparation 3 race *v* 4 cook 5 drive 6 make an effort 7 mix 8 speed 9 walk

scrap *n* → 1 discard 2 part 3 remnant 4 small amount 5 waste *v* 6 disuse 7 fight 8 separate 9 throw out *adj* 10 disused 11 partial 12 useless

scrape *n* → 1 dilemma 2 fight 3 rubbing *v* 4 be dissonant 5 have sex 6 make music 7 rub 8 smooth

scratch *n* → 1 disfigurement 2 dissonance 3 furrow 4 injury 5 quiet sound 6 rubbing 7 shallow 8 starting line 9 writing *v* 10 back out 11 be dissonant 12 cudgel 13 cut 14 disfigure 15 furrow 16 rub 17 touch 18 write *adj* 19 lucky

scream *n* → 1 humorist 2 shout *v* 3 laugh 4 shout

screw *n* → 1 distortion 2 gaoler 3 horse 4 income 5 look 6 machine 7 miser 8 nail 9 policeman 10 propellant 11 sexual intercourse 12 spiral 13 twist *v* 14 extort 15 fasten 16 force 17 have sex 18 spoil 19 twist *adj* 20 spinning

scruffy *adj* → 1 unkempt 2 untidy

seal *n* → 1 animal's coat 2 emblem 3 label 4 model 5 paving 6 plug *v* 7 assent to 8 authorise 9 close 10 coat 11 emblematise 12 fish 13 label 14 smooth

seam *n* → 1 furrow 2 joint 3 layer 4 deflect 5 furrow 6 join

second *n* → 1 angle 2 helper 3 inferior 4 moment 5 partner 6 singer 7 song 8 string instrument *v* 9 help 10 perform *adj* 11 additional 12 following 13 two *adv* 14 after

secondary *n* → 1 coming after 2 feather 3 inferior 4 partner 5 second *adj* 6 inferior 7 resultant 8 rocky 9 two 10 unimportant

section *n* → 1 armed forces 2 book part 3 coating 4 cut 5 diagram 6 lesson 7 musical band 8 part 9 railway 10 separation *v* 11 cut

secure v → 1 fasten 2 gain 3 imprison 4 steady adj 5 certain 6 composed 7 fastened 8 joined 9 protected 10 safe 11 steady

security n → 1 capital 2 composure 3 defence 4 insurance 5 safety 6 surety

seek v → 1 attempt 2 desire 3 pursue 4 search

seep n → 1 exit 2 flow 3 wetness v 4 discharge 5 flow

seize v → 1 arrest 2 capture 3 fasten 4 hold 5 meet an obstacle 6 use

selection n → 1 choice 2 competitor 3 conception 4 farm 5 written composition

sell n → 1 disenchantment 2 incentive 3 selling 4 trick v 5 encourage 6 trick

send n → 1 thrust v 2 excite 3 thrust 4 transport

senior n → 1 boss 2 lawyer 3 old people 4 pupil 5 sportsman adj 6 aged 7 important

sensation n → 1 emotion 2 excitement 3 good thing 4 news item 5 perception

sense n → 1 competence 2 direction 3 logic 4 meaning 5 mind 6 perception 7 realism 8 translation 9 understanding 10 wisdom v 11 know 12 perceive

sensitive adj → 1 cultivated 2 emotional 3 influenced 4 perceptive 5 reactive

sequel n → 1 coming after 2 drama 3 magazine 4 result

serious adj → 1 attentive 2 dangerous 3 important 4 sombre

serve n → 1 reprimand 2 supplies v 3 be adequate 4 be expedient 5 be of service 6 be sociable 7 cover 8 do one's duty 9 feed 10 help 11 obey 12 operate 13 satisfy 14 take the cloth 15 twist 16 work

service n → 1 help 2 prayer 3 repair 4 supply 5 twist 6 usefulness v 7 conceive 8 repair

set n → 1 accumulation 2 book 3 class 4 clique 5 direction 6 distortion 7 hanging 8 hardening 9 point of view 10 pose 11 position 12 similar thing 13 stage 14 surf 15 television v 16 command 17 cost 18 dance 19 decorate 20 descend 21 direct 22 flow 23 give birth 24 harden 25 make 26 make music 27 medicate 28 order 29 place 30 print 31 regularise 32 sharpen 33 steady 34 support adj 35 conventional 36 faithful 37 prepared 38 steady

setting n → 1 hairdressing 2 hardening 3 musical piece 4 placement 5 position 6 stage 7 surroundings

settle n → 1 couch v 2 account 3 agree 4 arrange 5 dismount 6 fall 7 finish 8 give 9 inhabit 10 make whole 11 mediate 12 order 13 pay 14 promise 15 rest 16 steady

severe adj → 1 callous 2 difficult 3 intense 4 precise 5 strict 6 violent

shade n → 1 darkener 2 grade 3 hiding 4 phantom 5 screen v 6 change 7 cover 8 darken 9 depict 10 graduate 11 hide 12 secure

shadow n → 1 black 2 companion 3 danger 4 drawing 5 friend 6 grade 7 imprecision 8 shade 9 small amount v 10 cloud 11 darken 12 depict 13 partner 14 pursue 15 secure

shake n → 1 drink 2 flutter 3 gap 4 moment 5 timber 6 turbulence 7 vibration v 8 agitate 9 agree 10 be frightened 11 elude 12 escape 13 extort 14 make music 15 mix 16 recline 17 rob 18 search 19 vibrate 20 weaken

shed n → 1 shelter 2 stable 3 toilet v 4 bare 5 disuse 6 repel 7 separate 8 shelter

shell n → 1 ammunition 2 animal part 3 bag 4 building 5 coating 6 covering 7 explosive 8 fruit 9 outside 10 roof 11 rowing boat 12 seclusion 13 skin v 14 fire on 15 pay

shield n → 1 armour 2 coating 3 defence 4 heraldry 5 rock outcrop 6 wall v 7 prohibit 8 secure

shock n → 1 illness 2 impact 3 psychic disturbance 4 surprise 5 violent outburst v 6 electrify 7 surprise adj 8 surprising

shop n → 1 factory v 2 betray 3 buy 4 report on

shortage n → 1 deficiency 2 insufficiency

shovel n → 1 digging implement 2 dwelling 3 room v 4 dig

show n → 1 appearances 2 display 3 entertainment 4 festival 5 luck 6 sign 7 situation 8 small amount v 9 appear 10 authenticate 11 be third 12 display 13 evidence 14 inform 15 perform 16 reveal 17 teach

shower n → 1 amount 2 bath 3 cleansing 4 covering 5 gathering 6 rainfall v 7 be generous 8 clean 9 give 10 rain 11 wet

shrewd adj → 1 cunning 2 sharp 3 unkind 4 wise

shriek n → 1 loud sound 2 mirth 3 shout v 4 be loud 5 laugh 6 shout 7 shrill

shrink n → 1 contraction 2 going backwards 3 psychologist v 4 be modest 5 contract 6 decrease 7 go back 8 lack courage

shudder n → 1 coldness 2 fright 3 turbulence v 4 be cold 5 be frightened 6 vibrate

shuffle n → 1 avoidance 2 walking v 3 dance 4 mix 5 tangle 6 untidy 7 walk

shut n → 1 closure 2 joint v 3 close 4 prohibit adj 5 closed

shy n → 1 reaction 2 throw v 3 be frightened 4 react 5 swerve 6 throw 7 worry adj 8 frightened 9 infertile 10 modest 11 reticent 12 solitary 13 unwilling

sick n → 1 vomit adj 2 angry 3 colourless 4 damaged 5 ill 6 infertile

silly n → 1 fool adj 2 close 3 foolish 4 stupid 5 unconscious 6 weak

sincere adj → 1 emotional 2 forthright 3 honest 4 truthful

single-minded adj → 1 artless 2 honest 3 persevering 4 serious

sink n → 1 bath 2 borehole 3 den of vice 4 hollow 5 toilet v 6 be tired 7 decrease 8 deteriorate 9 dig 10 eat 11 exclude 12 fall 13 hide 14 hollow 15 repose 16 ruin 17 slope 18 sound 19 weaken

situation n → 1 condition 2 job 3 position

skate n → 1 electric circuit 2 journey 3 man 4 sledge v 5 do easily 6 glide

sketch n → 1 act 2 comedy 3 diagram 4 drawing 5 essay 6 musical piece 7 narrative 8 portrait 9 written composition v 10 depict 11 narrate

skim n → 1 dirt v 2 be inattentive 3 look 4 move 5 neglect 6 read 7 throw

skip n → 1 boss 2 dancing 3 jump 4 train v 5 depart 6 escape 7 exclude 8 jump

skirt n → 1 bottom 2 dress 3 edge 4 pendant 5 shaft 6 woman v 7 border 8 flank 9 overtake

slack n → 1 period of inaction 2 powder 3 promiscuous person 4 waste v 5 be unwilling 6 decrease 7 idle 8 moderate 9 weaken adj 10 idle 11 inactive 12 lenient 13 neglectful 14 promiscuous 15 slow 16 weak adv 17 idly 18 limply 19 neglectfully

slam n → 1 closure 2 explosion 3 impact 4 reprimand v 5 close 6 disapprove of 7 explode 8 hit 9 slander

sleek v → 1 smooth adj 2 bright 3 courteous 4 smooth

slick n → 1 magazine 2 wheel v 3 smooth adj 4 bright 5 busy 6 competent 7 courteous 8 cunning 9 eloquent 10 oily 11 smooth

slight n → 1 insult v 2 belittle 3 insult 4 slander adj 5 ethereal 6 shallow 7 small 8 smallest 9 thin 10 unimportant 11 weak

sling n → 1 bribe 2 medication 3 propellant 4 tape 5 wire v 6 bribe 7 hang 8 lower 9 throw

slip n → 1 bedclothes 2 break 3 ceramics 4 children 5 error 6 escape 7 failure 8 fall 9 grammatical error 10 harbour 11 misdemeanour 12 misfortune 13 move 14 paint 15 record 16 saddlery 17 shaft 18 sharpener 19 underwear 20 wrong v 21 be immoral 22 be inattentive 23 deteriorate 24 err 25 fall 26 farm 27 give birth 28 glide 29 let oneself go 30 move 31 separate 32 speed 33 wane

slippery adj → 1 changeable 2 dishonest 3 elusive 4 escaped 5 oily 6 smooth 7 uncertain 8 unfaithful

slit n → 1 cut 2 gap 3 groin 4 opening v 5 cut 6 open 7 separate adj 8 gaping

sloppy *adj* → 1 dirty 2 emotional 3 foolish 4 sludgy 5 untidy 6 wet

slouch *n* → 1 hanging 2 incompetent 3 pose *v* 4 hang 5 repose 6 walk

slump *n* → 1 cheapness 2 failure 3 fall 4 misfortune 5 period of inaction *v* 6 be cheap 7 be out of luck 8 be unhappy 9 fail 10 fall

slur *n* → 1 denigration 2 faulty speech 3 musical phrase 4 musical score 5 slander *v* 6 dirty 7 glide 8 make music 9 mispronounce 10 slander 11 speak

sly *adj* → 1 badly-behaved 2 cunning 3 humorous 4 secretive

smack *n* → 1 corporal punishment 2 endearments 3 gesture 4 hit 5 narcotic 6 sailing ship 7 small amount 8 taste 9 watercraft *v* 10 click 11 hit 12 kiss *adv* 13 hurriedly 14 resonantly 15 straight

smart *v* → 1 pain *adj* 2 beautiful 3 busy 4 clothed 5 competent 6 cunning 7 eloquent 8 fashionable 9 intelligent 10 speedy 11 tasteful

smash *n* → 1 explosion 2 failure 3 hit 4 impact 5 performance 6 popularity 7 ruin 8 stroke *v* 9 break 10 collide 11 destroy

smear *n* → 1 denigration 2 slander *v* 3 coat 4 dirty 5 disgrace 6 slander

smother *n* → 1 cloud 2 fire 3 flood 4 cover 5 enclose 6 extinguish 7 flood 8 hide 9 keep secret 10 kill 11 oversupply 12 repress 13 suffocate 14 welcome

smudge *n* → 1 cloud 2 dirt 3 shapelessness *v* 4 blacken 5 dirty

smug *adj* → 1 arrogant 2 proud 3 smooth 4 tidy

snag *n* → 1 hindrance 2 knob 3 mouth 4 piercer 5 smallgoods *v* 6 hinder

snap *n* → 1 button 2 click 3 easy thing 4 good fortune 5 photograph 6 vitality *v* 7 break 8 call (of animals) 9 click 10 hit 11 photograph 12 speak *adj* 13 momentary *adv* 14 speedily

snatch *n* → 1 groin 2 lifting 3 move 4 part 5 robbery 6 sex object 7 takings *v* 8 capture 9 fluctuate

snivel *n* → 1 affectation 2 cry 3 secretion *v* 4 attitudinise 5 be unhappy 6 excrete 7 grieve 8 hiss 9 speak

snub *n* → 1 insult 2 repulsion 3 stoppage *v* 4 be unfriendly 5 humble 6 insult 7 repel 8 stop *adj* 9 short

soak *n* → 1 absorber 2 drinking session 3 heavy drinker 4 hollow 5 liquid 6 wetting *v* 7 cook 8 extract 9 liquefy 10 wet

soar *v* → 1 ascend 2 fly 3 prosper 4 succeed 5 tower

sober *adj* → 1 abstinent 2 colourless 3 realistic 4 sane 5 sombre

somersault *n* → 1 exercise 2 overturn 3 roll *v* 4 overturn 5 roll

sophisticated *adj* → 1 complex 2 composed 3 courteous 4 knowledgeable 5 mixed 6 tasteful

sorrow *n* → 1 grieving 2 misfortune 3 penitence 4 unhappiness *v* 5 be unhappy

sorry *adj* → 1 ashamed 2 bad 3 penitent 4 pitiable 5 pitying 6 unhappy

sort *n* → 1 character 2 class 3 example 4 method 5 woman *v* 6 class 7 differ 8 inquire into

sound *n* → 1 bay 2 channel 3 news *v* 4 appear 5 dive 6 examine 7 float 8 make music 9 measure 10 plumb the depths 11 practise medicine 12 publicise 13 speak *adj* 14 good 15 healthy 16 honest 17 logical 18 perfect 19 true

spare *n* → 1 equipment *v* 2 acquit 3 disuse 4 ease 5 forgive 6 give *adj* 7 abstinent 8 small 9 thin 10 thrifty

sparkle *n* → 1 artistry 2 fire 3 happiness 4 light *v* 5 be happy 6 bubble 7 excel 8 shine

special *n* → 1 bargain 2 policeman 3 textbook 4 train *v* 5 practise medicine *adj* 6 intense 7 particular 8 reputable

spell *n* → 1 allure 2 centre of activity 3 influence 4 interruption 5 interval 6 magic spell 7 period 8 rest *v* 9 rest 10 substitute

spend *v* → 1 give 2 pay 3 use up

spike *n* → 1 animal part 2 flower 3 fortification 4 inserter 5 nail 6 piercer *v* 7 be infertile 8 brew 9 jut 10 kill 11 sharpen

spill $n \to$ 1 dismissal 2 lighter 3 liquid 4 misplacement 5 part 6 plug 7 printwork v 8 discharge 9 disperse 10 flood 11 flow 12 misplace 13 reveal

spirited $adj \to$ 1 busy 2 capricious 3 courageous 4 energetic 5 living 6 predisposed

spite $n \to$ 1 ill will 2 unfriendliness v 3 be unfriendly 4 hinder 5 victimise

split $n \to$ 1 break 2 exercise 3 gap 4 part 5 share v 6 depart 7 gape 8 separate 9 share out adj 10 gaping 11 separate 12 shared

sponge $n \to$ 1 absorber 2 cleansing 3 extortionist 4 mineral 5 pulp 6 self-seeker 7 washer v 8 clean 9 dry 10 idle

spontaneous $adj \to$ 1 agreeable 2 capricious 3 liberated

spot $n \to$ 1 a drink 2 dilemma 3 disfigurement 4 lighting 5 multicolour 6 position 7 small amount v 8 clean 9 dirty 10 disfigure 11 disperse 12 find 13 see

spread $n \to$ 1 area 2 bedclothes 3 covering 4 dispersal 5 flood 6 flood 7 growth 8 meal 9 show 10 size 11 thickness v 12 coat 13 disperse 14 diverge 15 extend 16 flood 17 generalise 18 grow 19 open up 20 separate adj 21 thick

spring $n \to$ 1 cord 2 elastic 3 innovator 4 jump 5 morning 6 pliability 7 season 8 start v 9 appear 10 attack 11 bend 12 bounce 13 explode 14 flow out 15 flower 16 jump 17 liberate 18 separate adj 19 pliable 20 seasonal

sprinkle $n \to$ 1 dispersal 2 flow 3 rainfall 4 small amount v 5 disperse 6 rain 7 wet

spurt $n \to$ 1 busyness 2 ephemeral 3 flow 4 stream v 5 flow

square $n \to$ 1 area 2 armed forces 3 field 4 number 5 plane figure 6 protractor v 7 account 8 bend 9 compute 10 fit 11 level 12 pay 13 shape 14 swerve adj 15 bent 16 equal 17 erect 18 fair 19 great 20 honest 21 level 22 old 23 satisfactory adv 24 angularly 25 fairly 26 honestly 27 precisely

squash $n \to$ 1 drink 2 pressing 3 pulp 4 splash v 5 press 6 pulp 7 repress 8 silence 9 splash

squawk $n \to$ 1 birdcall 2 complaint 3 shout v 4 chirp 5 complain 6 shrill

squeal $n \to$ 1 complaint 2 shout v 3 complain 4 report on 5 shout 6 shrill

squeeze $n \to$ 1 copy 2 dilemma 3 endearments 4 friendship 5 gathering 6 pressing 7 restraint v 8 copy 9 extract 10 force 11 kiss 12 press

stab $n \to$ 1 attempt 2 cut 3 injury 4 kick 5 pat 6 perforation v 7 injure 8 open 9 pain 10 perforate 11 roughen

stable $n \to$ 1 animal dwelling 2 factory 3 fauna 4 gathering 5 pen v 6 inhabit 7 store adj 8 changeless 9 composed 10 serious 11 steady

stack $n \to$ 1 accumulation 2 arsenal 3 flight 4 impact 5 library 6 passageway 7 sound system 8 storage v 9 act unfairly 10 collide 11 gather 12 place 13 store

stain $n \to$ 1 denigration 2 dirt 3 dye 4 multicolour v 5 colour 6 disfigure 7 disgrace

stake $n \to$ 1 fortification 2 gambling equipment 3 ownership 4 participation 5 shaft v 6 fasten 7 gamble 8 support

stall $n \to$ 1 animal dwelling 2 factory 3 hindrance 4 pen 5 room 6 shop 7 stoppage v 8 avoid 9 imprison 10 inhabit 11 stop

stamina $n \to$ 1 durability 2 perseverance 3 persistence

stand $n \to$ 1 dissidence 2 point of view 3 pose 4 rack 5 shop 6 stable 7 stoppage v 8 be inactive 9 conceive 10 electioneer 11 erect 12 position 13 stop 14 tend to 15 undertake 16 wage war

standard $n \to$ 1 class 2 currency 3 example 4 flag 5 flower 6 fuel 7 morality 8 musical piece 9 ordinariness 10 perfect thing 11 rule 12 tester adj 13 model 14 ordinary

standing $n \to$ 1 condition 2 duration 3 grade 4 reputation adj 5 changeless 6 continual 7 erect 8 postural 9 unused

stark *adj* → 1 bare 2 hard 3 most 4 simple 5 strict 6 thorough *adv* 7 greatly 8 wholly

startle *n* → 1 surprise 2 turbulence *v* 3 agitate 4 surprise 5 worry

state *n* → 1 administrative area 2 condition 3 domain 4 excitement 5 formality 6 nation 7 the public *v* 8 assert 9 speak *adj* 10 formal 11 legislative 12 national 13 sports

statement *n* → 1 account 2 assertion 3 evidence 4 information 5 narrative

station *n* → 1 barracks 2 condition 3 factory 4 farm 5 grade 6 job 7 position 8 reputation 9 telecommunications station *v* 10 place 11 position

staunch *n* → 1 flow 2 stopper *v* 3 moderate 4 stop *adj* 5 dry 6 faithful 7 friendly 8 persevering 9 serious 10 strong

stay *n* → 1 cord 2 persistence 3 stoppage 4 support 5 timber 6 visit *v* 7 be present 8 continue 9 gamble 10 go slowly 11 help 12 inhabit 13 moderate 14 persist 15 restrain 16 satisfy 17 stop 18 strengthen 19 support 20 swerve 21 visit

steel *n* → 1 knife 2 lighter 3 metal 4 stocks and shares 5 sword *v* 6 harden 7 strengthen 8 work metal *adj* 9 durable 10 grey 11 hard 12 metallic

steep *n* → 1 liquid 2 slope 3 wetting *v* 4 cook 5 liquefy 6 wet *adj* 7 expensive 8 mountainous 9 sloping

step *n* → 1 click 2 gradation 3 length 4 move 5 stairs 6 support 7 walking *v* 8 measure 9 support 10 walk

stick *n* → 1 adhesive 2 bomb 3 club 4 difficulty 5 gambling equipment 6 hindrance 7 marijuana 8 musical instrument 9 person 10 propellant 11 stoppage 12 timber *v* 13 confuse 14 fasten 15 kill 16 perforate 17 place 18 puzzle 19 support

stiff *n* → 1 groin 2 heavy drinker 3 nonachiever 4 the dead *adj* 5 calamitous 6 difficult 7 drunk 8 excessive 9 formal 10 hard 11 intoxicating 12 lame 13 poor 14 steady 15 strict 16 stubborn 17 ugly 18 windy *adv* 19 hard

stifle *v* → 1 kill 2 repress 3 restrain 4 silence 5 suffocate

still *n* → 1 bottle 2 cleanser 3 photograph 4 pub *v* 5 brew 6 distil 7 moderate 8 silence *adj* 9 inactive 10 quiet 11 resting 12 silent *adv* 13 continually 14 inactively 15 in the future 16 nevertheless 17 now 18 silently

stint *n* → 1 period 2 restraint 3 share 4 stoppage *v* 5 be miserly 6 restrict 7 stop

stir *n* → 1 busyness 2 excitement 3 pat 4 perception 5 prison 6 quiet sound *v* 7 agitate 8 annoy 9 emotionalise 10 mix 11 move 12 publicise 13 spin

stock *n* → 1 agenda 2 ancestry 3 class 4 goods 5 gun part 6 handle 7 language 8 model 9 neckwear 10 reputation 11 storage 12 stupid person 13 support 14 timber *v* 15 farm 16 punish 17 restrain 18 store *adj* 19 customary 20 proverbial

stomach *n* → 1 abdomen 2 courage 3 desire 4 hunger 5 pride *v* 6 be angry with 7 eat

stone *n* → 1 abrasive 2 bead 3 building materials 4 fruit 5 grave 6 grey 7 jewel 8 rock 9 smoother *v* 10 kill 11 rub *adj* 12 hard 13 rocky

stony *adj* → 1 callous 2 hard 3 inactive 4 infertile 5 poor 6 rocky

stop *n* → 1 angle 2 bad debt 3 camera part 4 closure 5 cord 6 destination 7 discourager 8 obstacle 9 plug 10 restraints 11 stopper 12 tap 13 visit *v* 14 be inactive 15 be present 16 close 17 defeat 18 discourage 19 fill 20 hinder 21 interrupt 22 make music 23 obstruct 24 restrain 25 restrict

store *n* → 1 adequacy 2 computer record 3 much 4 reputation 5 shop 6 storage 7 place

storm *n* → 1 attack 2 explosion 3 rainfall 4 violent outburst 5 weather 6 wind *v* 7 be angry 8 be violent 9 blow 10 fire on 11 rain

strain *n* → 1 ancestry 2 character 3 class 4 condition 5 cramp 6 distortion 7 effort 8 gradation 9 injury 10 insistence 11 music 12 poetry 13 pressure 14 small amount 15 tiredness *v* 16 cook 17 distort 18 flow 19 hold 20 injure 21 tire

streak n → 1 addition 2 character 3 characteristics 4 jewel 5 layer 6 line 7 multicolour 8 period 9 powder 10 tall person 11 thin person v 12 line 13 speed 14 undress

stretch n → 1 direction 2 enlargement 3 imprisonment 4 period 5 racecourse 6 region v 7 become greater 8 execute 9 extend 10 limber adj 11 pliable

strike n → 1 failure 2 finding 3 industrial action 4 period of inaction 5 stroke 6 temperature v 7 arrive 8 be inactive 9 depart 10 find 11 fish 12 flower 13 hit 14 influence 15 ignite 16 make music 17 remove 18 signal 19 smooth 20 sound

strip n → 1 coating 2 colour 3 line 4 newspaper 5 pornography 6 sportswear 7 thinness v 8 bare 9 capture 10 farm 11 harvest 12 line 13 refuse 14 remove 15 rob 16 separate 17 take 18 undress

struggle n → 1 attempt 2 contest 3 difficulty v 4 fight 5 make an effort

strut n → 1 beam 2 walking v 3 show off 4 support 5 walk

stuff n → 1 cash 2 characteristics 3 equipment 4 essence 5 finished product 6 matter 7 raw materials 8 textiles v 9 close 10 conserve 11 cook 12 fill 13 gorge 14 have sex 15 insert 16 oversupply

stumble n → 1 error 2 fall 3 wrong v 4 bungle 5 confuse 6 err 7 fall

stump n → 1 bottom 2 remnant 3 walking v 4 confuse 5 defeat 6 electioneer 7 farm

sturdy adj → 1 durable 2 growing 3 hard 4 persevering 5 serious 6 strong

style n → 1 artistry 2 beauty 3 character 4 fashion 5 fine arts 6 flower 7 good taste 8 name 9 sharp point 10 show 11 structure v 12 clothe 13 name 14 regularise 15 shape

subdue v → 1 defeat 2 farm 3 lose colour 4 make peace 5 repress 6 silence 7 victimise

submit v → 1 assert 2 be meek 3 capitulate 4 compose oneself 5 guide 6 obey 7 offer 8 theorise

subordinate n → 1 inferior v 2 belittle adj 3 inferior 4 unimportant

subservient adj → 1 flattering 2 inferior 3 obedient 4 useable

subsidiary n → 1 inferior 2 music adj 3 additional 4 helpful 5 inferior 6 unimportant

substance n → 1 actuality 2 essence 3 importance 4 important thing 5 matter 6 meaning 7 property 8 raw materials 9 subject matter

substantial n → 1 actuality adj 2 essential 3 fundamental 4 great 5 tangible 6 wealthy

subtle adj → 1 accomplished 2 cunning 3 discriminating 4 thin 5 wise

succeed v → 1 accomplish 2 follow 3 get 4 prosper

sucker n → 1 absorber 2 animal offspring 3 artless person 4 extractor 5 piping 6 stem 7 victim

sudden n → 1 surpriser adj 2 momentary 3 speedy 4 surprising adv 5 surprisingly

suffer v → 1 dislike 2 feel pain 3 perceive 4 permit 5 persevere

suffocate v → 1 die 2 kill

suggest v → 1 assert 2 encourage 3 guide 4 imply 5 offer 6 predict

suit n → 1 class 2 dress 3 entreaty 4 flirtation 5 litigation 6 outfit v 7 fit 8 satisfy

sullen adj → 1 acrimonious 2 badly-behaved 3 cloudy 4 irritable 5 silent 6 slow 7 unhappy 8 unsociable

sum n → 1 addition 2 amount 3 computation 4 essence 5 whole v 6 compute adj 7 whole

summary n → 1 abridgment 2 essay 3 information adj 4 impermanent

super n → 1 fuel 2 income 3 manager 4 policeman 5 surplus v 6 fertilise adj 7 good 8 superior

supercilious adj → 1 arrogant 2 discourteous 3 disdainful

superficial adj → 1 apparent 2 deficient 3 inattentive 4 misjudged 5 outside 6 shallow 7 smallest 8 stupid 9 unimportant

supple v → 1 soften adj 2 beautiful 3 changeable 4 meek 5 pliable 6 soft

supplement n → 1 angle 2 more 3 newspaper v 4 add 5 make whole

suppose v → 1 be likely 2 conjecture 3 devise 4 expect 5 think

suppress v → 1 be reticent 2 hide 3 restrain 4 silence 5 stop 6 victimise

supreme adj → 1 authoritative 2 final 3 good 4 important 5 most 6 predominant 7 superior

sure adj → 1 certain 2 competent 3 faithful 4 inevitable 5 safe 6 steady adv 7 certainly interj 8 bullshit

surface n → 1 appearances 2 outside v 3 appear 4 arrive 5 clean 6 dig 7 smooth 8 wake up adj 9 apparent 10 land 11 outside 12 sea

surmount v → 1 accomplish 2 ascend 3 influence 4 predominate 5 surpass 6 top 7 tower

surrender n → 1 abandonment v 2 back out 3 capitulate 4 give

survey n → 1 agenda 2 essay 3 investigation 4 look v 5 assess 6 investigate 7 look 8 measure 9 question

survive v → 1 be 2 continue 3 escape 4 live 5 protract

suspect n → 1 accused v 2 conjecture 3 doubt adj 4 disreputable

suspend v → 1 be unable to pay 2 be uncertain 3 boycott 4 defer 5 dismiss 6 fasten 7 hang

sustain v → 1 authenticate 2 equip 3 help 4 persevere 5 protract 6 strengthen 7 support

swallow n → 1 eating v 2 absorb 3 believe 4 drink 5 eat 6 persevere

swamp n → 1 sludge 2 stream v 3 fall 4 fill 5 flood 6 oversupply 7 walk 8 weaken 9 wet

sway n → 1 authority 2 flutter 3 influence 4 power v 5 encourage 6 flutter 7 persuade 8 slope 9 vacillate

sweat n → 1 bodily discharge 2 exercise 3 toil 4 worry v 5 be angry with 6 excrete 7 extort 8 heat 9 manage 10 question 11 stick together 12 wet 13 work 14 worry

sweep n → 1 advance 2 bar 3 cleansing 4 cord 5 direction 6 gambling 7 hanging 8 move 9 propellant 10 removal 11 stroke 12 thrust v 13 advance 14 clean 15 curve 16 hang 17 hit 18 investigate 19 look 20 move 21 walk

swell n → 1 aristocrat 2 bulge 3 enlargement 4 fashionable person 5 increase 6 loudness 7 mound 8 outburst 9 push 10 surf v 11 be arrogant 12 become greater 13 bulge 14 flow 15 louden adj 16 fashionable 17 good 18 tasteful

swing n → 1 amusement park 2 flutter 3 pendant 4 rhythm v 5 be promiscuous 6 be punished 7 deflect 8 die 9 flutter 10 hang 11 have sex 12 innovate 13 make music 14 persuade 15 rotate 16 vacillate

switch n → 1 animal's coat 2 change 3 club 4 electric circuit 5 hairpiece 6 hit 7 railway 8 stick 9 telecommunications v 10 change 11 cudgel 12 divert 13 exchange 14 transport

symbol n → 1 emblem 2 sign v 3 represent 4 signify

sympathy n → 1 agreement 2 approval 3 congruity 4 emotionality 5 friendship 6 participation 7 pity

syndicate n → 1 company 2 corporation 3 council 4 judge

system n → 1 body 2 classification 3 combine 4 number system 5 order 6 plan 7 tangle 8 whole

tab n → 1 account 2 addition 3 computer 4 label 5 medication 6 steering wheel v 7 label

tack n → 1 cord 2 direction 3 food 4 method 5 move 6 nail 7 route 8 saddlery 9 stickiness 10 turn v 11 fasten 12 set sail 13 sew 14 swerve 15 turn

tackle n → 1 cord 2 equipment 3 impact 4 thread v 5 attempt 6 bowl over 7 undertake

tail n → 1 animal part 2 bottom 3 buttocks 4 extremity 5 groin 6 hair 7 line 8 meteor 9 musical score 10 pendant 11 qualification 12 rear 13 remnant 14 restraining order 15 sex object 16 stream v 17 be fastened 18 capture 19 cut off 20 direct 21 farm adj 22 rear

taint n → 1 colour 2 denigration 3 deterioration v 4 colour 5 dirty 6 disgrace 7 spoil

take-off n → 1 departure 2 flying 3 imitation 4 jump

tally n → 1 account 2 computation 3 list 4 score 5 stick v 6 account 7 compute 8 fit 9 mark 10 record

tame v → 1 defeat 2 moderate 3 repress 4 subdue adj 5 boring 6 cowardly 7 moderate

tap n → 1 beer 2 boom 3 cutter 4 drink 5 exit 6 pat 7 plug 8 pub 9 small amount 10 stopper 11 touch v 12 cash 13 cut 14 extract 15 hear 16 hit 17 touch 18 use

tarnish n → 1 colourlessness 2 deterioration 3 disfigurement 4 plating v 5 disgrace 6 dull 7 lose colour 8 spoil

tarry n → 1 visit v 2 be late 3 be present 4 expect 5 go slowly 6 idle 7 visit adj 8 coated

tart n → 1 prostitute 2 woman adj 3 sour

task n → 1 difficulty 2 job 3 obligation 4 punishment 5 tax 6 toil 7 undertaking 8 work v 9 tax 10 tire

team n → 1 ancestry 2 animal offspring 3 corporation 4 horse 5 offspring 6 sportsman v 7 transport

tear n → 1 angry act 2 break 3 cut 4 emotion 5 gap 6 pull 7 secretion v 8 break 9 depart 10 open 11 pain 12 pull 13 separate 14 speed

tease n → 1 annoyance 2 annoyer 3 flirt v 4 annoy 5 flirt 6 irritate 7 mock 8 separate 9 sew

technique n → 1 artistry 2 method

teem v → 1 abound 2 be fertile 3 conceive 4 discharge 5 flower 6 give birth 7 rain

tell n → 1 mound v 2 be important 3 command 4 compute 5 discriminate 6 narrate 7 operate 8 publicise 9 reveal 10 speak

temper n → 1 anger 2 character 3 condition 4 emotion 5 hardness 6 irritation 7 pliability v 8 combine 9 ease 10 harden 11 make peace 12 mix 13 moderate 14 quieten 15 strengthen

temperamental adj → 1 changeable 2 characteristic 3 emotional 4 irritable

tender n → 1 cash 2 offer 3 train 4 watercraft v 5 give 6 offer adj 7 brittle 8 loving 9 painful 10 soft 11 weak 12 youthful

tense adj → 1 contracted 2 worried

tension n → 1 electricity 2 excitement 3 pliability 4 pressure 5 worry

terminal n → 1 destination 2 electric circuit 3 finish 4 moulding 5 boundary 6 deadly 7 distant 8 final

terrible adj → 1 bad 2 enormous 3 frightening 4 intense

terrific adj → 1 frightening 2 good 3 intense

terrify v → frighten

terse adj → 1 concise 2 discourteous 3 irritable

thank v → be grateful

theatre n → 1 audience 2 auditorium 3 hall 4 room

theory n → 1 conjecture 2 idea 3 opinion

there adv → 1 here 2 particularly 3 then interj 4 hey

thick n → 1 solidity 2 stupid person adj 3 cloudy 4 dark 5 friendly 6 inactive 7 opaque 8 quiet 9 sludgy 10 solid 11 stupid adv 12 solidly 13 thickly

thing n → 1 actuality 2 affair 3 any 4 emotion 5 matter 6 point of view 7 undertaking

though adv → 1 conditionally 2 nevertheless conj 3 on condition that

thought n → 1 care 2 expected thing 3 idea 4 mind 5 opinion 6 plan 7 small amount 8 thinking

thrash n → 1 hit v 2 beat 3 defeat 4 set sail

threat n → 1 challenge 2 command 3 danger 4 force 5 menace 6 warning

thrill n → 1 excitement 2 perception 3 pleasure 4 vibration v 5 excite 6 feel emotion 7 vibrate

thrive v → 1 become greater 2 be healthy 3 be wealthy 4 flower 5 prosper

throb n → 1 ache 2 vibration v 3 feel emotion 4 pain 5 vibrate

throng n → 1 gathering 2 many v 3 abound 4 fill 5 gather

through adv → 1 across 2 regularly 3 thoroughly prep 4 across 5 at 6 during 7 inclusive of

thump *n* → 1 boom 2 explosion 3 impact *v* 4 be loud 5 boom 6 explode 7 fight 8 hit 9 rob 10 walk

thunder *n* → 1 boom 2 explosion 3 loud sound 4 menace 5 weather — *v* 6 be angry 7 be loud 8 be violent 9 boom 10 explode 11 menace

ticket *n* → 1 account 2 hallucinogen 3 label 4 legal order 5 list 6 public notice *v* 7 label

tight *adj* → 1 difficult 2 drunk 3 few 4 full 5 mean 6 steady 7 sticky 8 strict *adv* 9 hard 10 steadily

tilt *n* → 1 roof 2 slope 3 stroke *v* 4 attack 5 fight 6 slope

timid *adj* → 1 cowardly 2 frightened 3 unwilling

tinkle *n* → 1 quiet sound 2 ringing 3 telecommunications *v* 4 ring 5 urinate

tiny *adj* → small

tip *n* → 1 allowance 2 extremity 3 garbage dump 4 gift 5 gratefulness 6 guidance 7 idea 8 information 9 overturn 10 pat 11 prediction 12 sharp point 13 top *v* 14 give 15 hit 16 overturn 17 predict 18 slope

title *n* → 1 book 2 church 3 entitlement 4 evidence 5 justification 6 name 7 ownership 8 religious ministry 9 rights *v* 10 name

toast *n* → 1 a drink 2 applause 3 congratulation 4 tribute *v* 5 approve 6 brown 7 cook 8 drink alcohol 9 fire 10 offer 11 rejoice

toil *n* → 1 act of war 2 contest *v* 3 make an effort 4 persist 5 walk 6 work

tolerate *v* → 1 permit 2 persevere

tone *n* → 1 character 2 colour 3 fashion 4 fine arts 5 good taste 6 health 7 perceptivity 8 pitch 9 pliability 10 sound 11 speaking *v* 12 colour 13 photograph 14 sound

tongue *n* → 1 footgear 2 headland 3 knob 4 language 5 mouth 6 nonsense 7 resonator 8 rod 9 speaking *v* 10 contact 11 make music 12 scold 13 speak

tool *n* → 1 groin 2 knife 3 method 4 victim *v* 5 cut 6 drive 7 shape

top *n* → 1 apex 2 front 3 head 4 outside 5 perfect thing 6 shirt 7 spin 8 stroke *v* 9 arrive 10 ascend 11 close 12 cover 13 fertilise 14 jump 15 surpass *adj* 16 competent 17 desirable 18 good 19 high 20 important 21 most 22 outside 23 superior

topic *n* → subject matter

torment *n* → 1 annoyance 2 corporal punishment 3 pain 4 turbulence 5 victimisation *v* 6 act unkindly 7 agitate 8 annoy 9 pain

torture *n* → 1 corporal punishment 2 pain *v* 3 act unkindly 4 distort 5 pain 6 punish

toss *n* → 1 gambling 2 throw 3 turbulence *v* 4 create 5 flutter 6 gamble 7 lift 8 throw

total *n* → 1 addition 2 computation 3 score 4 whole *v* 5 compute *adj* 6 inclusive 7 unconditional 8 whole

touchy *adj* → 1 dangerous 2 emotional 3 fiery 4 irritable 5 perceptive

tough *n* → 1 violent person *adj* 2 brutal 3 callous 4 difficult 5 durable 6 hard 7 persevering 8 sludgy 9 stubborn 10 unpleasant *adv* 11 angrily

tour *n* → 1 journey 2 race 3 visit *v* 4 perform 5 travel 6 visit

tow *n* → 1 cord 2 pull *v* 3 pull *adj* 4 yellow

towards *prep* → 1 concerning 2 near

towel *n* → 1 drier *v* 2 beat 3 defeat 4 dry 5 rub

toy *n* → 1 amusement 2 flirt 3 unimportant thing *v* 4 amuse oneself

trace *n* → 1 harness 2 memory 3 psyche 4 remnant 5 sign 6 small amount 7 smell *v* 8 copy 9 decorate 10 find 11 map 12 press 13 write

track *n* → 1 direction 2 line 3 method 4 path 5 racecourse 6 railway 7 recording 8 route 9 transporter *v* 10 adjust 11 beat a path 12 extend 13 pursue

tragedy *n* → 1 drama 2 misfortune

tragic *adj* → 1 calamitous 2 distressing 3 dramatic

train *n* → 1 explosive 2 lighter 3 line 4 meteor 5 pendant 6 result 7 sequence 8 series *v* 9 direct 10 drive 11 prepare 12 study 13 teach

traitor *n* → 1 betrayer 2 disobeyer 3 enemy

trample n → 1 pressing v 2 press 3 walk

transfer n → 1 copy 2 defection 3 defector 4 label 5 transport v 6 transport

transform n → 1 linguistics 2 mathematical operation v 3 change

translucent adj → transparent

transparent adj → 1 bright 2 clear

trap n → 1 allure 2 carriage 3 danger 4 door 5 fishing tackle 6 fortification 7 mouth 8 opening 9 policeman 10 propellant 11 stratagem v 12 arrest 13 cover 14 hunt 15 obstruct

trash n → 1 bad person 2 bad thing 3 nonsense 4 remnant 5 waste v 6 subtract

treasure n → 1 good thing 2 wealth v 3 hide 4 respect

tree n → 1 ancestry 2 chemical agent 3 cross 4 number system 5 plant 6 shaft v 7 cause difficulties 8 hunt 9 pursue 10 shape

tremble n → 1 coldness 2 fright v 3 be cold 4 be excited 5 be frightened 6 vibrate

trend n → 1 direction 2 fashion 3 point of view v 4 tend to

trespass n → 1 advance 2 crime 3 entrance 4 evildoing 5 harm 6 wrong v 7 be immoral 8 contravene 9 enter 10 misbehave 11 wrong

trial n → 1 annoyance 2 attempt 3 contest 4 examination 5 pain 6 questioning 7 race 8 racing 9 test v 10 test adj 11 litigious 12 test

trick n → 1 behaviour 2 expedient 3 illusion 4 misdemeanour 5 stratagem adj 6 cunning

trim n → 1 clothes 2 condition 3 covering 4 display 5 equipment 6 hairdressing 7 tidiness 8 trimming v 9 change 10 clothe 11 cover 12 cut 13 decorate 14 defeat 15 exercise restraint 16 fly 17 make do 18 shape 19 smooth 20 subtract adj 21 equipped 22 good 23 tidy adv 24 tidily

trip n → 1 drug use 2 error 3 fall 4 hallucinogen 5 journey 6 misdemeanour 7 pleasure 8 wrong v 9 dance 10 enjoy 11 fall 12 hinder 13 take drugs 14 travel 15 walk 16 wrong

triumph n → 1 joy 2 success v 3 predominate 4 rejoice 5 succeed

troop n → 1 armed forces 2 crowd 3 gathering 4 many 5 theatrical company v 6 abound 7 display 8 tidy 9 walk

trouble n → 1 annoyance 2 annoyer 3 commotion 4 difficulty 5 effort 6 illness 7 misfortune 8 pain 9 turbulence 10 worry v 11 agitate 12 alarm 13 annoy 14 displease 15 pain

trudge v → walk

trunk n → 1 animal part 2 box 3 chest 4 post 5 railway 6 stem 7 stream

trust n → 1 belief 2 care 3 hope 4 obligation 5 reverence 6 surety v 7 believe 8 hope

trustworthy adj → 1 believable 2 faithful 3 honest

try n → 1 attempt v 2 assess 3 attempt 4 authenticate 5 bore 6 examine 7 liquefy 8 taste 9 test

tube n → 1 alcohol container 2 bladder 3 drinking vessel 4 electrical device 5 flower 6 neck 7 piping 8 railway 9 solid 10 surf 11 television

tuck n → 1 clothes 2 dive 3 fold 4 food 5 sword v 6 contract 7 cover 8 fold 9 insert

tumble n → 1 fall 2 jumble 3 roll v 4 disorder 5 fall 6 jump 7 lower 8 overturn 9 roll 10 wane

tumult n → 1 anarchy 2 commotion 3 loud sound 4 muddle 5 turbulence

tunnel n → 1 animal dwelling 2 bridge 3 channel 4 diggings 5 passageway 6 path v 7 dig 8 hollow 9 open

turmoil n → 1 anarchy 2 disorder 3 loud sound 4 muddle 5 turbulence

turn n → 1 celebration 2 change 3 circle 4 crucial moment 5 curve 6 exercise 7 fright 8 illness 9 party 10 period 11 point of view 12 shape 13 stocks and shares 14 twist 15 walk v 16 alternate 17 bend 18 be unpalatable 19 blunt 20 change 21 create 22 curve 23 defect 24 deteriorate 25 rotate 26 shape 27 swerve 28 translate

tutor n → 1 protector 2 teacher v 3 be strict 4 scold 5 teach

twin

twin n → 1 offspring 2 repetition 3 sibling 4 similar thing 5 two v 6 double 7 give birth adj 8 simultaneous 9 two

twinkle n → 1 light 2 moment 3 urination v 4 shine

twirl n → 1 spin 2 twist v 3 roll up 4 spin

ultimate n → 1 finish 2 good thing adj 3 distant 4 final 5 fundamental

unbalanced adj → 1 confused 2 mad 3 misplaced 4 prejudiced 5 psychologically disturbed 6 unequal

uncouth adj → 1 discourteous 2 ill-bred 3 incompetent 4 ugly

underhand adj → 1 cunning 2 secretive adv 3 in secret

underneath n → 1 bottom adv 2 below prep 3 under

unfold v → 1 display 2 explain 3 grow 4 open up 5 reveal

uniform n → 1 emblem of office 2 formal dress adj 3 boring 4 homogeneous 5 simple

union n → 1 combination 2 combine 3 joining 4 marriage 5 society 6 weave

unique adj → 1 nonconformist 2 one 3 strange 4 unrelated

unit n → 1 armed forces 2 flat 3 genetics 4 gradation 5 machine 6 one 7 train adj 8 one

unite v → 1 agree 2 associate 3 converge 4 cooperate 5 join 6 marry 7 stick together

universal adj → 1 cosmic 2 general

unnecessary adj → 1 surplus 2 useless

unravel v → 1 clarify 2 inquire into 3 separate 4 simplify 5 translate

unreal adj → 1 bad 2 delusive 3 good 4 intangible 5 unrealistic

unreasonable adj → 1 illogical 2 prejudiced 3 rash 4 stubborn

unruly adj → 1 anarchic 2 badly-behaved 3 disobedient

unsteady adj → 1 changeable 2 indecisive 3 irregular

unthinkable adj → impossible

until conj → while

untold adj → 1 infinite 2 many 3 uncertain

unusual adj → 1 nonconformist 2 rare 3 strange

venerate

up n → 1 ascent v 2 direct 3 increase 4 lift 5 surpass adj 6 advanced 7 ascending 8 erect 9 occurrent 10 operating 11 successful adv 12 erectly

upgrade n → 1 slope v 2 improve 3 promote

upright n → 1 piano adj 2 correct 3 erect 4 honest 5 postural adv 6 erectly

uprising n → 1 ascent 2 mutiny 3 revolution

uproar n → 1 commotion 2 loud sound 3 muddle

upset n → 1 disagreement 2 illness 3 jumble 4 losing 5 muddle 6 overturn v 7 defeat 8 disorder 9 displease 10 make unhappy 11 overturn adj 12 nauseous 13 overturned 14 unhappy 15 worried

urge n → 1 desire 2 incentive v 3 encourage 4 entreat 5 guide 6 persuade

usual adj → 1 conventional 2 customary 3 repetitive

utilise v → use

utter v → 1 circulate 2 expel 3 finance 4 publicise 5 speak 6 write adj 7 most 8 thorough 9 unconditional

vacant adj → 1 abandoned 2 absent 3 empty 4 unused

vague adj → 1 imprecise 2 uncertain

valid adj → 1 healthy 2 lawful 3 logical 4 true 5 useable

variety n → 1 choice 2 class 3 difference 4 something different adj 5 dramatic

vault n → 1 arch 2 grave 3 jump 4 room 5 treasury v 6 jump

vehemence n → 1 anger 2 emotion 3 enthusiasm 4 violence

veil n → 1 covering 2 disguise 3 headband 4 monasticism 5 wall v 6 hide

vein n → 1 blood vessel 2 character 3 diggings 4 leaf 5 line 6 mineral 7 multicolour 8 rock outcrop 9 stream v 10 channel 11 line

velvet n → 1 gambling equipment 2 profit 3 smooth object adj 4 smooth 5 soft

venerate v → 1 glorify 2 respect 3 revere 4 worship

vent n → 1 airway 2 exit 3 gap 4 means of escape v 5 discharge 6 display 7 expel 8 speak

venture n → 1 attempt 2 danger 3 gamble 4 trade 5 undertaking v 6 brave 7 risk

verge n → 1 apex 2 domain 3 edge 4 emblem of office 5 post 6 space v 7 come close 8 slope

verify v → 1 authenticate 2 be true 3 examine

vet v → 1 healer 2 serviceman v 3 examine 4 investigate

veteran n → 1 serviceman 2 specialist adj 3 accomplished 4 antique 5 old 6 vehicular

vex v → 1 agitate 2 anger 3 damage 4 displease 5 irritate 6 pain

vice n → 1 clip 2 holder 3 immorality 4 imperfection 5 wrong v 6 hold 7 press

vicious adj → 1 immoral 2 imperfect 3 poisonous 4 promiscuous 5 unkind 6 wrong

vindicate v → 1 acquit 2 justify 3 liberate 4 punish 5 retaliate

violate v → 1 be promiscuous 2 be violent 3 disobey 4 hold in low regard 5 ill-treat 6 profane 7 rape

virtue n → 1 correctness 2 courage 3 good 4 honesty 5 innocence 6 manliness 7 power 8 reverence

virtuoso n → 1 aesthete 2 expert 3 musician 4 specialist adj 5 accomplished 6 knowledgeable

vital adj → 1 energetic 2 enthusiastic 3 fundamental 4 important 5 living 6 necessary

vivid adj → 1 artistic 2 bright 3 colourful 4 energetic 5 intense 6 living 7 obvious 8 perceptional

voice n → 1 election 2 pitch 3 singer 4 speaking v 5 publicise 6 speak

void n → 1 emptiness 2 gap 3 nonbeing 4 space v 5 annihilate 6 cancel 7 deny 8 depart 9 empty 10 expel adj 11 empty 12 ineffectual 13 powerless

volume n → 1 book 2 loudness 3 much 4 size

vow n → 1 contract 2 religious ceremony v 3 assert 4 intend 5 promise 6 take the cloth

waddle n → 1 flutter 2 walking v 3 flutter 4 walk

wage n → 1 income 2 surety v 3 do 4 gamble

wail v → 1 cry 2 shout v 3 be loud 4 call (of animals) 5 grieve 6 shrill

wallow v → 1 binge 2 hollow 3 lake 4 show 5 swamp v 6 be pleased 7 get dirty 8 overindulge 9 roll

wander v → 1 walk 2 become confused 3 be inattentive 4 travel 5 waffle

wangle v → 1 dishonesty 2 expedient 3 stratagem v 4 beguile 5 make do 6 swindle

want n → 1 absence 2 deficiency 3 desire 4 insufficiency 5 necessities 6 poverty 7 will v 8 desire 9 fall short 10 necessitate

wanton n → 1 promiscuous person 2 sexual partner v 3 be promiscuous 4 let oneself go 5 overindulge adj 6 capricious 7 extravagant 8 growing 9 happy 10 immoral 11 liberated 12 overindulgent 13 rash 14 uncompromising 15 unfair

warm v → 1 enthuse 2 heat adj 3 acrimonious 4 busy 5 close 6 emotional 7 energetic 8 enthusiastic 9 findable 10 friendly 11 hot 12 kind 13 reddish

warp n → 1 cord 2 distortion 3 intolerance 4 soil 5 weave v 6 distort 7 pull 8 swerve

warrant n → 1 account 2 authentication 3 insistence 4 justification 5 legal order 6 permission 7 surety v 8 authorise 9 justify 10 permit

wash v → 1 airflow 2 channel 3 cleansing 4 coating 5 current 6 dirt 7 drink 8 dye 9 flow 10 liquid 11 medication 12 mineral 13 paint 14 painting 15 seaside 16 soil 17 splash 18 swamp 19 winemaking v 20 clean 21 colour 22 flow

waste n → 1 deterioration 2 dirt 3 discard 4 extravagance 5 harm 6 misuse 7 nature 8 neglectfulness 9 remnant 10 textiles 11 wasteland v 12 contract 13 destroy 14 fall into disuse 15 ill-treat 16 kill 17 squander 18 weaken adj 19 disused 20 excremental 21 infertile 22 natural 23 surplus 24 useless

watch   626   **wish**

watch n → 1 looker 2 seeing 3 timepiece v 4 attend to 5 care for 6 look 7 worship interj 8 lo

water n → 1 extinguisher 2 rainfall 3 urination v 4 excrete 5 mix 6 wet adj 7 liquid

wave n → 1 advance 2 curve 3 flutter 4 gesture 5 hairdressing 6 outburst 7 point of view 8 radiation 9 sea 10 surf 11 water v 12 curve 13 flutter 14 gesture 15 twist

waver n → 1 signaller v 2 flutter 3 lack courage 4 move 5 vacillate

wax n → 1 adhesive 2 angry act 3 fat 4 raw materials v 5 become greater 6 flower 7 illuminate 8 polish

way n → 1 access 2 advance 3 behaviour 4 characteristic 5 condition 6 custom 7 direction 8 method 9 move

wayward adj → 1 badly-behaved 2 capricious 3 changeable 4 moving

weary v → 1 bore 2 tire adj 3 bored 4 discontented 5 effortful 6 tired

web n → 1 combine 2 feather 3 skin 4 stratagem 5 textiles v 6 cover

wedge n → 1 angle 2 armed forces 3 atmospheric pressure 4 machine 5 nail 6 obstacle 7 part v 8 fill 9 obstruct 10 separate

weep n → 1 cry v 2 be unhappy 3 discharge 4 excrete 5 grieve 6 wet

welcome n → 1 courtesy 2 friendship 3 sociability v 4 be sociable 5 enjoy adj 6 pleasant 7 rightful

well n → 1 basin 2 diggings 3 excavation 4 room 5 spring 6 start v 7 discharge 8 flow adj 9 healthy adv 10 courteously 11 easily 12 satisfactorily 13 thoroughly interj 14 oh

wheeze n → 1 breathing 2 joke 3 stratagem v 4 breathe 5 shrill

whiff n → 1 absorption 2 breathing 3 cloud 4 outburst 5 shout 6 smell 7 tobacco v 8 absorb 9 breathe 10 smell out 11 smoke

whimper n → 1 animal call 2 cry 3 shout v 4 grieve 5 shout

whimsical adj → 1 capricious 2 changeable 3 humorous 4 indecisive

whine n → 1 animal call 2 click 3 complaint 4 cry 5 quiet sound 6 shout v 7 call (of animals) 8 complain 9 grieve 10 shrill 11 speak

whinge n → 1 complaint v 2 be ungrateful 3 complain

whip n → 1 club 2 cord 3 driver 4 gunfire 5 hit 6 incentive 7 leader 8 machine 9 move 10 percussion instrument 11 propellant v 12 agitate 13 cook 14 cover 15 cudgel 16 defeat 17 fish 18 scold 19 speed 20 spin 21 twist

whirl n → 1 rate 2 spin v 3 speed 4 spin 5 swerve 6 throw

whirr n → 1 click 2 vibration v 3 click 4 spin 5 vibrate

whisk n → 1 accumulation 2 cookware 3 rate v 4 agitate 5 capture 6 cook

wholesale v → 1 sell adj 2 inclusive 3 saleable 4 thorough adv 5 commercially 6 sizeably 7 wholly

whoop n → 1 challenge 2 shout v 3 chirp 4 encourage 5 shout

wicked adj → 1 annoying 2 bad 3 immoral 4 unpleasant 5 wrong

wide adj → 1 deflective 2 distant 3 open 4 spacious 5 thick adv 6 deflectively 7 open 8 remotely 9 thickly 10 thoroughly

wild adj → 1 animal-like 2 disorderly 3 enthusiastic 4 excited 5 foolish 6 liberated 7 muddled 8 natural 9 rash 10 untidy 11 violent adv 12 deflectively 13 naturally 14 violently

wilful adj → 1 capricious 2 disobedient 3 stubborn 4 uncompromising

wind n → 1 abdomen 2 airflow 3 bombast 4 breathing 5 burp 6 gas 7 point of view 8 pride 9 twist 10 wind instrument 11 flow 12 pursue 13 tangle 14 turn 15 twist

wing n → 1 addition 2 aeroplane 3 arm 4 bird part 5 building 6 combat troops 7 door 8 feather 9 flight 10 flower 11 fruit 12 knob 13 political spectrum 14 side 15 stage 16 stem v 17 fly 18 injure 19 perform

wipe v → 1 coat 2 dry 3 repel

wiry adj → 1 corded 2 hard 3 resonant 4 strong 5 thin

wish n → 1 desire 2 will v 3 desire 4 intend

withdraw $v \rightarrow$ 1 be modest 2 cancel 3 depart 4 extract 5 go back 6 make peace 7 remove

wither $v \rightarrow$ 1 contract 2 deteriorate 3 die 4 dry

witness $n \rightarrow$ 1 evidence 2 litigant 3 looker 4 testifier v 5 see 6 testify

wobble $n \rightarrow$ 1 vibration v 2 vacillate 3 vibrate

woman $n \rightarrow$ 1 lover 2 servant 3 sexual partner 4 spouse v 5 feminise

wonderful $adj \rightarrow$ 1 astonishing 2 good

wood $n \rightarrow$ 1 timber 2 wind instrument adj 3 angry

work $n \rightarrow$ 1 book 2 building 3 drama 4 effort 5 finished product 6 job 7 musical piece 8 undertaking v 9 accomplish 10 brew 11 make 12 make an effort 13 move 14 operate 15 sew 16 undertake 17 work metal

worn $adj \rightarrow$ 1 blunt 2 dilapidated 3 tired 4 used up

worry $n \rightarrow$ 1 annoyer v 2 agitate 3 alarm 4 annoy 5 discontent

worse $n \rightarrow$ 1 inferiority adj 2 deteriorating 3 inferior

worthy $n \rightarrow$ 1 famous person 2 person adj 3 highly regarded 4 reputable

wound $n \rightarrow$ 1 injury v 2 displease 3 injure 4 pain

wrap $n \rightarrow$ 1 cloak v 2 cover 3 fasten 4 fold 5 secure 6 surround 7 twist

wreck $n \rightarrow$ 1 casualty 2 damage 3 patient 4 psychotic 5 remnant 6 ruin 7 unfortunate 8 watercraft 9 weakling v 10 ruin 11 spoil

wretched $adj \rightarrow$ 1 bad 2 pitiable 3 poor 4 unfortunate 5 unhappy 6 unkempt

wriggle $n \rightarrow$ 1 circuitousness 2 move v 3 flutter 4 make do 5 move 6 twist 7 walk

writ $n \rightarrow$ 1 imprisonment 2 insistence 3 legal order 4 litigation 5 record 6 restraining order

write $v \rightarrow$ 1 mark 2 narrate 3 portray 4 send a message

writhe $n \rightarrow$ 1 circuitousness 2 distortion 3 move v 4 distort 5 feel pain 6 move 7 toss 8 twist

yarn $n \rightarrow$ 1 story 2 talk 3 thread 4 weave v 5 narrate 6 talk

yawn $n \rightarrow$ 1 bore 2 gap 3 opening 4 sleepiness v 5 become sleepy 6 gape 7 open up

yell $n \rightarrow$ 1 shout v 2 shout 3 speak

yellow $n \rightarrow$ 1 narcotic adj 2 cowardly

yelp $n \rightarrow$ 1 shout v 2 call (of animals) 3 shout

yield $n \rightarrow$ 1 amount 2 atomic radiation 3 finished product 4 profit v 5 abandon 6 be fertile 7 be lenient 8 capitulate 9 give 10 lose 11 pay

young $n \rightarrow$ 1 offspring adj 2 ignorant 3 inferior 4 new 5 youthful

youth $n \rightarrow$ 1 adolescent 2 innovator 3 man 4 start 5 youthfulness